McGraw-Hill/Irwin provides Solomon users with technology supplements that are second to none, including the Online Learning Center, ALEKS, and NetTutor™.

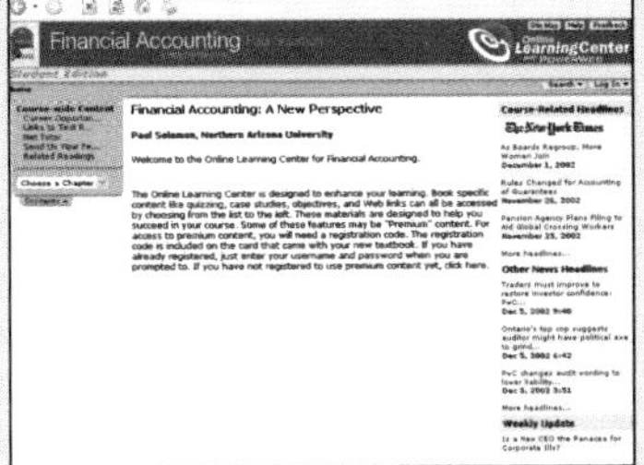

The **Online Learning Center** (OLC) is your classroom on the Web, a great place for both instructors and students to find resources that make learning financial accounting easier and more fun. For a list of OLC assets, see the box at right.

ALEKS® (Assessment and LEarning in Knowledge Spaces) delivers precise, qualitative diagnostic assessments of students' mathematical knowledge. ALEKS® interacts with the student much as a skilled human tutor would, moving between explanation and practice as needed, correcting and analyzing errors, defining terms and changing topics on request. By sophisticated modeling of a student's knowledge state, ALEKS® can focus clearly on what the student is most ready to learn next. When students focus on exactly what they are ready to learn, they build confidence, and a learning momentum that fuels success.

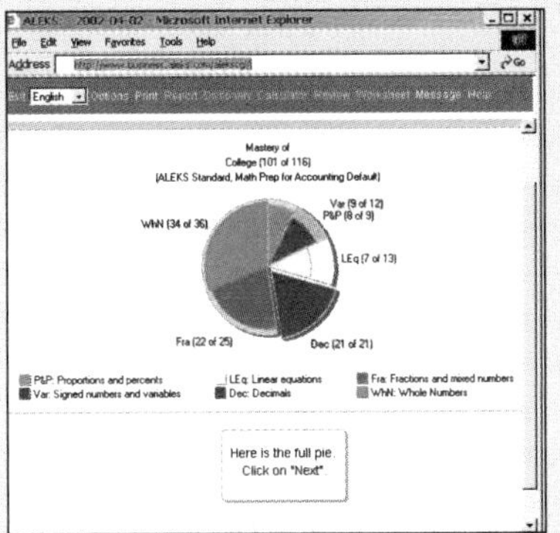

Learn more at http://www.business.aleks.com.

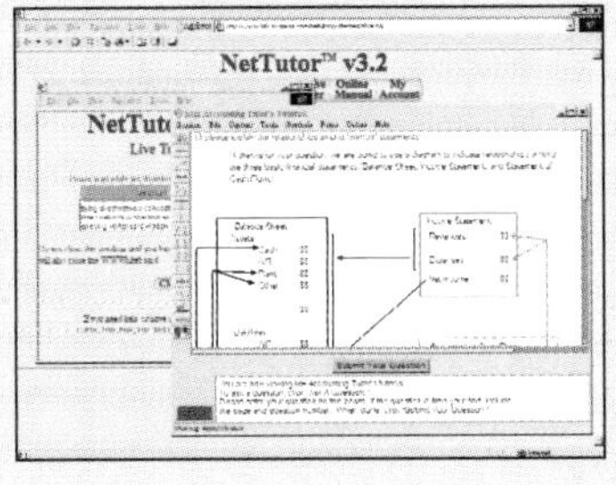

NetTutor™ allows your students to receive live, personalized tutoring via the Internet. Using NetTutor's™ powerful WWWhiteboard software, they can post a question and receive prompt, text-specific feedback from an expert in financial accounting. And they don't even need an appointment.

Information Center

Overview
T.O.C.
Author Biography
Preface
List of Print and Electronic Supplements
Link to Pageout
NetTutor™ Demo
Link to ALEKS®

Online Instructor Center

Instructor's Resource Guide
Solutions Manual
Chapter Powerpoint® Presentations
Excel Template Exercises and Solutions
Sample Syllabi
Links to Professional Resources

Online Student Center

Sample Study Guide Chapter
Complete List of Performance Objectives
List of Performance Objectives by Chapter
Glossary of Key Terms by Chapter
Flashcard Key Terms Review
Chapter PowerPoint® Presentations
Research Assignments
Interactive Sample Final Exam
Online Chapter Quizzes
Excel Template Exercises
Check Figures
Links to text-referenced Companies

Check back for additional content updates!

Financial Accounting

A New Perspective

Paul Solomon
Northern Arizona University

Boston Burr Ridge, IL Dubuque, IA Madison, WI New York San Francisco St. Louis
Bangkok Bogotá Caracas Kuala Lumpur Lisbon London Madrid Mexico City
Milan Montreal New Delhi Santiago Seoul Singapore Sydney Taipei Toronto

The McGraw-Hill Companies

FINANCIAL ACCOUNTING: A NEW PERSPECTIVE

Published by McGraw-Hill/Irwin, a business unit of The McGraw-Hill Companies, Inc., 1221 Avenue of the Americas, New York, NY, 10020.

This book is printed on acid-free paper.

domestic 1 2 3 4 5 6 7 8 9 0 DOW/DOW 0 9 8 7 6 5 4 3
international 1 2 3 4 5 6 7 8 9 0 DOW/DOW 0 9 8 7 6 5 4 3

ISBN 0-07-284034-X

Publisher: *Brent Gordon*
Sponsoring editor: *Steve DeLancey*
Developmental editor I: *Kelly Odom*
Marketing manager: *Katherine Mattison*
Senior producer, Media technology: *David Barrick*
Senior project manager: *Kimberly D. Hooker*
Production supervisor: *Gina Hangos*
Lead designer: *Pam Verros*
Senior Advertising designer: *Erwin Llereza*
Photo research coordinator: *Jeremy Cheshareck*
Photo researcher: *Jennifer Blankenship*
Lead supplement producer: *Becky Szura*
Senior digital content specialist: *Brian Nacik*
Cover photo: © *Masterfile*
Typeface: *10.5/12 Times Roman*
Compositor: *TechBooks*
Printer: *R. R. Donnelley*

Library of Congress Cataloging-in-Publication Data

Solomon, Paul, 1948–
Financial accounting : a new perspective / Paul Solomon.
p. cm.
Includes index.
ISBN 0-07-284034-X (alk. paper)—ISBN 0-07-121512-3 (international : alk. paper)
1. Accounting. I. Title.
HF5635 .S6892 2004
657—dc21 2002038900

INTERNATIONAL EDITION ISBN 0-07-121512-3

www.mhhe.com

This book is dedicated to the two most important women in my life—

- my mother, Edith (1912–2000), the first published author in our family whose love of language has inspired me, and
- my wife, Susan, an accomplished publishing professional in her own right, whose wise counsel and creative insights have had a great impact on this book, and whose support and love have sustained me.

Dear Colleagues:

Financial Accounting: A New Perspective embodies an approach to teaching that I have developed over my 30 plus years in the classroom. It truly is a new perspective, and here's why:

- It introduces concepts to students as they are ready for them by using what I call a *spiral approach,* which doesn't require students to master concepts in one presentation. Instead, students often have two or more opportunities to refine their understanding of particular concepts.
- It breaks the long-standing paradigm that other books use. For example, it begins not by talking about business and accounting in the abstract, but by introducing a realistic, concrete business case students can count on throughout the book as a controlled environment in which to learn new concepts.
- It motivates students by truly acknowledging them as business majors *first* — by taking them out of the preparer mode yet still emphasizing how they cannot be successful in business without accounting. Thus, students are more likely to stay in the course and ultimately become accounting majors.
- It discourages memorization in three ways: it uses the aforementioned spiral approach; it delays such topics as debits and credits and the accounting cycle, giving students more time to master basic concepts; and it uses the more intuitive organizing principle of three business activities — financing, investing, and operating — rather than a daunting list of balance sheet accounts.

My results from using this new perspective have been dramatic. How dramatic? Before I fully implemented this approach, I often complained to my colleagues that the quality of my students was declining. Then, the first time I used this new perspective, I was struck by how unusually bright and motivated my students appeared. Only after several weeks did it occur to me that it was the *course* that had changed not the quality of my students! When I changed my course perspective to one that was truly student-centered, my students' true abilities emerged. The evidence that my students are more motivated is clear: they tell me how much they enjoy the course because of its focus on business and those who admit to dropping or failing a previous course, remark how different it is from traditional instructor-centered courses. My attrition rate is lower, I have fewer complaints, students are more enthusiastic, and I enjoy teaching more!

I encourage you to try this new student-centered perspective on financial accounting!

Sincerely,

Paul Solomon

ABOUT THE AUTHOR

For over 30 years, **Paul Solomon** has dedicated himself to accounting education because he loves to teach accounting. This textbook embodies his special talent of being able to explain even the most difficult accounting concepts in ways students easily grasp and his passion and long-standing involvement in accounting education.

Paul teaches at Northern Arizona University and is a leading proponent of implementing a user-oriented first course in accounting. Prior to teaching at NAU, he was a tenured faculty member at San Jose State University.

While at San Jose State, Paul chaired a conference for ten years that allowed two- and four-year educators to meet and communicate on significant education issues. This conference became known as The California Colloquium on Accounting Education, his efforts for which were rewarded with the California Society of CPA's 1995 *Faculty Excellence Award.* In 1998, Paul's dedication and initiative culminated in his being awarded the coveted American Accounting Association's *Innovation in Accounting Education Award.*

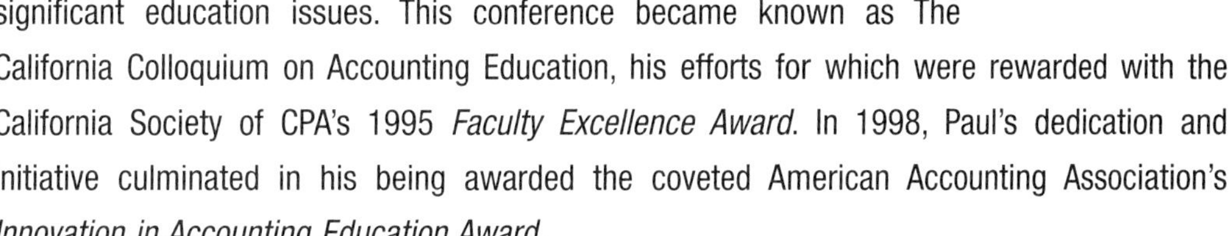

Paul earned his Ph.D. from the University of Minnesota in 1981 and was awarded the *Ernest Heilman Award* for Outstanding Graduate Student Teaching while studying for his doctorate. His professional experience includes positions at the General Accounting Office; Touche Ross and Company; Lybrand, Ross Brothers and Montgomery; and Haskins and Sells.

Today, Paul is closely involved in the American Accounting Association's focus on faculty development. He is the founder and chairman of the Colloquium on Change in Accounting Education, a national faculty conference. He travels extensively to present faculty workshops and to consult with individual accounting programs.

Paul lives with his wife Susan and four dogs — Cookie, Molly, Max, and Zachary — among the awe-inspiring red rocks of Sedona, Arizona.

Your students' outlook

Financial accounting

has long been the critical foundation for a student's introduction into accounting and the world of business at large. Over the past 25 years, Dr. Paul Solomon has refined a teaching method that engages students — piquing their interest in business and accounting — and helping them to be successful in their study of financial accounting.

Dr. Solomon knew that if students felt successful during their first weeks in the course, if they could immediately relate to the experiences of applying accounting information in a realistic business setting, they would recognize the value and application of accounting in all segments of their future business careers. With this achieved, Solomon could further inspire his students to continue on in their study of accounting. *Financial Accounting: A New Perspective* is the culmination of these efforts.

Throughout the development of this text, Solomon has strived to present financial accounting from a genuinely new perspective. The approach he found most successful was to introduce students to a business, and then bringing the more technical aspects of financial accounting and their application into that business. Solomon believes that if you explain accounting concepts to students using engaging, real world examples with which they are already familiar, you, the instructor, can then introduce the technical aspects of financial accounting and find that the students are motivated to understand how financial accounting analyzes and explains business activities.

on financial accounting is about to change...

Motivation. Cards & Memorabilia Unlimited is a running case — introduced at the beginning of Chapter One and continuing throughout the text — which will capture students' interest and keep them grounded as they discover the purpose and function of basic accounting concepts. As the needs of young entrepreneur Susan Newman and her developing business dictate, Solomon introduces relevant accounting tools, including financial statements, transaction analysis, ratios, and debits and credits. Students are able to understand why they are learning the material and how it will be relevant to their lives in the world of business.

Readability. Focus group participants and reviewers agree: one of Solomon's greatest strengths is its readability. Not only does the writing style enable students to better understand the concepts presented, but also the presentation captures students' interest, inspiring them to want to read on to learn more about what happens to Susan Newman and her new business.

Success. Paul Solomon has carefully developed this text to ensure students' understanding of financial accounting concepts. The use of performance objectives, similar to those the student will be expected to meet in the business world, reinforces the integral relationship between financial accounting and business. This book helps students understand the relevance of accounting by employing a learning system that includes an Online Learning Center, NetTutor, and real world articles from McGraw-Hill's proprietary technology PowerWeb.

Paul Solomon has demonstrated that students can be successful in financial accounting when they understand the relationship between the real world and the concepts they learn in the course. His book approaches these concepts in an engaging and easy to understand manner. By providing your students with this clear, new perspective on financial accounting, they too will be able to effectively grasp and master the accounting skills they'll need to be successful in the rest of their business classes as well as their future business careers.

Successful Learning starts with a clear perspective

Performance Objectives

Performance Objectives tie the text together and are vital to Paul Solomon's approach.

- "POs" are listed in the chapter openers, derived from text discussion so students can see why they are critical to their learning.
- Performance Objectives are revisited throughout the chaper when applicable and finally keyed to end-of-chapter material.
- Chapter openers remind students of previously learned POs that will then be re-applied in the current chapter.
- This constant reinforcement - the book's "spiral approach" - keeps the student focused on important chapter topics while helping them learn core text concepts, always building on what they have previously mastered.

CHAPTER THREE

3

Financial Statements and Their Relationships

Also be sure you have mastered the following Performance Objectives from previous chapters. They lay the foundation for the concepts you will learn in this chapter:

PO2
PO4
PO5
PO7

PERFORMANCE OBJECTIVES

In this chapter, you will learn the following new Performance Objectives:

PO10 **Prepare** an income statement that reports the results of operations of any entity.

PO11 **Differentiate** the balance sheet from the income statement by being able to:
a. **Distinguish between** transactions that do and do not affect the income statement.

You will be able to determine these and other facts about an entity when you strate mastery of Performance Objective 7, which you first encountered in Ch

YOUR PERFORMANCE OBJECTIVE 7

a. **Define** the terms *financing activities, investing activities,* and *operating acti*
b. **Classify** any accounting transaction into one of these activities or a noncas vesting and financing activity.
c. **Classify** any cash receipt or cash payment transaction into the appropriate ity as reported in the statement of cash flows.

Cards & Memorabilia Unlimited's Statement of Cash Flows

CARDS & MEMORABILIA UNLIMITED

You saw CMU's first statement of cash flows in Figure 2-8, which reported fects of Transactions A_1 through D for January 1 to January 6. Now let's c that statement with Figure 3-9, which reports the statement of cash flows for first year of business. Although Figure 3-9 represents the effect of all of Susan

Critical Thinking Problem

P3-1 Applying the Definitions of Asset, Liability, and Full Disclosure to Financial Reporting

YOUR PERFORMANCE OBJECTIVE 4 *(page 22)*

In this chapter, you read about the concept of *full disclosure* as it applied to reporting significant noncash transactions in the statement of cash flows. This concept has also influenced reporting requirements for another type of transaction, capital leases. Historically, companies leasing assets would simply report the cost of the lease payments each year as rent expense on the income statement. Over the past twenty-five years, the accounting profession has wrestled with how to properly account for the financial statement effects of leases. Currently, companies must report leases meeting certain criteria as both an asset and a liability. For example, if a company leases equipment and has the option to purchase the property at a price significantly below market value (a bargain purchase option) at the end of five years, the equipment must be recorded and classified as a property, plant, and equipment asset on the balance sheet. The company must also record a lease liability on its balance sheet. Although the company doesn't own the asset at the start of the lease, the asset is recorded and depreciated over its useful life.

a. Refer to the definitions provided for assets and liabilities in this chapter, and explain why

Financial Accounting: A New Perspective has pedagogy that reinforces the author's proven approach to teaching this course. The following pages describe how students can use this pedagogy to master text and course material.

HOW SHOULD CARDS & MEMORABILIA UNLIMITED PRESENT ITS FINANCIAL REPORTS?

Susan is facing an important decision—one every business owner must face. Precisely what information, how much detail, and what format should she use to communicate CMU's financial results to its various users? This is a difficult decision for Susan, who, as a new owner, has never before issued financial reports. When Susan asks George Wu for help, he suggests she educate herself about the types of financial information many businesses prepare annually. He remarks that although her business is a sole proprietorship, she might learn a lot by looking at the wide variety of information presented by corporations in what are called annual reports.

An **annual report** is a major product of the financial accounting system of a company. Its primary purpose is to communicate information about the company's financial condition and its results of operations to current and prospective investors. The annual report accomplishes this purpose like any other successful communication—by keeping the needs of its audience in mind. Thus, it reports the achievements and the financial activities of the company for the last year, as well as other information likely to be of interest to current and prospective investors. Annual reports come in many shapes and sizes; some are very colorful, some are not. But an examination of a variety of annual reports shows that almost all of them are divided into two parts that contain roughly the same content.

The first part of an annual report usually provides general information about the company and its performance. It often engages its audience by including summaries, photographs, charts and graphs, letters or messages from particular company officials, and descriptions about the company's products or activities. Almost all annual rep contain a letter to the stockholders from the president or the chief executive of (CEO), showcasing positive results and attempting to foster confidence among cu and prospective investors.

The second part of the annual report contains what is usually referred to as "financials"—the heart of the annual report. The specific contents of the financials usually the following items:

- **Management's Discussion and Analysis of Operations,** commonly called t **MD&A**—The annual report is a chance for the people who manage the comp to show the results of their business decisions. Thus, the MD&A section gives these managers a chance to showcase their successes and explain their failu
- **The Financial Statements**—The *balance sheet, income statement, statemen shareholders' equity,*[1] and *statement of cash flows* are the four financial statements you will learn about in this book. They are prepared by the company's counting staff to help create a complete picture of how the company has perf financially.
- **The Notes to the Financial Statements**—These serve the same purpose that footnotes do in a report. They document, support, or elaborate on specific items within the financial statements; they are prepared by the company's accounting staff.

[1] The term "shareholders' equity" is used in the annual report because the entity described is usually a corporation. But the term "owners' equity" will often be used in this book because it is a generic term applicable to all entities.

(continued on next page)

USER FOCUS **How Annual Reports Can Help You Get a Job**

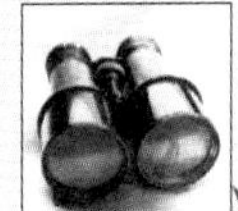

Suppose you are preparing for a job interview, and you want to learn as much as you can about the company so you can impress your interviewer. What information do you need, and where can you find it? A seldom used but excellent resource is a company's annual report. Although its primary audience is current and prospective investors, the annual report will help you because it is loaded with information that you can use for your interview.

The annual report is also a way to view the inner workings of the company. Eileen Ast has headed many annual report teams for large corporations, such as Harper/Collins and Conde Nast Publications. She advises that you do all you can to learn how to read and interpret annual reports. "An annual report is one sure vehicle you can use to gain a complete financial picture of a company. If you know how to read and interpret the financials, you can figure out exactly where a company is going. You can spot the problem areas." Other advice is offered by Bob Hill, a professional writer who works on the annual report for Easel Corporation, which publishes object-oriented design software tools. Bob says the savvy readers of annual reports go straight to the financials, and he ad-

Advantages of Using an Aging Schedule INSIGHT

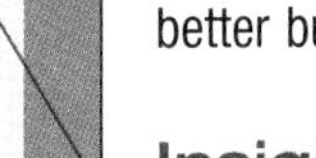

In estimating bad debts as a percentage of unpaid receivables, some businesses use a more detailed analysis called an *accounts receivable aging schedule.* An **aging schedule** divides a company's existing receivable balance into categories based on how long individual receivables have been unpaid. It is quite likely that you have seen such an aging schedule if you have ever received a medical bill. Such bills anticipate longer collection periods due to the time it often takes health insurance to pay its portion of the amount due.

The general premise underlying any aging schedule is that the probability that an unpaid receivable will never be collected increases with the length of time it has been outstanding. Thus, as shown below for our earlier $6,000 receivable balance, higher uncollectible percentages are assigned to those customer balances that have been outstanding for lengthier periods.

		Amount	×	Uncollectible Percentage	=	Estimated Uncollectible
Current	(0–30 days)	$4,400		.05		$220

Running Business Case

Cards & Memorabilia Unlimited (CMU) is a realistic case designed to help students gradually increase their understanding of financial accounting. By integrating the case *throughout* the book, students encounter key accounting concepts as they occur in the real world.

- Chapter opening text describes CMU events that will trigger the need for the accounting tools introduced in that particular chapter.
- After Chapter 1, the CMU icon appears throughout the text's margins to signal when the case is again being used.

User Focus

This feature helps students focus on the effective use of accounting information. Each User Focus explains how particular accounting information is relevant to students and how it can be used to make better business decisions.

Insight

This feature helps students gain further insight into important concepts.

Successful Learning
starts with a clear perspective

End of Chapter Material

Summary with Key Terms is an end of chapter narrative that includes all key terms introduced in that chapter, presented in the context of the chapter concepts. Numbers in parentheses following each key term cite the page number on which the term is first defined.

Making Business Decisions pose a variety of business challenges to demonstrate how students can use what they learn in the chapter to help make better business decisions.

Summary with Key Terms

The number in parentheses following each **key term** is the page number on which the term is defined.

In this chapter, you learned about the role the **annual report** (87) plays in communicating useful information about publicly traded companies. The financial information within an annual report is usually found in these sections: **Management's Discussion and Analysis (MD&A)** (87), the **Financial Statements** (87), the **Notes to the Financial Statements** (87), the **Report of Management (Management's Financial Responsibility)** (88), and the **Independent Auditors' Report** (88). The objective of the **auditing** (88) profession is to assure users that such information is fairly presented. Although an annual report is often used to communicate information about a corporation, it seldom communicates information about a sole proprietorship.

Although noncorporate entities rarely issue an annual report, almost every **entity** (90) is required to prepare financial statements guided by the principle of **full disclosure** (97). The first financial statement described is known as the statement of financial condition/position or balance sheet. A balance sheet is prepared at a point in time and includes three elements: **assets** (92), **liabilities** (93), and **owner's equity** (94). Some assets are related to liabilities. For example, a seller's **accounts receivable** (93) represents an **account payable** (93) to the customer. When a liability is created, **leverage** (94) describes the company's relative indebtedness. Owner's equity, or net worth as it is called in a personal balance sheet, is composed of the **owner's contribution** (94) and **retained earnings** (94) from profitable operations. Another synonym for owner's equity is net assets.

The **income statement** (95) reports the results of operations for a period of time and is composed of two elements: **revenue** (96) and **expense** (98). **Net income** (96), the difference between these two elements, is a measure of one's return on investment. Although most income statements report past revenues and expenses, you can also prepare a future-oriented income statement or **projected income statement** (96) sometimes called an operating budget. The linkage that exists between the balance sheet and the income statement is one example of how financial statements are related.

Making Business Decisions

YOUR PERFORMANCE OBJECTIVE 2
(page 18)

Jay Azuma, one of your close college friends, has started a new business, VideoValor—a video game company dedicated to nonviolent but very stimulating and challenging games. He has three products on the market, and his revenues are approaching two hundred thousand dollars after only one year in business. He also has one store from which he sells his products.

Last week, Jay called to ask if you might be interested in investing in his company. You do have $5,000 you could invest, so you tell him you need more information. Jay sends you some materials about VideoValor, including a set of financial statements.

In groups or on your own, as your instructor directs you, write a one-page document explaining in detail why (solely on the basis of the financial statements) you would or would not invest in VideoValor.

To help you make this decision, first answer the ten questions on pages 118–119 about the financial statements of VideoValor. For each response, describe in which financial statement you found the information and where.

VIDEOVALOR COMPANY
Income Statement
For the Year Ended January 31

Revenues:		
Sales revenue		$171,700
Expenses:		
Cost of goods sold	$59,620	
Rent expense	30,200	
Salaries expense	26,580	
Depreciation expense	12,400	
Delivery expense	7,450	
Miscellaneous expense	6,470	
Store supplies expense	2,220	
Interest expense	2,180	147,120
Net Income		$ 24,580

Questions

YOUR PERFORMANCE OBJECTIVE 4
(page 22)

3-1 Explain in your own words the meaning of key business terms.
a. Annual report
b. Liabilities
c. Leverage
d. Owner's equity
e. Net worth
f. Owner's contribution
g. Retained earnings
h. Income statement
i. Financial statement relationships
j. Statement of contributed capital
k. Statement of retained earnings
l. Dividends declared
m. Statement of cash flows
n. Interim reporting
o. Securities
p. Securities and Exchange Commission

3-2 What is contained in the section of an annual report known as the "financials"?

3-3 In an annual report, how does the Management's Discussion and Analysis (MD&A) section differ from the Notes to the Financial Statements section?

Reinforcement Exercises

YOUR PERFORMANCE OBJECTIVE 4
(page 22)

E3-1 Asking the Right Questions: A Group Activity
It's often said that knowing the right answer is not nearly as important as asking the right question. Asking the right question is a problem-solving skill that will help you make sound business decisions. In this exercise, you will review the vocabulary introduced in Chapter 3 by creating questions to match answers—similar to a popular TV show.

Required

a. Given an answer, what's the question?
Choose *three* of the following terms to serve as an answer. Create an appropriate question for each term. For example, if you choose the term *balance sheet*, you might create the question—*What financial statement shows the assets, liabilities, and owners' equity of an entity on a specific date?*

Full disclosure	Account payable	Revenue
Statement of cash flows	Retained earnings	Auditing
Account receivable	Contributed capital	Annual report
Dividends declared	Expense	Owners' equity

b. Are you sure that's the question?
Have each group member of your group read aloud the questions they developed in Requirement (a). As a group, decide whether each question is an accurate match for each answer. Once satisfied that all questions are appropriate, the group, as a whole, chooses the three best questions created within the group. Record the three questions chosen (with their answers) on separate pieces of paper or index cards and give them to your instructor.

Critical Thinking Problems

YOUR PERFORMANCE OBJECTIVE 4
(page 22)

P3-1 Applying the Definitions of Asset, Liability, and Full Disclosure to Financial Reporting
In this chapter, you read about the concept of *full disclosure* as it applied to reporting significant noncash transactions in the statement of cash flows. This concept has also influenced reporting requirements for another type of transaction, capital leases. Historically, companies leasing assets would simply report the cost of the lease payments each year as rent expense on the income statement. Over the past twenty-five years, the accounting profession has wrestled with how to properly account for the financial statement effects of leases. Currently, companies must report leases meeting certain criteria as both an asset and a liability. For example, if a company leases equipment and has the option to purchase the property at a price significantly below market value (a bargain purchase option) at the end of five years, the equipment must be recorded and classified as a property, plant, and equipment asset on the balance sheet. The company must also record a lease liability on its balance sheet. Although the company doesn't own the asset at the start of the lease, the asset is recorded and depreciated over its useful life.

a. Refer to the definitions provided for assets and liabilities in this chapter, and explain why you believe this method of reporting a leased asset and liability is appropriate.
b. Using the concept of *full disclosure*, explain why this method of reporting a leased asset and a liability is preferable to the older method of simply recording lease payments as an expense.

YOUR PERFORMANCE OBJECTIVE 5a
(page 57)

P3-2 Transaction Analysis
Seinfeld Company, a sole proprietorship, began business in January. Show the effect of each of the following transactions on the company's assets, liabilities, and owner's equity using a table similar to the following. The complete analysis of Transaction (a) is included as an example of a correct solution.

Questions are a short-answer testing vehicle and require content recall.

Reinforcement Exercises reinforce the concepts presented and examples used in the chapter. For easy reference, each exercise has a title, which identifies what it tests, and an associated Performance Objective.

Critical Thinking Problems are also individually titled and keyed to the Performance Objectives. They are more comprehensive in scope than the Reinforcement Exercises, requiring students to integrate concepts and skills.

Excel Spreadsheet Assignments extend specific problems and are located on the text Online Learning Center at www.mhhe.com/solomon. An Excel icon appears next to those problems that have corresponding spreadsheet assignments.

Research Assignments are referenced last in the end-of-chapter material. These assignments direct students to collect and use information outside the book—from the Internet, newspapers, periodicals, local businesses, friends, and colleagues. The actual assignments are found on the text's Online Learning Center at www.mhhe.com/solomon.

A New Perspective

Most students taking financial accounting today never knew a time when computers weren't commonplace. McGraw-Hill/Irwin has created technology tools that take advantage of this familiarity, using the Internet and multimedia to provide interactive assistance for the most challenging portions of the financial accounting course.

NetTutor™

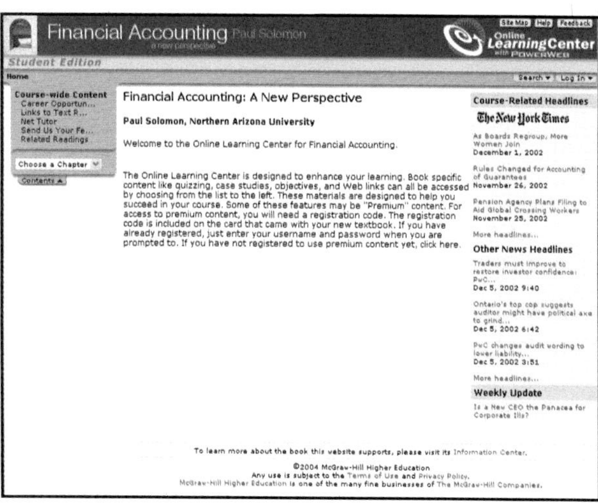

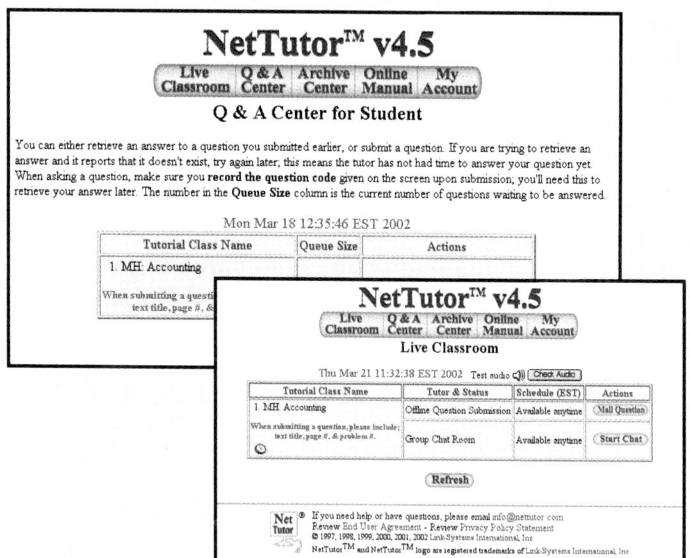

Online Learning Center

www.mhhe.com/solomon For instructors, the book's Online learning center contains the Instructor's Resource Guide, Solutions Manual, PowerPoint slides, Excel templates and solutions, Research Assignments, Sample Final Exam and solutions, and links to professional resources.

The student section of the site features all of the Performance Objectives and the Key Term definitions by chapter, a sample Study Guide Chapter, flashcards, PowerPoint slides, interactive quizzes and exercises, Excel template exercises, Research Assignments, and a Sample Final Exam.

In addition, students and instructors alike will appreciate the Online Learning Center's links to many of McGraw-Hill's most popular online technologies, including PageOut, NetTutor, and ALEKS.

NetTutor

Net Tutor is a breakthrough program that allows one-on-one assistance completely online. Qualified accounting tutors equipped with a copy of **Financial Accounting** work online with your students on specific problems or concepts from their text.

The **Live Tutor Center** via NetTutor's WWWhiteboard enables a tutor to hold an interactive, on-line tutorial session with a student or several students. The **Q&A Center** allows students to submit questions at any time and retrieve answers within 24 hours. Finally, the **Archive Center** allows students to browse for answers to previously asked questions. They can also search for questions pertinent to a particular topic, and can ask a follow-up question if they encounter an answer they do not understand.

Preface on Technology

ALEKS®

ALEKS® Math Prep for Accounting

Math Prep for Accounting provides coverage of the basic math skills needed to succeed in introductory financial accounting, including basic arithmetic, fractions, decimals, percents, and simple algebra concepts. Refreshing and improving these skills helps students perform better throughout the course.

For more information, visit the ALEKS website at www.business.aleks.com.

Online Course Management

No matter which online course solution you choose, you can count on the highest level of service. Our specialists offer free training and answer any question you have through the life of your adoption.

Instructor Advantage is a special level of service McGraw-Hill offers in conjunction with WebCT and Blackboard. A team of platform specialists is always available, either by toll-free phone or e-mail, to ensure everything runs smoothly. Instructor Advantage is available free to all McGraw-Hill customers.

Instructor Advantage Plus guarantees you a full day of on-site training by a Blackboard or WebCT specialist, for yourself and up to nine colleagues. Thereafter, you will enjoy the benefits of unlimited telephone and e-mail support throughout the life of your adoption. *Instructor Advantage* Plus is available to qualifying McGraw-Hill adopters (see your McGraw-Hill/Irwin representative for details).

Knowledge Gateway

Knowledge Gateway

Developed with the help of our partner Eduprise, the McGraw-Hill Knowledge Gateway is an all-purpose service and resource center for instructors teaching online. While training programs from WebCT and Blackboard will help teach you their software, only McGraw-Hill has services to help you actually *manage and teach* your online course, as well as run and maintain the software. To see how these platforms can assist your online course, visit www.mhhe.com/solutions.

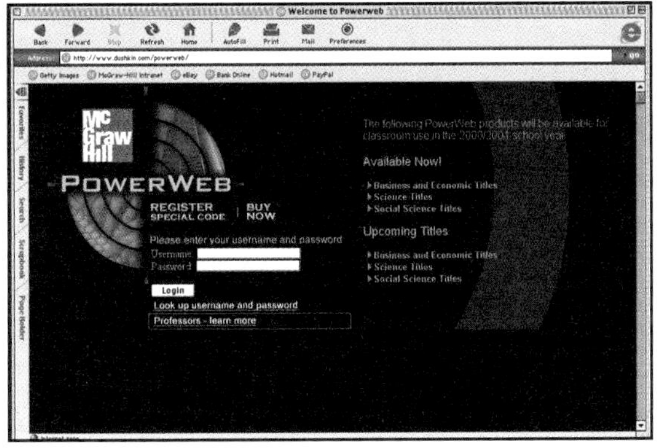

PowerWeb

Keeping your course current can be a job in itself, and now McGraw-Hill helps do that job for you. PowerWeb extends the learning experience beyond the core textbook by offering all of the latest news and developments pertinent to financial accounting, without the clutter and dead links of a typical online search.

PowerWeb offers timely articles and links culled by a real-world expert in financial accounting. PowerWeb users can also take advantage of self-grading quizzes, interactive glossaries and exercises, and study tips.

Visit the PowerWeb site at www.dushkin.com/powerweb to see firsthand what PowerWeb can mean to your course.

Supplements

INSTRUCTOR SUPPLEMENTS

Instructor's Resource Guide
(0072840374)
This teaching tool includes the following resources for each chapter: integrated performance objectives, a list of key terms, research assignments, and case study. It also suggests ways to use the text without teaching debits/credits.

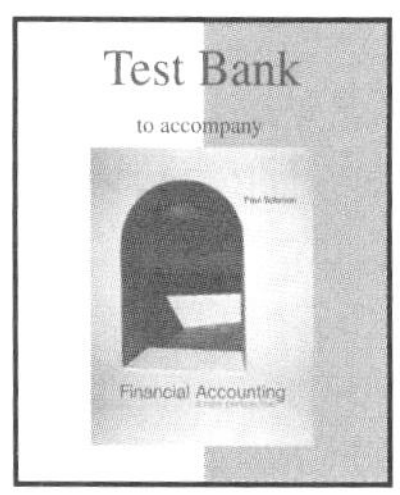

Test Bank
(0072840382)
A collection of true/false, matching, multiple choice, essay questions, and critical thinking problems to accompany every chapter in the text.

Solutions Transparencies
(0072840390)
The font used in the solutions acetates is large enough for the back row of any lecture hall. Masters of these transparencies are available in the Solutions Manual.

Solutions Manual
(0072840366)
This manual contains completely worked-out solutions to the text End of Chapter material. Each chapter begins with a content analysis, which outlines the difficulty level of each exercise or problem, approximates the length of time it will take to complete, and details to which Performance Objective it corresponds.

Instructor's Presentation CD-ROM
(0072840404)
This includes electronic versions of the Resource Guide, Solutions Manual, and Test Bank, Computerized Test Bank, as well as PowerPoint presentations and Excel problems and solutions.

Diploma Computerized Test Bank
(available on the Instructor's Presentation CD-ROM)
The text test bank is delivered in the latest version of Diploma, from Brownstone. It can be used to make different versions of the same test, change the answer order, edit and add questions, and conduct online testing. Technical support for this software is available at (800) 331-5094.

STUDENT SUPPLEMENTS

Study Guide
(0072840358)
This proactive learning tool is designed around the chapter performance objectives, giving students a deeper understanding of the course material while reinforcing what they are learning in the main text. It provides comprehensive reflective chapter overviews that require students to actively respond to chapter material. Additionally, it provides visual activities to synthesize key ideas, as well as traditional problem solving and reinforcement exercises.

Check Figures
Available online at www.mhhe.com/solomon, these provide key answers for selected problems.

PowerPoint Presentations Available online at www.mhhe.com/solomon, a complete set of slides covers many of the key concepts presented in each chapter.

Acknowledgements

Feedback and comments from accounting faculty colleagues are invaluable resources when developing and producing a first edition text. Dr. Solomon would like to acknowledge and thank the following people for their assistance with ***Financial Accounting: A New Perspective:***

Dennis Baker, California State University–Fresno
Suzanne Busch, California State University–Hayward
Carol Klinger, Cuny Queens College
Mallory McWilliams, San Jose State University
Dawn Massey, Fairfield University
Mary Maury, St. John's University
Debra Prendergast, Northwestern Business College
Kathy Otero, University of Texas–El Paso
Marilyn Okleshen, Minnesota State University–Mankato
Rebekah Sheely, Emporia State University
Joanne Sheridan, Montana State University–Billings
Tracy Smith, University of Memphis
Coleen Troutman, Bradley University
Joan Van Hise, Fairfield University
Suzanne Ward, University of Louisiana–Lafayette
Allan Young, DeVry University–Atlanta
Rodney Alsup, Kennesaw State University
Sandra Pelfrey – Oakland University
Kathleen Simons, Bryant College
Dean Crawford, SUNY College at Oswego
Bruce Cassel, Dutchess Community College
Betty McMechen, Mesa State College
Susan Kattelus, Eastern Michigan University
Peter Huey, Collin County Community College
Charles Stahl III, Madonna University

Dr. Solomon would also like to thank the following people for their contribution to his text:

Ken LeDeit, Silicon Valley Bank
Mary Mathews Stephans
Randall Ramian, Well Fargo Bank
Ed Whitford, Dee and Ed's Collectibles
Louis Jean Louis, Sportcard Mania
Charles Vincent, General Accounting Office
San Jose SCORE Office
Robert Knox, California Society of CPAs
Joseph Mori, San Jose State University
Charles Purdy, University of Minnesota
Urton Anderson, University of Texas-Austin
Glen Berryman, University of Minnesota

In addition, Dr. Solomon would like to express his utmost gratitude to the following individuals who helped shape, critique, and greatly add to the overall text presentation and supplements package:

Janet Cassagio, Nassau Community College
Jane Wiese, Valencia Community College
Patrick Reihing, Nassau Community College
Jayne Maas, Loyola College in Maryland
Gail B. Wright, Bryant College
Alice Sineath, Forsyth Technical Community College
Jason Fink, Indiana University
Jack Terry, ComSource, Inc.
Elizabeth Morgan
Beth Woods

And finally, Dr. Solomon is grateful for the outstanding support from the McGraw-Hill/Irwin book team. In particular, he would like to thank Brent Gordon, Publisher; Steve DeLancey, Sr. Sponsoring Editor; Kelly Odom, Developmental Editor; Katherine Mattison, Marketing Manager; Kimberly Hooker, Sr. Project Manager; Gina Hangos, Production Supervisor; Pam Verros, Lead Designer; Erwin Llereza, Senior Advertising Designer; Dan Wiencek, Advertising Copywriter; Becky Szura, Lead Supplements Producer; Jennifer Blankenship, Photo Researcher; and Jeremy Cheshareck, Photo Research Coordinator.

BRIEF CONTENTS

* Appendix 13–1 and Appendix 13–2 are available on the book's Online Learning Center, www.mhhe.com/solomon.

CONTENTS

CHAPTER 9

The Accounting Process: Manual and Computerized Systems 376

CHAPTER 10

Comparing Financial Statements by Entity and Industry 460

*Appendix 13–1 is available on the book's Online Learning Center, www.mhhe.com/solomon.

* Appendix 13–2 is available on the book's Online Learning Center, www.mhhe.com/solomon.

Financial Accounting

CHAPTER ONE

1

Introduction to a Business

Cards & Memorabilia Unlimited

PERFORMANCE OBJECTIVES

In this chapter, you will learn the following new Performance Objectives:

PO1 **Prepare** a simple operating budget and **explain** its usefulness.

PO2 **Identify** several ways in which accounting information is used to make business and personal decisions.

PO3 **Calculate** the return on equity ratio and **discuss** its usefulness and limitations in making decisions.

PO4 **Explain** in your own words the meaning of key business terms.

STARTING A NEW BUSINESS

Susan Newman was surfing the net, reading the day's news on her favorite news provider. As she skimmed the headlines, the title of an article caught her eye—*Do You Love Your Work?* She clicked the link and what she read excited her. For weeks Susan had been thinking about starting her own business—a trading card and sports memorabilia store. After reading this article, she had the encouragement she needed. She would turn what she loved into her work.

Susan's parents questioned her decision. After all, she had graduated from college over three years ago with a business marketing degree. She had landed a good job at Spacebar Software and was making good money. She'd been promoted to customer service manager after only two years. Her parents wondered why Susan would want to give up a secure, well-paying job; but as she described the shortcomings of her present job, they began to understand.

Susan explained that at Spacebar she seldom used the knowledge and skills she acquired at college. Further, she wanted to work with people. Her work environment was comfortable, but her promotion hadn't helped her all that much. She now made a little more money, but she interacted with customers less and was buried at a desk filling out reports.

The Web article excited her; it told her to identify what she really loved to do and then find a job that allowed her to do it. Susan had done just the opposite when she graduated. She chose a job to please her parents and impress her friends, rather than a job she really enjoyed. She loved collecting trading cards and sports memorabilia when she was growing up. Now as an adult, she would be able to integrate her childhood passion into how she made her living.

Microsoft Windows Update - Microsoft Internet Explorer

File Edit View Go Favorites Help

Back Forward Stop Refresh Home Search Favorites History Channels Fullscreen Mail Print

Address http://clinews.com

CLINEWS.COM

Trends in Business

Home
U.S.
World
Business
Weather
Women
Science
Technology
Health
Livestyles

Do You Love Your Work?

Do you begin your day excited about what awaits you at work? Do you love what you do for 40, 50, or more hours a week? If your answer is yes, you may be one of thousands of Americans who increasingly find happiness and fulfillment when they make their hobbies, their interests, or their passions their work. "I knew I had to make a change, but feared I'd just go from one unhappy job to another. When my great aunt died and left me

Done Internet zone

Start Microsoft Windows U...

Susan knew that trading cards and sports memorabilia were not just for kids any more. Rookie cards, autographed balls and uniforms were big business. Then there was the emergence of the nonsport card—cards for TV programs, infamous criminals, historical figures and events, and even cards for movies. The trading card and memorabilia industry had grown in interesting and exciting ways, and Susan could now be part of it (Figure 1-1).

(continued on next page)

(continued from previous page)

FIGURE 1-1

The latest development in this industry is the increasing popularity of sports memorabilia

Throughout this book, you will follow Susan Newman as she uses accounting to help her plan, open, operate, and expand her small business, Cards & Memorabilia Unlimited (CMU). Carefully read and understand the details of this case; it will help you learn not only about accounting but also about business. In other words, the case provides you with a real world context to which you can relate the accounting concepts presented in this textbook. The case reinforces the basic reason you are required to take this course—not to learn accounting as an end in itself but to develop the skills you will need for your career in business. In short, the case is a feature that will help you achieve success in this course. The CMU logo, shown here, will appear throughout this book whenever the case is used to reinforce accounting concepts. Since this chapter is entirely devoted to CMU, the logo will next appear in Chapter 2.

Planning a New Business

Although she was eager to start her new business, Susan decided to continue working at Spacebar until the end of the year. She would use November and December to write her business plan (see the *User Focus* later in this chapter and *Appendix 1–1*) and to make the necessary arrangements so that she could open for business in January of the coming year. Susan realized that before opening her business, she must do such things as research the industry, decide on a marketing strategy, secure a place to conduct business, and choose a form of business.

Researching the Industry

Susan began her research by speaking to both card manufacturers and card wholesalers as well as local card store owners who would talk to her about their business practices. In addition, she surfed the net for many hours to find as much information about the trading card and sports memorabilia industry as she could.

Choosing a Marketing Strategy

From her college marketing course, Susan knew that her marketing strategy should address four factors, commonly called the 4 P's[1]:

1. *Product* a good, service, or idea to meet consumers' needs.
2. *Price* what is paid for the product.
3. *Promotion* a means of communication between seller and buyer.
4. *Place* a means of getting the product into consumers' hands.

Susan had decided what her product would be, and she knew that the prices were somewhat established by trading card and sports memorabilia price guides. She wanted to keep her first year promotion costs low, so she decided to have posters printed. She also decided to contact reporters at three local newspapers to convince them to write feature or special interest stories about trading cards and sports memorabilia in general, and about her new business in particular. Before she tackled the last P, place, she decided to identify her consumers, select a company name, and find inventory suppliers.

Selecting a Target Market Susan knew that if she focused her sales and marketing efforts on the needs of a specific group of potential consumers, her *target market*, she could increase the chances that her business would succeed. While doing her research, she discovered that people who buy trading cards and sports memorabilia fall into two groups—collectors and investors.

Collectors are both adults and children who buy trading cards and sports memorabilia as a hobby. They buy cards for their favorite sport, favorite TV shows, or other interests (Figure 1-2). Typically, collectors enjoy building a collection of items they like, regardless of the monetary value.

Investors, on the other hand, are usually adults who buy not as a hobby but as a way to make money. They regularly consult price guides and buy only those items that they expect will increase in value. For example, Susan discovered that some investors who bought rookie baseball cards (cards of first-year, major league players) made more money than if they had invested the same amount of money in corporate bonds, common stocks, coins, or gold and silver during the same five-year period.

Susan had not collected cards for several years, and so she realized that she did not yet know enough to succeed with the investor type consumer. But she did feel confident that she could communicate her love of collecting. Thus, she decided initially to target the same type of consumer she had been—the collector or hobbyist. As she gained more experience, she would broaden her market to investors.

Naming the Business While doing her research, Susan had heard a story about how a trading card store owner had named his business *The Collection Agency* and then received countless calls from companies interested in reducing their uncollectible customer accounts! She knew from this story and her college marketing courses that deciding what to name a business was very important. After some deliberation, she decided to name her business Cards & Memorabilia Unlimited, or CMU for short, because "Cards and Memorabilia" left little doubt about the product she sold, and "Unlimited" conveyed the message that she would have a more than plentiful inventory.

When Susan told her father the name she had chosen, he recommended that she register it. He explained that she should go to the county clerk's office to verify that no other business within the county had registered the name Cards & Memorabilia

[1] E. Jerome McCarthy and William D. Perreault, Jr., *Basic Marketing: A Managerial Approach, 14th edition* (New York: McGraw Hill, 2002).

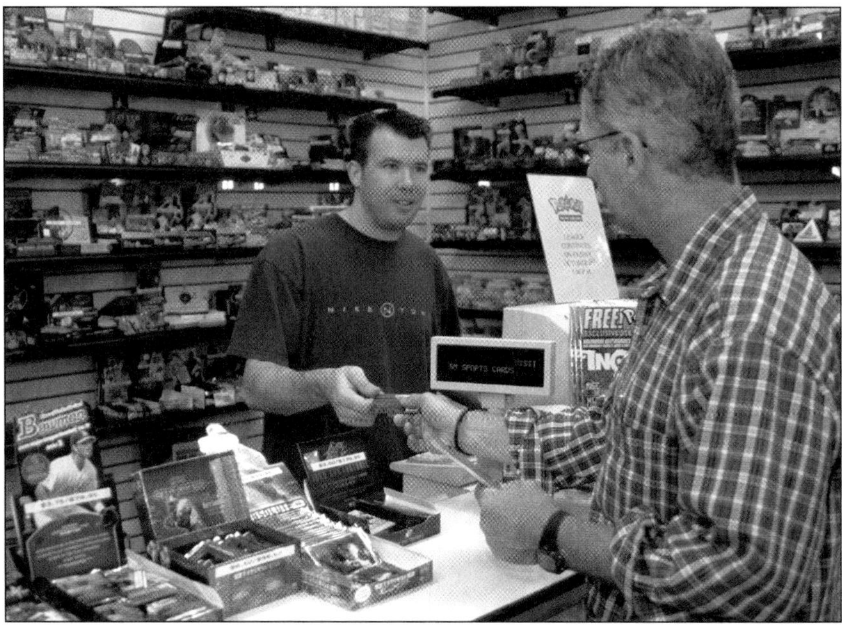

FIGURE 1-2

Trading card collectors often buy cards in shops such as this

Unlimited. When she went to register her company name, Susan learned that the procedure for registering a company name was not the same in all states.

Finding Suppliers While researching the trading card and sports memorabilia industry, Susan discovered that she could purchase her inventory of cards and memorabilia from four sources—manufacturers, wholesalers, retailers, and consumers (Figure 1-3).

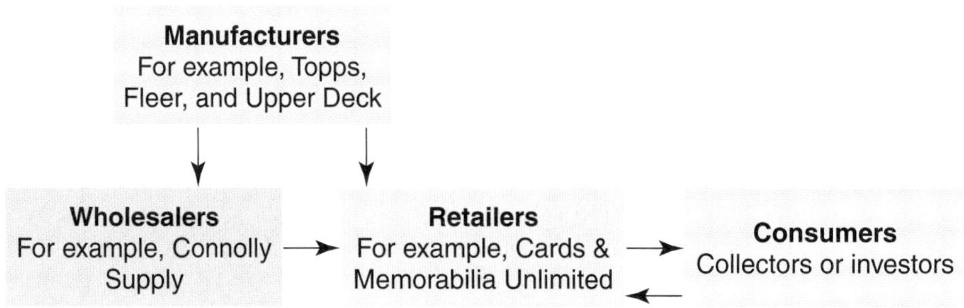

FIGURE 1-3

Trading card and sports memorabilia suppliers and how they distribute their product

Manufacturers, such as **Topps**, **Fleer**, and **Upper Deck**, sell their products at the lowest prices available. Susan wanted to be able to buy her inventory at these low prices, but she discovered that some manufacturers would not sell to her directly; to buy from those manufacturers directly, she must become a certified dealer. Susan decided that this option was fairly risky because acceptance as a certified dealer could take a long time and her application might be rejected. She concluded that she needed to have nonmanufacturer sources if she were to secure an immediate source of cards for her opening inventory.

Susan discovered that she could buy inventory from another type of supplier—a *wholesaler*—Connolly Supply. To avoid paying Connolly Supply sales tax on what she purchased, Susan had to prove CMU was a retail business that would charge sales tax to its customers. So she had to show Connolly Supply a *seller's permit*, also sometimes known as a *resale tax number*. To get this seller's permit, she applied to

FIGURE 1-4

A trading card and sports memorabilia show

a state government agency and submitted, among other items, personal financial information.

A third source of inventory is *retailers*, or *dealers*. Some retailers do not have stores and transact business with one another and with consumers at such places as weekend shows in hotels, flea markets, and other public gatherings (Figure 1-4). Other retailers have stores, such as Susan was planning to open, and/or websites (Figure 1-5). Susan decided that as soon as she established her retail operation, she would build a website to help sell her product.

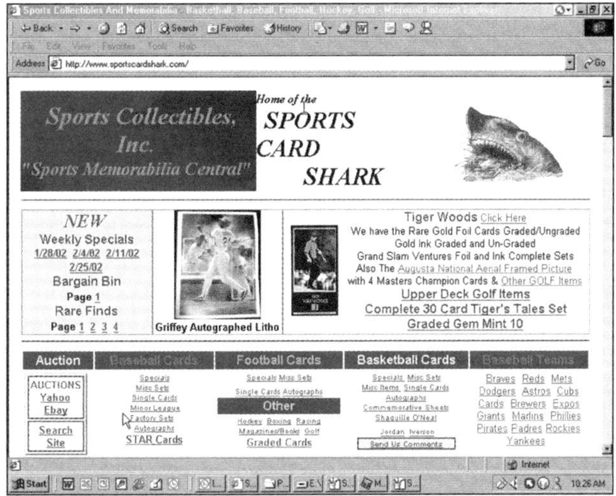

FIGURE 1-5

The homepage of Sports Collectibles, Inc., a card and memorabilia company that conducts business on the web

The fourth source of inventory, over-the-counter transactions between Susan and her consumers, was unavailable to her until she opened her store.

Thus, Susan decided to apply for certified dealer status with several of the major card and memorabilia manufacturers and, in the meantime, to purchase her opening inventory from Connolly Supply and from dealers selling via websites.

Securing a Place to Conduct Business

Susan could now turn her attention to the last of the four P's, place. Where should she locate her store? When she researched the locations of area trading card and sports memorabilia stores, she discovered a clear absence of stores in Rialto, a community 15 miles north of downtown Phoenix. Susan decided to locate her store in Rialto to capitalize on the absence of competition and its relatively high concentration of upper-middle class households.

In early November she had begun working with Mary Mathews, a commercial real estate agent, to find a retail space for CMU to rent. Susan decided she needed about 750 square feet of space to adequately display her inventory and provide comfortable seating for customers. After looking at several vacant properties with Mary, she found the location she wanted in late November; the rent was $1,000 a month. Mary assisted Susan in negotiating a lease. A **lease** is a contract calling for the **lessee**, or user of the property like Susan, to pay the **lessor**, or landlord or owner of the property, for the use of that property. Mary told Susan that the owner of the desired property needed assurance that Susan would be financially able to pay what she owed him, that is, monthly rent.

When Mary learned that Susan was applying for a bank loan the next day, she asked Susan to contact her as soon as the application process was completed. Mary explained that to complete the process of negotiating the lease, Susan would need to show the landlord some of the same financial statements that were submitted to the bank.

Choosing the Form of Business

As you will later learn in much greater detail, businesses are usually organized into one of three forms—a sole proprietorship, a partnership, or a corporation. A **sole proprietorship** is a business that is owned by only one person. A major advantage of this form of business is that it can be established rather easily. That is, the owner or *sole proprietor* often needs only a modest amount of cash and legal work to open his/her business. Although a sole proprietorship may employ more than one person, only the sole proprietor receives all income or losses and is liable for all business obligations. The proprietorship is the most popular form of business in the United States and often turns out to be the form of business initially used by such large and successful corporations as Wendy's and Ford Motor Company.

A **partnership** is a business owned by two or more persons. Partnerships are designed to attract more resources than sole proprietorships and have rules governing the relationships between co-owners, or *partners.* But the partnership and sole proprietorship have many similarities. For example, in both forms of business, the personal resources of the owner(s) are available to pay off business obligations. Likewise, both forms of business are very vulnerable to changes in ownership. That is, each is dissolved whenever the sole proprietor or a partner leaves or dies.

A **corporation** is a business owned by persons or organizations who have purchased what are called *shares of stock.* Unlike the sole proprietorship and the partnership, the corporation is legally separate from its owners, or *shareholders.* When these ownership interests or shares of stock are widely available to all investors through an organized stock exchange, they are said to be *publicly traded.* The greatest advantage of this form of business is a feature called limited liability. Essentially, **limited liability** refers to the right of shareholders to not be held personally liable for the obligations of the business, unlike owner(s) in the other forms of business. This and other features explain why the corporate form is preferred by most large U.S. businesses. As you will learn later, corporations can take many forms, including the closely held corporation and the limited liability corporation (LLC).

Susan is willing to accept personal liability for her business obligations, has enough resources to open her business, has no interested co-owners or employees, and does not want to deal with the legal complications and higher costs associated with a corporation. Thus, she decides to establish CMU as a sole proprietorship.

Financing a New Business

Susan must still make some important decisions. She must decide how much inventory to purchase and how much money she will need to furnish her store and to pay her rent and other recurring costs. These and other similar decisions are often referred to as *financing* decisions.

So Susan must determine how much money she needs to open and operate her business during the first year, and then she must find a source or sources to provide her the money. Before reading further, try to estimate how much money you think Susan needs to start her business, and then think about how a person in Susan's position might reasonably obtain this money.

Determining the Amount

Susan knew that **financing**, or obtaining money from outside the business, is one of the fundamental activities necessary for every business, but how much money did she need?

Her visits to over two dozen stores revealed that almost all of them were small and poorly decorated. Despite the higher costs, Susan decided to clearly differentiate her store from her competitors. Her reasoning was that a clean, tastefully decorated store would not only attract more customers but also encourage them to stay longer to pursue their hobby.

After pricing large screen TV's (to attract sports card and memorabilia collectors), cash registers, fax machines, copiers, and furniture, such as glass display cases, shelving, and tables and chairs, Susan realized that she needed at least $10,000. Moreover, to attract her target customers, she'd need a substantial inventory, which she estimated would cost somewhere between $12,500 and $15,500. Finally, Susan needed money for the first month's rent (estimated to be between $1,000 and $1,200) and rent-related expenses, such as utilities, janitorial, and so on. Mary Mathews, Susan's commercial real estate agent, told her to expect the monthly rent-related expenses to run between $0.25 to $0.35 a square foot. Therefore, these rental costs totaled somewhere between $1,188 [$1,000 + (750 square feet × $0.25)] and $1,463 [$1,200 + (750 square feet × $0.35)].

Figure 1-6 shows Susan's summary of all these costs. After studying her summary, Susan was tempted to conserve cash and try to get by with her high-end estimate. But what if she had underestimated costs? She knew she needed a margin of safety. As a result, she decided to initially seek financing of $30,000.

Item	Low Estimate	High Estimate
Office equipment	$10,000	$10,000
Card inventory	12,500	15,500
Rental costs	1,188	1,463
	$23,688	$26,963

FIGURE 1-6

Susan's estimate of her initial investment

Securing the Amount

Now that Susan knew approximately what amount of money she needed to finance her business, she began to consider how she might obtain money to invest in and operate her business. She was able to find three sources of financing for her business: her personal savings, some money from her uncle, and a bank loan.

Personal Savings Since graduating from college, Susan had saved over $14,000 by living with her parents. She had also raised $3,000 by selling some of her personal baseball card collection. Thus, Susan had a balance of about $17,000 in her savings account.

Money from Uncle When Susan's uncle learned of her plans, he offered her $15,000. He had no children of his own and explained that Susan had been like a daughter to him. He told her to forget about paying him back. Susan gratefully accepted her uncle's offer, but insisted that once her business was well-established, she wanted to pay him back.

Recall that Susan had estimated that she needed about $30,000 for her initial investment. With $32,000 available from her personal savings ($17,000) and her uncle ($15,000), Susan had achieved a margin of safety and decided to invest a total of $30,000 in her business at the beginning of the new year and retain the remaining $2,000 for her personal needs.

Bank Loan Although Susan had raised money to meet her immediate cash needs, she was worried that she would not have enough cash to operate CMU for the first year. She knew that her initial investment might be gone by the end of January, giving little or no financial protection for the remainder of her first year of business. As a result, she decided to apply for a bank loan.

Applying for a Bank Loan

In early December, Susan visited Central Bank and met with Phillip Strauss, a loan officer. She showed him her business plan (*Appendix 1–1*) and said she'd like a *line of credit*, a loan to draw on as needed rather than a loan of a single lump sum. Phillip advised her to apply for the maximum amount for which she could qualify. His reasoning was that there was no penalty for not borrowing the maximum amount, and that if she ever wanted to expand her business, she would be forced to apply for additional financing when interest rates might be higher. Based on this advice, Susan decided to apply for a $50,000 line of credit, the maximum amount for which she could qualify.

Business versus Personal Loan Decision Phillip told Susan that it is difficult for new businesses to obtain business loans from banks. Susan's college degree and three years of employment, for example, were insufficient to qualify her for the loan. Instead, the bank's business loan application required Susan to provide financial statements for the last three years of her business operation, prove that she had had five years' work experience in the same industry as that of the business, and project her business earnings for the next three years.

When Phillip realized that Susan could provide only the last of these three documents, he recommended that she apply, instead, for a personal line of credit. He explained that such a loan did not require her to have an existing business or past work experience in the cards and memorabilia industry. He explained that she could use personal loan funds for her business as long as it was a sole proprietorship. So Susan decided to fill out a personal loan application. Phillip then asked for her preference—an 8% interest rate on the line of credit or a 7.5% interest rate with a $250 fee payable when the line of credit was approved. Susan chose the 8% rate because she didn't plan to access the credit line unless absolutely necessary and wanted to conserve her business cash whenever possible.

Personal Loan Information Requirements Susan had to provide three pieces of information to obtain her personal line of credit. First, she had to fill out a loan application form entitled *Personal Financial Statement*, which she recognized was actually called a **balance sheet** in her accounting courses. This form required her to list the amounts of both the items she *owned*, called **assets**, and the items she *owed*, called **liabilities**. It then required Susan to calculate the difference between the amounts owned and the amounts owed to determine her **net worth** or **owner's equity**. Study how Susan filled out the bank loan application representing her balance sheet (Figure 1-7).

FIGURE 1-7

Susan's personal balance sheet

CENTRAL BANK LOAN APPLICATION

PERSONAL FINANCIAL STATEMENT

PERSONAL PROFILE

NAME: Susan Newman		AGE: 26	SOCIAL SECURITY NUMBER: 593-70-0210
STREET ADDRESS: 901 Ginger Way	CITY: Rialto	STATE: AZ	ZIP: 85000
HOME PHONE: (602) 555-3001	☐ OWN ☐ RENT $ ____ PER MONTH ☒ OTHER live with parents	AT CURRENT ADDRESS SINCE (MM/YY): 05 / 78	
☐ MARRIED ☐ SEPARATED ☒ UNMARRIED	NUMBER OF DEPENDENTS: 0	AGES OF DEPENDENTS: N/A	YEARS WITH COMPANY: N/A
SPOUSE'S NAME: N/A	SPOUSE'S OCCUPATION: N/A	SPOUSE'S SOCIAL SECURITY NUMBER: N/A	
SPOUSE EMPLOYED BY: N/A	HOW LONG WITH EMPLOYER? (SPOUSE) YRS. MOS.: N/A	SPOUSE'S WORK PHONE: ( ) N/A	

BANKING RELATIONSHIPS (Please list only your personal accounts.)

NAME OF BANK	ACCOUNT NUMBER	PERSONAL CHECKING	PERSONAL SAVINGS	CURRENT BALANCE
Central Bank	0321-62221	✓		$ 1,500
Central Bank	0321-52701		✓	$17,000

FINANCIAL STATEMENT

ASSETS	AMOUNT	LIABILITIES	AMOUNT
CASH IN CENTRAL BANK	$18,500	TOTAL REVOLVING CREDIT	$500
CASH IN OTHER BANKS	0	TOTAL INSTALLMENT LOANS	0
RETIREMENT ACCOUNTS (IRA, SEP. KEOGH, 401-K)	0	1ST MORTGAGE ON RESIDENCE	N/A
STOCK / BONDS / MUTUAL FUNDS (INCLUDE COPY OF BROKER'S STATEMENTS)	0	OTHER MORTGAGES ON RESIDENCE	N/A
RESIDENCE MARKET VALUE	N/A	MORTGAGE(S) ON OTHER REAL ESTATE	N/A
OTHER REAL ESTATE MARKET VALUE	N/A	OTHER LIABILITIES (PLEASE DESCRIBE)	N/A
OTHER ASSETS (PLEASE DESCRIBE) Personal Auto	10,000	OTHER LIABILITIES (PLEASE DESCRIBE)	
OTHER ASSETS (PLEASE DESCRIBE)			
TOTAL ASSETS	$28,500	**TOTAL LIABILITIES**	$500

NET WORTH (TOTAL ASSETS MINUS TOTAL LIABILITIES) $ 28,000

DO YOU GUARANTEE ANY OTHER DEBT? YES ____ NO ✓ IF YES, WHAT IS THE TOTAL: $ N/A

WHO IS THE BORROWER? N/A

NAME OF FINANCIAL INSTITUTION N/A

Next, Phillip asked Susan to provide copies of her last two *federal income tax returns* to provide evidence of her earning power. Susan also gave Mary Mathews copies of her current balance sheet and tax returns to help secure the lease. Finally, Phillip asked Susan to prepare a document as soon as possible describing how she thought her business would do during its first year—what is often called an **operating budget**.

Gaining Bank Loan Approval

Phillip explained that the bank would approve the line of credit for which Susan had applied if she could provide convincing evidence of her ability to repay the line of credit amount. Unfortunately, it was more difficult for Susan to provide this evidence for CMU than it would have been for a more mature business. This is because a bank can seize amounts owed from customers and sell enough equipment and inventory to repay a full loan more easily for a mature business. Central Bank's policy, based on its experience with many businesses, indicated that recovering a large percentage of the full cost of either Susan's business equipment or inventory was unlikely. Thus, the bank needed additional protection.

Collateral When Susan heard how difficult it was for a bank to recover a loan from a failed new business, she better understood its hesitancy in making a loan to her without collateral. **Collateral** is defined as things of value that a borrower pledges to the bank in case the borrower is unable to repay the loan. That is, collateral represents the bank's protection against a borrower's failure to repay its loan.

Subordinated Liability Phillip asked Susan to list the items her new business would own that might serve as collateral for the line of credit. He calculated that the bank would recover a minimum of $15,000 from this collateral if her business failed (Figure 1-8). Then, he explained that the bank did not have a clear path to recovering this amount. Phillip realized that her uncle's money was not really a loan, but was concerned that, if her business started to fail, Susan might sell her collateral and use the money received to pay back her uncle. Therefore, Phillip asked if Susan's uncle would be willing to delay his right to repayment, that is, *subordinate* his right, until Susan first repaid the bank's loan. A **subordinated liability** is a debt whose right to repayment is waived or given up until another loan has been repaid. That is, it is a liability whose repayment is made secondary or subordinated to another liability. When Susan called her uncle, he agreed without hesitation to subordinate his right to repayment.

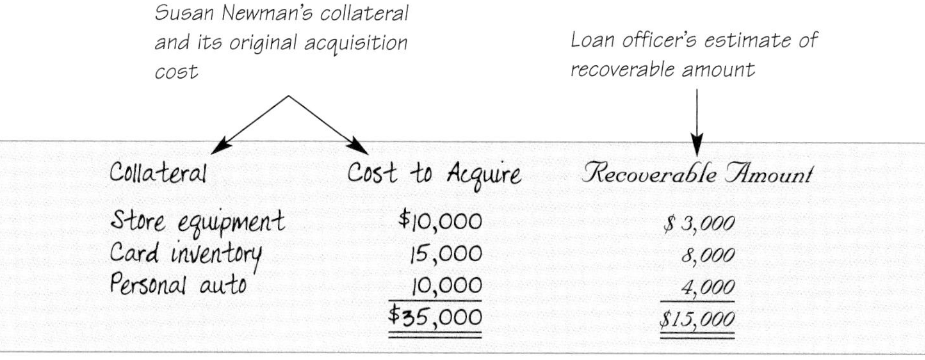

Collateral	Cost to Acquire	Recoverable Amount
Store equipment	$10,000	$ 3,000
Card inventory	15,000	8,000
Personal auto	10,000	4,000
	$35,000	$15,000

FIGURE 1-8

Susan Newman's list of collateral with loan officer's estimate of recoverable amount

Secured Liability Although she was pleased that her uncle had agreed to Phillip's request, Susan realized that she wanted more financial security for her business than just a $15,000 line of credit. When she explained this to Phillip, he asked her about her parents' home. Susan answered that last year her parents had finally paid off the mortgage; thus, they no longer owed money on their home, which was located in an area where comparable homes were selling for at least $200,000. Phillip told Susan that her line of credit would undoubtedly be approved for $50,000 if her parents "collateralized," or **secured**, her loan **liability** by pledging or promising the home they owned, an asset, to the bank as collateral for Susan's line of credit. He went on to describe the step-by-step process commonly called *taking a lien*. In simple terms, the bank would give Susan a line of credit if her parents gave the bank the legal right to sell their home if Susan did not repay her loan.

Susan was a little uneasy about asking her parents to take a lien on their home, but when she spoke with them and explained all the details, they assured her they would help. They agreed to have the bank take a $35,000 lien on their home that, even under a worst case scenario, represented only a small percentage of its full value.

Susan informed Phillip that her parents had agreed to collateralize their home. He told her he was confident her loan would be approved because he had also just received her credit report, which showed an excellent credit history. He estimated that formal loan approval would occur just after New Year's Day. He did remind her, however, that he still needed her operating budget to complete the loan package.

Writing a Business Plan

USER FOCUS

As you have seen, Susan Newman engaged in a great deal of decision making in just over two months of research and planning for her new business. Some of these decisions will likely determine whether or not CMU survives its first year of operations. For example, if Susan's decisions about the amount of financing or business location turn out to be poorly conceived, her business might fail no matter how much demand exists for her products or how well she manages the business.

Given the importance of the initial decision-making process to the success of a new business, what can people do to increase a new business's chances for success? One quite simple but valuable action you can take is to write a business plan, just as Susan did. Refer to *Appendix 1–1* to see the business plan for CMU. A **business plan** is a written document that includes specifics about a business such as a description of its goods and services and how they will be marketed, an analysis of its industry, an operating plan, and a realistic estimate of its revenues, expenses, and cash flows. A business plan is a valuable decision-making tool because the act of writing it forces you to consider business issues that you might otherwise have overlooked. It also requires you to provide financial information that can improve your chances of obtaining money from a loan or additional owner investment.

Preparing an Operating Budget

The very day that Phillip Strauss reminded Susan to complete her operating budget, Mary Mathews also asked Susan to submit one. Mary asked for this report because the landlord could not evaluate the money-making potential of Susan's business using Susan's personal balance sheet.

In general terms, a **budget** is a projection or future-oriented plan expressed in financial terms. Two budgets you will commonly encounter are a budgeted balance sheet and a budgeted income statement. If Susan prepared a budgeted or projected balance sheet, she would estimate what her assets and liabilities would be at a future point in time. Likewise, Susan's budgeted or projected income statement describes how she expects her business will perform during its first year. You will learn more about the income statement later. For now, just remember that an **income statement** is a financial statement that reports the results of operations. Another term often used for "projected income statement" is *operating budget*. The use of an operating budget is not, however, restricted to the first year of a business. It is also useful for planning future years, quarters, months, or weeks.

Estimating Sales Revenue

Susan began preparing this budget by estimating sales for her first year of business. She remembered from her accounting classes that **sales revenue**—money received or to be received from the sale of goods or services—is a more complete term than simply *sales* for purposes of income statement presentation.

To estimate first-year sales revenue, she decided to talk to several card and memorabilia store owners, who estimated her likely sales revenue to be from $50,000 to $80,000. Susan supplemented their estimates with advice from her good friend, George Wu, whom she had met in college. George was now a certified public accountant (CPA) working for a national public accounting firm.

George asked Susan to estimate both the cost of fully stocking her inventory and the number of times during the year that she expected to turn over or sell her complete inventory. When Susan answered that she expected to sell *nearly all* of her $15,000 inventory every four months or three times a year, he reasoned that she would probably have about $5,000 inventory remaining if she invested $15,000 each of three times. Thus, he concluded that the cost of acquiring the cards sold was $40,000 [($15,000 × 3) − $5,000]. George then asked her to estimate the average selling price she would set for each dollar invested in inventory. From her discussions with card dealers, Susan decided that her markup for each dollar invested in cards would be 60 cents, that is, a 60% markup on cost. Thus, for a card costing her $1.00, Susan will sell it for $1.60 ($1.00 + $0.60). Using that information, George provided her with an estimated sales figure of $64,000. His calculations were as follows:

Cost to acquire $15,000 of inventory three times		$45,000
Less cost to acquire inventory balance in store	−	5,000
Cost to acquire inventory sold (cost of goods sold)	=	$40,000
Markup of inventory to estimated selling price per dollar invested in inventory	×	1.60
Estimated sales revenue	=	$64,000

When Susan recognized that George's estimate was nearly identical to the $65,000 midpoint of the card store owners' range of estimates, she decided to use his $64,000 figure.

Estimating Expenses

Susan's next step in preparing her operating budget was to estimate what her first-year expenses might be. She still remembered from her college accounting course that the term *expense* was used in conjunction with the income statement. But she could not remember the distinction between the terms *cost* and *expense*, so she decided to calculate her expected costs for the year and simply refer to them as expenses. She then made a mental note to ask George to refresh her memory about the difference between these two terms.

Susan, however, had no trouble recalling the concept of opportunity cost and knowing not to include it in her list of expenses. Susan's most obvious opportunity cost was the cost of forgoing her $27,000 salary at Spacebar Software. An **opportunity cost** is the amount of profit sacrificed by deciding to apply a set of resources elsewhere. In this case, it is the salary Susan loses when she decides to leave her job and start a business. Financial reports prepared for those outside the firm do not generally include opportunity costs as expenses. For example, in Susan's situation, her former salary is not an actual or out-of-pocket cost of doing business at Cards & Memorabilia Unlimited. In addition, her salary is too subjective to be included, since an unemployed person opening up an identical business would have no comparable opportunity cost.

Susan created a list of expenses and categorized them. As Figure 1-9 shows, she estimated that her expenses for her first year in business would total $66,000. With this information, she was ready to create the first draft of her operating budget.

	Total
Inventory	
• George's estimate.	$40,000
Rent and Related Expenses	
• Rent is $1,000 per month. ($1,000 × 12 months)	12,000
• Monthly rent-related expenses on this property will be about $0.30 per square foot (750 × .30 × 12 months) per month.	2,700
Equipment	
• Cost of store-related equipment.	10,000
Other	
• Estimate of all other expenses, including advertising and business license.	1,300
	$66,000

FIGURE 1-9

Susan's list of estimated expenses

Distinguishing between Cost and Expense

As with her estimate of sales revenue, Susan asked George to look over her expense estimates and the first draft of her operating budget (Figure 1-10a). Before you read any further, study Figure 1-10a. Do you think Susan's first draft is ready to be submitted to the landlord?

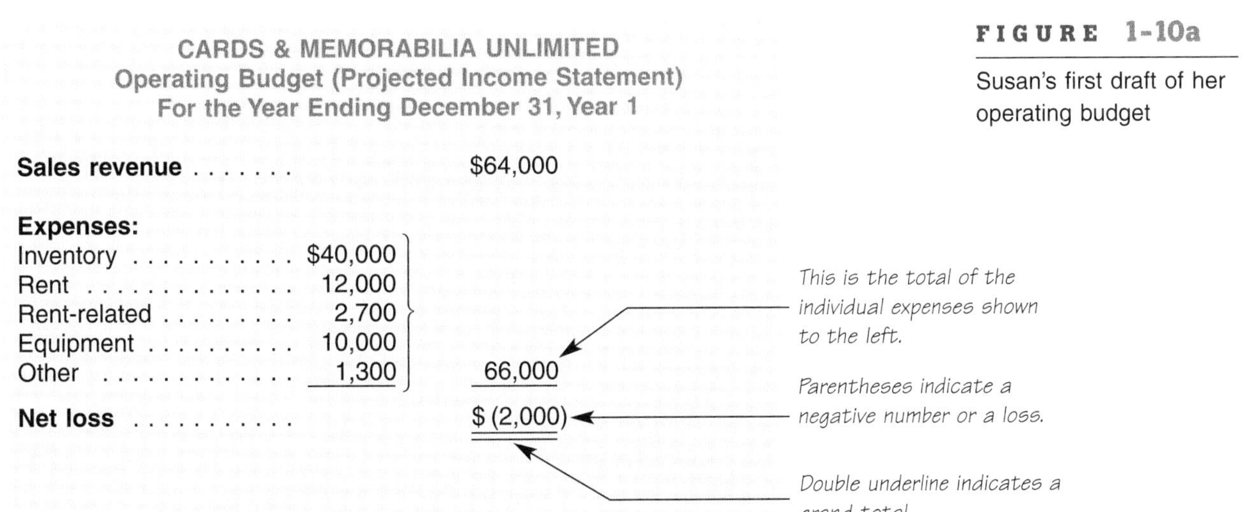

CARDS & MEMORABILIA UNLIMITED
Operating Budget (Projected Income Statement)
For the Year Ending December 31, Year 1

Sales revenue		$64,000
Expenses:		
Inventory	$40,000	
Rent	12,000	
Rent-related	2,700	
Equipment	10,000	
Other	1,300	66,000
Net loss		$ (2,000)

FIGURE 1-10a

Susan's first draft of her operating budget

Almost immediately, George questioned the $10,000 amount for equipment. He pointed out that while the equipment did *cost* Susan $10,000, it would be used for several years. That means its annual *expense* would be substantially less than $10,000. He explained that it was necessary to divide the $10,000 cost of the equipment by an estimate of the store equipment's useful years of service, or **useful life**. George advised

Susan that a useful life of five years was reasonable and corrected the first draft of Susan's operating budget accordingly (Figure 1-10b).

FIGURE 1-10b

Susan's operating budget with George's corrections

Recognizing the concept of depreciation reduces this expense by $8,000.

CARDS & MEMORABILIA UNLIMITED
Operating Budget (Projected Income Statement)
For the Year Ending December 31, Year 1

Sales revenue			$64,000	
Expenses:				
~~Inventory~~ *Cost of goods sold*	$40,000			
Rent	12,000			
Rent-related	2,700			
~~Equipment~~ *Depreciation*	~~10,000~~	*2,000*		
Other	1,300		~~66,000~~	*58,000*
Net ~~loss~~ *income*			**$ ~~(2,000)~~**	*6,000*

George's corrections change what was a negative evaluation to a positive one.

An $8,000 decrease in the total expenses changes a $2,000 net loss into a $6,000 net income.

Susan remembered that this calculation ($10,000/5), or $2,000, was called depreciation expense. **Depreciation** is the process of allocating a cost to the periods of time being benefited. George reminded Susan that a **cost** is a sacrifice of cash made now or in the future to acquire goods or services today, whereas an **expense** is the portion of that same cost that is used up to produce revenue during the year. In other words, an expense is an expired cost. Since Susan had purchased the equipment for the purpose of producing sales revenue, a portion of its cost had to be assigned or allocated to her expenses each year. That is, the $2,000 depreciation expense was the portion of the $10,000 equipment cost treated as "used up" in producing services or first-year revenues. He reminded her that he had used the same distinction between

INSIGHT

How Will Performance Objectives Help You Succeed in this Course?

A valuable feature of this textbook is its learning or performance objectives. They are designed to help you master accounting principles and will appear throughout the textbook whenever appropriate. Performance Objective 1 asks you to master the preparation of a simple operating budget and explain why it is useful.

YOUR PERFORMANCE OBJECTIVE 1
Prepare a simple operating budget and **explain** its usefulness.

Notice that performance objectives are expressed in behavioral terms. In this case you are asked to perform two behaviors—prepare and explain—to demonstrate your mastery. For this reason, these objectives are often called behavioral objectives. Pay careful attention to these behavioral performance objectives whenever they appear in this textbook. The **insight** you should gain here, is that if you use them to help you study, you will have a better chance of succeeding in this course.

cost and expense when he calculated her inventory expense. That is, he had assigned only $40,000 of the $45,000 cost of inventory to expense, because he recognized that the $5,000 unsold inventory had not yet produced sales revenue. The $5,000 amount was a cost of goods that had not been "used up" in the act of sale and, therefore, was not an expense.

Once George corrected her estimated expenses as shown by his recalculations in Figure 1-10b, Susan was ready to produce a final draft of her operating budget for the landlord and for Central Bank (Figure 1-10c). As shown in this figure, inventory expense is customarily called **cost of goods sold** and the difference between revenues and expenses is called **net income**.

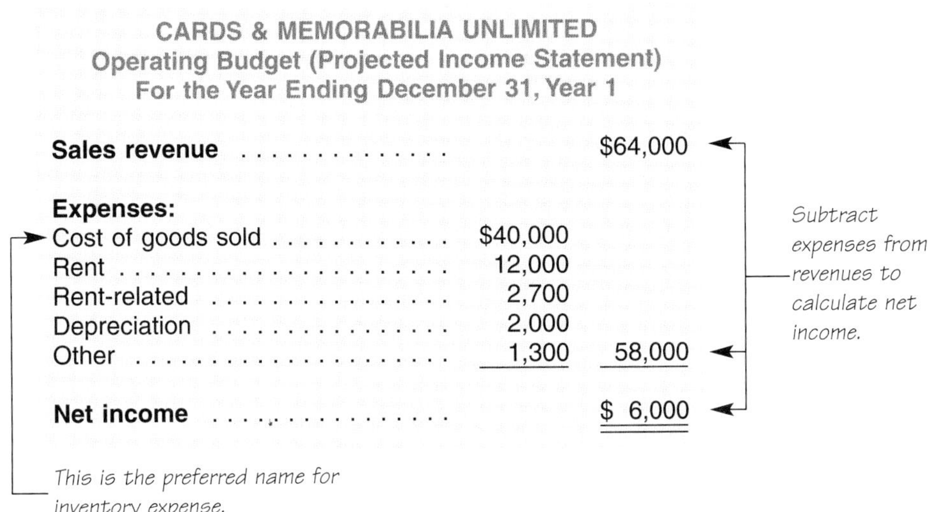

CARDS & MEMORABILIA UNLIMITED
Operating Budget (Projected Income Statement)
For the Year Ending December 31, Year 1

Sales revenue		$64,000
Expenses:		
Cost of goods sold	$40,000	
Rent	12,000	
Rent-related	2,700	
Depreciation	2,000	
Other	1,300	58,000
Net income		$ 6,000

Subtract expenses from revenues to calculate net income.
This is the preferred name for inventory expense.

FIGURE 1-10c

Susan's final operating budget

What Is Accounting and How Is It Used in Business?

Although this chapter has introduced a good deal of information about business, you might think it has discussed little about accounting, the subject of this textbook and course. Thus, it is important to now ask the question, "What is accounting and how is it used in business?" This section will answer that question by first defining the term *accounting*, describing how it is used in business, distinguishing between financial and managerial accounting, and explaining how Susan's operating budget can be viewed as both a financial and managerial accounting report.

What Is Accounting?

Accounting is a measurement and reporting information system that helps users of that information make business decisions. It does so by communicating relevant information about the financial activities of an entity through the preparation and distribution of various accounting reports. One such report is the operating budget just introduced.

How Is Accounting Used in Business?

This chapter describes how accounting is useful in making both business and personal financial decisions. Recall how Susan's loan officer and landlord asked her for financial information that they could analyze to decide whether or not to lend her money or lease property to her. Both individuals used accounting information—Susan's balance sheet and projected income statement (operating budget)—to make their respective business decisions. Likewise, Susan, as owner-manager, will use this same accounting information to help her make decisions that can increase her company's chances for success. For example, Susan used her estimate of sales revenue to decide how much inventory to buy. Performance Objective 2 underscores how important it is that you are able to express the usefulness of accounting in concrete ways:

YOUR PERFORMANCE OBJECTIVE 2
Identify several ways in which accounting information is used to make business and personal decisions.

You will apply Performance Objective 2 throughout this course.

INSIGHT

One Way to Learn and Retain Accounting Concepts

You probably know from many of the other courses you have taken, that it is usually easier to understand and master concepts when you can apply them to your life. Thus, whenever you read about a new accounting concept in this book, try to look for ways that this concept applies to you. For example, consider Performance Objective 1. You would be more likely to master this objective if you prepared your own personal operating budget, as you will do in Exercise 1-5, before you prepare such a budget for a company with which you are not familiar. The **insight** you should gain here is that whenever you think a concept is difficult, first think about how you might apply this concept to your life. This will help you more easily learn and retain the material in this course.

How Do You Distinguish between Financial and Managerial Accounting?

Although this book is designed primarily for the study of financial accounting, you might very well have heard people mention managerial accounting. To understand the difference between financial and managerial accounting, let's begin with their definitions. **Financial accounting** is the process of collecting, measuring, processing, and communicating the financial effects of business transactions to facilitate decision making by those outside the entity. In contrast, **managerial accounting** is the process of collecting, measuring, processing, and communicating both quantitative and qualitative information for the internal use of management in planning and controlling activities.

As you can see from their definitions, a primary difference between these accounting perspectives is based on whether the decision maker is outside the company, an external user, or is a decision maker who works for the company, an internal user. For example, when both the loan officer and the landlord evaluated the creditworthiness of Cards & Memorabilia Unlimited, they were outside the company; thus, they were using financial accounting information. In contrast, when Susan evaluated CMU's prospects for success by estimating its net income (Figure 1-10c), she was viewing the firm as owner-manager and was, therefore, using managerial accounting information. Another difference you will discover is that external users tend to rely more on objective and verifiable information, or actual, past results, while internal users more often rely on subjective, internally generated information, and future projections.

To summarize, remember that financial accounting measures and reports information for *external users*—decision makers outside a company—while managerial accounting measures and reports information for *internal users*—decision makers inside the company.

Financial and Managerial Uses of an Operating Budget

INSIGHT

Some accounting reports have both financial and managerial uses. A good example is the operating budget prepared by Susan Newman (Figure 1-10c). It is traditionally thought of as a managerial accounting report. It may be treated, however, as a financial accounting report when used by such external decision makers as Susan's loan officer and landlord.

Susan did not think of creating this budget for herself; her loan officer and landlord required her to prepare it. But this budget helped Susan, too, because such a forecast of revenues and expenses is a useful managerial decision-making tool. For example, she can obtain valuable feedback about CMU's performance by comparing planned revenues and expenses to actual revenues and expenses. If this feedback is unfavorable, Susan might be able to modify her initial decisions and, therefore, better control CMU's operations.

The insight you should gain here is that a budget is fundamentally an accounting report that has value in making both financial and managerial decisions. Distinguishing between the uses of financial and managerial accounting will help you use accounting information to make sound business decisions.

Forecasting the Success of a New Business

Susan's bank and landlord asked for her operating budget so that they could forecast CMU's future success. Central Bank wanted to be reasonably sure that CMU could repay any amounts borrowed through its line of credit, and Susan's landlord wanted to be reasonably sure that CMU could pay its monthly rent in full and on time. Since Susan's company was new, both the bank and the landlord had to depend on a forecast, her operating budget, to determine the success of the new business.

Susan, herself, was interested in forecasting the success of her new business. Although her perspective was that of an owner, rather than that of a lender or landlord, she was keenly interested in measuring her likely success. Let's now examine how an owner such as Susan evaluates both the financial and nonfinancial success of her business.

The Financial Rewards of Business Ownership

A general measure of business profitability is return *on* investment, which should not be confused with return *of* investment. Although return *on* investment may take many forms, you will soon see how a specific form known as *return on equity* can be applied to measure CMU's expected first year profitability.

Return on Investment (ROI) Susan noticed that when George reduced her expenses from $10,000 to $2,000, her income increased by $8,000. Obviously, she preferred an operating budget that showed a $6,000 net income, or revenues in excess of expenses, to one showing a \$2,000 **net loss**, or expenses in excess of revenues. If she does earn the projected \$6,000 net income, it will be considered a "return" on the \$30,000 investment that Susan made in her business at the beginning of the year. That is, the \$6,000 will be her **return *on* investment**. In contrast, if Susan ever decides to remove some of her original investment in her business, what she removes, up to the original \$30,000, will be referred to as a **return *of* investment**.

Although net income is a popular measure of success, it does have some limitations. One such limitation is that net income does not allow you to easily compare the profitability of different-sized businesses. That is, CMU's projected net income of \$6,000 might actually be a return that is superior to a larger company's net income of \$60,000. So when Susan expressed concern about her business earning such a small amount in its first year, George advised her to combine her dollar return—measured using net income—with her original investment figure to better measure performance. This is known as **rate of return on investment** (**ROI**), a ratio that is calculated as follows:

$$\text{Rate of Return on Investment} = \frac{\text{Net Income}}{\text{Investment}}$$

When Susan initially saw the \$6,000 amount, it is not surprising that she thought that \$6,000 was not a good return; she certainly couldn't live on \$6,000 a year. But after thinking about the concept of ROI, Susan evaluated the \$6,000 as a percentage of her \$30,000 investment and asked herself, "What investment alternative do I have that in one year will return more than 20% (\$6,000/\$30,000) on my \$30,000?" When she realized that she had no investment opportunities to match this rate of return, she perceived the \$6,000 differently and became more enthusiastic about her prospects with CMU. Moreover, Susan knew that her financial needs would be minimal because she would continue to live with her parents, who had promised to help her financially during her first few years of business.

Return on Equity (ROE) As you will learn later, the investment denominator in the ROI ratio can be expressed in several ways. For now, let's examine Susan's specific measure of investment, known as equity. Although we will define the term more fully later, **equity** is the amount invested or contributed by an owner to finance a business. In this chapter, for example, Susan's equity in her business was \$30,000. When the projected net income from her operating budget is divided by this amount of equity, the result is Susan's **rate of return on equity** (**ROE**) or more simply, **return on equity**:

$$\text{Return on Equity} = \frac{\text{Net Income}}{\text{Equity}} = \frac{\$6{,}000}{\$30{,}000} = 20\%$$

Performance Objective 3 encourages you to use this ratio properly to reap its benefits in business decision making.

YOUR PERFORMANCE OBJECTIVE 3

Calculate the return on equity ratio and **discuss** its usefulness and limitations in making decisions.

This rate of return measurement is useful in decision making because it enables investors to compare the performance of investments that differ in size. For example, if Susan earns \$6,000 net income on an equity investment of \$50,000 instead of \$30,000, using only the absolute return of \$6,000 does not help her distinguish between these investments. Using a *relative* or percentage return on equity investment helps Susan see that earning \$6,000 on a \$30,000 investment (20%) is clearly preferable to earning \$6,000 on a \$50,000 investment (12%). Thus, it should be clear that using a *relative* or percentage return on equity is a more reliable basis for making business decisions than using an absolute return on investment, such as the $6,000. A limitation, however, is that it does not consider the concept of opportunity cost, as discussed in the following Insight.

Financial and Managerial Uses of the Return on Equity

INSIGHT

Just as a budget can be used to make both financial and managerial decisions, so too can a return on equity. Consider, for example, Susan's 20% rate of return on equity just calculated. If Susan uses it to inform *external users*, such as the bank, about her business's expected profitability, it is a financial accounting ratio. If, however, Susan uses it as an owner-manager to evaluate her business's profitability, it is a managerial accounting ratio.

Susan's calculation of her business's rate of return on equity for managerial purposes differs from her earlier calculation of the same business's ratio for financial accounting purposes. To adapt this ratio to a managerial setting, she needs to subtract the opportunity cost of starting her own business from her net income, as shown here.

$$\text{Return on Equity} = \frac{\text{Net Income} - \text{Opportunity Cost}}{\text{Equity}} = \frac{\$6{,}000 - \$27{,}000}{\$30{,}000}$$

$$= \frac{-\$21{,}000}{\$30{,}000} = -70\%$$

The reason for this adjustment is that financial accounting does not include opportunity costs while managerial accounting does. Susan's salary of $27,000, or opportunity cost, was not recorded earlier because it is not an actual or out-of-pocket cost of doing business at CMU. Also, it is too subjective a cost from the perspective of an external user of such information. The fact that opportunity costs are not included in the accounting records, however, does not mean that they are not useful in the economic decision making of an owner-manager such as Susan. When Susan included opportunity cost in her return on equity calculation, she realized that her small business profit did not nearly offset the salary she had earned by applying her resources to a salaried position. Yet, Susan decided to open her business in January, a clear indication that her decision-making process also involved some nonfinancial considerations as discussed next.

The **insight** you should gain here is that the same ratio may be calculated differently for managerial accounting purposes than for financial accounting purposes because of their different treatments of the concept of opportunity cost.

The Nonfinancial Rewards of Business Ownership

As Susan made final preparations to open her business in January, she realized that she had already begun to reap the rewards she had hoped to obtain from business ownership. In researching and planning for the new business, for example, she had applied much of what she had learned in college. She also had learned many new things about how to start a business.

Susan found it remarkable how her attitude about accounting had changed in just a few weeks. While in college, she thought her accounting courses were boring and overly concerned with minute details. Now that she understood how important financial statement information is to the establishment and survival of any business, she began to appreciate the value of her accounting classes.

Of course, there were trade-offs involved in owning a business. She'd have to work many more hours during the week, and she knew she might be under more stress. Every day she would have to face the financial risk she had undertaken and the possibility that her business might not survive.

Despite these worries and the discovery that her projected return on equity was negative, Susan was convinced that the risk-to-reward ratio was in her favor. At CMU she would be her own boss with greater control over the time and direction of the business. She would be able to interact with customers on a daily basis in a stimulating environment. Above all else, Susan would be doing what she loved to do.

Learning Business Terminology: An Immediate Benefit of This Course

Accounting is often described as the "language of business" because its precise terminology is the foundation of business communications. After reading only one chapter in this book, you have seen how accounting has expanded your business vocabulary and, thus, your understanding of business by exposing you to terms such as *limited liability*, *financing*, *lease*, *collateral*, *balance sheet*, *assets*, *income statement*, *revenue*, *expense*, *depreciation*, *cost of goods sold*, *net income*, and *budget*. To continue to master this terminology, always consult the *Summary with Key Terms* located at the end of each chapter and, for each term, master Performance Objective 4:

YOUR PERFORMANCE OBJECTIVE 4
Explain in your own words the meaning of key business terms.

APPENDIX

1-1

Cards & Memorabilia Unlimited's Business Plan

Susan planned her new business in November and December. She knew if her plan was well conceived and well written, it would not only help her secure funding for her business, but it would also increase the chances that her business would be successful.

She decided to use *BizPlanBuilder*™, a strategic business and marketing plan software package. This appendix contains Susan's entire business plan.

DECEMBER YEAR 0

Business Plan Copy Number 1

This document contains confidential and proprietary information belonging exclusively to Cards & Memorabilia Unlimited.

Susan Newman, Owner
901 Ginger Street
Rialto, Arizona 85000
(602) 555-3001

TABLE OF CONTENTS

EXECUTIVE SUMMARY

Cards & Memorabilia Unlimited will open for business in January of Year 1 to take advantage of the sustained and growing interest in trading cards and sports memorabilia.

Today, trading card and sports memorabilia collectors living in the Phoenix area are at a disadvantage. They do not have access to retail establishments that stock a large, diverse inventory and offer a pleasant environment in which to meet for trading and talking. Cards & Memorabilia Unlimited will fill this void.

My initial objective is to build the business and the customer base over the next two years, so that by Year 3 Cards & Memorabilia Unlimited will be in suitable condition for further expansion. In the third year of business, I plan to expand to investors. By the fifth year of business, my objective is to be the largest trading card and sports memorabilia dealer in the greater Phoenix area. Cards & Memorabilia Unlimited franchises will be offered at that time. To accomplish these objectives, I have developed a comprehensive plan for marketing activities and customer services.

In this business plan, I will show the background research I have done to support the establishment of Cards & Memorabilia Unlimited and describe in detail the financial and operational plans for the business.

Pgs. 2–3

CURRENT MARKET ENVIRONMENT

The demand for professional sports-related apparel, gifts, souvenirs, and memorabilia has increased rapidly over the past five years. It is common to see TV commercials advertising official NFL athletic wear, athletic shoes endorsed by sports stars, and trading cards. In towns throughout the United States, trading card shows in hotels and convention centers have become commonplace. Recent sporting events, such as the Sammy Sosa/Barry Bonds home run race has sparked renewed interest in trading cards and sports memorabilia. A recent *USA Today* article reports that Bonds's rookie card has gone from $8 three years ago to over $100 today. A query on any search engine on the Internet results in thousands of sites associated with cards, autographed uniforms and balls, and so on.

Most trading card manufacturers are thriving, and their market is growing at a rapid rate. Forecasters predict this industry will double by 2010. The overall market potential for trading cards is estimated to be $1.8 billion by 2006, with the area of greatest growth being baseball cards. The sports memorabilia market is currently estimated to be $750 million.[1]

All this potential business exists, and yet *The Phoenix Democrat* and my own market research indicates that in greater Phoenix there is currently only one card store for every 9,000 collectors.[2] The market conditions are ripe for a business such as Cards & Memorabilia Unlimited.

[1] These numbers are an average derived from recent articles in *USA Today, Investment Monthly*, and the annual reports of *Topps* and *Upper Deck*.

[2] See the articles in the Sports section of *The Phoenix Democrat*, July 9, Year 0 and September 17, Year 0. I would be pleased to provide the notes I took from my in-person and telephone interviews of 24 store owners in Arizona, Colorado, and Utah. Also, I researched store locations in the greater Phoenix area by using telephone yellow pages and business-to-business directories.

OBJECTIVE

My objective is to make Cards & Memorabilia Unlimited the leading seller of trading cards and sports memorabilia in the greater Phoenix area by Year 5. I hope to achieve this objective by transferring my business skills, my passion for spectator sports, and my hobby of collecting trading cards and sports memorabilia into a highly profitable entity that provides services and products not found in any other retail establishment in greater Phoenix. I plan to achieve this objective by:

- Targeting my customers.
- Providing unique products and services that my competitors do not provide.
- Choosing an excellent location.
- Designing and managing reliable inventory controls.
- Using the latest technology.
- Conducting a strong advertising and promotion campaign.
- Using financial management tools and techniques.

MANAGEMENT

Cards & Memorabilia Unlimited's legal form of ownership will be a sole proprietorship with me as the owner-manager. I will also be the only full-time employee for the first year of business to minimize expenses.

I have a degree in business administration from Phoenix State University. Among the courses I took there were two that will particularly help me start and manage a small business—Small Business Management and Entrepreneurship. In the latter course, I was awarded the "Entrepreneur Prize" for my project on starting a new business.

My full-time work experience includes three years at Spacebar Software, where I began as a customer service representative. At the end of my second year on this job, I was named Service Representative of the Year. Then I was promoted to customer service manager after only twenty-six months as a service representative. In this management position I used a variety of marketing, management, and financial skills. Within seven months of my working as a manager, Spacebar's customer service ratings jumped from 5 to 7 on a 10-point scale.

In addition, I possess strong computer information systems skills and knowledge. I plan to use technology in all aspects of my financing, investing, and operating activities, and I plan to capitalize on e-commerce for advertising and retailing my inventory.

Pgs. 4–5

MARKET ANALYSIS

5-1 Targeted Customers

In the first two years of business, Cards & Memorabilia Unlimited will target customers who are collectors. These customers range widely in age—from the elementary school child to the retiree. Collectors are usually from middle to upper-middle class suburban neighborhoods and cross racial and ethnic lines. Collectors are almost always sports enthusiasts, and the vast majority are male.

5-2 Focus Groups

Based on this profile of the typical card collector, I conducted two focus groups—one with collectors from 9 to 22 years old and one with collectors from 25 to 65 years old. Each group contained 8 people plus a moderator. All group members lived within a 20-mile radius of Rialto.

The groups were asked open-ended questions to discover their buying behavior, the types of information they desire, and their attitudes toward card and memorabilia stores, conventions, and websites.

From the focus group I learned that card and memorabilia collectors are becoming more sophisticated; they are media driven and technologically astute. Their purchase decisions are sometimes practical but often emotional. They do use the Internet, but they also want the face-to-face interaction when trading and buying cards and collectibles. They want to shop in an atmosphere more pleasant than a 9 × 12 storefront containing nothing but display cases of cards. They want upscale environments that offer trading cards and sports memorabilia as well as other amenities that allow them to make more informed buying decisions.

5-3 The Competition

Trading card and sports memorabilia stores within a 40-mile radius of Rialto and their locations are:

All American Cards	Gridley
Baseball Cards & Souvenirs	Phoenix

Brian's Books	Phoenix
C & M's Cards & Collectibles	Phoenix
Canyon Cards & Collectibles	Blanca
Collector's Corner II	Blanca
Jim's Card Collection	Felicity
Triple Play Sports Cards	Phoenix
Sports Cards of Phoenix	Phoenix
Stamps in the Attic	Helio
What's Hot Comics and Cards	Helio

These establishments are significantly different from my plan for Cards & Memorabilia Unlimited. First, all of these stores are between 200 and 500 square feet—with the exception of Collector's Corner II and Brian's Books. Both of these carry a more diverse inventory, including coins, stamps, and dolls. Second, all of these stores lack seating for customers. Third, only one of these stores offers any form of customer service; What's Hot Comics and Cards has a small collection of catalogues and pricing guides that customers can use. Finally, most of these stores limit their advertising to occasional ads in local newspapers.

In conclusion, my analysis of the market indicates that many customer needs are not being met by existing retail stores.

Pgs. 5–6

DESCRIPTION OF CARDS & MEMORABILIA UNLIMITED

6-1 Location

I have decided to establish the business in Rialto, an affluent, middle to upper-middle class community. As such, its residents have ample discretionary income. The closest card and memorabilia store to the location I have selected is about five miles away in Helio.

The retail space I intend to lease is in a small strip mall. This mall also houses a sports bar and restaurant, and a sporting goods store. Customers can gain easy access to the mall from both Highway 51 and Rialto Boulevard; the parking lot provides more than ample space for customers. I will be able to secure signage near the top of the mall marquee for no charge. I have obtained a commitment in writing from the landlord of the mall that he will not lease space in the mall to any other trading card or sports memorabilia businesses.

6-2 Physical Plant and Furnishings

The space itself is about 750 square feet and is pleasant and well lighted. I will decorate and furnish this space to create a warm, friendly environment with comfortable seating and a television for viewing ESPN and other sports channels. In addition, I will have tables with comfortable chairs and an area with shelves to house collector's notebooks, plastic sleeves, and other trading card paraphernalia.

6-3 Inventory

I will stock a wide variety of trading cards—sports cards and cards for TV shows, movies, comic book characters, famous personalities, and so on, as well as sports memorabilia. In this way, customers will perceive Cards & Memorabilia Unlimited as having a lot to choose from and as the best place to spend time shopping and trading. By the end of its third year of business, Cards & Memorabilia Unlimited will have one of the most complete inventories of any trading card and sports memorabilia store in Arizona.

6-4 Technology

I will use technology to give customers easy access to Cards & Memorabilia Unlimited's inventory. Details about card sets, individual rare cards, uniforms, autographs, photographs, and so on will be entered into a database. Each record will contain all relevant data. For example, card set data will include the date the set or card was manufactured, its manufacturer, and where it is kept in the store. Additionally, data available for management decisions (hidden from customer access) include the date the card was purchased and the historical cost of the card. Thus, this database will eliminate many of the problems currently encountered by card and memorabilia retailers—problems such as how to remember what is in stock, stock locations, and how much money is invested in the item.

Besides the traditional print-based catalogues, magazines, and price guides, Cards & Memorabilia Unlimited will offer electronic resources to help customers do such things as browse through inventory. I will launch a CMU Web page in April Year 1 that will list my inventory and advertise my services.

MARKETING STRATEGY

7-1 Overall Strategy

Cards & Memorabilia Unlimited's marketing strategy is to enhance, promote, and support the unique atmosphere and services offered to customers. All communications with the market will present an image consistent with this strategy.

7-2 Advertising and Promotion

I believe one initial key to success is extensive promotion. I plan to reach potential customers by developing an advertising campaign that will emphasize Cards & Memorabilia Unlimited's image.

Newspaper Stories I already have commitments from *The Phoenix Democrat*, *The Rialto Sun*, and *The Arizona Transcript* to run special interest stories about Cards & Memorabilia Unlimited, each with a different "angle."

Fliers I will use fliers to convey the look and feel of Cards & Memorabilia Unlimited—a great place to visit for trading cards, sports memorabilia, fun, and friendships with other collectors. For the first year of business I will use my knowledge of desktop publishing to produce fliers so I can keep expenses to a minimum.

Press Releases I will write a press release for the grand opening, which I have scheduled for February 9, one month after the actual opening on January 9. I will send this press release to all newspapers within a 40-mile radius of Rialto. With this release I will include an attractive 8 × 10 black and white photo of the store interior showing customers sitting and enjoying the facilities in the store.

Trade Shows I will use trade shows to reach out to new customers, but I will limit my attendance to the four largest shows in the western United States. By way of summary, here is my preliminary advertising and promotion schedule:

7-3 Preliminary Advertising and Promotion Schedule

Item	Date	Recipients
Fliers	January 3–8	8,000 Rialto, Helio, Blanca, and selected Phoenix residents
Press release	Mail, January 5	60 editors of newspapers, newsletters, and list serves
Rialto Sun article	Week of January 6th	23,000 readers
Arizona Transcript article	Week of January 6th	75,000 readers
Phoenix Democrat article	Week of January 15th	500,000 readers
NCTCA Show, Phoenix	March 20th	4,000 attendees
CCD, Denver	May 24	2,000 attendees
ACC Fair, San Francisco	August 8	5,500 attendees
Pacific West Cards and Collectibles, Seattle	November 8	2,000 attendees

My research indicates that an organized advertising campaign such as described here has never been used by any of the competition.

7-4 Public Relations
I will develop a sustained public relations effort with ongoing contact with Rialto community groups, such as Little League, Rialto Hoops, and the Chamber of Commerce. During the first year, I will sponsor a Little League team and a soccer team. My goal is to position Cards & Memorabilia Unlimited as a healthy outlet for children and adults alike.

FINANCIALS

8-1 Resources
I have provided a current personal balance sheet on the next page.

CENTRAL BANK LOAN APPLICATION

PERSONAL FINANCIAL STATEMENT

PERSONAL PROFILE

NAME		AGE	SOCIAL SECURITY NUMBER
Susan Newman		26	593-70-0210
STREET ADDRESS: 901 Ginger Way	CITY: Rialto	STATE: AZ	ZIP: 85000
HOME PHONE: (602) 555-3001	☐ OWN ☐ RENT $ ____ PER MONTH ☒ OTHER live with parents		AT CURRENT ADDRESS SINCE (MM/YY): 05 / 78
☐ MARRIED ☐ SEPARATED ☒ UNMARRIED	NUMBER OF DEPENDENTS: 0	AGES OF DEPENDENTS: N/A	YEARS WITH COMPANY: N/A
SPOUSE'S NAME: N/A	SPOUSE'S OCCUPATION: N/A		SPOUSE'S SOCIAL SECURITY NUMBER: N/A
SPOUSE EMPLOYED BY: N/A	HOW LONG WITH EMPLOYER? (SPOUSE) YRS. MOS. N/A		SPOUSE'S WORK PHONE: ( ) N/A

BANKING RELATIONSHIPS (Please list only your personal accounts.)

NAME OF BANK	ACCOUNT NUMBER	PERSONAL CHECKING	PERSONAL SAVINGS	CURRENT BALANCE
Central Bank	0321-62221	✓		$ 1,500
Central Bank	0321-52701		✓	$17,000

FINANCIAL STATEMENT

ASSETS	AMOUNT	LIABILITIES	AMOUNT
CASH IN CENTRAL BANK	$18,500	TOTAL REVOLVING CREDIT	$500
CASH IN OTHER BANKS	0	TOTAL INSTALLMENT LOANS	0
RETIREMENT ACCOUNTS (IRA, SEP. KEOGH, 401-K)	0	1ST MORTGAGE ON RESIDENCE	N/A
STOCK / BONDS / MUTUAL FUNDS (INCLUDE COPY OF BROKER'S STATEMENTS)	0	OTHER MORTGAGES ON RESIDENCE	N/A
RESIDENCE MARKET VALUE	N/A	MORTGAGE(S) ON OTHER REAL ESTATE	N/A
OTHER REAL ESTATE MARKET VALUE	N/A	OTHER LIABILITIES (PLEASE DESCRIBE)	N/A
OTHER ASSETS (PLEASE DESCRIBE) Personal Auto	10,000	OTHER LIABILITIES (PLEASE DESCRIBE)	
OTHER ASSETS (PLEASE DESCRIBE)			
TOTAL ASSETS	$28,500	**TOTAL LIABILITIES**	$500

NET WORTH (TOTAL ASSETS MINUS TOTAL LIABILITIES) $ 28,000

DO YOU GUARANTEE ANY OTHER DEBT? YES ____ NO ✓ IF YES, WHAT IS THE TOTAL: $ N/A

WHO IS THE BORROWER? N/A

NAME OF FINANCIAL INSTITUTION N/A

8-2 Objectives

I have provided a summary of my financial objectives by including:

Projected Income Statement

CARDS & MEMORABILIA UNLIMITED
Operating Budget (Projected Income Statement)
For the Year Ending December 31, Year 1

Sales revenue		$64,000
Expenses:		
Cost of goods sold	$40,000	
Rent	12,000	
Rent-related	2,700	
Depreciation	2,000	
Other	1,300	58,000
Net income		$ 6,000

Return on Equity Projection Based on a market share of trading card and sports memorabilia business in the greater Phoenix area, I estimate that by the end of the first year of business, Cards & Memorabilia Unlimited's return on equity will be 20%. Further, I project that sales will increase 25% for each of Years 2 through 5.

CONCLUSION

This business plan reflects conservative financial planning and my strong desire to succeed with this business. Cards & Memorabilia Unlimited will meet customer needs not currently met by any other trading card and sports memorabilia store in the Phoenix area. By providing a variety of goods and services to meet these needs, I hope to build a loyal customer base. I will use computer technology to help me make managerial and financial decisions and to plan for solid, sustained financial growth.

Cards & Memorabilia Unlimited will open for business on January 9, Year 1.

Page 9

Summary with Key Terms

The number in parentheses following each **key term** is the page number on which the term is defined.

In this chapter, you read about Susan Newman and some of the initial steps she took to start her small business, Cards & Memorabilia Unlimited.

After researching the trading card and sports memorabilia industry, Susan decided that her target market would be collectors, rather than investors. To support this decision, she planned to stock trading cards and sports memorabilia for her customers. She then registered the name Cards & Memorabilia Unlimited at her county clerk's office and searched for a suitable location. When she found a place to conduct her business, she became a **lessee** (8) by entering into a **lease** (8) agreement with a landlord or **lessor** (8). Another decision Susan made was to organize her business as a **sole proprietorship** (8) rather than as a **partnership** (8) or **corporation** (8), despite the fact that this single-owner form of business did not provide **limited liability** (8).

Next, Susan focused on **financing** (9) her new business by determining how much money to obtain and from whom to obtain it. One source of financing Susan decided to apply for was a bank loan called a line of credit. To obtain this loan, Susan submitted to her loan officer both a **business plan** (13) and a personal financial statement called a **balance sheet** (11). A balance sheet's elements include **assets** (11), **liabilities** (11), and **net worth** (11), or **owner's equity** (11). The loan officer convinced Susan that she would have to provide **collateral** (12) for the loan. To do so, she first had to receive permission from Susan's uncle to make his loan a **subordinated liability** (12) to the bank's line of credit so that the bank had a priority claim against Susan's collateral. Susan was finally able to obtain her loan when her parents agreed to make it a **secured liability** (12) by pledging their home as an asset that the bank could use—place a lien on—if Susan did not repay the loan.

Both the loan officer and the landlord or lessor also asked Susan to submit a **budget** (13), specifically an **operating budget** (11), that reports how she expected her business to perform in its first year of operation. The primary measure of success reported in this future-oriented financial statement, known as an **income statement** (13), was **net income** (17), the excess of **sales revenue** (14) over **expense** (16). While preparing her list of expenses, Susan recalled the concept of **opportunity cost** (14) and remembered not to include it in her accounting records.

Had Susan expected the amount of expenses to exceed the amount of revenues, the difference would have been a **net loss** (20). While preparing this financial statement, Susan had to calculate both **cost of goods sold** (17) and **depreciation expense** (16), which allowed her to refresh her memory about the term **useful life** (15) and the distinction between a **cost** (16) and an **expense** (16).

In a discussion of the financial rewards of business ownership, you learned how to distinguish between a **return *on* investment** (20) and a **return *of* investment** (20). You also learned that Susan's expected return *on* investment or net income of $6,000 can be paired with her initial investment of $30,000 to produce a **rate of return on investment (ROI)** (20) of 20%. Technically, the term **equity** (20) better describes Susan's ownership contribution of $30,000. Thus, this ratio is commonly called a **rate of return on equity** (or **return on equity**) (20).

You also learned a definition of **accounting** (17), how **financial accounting** (18) may be distinguished from **managerial accounting** (18), and how an operating budget can be thought of as both a financial and managerial accounting report.

Making Business Decisions

YOUR PERFORMANCE OBJECTIVE 2
(page 18)

Decision making is an activity common to all types of business. Good decision-making skills are essential for your success in business. For example, consider all the decisions made in the Cards & Memorabilia Unlimited case study. Imagine the different outcomes that would have occurred if Susan had made different decisions from those described in this chapter. What if Susan had decided to start her business in November and not January? What if she had decided to name her business *Collectibles Unlimited* and focus on a different target market? What if she did not apply for a line of credit?

How do you learn to make good business decisions? You can start by identifying what decisions need to be made, when they need to be made, what information should be gathered before they are made, and who should make the decisions. You might learn to make good decisions by first making some bad decisions and learning from your mistakes. Or sometimes you can learn by observing and critiquing other people's decisions. In this *Making Business Decisions* assignment, you'll do just that. You'll identify and then critique the decisions made in the Cards & Memorabilia Unlimited case study.

Use the following three-column format to:

- Identify and describe each decision made in the case study and identify the decision maker.
- List the decisions in the order they occurred in the chapter.
- Assign each decision a number.
- Describe what information was gathered to make the decision.
- Analyze the decision. Was it a good decision? Why or why not? What other decision(s), if any, should have been made?

The first decision has been done for you.

The Decision	Information Gathered	Analysis
1. Susan decides she wants to leave her job.	She is unhappy at her job. She does not use the knowledge and skills she learned at college, and she wants to work more with people.	Susan is making a good decision to work in a job she will enjoy more, but if the economy should deteriorate, she is taking a big risk leaving a secure, steady-paying job.
2.		
3.		

Questions

(Questions 1 through 20 test your mastery of Performance Objective 4)

YOUR PERFORMANCE OBJECTIVE 4
(page 22)

1-1 Explain in your own words the meaning of key business terms.

a. Financing
b. Collateral
c. Balance sheet
d. Budget
e. Operating budget
f. Income statement
g. Revenue
h. Useful life
i. Equity
j. Return on equity

1-2 Explain what is meant by registering a business name.

1-3 Distinguish among a lease, a lessee, and a lessor.

1-4 Distinguish among businesses organized as sole proprietorships, partnerships, and corporations.

1-5 Distinguish between assets and liabilities.

1-6 How have you used the concept of collateral (other than a bank loan) in your everyday life?

1-7 Explain what is meant by a subordinated loan or liability.

1-8 Distinguish *financial accounting* from *managerial accounting.*

1-9 Describe the nature of sales revenue in each of the following businesses:

a Movie theater
b. Amusement park
c. Beauty salon
d. Health club
e. Nursing home
f. Computer manufacturer
g. Computer retailer
h. College bookstore
i. TV network
j. Automobile dealership

1-10 Calculate Susan's depreciation expense, assuming her equipment's estimated useful life was 10 rather than 5 years.

1-11 Distinguish between the terms *cost* and *expense.* Provide an example of this distinction drawn from your everyday life.

1-12 How is cost of goods sold related to inventory?

1-13 Which expenses, if any, would differ if you were operating a small restaurant instead of a cards and memorabilia store?

1-14 What is the difference between *net income* and *net loss?*

1-15 Distinguish *net income* from *net worth.*

1-16 Would it be possible to prepare a budgeted balance sheet? Why or why not?

1-17 Use an example not used in this chapter to distinguish between "return *on* investment" and "return *of* investment."

1-18 Distinguish between "return on investment" and "rate of return on investment."

1-19 You might have wondered why Susan decided to sell some of her personal baseball card collection to help finance her business rather than simply contributing the cards to her business inventory. Discuss some plausible reasons for her decision. One reason might be that her marketing strategy did not include cards older than 10 years. What would you have done?

1-20 In this chapter, you learned that financial accounting measures and reports information for external users of accounting information, while managerial accounting measures and reports information for internal users. In your groups, respond to the following:

a. What is meant by the phrase *a user of accounting information?* Differentiate between an internal and external user.
b. Can a user of accounting information be both an internal and external user? Explain.
c. List at least three external and three internal users of accounting information.

Appendix Questions

AQ1-1 Do you think Susan has made a convincing case for placing her store in Rialto, Arizona? Why or why not?

AQ1-2 Do you think Susan has taken on too much work for herself? Give all your reasons in detail.

AQ1-3 Discuss the quality of Susan's advertising and promotion campaign. How would you change or improve upon it?

AQ1-4 Suppose you were helping Susan plan for the grand opening celebration of her store. Based on information in this business plan, how many people do you think will attend? Give detailed reasons for your answer.

AQ1-5 Suppose you were helping Susan plan for her focus groups. Write five questions that you think she should ask her focus group participants.

Reinforcement Exercises

E1-1 Asking the Right Questions: A Group Activity

YOUR PERFORMANCE OBJECTIVE 4 *(page 22)*

It is often said that knowing the right answer is not nearly as important as asking the right question. Asking the right question is a problem-solving skill that will help you make sound business decisions. In this exercise, you will review the vocabulary introduced in Chapter 1 by creating questions to match answers—similar to a popular TV show.

Required

a. Given an answer, what's the question?
   Choose *three* of the following terms to serve as an answer and create an appropriate question for each term. For example, if you choose *balance sheet*, you might create the question—*What financial statement shows the assets, liabilities, and owner's equity of an entity on a specific date?*—although now you can't use this question!

Operating budget	Sales revenue	Expense
Cost	Return of investment	Return on equity
Return on investment	Business plan	Financing
Collateral	Balance sheet	Net income

b. Are you sure that's the question?
   Have each group member within your small group read aloud the questions they developed in Requirement (a). As a group, decide whether each question is an accurate match for each answer.
   Once satisfied that all questions are appropriate, the group, as a whole, chooses the three best questions created within the group. Record the three questions chosen (with their answers) on separate pieces of paper or index cards and give them to your instructor.

c. What's the answer?
   To ensure that you have learned the vocabulary terms listed in requirement (a) your instructor will now quiz you on the questions written by all of your classmates.

E1-2 Preparing Your Own Balance Sheet

Prepare a balance sheet showing the items you own (your assets), the items you owe (your liabilities), and the difference between them (your net worth) by using the personal financial statement form or loan application form shown on page 36. Then answer questions (a) through (d). If you feel uncomfortable disclosing your personal financial information, use fictitious item names and numbers.

Required

a. In what ways is your financial statement information comparable to the information provided by Susan Newman?
b. In what ways, if any, does your financial statement information differ from the information provided by Susan?
c. What items, if any, are you uncertain about how to measure?
d. Which items listed under assets qualify as collateral? Why?

E1-3 Evaluating a Personal Loan Application

Carefully study the loan application shown on page 37 on your own or in a group.

Required

a. Which financial statement described in Chapter 1 does this loan application represent?
b. Write a brief summary explaining what Jason Hammer owns, what he owes to others, and what his net worth represents.
c. Assume Jason Hammer has applied for a $75,000 line of credit. Answer the following questions:

PERSONAL FINANCIAL STATEMENT

PERSONAL PROFILE

NAME		AGE	SOCIAL SECURITY NUMBER	
STREET ADDRESS	CITY		STATE	ZIP
HOME PHONE ( )	☐ OWN ☐ RENT $ ______ PER MONTH ☐ OTHER ______		AT CURRENT ADDRESS SINCE (MM/YY): ____ / ____	
☐ MARRIED ☐ SEPARATED ☐ UNMARRIED	NUMBER OF DEPENDENTS	AGES OF DEPENDENTS	YEARS WITH COMPANY	
SPOUSE'S NAME	SPOUSE'S OCCUPATION		SPOUSE'S SOCIAL SECURITY NUMBER	
SPOUSE EMPLOYED BY	HOW LONG WITH EMPLOYER? (SPOUSE) YRS. MOS.		SPOUSE'S WORK PHONE ( )	

BANKING RELATIONSHIPS (Please list only your personal accounts.)

NAME OF BANK	ACCOUNT NUMBER	PERSONAL		CURRENT BALANCE
		CHECKING	SAVINGS	

FINANCIAL STATEMENT

ASSETS	AMOUNT	LIABILITIES	AMOUNT
CASH IN YOUR PRIMARY BANK		TOTAL REVOLVING CREDIT	
CASH IN OTHER BANKS		TOTAL INSTALLMENT LOANS	
RETIREMENT ACCOUNTS (IRA, SEP. KEOGH, 401-K)		1ST MORTGAGE ON RESIDENCE	
STOCK / BONDS / MUTUAL FUNDS (INCLUDE COPY OF BROKER'S STATEMENTS)		OTHER MORTGAGES ON RESIDENCE	
RESIDENCE MARKET VALUE		MORTGAGE(S) ON OTHER REAL ESTATE	
OTHER REAL ESTATE MARKET VALUE		OTHER LIABILITIES (PLEASE DESCRIBE)	
OTHER ASSETS (PLEASE DESCRIBE)		OTHER LIABILITIES (PLEASE DESCRIBE)	
OTHER ASSETS (PLEASE DESCRIBE)			
TOTAL ASSETS		**TOTAL LIABILITIES**	

NET WORTH (TOTAL ASSETS MINUS TOTAL LIABILITIES) $ ______

DO YOU GUARANTEE ANY OTHER DEBT? YES ____ NO ____ IF YES, WHAT IS THE TOTAL: $ ______

WHO IS THE BORROWER? ______

NAME OF FINANCIAL INSTITUTION ______

1. If you were a bank loan officer, what questions would you have regarding the information presented on Jason's personal financial statement? Explain why you would have each of these questions.
2. What information *not* contained in this financial statement would you need or want to know about Jason before agreeing or not agreeing to lend him money? In each case, explain why.

YOUR PERFORMANCE OBJECTIVE 4
(page 22)

E1-4 Explaining Cost, Expense, and Cost of Goods Sold

You have just opened a store called Rocky Mountain Outfitters. Your inventory includes a wide assortment of such camping and hiking gear as tents, backpacks, hiking shoes, lanterns, and cooking utensils. You have purchased $25,000 worth of inventory to start your business and expect to purchase an additional $15,000 of inventory before the end of the first year. You also expect your sales to be $60,000 and your inventory at the end of the year to amount to $10,000.

Required

a. Distinguish between the terms *cost* and *expense,* using this example.
b. What is the amount of the expense called "Cost of Goods Sold"?

LOAN APPLICATION

PERSONAL PROFILE

NAME	AGE	SOCIAL SECURITY NUMBER	
JASON HAMMER	28	921-00-9999	
STREET ADDRESS: 501 Circle Drive	CITY: San Jose	STATE: CA	ZIP: 95101
HOME PHONE: (408) 555-1321	☒ OWN ☐ RENT $ ____ PER MONTH ☐ OTHER ____	AT CURRENT ADDRESS SINCE (MM/YY): 2 / 98	
☐ MARRIED ☐ SEPARATED ☒ UNMARRIED	NUMBER OF DEPENDENTS: 1 / AGES OF DEPENDENTS: 3	YEARS WITH COMPANY: 2	
SPOUSE'S NAME	SPOUSE'S OCCUPATION	SPOUSE'S SOCIAL SECURITY NUMBER	
SPOUSE EMPLOYED BY	HOW LONG WITH EMPLOYER? (SPOUSE) YRS. MOS.	SPOUSE'S WORK PHONE ( )	

BANKING RELATIONSHIPS (Please list only your personal accounts.)

NAME OF BANK	ACCOUNT NUMBER	PERSONAL CHECKING	PERSONAL SAVINGS	CURRENT BALANCE
Wells Fargo Bank	118-67242	✓		$ 560
Union Savings Bank	14-76429		✓	4,310

FINANCIAL STATEMENT

ASSETS	AMOUNT	LIABILITIES	AMOUNT
CASH IN YOUR PRIMARY BANK	$ 560	TOTAL REVOLVING CREDIT	$ 3,900
CASH IN OTHER BANKS	4,310	TOTAL INSTALLMENT LOANS	N/A
RETIREMENT ACCOUNTS (IRA, SEP. KEOGH, 401-K)	-0-	1ST MORTGAGE ON RESIDENCE	122,800
STOCK / BONDS / MUTUAL FUNDS (INCLUDE COPY OF BROKER'S STATEMENTS)	1,300	OTHER MORTGAGES ON RESIDENCE	N/A
RESIDENCE MARKET VALUE	165,000	MORTGAGE(S) ON OTHER REAL ESTATE	N/A
OTHER REAL ESTATE MARKET VALUE	N/A	OTHER LIABILITIES (PLEASE DESCRIBE)	N/A
OTHER ASSETS (PLEASE DESCRIBE) Personal Auto	9,500	OTHER LIABILITIES (PLEASE DESCRIBE)	N/A
OTHER ASSETS (PLEASE DESCRIBE) Home Furnishings	12,900		
TOTAL ASSETS	$193,570	**TOTAL LIABILITIES**	$126,700

NET WORTH (TOTAL ASSETS MINUS TOTAL LIABILITIES) $ 66,870

DO YOU GUARANTEE ANY OTHER DEBT? YES ____ NO X IF YES, WHAT IS THE TOTAL: $ ____

WHO IS THE BORROWER? ____

NAME OF FINANCIAL INSTITUTION ____

E1-5 Preparing Your Own Operating Budget

YOUR PERFORMANCE OBJECTIVE 1 *(page 16)*

Prepare an operating budget for your next college term (quarter or semester) showing your projected revenues and expenses. Examples of revenues might include your earnings from a part-time job or support from your family. Examples of expenses might include your tuition, books, and living expenses. When you complete this financial report, answer questions (a) through (d). If you feel uncomfortable disclosing personal financial information, use fictitious item names and numbers.

YOUR PERFORMANCE OBJECTIVE 3 *(page 20)*

Required

a. In what ways is your operating budget comparable to Susan Newman's operating budget?
b. In what ways, if any, does your operating budget differ from Susan's operating budget?
c. What items, if any, are you uncertain about how to measure?
d. Explain how preparing such a budget might be useful to you.

E1-6 Evaluating Companies by Their ROI

The following information is from three different companies:

	Witt Company	Paine Company	Scott Company
Original investment	$21,000	$62,000	$158,000
Net income	3,045	8,990	22,910

Required

a. In your own words, describe what is meant by rate of return on investment (ROI).
b. Calculate the ROI for each company.
c. Compare and contrast the results of the ROI calculated for all three companies. Is one company performing better than the others? Explain your answer.
d. Assume the net income for each of the three companies was $3,000 higher than shown. How would the results obtained in question (b) and your response to question (c) be affected by this change?

Critical Thinking Problems

YOUR PERFORMANCE OBJECTIVE 2 *(page 18)*

P1-1 Evaluating Business Loan Applications

As a loan analyst for Heritage Bank, you are asked to evaluate business loan applications and then make your recommendations to the bank's loan committee. Today, you are looking at three loan applications for a $60,000 business line of credit.

Required

a. Based solely on the information presented below, which, if any, of the applications would you recommend?
b. Explain in detail your reasons for accepting or rejecting each application. Include in your explanation any assumptions you felt were necessary to make.

	Application 1	Application 2	Application 3
Industry	Restaurant	Architecture	Pest Control
Past industry experience	5 years	2 years	None
Past work experience	5 years	10 years	15 years
Academic background	High school degree	Graduate degree	Undergraduate degree
Recoverable amounts of items owned	$50,000	$150,000	$75,000
Amounts of items owed	$20,000	$75,000	$25,000
Other data	Rents Married 2 children	Home owner Married No children	Lives with parents Single No children

P1-2 Ethical and Legal Implications of Withdrawing Assets from a Business

Recall that Susan Newman's uncle gives her $15,000 to start her business and agrees to subordinate his right to repayment to the bank. Assume that Susan purchases equipment, furniture, and fixtures for use in her new business, including two VCRs. Six months later she realizes that she does not need one of the VCRs. Her uncle's birthday is next week, so Susan decides to give him the extra VCR as a gift.

The objective of this assignment is to consider the ethical and legal implications of withdrawing assets from a business.

Required

a. In your own words, describe the meaning of a subordinated liability.
b. Is the gift given to Susan's uncle in violation of the agreement he made to subordinate his right to repayment? Explain in detail why or why not.
c. If Susan withdrew cash from the business and then used the cash to purchase a new VCR for her uncle, would this be a violation of the agreement? Explain in detail why or why not.

d. If either amount described in question (b) or question (c) is in violation of the agreement, does Susan have to notify the bank? If she does not, how would the bank find out about the amount? Who are the stakeholders (those liable to be harmed or to benefit) in this situation?

P1-3 The Ethics of Financial Information Presentation

People in the public limelight are often prosecuted or censured for unethical presentations on personal financial statements. In this problem you'll explore what is fraudulent or misleading information. In other words, you'll clarify what is ethical and unethical in presenting financial information.

Required

a. Study the information requested on the Personal Financial Statement shown below. What's another name for this financial statement?

b. In groups or on your own, assume you are applying for a loan with this bank. Assume also that you know you need more money than the bank is likely to approve for a person

PERSONAL FINANCIAL STATEMENT

PERSONAL PROFILE

NAME		AGE	SOCIAL SECURITY NUMBER
STREET ADDRESS	CITY	STATE	ZIP
HOME PHONE ( )	☐ OWN ☐ RENT $ ______ PER MONTH ☐ OTHER ______	AT CURRENT ADDRESS SINCE (MM/YY): ____ / ____	
☐ MARRIED ☐ SEPARATED ☐ UNMARRIED	NUMBER OF DEPENDENTS	AGES OF DEPENDENTS	YEARS WITH COMPANY
SPOUSE'S NAME	SPOUSE'S OCCUPATION		SPOUSE'S SOCIAL SECURITY NUMBER
SPOUSE EMPLOYED BY	HOW LONG WITH EMPLOYER? (SPOUSE) YRS. MOS.		SPOUSE'S WORK PHONE ( )

BANKING RELATIONSHIPS (Please list only your personal accounts.)

NAME OF BANK	ACCOUNT NUMBER	PERSONAL CHECKING	PERSONAL SAVINGS	CURRENT BALANCE

FINANCIAL STATEMENT

ASSETS	AMOUNT	LIABILITIES	AMOUNT
CASH IN YOUR PRIMARY BANK		TOTAL REVOLVING CREDIT	
CASH IN OTHER BANKS		TOTAL INSTALLMENT LOANS	
RETIREMENT ACCOUNTS (IRA, SEP. KEOGH, 401-K)		1ST MORTGAGE ON RESIDENCE	
STOCK / BONDS / MUTUAL FUNDS (INCLUDE COPY OF BROKER'S STATEMENTS)		OTHER MORTGAGES ON RESIDENCE	
RESIDENCE MARKET VALUE		MORTGAGE(S) ON OTHER REAL ESTATE	
OTHER REAL ESTATE MARKET VALUE		OTHER LIABILITIES (PLEASE DESCRIBE)	
OTHER ASSETS (PLEASE DESCRIBE)		OTHER LIABILITIES (PLEASE DESCRIBE)	
OTHER ASSETS (PLEASE DESCRIBE)			
TOTAL ASSETS		**TOTAL LIABILITIES**	

NET WORTH (TOTAL ASSETS MINUS TOTAL LIABILITIES) $ ____________

DO YOU GUARANTEE ANY OTHER DEBT? YES ____ NO ____ IF YES, WHAT IS THE TOTAL: $ ____________

WHO IS THE BORROWER? ____________

NAME OF FINANCIAL INSTITUTION ____________

in your financial situation. List all of the items on this application that, were you not honest, you could "fudge" or not reveal all the details so you could get your loan approved for more money.

c. In groups or on your own, answer the following questions:
   1. Do you think it is a common practice for people to provide false, misleading, or incorrect information on a personal financial statement? Explain.
   2. How can someone determine if the information provided is true or false? What measures should the bank take to ensure the information is accurate?
   3. What can happen if the bank does not initially discover the false information and grants the loan but later discovers the borrower's dishonesty?
   4. Who are the stakeholders (those who would be harmed or benefit) if the loan is granted under false pretenses?
   5. What recourse would the bank have if the false information is not detected and the borrower defaults on the loan?
   6. Suppose a friend asks you for advice. He needs a loan to help him pay for his child's doctor bills. He also tells you that he is quite certain that he will be granted a loan only if he provides false information. What advice would you give your friend? What reasons could you give him *not* to provide false information?

P1-4 Including Foreign Assets on Your Personal Balance Sheet

Suppose you are applying for a small business loan and your banker asks you to prepare a personal balance sheet. While making a list of your assets, you remember a relative who deposited money in a bank account in your name in Mexico many years ago. The balance in the account is now 18,500 pesos. The current equivalent to U.S. dollars is 9.2088 pesos to $1. In other words, for every dollar, you get 9.2088 pesos; conversely, for every peso, you get about 11 cents.

The objective of this assignment is to consider whether you should include certain assets on your personal balance sheet and, if so, how much should you show?

Required

Answer the following questions in groups or on your own:

a. What is the balance in this bank account in U.S. dollars?
b. Do you think you should include this amount on your personal balance sheet? Why or why not? If so, would you consider it part of the amount shown as cash in savings accounts, as an investment, or somewhere else? Should the amount be shown as U.S. dollars or pesos?
c. Is it important for you to disclose to your banker that this amount is in a foreign bank account? Explain your answer.
d. Do you think it would be difficult to protect or to withdraw the funds in the Mexican bank account? Why or why not? What other problems do you think you might encounter in managing this bank account?

YOUR PERFORMANCE OBJECTIVE 3
(page 20)

P1-5 Return on Equity and Ethics

Nancy Polizzio has owned and operated a moderately successful exercise gym for the past four years. The gym space she rents is part of a larger building. The person who rents the adjacent space recently told her that his company would be moving out within the next 6 to 12 months. Nancy believes that she could improve her profits by expanding into this space and offering additional exercise rooms and activities. She then finds out from the landlord that she might be able to rent this space if she provides him additional financial information and is able to obtain additional bank financing. Nancy realizes that both the landlord and bank will want to assess her financial position by looking at the gym's financial statements, including the net income and rate of return on equity. The following information is available for each year Nancy has been in business:

	Year 1	Year 2	Year 3	Year 4
Net income	$ 3,500	$ 8,200	$12,100	$12,300
Year-end capital	42,500	46,700	50,800	54,100

Nancy started the business four years ago by investing $40,000. During the current year, in anticipation of expanding her business, she purchased $30,000 in additional equipment, using $10,000 cash and signing a five-year note with the equipment company for $20,000. Nancy estimates that the new equipment has a useful life of six years. Just before the end of the year, she estimates her income before depreciation expense on the new equipment will be $12,600 for the year. Nancy withdrew $8,000 in cash from the business during the year for personal living expenses.

The objective of this assignment is to reinforce the concept of return on equity and consider the ethical implications of presenting misleading or false financial information.

Required

In groups or on your own:

a. Calculate Nancy's rate of return on equity for each of the four years she has been in business. Comment briefly on whether you think Nancy is doing better or worse each year.
b. Calculate Nancy's net income for Year 5.
c. Calculate Nancy's year-end capital balance and her rate of return on equity for Year 5. Explain why this year is better or worse than the previous years.
d. Nancy is concerned with how the results for Year 5 will affect her expansion plans. Having some experience with accounting, she is considering two options:

   Option A: Even though the estimated useful life of the new equipment is 6 years, she is considering using a 10-year useful life to calculate depreciation.

   Option B: Assuming she has adequate cash, she is thinking of withdrawing $10,000 in cash as a personal living expense and reinvesting an equal amount ($10,000) in the business sometime during the second month of Year 6.

   1. Determine the effect *each* option will have on Nancy's net income and rate of return on equity for Year 5.
   2. Is either option proper? Why or why not?
   3. What impact do you think these options would have on the way the landlord and loan officer view Nancy's financial status?

Required

On your own:

a. Write a brief description of how rate of return on equity is calculated and how it can be used to make business decisions.
b. Briefly describe the difference between cost and expense. Then explain whether depreciation is a cost or an expense of doing business.
c. Briefly describe the difference between return on investment and return of investment. Then explain whether the amounts Nancy withdrew from the business for personal living expenses were a return of investment or return on investment.

Appendix Critical Thinking Problems

AP1-1 Would You Invest in CMU?

YOUR PERFORMANCE OBJECTIVE 2 *(page 18)*

Suppose you were a friend of Susan's and you had $5,000 that you could invest in Cards & Memorabilia Unlimited. Would you invest $5,000 in Susan's business based on this business plan or would you invest the money in the stock market? Give detailed reasons for your answer.

AP1-2 Evaluating Susan's Business Plan

List what you consider to be the strengths and weaknesses of Susan's business plan.

AP1-3 Creating an Advertisement

Susan has asked you to help her create an advertisement that she plans to run in *The Phoenix Democrat* announcing her grand opening. The ad will be 4 inches by 4 inches square and can contain one piece of black and white art. Create the ad for Susan. You may use the computer or write/sketch it by hand.

AP1-4 Providing Written Feedback to Susan

Susan has created the first draft of the flier she plans to distribute in the Phoenix area. She shows it to you and asks for your feedback. Write Susan a note making suggestions for what to change and what to retain on this flier. Be very specific. Comment on size, font, layout, graphics, text, and other aspects of the flier.

Cards & Memorabilia Unlimited
Cards • Supplies • Photographs •
Autographed Equipment • and much more

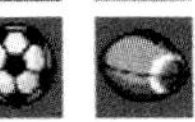

We're pleased to announce the
Grand Opening.
Come and see the greatest selection in the
greater Phoenix area. Bring your friends!
Receive 10% off your first purchase!
M-F 10-6 Sat 10-3
Located in the Village Mountain Plaza across
from Rialto Video

Research Assignments

A wide variety of interesting Research Assignments for this chapter are available for the following topics at www.mhhe.com/solomon:

R1-1 Why Write a Business Plan?
R1-2 What Tools Are Available to Write a Business Plan?
R1-3 What Do You Think of Susan's Business Plan?
R1-4 Would You Invest in Cards & Memorabilia Unlimited?
R1-5 Learning More about the Trading Card and Sports Memorabilia Business
R1-6 Investigating a Trading Card and/or Sports Memorabilia Store (PO 2)
R1-7 How Do You Register a Business Name in Your County?
R1-8 How Does Your Local Bank Decide to Grant Loans?
R1-9 Interviewing a Business Professional (PO 2)
R1-10 Finding Financial Statements on the Internet (PO 2)

Appendix Research Assignments

AR1-1 Writing Your Own Business Plan
AR1-2 Trading Card and Sports Memorabilia Business Locations
AR1-3 Trading Cards and Sports Memorabilia on the Internet

CHAPTER TWO

Analyzing the Transactions of a Business

Also be sure you have mastered the following Performance Objectives from previous chapters. They lay the foundation for the concepts you will learn in this chapter:

PO2
PO4

PERFORMANCE OBJECTIVES

In this chapter, you will learn the following new Performance Objectives:

PO5 **Apply** the fundamental accounting equation, Assets = Liabilities + Owner's Equity, to:

a. **Analyze** the effects of accounting transactions on the elements of the balance sheet.
b. **Prepare** a balance sheet that reports the financial condition of any entity.

PO6 **Identify** and **apply** the three conditions necessary for a transaction to qualify as an accounting transaction and, therefore, be recorded in an accounting information system.

PO7
a. **Define** the terms *financing activities*, *investing activities*, and *operating activities*.
b. **Classify** any accounting transaction into one of these activities or a noncash investing and financing activity.
c. **Classify** any cash receipt or cash payment transaction into the appropriate activity as reported in the statement of cash flows.

PO8 **Explain** what role ethics plays in the preparation of financial statements.

PO9 **Identify** the types of decisions investors and creditors make and **describe** what information in the financial statements and/or related disclosures meets the information needs of each group.

CARDS & MEMORABILIA UNLIMITED: THE LARGE ROLE OF SMALL BUSINESS

You might not be surprised to learn that in the United States today, virtually all businesses, large and small, are expected to follow the same set of accounting rules and produce the same types of financial statements. But you might be surprised by the answers to the following questions: Which type of business—large or small—accounts for 99.7% of all U.S. employers? Which type of business—large or small—accounts for 53% of the U.S. private workforce? Which type of business generates 47% of all U.S. sales? Which type of business represents 96% of all U.S. exporters?

If you answered "small" to *all* of these questions, you would be correct. Surprised? Consider the following facts. According to the U.S. Small Business Administration, on any given day approximately 30% of Americans are thinking of starting a small business. Small businesses provide 67% of workers with their first jobs and initial on-the-job training in basic skills. Further, small businesses generate more than half of the nation's gross domestic product and are the principal source of new jobs in the U.S. economy.

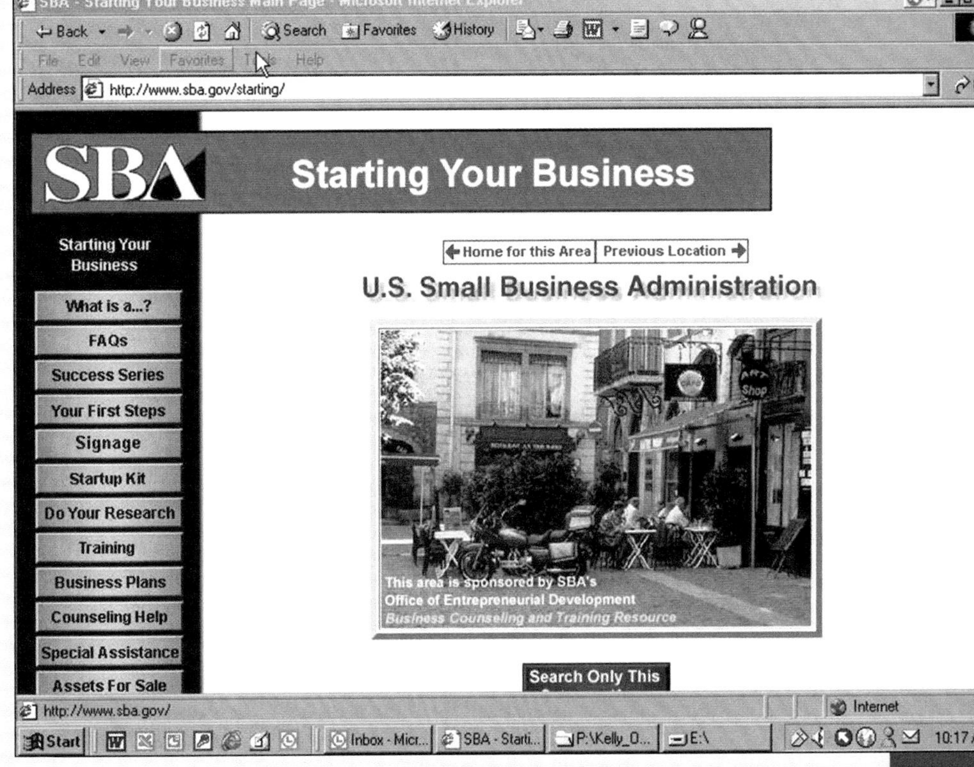

And what is a small business? According to the Small Business Administration, a business is considered small if it is "independently owned and operated," if it is not "dominant in its field," and if it reports revenues of less than $500,000.

Looking at these facts, you might conclude that sometime in your career you are likely to work for a small business. Many people start their careers by working in a big business to "learn the ropes" of a particular industry and then move to a small business or even start their own to compete with larger businesses in the same industry.

The Cards & Memorabilia Unlimited case is purposely developed as a small business because today the ultimate goal of many students, maybe even you, is to start their own businesses. In fact, only a small percentage of your classmates will work for Fortune 500 firms. What's more, you will find it easier to first learn accounting concepts in a small business setting. The numbers are smaller, the scope of the business decisions is smaller, and you are more likely to identify with many of the decisions a small business owner makes than with someone who makes multimillion dollar decisions at a Fortune 500 firm.

So in this chapter you'll get your first look at how accounting records business events by following Susan Newman and her first few business transactions as the owner of Cards & Memorabilia Unlimited. And you'll learn that no matter what their size, virtually all businesses follow the same set of accounting rules and produce the same types of financial statements. When it comes to accounting, there's little difference between the large and the small business.

Financial Statements: The Reported Effects of Business Events

In Chapter 1 you learned how Susan planned to conduct her first year of business at Cards & Memorabilia Unlimited. Recall that she was unable to provide the bank or the landlord financial statements from the business in November or December because she had not yet begun to conduct business. But in January of her first year of conducting business, she will be able to report the effects of business events or transactions engaged in by her business. That is, the recorded effects of these transactions will be reported in *financial statements*, reports whose information gives a picture of the financial "health" of a business. The concept of financial statements is not entirely new to you; you were exposed to two of them in Chapter 1. The application form Susan filled out to apply for a line of credit (Figure 1-7) was actually a *balance sheet*. Also, you saw Susan's projected *income statement* or operating budget for CMU (Figure 1-10c). Before you examine these and other financial statements in more detail, let's consider two essential questions that establish a foundation for how to evaluate all businesses.

Two Questions to Ask When Evaluating a Business

Every business decision maker is a potential user of accounting information. For example, when Phillip Strauss, Susan's loan officer, finished "packaging" her loan application, he presented it to Ken Ledeit, the loan analyst at Central Bank. Ken's job was to decide whether or not to recommend that the bank's loan committee grant Susan a $50,000 line of credit. To properly evaluate Susan's financial condition, Ken needed to know whether she would have enough cash available to repay his bank. If he authorized loaning Susan money that she was unable to repay, his decision might have severe consequences for both Susan and his bank.

Another business decision maker who used accounting information was Susan's commercial real estate agent, Mary Mathews. Mary was interested in Susan's financial condition to determine the amount of rent Susan could afford. Mary needed this information to match Susan with a property that was not too expensive.

Notice, both Ken Ledeit and Mary Mathews needed answers to two questions when they evaluated Susan's financial condition. First, they asked, *"What things of value are owned or controlled?"* And second, they asked, *"What are the claims against or sources of these things of value?"* Notice that the phrases *claims against* and *sources of* are similar. That is, an owner can be said to have a claim against things of value and also be the source of things of value. Generally, we will use the phrase *sources of* in this book to describe who provides things of value.

The answers to these simple questions provide not only information Ken and Mary can use in their decisions but also information Susan can use to record her initial transactions at Cards & Memorabilia Unlimited. You can answer the first question by listing what Susan owns in what might be called a "Things of Value Report." You can then answer the second question by listing the claims of various parties against Susan's things of value in what might be called a "Sources of Things of Value Report." Taken together, these reports provide valuable feedback to Ken, Mary, and Susan about the initial financial condition of CMU.

Distinguishing between Activities and Transactions

Before you prepare Susan's things of value report and her sources of things of value report, you must learn how a **business activity** differs from a business transaction.

Start by thinking of moving from the general (an activity) to the specific (a transaction). That is, a business activity is one of the three fundamental actions taken by an entity to ensure its growth and survival. These fundamental actions include financing activities, investing activities, and operating activities as shown in Figure 2-1. On a global level, therefore, all business actions can be divided into three types of action or activity. On a more detailed level, however, you can identify a smaller, more basic unit of business activity called a transaction. Each of the three fundamental business activities generates its own unique transactions. For now, let's define a **business transaction** as simply an event involving a transfer or exchange between two parties. In general, there are three types of such exchanges—financing transactions, investing transactions, and operating transactions.

FIGURE 2-1 The nature of and relationships among the three fundamental business activities

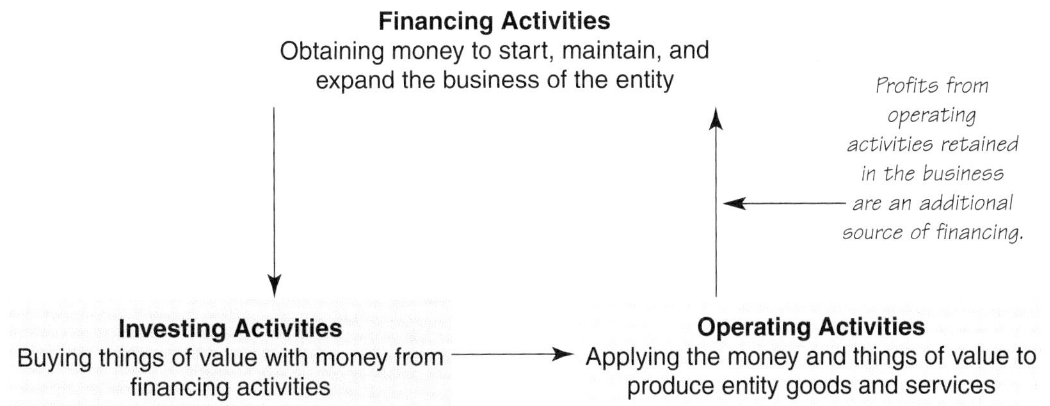

For simplicity, Susan's first year of business is divided into transactions labeled A_1 through Z. You can find a complete list of these transactions in Appendix C. Since you will be working with CMU's transactions throughout this textbook, take the time now to scan them. In this chapter, we will cover the first four transactions as shown in Figure 2-2. Don't forget that these and all transactions can be classified into one of the three essential business activities. As you learn about these activities and transactions, you will discover you have already engaged in many of them. That's right, you have been involved in each activity and many of these transactions in your personal, day-to-day experiences.

Now that you understand the essential difference between an activity and a transaction, you're ready to apply what you've just learned to four examples—the first four transactions of CMU in early January.

FIGURE 2-2 Transactions A_1, B, C_1, and D for Cards & Memorabilia Unlimited

A_1	01/02	—	$30,000 cash is contributed by the owner who opens a business checking account.
B	01/02	—	$6,000 cash is withdrawn from the checking account to open a business savings account.
C_1	01/04	—	$10,000 worth of store equipment is acquired with a credit card.
D	01/06	—	$15,000 cash is paid to acquire merchandise inventory.

Transaction A_1—A Financing Activity Transaction

If you have ever borrowed money and then repaid it, you have initiated and completed a financing activity. In this financing activity, the relevant entity is you, a legal person. Likewise, if you and a friend share the cost and the driving on a spring break vacation, the two of you are engaged in a travel venture *financed* with personal contributions. In this financing activity, the relevant entity is a social partnership composed of you and your friend.

In general, **financing activities** are transactions in which an entity obtains money for starting, maintaining, and expanding the scale of its operation. You initiate financing activities with transactions that obtain money and other resources for the entity from lenders and owners. Figures 2-3a and 2-3b describe two typical financing activities that corporations use to acquire resources or **capital** from lenders and owners through various financial markets. Figure 2-3a illustrates a borrowing transaction initiated by Sprint Capital Corporation. Those who invest in these "new issues" are called **lenders**. When Sprint borrows, it creates a claim held by lenders against its things of value. Figure 2-3b illustrates a common stock financing transaction that Cheap Tickets, Inc., uses to obtain money from its potential owners or shareholders.

Financing activities are completed by transactions that repay lenders or owners, the outside sources of this money. That is, financing activities don't end with the creation of claims against things of value; they also include transactions that eliminate the claims. Now let's examine Cards & Memorabilia Unlimited's first financing activity.

FIGURE 2-3a

A financing activity transaction in which Sprint Capital Corporation raises money by borrowing

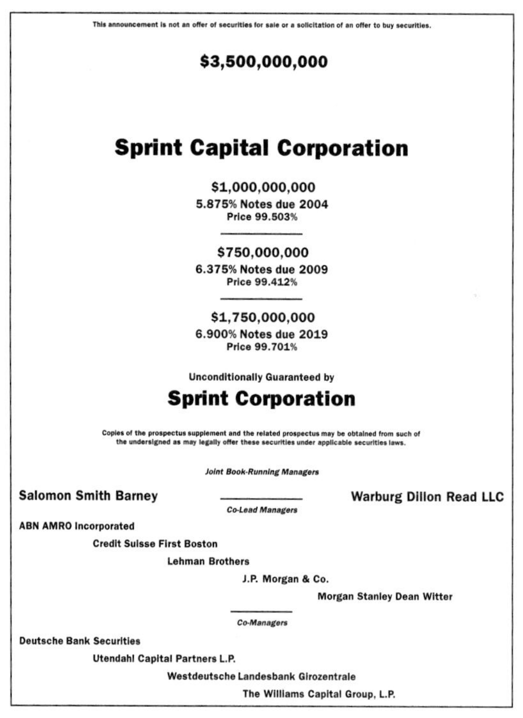

This announcement is not an offer of securities for sale or a solicitation of an offer to buy securities.

$3,500,000,000

Sprint Capital Corporation

$1,000,000,000
5.875% Notes due 2004
Price 99.503%

$750,000,000
6.375% Notes due 2009
Price 99.412%

$1,750,000,000
6.900% Notes due 2019
Price 99.701%

Unconditionally Guaranteed by

Sprint Corporation

Copies of the prospectus supplement and the related prospectus may be obtained from such of the undersigned as may legally offer these securities under applicable securities laws.

Joint Book-Running Managers

Salomon Smith Barney
Warburg Dillon Read LLC

Co-Lead Managers

ABN AMRO Incorporated
Credit Suisse First Boston
Lehman Brothers
J.P. Morgan & Co.
Morgan Stanley Dean Witter

Co-Managers

Deutsche Bank Securities
Utendahl Capital Partners L.P.
Westdeutsche Landesbank Girozentrale
The Williams Capital Group, L.P.

Transaction On Monday, January 2, Susan Newman contributes $30,000 of cash to finance her business. This transaction occurs when Susan deposits $30,000 in a business checking account.

Explanation This transaction is a financing activity because it provides $30,000 cash to CMU from its owner, Susan Newman. Recall, Susan had accumulated this amount by combining $15,000 of personal savings with $15,000 from her uncle that she deposited in her personal checking account. Thus, this transaction is made up of Susan's transfer of $15,000 from her personal savings account and a transfer of $15,000 from her personal checking account into a new business checking account.

This is not an offer to sell nor a solicitation of offers to buy any of these securities.
This offer is made only by the Prospectus.

3,500,000 Shares

CHEAP TICKETS INC.

www.cheaptickets.com

Common Stock

Price $15 Per Share

Copies of the Prospectus may be obtained within any State from any Underwriter who may lawfully offer these securities within such State.

William Blair & Company   Dain Rauscher Wessels
a division of Dain Rauscher Incorporated

BT Alex. Brown Incorporated   Donaldson, Lufkin & Jenrette   Goldman, Sachs & Co.

Hambrecht & Quist   Lehman Brothers   NationsBanc Montgomery Securities LLC

PaineWebber Incorporated   Salomon Smith Barney

Adams, Harkness & Hill, Inc.   Everen Securities, Inc.   Fahnestock & Co. Inc.

Jefferies & Company, Inc.   Josephthal & Co. Inc.   McDonald Investments Inc.

Needham & Company, Inc.   Raymond James & Associates, Inc.

Southeast Research Partners, Inc.   Sutro & Co. Incorporated   C.E. Unterberg, Towbin

U.S. Bancorp Piper Jaffray   Volpe Brown Whelan & Company

FIGURE 2-3b

A financing activity transaction in which Cheap Tickets, Inc. raises money by issuing common stock

This transfer marks the beginning of Susan's business, even though her store's grand opening is not scheduled until a week later, Monday, January 9.

To help yourself become an active rather than a passive learner, reread Transaction A_1, and try to answer the following two questions before you continue reading: *What things of value are owned?* and *What are the sources of these things of value?* Before you check these answers, fill in these two reports.

CARDS & MEMORABILIA UNLIMITED
Things of Value Report
January 2

______________	$______
	$______

CARDS & MEMORABILIA UNLIMITED
Sources of Things of Value Report
January 2

______________	$______
	$______

Now let's consider the correct answers on page 50.

Analysis Your answer to the first question—What things of value are owned?—should be $30,000 of cash to reflect Susan's increase in her business checking account. You will find this increase in her Things of Value Report below. To record transaction effects accurately, we express them in what are called accounts. An **account** is simply a financial record that documents increases and decreases. For example, the account entitled Cash is increased by $30,000 as a result of Transaction A_1. Every account is assigned its own unique **account title**, and it is important to know what names to assign to various accounts.[1]

The answer to the second question—*What are the sources of these things of value?*—is Susan, who, as owner, has provided the entire amount of cash. Suppose, for example, that Susan has a complete change of heart about opening her business and transfers the entire $30,000 back to her personal checking account. Susan, as owner and sole contributor to her business, can withdraw the entire amount because she has a valid claim against it. As shown in the following Sources of Things of Value Report, Susan's claim as owner is represented by a specific account called "Susan Newman, Capital." Finally, note that both reports have the same $30,000 total which, you will soon learn, is not a coincidence.

The two reports properly filled out are shown here:

CARDS & MEMORABILIA UNLIMITED
Things of Value Report
January 2

Cash	$30,000
	$30,000

CARDS & MEMORABILIA UNLIMITED
Sources of Things of Value Report
January 2

Susan Newman, capital	$30,000
	$30,000

Before you examine a transaction classified as an investing activity, be certain you do not make a common error associated with owner contributions or "investments" in an entity. Quite simply, the mistake is to label such transactions (Transaction A_1, for example) as investing activities rather than financing activities. Although these transactions often use the terms "invest" or "investing" and are clearly investing activities from the owner's personal perspective, they are financing activities from the entity's perspective. The way to avoid this mistake is to think about the event from the business entity's perspective. Since financial statements generally report the effects of an entity apart from the personal transactions of that entity's owners, Transaction A_1 and others like it are classified as financing activities. That is, whenever an entity obtains money from creditors or owners, the transaction is classified as a financing activity.

Transaction B—An Investing Activity Transaction

If you have ever acquired anything that has long-term value, such as an automobile or stocks and bonds, and then sold it, you have initiated and completed an investing activity. In general, **investing activities** are transactions in which an entity acquires things of value that it uses to develop, produce, and sell its products and/or services. You usually initiate investing activities by applying the money obtained from financing activity transactions to long-term, nonoperating activity transactions, such as making loans or buying securities and productive equipment. You complete investing activities with transactions that either collect on the loans you have made or sell the investment securities or productive equipment. Now let's examine an example of Cards & Memorabilia Unlimited's investing activity.

[1] Consult Appendix B if you need help in assigning names to accounts.

CARDS & MEMORABILIA UNLIMITED

Transaction On Monday, January 2, Susan Newman withdraws $6,000 from her business checking account to open a business savings account.

Explanation Although Susan initially opens a business checking account in the amount of $30,000, she quickly transfers $6,000 of it into a business savings account that earns a 5% annual interest rate. Susan makes this transfer because she has a $50,000 credit line available as an emergency source of financing, and she wants to earn a return on otherwise idle funds.

This transaction is an investing activity because it applies $6,000 cash obtained from a financing activity transaction (A_1) to a nonoperating, interest-bearing use within the entity. In essence, CMU has made a loan to the bank in exchange for future interest and a right to reclaim the $6,000. Answer the same two questions asked in Transaction A_1, and then decide how to fill in the following reports. *Hint*: Although interest is earned with the passage of time, don't let it distract you. It is too early to record this interest on January 2.

CARDS & MEMORABILIA UNLIMITED
Things of Value Report
January 2

Cash	$30,000
	$?

CARDS & MEMORABILIA UNLIMITED
Sources of Things of Value Report
January 2

Susan Newman, capital	$30,000
	$?

You are correct if you decided only the Things of Value Report should be changed. You are also correct if you realized that the final balance in both reports should remain unchanged! Let's analyze how this apparent contradiction can be explained.

Analysis Your answer to the first question—What things of value are owned?—should still be $30,000 cash. The difference now is that this amount is divided into two separate accounts—a cash checking account of $24,000 and a cash savings account of $6,000. For reporting purposes, however, these two distinct cash accounts will normally be combined into one general cash account. Although the change in cash is relevant to Susan, it is seldom important enough to other users of financial information to warrant separate disclosure.

Since the *total* amount reported for things of value remains unchanged, the *total* amount for the *sources* of these things of value also remains unchanged. That is, Susan, as owner, has still provided the entire $30,000 amount of cash. Since this transaction has served only to move $6,000 from one type of cash account to another (checking to savings), it represents what is often called a *reclassification*. For simplicity, this textbook will present the reports prepared after Transaction B as identical to those you viewed after Transaction A_1.

Transaction C_1—An Investing Activity Transaction

Transaction On Wednesday, January 4, Susan acquires $10,000 worth of store equipment (large-screen TV, cash register, fax machine, copier, furniture, and fixtures) by using a credit card from one of her suppliers, Office Mart, Inc. Although this credit card bears an 18% interest rate, no interest will be incurred because Susan will pay the debt within 30 days. Each piece of store equipment has an estimated useful life of five years.

Explanation This transaction is an investing activity because it applies the money obtained from Transaction A_1 (a financing activity transaction) to purchase productive equipment (a long-term, nonoperating activity transaction).

The total cost of $10,000 includes not only the individual prices of each piece of store equipment, which totaled $9,234.34, but also such incidental costs as a $715.66 sales tax (calculated on the basis of a 0.0775% rate) and a $50 delivery charge. While you might be tempted to treat these incidental costs as other than store equipment, a generally accepted accounting principle is to treat the entire $10,000 as store equipment. The justification for such an approach is that the cost of store equipment should include all necessary costs to obtain it and to get it into position for its intended use. This practice also simplifies the work of the accountant.

When debt is incurred as in Transaction C_1, a **creditor**—a person or institution lending money or extending credit—is the source of the amount of money borrowed or credit extended by the entity. Recall that in Transaction A_1, the owner, Susan Newman, was the source of cash received. That is, she had a claim against the business. Show how you think the following reports would look immediately after Transaction C_1 has occurred.

CARDS & MEMORABILIA UNLIMITED
Things of Value Report
January 4

Cash	$30,000
____________	______
	$

CARDS & MEMORABILIA UNLIMITED
Sources of Things of Value Report
January 4

____________	$
Susan Newman, capital	30,000
	$

Compare your answer with the correct answer.

CARDS & MEMORABILIA UNLIMITED
Things of Value Report
January 4

Cash	$30,000
Store equipment	10,000
	$40,000

CARDS & MEMORABILIA UNLIMITED
Sources of Things of Value Report
January 4

Accounts payable	$10,000
Susan Newman, capital	30,000
	$40,000

Analysis The $10,000 worth of store equipment is a thing of value apart from cash. Thus, this account is titled Store Equipment. The corresponding source of the store equipment is Office Mart, a supplier or creditor. The amount owed to this source of store equipment is accounted for using the accounts payable account. **Accounts Payable** is an account title used to identify short term claims held by suppliers or other creditors. Notice also that the Things of Value Report and the Sources of Things of Value Report have the same $40,000 total. That is, these balances are equal. Now, take a look at Transaction D.

Transaction D—An Operating Activity Transaction

If you ever had a lemonade stand as a child, you incurred costs to produce a product that you then sold. In other words, you initiated and completed an operating activity. In general, an **operating activity** is a transaction in which an entity develops, produces, and sells its products and/or services. You initiate operating activities with transactions that apply the money obtained from financing activities to the purchase or production of goods and services. You complete operating activities with transactions in which goods are sold and services are performed.

Transaction On Friday, January 6, Susan acquires $15,000 worth of merchandise inventory by paying cash (Susan writes a check from the business checking account) to a wholesale trading card distributor.

Explanation This transaction is an operating activity because it applies the money obtained from a financing activity transaction to the purchase of goods that will be resold.

Unlike Transaction C_1, the $15,000 does not include sales tax. The wholesaler, which is not licensed to sell to the general public, is not required to collect a sales tax. Instead, it is the retailer who is responsible for collecting the tax. To assure the taxing authority that the retail seller will collect the sales tax, the wholesaler requires Susan to provide her resale tax number as proof of her retail operation. Once Susan provides this documentation, she becomes officially responsible for collecting the sales tax, and the wholesaler becomes legally able to sell its products to Cards & Memorabilia Unlimited.

Again, show the impact of Transaction D on both reports before checking the answer.

CARDS & MEMORABILIA UNLIMITED
Things of Value Report
January 6

Cash	$?
____________________	
Store equipment	10,000
	$?

CARDS & MEMORABILIA UNLIMITED
Sources of Things of Value Report
January 6

Accounts payable	$10,000
Susan Newman, capital	30,000
	$?

Now let's look at the answer to Transaction D.

CARDS & MEMORABILIA UNLIMITED
Things of Value Report
January 6

Cash ($30,000 − $15,000)	$15,000
Merchandise inventory	15,000
Store equipment	10,000
	$40,000

CARDS & MEMORABILIA UNLIMITED
Sources of Things of Value Report
January 6

Accounts payable	$10,000
Susan Newman, capital	30,000
	$40,000

Analysis The trading card inventory is treated as a thing of value because it is reasonable to assume that these cards could be resold for at least $15,000 cash. The account title often used to describe such inventory held for resale is Merchandise Inventory. When she acquired the inventory, Susan decreased the $30,000 balance in her cash account ($24,000 in her business checking account plus $6,000 in her business savings account) by writing a $15,000 check. Thus, her January 6 cash balance is $30,000 minus $15,000, or $15,000. Notice, unlike Transactions A_1 and C_1, this transaction has no effect on the Sources of Things of Value Report. In fact, transactions can affect only things of value (as in Transactions B and D), only sources of things of value (as in Transaction J_2 in Chapter 4), or both the things of value and sources of things of value (as in Transactions A_1 and C_1). Although particular transactions affect these two reports in different ways, every accounting transaction will *always* maintain the equality between the two reports.

INSIGHT

The Notion of an Accounting Information System

In an actual business, an accountant would not use the process we just used to produce financial reports. Instead, he or she would enter the preceding four transactions into what is called the business's accounting information system. Accountants use the rules and procedures included in accounting information systems to help process raw business transactions into polished financial statements. As a result, it is important for you to have an elementary notion of how an accounting information system works before you study it in greater detail in Chapter 10. Let's begin with its definition.

An **accounting information system (AIS)** is a system that captures, processes, and reports information about accounting transactions for the purpose of helping management make business decisions. Let's apply each component of this definition to the preceding group of four transactions.

- *Captures.* Given all the transactions a business can undertake, how would you know which of CMU's transactions to include in an accounting information system, what specific information you need to include, and what specific information you can ignore? The accounting information system provides criteria to help the accountant decide to record, for example, Susan's purchase of store equipment but not to record her signing of the store lease.

- *Processes.* Once a transaction has been captured by an accounting information system, it may advance through several processing steps. These may include:
  - –Gathering and maintaining its supporting documentation—a checking account withdrawal slip and a savings account deposit slip for Transaction B.
  - –Determining the correct dollar amount to record in the company's financial records—a $10,000 increase to the store equipment account in Transaction C_1 despite the fact that its invoice cost was less than $9,250.
  - –Determining in what accounts the effects of each transaction should be shown—distributing the financial effects of Transaction D into the merchandise inventory and cash accounts.
- *Reports.* Once an accounting transaction has been processed so that its effects are reflected in assets, liabilities, and owner's equity, the accounting information system presents the information in financial reports. In this chapter, those reports were referred to as the Things of Value Report and the Sources of Things of Value Report. In the following sections, you will learn about three reports produced by an accounting information system.

The insight you should gain here is that businesses don't construct financial reports simply by employing transaction analysis as we did in this chapter. Although the financial reports constructed for Cards & Memorabilia Unlimited are accurate, the process was simplified to make your learning easier. In the real world, all businesses use an accounting information system to capture, process, and report meaningful information from transactions and the business decisions that created them.

Reporting the Effects of Transactions: A First Look at the Balance Sheet

As you may have already discovered, when you combine the Things of Value Report with the Sources of Things of Value Report, you produce what is most often called the balance sheet. Because the **balance sheet** is a financial statement that reports the financial position of an entity at a *point in time*, it sometimes is called a *statement of financial position* or a *statement of financial condition.*

A balance sheet may be prepared after a single transaction, as was done with Transaction A_1, or after any number of transactions. Recall, for example, that you were asked to prepare a new balance sheet after each of the four transactions A_1, B, C_1, and D. Figure 2-4 provides your first look at the balance sheet for Cards & Memorabilia Unlimited. As you study this balance sheet, consider what information it provides and see if you can identify its primary characteristics. You will be required to prepare more balance sheets as Susan's business grows and when you work on end-of-chapter exercises and problems.

CARDS & MEMORABILIA
UNLIMITED

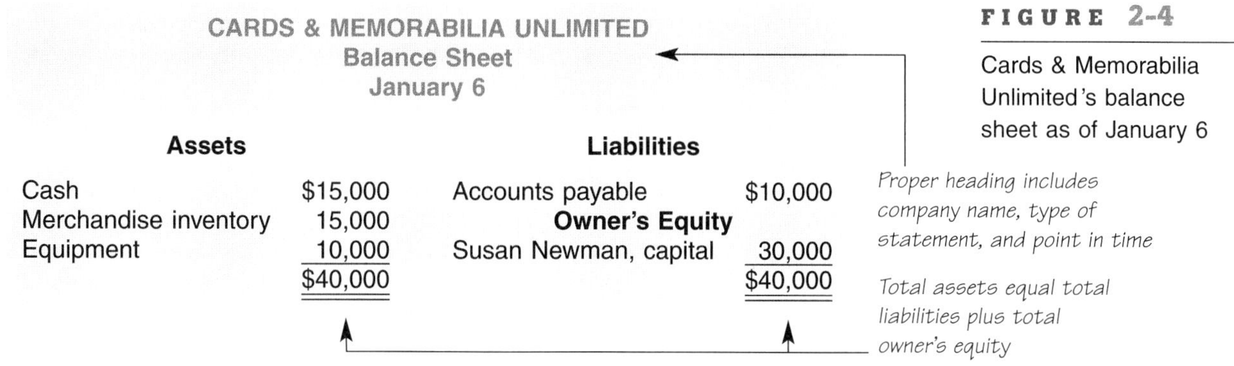

CARDS & MEMORABILIA UNLIMITED
Balance Sheet
January 6

Assets		Liabilities	
Cash	$15,000	Accounts payable	$10,000
Merchandise inventory	15,000	**Owner's Equity**	
Equipment	10,000	Susan Newman, capital	30,000
	$40,000		$40,000

Proper heading includes company name, type of statement, and point in time
Total assets equal total liabilities plus total owner's equity

FIGURE 2-4 Cards & Memorabilia Unlimited's balance sheet as of January 6

What Information Does a Balance Sheet Provide?

As you have just learned, a balance sheet answers two questions about the financial condition of a business. First, you can identify the **assets** of a business when you answer the question, "What things of value does the business own?" Three assets were identified for Cards & Memorabilia Unlimited: cash, merchandise inventory, and store equipment. Second, you can identify liabilities and owner's equity when you answer the question, "What are the claims against or sources of a business's things of value?" There are two distinct types of asset sources or claims against assets. A **liability**, such as accounts payable, is a source of assets provided by creditors. By law, it has priority over all other asset sources. This means whenever an entity decides to close and liquidate (sell its assets and convert them to cash), its recoverable cash must first be distributed to the creditors. The remaining source of an entity's assets provided by an owner (or owners) is known as owner's equity, or simply as equity. Stated another way, **owner's equity** is the claim against assets held by the owner. An example is the account Susan Newman, Capital representing the claim against assets Susan has as CMU's owner.

What Are a Balance Sheet's Characteristics?

A balance sheet should always have a heading. The heading in Figure 2-4's balance sheet, for example, tells you first, the name of the company (Cards & Memorabilia Unlimited); second, the type of financial statement reported (balance sheet); and third, the point in time (January 6) the balance sheet represents. In addition to a heading, a balance sheet must always contain three elements: assets, liabilities, and owner's equity. Note, the balance sheet in Figure 2-4 has two sides—the asset heading on the left side, and the liabilities and owner's equity headings on the right side. Sometimes balance sheets put all three of these elements in a single column.

As you learned earlier, the balance sheet is formed by combining a report of assets with a report of the sources of assets. Since there was always an equality between each of these reports after each of Transactions A_1 through D, it is logical to expect that the balance sheet captures this same equality. It does. This balance sheet equation is the single most important characteristic of a balance sheet.

The Fundamental Accounting Equation

After each transaction (A_1, B, C_1, and D), the entity's total assets always equaled the total of its sources of assets. That is, sources of assets are neither smaller nor larger than assets at any point in time. This simple but powerful concept is expressed in equation form as:

$$\text{Assets} = \text{Sources of Assets}$$

This equation represents the two key questions answered by a balance sheet.

Since sources of assets are either liabilities or owner's equity, we can rewrite the equation as:

$$\text{Assets} = \text{Liabilities} + \text{Owner's Equity}$$

This equation makes sense, because an entity gets its assets by either borrowing from creditors or from contributions by owners. This equation is called the **fundamental accounting equation** and is the basis of much of what you will learn in this course. Consider the following performance objective, which tests both your understanding of this equation and your ability to apply it.

YOUR PERFORMANCE OBJECTIVE 5

Apply the fundamental accounting equation [Assets = Liabilities + Owner's Equity] to:

a. **Analyze** the effects of accounting transactions on the elements of the balance sheet.
b. **Prepare** a balance sheet that reports the financial condition of any entity.

In fact, you have already analyzed the effects of accounting transactions on the balance sheet (Performance Objective 5a) when you analyzed Transactions A_1, B, C_1, and D. Further, you prepared balance sheets that reported the financial condition of Cards & Memorabilia Unlimited (Performance Objective 5b) after each transaction.

Because the fundamental accounting equation includes all three elements of the balance sheet, it is often referred to as the **balance sheet equation**. In Figure 2-4, for example, notice that the total assets ($40,000) equal the total liabilities plus the owner's equity ($40,000). In fact, every balance sheet expresses the fundamental accounting equation.

The balance sheet equation is valid for all entities, including the sole proprietorship form used by Cards & Memorabilia Unlimited. Sometimes the title used to identify owner's equity is different. For example, in the balance sheet equations shown below for an individual and a sole proprietorship, it is called "net worth" for one and "capital" for the other.

Individual	Assets = Liabilities + Net Worth
Sole Proprietorship	Assets = Liabilities + Capital

An equivalent version of the fundamental accounting equation expresses the idea that owners are entitled to the assets remaining after the claims of the creditors have first been satisfied. Thus, we can say that:

Assets − Liabilities = Owner's Equity

For example, in Figure 2-4, if Cards & Memorabilia Unlimited repays its $10,000 liability with a portion of the $40,000 of assets available, Susan Newman will be able to claim $30,000 of the remaining assets. When you subtract liabilities from assets, the difference is called **net assets**. If you glance at the preceding version of the fundamental accounting equation, you will see net assets not only equal assets minus liabilities but also equal owner's equity. That is:

Assets − Liabilities = Net Assets = Owner's Equity

In other words, Susan, as owner, is entitled to the net assets of Cards & Memorabilia Unlimited.

The effects of all transactions, not just the effects of Transactions A_1, B, C_1, and D, maintain the equality of the fundamental accounting equation. This important concept will become apparent as we now take a more comprehensive look at transactions and how they are analyzed.

Transaction Analysis

When we analyzed Transactions A_1, B, C_1, and D earlier in this chapter, we used a very elementary form of what is called transaction analysis. **Transaction analysis** is a process that identifies the effects specific transactions have on the fundamental accounting equation, that is, on an entity's assets, liabilities, and owner's equity. In other words, it is a fundamental skill you *must* have to fully understand how transactions affect an entity's financial statements. Before you can apply transaction analysis, however, you must be able to determine which transactions qualify for inclusion in the accounting information system.

What Conditions Must a Transaction Meet to Enter an Accounting Information System?

As you might expect, an accounting information system does not include the effects of every transaction. For example, suppose Susan hires a part-time employee to work on weekends. This event is a transaction because Susan and the employee have exchanged something of value—their mutual promises to provide a job and perform work, respectively. This transaction, an oral contract, does not, however, qualify for inclusion in the accounting information system. To enter an accounting information system, transactions must meet *all* of the following three conditions:

1. The event must be measurable in dollars (quantifiable).
2. The event must be related to the entity being measured.
3. The event must affect the entity's current financial position.

Although it is essential that you remember these conditions, do not simply memorize them. You need to be able to understand their meaning so that you can determine whether the transactions of any business have been treated properly. The consequence of improper treatment of transactions—misstatement of amounts reported in financial statements and potentially harmful decisions—is very serious. To ensure that you do understand what is proper treatment of transactions, let's look at each of these conditions in more detail.

An exchange of dollars between two parties is one example of the money measurement concept.

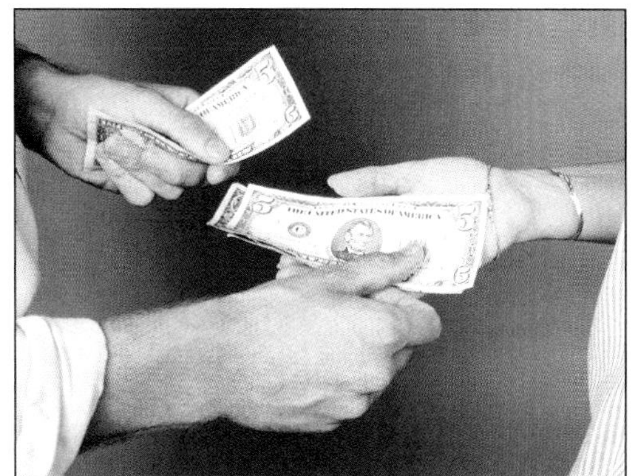

The Money Measurement Concept The first condition, the event must be measurable in dollars, is derived from the money measurement concept. The **money measurement concept** says the financial statements report only the effects of those transactions that can be expressed in monetary or financial terms. Thus, the accounting information system records financial transactions—those that can be stated in dollar amounts—rather than nonfinancial transactions. For example, on January 1, Susan's uncle gave her a check for $15,000 to help her finance her business. Susan didn't want to take any chances, so later that day, she deposited her uncle's check into her personal checking account. Such a transfer or exchange represents a measurable transaction because there is a transfer of a specific amount of money between two parties. If Susan's uncle had promised to help her but did not give her a check, the event would not be quantifiable or measurable in dollars because no money was actually transferred; therefore, no amount could be measured. Since meeting this condition alone is not enough to record a transaction, consider another necessary condition.

The Entity Concept The second condition, the event must be related to the entity being measured, is derived from the entity concept. The **entity concept** says the financial statements report only the effects of an entity's transactions rather than the personal transactions of the entity's owners. That is, the accounting information system records only those transactions that involve a promise or exchange related to the entity. For example, the January 1 transaction in which Susan received a $15,000 check does not qualify because the $15,000 is not received by the entity—in this case, Cards & Memorabilia Unlimited. Quite simply, it is a personal transaction of Susan, CMU's owner, with her uncle who has no business relationship with CMU. Thus, to

qualify as a recordable transaction, the event must affect the business of the entity, not the personal transactions engaged in by its owners. Also, since Susan did not open her business until Monday, January 2, the entity Cards & Memorabilia Unlimited did not exist when she deposited the personal loan on January 1.

To appreciate why an accounting information system requires more information than the effects of a transaction that is both measurable and related to the entity, consider the following example. On Tuesday, January 3, Susan learns that Central Bank had approved her $50,000 line of business credit. This agreement specifies Susan may borrow amounts up to $50,000 at any time as long as she pays an annual interest rate of 8% and carries a zero loan balance for at least 30 consecutive days each year. Clearly, this event is measurable in dollars—$50,000 by the terms of the agreement—and is related to the entity—the agreement clearly applies to CMU. Should this transaction be recorded? If you say "yes," you have probably been misled by the $50,000. Although the bank has authorized this dollar amount, an actual transfer or exchange of money did not occur on January 3. Susan neither borrowed money on January 3, nor did she decide how much money to borrow in the future. That is, her assets have not been affected by this transaction. This transaction illustrates that an accounting information system will not include events that satisfy *only* the two conditions discussed so far.

Effect on Current Financial Position An event must be both measurable in dollars and related to the entity being measured to be entered into an accounting information system. But satisfying these two conditions alone is insufficient, as you just saw. To see why a third condition is needed, consider another example. In late December, Susan receives a call from Mary Mathews telling her the landlord has agreed to rent her the store location she wants. On Thursday, January 5, Susan signs a 36-month lease for store space. The contract requires payments of $1,000 per month plus a security deposit of $2,000 (including damage deposit and last month's rent), payable on Monday, January 9, the first date of occupancy. The contract also provides the first month rent-free as an incentive to sign the lease. Although unusual, this concession of free rent is understandable given the high rate of unoccupied office and store space in Rialto at the time.

This event does involve definite amounts due that are measurable. Furthermore, this transaction is related to the entity because the store space is specifically designated for CMU. Although this transaction satisfies the first two conditions discussed so far, it is properly excluded from the accounting information system because it has no effect on the financial position of the business on January 5, the day Susan signed the lease. On that date, there is no change in assets, liabilities, or owner's equity as a result of Susan signing the lease. Thus, the final condition for an event to be entered into an accounting information system is that the event must affect the current financial position of the business.

Accounting Transactions A transaction that meets all three conditions necessary for entry into an accounting information system is called an accounting transaction. An **accounting transaction** is a financial event that is usually supported by a business document, such as a check or a sales invoice, and results in measurable changes (increases and decreases) in the assets and/or sources of assets of an entity as of the current date. Use the following performance objective to help you determine which transactions qualify as accounting transactions:

YOUR PERFORMANCE OBJECTIVE 6

Identify and **apply** the three conditions necessary for a transaction to qualify as an accounting transaction and, therefore, be recorded in an accounting information system.

Your first step in meeting this objective is to *identify* the three conditions a transaction must satisfy. Once again, the transaction or event must:

1. Be measurable in dollars.
2. Be related to the entity being measured.
3. Affect the entity's current financial position.

Figure 2-5 illustrates how you could apply these conditions to analyze Susan's first week of transactions. Study it carefully. Be certain you understand why only four of seven transactions—what we've already seen as Transactions A_1, B, C_1, and D—qualify as accounting transactions and, therefore, are recorded in the accounting information system.

FIGURE 2-5

Which of these CMU transactions may be entered into an accounting information system?

			Conditions		
Date		**Transaction**	**Measurable in Money**	**Related to Entity**	**Affects Current Financial Position**
1/01		Susan deposits her uncle's money	Yes	No	No
1/02	**A_1**	**Susan invests cash in the business**	**Yes**	**Yes**	**Yes**
1/02	**B**	**Cash is transferred from checking account to a savings account**	**Yes**	**Yes**	**Yes**
1/03		Bank approves a line of credit	Yes	Yes	No
1/04	**C_1**	**Equipment is acquired on credit**	**Yes**	**Yes**	**Yes**
1/05		Lease for store space is signed	Yes	Yes	No
1/06	**D**	**Inventory is purchased with cash**	**Yes**	**Yes**	**Yes**

Note: The transactions that properly enter the accounting information system are indicated in boldface type.

The Effects of Transaction Analysis on the Fundamental Equation

Since transaction analysis identifies the effect of specific transactions on the fundamental accounting equation, look at Figure 2-6 to consider the effect transactions A_1, B, C_1, and D had on the fundamental accounting equation. Study this figure to be sure you understand how each transaction affects CMU's assets, liabilities, and owner's equity.

As you now know from your study of the three conditions discussed in the preceding sections, you must use transaction analysis whenever you determine if an event qualifies as an accounting transaction. Since you will use this process of transaction analysis throughout this course, review the relevant performance objective introduced earlier:

YOUR PERFORMANCE OBJECTIVE 5a

Apply the fundamental accounting equation, Assets = Liabilities + Owner's Equity, to **analyze** the effects of accounting transactions on the elements of the balance sheet.

FIGURE 2-6

Transaction analysis of Cards & Memorabilia Unlimited's initial transactions

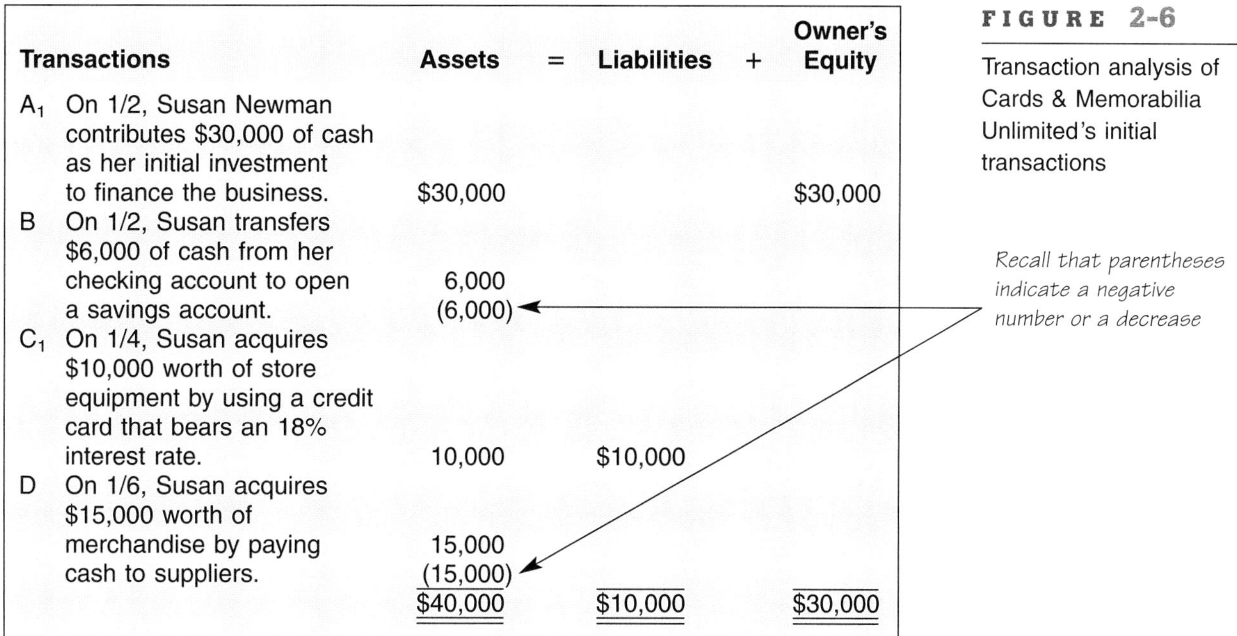

Transactions	Assets	=	Liabilities	+	Owner's Equity
A_1 On 1/2, Susan Newman contributes $30,000 of cash as her initial investment to finance the business.	$30,000				$30,000
B On 1/2, Susan transfers $6,000 of cash from her checking account to open a savings account.	6,000 (6,000)				
C_1 On 1/4, Susan acquires $10,000 worth of store equipment by using a credit card that bears an 18% interest rate.	10,000		$10,000		
D On 1/6, Susan acquires $15,000 worth of merchandise by paying cash to suppliers.	15,000 (15,000)				
	$40,000		$10,000		$30,000

Recall that parentheses indicate a negative number or a decrease

Now, explore further what it means to analyze the effect of accounting transactions on the elements of the balance sheet. Recall that the balance sheet equation is maintained for each of Transactions A_1, B, C_1, and D. Also, you might have noticed that each of these transactions resulted in two effects on the equation. Does the analysis of every transaction produce two effects? Could transaction analysis ever produce one or more than two effects and still maintain the equation?

What Is the Dual Effect Concept?

Perhaps you have already realized that every transaction must have at least two effects. For example, if assets increase, there must be a corresponding claim to those assets, as in Transactions A_1 and C_1, or an offsetting decrease to another asset, as in Transactions B and D. Simply stated, a single effect will cause the fundamental accounting equation to be out of balance.

Could an accounting transaction have more than two effects? What if, in Transaction A_1, Susan had invested $25,000 cash and $5,000 worth of card inventory instead of $30,000 cash? In this case, two effects include the increase in two assets, cash and trading cards inventory. A third effect, of course, is the increase of $30,000 in Susan's capital account or owner's equity.

Thus, the **dual effect concept** states that every recorded transaction must have *at least two* effects on the fundamental accounting equation. There are nine dual effects that are logically possible as shown in Figure 2-7. Study this figure carefully. Note, eight of the nine possible types of dual effects are illustrated by Transactions A_1 through Z of Cards & Memorabilia Unlimited.

FIGURE 2-7 All possible dual effects of transactions on the fundamental accounting equation

Dual Effects on Balance Sheet Elements	Effect on Equation	CMU Transactions (Appendix C)
1. Increase one asset account and decrease another	No change	B, D, E, H, V
2. Increase one liability account and decrease another	No change	J_2
3. Increase one owner's equity account and decrease another	No change	None
4. Increase an asset account and increase a liability account	Equality maintained	C_1, F, G, I and L
5. Decrease an asset account and decrease a liability account	Equality maintained	C_2, J_1, and K_1
6. Increase an asset account and increase an owner's equity account	Equality maintained	A_1, M, N, O_1, A_2, and O_2
7. Decrease an asset account and decrease an owner's equity account	Equality maintained	P, Q_1, R, S, K_2, T, U, W, Q_2
8. Increase a liability account and decrease an owner's equity account	No change	X and Y
9. Decrease a liability account and increase an owner's equity account	No change	Z

Since the fundamental accounting equation must stay in balance after the analysis of one transaction's effects, it is easy to understand how the balance sheet, which usually shows the effect of many transactions, got its name. The balance sheet represents the accumulated equality or "balance" between assets and their sources.

INSIGHT

"Give and Get"—Another Way to Look at Transaction Analysis

If you are not yet comfortable with how to perform transaction analysis, you might find the concept of "give and get" helpful. Recall that a *business transaction* is an event involving a transfer or exchange between two parties. If you focus on the idea of an exchange between two parties, you can see that each party *gives* something of value to *get* something of equal value. You can use this idea to help you analyze transactions such as A_1, B, C_1, and D. For example, in Transaction A_1, Cards & Memorabilia Unlimited *gives* Susan a $30,000 claim against assets in exchange for *getting* $30,000 of cash. You can represent this transaction as well as Transactions B, C_1, and D in the following way:

Transaction	Assets	=	Liabilities	+	Owner's Equity
A_1	**Get** cash	=			**Give** owner a claim to cash
B	**Get** cash–savings **Give** cash–checking				
C_1	**Get** store equipment	=	**Give** supplier a promise to pay		
D	**Get** inventory **Give** cash				

In Transaction B, CMU *gets* a $6,000 savings account in exchange for *giving* up $6,000 of cash from its checking account. In Transaction C1, CMU *gets* $10,000 of store equipment in exchange for *giving* a promise to its supplier that it will pay $10,000 in the future. Likewise, in Transaction D, CMU *gets* $15,000 of inventory in exchange for *giving* its supplier $15,000 in cash.

The insight you should gain here is that each of these four transactions represents the idea of an exchange. In each, the entity (CMU, in this case) *gives* something of value (a claim to cash, checking account cash, a promise to pay cash, and cash) to *get* something else of value (cash, savings account cash, store equipment, and inventory).

Reporting the Effects of Transactions: A First Look at the Income Statement

In Chapter 1 you learned an income statement is a financial statement that reports the results of operations. In fact, an income statement generally reports operating activities that have been *completed*. Since CMU has *initiated* only a single operating activity transaction by January 6 (Transaction D), no income statement may be prepared at this time. When the merchandise obtained in this transaction is sold, however, both a revenue and an expense may be reported in an income statement. You have already seen a form of CMU's income statement when you looked at CMU's operating budget in Figure 1-10c. You will learn more about the measurement of these income statement elements in Chapter 3.

Reporting the Effects of Business Activities: A First Look at the Statement of Cash Flows

Both the balance sheet and income statement are constructed by accumulating the effects of business transactions. In contrast, the financial statement known as the statement of cash flows is organized by using activities as well as transactions. Specifically, the **statement of cash flows** reports the cash receipts or inflows and cash payments or outflows of an entity's operating, investing, and financing activities for a period of time. Using Transactions A_1, B, C_1, and D, you'll first learn how these transactions are classified into activities. Then you will discover how to determine which transactions belong in a statement of cash flows.

Classifying Transactions into Activities

Each of CMU's first four transactions can be classified into one of the three types of business activities described earlier in this chapter—financing, investing, and operating. Transaction A_1, Susan's $30,000 contribution to her business, is a cash financing activity that enables her to start her business. Transaction B, a $6,000 transfer of cash between her checking and savings accounts, is not reported in the statement of cash flows, as you will learn in Chapter 8. Transaction C_1, her $10,000 credit purchase of store equipment, is a noncash investing activity that enables CMU to acquire business equipment. Transaction D, her $15,000 cash purchase of inventory, is a cash operating activity that enables her to resell merchandise at a price higher than its cost. These CMU transactions, therefore, conveniently illustrate the three fundamental activities of any business.

The financial effects of Transactions A_1, B, C_1, and D are not all limited to the balance sheet. Figure 2-8 shows that two of the four transactions—Transaction A_1 (a financing activity) and Transaction D (an operating activity)—are included in the statement of cash flows because they involve cash flows. As you study Figure 2-8, make sure you can now perform each of the steps described in Performance Objective 7:

FIGURE 2-8 Cards & Memorabilia Unlimited's statement of cash flows prepared from transactions A_1 and D

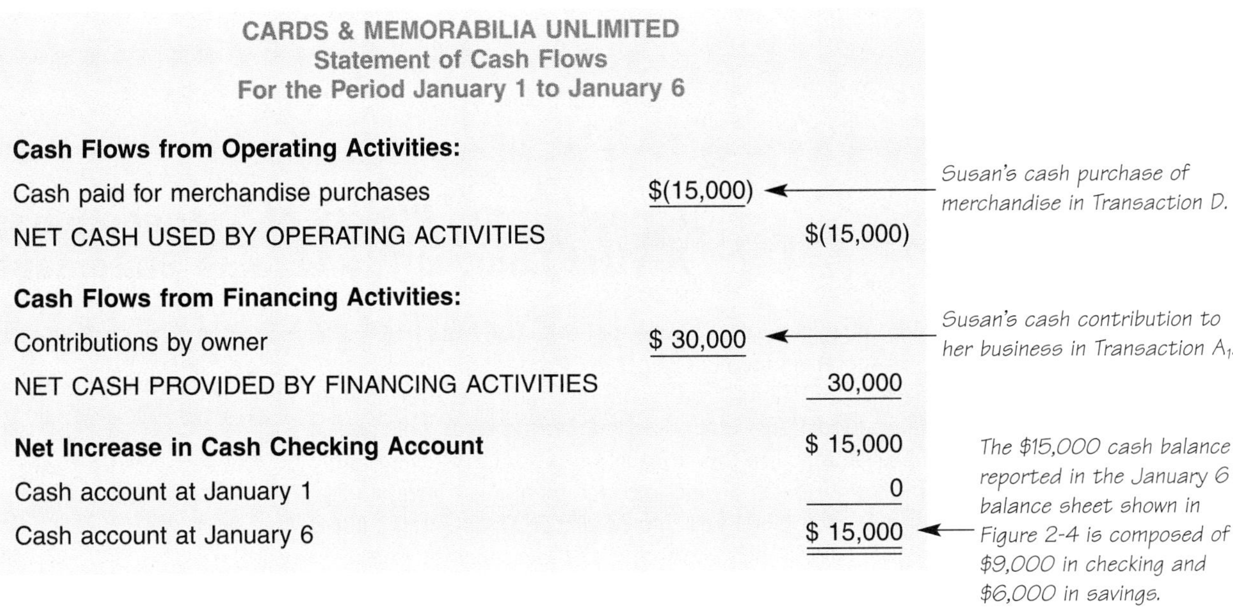

CARDS & MEMORABILIA UNLIMITED
Statement of Cash Flows
For the Period January 1 to January 6

Cash Flows from Operating Activities:		
Cash paid for merchandise purchases	$(15,000)	
NET CASH USED BY OPERATING ACTIVITIES		$(15,000)
Cash Flows from Financing Activities:		
Contributions by owner	$ 30,000	
NET CASH PROVIDED BY FINANCING ACTIVITIES		30,000
Net Increase in Cash Checking Account		$ 15,000
Cash account at January 1		0
Cash account at January 6		$ 15,000

YOUR PERFORMANCE OBJECTIVE 7

a. **Define** the terms *financing activities*, *investing activities*, and *operating activities*.
b. **Classify** any accounting transaction into one of these activities or a noncash investing and financing activity, and
c. **Classify** any cash receipt or cash payment transaction into the appropriate activity as reported in the statement of cash flows.

What Is Accounting's Role in Society?

In Chapter 1 you saw how valuable accounting and its reports can be to various business decision makers. For example, you saw how bankers, landlords, and owner-managers all used accounting information to make their respective resource allocation decisions. If you extrapolate from this simple CMU case to the untold millions of such decisions occurring daily within our economy, you can imagine the central role accounting plays in the economic well-being of our society.

Essentially, accounting provides feedback to decision makers about the relative financial success of both business and nonbusiness entities. Examples of business entities include *merchandisers*, who sell goods produced by other companies; *manufacturers*, who sell goods they produce; and *service companies*, who sell services rather than goods. Nonbusiness entities include both government and other not-for-profit organizations, such as charitable and religious organizations. Although nonbusiness entities do not have a profit motive, they rely just as much on accounting information as business entities to get the maximum benefit from their scarce resources. The Internal Revenue Service (IRS), for example, is a government organization that relies heavily on accounting information to make decisions affecting the financing ability of the U.S. government.

Because accounting plays a critical role in providing financial information for decision making at all levels of our society, it is essential that preparers of accounting

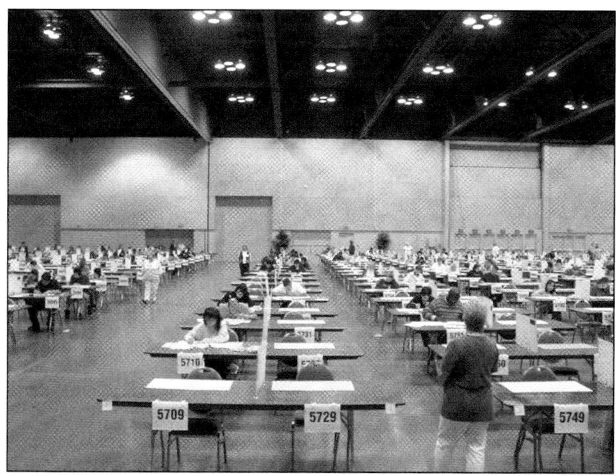

Certified Public Accountants must pass a stringent examination in the state where they will practice accounting.

information employ high ethical standards in their work. This has led to the establishment of an entire industry known as the public accounting profession. Firms in this profession examine the financial statements and underlying accounting systems of businesses to determine whether or not their statements fully and fairly disclose their financial condition and results of operations. Recently, the ethical standards of the public accounting profession in the United States have been questioned in light of the well-publicized Enron scandal. Enron's public accounting firm, Arthur Andersen, was found guilty of obstructing justice in the federal investigation of its audit client, Enron Corporation.

An **audit** is the systematic examination conducted by individual auditors, at least one of whom must be a **certified public accountant (CPA)**. At the completion of this independent examination, the auditors express an opinion on the integrity of the entity's financial statements. Because companies normally receive positive feedback on their financial statements—often referred to as a "clean" opinion—an adverse opinion can have a devastating effect on a company's ability to attract financing. This **Independent Auditors' Report** or *Report of the Independent Accountants* (Figure 2-9) is always included in the company's annual report, which is covered in Chapter 3.

Your understanding of the critical role accountants play in our society's need for fair presentation of financial information is expressed by the following performance objective:

YOUR PERFORMANCE OBJECTIVE 8
Explain what role ethics plays in the preparation of financial statements.

Why Study Accounting?

USER FOCUS

Most likely you and the more than 300,000 of your fellow students across the country who are starting this course have enrolled in accounting because it is a required part of your academic program. That's not unusual. Everyone pursuing a college degree takes courses they might not take if these courses were not required. It is perfectly natural if you question whether this course is relevant to your life as well as your career.

This textbook's purpose is not solely to educate accounting majors. Instead, its simple premise is that accounting plays an indispensable role in all business decision making.

If asked, many former accounting students will tell you that they regret not studying harder in this course. To maximize your success with this textbook and the course it supports, it is important that you learn now, not later, about the real benefits you will reap from a serious study of accounting.

FIGURE 2-9

An independent auditors' report for Wal-Mart Stores, Inc.

REPORT OF INDEPENDENT AUDITORS

The Board of Directors and Shareholders,
Wal-Mart Stores, Inc.

We have audited the accompanying consolidated balance sheets of Wal-Mart Stores, Inc. as of January 31, 2002 and 2001, and the related consolidated statements of income, shareholders' equity and cash flows for each of the three years in the period ended January 31, 2002. These financial statements are the responsibility of the Company's management. Our responsibility is to express an opinion on these financial statements based on our audits.

We conducted our audits in accordance with auditing standards generally accepted in the United States. Those standards require that we plan and perform the audit to obtain reasonable assurance about whether the financial statements are free of material misstatement. An audit includes examining, on a test basis, evidence supporting the amounts and disclosures in the financial statements. An audit also includes assessing the accounting principles used and significant estimates made by management, as well as evaluating the overall financial statement presentation. We believe that our audits provide a reasonable basis for our opinion.

In our opinion, the financial statements referred to above present fairly, in all material respects, the consolidated financial position of Wal-Mart Stores, Inc. at January 31, 2002 and 2001, and the consolidated results of its operations and its cash flows for each of the three years in the period ended January 31, 2002, in conformity with accounting principles generally accepted in the United States.

Ernst & Young LLP

Tulsa, Oklahoma
March 22, 2002

This term implies that the financial statements reflect high ethical standards.

What Are the Benefits of Learning about Accounting?

You can derive several benefits from learning about accounting. Some of these benefits will help you as a businessperson and some will help you in your personal life.

Introduces Business Terminology and Activities

As you learned in Chapter 1, accounting is the "language of business." No matter what your major, this course will help you because it will introduce you to the terminology and transactions normally encountered in business. As your business vocabulary expands from your study of accounting, so too will your understanding of business.

Aside from business terminology, accounting exposes you to a multitude of business transactions. As you just learned, you can divide business transactions into three activities: financing, investing, and operating. Recall, for example, that Susan decided to *finance* her business with personal savings, her uncle's money, and a bank line of credit. With a portion of these resources, she first *invested* in a savings account to earn a return on otherwise idle cash. Next, she invested in store equipment to be used as a basis for the sale of goods and services. Finally, she purchased inventory for the day-to-day operations of her business. You also saw how Susan had to estimate the expenses associated with *operating* activities when she developed an operating budget.

Moreover, the Cards & Memorabilia Unlimited case is specifically designed to introduce all the functional areas normally encountered in both a standard business curriculum and in a company, including marketing, finance, management, production, and management information systems. Since this accounting textbook is designed as a means to teach you about accounting's role in business, rather than to teach you accounting as an end in itself, you will learn a lot about business if you conscientiously study its content.

Facilitates Business Decision Making

Accounting information helps people and businesses make better business decisions. Here are some of the users of accounting information and the concrete ways in which such information enables them to make better decisions.

Current Investors The owners or current investors in corporations usually hold ownership shares (stock) in corporations and are very interested in the earnings performance of those corporations. In particular, investors are often interested in feedback about return on their investment through dividends and increases in stock price. They can calculate at least a rough measure of this return by consulting reports issued periodically by the corporation—news releases, fact sheets, quarterly earnings announcements, and interim financial statements, as well as financial statements included in annual reports. Since it is likely that at one time or another, or even now, you will be such a decision maker, this book includes numerous examples of financial accounting information that is of interest to investors, as illustrated in Figures 2-10a and 2-10b.

FIGURE 2-10a Financial accounting information of interest to investors—Wal-Mart Stores, Inc. financial highlights

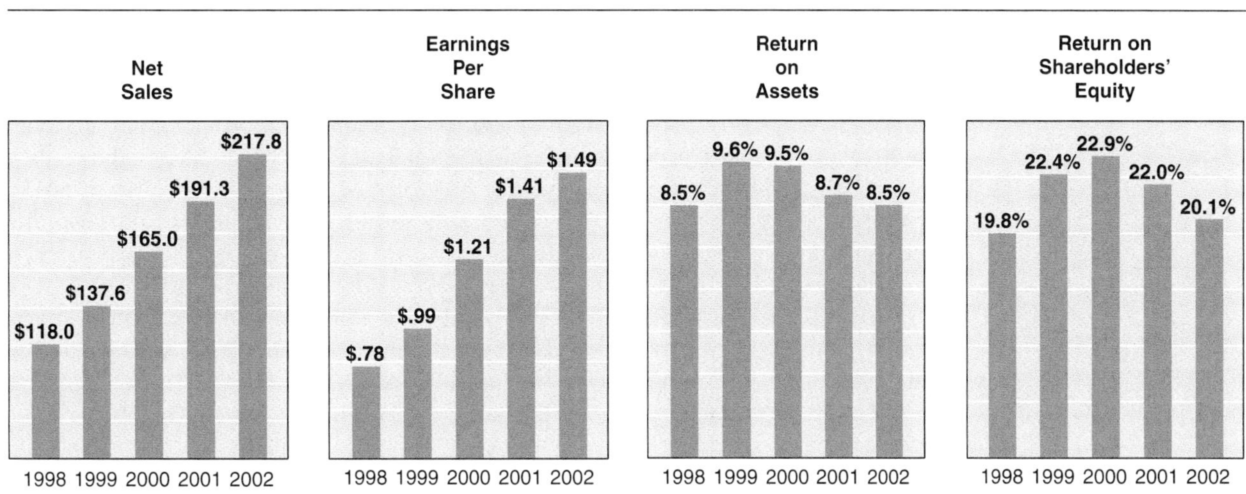

Potential Investors If you were trying to make a decision about whether to invest in a particular company, you might want to perform a detailed analysis of the financial statements of several other companies in the same industry to evaluate the quality of your prospective investment. Or you might study what are called the **notes**, the explanations accompanying those financial statements, which provide detailed information unavailable in the financial statements alone (Figure 2-11). In this book you will learn about all the standard measures you can use to analyze financial

FIGURE 2-10b

Financial accounting information of interest to investors—Novell, Inc.'s comparative income statement

NOVELL, INC.
Consolidated Unaudited Condensed Statements of Income
(In thousands, except per share data)

	First Fiscal Quarter Ended	
	Jan. 31 Year 2	Jan. 31 Year 1
Net sales	**$285,806**	**$252,042**
Cost of sales	64,120	57,087
Gross profit	**$221,686**	**$194,955**
Operating expenses		
Sales and marketing	$105,337	$104,211
Product development	54,005	60,238
General and administrative	25,994	25,574
Total operating expenses	$185,336	$190,023
Income (loss) from operations	**$ 36,350**	**$ 4,932**
Other income, net	3,786	14,643
Income (loss) before taxes	$ 40,136	$ 19,575
Income taxes	11,238	5,481
Net income (loss)	**$ 28,898**	**$ 14,094**

Investors might be interested to see net income has doubled.

statements; you will also learn how to incorporate the notes to financial statements in your analysis.

Creditors A **creditor** is a person or business that lends money to a borrower or extends credit to a customer. In either case, money is then owed to the creditor. Central Bank and Connolly Supply are both examples of Cards & Memorabilia Unlimited's creditors.

In Chapter 1, Phillip Strauss, the loan officer, asked Susan to provide accounting information to support her loan application. In succeeding chapters, you will learn about the ratio analysis the bank used to approve her application, as well as other evaluation tools this type of creditor commonly uses.

Credit managers often decide whether or not to extend credit to customers by consulting a credit report, which is based on accounting information. In addition, credit managers might decide to make changes in their credit terms, such as how much of a penalty they will charge on overdue bills or how long they will allow a bill to go unpaid before they turn it over to a collection agency. They would base this decision on such measures as the average collection period, which in turn is based on accounting elements such as amounts owed by customers and sales revenue.

In your business career, it is highly likely that someone will owe money to you or to your company. In other words, you will almost certainly be a creditor at one time or another. As a creditor, you will need to make decisions about whether or not to extend credit or how to increase the chances of collecting amounts owed to you or your company. In either case, a knowledge about accounting information will be essential to help you make a good business decision as a creditor.

Accounting is an important resource in meeting the information needs of both investors and creditors, as the following performance objective emphasizes:

YOUR PERFORMANCE OBJECTIVE 9

Identify the types of decisions investors and creditors make and **describe** what information in the financial statements and/or related disclosures meets the information needs of each group.

FIGURE 2-11 An example of notes to financial statements for The Walt Disney Company

Notes to Consolidated Financial Statements

The Walt Disney Company and Subsidiaries

(Tabular dollars in millions, except per share amounts)

Note 1. Description of the Business and Summary of Significant Accounting Policies

The Walt Disney Company, together with its subsidiaries (the "company"), is a diversified international entertainment organization with operations in the following businesses.

Creative Content

The company produces and acquires live-action and animated motion pictures for distribution to the theatrical, home video and television markets. The company also produces original television programming for the network and first-run syndication markets. The company distributes its filmed product through its own distribution and marketing companies in the United States and most foreign markets.

The company licenses the name "Walt Disney," as well as the company's characters, visual and literary properties and songs and music, to various consumer manufacturers, retailers, show promoters and publishers throughout the world. The company also engages in direct retail distribution principally through the Disney Stores, and produces books and magazines for the general public in the United States and Europe. In addition, the company produces audio and computer software products for the entertainment market, as well as film, video and computer software products for the educational marketplace.

Buena Vista Internet Group ("BVIG") coordinates the company's internet initiatives. BVIG develops, publishes and distributes content for narrow-band on-line services, the interactive software market, interactive television platforms, internet web sites, including Disney.com, Disney's Daily Blast, ESPN.com, ABCNews.com and the Disney Store Online, which offers Disney-themed merchandise over the Internet.

Broadcasting

The company operates the ABC Television Network, which has affiliated stations providing coverage to U.S. television households. The company also owns television and radio stations, most of which are affiliated with either the ABC Television Network or the ABC Radio Networks. The company's cable and international broadcast operations are principally involved in the production and distribution of cable television programming, the licensing of programming to domestic and international markets and investing in foreign television broadcasting, production and distribution entities. Primary domestic cable programming services, which operate through subsidiary companies and joint ventures, are ESPN, the A&E Television Networks, Lifetime Entertainment Services and E! Entertainment Television. The company provides programming for and operates cable and satellite television programming services, including the Disney Channel and Disney Channel International.

Theme Parks and Resorts

The company operates the Walt Disney World Resort® in Florida, and Disneyland Park,® the Disneyland Hotel and the Disneyland Pacific Hotel in California. The Walt Disney World Resort includes the Magic Kingdom, Epcot, Disney-MGM Studios and Disney's Animal Kingdom, thirteen resort hotels and a complex of villas and suites, a retail, dining and entertainment complex, a sports complex, conference centers, campgrounds, golf courses, water parks and other recreational facilities. In addition, the resort operates Disney Cruise Line from Port Canaveral, Florida. Disney Regional Entertainment designs, develops and operates a variety of new entertainment concepts based on Disney brands and creative properties, operating under the names Club Disney, ESPN Zone and DisneyQuest. The company earns royalties on revenues generated by the Tokyo Disneyland® theme park near Tokyo, Japan, which is owned and operated by an unrelated Japanese corporation. The company also has an investment in Euro Disney S.C.A., a publicly-held French entity that operates Disneyland Paris. The company's Walt Disney Imagineering unit designs and develops new theme park concepts and attractions, as well as resort properties. The company also manages and markets vacation ownership interests in the Disney Vacation Club. Included in Theme Parks and Resorts are the company's National Hockey League franchise, the Mighty Ducks of Anaheim, and its ownership interest in the Anaheim Angels, a Major League Baseball team.

Government Taxing Authorities and Regulatory Agencies As described earlier, taxing authorities such as the Internal Revenue Service (IRS), and its state and local counterparts, use accounting information. Interestingly enough, the personal tax return (1040), which most Americans fill out every year, is really an income statement that conforms to the special rules of the IRS. Likewise, all federal government agencies from the Securities and Exchange Commission (SEC) to the Federal Communications Commission (FCC) require businesses under their regulation to submit financial information. If you work in a government agency or in a company that conducts business with such agencies, you will undoubtedly come into contact with this massive financial reporting system.

Even if you do not work for or with the government, a knowledge of financial accounting can help you better understand many of today's headlines and become an informed citizen. For example, the General Accounting Office (GAO), whose mission is to serve as the watchdog for Congress, played an important role in exposing the full extent of the Savings and Loan Scandal of the 1980s, when ordinary citizens lost millions of dollars of their savings. In addition, the GAO brought to light the House Banking Scandal in the early 1990s, in which congressmen wrote checks in excess of their available balances. To fully comprehend these investigations, you would need an understanding of financial accounting.

Other Not-for-Profit Organizations People who contribute to not-for-profit organizations want assurances that their contributions are primarily being used to support essential services, not to finance the growth of its administration. For example, the 1991 investigation into the United Way Agency questioned whether an unacceptably high percentage of donations had been used for purely administrative purposes. A primary focus of this investigation was an analysis of the financial records and financial statements of the United Way. Another example of how financial accounting information was used to make decisions was the probe into televangelist organizations in which donations intended to help the sick and needy were used to finance the personal excesses of the televangelists.

Union Negotiators In attempting to improve the pay of its workers, a union must analyze the financial statements of the business with which it is negotiating. Union members are better able to understand the respective positions of both the union and management if they are able to analyze financial accounting information. For members of the actual union negotiation team, such knowledge would be essential.

Media Investigators Investigative reports from newspapers, such as *The New York Times* and *The Wall Street Journal*, as well as popular television programs, such as *60 Minutes*, *20/20*, and *A Current Affair*, frequently focus on the financial wrongdoing of businesses or famous people. Since the basis for such investigations is the analysis of financial records and/or financial statements, people who plan to be journalists, as well as their audience, will clearly benefit from an understanding of financial accounting.

Facilitates Your Growth as a Business Professional

When you enter the business world, you will discover that most businesspeople assume that you have a working knowledge of accounting. Whether you work in marketing, human resources, production, technical support, or another area, you will almost certainly encounter accounting reports that are important to understand. If you become a manager, you will be expected to analyze and understand the financial condition and results of operations of not only your own company but also that of your competitors, suppliers, or customers. Understanding financial accounting will increase your mastery of business and, thus, your development as a business professional.

Facilitates Personal Decision Making

Important reasons for pursuing a college education are to become a more informed and responsible citizen and to improve the quality of your life. Both of these objectives are facilitated by studying financial accounting. That is, this text will prepare you to make important personal financial decisions and provide specific tools that will make you a more informed person.

Managing Your Money with a Cash Budget and a Bank Reconciliation In Chapter 8, you will become acquainted with a tool known as a **cash budget**, which businesses use to plan their cash needs. A cash budget is prepared by projecting the future cash receipts and cash payments of an entity. You will also learn how to use a tool businesses use to determine how much cash they actually have on hand at any point in time. Known as a **bank reconciliation**, this tool's simplicity masks its powerful contribution to a business's internal control over cash. You will want to learn how to use both tools because each will give you much more confidence in your ability to manage your money. If you have ever been uncertain about whether you can truly afford to buy goods and services or if you have struggled to reconcile your checkbook balance to the balance found on the bank statement, you will appreciate how powerful these tools can be.

Preparing for a Job Interview Using Financial Analysis In Chapter 1, you were introduced to a specific tool of financial statement analysis known as rate of return on investment. Such tools of analysis are a means of improving business decision making, but you can also use them to help you prepare for employment interviews and, thus, improve your attractiveness as a job candidate. Taking the time to analyze a company's financial statements and mode of operation enables you to avoid interviews with less desirable companies while being a more confident and knowledgeable interviewee with companies with whom you interview. If you can demonstrate that you have prepared for your interview by analyzing and interpreting the financial accounting information of the interviewer's company, you will send a powerful message about your potential for success on the job itself. This textbook will prepare you to conduct such an analysis.

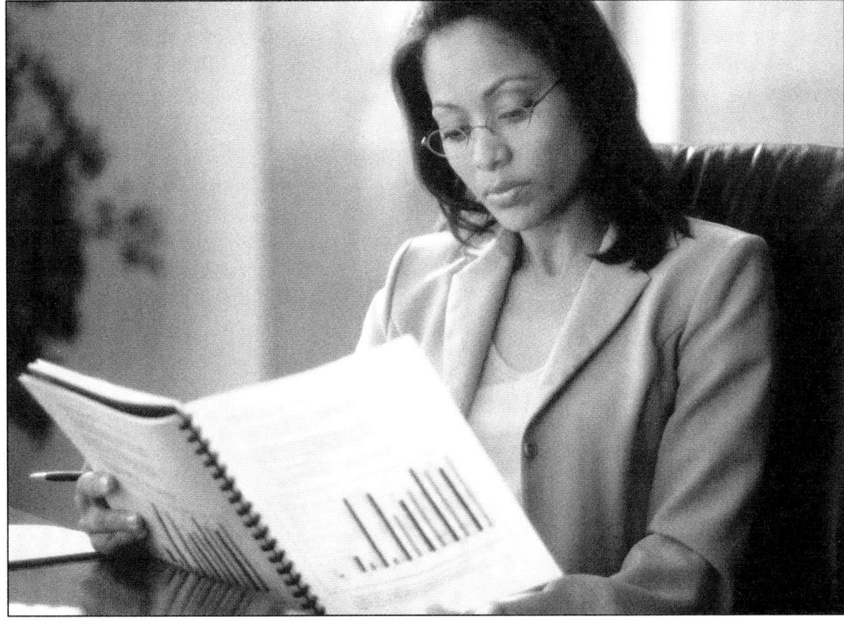

Annual reports are valuable sources of information when preparing for a job interview.

Introduces the Time Value of Money Concept

This book first introduces the **time value of money** concept, sometimes called the *mathematics of finance* or the *compound interest concept*, in *Appendix 12–1* and then applies this concept to both business and personal decision-making situations in Chapter 13. In its simplest form, the concept states that a dollar received today is not the same as a dollar received in the future. Although this concept is applied in the measurement of long-term liabilities, its most relevant applications to your personal decision making include the following three situations, which you will almost undoubtedly encounter one or more times during your life.

Planning for Retirement and Other Major Needs In *Appendix 12–1* you will study tools that financial planners use to determine how much money to set aside for such events as a child's college education or someone's retirement. You will also learn how a pension plan works in Chapter 13. Studying such tools as future value, present value, and annuities will enable you to make financial decisions that affect the rest of your life.

Understanding How an Installment Loan Works In today's world, it is essential that you understand how such transactions as automobile loans, long-term promissory notes, and home loans actually work. You will study all of these installment loans as applications of the present value concept in Chapter 13.

Determining Whether to Lease or to Purchase Determining whether it is preferable financially to lease property or to purchase the property outright is a classic decision situation that both businesses and individuals often encounter. This application of the present value concept is presented in *Appendix 13–1*.

Summary with Key Terms

The number in parentheses following each **key term** is the page number on which the term is defined.

In this chapter, you learned how the recorded effects of transactions and fundamental business activities are reported in financial statements. To facilitate this understanding, you learned the distinction between a **business activity** (46) and a **business transaction** (47).

You then learned about the first four transactions of Cards & Memorabilia Unlimited. Transaction A_1, a **financing activity** (48), involved the obtaining of **capital** (48) from Susan Newman, the owner. A financing activity also occurs when a business obtains capital from **lenders** (48) or other creditors. Transactions B and C_1 were both examples of an **investing activity** (50), while Transaction D illustrated an **operating activity** (53).

Each effect of a transaction is recorded in an **account** (49), a financial record that documents increases and decreases. In Transaction C_1, for example, you learned that an obligation to a **creditor** (52) can be represented by the unique **account title** (50) **Accounts Payable** (53). The **dual effect concept** (61) underlies this important technique. You then discovered some of the primary characteristics of a **balance sheet** (55), such as the fact that it is composed of **assets** (56), **liabilities** (56), and **owner's equity** (56). You used the technique of **transaction analysis** (57) to analyze Transactions A_1–D and prepare four separate balance sheets. Every balance sheet represents the **fundamental accounting equation** (56), which establishes the relationship between the elements of the balance sheet. One variation of this **balance sheet equation** (57) is the idea that **net assets** (57) equals owner's equity.

You then learned the conditions a transaction must meet to enter the **accounting information system (AIS)** (54). The first condition—the event must be measurable in dollars—is derived from the **money measurement concept** (58). The second condition—the event must be related to the entity being measured—is derived from the **entity concept** (58). A transaction that meets these conditions as well as the third condition—the event affects the entity's current financial position—is an **accounting transaction** (59).

Although this chapter focused on how a balance sheet is produced by recording the effects of transactions, it also provided your first look at the **statement of cash flows** (63). Unlike a balance sheet, this statement is produced by recording the effects of business activities as well as business transactions.

In this chapter, you learned the importance of the **audit** (65) conducted by the **certified public accountant**, or **CPA** (65), and reported in the **Independent Auditors' Report** (65). You also learned about the many ways you will be able to use accounting in your business and personal life. These include understanding the **notes** (67) to financial statements, preparing both a **cash budget** (71) and a **bank reconciliation** (71), and applying the **time value of money** (71) to several business and personal transactions.

Making Business Decisions

YOUR PERFORMANCE OBJECTIVE 2
(page 18)

Every day, individuals in businesses make decisions that result in accounting transactions. These transactions can, sometimes individually and sometimes in combination, have far-reaching effects on the financial health of those businesses. Dan and Lisa Wallace are two such businesspeople. They began their Web site development service business, Wallace Computer Web Services, in their home just one year ago. Advertising over the Internet, their revenue has grown remarkably, to the point where they are now billing about $5,000 per month.

Consider the following transactions that occurred at Wallace Computer Web Services (hereafter, the entity):

1. A $10,000 business line of credit is approved by the entity's bank. Borrowing on the line of credit is available immediately at an 8% interest rate.
2. The Wallaces contribute $15,000 cash to finance their business. This transaction occurs when they deposit $15,000 in a new business checking account.
3. A combination desk-worktable is purchased for $525 by check from Office Station.
4. A credit card is used to purchase $400 worth of bookkeeping software from an online software retail company.
5. The entity receives a $225 check in payment of an existing customer balance on April 15, and this check is deposited in the company checking account.
6. A lease agreement is signed for the monthly rental of a digital camera to be used in creating images that will be uploaded to customers' websites. The first monthly payment of $35 is due at the end of this month.
7. The entity opens a money market account and deposits $1,500 into this account on June 10.
8. An advance of $2,000 on services to be performed by the entity during the next year is received from a corporate client.
9. An agreement is signed with another client for periodic maintenance of its website for $300 per month, starting next month.
   a. For each of these transactions, answer the following three questions:
      (1) Does this transaction qualify as an accounting transaction—that is, does it enter the accounting information system? Why or why not?
      (2) Describe the effect of any accounting transactions on each of the three financial statements.
      (3) Suppose that you are one of the Wallaces. Describe the decision-making process you would likely have used for each transaction. In other words, describe what alternative decisions you likely considered and your justification for making the particular decision you did make, and list the potentially favorable and unfavorable effects of these transactions on the financial statements.
   b. Since the entity is organized as a partnership, describe any differences you might expect to find in its financial statements when you compare them to those of Cards & Memorabilia Unlimited, the sole proprietorship described in this chapter.

Questions

YOUR PERFORMANCE OBJECTIVE 4
(page 22)

2-1 Explain in your own words the meaning of key business terms:

a. Capital
b. Account title
c. Accounts Payable
d. Dual effect concept
e. Balance sheet
f. Assets
g. Liabilities
h. Owner's equity
i. Transaction analysis
j. Fundamental accounting equation
k. Balance sheet equation
l. Net assets
m. Statement of cash flows
n. Audit
o. Certified public accountant (CPA)
p. Independent Auditors' Report
q. Notes
r. Bank reconciliation
s. Time value of money

2-2 What are the two questions that every balance sheet is designed to answer?

2-3 List 10 typical things of value a business might own.

2-4 Distinguish between a business activity and a business transaction.

2-5 Distinguish between a lender and a creditor.

2-6 Business transactions can be classified into three major activities: financing, investing, and operating. Define these activities. Then choose a specific business, and give one example of each activity from this business.

2-7 Explain why an owner's investment in a business is considered a financing activity and not an investing activity.

2-8 Explain why the amount of asset sources always equals the amount of assets.

2-9 Discuss whether or not the fundamental accounting equation is valid for all forms of businesses.

2-10 Given that no liability or owner's equity accounts were affected by Transaction D, how can it be argued that the fundamental accounting equation is maintained?

2-11 Identify an accounting information system (AIS) of a company with which you have interacted either as an employee or as a customer. Choose a transaction you have experienced and apply each component of the AIS definition by illustrating how the component relates to that transaction.

2-12 What is the money measurement concept? Discuss how this concept affects the information presented in financial statements.

2-13 What is the business entity concept? Discuss the importance of this concept in preparing financial statements.

2-14 Using the three conditions that a transaction must satisfy to be recorded, discuss how each of the following events should be treated:

a. The founder and president of your company is seriously ill.
b. A major worker strike has begun at all your warehouse facilities.
c. An attorney's client pays cash, a retainer, prior to the attorney providing agreed-upon services.
d. A company contracts to provide its employees with health care coverage for the first time.
e. The Environmental Protection Agency has shut down a manufacturer's main production facility because of a toxic spill.
f. A new employee is hired.

2-15 Distinguish between transactions and accounting transactions.

2-16 Provide an example of a personal transaction for each of the nine dual effects shown in Figure 2-7.

2-17 Write a one-page paper in which you discuss accounting's role in society.

2-18 List at least ten decision makers who use financial accounting information.

2-19 What decisions can financial accounting help you make?

2-20 In Chapter 1, you learned that financial accounting measures and reports information for external users of accounting information, while managerial accounting measures and reports information for internal users. In groups or on your own as assigned by your instructor, answer the following question:

For each of the following users of accounting information, identify if this user is an internal or external user and explain how this user uses accounting information.

a. Sole proprietors
b. Partners
c. Present investors (stockholders)
d. Potential investors
e. Creditors
f. Employees
g. Managers
h. Officers of a corporation.
i. Board of directors of a corporation
j. Government taxing authorities and regulatory agencies
k. Other not-for-profit organizations
l. Union negotiators
m. Union members
n. Media investigators

Reinforcement Exercises

YOUR PERFORMANCE OBJECTIVE 4
(page 22)

E2-1 Asking the Right Questions: A Group Activity

It's often said that knowing the right answer is not nearly as important as asking the right question. Asking the right question is a problem-solving skill that will help you make sound business decisions. In this exercise, you will review the vocabulary introduced in Chapter 2 by creating questions to match answers—similar to a popular TV show.

Required

a. Given an answer, what's the question?
Choose *three* of the following terms to serve as an answer and create an appropriate question for each term. For example, if you choose the term *balance sheet*, you might create the question—*What financial statement shows the assets, liabilities, and owner's equity of an entity on a specific date?*—although now you can't use this question!

Operating activity	Financing activity	Investing activity
Balance sheet	Asset	Accounting information system
Liability	Owner's equity	Transaction
Entity concept	Net assets	Accounting transaction

b. Are you sure that's the question?
Have each group member within your small group read aloud the questions they developed in Requirement (a). As a group, decide whether each question is an accurate match for each answer. Once satisfied that all questions are appropriate, the group, as a whole, chooses the three best questions created within the group. Record the three questions chosen (with their answers) on separate pieces of paper or index cards and give them to your instructor.

c. What's the answer?
To ensure that you have learned the vocabulary terms listed in Requirement (a), your instructor will now quiz you on the questions written by all of your classmates.

E2-2 Applying the Fundamental Accounting Equation

YOUR PERFORMANCE OBJECTIVE 5a *(page 60)*

Answer each of the following questions:

a. Sarah Torres has assets of $26,000 and owner's equity of $11,250. What is the amount of her liabilities?
b. John Burkett has liabilities of $12,600 and owner's equity of $7,900. What is the amount of his assets?
c. Judith Deshaies has assets of $37,500 and liabilities of $17,250. What is the amount of her owner's equity?
d. Bill Swift started September with assets of $75,000 and liabilities of $45,000. During the month of September, his owner's equity increased by $12,000 and his liabilities decreased by $5,000. What is the amount of his assets at the end of September?
e. Trevor Wilson's liabilities are equal to one-third of his total assets and his owner's equity totals $9,000. What is the amount of his total liabilities at the end of the year?

E2-3 Applying the Fundamental Accounting Equation

YOUR PERFORMANCE OBJECTIVE 5a *(page 60)*

At the beginning of the year, Kronzek Company had total assets of $70,000 and total liabilities of $50,000. Answer the following questions:

a. If total assets increased $15,000 during the year and total liabilities decreased $8,000, what is the amount of owner's equity at the end of the year?
b. If total liabilities increased $10,000 during the year and owner's equity decreased $7,000, what is the amount of total assets at the end of the year?
c. If total assets decreased $9,000 and owner's equity increased $12,000 during the year, what is the amount of total liabilities at the end of the year?

E2-4 Transaction Analysis

YOUR PERFORMANCE OBJECTIVE 5a *(page 60)*

Analyze the effects of the following transactions for Nate's Auto Parts, a sole proprietorship. The example below illustrates how to properly record Transaction a. Use + for increase, − for decrease, and NE for no effect if the account is unaffected by the transaction.

Transaction	Assets	=	Liabilities	+	Owner's Equity
a.	+100,000	=	NE		+100,000

Transactions

a. The owner, Morris Mesonznick, makes a cash contribution of $100,000 to start the business.
b. $15,000 is borrowed from the bank.
c. $5,000 of the bank loan is repaid.
d. Used auto parts are purchased for $25,000 cash.

e. Office supplies of $6,000 are purchased on account.
f. Morris withdraws $8,000 to pay personal expenses.
g. $25,000 worth of equipment is purchased by signing a three-year note.
h. Monthly rent of $1,500 is prepaid.
i. A portion of the equipment is sold for $4,000 (no gain or loss).
j. Cash of $3,000 is received from customers before auto parts are delivered.

YOUR PERFORMANCE OBJECTIVE 5a *(page 60)*

E2-5 Transaction Analysis

Analyze the effects of the following transactions for Stravinsky Company, a sole proprietorship. The example below illustrates how to properly record Transaction b. Use + for increase, − for decrease, and NE for no effect if the account is unaffected by the transaction.

Transaction	Assets	=	Liabilities	+	Owner's Equity
b.	+50,000 −10,000	=	+40,000		NE

Transactions

a. The owner, Igor Stravinsky, makes a cash contribution of $40,000 to start the business.
b. Land is purchased for $50,000, $10,000 of which is paid in cash. A note payable is signed for the balance.
c. Inventory is purchased for $20,000 on credit.
d. A $7,500 liability is paid off.
e. A $30,000 line of credit is obtained from a local bank. No amount has yet been borrowed.
f. Igor wants to make an additional investment in the company in the future and arranges a $10,000 personal bank loan.
g. Cash of $22,500 is borrowed on the line of credit.
h. Igor withdraws $5,000 for personal expenses.
i. Igor invests the $10,000 described in Item f in his company.

YOUR PERFORMANCE OBJECTIVE 5a *(page 60)*

E2-6 Transaction Analysis

Analyze the effects of the following transactions for Metaphor Company, a sole proprietorship. The example below illustrates how to properly record Transaction c. Use + for increase, − for decrease, and NE for no effect if the account is unaffected by the transaction.

Transaction	Assets	=	Liabilities	+	Owner's Equity
c.	+24,500	=	+24,500		NE

Transactions

a. Made a $75,000 cash investment to start the business.
b. Borrowed $10,000 through a bank loan.
c. Purchased $24,500 worth of merchandise on account.
d. Purchased several items of office equipment for $20,000.
e. Paid $16,500 of the account payable incurred in Item c.
f. Contributed land worth $25,000 to the business.
g. Repaid $2,000 of the bank loan.
h. Paid a yearly insurance premium of $5,000 in advance.
i. Doctors inform the owner that he has a terminal illness and has less than six months to live.

YOUR PERFORMANCE OBJECTIVE 5a *(page 60)*

E2-7 Transaction Analysis

Wilkens Lawn Care Company entered into these transactions in January:

a. Made a $65,000 cash investment to start the business.
b. Purchased lawn care equipment for $4,000 cash.
c. The owner, Jim Wilkens, withdrew $3,000 for his personal use.
d. Customers paid $1,500 for scheduled services in February.
e. Purchased lawn supplies of $2,000 on account.

f. Received $6,000 cash from bank loan.
g. Repaid bank loan in full.
h. Replaced 30-day accounts payable (Item e) with a 90-day note.

Required
For each of the lettered transactions above, indicate by number which dual effect below will result.

1. Increase one asset and decrease another.
2. Increase one liability and decrease another.
3. Increase one owner equity and decrease another.
4. Increase an asset and increase a liability.
5. Decrease an asset and decrease a liability.
6. Increase an asset and increase an owner equity.
7. Decrease an asset and decrease an owner equity.
8. Increase a liability and decrease an owner equity.
9. Decrease a liability and increase an owner equity.

E2-8 Preparing a Balance Sheet
Prepare a balance sheet for Limbaugh Company as of December 31, given the following data:

YOUR PERFORMANCE OBJECTIVE 5b
(page 57)

Cash	$2,150
Accounts receivable	700
Supplies inventory	1,050
Ditto copier machine	2,100
Land	4,000
Accounts payable	1,000
Bank loan payable	2,000
Taxes payable	600
Larry Limbaugh, capital	?

E2-9 Preparing a Balance Sheet
Prepare a balance sheet for Stern Company as of December 31, given the following data:

YOUR PERFORMANCE OBJECTIVE 5b
(page 57)

Cash	$ 1,600
Personal CD collection	4,000
Wig inventory	2,000
Recording equipment	$ 2,100
Building	5,000
Interest payable	1,000
Libel suit payable	12,000
Salaries payable	2,500
Fred Stern, capital	?

E2-10 Preparing a Balance Sheet
Prepare a balance sheet for Biggs Short and Small Clothiers as of December 31, given the following data:

YOUR PERFORMANCE OBJECTIVE 5b
(page 57)

Cash	$?
Accounts receivable	30,000
Inventories	45,000
Plant assets	187,500
Accounts payable	20,000
Salaries payable	5,000
Mortgage loan payable	50,000
Stanley Biggs, capital	212,500

YOUR PERFORMANCE OBJECTIVE 5b
(page 57)

E2-11 Preparing a Balance Sheet
Prepare a balance sheet for Maria Puente Senior Residence Hall as of December 31, given the following data:

Accounts payable	$?
Accounts receivable	8,120
Bonds payable	40,200
Land	18,000
Building	65,760
Equipment	4,450
Cash on hand and in bank	6,600
Supplies inventory	11,200
Notes payable—due in 3 years	9,000
Salaries payable	1,770
Maria Puente, capital	49,860

YOUR PERFORMANCE OBJECTIVE 6
(page 59)

E2-12 Identifying Accounting Transactions
Fill in the table below with "yes" or "no" answers for the following transactions of a sole proprietorship.

	Conditions		
Transaction	**Measurable in Money**	**Related to Entity**	**Affects Current Financial Position**
a. The owner receives $5,000 as an inheritance from a relative.	________	________	________
b. The bank approves a $20,000 line of credit for the business.	________	________	________
c. A lease for store space is signed agreeing that monthly payments of $3,000 will be paid on the first day of each month.	________	________	________
d. A telephone bill of $135 is paid.	________	________	________
e. An employee is hired at a monthly salary of $600.	________	________	________

YOUR PERFORMANCE OBJECTIVE 7
(page 64)

E2-13 Determining How a Transaction Affects the Statement of Cash Flows
Identify whether the transactions described in Exercise 2-4 are investing, financing, or operating activities. For each transaction, write a brief statement supporting your choice.

YOUR PERFORMANCE OBJECTIVE 7
(page 64)

E2-14 Determining How a Transaction Affects the Statement of Cash Flows
Identify whether the transactions described in Exercise 2-5 are investing, financing, or operating activities. For each transaction, write a brief statement supporting your choice.

YOUR PERFORMANCE OBJECTIVE 7
(page 64)

E2-15 Determining How a Transaction Affects the Statement of Cash Flows
Identify whether the transactions described in Exercise 2-6 are investing, financing, or operating activities. For each transaction, write a brief statement supporting your choice.

E2-16 Determining How a Transaction Affects the Statement of Cash Flows
Identify whether the transactions described in Exercise 2-7 are investing, financing, or operating activities. For each transaction, write a brief statement supporting your choice.

YOUR PERFORMANCE OBJECTIVE 8
(page 65)

E2-17 Distinguishing between *Ethics* and *Morals*
Describe the difference in meaning, if any, between the terms *ethics* and *morals.* Discuss what role, if any, *morals* play in the preparation of financial statements.

Critical Thinking Problems

P2-1 How You Can Use Financial Accounting Information

YOUR PERFORMANCE OBJECTIVE 2 *(page 18)*

A close friend, who just completed a financial accounting course at another school, learns that you are now taking this course. She tells you how much she disliked the course and asks you how this course could possibly be relevant to you. Explain to your friend how learning about financial accounting information will help you with the following aspects of your life:

a. Your business school coursework
b. Your career if you were to become a:
   1. Politician
   2. Health care professional
   3. Marketing manager
   4. Loan officer
   5. Real estate agent
   6. Production manager
   7. Professional athlete or entertainer
c. Your personal life

P2-2 Transaction Analysis

YOUR PERFORMANCE OBJECTIVE 5a *(page 60)*

For each of the following dual effects, describe one or more accounting transaction(s) that will have the stated effect on the elements of the fundamental accounting equation. For added realism, assume your business is a partnership with three equal partners.

a. Increase one asset account and decrease another asset account.
b. Increase one liability and decrease another.
c. Increase one owner equity and decrease another.
d. Increase an asset and increase a liability.
e. Decrease an asset and decrease a liability.
f. Increase an asset and increase an owner equity.
g. Decrease an asset and decrease an owner equity.
h. Increase a liability and decrease an owner equity.
i. Decrease a liability and increase an owner equity.

P2-3 Transaction Analysis

YOUR PERFORMANCE OBJECTIVE 5a *(page 60)*

In this problem, you will reverse the order of Performance Objective 5a. That is, you need to describe what specific accounting transactions produced each of the following ten effects on the fundamental accounting equation. Note that some cases have more than one possible explanation. Note also that NE stands for "no effect."

Transaction	Assets	=	Liabilities	+	Owner's Equity
a.	+6,000		NE		+7,000
	+1,000				
b.	+4,000		+3,200		NE
	−800				
c.	−5,300		−5,300		NE
d.	NE		+800		NE
			−800		
e.	−10,000		NE		−10,000
f.	+12,500		+12,500		NE
g.	NE		NE		+7,500
					−7,500
h.	+12,000		NE		NE
	−12,000				
i.	+4,800		NE		+4,800
j.	NE		−3,600		+3,600

P2-4 Preparing a Balance Sheet

YOUR PERFORMANCE OBJECTIVE 5b *(page 57)*

From the transactions listed in Exercise 2-4, prepare a balance sheet, using the format shown in Figure 2-4.

YOUR PERFORMANCE OBJECTIVE 5b
(page 57)

P2-5 Preparing a Balance Sheet
From the transactions listed in Exercise 2-5, prepare a balance sheet, using the format shown in Figure 2-4.

YOUR PERFORMANCE OBJECTIVE 5b
(page 57)

P2-6 Preparing a Balance Sheet
From the transactions listed in Exercise 2-6, prepare a balance sheet, using the format shown in Figure 2-4.

P2-7 Preparing a Balance Sheet
From the transactions listed in Exercise 2-7, prepare a balance sheet, using the format shown in Figure 2-4.

YOUR PERFORMANCE OBJECTIVE 6
(page 59)

P2-8 Identifying Accounting Transactions
Tina Triassic, owner of Velociraptor Cutlery, has asked you to review the following events for her business that began on July 1. State whether each event is an accounting transaction that should be entered in Velociraptor's accounting information system, and for each event, explain how you reached your decision.

a. Tina received $15,000 in severance pay from her previous employer, Tyrannosaur Wrecking Company.
b. Tina deposited $10,000 of the severance pay in a business checking account for Velociraptor.
c. Tina hires Dennis Nedry as her assistant at a monthly salary of $2,000 on July 1. He will begin work on August 1 and will receive his first paycheck on August 15.
d. Tina negotiates a bank line of credit in the amount of $25,000. Currently, Tina has not used this line of credit.
e. Tina borrows $20,000 by using the line of credit.
f. Tina orders $12,000 of fine knife sets on September 1 that will be received in a month. All invoices are due and payable one month after delivery.
g. The fine knife sets are delivered.
h. Tina withdraws $4,000 from the business for her personal use.

YOUR PERFORMANCE OBJECTIVE 6
(page 59)

P2-9 Identifying Accounting Transactions
Richard Kimbrough opens the Fugitive Memorabilia Shop on March 1. State whether each event is an accounting transaction that should be entered in the Fugitive's accounting information system and how you reached your decision.

a. Richard personally borrows $50,000 from a local bank to open his business. His home is used as collateral to obtain the loan.
b. Richard opens a business checking account by depositing $20,000.
c. Richard signs a three-year lease to acquire store space for his business. He pays $5,000 to landlord Lee Jones as a deposit at the time of the signing.
d. Richard signs a $1,000,000 contract for the movie rights to his life story with Rockcastle Entertainment. Harry Ford is selected to portray Richard in the upcoming movie.
e. Richard goes to the bank and exchanges $100 cash for an equal amount of quarters.
f. Richard receives a $500 order from a customer for the Waterslide Game and the Do-It-Yourself Medical Emergency Kit.
g. Richard sends a $300 check to an insurance company for property insurance. The period of coverage begins next month.
h. Richard is charged with criminal fraud and jailed. Business falters dramatically due to the negative publicity.

YOUR PERFORMANCE OBJECTIVE 7
(page 64)

P2-10 Preparing a Statement of Cash Flows
From the transactions listed in Exercise 2-4, prepare a statement of cash flows, using the format shown in Figure 2-8.

P2-11 Preparing a Statement of Cash Flows
From the transactions listed in Exercise 2-5, prepare a statement of cash flows, using the format shown in Figure 2-8.

YOUR PERFORMANCE OBJECTIVE 7
(page 64)

P2-12 Preparing a Statement of Cash Flows
From the transactions listed in Exercise 2-6, prepare a statement of cash flows, using the format shown in Figure 2-8.

P2-13 Preparing a Statement of Cash Flow

From the transactions listed in Exercise 2-7, prepare a statement of cash flows, using the format shown in Figure 2-8.

YOUR PERFORMANCE OBJECTIVE 7 *(page 64)*

P2-14 Determining How a Transaction Affects the Statement of Cash Flows and Preparing a Statement of Cash Flows

Mark Perkins has just opened a pet store called *The Animal Kingdom.* He has prepared the following Things of Value/Sources of Value Reports detailing the first five transactions that occurred in the business:

YOUR PERFORMANCE OBJECTIVE 7 *(page 64)*

THE ANIMAL KINGDOM
Things of Value Report
April 1

Cash	$32,000

THE ANIMAL KINGDOM
Sources of Things of Value Report
April 1

Mark Perkins, capital	$32,000

THE ANIMAL KINGDOM
Things of Value Report
April 2

Cash	$15,000
Equipment	17,000
	$32,000

THE ANIMAL KINGDOM
Sources of Things of Value Report
April 2

Mark Perkins, capital	$32,000

THE ANIMAL KINGDOM
Things of Value Report
April 3

Cash	$15,000
Equipment	27,000
	$42,000

THE ANIMAL KINGDOM
Sources of Things of Value Report
April 3

Loan payable	$10,000
Mark Perkins, capital	32,000
	$42,000

THE ANIMAL KINGDOM
Things of Value Report
April 4

Cash	$15,000
Merchandise inventory	8,500
Equipment	27,000
	$50,500

THE ANIMAL KINGDOM
Sources of Things of Value Report
April 4

Accounts payable	$ 8,500
Loan payable	10,000
Mark Perkins, capital	32,000
	$50,500

THE ANIMAL KINGDOM
Things of Value Report
April 5

Cash	$17,500
Merchandise inventory	8,500
Equipment	27,000
	$53,000

THE ANIMAL KINGDOM
Sources of Things of Value Report
April 5

Accounts payable	$ 8,500
Loan payable	10,000
Mark Perkins, capital	34,500
	$53,000

Required

a. In groups or on your own as assigned by your instructor, carefully study all five reports.
b. For each transaction shown, write a description of what possibly took place, and explain why you believe it was an operating, investing, or financing activity.
c. Prepare a balance sheet for *The Animal Kingdom* as of April 5.
d. Prepare a statement of cash flows for *The Animal Kingdom* for the period April 1–April 5.

YOUR PERFORMANCE OBJECTIVE 8
(page 65)

P2-15 Distinguishing between *Ethics* and *Integrity*

Figure P2-15 is an excerpt from the American Institute of CPA's Code of Professional Conduct on the meaning of the term "integrity." With this information, write a one-page paper in which you compare and contrast the terms *ethics* and *integrity.* Suppose a client asked you to overstate the value of assets reported on his company's balance sheet. Apply these terms to this situation.

YOUR PERFORMANCE OBJECTIVE 9
(page 68)

P2-16 Understanding the Independent Auditors' Report

Figure 2-9 presents an example of an Independent Auditors' Report. This report is actually a letter to a company's board of directors and stockholders from the independent accounting firm hired to audit the company's annual financial statements.

FIGURE P2-15

Section 54–Article III: Integrity

To maintain and broaden public confidence, members should perform all professional responsibilities with the highest sense of integrity.

.01 Integrity is an element of character fundamental to professional recognition. It is the quality from which the public trust derives and the benchmark against which a member must ultimately test all decisions.

.02 Integrity requires a member to be, among other things, honest and candid within the constraints of client confidentiality. Service and the public trust should not be subordinated to personal gain and advantage. Integrity can accommodate the inadvertent error and the honest difference of opinion; it cannot accommodate deceit or subordination of principle.

.03 Integrity is measured in terms of what is right and just. In the absence of specific rules, standards, or guidance, or in the face of conflicting opinions, a member should test decisions and deeds by asking: "Am I doing what a person of integrity would do? Have I retained my integrity?" Integrity requires a member to observe both the form and the spirit of technical and ethical standards; circumvention of those standards constitutes subordination of judgment.

.04 Integrity also requires a member to observe the principles of objectivity and independence and of due care.

Required

a. Carefully read the three paragraphs composing this letter and, in your own words, write a description of the work the auditors performed, as explained in each paragraph.
b. In small groups, rewrite the auditors' letter in simple terms by using Figure 2-9 and your descriptions in (a). Be careful to describe fully what the auditors actually claim they have done.
c. The letter in Figure 2-9 refers to "generally accepted auditing standards" and "generally accepted accounting principles." From the information contained in this letter and in Chapter 2, describe what these terms mean and whether you think they are important to users of financial information. Be prepared to share your responses aloud with the entire class.
d. After completing the group work, write your own response as to whether you agree or disagree with the following statement:

   As a potential investor, if a U.S. company's audited annual report contains a "clean opinion," I am assured that the information is accurate, complete, and comparable to other companies in the same industry and I can rely on it to make investment decisions.

P2-17 Comprehensive Problem

YOUR PERFORMANCE OBJECTIVES 4, 5, 7, 8 *(pages 22, 57, 64, 65)*

Although some of the accounting terms and procedures we use today date back more than five hundred years, the accounting process is constantly evolving. In its current form, the balance sheet dates back over forty years; but the practice of reporting information about operating, investing, and financing activities is less than ten years old. The objective of this critical thinking problem is to consider the type of information disclosed on a balance sheet and why companies now report additional information.

Required

a. Briefly describe what is meant by a "balance sheet."
b. Briefly describe what is meant by "operating, investing, and financing activities."
c. Carefully study the balance sheet at the top of the following page and answer Questions (1), (2), and (3).
   1. From your examination of the balance sheet, can you answer the following questions? Why or why not?
      (a) How long has *The Book Loft* been in business?
      (b) Did the company's cash increase or decrease this year?
      (c) Did the company's total liabilities increase or decrease this year?
      (d) What assets did the company buy in exchange for the loan payable?
      (e) How much store equipment was purchased this year?

(f) Did the owner invest any additional money in the business this year?
(g) Can you explain what operating, investing, and financing activities took place during the year?

2. Based on your responses to Question (1), list the strengths and weaknesses of a balance sheet.

THE BOOK LOFT
Balance Sheet
December 31

Assets		Liabilities	
Cash	$11,000	Accounts payable	$13,000
Merchandise inventory	47,000	Loan payable	22,000
Store equipment	34,000		$35,000
		Owner's Equity	
		Phil Banks, capital	57,000
	$92,000		$92,000

3. Explain why you believe it would be important for an external user of accounting information to know what operating, investing, and financing activities took place during a given year.

Research Assignments

A wide variety of interesting Research Assignments for this chapter are available for the following topics at www.mhhe.com/solomon:

R2-1 **Visit the Small Business Administration Website**
R2-2 **Working at the Small Business Administration**
R2-3 **What Internet Resources Are Available to Help Small Businesses?**
R2-4 ***The Wall Street Journal*****'s Interest in Small Business**
R2-5 **How Do You Obtain Financing to Start a Small Business?**
R2-6 **Financial Statements on the Internet**
R2-7 **The CPA Profession**
R2-8 **Ethics and the Enron Scandal (PO 8)**
R2-9 **User Interview—Investor Decisions (PO 9)**
R2-10 **User Interview—Creditor Decisions (PO 9)**

CHAPTER THREE

3

Financial Statements and Their Relationships

Also be sure you have mastered the following Performance Objectives from previous chapters. They lay the foundation for the concepts you will learn in this chapter:

PO2
PO4
PO5
PO7

PERFORMANCE OBJECTIVES

In this chapter, you will learn the following new Performance Objectives:

PO10 **Prepare** an income statement that reports the results of operations of any entity.

PO11 **Differentiate** the balance sheet from the income statement by being able to:

a. **Distinguish between** transactions that do and do not affect the income statement.
b. **Classify** account titles into asset, liability, owners' equity, and income statement accounts.

PO12 **Prepare** a statement of owners' equity that reports the changes in owner equity accounts for any entity.

PO13 **Link** the following related financial statements—balance sheet, income statement, and statement of owners' equity—by being able to **calculate** missing amounts in each of them.

PO14 **Navigate** through and **locate** information in an annual report, so that you can make informed decisions about that entity's financing, investing, and operating activities.

PO15 **Describe** how information sources other than the corporate annual report (e.g., quarterly reports and SEC Form 10-K) can be used to learn more about the nature of an entity's business.

HOW SHOULD CARDS & MEMORABILIA UNLIMITED PRESENT ITS FINANCIAL REPORTS?

Susan is facing an important decision—one every business owner must face. Precisely what information, how much detail, and what format should she use to communicate CMU's financial results to its various users? This is a difficult decision for Susan, who, as a new owner, has never before issued financial reports. When Susan asks George Wu for help, he suggests she educate herself about the types of financial information many businesses prepare annually. He remarks that although her business is a sole proprietorship, she might learn a lot by looking at the wide variety of information presented by corporations in what are called annual reports.

An **annual report** is a major product of the financial accounting system of a company. Its primary purpose is to communicate information about the company's financial condition and its results of operations to current and prospective investors. The annual report accomplishes this purpose like any other successful communication—by keeping the needs of its audience in mind. Thus, it reports the achievements and the financial activities of the company for the last year, as well as other information likely to be of interest to current and prospective investors. Annual reports come in many shapes and sizes; some are very colorful, some are not. But an examination of a variety of annual reports shows that almost all of them are divided into two parts that contain roughly the same content.

The first part of an annual report usually provides general information about the company and its performance. It often engages its audience by including summaries, photographs, charts and graphs, letters or messages from particular company officials, and descriptions about the company's products or activities. Almost all annual reports contain a letter to the stockholders from the president or the chief executive officer (CEO), showcasing positive results and attempting to foster confidence among current and prospective investors.

The second part of the annual report contains what is usually referred to as the "financials"—the heart of the annual report. The specific contents of the financials are usually the following items:

- **Management's Discussion and Analysis of Operations,** commonly called the **MD&A**—The annual report is a chance for the people who manage the company to show the results of their business decisions. Thus, the MD&A section gives these managers a chance to showcase their successes and explain their failures.
- **The Financial Statements**—The *balance sheet, income statement, statement of shareholders' equity,*[1] and *statement of cash flows* are the four financial statements you will learn about in this book. They are prepared by the company's accounting staff to help create a complete picture of how the company has performed financially.
- **The Notes to the Financial Statements**—These serve the same purpose that footnotes do in a report. They document, support, or elaborate on specific items within the financial statements; they are prepared by the company's accounting staff.

[1] The term "shareholders' equity" is used in the annual report because the entity described is usually a corporation. But the term "owners' equity" will often be used in this book because it is a generic term applicable to all entities.

(continued on next page)

(continued from previous page)

- **The Report of Management,** also known as **Management's Financial Responsibility**—This report has become a regular feature in many annual reports. It asserts that the company's managers, not the public accounting firm that evaluates the accuracy and fairness of the financial statements, are responsible for the financial information contained in the annual report.
- **The Independent Auditors' Report**—Recall from Chapter 2 that this report is written by the public accounting firm that has audited the financial statements. **Auditing** is a process in which the fairness of the financial statements is evaluated. It involves an examination of *selected* accounting records rather than a detailed inspection of all the accounting records.

In most corporations, a project team made up of individuals with different expertise creates the annual report. Besides the accounting staff, this team usually includes the company's top financial managers, president and/or CEO, head of the public relations or marketing communications department, a graphic designer and/or an artist, and a writer. Someone, usually the head of public relations or marketing communications, is appointed to head the team.

The team might meet several times to discuss the theme or "look" they want the annual report to have. As an example, the theme of Merck's 2001 annual report is "Poised for a New Generation of Breakthroughs." This theme appears on the cover (Figure 3-1) and is reinforced in the Chairman's Message.

Once a theme is determined, the team members work on their respective parts. For example, a writer or other marketing communications specialist usually drafts the letter to the stockholders and then works with the president or CEO to revise it until it meets his or her approval. The designer's job, on the other hand, is not to create any of the content but to find ways to present content so that it is attractive, eye-catching, and yet easy to read. Creating, designing, and finalizing the annual report is a complex task that takes many hours of work.

A company's public relations or marketing communications department usually produces the annual report because it is often considered an extension of corporate public relations. An annual report is an opportunity to build the corporate image and to communicate the personality of the company to current and prospective investors.

Now that you have learned about the purpose and content of annual reports, you may be wondering if Susan Newman will need to produce an annual report to summarize Cards & Memorabilia Unlimited's first year of business. Susan would likely prepare such a report if her business was organized as a corporation and was publicly traded. As you learned in Chapter 1, a corporation is a business owned by individuals or organizations that have purchased shares of stock. A publicly traded corporation is one whose shares of stock are bought and sold on an organized market such as the New York Stock Exchange. Almost all publicly traded corporations issue annual reports. A corporation that is *closely held*, however, is not interested in expanding its ownership group beyond selected individuals such as family members and is not generally required to issue an annual report.

CMU is a sole proprietorship, not a corporation. In other words, the business is owned by only one person. Since Susan does not want to share ownership at this time, she has no need to issue an annual report. So the answer to the question is "No." CMU does not need to issue an annual report, but it should prepare financial statements.

Since the primary objective of this textbook is to develop your ability to intelligently read and understand financial statements, we'll use the relatively simple Cards & Memorabilia Unlimited case for your first exposure to the details underlying

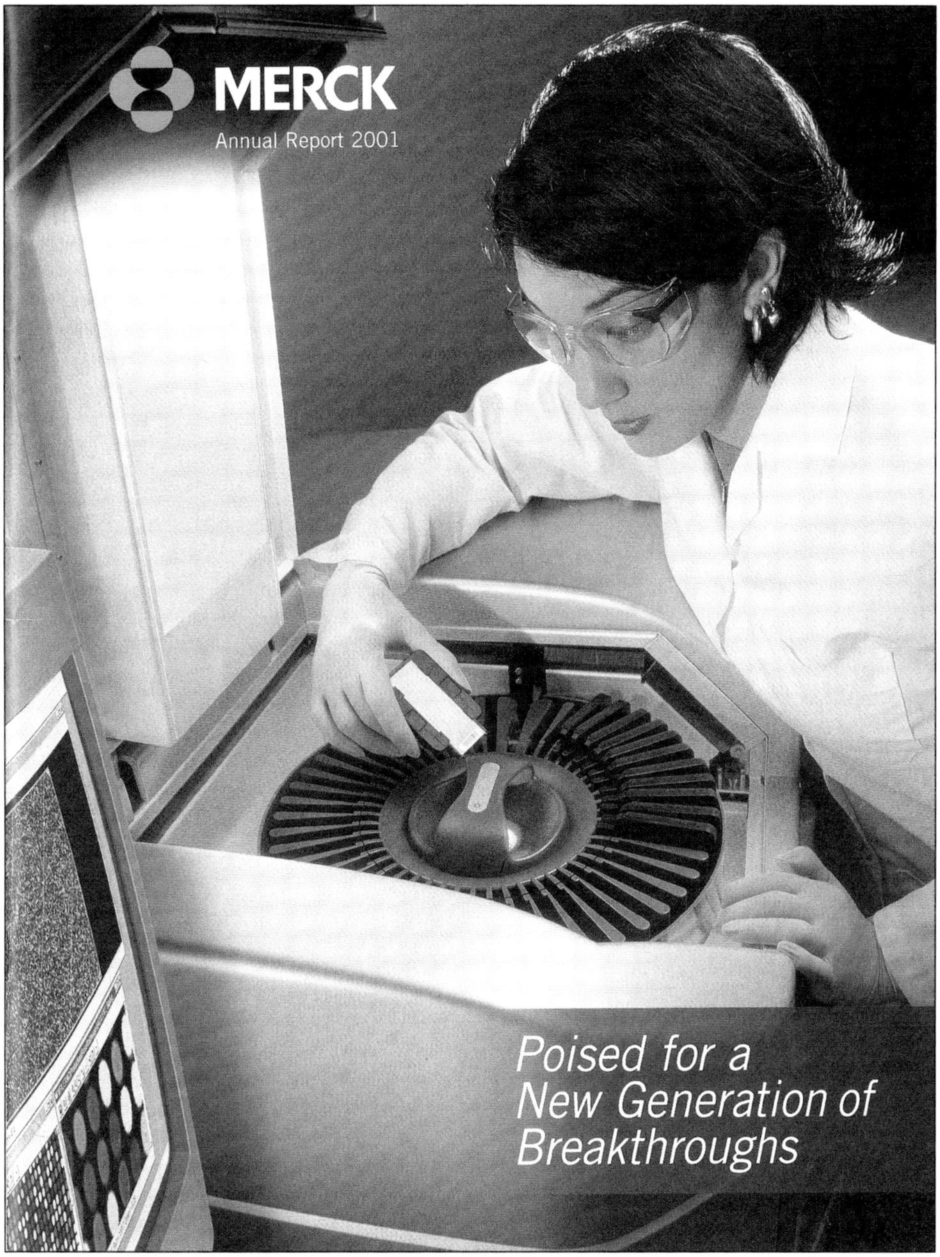

FIGURE 3-1

The cover of Merck's 2001 annual report showcases its "Breakthroughs" theme

financial statements. We'll temporarily jump ahead one year and examine CMU's first full year of operation. You'll examine CMU's balance sheet after a full year of transactions and then investigate three additional financial statements. Finally, you'll learn how all four financial statements relate to each other.

An Overview of the Financial Statements

Susan knew from her business school coursework that most businesses are required to prepare four financial statements managers and investors use to make business decisions. These financial statements are: the balance sheet (statement of financial position or condition), the income statement, the statement of owner's equity, and the statement of cash flows.

USER FOCUS

How Annual Reports Can Help You Get a Job

Suppose you are preparing for a job interview, and you want to learn as much as you can about the company so you can impress your interviewer. What information do you need, and where can you find it? A seldom used but excellent resource is a company's annual report. Although its primary audience is current and prospective investors, the annual report will help you because it is loaded with information that you can use for your interview.

The annual report is also a way to view the inner workings of the company. Eileen Ast has headed many annual report teams for large corporations, such as Harper/Collins and Conde Nast Publications. She advises that you do all you can to learn how to read and interpret annual reports. "An annual report is one sure vehicle you can use to gain a complete financial picture of a company. If you know how to read and interpret the financials, you can figure out exactly where a company is going. You can spot the problem areas." Other advice is offered by Bob Hill, a professional writer who works on the annual report for Easel Corporation, which publishes object-oriented design software tools. Bob says the savvy readers of annual reports go straight to the financials, and he advises you to "look at the notes to the financial statements. They are loaded with valuable information; they tell you so much more than the statements alone."

So let's go back to where we started—looking for a job. One of the things you might want to do when you look for a job is to analyze the annual reports of potential employers. You can usually find annual reports at the company's website or obtain a free copy by calling the company's investor relations department. Using the annual report, you can identify companies that are financially successful. After all, your career and job security rests at least in part with the current and future financial success of the company that employs you. Thus, before your interview with a prospective employer, study the company's annual report so that you are able to demonstrate both your interest in and knowledge of the company.

After you get a job, the annual report can continue to be a helpful source of information. For example, if you become a manager, the annual report can guide your managerial decision making. Or if, as an employee, you are awarded stock in the company, the annual report might help you determine the likely future value of the stock. Or if you are thinking of investing in the company, the annual report might help you make sound investment decisions. Thus, no matter what your role—prospective employee, employee, manager, investor—the annual report is an invaluable business decision-making tool.

A person or a business prepares these financial statements. But what about not-for-profit and government organizations? Are they also required to prepare financial statements? The answer is Yes. And so, for the sake of convenience, we will use the term **entity** to mean a person, sole proprietorship, partnership, corporation, or any other organization.

You have already learned that a balance sheet reports what an entity owns and owes at a particular *point in time*. Because a balance sheet provides a "photograph" of an entity at a specific point in time, it is sometimes called a *statement of financial position* or a *statement of financial condition.* In contrast, an income statement provides a "motion picture" of how profitable the entity is for a specific period of time. Just as a motion picture captures a passage of time in the lives of its characters, so too does an income statement capture the continuous action involved in reporting the results of operations for a period of time. Recall from Chapter 1 that Susan's expected $6,000 excess of revenue over expenses was referred to as *net income.* Another way of thinking about this is to say a balance sheet is used to evaluate the *condition* of an entity, whereas an income statement is used to evaluate the *performance* of an entity.

You have also been introduced to the last statement in Chapter 2—the statement of cash flows. This statement reports the cash effects of an entity's financing, investing, and operating activities.

You have not yet, however, read about the statement of owner's equity. This statement reports the change in the owner's investments in the business and the change in the earnings retained in the business.

The Balance Sheet

Now that you've seen an overview of the four financial statements, let's concentrate on a more in-depth treatment of the first of these statements, the balance sheet. You prepared balance sheets in Chapter 2 after each of Transactions A_1 through D. (Remember, these and all CMU transactions are listed in Appendix C.) Recall Performance Objective 5b.

YOUR PERFORMANCE OBJECTIVE 5b
Prepare a balance sheet that reports the financial condition of any entity.

To satisfy this objective, you have to do more than state the definition of a balance sheet. You must also be able to actually prepare a balance sheet. To do this, you must first learn what information the balance sheet provides to decision makers.

What Information Does a Balance Sheet Provide?

The balance sheet provides decision makers information about what assets are held by the business and how the business obtained those assets. A balance sheet can also help you make better decisions by telling you which liabilities should be paid first. Balance sheets do this when they classify liabilities as *current* and *noncurrent*. This distinction is helpful to decision makers because it identifies the accounts that should be paid promptly. For now, remember that the distinction between current and noncurrent assets and between current and noncurrent liabilities is one year. That is, businesses generally consider an asset to be current when it is to be held for one year or less and a liability to be current when it is due in one year or less.

Recall that a balance sheet also informs you which claims against assets will be paid first in case the business fails. That is, by law, the claims of the business creditors must be settled before the claims of the owners can be addressed. Of course, this information would be especially significant to you if you were either a creditor or an owner. Later, you will learn what additional information the balance sheet provides.

Cards & Memorabilia Unlimited's End-of-Year Balance Sheet

Cards & Memorabilia Unlimited's financial condition at the end of its first year of business is shown in Figure 3-2, which represents the effects of Transactions A_1 through Z as of December 31. Notice that this balance sheet includes the current/noncurrent distinction for both assets and liabilities. This balance sheet might appear complex to you, but don't worry. For now, we're just going to concentrate on the three elements that comprise all balance sheets.

What Are the Primary Elements of a Balance Sheet?

In Chapter 2, you gained some *insight* into the elements of a balance sheet—assets, liabilities, and owner's equity. Let's now examine these elements in more detail by again looking at CMU's balance sheet as of January 6 in Figure 3-3.

FIGURE 3-2 Cards & Memorabilia Unlimited's balance sheet as of December 31

CARDS & MEMORABILIA UNLIMITED
Balance Sheet
December 31

Assets			**Liabilities and Owner's Equity**		
Current Assets			**Current Liabilities**		
Cash checking		$32,000	Accounts payable		$ 350
Cash savings		6,275	Salaries payable		750
Accounts receivable		5,000	Advances from customers*		2,000
Interest receivable		25	Notes payable		6,000
Merchandise inventory		13,000	Total current liabilities		9,100
Total current assets		56,300			
Investments			**Noncurrent Liability**		
Security deposit receivable		2,000	Notes payable		4,000
Property, Plant, and Equipment			**Owner's Equity**		
Store equipment	$19,000		Contributed capital	$40,000	
Less: Accumulated depreciation	2,300	16,700	Retained earnings	21,900	61,900
Total assets		$75,000	**Total liabilities and owner's equity**		$75,000

*Also referred to as "Unearned revenue" or "Deferred revenue"

What Are Assets? In Chapter 2, we defined assets as things of value that are owned by an entity. But this definition is somewhat simplistic. Now you are ready for a more complete definition—including the fact that assets have value because they will benefit the entity in the future. In other words, **assets** *are things of value owned by an entity that provide future economic benefits.* Something is considered to be an asset if it can reasonably be expected to provide at least *one* of the following economic benefits:

1. *Purchasing power.* If items, such as cash or traveler's checks, can be used to acquire resources, they are said to have purchasing power.

FIGURE 3-3 Cards & Memorabilia Unlimited's balance sheet as of January 6

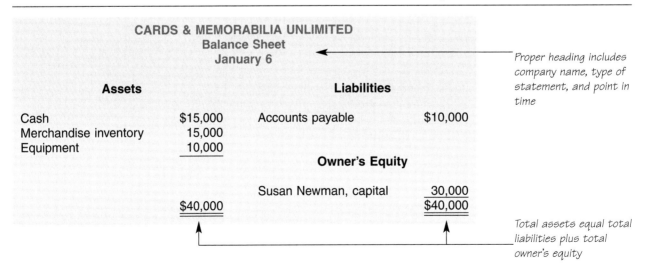

CARDS & MEMORABILIA UNLIMITED
Balance Sheet
January 6

Proper heading includes company name, type of statement, and point in time

Assets		**Liabilities**	
Cash	$15,000	Accounts payable	$10,000
Merchandise inventory	15,000		
Equipment	10,000		
		Owner's Equity	
		Susan Newman, capital	30,000
	$40,000		$40,000

Total assets equal total liabilities plus total owner's equity

2. *A claim to purchasing power.* If an item, such as accounts receivable (defined below), can be quickly converted to cash, it is said to have a claim to purchasing power.
3. *Salability.* Salability is the ability to convert inventory into accounts receivable and ultimately cash through a sale.
4. *Possession of productive services or rights.* Possessing tangible and intangible assets provides indirect benefits by allowing the entity to more easily store and promote the sale of inventory, which leads to more direct benefits, such as cash. Tangible assets are those having physical substance, such as supplies, land, buildings, and equipment. Intangible assets are those that might be invisible to the human eye, such as a patent or a copyright.

Notice that in this list of economic benefits, all noncash assets are eventually converted indirectly or directly into cash. That is, to identify an item as an asset, you must be able to show that, ultimately, it can be converted into cash. For example, if an item is expected to indirectly produce future cash, such as a patent that grants the right to produce a computerized video game, that item is an asset. Or if an item is expected to directly produce future cash, such as when the video game inventory is sold for cash, that item is also an asset. A synonym sometimes used for asset is "economic resource."

An asset that you encountered for the first time in Figure 3-2 and that you will encounter throughout this book is accounts receivable. **Accounts receivable** represent amounts from credit sales to customers that have not yet been collected. The concept of accounts receivable is commonplace in business. If, for example, Susan sells some cards to a customer who promises to pay her in the future, Susan has a claim to cash or purchasing power, which represents an account receivable.

Try now to apply the definition of asset to Transactions A_1, B, C_1, and D. Would you agree that Susan's cash checking, cash savings, store equipment, and merchandise inventory, respectively, are economic resources that will provide her business with future economic benefits? The cash obtained in Transaction A_1, for example, provides immediate purchasing power that Susan uses to buy additional assets in Transactions B, C_1, and D. Likewise, when Susan sells any portion of her inventory, obtained in Transaction D, she will receive future economic benefit in the form of cash. Finally, the equipment obtained in Transaction C_1 is an asset because it makes it easier for Susan to sell her inventory and, in turn, to receive cash.

What Are Liabilities? As you've seen before, **liabilities** are claims creditors have against assets. In Transaction C_1, for example, Susan obtained an asset—store equipment—by promising to pay a supplier in the future. From Susan's perspective, this creditor's claim against her assets, payable in the future, is her liability. Sometimes people use the words *debt* or *obligation* instead of liability. The specific liability account title in Transaction C_1 is **Accounts Payable**. From the supplier's perspective, Transaction C_1 creates an asset, an account receivable.

Keep in mind that all liabilities arise from one of the following transactions:

1. *Borrowing money.* If Susan's line of credit is approved, any amount borrowed is considered a liability.
2. *Purchasing goods or services on account.* Recall Transaction C_1 and the Accounts Payable account.
3. *Incurring obligations to employees or to the government.* A liability to employees is often called Wages Payable or Salaries Payable, and one liability to the government is called Income Tax Payable.
4. *Receiving cash from a customer for whom services are not yet performed or goods not yet delivered.* You can actually owe your customers if they have already

paid you for the goods or services you have not yet provided. This type of liability is sometimes given the account title Advances from Customers.

When a significant portion of a company's assets have been obtained with one or more of these liability transactions, the company is said to be *leveraged*. The term **leverage**, therefore, refers to the relative use of credit rather than cash to finance asset purchases. In Figure 3-2, for example, Cards & Memorabilia Unlimited is not heavily leveraged because only $13,100 ($9,100 + $4,000) of its $75,000 claims against assets are liabilities. This fact is important to Susan because the creditor's claims or liabilities are a *priority* claim against assets. That is, if CMU fails at the end of the first year of business, Susan will be obligated to repay her creditors only $13,100 *before* she tries to recover the remaining $61,900 of assets shown on her balance sheet.

What Is Owner's Equity? Exactly what do we mean by the term *owner's equity*? In fact, you have observed the owner's equity concept in each of the preceding two chapters. In Figure 1-7, for example, the difference between Susan Newman's assets (items owned) and liabilities (items owed) represented owner's equity. Likewise, in Figure 2-4, you learned that when the priority claims of creditors or liabilities of $10,000 were subtracted from CMU's assets of $40,000, the remaining or residual amount represented the claim, interest, or equity of the owner. In each case, the difference between assets and liabilities represented the claims against assets held by the owner or simply owner's equity. Thus, we can define **owner's equity** as the residual or leftover claim or interest of the owners in the assets of the entity after they have paid their liabilities. Another term, introduced in Chapter 2 and used in place of owner's equity, is *net assets*; that is, net assets represent the subtraction of liabilities from assets, which equals owner's equity.

Unfortunately, the number of synonyms for the owner's equity concept can be challenging to remember. For example, the "net worth" title found in Figure 1-7's balance sheet describing Susan's personal owner's equity has been replaced in Figure 3-3 with "Susan Newman, capital," a title that details Susan's sole proprietorship owner's equity. In annual reports, however, the term *shareholders'* (or *stockholders'*) *equity* is used because the entity is usually a corporation. Although you might find the sheer number of these owner equity titles frustrating, they do serve an important function. They allow you to distinguish between the personal equity of an individual, the business equity of a sole proprietor or partner, and the corporate equity of shareholders.

Differences in punctuation also deserve your attention. For example, this book uses the singular form "owner's equity" when dealing with a sole proprietorship such as Cards & Memorabilia Unlimited and the plural form "owners' equity" when dealing with all other business entities.

What Are the Two Components of Owners' Equity? No matter what form of entity you might encounter, the owners' equity concept has two and only two components. The first component consists of **owner's** or **owners' contributions** to finance the business. In Figure 3-3's balance sheet as of January 6, for example, this component is represented by Susan's contribution of $30,000. In Figure 3-2's end-of-year balance sheet, however, this same component is represented by the $40,000 amount next to the account title Contributed Capital.[2] An additional owner contribution made late in the year accounts for the $10,000 increase in this component. The second component consists of **retained earnings**, the earnings from profitable operations retained in the business. In Figure 3-3, retained earnings does not yet apply to the CMU case because Susan's operations did not begin until January 9. Note in Fig-

[2] The justification for using this title will be explained later in this chapter.

ure 3-2 that this component is reported in a separate account amounting to $21,900. We will reexamine these very important components and the titles used to express them in more depth later in this chapter.

The Income Statement

Now that you have learned more about what information a balance sheet provides and the nature of its three elements, we'll turn our attention to the income statement, the second of the four financial statements included in the annual report.

Cards & Memorabilia Unlimited's Income Statement

Figure 3-4 is the income statement for Cards & Memorabilia Unlimited. An **income statement** is a financial statement that reports the results of an entity's operations for a *period of time*. Income statements may be prepared for persons, sole proprietorships, partnerships, corporations, and other organizations. As with the balance sheet, you will learn how to prepare an income statement. Examine the following performance objective:

YOUR PERFORMANCE OBJECTIVE 10
Prepare an income statement that reports the results of operations of any entity.

To satisfy this objective, you will have to do more than just identify the elements of an income statement; you will also have to actually prepare an income statement. To do this, you must first learn what information the income statement provides.

What Information Does an Income Statement Provide?

As you learned in Chapter 1, business decision makers, such as investors and owners, want to know how well a business will perform over a given period of time. When Susan Newman was planning her business, for example, she wanted to know what

FIGURE 3-4

Cards & Memorabilia Unlimited's income statement for the year ended December 31

CARDS & MEMORABILIA UNLIMITED
Income Statement
For the Year Ended December 31

Revenues:		
Sales revenue	$86,600	
Service revenue	600	
Interest revenue	300	$87,500
Expenses:		
Cost of goods sold	30,000	
Rent expense	11,000	
Salaries expense	8,750	
Depreciation expense	2,600	
Miscellaneous expense	4,600	
Interest expense	200	
Loss on equipment sale	350	57,500
Net income		$30,000

Net income represents an excess of revenues over expenses.

rate of *return* she would earn *on* her *equity* investment (ROE). She used net income as a short-run measure, that is, a one-year measure of her ROE; and she discovered her projected rate of return on equity was 20%. Now that Susan has completed her first year of business, she can compare her projected rate of return to her actual rate of return and, thereby, evaluate Cards & Memorabilia Unlimited's performance. Recall that Susan projected her rate of return on equity by dividing her projected net income by her initial investment, a $30,000 contribution (Transaction A_1). You can see from Figure 3-4 that CMU's actual net income for the first year of business is $30,000. Thus, we have:

$$\text{Rate of Return on Equity} = \frac{\$30{,}000}{\$30{,}000} = 100\%$$

Using the income statement as a performance measure, Cards & Memorabilia Unlimited's first year of operations was five times more profitable than Susan's forecast of a year earlier! While a skeptic might argue that this proves there's no point in planning since the actual results are so different, more careful thought yields a different conclusion—namely, Susan's less profitable forecast motivated her to make decisions during the year that increased her profitability to the present level.

Now that you have seen at least one way in which a decision maker can use the income statement, let's look more closely at the elements of an income statement.

What Are the Primary Elements of an Income Statement?[3]

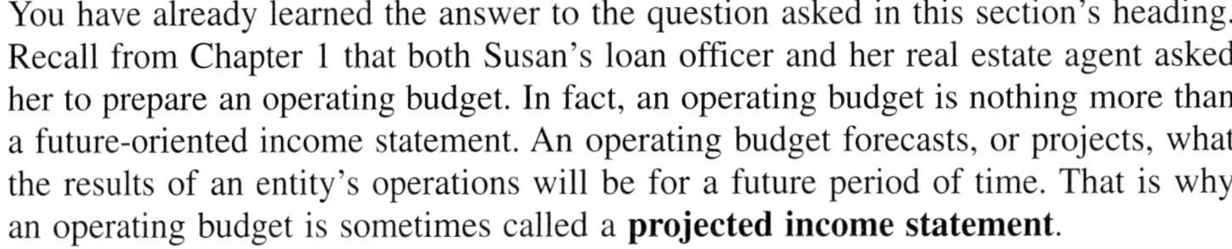

You have already learned the answer to the question asked in this section's heading. Recall from Chapter 1 that both Susan's loan officer and her real estate agent asked her to prepare an operating budget. In fact, an operating budget is nothing more than a future-oriented income statement. An operating budget forecasts, or projects, what the results of an entity's operations will be for a future period of time. That is why an operating budget is sometimes called a **projected income statement**.

Review Figure 1-10c. You will see that Susan prepared her projected income statement by first estimating her **revenue**, that is, money received or receivable from selling goods and providing services. She next estimated her expenses, that is, the cost of goods or services used up during the year to produce the revenue. Then, Susan subtracted her estimated expenses from her estimated revenue. She knew if her revenues exceeded her expenses, Cards & Memorabilia Unlimited would have a net income. If her expenses exceeded her revenues, however, Cards & Memorabilia Unlimited would have a net loss. Thus, whether future-oriented or past-oriented, whether showing a **net income** or a net loss, every income statement contains two elements: revenues and expenses. Let's now take a closer look at each of these elements.

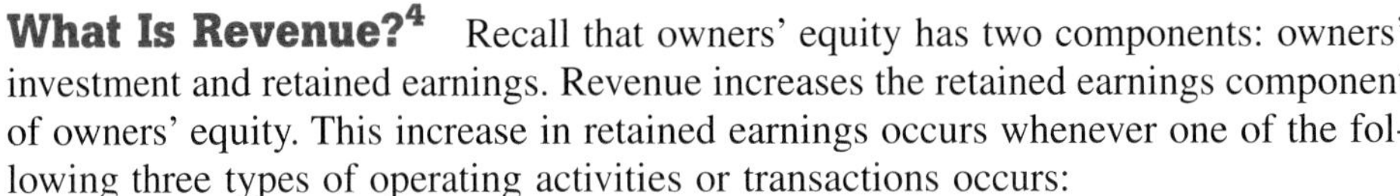

What Is Revenue?[4] Recall that owners' equity has two components: owners' investment and retained earnings. Revenue increases the retained earnings component of owners' equity. This increase in retained earnings occurs whenever one of the following three types of operating activities or transactions occurs:

- *Merchandise sales.* Sales of merchandise, or simply sales revenue, is the product of a sales price times a sales quantity. For example, on January 9, Susan's first day of business, customers purchased $680 worth of goods—$315 from the

---

[3] To reduce complexity, gains and losses will be discussed in Chapter 6.

[4] "Elements of Financial Statements," *Statement of Financial Accounting Concepts No. 6* (Stamford, Conn.: Financial Accounting Standards Board, 1985), paragraphs 78–79.

Sale of merchandise is an example of revenue, which increases the retained earnings component of owners' equity.

sale of three boxes of Fleer Ultra basketball cards at $105 a box, $125 from the sale of two boxes of Upper Deck basketball cards at $62.50 a box, $190 worth of individual card sales, and $50 from the sale of supplies, such as card albums and price guides. On January 9, the $680 was made up of $270 of cash sales and $410 of credit card sales.

- *Services rendered.* Product sales are Cards & Memorabilia Unlimited's primary form of revenue; but in its first year of operation, Cards & Memorabilia Unlimited earned a small amount of service revenue. The source of this $600 revenue was Susan's salary for teaching a trading card investment course at a local community college. As with product sales, service revenue can arise from both cash and credit sales. Note in Figure 3-4, the $600 could have been included under sales revenue rather than creating a "service revenue" account title, because $600 is relatively insignificant. However, Susan decided to report it as shown in keeping with a broad principle of financial accounting known as full disclosure. The principle of **full disclosure** means that financial statements and related notes should report all information about the entity that might affect the decisions of financial statement users. In this case, Susan is a user who desires this level of detail.
- *Interest or dividends received or receivable.* Another way an entity can earn revenue is by receiving either interest and dividends or the right to interest and dividends. Interest and dividends are derived from investing activities. An example of interest revenue is the return from loans made for a specific period of time to individuals and organizations outside the business. An example of dividend revenue is cash distributions received from investments in the stock of other companies. Both of these examples illustrate investments made outside the company, that is, external investments. These investments are different from the investment of an owner in the business itself, such as Transaction A_1. You will see in later chapters that Cards & Memorabilia Unlimited earned $300 in interest revenue from a savings account it held the entire year. It did not earn any dividends.

To help you initially understand the concept of revenue, you might think of revenue as an accomplishment. For example, you might consider the grade you earn and the amount of learning your effort produces in this course to be two forms of accomplishment or favorable consequences. That is, the sense of well-being you feel by "earning" a good grade might be considered psychological revenue.

Use the following three facts about the proper treatment of revenue in financial statements to help you build your knowledge about revenue and avoid mistakes students commonly make.

1. *Revenues are not equivalent to assets.* Revenue usually enters a company in the form of assets, such as cash or accounts receivable. But don't assume revenues are equivalent to assets. Instead, remember *when a revenue is recorded, it is accompanied by an asset.* For example, when Susan received $680 from her first day of sales, her cash account increased by $270, her accounts receivable account increased by $410, and her sales revenue account increased by $680:

Date	Transaction	Assets		= Liability	+ Owner's Equity
		Cash	Accounts Receivable		Sales Revenue
1/09	Cash and credit sales are made to customers	+$270	+$410		+$680

Although the $680 of sales revenue does enter the business in the form of assets ($270 cash and $410 of accounts receivable), we cannot say the revenue itself is an asset. Instead, the revenue represents an increase to owner's equity, Susan's claim against her assets. Under the dual aspect concept, Susan has both $680 of assets ($270 + $410) and $680 of claims against assets at the close of business on January 9 that she did not have at the opening of business on the same day. In other words, this sales transaction is recorded by increasing both the assets and the source of those assets, revenue. Since revenue increases the retained earnings component of owner's equity, both assets and owner's equity are increased by $680. Notice once again, therefore, how this transaction maintains the fundamental accounting equation introduced in Chapter 2.

2. *Revenue is not recorded when cash is received from borrowing or from an owner's contributions.* An example of borrowing is the $5,000 cash Susan receives from a business credit line in Transaction F (refer to Appendix C), which you will study in more detail in Chapter 4. An example of an owner's contribution is the $30,000 cash received from Susan in Transaction A_1. Restated, revenue is derived from operating activities rather than from financing activities.
3. *Revenue may be recorded by reducing a liability.* For example, in both November and December of her first year of business, you'll learn that Susan will deliver $2,000 of cards to customers who have already paid her (Transaction I in Appendix C). When she does this, Susan will reduce her Advances from Customers liability account—recall this account title from earlier in this chapter—and increase her Sales Revenue account by a total of $4,000. Or, if one of Susan's creditors is willing to accept payment in the form of cards, she will reduce the liability at the same time that she increases her sales revenue.

What Is Expense?[5] The second element of an income statement is expense. An expense represents a decrease in the retained earnings component of owners' equity. This decrease in retained earnings occurs whenever an asset is used up or a liability is incurred as the result of an operating activity. But the definition of expense you are most likely to remember and use is that an **expense** represents the cost of goods or services used up or consumed to produce revenue. In other words, an expense is essentially an expired asset.

To help you initially understand the concept of expense, you might think of expense as an effort. For example, the expense you incur by taking this class is the personal time and effort you consume learning about financial accounting. Other

[5] "Elements of Financial Statements," *Statement of Financial Accounting Concepts No. 6* (Stamford, Conn.: Financial Accounting Standards Board, 1985), paragraphs 80–81.

examples of expenses are cost of goods sold and depreciation expense. Recall from Chapter 1 that cost of goods sold represents the cost of merchandise that has been used up or removed from the company through sale. Depreciation expense represents the cost of depreciable assets that has been consumed in the operation of the business.

Distinguishing between Transactions that Do and Do Not Affect the Income Statement

Now that you have learned about the balance sheet and the income statement, you might be wondering how you will know whether or not a particular transaction affects the income statement. The key to making this distinction is to determine whether the transaction affects a revenue or expense account. For example, the effects of Transaction D, the cash purchase of inventory, are reported in the balance sheet because only balance sheet accounts are recorded. If the same inventory is sold, however, both an asset (cash or accounts receivable) and a revenue are recorded. Thus, this transaction affects the income statement. Likewise, the related transaction in which the inventory asset is converted into an expense called cost of goods sold also affects the income statement.

From this example, it can be said that the income statement generally includes the effects of transactions resulting in either a revenue or expense. In this course, you will soon be expected to distinguish between transactions that affect only the balance sheet and those that affect the balance sheet and income statement, as stated in Performance Objective 11:

YOUR PERFORMANCE OBJECTIVE 11

Differentiate the balance sheet from the income statement by being able to:

a. **Distinguish** between transactions that do and do not affect the income statement.
b. **Classify** account titles into asset, liability, owners' equity, and income statement accounts.

You might be wondering how revenue and expense accounts, which are found only in an income statement, affect owners' equity, an account found only in a balance sheet. You will be able to resolve this apparent contradiction once you learn about the next financial statement, the statement of owners' equity.

The Statement of Owners' Equity

Recall from earlier in this chapter, the owners' equity concept has two components—the owners' investment and retained earnings from profitable operations. Thus, the **statement of owners' equity**—called the **statement of shareholders' equity** when the entity is a corporation—reports both changes in owner investments in the business and changes in retained earnings for the business. The underlying meaning of this definition is that the statement of owners' equity reports change—both the change in the amount of assets financed by owner contributions and the change in the amount of assets financed by retained earnings. Another important function of this statement is to link the income statement to the balance sheet.

What Accounts Are Found in a Statement of Owners' Equity?

Both the sole proprietorship and partnership customarily combine and report together the owner's investment and retained earnings in a single account titled Capital. That

is, the specific owner's name followed by the term *Capital* is the account title typically used to represent owner's equity in a sole proprietorship or partnership. In Susan's sole proprietorship, for example, the account title Susan Newman, Capital is a technically correct name for the account that accumulates owner's investment and retained earnings. Despite its popularity, the use of the capital account title is undesirable for two reasons: it fails to disclose the relative amounts of each owner's equity component, and it is inconsistent with the owner's equity presentations used in other forms of entity. Figure 3-2, for example, separates Susan Newman's owner equity into both the amount invested ($40,000) and the amount retained in the business from profitable operations ($21,900). Clearly, this presentation is more informative than lumping them into one account entitled Susan Newman, Capital, and totaling $61,900. Likewise, presenting both components of owner's equity in Figure 3-2 allows us to more easily compare the owners' equity of businesses no matter what their form.

Because of these limitations of the "capital" account, this book will seldom combine these two components into one account. Instead, we will separate them using two account titles—Contributed Capital and Retained Earnings—to help you identify more clearly the activity of each individual component. The account title Contributed Capital represents the owner's(s') investment activity; the account title Retained Earnings represents the earnings from profitable operations retained in the business.

What Is Contributed Capital? **Contributed Capital** is an owners' equity account title that reports the asset contributions of owners. During its first year of business, CMU engaged in two transactions that affected its contributed capital account—a cash contribution of $30,000 to start the business (Transaction A_1) and an additional noncash owner contribution of $10,000 made late in the year (Transaction A_2). This account will increase by the amount of any additional owners contributions made on behalf of CMU.

What Is Retained Earnings? **Retained Earnings** is an owners' equity account title that reports earnings from profitable operations retained in the business. It consists of cumulative net income less any net losses and asset withdrawals. If, for example, Cards & Memorabilia Unlimited had been in business for three years, retained earnings would be determined by considering, for the entire three-year period, all net income, any net losses, and any withdrawals. Since retained earnings is part of owners' equity, its $21,900 balance is included on the December 31 balance sheet of CMU in Figure 3-2. Since CMU did not have a net loss, this balance was determined by subtracting total withdrawals from total net income as shown here:

- *A $30,000 net income.* As shown in Figure 3-4, this income statement amount represents an excess of increases (revenues) over decreases (expenses) to retained earnings. The $30,000 net income amount, therefore, increases retained earnings from zero to $30,000. In general, net income increases retained earnings.
- *An $8,100 owner withdrawal.* Susan withdrew cash from her business several times during the year to pay for personal costs. Unlike net income, these withdrawals (Transaction W) decreased the retained earnings account from $30,000 to $21,900. The essential idea underlying this subtraction is that if assets are reduced by $8,100, the sources of those assets must also be reduced by $8,100. The effect of this summary withdrawal transaction on the fundamental equation is:

Transaction W	Assets	=	Liabilities	+	Owner's Equity
$8,100 cash is withdrawn from the business by the owner throughout the year.	(8,100)				(8,100)

No retained earnings account was reported in the January 6 balance sheet shown in Figure 3-3 because no revenue, expense, or withdrawal transactions occurred until January 9.

How Is a Statement of Owners' Equity Presented?

When Susan asked George Wu for help in preparing her financial statements at the end of the year, he suggested two formats she might use for her statement of owner's equity. The first of these presentations is shown in Figure 3-5. This format simply reports the changes in Susan's capital account for a period of time. Although you just learned why use of a single capital account is not recommended, it is presented here so that you can better understand how it differs from the preferred format presented in Figure 3-6. This presentation determines the end-of-period capital account balance (C_E) by adding net income and owner contributions to the beginning-of-period capital account balance and then subtracting owner withdrawals as shown below:

$$\begin{array}{lclclclcl} \text{Ending} & & \text{Beginning} & & & & & & \\ \text{Capital} & = & \text{Capital} & + & \text{Contributions} & + & \text{Net Income} & - & \text{Withdrawals} \\ C_E & = & \$0 & + & \$40{,}000 & + & \$30{,}000 & - & \$8{,}100 \quad = \underline{\underline{\$61{,}900}} \end{array}$$

FIGURE 3-5

Cards & Memorabilia Unlimited's statement of owner's equity for the year ended December 31

CARDS & MEMORABILIA UNLIMITED
Statement of Owner's Equity
For the Year Ended December 31

Balance at January 1	$ 0
Add: Owner contributions	40,000
Net income	30,000
Deduct: Owner withdrawals	(8,100)
Balance at December 31	$61,900

This statement is traditionally called a statement of capital.

Now, let's examine the second of these statement of owner's equity presentations, the three-column format shown in Figure 3-6. This format is equivalent in concept but different in form to that of Figure 3-5. Note the use of its three columns: one for the activity or change in the contributed capital account, one for the activity or change in the retained earnings account, and a column titled Owner's Equity that combines these account changes. Essentially, this more detailed statement of owner's equity format includes two statements: a statement of contributed capital and a statement of retained earnings.

FIGURE 3-6

A more detailed version of Cards & Memorabilia Unlimited's statement of owner's equity for the year ended December 31

In the annual report, this statement is usually called a statement of shareholders' equity (or statement of stockholders' equity).

CARDS & MEMORABILIA UNLIMITED
Statement of Owner's Equity
For the Year Ended December 31

	Contributed Capital	Retained Earnings	Owner's Equity
Balance at January 1	$ 0	$ 0	$ 0
Add: Owner contributions	40,000		40,000
Net income		30,000	30,000
Deduct: Owner withdrawals		(8,100)	(8,100)
Balance at December 31	$40,000	$21,900	$61,900

What Is a Statement of Contributed Capital? A **statement of contributed capital** is a financial statement that reports changes in an owner's contributed capital accounts for a period of time. This statement determines the end-of-year contributed capital account (CC_E) balance by adding owner contributions to the beginning-of-year contributed capital account balance. This equation and Susan's column amount in Figure 3-6, respectively, are:

$$\begin{array}{ccccccc} \text{Ending} & & \text{Beginning} & & & & \\ \text{Contributed Capital} & = & \text{Contributed Capital} & + & \text{Contributions} & & \\ CC_E & = & \$0 & + & \$40{,}000 & = & \underline{\underline{\$40{,}000}} \end{array}$$

What Is a Statement of Retained Earnings? A **statement of retained earnings** is a financial statement that reports the changes in the retained earnings account for a period of time. This statement determines the end-of-year retained earnings account balance (RE_E) by adding net income to and subtracting withdrawals from the beginning-of-year retained earnings account balance. In a corporation, **dividends declared**, or distributions of assets to shareholders, are equivalent in concept to asset withdrawals. This equation and Susan's column amount in Figure 3-6, respectively, are:

$$\begin{array}{ccccccccc} \text{Ending} & & \text{Beginning} & & & & & & \\ \text{Retained Earnings} & = & \text{Retained Earnings} & + & \text{Net Income} & - & \text{Withdrawals} & & \\ RE_E & = & \$0 & + & \$30{,}000 & - & \$8{,}100 & = & \underline{\underline{\$21{,}900}} \end{array}$$

Combining Statements into a Statement of Owner's Equity When these two statements are combined in the third column of the statement of owner's equity, the resulting equation and Susan's amounts, respectively, are:

$$\begin{aligned} CC_E + RE_E &= (\text{Beginning Contributed Capital} + \text{Contributions}) \\ &\quad + (\text{Beginning Retained Earnings} + \text{Net Income} - \text{Withdrawals}), \text{ or} \\ CC_E + RE_E &= (\$0 + \$40{,}000) + (\$0 + \$30{,}000 - \$8{,}100) = \underline{\underline{\$61{,}900}} \end{aligned}$$

Note that the $61,900 is reported in the statement of owner's equity (Figures 3-5 and 3-6) as well as in the balance sheet (Figure 3-2).

Now that you have learned about the statement of owners' equity, you know you will be able to demonstrate your knowledge by mastering Performance Objective 12:

YOUR PERFORMANCE OBJECTIVE 12

Prepare a statement of owners' equity that reports the changes in owner equity accounts for any entity.

INSIGHT

Distinguishing between Two Types of Dividend Transactions

To help you develop business literacy, you must be able to distinguish between the declaration and payment of a dividend and the receipt of a dividend. When an entity declares it will *pay* a cash dividend to its owners at a future date, both dividends payable (a liability account) and dividends declared (an account that reduces retained earnings) are recorded. When instead an entity *receives* a dividend in cash from an investment it holds in another entity, both cash and a dividend revenue increase. The insight you should gain here is that a dividend can result in a decrease to retained earnings, titled Dividends Declared, or an increase to a revenue, titled Dividend Revenue, depending on whether it is paid or received.

Financial Statement Relationships

You've now learned about three financial statements—the balance sheet, the income statement, and the statement of owners' equity. Although these three statements report different information, they are related. The following section explains why and how.

Evidence of a Relationship

Evidence of a relationship among these three financial statements is the fact that many individual transactions affect all three of these statements at the same time. For example, since Cards & Memorabilia Unlimited's January 9 sales of $680 simultaneously affect both balance sheet and income statement accounts, it logically follows that there *is* a relationship between these two financial statements. That is, if both the balance sheet (through cash and accounts receivable) and the income statement (through sales revenue) increase by $680, the two statements are not completely independent. Moreover, as you record sales revenue, you are also increasing retained earnings, a primary component of the statement of owners' equity.

A similar example of a financial statement relationship is illustrated by the following equation derived from Susan's statement of retained earnings:

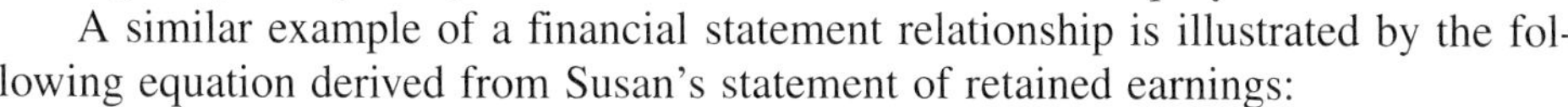

$$RE_E = \text{Beginning Retained Earnings} + \text{Net Income} - \text{Withdrawals}$$
$$RE_E = \$0 + \$30{,}000 - \$8{,}100 = \underline{\underline{\$21{,}900}}$$

Notice that the $30,000 net income derived from the income statement helps, in part, to explain the $21,900 change in retained earnings, the result of change in one balance sheet account over time. Thus, you can say that the income statement links the balance sheet at the beginning of the period with the balance sheet at the end of the same period.

As you have now seen, there is clear evidence of a relationship among the financial statements introduced so far. Your next task is to better comprehend how this relationship works and why it is important.

How Does a Statement of Owners' Equity Link an Income Statement to a Balance Sheet?

Recall that the statement of owners' equity reports both the change in the amount of assets financed by owner contributions and the change in the amount of assets financed by earnings retained in the business. This statement also links the income statement to the balance sheet. Figure 3-7 illustrates how they are linked by combining summarized versions of Figures 3-2, 3-4, and 3-6 from CMU. Study this figure and see how the statement of owner's equity specifically links the income statement to the balance sheet through the retained earnings account.

The Role of the Retained Earnings Account Although withdrawals made or dividends declared can reduce the retained earnings account reported in the balance sheet, net income is usually the primary cause of change in the retained earnings account. In other words, the entity's earnings activities, which are reported in the income statement as either net income or net loss, usually play the greatest role in explaining changes in the retained earnings account. Since the ending balance of retained earnings in the balance sheet is affected by the income statement and the changes in retained earnings are described in the statement of owners' equity, it is clear that the retained earnings account is at the center of this relationship. That is,

FIGURE 3-7 How the statement of owner's equity links the income statement to the balance sheet

FIGURE 3-4
CARDS & MEMORABILIA UNLIMITED
Income Statement
For the Year Ended December 31

Revenues	$87,500
Expenses	57,500
Net Income	$30,000

FIGURE 3-2
CARDS & MEMORABILIA UNLIMITED
Balance Sheet
December 31

Assets		Liabilities & Owner's Equity	
Cash	$38,275	Accounts payable	$ 350
Accounts receivable	5,000	Salaries payable	750
Interest receivable	25	Advances from customers	2,000
Merchandise inventory	13,000	Notes payable	6,000
Current assets	56,300	Current liabilities	9,100
Security deposit receivable	2,000	Notes payable	4,000
Store equipment	19,000	Contributed capital	40,000
Less: Accumulated depreciation	(2,300)	Retained earnings	21,900
Book value of equipment	$16,700		61,900
Total Assets	$75,000	Total Liabilities & Owner's Equity	$75,000

FIGURE 3-6
CARDS & MEMORABILIA UNLIMITED
Statement of Owner's Equity
For the Year Ended December 31

	Contributed Capital	Retained Earnings	Owner's Equity
Balance at January 1	$ 0	$ 0	$ 0
Add: Owner contributions	40,000		40,000
Net income		30,000	30,000
Deduct: Owner withdrawals		(8,100)	(8,100)
Balance at December 31	$40,000	$21,900	$61,900

the retained earnings account links the income statement to the balance sheet. Because this account plays such an important role in linking the income statement to the balance sheet, most entities issue a separate report or statement of retained earnings, as described earlier. Don't forget: The relationship among these financial statements and the special role played by the retained earnings account are shown in Figure 3-7.

The Expansion of the Fundamental Accounting Equation You now know that the statement of owners' equity links the income statement to the balance sheet and provides updated information about owner contributions and withdrawals. You have also learned that the "linkage device" is the owners' equity account Retained Earnings.

Perhaps not as obvious, but equally true, is that the fundamental accounting equation underlying the balance sheet can be expanded to include the effects of both the income statement and the statement of owners' equity. This fact is demonstrated algebraically and numerically in the series of fundamental accounting equations shown in Figure 3-8. Study this figure carefully and be certain you understand how the retained earnings account links the income statement to the balance sheet.

You will demonstrate mastery of these financial statement relationships when you can satisfy Performance Objective 13:

> **YOUR PERFORMANCE OBJECTIVE 13**
> **Link** the following related financial statements—balance sheet, income statement, and statement of owners' equity—by being able to **calculate** missing amounts in each of them.

If you understand these financial statement relationships, you will have acquired an invaluable financial analysis tool. For example, if you discover a business transaction was not properly recorded, you will be able to immediately discern the effects of this error on all the financial statements affected. In other words, you will be able to visualize how individual business transactions generate ripple effects on the information presented in the financial statements. You will also be able to overcome the effects of incomplete information. For example, suppose the net income amount (NI) in the third equation and the revenue amount (R) in the fourth equation were missing in Figure 3-8. You would now be able to figure out the missing information by calculating as follows:

$$\$75{,}000 = \$13{,}100 + \$0 + \$40{,}000 + \$0 + NI - \$8{,}100 \qquad NI = \$30{,}000$$
$$\$75{,}000 = \$13{,}100 + \$0 + \$40{,}000 + \$0 + R - \$57{,}500 - \$8{,}100 \qquad R = \$87{,}500$$

These calculations are examples of how you will be expected to demonstrate your mastery of Performance Objective 13. Several exercises and problems at the end of the chapter provide further practice in mastering this objective.

FIGURE 3-8 Expansion of fundamental accounting equation for Cards & Memorabilia Unlimited

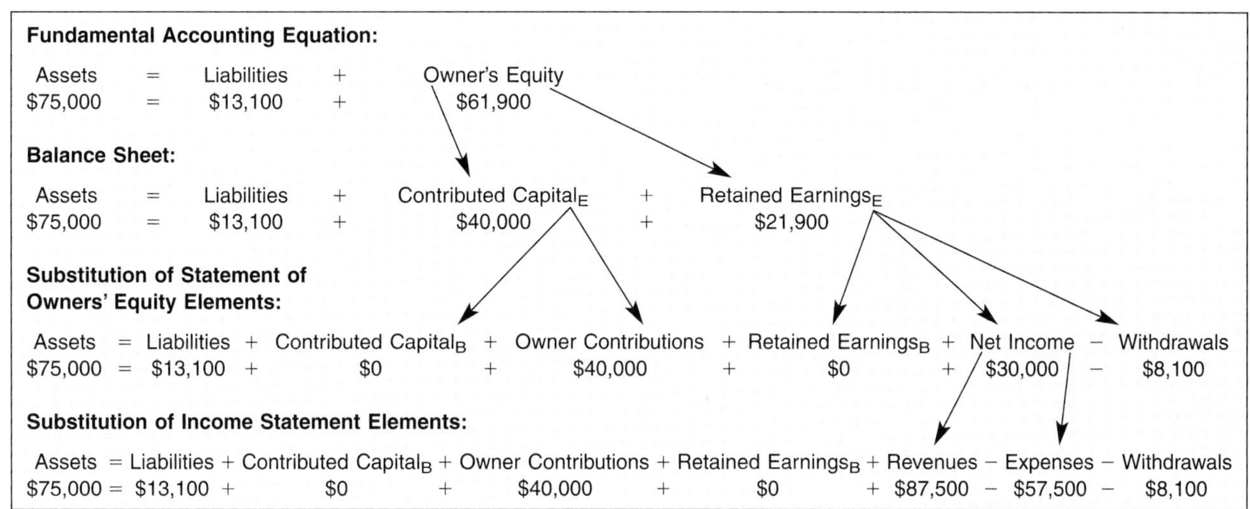

Fundamental Accounting Equation:
Assets = Liabilities + Owner's Equity
$75,000 = $13,100 + $61,900
Balance Sheet:
Assets = Liabilities + Contributed Capital$_E$ + Retained Earnings$_E$
$75,000 = $13,100 + $40,000 + $21,900
Substitution of Statement of Owners' Equity Elements:
Assets = Liabilities + Contributed Capital$_B$ + Owner Contributions + Retained Earnings$_B$ + Net Income − Withdrawals
$75,000 = $13,100 + $0 + $40,000 + $0 + $30,000 − $8,100
Substitution of Income Statement Elements:
Assets = Liabilities + Contributed Capital$_B$ + Owner Contributions + Retained Earnings$_B$ + Revenues − Expenses − Withdrawals
$75,000 = $13,100 + $0 + $40,000 + $0 + $87,500 − $57,500 − $8,100

The Statement of Cash Flows

The fourth and final financial statement included in every annual report is the statement of cash flows. The **statement of cash flows** classifies cash receipts and cash payments into operating, investing, and financing activities. Familiarity with this statement will provide you with the tools to answer such questions as:

- How have U.S. automakers financed major retooling of their production processes to compete against foreign automakers?
- How was a company like Texaco able to pay $5.5 billion to Pennzoil several years ago in settlement of their legal dispute and still survive?

- How are companies able to be profitable in the same year they experience serious cash flow problems?
- How are companies able to acquire costly noncurrent assets in the same year they report a net loss?

Answers to questions like these are not found in the balance sheet, income statement, or statement of owners' equity because those financial statements do not report the cash effects of operating, investing, and financing activities. Let's now take a closer look at the specific information needs satisfied by a statement of cash flows.

What Information Does a Statement of Cash Flows Provide?

The primary purpose of the statement of cash flows is to provide relevant information about the cash inflows and outflows of a business during a specified period of time. This information is useful to current and potential investors and creditors because it helps them determine such information as:

- The entity's ability to generate future cash flows.
- The entity's ability to meet its obligations, pay dividends, and satisfy its needs for outside financing.
- The reasons for differences between net income and cash flow.
- Both the cash and noncash aspects of the entity's investing and financing activities during the specified period.

You will be able to determine these and other facts about an entity when you demonstrate mastery of Performance Objective 7, which you first encountered in Chapter 2:

YOUR PERFORMANCE OBJECTIVE 7

a. **Define** the terms *financing activities, investing activities,* and *operating activities.*
b. **Classify** any accounting transaction into one of these activities or a noncash investing and financing activity.
c. **Classify** any cash receipt or cash payment transaction into the appropriate activity as reported in the statement of cash flows.

Cards & Memorabilia Unlimited's Statement of Cash Flows

You saw CMU's first statement of cash flows in Figure 2-8, which reported the effects of Transactions A_1 through D for January 1 to January 6. Now let's compare that statement with Figure 3-9, which reports the statement of cash flows for CMU's first year of business. Although Figure 3-9 represents the effect of all of Susan's first-year transactions, you can clearly recognize the cash effect of three transactions with which you are already familiar. Susan's cash contribution in Transaction A_1 is reported in the financing activity section. Her cash purchase of merchandise in Transaction D is reported in the operating activity section. Also, note that the zero balance in cash checking increased during the year to \$38,275, a figure that you can derive from her balance sheet in Figure 3-2. To do so, simply add together the balances in her cash checking (\$32,000) and her cash savings (\$6,275) accounts.

You might have noticed an additional section at the bottom of the statement entitled "Supplemental schedule of noncash investing and financing activities." Although you will learn more about this section in Chapter 8, you should recognize that this section is reserved for noncash transactions that represent *significant* financing and/or investing activities. This section is reserved, therefore, for transactions whose omission would interfere with the full disclosure principle introduced earlier in this chapter. That is, not reporting the purchase of computer equipment with a note, as shown

FIGURE 3-9 Cards & Memorabilia Unlimited's statement of cash flows for its first year of business

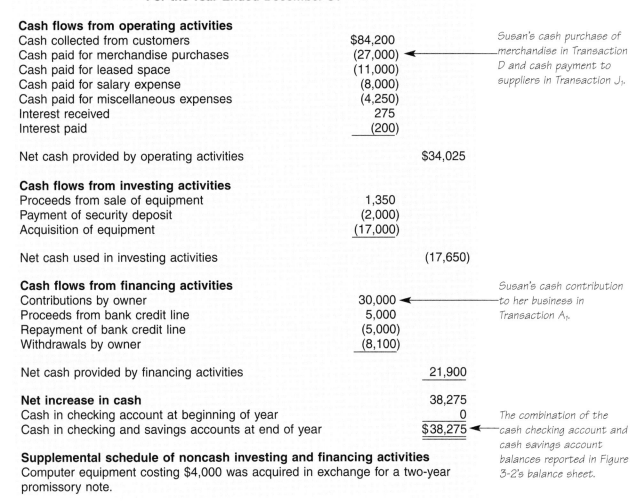

CARDS & MEMORABILIA UNLIMITED
Statement of Cash Flows
For the Year Ended December 31

Cash flows from operating activities		
Cash collected from customers	$84,200	
Cash paid for merchandise purchases	(27,000)	
Cash paid for leased space	(11,000)	
Cash paid for salary expense	(8,000)	
Cash paid for miscellaneous expenses	(4,250)	
Interest received	275	
Interest paid	(200)	
Net cash provided by operating activities		$34,025
Cash flows from investing activities		
Proceeds from sale of equipment	1,350	
Payment of security deposit	(2,000)	
Acquisition of equipment	(17,000)	
Net cash used in investing activities		(17,650)
Cash flows from financing activities		
Contributions by owner	30,000	
Proceeds from bank credit line	5,000	
Repayment of bank credit line	(5,000)	
Withdrawals by owner	(8,100)	
Net cash provided by financing activities		21,900
Net increase in cash		38,275
Cash in checking account at beginning of year		0
Cash in checking and savings accounts at end of year		$38,275

Supplemental schedule of noncash investing and financing activities
Computer equipment costing $4,000 was acquired in exchange for a two-year promissory note.

Susan's cash purchase of merchandise in Transaction D and cash payment to suppliers in Transaction J_1. (→ Cash paid for merchandise purchases)

Susan's cash contribution to her business in Transaction A_1. (→ Contributions by owner)

The combination of the cash checking account and cash savings account balances reported in Figure 3-2's balance sheet. (→ $38,275)

at the bottom of Figure 3-9, is an omission that might affect investor or creditor decisions about the company.

What Are the Primary Activities in a Statement of Cash Flows?

The Cards & Memorabilia Unlimited case has familiarized you with the three activities in which all businesses engage. It has also introduced you to these fundamental activities in the order they naturally occur in a business, that is financing, investing, and operating. But as you read about the statement of cash flows, keep in mind that it reports these three activities in reverse order—operating, investing, and financing—quite possibly reflecting their relative order of importance to most decision makers. Although you learned about the nature of each of these activities in Chapter 2, let's review.

You initiate financing activities when you obtain money and other resources from creditors and owners. Financing activities are completed when you repay or otherwise settle amounts owed to creditors and provide owners with a return on, and a return of, their investment.

You initiate investing activities when you either make loans or buy such assets as investment securities, land, buildings, or equipment. Investing activities are completed when you either collect on the loans you have made or sell investment securities or property, plant, and equipment.

You initiate operating activities when you either purchase or produce goods and services for sale. Operating activities are usually considered to be completed when goods are delivered or sold and services are performed.

How Is a Statement of Cash Flows Related to Other Financial Statements?

Recall that the statement of owners' equity links the income statement to the balance sheet. Also, the statement of cash flows has a relationship to both the balance sheet and the income statement. Let's explore this relationship by first seeing how the three statement of cash flow activities are related to balance sheet accounts.

First, when you initiate financing activities, you simultaneously create accounts found in the noncurrent liability (creditors') and owner equity (owners') sections of the balance sheet. For example, Contributed Capital, an owner's equity account within the balance sheet, was created by Transaction A_1, a financing activity. Second, when you initiate investing activities, you simultaneously create accounts found in the noncurrent asset section of the balance sheet. For example, Store Equipment, a noncurrent asset account within the balance sheet, was created by Transaction C_1, an investing activity. Third, when you initiate operating activities, you simultaneously create accounts found in the current asset and current liability sections of the balance sheet. For example, Merchandise Inventory, a current asset account within the balance sheet, was created by Transaction D, the initiation of an operating activity.

Now that you know how financing, investing, and operating activities affect specific balance sheet accounts, you might be wondering how the statement of cash flows relates to the income statement. The answer is that the statement of cash flows shows how operations affected cash for the period. This idea is illustrated in Figure 3-9. That is, each of the line items listed under Cash Flows from Operating Activities is directly related to revenue and expense accounts. For example, collections of credit sales to customers are related to sales revenue, salary payments are related to salary expense, and interest payments are related to interest expense. Additional evidence of this re-

FIGURE 3-10 How a statement of cash flows is related to a balance sheet and an income statement

Statement of Cash Flows	Balance Sheet	Income Statement
Operating activities	*Current asset and current liability accounts*	*Revenue and expense accounts*
Cash collected from customers	Accounts receivable	Sales revenue
Cash paid for merchandise purchases	Merchandise inventory	Cost of goods sold
Cash paid for leased space	Prepaid rent	Rent expense
Cash paid for salary expense	Salaries payable	Salary expense
Cash paid for miscellaneous expenses	Accounts payable	Miscellaneous expense
Interest paid	Interest payable	Interest expense
Investing activities	*Noncurrent asset accounts*	*Gains and losses on sales of noncurrent assets*
Financing activities	*Noncurrent liability and owners' equity accounts*	Generally no effect

lationship is the fact that a cash sale, an operating activity transaction, simultaneously affects the income statement (through sales revenue) and the statement of cash flows (through cash collected from customers). These relationships are illustrated in Figure 3-10.

Figure 3-10 shows how operating activities affect the balance sheet through current asset and current liability accounts, investing activities affect the balance sheet through noncurrent asset accounts, and financing activities affect the balance sheet through noncurrent liability and owner equity accounts. Also note in this figure that revenues and expenses reported in the income statement generally result from operating activities whose effects are eventually reported in both the balance sheet and statement of cash flows. For example, when a cash sale is made to a customer, there is a simultaneous increase in sales revenue reported in the income statement, cash reported in the balance sheet, and cash collected from customers reported in the statement of cash flows. This example confirms, therefore, that the statement of cash flows is related to both the income statement and balance sheet.

Merck & Co.: An Illustration of Corporate Financial Statements

Although you are learning about financial statements and their relationships by studying the sole proprietorship known as Cards & Memorabilia Unlimited, you will probably more often encounter corporate financial statements when you make both personal and business financial decisions. Accordingly, this section provides you the opportunity to compare the key differences between the financial statements of a proprietorship and those of a corporation.

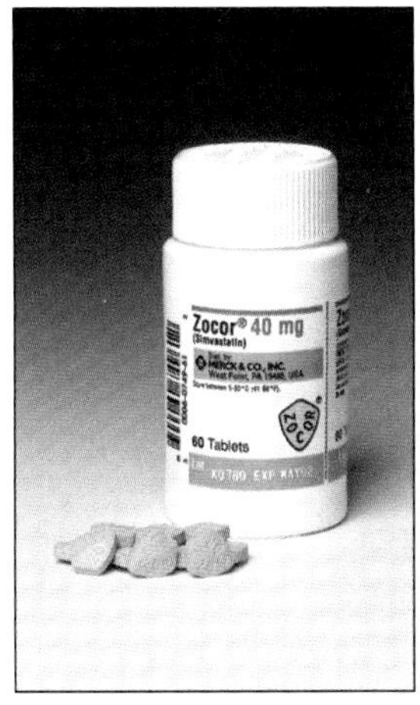

Merck & Company, Inc. discovers, develops, manufactures, and markets pharmaceutical products and services, such as Zocor, a drug designed to reduce cholesterol levels.

Annual Financial Statements

First, let's examine the annual financial statements of Merck & Co., Inc. a large pharmaceutical corporation. As Figures 3-11a through 3-11-d show, Merck's financial statement elements are identical to Cards & Memorabilia Unlimited's. For example, both balance sheets are composed of assets, liabilities, and owners' equity; both income statements are composed of revenues, expenses, and net income; both companies have a statement of retained earnings; and both statements of cash flows are composed of operating, investing, and financing activities.

You might also have identified attributes of Merck's financial statements that do not appear in Cards & Memorabilia Unlimited's financial statements. The most noteworthy examples are:

- Financial statements are *consolidated*. That is, the information presented represents several companies, called subsidiaries, which together make up the entire Merck organization.
- Numbers are expressed in millions of dollars.
- The balance sheet is comparative; that is, the two most recent balance sheets are presented.
- Owners' equity in the balance sheet is composed of two accounts titled "Common Stock" and "Other Paid-In Capital" rather than "Susan Newman, Capital" or "Contributed Capital."
- The income statement presents earnings-per-share information, which is never reported in a proprietorship because a proprietorship does not issue shares of stock.
- The income statement subtracts income tax expense ("Taxes on Income")—an account that is never reported in a proprietorship.
- The statement of retained earnings subtracts dividends declared rather than withdrawals.

FIGURE 3-11a Merck's balance sheet

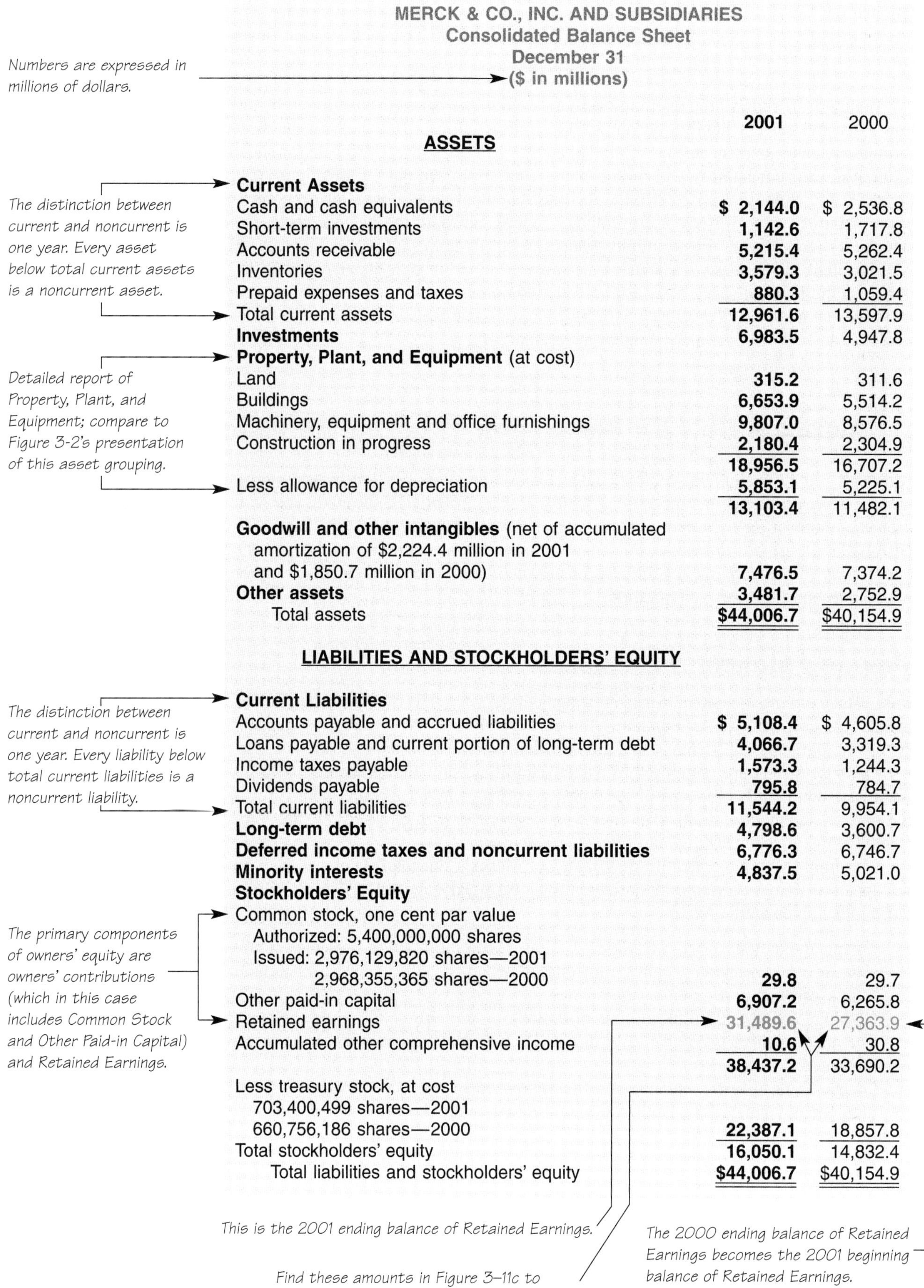

Numbers are expressed in millions of dollars.
The distinction between current and noncurrent is one year. Every asset below total current assets is a noncurrent asset.
Detailed report of Property, Plant, and Equipment; compare to Figure 3-2's presentation of this asset grouping.
The distinction between current and noncurrent is one year. Every liability below total current liabilities is a noncurrent liability.
The primary components of owners' equity are owners' contributions (which in this case includes Common Stock and Other Paid-in Capital) and Retained Earnings.
This is the 2001 ending balance of Retained Earnings.
Find these amounts in Figure 3–11c to discover a financial statement relationship.
The 2000 ending balance of Retained Earnings becomes the 2001 beginning balance of Retained Earnings.

MERCK & CO., INC. AND SUBSIDIARIES
Consolidated Balance Sheet
December 31
($ in millions)

	2001	2000
ASSETS		
Current Assets		
Cash and cash equivalents	$ 2,144.0	$ 2,536.8
Short-term investments	1,142.6	1,717.8
Accounts receivable	5,215.4	5,262.4
Inventories	3,579.3	3,021.5
Prepaid expenses and taxes	880.3	1,059.4
Total current assets	12,961.6	13,597.9
Investments	6,983.5	4,947.8
Property, Plant, and Equipment (at cost)		
Land	315.2	311.6
Buildings	6,653.9	5,514.2
Machinery, equipment and office furnishings	9,807.0	8,576.5
Construction in progress	2,180.4	2,304.9
	18,956.5	16,707.2
Less allowance for depreciation	5,853.1	5,225.1
	13,103.4	11,482.1
Goodwill and other intangibles (net of accumulated amortization of $2,224.4 million in 2001 and $1,850.7 million in 2000)	7,476.5	7,374.2
Other assets	3,481.7	2,752.9
Total assets	$44,006.7	$40,154.9
LIABILITIES AND STOCKHOLDERS' EQUITY		
Current Liabilities		
Accounts payable and accrued liabilities	$ 5,108.4	$ 4,605.8
Loans payable and current portion of long-term debt	4,066.7	3,319.3
Income taxes payable	1,573.3	1,244.3
Dividends payable	795.8	784.7
Total current liabilities	11,544.2	9,954.1
Long-term debt	4,798.6	3,600.7
Deferred income taxes and noncurrent liabilities	6,776.3	6,746.7
Minority interests	4,837.5	5,021.0
Stockholders' Equity		
Common stock, one cent par value Authorized: 5,400,000,000 shares Issued: 2,976,129,820 shares—2001 2,968,355,365 shares—2000	29.8	29.7
Other paid-in capital	6,907.2	6,265.8
Retained earnings	31,489.6	27,363.9
Accumulated other comprehensive income	10.6	30.8
	38,437.2	33,690.2
Less treasury stock, at cost 703,400,499 shares—2001 660,756,186 shares—2000	22,387.1	18,857.8
Total stockholders' equity	16,050.1	14,832.4
Total liabilities and stockholders' equity	$44,006.7	$40,154.9

FIGURE 3-11b Merck's income statement

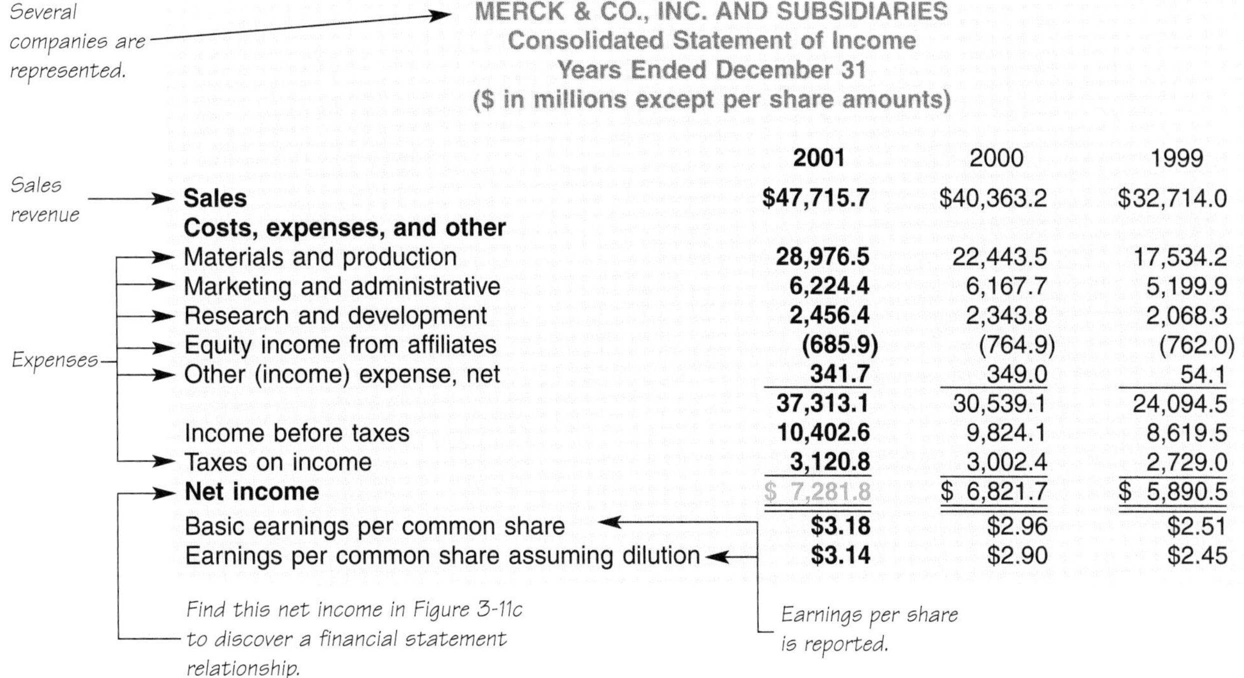
Several companies are represented.
Sales revenue
Expenses
Find this net income in Figure 3-11c to discover a financial statement relationship.
Earnings per share is reported.

MERCK & CO., INC. AND SUBSIDIARIES
Consolidated Statement of Income
Years Ended December 31
($ in millions except per share amounts)

	2001	2000	1999
Sales	**$47,715.7**	$40,363.2	$32,714.0
Costs, expenses, and other			
Materials and production	**28,976.5**	22,443.5	17,534.2
Marketing and administrative	**6,224.4**	6,167.7	5,199.9
Research and development	**2,456.4**	2,343.8	2,068.3
Equity income from affiliates	**(685.9)**	(764.9)	(762.0)
Other (income) expense, net	**341.7**	349.0	54.1
	37,313.1	30,539.1	24,094.5
Income before taxes	**10,402.6**	9,824.1	8,619.5
Taxes on income	**3,120.8**	3,002.4	2,729.0
Net income	$ 7,281.8	$ 6,821.7	$ 5,890.5
Basic earnings per common share	**$3.18**	$2.96	$2.51
Earnings per common share assuming dilution	**$3.14**	$2.90	$2.45

FIGURE 3-11c Merck's statement of retained earnings

Several companies are represented.

MERCK & CO., INC. AND SUBSIDIARIES
Consolidated Statements of Retained Earnings
Years Ended December 31
($ in millions)

	2001	2000	1999
Balance, January 1	$27,363.9	$23,447.9	$20,186.7
Net income	7,281.8	6,821.7	5,890.5
Common stock dividends declared	(3,156.1)	(2,905.7)	(2,629.3)
Balance, December 31	$31,489.6	$27,363.9	$23,447.9

Find this net income in Figure 3-11b to discover a financial statement relationship.

This balance is the result of adding net income to the beginning balance of retained earnings and then subtracting dividends declared.

FIGURE 3-11d Merck's statement of cash flows

MERCK & CO., INC. AND SUBSIDIARIES
Consolidated Statement of Cash Flows
Years Ended December 31
($ in millions)

	2001	2000	1999
Cash flows from operating activities			
Income before taxes	**$ 10,402.6**	$ 9,824.1	$ 8,619.5
Adjustments to reconcile income before taxes to cash provided from operations before taxes:			
Depreciation and amortization	**1,463.8**	1,277.3	1,144.8
Other	**(359.5)**	(222.8)	(496.6)
Net changes in assets and liabilities:			
Accounts receivable	**(9.2)**	(885.8)	(1,021.4)
Inventories	**(557.5)**	(210.1)	(223.0)
Accounts payable and accrued liabilities	**458.3**	(37.7)	673.0
Noncurrent liabilities	**(261.9)**	(94.3)	(150.9)
Other	**246.6**	204.3	69.9
Cash provided by operating activities before taxes	**11,383.2**	9,855.0	8,615.3
Income taxes paid	**(2,303.3)**	(2,167.7)	(2,484.6)
Net cash provided by operating activities	**9,079.9**	7,687.3	6,130.7
Cash flows from investing activities			
Capital expenditures	**(2,724.7)**	(2,727.8)	(2,560.5)
Purchase of securities, subsidiaries and other investments	**(34,780.4)**	(28,637.1)	(42,211.2)
Proceeds from sale of securities, subsidiaries and other investments	**33,383.0**	27,667.5	40,308.7
Proceeds from relinquishment of certain AstraZeneca product rights	**—**	92.6	1,679.9
Other	**(190.2)**	(36.5)	(33.9)
Net cash used by investing activities	**(4,312.3)**	(3,641.3)	(2,817.0)
Cash flows from financing activities			
Net change in short-term borrowings	**259.8**	905.6	2,137.9
Proceeds from issuance of debt	**1,694.4**	442.1	11.6
Payments on debt	**(11.0)**	(443.2)	(17.5)
Proceeds from issuance of preferred units of subsidiary	**—**	1,500.0	—
Purchase of treasury stock	**(3,890.8)**	(3,545.4)	(3,582.1)
Dividends paid to stockholders	**(3,145.0)**	(2,798.0)	(2,589.7)
Proceeds from exercise of stock options	**300.6**	640.7	322.9
Other	**(279.2)**	(149.2)	(152.5)
Net cash used by financing activities	**(5,071.2)**	(3,447.4)	(3,869.4)
Effect of exchange rate changes on cash and cash equivalents	**(89.2)**	(83.7)	(28.6)
Net (decrease) increase in cash and cash equivalents	**(392.8)**	514.9	(584.3)
Cash and cash equivalents at beginning of year	**2,536.8**	2,021.9	2,606.2
Cash and cash equivalents at end of year	**$ 2,144.0**	$ 2,536.8	$ 2,021.9

This statement is composed of three activities.

These ending cash balances are also found at the very top of the balance sheet—evidence of a financial statement relationship.

Quarterly Financial Statements and Interim Reporting

Corporations whose stock is publicly traded on a stock exchange usually issue one or more quarterly financial statements to their stockholders and other interested parties. Merck is no exception, as Figure 3-12 illustrates. Although some companies issue a

FIGURE 3-12 Merck's quarterly income statement

MERCK & CO., INC. AND SUBSIDIARIES
Quarterly Income Statement
Quarter Ended March 31
($ in millions except earnings per common share)

	2002	2001	Percentage Change
Sales	$12,169.3	$11,345.1	7%
Costs, expenses, and other			
Materials and production	7,980.7	7,046.5	13*
Marketing and administrative	1,464.8	1,506.2	−3
Research and development	530.3	547.4	−3
Equity income from affiliates	(171.8)	(178.6)	−4
Other (income) expense, net	43.8	56.1	
Income before taxes	2,321.5	2,367.5	−2
Taxes on income	696.5	710.2	
Net income	1,625.0	1,657.3	−2
Basic earnings per common share	$0.72	$0.72	—
Earnings per common share assuming dilution	$0.71	$0.71	—
Average shares outstanding	2,271.3	2,303.7	
Average shares outstanding assuming dilution	2,294.8	2,345.9	

*The increase in materials and production costs for the three months ended March 31, 2002, is primarily driven by growth in the Merck-Medco business.

full set of quarterly financial statements, the great majority, including Merck, issue a quarterly income statement.

Issuing quarterly financial information is part of a process often referred to as **interim reporting**, the issuing of financial information for periods shorter than the annual accounting period. Interim reporting exists for at least two reasons. First, most corporations are required to issue quarterly financial information by both the stock exchange, which trades their securities, and by the Securities and Exchange Commission, which regulates their securities. **Securities** are financing instruments, which include stocks and bonds. In addition to these formal requests, users of financial information informally request quarterly financial information. That is, for financial information to be useful, business decision makers need to receive it more frequently than once a year. These users have come to rely on the quarterly "financials" for early signs of important changes in a company's performance. Quarterly earnings releases, such as Merck's, therefore, satisfy both formal and informal demands for regular, timely financial reporting.

Sometimes users can misinterpret the information presented in some quarterly financial statements if they do not take revenue seasonality into account. For example, the quarter ending December 31 for retailers such as Sears produces significantly higher revenues than any other quarter, because of Christmas sales. If decision makers viewed the performance of that quarter as representative of the performance in all quarters, they might reach some inaccurate conclusions about how Sears performs over an entire year. Fortunately, the accounting profession has reduced the chance of such potential errors in decision making by treating each interim period as an integral part of the annual period.[6] This means that if 50% of a retailer's annual sales

[6] "Interim Financial Reporting," *Opinions of the Accounting Principles Board No. 28* (New York: AICPA, 1973).

occur in one quarter, 50% of that retailer's annual expenses would be allocated to that period to avoid overstated projections of sales revenue and profit for the annual period.

The reporting philosophy that each interim period is an integral part of the annual period is also evident from the practice of not reporting a particular three-month period in isolation. For example, as you can see in Figure 3-12, Merck compares the three months ending March 31 to the same period one year earlier in its income statement to avoid a misleading focus on seasonal factors.

Corporate Financial Statement Relationships

Corporate financial statement relationships are displayed both algebraically and numerically in the series of fundamental accounting equations found in Figure 3-13. Notice that the second numerical equation is derived from Merck's balance sheet found in Figure 3-11a. Likewise, the third and fourth numerical equations incorporate the statement of retained earnings information (Figure 3-11c) and the income statement information (Figure 3-11b). Study Figure 3-13 carefully. It demonstrates how you are now able to identify the financial statement relationships of any entity whose financial condition and performance are presented in an annual report.

Notice that the financial statement relationships of Merck in Figure 3-13 illustrate the same financial statement relationships displayed in Figure 3-8 for Cards & Memorabilia Unlimited. A major difference, however, is that in a corporation, the owner contributions element is represented by corporate stock accounts such as "Common Stock" and the earnings element is represented by the retained earnings account. Collectively, these accounts comprise Shareholders' Equity. In the case of Merck, another account called Treasury Stock is also included in its owners' equity section. Essentially, this account represents shares of stock that have been reacquired by the corporation and taken out of circulation for the present time. This account is subtracted from the combination of common stock and retained earnings.

FIGURE 3-13 Expansion of Merck's fundamental accounting equation for year 3 (in millions of dollars)

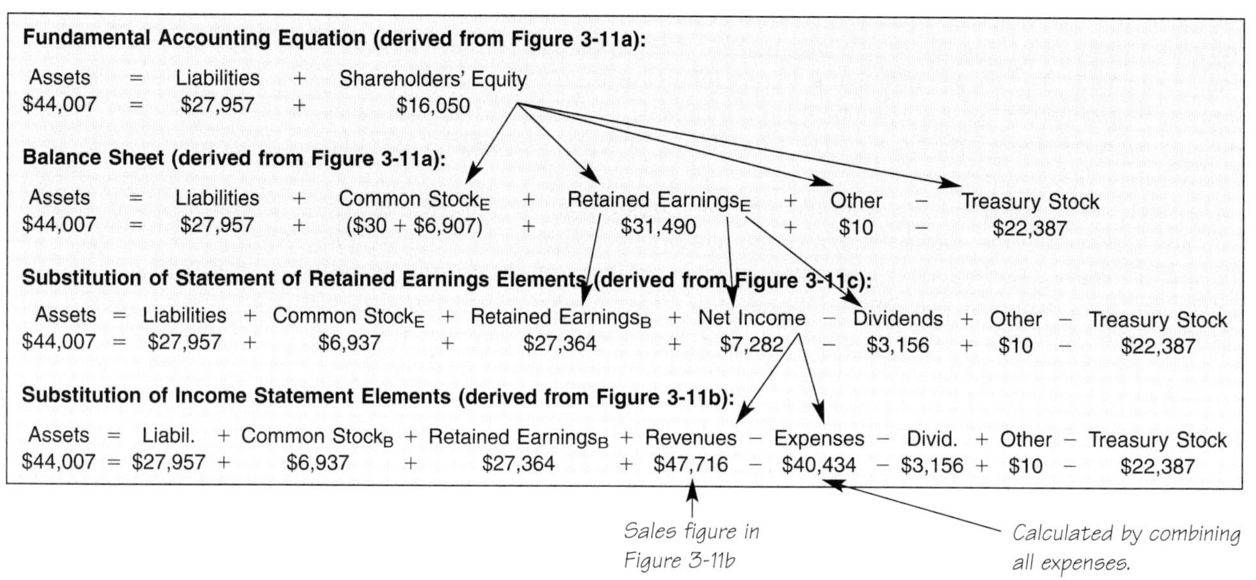

Conclusion

You have accomplished a great deal by reading this chapter. You are now able to recognize some of the essential information found in the financial statements included in most annual reports. That is, you should be able to demonstrate your mastery of Performance Objective 14:

YOUR PERFORMANCE OBJECTIVE 14
Navigate through and **locate** information in an annual report, so that you can make informed decisions about that entity's financing, investing, and operating activities.

Although in future chapters you will add significant depth to this understanding, you already possess the ability to look at the annual reports of prospective employers, for example, and be well informed about the nature and financial health of their businesses. Before you turn to the end-of-chapter material, however, read the following *Insight*. It will further refine your understanding of annual reports and the financial statements contained in them.

Distinguishing between Two Types of Annual Reports

INSIGHT

Companies that are publicly traded (that is, sell stocks or bonds to the public) must issue not only an annual report to shareholders, but also an annual report to the Securities and Exchange Commission (SEC). In this Insight you learn the key differences between the annual report prepared for shareholders, which was introduced earlier in this chapter, and the annual report prepared for the SEC, known as the 10-K report.

The **Securities and Exchange Commission (SEC)** is a federal regulatory agency established in 1934 by Congress to ensure that investors receive full and fair disclosure of financial information. Certain companies are required to register with the SEC and provide financial information including the preparation and filing of an annual report, known as **Form 10-K**, as well as a quarterly report, or **Form 10-Q**. These two reports are the primary SEC vehicles to help investors evaluate their risks and rewards of investment.

To simplify financial reporting, to remove inconsistencies between the two forms of annual reports, and to reduce the mass of paperwork companies must file, the SEC encourages companies to provide essentially the same information in the 10-K report as in the annual report to shareholders. For example, the requirements for the form and content of financial statements are generally the same, as are the management discussion and analysis section and the selected financial data summary. As a result, many companies no longer include a "Financials" section in the 10-K, instead referring interested users to study this information in its annual report to shareholders.

Despite these moves to standardization, some differences remain. This might be attributed to the fact that the audience for the annual shareholders' report is less sophisticated than the audience who views Form 10-K. For example, the austere tone of Nike Corporation's 10-K report pales in comparison to that of its annual shareholder's report that proclaims, "We are innovators. We are athletes. We are risk-takers. We are communicators. We are leaders." Likewise, if you were to examine any company's Form 10-K, you would be struck by how dull it appears in comparison to the high impact, marketing-oriented annual report to shareholders. The 10-K doesn't have color photographs, modern graphics, or high-quality glossy paper stock. Instead, it usually includes a wealth of much more detailed information about the company's past, present, and future prospects.

(continued)

For example, Wal-Mart's 58-page, 2001 10-K report includes sections on company history, current development of business, and detailed descriptions of the merchandise, operations, competition, and distribution of its three operating segments—Wal-Mart Stores, Sam's Club, and International. Also included are properties, detailed descriptions of its legal proceedings, and thumbnail sketches of the executive officers. It even informs readers that the seasonal nature of its industry causes it to experience its highest volume of sales in its fourth quarter (November to January).

The **insight** you should gain here is both types of annual reports are valuable to decision makers for different reasons. When you look for a job, for example, use the annual report to shareholders to decide with which companies you interview. When you are ready to prepare specific questions for the interview, however, you will have an advantage over other candidates if you carefully study the 10-K report, because it contains more detailed information about the company not readily found elsewhere.

Now you have seen that users of financial statements often rely on more than just a corporate annual report to make business decisions. For example, companies' quarterly reports and SEC 10-K reports can also provide valuable information to supplement the corporate annual report. Thus, your mastery of Performance Objective 15 will enable you to use all resources available to you to become a better business decision maker.

YOUR PERFORMANCE OBJECTIVE 15

Describe how information sources other than the corporate annual report (e.g., quarterly reports and SEC Form 10-K) can be used to learn more about the nature of an entity's business.

Summary with Key Terms

The number in parentheses following each **key term** is the page number on which the term is defined.

In this chapter, you learned about the role the **annual report** (87) plays in communicating useful information about publicly traded companies. The financial information within an annual report is usually found in these sections: **Management's Discussion and Analysis (MD&A)** (87), the **Financial Statements** (87), the **Notes to the Financial Statements** (87), the **Report of Management (Management's Financial Responsibility)** (88), and the **Independent Auditors' Report** (88). The objective of the **auditing** (88) profession is to assure users that such information is fairly presented. Although an annual report is often used to communicate information about a corporation, it seldom communicates information about a sole proprietorship.

Although noncorporate entities rarely issue an annual report, almost every **entity** (90) is required to prepare financial statements guided by the principle of **full disclosure** (97). The first financial statement described is known as the statement of financial condition/position or balance sheet. A balance sheet is prepared at a point in time and includes three elements: **assets** (92), **liabilities** (93), and **owner's equity** (94). Some assets are related to liabilities. For example, a seller's **accounts receivable** (93) represents an **account payable** (93) to the customer. When a liability is created, **leverage** (94) describes the company's relative indebtedness. Owner's equity, or net worth as it is called in a personal balance sheet, is composed of the **owner's contribution** (94) and **retained earnings** (94) from profitable operations. Another synonym for owner's equity is net assets.

The **income statement** (95) reports the results of operations for a period of time and is composed of two elements: **revenue** (96) and **expense** (98). **Net income** (96), the difference between these two elements, is a measure of one's return on investment. Although most income statements report past revenues and expenses, you can also prepare a future-oriented income statement or **projected income statement** (96) sometimes called an operating budget. The linkage that exists between the balance sheet and the income statement is one example of how financial statements are related.

A **statement of owners' equity** (99) or **statement of shareholders' equity** (99) for a corporation reports both the change in the owners' investment and the change in owners' retained earnings from profitable operations. **Contributed Capital** (100) is an owners' equity account that reports the asset contributions of owners. **Retained Earnings** (100) is an owners' equity account that reports earnings from profitable operations retained in the business. Changes in contributed capital can be accounted for in a **statement of contributed capital** (102). Changes in retained earnings can be accounted for in a **statement of retained earnings** (102). Both the account and the statement are increased by net income and decreased by owner withdrawals and any net loss. Owner withdrawals in a corporation are accumulated in a **dividends declared** (102) account.

The last financial statement introduced is the **statement of cash flows** (105), which describes the cash effects of operating activities, investing activities, and financing activities.

Interim reporting (113) serves the needs of decision makers who cannot afford to wait for the financial information available from the annual report. Interim or quarterly reports are issued by corporations whose **securities** (113) are traded by stock exchanges and regulated by the **Securities and Exchange Commission (SEC)** (115). The *Insight* section of this chapter described the distinctions between the shareholders' annual report and the annual report to the SEC on **Form 10-K** (115). Although the 10-K Report provides some of the same information as the shareholders' annual report, decision makers should be aware of the unique information it provides. **Form 10-Q** (115) is the quarterly report that is submitted to the SEC.

Making Business Decisions

YOUR PERFORMANCE OBJECTIVE 2
(page 18)

Jay Azuma, one of your close college friends, has started a new business, VideoValor—a video game company dedicated to nonviolent but very stimulating and challenging games. He has three products on the market, and his revenues are approaching two hundred thousand dollars after only one year in business. He also has one store from which he sells his products.

Last week, Jay called to ask if you might be interested in investing in his company. You do have $5,000 you could invest, so you tell him you need more information. Jay sends you some materials about VideoValor, including a set of financial statements.

In groups or on your own, as your instructor directs you, write a one-page document explaining in detail why (solely on the basis of the financial statements) you would or would not invest in VideoValor.

To help you make this decision, first answer the ten questions on pages 118–119 about the financial statements of VideoValor. For each response, describe in which financial statement you found the information and where.

VIDEOVALOR COMPANY
Income Statement
For the Year Ended January 31

Revenues:		
Sales revenue		$171,700
Expenses:		
Cost of goods sold	$59,620	
Rent expense	30,200	
Salaries expense	26,580	
Depreciation expense	12,400	
Delivery expense	7,450	
Miscellaneous expense	6,470	
Store supplies expense	2,220	
Interest expense	2,180	147,120
Net Income		$ 24,580

VIDEOVALOR COMPANY
Statement of Owner's Equity
For the Year Ended January 31

	Contributed Capital	Retained Earnings	Owner's Equity
Balance at February 1	$ 0	$ 0	$ 0
Add: Owner contributions	55,000		55,000
Net income		24,580	24,580
Deduct: Owner withdrawals		(18,000)	(18,000)
Balance at January 31	$55,000	$ 6,580	$61,580

VIDEOVALOR COMPANY
Balance Sheet
January 31

Assets		Liabilities and Owner's Equity	
Current Assets		**Current Liabilities**	
Cash	$ 7,620	Accounts payable	$ 23,740
Accounts receivable	18,170	Salaries payable	4,130
Inventory	41,600		
Store supplies	2,160	Total current liability	27,870
Prepaid rent	5,400		
		Noncurrent Liabilities	
Total current assets	74,950	Notes payable	$ 43,400
Property, Plant, and Equipment		Total liabilities	71,270
Store equipment	21,900		
Less: Accumulated depreciation	(3,600)	**Owner's Equity**	
	18,300	Contributed capital	55,000
		Retained earnings	6,580
Delivery equipment	48,400		
Less: Accumulated depreciation	(8,800)	Total owner's equity	61,580
	39,600		
Total property, plant, & equipment	57,900		
Total assets	$132,850	Total liabilities and owner's equity	$132,850

1. Is VideoValor Company a sole proprietorship, partnership, or corporation?
2. Does the company appear to be a service firm, a retailer, or a manufacturer?
3. Did the company have a net income or net loss for its first year of operations?
4. What is the company's largest current asset? Does this seem appropriate for this type of business?
5. Did the owner(s) contribute or withdraw money from the company this year?
6. Did the company buy any noncurrent assets this year? If yes, how did it pay for them?
7. What is the company's largest expense for the year? Does this seem appropriate for this type of business?
8. Does the company own or rent the space it occupies?

VIDEOVALOR COMPANY
Statement of Cash Flows
For the Year Ended January 31

Cash flows from operating activities:		
Cash collected from customers	$153,530	
Cash paid for merchandise	(77,480)	
Cash paid for leased space	(35,600)	
Cash paid for salaries	(22,450)	
Cash paid for delivery expense	(7,450)	
Cash paid for miscellaneous expense	(6,470)	
Cash paid for store supplies	(4,380)	
Cash paid for interest	(2,180)	
Net cash used by operating activities		$ (2,480)
Cash flows from investing activities:		
Cash paid for store equipment	$ (21,900)	
Net cash used for investing activities		$(21,900)
Cash flows from financing activities:		
Contributions by owner	$ 55,000	
Repayment of note payable	(5,000)	
Withdrawals by owner	(18,000)	
Net cash provided by financing activities		32,000
Net increase in cash		$ 7,620
Cash balance at beginning of year		0
Cash balance at end of year		$ 7,620
Supplemental schedule of noncash investing and financing activities:		
Delivery equipment acquired by issuance of note payable		$ 48,400

9. Does the company have any long-term debt? If yes, did it pay any of this debt off during the year? Did it pay any interest on this debt?
10. Who provided the largest source of assets for this company—investors or creditors?

Finally, write your one-page document explaining in detail why (solely on the basis of the financial statements) you would or would not invest in VideoValor.

Questions

YOUR PERFORMANCE OBJECTIVE 4
(page 22)

3-1 Explain in your own words the meaning of key business terms.

a. Annual report
b. Liabilities
c. Leverage
d. Owner's equity
e. Net worth
f. Owner's contribution
g. Retained earnings
h. Income statement
i. Financial statement relationships
j. Statement of contributed capital
k. Statement of retained earnings
l. Dividends declared
m. Statement of cash flows
n. Interim reporting
o. Securities
p. Securities and Exchange Commission

3-2 What is contained in the section of an annual report known as the "financials"?

3-3 In an annual report, how does the Management's Discussion and Analysis (MD&A) section differ from the Notes to the Financial Statements section?

3-4 In an annual report, how does The Report of Management differ from The Independent Auditors' Report?
3-5 What benefits does an annual report provide to the company that issues it?
3-6 Describe the different types of benefits an asset can provide.
3-7 Distinguish between an account receivable and an account payable.
3-8 List several measurable assets you possess as an individual.
3-9 List several liabilities you now owe or have owed as an individual.
3-10 Explain how an income statement can provide information about an investor's return on equity.
3-11 Distinguish between a revenue and an expense.
3-12 Distinguish between revenue and net income.
3-13 Explain why revenues are not equivalent to assets.
3-14 Explain why borrowing money does not create revenue.
3-15 Distinguish between net income and net loss.
3-16 Distinguish between an income statement and a projected income statement.
3-17 Distinguish between the owners' contribution and the earnings retained in the business from profitable operations.
3-18 What is the primary role of the retained earnings account?
3-19 Explain how the statement of cash flows can be linked to both the balance sheet and the income statement.
3-20 Discuss under what circumstances quarterly financial statements might be used in place of annual financial statements.
3-21 What are the key differences between the expanded fundamental equation of a noncorporate entity (line 4 of Figure 3-8) and that of a corporation (line 4 of Figure 3-13)?
3-22 Compare and contrast the annual report to shareholders and the annual report to the SEC on Form 10-K.
3-23 List the financial statements that every business must prepare.
3-24 Discuss why the distinction between a point in time and a period of time is important when preparing financial statements.
3-25 Using transaction information found in the inside back cover of your textbook, explain how the contributed capital account increased from a reported $30,000 as of January 6 in Figure 3-3 to a reported $40,000 as of December 31 in Figure 3-2.

Reinforcement Exercises

YOUR PERFORMANCE OBJECTIVE 4
(page 22)

E3-1 Asking the Right Questions: A Group Activity
It's often said that knowing the right answer is not nearly as important as asking the right question. Asking the right question is a problem-solving skill that will help you make sound business decisions. In this exercise, you will review the vocabulary introduced in Chapter 3 by creating questions to match answers—similar to a popular TV show.

Required

a. Given an answer, what's the question?
Choose *three* of the following terms to serve as an answer. Create an appropriate question for each term. For example, if you choose the term *balance sheet*, you might create the question—*What financial statement shows the assets, liabilities, and owners' equity of an entity on a specific date?*

Full disclosure	Account payable	Revenue
Statement of cash flows	Retained earnings	Auditing
Account receivable	Contributed capital	Annual report
Dividends declared	Expense	Owners' equity

b. Are you sure that's the question?
Have each group member of your group read aloud the questions they developed in Requirement (a). As a group, decide whether each question is an accurate match for each answer. Once satisfied that all questions are appropriate, the group, as a whole, chooses the three best questions created within the group. Record the three questions chosen (with their answers) on separate pieces of paper or index cards and give them to your instructor.

c. What's the answer?
To ensure that you have learned the vocabulary terms listed in Requirement (a), your instructor will now quiz you on the questions written by all of your classmates.

E3-2 Transaction Analysis
Use transaction analysis to determine the effect of each of the following transactions on the fundamental accounting equation:

YOUR PERFORMANCE OBJECTIVE 5a
(page 57)

	Assets	=	Liabilities + Owner's Equity
Example:			
Acquired supplies for $20,000 on account.	20,000		20,000
a. Owner contributed $30,000 to business.	______		______
b. Purchased equipment for $12,000 cash.	______		______
c. Owner withdrew $10,000 from business.	______		______
d. Recorded $20,000 in credit sales to customers.	______		______
e. Acquired $13,000 of inventory on account.	______		______
f. Paid $8,000 owed to suppliers.	______		______
g. Received $12,000 owed from customers.	______		______

E3-3 Transaction Analysis
Indicate whether the following transactions of the Mozart Company, a piano retailer, would increase, decrease, or have no effect on the company's total assets, liabilities, and owner's equity. Use "+" for increase, " − " for decrease, and "NE" for no effect if none of the accounts is affected by the transaction. Use the form shown below, which shows a correct analysis of Transaction (b).

YOUR PERFORMANCE OBJECTIVE 5a
(page 57)

Transaction	Assets	=	Liabilities	+	Owner's Equity
b.	+100,000 −20,000		 +80,000		

Transactions

a. Amadeus Wolfgang Mozart, the sole proprietor, begins business by contributing $120,000 cash.
b. A building is purchased for $100,000, $20,000 of which is paid in cash. A note payable is signed for the balance.
c. Piano inventory is purchased for $30,000 on credit from European Upright Piano Supply.
d. Payment of $10,000 is made to European Upright Piano Supply for an amount owed.
e. A $50,000 line of credit is obtained from a local bank. No amount has yet been borrowed.
f. Amadeus, the sole owner, wants to make an additional investment in the company in the future and arranges a $15,000 personal bank loan.
g. The line of credit is used to borrow $12,000.
h. Amadeus takes a baby grand piano home for his personal use. The piano costs $5,000.
i. Amadeus invests the $15,000 from Transaction (f) in the company.
j. Ludwig van Beethoven becomes a partner by investing $10,000.

E3-4 Preparing a Balance Sheet
From the transactions listed in Exercise 3-2, prepare a balance sheet using the format shown in Figure 3-3 of this textbook.

YOUR PERFORMANCE OBJECTIVE 5b
(page 57)

E3-5 Preparing a Balance Sheet
From the transactions listed in Exercise 3-3, prepare a balance sheet using the format shown in Figure 3-3 of this textbook.

YOUR PERFORMANCE OBJECTIVE 5b
(page 57)

E3-6 Preparing an Income Statement
Sidney Hemingway, an attorney, worked three years for a prestigious Los Angeles law firm after graduating from law school. On January 1, she begins business as a sole proprietor in her

YOUR PERFORMANCE OBJECTIVE 10 *(page 95)*

hometown. During her first year of practice, she receives legal fees of $137,000 for her services and incurs the following expenses:

Secretarial salaries	$40,000
Office rent	12,000
Heat and electricity	6,000
Telephone	1,500
Duplicating services	1,000
Office supplies	760
Professional dues	440
Investigative services	1,700
Travel and entertainment	3,600
Total expenses	$67,000

Required

a. Prepare an income statement for Sidney's law firm for the year ended December 31.
b. Compare this income statement to Merck's in Figure 3-11b. Explain why no earnings per share is presented on Sidney's income statement.

YOUR PERFORMANCE OBJECTIVE 10 *(page 95)*

E3-7 Preparing an Income Statement

The following information is from the Royko Company, an automobile repair business:

Cost of repair parts used	$ 67,800
Accounts receivable from customers	11,400
Wages earned by employees	82,600
Charges to customers for repair work	303,000
Cost of repair parts inventory	85,200
Rental cost of garage	31,200
Cost of telephone and electric service used	2,800
Accounts payable to parts suppliers	16,200

Required

Prepare an income statement for this year using the relevant data.

YOUR PERFORMANCE OBJECTIVE 11a *(page 99)*

E3-8 Differentiating between the Balance Sheet and the Income Statement

Identify which of the following transactions affect revenues or expenses, rather than only changes in asset and liability accounts.

a. Office supplies are purchased for cash.
b. Office supplies are purchased on account.
c. Office supplies previously purchased are used.
d. Office supplies previously purchased on account are paid.
e. A previously unrecorded electric bill is received and paid.
f. Services are provided to a customer in return for cash.
g. Services are provided to a customer who is then billed.
h. Collection from the customer previously billed is received.
i. Cash is borrowed from the bank.
j. Accumulated interest on the loan is accounted for and paid.
k. The bank loan is repaid.

YOUR PERFORMANCE OBJECTIVE 11b *(page 99)*

E3-9 Classifying Account Titles

Classify the following items as assets, liabilities, owners' equity, or as a non-balance-sheet account. If you think the item does not belong in the balance sheet, state your reason.

a. Cash in business account
b. Capital account
c. Office equipment
d. Accounts payable
e. Merchandise inventory
f. Cash in personal account
g. Security deposit receivable
h. Credit line payable
i. Advances from customers
j. Prepaid insurance
k. Value of college education
l. A trademark
m. Petty cash
n. Notes payable—current
o. Salaries expense
p. A firm's excellent customers

E3-10 Classifying Account Titles

YOUR PERFORMANCE OBJECTIVE 11b (page 99)

Classify the following items as assets, liabilities, owner's equity, or as a non-balance-sheet account. If you think the item does not belong in the balance sheet, state your reason.

a. Cash in bank
b. Owner withdrawals
c. Machinery
d. Cost of goods sold
e. Cash on hand
f. Cash of owner's spouse
g. Unfilled customer orders
h. Notes receivable
i. Unfilled purchase orders
j. Prepaid rent
k. Advances to employees
l. Good credit standing
m. A patent
n. Supplies inventory
o. Notes payable—noncurrent
p. Salaries payable
q. Potential liability under lawsuit (case has not yet gone to trial)

E3-11 Determining the Effect of Transactions on the Statement of Cash Flows

YOUR PERFORMANCE OBJECTIVE 7 (page 64)

Explain whether each transaction listed in Exercise 3-8 affects the current year's statement of cash flows. Be specific as to why the transaction would or would not be included in the statement.

E3-12 Preparing a Statement of Owner's Equity

YOUR PERFORMANCE OBJECTIVE 12 (page 102)

At the beginning of the current year, the owner's equity section of the Thompson Company balance sheet contained a contributed capital account and a retained earnings account with balances of $85,000 and $52,000, respectively. During the year, the following events occurred:

a. The company's net income amounted to $18,400.
b. Withdrawals of cash by Jim Thompson, the sole proprietor, amounted to $2,800.
c. Jim Thompson invested an additional $12,000 cash in his company.

Required

Prepare the statement of owner's equity for Thompson Company at the end of the year.

E3-13 Calculating Missing Owner's Equity Amounts

YOUR PERFORMANCE OBJECTIVE 12 (page 102)

Given the following data about a company over a period of three years, calculate the missing amounts:

	Year 1	Year 2	Year 3
Owner's equity, 1/1	$ 2,000	$?	$19,000
Owner investments for the year	10,000	6,000	0
Revenues for the year	16,000	?	?
Expenses for the year	?	10,000	16,000
Net income for the year	12,000	?	8,000
Owner withdrawals for the year	?	4,000	6,000
Owner's equity, 12/31	10,000	?	?

E3-14 Calculating Missing Owner's Equity Amounts

YOUR PERFORMANCE OBJECTIVE 12 (page 102)

Calculate the missing amounts for each of the *unrelated* cases below. Provide numerical support for each answer.

	Case 1	Case 2		Case 3	Case 4
Beginning capital, 1/1	$66,000	$?	RE, 1/1	$?	$40,000
Ending capital, 12/31	66,000	64,000	RE, 12/31	90,000	50,000
Owner contribution	?	17,000	Net income	36,000	?
Net income	(12,000)	40,000	Dividends	11,000	2,000
Withdrawals	8,000	15,000			

Note: A number in parentheses opposite net income indicates a net loss. The abbreviation RE stands for Retained Earnings.

YOUR PERFORMANCE OBJECTIVE 12 (page 102)

E3-15 Calculating Missing Retained Earnings Amounts
Calculate the missing amounts affecting retained earnings for the current year in each of the following *unrelated* cases:

	A	B	C	D	E
Beginning retained earnings	$30,000	$?	$64,000	$15,000	$8,000
Net income	10,000	25,000	36,000	?	(6,000)
Dividends declared	4,000	15,000	?	6,000	?
Ending retained earnings	?	100,000	94,000	18,000	2,000

YOUR PERFORMANCE OBJECTIVE 12 (page 102)

E3-16 Calculating Missing Retained Earnings Amounts
Calculate the missing amounts affecting retained earnings for each of the three consecutive years below.

	Year 1	Year 2	Year 3
Retained earnings, beginning balance	$4,750	$5,000	$?
Net income	?	?	1,200
Dividends declared	750	600	?
Retained earnings, ending balance	$?	$4,800	$4,900

YOUR PERFORMANCE OBJECTIVE 13 (page 105)

E3-17 Financial Statement Relationships
Given the following financial data about four companies (1, 2, 3, and 4), calculate the missing amounts identified by letters:

	Companies			
	1	2	3	4
Assets, 1/1	$120	$ 200	$160	J
Liabilities, 1/1	50	D	40	$ 200
Owners' equity, 1/1	A	140	H	800
Assets, 12/31	140	E	G	1,200
Liabilities, 12/31	52	58	32	K
Owners' equity, 12/31	B	148	I	840
Revenues	700	1,000	800	L
Expenses	674	F	760	3,000
Owner withdrawals for the year	C	10	16	30

YOUR PERFORMANCE OBJECTIVE 13 (page 105)

E3-18 Financial Statement Relationships
Calculate the missing amounts affecting the financial statement elements in each of the *unrelated* cases below.

	Year-End Amounts						
	Total Assets	Total Liabilities	Capital Stock	Retained Earnings 1/1	Net Income (Loss)	Dividends Declared	Retained Earnings 12/31
a.	$160	?	$30	$44	$30	$14	$?
b.	?	$130	40	?	40	10	60
c.	240	140	?	60	?	8	40

E3-19 Financial Statement Relationships

The following data pertain to the Stokes Company for the current year:

YOUR PERFORMANCE OBJECTIVE 13 (page 105)

	January 1	December 31
Total assets	$10,000	$12,400
Total liabilities	4,000	5,500

During the year, sales were $30,400, owner withdrawals were $400, and operating expenses (exclusive of cost of goods sold) were $15,000. There were no additional owner investments during the year.

Required

Calculate net income, cost of goods sold, and owners' equity on January 1.

E3-20 Financial Statement Relationships

The following data pertain to the Rossi Company for the current year:

YOUR PERFORMANCE OBJECTIVE 13 (page 105)

	January 1	December 31
Total assets	$15,000	$20,000
Total liabilities	8,500	10,000

During the year, sales were $50,000 and cost of goods sold was $42,000. In addition, $1,000 of owner investments and $200 of owner withdrawals were made during the year.

Required

Calculate net income and the total of all other expenses excluding cost of goods sold for the current year.

Critical Thinking Problems

P3-1 Applying the Definitions of Asset, Liability, and Full Disclosure to Financial Reporting

YOUR PERFORMANCE OBJECTIVE 4 (page 22)

In this chapter, you read about the concept of *full disclosure* as it applied to reporting significant noncash transactions in the statement of cash flows. This concept has also influenced reporting requirements for another type of transaction, capital leases. Historically, companies leasing assets would simply report the cost of the lease payments each year as rent expense on the income statement. Over the past twenty-five years, the accounting profession has wrestled with how to properly account for the financial statement effects of leases. Currently, companies must report leases meeting certain criteria as both an asset and a liability. For example, if a company leases equipment and has the option to purchase the property at a price significantly below market value (a bargain purchase option) at the end of five years, the equipment must be recorded and classified as a property, plant, and equipment asset on the balance sheet. The company must also record a lease liability on its balance sheet. Although the company doesn't own the asset at the start of the lease, the asset is recorded and depreciated over its useful life.

a. Refer to the definitions provided for assets and liabilities in this chapter, and explain why you believe this method of reporting a leased asset and liability is appropriate.
b. Using the concept of *full disclosure,* explain why this method of reporting a leased asset and a liability is preferable to the older method of simply recording lease payments as an expense.

P3-2 Transaction Analysis

YOUR PERFORMANCE OBJECTIVE 5a (page 57)

Seinfeld Company, a sole proprietorship, began business in January. Show the effect of each of the following transactions on the company's assets, liabilities, and owner's equity using a table similar to the following. The complete analysis of Transaction (a) is included as an example of a correct solution.

	Assets						=	Liabilities			+	Owner's Equity
	Cash	Merchandise Inventory	Prepaid Insurance	Land	Building	Equipment		Accounts Payable	Advances from Customers	Mortgage Payable		H. Seinfeld, Capital
a.	+80,000	+20,000										$100,000
b.												
c.												
d.												
e.												
f.												
g.												
h.												
i.												
j.												

Transactions

a. Harry Seinfeld invests $80,000 of cash and $20,000 worth of inventory to start the business.
b. Land and building costing $45,000 are acquired by paying $12,500 cash and assuming a 20-year, 8% mortgage for the balance. The land is reported at $15,000 and the building at $30,000 on the balance sheet.
c. Merchandise inventory costing $36,000 is acquired on account from various suppliers.
d. A $7,200 check is issued for 36 months of insurance coverage.
e. Equipment costing $16,000 is acquired for cash.
f. A payment of $200 is made to National Express Service for delivering the equipment.
g. Cash of $10,000 is received from customers for merchandise to be delivered in one month.
h. Inventory costing $1,000 that was purchased in (c) is returned as defective to the supplier.
i. Invoices totaling $24,000 from the purchases in (c) are paid after deducting a 2% discount for prompt payment. Seinfeld treats cash discounts as a reduction in inventory cost.
j. The remaining invoices from the purchases in (c) are paid after the discount period has ended.

YOUR PERFORMANCE OBJECTIVE 5b
(page 57)

P3-3 Calculating Missing Balance Sheet Amounts

Calculate the missing balance sheet amounts in each of the four *unrelated* cases below.

	Case A	Case B	Case C	Case D
Current assets	$120	$?	$?*	$?†
Noncurrent assets	80	100	68	?
Total assets	?	?	100	?
Current liabilities	100	30	?*	?†
Noncurrent liabilities	20	?	?	32
Owner's equity	?	50	58	28
Total liabilities & owner's equity	?	140	?	110

*Current Assets − Current Liabilities = $14
†Current Assets − Current Liabilities = $16

YOUR PERFORMANCE OBJECTIVE 5b
(page 57)

P3-4 Preparing Your Personal Balance Sheet

Refer to Exercise 1-2, which asks you to prepare a personal balance sheet. Once you have completed this personal balance sheet, answer the following questions:

a. How did you measure your noncash personal assets? That is, did you use the cost paid to acquire the asset, its current replacement cost, its current market value (i.e., selling price), or some other measurement? Explain how you decided to use the measurement you chose.
b. Should an individual divide his/her assets and liabilities into current and noncurrent categories as do businesses? Why or why not?
c. What is meant by the term "revolving credit" under liabilities?

d. How does the presentation of owner's equity found in your balance sheet differ from that found in the balance sheets of businesses?

P3-5 Preparing a Balance Sheet

Select a type of business with which you are familiar, such as a video rental store or a bookstore. Make a list of both the asset and liability account titles you believe would be found on the balance sheet of this type of business.

YOUR PERFORMANCE OBJECTIVE 5b
(page 57)

P3-6 Improving a Balance Sheet Presentation

The following presentation was actually used to represent the balance sheet for a local chapter of the Rotary International Service Club:

YOUR PERFORMANCE OBJECTIVE 5b
(page 57)

Balance Sheet
As of 5/31

Assets	
Checking	$ 3,043
Savings	10,207
Total cash	$13,250
Due to Rotary Foundation	$ 199
Equity	
Accounts receivable	$ 3,718
Due to Littleton Resort	2,800
Due to Best Eastern	1,000
Total accounts payable	$ 3,800
Net available	$12,969

Required

a. Using your understanding of correct balance sheet format and proper account title classification, revise this statement.

b. Does the fact that this service club is operated as a not-for-profit organization help to explain the format used above? Explain why or why not.

P3-7 Determining How a Transaction Affects the Balance Sheet

Refer to Transactions (a) through (j) in Problem 3-2 to complete this problem. For each transaction, list the balance sheet classification affected. Choose from the following balance sheet classifications: current assets; property, plant, and equipment; current liabilities; noncurrent liabilities; owner's equity; and no effect. Remember, most balance sheet transactions will affect at least two classifications. The first transaction is completed for you as an example.

YOUR PERFORMANCE OBJECTIVE 5
(page 57)

Transaction	Balance Sheet Classification
a.	Current assets and owner's equity
b.	
c.	
and so on . . .	

P3-8 Balance Sheet Analysis

Using the balance sheet for VideoValor in this chapter's *Making Business Decisions* case, answer these questions:

a. How was the year-end retained earnings balance calculated?

YOUR PERFORMANCE OBJECTIVE 5b
(page 57)

b. Although the company purchased store equipment for $21,900 during the year, the balance sheet reports the amount of this asset account to be $18,300 at the end of the year. Why did the equipment go down in amount and how did the company report this decrease?

YOUR PERFORMANCE OBJECTIVE 7 *(page 64)*

P3-9 Determining How a Transaction Affects the Statement of Cash Flows
Refer to Transactions (a) through (j) in Problem 3-2 to complete this problem. For each transaction, list the statement of cash flow activity affected. Choose from the following categories: operating, investing, financing, noncash activity, and no effect. The first transaction is completed for you below.

Transaction	Statement of Cash Flow Categories
a.	Financing and noncash activity
b.	
c.	
and so on . . .	

YOUR PERFORMANCE OBJECTIVE 7 *(page 64)*

P3-10 Statement of Cash Flow Analysis
Using the financial statements for VideoValor in this chapter's *Making Business Decisions* case, answer these questions about the statement of cash flows.

a. What were the company's two largest sources or inflows of cash for the year?
b. What were the company's four largest uses or outflows of cash for the year? Does this seem appropriate for this type of business?
c. Did the company have a net cash inflow or outflow from operating its business this year? Does this seem appropriate for this type of business?

YOUR PERFORMANCE OBJECTIVE 10 *(page 95)*

P3-11 Evaluating an Accounting-Related Newspaper Article and Preparing an Income Statement
Read the following news report excerpt that appeared several years ago:

Apple Sales Rise; Profits Drop 75%

Apple Computer Inc. reported that profits dropped 75 percent in the quarter ended December 31 as sales grew 23 percent—reflecting the company's decision to gain market share by lowering prices, even at the expense of a weakened bottom line.

For the first quarter of this year, Apple's sales advanced to 2.5 billion from 2 billion in the same period a year earlier. But net income fell to $40 million, or 34 cents a share, from $161.3 million, or $1.33 a share.

Required

a. Discuss how a business like Apple can experience a drop in profits when its revenues increase.
b. Prepare a condensed income statement (revenue, expense, and net income) for the first quarter of both this year and last year.
c. Approximately how many shares of common stock do Apple Corporation shareholders own?

YOUR PERFORMANCE OBJECTIVE 10 *(page 95)*

P3-12 Preparing an Income Statement
Select a type of business with which you are familiar, such as a video rental store or a movie theater. List the revenues and the expenses you would expect to find in its income statement.

YOUR PERFORMANCE OBJECTIVE 11 *(page 99)*

P3-13 Classifying Account Titles
The fundamental accounting equation in the March 31 balance sheet of Aurora Supply Company does not balance. The account balances provided are correct, but the account classifications contain many errors. Identify and list all the errors and determine the correct accounting equation in dollars for the March 31 balance sheet.

AURORA SUPPLY COMPANY
Balance Sheet
March 31

Assets		Liabilities and Owner's Equity	
Current Assets		**Current Liabilities**	
Cash	$ 4,500	Accounts receivable	$ 12,400
Accounts payable	8,900	Salaries payable	2,700
Equipment	32,000	Accumulated depreciation,	
Advances from customers	3,100	equipment	9,000
Total current assets	48,500	Total current liabilities	24,100
Property, Plant, and Equipment		**Noncurrent Liabilities**	
Land	45,000	Note payable (due in	
Inventory	21,300	six months)	18,400
Building	160,000	Note payable (due in	
Accumulated depreciation,		five years)	72,500
building	(44,000)	Contributed capital	65,000
Total property, plant,		Total noncurrent liabilities	155,900
and equipment	182,300	Total liabilities	180,000
		Owner's Equity	
		Retained earnings	51,600
Total assets	$230,800	Total liabilities and	
		owner's equity	$231,600

P3-14 Financial Statement Relationships

YOUR PERFORMANCE OBJECTIVE 13 *(page 105)*

Given the following financial data for Santa Cruz Co., calculate the missing amounts:

	December 31
Revenue	$ 7,800
Expenses	4,600
Dividends declared and paid	1,600
Net income	?
Assets—beginning of period	16,000
Assets—end of period	20,000
Liabilities—beginning of period	5,200
Liabilities—end of period	5,600
Capital stock—beginning of period	6,000
Capital stock—end of period	?
Retained earnings—beginning of period	?
Retained earnings—end of period	?

P3-15 Financial Statement Relationships

YOUR PERFORMANCE OBJECTIVE 13 *(page 105)*

The following financial statement information represents three calendar-year businesses (I, II, and III).

	I	II	III
Assets, 1/1	$ 60	$100	$ 80
Liabilities, 1/1	25	D	20
Assets, 12/31	70	E	G
Liabilities, 12/31	26	29	16
Owners' equity, 1/1	A	70	H
Owners' equity, 12/31	B	74	I
Revenues, year	350	500	400
Expenses, year	337	F	380
Dividends declared, year	C	5	8

Required

Using your understanding of financial statement relationships, calculate the missing amounts that are labeled with the letters A through I. Reproduce the following table and insert your answers along with *complete* numerical support.

	Answer	Numerical Support
A	________	________________________
B	________	________________________
and so on . . .		

YOUR PERFORMANCE OBJECTIVE 13 (page 105)

P3-16 Financial Statement Relationships

Link the following related financial statements—balance sheets, income statement, and statement of owner's equity—by being able to calculate the missing amounts in each of them.

Balance Sheets

	1/01	12/31
Assets	$600	$750
Liabilities	250	?
Owner's equity	?	560

Income Statement

For Year Ending 12/31	
Revenues	$880
Expenses	?
Net income	$?

Statement of Owner's Equity
For Year Ending 12/31

Balance at January 1		$?
Add: Owner contribution	$ 85	
Net income	?	?
Subtotal		$?
Deduct: Withdrawals		75
Balance at December 31		$?

YOUR PERFORMANCE OBJECTIVE 13 (page 105)

P3-17 Financial Statement Relationships

The Cochran Corporation has misplaced certain records during the current year. It is your job to assist Cochran's bookkeeper in determining the missing amounts in the financial statements below.

Balance Sheet
Beginning of Current Year

Cash	$ 30	Current liabilities	$ 20
Inventory	?		
Equipment	?	Common stock	?
Less: Accumulated depreciation	(5)	Retained earnings	45
Total assets	$115	Total liabilities & owners' equity	$?

Income Statement
For Current Year Ending 12/31

Sales revenue (all cash)		$?
Less expenses:		
Cost of goods sold	$30	
Depreciation expense	?	
Salary expense	12	?
Net income		$?

Balance Sheet
End of Current Year

Cash	$60	Current liabilities	$?
Inventory	20		
Equipment	?	Common stock	50
Less: Accumulated depreciation	(?)	Retained earnings	60
Total assets	$?	Total liabilities & owners' equity	$?

Additional Information

a. Ten dollars of inventory purchases were made during the current year.
b. Equipment was neither purchased nor sold during the current year.
c. Dividends of $20 were declared during the current year.
d. No credit sales were made during the current year.
e. Unpaid salaries at year-end equal 1/12 of the current year's salary expense.
f. Current liabilities, other than salaries, equal $9 at year-end.

Required

a. Calculate the missing amounts (indicated by question marks) for the financial statements.
b. Provide numerical support for the following items:
inventory, beginning of current year; net income; and current liabilities, end of current year.

P3-18 Financial Statement Relationships

YOUR PERFORMANCE OBJECTIVE 13 (page 105)

The Darden Company has misplaced some of its records during the current year. It is your job to assist Darden's bookkeeper in determining the missing amounts in the financial statements below.

Balance Sheet
January 1

Cash	$ 30	Current liabilities	$?
Inventory	40		
Equipment	50	Contributed capital	50
Less: Accumulated depreciation	(5)	Retained earnings	?
Total assets	$115	Total sources of assets	$?

Income Statement
For Year Ending December 31

Sales revenue (all cash)		$ 85
Less expenses:		
Cost of goods sold	$?	
Depreciation expense	8	
Salary expense	12	?
Net income		$?

Balance Sheet
December 31

Cash	$ 63	Current liabilities	$?
Inventory	20		
Equipment	50	Contributed capital	50
Less: Accumulated depreciation	(?)	Retained earnings	?
Total assets	$?	Total sources of assets	$?

Additional Information

a. Ten dollars of inventory purchases were made during the current year.
b. No credit sales were made during the current year.
c. Dividends of $20 were declared during the current year.
d. Current liabilities, other than salaries, equal $9 at year-end.
e. Unpaid salaries at year-end equal 1/12 of the current year's salary expense.

Required

a. Calculate the missing amounts (indicated by question marks) for the financial statements.
b. Provide numerical support for the following items: current liabilities, December 31; cost of goods sold; retained earnings, January 1; and accumulated depreciation, December 31.

YOUR PERFORMANCE OBJECTIVES 7, 10, 11, 13
(pages 64, 95, 99, 105)

P3-19 Comprehensive Problem: Financial Statement Relationships
Calculate the missing amounts below by using your understanding of financial statement relationships. The first four items listed represent changes in amount rather than absolute amounts.

Increase in total assets	$240
Decrease in total liabilities	45
Increase (decrease) in owners' equity	?
Increase in capital stock	120
Beginning retained earnings balance	315
Ending retained earnings balance	?
Net income	?
Dividends declared	200

YOUR PERFORMANCE OBJECTIVES 7, 10
(pages 64, 95)

P3-20 Comprehensive Problem: Analyzing Financial Statements
When you studied the VideoValor financial statements in the *Making Business Decisions* case in this chapter, you might have noticed that some numbers on the statements don't seem to correlate. For example, why is *sales revenue* different from *cash collected from customers*?

Required
Answer these questions.
a. Why is sales revenue different from cash collected from customers?
b. Why is salaries expense different from cash paid for salaries?
c. Find one more example of some numbers on the statements that don't seem to correlate and explain it.
d. Does the company employ any sales help? How can you tell?
e. Does the company sell goods on credit? How can you tell?
f. If you were a supplier, would you sell $20,000 of merchandise on credit to this company? Why or why not?

YOUR PERFORMANCE OBJECTIVES 2, 4, 7, 11
(pages 18, 22, 64, 99)

P3-21 Comprehensive Problem
Frank Karliner opened a retail stationery store, called *All the Write Stuff*, about four weeks ago. He is planning to meet with his accountant next week to review how the business did for its first month of operations. Frank has asked you to explain some unfamiliar terms that the accountant has used to discuss his transactions. Frank has prepared the following report to present to the accountant:

ALL THE WRITE STUFF
May Report

Deposits made into the business checking account:

5/3	Transferred $21,000 from my personal accounts to the new business.
5/8	Borrowed $3,000 from my sister to help pay my bills. Deposited the money in the business checking account and promised to pay her back within three months.
5/29	Collected $4,100 from customers and made deposits on 5/14, 5/19, and 5/28 into the checking account.

Checks written from the business checking account:

5/4	Check for $6,000 to my landlord, representing rent for the month of May, plus a two-month security deposit.
5/5	Check for $8,500 for fixtures and equipment for the store.
5/9	Bought $18,300 worth of inventory for the store, paying $6,100 by check and promising to pay the balance due in equal installments at the end of the next two months.
5/19	Check for $2,300 for more inventory to replace the stuff I sold so far.
5/26	Check for $210 to pay the utility bill.

Other items:

5/20	Returned $130 worth of Mother's Day greeting cards to the supplier because they didn't sell. He told me I could deduct the amount from what I owe him.
5/31	Counted $650 cash from customers that I haven't deposited yet.

Required

In small groups, complete (a) through (c).

a. For each date listed in the first column, complete a table like the one below.
Column 2: Identify whether the accounts involved in the transaction are assets, liabilities, owner's equity, revenue, or expense items. Remember, every transaction will affect at least two accounts.
Column 3: Identify whether the transaction described will affect the balance sheet, income statement, or both statements.
Column 4: Identify whether the transaction described is an operating, investing, or financing activity.

1	2	3	4
Date	**Types of Accounts**	**Financial Statement**	**Type of Activity**
5/3			
5/8			
5/29			
5/4			

b. Using specific examples from the table, write a detailed summary describing how you determined which responses to list in which column. For example, how did you decide something was an asset or an operating activity? Include in this summary a reference to any items with which you had difficulty or could have more than one answer.

c. Write a brief explanation of why you think it would be important to classify the transactions into the three categories shown in the table columns.

d. On your own, make a list of items you would discuss with Frank so that you could define and explain to him how the accountant would use the information in (a) through (c) to determine how Frank's business is doing.

Research Assignments

A wide variety of interesting Research Assignments for this chapter are available for the following topics at www.mhhe.com/solomon:

R3-1 Preparing the Statement of Retained Earnings (PO 12)
R3-2 Preparing the Statement of Retained Earnings (PO 12)
R3-3 Financial Statement Relationships (PO 13)
R3-4 Financial Statement Relationships (PO 13)
R3-5 Navigating the Contents of an Annual Report (PO 14)
R3-6 Navigating the Contents of an Annual Report (PO 14)
R3-7 Navigating the Contents of an Annual Report (PO 14)
R3-8 Evaluating the Attributes of Different Annual Reports (PO 14)
R3-9 Distinguishing between Financial Reports for Different Periods (PO 15)
R3-10 Distinguishing between Two Types of Annual Reports (PO 15)

CHAPTER FOUR

4

The Balance Sheet

PERFORMANCE OBJECTIVES

In this chapter, you will not encounter new Performance Objectives. Instead, you will use the following Performance Objectives from previous chapters. They lay the foundation for the concepts you will learn in this chapter:

PO2 **Identify** several ways in which accounting information is used to make business and personal decisions.

PO4 **Explain** in your own words the meaning of key business terms.

PO5 **Apply** the fundamental accounting equation, Assets = Liabilities + Owner's Equity, to:

a. **Analyze** the effects of accounting transactions on the elements of the balance sheet.
b. **Prepare** a balance sheet that reports the financial condition of any entity.

PO7

a. **Define** the terms *financing activities, investing activities,* and *operating activities.*
b. **Classify** any accounting transaction into one of these activities or a noncash investing and financing activity.
c. **Classify** any cash receipt or cash payment transaction into the appropriate activity as reported in the statement of cash flows.

PO8 **Explain** what role ethics plays in the preparation of financial statements.

PO9 **Identify** the types of decisions investors and creditors make and **describe** what information in the financial statements and/or related disclosures meets the information needs of each group.

PO11 **Differentiate** the balance sheet from the income statement by being able to:

a. **Distinguish between** transactions that do and do not affect the income statement.
b. **Classify** account titles into asset, liability, owners' equity, and income statement accounts.

PO12 **Prepare** a statement of owners' equity that reports the changes in owner equity accounts for any entity.

PO13 **Link** the following related financial statements—balance sheet, income statement, and statement of owners' equity—by being able to **calculate** missing amounts in each of them.

PO14 **Navigate** through and **locate** information in an annual report, so that you can make informed decisions about that entity's financing, investing, and operating activities.

THE HISTORY OF THE BALANCE SHEET: FROM ITALY, TO ENGLAND, TO CARDS & MEMORABILIA UNLIMITED

In 1586 an Italian named Don Angelo Pietra, a Benedictine monk, published an accounting book entitled, *Indrizzo Degli Economi.*[1] This was the first book ever to mention financial statements, even though they had been used for more than two hundred years. Pietra was the first known advocate of the entity concept you learned about in Chapter 2. He believed an entity's transactions should be separate and distinct from its owner's transactions. He also believed that accounting should reveal all changes in an entity's financial condition, not just changes in owner's equity. And so he encouraged the preparation of what we now call the income statement, statement of owner's equity, and the balance sheet.

The work of Pietra was not the only development enabling the balance sheet to evolve beyond simply showing customer receivables and assisting businessmen in making decisions about collecting bad debts. During the 17th century, a French government ordinance required merchants to report every two years their fixed and movable properties as well as their debts receivable and payable. This rule was enacted to aid potential bankruptcy proceedings by providing a clearer picture of the entity's financial condition. Another influence was the need by owners for a separate schedule of resources and debts whenever their relative ownership changed. Finally, with the growth of companies during the Industrial Revolution, creditors and shareholders needed a statement that would help them evaluate the financial condition of their investments.

Thus, by the mid 1600s, the balance sheet had become not only the most important financial statement but also often the only one a business would prepare. Users wanted to know more about assets and capital rather than revenue and expenses. A well-known example of a typical 17th century balance sheet is the personal balance sheet or "estate" of Englishman Derrick Roose.

INDRIZZO
DEGLI ECONOMI.
O SIA ORDINATISSIMA
INSTRVTTIONE DA REGOLATAMENTE
FORMARE QVALVNQVE SCRITTVRA
IN VN LIBRO DOPPIO,
AGGIVNTOVI L'ESSEMPLARE DI VN LIBRO
NOBILE, COL SVO GIORNALE, AD VSO DELLA
CONGREGATION CASSINESE, DELL'ORDINE
DI S. BENEDETTO.
CON DVE TAVOLE, L'VNA DE' CAPITOLI, ET L'ALTRA
DELLE COSE PIV DEGNE, A PIENO
INTENDIMENTO DI CIASCVNO.
Opera nuoua, non meno vtile che necessaria, a Religiosi, che viuono delle proprie
Rendite, & ad ogni Padre di Famiglia, che si diletti
del Libro Doppio.
Composta da Don Angelo Pietra Genouese Monaco, & indegno seruo di Giesu Christo.
IN MANTOVA, Per Francesco Osanna. Con licenza de' Superiori. MDLXXXVI.

THE ESTATE OF DERRICK ROOSE
Made up on the last day of December 1600

Estate of Capital debit	£ s d	Estate of Capital credit	£ s d
(list of liabilities)	51- 8-0	(list of assets)	3191-17-1
Balance debit, to close the statement	3140- 9-1		
Total	3191-17-1	Total	3191-17-1
The remainder (Capital) at year end is			3140- 9-1
At the beginning of the year it was			2153- 3-8
Increase during the year			987- 5-5

Symbol for English pound
Symbol for English shilling
Symbol for English pence

This increase in capital is equal to net income.

You will not be able to calculate the respective increases in shillings or pence unless you are familiar with the British system of currency. Refer to Critical Thinking Problem 4-22 at the end of this chapter.

[1] The following description of the history of the balance sheet is based on the article, "Balance Sheet," appearing in *The History of Accounting, An International Encyclopedia,* Edited by Michael Chatfield and Richard Vangermeersch, Garland Publishing, Inc., 1996, pp. 60–64.

(continued on next page)

(continued from previous page)

Notice that although assets and liabilities are separated, they are placed in exactly the opposite position from today's balance sheet. Also, unlike current balance sheets, what is actually net income is reported as the net change in capital during the year.

During the 18th and 19th centuries, the format and continued importance of the balance sheet was greatly influenced by various government acts, especially those passed by England's Parliament. The intention of these acts was no longer solely to assist businessmen but to better allocate society's resources by improving investor decisions. For example, the Companies Act of 1844 required that corporate stockholders must receive an audited balance sheet. The Companies Acts of 1855 and 1856 included a model balance sheet, a representation of which is shown here:

BALANCE SHEET of the ____________ Company
Made up to ____________ 1856

Capital and Liabilities		Property and Assets	
I. Capital from stock sales		III. Property	
a. Shares outstanding		a. Immovable	
b. Price per share		b. Movable	
II. Debts and Liabilities		IV. Debts owing to the firm	
a. Long-term liabilities		a. Notes Receivable	
b. Short-term debts		b. Accounts Receivable	
VI. Reserve for Contingencies		c. Bad debts	
VII. Profit available for dividends		V. Cash and Investments	
	_____		_____
	_____		_____
Contingent Liabilities			

Notice that this balance sheet groups related items into subtotals and places debts opposite asset accounts expected to be used in payment of those debts. In other words, this balance sheet encourages interpretation, a dramatic departure from earlier balance sheets in which account balances were listed in a more random order.

Do you see that this balance sheet's placement of assets on the right, liabilities on the left, and capital on the top left is nearly a complete reversal of the modern American balance sheet? One explanation for this difference between American and British balance sheets is that American 19th century corporations were generally smaller than their British counterparts and financed their growth more with short-term bank loans than issuances of stock. As a result, their balance sheets were influenced more by the needs of bankers, who wanted to first determine if the business had the ability to repay its maturing loans. This banking influence led to the practice of placing current assets and current liabilities at the top of the American balance sheet.

Now that you've gained some appreciation of the historical development of the balance sheet, let's look at a modern version, that of Cards & Memorabilia Unlimited.

More Balance Sheet Transactions at Cards & Memorabilia Unlimited

In Chapter 2, you learned how to use the fundamental accounting equation to analyze the effects of accounting transactions on the elements of the balance sheet. Recall Performance Objective 5, which has now been reworded:

YOUR PERFORMANCE OBJECTIVE 5a
Analyze the effects of accounting transactions on the fundamental accounting equation, that is, the primary elements of the balance sheet.

In an effort to meet this performance objective, we analyzed the effects of Susan's first four transactions—Transactions A_1, B, C_1, and D—on the balance sheet equation. Before you read the next section, review Figure 4-1 to be certain you understand this transaction analysis.

FIGURE 4-1

Transaction analysis of Cards & Memorabilia Unlimited's initial transactions

Transactions	Assets	=	Liabilities	+	Owner's Equity
A_1 On January 2, Susan Newman contributes $30,000 of cash as her initial investment to finance the business.	$30,000				$30,000
B On January 2, Susan transfers $6,000 of cash from her checking account to open a savings account.	6,000 (6,000)				
C_1 On January 4, Susan acquires $10,000 worth of store equipment by using a credit card that bears an 18% interest rate.	10,000		$10,000		
D On January 6, Susan acquires $15,000 worth of merchandise by paying cash to suppliers.	15,000 (15,000)				
	$40,000		$10,000		$30,000

Transaction Identification and Explanation

Let's now examine several more transactions of Cards & Memorabilia Unlimited that affect Susan's balance sheet—Transactions E through L. We'll use transaction analysis to determine the specific effects (increase/decrease) of each transaction on the balance sheet. Try to determine the effect of each transaction on the fundamental accounting equation yourself *before* you check the answers provided on pages 140 to 143. Because transaction analysis is so important in this course, it is essential that you can perform it confidently.

Transaction E: $2,000 cash is paid to the landlord on January 9 to obtain access to leased store space. The 36-month lease was signed on January 5.

Explanation: A security deposit protects the landlord from potential loss; in this case, it is comprised of a $1,000 damage deposit and a $1,000 amount for the final month's rent. Normally, a security deposit also includes first month's rent, but Susan was able to negotiate a free first month because of low demand for commercial real estate. Try to analyze this transaction before looking at the answer.

Transaction E	Assets	=	Liabilities	+	Owner's Equity
On January 9, a $2,000 security deposit is paid to lease store space.					

As you might recall, CMU began to record sales revenue on January 9, the first day it was open for business. None of these sales transactions are recorded in this section, however, because the primary purpose of this chapter is to present transactions that directly affect the balance sheet. Chapter 6 will present all first-year transactions that affect the income statement, including sales revenue and various expenses. As a result, Transactions A_1 through Z are not always presented in chronological order.

Proceed through the rest of this section by first reading each transaction—C_2 through L—and its explanation and then analyze the transaction before checking its answer.

Transaction C_2: $10,000 cash is paid in full on February 3 to settle the credit card obligation made on January 4.

Explanation: In Transaction C_1, Susan has approximately one month to pay the credit card balance incurred on January 4. Note that Susan makes this payment in time to avoid interest or late charges.

Transaction C_2	Assets	=	Liabilities	+	Owner's Equity
On February 3, $10,000 cash is paid in full to settle the credit card obligation made on January 4.					

Transaction F: $5,000 cash is borrowed on July 1 with a bank credit line bearing interest at an 8% rate.

Explanation: Although Susan was able to finance her operations for one-half year without borrowing money, she now needs to access her bank credit line.

Transaction F	Assets	=	Liabilities	+	Owner's Equity
On July 1, $5,000 cash is borrowed with a bank credit line bearing interest at an 8% rate.					

Transaction G: On the first day of each month from July through December, $18,000 worth of additional merchandise is acquired on account.

Explanation: Unlike Transaction D, in which merchandise was acquired in exchange for cash, CMU acquires merchandise by promising to make future payments on its charge account with the supplier. These six acquisitions on account amount to approximately $3,000 each.

Transaction G	Assets	=	Liabilities	+	Owner's Equity
From July 1 to December 1, $18,000 worth of additional merchandise is acquired on account.					

Transaction H: On July 1, $7,000 cash is paid to acquire a used van with a 5–year useful life for the business.

Explanation: After six months of business, Susan realizes she needs a business vehicle that she can use for large purchases and deliveries.

Transaction H	**Assets**	**=**	**Liabilities**	**+**	**Owner's Equity**
On July 1, $7,000 cash is paid to acquire a used van with a 5-year useful life for the business.					

Transaction I: On November 1, $6,000 cash is collected from customers before any goods or services are provided.

Explanation: CMU receives sales orders from several customers for some soon to be published cards and receives $6,000 cash in advance. When $2,000 worth of these cards are received from manufacturers at the end of both November and December, they will be delivered immediately to the appropriate customers.

Transaction I	**Assets**	**=**	**Liabilities**	**+**	**Owner's Equity**
On November 1, $6,000 cash is collected from customers before any goods or services are provided.					

Transaction J_1: From July 31 to November 30, $12,000 cash is paid to reduce accounts payable.

Explanation: Recall from Transaction G that about $3,000 worth of inventory is acquired on account in each of the months July through December. When CMU acquires inventory on account from its suppliers, however, it is obligated to pay amounts owed within 30 days. CMU pays off the July, August, and September accounts payable balances on time. To conserve cash needed for other purposes, however, Susan asks permission from her supplier to pay only $1,500 at the end of both October and November and then pay the remaining balance owed in full at the end of December. In the interest of maintaining good customer relations, the supplier grants Susan's request. Note that the three payments of $3,000 and two payments of $1,500 amount to a total payment of $12,000.

Transaction J_1	**Assets**	**=**	**Liabilities**	**+**	**Owner's Equity**
From July 31 to November 30, $12,000 cash is paid to reduce accounts payable.					

Transaction J_2: On December 31, $6,000 of accounts payable is converted to a 6% interest-bearing note payable due on March 31.

Explanation: With a $3,000 balance due from October and November, and the entire $3,000 balance due from December's acquisition of inventory, Susan decides it is in her best interest to conserve cash a short time longer. As a result, she renegotiates with the inventory supplier to postpone payment due on the $6,000 account payable. Essentially, CMU pays 6% interest in return for extending the due date from December 31 to March 31.

Note that the account payable is replaced by a more formal promise to pay or promissory note, a written acknowledgment of a borrower's or customer's promise to pay the amount owed.

Transaction J_2	**Assets**	**=**	**Liabilities**	**+**	**Owner's Equity**
On December 31, $6,000 of accounts payable is converted to a 6% interest-bearing note payable due on March 31.					

Transaction K_1: On December 31, $5,000 cash is paid in full to settle the credit line loan made on July 1.
Explanation: If you restudy Transaction F, you will see that Susan owed $5,000 on this loan from July 1 to December 31.

Transaction K_1	**Assets**	**=**	**Liabilities**	**+**	**Owner's Equity**
On December 31, $5,000 cash is paid in full to settle the credit line loan made on July 1.					

Transaction L: On December 31, $4,000 worth of a computer and printer is acquired by signing a two-year promissory note. The note bears interest at 12% and is payable in equal monthly installments.
Explanation: After processing all of her first-year transactions manually, Susan decides she will convert her manual accounting information system to a computerized one for her second year of operations. To accomplish this task, she purchases a computer and printer.

Transaction L	**Assets**	**=**	**Liabilities**	**+**	**Owner's Equity**
On December 31, $4,000 worth of a computer and printer is acquired by signing a two-year promissory note.					

Transaction Analysis

Compare the answers you have for the preceding transactions to the answers in this section. This will give you immediate feedback on how well you understand the technique of transaction analysis.

Transaction E	**Assets**	**=**	**Liabilities**	**+**	**Owner's Equity**
On January 9, a $2,000 security deposit is paid to lease store space.	2,000 (2,000)				

Analysis: Whenever you pay cash, you must decrease the asset account Cash. But in this transaction, CMU has the right to receive $2,000 in 36 months as long as the last month's rent is paid and the property is not damaged. Since the security deposit represents a receivable, CMU uses the asset account title Security Deposit Receivable. Notice that one asset, a receivable,

increases while another asset, cash, decreases by the same amount. Since neither assets nor sources of assets change as a result of this transaction, the equality between assets and sources of assets is maintained.

Transaction C_2	**Assets**	=	**Liabilities**	+	**Owner's Equity**
On February 3, $10,000 cash is paid in full to settle the credit card obligation made on January 4.	(10,000)		(10,000)		

Analysis: Both the asset account Cash and the liability account Accounts Payable are decreased by $10,000 as a result of this transaction. The response to the question, "What is the current balance in the Accounts Payable account?" is "It is now zero." That is, this account's balance increased from zero to $10,000 in Transaction C_1 and decreased from $10,000 to zero as a result of Transaction C_2.

Transaction F	**Assets**	=	**Liabilities**	+	**Owner's Equity**
On July 1, $5,000 cash is borrowed with a bank credit line bearing interest at an 8% rate.	5,000		5,000		

Analysis: This transaction has two effects. Both the asset account Cash and the liability account Credit Line Payable are increased because cash borrowed today is payable in the future. Since interest is incurred with the passage of time, you do not need to calculate interest on July 1.

Transaction G	**Assets**	=	**Liabilities**	+	**Owner's Equity**
From July 1 to December 1, $18,000 worth of additional merchandise is acquired on account.	18,000		18,000		

Analysis: The merchandise inventory account, an asset, should be increased by $18,000 because Cards & Memorabilia Unlimited now holds resources with future economic benefits. The equation is maintained by increasing the liability account Accounts Payable to reflect the supplier's claim against the asset acquired.

Transaction H	**Assets**	=	**Liabilities**	+	**Owner's Equity**
On July 1, $7,000 cash is paid to acquire a used van with a 5-year useful life for the business.	7,000 (7,000)				

Analysis: You must increase the Store Equipment account, an asset, but decrease the asset account Cash to recognize that cash has been paid. Again, the equality between assets and sources of assets is maintained even though no liabilities or owner's equity accounts are affected by this transaction.

Transaction I	Assets	=	Liabilities	+	Owner's Equity
On November 1, $6,000 cash is collected from customers before any goods or services are provided.	6,000		6,000		

Analysis: This transaction increases both the asset account Cash and the liability account called Advances from Customers. CMU incurs a liability because it has a future obligation to deliver the cards to these customers.

Transaction J_1	Assets	=	Liabilities	+	Owner's Equity
From July 31 to November 30, $12,000 cash is paid to reduce accounts payable.	(12,000)		(12,000)		

Analysis: In concept, this transaction is identical to Transaction C_2 except for the amounts. That is, both the asset account Cash and the liability account Accounts Payable are decreased as a result of this transaction. Notice that the balance in the accounts payable account is now $6,000, since $18,000 (Transaction G) reduced by $12,000 is $6,000.

Note: If you have discovered CMU's cash balance now totals a negative $5,000, you are to be commended for your attention to detail. Nevertheless, CMU did not experience a negative cash balance during the year. How could this happen? Think about this, and you'll find the answer in an *Insight* at the end of this chapter.

Transaction J_2	Assets	=	Liabilities	+	Owner's Equity
On December 31, $6,000 of accounts payable is converted to a 6% interest-bearing note payable due on March 31.			(6,000) 6,000		

Analysis: This transaction simply replaces an informal promise to pay (accounts payable) with a more formal promise to pay (notes payable). Notice that the fundamental accounting equation is maintained, because one liability decreases while another liability increases by the same amount. Another term used to describe such a transaction is a *reclassification entry.*

Transaction K_1	Assets	=	Liabilities	+	Owner's Equity
On December 31, $5,000 cash is paid in full to settle the credit line loan made on July 1.	(5,000)		(5,000)		

Analysis: The asset account Cash decreases when cash is paid, while the liability recorded in Transaction F decreases.

Transaction L	Assets	=	Liabilities	+	Owner's Equity
On December 31, $4,000 worth of a computer and printer is acquired by signing a two-year promissory note.	4,000		4,000		

Analysis: As in Transactions C_1 and H, Susan has once again acquired equipment. Although each acquisition involves different types of equipment, a single asset account, Store Equipment, will be used for simplicity. The source of this asset is expressed by increasing a liability account entitled Notes Payable. While the maturity dates of the notes payable introduced in Transactions J_2 and L differ significantly, the same liability account is used in the interest of simplicity.

How Transaction Analysis Helps You Prepare a Balance Sheet

Preparing a balance sheet after each and every accounting transaction, as we did in Chapter 2, requires too much time and expense to be used in a real business. A more practical approach is to present the collective effects of a large number of transactions at a specific point in time, as is done in Figure 4-2, CMU's balance sheet for

FIGURE 4-2 Deriving a balance sheet from transaction analysis using CMU

Details of transactions

A_1	1/2	$30,000 cash is contributed by the owner who opens a business checking account.
B	1/2	$6,000 cash is withdrawn from the checking account to open a business savings account.
C_1	1/4	$10,000 worth of store equipment is acquired with a credit card.
D	1/6	$15,000 cash is paid to acquire merchandise inventory.
E	1/9	$2,000 cash is paid to the landlord for the security deposit on the store lease.
C_2	2/3	$10,000 cash is paid in full to settle the credit card obligation made on January 4.
F	7/1	$5,000 cash is borrowed with a bank credit line bearing interest at an 8% rate.
G	7/1–12/1	$18,000 worth of additional merchandise is acquired on account.
H	7/1	$7,000 cash is paid to acquire a used van with a 5-year useful life for the business.
I	11/1	$6,000 cash is collected from customers before any goods or services are provided.
J_1	7/31–11/30	$12,000 cash is paid to reduce accounts payable.
J_2	12/31	$6,000 of accounts payable is converted to a 6% interest-bearing note payable due on March 31.
K_1	12/31	$5,000 cash is paid in full to settle the credit line loan made on July 1.
L	12/31	$4,000 worth of a computer and printer is acquired by signing a 2-year promissory note.

Analysis of transactions

	Assets				=	Liabilities				+	Owner's Equity	
	Cash	Receivables	Merchandise Inventory	Store Equipment (Net)		Accounts Payable	Credit Line Payable	Advances from Customers	Notes Payable		Contrib. Capital	Retained Earnings
A_1	30,000										30,000	
B	6,000											
	(6,000)											
C_1				10,000		10,000						
D	(15,000)		15,000									
E	(2,000)	2,000										
C_2	(10,000)					(10,000)						
F	5,000						5,000					
G			18,000			18,000						
H	(7,000)			7,000								
I	6,000							6,000				
J_1	(12,000)					(12,000)						
J_2						(6,000)			6,000			
K_1	(5,000)						(5,000)					
L				4,000					4,000			
A_1-L	(10,000)	2,000	33,000	21,000	=	0	0	6,000	10,000	+	30,000	
M – Z	48,275	5,025	(20,000)	(4,300)		1,100		(4,000)	0		10,000	21,900
A_1-Z	38,275	7,025	13,000	16,700		1,100	0	2,000	10,000		40,000	21,900
		$75,000			=		$13,100			+	$61,900	

FIGURE 4-3 Cards & Memorabilia Unlimited's balance sheet as of December 31

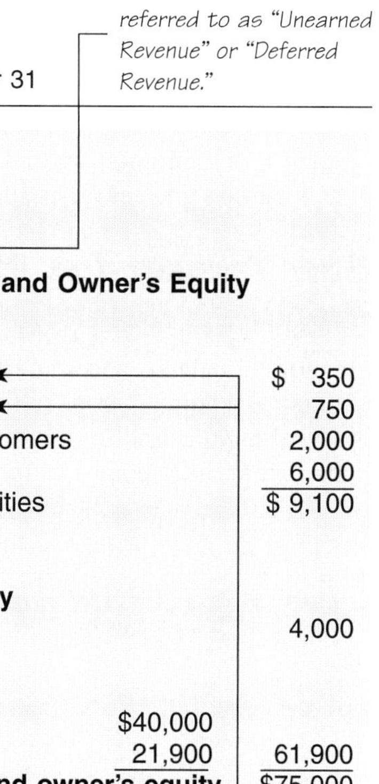

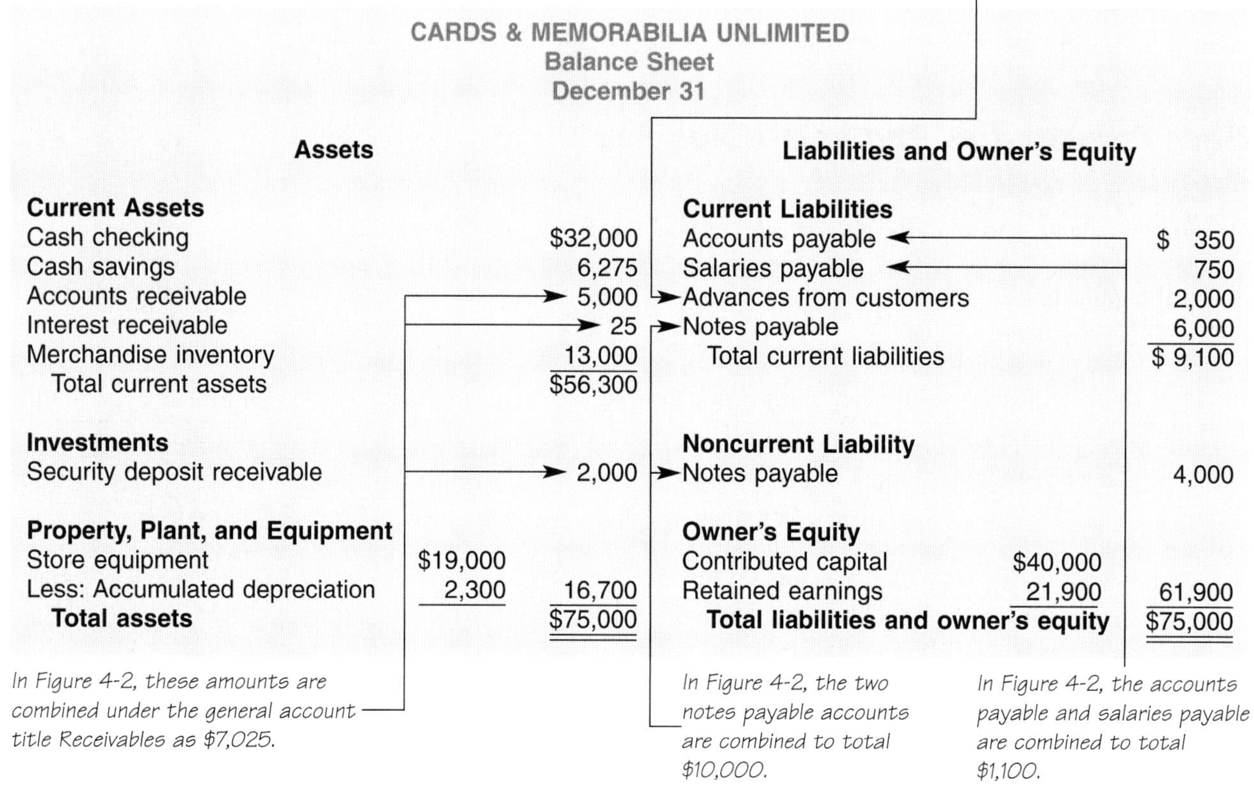

CARDS & MEMORABILIA UNLIMITED
Balance Sheet
December 31

Assets			**Liabilities and Owner's Equity**		
Current Assets			**Current Liabilities**		
Cash checking		$32,000	Accounts payable		$ 350
Cash savings		6,275	Salaries payable		750
Accounts receivable		5,000	Advances from customers		2,000
Interest receivable		25	Notes payable		6,000
Merchandise inventory		13,000	Total current liabilities		$ 9,100
Total current assets		$56,300			
Investments			**Noncurrent Liability**		
Security deposit receivable		2,000	Notes payable		4,000
Property, Plant, and Equipment			**Owner's Equity**		
Store equipment	$19,000		Contributed capital	$40,000	
Less: Accumulated depreciation	2,300	16,700	Retained earnings	21,900	61,900
Total assets		$75,000	**Total liabilities and owner's equity**		$75,000

In Figure 4-2, these amounts are combined under the general account title Receivables as $7,025.
In Figure 4-2, the two notes payable accounts are combined to total $10,000.
In Figure 4-2, the accounts payable and salaries payable are combined to total $1,100.

December 31. This balance sheet presents the transaction analysis for each of the first 14 transactions of Cards & Memorabilia Unlimited—Transactions A_1 through L—and the combined transaction analysis of Transactions M through Z. Although Figure 4-2 does not look like a traditional balance sheet, it does include the same totals found in CMU's balance sheet for December 31 (Figure 4-3). Figure 4-2 presents the effects of A_1 through Z on the fundamental accounting equation and also breaks down each element into accounts. For example, notice how the $75,000 total of the four asset accounts equals the total of the four liability accounts, $13,100, plus the total of the two owner's equity accounts, $61,900.

The fact that the 14 transactions shown in Figure 4-2 affect only the balance sheet is not coincidental. Transactions A_1 through L were designed as an instructional tool to help you concentrate on the balance sheet. In Chapters 6 and 7, you will learn how Transactions M through Z affect not only the balance sheet but also the income statement. You might notice some new terms in Figures 4-2 and 4-3. These terms will be explained throughout this chapter.

A Classified Balance Sheet Presentation

As you have learned, a balance sheet contains information that is often used to make business decisions, such as whether to loan money or lease property to an entity. If the balance sheet presents this information so that decision makers are better able to interpret it, the usefulness of the balance sheet is enhanced. For example, compare the balance sheets presented in Figure 4-2 and Figure 4-3. Besides the fact that Figure 4-2 presents the detailed effects of many transactions, whereas Figure 4-3 does not present specific transactions, what difference do you notice? One difference is that, unlike Figure 4-2, Figure 4-3 classifies assets and liabilities into *current* and *non-current* categories. For now, we'll use the word *current* to describe all accounts that are expected to be turned into cash, sold, exchanged, or discharged within one year. This difference is one of many ways in which the information contained in the balance sheet can be presented in useful subcategories. When a balance sheet has such subcategories, as is almost always the case in annual reports, we usually refer to that balance sheet as a classified balance sheet. A **classified balance sheet**, such as that shown in Figure 4-3, organizes its accounts into categories that allow its readers to more easily grasp the entity's financial position and, therefore, make better decisions. Since annual reports are usually prepared by corporations, we will concentrate on corporate balance sheet illustrations for the remainder of this chapter. For this reason, let's now examine how the balance sheets of corporations differ from those of CMU and other noncorporate entities.

How Do Corporate Balance Sheets Differ from Noncorporate Balance Sheets?

INSIGHT

There are two primary differences between the balance sheets of corporations and those of entities that are not corporations, such as sole proprietorships and partnerships. First, corporate balance sheets are usually more detailed than noncorporate balance sheets. For this reason, they are more likely to be classified. This should not surprise you since the typical corporation is larger than the typical noncorporation and requires more detail to adequately report the scope of its operations and its many transactions.

Second, the owners' equity section of a corporate balance sheet is easily distinguishable from the owners' equity section of a noncorporate balance sheet, as illustrated in Figure 4-4. In this figure, owners' equity is divided into two conceptual components: the owners' investment to finance the business and the retained earnings from profitable operations. As you have seen, both sole proprietorships and partnerships usually combine these two components into a single account title composed of the owner's name followed by the term "Capital" such as Susan Newman, Capital. In contrast, corporations use at least one account to represent each component, a generic capital stock account (common or preferred) and a retained earnings account.

FIGURE 4-4 Distinguishing between different entities by using owners' equity account titles

	Owners' Equity Components			
	Investment		Earnings	
Business Entity	**Traditional**	**Recommended**	**Traditional**	**Recommended**
Sole proprietorship:	Capital	**Contributed Capital**	Capital	**Retained Earnings**
Partnership:	Capital	**Contributed Capital**	Capital	**Retained Earnings**
Corporation:	Capital Stock	**Capital Stock**	Retained Earnings	**Retained Earnings**

A partnership is distinguished from a sole proprietorship because it has separate contributed capital and retained earnings accounts for each partner. For example, a partnership would have at least two contributed capital accounts, such as Contributed Capital–Smith and Contributed Capital–Jones.

In this textbook we maintain these conceptual components by assigning a separate account title to each component no matter what form of business entity we encounter. In both a sole proprietorship and partnership, for example, we will use the account title Con-

(continued)

tributed Capital to represent the owners' investment and the account title Retained Earnings to represent the earnings from profitable operations retained in the business.

The **insight** you should gain here is that by knowing what to look for, you will be able to determine quickly whether a balance sheet reports on a corporate or noncorporate entity. Ask yourself, "Is it classified?" Then look at the account titles in the owners' equity section. If you see a form of the capital stock account title, there is no question you are looking at a corporate balance sheet.

Account Categories and Titles Usually Found in Corporate Balance Sheets

Corporate balance sheets generally contain two asset categories: current assets and noncurrent assets, which include investments; property, plant, and equipment; intangible assets; and other assets. Corporate liabilities generally contain two categories: current liabilities and noncurrent or long-term liabilities. Corporate owners' equity, referred to as stockholders' or shareholders' equity, generally includes two categories: contributed capital and retained earnings. Most of these categories contain two or more account titles. For example, Cash and Merchandise Inventory are two current asset account titles, while Common Stock and Preferred Stock are two contributed capital titles (each account will be explained later).

Why do you need to know about these account categories and titles? Because, to intelligently read financial statements, you must be able to distinguish between the

FIGURE 4-5

Some categories and account titles found in a typical classified balance sheet

Balance Sheet Element	Account Classification	Characteristic Account Title(s)
Assets	Current Assets	Cash and Cash Equivalents Marketable Securities Accounts and Notes Receivable Less: Allowance for Uncollectibles Inventories Prepayments
	Noncurrent Assets	Investments Property, Plant, and Equipment Less: Accumulated Depreciation Intangible Assets Other Assets
Liabilities	Current Liabilities	Accrued Liabilities Advances from Customers Current Portion of Long-Term Debt
	Noncurrent Liabilities	Mortgages Payable Notes Payable Bonds Payable Capital Lease Obligations Warranty Liabilities Pension Obligations Deferred Income Taxes
Owners' Equity	Contributed Capital	Capital Stock Additional Paid-In Capital
	Retained Earnings	Retained Earnings Less: Treasury Stock

account categories and titles found on balance sheets and the account categories and titles found on the other financial statements. Recall that this ability to distinguish account titles is part (b) of Performance Objective 11:

YOUR PERFORMANCE OBJECTIVE 11b
Differentiate the balance sheet from income statement by being able to **classify** account titles into asset, liability, owners' equity, and income statement accounts.

Next, you will learn about the nature of typical account titles included in the categories listed above. To guide you through the numerous account titles that follow, refer often to Figure 4-5. This figure summarizes the typical categories and specific accounts used in presenting the three elements of the balance sheet. As you read through these accounts, be sure you are able to apply part (b) of Performance Objective 11.

Why Are Account Titles Useful to You?

USER FOCUS

The next several pages of this textbook contain detailed descriptions of account titles. It is no exaggeration to say that these pages are among the most important you will read in this textbook. Why? The answer is really quite simple. Account titles are significant elements in every financial statement. Since this textbook's primary objective is to help you intelligently read them, the degree to which you are familiar with account titles dictates how well you will understand financial statements. Underscoring the critical importance to your success of learning these titles is *Appendix B*—a special tool prepared to help you better understand account titles. Use this appendix whenever you are uncertain about an account title or its content.

So what can you do now to make your study of account titles less burdensome? First, relax, because the titles you will now study include only those typically found on the balance sheet. We'll cover the typical income statement account titles in Chapter 7. Second, look for repeating patterns in account titles. For example, the typical liability account title includes the words *payable, liability,* or *obligation.* With this tip and knowing there are relatively few owners' equity titles, you can focus on the more numerous asset account titles. Also, you have a helpful tool in *Appendix B,* so don't forget to use it!

Finally, the most effective way to learn account titles is to see them in a real-world environment. For example, rather than memorizing the titles, find them in the annual report balance sheet of a company in which you have a special interest. In this way, you'll be more likely to remember these and related titles. Actively apply these account titles to your daily life. If a relative or friend works in "accounts receivable," ask him/her about it!

What Are Typical Current Asset Account Titles?

Recall that an account is the detailed record of the changes that have occurred in particular assets, liabilities, and owner equities. Typical current asset account titles listed in order of their **liquidity**—how easily convertible they are to cash—include Cash and Cash Equivalents, Marketable Securities, Accounts and Notes Receivable, Inventories, and various prepaid items. The degree to which a company holds liquid assets indicates its **solvency**, that is, its ability to meet liabilities whose balances are either due or payable in the near future. So you can begin evaluating the financial health of a company by first examining the amount and distribution of its current assets. Let's now examine in greater detail the current asset accounts you are likely to find in corporate balance sheets.

Cash and Cash Equivalents As you have already learned, the **cash** account is used to accumulate the cash effects (increases and decreases) of an entity's transactions. Cash may be divided into two accounts: (1) a cash on hand account, which consists of money—such as currency, coins, money orders, and checks waiting to be deposited—in a cash register, a petty cash box,[2] or safe and (2) a cash in bank account, which consists of money deposited in bank accounts that can be withdrawn quickly. In summary, cash represents money and any other medium of exchange that a bank will accept for deposit.

Most balance sheets today include **cash equivalents**, that is, highly liquid, interest-bearing investments that have maturities of three months or less when purchased. Examples include time deposits or savings accounts, certificates of deposit, money market funds, treasury bills, and commercial paper (short-term, unsecured promissory notes of large firms payable to investors). No collateral is provided on commercial paper as protection against loss. Another useful description of cash equivalents is that they are highly liquid marketable securities.

Because cash equivalents are almost as liquid as cash, annual reports usually combine cash and cash equivalents. For example, Ford Motor Company listed nearly $8 billion cash and cash equivalents at the end of 1997! Was it a good business decision to have that much cash in light of the fact that this same combination decreased to about $4 billion at the end of 2001? Holding significant amounts of assets in an account that is unproductive is not good cash management because neither interest nor dividends are earned. Thus, if investors or employees of Ford want to evaluate its cash management, they will want to determine what portion of Ford's cash account was composed of cash equivalents.

Marketable Securities **Marketable securities** are temporary or short-term investments of idle cash. This asset includes many of the same items associated with cash equivalents, as well as investments in shares of corporate stock (equity securities), corporate or government bonds, and certificates of deposit (debt securities). They are said to "mature," that is pay cash, on a specific date. Also, they have maturities of greater than three months to one year. In contrast, cash equivalents have maturities of three months or less at date of purchase. To qualify as a marketable security, the security must have a ready *market value* derived from a securities exchange such as the New York Stock Exchange, American Stock Exchange, or NASDAQ (National

NASDAQ® is the world's largest electronic stock market and lists the securities of nearly 4100 of the world's leading companies.

[2] Many businesses operate what is called a *petty cash fund* to avoid the inconvenience and expense of writing a check for such inexpensive items as taxi fares, newspapers, and small amounts of supplies. A check is written to establish such a fund and to replenish it either at the end of a period or when the fund itself becomes low.

FIGURE 4-6

The Coca-Cola Company's balance sheet presentation of cash equivalents, marketable securities, and investments

THE COCA-COLA COMPANY AND SUBSIDIARIES
Consolidated Balance Sheets
December 31
(In millions except share data)

	Year 2	Year 1
Assets		
Current		
Cash and cash equivalents	**$ 1,648**	$ 1,737
Marketable securities	**159**	106
	1,807	1,843
Trade accounts receivable, less allowances of $10 in year 1 and $23 in year 2	**1,666**	1,639
Inventories	**890**	959
Prepaid expenses and other assets	**2,017**	1,528
Total Current Assets	**6,380**	5,969
Investments and Other Assets		
Equity method investments		
Coca-Cola Enterprises Inc.	**584**	184
Coca-Cola Amatil Limited	**1,255**	1,204
Coca-Cola Beverages plc	**879**	—
Other, principally bottling companies	**3,573**	3,049
Cost method investments, principally bottling companies	**395**	457
Marketable securities and other assets	**1,863**	1,607
	8,549	6,501
Property, Plant, and Equipment		
Land	**199**	183
Buildings and improvements	**1,507**	1,535
Machinery and equipment	**3,855**	3,896
Containers	**124**	157
	5,685	5,771
Less allowances for depreciation	**2,016**	2,028
	3,669	3,743
Goodwill and Other Intangible Assets	**547**	668
	$19,145	$16,881

Figure 4-7 indicates $1,227 of this amount represents cash equivalents. Thus, $421 represents cash.

Figure 4-7 splits this amount into two categories ($79 and $80).

Figure 4-7 indicates $216 ($92 and $124) of this amount represents marketable securities. Thus, $1,647 represents other assets.

The classification system described in the next Insight applies to cash equivalents, marketable securities, and noncurrent investments.

Association of Securities Dealers Automated Quotations). In other words, the security must be able to be sold quickly at an established price. Although the detailed accounting for marketable securities and investments will be covered in Chapter 12, the following *Insight* describes the underlying classification system for the balance sheet presentation of cash equivalents, marketable securities, and investments shown in Figure 4-6.

Accounts and Notes Receivable Both **accounts receivable** and **notes receivable** generally represent the amount of money a company expects to collect from its customers. These receivables arise from sales of products or services for which the customer promises to pay in the future. Such sales are often referred to as *credit sales* or *sales on account*. The primary distinction between accounts receivable and notes receivable is that the note receivable represents a more formal promise to pay than does the account receivable. That is, a note receivable is recorded when a

INSIGHT How Investments in Securities Are Presented on the Balance Sheet

As recently as May 1993, the accounting profession created a new classification system to account for and report most investments in debt securities and equity securities. As a result, these securities are now classified into one of three categories: trading, available for sale, or held to maturity. The Coca-Cola Company, for example, uses the last two of these categories to describe its security investments in Figure 4-7. A business must decide in which category a security belongs before it can properly place it in a classified balance sheet and report its dollar amount. This classification system applies to both of the current assets we've already discussed, namely cash equivalents and marketable securities, as well as to the noncurrent investment asset, which will soon be explained.

Trading securities are those the company intends to actively trade to profit from short-term differences in price. Because they are held for only a short period of time, trad-

FIGURE 4-7 Footnote explanation of how The Coca-Cola Company accounts for cash equivalents, marketable equity securities, and investments

THE COCA-COLA COMPANY AND SUBSIDIARIES
Notes to Consolidated Financial Statements

Note 8: Financial Instruments

Certain Debt and Marketable Equity Securities—Investments in debt and marketable equity securities, other than investments accounted for by the equity method, are categorized as either trading, available for sale or held to maturity. On December 31, Year 1, we had no trading securities. Securities categorized as available for sale are stated at fair value, with unrealized gains and losses, net of deferred income taxes, reported as a component of accumulated other comprehensive income. Debt securities categorized as held to maturity are stated at amortized cost.

On December 31, Year 1, available-for-sale and held-to-maturity securities consisted of the following (in millions):

December 31, Year 1	Cost	Gross Unrealized Gains	Gross Unrealized Losses	Estimated Fair Value
Available-for-sale securities				
Equity securities	$ 304	$67	$(48)	$ 323
Collateralized mortgage obligations	89	—	(1)	88
Other debt securities	11	—	—	11
	$ 404	$67	$(49)	$ 422
Held-to-maturity securities				
Bank and corporate debt	$1,339	$—	$ —	$1,339
Other debt securities	92	—	—	92
	$1,431	$—	$ —	$1,431

On December 31, Year 1, these investments were included in the following captions in our consolidated balance sheets (in millions):

December 31, Year 1	Available-for-Sale Securities	Held-to-Maturity Securities
Cash and cash equivalents	$ —	$1,227
Current marketable securities	79	80
Cost method investments, principally bottling companies	251	
Marketable securities and other assets	92	124
	$422	$1,431

The contractual maturities of these investments as of December 31, Year 1, were as follows (in millions):

	Available-for-Sale Securities		Held-to-Maturity Securities	
	Cost	Fair Value	Amortized Cost	Fair Value
Year 2	$ 7	$ 7	$1,307	$1,307
Year 3 to Year 6	4	4	124	124
Collateralized mortgage obligations	89	88	—	—
Equity securities	304	323	—	—
	$404	$422	$1,431	$1,431

Notice that the $422 and $1,431 amounts are each analyzed in three schedules

These three amounts are classified as noncurrent investments

Combined on the balance sheet

Excludes cash

ing securities are classified as current assets. They are usually held by businesses whose normal operations involve buying and selling securities, such as banks and insurance companies. Thus, you will not see many illustrations of trading securities in this textbook. When you do, remember the market value of trading securities must be reported on the balance sheet.

Available-for-sale securities are those debt ($88 + $11 in Figure 4-7) or equity securities ($323 in Figure 4-7) the company intends to sell in the future but does not actively trade to profit from short-term differences in price. They can be classified as either current or noncurrent assets. Although the company must disclose both the cost and market value of available-for-sale securities, their market value must be reported on the balance sheet.

Held-to-maturity securities are those debt securities the company has both the intent and ability to hold to maturity. Because equity securities, by definition, do not have maturity dates, they cannot be classified as held-to-maturity. Held-to-maturity securities can be classified as either current or noncurrent assets. Although the company must disclose both the cost and market value of these securities, their cost must be reported on the balance sheet.

The insight you should gain here is that if you want to understand how securities are reported on the balance sheet, you must familiarize yourself with these three categories for classifying investments in securities. First, this classification system helps you determine whether the security is classified as current or noncurrent. Then, it provides guidance as to what balance sheet amount should be reported for this security.[3]

[3]"Accounting for Certain Investments in Debt and Equity Securities," *Statement of Financial Accounting Standards No. 115,* Financial Accounting Standards Board, May 1993.

promissory note is received. A *promissory note* is a written promise to pay a fixed amount of money by a certain date.

As you might have guessed, every account receivable and note receivable reported for one entity has a corresponding account payable and note payable reported for another entity. For example, when Susan Newman bought a computer and printer in exchange for a note payable in Transaction L, the store selling her this computer hardware recorded an increase in a note receivable.

Since not all credit sales are expected to be collected, an estimate of the uncollectible amount is generally deducted from the related receivable to derive a more realistic measurement of what is referred to as the *net receivable*. Any such account that reduces another account is referred to as a **contra account**. In this case, the contra asset account is titled **Allowance for Uncollectible Accounts** and is placed immediately below and subtracted from its **primary asset account**, which in this case is Accounts Receivable. The word *net* is used in accounting to indicate the result of subtracting a contra account's balance from the primary account's balance.

Primary account	⟶	Accounts Receivable	$xxx,xxx
Contra asset account	⟶	Allowance for Uncollectibles	(x,xxx)
		Net Accounts Receivable	$xxx,xxx

The dollar value of accounts receivable is especially significant for such large retailers as Sears and JCPenney. Sears, for example, reported over $17 billion of net credit card receivables in 2000, which represented more than 60% of its current assets and nearly 47% of its total assets.

A company's notes receivable account might have to be split into current and noncurrent portions for proper presentation on the balance sheet. In the 1993 annual report of the Boston Celtics in Figure 4-8a, for example, both the current (due within one year) and noncurrent (due in more than one year) notes receivable from players

FIGURE 4-8a

An example of a company's notes receivable that includes both current and noncurrent portions

BOSTON CELTICS LIMITED PARTNERSHIP AND SUBSIDIARIES
Notes to Consolidated Financial Statements
June 30, 1993 and 1992

Note D—Notes Receivable from Players

Notes receivable from players are comprised of:

	1993	1992
Note receivable, with 10% interest, due October 1992		$200,000
Note receivable, without interest, due August 1992		125,000
Note receivable, with 10% interest, due August 1992		260,000
Note receivable, with 9% interest, due in four annual installments of principal beginning October 1993	$165,286	165,286
	165,286	750,286
Less portion due within one year	42,857	585,000
	$122,429	$165,286

are shown. When the entire amount of notes receivable is noncurrent, the presentation is much simpler, as shown by the line item and footnote taken from the 1998 annual report of this partnership in Figure 4-8b.

FIGURE 4-8b

An example of a noncurrent notes receivable balance sheet presentation with supporting documentation

CELTICS BASKETBALL HOLDINGS, LIMITED PARTNERSHIP AND SUBSIDIARY
Consolidated Balance Sheet
June 30, 1998

Note Receivable (See Note C)	$6,610,017

Note C—Notes Receivable

Notes receivable represents a convertible note due from an unrelated company which has been classified as held-to-maturity and is carried at amortized cost, which approximates market value. This note, which is comprised of $6,000,000 face value and accrued interest of $610,017, bears interest at LIBOR plus 1%, with quarterly interest payments beginning in May 1999 and quarterly payments of principal plus interest beginning February 2002 through the maturity of the note in January 2007. The note is secured by substantially all of the assets of this company. There were no unrealized gains or losses on this investment at June 30, 1998.

Inventories Later in this course, you will learn about the typical inventories of a manufacturer. For now, focus your attention on goods being held for sale by retailers, such as Cards & Memorabilia Unlimited. Such **merchandise inventory** represents completed products that a company has on hand for resale to its customers. Inventories often represent an entity's largest asset. This was true of Apple Computer Inc. which reported over $1.75 billion worth of inventories in its September 29, 1995 balance sheet. In its September 25, 1999, balance sheet, however, Apple reported only $20 million! This is a good example of information you can find in the balance sheet that can signal very meaningful changes in a company's financial condition. You might want to ask whether this significant drop in the amount of inventory signals a problem or just represents a change in how Apple handles its inventory of computers and computer-related products. Research Assignment 10 in Chapter 5 will give you an opportunity to find out the answer to this question.

Prepayments The account title **Prepayments** represents payments made to obtain insurance coverage (prepaid insurance), use of facilities (prepaid rent), and supplies (prepaid supplies) that will be used up in future periods. A less used account title is *Prepaid Expenses*. This title is misleading because the acquisition of future benefits through payment represents an asset, not an expense. For example, you would decrease the asset, prepaid insurance, and simultaneously increase insurance expense only as your insurance coverage was used up with the passage of time.

Although these prepayments produce benefits that often last beyond the typical one-year current/noncurrent cutoff, they are generally classified as current assets. The argument used to justify this practice is that these prepayments *are current* in the sense that if you hadn't made them earlier, you would now have to sacrifice a current asset, cash, to obtain their benefits.

What Are Typical Noncurrent Asset Account Titles?

As you already know, the characteristic common to all noncurrent assets is that they require more than one year to be converted to cash, sold, or consumed. The investments, intangible assets, and other asset categories don't consistently appear in publicly disclosed balance sheets. But you can expect to nearly always find specific account titles included in the property, plant, and equipment category.

Investments **Investments** include assets that are acquired in the hope that they will provide dividends, increases in market value, or interest. Investments include common or preferred stock, notes, or bonds issued by other entities. Since you will learn about the equity method in Chapter 12, consider only the last two lines under the investments and other assets heading in Figure 4-6. As we saw earlier, this asset can include both available-for-sale and held-to-maturity securities. In Figure 4-7, for example, The Coca-Cola Company reports $251 million and $92 million under available-for-sale securities and $124 million for the held-to-maturity securities. An asset can be included in Investments only if the entity acquiring it does not use it in normal business operations and does not intend to hold it as a current asset. These investments are increasingly being referred to as *financial instruments.* In addition, land held for speculative purposes is sometimes included in Investments.

Property, Plant, and Equipment The asset category **Property, Plant, and Equipment**, sometimes referred to as *Fixed Assets* or simply *Plant Assets*, includes accounts that have three characteristics in common. They are:

1. Noncurrent—that is, they have relatively long lives.
2. Tangible—that is, they have physical substance.
3. Acquired to be actively used in the operation of the business rather than held as an investment or for resale.

Account titles included in this general category may be divided into the following types:

- *Property, plant, and equipment subject to depreciation*, such as buildings, equipment, furniture, and fixtures.
- *Natural resources subject to depletion*, such as oil and gas reserves, mineral deposits, and timber tracts.
- *Property not subject to depreciation or depletion*, such as land.

When dealing with depreciable assets, it is customary for entities to estimate how long their future benefits will last by calculating an estimated useful life. Recall from Chapter 1 that **depreciation** is the process of allocating the cost of such assets to the periods of time being benefited or the estimated useful life. When Susan assigned an estimated useful life of five years to the store equipment acquired in Transaction C_1, for example, depreciation expense for each year was calculated to be $2,000 ($10,000/5).

Now that you have reviewed how the depreciation concept works, let's look at an account title called Accumulated Depreciation that accompanies every depreciable asset. As its straightforward account title implies, **Accumulated Depreciation** is the cumulative amount of depreciation calculated at different points along a depreciable asset's useful life. For example, Figure 4-9 illustrates the scheduled amounts in this account for the store equipment acquired in Transaction C_1. As you can see by carefully studying this figure, the Accumulated Depreciation account, like the Allowance for Uncollectibles account described earlier, is a contra account. That is, it reduces its primary asset account, Store Equipment, from its original cost to what is called book value. **Book value** is the difference between a depreciable asset's original cost and the amount of its cost consumed with the passage of time known as accumulated depreciation.

FIGURE 4-9

The scheduled balances in the depreciation expense and store equipment—accumulated depreciation accounts created by transaction C_1

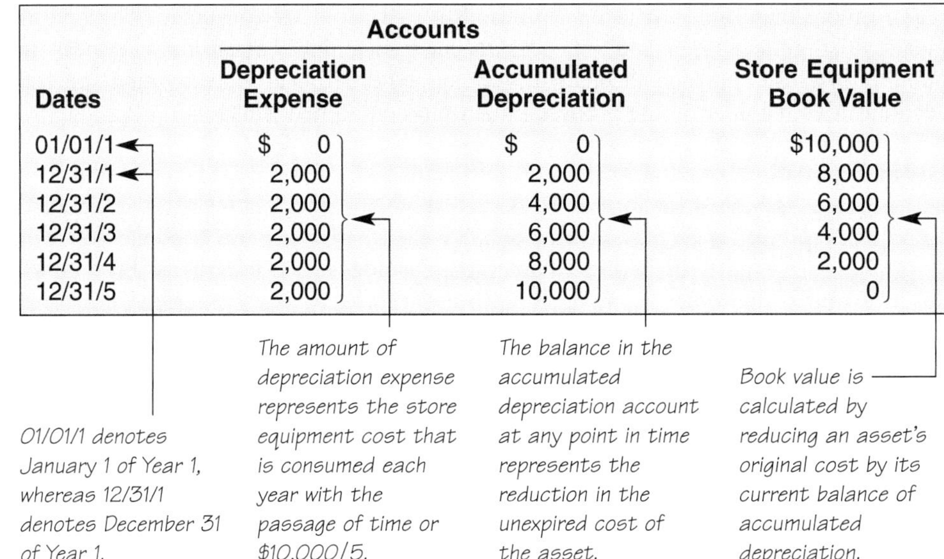

	Accounts		
Dates	Depreciation Expense	Accumulated Depreciation	Store Equipment Book Value
01/01/1	$ 0	$ 0	$10,000
12/31/1	2,000	2,000	8,000
12/31/2	2,000	4,000	6,000
12/31/3	2,000	6,000	4,000
12/31/4	2,000	8,000	2,000
12/31/5	2,000	10,000	0

Figure 4-10 shows how primary and contra accounts are presented for CMU, and then for the global giant, IBM. Despite the huge dollar difference and the fact that CMU's report represents a single account rather than the thousands of accounts summarized in IBM's report, there is no essential difference between how the depreciation concept is reported by each company.

Essentially, you account for all property, plant, and equipment accounts (other than land) by first setting up a contra account and then subtracting its balance from the primary account balance. You might wonder why, in the case of CMU, depreciable assets themselves ($10,000 in Figure 4-10) are not simply reduced by the amount of depreciation ($2,000), rather than using this more complicated method. After all, when you make a cash payment, you simply decrease your cash account directly.

In fact, reporting the effect of depreciation in a contra asset account actually enhances the decision making of those who study the balance sheet. This practice allows an entity to report the original cost of its depreciable assets and, therefore, allows you to evaluate the relative size of the entity's investment in such assets. In contrast, decreasing the primary account directly for depreciation produces a zero balance after the useful life has expired ($10,000 cost minus $10,000 accumulated depreciation). This would require its removal from the balance sheet, despite the fact that it might still be in service after its estimated useful life has expired. The primary/contra

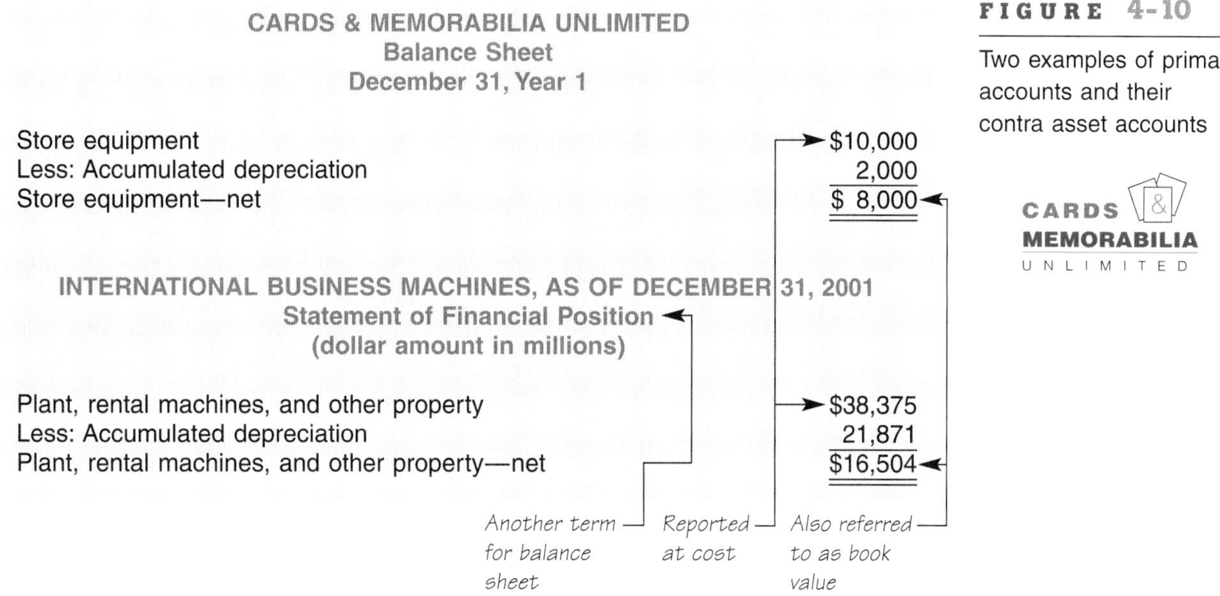

CARDS & MEMORABILIA UNLIMITED
Balance Sheet
December 31, Year 1
Store equipment $10,000
Less: Accumulated depreciation 2,000
Store equipment—net $ 8,000
INTERNATIONAL BUSINESS MACHINES, AS OF DECEMBER 31, 2001
Statement of Financial Position
(dollar amount in millions)
Plant, rental machines, and other property $38,375
Less: Accumulated depreciation 21,871
Plant, rental machines, and other property—net $16,504
Another term for balance sheet
Reported at cost
Also referred to as book value

FIGURE 4-10

Two examples of primary accounts and their contra asset accounts

CARDS & MEMORABILIA UNLIMITED

approach, however, avoids potentially misleading results and allows you to roughly determine the relative age of a company's investment in depreciable assets. For example, decision makers might find it useful to know that a greater portion of IBM's depreciable assets have been consumed than those of CMU's, 56.5% ($21,741/$38,455) compared to 20% ($2,000/$10,000).

For some companies, natural resources, also called wasting assets, are such a significant asset, that they are reported in an account separated from property, plant, and equipment. For example, in its 2001 balance sheet, Weyerhaeuser Company reported nearly $1.8 billion of timber and timberlands. This asset is subject to what is called depletion. The concept of **depletion** is very similar to depreciation, except that it represents the cost of natural resources allocated to expense instead of the cost of depreciable assets allocated to expense. As you might guess, the contra asset account, Accumulated Depletion, is similar in concept to the accumulated depreciation account. The few companies that report natural resources nearly always combine their accumulated depletion and accumulated depreciation accounts on the balance sheet. Likewise, such companies also combine their depletion expense and depreciation expense accounts. Both practices make it very difficult for annual report users to determine what proportion of property, plant, and equipment is composed of natural resources.

The final type of property, plant, and equipment account is tangible property that is neither subject to depreciation nor depletion. Land, for example, is considered to have an unlimited useful life and, therefore, no depreciation or depletion calculation is possible.

Intangible Assets **Intangible assets** differ in only one major respect from assets included in Property, Plant, and Equipment: they do not have their value tied to physical substance. Examples of intangible assets include patents, copyrights, trademarks, franchises, computer programs, certain types of property leases, and goodwill. Goodwill is perhaps the most common intangible asset. **Goodwill** represents the cost of acquiring another company over and above the total market price of that company's individual assets less liabilities (net assets). In 1999, for example, Ford Motor Company purchased a majority interest in Volvo, a Swedish manufacturer of luxury cars, and reported goodwill of $2.5 billion on its balance sheet! Some intangible assets are subject to a process known as amortization. This means that as the future benefits of such assets are used up or consumed, the cost of the intangible asset is allocated to expense. The term **amortization** is identical in concept to depreciation and depletion, except that it represents the cost of intangible assets rather than the cost of tangible depreciable assets or natural resources.

Other Assets The account titled **Other Assets** represents assets that do not conveniently fit into any other category (recall this account title in The Coca-Cola Company balance sheet in Figure 4-6). Examples are idle land held for future use and **organization costs**, or costs associated with beginning a business. An organization cost for CMU is the fee it pays for obtaining a business license. For a corporation, however, such costs will typically include legal costs, incorporation fees, and costs of printing stock certificates.

What Are Typical Current Liability Account Titles?

Current liability account titles are generally listed on the right side of the balance sheet in the order of their due dates, with the earliest due date listed first. Figure 4-11 shows some typical current liabilities and their appropriate account titles. Note that some balance sheets summarize these amounts a company owes to employees and others for services provided by using the term **accrued liabilities**.

FIGURE 4-11

Typical accrued liabilities and their specific account titles

Money Owed For	Account Title
Services from suppliers	Accounts Payable
Supplies from suppliers	Accounts Payable
Merchandise and raw materials from suppliers	Accounts Payable
Wages and salaries to employees	Wages or Salaries Payable
Taxes to government units	Taxes Payable or Estimated Tax Liability
Interest on loans	Interest Payable

Not all current liabilities represent cash owed to creditors for goods or services provided. Suppose, for example, a seller has not fulfilled its half of the exchange and "owes" goods or services to the customer who has paid in advance. These liabilities are called **advances from customers** (Transaction I), **deferred revenues**, or **unearned revenues**.

When a company has noncurrent liabilities, such as notes payable or bonds payable, it will often report the portion of the liability that will be repaid within the standard cutoff of one year as a current liability. Such liabilities are often summarized under the account title **Current Portion of Long-Term Debt**.

What Are Typical Noncurrent Liability Account Titles?

The noncurrent liability account titles that might be found on the balance sheet include Mortgages Payable, Notes Payable, Bonds Payable, Capital Lease Obligations, Deferred Income Taxes, Warranty Liabilities, and Pension Obligations. A **mortgage payable** is a special form of promissory note or **note payable** in which the borrower gives up its unrestricted ownership of property to a lender in return for a loan from that lender. A **bond payable** differs from a note payable in that the promise to pay is included in a more formal legal document or instrument; the amounts owed are to numerous parties rather than one company; and the term of the loan is often longer than that of a typical note payable.

When property is leased under a contract that is essentially equivalent to an exclusive purchase of the asset, as when a mining company leases land from the government for 99 years, the agreement is treated as a **capital lease**; and both an asset and **Capital Lease Obligations**, a related liability, must be reported on the balance sheet. A lease obligation such as Transaction E, however, is not reported on the balance sheet. Such a lease is referred to as an **operating lease**. A lessee usually prefers an operating lease because it is a form of financing commonly described as **off-balance-sheet financing**. That is, Susan gains access to property without being required to report the obligation on her balance sheet. The distinction between capital and operating leases is covered in Appendix 13–1(which you will find at www.mhhe.com/solomon).

The account title Deferred Income Taxes arises from the fact that the income taxes owed to the state and federal governments are not identical to the income tax expense reported in the annual report. That is, many companies are able to calculate revenues and expenses on their tax return in such a way as to allow them to postpone or *defer* taxes. When such a temporary difference between income tax payable and income tax expense occurs, it is captured in a special liability account called **Deferred Income Taxes**.

The account title **Warranty Liabilities** represents estimated amounts owed to customers for product defects, whereas the account title **Pension Obligations** represents the present value of estimated future retirement payments to present and retired employees.

What Are Typical Owners' Equity Account Titles?

Two contributed capital account titles found in stockholders' equity or shareholders' equity are the Capital Stock and Additional Paid-in Capital accounts. The earnings from profitable operations retained in the business are represented by the Retained Earnings account.

Capital Stock When the owners of a corporation contribute cash or other assets to the business, they receive **capital stock** or ownership shares in exchange. Capital stock generally is divided into two types: common and preferred. **Common stock** carries both voting rights and the right to share in corporate profits whenever dividends are declared by the board of directors. Although **preferred stock** does not usually carry voting rights, it provides owners of this type of stock a preferred status with respect to dividends and assets if the corporation goes out of business. The number of individual units of capital stock or *shares* one receives in exchange for an investment is documented with a *stock certificate*, an example of which is shown in Figure 4-12.

Each share of both common and preferred stock is often assigned an arbitrary value called **par** or **stated value**, which is listed in the owners' equity section of the balance sheet. Although this arbitrary value has some legal significance, it is important that you know about par and stated value now because it allows you to determine the actual dollar amount recorded in these accounts. For example, if you multiply the $0.75 par value shown in the 2001 balance sheet of ChevronTexaco Corporation by the 1,137,021,057 shares of common stock issued, you will see how the preparers of the 2001 annual report calculated the reported common stock dollar amount of $853 million.

Additional Paid-In Capital **Additional Paid-In Capital**, also called **Capital Paid in Excess of Par Value**, is the title of the account that measures the amounts invested by owners of common or preferred stock that are in excess of par or stated

FIGURE 4-12

A stock certificate for one share of The Walt Disney Company

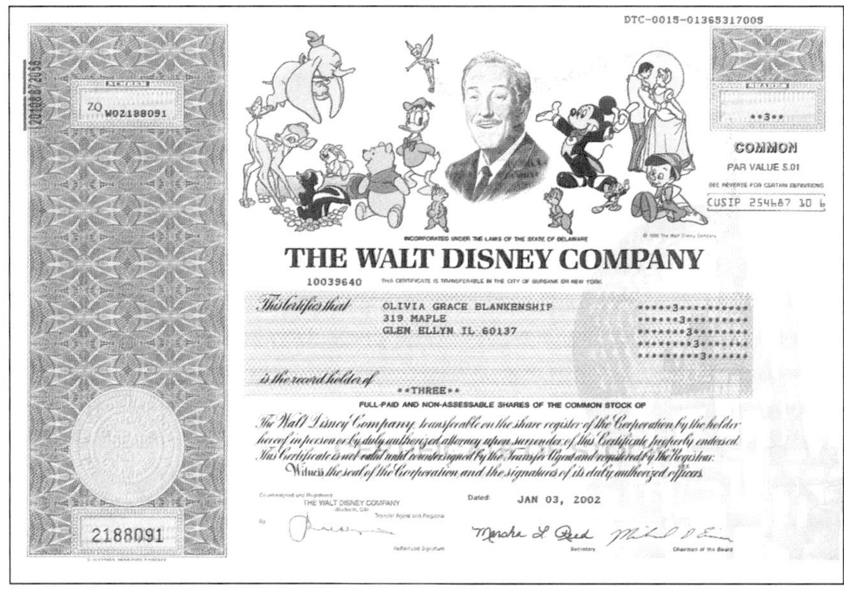

value. For example, if you were to buy 100 shares of $1 par value common stock at $10 per share, the company would increase its cash account by $1,000 (100 shares × $10 per share), its common stock account by $100 (100 shares × $1 par value), and its additional paid-in capital account by $900 (100 shares × $9 paid in excess of par value). In its July 31, 2001, balance sheet, for example, Intuit Inc., a software developer, listed both Common Stock and Additional Paid-In Capital account titles. The common stock was composed of 210,526,239 shares at $0.01 par value, or approximately $2,105,000, whereas the additional paid-in capital is reported at the excess over par of $1,723,385,000.

Retained Earnings **Retained Earnings** is an account title that represents the second component of shareholders' equity, namely earnings from profitable operations retained in the business. As you learned in Chapter 3, retained earnings consists of accumulated earnings or net income reduced by any net losses and dividends declared to date. In its September 30, 2001, balance sheet, for example, The Walt Disney Company reported that its retained earnings balance of over $12 billion—$12,171,000,000—was composed of a $12,767,000,000 September 30, 2000 balance minus $158,000,000 of net loss minus $438,000,000 of dividends.

Treasury Stock Recall that you briefly learned about this account in Chapter 3 when we discussed Merck's annual report. Essentially, **treasury stock** represents shares of stock that have been reacquired by the corporation and taken out of circulation for the present time. The cost of repurchasing these shares is subtracted from stockholders' equity as a whole. For example, The Walt Disney Company's September 30, 2001, balance sheet reports just such a subtraction of $1.395 billion in its stockholders' equity section from the repurchase of 81.4 million shares. Although corporations reacquire their stock for many different reasons, one incentive is to hold these shares for reissuance as employee stock options.

You have just completed a fairly comprehensive description of the account titles found in the classified balance sheets of major companies. To help you reinforce what you have just learned, Figure 4-13 presents a model classified balance sheet. Look at this figure carefully, and resist the temptation to skim its content. Take time to reacquaint yourself with the account titles and their placement.

FIGURE 4-13 A model classified balance sheet

IDEALISTIC COMPANY
Balance Sheet (in thousands)
December 31

Assets			Liabilities and Owners' Equity	
Current Assets			**Current Liabilities**	
Cash and cash equivalents		$ 75,000	Accounts payable	$ 80,000
Marketable securities		20,000	Loans payable	25,000
Accounts and notes receivable		60,000	Salaries and wages payable	15,000
Less: Allowance for uncollectibles		(3,000)	Taxes payable	18,000
Merchandise inventory		135,000	Current portion of long-term debt	7,000
Prepaid assets		13,000	Deferred revenues	5,000
Total current assets		$300,000	Total current liabilities	$150,000
Investments		$ 55,000	**Noncurrent Liabilities**	
			Notes payable	$100,000
			Capital lease obligations	125,000
Property, plant, & equipment	$250,000		Deferred income taxes	50,000
Less: Accumulated depreciation	50,000	$200,000	Contingencies (see Note 10)	
				$275,000
Intangible Assets			**Shareholders' Equity**	
Capital leases	$125,000		Common stock, $2 par, 100,000 shares	$200,000
Patents net of amortization	45,000	$170,000	Capital paid in excess of par value	50,000
			Retained earnings	100,000
			Less treasury stock, at cost	(25,000)
Other assets		$ 25,000		$325,000
Total assets		$750,000	Total liabilities and shareholders' equity	$750,000

How Did CMU Avoid a Negative Cash Balance during the Year?

INSIGHT

If you study Figure 4-2's cash column, you will see that CMU's cash account had a $5,000 negative balance after recording the effects of Transaction J_1. Earlier in this chapter, however, you were told CMU did not experience a negative cash balance during the year. How could this happen?

The explanation requires you to look at a transaction not yet covered but available to you in the first-year CMU transactions shown in Appendix C. This transaction is M, representing daily cash sales. As you saw in Chapter 3, cash sales began on January 9, so it is reasonable to assume that at least $5,000 of the $63,200 of annual cash sales entered the business by July 31. The **insight** you should gain here is that, in reality, CMU did not experience a negative cash balance during the year. In this chapter, we have isolated the balance sheet transactions for instructional purposes. But in "real life," income statement transactions would not have been delayed.

Summary with Key Terms

The number in parentheses following each **key term** is the page number on which the term is defined.

In this chapter, you examined in detail the financial statement known as the balance sheet. To broaden your background, the chapter began with a brief history of the balance sheet followed by a return to Cards & Memorabilia Unlimited to analyze the effects of Transactions E–L on its balance sheet.

Generally, an annual report contains a **classified balance sheet** (145) that divides accounts into current assets and noncurrent assets and current liabilities and noncurrent liabilities. These categories enable decision makers to better evaluate the business's **solvency** (147) or its relative ability to meet maturing liabilities by converting noncash assets into cash. Current asset account titles listed in the order of their **liquidity** (147) include **Cash** (148), **Cash Equivalents** (148), **Marketable Securities** (148), **Accounts Receivable** and **Notes Receivable** (149), **Merchandise Inventory** (152), and **Prepayments** (153). Noncurrent asset account titles include **Investments** (153), **Property, Plant, and Equipment** (153), **Intangible Assets** (155), and **Other Assets** (156). Two intangible asset account titles described were **Goodwill** (155) and **Organization Costs** (156).

In an *Insight*, you learned that investments in debt and equity securities can be classified into one of three categories. **Trading securities** (150) are treated as current assets and are reported at market value. **Available-for-sale securities** (151) are included in either the current or noncurrent sections of the balance sheet and are also reported at market value. Finally, **held-to-maturity securities** (151) apply only to debt securities, are included in either the current or noncurrent sections of the balance sheet, and are reported at their cost.

A special category is that of the **contra** asset **accounts** (151). Examples of contra asset account titles include **Allowance for Uncollectible Accounts** (151), **Accumulated Depreciation** (154), and Accumulated Depletion. When the total amount of either **depreciation** (153), **depletion** (155), or **amortization** (156) accumulated in a contra account is subtracted from the cost of its **primary asset account** (151), the result is **book value** (154).

Current liability accounts often include a general account category called **accrued liabilities** (156), as well as the account titles **Advances from Customers** (156)—also often called **Deferred Revenue** (156) or **Unearned Revenue** (156)—and the **Current Portion of Long-Term Debt** (156). Noncurrent liability account titles include **Mortgages Payable** (156), **Notes Payable** (156), **Bonds Payable** (156), **Capital Lease Obligations** (157), **Deferred Income Taxes** (157), **Warranty Liabilities** (157), and **Pension Obligations** (157). In addition, the essential distinction between the **operating lease** (157), one form of **off-balance-sheet financing** (157), and the **capital lease** (157) was introduced. Finally, owners' equity account titles include the generic **Capital Stock** (157) (which is divided into both **Common Stock** (157) and **Preferred Stock** (157), **Additional Paid-In Capital** (157) or **Capital Paid in Excess of Par Value** (157), **Retained Earnings** (158) and **Treasury Stock** (158). In this section, the terms **par value** (157) and **stated value** (157) were briefly introduced.

Making Business Decisions

YOUR PERFORMANCE OBJECTIVE 2
(page 18)

After working for a large advertising agency for nearly 10 years, Lily Duchamp and Rita Malvino have decided to open their own advertising agency, Duchamp & Malvino. Their business will provide radio, TV, Web, and print advertising for small to mid-sized companies in the greater Los Angeles area. Currently, they have six clients lined up, 1500 square feet of office space, an assistant, and an accountant, Jennifer Bauman, who is setting up their accounting information system.

Today, Jennifer is interviewing Lily and Rita about the nature of their business to help her better design their accounting information system. Jennifer realizes that she must devote some of the meeting time to explaining the nature of account titles when she hears Lily's and Rita's questions.

"Where do account titles come from and who decides what account titles a business will have?" asks Lily.

"How are these account titles managed and what's to stop me from using the title Advances from Clients for money received from clients prior to service and Lily using the title Unearned Client Revenue?" asks Rita.

"Well, you certainly are full of questions today," Jennifer remarks. "And I will answer all of them. First, the vehicle that the accounting profession uses to manage account titles is called the *chart of accounts.* It's a complete list of an entity's accounts organized with a unique assigned number for each account. For balance sheet accounts, asset account titles are listed first, liability account titles second, and then owners' equity account titles. Other accounts track particular kinds of revenues and expenses. There are some generally accepted account titles and numbering systems that accountants use,[4] but most companies will also customize some titles to reflect unique characteristics of their industry. In advertising, for example, the liability account you asked about is sometimes titled Client Advance Payments.

"Although I could do it for you myself, I believe you will benefit most if one of you sets up an initial chart of accounts. Even with your lack of accounting experience, this process is sure to provide you with a greater grasp of your business, and it might even be fun."

When Rita expresses interest, Jennifer says, "You give it a try, and then I'll take a look at it to help you finalize your chart of accounts."

Required

1. Find out as much as you can about advertising agencies from the Web, friends, family members, or actual professionals. Keep detailed notes as you might need them for Research Assignment 4-1. Then decide what advertising specialties you'd like Duchamp & Malvino to pursue. That is, would you prefer they engage in all or only some of the following: art work, graphic design, copywriting services, media selection and insertion, market research, public relations, direct mail, or Internet services?
2. Make a list of the departments you believe Duchamp & Malvino must establish. For example, an advertising agency might have a campaign department, an art department, various production services such as photography and printing, and an account executives department for employees who represent the agency to clients.
3. Based on the list you created in (2), decide whether to departmentalize by client account or by advertising function. New agencies, for example, may departmentalize by individual clients, whereas larger, more mature agencies may departmentalize by advertising functions such as art, media, or production.
4. Based on your decisions above, determine what account titles Rita should include in her chart of accounts for Duchamp & Malvino. Do not include the numbering scheme because you'll learn more about that in Chapter 9. For now, make a list of what you think the balance sheet account titles should be by setting up three distinct account groups: assets, liabilities, and owners' equity.

Questions

YOUR PERFORMANCE OBJECTIVE 4 (page 22)

4-1 Explain in your own words the meanings of these key business terms.

Current asset terms:

a. Cash
b. Cash equivalents
c. Marketable securities
d. Accounts and notes receivable (distinguish between)
e. Allowance for uncollectible accounts
f. Merchandise inventories
g. Prepayments

Noncurrent asset terms:

h. Investments
i. Property, plant, and equipment
j. Accumulated depreciation and accumulated depletion (distinguish between)
k. Goodwill
l. Organization costs

Current liability terms:

m. Accrued liabilities
n. Advances from customers
o. Current portion of long-term debt

[4] For example, see *Portfolio of Accounting Systems for Small and Medium-Sized Businesses,* National Society of Public Accountants, Prentice Hall, 1992.

Noncurrent liability terms:
p. Mortgage payable
q. Notes payable
r. Bonds payable
s. Capital lease obligations
t. Deferred taxes
u. Warranty liabilities
v. Pension obligations
Shareholders' equity terms:
w. Capital stock
x. Common stock
y. Preferred stock
z. Additional paid-in capital or capital paid in excess of par value
aa. Retained earnings
bb. Treasury stock

4-2 Explain why owner's equity is not affected in Transactions B through L of Cards & Memorabilia Unlimited.

4-3 Explain why Cards & Memorabilia Unlimited did not actually experience a negative cash balance immediately after recording Transaction J_1.

4-4 What is a classified balance sheet?

4-5 Explain two ways in which you can distinguish between a corporate balance sheet and a noncorporate balance sheet.

4-6 Explain why it is important to distinguish between the terms current and noncurrent when examining a balance sheet.

4-7 On what basis are assets organized?

4-8 On what basis are liabilities organized?

4-9 Distinguish between the terms "solvency" and "liquidity."

4-10 Explain why the *held-to-maturity security* classification does not include equity securities.

4-11 Distinguish between *trading securities* and *available-for-sale securities.*

> Use an annual report (your instructor will assign a specific one or allow you to choose one) to answer Questions 4-12 through 4-16.

4-12 Find the current assets.
a. List the current asset accounts reported on the balance sheet.
b. What accounts listed in this chapter are not found in this report's balance sheet?
c. What current asset accounts shown in this report's balance sheet were not discussed in this chapter?

4-13 Find the noncurrent assets.
a. List the noncurrent asset accounts reported on the balance sheet.
b. What accounts listed in this chapter are not found in this report's balance sheet?
c. What noncurrent asset accounts shown in this report's balance sheet were not discussed in this chapter?

4-14 Find the current liabilities.
a. List the current liability accounts reported on the balance sheet.
b. What accounts listed in this chapter are not found in this report's balance sheet?
c. What current liability accounts shown in this report's balance sheet were not discussed in this chapter?

4-15 Find the noncurrent liabilities.
a. List the noncurrent liability accounts reported on the balance sheet.
b. What accounts listed in this chapter are not found in this report's balance sheet?
c. What noncurrent liability accounts shown in this report's balance sheet were not discussed in this chapter?

4-16 Find the owners' equity section.
a. List the owners' equity accounts reported on the balance sheet.
b. What accounts listed in this chapter are not found in this report's balance sheet?
c. What owners' equity accounts shown in this report's balance sheet were not discussed in this chapter?

4-17 What is a contra account? How is it related to a primary account? Provide at least one example of a contra account and its primary account.
4-18 How is an asset's book value calculated?
4-19 Distinguish between depreciation, depletion, and amortization.
4-20 Explain the justification for reporting organization costs as an asset.
4-21 Name at least five current liability accounts that can be included in the accrued liabilities category.
4-22 Distinguish between the account titles Advances from Customers, Deferred Revenue, and Unearned Revenue.
4-23 What is off-balance-sheet financing?
4-24 Evaluate this statement—All leases are reported in the liability section of the balance sheet.
4-25 Distinguish between par value and stated value.

Reinforcement Exercises

E4-1 Asking the Right Questions: A Group Activity

YOUR PERFORMANCE OBJECTIVE 4
(page 22)

It's often said that knowing the right answer is not nearly as important as asking the right question. Asking the right question is a problem-solving skill that will help you make sound business decisions. In this exercise, you will review the vocabulary introduced in Chapter 4 by creating questions to match answers—similar to a popular TV show.

Required

a. Given an answer, what's the question?
Choose *three* of the following terms to serve as an answer. For each term, create an appropriate question. For example, if you choose the term *balance sheet,* you might create the question—*What financial statement shows the assets, liabilities, and owners' equity of an entity on a specific date?*

Solvency	Depreciation	Par value
Liquidity	Operating lease	Accrued liabilities
Book value	Cash equivalents	Contra accounts
Investments	Market value	Marketable securities

b. Are you sure that's the question?
Have each member of your group read aloud the questions they developed in Requirement (a). As a group, decide whether each question is an accurate match for an answer. Once satisfied that all questions are appropriate, the group, as a whole, chooses the three best questions created within the group. Record the three questions chosen (with their answers) on separate pieces of paper or index cards and give them to your instructor.

c. What's the answer?
To ensure that you have learned the vocabulary terms listed in Requirement (a), your instructor will now quiz you on the questions written by all of your classmates.

E4-2 Transaction Analysis

YOUR PERFORMANCE OBJECTIVE 5a
(page 137)

The following selected transactions of Stober Subway Sandwiches represent important business activity during February. Analyze the effects of these transactions on the elements of Stober's balance sheet by using the form provided. Transaction (a) is filled in for you. Use the abbreviation NE for "no effect" if none of the accounts are affected by the transaction.

		Fundamental Equation			
Trans-action	Asset Account Title	Assets	= Liabilities	+ Owner's Equity	Sources of Assets Account Title
a.	Food Inventory	6,000			
	Cash	(2,000)	4,000		Accounts Payable

Transactions

a. Food inventory costing $6,000 is purchased. Cash of $2,000 is paid with the balance payable in 30 days.
b. Stober pays suppliers $3,000 on account.
c. Tom Stober, the owner, contributes $10,000 to his business to finance the purchase of a delivery truck and other costs.
d. A delivery truck costing $5,500 is purchased with cash.
e. Stober Subway Sandwiches pays $5,000 of the $25,000 amount owed the bank. *Hint:* Use the Bank Loan Payable account.
f. Employees are paid $2,000 for amounts owed to them.
g. Tom Stober withdraws $1,500 cash to finance his vacation.

YOUR PERFORMANCE OBJECTIVE 5a
(page 137)

E4-3 Transaction Analysis

The following selected transactions of Lovitz Apparel Company represent important business activity during April. Analyze the effects of these transactions on the elements of Lovitz's balance sheet by using the form provided. Transaction (a) is filled in for you. Use NE for no effect if none of the accounts are affected by the transaction.

		Fundamental Equation					
Trans-action	Asset Account Title	Assets	=	Liabilities	+	Owner's Equity	Sources of Assets Account Title
a.	Land	50,000					
	Cash	(10,000)		40,000			Note Payable

Transactions

a. Land costing $50,000 is acquired by making a $10,000 down payment and issuing a note payable for the balance.
b. The company buys equipment costing $20,000 on credit.
c. The company arranges for a $50,000 line of credit from the bank. No amounts have yet been borrowed.
d. The proprietor, Jon Lovitz, arranges a personal bank loan of $10,000 to increase his financing in the company.
e. Jon Lovitz transfers $8,000 from his personal savings account to his business checking account.
f. The company borrows $25,000 from its line of credit.
g. Inventory costing $10,000 is acquired on credit.
h. The company pays its inventory supplier $10,000.
i. Jon Lovitz withdraws $6,000 from his business checking account for personal use.

YOUR PERFORMANCE OBJECTIVE 5a
(page 137)

E4-4 Transaction Analysis

The following selected transactions of Fabio's Tanning Salon represent important business activity during June. Analyze the effects of these transactions on the elements of Fabio's balance sheet by using the form provided. Transaction (a) has been filled in for you. Use NE for no effect if none of the accounts are affected by the transaction.

	Fundamental Equation							
	Assets		=	Liabilities		+	Owner's Equity	
Trans-action	Increase	Decrease		Increase	Decrease		Increase	Decrease
a.	20,000						20,000	

Transactions

a. Fabio invests an additional $20,000 in his tanning salon business.
b. Fabio purchases tanning booth equipment for $40,000. He pays $15,000 in cash and issues a note for the balance.
c. Shortly after the purchase in (b), Fabio takes home a tanning booth costing $5,000 for his personal use.
d. The salon receives advances from customers of $10,000. This cash represents future tanning sessions that customers will receive over the next three months.

e. A six-month premium of $3,000 for specialized liability insurance is paid.
f. Various tanning supplies are purchased for $2,200 on account.
g. A payment of $1,200 is made to tanning suppliers.
h. A tanning booth that was acquired for $5,000 is deemed unnecessary and is sold at its original cost for cash.

E4-5 Transaction Analysis

YOUR PERFORMANCE OBJECTIVE 5a (page 137)

Martha Stewart and Rod Stewart form an entertainment corporation and engage in the following transactions during their first month of business. Analyze the effects of these transactions on the elements of the corporate balance sheet by using the form provided. Transaction (a) has been filled in for you. Use NE for no effect if none of the accounts are affected by the transaction.

		Fundamental Equation					
Trans-action	Asset Account Title	Assets	=	Liabilities	+	Owner's Equity	Sources of Assets Account Title
a.	Cash	10,000				10,000	Common Stock

Transactions

a. One thousand shares of common stock are issued—500 shares to Martha Stewart and 500 shares to Rod Stewart—at $10.00 per share.
b. The company pays $800 in advance for the first month's rent of office space.
c. The company borrows $5,000 from a bank in exchange for a two-year promissory note.
d. Furniture and fixtures are purchased for $6,000 by paying $1,500 in cash and charging the balance to a credit card.
e. Office supplies are purchased for $850 cash.
f. The company pays $1,500 to reduce the credit card obligation incurred in (d).
g. An advance of $4,000 is received from a studio for a script.

E4-6 Transaction Analysis

YOUR PERFORMANCE OBJECTIVE 5a (page 137)

Several August transactions from Jeopardy Company, a proprietorship, are analyzed below. Describe in one sentence the most reasonable explanation for each transaction, referring to each transaction by its letter name.

	Fundamental Equation					
	Assets		Liabilities		Owner's Equity	
Trans-action	Increase	Decrease	Increase	Decrease	Increase	Decrease
a.	100,000				100,000	
b.	40,000		40,000			
c.			5,000	5,000		
d.	7,000	7,000				
e.		3,600		3,600		
f.		12,000				12,000

E4-7 Transaction Analysis

YOUR PERFORMANCE OBJECTIVE 5a (page 137)

Carl Canola decides to start a business that sells a variety of popcorn and popcorn accessories. The business, called Popcorn Mania, engages in the following transactions during January, the first month of operations. Analyze the effects of these transactions on the elements of Popcorn Mania's balance sheet by using the form provided:

	Assets				=	Liabilities			+	Owner's Equity	
	Cash	Prepaid Rent	Product Inventory	Store Equipment		Accounts Payable	Adv. from Customers	Bank Loan Payable		Contributed Capital	Retained Earnings
a.											

Transactions

a. Carl invests $98,000 cash and $2,000 of his personal popcorn poppers to finance his business.
b. A $20,000 purchase of store equipment on January 2 is financed with a one-year bank loan that bears an annual interest rate of 10%.
c. Carl leases a small store at an annual rental of $12,000. Rent for the first six months is paid in advance.
d. A variety of popcorn accessories costing $15,000 are purchased from a supplier on account.
e. Popcorn accessories in the amount of $25,000 are purchased from suppliers for cash.
f. The company receives cash advances from customers totaling $5,000 for the yet to be delivered Nonfat Coconut Oil Popper.
g. An $8,000 installment is paid on the bank loan.
h. A single case of popcorn poppers purchased in Transaction (d) and costing $750 arrived in damaged condition. The poppers were capable of shocking users and so were returned to the supplier for full credit. *Hint:* These poppers were intended for resale.
i. The company pays $7,250 of the remaining account payable.
j. Carl withdraws $10,000 of cash from his business.

YOUR PERFORMANCE OBJECTIVE 5b
(page 57)

E4-8 Preparing a Balance Sheet
Prepare an unclassified balance sheet for Stober Subway Sandwiches as of January 31, given the following data.

Cash	$ 8,000
Food inventory	15,000
Equipment	50,000
Accounts payable	7,000
Salaries payable	3,000
Bank loan payable	25,000
Contributed capital	?
Retained earnings	28,000

YOUR PERFORMANCE OBJECTIVE 5b
(page 57)

E4-9 Preparing a Balance Sheet
Prepare an unclassified balance sheet for Lovitz Apparel Company as of March 31, given the following data:

Cash	$20,000
Inventory	12,000
Equipment	31,000
Accounts payable	5,500
Salaries payable	2,000
Note payable	10,000
Contributed capital	21,500
Retained earnings	?

YOUR PERFORMANCE OBJECTIVE 5b
(page 57)

E4-10 Preparing a Balance Sheet
Prepare an unclassified balance sheet for Fabio's Tanning Salon as of May 31, given the following data:

Cash	$55,000
Tanning supplies	16,000
Tanning booth equipment	25,000
Accounts payable	7,500
Salaries payable	2,500
Note payable	10,000
Contributed capital	80,000
Retained earnings	?

E4-11 Preparing a Balance Sheet
Prepare an unclassified balance sheet for Stewart & Stewart Corporation on the basis of your transaction analysis in Exercise 4-5.

YOUR PERFORMANCE OBJECTIVE 5b
(page 57)

E4-12 Preparing a Balance Sheet
Prepare an unclassified balance sheet for Popcorn Mania on the basis of your transaction analysis in Exercise 4-7.

YOUR PERFORMANCE OBJECTIVE 5b
(page 57)

E4-13 Preparing the Owners' Equity Section of a Balance Sheet
A local business has assets of $750,000 and liabilities of $500,000. Present the owners' equity section of the business balance sheet under the following independent assumptions:

a. The business is a sole proprietorship owned by Clair Janes.
b. The business is a partnership. Clair Janes has a 35% interest, Donald Roark has a 40% interest, and Robert Walker has a 25% interest.
c. The business is a corporation. Outstanding common stock was originally issued for $180,000, of which $100,000 represented par value. The remaining owners' equity represents accumulated earnings retained in the business.

YOUR PERFORMANCE OBJECTIVE 5b
(page 57)

E4-14 Classifying Transactions into Statement of Cash Flow Activities
Using the discussion found on pages 140–141 and the information found in Figure 3-9, classify CMU Transactions E, C_2, and F into the appropriate activity as reported in the statement of cash flows.

YOUR PERFORMANCE OBJECTIVE 7c
(page 64)

E4-15 Classifying Transactions into Statement of Cash Flow Activities
Using the discussion found on pages 141–142 and the information found in Figure 3-9, classify CMU Transactions H, I, J_1, and K_1 into the appropriate activity as reported in the statement of cash flows.

E4-16 Classifying Account Titles
For each of the following accounts, indicate whether it is a current asset (CA), noncurrent asset (NA), current liability (CL), or noncurrent liability (NL):

a. Prepaid Rent
b. Accounts Payable
c. Merchandise Inventory
d. Store Equipment
e. Organization Costs
f. Cash Equivalents
g. Advances from Customers
h. Notes Payable
i. Current Maturities of Noncurrent Debt
j. Notes Receivable

YOUR PERFORMANCE OBJECTIVE 11b
(page 99)

E4-17 Classifying Account Titles
For each of the following accounts, indicate whether it is an asset, a liability, owners' equity, revenue, or an expense:

a. Cost of Goods Sold
b. Organization Costs
c. Accumulated Depreciation
d. Treasury Stock
e. Allowance for Uncollectibles
f. Common Stock
g. Amortization Expense
h. Service Revenue
i. Current Portion of Long-Term Debt
j. Capital Lease Obligation
k. Rent Expense
l. Capital Paid in Excess of Par Value
m. Susan Newman, Drawing

YOUR PERFORMANCE OBJECTIVE 11b
(page 99)

E4-18 Classifying Account Titles
Below are classifications frequently found on classified balance sheets within annual reports. Place the letter of the correct classification next to each of the numbered accounts.

a. Current Assets
b. Investments
c. Property, Plant, and Equipment
d. Intangible Assets
e. Other Assets
f. Current Liabilities
g. Noncurrent Liabilities
h. Shareholders' Equity
i. Nonbalance-sheet account

1. Loans Payable
2. Prepaid Rent
3. Salaries Expense
4. Common Stock
5. Merchandise Inventory
6. Property Taxes Payable

YOUR PERFORMANCE OBJECTIVE 11b
(page 99)

7. Retained Earnings
8. Marketable Securities
9. Undeposited Cash
10. Interest Revenue
11. Mortgage Payable
12. Cost of Goods Sold
13. Accumulated Depreciation
14. Deferred Revenue

YOUR PERFORMANCE OBJECTIVE 13 (page 105)

E4-19 Financial Statement Relationships
Calculate retained earnings as of February 28 using the information found in Exercises 4-2 and 4-8. *Hints:* The January 31 retained earnings account balance represents the beginning retained earnings balance for February and February's withdrawals are given.

YOUR PERFORMANCE OBJECTIVE 13 (page 105)

E4-20 Financial Statement Relationships
Calculate retained earnings as of April 30 using the information found in Exercises 4-3 and 4-9. *Hints:* The March 31 retained earnings account balance represents the beginning retained earnings balance for April and April's withdrawals are given.

YOUR PERFORMANCE OBJECTIVE 13 (page 105)

E4-21 Financial Statement Analysis

a. Calculate how much of the $1,648,000,000 in The Coca-Cola Company cash and cash equivalents account is cash, using information found in Figures 4-6 and 4-7.
b. Calculate how much of the $1,863,000,000 in the Coca-Cola Company marketable securities and other assets account is marketable securities, using information found in Figures 4-6 and 4-7.

Critical Thinking Problems

YOUR PERFORMANCE OBJECTIVE 4 (page 22)

P4-1* Definition of an Asset
Use the following asset definition as well as the three essential conditions listed in the footnote at the bottom of this page to decide whether the events listed below give rise to an asset. **Assets**—resources that result from *past* transactions or events and that are expected to provide *future* economic benefits to the entity that holds them. If you believe an asset should be recognized, state its account title and amount.

a. A contract is signed by a company to buy a complete supply of inventory for next year.
b. A contract is signed by a company to buy $12,000 of inventory that will be delivered in the future.
c. Assume the contract in (b) is accompanied by a $4,000 payment.
d. Assume the contract in (b) results in delivery of the inventory in exchange for the $12,000 payment.
e. A merchandise order for $10,000 is received from a customer.
f. Assume the order in (e) is accompanied with $10,000 cash.
g. A $5,000 note due in six months is received from a customer for a sale of merchandise.
h. A good reputation developed with customers is estimated by company executives to be worth $25,000 in future benefits.
i. Manufacturing equipment is acquired by agreeing to pay a total of $27,000 over three years. Legal ownership of the equipment will transfer to the company after the last payment is made.
j. The rights to 50 acres of land are donated by a local government to attract your company.

YOUR PERFORMANCE OBJECTIVE 4 (page 22)

P4-2* Definition of a Liability
Use the following liability definition as well as the three essential conditions listed in the footnote at the bottom of this page to decide whether the following events give rise to a liability. **Liabilities** are resources that are *presently* owed to an entity and that are expected to be pro-

* Both P4-1 and P4-2 ask you to use the three essential conditions needed (introduced in Chapter 2) before recording any transaction. Thus, these three conditions are listed below to serve as a convenient reference for you.

1. The event must be measurable in dollars.
2. The event must be related to the entity being measured.
3. The event must affect the entity's current financial position.

vided in the *future* in return for resources received in the *past*. If you believe a liability should be recognized, state its account title and amount.

a. A new president of the company is hired under a contract whose terms begin next month and call for an annual salary of $100,000.
b. Cash of $50,000 is received from customers for products to be delivered in the future.
c. A $5,000 note due in six months is given to a supplier in exchange for inventory received.
d. A pension obligation of $35,000 is payable to a vice-president ten years from today in return for past and current service.
e. A contract is signed by a company to have its corporate offices remodeled for $30,000.
f. A contract is signed by a company to have its corporate offices remodeled for $30,000. Assume a $5,000 down payment is made.
g. Merchandise inventory is purchased by agreeing to pay $6,000 to the supplier within 30 days.
h. Cash of $100,000 is received in exchange for the issuance of long-term bonds.
i. Cash of $100,000 is received in exchange for the issuance of preferred stock.
j. A company signs an agreement with its employees' labor union, promising to provide enhanced medical and dental benefits, as well as increasing wages by 4%.

P4-3 Transaction Analysis

YOUR PERFORMANCE OBJECTIVE 5a (page 137)

You have seen different transaction analysis formats in Exercises 4-2, 4-4, and 4-7. Compare and contrast these formats in terms of their simplicity and usefulness.

Note: For each of Problems 4-4 to 4-8, you are to prepare a spreadsheet presentation of its transactions, where rows represent transactions and columns represent transaction number and account titles. Use the same form shown in Appendix C for Cards & Memorabilia Unlimited's analysis of transactions. Do not, however, expect your columns to be identical to those in Appendix C.

P4-4 Spreadsheet Transaction Analysis

YOUR PERFORMANCE OBJECTIVE 5a (page 137)

Use a spreadsheet to represent the transactions found in Exercise 4-2.

P4-5 Spreadsheet Transaction Analysis

Use a spreadsheet to represent the transactions found in Exercise 4-3.

P4-6 Spreadsheet Transaction Analysis

YOUR PERFORMANCE OBJECTIVE 5a (page 137)

Use a spreadsheet to represent the transactions found in Exercise 4-4.

P4-7 Spreadsheet Transaction Analysis

YOUR PERFORMANCE OBJECTIVE 5a (page 137)

Use a spreadsheet to represent the transactions found in Exercise 4-5.

P4-8 Spreadsheet Transaction Analysis

Use a spreadsheet to represent the transactions found in Exercise 4-7.

P4-9 Transaction Analysis

YOUR PERFORMANCE OBJECTIVE 5a (page 137)

The December 31 balance sheet of Traebec & Associates, Inc., a talent agency, is shown below in equation form. It is followed by January Transactions (a) through (h) whose effect on the fundamental accounting equation is also shown. Describe the most reasonable explanation in one sentence for each transaction.

	Assets					=	Liabilities			+	Shareholders' Equity	
	Cash	Accounts Receivable	Prepaid Insurance	Office Supplies	Equipment		Accounts Payable	Salaries Payable	Note Payable		Capital Stock	Retained Earnings
	$11,000	$14,000	$800	$1,400	$15,300		$6,000	$1,600	$5,000		$25,000	$4,900
a.	(1,200)				6,000				4,800			
b.				(400)			(400)					
c.	5,000										5,000	
d.	(5,000)								(5,000)			
e.	7,000	(7,000)										
f.	(3,000)						(3,000)					
g.	(1,600)							(1,600)				
h.				800			800					

YOUR PERFORMANCE OBJECTIVE 5b *(page 57)*

P4-10 Preparing a Balance Sheet

Prepare a classified balance sheet for Stober Subway Sandwiches as of February 28, given the opening account balances as of January 31, shown in Exercise 4-8, and the February transactions described in Exercise 4-2.

YOUR PERFORMANCE OBJECTIVE 5b *(page 57)*

P4-11 Preparing a Balance Sheet

Prepare a classified balance sheet for Lovitz Apparel Company as of April 30, given the opening account balances as of March 31, shown in Exercise 4-9, and the April transactions described in Exercise 4-3.

YOUR PERFORMANCE OBJECTIVE 5b *(page 57)*

P4-12 Preparing a Balance Sheet

Prepare a classified balance sheet for Fabio's Tanning Salon as of June 30, given the opening account balances as of May 31, shown in Exercise 4-10, and the June transactions described in Exercise 4-4.

YOUR PERFORMANCE OBJECTIVE 5b *(page 57)*

P4-13 Preparing a Balance Sheet

Prepare a classified balance sheet for Traebec & Associates as of January 31, given the opening account balances and the January transactions described in Problem 4-9.

YOUR PERFORMANCE OBJECTIVES 8, 9 *(pages 65, 68)*

P4-14 Ethical Issue

Knowing that investors and creditors are less concerned about a noncurrent liability than a current liability, why don't all companies simply reclassify all of their liabilities as noncurrent?

YOUR PERFORMANCE OBJECTIVE 9 *(page 68)*

P4-15 Users' Decision Process

The following statements are excerpts from an article by Donald J. Swanz, entitled "Doing Business in China," (*The CPA Journal*, March 1995, pages 42–45 & 49).

> The *China Daily* in its Bejiing edition of May 28, 1993, states "... the country's current accounting system remains an obstacle. Different types of enterprises run by different government departments have different ways of accounting." According to a report from the State Economic & Trade Commission, China now has more than 70 accounting systems.
>
> A unified system in more than name only must be implemented; one that will correlate with the political/economic transition underway. For example, government enterprise is now profit driven.
>
> Chinese auditing standards remain a weak point, as only vague official guidelines are in place. They are often expedited regardless of entity size and avoid the confrontation and probing style of Western audits because of Eastern ideas of 'saving face' and respect for seniority.

In your groups, respond to the following questions and then have a representative share your responses aloud with the entire class:

a. Based on the excerpts, explain how you think accounting and auditing in China differ from accounting and auditing in the United States.
b. How do you think Chinese accounting and auditing methods would affect the decision-making process for users of financial information?

YOUR PERFORMANCE OBJECTIVE 11b *(page 99)*

P4-16 Classifying Account Titles

For each of the accounts shown below, indicate whether it is a current asset (CA), noncurrent asset (NA), current liability, (CL) or noncurrent liability (NL).

a. Petty Cash
b. Undeposited Cash or Cash on Hand
c. Finished Goods Inventory
d. Store Equipment
e. Organization Costs
f. Advances to Employees
g. Advances from Customers
h. Notes Payable
i. Current Maturities of Noncurrent Debt
j. Rent Receivable

YOUR PERFORMANCE OBJECTIVE 11b *(page 99)*

P4-17 Creating a Chart of Accounts

Using titles introduced in this chapter and *Appendix B*, create no more than 15 account titles that you would expect to find on a balance sheet of a small bookstore. Divide the accounts you choose into assets, liabilities, and owners' equity.

P4-18 Creating a Chart of Accounts
Using titles introduced in this chapter and *Appendix B*, create no more than 15 account titles that you would expect to find on a balance sheet of a three-partner law firm. Divide the accounts you choose into assets, liabilities, and owners' equity.

YOUR PERFORMANCE OBJECTIVE 11b
(page 99)

P4-19 Creating a Chart of Accounts
Using titles introduced in this chapter and *Appendix B*, create no more than 15 account titles that you would expect to find on a balance sheet of a family-owned, single screen movie theater. Divide the accounts you choose into assets, liabilities, and owners' equity.

YOUR PERFORMANCE OBJECTIVE 11b
(page 99)

P4-20 Creating a Chart of Accounts
Using titles introduced in this chapter and *Appendix B*, create no more than 15 account titles that you would expect to find on a balance sheet of a restaurant. Divide the accounts you choose into assets, liabilities, and owners' equity.

YOUR PERFORMANCE OBJECTIVE 11b
(page 99)

P4-21 Creating a Chart of Accounts
Refer to this chapter's *Making Business Decisions*. Assume that Jennifer is planning to use QuickBooks®, an accounting software package, for the agency's transactions. QuickBooks provides the following list of balance sheet account types in its chart of accounts. Write an essay in which you compare and contrast the following list of account types to those described in this chapter.

Bank account	Other asset	Current liability
Accounts receivable	Accounts payable	Long-term liability
Other current asset	Credit card	Equity
Fixed asset		

YOUR PERFORMANCE OBJECTIVE 11b
(page 99)

P4-22 Foreign Currency Translation
Refer to the balance sheet of Derrick Roose found at the very beginning of this chapter. Given that there are 20 shillings in a pound and 12 pence in a shilling, verify that the calculation of the change in capital is correct by showing your calculations.

YOUR PERFORMANCE OBJECTIVE 12
(page 102)

P4-23 Financial Statement Analysis
Darcy Hannah owns Roxanne's, a beauty parlor catering to the rich and famous. Her latest balance sheet, shown as follows, was submitted to Hanks Bank as part of her application for a business expansion loan.

YOUR PERFORMANCE OBJECTIVES 5, 6
(pages 57, 59)

ROXANNE'S
Balance Sheet
December 31

Assets		Liabilities	
Cash	$ 11,000	Accounts payable	$ 10,000
Accounts receivable	2,725	Automobile loan	6,500
Cosmetic supplies	1,050	Salaries payable	7,700
Wig inventory	25,000	Home mortgage	120,000
Equipment	4,000		$144,200
Personal residence	200,000		
Aston Spumoni roadster	16,500	Owner's Equity	
		Darcy Hannah, Capital	116,075
	$260,275		$260,275

Additional Information

a. Of the cash listed on the balance sheet, $1,200 represents cash in Darcy's fiancee's personal account and $800 represents cash in Darcy's personal account.
b. Although the original cost of wigs was $15,000, Darcy decides a more meaningful measure of value to report on the balance sheet is the current cost of their replacement.
c. Of the accounts payable, $5,000 represents employee training amounts owed to the Bakker School of Cosmetology.

d. The volume of Darcy's business has increased significantly since she purchased the state-of-the-art Makeover Machine for $15,000. Darcy does not include this asset on her balance sheet because she financed its entire cost with a bank loan, giving the bank legal ownership. On December 31, Darcy has repaid $5,000 of the loan balance.

Required

1. Do you find any error(s) on this balance sheet?
2. If you do:
   a. Identify the error(s).
   b. Explain why you believe they are error(s).
   c. Prepare a corrected balance sheet.

Research Assignments

A wide variety of interesting Research Assignments for this chapter are available for the following topics at www.mhhe.com/solomon:

R4-1 Making Business Decisions (PO 2)
R4-2 Examining Older Balance Sheets (PO 5b)
R4-3 Noncorporate Balance Sheet (PO 5b)
R4-4 Classified Balance Sheet (PO 5b)
R4-5 Obtaining a Chart of Accounts (PO 11b)
R4-6 Statement of Shareholders' Equity (PO 12)
R4-7 Classified Balance Sheet Assets (PO 14)
R4-8 Balance Sheet Investment Security Disclosures (PO 14)
R4-9 Classified Balance Sheet Liabilities and Shareholders' Equity (PO 14)

CHAPTER FIVE

Using the Balance Sheet to Make Decisions

PERFORMANCE OBJECTIVES

In this chapter, you will learn the following new Performance Objectives:

PO3 **(Expanded form of earlier version) Calculate** at least one financial statement ratio within each of the following five categories, **interpret** its meaning, and **discuss** its usefulness and limitations in making decisions:

a. Liquidity—e.g., current ratio and acid test ratio.
b. Activity or turnover—e.g., average collection period.
c. Financial leverage—e.g., debt to equity ratio.
d. Profitability—e.g., return on equity and profit margin ratio.
e. Valuation—e.g., price earnings ratio and dividend yield.

PO16 **Describe** how the amounts reported on the income statement and balance sheet are determined by:

a. **Distinguishing** among the following valuation methods: historical cost, replacement cost, fair market value, and the present value of future cash flows.
b. **Identifying** the generally accepted valuation method for each of the major asset and liability accounts.

PO17 **Identify** several limitations of the financial statements found in the annual report.

Also be sure you have mastered the following Performance Objectives from previous chapters. They lay the foundation for the concepts you will learn in this chapter:

PO2
PO4
PO5
PO7c
PO8
PO9
PO11b
PO13
PO14
PO15

KEN LEDEIT, BANK LOAN ANALYST

My name is Ken LeDeit, and I am a loan analyst for a bank. I graduated from college with a bachelor's degree in Finance and a minor in Communications. I took an introductory accounting course, but only because it was required. Although the course was challenging, I really didn't expect that it would be valuable, because, after all, accounting was not my major. Since I began working for the bank, however, my thinking has quickly changed. I use financial accounting information *every day* in my job. Let me tell you how.

When individuals apply for a business loan from my bank, a loan officer helps them assemble information about their personal or business financial condition. This information might include income statements, balance sheets, operating budgets, income tax returns, and descriptions of collateral. After assembling this information, the loan officer forwards it to me for analysis. I use a specialized software package to perform various calculations that help me evaluate how risky it will be to lend money to the applicant. I also consider factors such as the applicant's character, the stability and economic state of the industry in which his/her business operates, the applicant's experience in the industry, and the size of the company. After my analysis, I write a 5- to 10-page report in which I recommend that the bank either approve or reject the person's loan application. I submit this report to a committee to whom I later make an oral presentation.

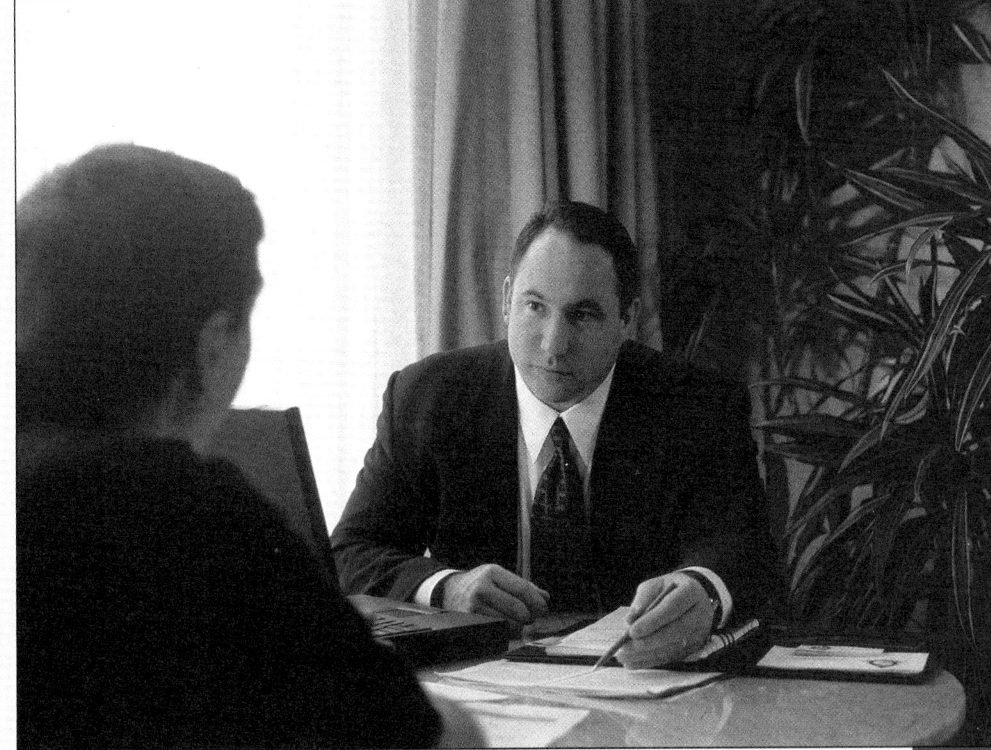

So you can see that a loan's approval or rejection depends upon my ability to analyze and properly interpret financial information. When I started as a loan analyst, I quickly realized that I needed to learn more about financial accounting. I needed to be able to analyze financial statements more efficiently and accurately; if I didn't, my chance for success—promotions, raises, and the like—would be greatly diminished. So I enrolled as a part-time student and took an evening accounting class.

If, as a student, I had realized how much financial accounting would help me in my job, I would have paid more attention in class and done more of the homework. Take it from me—the reality is that if you're a business major or plan to go into any type of business, you're going to need to know about accounting; and it's a lot easier to learn what you need to know now, rather than later. The people who work hard and pay attention in your accounting class today will be the people against whom you'll compete tomorrow. If you don't master financial accounting concepts now, don't expect to advance as rapidly as those who have. No matter what your major, if you're going into business, you'll need this course.

Using a Classified Balance Sheet to Make Better Decisions

In preceding chapters, you learned a balance sheet contains information that can be used to make business decisions, such as whether to loan money or lease property to an entity. But what you have not yet learned is how to interpret the information presented in a balance sheet to make these and other important decisions. Your starting point in this process is the classified balance sheet. Let's once again use CMU's classified balance sheet (Figure 5-1) introduced in Chapter 3. As you have seen, the accounts in a classified balance sheet are organized into categories so that users can more easily understand the entity's financial position and, therefore, make better decisions. Let's explore why this is true.

FIGURE 5-1 Cards & Memorabilia Unlimited's classified balance sheet as of December 31

CARDS & MEMORABILIA UNLIMITED
Balance Sheet
December 31

Assets			Liabilities and Owner's Equity		
Current Assets			**Current Liabilities**		
Cash checking		$32,000	Accounts payable		$ 350
Cash savings		6,275	Salaries payable		750
Accounts receivable		5,000	Advances from customers		2,000
Interest receivable		25	Notes payable		6,000
Merchandise inventory		13,000	Total current liabilities		$ 9,100
Total current assets		$56,300			
Investments			**Noncurrent Liability**		
Security deposit receivable		2,000	Notes payable		4,000
Property, Plant, and Equipment			**Owner's Equity**		
Store equipment	$19,000		Contributed capital	$40,000	
Less: Accumulated depreciation	(2,300)	16,700	Retained earnings	21,900	61,900
Total assets		$75,000	**Total liabilities & owner's equity**		$75,000

Why Distinguish between Current and Noncurrent?

In Chapter 3, you learned that the basic distinction between current and noncurrent assets and between current and noncurrent liabilities is one year. In Chapter 4, "current" was used to describe all accounts expected to be turned into cash, sold, exchanged, or discharged within one year. We all use the current versus noncurrent concept to make everyday decisions. For example, you might be using your energy (a type of current asset) to read this chapter because it is due tomorrow (a type of current liability), instead of beginning another course's assignment that is not due for several days (a noncurrent liability). Allocating your resources to meet the immediate assignment is a wise decision, as long as you do not continually postpone work on the other assignment. Thus, you can see how your decisions can often be directly influenced by whether an item is current or noncurrent.

Such a conclusion is just as valid in a financial setting. Knowing that a particular liability is current helps decision makers because it alerts them to accounts whose prompt payment is a priority. In Transaction C_2, for example, Susan decides to pay the total credit card liability incurred in Transaction C_1 because she knows that this balance is due and payable within the next month. On the other hand, she decides not to repay the note payable in Transaction L immediately, because she knows its balance is payable in monthly installments over a two-year period. Notice that both of these decisions were influenced by the current/noncurrent liability classification. The definition of current and noncurrent might differ from one person to another. So, to eliminate inconsistency when using balance sheets to make decisions, we will now introduce a uniform treatment for these terms.

How to Distinguish between Current and Noncurrent

The definitions of both current assets and current liabilities involve the concept of the operating cycle. In simple terms, the **operating cycle** is the average length of time it takes a business to move or cycle through three phases of operations: purchasing, selling, and collecting. Since this cycle is initiated with the payment of cash (purchasing) and completed with the receipt of cash (collecting), it is said that the operating cycle is the average length of time it takes to go from "cash back to cash." For example, suppose it takes Cards & Memorabilia Unlimited an average of 20 days after payment to receive merchandise inventory, 45 more days for that inventory to be sold, and 25 more days to collect outstanding customer balances. The length of this operating cycle is 90 days (20 + 45 + 25). This is the average number of days it takes Cards & Memorabilia Unlimited to generate a return of cash from an investment of cash. Assuming a 360-day year for simplicity, Cards & Memorabilia Unlimited will experience four (360 days/90 days) operating cycles a year.

As you can see, the operating cycle is aptly named. The word "operating" refers to the normal phases of purchasing, selling, and collecting that are included in the term "operating activities." The word "cycle" is appropriate because purchasing, selling, and collecting are repetitive phases in the operation of a business. The operating cycle is shown in greater detail in Figure 5-2. Pay careful attention to this figure's description of the three phases.

Although the great majority of businesses have operating cycles lasting less than one year, there are exceptions. Consider, for example, that distillers or manufacturers of alcohol, publishers, construction companies, tobacco or timber growers, and cattle breeders might require several years of preparation or storage. Also, the operating cycle of a company that sells on an installment basis might extend for several years. One example is sales by land development companies.

As you will learn in Chapter 11, shortening each phase of the operating cycle (for example, cutting in half the length of time a box of trading cards sits on the shelf) has the effect of reducing the amount of assets required to operate the business. Although no retailer wants to incur customer ill will due to inventory shortages, all retailers prefer to *turn over* large inventory and receivable balances into cash for reinvestment and liquidity needs. Thus, in future chapters, you will learn how operating cycle information that we derive from financial statements can be used to make decisions about an entity's resource needs.

Next, you will learn how understanding the operating cycle will help you better understand the definitions of both current assets and current liabilities.

Current Assets **Current assets** are cash and noncash assets that are expected to be converted into cash, sold, or consumed within one year or the operating cycle of the business, whichever is longer.[1] Most businesses use one year as the dividing line between current and noncurrent. For example, if the operating cycle is 90 days,

[1] "Restatement and Revision of Accounting Research Bulletins," *Accounting Research Bulletin No. 43* (New York, N.Y.: Committee on Accounting Procedure, 1953), Chapter 3, Section A.

FIGURE 5-2

The operating cycle

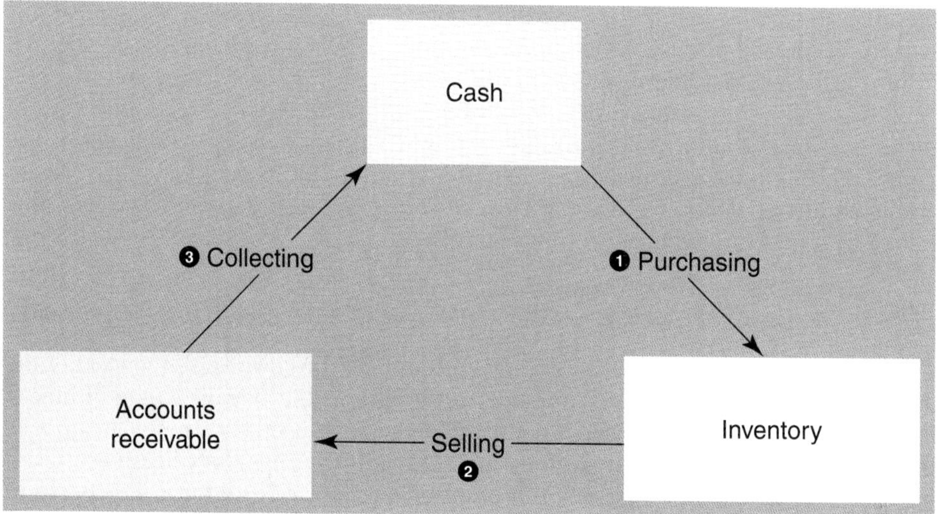

❶ **Purchasing phase:** The first phase of the operating cycle begins at the moment cash is used to acquire merchandise inventory. It ends when this inventory is received from a supplier and is ready for sale.

❷ **Selling phase:** The second phase of the operating cycle begins when the inventory is received and ready for sale. It ends with the sale, that is, delivery of the product to the customer.

❸ **Collecting phase:** The third phase of the operating cycle begins when the customer receives the product. It ends when the seller receives cash, either immediately or later when an account receivable is collected from customers.

as we saw with CMU, the longer of one year or 90 days is clearly one year. Thus, noncash assets converted into cash, sold, or consumed within one year are classified as current. Assets that require more than this amount of time are considered noncurrent. If you are told, however, that a winery's operating cycle is two years in length, two years would be the cutoff between current and noncurrent. That is, a 2003 Cabernet Sauvignon wine that was bottled on May 15 of 2003 would be classified as a current asset until May 16 of 2005.

On a balance sheet, current and noncurrent assets are listed in order of their liquidity. **Liquidity** is a measure of the availability of cash, that is, how quickly a noncash asset can be turned into cash. Cash is the most liquid of assets; noncash assets that are difficult to transform into cash are least liquid. Generally speaking, creditors and other users of the balance sheet regard liquidity as a sign of financial health.

Current Liabilities **Current liabilities** are defined as obligations that will be eliminated within one year or the operating cycle of the business, whichever is longer. These liabilities are generally settled either by payment from current assets, such as cash, or by the creation of other current liabilities. Once again, most businesses use one year as the division between current and noncurrent.

As with assets, both current and noncurrent liabilities appear in the balance sheet in order of liquidity or scheduled payment date. Thus, accounts payable due in 30 days are listed before a 90-day note payable. The higher the amount of current liabilities a company has incurred, the less attractive that company appears to potential lenders. That is, a company is more likely to receive financing from creditors if the majority of its indebtedness is from noncurrent liabilities. Of course, a company with no balance sheet debt is in an even stronger position to borrow money.

Using Balance Sheet Ratios to Make Better Decisions

CARDS & MEMORABILIA UNLIMITED

Sometimes a classified balance sheet enables you to discover important financial relationships simply by observing the distinction between current and noncurrent for both assets and liabilities. Quite often, however, you will have to use various financial analysis tools to reveal financial relationships that are not so clearly visible. One of these tools is the use of ratios.

A **ratio** is a percentage or decimal that shows the relationship of one number to another. Ratios are useful decision-making tools because they conveniently summarize information in a form that is more easily understood, interpreted, and compared. In particular, decision makers use ratios because they illuminate relationships among different elements in the financial statements.

Recall, for example, how Susan Newman used a profitability ratio called rate of return on equity or return on equity (ROE) to measure Cards & Memorabilia Unlimited's performance. In Chapter 1, she divided her projected net income by her initial owner investment to estimate her company's first-year performance. In Chapter 3, she calculated this same ratio with actual results to evaluate whether her company's performance had failed to match or had surpassed its projected return on equity.

We'll now look at two additional types of ratios derived from the balance sheet and frequently used by decision makers—liquidity ratios and leverage ratios.

How Are Liquidity Ratios Used to Determine Solvency?

Now that you can classify assets and liabilities into current and noncurrent categories, you can evaluate a company's **solvency**—its ability to meet obligations that mature or come due in the current period. A popular but somewhat misleading measure of solvency is working capital. **Working capital** is simply current assets minus current liabilities. Although easy to calculate, working capital has limitations. One such limitation is that working capital measures only a company's *absolute* ability to meet its maturing debts. For example, it does not distinguish between Company A with $2,000,000 of current assets and $1,000,000 of current liabilities and Company B with $101,000,000 of current assets and $100,000,000 of current liabilities. Each of these companies has $1,000,000 more current assets than current liabilities, but Company B is clearly not as solvent as Company A. Another limitation of working capital in evaluating solvency is its failure to consider the *liquidity* of an entity's current assets—how easily they can be converted to cash. For example, consider two companies that are identical in all respects except one. Company C holds $2,000,000 in cash and $500,000 in merchandise inventory, whereas Company D holds $500,000 in cash and $2,000,000 in merchandise inventory. Which company is more solvent? The answer is that Company C is likely to be more solvent than Company D because inventory is among the most difficult of current assets to fully liquidate. Yet, the working capital measure fails to detect any difference in solvency between these two companies.

A more useful measure of solvency is the liquidity ratio. A **liquidity ratio** measures a company's *relative* ability to meet its maturing current debts, that is, its solvency. Two of the more commonly used liquidity ratios are the current ratio and the acid test or quick ratio. The current ratio is a relatively optimistic measure, whereas the acid test ratio is a more conservative measure. We'll now illustrate both of these ratios using Cards & Memorabilia Unlimited. Then we'll see how Ken LeDeit used banking industry liquidity ratios to recommend that Susan's loan application be accepted.

Current Ratio The **current ratio** is aptly named because it is calculated by simply dividing *current* assets by *current* liabilities:

$$\text{Current Ratio} = \frac{\text{Current Assets}}{\text{Current Liabilities}}$$

A high ratio is a ratio in which the numerator, current assets, is significantly higher than the denominator, current liabilities. In general, a high ratio is desirable because it indicates that creditors will be paid in full and on time; but too high a ratio might indicate that the company is holding excessive amounts of cash, accounts receivable, and inventory. So how do you know when a current ratio amount is neither too high nor too low? An often-used rule of thumb is that a current ratio should be 2.0 or greater. For example, let's now use the current ratio to reevaluate the solvency of Company A and Company B from our earlier working capital example. Notice how much more solvent Company A appears to be than Company B on the basis of A's current ratio of 2.0 ($2,000,000/$1,000,000) and B's current ratio of 1.01 ($101,000,000/$100,000,000). Nevertheless, it would be a mistake to discontinue your analysis here, since a ratio of 2.0 is not that impressive in some industries. In fact, no matter what kind of ratio you use, you should always compare it first to the industry average and then to the corresponding ratios of similar companies in the same industry. Likewise, you should also determine whether your company's ratio has changed much when compared to its ratios of past years. Upon such further analysis, you may discover that the current ratio has been declining steadily for years! Comparing your company's ratio in the present to those it calculated in the past and to those of other companies in the same industry is a must.

If you want to conduct effective financial analysis, you must do more than simply calculate a single ratio at a single point in time. A current ratio can provide *insight* about liquidity, but it should never be the only tool you use to evaluate a company's well-being. For example, such communication companies as Airtouch Communications Inc. and BellSouth Telecommunications Inc. have current ratios ranging from 0.86 to as low as 0.65 because of almost no inventories. Concluding that either company is insolvent, however, is unwarranted. In fact, more extensive analysis shows that both of these companies are solvent. Airtouch, for example, had cash flows from operations totaling $1.9 billion in 1998!

We can calculate Cards & Memorabilia Unlimited's current ratio by examining its end-of-year classified balance sheet shown in Figure 5-1:

$$\text{Current Ratio} = \frac{\$56{,}300}{\$9{,}100} = 6.187$$

This current ratio indicates that Susan has adequate resources to meet her current obligations. However, closer study of her assets indicates that nearly 25% ($13,000/$56,300) is composed of merchandise inventory. Thus, Cards & Memorabilia Unlimited's case clearly illustrates the primary limitation of the current ratio—it assumes that noncash current assets can be easily converted into cash to cover current liabilities. In many businesses, however, inventories and some receivables are neither quickly converted to cash nor likely to be realized in their full amount. It is highly unlikely, for example, that Susan will recover $13,000 of cash if she is forced to liquidate her inventory. If such a forced sale occurs, she will be less able to fully meet her current obligations from current assets. The next ratio is designed to overcome this limitation.

Acid Test or Quick Ratio The **acid test** or **quick ratio** has the same denominator as does the current ratio—current liabilities. Its numerator, however, differs from the current ratio numerator by eliminating any current assets that are not near cash (liquid) in nature, such as inventories and prepayments. Thus, this ratio is a more conservative measure of liquidity than the current ratio.

$$\text{Acid Test Ratio} = \frac{\text{Current Assets} - (\text{Inventories} + \text{Prepaid Assets})}{\text{Current Liabilities}}$$

As the name *acid test* suggests, this ratio is more certain and dependable than the current ratio. The word *quick* also accurately describes this ratio because the numerator is calculated by considering only cash, marketable securities, and net receivables, rather than all current assets.

We can calculate Cards & Memorabilia Unlimited's acid test ratio by again referring to its balance sheet in Figure 5-1:

$$\text{Acid Test Ratio} = \frac{\$43,300}{\$9,100} = 4.758$$

Although this ratio is still relatively high, its substantial decrease from the current ratio of 6.2 reflects a more realistic treatment of inventory.

Bank Ratios Used in Approving Susan's Loan Application When Central Bank loan analyst Ken LeDeit received Susan's completed loan application, he discovered that he was unable to use the standard business ratios he normally used. This was because Susan's business had not yet begun, forcing Ken to evaluate her financial condition as an individual. If you review Chapter 1, you will discover that Figure 5-3 roughly represents Susan's personal financial condition.

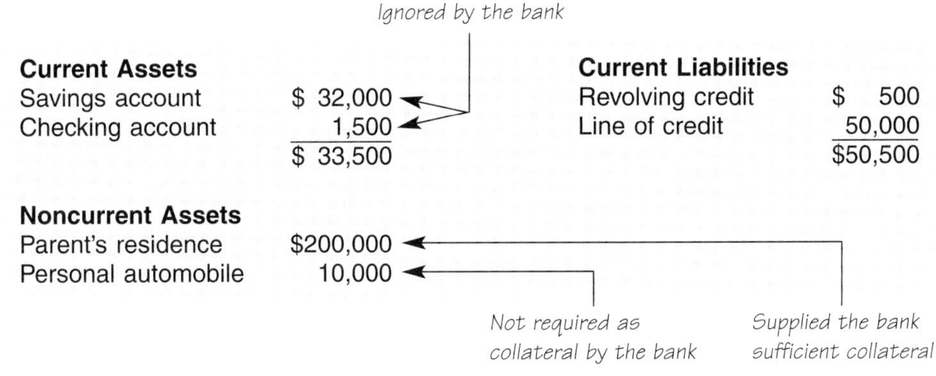

FIGURE 5-3

Susan's personal financial condition at the start of her business

When evaluating Susan's financial condition, the bank ignored her savings and checking accounts because it did not have control over either balance. Once Susan's parents agreed to put up their home as collateral, the bank recognized that it had more than adequate protection and didn't ask Susan to put up her personal automobile as collateral. You might recall that Susan applied for a \$50,000 line of credit based on a market value for her parents' home of at least \$200,000. The money from Susan's uncle was effectively ignored not only because it had no definite due date but also because it was subordinated or restricted from being paid until Susan repaid the line of credit.

Ultimately, Ken LeDeit calculated two ratios often used by banks. The first was an optimistic ratio called *loan to value* that involved dividing the \$50,000 maximum *loan* liability by the \$200,000 market *value* of the collateral:

$$\text{Loan to Value} = \frac{\$50,000}{\$200,000} = 25\%$$

Because Central Bank normally makes loans whenever this percentage is below 75%, Ken decided to recommend this loan application to his bank's loan committee. To play it safe, however, he also calculated a *loan to liquidation value* to reflect two facts—first, the bank might initially recover less than $200,000 from the sale of the collateral because of real estate market fluctuations; and second, the bank would definitely net less than $200,000 because of unavoidable selling costs. Since Ken's bank uses a factor of 70% for homes with market values under a million dollars, the liquidation value is $140,000 ($200,000 × 0.70). So this ratio's calculation is:

$$\text{Loan to Liquidation Value} = \frac{\$50{,}000}{\$140{,}000} = 35.7\%$$

Notice how these bank ratios parallel the behavior of the current and acid test ratios, respectively, when their numerators and denominators are reversed. For example, the more optimistic loan to value ratio becomes 4.0 ($200,000/50,000), while the more conservative loan to liquidation value ratio is reduced to 2.8 ($140,000/$50,000), reflecting a decrease in the somewhat unrealistic selling price numerator. Although Ken LeDeit's ratios appear different from the current and acid test ratios, all of these ratios compare a measure of assets to a measure of liabilities.

How Is a Leverage Ratio Used to Evaluate Financial Risk?

A **leverage ratio** measures the extent to which an entity has been financed by debt. What do we mean by "financed by debt"? You have learned that every business has two sources of financing available. In a corporation, for example, resources or assets can be acquired by incurring liabilities (debt financing) or by issuing shares of capital stock (equity financing). The cost of debt financing is interest payments, whereas the cost of equity financing is dividends. Unfortunately, a business cannot simply compare the dollar cost of interest payments to the dollar cost of dividend payments in deciding which source of financing is best. One reason is because the tax consequence of using debt is different from the tax consequence of using equity. In fact, the present U.S. tax system encourages the use of debt financing rather than equity financing. The preference of debt over equity financing occurs because corporations can deduct interest expense but not dividends when they prepare their income taxes.

Thus, corporate managers usually prefer a financing cost that provides a tax break, such as debt, to a financing cost that does not. This preference tends to increase the use of debt financing, which might burden the company with interest payments. In fact, as a company increases its use of debt financing, it also increases the probability of encountering financial distress because it must make principal and interest payments at specific dates. That is, if the company misses a payment date, technical bankruptcy occurs. This relationship between an increase in a corporation's indebtedness and the increase in its probability of financial distress is referred to as **financial risk**. Equity financing does not entail financial risk because dividends require no specific repayment. Debt financing is advantageous because of the deductibility of interest payments but disadvantageous because of financial risk. You can monitor this risk, however, by measuring how *leveraged*—the extent to which a business's assets are financed by debt—the business has become.

Two ratios commonly used to evaluate the amount of financial risk borne by a particular entity are the *debt to assets ratio*, which derives all its elements from the balance sheet, and the *number of times interest earned ratio*, which most often derives all its elements from the income statement. We'll delay our discussion of this latter ratio until Chapter 7.

Debt to Assets Ratio The **debt to assets ratio** is a leverage ratio that indicates the long-run solvency of the business. That is, it describes the relative amount of financial risk incurred by the entity. Notice that the method of calculating this ratio is fairly evident from its title:

$$\text{Debt to Assets} = \frac{\text{Total Liabilities}}{\text{Total Assets}}$$

For Cards & Memorabilia Unlimited, this ratio is calculated as follows:

$$\frac{\$13{,}100}{\$75{,}000} = 0.175$$

Thus, more than one-sixth (0.175) of Cards & Memorabilia Unlimited's financing is debt, and nearly five-sixths is equity. Rarely would business decision makers consider a 0.175 debt to assets ratio very risky.

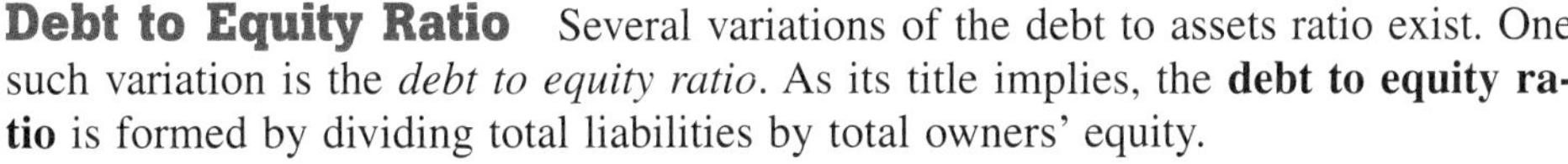

Debt to Equity Ratio Several variations of the debt to assets ratio exist. One such variation is the *debt to equity ratio*. As its title implies, the **debt to equity ratio** is formed by dividing total liabilities by total owners' equity.

$$\text{Debt to Equity} = \frac{\text{Total Liabilities}}{\text{Total Owners' Equity}}$$

For Cards & Memorabilia Unlimited, this ratio is calculated from the information in Figure 5-1 as follows:

$$\frac{\$13{,}100}{\$61{,}900} = 0.212$$

This ratio again confirms that CMU is not highly leveraged.

You have now learned about three categories of ratios. Prior to reading this chapter, you were introduced to a specific type of profitability ratio called return on equity. In this chapter, you learned about two liquidity ratios and two leverage ratios. To recognize that you are now able to calculate more than the return on equity, Performance Objective 3 has been modified as shown here. (You'll learn about Performance Objectives 3b and 3e later.)

YOUR PERFORMANCE OBJECTIVE 3

Calculate at least one financial statement ratio within each of the following five categories, **interpret** its meaning, and **discuss** its usefulness and limitations in making decisions:

a. Liquidity—e.g., current ratio and acid test ratio
b. Activity or turnover—e.g., average collection period
c. Financial leverage—e.g., debt to equity ratio
d. Profitability—e.g., return on equity and profit margin ratio
e. Valuation—e.g., price earnings ratio and dividend yield

Using Information Not Found in the Balance Sheet to Make Decisions

Suppose you wanted to find out as much as you could about a company's balance sheet. What would you do? If your answer is that you'd look at the balance sheet in its annual report, you'd be only partly right. And that's because some very valuable information about the balance sheet is not itself found in the balance sheet. Instead, this information is found in two distinctly different annual report sections to which you were introduced at the beginning of Chapter 3. These are Management's Discussion and Analysis of Operations, commonly called the MD&A, and the notes to

FIGURE 5-4 Liquidity and capital resources section of MD&A for Federal Express

MANAGEMENT'S DISCUSSION AND ANALYSIS

FINANCIAL CONDITION

LIQUIDITY

Cash and cash equivalents totaled $121 million at May 31, 2001, compared to $68 million at May 31, 2000. Cash flows from operating activities during 2001 totaled $2.0 billion, compared to $1.6 billion for 2000 and $1.8 billion for 1999.

CAPITAL RESOURCES

As mentioned previously, our operations are capital intensive, characterized by significant investments in aircraft, vehicles, computer and telecommunications equipment, package-handling facilities and sort equipment. The amount and timing of capital additions depend on various factors, including volume growth, domestic and international economic conditions, new or enhanced services, geographical expansion of services, competition, availability of satisfactory financing and actions of regulatory authorities.

The following table compares capital expenditures (including equivalent capital, which is defined below) for the years ended May 31 (in millions):

	2001	2000	1999
Aircraft and related equipment	**$ 756**	$ 469	$ 606
Facilities and sort equipment	**353**	437	466
Information and technology equipment	**406**	378	366
Other equipment	**378**	343	332
Total capital expenditures	**1,893**	1,627	1,770
Equivalent capital, principally aircraft-related	–	365	561
Total	**$1,893**	$1,992	$2,331

We finance a significant amount of aircraft and certain other equipment needs using long-term operating leases. We believe the determination to lease versus buy equipment is a financing decision, and both forms of financing are considered when evaluating the resources committed for capital. The amount we would have expended to purchase these assets had we not chosen to obtain their use through operating leases is considered equivalent capital in the table above. Capital expenditures (including equivalent capital) over the past two years have been reduced in response to lower U.S. domestic volume growth at FedEx Express. This trend of lower U.S. domestic volume growth, along with the current year economic slowdown and its effects on IP volume growth, has resulted in future excess airlift capacity. During the fourth quarter of 2001, we began the process of reducing certain planned aircraft programs, which is expected to result in lower capital expenditures in future periods (see Note 15 to our financial statements). For 2002, we expect capital spending, including equivalent capital, to approximate the level of 2001 capital expenditures. We plan to continue to make strategic capital investments, particularly in information technology and ground network expansion, in support of our long-term growth goals. For information on our purchase commitments, see Note 13 to our financial statements.

We have historically financed our capital investments through the use of lease, debt and equity financing in addition to the use of internally generated cash from operations. Generally, our practice in recent years with respect to funding new wide-bodied aircraft acquisitions has been to finance such aircraft through long-term lease transactions that qualify as off-balance sheet operating leases under applicable accounting rules. We have determined that these operating leases have provided economic benefits favorable to ownership with respect to market values, liquidity and after-tax cash flows. In the future, other forms of secured financing may be pursued to finance aircraft acquisitions when we determine that it best meets our needs. Historically we have been successful in obtaining investment capital, both domestic and international, for long-term leases on acceptable terms, although the marketplace for such capital can become restricted depending on a variety of economic factors beyond our control. See Note 4 to our financial statements for additional information concerning our debt facilities.

the financial statements. Let's now examine these annual report sections more closely to find out how each can help you make better decisions about the business you are studying. Since the MD&A normally precedes both the financial statements and the notes to the financial statements in an annual report, we'll examine it first.

How You Can Use the MD&A to Enhance Your Analysis of the Balance Sheet

No matter what company's annual report you study, the structure of its **Management's Discussion and Analysis of Operations** or Financial Review section is often quite the same. The MD&A generally begins with a relatively lengthy discussion about the results found on the income statement. This section, usually entitled Results of Operations, will be discussed in Chapter 7. The next section of the MD&A relates directly to the balance sheet and is usually called Liquidity and Capital Resources. Figure 5-4 presents a somewhat brief illustration of this information for FedEx Corporation under the heading Financial Condition. Notice that the Liquidity discussion focuses on current assets. In contrast, the first two paragraphs of the Capital Resources section focus on noncurrent assets while the next two paragraphs focus on various types of liabilities used to finance asset purchases. In recent years, companies have expanded the MD&A to include additional discussions deemed important. For example, many 1999 annual reports contained a discussion about the company's Y2K preparations in the MD&A section.

Annual Report Discussions of Liquidity and Leverage

USER FOCUS

In an earlier section of this chapter, you learned how to evaluate a company's solvency and financial risk by calculating liquidity and leverage ratios from the balance sheet. But most companies also provide related feedback in their annual report's MD&As. In Merck's 2001 Analysis of Liquidity and Capital Resources narrative shown in Figure 5-5, for example, there is a three-year listing of working capital and the debt to assets ratio (note that liabilities plus equity equal assets), as well as a discussion of those transactions affecting its solvency and financial risk. Since such information is present in almost all annual reports, it is essential that you supplement your ratio calculations with a careful reading of the liquidity and leverage discussion found in the MD&A section.

FIGURE 5-5

Liquidity and leverage ratios included in the MD&A for Merck & Co., Inc.

Analysis of Liquidity and Capital Resources

Cash provided by operations continues to be the Company's primary source of funds to finance operating needs and capital expenditures. In 2001, cash flows from operations were $9.1 billion, reflecting the continued growth of the Company's earnings. This cash was used to fund capital expenditures of $2.7 billion, to pay Company dividends of $3.1 billion and to partially fund the purchase of treasury shares. At December 31, 2001, the total of worldwide cash and investments was $10.3 billion, including $3.3 billion in cash, cash equivalents and short-term investments, and $7.0 billion of long-term investments. The above totals include $1.1 billion in cash and investments held by Banyu Pharmaceutical Co., Ltd., in which the Company has a 50.87% ownership interest.

Selected Data

($ in millions)	**2001**	2000	1999
Working capital	**$1,417.4**	$3,643.8	$2,500.4
Total debt to total liabilities and equity	**20.1%**	17.2%	16.7%
Cash provided by operations to total debt	**1.0:1**	1.1:1	1.0:1

(continued)

Working capital levels are more than adequate to meet the operating requirements of the Company. The ratio of total debt to total liabilities and equity was affected by incremental borrowings used to fund capital expenditures, treasury stock repurchases and other corporate initiatives. The ratio of cash provided by operations to total debt, although impacted by these incremental borrowings, reflects the ability of the Company to cover its debt obligations.

How You Can Use the Notes to the Financial Statements to Enhance Your Analysis of the Balance Sheet

With few exceptions, the notes follow the financial statements in an annual report. Most annual reports contain from 15 to 20 **notes** or **footnotes**, information that documents, supports, or elaborates on specific items within the financial statements. The first few notes are often general in nature. A good example is the Summary of Significant Accounting Policies, described in more detail in the first of three sections that follow our discussion here. Then, notes relating directly to the balance sheet are shown. Good examples are more detailed presentations of the inventory and property, plant, and equipment balance sheet accounts. Finally, information about the income statement is generally provided in the last part of the notes section. You will learn more about these notes in Chapter 7. In the next three sections, we examine (1) a note usually entitled the Summary of Significant Accounting Policies, (2) the various notes providing underlying detail for asset, liability, and owners' equity accounts reported on the balance sheet, and (3) a note entitled Commitments and Contingencies.

Summary of Significant Accounting Policies Until recently, the Summary of Significant Accounting Policies was the first note shown in the notes section of annual reports. Today, however, the first note is often a condensed version of the 10-K description of the business and its accounting policies. In the 1998 annual report of Merck & Co., Inc., shown in Figure 5-6, the first note entitled Nature of Operations provides a thumbnail sketch of Merck's business and is followed by a second note entitled Summary of Accounting Policies. The **Summary of Significant Accounting Policies** includes the essential accounting principles used by a particular business. Some examples from Figure 5-6 include methods used to combine Merck and the companies it owns called principles of consolidation, the definition of cash equivalents, and the particular methods or principles used to account for both inventories and depreciation. Often, this particular note is two to three pages long and covers a wide range of information about the nature of the particular business you are studying. Don't worry if you don't recognize such terms as *LIFO* or *FIFO* under Inventories. These and other terms unfamiliar to you will be covered in future chapters.

Figure 5-7 is designed to give you an even greater appreciation of the type of information found in this section. A check mark under a company column indicates that this company discloses the particular policy listed in that row. Notice that both general accounting policies and more specific policies relating to the balance sheet of several well-known companies are listed. As you look over this figure, it should be apparent that scanning the accounting policies note is a valuable way to initially familiarize yourself with a new company and its balance sheet.

Notes Providing Underlying Detail for Balance Sheet Accounts Figure 5-8 shows notes describing five balance sheet accounts—a partial presentation of Nordstrom's accounts receivable, Cisco Systems's inventories, Dreyers property, plant, and equipment, ADP's debt, and Microsoft's common stock. In each case, notice how much more detailed the information presented is in these notes compared

FIGURE 5-6 The summary of significant accounting policies for Merck & Co. Inc.

Notes to Consolidated Financial Statements

Merck & Co., Inc. and Subsidiaries
($ in millions except per share amounts)

1. Nature of Operations

Merck is a global research-driven pharmaceutical company that discovers, develops, manufactures and markets a broad range of human and animal health products, directly and through its joint ventures, and provides pharmaceutical benefit services through Merck-Medco Managed Care (Merck-Medco). Human health products include therapeutic and preventive agents, generally sold by prescription, for the treatment of human disorders. Pharmaceutical benefit services primarily include sales of prescription drugs through managed prescription drug programs as well as services provided through programs to manage patient health and drug utilization.

Merck sells its human health products and provides pharmaceutical benefit services primarily to drug wholesalers and retailers, hospitals, clinics, government agencies, corporations, labor unions, retirement systems, insurance carriers, managed health care providers such as health maintenance organizations and other institutions.

2. Summary of Accounting Policies

Principles of Consolidation – The consolidated financial statements include the accounts of the Company and all of its subsidiaries in which a controlling interest is maintained. For those consolidated subsidiaries where Merck ownership is less than 100%, the outside stockholders' interests are shown as Minority interests. Investments in affiliates over which the Company has significant influence but not a controlling interest are carried on the equity basis.

Foreign Currency Translation – The U.S. dollar is the functional currency for the Company's foreign subsidiaries.

Cash and Cash Equivalents – Cash equivalents are comprised of certain highly liquid investments with original maturities of less than three months.

Inventories – The majority of domestic inventories are valued at the lower of last-in, first-out (LIFO) cost or market. Remaining inventories are valued at the lower of first-in, first-out (FIFO) cost or market.

Revenue Recognition – Revenues from sales of Merck human health products are recognized upon shipment of product. Revenues generated by Merck-Medco's pharmaceutical benefit services, comprised principally of sales of prescription drugs, are recognized, net of certain rebates, upon dispensing of product. Specifically, revenues from plan member orders dispensed at Merck-Medco's mail service pharmacies are recognized when the product is shipped, while revenues from orders dispensed by retail network pharmacies are recognized when the prescription is filled. For the majority of the retail business, Merck-Medco assumes financial risk through having independent contractual arrangements to bill plan sponsors and pay the retail network pharmacy providers. In such cases, revenues are recognized based on the prescription drug price negotiated with the plan sponsor. When Merck-Medco acts solely as a liaison to reimburse retail pharmacies on the plan sponsor's behalf, no financial risk has been assumed, and therefore, revenues are recognized only for the amount of the administrative fee received from the plan sponsor.

Merck-Medco has contracts with multiple pharmaceutical manufacturers that offer rebates on drugs included on Merck-Medco formularies. These rebates are recognized as a credit to cost of sales in the period earned based upon the dispensed volume of specific drugs stipulated in the contracts.

Depreciation – Depreciation is provided over the estimated useful lives of the assets, principally using the straight-line method. For tax purposes, accelerated methods are used. The estimated useful lives primarily range from 10 to 50 years for Buildings, and from 3 to 15 years for Machinery, equipment and office furnishings.

Goodwill and Other Intangibles – Goodwill of $4.1 billion in 2001 and $3.8 billion in 2000 (net of accumulated amortization) represents the excess of acquisition costs over the fair value of net assets of businesses purchased and is amortized on a straight-line basis over periods up to 40 years. Under Statement No. 142, Goodwill and Other Intangible Assets (FAS 142), goodwill associated with acquisitions subsequent to June 30, 2001 is not amortized. (See Note 3.) Effective January 1, 2002, goodwill existing at June 30, 2001 will no longer be amortized, but rather, evaluated for impairment on an annual basis using a fair value based test. Other acquired intangibles principally include customer relationships of $2.5 billion in 2001 and 2000 (net of accumulated amortization) that arose in connection with the acquisition of Medco Containment Services, Inc. (renamed Merck-Medco) and patent rights approximating $.6 billion in 2001 and $.7 billion in 2000 (net of accumulated amortization) acquired as part of the restructuring of Astra Merck Inc. (AMI). (See Note 4.) These acquired intangibles are recorded at cost and are amortized on a straight-line basis over their estimated useful lives of up to 40 years. The weighted average amortization period for other intangibles was 29 years at December 31, 2001 and 2000. The Company reviews other intangibles to assess recoverability from future operations using undiscounted cash flows derived from the lowest appropriate asset groupings, generally the subsidiary level. Impairments are recognized in operating results to the extent that carrying value exceeds fair value, which is determined based on the net present value of estimated future cash flows.

Stock-Based Compensation – Employee stock-based compensation is recognized using the intrinsic value method. For disclosure purposes, pro forma net income and earnings per share impacts are provided as if the fair value method had been applied.

Use of Estimates – The consolidated financial statements are prepared in conformity with accounting principles generally accepted in the United States (GAAP) and, accordingly, include amounts that are based on management's best estimates and judgments. Estimates are used in determining such items as provisions for rebates, returns and allowances, depreciable/amortizable lives, pension and other postretirement benefit plan assumptions, and amounts recorded for contingencies, environmental liabilities and other reserves. Because of the uncertainty inherent in such estimates, actual results may differ from these estimates. The Company is not aware of reasonably likely events or circumstances which would result in different amounts being reported that would have a material impact on results of operations or financial condition.

FIGURE 5-7 Typical disclosures found in the summary of significant accounting policies of six corporations

General Information Items:	Chevron	Coca-Cola	Disney	FedEx	Nordstrom	Seagate
The Company or Nature of Operations		√			√	√
Principles of Consolidation or Basis of Consolidation or Basis of Presentation or Subsidiary and Affiliated Companies	√	√	√	√	√	√
Foreign Currency Translation	√			√		
Use of Estimates or Accounting Estimates		√	√	√		√
Recent Pronouncements or Accounting Changes		√	√	√	√	√
Reclassifications			√	√		
Environmental Expenditures	√					
Balance Sheet Information: Cash and Cash Equivalents		√	√	√	√	√
Customer Accounts Receivable					√	
Inventories	√	√	√	√	√	√
Property, Plant, & Equipment	√	√		√	√	√
Marketable Securities or Investments	√	√	√	√		√
Goodwill & Other Intangibles		√	√	√		
Capitalized Interest				√	√	√

to typical balance sheet presentations of these same accounts. Looking at these and similar notes is a must if you want to have more than just a superficial look at the balance sheet.

Commitments and Contingencies A critical balance sheet disclosure usually found only in the notes is Commitments and Contingencies. You might remember seeing Contingencies as a liability in Figure 4-13. You might also have noticed that no amounts appeared next to this title. What does this absence of numbers mean? To answer this question, let's first examine commitments, since they are not the same as contingencies. As its name implies, a **commitment** is a transaction in which a business signs a contract promising to pay certain amounts in the future in return for future benefits. Such an obligation involves what is called an executory contract.

A common form of commitment is cash payments that must be made under the terms of noncancelable lease arrangements. Apple Computer, Inc., for example, has a relatively small amount of noncurrent liabilities in its balance sheet dated September 30, 2000. To the uninformed, this fact might indicate that Apple has a "clean" balance sheet, with little long-term debt. A closer look at the note entitled "Commitments and Contingencies," however, reveals that its reported position is somewhat misleading. As shown in Figure 5-9, it is clear that Apple's potential noncurrent liabilities are greater than one might determine from looking at the balance sheet alone. In 2000, for example, the company paid approximately $93,000,000 to lease facilities and equipment under operating leases, a type of lease you read about in the preceding chapter. Essentially, these leases are future obligations arising out of

FIGURE 5-8 Five representative notes providing underlying detail for balance sheet accounts

NORDSTROM, INC.

Note 8: Accounts Receivable

The components of accounts receivable are as follows:

January 31,	2001	2000
Customers	$716,218	$611,858
Other	22,266	20,969
Allowance for doubtful accounts	(16,531)	(15,838)
Accounts receivable, net	$721,953	$616,989

CISCO SYSTEMS, INC.

5. Balance Sheet and Cash Flow Details

The following tables provide details of selected balance sheet items (in millions):

	July 28, 2001	July 29, 2000
Inventories, net:		
Raw materials	$ 662	$ 145
Work in process	260	472
Finished goods	669	496
Demonstration systems	93	119
Total	$1,684	$1,232

DREYERS GRAND ICE CREAM, INC.

Note 4: Property, Plant, and Equipment

Property, plant, and equipment at December 30, 2000 and December 25, 1999 consisted of the following:

(In thousands)	2000	1999
Machinery and equipment	$237,412	$197,635
Buildings and improvements	89,984	90,030
Capital leased assets		12,216
Office furniture and fixtures	6,463	6,481
	333,859	306,362
Less: Accumulated depreciation and amortization	165,472	134,778
	168,387	171,584
Land	15,634	15,436
Construction in progress	6,812	10,372
	$190,833	$197,392

During 2000, the capital lease agreement covering certain equipment expired and the associated capital lease obligation was repaid. The agreement specified that title to the leased assets passed to the Company at the expiration date. Accordingly, the $12,216,000 of original cost of these assets was reclassified to machinery and equipment. Accumulated amortization under the capital leased assets was $7,748,000 at December 25, 1999.

Interest capitalized was $527,000, $256,000, and $1,244,000 in 2000, 1999, and 1998, respectively.

Depreciation expense for property, plant and equipment, including amortization expense for capital leased assets was $32,204,000, $31,607,000, and $32,375,000 in 2000, 1999, and 1998, respectively.

AUTOMATIC DATA PROCESSING, INC.

Note 7: Debt

Components of long-term debt are as follows:

(In thousands) June 30,	2001	2000
Zero coupon convertible subordinated notes (5.25% yield)	$ 62,312	$ 86,639
Industrial revenue bonds (with fixed and variable interest rates from 2.85% to 3.5%)	36,449	36,858
Other	12,681	11,713
	111,442	135,210
Less current portion	(1,215)	(3,193)
	$110,227	$132,017

The zero coupon convertible subordinated notes have a face value of approximately $108 million at June 30, 2001 and mature February 20, 2012, unless converted or redeemed earlier. At June 30, 2001, the notes were convertible into approximately 2.8 million shares of the Company's common stock. The notes are callable at the option of the Company, and the holders of the notes can convert into common stock at any time or require redemption in certain years. During fiscal 2001 and 2000, approximately $50 million and $31 million face value of notes were converted, respectively. As of June 30, 2001 and 2000, the quoted market prices for the zero coupon notes were approximately $139 million and $208 million, respectively. The fair value of the other debt, included above, approximates its carrying value.

Long-term debt repayments at June 30, 2001 are due as follows:

(In thousands)	
2003	$ 1,485
2004	290
2005	281
2006	822
2007	173
Thereafter	107,176
	$110,227

During fiscal 2001 and 2000, the average interest rate for notes payable was 5.9% and 5.0%, respectively.

Interest payments were approximately $10 million in fiscal 2001, $10 million in fiscal 2000 and $12 million in fiscal 1999.

MICROSOFT

Common Stock

Shares of common stock outstanding were as follows:

In Millions/Year Ended June 30	1999	2000	2001
Balance, beginning of year	4,940	5,109	5,283
Issued	213	229	189
Repurchased	(44)	(55)	(89)
Balance, end of year	5,109	5,283	5,383

Repurchase Program

The Company repurchases its common shares in the open market to provide shares for issuance to employees under stock option and stock purchase plans. During 1998, the Company executed two forward settlement structured repurchase agreements with an independent third party totaling 42 million shares of stock and paid cash for a portion of the purchase price. In 1999, the Company settled the agreements by returning 28 million shares of stock, based upon the stock price on the date of settlement. The timing and method of settlement were at the discretion of the Company. The differential between the cash paid and the price of Microsoft common stock on the date of the agreement was originally reflected in common stock and paid-in-capital. In 2001, the Company entered into a structured stock repurchase transaction giving it the right to acquire 5.1 million of its shares (2.55 million shares in October 2001 and 2.55 million shares in June 2002) in exchange for an up-front net payment of $264 million.

INSIGHT

The Concept of an Executory Contract

Consider a 10-year, $100 million contract signed by a sports franchise to acquire the services of a sports superstar. When this contract is signed, it represents an **executory contract,** one in which both parties promise to perform certain duties as outlined in the contract between them. Since the franchise will receive the benefits of this contract in the future, accounting treats the obligation as an executory contract and generally does not require the business to recognize a liability. However, when the franchise begins to either pay the player or receive player services, the business can record a portion (for example, $10,000,000) of the 100-million-dollar transaction. That is, when either event occurs, the contract is said to be *partially executed* and a liability may be recorded. Essentially, accounting does not record a liability *until* the business incurs an obligation for a past or current benefit received.

When a sports star, such as Alex Rodriguez (A-Rod), signs a contract with a sports franchise, this is an executory contract and does not usually require the franchise to recognize a liability.

The concept of an executory contract should not be entirely new to you. In Chapter 2, for example, you learned that a transaction must affect the entity's current financial position before it can be recorded. When the multimillion dollar contract is signed, neither the current financial position of the business nor that of the player is affected. That is, the contract is unexecuted—neither side has performed.

For another perspective on why accounting doesn't have to report certain liability transactions in the balance sheet, let's reconsider our definition of a liability. In Chapter 3, for example, we defined liabilities as claims of creditors against assets and as debts or obligations. The generally accepted and more technical definition, however, is that **liabilities** are probable future sacrifices of economic benefits arising from *present obligations of a particular entity* to transfer assets or provide services to other entities in the future *as a result of past transactions or events.*[2] The italicized phrases, *present obligations of a particular entity* and *as a result of past transactions or events,* mean that you must have a present obligation for services performed to record a liability. That is, you are not required to record a liability when you have a future contractual obligation to make payments.

The **insight** you should gain here is that since commitments usually represent executory contracts, they are not initially reported on the balance sheet as liabilities. Therefore, if you want to know the amount of a company's future cash obligations, you have to look beyond the liability section and consult the notes to the financial statements for such executory contracts.

[2]"Elements of Financial Statements," *Statement of Financial Accounting Concepts No. 6* (Stamford, Conn.: Financial Accounting Standards Board, 1985), para. 35.

executory contracts. Since these obligations are not customarily reported as balance sheet liabilities, they represent a popular form of off-balance-sheet financing. A further reading of this footnote indicates that the company is obligated for future lease payments of $255,000,000 beyond 2000. Do you think that Apple's insertion of this financial information in the notes section of its annual report is an unethical practice?

FIGURE 5-9

An example of a note about commitments in an annual report of Apple Computer, Inc.

Apple Computer, Inc.

Note 9—Commitments, Contingencies, and Related Party Transactions

LEASE COMMITMENTS: The Company leases various facilities, equipment, and data transmission capacity under noncancelable operating lease arrangements. The major facilities leases are for terms of 5 to 10 years and generally provide renewal options for terms of 3 to 5 additional years. Rent expense under all operating leases was approximately $93 million, $61 million, and $63 million in 2000, 1999, and 1998, respectively. Future minimum lease payments under noncancelable operating leases having remaining terms in excess of one year as of September 30, 2000, are as follows (in millions):

2001	$ 61
2002	55
2003	40
2004	30
2005	18
Later Years	51
Total minimum lease payments	$ 255

In fact, most informed users of financial statements would *not* consider Apple guilty of an unethical financial reporting practice—it has simply followed generally accepted accounting principles to deal with the effects of executory contracts. Why? Because the occupancy of leased facilities and rental of equipment for years beyond 2000 does not represent a *past* transaction. If Apple is "guilty" of anything, it's of cleverly structuring the financing of its facilities and equipment to avoid reporting a large liability on its balance sheet. Clearly, Apple would be guilty of an unethical practice if it failed to disclose this "in substance" liability in the notes.

Like commitments, *contingencies* are special types of liabilities that are rarely reported on the balance sheet itself, but they might be disclosed in the notes to the financial statements. Unlike the future obligation under a commitment, however, a contingency may never materialize. Using a key word from the liability definition introduced previously, one can say that the chance that a contingency will become a liability is less than *probable*. In other words, a **contingent liability** is a potential future obligation arising from past events that is contingent on the outcome of a future event, such as a lawsuit. The uncertainty of such a liability ever occurring prevents it from normally being disclosed on the balance sheet. For example, the 2000 annual report of The Walt Disney Company reported the following contingency information under the heading Commitments and Contingencies:

> *The Company, together with, in some instances, certain of its directors and officers, is a defendant or co-defendant in various legal actions involving copyright, breach of contract, and various other claims incident to the conduct of its businesses. Management does not expect the Company or the Internet Group to suffer any material liability by reason of such actions, nor does it expect that such actions will have a material effect on the Company's or the Internet Group's liquidity or operating results.*

Now that you understand more about commitments and contingencies, it's important to realize that you cannot take the balance sheet at face value. Be watchful for company disclosures about transactions that might obligate it in the future, even though it does not have to report these transactions at present. Because valuable information often awaits you in such other parts of the annual report as the MD&A and the notes, be sure you look beyond the financial statement. Now, let's return to the balance sheet to learn how monetary amounts are assigned to assets.

How Are Assets on a Balance Sheet Measured?

To learn how assets are measured on the balance sheet, you must first determine whether you are looking at a business or personal balance sheet. A broad interpretation of the entity concept introduced in Chapter 2 is that a business balance sheet accounts for the affairs of the business, whereas a personal balance sheet accounts for the nonbusiness affairs of the owner(s). Since a business entity and a personal entity are so different, it follows that some of their assets are not measured in the same way. Keep this difference in mind as you discover how assets are measured in different entities—a discovery that is critical to effectively using the balance sheet as a business decision-making tool.

Alternative Ways to Measure Assets

The appropriate measure of an asset's value, sometimes referred to as *asset valuation*, has long concerned the accounting profession. Accounting scholars often use the concepts of entry and exit prices to illuminate this subject. For example, when goods (such as inventory) and services are acquired, they are said to "enter" the business and their purchase prices are called *entry prices*. When those same goods and services are sold or otherwise disposed of, they are said to "exit" the business and their selling or liquidation prices are called *exit prices*. This perspective creates at least four ways to measure assets: historical cost, a past entry price; replacement cost or current cost, a current entry price; fair market value, a current exit price; and the present value of future cash flows, a calculation involving future exit prices. Let's take a closer look at each of these entry and exit prices.

Entry Prices Many people who have taken an accounting course mistakenly believe that *all* assets are reported on the balance sheet at their **historical cost**, the price paid to acquire them. Historical cost is a past entry price measurement and is also called *original cost* or *acquisition cost*. The historical cost concept states that assets are ordinarily recorded in the accounting records at cost and later reported in the balance sheet at cost. This asset measure can be illustrated by looking at an example from Cards & Memorabilia Unlimited. Assume that in October 2001, you purchased a single pack of year 2001 cards manufactured by Upper Deck for $4.50 from CMU. If you were fortunate enough to find a card for baseball superstar Mark McGwire in the standard pack of 10 cards, you might argue that your historical cost for this card, including sales tax at 8%, is approximately fifty cents [($4.50 × 1.08)/10].

Assume that in April 2002, you give the Mark McGwire card to a friend as a gift. You might be curious to find out this card's **replacement cost** or **current cost**, the cost you would pay to *replace* the card you purchased in October 2001. Undoubtedly, this current entry price will be higher in April when the new baseball season is in full stride and the supply of his 2001 card has diminished. Also, it is less likely you will find a Mark McGwire card in a still unopened 2001 pack in the 2002 card season. Assume that the April price guide indicates you have to pay approximately $4.50 to *replace* the same card you bought in October for 50 cents. In this case, $4.50 represents the replacement cost required to buy the card you once owned. Many managers seek replacement cost information to help them set their prices high enough to both cover the current cost of replacing their inventory and earn a reasonable profit.

Exit Prices Individuals who are unfamiliar with business financial statements often assume that assets are reported on the balance sheet at a current exit price measure called **fair market value** or *fair value*, the expected selling price of those assets. This assumption is not unreasonable if you consider how people inquire about personal assets, such as cars or homes. They ask questions such as, "What's it worth?" or "How much could you sell that for now?" This asset measure can be illustrated by returning to our Cards & Memorabilia Unlimited example and assuming that instead of giving the Mark McGwire card as a gift, you decide to immediately sell it. One rule of thumb is to expect to receive about 60% of the single card "out of pack" price guide selling price. Thus, if the full retail selling price of this card is $4.00, you would receive $2.40 ($4.00 × 60%). Despite this guideline, you would discover there is no single fair market value but a range of market values for this card. For example, five different card stores might very well offer you five different prices. Thus, one measure of this card's fair market value would be to take the average of the five different price quotes from different dealers. The fair market value would also depend on whether you sell the card to a dealer, such as Susan, or to another collector. If you sold the card to a dealer in the St. Louis area, where McGwire is particularly popular, you could expect to receive more than $2.40. You would probably receive more than $2.40 if you sold the card to another collector, since we now know the collector might have to pay as much as $4.50 to buy this card from a store.

Finally, accounting educators and theoreticians often focus on the "future economic benefits" portion of the asset definition to argue that many assets should be reported on the balance sheet at a future exit price measure called the **present value of future cash flows**. This measure is calculated by converting a set of estimated future dollar amounts into a single present value amount that can be recorded by the company. This valuation method will be discussed in *Appendix 12–1* and Chapter 13.

Now that you have read about each of these alternative measures of an asset, you should recognize how no single measure of an asset is superior to all others. Even if you decide to use fair market value, for example, you still have to decide *which* fair market value to use. Thus, even the same person might use different asset measurements for different decisions. To help you master these alternative valuation methods, use Performance Objective 16 shown here.

YOUR PERFORMANCE OBJECTIVE 16

Describe how the amounts reported on the income statement and balance sheet are determined by:

a. **Distinguishing** among the following valuation methods: historical cost, replacement cost, fair market value, and the present value of future cash flows.
b. **Identifying** the generally accepted valuation method for each of the major asset and liability accounts.

You might also refer to Figure 5-10, which appears later in this chapter, to help you master Performance Objective 16b.

As you will soon discover, personal balance sheets report some assets differently than do business balance sheets, and business balance sheets use a combination of all four valuation methods described above. So now that you understand these methods of asset measurement, let's explore how personal balance sheets differ from business balance sheets in reporting assets. Then, we'll take an initial look at the values used by businesses of today in reporting each of their major asset categories.

The Moment When All Valuation Methods
Are Equivalent

When you buy an asset from a seller, such as buying the Mark McGwire card for $4.50 from a dealer in April 2002, there is a single exchange price. Interestingly, this single price represents your asset's historical cost, its current cost, its fair market value, and its present value of future cash flows. In theory, this interesting result exists only for an instant—the moment you purchase the asset. At this instant, all valuation methods, by definition, are equivalent. This fact—that assets are initially recorded at their current fair market value—does not contradict the historical cost concept. Although all valuation methods are equivalent at the moment of purchase, each method diverges from all the others as time passes, except by coincidence. For example, the current fair market value of most assets begins to differ from its historical cost *immediately* after purchase. Thus, the fair market value of the Mark McGwire card will likely increase over time and will be different from the amount you paid for it.

The **insight** you should gain here is that these valuation methods generate an equivalent amount when an asset is *recorded* but different amounts when that asset is *reported*. These methods, therefore, are useful only when the asset is *reported* on the balance sheet. Be sure you understand this distinction between *recording* and *reporting*, because it is an important one that we will revisit in future chapters.

Asset Valuation: Personal Balance Sheet

Personal balance sheets, sometimes referred to as personal financial statements, present the financial condition of either an individual, a husband and wife, or a family. In the personal balance sheet, the term "estimated current value," or fair market value, has been the basis used to measure personal assets since 1983, when it replaced historical cost. The authority for such accounting rules is called **generally accepted accounting principles**, or **GAAP**—the principles, rules, and procedures that define currently accepted accounting practice in the United States. Although the Financial Accounting Standards Board and its predecessors are the primary source of these acceptable methods, the American Institute of Certified Public Accountants' (AICPA) Statements of Position also may contribute to this framework.

Users of the personal balance sheet depend on this statement to decide whether to grant credit (recall how Susan Newman was required to prepare one to obtain a bank line of credit and rental space for her business) or any of the uses described in the following AICPA Statement of Position:

> *The primary focus of personal financial statements is a person's assets and liabilities, and the primary users of personal financial statements normally consider estimated current value information to be more* relevant *for their decisions than historical cost information. Lenders require estimated current value information to assess collateral and most personal loan applications require estimated current value information. Estimated current values are required for estate, gift, and income tax planning, and estimated current value information is often required in federal and state filings of candidates for public office.*[3]

This **estimated current value** or fair market value of an asset is defined as the amount derived from an exchange of an asset between buyer and seller known as an *arm's-length bargaining transaction*. In such a transaction, it is assumed that both the

---

[3] "Accounting and Financial Reporting for Personal Financial Statements," *Statement of Position 82-1,* American Institute of Certified Public Accountants, October 1, 1982, para. 3.

buyer and seller are well informed and willing, and neither is compelled to buy or sell. When Susan prepared her personal financial statement in Chapter 1 (Figure 1-7), she estimated the market value of her personal automobile by using recent sales transaction information for identical autos. This information is compiled in what is generally called the "Blue Book" and is available at your library or local car dealership.

Asset Valuation: Business Balance Sheet

In contrast to personal balance sheets, business balance sheets employ a variety of ways to measure assets, as illustrated in Figure 5-10. This figure illustrates that business balance sheets use more than historical cost, a past entry price. For example, cash is reported at its current monetary value. Inventories, as you'll learn in Chapter 11, may be measured using a current entry price we call replacement cost. Accounts receivable are reported at the selling price of goods or services, a current exit price we call fair market value. Likewise, depending on classification, marketable securities may also be reported at fair market value. And investments in bonds and long-term notes receivable are reported at the present value of future cash flows. Nevertheless, it is safe to say the majority of assets are valued at historical cost.

FIGURE 5-10 How characteristic assets are measured and reported on the balance sheet

Asset Category	Asset Account Title(s)	Measurement Method
Current Assets	Cash	Current monetary worth
	Marketable Securities	Fair market value or cost
	Accounts and Notes Receivable	Fair market value less an allowance for uncollectibles
	Inventories	Lower of cost or replacement cost
Investments	Investments in Stock	Fair market value
	Investments in Bonds	Present value of future cash flows
	Long-Term Notes Receivable	Present value of future cash flows
Property, Plant, and Equipment	Buildings, Equipment, etc.	Cost less accumulated depreciation
Intangibles	Patents, Goodwill, etc.	Cost less accumulated amortization

Notes:
1. The measurement methods for current assets shown above will be described in Chapters 11 and 12.
2. The measurement methods for noncurrent assets shown above will be described in Chapters 12 and 13.

Now, let's turn to some basic arguments that business decision makers use to decide what asset measurement method should be used for particular assets. That is, to help you decide how to value particular assets, you should first decide what you value more—the *relevance* or *reliability* of accounting information.

Key Qualitative Characteristics of Accounting Information An important qualitative characteristic of accounting information is **relevance**, the ability of accounting information to make a difference in a decision.[4] For example, the current fair market value of a home is probably more relevant information to an owner interested in selling it than its purchase price or historical cost over ten years ago. In fact, you just learned that fair market value is considered more relevant than

[4] "Qualitative Characteristics of Accounting Information," *Statement of Financial Accounting Concepts No. 2* (Stamford, Conn.: Financial Accounting Standards Board, 1980), p. 15.

historical cost for making personal balance sheet decisions. Why, then, is historical cost the primary basis of measurement for business assets? At least three arguments have been used to justify its use for decision making in a business:

- *Market values are difficult to estimate; they are too subjective.* Consider once again the Mark McGwire trading card example. Although a price guide helps you determine a precise market value for the card, estimating a market value is still difficult, because there is substantial disagreement about the card's value. Market values do not generally meet the test of reliability, one of the most important qualitative characteristics of accounting information. **Reliability** is the degree to which a user of financial statements can depend upon or have confidence in the information.[5] A primary ingredient of reliability is *verifiability*, a condition in which the amount recorded for an asset is traceable to an underlying business document. It is argued, therefore, that the historical cost of an asset, unlike its market value, is relatively easy to measure accurately and is subject to independent or objective verification.
- *The reporting of market values is too costly.* Consider, for example, that measuring assets at fair market value requires revaluation each time a balance sheet is prepared, rather than the single measurement required by historical cost.
- *Market value information about most assets is irrelevant because assets are acquired to be used rather than sold.* That is, if you accept the **going concern concept**—every entity will continue indefinitely and is not about to be sold—you will not need to measure asset market values, such as those falling under the category Property, Plant, and Equipment. According to this argument, market value measurements are unnecessary because there is no interest in selling prices.

In conclusion, accounting information should be both relevant and reliable if it is to be useful for decision making. Unfortunately, however, there is sometimes a trade-off between these two attributes. For example, you have already seen in the Mark McGwire example how fair market value information about an asset is more relevant but less reliable than historical cost information about the same asset. With notable exceptions, therefore, business assets are reported at historical cost because market value measures are difficult to estimate, subjective, costly, and often unnecessary.

INSIGHT

Limitations of the Balance Sheet

Despite the wealth of information you can discover in a balance sheet, it does have several significant limitations. One, discussed earlier in this chapter, is that current accounting principles do not require reporting all obligations in the liability section of a balance sheet. Four additional limitations are that the balance sheet does not report the following items:

1. *The current market value of most purchased assets.* As you have seen, an asset's current value is believed to be more relevant in making decisions than its historical cost. But since the assets whose market values differ most from cost, such as buildings, machinery, and equipment, were not acquired to be resold, a traditional argument is that this limitation does not destroy the balance sheet's usefulness.
2. *Qualitative information.* Recall from the money measurement concept introduced in Chapter 2 that financial statements show quantitative rather than qualitative informa-

[5] "Qualitative Characteristics of Accounting Information," *Statement of Financial Accounting Concepts No. 2* (Stamford, Conn.: Financial Accounting Standards Board, 1980), p. 15.

tion. This means that the balance sheet does not provide a complete report about the business. For example, information that the president's health is failing, that a strike might be about to begin, or that the company is about to sign a very profitable contract are not captured in the balance sheet.

3. *The effects of general price level changes.* The money measurement concept assumes that the dollar is a stable unit of measure because it is the common denominator for conducting economic activity. Although inflation has declined in recent years, no reasonable person can argue that the dollar is a stable unit of measure. For example, today the purchasing power of the dollar is less than one-fifth of its 1949 level. If you do not use purchasing power as the unit of measure, you cannot validly add, subtract, and compare current dollars on financial statements with dollars of previous years. If, for example, prices have increased by 50% in the last decade, you cannot validly compare the amount of today's building account reported on the balance sheet with the amount of the building account reported ten years ago:

Building account reported 10 years earlier	\$80,000
Current building account	\$100,000

Without adjustment, it appears that the investment in this asset has increased. However, an approach known as **inflation accounting** produces just the opposite result. The key is to realize that if prices are now 50% higher—you need \$150 today to buy the same goods that cost you \$100 ten years earlier—the purchasing power of the dollar has been cut in half. In this case, the purchasing power adjustment is calculated as follows:

Old building account restated in current year dollars (\$80,000 × 150/100, or \$80,000 × 1.50)	\$120,000
Current building account	\$100,000

Notice that when measured in equal units of purchasing power, the *real* investment in this asset has decreased rather than increased. This example illustrates how important it is for you, as a decision maker, to use purchasing power adjustments when comparing dollar amounts widely separated over time. The fact that these adjustments are not reflected in the balance sheet does not prevent you from using your own inflation analysis when needed to make better business decisions.

4. *The value of human resources as an asset.* Despite the assertion of countless company presidents that "people are our most valuable resource," balance sheets do not include the value of a company's employees as assets. Should human resources be reported as assets? Not if we use our definition of an asset introduced in Chapter 3. There, we defined assets as things of value owned by an entity that provide future economic benefits. Under this definition, it can be argued that a person's value should not be reported on a balance sheet unless he or she is a slave. The generally accepted and more technical definition, however, is that **assets** are probable future economic benefits obtained or controlled by a particular entity as a result of *past transactions or events.*[6] This definition seems to allow for reporting human resources as assets since human workers do provide future economic benefits for particular companies. In the early 1970s, for example, the R. G. Barry Corporation, a Columbus, Ohio, comfort footware manufacturer, did report its human resources as an asset on a supplemental balance sheet included in its annual report. Although this innovative presentation shown in Figure 5-11 did attract favorable attention, other companies failed to adopt the approach, and after issuing its 1973 annual report, R. G. Barry

[6] "Elements of Financial Statements," *Statement of Financial Accounting Concepts No. 6* (Stamford, Conn.: Financial Accounting Standards Board, 1985), para. 25.

FIGURE 5-11

An actual presentation of human resources as a balance sheet asset for R. G. Barry Corporation

THE TOTAL CONCEPT
R. G. Barry Corporation and Subsidiaries
Pro-Forma
(Conventional and Human Resource Accounting)*

BALANCE SHEET	1972 Conventional and Human Resource	1972 Conventional Only
Assets		
Total Current Assets	$16,408,620	$16,408,620
Net Property, Plant and Equipment	3,371,943	3,371,943
Excess of Purchase Price over Net Assets Acquired	1,288,454	1,288,454
Deferred Financing Costs	183,152	183,152
Net Investments in Human Resources	1,779,950	—
Other Assets	232,264	232,264
	$23,264,383	$21,484,433
Liabilities and Stockholders' Equity		
Total Current Liabilities	3,218,204	3,218,204
Long Term Debt, Excluding Current Installments	7,285,000	7,285,000
Deferred Compensation	116,533	116,533
Deferred Federal Income Tax Based Upon Full Tax Deduction for Human Resource Costs	889,975	—
Stockholders' Equity:		
Capital Stock	1,818,780	1,818,780
Additional Capital in Excess of Par Value	5,047,480	5,047,480
Retained Earnings:		
Financial	3,998,436	3,998,436
Human Resources	889,975	—
	$23,264,383	$21,484,433

STATEMENT OF INCOME		
Net Sales	$39,162,301	$39,162,301
Cost of Sales	25,667,737	25,667,737
Gross Profit	13,494,564	13,494,564
Selling, General and Administrative Expenses	10,190,773	10,190,773
Operating Income	3,303,791	3,303,791
Interest Expense	549,225	549,225
Income before Federal Income Taxes	2,754,566	2,754,566
Net Increase in Human Resource Investment	218,686	—
Adjusted Income before Federal Income Taxes	2,973,252	2,754,566
Federal Income Taxes	1,414,343	1,305,000
Net Income	$ 1,558,909	$ 1,449,566

*The information presented on this page is provided only to illustrate the informational value of human resource accounting for more effective internal management of the business. The figures included regarding investments and amortization of human resources are unaudited and you are cautioned for purposes of evaluating the performance of this company to refer to the conventional certified accounting data further on in this report.

discontinued this presentation. At least two obstacles have prevented the value of human resources from being included in the balance sheet. One obstacle has been the difficulty in measuring human resources. Another stems from the cultural belief in the inherent worth of human life and the strong revulsion associated with placing a dollar value on people.

The insight you should gain here is that while a balance sheet is a valuable source of information about the financial condition of an entity, it is incomplete. Your analysis should be derived from several sources of financial information, including the income statement, as you will see in Chapter 6. It is not enough, however, to simply understand the content of the other primary financial statements. Instead, you will need to familiarize yourself with their limitations just as you did about the limitations of the balance sheet. This will be accomplished by mastering Performance Objective 17, shown below.

YOUR PERFORMANCE OBJECTIVE 17
Identify several limitations of the financial statements found in the annual report.

Summary with Key Terms

The number in parentheses following each **key term** is the page number on which the term is defined.

In this chapter, you examined balance sheet information found in the annual report that helps you make decisions. First, you learned how the format of a classified balance sheet can help you better interpret the content of its information. A classified balance sheet divides accounts into **current assets** (177) and noncurrent assets, **current liabilities** (178) and noncurrent liabilities. These categories help you evaluate the **liquidity** (178) of the assets as well as the **solvency** (179) of the business. The concept of the **operating cycle** (177) is used to determine which accounts are current and noncurrent. The word "operating" refers to the purchasing, selling, and collecting phases normally associated with the term "operating activities."

Next, you examined the meaning of the term **ratio** (179), a popular measure known as **working capital** (179), and two more useful measures designed to measure solvency. These **liquidity ratios** (179) are the **current ratio** (180) and the **acid test** or **quick ratio** (180). Cards & Memorabilia Unlimited's bank loan, however, was evaluated by using related but slightly different ratios called *loan to value* and *loan to liquidation value*. Two **leverage ratios** (182), the **debt to assets ratio** (182) and the **debt to equity ratio** (183), were then introduced as a means of evaluating an entity's **financial risk** (182).

You then learned about two important non-balance-sheet sections of the annual report. These were **Management's Discussion and Analysis of Operations** (185) or MD&A and the **notes** (186) or **footnotes** (186) to the financial statements. Three examples of important disclosures found in the notes include the **Summary of Significant Accounting Policies** (186), **commitments** (188) and **contingent liabilities** (191). The concept of an **executory contract** (190), described in an *Insight* of this chapter, underlies commitments.

The primary way in which personal balance sheets differ from business balance sheets centers around asset measurement. Personal balance sheets essentially use a **fair market value** (193) measure called **estimated current value** (194). Under current **generally accepted accounting principles**, or **GAAP** (194), business balance sheets use at least four measures including **historical cost** (192), **replacement cost** (192) or **current cost** (192), fair market value, and the **present value of future cash flows** (193). One effective argument for the use of historical cost has been the **going concern concept** (196). Discussions of which measure to use generally revolve around the trade-off between the **relevance** (195) and **reliability** (196) of accounting information. Both the definitions of **asset** (197) and **liability** (190) were refined in this chapter to support the more in-depth discussion of the balance sheet.

The final *Insight* section of this chapter described four limitations of the balance sheet. Two of these limitations result from using the money measurement concept. A potential solution to the problem that the dollar is assumed to be a stable unit of measure is called **inflation accounting** (197) and was briefly described.

Making Business Decisions

YOUR PERFORMANCE OBJECTIVE 2
(page 18)

[*This case was written by Ken LeDeit, the loan analyst featured in this chapter.*]

You are a bank loan analyst at Times Commercial Bank. In a meeting with a loan officer, you examined Mr. Charles Liu's application for a $2 million line of credit.

Mr. Liu owns Active Sports Inc., a sporting goods equipment wholesaler and distributor based in Indianapolis. He founded this company three years ago, and for the last two years its sales have doubled. He has decided to apply for a line of credit to support his company's high growth rate.

The loan officer has also told you that, as a wholesaler and distributor, Active Sports buys specialized and/or customized high-quality sporting goods, such as football equipment, tennis equipment, golf clubs, and so on, from small independent sporting goods manufacturers. It then resells this product to sporting goods retailers across the United States and Canada. By creating a niche in the sporting goods market, Active Sports does not have to compete against the much larger sporting goods companies. When you ask the loan officer about Mr. Liu's work experience, he tells you that before founding Active Sports, Mr. Liu was the vice-president of sales and marketing for seven years for one of the largest international sporting goods companies. Mr. Liu provides the following financial information:

	2003	2004	2005	2006
	Actual	Actual	Actual	Projection
Sales	$3,000,000	$6,000,000	$12,000,000	$24,000,000
Net income	150,000	300,000	450,000	550,000

	2003	2004	2005	2006
Current ratio	2.0	1.9	1.9	2.1
Quick ratio	0.5	0.4	0.2	0.4
Debt to equity ratio	3.0	4.0	5.0	4.0

Required

Use the preceding information about Active Sports to answer the following questions:

1. Is Mr. Liu's reason for applying for a line of credit—to support his company's high growth rate—legitimate?
2. Discuss how Mr. Liu's particular background affects your decision to grant Active Sports a $2 million line of credit.
3. Mr. Liu's projections do not include plans to contribute additional funds himself (equity financing). How would your analysis be affected if Mr. Liu's plans did include such equity financing in 2005 or 2006?
4. Mr. Liu projects a stable current ratio. His quick or acid test ratio, however, is quite low. What is the reason for such a difference? Can you think of any reasons why such a low ratio may not be cause for concern?
5. Evaluate Mr. Liu's debt to equity ratio. For example, you might consult a firm such as Robert Morris and Associates, which provides typical ranges for key ratios by industry. Given the company's 2006 sales and income projection, is it probable to expect a decrease in this ratio?
6. Using all of this information about Active Sports, explain why you think your bank should or should not make the loan.

Questions

YOUR PERFORMANCE OBJECTIVE 4
(page 22)

5-1 Explain in your own words the meaning of key business terms.

a. current assets
b. current liabilities
c. ratio
d. current ratio
e. quick or acid test ratio
f. present value of future cash flows
g. going concern concept
h. money measurement concept
i. inflation accounting

5-2 Explain why it is important to distinguish between current and noncurrent when examining a balance sheet.

5-3 Distinguish between the terms *operating cycle* and *operating activity.*
5-4 Using Figure 5-2, identify the three phases of the operating cycle and explain how each phase is different.
5-5 Compare and contrast working capital and the current ratio.
5-6 What is the primary limitation of working capital?
5-7 Compare and contrast the current ratio and the acid test ratio.
5-8 What is the primary limitation of the current ratio?
5-9 Compare and contrast the loan to value ratio and the current ratio.
5-10 Compare and contrast the loan to liquidation value to the acid test ratio.
5-11 Distinguish between a liquidity ratio and a leverage ratio.
5-12 Describe one advantage and one disadvantage of debt financing.
5-13 Explain what is meant by the term *financial risk* by applying it to your personal financial situation.
5-14 Compare and contrast the debt to assets ratio and the debt to equity ratio.
5-15 Distinguish between Management's Discussion and Analysis of Operations and the notes to the financial statements.
5-16 Compare and contrast financial statements with the notes to financial statements.
5-17 Describe the content of the Summary of Significant Accounting Policies.
5-18 Distinguish between commitments and contingent liabilities.
5-19 Identify from your own experience a transaction you have entered into that was, in concept, an executory contract.
5-20 Distinguish between entry prices and exit prices.
5-21 Distinguish between historical cost, fair market value, and current cost as measurements of assets.
5-22 Explain the meaning of the following sentence: "All asset valuation methods are equivalent at the moment an asset is purchased."
5-23 What are generally accepted accounting principles or GAAP?
5-24 Explain the meaning of an arm's-length bargaining transaction.
5-25 Describe the ways in which personal and business balance sheets differ.
5-26 Describe the reasons that business balance sheets do not use fair market value as the exclusive method for measuring assets.
5-27 Describe the significance of the going concern concept.
5-28 Distinguish between the terms *reliability* and *relevance.* How do these characteristics complement one another? Why is there often a trade-off between them?
5-29 Describe the major limitations of a balance sheet.
5-30 Argue for reporting the value of human resources on the balance sheet.
5-31 Argue against reporting the value of human resources on the balance sheet.

Reinforcement Exercises

E5-1 Ratio Analysis

Presented below are the balance sheets of Kilauea Caldera Hot Waterslide Park for the current year.

Balance Sheets
January 1 and December 31

Assets	Jan. 1	Dec. 31	Liabilities and Stockholders' Equity	Jan. 1	Dec. 31
Cash	$ 2,500	$ 2,000	Accounts payable	$ 2,000	$ 3,000
Marketable securities	1,500	3,400	Taxes payable	4,000	2,000
Accounts receivable, net	6,000	4,000	Bonds payable	8,000	8,000
Inventory	4,000	6,000	Preferred stock—6%	2,000	2,000
Prepaid assets	1,000	3,000	Common stock, par value $10	5,000	5,000
Buildings and equipment	22,000	22,000	Retained earnings	1,000	4,400
Less: Accumulated depreciation	(15,000)	(16,000)			
Total assets	$22,000	$24,400	**Total liabilities and stockholders' equity**	$22,000	$24,400

YOUR PERFORMANCE OBJECTIVE 3 (page 183)

Required

Calculate the following ratios for the current year:

a. Current ratio
b. Acid test (quick) ratio
c. Debt to assets ratio
d. Debt to equity ratio
e. Return on equity ratio (assume net income amounts to $3,600)

YOUR PERFORMANCE OBJECTIVE 3 (page 183)

E5-2 Ratio Analysis

Rostenkowski Company presents the following condensed and incomplete comparative balance sheet:

ROSTENKOWSKI COMPANY
Comparative Balance Sheet
December 31, 2003 and 2004

	12/31/03	12/31/04
Current assets	$ 78,000	$?
Noncurrent assets	?	?
Total assets	$298,000	$320,000
Current liabilities	$ 61,000	?
Noncurrent liabilities	?	85,000
Total liabilities	$128,000	$?
Common stock	$?	$120,000
Retained earnings	50,000	65,000
Total owners' equity	$170,000	$185,000
Total liabilities and owners' equity	$298,000	$320,000

Required

a. Calculate the missing amounts in these balance sheets.
b. Calculate the debt to assets ratio.
c. Calculate the debt to equity ratio.
d. What information would you need to calculate the acid test ratio?

Hint: The current ratio at the end of 2004 is 1.40.

Use an annual report (your instructor will assign a specific one or allow you to choose one) to answer Exercises 5-3 through 5-6.

YOUR PERFORMANCE OBJECTIVE 3 (page 183)

E5-3 Ratio Analysis

Calculate the current ratio for the company. Is this ratio increasing or decreasing?

E5-4 Ratio Analysis

Calculate the acid test ratio for the company. Is this ratio increasing or decreasing?

YOUR PERFORMANCE OBJECTIVE 3 (page 183)

E5-5 Ratio Analysis

Calculate the debt to assets ratio for the company. Is this ratio increasing or decreasing?

E5-6 Ratio Analysis

Calculate the debt to equity ratio for the company. Is this ratio increasing or decreasing?

YOUR PERFORMANCE OBJECTIVE 3 (page 183)

E5-7 Ratio Analysis

Refer to the model classified balance sheet of Idealistic Company presented in Chapter 4 (Figure 4-13) and repeated on the next page to respond to this problem.

Required

Using the classified balance sheet for Idealistic Company, calculate the following ratios:

a. Current ratio
b. Acid test (quick) ratio
c. Debt to assets ratio
d. Debt to equity ratio

IDEALISTIC COMPANY
Balance Sheet (in thousands)
December 31

Assets			**Liabilities and Shareholders' Equity**	
Current Assets			**Current Liabilities**	
Cash and cash equivalents		$ 75,000	Accounts payable	$ 80,000
Marketable securities		20,000	Loans payable	25,000
Accounts and notes receivable		60,000	Salaries and wages payable	15,000
Less: Allowance for uncollectibles		(3,000)	Taxes payable	18,000
Merchandise inventory		135,000	Current portion of long-term debt	7,000
Prepaid assets		13,000	Deferred revenues	5,000
Total current assets		$300,000	Total current liabilities	$150,000
Investments		$ 55,000	**Noncurrent Liabilities**	
			Notes payable	$100,000
			Capital lease obligations	125,000
Property, plant, & equipment	$250,000		Deferred income taxes	50,000
Less: Accumulated depreciation	50,000	$200,000	Contingencies (see Note 10)	
				$275,000
Intangible Assets			**Shareholders' Equity**	
Capital leases	$125,000		Common stock, $2 par, 100,000 shares	$200,000
Patents net of amortization	45,000	$170,000	Capital paid in excess of par value	50,000
			Retained earnings	100,000
			Less treasury stock, at cost	(25,000)
Other assets		$ 25,000		$325,000
Total assets		$750,000	**Total liabilities and shareholders' equity**	$750,000

YOUR PERFORMANCE OBJECTIVE 4 *(page 22)*

E5-8 Asking the Right Questions: A Group Activity
It's often said that knowing the right answer is not nearly as important as asking the right question. Asking the right question is a problem-solving skill that will help you make sound business decisions. In this exercise, you will review the vocabulary introduced in Chapter 5 by creating questions to match answers—similar to a popular TV show.

Required

a. Given an answer, what's the question?
Choose *three* of the following terms to serve as an answer. Create an appropriate question for each term. For example, if you choose the term *balance sheet*, you might create the question—*What financial statement shows the assets, liabilities, and owners' equity of an entity on a specific date?*

Current assets	Current ratio	Current liabilities
Operating cycle	Operating lease	Operating activity
Commitments	Working capital	Financial risk
Leverage ratio	Fair market value	Historical cost

b. Are you sure that's the question?
Have each member of your group read aloud the questions they developed in Requirement (a). As a group, decide whether each question is an accurate match for an answer. Once satisfied that all questions are appropriate, the group, as a whole, chooses the three best questions created within the group. Record the three questions chosen (with their answers) on separate pieces of paper or index cards and give them to your instructor.

c. What's the answer?
To ensure that you have learned the vocabulary terms listed in Requirement (a), your instructor will now quiz you on the questions written by all of your classmates.

YOUR PERFORMANCE OBJECTIVE 5a
(page 137)

E5-9 Transaction Analysis
Analyze the effect of the following transactions of Travolta Disco Novelties, a sole proprietorship, on the elements of the balance sheet using the format below. If you believe any of the following transactions should not be recorded, write NE for no effect and your reason.

		Fundamental Equation					
Transaction	Asset Account Title	Assets	=	Liabilities	+	Owner's Equity	Sources of Assets Account Title
a.							

Transactions

a. Tony Manero invested $100,000 cash in the company.
b. Paid $1,200 to Stallone Brothers Mutual for a two-year insurance policy.
c. Purchased a building (Odyssey Disco) for $50,000, paying 20% down and signing a mortgage note for the balance.
d. Placed an order for merchandise amounting to $5,000.
e. Purchased merchandise on account for $4,000.
f. Paid $2,500 owed on merchandise purchased in Transaction (e).
g. Gave the supplier of the merchandise purchased in (e) a 60-day note for the balance owed. Assume that the supplier accepted this note.
h. Tony Manero withdrew $10,000 in cash from the company.
i. Credit sales of merchandise to customers amount to $5,500.
j. Received $3,500 of cash in advance from Stephanie Mangano & Associates for next month's rental of office space in the Odyssey Disco.
k. Returned $500 of merchandise purchased in Transaction (e) that has not yet been paid for. Refer to Transaction (g) to determine the account title.
l. Collected $3,000 from a customer (O. Welles) on account.
m. The cost of merchandise sold is determined to be $2,800.

YOUR PERFORMANCE OBJECTIVE 5b
(page 57)

E5-10 Preparing a Balance Sheet
Using the transactions in Exercise 5-9, prepare an unclassified balance sheet.

YOUR PERFORMANCE OBJECTIVE 5b
(page 57)

E5-11 Preparing a Balance Sheet
Here is a list of balance sheet account titles taken in random order from a recent balance sheet of Microsoft Corporation (in millions):

Accrued compensation (a current liability)	$ 359
Cash and short-term investments	13,927
Retained earnings	7,622
Income taxes payable	915
Equity investments	4,703
Accounts receivable	1,460
Other current liabilities	809
Commitments and contingencies	0
Other current assets	502
Common stock and paid-in capital	8,025
Property and equipment	1,505
Accounts payable	759
Other assets	260
Unearned revenue	2,888
Convertible preferred stock	980

Required
Prepare a classified balance sheet that reports the financial condition of Microsoft Corporation.

E5-12 Preparing a Balance Sheet

YOUR PERFORMANCE OBJECTIVE 5b (page 57)

Here is a list of balance sheet account titles taken in random order from a recent balance sheet of Blockbuster Entertainment Corporation (in thousands):

Capital in excess of par value	$244,592
Current portion of long-term senior debt	501
Cash and cash equivalents	48,398
Retained earnings	223,002
Merchandise inventories	75,629
Subordinated convertible debt	109,645
Accounts receivable, less allowance	31,770
Accrued liabilities	30,025
Other current assets	6,797
Common stock	16,210
Videocassette rental inventory, net	232,171
Income taxes payable	15,303
Property and equipment, net	237,831
Other liabilities	22,538
Intangible assets, net	103,314
Commitments and contingencies	0
Other assets	68,215
Accounts payable	118,309
Long-term senior debt, less current portion	24,000

Required

Prepare a classified balance sheet that reports the financial condition of Blockbuster Entertainment Corporation.

E5-13 Preparing a Balance Sheet

YOUR PERFORMANCE OBJECTIVE 5b (page 57)

Here is a list of balance sheet account titles taken in random order from a past balance sheet of United Airlines Corporation (in millions):

Other shareholders' equity	$ 1,145
Cash and cash equivalents	647
Inventories, net	290
Short-term borrowings	431
Receivables, net	1,120
Advance ticket sales	1,080
Other current liabilities	2,985
Common stock	127
Minority interest	37
Postretirement insurance and health care benefit liability	1,016
Operating property and equipment	11,371
Other liabilities	1,549
Intangible assets, net	859
Accumulated depreciation and amortization:	
Operating property and equipment	4,699
Commitments and contingent liabilities	0
Other assets	1,053
Accounts payable	666
Long-term debt	2,652
Short-term investments	1,269
Prepaid expenses and other current assets	294
Leased operating property and equipment	1,132
Accumulated amortization: Leased assets	383
Convertible preferred stock	30
Deferred pension liability	394
Long-term obligations under capital leases	841

Required

Prepare a classified balance sheet that reports the financial condition of United Airlines Corporation.

YOUR PERFORMANCE OBJECTIVE 7c
(page 64)

E5-14 Classifying Transactions into Statement of Cash Flows Activities
Classify the transactions in Exercise 5-9 into the appropriate activity as described in PO 7b and then indicate which of these transactions will be reported in the statement of cash flows as described in PO 7c.

YOUR PERFORMANCE OBJECTIVE 11b
(page 99)

E5-15 Classifying Account Titles
For each of the following accounts, indicate whether it is an asset, liability, owner equity, revenue, or expense.

a. Preferred Stock
b. Deferred Revenue
c. Accumulated Depreciation
d. Investment in Subsidiary
e. Petty Cash
f. Dividend Revenue
g. Amortization Expense
h. Land Held for Future Use
i. Capital Lease Obligation
j. Capital Lease
k. Contingencies
l. Patents
m. Susan Newman, Drawing
n. Interest Revenue

YOUR PERFORMANCE OBJECTIVE 13
(page 105)

E5-16 Financial Statement Relationships
To work on this exercise, you must refer to the information found in Exercise 5-2. Assume that you are provided with the following additional information:

	For the Year Ended	
	12/31/03	12/31/04
Net income	$20,000	$?
Dividends declared	7,000	8,000

Required
Calculate the following items:
a. Net income for the year ended December 31, 2004.
b. Retained earnings on January 1, 2003.

Obtain an annual report and a 10-K report from the same company (your instructor will assign a specific company or allow you to choose one) to answer Exercises 5-17 and 5-18.

YOUR PERFORMANCE OBJECTIVE 15
(page 116)

E5-17 Distinguishing between Two Types of Annual Reports
Study the MD&A (Management's Discussion and Analysis of Operations) from the annual report to shareholders and the 10-K of the same company. What similarities and differences do you observe? Be specific.

YOUR PERFORMANCE OBJECTIVE 15
(page 116)

E5-18 Distinguishing between Two Types of Annual Reports
Study the notes or footnotes to the financial statements from the annual report to shareholders and the 10-K of the same company. What similarities and differences do you observe? Be specific.

YOUR PERFORMANCE OBJECTIVE 16
(page 193)

E5-19 Distinguishing among Asset Valuation Methods
Using a specific example from your own experience, distinguish among the following asset valuation methods: historical cost, replacement cost, and fair market value.

YOUR PERFORMANCE OBJECTIVE 16
(page 193)

E5-20 Identifying Generally Accepted Asset Valuation Methods
Identify the current generally accepted valuation methods for each of the following asset accounts reported on the balance sheet.

a. Merchandise Inventory
b. Accounts Receivable
c. Building
d. Investments—Trading Securities
e. Investments—Available for Sale
f. Investments—Held to Maturity
g. Investment in Bonds

Critical Thinking Problems

P5-1 Ratio Analysis

YOUR PERFORMANCE OBJECTIVE 3
(page 183)

Calculate the following ratios by referring to the balance sheet information for Microsoft Corporation presented in Exercise 5-11. Whenever possible, try to interpret their meaning.

a. Current
b. Acid test
c. Debt to assets
d. Debt to equity

P5-2 Ratio Analysis

YOUR PERFORMANCE OBJECTIVE 3
(page 183)

Calculate the following ratios by referring to the balance sheet information for Blockbuster Entertainment Corporation presented in Exercise 5-12. Whenever possible, try to interpret their meaning.

a. Current
b. Acid test
c. Debt to assets
d. Debt to equity

P5-3 Ratio Analysis

YOUR PERFORMANCE OBJECTIVE 3
(page 183)

Calculate the following ratios by referring to the balance sheet information for United Airlines Corporation presented in Exercise 5-13. Whenever possible, try to interpret their meaning.

a. Current
b. Acid test
c. Debt to assets
d. Debt to equity

P5-4 Ratio Analysis

YOUR PERFORMANCE OBJECTIVE 3
(page 183)

Refer to the model classified balance sheet of Idealistic Company presented in Chapter 4 (Figure 4-13) and repeated on page 203 to respond to this problem.

Idealistic Company is planning to purchase a new building at a cost of $20,000,000. The company is considering several different payment options. For each independent assumption listed, determine the effect the option would have on the balance sheet, and prepare a schedule showing the impact of each option on each of the ratios calculated in Exercise 5-7.

a. The company purchases the building for cash.
b. The company exchanges its marketable securities for the building.
c. The company issues a short-term note payable for the building.
d. The company issues a long-term note payable for the building.
e. The company issues one million shares of common stock in exchange for the building.
f. The company leases the building and the lease agreement is considered an operating lease.
g. Compare the results obtained in parts (a) through (f). Write a summary describing how each option would affect the company's ratios. As a result of your analysis, do you find one option preferable to the others? Explain.

P5-5 Commitments and Off-Balance-Sheet Financing

YOUR PERFORMANCE OBJECTIVE 3
(page 183)

In 1993, Apple Computer, Inc., had little or no debt, but the notes to the financial statements disclosed that the company had paid $170 million in lease payments and was committed to paying an additional $520 million in lease payments beyond 1998. By 1998, Apple reduced its lease payments to about $63 million and reduced its estimated future lease payments beyond 1998 to $171 million. Between 1993 and 1998, long-term debt increased by $949 million, while total assets increased by only $193 million.

a. Considering long-term debt does not include lease obligations, what other types of long-term liabilities could Apple have incurred since 1993?
b. How does this affect its previous use of off-balance-sheet financing?
c. How does this increase in long-term debt affect the current ratio, return on equity, and debt to total assets calculations?

P5-6 An Ethical Issue: Manipulating a Ratio

YOUR PERFORMANCE OBJECTIVE 8
(page 65)

You are the controller of a company and are responsible for preparing its financial statements. The treasurer, who is responsible for securing financing for the company, has approached you, stating that she is concerned about some of the numbers she has seen on the preliminary financial statements. The company has certain long-term debt obligations that require it to maintain a current ratio of 2:1, or the loans become immediately payable. Based on the preliminary numbers, the current ratio will be 1.95:1. The treasurer asks if it would be possible to reclassify some long-term assets as current, that is, long-term investments as marketable securities, or to reclassify some current liabilities as long-term. She believes these reclassifications can be defended by saying that the company's plans for its investments have changed or that its operating cycle has lengthened over time. Considering this request, respond to the following:

a. Why does the treasurer want you to reclassify items?
b. What affect will the reclassification have on the current ratio?
c. Identify the stakeholders (those who could be helped or harmed) if you were to make these changes.
d. What alternative ideas could you suggest to the treasurer?
e. Should you agree to make these changes? Explain why or why not.

YOUR PERFORMANCE OBJECTIVE 8
(page 65)

P5-7 An Ethical Issue: Manipulating a Classified Balance Sheet

Erica Quandary, a close personal friend, operates Health Nut Veggies, a small vegetarian restaurant. Erica's selection of low-fat entrees has attracted a loyal following of health-conscious customers. Because the success of her restaurant has been accompanied by the reputation of long waits for a table, she now wants to expand her seating capacity. When she discovers you are taking this course, she asks you to help her prepare financial statements that she can use to apply for a $100,000 business expansion loan.

Erica explains that restaurants have a particularly difficult time obtaining bank loans because of their high failure rate and the unwillingness of most banks to treat restaurant inventory as collateral. She confides to you that despite the critical acclaim her restaurant has received, she is pessimistic about her chances of obtaining a loan. She tells you that "My only hope is if the bank finds my financials to be as squeaky clean as my kitchen."

In your analysis of her financial records, you discover two troubling items. The first is a note payable to Jalapeño Hummous that is due in 90 days, but Erica has included it in her long-term liabilities. When you question Erica about this discrepancy, she insists that the bank will deny her the loan if this $5,000 liability is reported in the current liability section of the balance sheet. You also discover in conversation with Erica's attorney that a customer has filed a food poisoning lawsuit that has a reasonable chance of success. The customer claims that his breathing was so impaired from the restaurant's jalapeño sauce that he lost consciousness and suffered mild but measurable brain damage. The most compelling evidence against Erica, the attorney bitterly complains, is an excerpt from the restaurant's own menu that claims "Our jalapeño sauce will take your breath away." The customer is asking $10,000 in damages.

Required

a. Explain how your decision to classify the note payable as either current or noncurrent could be the critical factor in whether the bank makes a loan to your friend.
b. What decision will you make about how to classify the note payable? Give specific reasons to support your position.
c. Can you suggest any action by Erica that might help her avoid the ethical dilemma posed by the note?
d. How should the pending lawsuit be reported? Do you have a moral obligation to do whatever is necessary to help Erica obtain the loan? That is, should you not disclose the potential liability?
e. Would either of your decisions in (b) and (d) above be different if you were Erica or if you were a certified public accountant retained by Erica to evaluate the full and fair disclosure of her financial statements?

YOUR PERFORMANCE OBJECTIVE 11b
(page 99)

P5-8 Classifying Account Titles

Below are classifications frequently found on classified balance sheets within annual reports. Place the letter of the correct classification next to each of the numbered accounts.

a. Current assets
b. Investments
c. Property, plant, and equipment
d. Intangible assets
e. Other assets
f. Current liabilities
g. Noncurrent liabilities
h. Shareholders' equity
i. Non-balance-sheet account

1. Cash in savings account
2. Prepaid rent
3. Salaries expense
4. Goodwill
5. Contingencies
6. Organization costs
7. Undeposited cash
8. Allowance for uncollectibles
9. Investments in commercial paper
10. Land held for future use
11. Petty cash
12. Copyright held by business
13. Notes receivable, due in three years
14. Notes receivable, due in 60 days
15. Accumulated depletion
16. Property and equipment under capital leases
17. Treasury stock
18. Current maturities of long-term debt
19. Advances from customers
20. Advances to employees
21. Sales
22. Customer goodwill

P5-9 Analyzing the Balance Sheet

YOUR PERFORMANCE OBJECTIVE 14 *(page 115)*

Answer the following questions by referring to the balance sheet information for Microsoft Corporation in Exercise 5-11:

a. Describe in your own words what the current liability account Accrued Compensation represents.
b. Why is the inventories account plural? That is, what different types of inventory do you think this software manufacturer maintains?
c. How do you interpret the fact that the commitments and contingencies account has no balance?
d. Distinguish Common Stock from Paid-In Capital.
e. What contra asset accounts are apparently in use from the balance sheet of Microsoft Corporation?

P5-10 Analyzing the Balance Sheet

YOUR PERFORMANCE OBJECTIVE 14 *(page 115)*

Answer the following questions by referring to the balance sheet information for Blockbuster Entertainment Corporation in Exercise 5-12:

a. Although you have not been specifically introduced to the long-term senior debt, less current portion, or the subordinated convertible debt accounts, what do you think each account represents? *Hint*: The term *subordinated* was defined in Chapter 1.
b. How are the accounts Current Portion of Long-Term Senior Debt and Long-Term Senior Debt, Less Current Portion related?
c. How do you interpret the fact that the commitments and contingencies account has no balance?
d. What contra asset accounts are apparently in use from the balance sheet of Blockbuster Entertainment Corporation?
e. What types of intangible assets would you expect to find if you conducted a detailed analysis of this company's business?

P5-11 Analyzing the Balance Sheet

YOUR PERFORMANCE OBJECTIVE 14 *(page 115)*

Answer the following questions by referring to the balance sheet information for United Airlines Corporation (UAL) in Exercise 5-13:

a. Some large corporations have thousands of individual accounts. As a result, financial statements presented in annual reports are usually highly condensed. Given the fact that the balance sheet already includes a common stock account as well as a convertible preferred stock account, what do you think the other shareholders' equity account represents?
b. Describe in your own words what the advance ticket sale account represents. What other account titles might be acceptable alternatives?
c. How do you explain the fact that the commitments and contingent liabilities account has no balance?
d. Although you have not been specifically introduced to any of the following accounts, what do you think each represents?
    1. Minority Interest
    2. Deferred Pension Liability
    3. Convertible Preferred Stock
    4. Postretirement Insurance and Health Care Benefit Liability

e. What types of intangible assets would you expect to find if you conducted a detailed analysis of UAL's business?
f. Clearly distinguish between the operating property and equipment accounts presented in the balance sheet of UAL.
g. Distinguish between the contra asset accounts Accumulated Depreciation and Accumulated Amortization. Why can't both accounts simply be called Accumulated Depreciation in the interest of simplicity?

YOUR PERFORMANCE OBJECTIVES 14, 16
(pages 115, 193)

P5-12 Comprehensive Problem: Analyzing Financial Statements Using the Notes
Sony Corporation is a Japanese company in the electronics and entertainment industries. Approximately 30% of Sony's revenues are earned through subsidiaries in the United States. All financial information included in Sony's annual report is shown in Japanese yen. In most parts of the report, including the financial statements, a column is added showing the amounts in U.S. dollars, for the current year only. The following excerpts are taken from recent notes to the financial statements:

2. Summary of significant accounting policies:
The parent company and its subsidiaries in Japan maintain their records and prepare the financial statements in accordance with the accounting principles generally accepted in Japan, while its foreign subsidiaries maintain their records and prepare their financial statements in conformity with accounting principles generally accepted in the countries of their domicile. Certain adjustments and reclassifications . . . have been incorporated in the accompanying consolidated financial statements to conform with accounting principles generally accepted in the United States of America (U.S. GAAP). These adjustments were not recorded in the statutory books of account.

The preparation of financial statement in conformity with U.S. GAAP requires management to make estimates and assumptions that affect the reported amounts of assets and liabilities and disclosures of contingent assets and liabilities at the date of the financial statements and the reported amounts of revenues and expenses during the reporting period. Actual results could differ from those estimates.

Translation of foreign currencies
All asset and liability accounts of foreign subsidiaries and affiliates are translated into Japanese yen at appropriate year-end current rates, and all income and expense accounts are translated at rates that approximate those rates prevailing at the time of the transactions. The resulting translation adjustments are accumulated as a component of stockholders' equity.

Foreign currency receivables and payables are translated at appropriate year-end rates, and the resulting translation gains and losses are taken into income currently.

3. U.S. dollar amounts:
U.S. dollar amounts presented in the financial statements are included solely for the convenience of the reader. These translations should not be construed as representations that the yen amounts actually represent, or have been or could be converted into U.S. dollars. As the amounts shown in U.S. dollars are for convenience only, the rate of −124 = U.S.$1, the approximate current rate at March 31 has been used for the purpose of presentation of the U.S. dollar amounts in the accompanying financial statements.

Required

a. In your own words, explain what these notes tell the reader about Sony's financial statements. Specifically, in simple terms, explain how Sony prepares its financial statements, how it handles foreign currency translations, and how it reports U.S. dollar amounts.
b. In this chapter, you learned that business balance sheets measure assets using a combination of historical cost, current cost, fair market value, and present value of future cash flows. Based on your interpretation of these notes, what methods is Sony using to value the numbers presented on its balance sheet? Explain how you determined each method was chosen. How do these methods affect the relevance and reliability of the statements?

YOUR PERFORMANCE OBJECTIVES 3, 5, 12
(pages 183, 57, 102)

P5-13 Comprehensive Problem: Balance Sheet Analysis
Analyze the following comparative balance sheet for the Mason Company.

Required
Answer the following questions based on your analysis.

a. Is Mason Company a proprietorship or a corporation?
b. Has there been any owner financing during 2004, and if so, how much?
c. Has the current ratio increased, decreased, or remained the same?

MASON COMPANY
Comparative Balance Sheet
For the Years Ending December 31, 2003 and 2004

	12/31/04	12/31/03	Change
Cash	$ 6,800	$ 4,000	$2,800
Accounts receivable	7,000	8,000	(1,000)
Equipment	10,000	10,000	0
Less: Accumulated depreciation	(3,500)	(3,000)	(500)
Total assets	$20,300	$19,000	$1,300
Salaries payable	$ 1,800	$ 1,600	$ 200
Contributed capital	13,600	12,000	1,600
Retained earnings	4,900	5,400	(500)
Total liabilities & owner's equity	$20,300	$19,000	$1,300

d. Assume that the owner's withdrawals were $200 during 2004. Did Mason Company earn a net income or incur a net loss during 2004, and if so, how much?
e. The December 31, 2003 balance sheet discloses a retained earnings balance of $5,400. From this fact, which of these conclusions is correct?
   1. The company earned a $5,400 net income during 2003.
   2. The company had $5,400 of cash available for expansion at the end of 2003.
   3. No withdrawals were made in 2003.
   4. The company earned net income during 2003, but the amount cannot be determined from the available information.
   5. None of conclusions 1–4 can be drawn from the information provided.
f. No equipment has been acquired or sold since Mason began business. What was the depreciation expense for 2004?
g. Assume that the equipment's entire cost will be depreciated over its useful life. What was the originally estimated useful life of the equipment?
h. As of December 31, 2004, how long has Mason held the equipment?

P5-14 Comprehensive Problem: Balance Sheet Analysis
Analyze the following comparative balance sheet for the Dixon Company.

YOUR PERFORMANCE OBJECTIVES 3, 5, 12
(pages 183, 57, 102)

DIXON COMPANY
Comparative Balance Sheet
For the Years Ending December 31, 2003 and 2004

	12/31/04	12/31/03	Change
Cash	$ 5,200	$ 4,000	$1,200
Accounts receivable	9,000	8,000	1,000
Equipment	10,000	10,000	0
Less: Accumulated depreciation	(4,000)	(3,000)	(1,000)
Total assets	$20,200	$19,000	$1,200
Salaries payable	$ 1,400	$ 1,600	$ (200)
Capital stock	14,000	12,000	2,000
Retained earnings	4,800	5,400	(600)
Total liabilities & owner's equity	$20,200	$19,000	$1,200

Required
Answer the following questions based on your analysis.
a. Is Dixon Company a proprietorship or a corporation?
b. Has there been any owner financing during 2004, and if so, how much?
c. Has the current ratio increased, decreased, or remained the same?
d. Assume that cash dividends paid were $200 during 2004. Did Dixon Company earn a net income or incur a net loss during 2004, and if so, how much?
e. The December 31, 2003 balance sheet discloses a retained earnings balance of $5,400. From this fact, which of these conclusions is correct?
   1. The company earned a $5,400 net income during 2003.
   2. The company had $5,400 of cash available for expansion at the end of 2003.
   3. No dividends were paid in 2003.
   4. The company earned net income during 2003, but the amount cannot be determined from the available information.
   5. None of conclusions 1–4 can be drawn from the information provided.
f. No equipment has been acquired or sold since Dixon began business. What was the depreciation expense for 2004?
g. Assume that the equipment's entire cost will be depreciated over its useful life. What was the originally estimated useful life of the equipment?
h. As of December 31, 2004, how long has Dixon held the equipment?

YOUR PERFORMANCE OBJECTIVES 3, 5b, 9
(pages 183, 57, 68)

P5-15 Comprehensive Problem: Balance Sheet Analysis
Use the information in P5-13 and P5-14 to solve this problem. Assume that the numbers contained in the preceding problems were shown in thousands. For example, Mason Company had $6,800,000 in cash on 12/31/04. You are working as an intern for a bank loan officer. Both Mason Company and Dixon Company have submitted loan applications for $5,000,000. You have been asked to review the financial information submitted by each company. Write a one-page memo to the loan officer explaining to which company you would prefer to extend credit. In your response, be specific as to your reasons for choosing one company over the other. Consider items such as return on equity, debt to total assets, current ratio, form of business organization, and liquidity in your explanation.

YOUR PERFORMANCE OBJECTIVES 6, 14
(pages 59, 115)

P5-16 Comprehensive Problem: Financial Statement Analysis
On October 15, 1990, UAL Corporation, the parent or holding company for United Airlines Corporation, announced the largest widebody aircraft order in commercial aviation history—68 of the long-awaited Boeing 777's and 60 Boeing 747-400's—with an estimated value of $22 billion. This agreement, equally split between firm orders and options, required that the first of these new planes be delivered at the beginning of 1995. Although the Boeing Company's management was pleased with this order, they recognized, as they stated in their 1989 annual report, that a downturn in economic conditions could result in customers' asking to renegotiate the terms of firm orders or to cancel them totally.
a. Should this announcement be included in the annual report of UAL and of Boeing? If you think it should, when and where should it be reported? Write your suggestion for how the announcement should be worded.
b. Should the accounting for firm orders differ from the accounting for options? Why? And if you think they should, explain how.
c. How should advance payments on these aircraft be recorded?
d. UAL's 1992 annual report reported a total net loss of $957 billion. As a result, on December 14, 1992, United announced that it was involved in discussions with Boeing about revising the terms of the 1990 order described previously. Should this announcement be reported in either company's financial statements? Why? If you think it should, explain why and where it should be reported. Write your suggestion for how the announcement should be worded.
e. Can you think of an industry in which firm orders would be treated differently from options? If so, name that industry and give reasons for the difference in treatment. If you do not think that other industries would treat firm orders differently, explain why not.

YOUR PERFORMANCE OBJECTIVES 5b, 14
(pages 57, 115)

P5-17 Comprehensive Problem: Balance Sheet Analysis
The Philips Group balance sheet is derived from an annual report of Philips Electronics N.V., a global consumer electronics company. This company employs over a quarter of a million

people and has affiliated companies throughout Europe, North and South America, Australia, Africa, and Asia. List the key differences between this Netherlands balance sheet and the balance sheets of U.S. companies.

PHILLIPS GROUP
Consolidated Balance Sheets
December 31 (in millions of guilders)

Assets		**Equity and Liabilities**		
Fixed Assets:		*Group Equity:*		
Intangible fixed assets	2,290	Stockholders' equity	12,683	
Tangible fixed assets	12,954	Other group equity	1,752	14,435
Unconsolidated companies	1,218			
Other noncurrent financial assets	1,763	*Provisions:*		
		Long-term		6,002
	18,225	Short-term		3,100
Current Assets:				
		Long-term debt		6,179
Inventories	10,443			
Receivables	16,629	*Current Liabilities:*		
		Short-term debt		3,093
		Other liabilities		14,891
Cash and cash equivalents	2,824			
		Dividend payable		421
	29,896			
Total	48,121	Total		48,121

P5-18 Deciding What Asset Valuation Method(s) to Use

YOUR PERFORMANCE OBJECTIVE 16 *(page 193)*

In this chapter, one of the reasons cited for using historical cost in business balance sheets is the "going concern concept." Recall that this concept states that *every entity will continue indefinitely and is not about to be sold.* Assume you are preparing a balance sheet for a company that is about to be sold. Which valuation methods would you think are most appropriate to use? Would using a variety of methods be appropriate? Provide specific examples of each type of valuation you would use, and explain why you think it would be an appropriate measure.

P5-19 Deciding Whether the $15,000 Received from Susan's Uncle Is a Contingent Liability

YOUR PERFORMANCE OBJECTIVES 4, 6 *(pages 22, 59)*

Recall from Chapter 1 that when Susan's uncle learned of her plans to start her own business, he offered her $15,000 and told her to forget about paying him back. Susan gratefully accepted her uncle's offer, but insisted that once her business was well established, she wanted to pay him back.

a. Discuss why the $15,000 was not recorded as a liability by Susan. In your discussion, use the liability definition found in this chapter's *Insight* on executory contracts.
b. Did the fact that Susan's uncle agreed to subordinate this amount affect the bank's decision to not treat it as a liability? Why or why not?
c. Does the $15,000 represent an executory contract? Why or why not?
d. Does the $15,000 represent a contingent liability? Why or why not?

Research Assignments

A wide variety of interesting Research Assignments for this chapter are available for the following topics at www.mhhe.com/solomon:

R5-1 Finding Liquidity and Leverage Ratios in an Annual Report (PO 3)
R5-2 Calculating Liquidity Ratios (PO 3a)
R5-3 Calculating Leverage Ratios (PO 3b)

R5-4 How Do Loan Analysts Use Accounting Information? (PO 9)
R5-5 Using the MD&A to Make Balance Sheet Decisions (PO 14)
R5-6 Using the Notes to Learn More About Assets (PO 14)
R5-7 Using the Notes to Learn More About Liabilities (PO 14)
R5-8 Using the Notes to Learn More About Shareholders' Equity (PO 14)
R5-9 Commitments and Contingencies (PO 14)
R5-10 Investigating a Significant Reduction in Inventories (PO 14)

CHAPTER SIX

6

The Income Statement

Also be sure you have mastered the following Performance Objectives from previous chapters. They lay the foundation for the concepts you will learn in this chapter:

PO2
PO4
PO5
PO9
PO10
PO11
PO13
PO14

PERFORMANCE OBJECTIVES

In this chapter, you will learn the following new Performance Objective:

PO18 **Distinguish between** the accrual and cash basis of income measurement by being able to:

a. **Prepare** both an accrual basis and a cash basis income statement from the same set of facts.
b. **Explain** why the accrual basis generally provides a more precise income measurement than does the cash basis.
c. **Convert** a cash basis income statement into an accrual basis income statement.
d. **Describe** transactions in which cash flows precede, coincide with, or follow the period in which both revenues and expenses are recognized under the accrual basis.

THE HISTORY OF THE INCOME STATEMENT: FROM ITALY, TO THE AMERICAN RAILROADS, TO CARDS & MEMORABILIA UNLIMITED

Unlike the balance sheet, which existed as early as the 16th century, the income statement did not formally appear until the early 19th century. Nevertheless, the concept of reporting an entity's revenues and expenses for a specified time period had been encouraged several centuries before. For example, the man known as the first accountant, Luca Pacioli, in his historic work *Summa de Arithmetica* (1494), described the so-called *income account* as the place to record profits and losses from different ventures, trips, inventory items, and miscellaneous income. Likewise, the Englishman Simon Stevin (1607), the Scotsman Robert Colinson (1683), and the American James Arlington Bennett (1820) all used and referred to this income account. Despite their efforts, the income account was not translated into the income statement that we know today until the early 1800s.

Surprisingly, it was the U.S. railroads of the 1830s that were most responsible for popularizing the use of the income statement. To understand why railroads were so instrumental, you must first understand how critical they were to the economy of the United States. Long forgotten railroads that have since passed into history were, in fact, the economic backbone of this country. Although only railroad buffs might recognize the names Baltimore & Ohio (usually called the B&O), the Pennsylvania Railroad, and the Chesapeake & Ohio, these railroads moved people and products faster and more efficiently than ever before. Since they were the lifeblood of the communities on their lines, their financial condition was of interest to all the towns they linked. As a result, their securities were publicly traded and carefully scrutinized by U.S. investors and economic analysts during the 1800s. In addition, state and federal government officials were interested in their financial information for regulatory purposes. For all of these reasons, the financial statements of U.S. railroads were widely published.

Source: The following history of the income statement is based on the article "Income Statement/Income Account," appearing in *The History of Accounting, An International Encyclopedia,* edited by Michael Chatfield and Richard Vangermeersch, Garland Publishing, Inc., 1996, pp. 315–318.

(continued on next page)

(continued from previous page)

The income statement for the B&O Railroad for the year ended September 30, 1832.

[M. No. 5.]

A detailed statement of the Receipts, Expenses and net Revenue of Transportation on the Baltimore and Ohio Rail Road from the 1st October, 1831, to the 30th September, 1832.

During the month of	PASSENGERS.			TONNAGE.			TOTAL.		
	Receipts.	Expenses.	Net Revenue.	Receipts.	Expenses.	Net Revenue.	Receipts.	Expenses.	Net Revenue.
October, 1831.	$2,650 85	$1,449 07	$1,201 78	$ 797 65	$ 285 50	$ 512 15	$3,448 50	$1,734 57	$1,713 93
November,	3,438 77	1,628 32	1,810 45	1,166 37	595 —	570 37	4,605 14	2,224 32	2,380 82
December,	3,497 03	2,715 75	781 28	2,264 72	2,099 62	165 10	5,761 75	4,815 37	946 38
January, 1832.	2,873 91	2,743 64	130 27	4,995 02	4,479 04	515 98	7,868 93	7,222 68	646 25
February,	3,338 37	2,603 19	737 18	7,205 78	4,933 86	2,271 92	10,544 15	7,537 05	3,007 10
March,	5,299 97	2,708 54	2,591 43	8,406 58	5,005 80	3,400 78	13,706 55	7,714 34	5,992 21
April,	7,049 73	2,885 32	4,164 41	7,949 04	3,666 86	4,282 18	14,998 77	6,552 18	8,456 59
May,	8,240 25	2,949 00	5,291 25	8,243 14	3,394 49	4,848 65	16,483 39	6,343 49	10,139 90
June,	8,661 29	3,019 00	5,642 29	5,887 36	3,025 55	2,861 81	14,548 65	6,044 55	8,504 10
July,	8,614 39	3,035 55	5,578 84	5,393 67	3,062 39	2,331 28	14,008 06	6,097 94	7,900 12
August,	8 691 23	3,054 08	5,637 15	7,377 23	3,433 39	3,943 84	16,068 16	6,487 47	9,580 99
September.	5,554 53	3,061 32	2,486 21	9,340 82	3,692 19	5,648 63	14,895 35	6,760 51	8,134 84
Totals,	$67,910 32	$31,859 78	$36,050 54	$69,027 38	$37,674 69	$31,352 69	$136,937 70	$69,534 47	$67,403 23

Total amount of revenue brought down, - - - - - - - - -			$136,937.70
Ditto expenses, - - - - - - - - -		69,534.47	
In addition to the above there are the following charges for repairs, viz:			
By the Superintendent of Construction, for repairs of the Railroad,	2,067.97		
By the Superintendent of Machinery, for repairs of carriages and machinery,	4,071.99	6,139.96	75.674.43
Net Revenue,			$61,263.27

In spite of the widespread acceptance and use of the income statement by American railroads, it took another hundred years for income statements to become regularly included in the annual reports of a majority of this country's major businesses. One study of 20 U.S. industrial companies, for example, shows 1930 was the first year in which all 20 of these companies prepared and published income statements! Given the importance of earnings information to worldwide financial markets, it is truly amazing how long businesses failed to prepare income statements and communicate their useful information to investors. Today, of course, businesses around the world report income information on at least a quarterly basis.

Now that you've gained some appreciation of the historical development of the income statement, let's look at a modern version, that of Cards & Memorabilia Unlimited.

In Chapters 4 and 5, you learned about the balance sheet by focusing on only those transactions that affected it (Transactions A_1 through L). In this chapter, you will learn about operating activity transactions and about the income statement that reports them. Once again, you'll examine the transactions of Cards & Memorabilia Unlimited to focus on essential income statement concepts. We'll begin by taking a closer look at revenues and expenses—the elements of an income statement.

What Are the Elements of an Income Statement?

An **income statement** is a financial statement that reports the results of operations for a period of time. Although it may be prepared for an individual or nonbusiness entity, the income statement is most often associated with a business entity. Income statements can report either the expected operating results of a future period or the actual operating results of a past period as illustrated in Figure 6-1. Recall that the first income statement shown in this figure—the operating budget or projected in-

CARDS & MEMORABILIA UNLIMITED
Operating Budget (Projected Income Statement)
For the Year Ending December 31

Sales revenue		$64,000
Expenses:		
Cost of goods sold	$40,000	
Rent	12,000	
Rent-related	2,700	
Depreciation	2,000	
Other	1,300	58,000
Net income		$ 6,000

CARDS & MEMORABILIA UNLIMITED
Income Statement
For the Year Ending December 31

Revenues:		
Sales revenue	$86,600	
Service revenue	600	
Interest revenue	300	$87,500
Expenses:		
Cost of goods sold	$30,000	
Rent expense	11,000	
Salaries expense	8,750	
Depreciation expense	2,600	
Miscellaneous expense	4,600	
Interest expense	200	
Loss on equipment sale	350	57,500
Net income		$30,000

FIGURE 6-1

Two income statements with which you are already familiar

come statement—was presented in Chapter 1, and this figure's second income statement was presented in Chapter 3. Notice that this second income statement represents CMU's actual operating results for its first year of business. As you work through this chapter's description of CMU's operating activity transactions, you will learn how this income statement emerged. Recall Performance Objective 10:

YOUR PERFORMANCE OBJECTIVE 10
Prepare an income statement that reports the results of operations of any entity.

An income statement enables decision makers to evaluate the operating performance of an entity. Since you already know that the primary elements of the income statement are revenues and expenses, we'll now examine these two elements more closely. Then, you'll learn about two additional elements often reported in an income statement—gains and losses.

Revenue

Revenue represents an increase in the portion of owners' equity known as retained earnings. Recall from Chapter 3 that this increase in retained earnings results from merchandise sold, services rendered, or interest or dividends received or receivable. Revenue is not recorded when cash is received from a loan or from owner contributions. Revenue is derived from operating activities rather than from financing or investing activities. Though you can think of revenue as an accomplishment, don't confuse revenue with assets. Instead, think of revenue as the source of an asset; that is, when a revenue is recorded, it is accompanied by assets, such as cash or accounts receivable.

Expense

An expense represents a decrease in the portion of owners' equity known as retained earnings. This decrease in retained earnings arises from an ongoing major or central operating activity or transaction in which an asset is used up or a liability is incurred. You might think of an expense as an effort, but the definition you are most likely to remember and apply is that of an **expense** representing the cost of goods or services that are used up or consumed to produce revenue. An expense is essentially an expired asset. For example, cost of goods sold, an expense, is recorded when inventory, an asset, is removed or expires because it is sold.

Gains and Losses

Gains and losses usually occupy less room on an income statement than revenues and expenses. But don't let that fool you. Gains and losses usually represent a critical part of one's reading and analysis of an income statement.

Gains are increases and **losses** are decreases in retained earnings that result from *peripheral* or *incidental* transactions of a company. For example, suppose a retailer sells for $10,000 unneeded land that originally cost $7,000. Unlike revenue from selling merchandise inventory, the $3,000 gain ($10,000 selling price less $7,000 cost) recorded for this sale of land does not represent the retailer's primary operating activity. Hence, the sale of the land is a peripheral or incidental transaction.[1]

Gains and losses arise from transactions and events that do not result in either revenues or expenses. That is, gains and losses are customarily derived from the nonoperating sale or disposal of investments and other noncurrent assets and liabilities, whereas revenues and expenses are customarily derived from such operating activities as rendering services, producing goods, and/or delivering goods. Referring to our example, the $3,000 gain arises from a sale of the noncurrent asset known as land.

In a gain, the increase in retained earnings is accompanied either by a net increase in assets or by a decrease in a liability; whereas in a loss, the decrease in retained earnings is accompanied by either a net decrease in assets or an increase in a liability. You calculate the amount of such a gain or loss on land by comparing the selling price of an asset, if any, to its original cost. Again in our example, the $3,000 increase in retained earnings is accompanied by a $10,000 increase in cash and a $7,000 decrease in land.

CARDS & MEMORABILIA UNLIMITED

When depreciable assets are sold, the calculation of a gain or loss is actually more complicated than this land sale illustration. Assume, for example, that on December 31 of the company's first year of operations, Cards & Memorabilia Unlimited sells all of the store equipment it purchased in Transaction C_1. As described in Figure 4-9, this asset's book value (original cost less accumulated depreciation) at the end of its first year of use is now $8,000 [$10,000 − ($10,000/5)]. Assume further that one-half of the equipment was sold for $6,000 and the other half was sold for $3,000. The resulting gain and loss would be calculated as follows:

---

[1] "Elements of Financial Statements," *Statement of Financial Accounting Concepts No. 6* (Stamford, Conn.: Financial Accounting Standards Board, 1985), paragraphs 82–89.

Selling price	$6,000	Selling price	$3,000
Asset book value	−4,000*	Asset book value	−4,000*
Gain on sale	$2,000	Loss on sale	$(1,000)

*1/2 ($10,000 cost − $2,000 accumulated depreciation)

Two characteristics that gains and losses have in common with revenues and expenses are that they both affect retained earnings and are reported in an income statement. But there are three important differences between them. First, as you've already seen, gains and losses result from a company's peripheral or incidental transactions, whereas revenues and expenses result from a company's major or central operations or activities. Second, the amount of a gain or loss is the result of reducing one number by some other number, whereas revenues and expenses represent numbers not reduced by any significant items. In other words, gains and losses are *net inflows and outflows*, whereas revenues and expenses are *gross inflows and outflows*. For example, the $3,000 gain on the land sale and reported in the income statement is the *net* result of subtracting the cost or book value of an asset from its selling price. In contrast, when sales revenue is reported in the income statement, it is not reduced by any significant items. It essentially stands alone as a gross inflow of resources that ultimately produces *net* income only when it is reduced by other gross amounts, such as cost of goods sold. Third, unlike revenues and expenses, gains and losses often occur because they are based on an accounting estimate. Assume, for example, that Susan had overestimated her store equipment's useful life (10 years rather than 5 years) and then sold equipment costing $10,000 at the end of two years for $7,000. Susan's accumulated depreciation amount would be understated ($2,000 rather than $4,000), causing the asset's book value to be overstated ($8,000 rather than $6,000), resulting in the reporting of a loss rather than a gain. This error in estimation is shown here:

Correct Calculation		**Incorrect Calculation**	
Book value: $10,000 − 2($10,000/5) =	$6,000	$10,000 − 2($10,000/10) =	$ 8,000
Selling price	7,000	Selling price	7,000
Less book value	−6,000	Less book value	−8,000
Gain	$1,000	Loss	$(1,000)

Revenue Transactions

Recall that revenues represent claims against two assets that an entity receives—cash and accounts receivable. That is, entities increase cash whenever making a *cash sale* and increase accounts receivable whenever making a *credit sale* or *sale on account*. Today, however, the easy availability and popularity of credit cards has added a variation of these revenue transactions called the *credit card sale*. We'll examine this transaction in an *Insight*, but we will begin our study of revenue transactions with cash sales.

Cash Sales

A **cash sale** is a revenue transaction in which goods or services are exchanged for cash (coin, currency, or customer check) that is received immediately. For example, when the retail giant Sears makes a cash sale, it increases both an asset called Cash and an owners' equity account (more specifically, the retained earnings account) called Sales Revenue. At the moment a sale is made, the Sales Revenue account increases, which in turn increases retained earnings and owners' equity. Assume, for example, that Sears sells men's underwear for $20 to a customer who pays in cash. The effects of such a cash sale on the fundamental accounting equation would be:

Revenue Transaction	Assets	=	Liabilities	+	Owners' Equity
A cash sale is made.	+ Cash 20				+ Sales Revenue 20

Credit Sales

A **credit sale** is a revenue transaction in which goods or services are exchanged for a customer's promise to pay the existing balance within a specified period of time, such as 30 days. Sears customers, for example, who hold the Sears credit card represent potential credit sales to the retailer. Accounts of customers who are unwilling or unable to pay their account balances at some point after they are due are known as *uncollectible* or *doubtful accounts*, or simply *bad debts*.

When Sears makes a credit sale, it increases both its asset Accounts Receivable and its owners' equity account (more specifically, retained earnings) called Sales Revenue. Assume, for example, that Sears sells a television at a total price of $379 and accepts the customer's Sears credit card for payment. The effects of such a credit sale on the fundamental accounting equation are:

Revenue Transaction	Assets	=	Liabilities	+	Owners' Equity
A credit sale is made.	+ Accounts Receivable 379.00				+ Sales Revenue 379.00

INSIGHT

How to Account for Credit Card Sales

Suppose a customer uses a Visa card to buy a $289 lawn mower. What will be the effect of this transaction on the fundamental accounting equation? This **credit card sale**, like the earlier cash and credit sales, results in an increase to sales revenue and, therefore, an increase to retained earnings and owners' equity, respectively. But which asset—cash or accounts receivable—must you increase to equal the corresponding increase in owners' equity? You might be surprised to learn that retailers usually treat sales resulting from credit cards as increases to cash rather than increases to accounts receivable.

To see why credit card sales are considered "liquid" enough to be considered equivalent to cash, let's look at an example. When Sears makes a sale to a customer who uses a Visa card, the Sears sales clerk electronically notifies the credit card company. In addition, Sears will also deposit the credit card slip along with its daily deposits of checks and currency to a bank. Within one or, at most, two days from the date of the sale, Visa Corporation, working through an affiliated bank, electronically increases Sears' bank account by $289 less a 2% merchant fee. Although this credit card sale does not provide immediate cash to Sears, neither do customer checks to be deposited in a bank. The effects of such a credit card sale on the fundamental accounting equation are:

Revenue Transaction	Assets	=	Liabilities	+	Owners' Equity
A credit card sale is made.	+ Cash 283.22				+ Sales Revenue 283.22

Notice that the cash account and the sales revenue account are increased by 98% of the $289.00 or $283.22. Although $283.22 represents the net amount that Sears will realize from this sale, can you detect one disadvantage in the preceding analysis? It is that the $5.78

($289.00 less $283.22 or $289 × .02) merchant fee, an important piece of information, is not recorded directly. To formally recognize this reduction in revenue or sales discount that reimburses Visa for its service, an equivalent but more complete transaction analysis follows:

Revenue Transaction	Assets	=	Liabilities	+	Owners' Equity
A credit card sale is made.	+ Cash 283.22				+ Sales Revenue 289.00 + Sales Discount (5.78)

Notice that the sales contra account called Sales Discount is increased by $5.78 in conjunction with the increase of $289.00 to its companion account, Sales Revenue. The function of this contra account is to reduce the gross sales figure of $289.00 and provide management with important information about the net sales realized from the transaction ($283.22). In this way, the cost of the merchant fee ($5.78) is more apparent.

An Alternative Analysis

Although the idea of the sales discount contra account is conceptually sound, a simpler, acceptable alternative is to treat the credit card merchant fee as a miscellaneous expense, rather than as a reduction of sales revenue. To demonstrate the validity of this approach, again consider the lawn mower sale:

Revenue Transaction	Assets	=	Liabilities	+	Owners' Equity
A credit card sale is made.	+ Cash 283.22				+ Sales Revenue 289.00 + Miscellaneous Expense (5.78)

Notice that this analysis shows both gross sales of $289.00, net sales of $283.22, and the cost of accepting a non-Sears credit card of $5.78. Treating this reduction in sales revenue as a miscellaneous expense provides essential information in a simplified manner.

Exceptions to the General Rule

The great majority of credit card sales are equivalent to cash sales; but some credit card sales are equivalent to credit sales and, thus, increase an account receivable. This happens when:

- *The seller makes credit card sales without the customer's signature.* The seller may accept a customer's credit card number over the phone and therefore does not get a customer signature. This significantly delays the ability of the credit card company to process the sale as quickly as in-store sales.
- *The seller has what is called a "limit account."* If the seller exceeds an agreed-upon dollar limit on credit card sales, the credit card company processes sales over the limit significantly more slowly than sales under or equal to the limit.
- *The seller agrees to wait for payment for 15 or 30 days in return for a lower merchant fee.*

In each of these cases, the seller has an account receivable that will be collected in one to four weeks. Thus, such sales are equivalent to the traditional credit sale.

The **insight** you should gain here is that credit card sales are generally treated as equivalent to cash sales in today's world of electronic processing. However, in those cases where the business does not have the technological means to receive cash electronically, credit card sales are equivalent to credit sales and, therefore, increase accounts receivable. Because technology is changing the world we live in so rapidly, however, it is highly likely that all credit card sales will soon be treated as equivalent to cash sales.

Revenue Transactions at Cards & Memorabilia Unlimited

Now that you have a basic understanding of revenue, we'll take a closer look at how revenue is reported on the income statement of Cards & Memorabilia Unlimited. Note that CMU honors three credit cards—Visa, Mastercard, and American Express.

Revenue Identification and Explanation Transactions M, N, and O_1 each represent a summary of several separate transactions that occurred during the first year of business. Transaction M, for example, summarizes the effect of thousands of individual cash sales totaling $63,200, which occurred from January 9 to December 31. Once again, don't look at the answers on pages 225 to 226 *before* you have attempted your analysis of the effects of these transactions, so you'll know exactly how well you really understand revenue.

Transaction M: $63,200 of cash sales are made to customers throughout the year.

Explanation: CMU experienced thousands of individual sale transactions in which merchandise was sold to customers in exchange for either coin and currency, check, or credit card charges. Susan divided her customer checks into two piles at the end of each business day. In one pile she'd put checks from customers whom she believed posed little or no risk of passing a bad check; this pile consisted of more than three-fourths of all checks. She deposited these checks in her bank account. In the second pile Susan put the checks with which she was not as confident. She deposited these checks with a check guarantee service, from which she received the face amount of the checks in return for a service charge. We will treat this service charge as a miscellaneous expense in Transaction T. Try to analyze this transaction before looking at the answer.

Transaction M	Assets	=	Liabilities	+	Owner's Equity
$63,200 of cash sales are made to customers throughout the year.					

Now let's look at Transaction N.

Transaction N: $20,000 of revenue is earned on account—$19,400 for customer credit sales throughout the year and $600 for teaching a course.

Explanation: CMU entered into hundreds of individual sales transactions in which merchandise was given to customers in exchange for three forms of assurance that the amount owed would soon be paid. Such sales "on account" consisted of Visa/Mastercard credit card sales above a $3,000 account limit per month set by Visa and Mastercard with CMU, American Express sales imprinted manually, and special arrangements Susan established between CMU and particularly reliable customers. The distinction between these credit sales and the cash sales in Transaction M involves the timing of cash received from customers. In a cash sale, the collection of cash is immediate, whereas in a credit sale, collection is delayed.

Transaction N	Assets	=	Liabilities	+	Owner's Equity
$20,000 of revenue is earned on account (credit sales) throughout the year.					

Finally, let's look at the last revenue identified for now, Transaction O_1.

Transaction O_1: $275 interest is earned from January 2 to December 2 on $6,000 of savings bearing 5% interest.

Explanation: Recall that in Transaction B, Susan transferred $6,000 into a business interest-bearing savings account. She decided to do so because her $50,000 credit line provided an emergency source of financing, and she desired to earn a return on otherwise idle funds. Each month, Susan earned $25 simple interest on her $6,000 savings account ($6,000 × .05 × 1/12). This cash was added to her account on the second day of each month for each of the months between February and December for a cash increase of $275 ($25 × 11) during the calendar year.

Transaction O_1	**Assets**	**=**	**Liabilities**	**+**	**Owner's Equity**
$275 interest is earned from January 2 to December 2 on $6,000 of savings bearing 5% interest.					

Revenue Analysis Let's now analyze Transaction M.

Transaction M	**Assets**	**=**	**Liabilities**	**+**	**Owner's Equity**
$63,200 of cash sales are made to customers throughout the year.	63,200				63,200

Analysis: The first of this transaction's two (dual) effects is on the cash account. When you receive cash from any source, you must increase the cash asset. Whenever you increase an asset, you must decrease another asset or increase a liability or owner's equity in an equal amount. Since neither an asset other than cash nor a liability is affected, the second of this transaction's two effects must increase owners' equity. This answer can be reconciled with the fact that sales revenue increases the portion of owners' equity called retained earnings.

Next, let's analyze Transaction N.

Transaction N	**Assets**	**=**	**Liabilities**	**+**	**Owner's Equity**
$20,000 of revenue is earned on account (credit sales) throughout the year.	20,000				19,400 600

Analysis: The analysis of this transaction is identical to Transaction M's except that the Accounts Receivable account, not the Cash account, is increased, and two types of revenue are affected. Note that $600 is recorded in a Service Revenue account, whereas $19,400 is recorded in a Sales Revenue account. Distinguishing between these types of revenues is important because it provides an owner/manager such as Susan useful feedback about the company's revenue sources. Remember that when you record increases to revenues, you also increase Retained Earnings, a specific owners' equity account.

Finally, let's analyze Transaction O_1.

Transaction O_1	Assets	=	Liabilities	+	Owner's Equity
$275 interest is earned from January 2 to December 2 on $6,000 of savings bearing 5% interest.	275				275

Analysis: This transaction's first effect is on the Cash account. When you receive cash from any source, you must increase the cash asset. Since the source of this cash is interest earned on a savings account balance, this transaction's second effect is to increase owners' equity, specifically the Interest Revenue account. This answer can be reconciled with the fact that interest revenue increases the portion of owners' equity called retained earnings.

Expense Transactions

The preceding analysis of Transactions M, N, and O_1 shows that when a company earns revenue, an increase to owners' equity is recorded. Likewise, the opposite is true in every expense transaction; an expense is recorded as a decrease to owners' equity. How do you decide if a cost should be recorded as an asset or an expense? We'll answer this question and then examine seven expense transactions for CMU.

Asset versus Expense

Recall from Chapter 1 that a **cost**, sometimes also called an **expenditure**, represents the amount of sacrifice made to obtain goods and services. So, when Susan purchased store equipment in Transaction C_1, $10,000 was the *cost* of the store equipment. Also in Chapter 1 we carefully distinguished a cost from an expense. An expense represents the cost of goods and services that is used up to produce revenue. Usually, an expense is recorded sometime after the occurrence of the related cost or expenditure. Using the store equipment example, $2,000 of the $10,000 cost is used up at the end of the first year of a five-year useful life. Thus, an expenditure or cost is not the same as an expense.

Assume that you have just made a $3,500 expenditure for goods or services by incurring a liability. Your expenditure must either be (1) recorded as an increase to an asset or (2) recorded as an increase to an expense as shown here:

		Fundamental Accounting Equation					
	Account Title	Assets	=	Liabilities	+	Owners' Equity	Source of Asset Account Title
(1)	Some Asset	3,500		3,500			Some Liability
(2)						(3,500)	Some Expense
				3,500			Some Liability

Alternatively, this expenditure could have been incurred by decreasing an asset, rather than by increasing a liability.

The real question, however, is a classic accounting question, "Should an asset or an expense be recorded to accompany the liability increase or asset decrease?" In Transaction C_1, we decided to record the store equipment expenditure as an asset rather than as an expense. But how did we know which account—asset or expense—to record? Fortunately, there is a very specific process you can use to help you decide when to **capitalize**, that is, when to record an expenditure as an asset and when to expense an expenditure. Figure 6-2 presents this process in a flowchart. Study this figure by beginning at the top of the chart with any expenditure and working your way through the flowchart to the presentation of the financial statements.

FIGURE 6-2 Deciding whether an expenditure is an asset or an expense

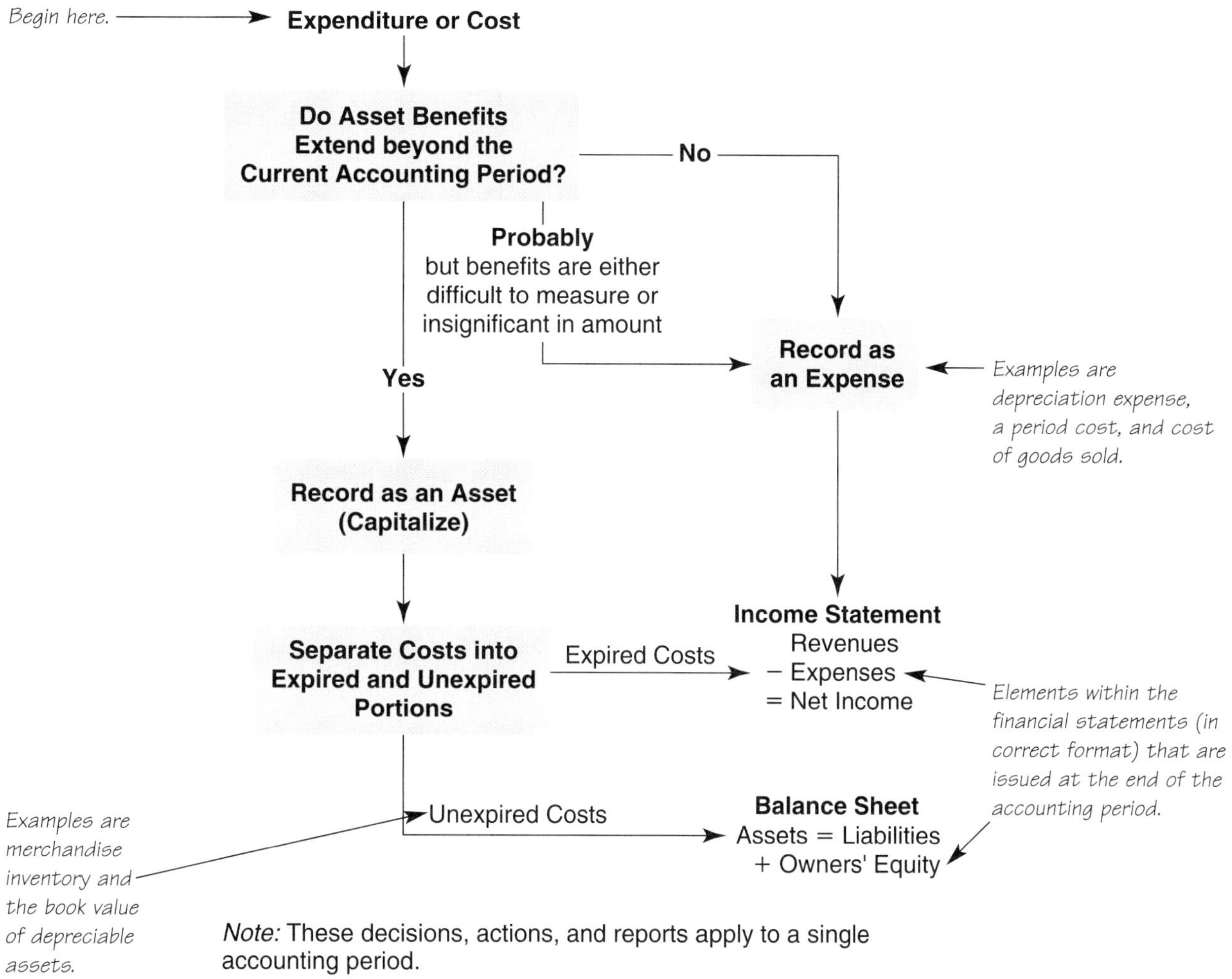

Begin here. → **Expenditure or Cost**

Do Asset Benefits Extend beyond the Current Accounting Period?

- **No** → **Record as an Expense**
- **Probably** but benefits are either difficult to measure or insignificant in amount → **Record as an Expense**
- **Yes** → **Record as an Asset (Capitalize)**

Record as an Expense ← *Examples are depreciation expense, a period cost, and cost of goods sold.*

Record as an Expense → **Income Statement**

Record as an Asset (Capitalize) → **Separate Costs into Expired and Unexpired Portions**

Separate Costs into Expired and Unexpired Portions

- Expired Costs → **Income Statement**: Revenues − Expenses = Net Income
- Unexpired Costs → **Balance Sheet**: Assets = Liabilities + Owners' Equity

Examples are merchandise inventory and the book value of depreciable assets. → Unexpired Costs

Elements within the financial statements (in correct format) that are issued at the end of the accounting period. → Expenses (Income Statement) and Assets = Liabilities + Owners' Equity (Balance Sheet)

Note: These decisions, actions, and reports apply to a single accounting period.

To interpret Figure 6-2 effectively, think of an **accounting period** as the length of time covered by an income statement and reported in its heading. An accounting period can be any length of time. However, the most commonly used accounting periods are monthly, quarterly, and annually. For example, many entities prepare monthly income statements to help their managers make timely decisions. Entities reporting to the Securities and Exchange Commission (SEC) prepare both quarterly and annual income statements. Nevertheless, it is increasingly common for many managers to now prepare daily spreadsheets to monitor their income statements. In practice, entities choose the length of their accounting periods on the basis of how often managers, investors, and other users require information about that entity's performance. Thus, activities shown in Figure 6-2 could represent *any* time period.

All entities, including CMU, prepare income statements for their **fiscal year**, which is any 12-month period. The fiscal year of most entities coincides with the **calendar year**, beginning on January 1 and ending on December 31. The type of fiscal year advocated by the accounting profession, as well as the SEC, however, is the **natural business year**, the period of 12 consecutive months that ends when an entity

reaches its lowest point of business activity. The Walt Disney Company, for example, uses a natural business year by ending its fiscal year on September 30, a point in time between its peak activities of summer and Christmas vacations.

Now that you understand the concept of an accounting period, reconsider Figure 6-2. If the benefits from the expenditure are expected to last for *more than* one accounting period, the expenditure is capitalized. Let's use Transaction C_1, an expenditure made to acquire store equipment, to work through Figure 6-2. Does this asset's benefits extend beyond the current accounting period, which for CMU is one year? Since the store equipment's estimated life is five years, the asset benefits do extend beyond the current accounting period. Thus, you select the Yes answer in the flowchart and capitalize the $10,000 expenditure. At the end of the current accounting period, the amount of cost consumed in operations with the passage of time (a period cost) is recorded as depreciation expense.

Now let's consider Transaction P, the payment of $1,000 rent each month. Is each of the monthly rent payments an expense or an asset? If you consider the February 1 payment, for example, you will realize that the benefits of this expenditure extend through the month of February only, so you'd select the answer "No" in the flowchart. This particular expenditure does not extend beyond the current accounting period of one year—or one month for that matter—and must be recorded as rent expense. If, however, the rent paid on February 1 was for a period of 24 months, the benefits of that expenditure would extend beyond one year; and you would record an asset called "Prepaid Rent," rather than rent expense.

What if CMU's financial statements were prepared on a monthly basis and the payment on February 1 covered three months? Would your answer change? Why? You are correct if you answered "Yes" to this question. Three months' occupancy represents benefits that extend beyond the current period defined as one month and therefore should be capitalized.

Another advantage of using the flowchart in Figure 6-2 is that it provides a more efficient way to record transactions. Consider Transaction P again. Since the benefits of the 11 rent payments of $1,000 each do not provide benefits beyond the current year, the figure helps you to avoid an unnecessary capitalization by having you record the expense immediately.

You will maximize your understanding of Figure 6-2 if you trace different expenditures, such as inventory, equipment, insurance, advertising, employee services, and so on, through its flowchart. Since deciding whether to record an asset or an expense involves a choice between the balance sheet or income statement, Performance Objective 11(a) is once again applicable in guiding your study:

YOUR PERFORMANCE OBJECTIVE 11a

Differentiate the balance sheet from the income statement by being able to **distinguish between** transactions that do and do not affect the income statement.

Expense Transactions at Cards & Memorabilia Unlimited

As you might suspect, expenses have not only the opposite effect on net income as revenues but also the opposite effect on owner's equity. For example, when a revenue is realized, owner's equity increases; but when an expense is incurred, it decreases the retained earnings component of owner's equity. In other words, expenses are inversely related to owner's equity.

Let's now take a closer look at the relationships between expenses and net income, and expenses and owner's equity by looking at seven transactions that represent important expense activity of Cards & Memorabilia Unlimited for its first year of business.

Expense Identification and Explanation

Transaction P: $1,000 cash is paid for office rent due the first day of each month beginning February 1.

Explanation: Since the lease agreement provided for a free first month of rent, Susan issued eleven separate rent checks on the first day of each month, beginning February 1. This transaction summarizes the effect of these 11 payments. *Hint*: Record the entire year's amount.

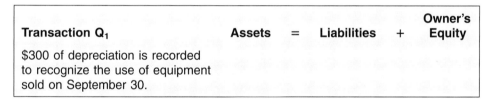

Transaction P	Assets	=	Liabilities	+	Owner's Equity
$1,000 cash is paid for office rent due the first day of each month beginning February 1.					

Study this section carefully so that you will understand the analysis of Transaction Q_1 and Transaction R described later in this chapter.

Transaction Q_1: $300 of depreciation is recorded to recognize the use of equipment sold on September 30.

Explanation: When Susan began to redecorate her store in September, she discovered that she had furniture she no longer needed. She also decided that she did not need her fax machine because the computer she planned to purchase at the end of the year included a fax modem (Transaction L). As a result of these decisions, she sold the extra furniture and the fax machine on September 30. The combined original cost of these pieces of store equipment was $2,000. Whenever depreciable assets are sold, it is customary to record the expiration or depreciation of the asset sold.

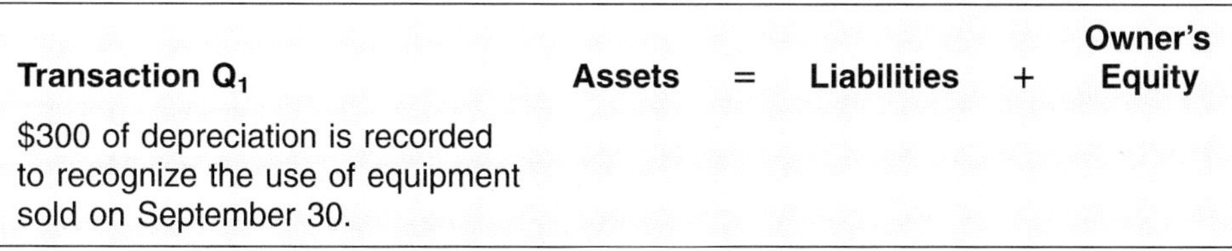

Transaction Q_1	Assets	=	Liabilities	+	Owner's Equity
$300 of depreciation is recorded to recognize the use of equipment sold on September 30.					

Transaction R: $2,000 worth of the store equipment bought on January 4 for $10,000 (Transaction C_1), is sold for $1,350 on September 30.

Explanation: Susan must record not only the proper amount of depreciation on the $2,000 of store equipment that she sold on September 30 (Transaction Q_1) but also record the effects of the sale itself. This sales transaction requires that you remove both the cost and accumulated depreciation of the store equipment sold, account for the cash received, and calculate any applicable gain or loss.

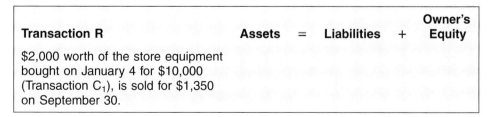

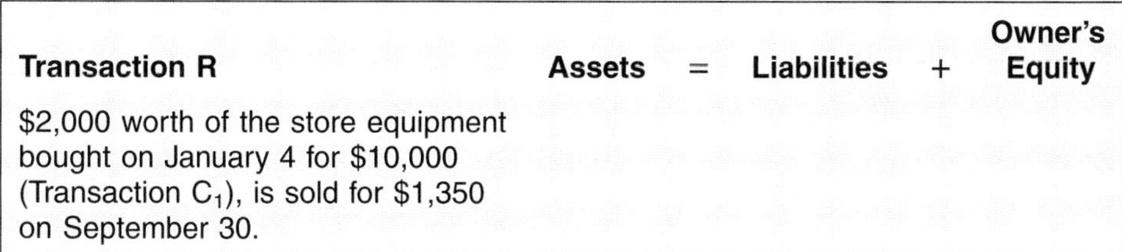

Transaction R	Assets	=	Liabilities	+	Owner's Equity
$2,000 worth of the store equipment bought on January 4 for $10,000 (Transaction C_1), is sold for $1,350 on September 30.					

Transaction S: $8,000 cash is paid to employees for work performed through the year's last payday of December 5. The next payday is January 4.

Explanation: As her first year in business progressed, Susan worked longer hours than she had at Spacebar Software. As a new small business owner, she was unable to afford full-time help. Also, she operated seven days a week to maximize her chances for sales. The store's hours of business during the first year of operation were:

Sunday:	12:00 Noon–6:00 P.M.
Thursday:	10:00 A.M.–9:00 P.M.
All other days:	10:00 A.M.–7:00 P.M.

Although family and friends had worked in the store during busy times and in her absence, Susan hired two part-time employees in early February to provide much needed relief. She paid Steve Wheeler, a high school trading card enthusiast, $5 an hour for sales work and Peter Nguyen, a business management major, $7 an hour for sales work and other duties. Susan paid her employees by check on the first Friday of each month. Her payment on Friday, December 5 brought Steve's and Peter's combined salaries paid in cash for the year to a total of $8,000. Like Transaction P, this transaction summarizes the effect of all payments of the same type, in this case payments Susan made to her employees during her first year of business.

Transaction S	Assets	=	Liabilities	+	Owner's Equity
$8,000 cash is paid to employees for work performed through the year's last payday of December 5.					

Transaction K_2: $200 cash is paid for interest due on $5,000 borrowed on July 1 at 8% (Transaction F) and repaid on December 31 (Transaction K_1).

Explanation: Recall that $5,000, bearing interest at an annual rate of 8%, was borrowed from the credit line for a period of six months (July 1–December 31). The interest cost of the borrowed funds is calculated as follows:

$$\textbf{Interest} = \$5{,}000 \times 0.08 \times 6/12 = \$200$$

Since interest is incurred with the passage of time, the $200 interest payment represents an expense of borrowing. Technically, K_1 and K_2 represent a single transaction in which interest ($200) and principal ($5,000) are repaid at the same time. However, this transaction has been divided into two parts so that you can more easily distinguish between a pure balance sheet transaction (K_1) and a transaction affecting the income statement (K_2).

Transaction K_2	Assets	=	Liabilities	+	Owner's Equity
$200 cash is paid for interest due on $5,000 borrowed on July 1 at 8% (F) and repaid on December 31 (K_1).					

Transaction T: $4,250 cash is paid for miscellaneous expenses incurred throughout the year.

Susan included several items in her miscellaneous expense category, such as license fees, supplies, advertising, rent-related expenses, and check guarantee and credit card fees. Here is more detail for each of these expenses:

a. *License Fees:* Costs include $87.75 for a business license[2] issued by the city of Rialto.
b. *Supplies:* This category includes items such as copier paper, stationery, and plastic protective sleeves for cards displayed and sold.
c. *Advertising:* Susan spent about $500 on a small weekly advertisement in the sports section of the local newspaper and on occasional advertisements on a local cable sports network.
d. *Rent-Related Expenses:* Recall from Chapter 1 that Susan's projected operating budget contained expenses that were separate from the monthly rent and were estimated to run about $0.30 per square foot per month. These expenses included utilities, property taxes, property insurance, and common area maintenance totaling $2,645.
e. *Check Guarantee and Credit Card Fees:* These totaled just over $1,250 and included: a 5% charge on guaranteeing risky checks; a 4% charge per dollar for American Express sales; and Visa/Mastercard charges of 2% per dollar of sales, $0.20 per transaction, and $7.50 per month for an activity statement.

Transaction T	Assets	=	Liabilities	+	Owner's Equity
$4,250 cash is paid for miscellaneous expenses incurred throughout the year.					

Transaction U: $30,000 of cost of goods sold (i.e., Transactions M, N, and Z) is determined by taking a physical count of inventory on December 31.

Explanation: On December 31, Susan closed her business to take a physical count of all trading cards and sports memorabilia on hand. By estimating the original costs of the cards and memorabilia still in her inventory, Susan was able to determine that the ending balance in her merchandise inventory account totaled approximately $13,000. Since the consumption or sale of an asset creates an expense, she used the following calculation to determine the cost of goods sold expense amount to report in her income statement:

Beginning merchandise inventory	$ 0
Merchandise acquisitions	43,000
Cost of merchandise (goods) for sale	$43,000
Less: Ending merchandise inventory	(13,000)
Cost of merchandise (goods) sold	$30,000

The beginning inventory is zero simply because no inventory existed at the end of the preceding year to carry forward to the beginning of this year. The $43,000 acquisition cost results from adding Transactions D, G, and A_2. Susan made this particular cost of goods sold measurement by using what is called the **periodic inventory system**. That is, the $30,000 amount represents a periodic calculation that is made only once at the end of the period, rather than a perpetual calculation that is made many times during

[2] This cost includes a $75.00 base fee plus a charge of 2 cents per square foot (for businesses having up to 5,000 square feet of space) reduced by 15% for unusable space. The total charge was calculated as $75 + (750 × $0.02 × .85) = $87.75.

the period. Had Susan calculated her cost of goods sold figure by recording costs every time a sale was made, she would have been using what is called the **perpetual inventory system**. While this system is advantageous to use in some business settings, it would be much too time consuming and expensive an approach to use in the trading card industry.

Transaction U	Assets	=	Liabilities	+	Owner's Equity
$30,000 of cost of goods sold (i.e., Transactions M, N, and Z) is determined by taking a physical count of inventory on December 31.					

Expense Analysis Now, we'll analyze each of CMU's expense transactions.

Transaction P	Assets	=	Liabilities	+	Owner's Equity
$1,000 cash is paid for office rent due the first day of each month beginning February 1.	(11,000)				(11,000)

Analysis: The first effect of this transaction on the fundamental equation is to decrease the Cash account by a total of $11,000. Since each of the rent payments represents a cost that is used up each month in providing a place to conduct business, the second effect involves an increase in the Rent Expense account. Once again, recording an increase in any expense decreases the Retained Earnings account, which also decreases owners' equity.

Transaction Q_1	Assets	=	Liabilities	+	Owner's Equity
$300 of depreciation is recorded to recognize the use of equipment sold on September 30.	(300)				(300)

Analysis: Although you were told that $300 is the portion of the asset cost consumed with the passage of time, let's verify that this amount is correct. To do so, note that the $2,000 of assets sold were used for 9 months (January 1–September 30) of the expected 60 months (5 years × 12 months a year) of useful life. Thus, exactly 9/60 of the $2,000 cost has been used up by September 30. That is, $300 [($2,000/5) × 3/4] of the $2,000 cost represents the use of nine months of service. To recognize depreciation on the asset sold, we increase the Depreciation Expense account and simultaneously increase the Accumulated Depreciation account, a contra-asset to the Store Equipment account, in the amount of $300.

Transaction R	Assets	=	Liabilities	+	Owner's Equity
$2,000 worth of the store equipment bought on January 4 for $10,000 (Transaction C_1), is sold for $1,350 on September 30.	1,350 (1,700)				(350)

Analysis: The first effect of this equipment sale on the fundamental equation is to increase the Cash account by $1,350, an amount sometimes called the *cash proceeds.* In exchange for these cash inflows, however, the business gives up an asset whose book value—its original cost less any accumulated depreciation at the time of sale—is $1,700. The book value is $1,700 rather than $2,000 because a portion of the asset ($300 from Transaction Q_1) has been used up in the period between the asset purchase and the asset sale. Thus, the book value or unexpired cost of the asset equals $1,700 ($2,000 − $300) at the time of its sale. CMU must remove the asset's book value simply because it no longer holds the asset. Now that the increase in cash proceeds and the decrease in the book value of the asset have been recorded, you must record any gain or loss that results from making the sale. Recall that both of these income statement components are calculated by subtracting an asset's book value from its selling price. The calculation for our present example is as follows:

Sale calculation:		Since a loss is similar in nature to
Selling price	$1,350	an expense, the effect on the fundamental
− Book value	(1,700)	equation is to decrease owners' equity by
= Loss on sale	$ (350)	$350 as shown in this analysis.

In other words, an asset with a $1,700 book value was exchanged for cash of $1,350, resulting in a loss on the exchange of $350.

Transaction S	**Assets**	**=**	**Liabilities**	**+**	**Owner's Equity**
$8,000 cash is paid to employees for work performed through the year's last payday of December 5.	(8,000)				(8,000)

Analysis: This summary transaction's first effect on the fundamental equation is to decrease the Cash account by $8,000. But should an asset or expense be recorded in conjunction with this cash decrease? We'll use Figure 6-2 to help with the answer. The $8,000 paid to employees represents services received as of 12/5 and should be recorded as salaries expense. If, however, any portion of the $8,000 had been paid to acquire employee services that were not performed by the end of the year—that is, extended beyond the current accounting period—an asset titled Prepaid Employee Services might be recorded.

Transaction K_2	**Assets**	**=**	**Liabilities**	**+**	**Owner's Equity**
$200 cash is paid for interest due on $5,000 borrowed on July 1 at 8% (F) and repaid on December 31 (K_1).	(200)				(200)

Analysis: An obvious effect of this transaction on the fundamental equation is to decrease the Cash account by $200. You can deduce another effect through process of elimination. Specifically, you know that the $200 cash decrease may be accompanied by either an asset increase, a liability decrease, or a decrease in owners' equity. First, you are not increasing an asset account such as interest receivable, because in this transaction you are paying, not receiving, interest. Second, you cannot reduce a liability such as interest payable, because no such account exists from an earlier transaction. Finally, since interest expense, like all expenses, reduces retained earnings, you are, in fact, reducing owners' equity. By recording interest expense for the six months beginning July 1 and ending December 31, you properly report the incurrence of interest with the passage of time.

Transaction T	Assets	=	Liabilities	+	Owner's Equity
$4,250 is paid for miscellaneous expenses incurred throughout the year.	(4,250)				(4,250)

Analysis: Once again, the Cash account is decreased and an expense account increases, which simultaneously decreases the retained earnings component of owners' equity. Since most businesses incur expenses that are not fully paid for at the end of the year, it is unrealistic to assume that Susan has paid all of her expenses in full by the last day of the year. Thus, it is reasonable to expect that Susan's miscellaneous expense totals more than $4,250. To determine how much more miscellaneous expense to record, Susan will have to discover an additional transaction that affects miscellaneous expense. Think about what additional transaction or adjustment might be needed, and we will revisit this issue shortly.

Transaction U	Assets	=	Liabilities	+	Owner's Equity
$30,000 of cost of goods sold (i.e., Transactions M, N, and Z) is determined by taking a physical count of inventory on December 31.	(30,000)				(30,000)

Analysis: If you study the calculation underlying the cost of goods sold amount in Transaction U, you will see that the asset, merchandise inventory, decreased by the $30,000 cost of merchandise that was sold. Since this amount represents the cost of goods used up in the production of revenue (through sales), the expense account Cost of Goods Sold is increased,[3] thereby decreasing Retained Earnings, an owner equity account. Technically, a sales transaction includes both revenue and expense components, as shown in Figure 6-3.

FIGURE 6-3

The two components of a sales transaction

Component	Accounts Affected	Measurement Basis	Example
Revenue	Sales revenue	Selling price	A card costing $5 is sold
Expense	Cost of Goods Sold	Historical cost	for $7, a $2 profit.

[3] More procedurally oriented textbooks describe an equivalent periodic inventory process in which the financial effect of the cost of goods sold calculation is recorded without using a formal cost of goods sold account. While this indirect worksheet approach has been used for many years, the direct approach used here accomplishes the same effect with fewer details so that you can learn the concept more easily.

Collections of Credit Sales

As you learned from looking at the credit sales in Transaction N, Susan does not collect cash from every card sale. Since the majority of her credit sales were made during December's heavy Christmas season and such customers have up to 30 days to pay, she does not expect to collect all of these credit sales by December 31. Thus, as Transaction V shows, Susan receives only $15,000 of this year's $20,000 of credit sales by year-end.

Transaction V	Assets	=	Liabilities	+	Owner's Equity
$15,000 cash is collected from customers throughout the year for amounts owed.	15,000 (15,000)				

Note that the effect of making the credit sales in Transaction N *and not* the effect of collecting credit sales in Transaction V is reported in the income statement. Generally, the sale event rather than the cash collection event is what triggers the reporting of revenue in the income statement. This income measurement approach is known as the accrual basis, about which you will soon learn.

Income Statement of Cards & Memorabilia Unlimited

Each of transactions M through U affected the income statement of Cards & Memorabilia Unlimited during its first year of operations. The effects of these transactions on the fundamental accounting equation are summarized in Figure 6-4. When you compare the income statement effects of these transactions to CMU's actual income statement in Figure 6-5, however, you will discover some discrepancies. Figure 6-4 records lesser amounts for sales revenue, interest revenue, salaries expense, depreciation expense and miscellaneous expense. Let's focus again on the amount of miscellaneous expense. Although $4,250 was just recorded in Transaction T and is reflected in Figure 6-4, $4,600 is reported in Figure 6-5. If $350 of additional miscellaneous expense was recorded during the year, how do we account for the missing transaction? One plausible answer is to reason that $350 of miscellaneous expense was not paid in cash but was instead unpaid at year-end. Here is how this potential transaction would be recorded:

		Fundamental Accounting Equation					
Date	Asset Account Title	Assets	=	Liabilities	+	Owner's Equity	Source of Asset Account Title
12/31						(350)	Miscellaneous Expense
				350			Accounts Payable

Although you will have to wait until Chapter 7 to discover whether the preceding transaction or adjustment is correct, it should be obvious to you that some adjustments are needed to reconcile these differences. If your curiosity is aroused, the *Making Business Decisions* case at the end of this chapter will allow you to explore this issue in more depth.

FIGURE 6-4 Effects of CMU's income statement transactions on its fundamental accounting equation

Details of Transactions

M	Daily	$63,200 of cash sales are made to customers throughout the year.
N	Daily	$20,000 of revenue is earned on account—$19,400 for customer credit sales throughout the year and $600 for teaching a course.
O_1	12/02	$275 interest is earned from 1/2 − 12/2 on $6,000 of savings bearing 5% interest.
P	Monthly	$1,000 cash is paid for office rent due the first day of each month beginning February 1.
Q_1	09/30	$300 of depreciation is recorded to recognize the use of equipment sold on September 30.
R	09/30	$2,000 worth of the store equipment bought on January 4 for $10,000 is sold for $1,350.
S	12/05	$8,000 cash is paid to employees for work performed through the year's last payday.
K_2	12/31	$200 cash is paid for interest due on $5,000 borrowed on 7/1 at 8% and repaid on 12/31.
T	Daily	$4,250 cash is paid for miscellaneous expenses incurred throughout the year.
U	12/31	$30,000 of cost of goods sold is determined by taking a physical count of inventory.

Analysis of Transactions

	Assets						=	Liabilities			+	Owners' Equity		
	Cash	Accts. Rec.	Mdse. Inven.	Other Rec.	Store Equip.	Accum. Depr.		Accts. Pay.	Advn. from Cust.	Notes Pay.		Contrib. Capital	Retained Earnings	Name of Income Statement Account
Balance	$(10,000)	0	$33,000	$2,000	$21,000	0		0	$6,000	$10,000		$30,000		
M	63,200												$63,200	Sales Revenue
N		$20,000											19,400	Sales Revenue
													600	Service Revenue
O_1	275												275	Interest Revenue
P	(11,000)												(11,000)	Rent Expense
Q_1						$(300)							(300)	Depreciation Expense
R	1,350				(2,000)	300*							(350)	Loss on Sale
S	(8,000)												(8,000)	Salary Expense
K_2	(200)												(200)	Interest Expense
T	(4,250)												(4,250)	Miscellaneous Expense
U			(30,000)										(30,000)	Cost of Goods Sold
Balance	$ 31,375	$20,000	$ 3,000	$2,000	$19,000	0	=	0	$6,000	$10,000	+	$30,000	$29,375	
			$75,375				=		$16,000		+		$59,375	

*By reducing the amount of the accumulated depreciation account, this transaction actually increases the assets.

FIGURE 6-5

Cards & Memorabilia Unlimited's accrual basis income statement

CARDS & MEMORABILIA UNLIMITED
Income Statement
For the Year Ended December 31

Revenues:		
Sales revenue	$86,600	
Service revenue	600	
Interest revenue	300	$87,500
Expenses:		
Cost of goods sold	30,000	
Rent expense	11,000	
Salaries expense	8,750	
Depreciation expense	2,600	
Miscellaneous expense	4,600	
Interest expense	200	
Loss on equipment sale	350	57,500
Net income		$30,000

Distinguishing between the Cash and Accrual Bases of Income Measurement

An entity can measure income in one of two ways: the cash basis or the accrual basis. As its name implies, the **cash basis** recognizes revenue and expense at the time of cash inflows or receipts and cash outflows or payments, respectively. The accrual basis, however, recognizes income independent of the time when cash is received or cash is paid out.

Like many U.S. businesses, Cards & Memorabilia Unlimited uses the accrual basis of income (Figure 6-5) because it is a more accurate and, therefore, more useful measure of income. In fact, the accrual basis is mandatory for any business that produces or purchases merchandise for resale. As a result, published financial statements of U.S. corporations are almost always prepared using the accrual rather than the cash basis of income measurement.

Some service businesses, however—those employing professionals such as lawyers and accountants, for example—use the cash basis because they don't produce or purchase merchandise for resale and expect to collect cash from clients in a prompt and predictable manner. But even in these cases, such businesses do have depreciable assets, such as computers or office equipment, and so must calculate depreciation, an accrual basis measurement. As a result, these businesses really use a combination of the cash and accrual bases, known as the *modified cash basis*.

Initially, you might have difficulty applying the accrual basis to the measurement of income. Like many students, you might mistakenly apply the cash rather than the accrual basis to an income measurement situation. Use Performance Objective 18 to help you better understand the key differences between the cash and accrual bases.

YOUR PERFORMANCE OBJECTIVE 18

Distinguish between the accrual and cash basis of income measurement by being able to:

a. **Prepare** both an accrual basis and a cash basis income statement from the same set of facts.
b. **Explain** why the accrual basis generally provides a more precise income measurement than does the cash basis.
c. **Convert** a cash basis income statement into an accrual basis income statement.
d. **Describe** transactions in which cash flows precede, coincide with, or follow the period in which both revenues and expenses are recognized under the accrual basis.
e. **Explain** how accrual basis net income differs from both the net cash flow from operating activities and the change in the cash balance for the period.

Note that Performance Objective 18(e) will be discussed in a Chapter 7 *Insight*. Now, let's take a closer look at the cash basis.

Cash Basis of Income Measurement

As you study the general rules for measuring cash basis income, you will see that one of its primary advantages is simplicity; but you will also learn how the deficiencies of the cash basis far outweigh its benefits.

General Rules

The cash basis recognizes or records revenue and expense if and only if there is a receipt of and a payment of cash related to operating activities. Thus, revenue from selling goods and providing services is recorded in the period when cash is received. However, as you have already learned, you are never allowed to record revenue from financing activities. Examples include the receipt of cash from an owner contribution to the entity (recall Susan's $30,000 contribution in Transaction A_1) or from a loan (recall Susan's borrowing funds from her bank line of credit in Transaction F). Expense is recorded in the period when cash payments, sometimes called disbursements, are made for merchandise, salaries, insurance, taxes, and similar items.

Illustration

Now that you have studied the rules for measuring income under the cash basis, we can apply them to the transactions of Cards & Memorabilia Unlimited. Compare the income statement Susan prepared using the cash basis to the income statement she prepared using the accrual basis in Figure 6-6. When you do, you will see how they differ. To better understand this difference, let's first explore your own personal experience.

FIGURE 6-6 Cards & Memorabilia Unlimited's accrual basis and cash basis income statements

CARDS & MEMORABILIA UNLIMITED
Income Statements
For the Year Ending December 31

ACCRUAL BASIS			CASH BASIS		
Revenues:					
Sales revenue	$86,600		Cash sales (Transaction M)	$63,200	
Service revenue	600		Cash collections (Transactions I & V)	21,000	
Interest revenue	300	$87,500	Cash collection from equipment sale (Transaction R)	1,350	
			Interest collections (Transaction O_1)	275	$85,825
Expenses:					
Cost of goods sold	30,000		Merchandise payments (Transactions D & J_1)	27,000	
Rent expense	11,000		Rent payments (Transaction P)	11,000	
Salaries expense	8,750		Salary payments (Transaction S)	8,000	
Depreciation expense	2,600		Equipment payment (Transaction C_1)	10,000	
Miscellaneous expense	4,600		Miscellaneous payments (Transaction T)	4,250	
Interest expense	200		Interest payments (Transaction K_2)	200	60,450
Loss on equipment sale	350	57,500			
Net income		$30,000	**Net income**		$25,375

Intuitive Attractiveness

Although it is likely that you had never prepared an income statement before taking this course, you, like most individuals, intuitively conduct your personal financial transactions under the cash basis of income measurement. If you find this statement difficult to believe, ask yourself the following questions in the context of your present job or any of your past jobs:

1. *When do you think you earn your salary?* Most people think they have earned their salary at the moment they are paid, rather than when they perform their job on a day-to-day basis. It is unlikely, for example, that you actually calculate your salary or think you have earned the daily amount of your salary when you complete your work. It is more likely that you recognize your salary as a reward only when you receive it. If you experience a sense of well-being when you are paid, it is probable that you are intuitively applying the cash basis. Most of us intu-

itively recognize revenue when we receive cash rather than when we provide services to our employer.

2. *When do you think you incur expenses?* Most people do not feel anxious as they purchase items with a credit card. When the bills arrive several weeks later, however, they might well experience some real discomfort. That discomfort is their intuitive recognition of an expense they chose to ignore in the pleasure of the earlier moment. If your use of credit cards has ever resulted in your temporary or more permanent financial distress, it is probable that you were intuitively applying the cash basis of recognizing expenses. Had you used the accrual basis, you would have recognized the cost at the time of purchase and probably reduced your spending. Thus, under the cash basis, you recognize expense when you pay cash rather than when you acquire or consume resources.

As the answers to Questions 1 and 2 show, most of us intuitively use a rough version of the cash basis in our personal financial dealings. Clearly, the simplicity of the cash basis makes it much more attractive for us to use than the relatively unfamiliar accrual basis. It is also the basis of income measurement used by most individuals in calculating their personal income taxes. Why, then, do most business firms use the accrual basis instead? Let's examine some of the deficiencies of the cash basis to resolve this apparent dilemma.

Deficiencies

When comparing the income statements in Figure 6-6, you will discover that although both were prepared from the same set of facts, Susan's cash basis income statement reports significantly lower income than her accrual basis income statement. In addition, cash basis expense amounts, such as cash purchases of inventory and equipment, bear little resemblance to the corresponding accrual basis expense amounts in the cost of goods sold and depreciation expense accounts. If you understand each basis of income measurement, you will be able to satisfy Performance Objective 18(a):

YOUR PERFORMANCE OBJECTIVE 18a
Prepare both an accrual basis and a cash basis income statement from the same set of facts.

Generally speaking, the cash basis does not accurately measure the performance of an entity. Consider the operations of CMU, for example. The most significant operating event of this business is the sale of trading cards and sports memorabilia. Susan must determine the difference, or margin, between the selling price and the cost of the cards sold to evaluate the wisdom of her pricing. Unfortunately, the cash basis does not provide this evaluation because cash purchases are treated as an expense *whether or not the cards are sold*. In the case of Transaction D, for example, Susan would be forced to recognize the $15,000 cash payment as an expense before the cards were even sold. From this example, you can see how the cash basis is deficient. It uses activities—the receipt or disbursement of cash, which by themselves have little economic significance—to trigger the recognition of revenue and expense. Moreover, the cash basis allows managers to easily manipulate the timing of when revenue and expense transactions are recorded, which could result in a misleading income statement. Once again, if you understand how the cash and accrual bases differ, you will satisfy Performance Objective 18(b):

YOUR PERFORMANCE OBJECTIVE 18b
Explain why the accrual basis generally provides a more precise measurement of income than does the cash basis.

Since the accrual basis is generally preferable to the cash basis, it is quite common for small businesses that initially use a cash basis income statement for the sake of simplicity to later convert to an accrual basis income statement. Since working through this conversion process is an excellent way to better comprehend the differences between these income measurement systems, you are encouraged to master Performance Objective 18(c):

YOUR PERFORMANCE OBJECTIVE 18c
Convert a cash basis income statement into an accrual basis income statement.

Accrual Basis of Income Measurement

The **accrual basis** is a system of income measurement in which revenues and expenses are recorded in the time period when significant economic events—including the passage of time—occur, rather than when cash is actually received or paid (that is, cash flows). In other words, the accrual basis reflects revenues and expenses in the period in which critical events take place. To confirm that cash flows are not the basis upon which revenue and expense is recognized, use Performance Objective 18(d):

YOUR PERFORMANCE OBJECTIVE 18d
Describe transactions in which cash flows precede, coincide with, or follow the period (e.g., a month) in which both revenues and expenses are recognized under the accrual basis.

This objective describes four potential types of transactions (two revenue transactions and two expense transactions) in which net income is recognized in a different period from (that is, does not *coincide with*) the related cash flow. One such transaction, called a *deferred expense*, occurs whenever a cash outflow precedes the recognition of an expense (you purchase inventory for cash in January and sell it in February). Although cash is paid immediately, it is the use or sale of inventory, *not its purchase*, which serves as a catalyst for recognizing the cost of goods sold. A second such transaction, called an *accrued revenue*, occurs whenever a cash inflow follows the recognition of revenue (you earn a commission in December but don't collect it until January). These and the other two logically possible transactions, a *deferred revenue* and an *accrued expense*, are further explored in Problem 6-19 and in the significant discussion of adjustments in the next chapter.

Revenue Recognition

Under the accrual basis, two events that create revenues are the sale of goods and the rendering of services. For example, Susan recorded $20,000 of credit sales during her first year of business—$5,000 of which ($20,000 − $15,000) was uncollected at the end of the year. Under the cash basis, the critical revenue-producing or generating event is the $15,000 of cash collected. But, CMU uses the accrual basis, so the critical event is the sale of cards. Therefore, Susan recorded all $20,000 as revenue in her first year. Likewise, she recorded $63,200 of cash sales as revenue, not because cash was received, but because the critical revenue-generating event—selling the merchandise—had occurred. This CMU example demonstrates the key concept or rule underlying revenue recognition for the accrual basis:

Revenue Recognition Rule: Revenue is earned or realized in that period when goods are sold or services are performed.

Although less significant than card and memorabilia sales, don't forget that CMU did provide services when Susan taught her course on how to collect trading cards and memorabilia. This revenue is listed under Service Revenue on the accrual basis income statement in Figure 6-6.

Expense Recognition

Unlike the cash basis, the accrual basis does not record an expense on the basis of when cash is paid or disbursed. Examples of accrual basis events that do create expenses include:

- *The delivery of goods to customers* (Transaction U), rather than merchandise payments for those goods (Transactions D and J_1).
- *The use of equipment* (Transaction Q_1) or depreciation rather than the payment of $10,000 to purchase the equipment (Transaction C_1).
- *The performance of services by* Susan's *employees* amounting to $8,750 (refer to Figure 6-6), as opposed to her payment of $8,000 cash (Transaction S). In this case, the critical expense-generating event was the use or consumption of her employee resources.
- Susan's monthly *occupancy of* the *leased space*, rather than the signing of the lease on January 5 or each month's payment (Transaction P).

These examples illustrate the key concept or rule underlying expense recognition for the accrual basis:

Expense Recognition Rule:	Expense is incurred in that period when a cost is used to produce revenue or is consumed with the passage of time.

Recall that an expense is that portion of a cost that is used up during the year to produce revenue. When you consider this definition, you will find that expenses can generally be derived from three types of costs:

1. ***Product costs:*** Costs whose expiration is associated with the sale of a product. The primary examples of this direct cause and effect relationship are cost of goods sold and sales commissions. Transaction U, for example, represents the direct linkage between the cost of merchandise sold and the revenue generated from the sale of that merchandise in Transactions M and N. Likewise, if Susan paid her employees a commission based on sales, the sales commission expense would be considered a product cost because of its direct link to specific sales. It would then be reported in the same accounting period as the related sales revenue.
2. ***Period costs:*** Costs whose expiration is associated with the passage of a specific time period. Examples include rent and administrative costs, such as insurance and depreciation, which are incurred regardless of the level of product sales. In Transaction C_1, for example, the $10,000 cost of office equipment is estimated to benefit five years of operations. Therefore, through a systematic and rational process known as depreciation, the cost of this depreciable asset is allocated to expense with the passage of time by dividing $10,000 by 5.
3. ***Uncertain costs:*** Costs whose expiration is assumed because their traceability to a specific product or a specific time period is uncertain and, therefore, difficult to measure. These costs are recorded in their period of incurrence. Examples include advertising, and research and development.

Matching Concept

As you just learned, both product and period costs allow you to associate expenses with revenues of a period. The term used to describe this association is "matching."

The **matching concept** actually describes a two-step process. The first step involves assigning revenues to the accounting period in which goods are sold or services are performed (revenue recognition rule). The second step involves assigning expenses to the accounting period in which costs are used to produce revenue or are consumed with the passage of time (expense recognition rule). In short, the matching concept is the idea that revenues earned and expenses incurred in generating those revenues should be reported in the same accounting period and in the same income statement. The matching concept demonstrates the clearest distinction between the cash and accrual bases. The matching concept is conspicuously absent from the cash basis; but it is the foundation for the accrual basis of income measurement.

An Owner Withdrawal Transaction

Since owner withdrawals[4] are reported in the statement of owner's equity rather than in an income statement, you might wonder why such a transaction is discussed here. There are two reasons. First, this is a convenient place to describe Transaction W since it is the only remaining CMU transaction that does not affect the income statement. Transactions O_2, X, Y, Q_2, and Z appear in the next chapter and are all income statement transactions. Second, since withdrawals are often confused with expenses, it is important that you learn how they differ.

Susan withdrew cash from her business frequently during the year for personal living expenses. These withdrawals are summarized in a single transaction, Transaction W. Since both the sole proprietorship and the partnership forms of business are *not* legally separate from their owner(s), it is unnecessary to formally declare a withdrawal, as is required when a corporation declares a dividend.

The essential idea behind this transaction is that if you reduce assets (an \$8,100 cash decrease), so too must you reduce the source of those assets (an \$8,100 decrease to retained earnings). The effect of Transaction W on the fundamental accounting equation is:

Transaction W	Assets	=	Liabilities	+	Owner's Equity
\$8,100 cash is withdrawn from the business by the owner throughout the year.	(8,100)				(8,100)

Since Susan has decided not to reinvest \$8,100 of her \$30,000 first-year earnings, her retained earnings account must now be decreased from \$30,000 to \$21,900. You can reconfirm this amount by consulting Figures 3-5 to 3-7. If you understand this transaction's effects on the fundamental equation, you are ready to learn about an exciting late year development in the business operation of Cards & Memorabilia Unlimited.

An Owner Investment Transaction—CMU Becomes a Partnership

Recall from Transaction S that Susan Newman worked many hours at CMU because she could not afford full-time employees and because she wanted to operate seven days a week to maximize her sales. By Thanksgiving, Susan knew that her hard work

[4] Owners who frequently withdraw cash and other assets often use a *drawing* account, as in "taking a draw against the business."

had paid off. She was, however, exhausted from the strain of 60-hour work weeks. Susan decided it was time to search for a partner.

Her search ended less than a month later when Martha Perez joined CMU. Martha was a free-lance computer programmer and nonsports card enthusiast whose personal collection was worth over $30,000. She was a CMU customer whose valuable insights into nonsports cards had particularly impressed Susan. One day Susan told Martha she was looking for a partner, and they began to talk. By December 24th, they had signed a partnership agreement giving Martha a 25% interest in CMU.

They agreed that Martha would pursue her interest and take primary responsibility for nonsports cards; Susan would handle sports cards and be able to spend more time with sports memorabilia. They also agreed that Martha's initial contribution to the partnership would be entirely in the form of cards, valued at $10,000 as of December 24. The effect of this event, Transaction A_2, on the fundamental equation is:

Transaction A_2	Assets	=	Liabilities	+	Owners' Equity
$10,000 worth of merchandise is contributed by Martha Perez for an interest in the business.	10,000				10,000

Transaction A_2 is conceptually identical to Transaction A_1. The only difference is that merchandise inventory rather than cash is increased. If you understand this transaction's effects on the fundamental equation, you are ready to explore a common misconception about withdrawals and the income statement.

An Owner Withdrawal or Dividend Is Not an Expense

INSIGHT

One question Susan struggled with when she took her introductory accounting course was why withdrawals or dividends were not considered expenses. When Susan asked her instructor to explain the difference, he recited the following definitions and pointed out how the definitions of both withdrawals and dividends were obviously different from the definition of an expense. That is, neither a withdrawal nor a dividend was paid to produce revenue.

- ***Expense:*** A cost of goods or services that is used up or consumed to produce revenue
- ***Withdrawal:*** A disinvestment by a proprietor or partner in the form of assets
- ***Dividend:*** A distribution of assets to corporate shareholders that is equivalent in concept to that of a proprietor's or partner's withdrawal

Although Susan could see that these terms had different definitions, she felt too embarrassed to pursue the question further. To pass exams, she had memorized that neither withdrawals nor dividends were expenses despite never really understanding why. But as the sole owner of a business, she could no longer afford not to understand the distinction.

So, she asked her friend George Wu why her $8,100 withdrawal could not properly be reported as salary expense in the income statement. After reassuring Susan that it was not uncommon for accounting majors to ask the same question, George drew the following diagram to help explain his answer:

(continued)

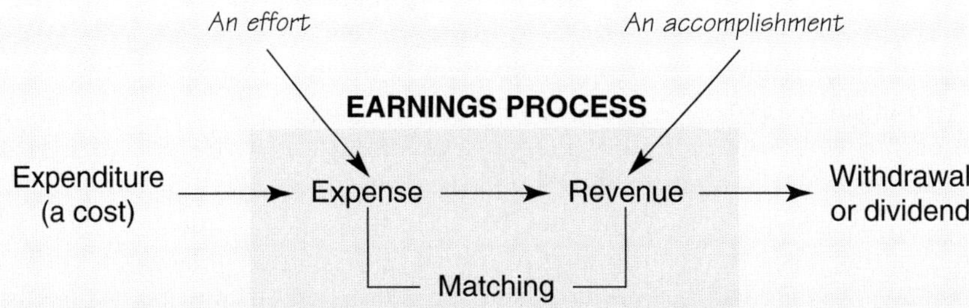

Using this diagram, George first cautioned Susan not to confuse an expenditure with an expense. He pointed out that an expenditure is a transaction in which an asset is decreased or a liability is increased in acquiring goods or services. An expense, however, is recorded only when these same goods or services are used to produce revenue. To help her visualize these concepts, George asked Susan to imagine an expenditure in which she acquired office equipment (Transaction C_1) or inventory (Transaction D). When he asked her when she should properly recognize depreciation expense and cost of goods sold respectively, she answered, "Not until I have used the office equipment or sold the inventory."

Still using the diagram, George focused Susan's attention on the distinction between an expense and a withdrawal or dividend. He pointed out that a proprietor or partner's withdrawal as well as a corporation's dividend declaration are financing decisions that are not themselves part of the earnings process. In the diagram you can see that a withdrawal or dividend is outside the box that contains the expense. That is, an expense is *an element of* the earnings process, whereas a withdrawal or a dividend is *a potential outcome of* the earnings process.

The source of the confusion might well be the fact that withdrawals, dividends, and expenses all reduce owners' equity. Having the same effect on a third account, however, does not prove they are identical. As you learned earlier, a withdrawal or dividend is reported in a statement of owners' equity, whereas an expense is reported in an income statement. Just as you now know that an owner investment does not represent revenue, it follows that an owner withdrawal does not represent expense. Instead, as explained in Chapter 1, an owner withdrawal is a return of investment to an owner.

The **insight** you should gain here is that owner withdrawals and dividends declared must be excluded from the income statement, a report of an entity's operating activities, because they represent financing activities. If an owner-manager's withdrawals—a financing activity—were reported in the income statement, imagine how the ability of decision makers to evaluate the entity's earning power would be hampered. Income could be manipulated because, unlike regular salaried employees, owners may set their salary/withdrawal at any amount they choose. That is, if owner-managers wanted to report a higher net income, they could do so by simply reducing their withdrawals.

Thus, the income statements of proprietorships and partnerships do not include a salary expense for the managerial services provided by owner(s). This practice ensures that net income is a useful measure of the owners' return on investment and that owners cannot easily manipulate income. Remember that the income statement is used to evaluate operating activity decisions and the statement of owners' equity is used to evaluate owners' financing activity decisions.

Classifying the Effects of Transactions in Accounts

Now that you have analyzed almost all of CMU's first year transactions, you are ready to learn some elementary steps in the process most entities use to convert transactions into financial statements. To thoroughly understand this process, you should try to prepare CMU's income statement and balance sheet from your analysis of the effects of Transactions A_1 through W, an analysis summarized in Appendix C. Before you begin, however, you will want to read the following time-saving approaches. Both the formal ledger account approach and the T-account approach are designed to classify the effects of each transaction into distinct accounts whose year-end balances are reported in the financial statements.

Formal Ledger Account Approach

The **ledger** is a collection of related accounts representing the effects of all transactions affecting the entity. For the most part, the accounts in a ledger are the same accounts normally found in the entity's balance sheet and income statement. Although almost every business today uses a computerized ledger system, in the manual accounting systems of the past, each ledger account was assigned one or more pages in a binder.

Consider, for example, Transaction V, in which Susan collected cash on amounts owed by customers. After recording this transaction in its chronological order, you would classify the effects this transaction has on particular accounts: namely, Cash and Accounts Receivable. The effect of Transaction V and other transactions on the Cash account found in CMU's balance sheet is shown in Figure 6-7(a). Note that this ledger records only the cash effects of Transactions A_1 to Z.

T-Account Approach

Although the ledger account approach is used in a standard manual accounting system (not computerized), it is not as efficient as the equivalent T-account approach. A **T-account** is a streamlined version of a ledger account. It allows you to quickly accumulate a transaction's effect on a particular account.

FIGURE 6-7(a) Recording the effects of cash transactions in a ledger account

		Cash		
Transaction	**Date**	**Increase**	**Decrease**	**Balance**
A_1	01/02	$30,000		$30,000
B	01/02	6,000	$ (6,000)	30,000
D	01/06		(15,000)	15,000
E	01/09		(2,000)	13,000
C_2	02/03		(10,000)	3,000
F	07/01	5,000		8,000
H	07/01		(7,000)	1,000
I	11/01	6,000		7,000
J_1	07/31–11/30		(12,000)	(5,000)*
K_1	12/31		(5,000)	(10,000)
M	Daily	63,200		53,200
O_1	12/02	275		53,475
P	Monthly		(11,000)	42,475
R	09/30	1,350		43,825
S	12/05		(8,000)	35,825
K_2	12/31		(200)	35,625
T	12/31		(4,250)	31,375
V	Daily	15,000		46,375
W	Daily		(8,100)	38,275

*Note the $5,000 negative balance adjacent to Transaction J_1. Do not assume that CMU experienced an overdraft, that is insufficient funds in cash or in the checking account. No overdraft actually occurred because cash received from cash sales in Transaction M began flowing in as early as January 9.

Asset T-Account Figure 6-7(b) illustrates the Cash T-account for Cards & Memorabilia Unlimited. Notice that this approach retains all the features of the formal ledger account with the exception of the individual transaction dates and the availability of the continuous balance. The title is centered at the top of the figure. The letter of each transaction that affected this account is labeled in parentheses. Once again, increases are placed to the left of decreases. That is, increases to the Cash account are shown on the left side of the account; decreases are shown on the right side of the account. This same format is used for all asset accounts.

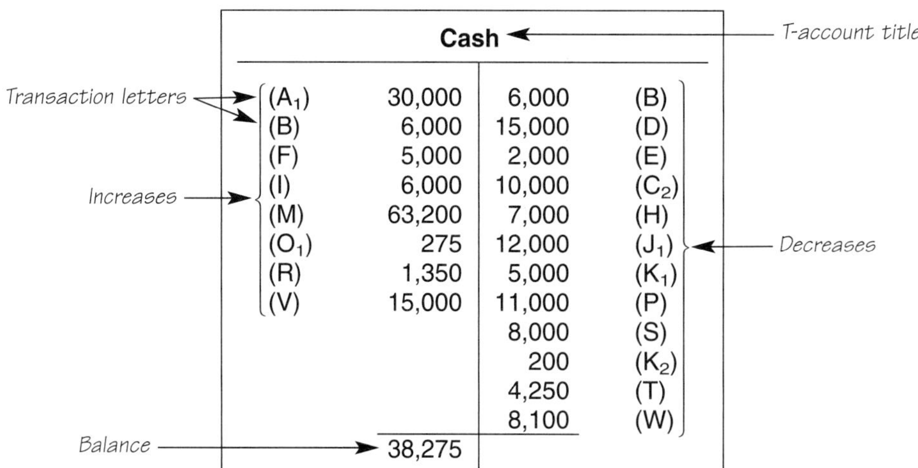

FIGURE 6-7(b)
Recording the effects of cash transactions in a T-account

Sources of Assets T-Account From algebra you know that quantities on one side of an equation reverse their sign when transferred to the opposite side of the equation. Thus, in contrast to the rules for an asset T-account, increases in a sources of assets T-account (Figure 6-7(c)) are shown on the right side of the account; decreases are shown on the left side of the account. This format is illustrated below for CMU's Accounts Payable T-account.

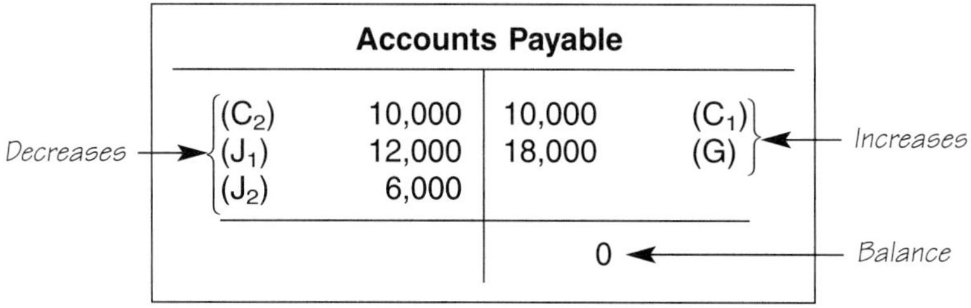

FIGURE 6-7(c)
Recording the effects of accounts payable transactions in a T-account

This format is used for all liability and owners' equity accounts. In Chapter 9, you will learn more about how an accounting system records transactions to produce financial statements. For now, end of chapter exercises will give you a chance to prepare the T-accounts that classify all the effects of CMU's transactions A_1 through A_2 and to use these T-accounts to prepare the balance sheet (Problem 6-4) and income statement (Problem 6-6) at December 31.

The Income Statement Known as Schedule C

INSIGHT

Review Cards & Memorabilia Unlimited's income statement (Figure 6-5). A distinctive feature of all proprietorship and partnership income statements is the absence of income tax expense. Sole proprietorships and partnerships are exempt from income taxes because these forms of entity are not legally separate from their owner(s), as are corporations.

Do not assume, however, that the income of these entities is not taxed. It is, but not in the entities' financial statements. Instead, the entities' net income is taxed when the individual owner(s) file individual tax returns (Form 1040 or Form 1065). Because the net income of the entity must "pass through" the entity to the owner before it is legally subject to income tax, such entities are often referred to as "pass through entities."

Taxing agencies require the owner(s) to use a special income statement, called a *tax return schedule* rather than an income statement. The Internal Revenue Service, for example, requires taxpayer-owners to prepare the income statement known as **Schedule C** (Figure 6-8) and file it with the Form 1040 individual income tax return. Schedule C is relatively easy to fill out. In Susan's case she would simply transfer each revenue and expense listed in Figure 6-5 to the appropriate lines of this schedule. For example, she would enter the $86,600 of sales revenue on line 1 and the $30,000 of cost of goods sold on line 4, resulting in gross profit of $56,600 on line 5. You will have an opportunity to fill out this form in Exercise 6-11.

The first insight you should gain here is that this tax return schedule, which is called Schedule C, is an income statement. You can verify this by noting how easy it is to transfer the information on Cards & Memorabilia Unlimited's income statement to Schedule C. Although most people, including accountants, don't think of tax returns as income statements, tax returns, such as the IRS's Form 1040, and supporting schedules, such as Schedule C, are clearly special versions of the income statement.

The second insight you should gain here is that many small proprietorships and partnerships do the opposite of what you might expect. They use the preparation of this tax return by their accountant as the basis for the income statement that they use for financial reporting purposes. These small businesses usually have few owners to report to, so the legal requirement to fill out a Schedule C is often the most compelling reason to prepare an income statement. As a result, many small businesses use a tax basis income statement.

The third insight you should gain here is that many small businesses prepare their tax returns on a cash rather than an accrual basis for ease of preparation. For example, notice that Line F of Schedule C asks you to specify which method—cash, accrual, or other—you use. Because small businesses often use the cash basis, the terms "tax basis" and "cash basis" are often used interchangeably.

The last insight you should gain here is that when lenders ask to see a proprietor's (or partners') tax return, they usually focus their attention on the borrower's Schedule C. From all these insights, you can see that Schedule C is a type of income statement you might well encounter in the future.

(continued)

FIGURE 6-8 The income statement known as Schedule C

SCHEDULE C (Form 1040)

Department of the Treasury
Internal Revenue Service (99)

Profit or Loss From Business

(Sole Proprietorship)

▶ Partnerships, joint ventures, etc., must file Form 1065 or Form 1065-B.

▶ Attach to Form 1040 or Form 1041. ▶ See Instructions for Schedule C (Form 1040).

OMB No. 1545-0074
2001
Attachment Sequence No. 09

Name of proprietor | Social security number (SSN)

A Principal business or profession, including product or service (see page C-1 of the instructions) | B Enter code from pages C-7 & 8 ▶

C Business name. If no separate business name, leave blank. | D Employer ID number (EIN), if any

E Business address (including suite or room no.) ▶
City, town or post office, state, and ZIP code

F Accounting method: (1) ☐ Cash (2) ☐ Accrual (3) ☐ Other (specify) ▶

G Did you "materially participate" in the operation of this business during 2001? If "No," see page C-2 for limit on losses . ☐ Yes ☐ No

H If you started or acquired this business during 2001, check here . . . ▶ ☐

Part I Income

1	Gross receipts or sales. **Caution.** If this income was reported to you on Form W-2 and the "Statutory employee" box on that form was checked, see page C-2 and check here ▶ ☐	1	
2	Returns and allowances	2	
3	Subtract line 2 from line 1	3	
4	Cost of goods sold (from line 42 on page 2)	4	
5	**Gross profit.** Subtract line 4 from line 3	5	
6	Other income, including Federal and state gasoline or fuel tax credit or refund (see page C-3)	6	
7	**Gross income.** Add lines 5 and 6 ▶	7	

Part II Expenses. Enter expenses for business use of your home **only** on line 30.

8	Advertising	8		19	Pension and profit-sharing plans	19	
9	Bad debts from sales or services (see page C-3)	9		20	Rent or lease (see page C-4):		
				a	Vehicles, machinery, and equipment	20a	
10	Car and truck expenses (see page C-3)	10		b	Other business property	20b	
11	Commissions and fees	11		21	Repairs and maintenance	21	
12	Depletion	12		22	Supplies (not included in Part III)	22	
13	Depreciation and section 179 expense deduction (not included in Part III) (see page C-3)	13		23	Taxes and licenses	23	
				24	Travel, meals, and entertainment:		
				a	Travel	24a	
14	Employee benefit programs (other than on line 19)	14		b	Meals and entertainment		
15	Insurance (other than health)	15		c	Enter nondeductible amount included on line 24b (see page C-5)		
16	Interest:						
a	Mortgage (paid to banks, etc.)	16a		d	Subtract line 24c from line 24b	24d	
b	Other	16b		25	Utilities	25	
17	Legal and professional services	17		26	Wages (less employment credits)	26	
18	Office expense	18		27	Other expenses (from line 48 on page 2)	27	

28	**Total expenses** before expenses for business use of home. Add lines 8 through 27 in columns ▶	28	
29	Tentative profit (loss). Subtract line 28 from line 7	29	
30	Expenses for business use of your home. Attach **Form 8829**	30	
31	**Net profit or (loss).** Subtract line 30 from line 29. • If a profit, enter on **Form 1040, line 12,** and **also** on **Schedule SE, line 2** (statutory employees, see page C-5). Estates and trusts, enter on Form 1041, line 3. • If a loss, you **must** go to line 32.	31	

32 If you have a loss, check the box that describes your investment in this activity (see page C-6).
• If you checked 32a, enter the loss on **Form 1040, line 12,** and **also** on **Schedule SE, line 2** (statutory employees, see page C-5). Estates and trusts, enter on Form 1041, line 3.
• If you checked 32b, you **must** attach **Form 6198.**

32a ☐ All investment is at risk.
32b ☐ Some investment is not at risk.

For Paperwork Reduction Act Notice, see Form 1040 instructions. Cat. No. 11334P **Schedule C (Form 1040) 2001**

Part III **Cost of Goods Sold** (see page C-6)

33 Method(s) used to value closing inventory: a ☐ Cost b ☐ Lower of cost or market c ☐ Other (attach explanation)

34 Was there any change in determining quantities, costs, or valuations between opening and closing inventory? If "Yes," attach explanation . . . ☐ **Yes** ☐ **No**

35	Inventory at beginning of year. If different from last year's closing inventory, attach explanation	35	
36	Purchases less cost of items withdrawn for personal use	36	
37	Cost of labor. Do not include any amounts paid to yourself	37	
38	Materials and supplies	38	
39	Other costs	39	
40	Add lines 35 through 39	40	
41	Inventory at end of year	41	
42	**Cost of goods sold.** Subtract line 41 from line 40. Enter the result here and on page 1, line 4	42	

Part IV **Information on Your Vehicle.** Complete this part **only** if you are claiming car or truck expenses on line 10 and are not required to file Form 4562 for this business. See the instructions for line 13 on page C-3 to find out if you must file.

43 When did you place your vehicle in service for business purposes? (month, day, year) ► .... / .... / ....

44 Of the total number of miles you drove your vehicle during 2001, enter the number of miles you used your vehicle for:

a Business .... **b** Commuting .... **c** Other ....

45 Do you (or your spouse) have another vehicle available for personal use? . . . ☐ **Yes** ☐ **No**

46 Was your vehicle available for personal use during off-duty hours? . . . ☐ **Yes** ☐ **No**

47a Do you have evidence to support your deduction? . . . ☐ **Yes** ☐ **No**

b If "Yes," is the evidence written? . . . ☐ **Yes** ☐ **No**

Part V **Other Expenses.** List below business expenses not included on lines 8–26 or line 30.

48 Total other expenses. Enter here and on page 1, line 27	48	

Schedule C (Form 1040) 2001

Summary with Key Terms

The number in parentheses following each **key term** is the page number on which the term is defined.

In this chapter, you examined in detail the financial statement known as the income statement. An **income statement** (218) includes four elements: **revenue** (219), **expense** (220), **gains** (220), and **losses** (220). A revenue transaction can be a **cash sale** (221) or a **credit sale** (222). In the first *Insight* section of this chapter, you learned that generally a **credit card sale** (222) is treated as equivalent to a cash sale. Identifying expense transactions, however, is normally more difficult than identifying revenue transactions. For example, you often must decide whether a **cost** (226) or **expenditure** (226) should be recorded as an asset or as an expense. This decision process involves a careful definition of the **accounting period** (227), which, if defined as an annual or **fiscal year** (227), may follow a **calendar year** (227) basis or a **natural business year** (227) basis. When you record an expenditure as an asset, you are said to **capitalize** (227) the expenditure. You recognize an expense when you have used up the cost of goods or services to produce revenue. Expenses are usually derived from either **product costs** (241) or **period costs** (241). Occasionally, an expense may also be derived from **uncertain costs** (241). Deciding when to expense a cost or an expenditure is also affected by such other factors as whether the entity uses a **periodic inventory system** (231) or a **perpetual inventory system** (232).

Another essential distinction you learned about was that between the **cash basis** (237) and the **accrual basis** (240) of income measurement. Most entities use the accrual basis for purposes of measuring income because it incorporates the **matching concept** (242), a set of rules designed to include revenues and expenses in the proper reporting period. Although the cash basis is easier to use, its single greatest disadvantage is its failure to incorporate the matching concept.

Another *Insight* section of this chapter discussed a common misconception—that owner **withdrawals** (243) or **dividends** (243) are identical to expense. In truth, both withdrawals and dividends are financing activities, whereas an expense is an operating activity.

You then learned some approaches for processing the effects of recorded transactions into a **ledger** (245) and then the financial statements. One such approach is to use a **T-account** (245) that allows you to more rapidly process transactions as well as more efficiently analyze both balance sheet and income statement accounts.

The last *Insight* section of this chapter described how the tax return schedule, **Schedule C** (247), is really a special income statement that doubles as both a tax return and annual income statement. The result is that entities often use the cash basis when preparing their income statements because they used it on their tax returns and do not wish to be inconvenienced by the accrual basis.

Making Business Decisions

YOUR PERFORMANCE OBJECTIVE 2
(page 18)

One of the more important decisions an accountant must make is to determine what adjustments are needed at the end of an accounting period. An example, whose analysis is illustrated below, is our discovery that CMU needed to adjust its Miscellaneous Expense account by $350 at the end of the year to correctly measure net income.

Miscellaneous expense in Figure 6-5	$4,600
Miscellaneous expense in Figure 6-4 (Transaction T)	4,250
Adjustment needed	$ 350

Adjustment recorded:

		Fundamental Accounting Equation					
Date	Asset Account Title	Assets	=	Liabilities	+	Owners' Equity	Source of Asset Account Title
12/31						(350)	Miscellaneous Expense
				350			Accounts Payable

As you will learn in Chapter 7, CMU needs four additional adjustments to properly measure net income for its first year of business. See if you can correctly decide what two transaction adjustments should be made by using the following information that is available to Susan Newman and Martha Perez at the end of their first year of business. Be sure to use the format provided to make your decisions.

YOUR PERFORMANCE OBJECTIVE 2
(page 18)

1. Sales revenue:

Sales revenue balance in Figure 6-5	$86,600
Sales revenue balance in Figure 6-4 (Transactions M and $19,400 from N)	82,600
Adjustment needed	$ 4,000
Advances from customers balance at 11/01 (Transaction I)	$ 6,000
Advances from customers balance in 12/31 balance sheet in Figure 5-1	2,000
Adjustment needed	$ 4,000

Adjustment recorded:

		Fundamental Accounting Equation					
Date	Asset Account Title	Assets	=	Liabilities	+	Owners' Equity	Source of Asset Account Title
12/31							

2. Salaries expense:

Salaries expense balance in Figure 6-5	$8,750
Salaries expense balance in Figure 6-4	8,000
Adjustment needed	$ 750
Salaries payable balance in 12/31 balance sheet in Figure 5-1	$ 750

Adjustment recorded:

		Fundamental Accounting Equation					
Date	Asset Account Title	Assets	=	Liabilities	+	Owners' Equity	Source of Asset Account Title
12/31							

Since an accountant has to uncover the information you were just provided for the Sales Revenue and Salaries Expense accounts, see if you can find similar background information so that you can decide the last two adjustments needed, given the following hints:

3. Compare the interest revenue amount in Figure 6-5 to that found in Figure 6-4.
4. Compare the depreciation expense amount in Figure 6-5 to that found in Figure 6-4.

Questions

YOUR PERFORMANCE OBJECTIVE 4
(page 22)

6-1 Explain in your own words the meaning of key business terms.

a. Revenue
   1. Cash sale
   2. Credit sale
   3. Credit card sale
b. Expense
c. Gain
d. Loss
e. Cost or expenditure
f. Accounting period
   1. Fiscal year
   2. Calendar year
   3. Natural business year
g. Capitalize
h. Cash basis
i. Accrual basis
j. Matching concept
k. Ledger
l. T-account
m. Schedule C

6-2 Compare and contrast an income statement and a balance sheet.
6-3 Distinguish between the terms *revenue* and *gain.*
6-4 Distinguish between the terms *expense* and *loss.*
6-5 Distinguish between the nouns *cost* and *expense.* Provide one example of this distinction.
6-6 Distinguish between the verbs *capitalize* and *expense.*
6-7 Distinguish between the terms *product cost* and *period cost.*
6-8 Describe why you do not record revenue for collections of credit sales.
6-9 Distinguish between the terms *periodic inventory system* and *perpetual inventory system.* Which system has this text used?
6-10 Distinguish between the terms *net income* and *net loss.*
6-11 Describe the general rules for recognizing revenue and expense under the cash basis of income measurement.
6-12 What are the advantages and disadvantages of the cash basis of income measurement?
6-13 Describe the revenue recognition rules for the accrual basis.
6-14 Describe the expense recognition rules for the accrual basis.
6-15 Describe the distinction between how the cash basis and the accrual basis recognize revenue.
6-16 Explain why the accrual basis generally provides a more precise measurement of income than does the cash basis.
6-17 Explain why withdrawals or dividends are not expenses.
6-18 Explain why the income statements of proprietorships and partnerships do not include a salary expense for the managerial services that owners provide.
6-19 Explain why increases to asset accounts must be placed on the side opposite to increases in either liability or owner equity accounts in a T-account.
6-20 Why is income tax expense not found in the income statements of sole proprietorships or partnerships?
6-21 Explain how a tax return is really a special type of income statement.
6-22 Identify at least two reasons why many small businesses use the cash basis of income measurement.

Reinforcement Exercises

YOUR PERFORMANCE OBJECTIVE 4 *(page 22)*

E6-1 Asking the Right Questions: A Group Activity

It's often said that knowing the right answer is not nearly as important as asking the right question. Asking the right question is a problem-solving skill that will help you make sound business decisions. In this exercise, you will review the vocabulary introduced in Chapter 6 by creating questions to match answers—similar to a famous TV show.

Required

a. Given an answer, what's the question? Choose *three* of the following terms to serve as an answer. Create an appropriate question for each term. For example, if you choose the term *balance sheet,* you might create the question—*What financial statement reports the assets, liabilities, and owners' equity of an entity on a specific date?*

Expenditure	Capitalize	Revenue
Accrual basis	Product cost	Gain
Cash basis	Period cost	Expense
Dividend	T-account	Loss

b. Are you sure that's the question? Have each member of your group read aloud the questions they developed in Requirement (a). As a group, decide whether each question is an accurate match for an answer. Once satisfied that all questions are appropriate, the group, as a whole, chooses the three best questions created within the group. Record the three questions chosen (with their answers) on separate pieces of paper or index cards and give them to your instructor.

c. What's the answer? To ensure that you have learned the vocabulary terms listed in Requirement (a), your instructor will now quiz you on the questions written by all of your classmates.

YOUR PERFORMANCE OBJECTIVE 5a *(page 137)*

E6-2 Transaction Analysis: Inventory

Merchandise inventory costing $6,000 is sold on account, for $8,100.

Required

a. Why is information about whether the company uses the periodic or perpetual inventory system relevant to your treatment of this transaction? (See pages 231–232 to review the meaning of these terms.)
b. Analyze the effects of this transaction on the fundamental accounting equation.
c. When should you recognize this transaction's income or loss?

NOTE: Both revenue and expense transactions have effects on the fundamental accounting equation. Thus, both revenue and expense transactions also affect the balance sheet.

E6-3 Transaction Analysis: Revenues

YOUR PERFORMANCE OBJECTIVE 5a *(page 137)*

Analyze the effects of the following transactions on the fundamental accounting equation:

a. $50,000 of cash sales are made.
b. $100,000 of sales are made on account.
c. $10,000 of goods already paid for by customers are delivered.
d. $15,000 of credit card sales are made.
e. Services valued at $20,000 are provided to customers.

E6-4 Transaction Analysis: Expenses

YOUR PERFORMANCE OBJECTIVE 5a *(page 137)*

Analyze the effects of the following transactions on the fundamental accounting equation assuming a monthly income statement is prepared:

a. Paid monthly salaries of $3,000 to employees on the last day of the month for services rendered.
b. This month's cost of goods sold was determined to be $22,400.
c. Office supplies purchased for $550 cash are used during the month.
d. Paid the monthly utility bill of $120.
e. Incurred $75 of monthly gasoline charges on a delivery truck.

E6-5 Transaction Analysis: Gains and Losses

YOUR PERFORMANCE OBJECTIVE 5a *(page 137)*

In this chapter you learned that gains and losses, like revenues and expenses, increase and decrease owners' equity, respectively. Since you must measure the amount of a gain or loss before you can record its effects on the fundamental accounting equation, it is useful to develop your skill. Thus, calculate the amount of gain or loss and then record its effects on the fundamental equation in each case below. Use Transaction R for reference.

Case 1: Land costing $10,000 is sold for $12,000.
Case 2: Land costing $10,000 is sold for $10,000.
Case 3: Land costing $10,000 is sold for $8,000.
Case 4: Equipment costing $10,000 and having a book value of $7,000 is sold for $8,500.
Case 5: Equipment costing $10,000 and with accumulated depreciation of $7,000 is sold for $2,400.

E6-6 Preparing a Balance Sheet

YOUR PERFORMANCE OBJECTIVE 5b *(page 57)*

Using Transactions A_1 through A_2 presented thus far and found in Appendix C, prepare a balance sheet for Cards & Memorabilia Unlimited.

E6-7 Income Statement Transaction Analysis

YOUR PERFORMANCE OBJECTIVE 5b *(page 57)*

Ballesteros Company prepared Balance Sheet A after Transaction A, Balance Sheet B after Transaction B, and so on, as follows:

	A	B	C	D	E	F	G	H	I
Assets									
Cash	$ 20	$ 50	$ 50	$ 40	$ 40	$ 40	$ 74	$ 50	$ 50
Receivables	40	40	86	86	86	86	102	102	102
Inventory	60	60	60	60	20	20	20	20	20
Machinery	80	80	80	80	80	80	80	80	70
	$200	$230	$276	$266	$226	$226	$276	$252	$242
Liabilities and Owners' Equity									
Payables	$100	$100	$100	$100	$100	$115	$115	$115	$115
Owner's equity	100	130	176	166	126	111	161	137	127
	$200	$230	$276	$266	$226	$226	$276	$252	$242

YOUR PERFORMANCE OBJECTIVE 10 (page 95)

Required

Identify the eight income statement transactions that caused these changes. *Hint:* Use transaction analysis to aid you in your reasoning process.

E6-8 Preparing an Income Statement

Using the transaction analysis of CMU Transactions M through U presented in Figure 6-4, prepare an income statement.

YOUR PERFORMANCE OBJECTIVE 10 (page 95)

E6-9 Preparing Income Statements

Trevino Company prepared Income Statement A after Transaction A, Income Statement B after Transaction B, and so on, as follows:

	A	B	C	D	E	F	G	H
Revenues:								
Cash sales	$425	$600	$600	$600	$600	$600	$600	$600
Credit sales	165	195	195	195	195	195	195	195
Rent	105	105	125	125	125	125	125	125
Interest	60	60	60	60	60	60	70	70
	$755	$960	$980	$980	$980	$980	$990	$990
Expenses:								
Cost of goods sold	$360	$360	$360	$490	$490	$490	$490	$490
Salaries	200	200	200	200	200	235	235	235
Depreciation	100	100	100	100	100	100	100	125
Miscellaneous	65	65	65	65	85	85	85	85
	$725	$725	$725	$855	$875	$910	$910	$935
Net income	$ 30	$235	$255	$125	$105	$ 70	$ 80	$ 55

Required

Identify the seven income statement transactions that caused these changes. *Hint:* Use transaction analysis to aid you in your reasoning process.

YOUR PERFORMANCE OBJECTIVE 10 (page 95)

E6-10 Preparing an Income Statement

Myrna Beecoff is a production consultant for a textbook publisher. Each of the following transactions engaged in during the month of August affected her owner's equity account.

	Cash	Accts. Rec.	Supplies	Office Equip.	=	Accts. Pay.	Beecoff, Capital	Owner's Equity Title
a.	+2,600	+1,900			=		+4,500	Fees Revenue
b.	−1,000				=		−1,000	Withdrawals
c.					=	+400	−400	Utilities Expense
d.	−1,675				=	+465	−2,140	Salaries Expense
e.	−1,300				=		−1,300	Rent Expense
f.			−215		=		−215	Supplies Expense
g.	+1,550				=		+1,550	Royalty Revenue
h.				−200	=		−200	Depreciation Expense

Required

Prepare an income statement based on these transactions. *Hint:* Use transaction analysis to aid you in your reasoning process.

YOUR PERFORMANCE OBJECTIVE 10 (page 95)

E6-11 Preparing an Income Statement: Schedule C

It's been said that the only things one can count on in life are death and taxes; and for some people, the agony of paying taxes is surpassed only by the agony of filling out a tax return. Now that you have learned how to prepare an income statement, you will find that filling out a tax return is not as difficult as it once was. With this in mind, fill out the Schedule C, opposite page, for Susan's sole proprietorship using the income statement in Figure 6-5 as a source of information. Be creative if certain tax return items force you to allocate some of your expense account amounts.

SCHEDULE C (Form 1040)

Department of the Treasury
Internal Revenue Service (99)

Profit or Loss From Business

(Sole Proprietorship)

▶ **Partnerships, joint ventures, etc., must file Form 1065 or Form 1065-B.**

▶ **Attach to Form 1040 or Form 1041.** ▶ **See Instructions for Schedule C (Form 1040).**

OMB No. 1545-0074

2001

Attachment Sequence No. **09**

Name of proprietor | **Social security number (SSN)**

A Principal business or profession, including product or service (see page C-1 of the instructions) | **B Enter code from pages C-7 & 8** ▶

C Business name. If no separate business name, leave blank. | **D Employer ID number (EIN), if any**

E Business address (including suite or room no.) ▶
City, town or post office, state, and ZIP code

F Accounting method: **(1)** ☐ Cash **(2)** ☐ Accrual **(3)** ☐ Other (specify) ▶

G Did you "materially participate" in the operation of this business during 2001? If "No," see page C-2 for limit on losses . ☐ **Yes** ☐ **No**

H If you started or acquired this business during 2001, check here . . . ▶ ☐

Part I Income

		Line	Amount
1	Gross receipts or sales. **Caution.** If this income was reported to you on Form W-2 and the "Statutory employee" box on that form was checked, see page C-2 and check here . . . ▶ ☐	1	
2	Returns and allowances	2	
3	Subtract line 2 from line 1	3	
4	Cost of goods sold (from line 42 on page 2)	4	
5	**Gross profit.** Subtract line 4 from line 3	5	
6	Other income, including Federal and state gasoline or fuel tax credit or refund (see page C-3)	6	
7	**Gross income.** Add lines 5 and 6 ▶	7	

Part II Expenses. Enter expenses for business use of your home only on line 30.

		Line	Amount			Line	Amount
8	Advertising	8		19	Pension and profit-sharing plans	19	
9	Bad debts from sales or services (see page C-3)	9		20	Rent or lease (see page C-4):		
				a	Vehicles, machinery, and equipment	20a	
10	Car and truck expenses (see page C-3)	10		b	Other business property	20b	
				21	Repairs and maintenance	21	
11	Commissions and fees	11		22	Supplies (not included in Part III)	22	
12	Depletion	12		23	Taxes and licenses	23	
13	Depreciation and section 179 expense deduction (not included in Part III) (see page C-3)	13		24	Travel, meals, and entertainment:		
				a	Travel	24a	
				b	Meals and entertainment		
14	Employee benefit programs (other than on line 19)	14		c	Enter nondeductible amount included on line 24b (see page C-5)		
15	Insurance (other than health)	15					
16	Interest:						
a	Mortgage (paid to banks, etc.)	16a		d	Subtract line 24c from line 24b	24d	
b	Other	16b		25	Utilities	25	
17	Legal and professional services	17		26	Wages (less employment credits)	26	
18	Office expense	18		27	Other expenses (from line 48 on page 2)	27	

		Line	Amount
28	**Total expenses** before expenses for business use of home. Add lines 8 through 27 in columns ▶	28	
29	Tentative profit (loss). Subtract line 28 from line 7	29	
30	Expenses for business use of your home. Attach **Form 8829**	30	
31	**Net profit or (loss).** Subtract line 30 from line 29. • If a profit, enter on **Form 1040, line 12,** and **also** on **Schedule SE, line 2** (statutory employees, see page C-5). Estates and trusts, enter on Form 1041, line 3. • If a loss, you **must** go to line 32.	31	

32 If you have a loss, check the box that describes your investment in this activity (see page C-6).
- If you checked 32a, enter the loss on **Form 1040, line 12,** and **also** on **Schedule SE, line 2** (statutory employees, see page C-5). Estates and trusts, enter on Form 1041, line 3.
- If you checked 32b, you **must** attach **Form 6198.**

32a ☐ All investment is at risk.
32b ☐ Some investment is not at risk.

For Paperwork Reduction Act Notice, see Form 1040 instructions. Cat. No. 11334P **Schedule C (Form 1040) 2001**

Schedule C (Form 1040) 2001 Page **2**

Part III Cost of Goods Sold (see page C-6)

33 Method(s) used to value closing inventory: **a** ☐ Cost **b** ☐ Lower of cost or market **c** ☐ Other (attach explanation)

34 Was there any change in determining quantities, costs, or valuations between opening and closing inventory? If "Yes," attach explanation . . . ☐ **Yes** ☐ **No**

35	Inventory at beginning of year. If different from last year's closing inventory, attach explanation	35	
36	Purchases less cost of items withdrawn for personal use	36	
37	Cost of labor. Do not include any amounts paid to yourself	37	
38	Materials and supplies	38	
39	Other costs	39	
40	Add lines 35 through 39	40	
41	Inventory at end of year	41	
42	**Cost of goods sold.** Subtract line 41 from line 40. Enter the result here and on page 1, line 4	42	

Part IV Information on Your Vehicle.

Complete this part **only** if you are claiming car or truck expenses on line 10 and are not required to file Form 4562 for this business. See the instructions for line 13 on page C-3 to find out if you must file.

43 When did you place your vehicle in service for business purposes? (month, day, year) ▶ ______/______/______.

44 Of the total number of miles you drove your vehicle during 2001, enter the number of miles you used your vehicle for:

a Business ______________ **b** Commuting ______________ **c** Other ______________

45 Do you (or your spouse) have another vehicle available for personal use? . . . ☐ **Yes** ☐ **No**

46 Was your vehicle available for personal use during off-duty hours? . . . ☐ **Yes** ☐ **No**

47a Do you have evidence to support your deduction? . . . ☐ **Yes** ☐ **No**

b If "Yes," is the evidence written? . . . ☐ **Yes** ☐ **No**

Part V Other Expenses.

List below business expenses not included on lines 8–26 or line 30.

48 **Total other expenses.** Enter here and on page 1, line 27	48	

Schedule C (Form 1040) 2001

E6-12 Capitalize or Expense?

YOUR PERFORMANCE OBJECTIVE 11a *(page 99)*

Determine which of the following transactions represent revenues or expenses rather than only changes in asset and liability accounts.

a. Office supplies are purchased for cash.
b. Office supplies are purchased on account.
c. Office supplies previously purchased are used.
d. Office supplies previously purchased on account are paid.
e. A previously unrecorded electric bill is received and paid.
f. Services are provided to a customer in return for cash.
g. Services are provided to a customer who is then billed.
h. Collection from the customer previously billed is received.
i. Cash is borrowed from the bank.
j. Accumulated interest on the loan is accounted for and repaid.
k. The bank loan is repaid.

E6-13 Capitalize or Expense Inventory Purchases?

YOUR PERFORMANCE OBJECTIVE 11a *(page 99)*

Assume that you have just purchased merchandise inventory. Given the following circumstances, use Figure 6-2 to decide whether you should capitalize or expense this expenditure. Include your reasoning to support your decision.

a. You expect to sell the entire amount of merchandise within one month, and monthly financial statements are prepared.
b. You expect to sell the entire amount of merchandise within two months, and monthly financial statements are prepared.
c. You expect to sell the entire amount of merchandise within six months, and yearly financial statements are prepared.
d. You expect to sell the entire amount of merchandise within fifteen months, and yearly financial statements are prepared.

E6-14 Capitalize or Expense Insurance Premiums?

YOUR PERFORMANCE OBJECTIVE 11a *(page 99)*

Assume that you paid automobile insurance premiums on January 1 that provide future coverage. Given the following circumstances, use Figure 6-2 to decide whether you should capitalize or expense this expenditure. Include your reasoning to support your decision.

a. Your coverage expires in six months, and monthly financial statements are prepared.
b. Your coverage expires in three months, and quarterly financial statements are prepared.
c. Your coverage expires in six months, and quarterly financial statements are prepared.
d. Your coverage expires in six months, and yearly financial statements are prepared.

E6-15 Capitalize or Expense Advertising Costs?

YOUR PERFORMANCE OBJECTIVE 11a *(page 99)*

Assume that you have just purchased advertising on January 1. Given the following circumstances, use Figure 6-2 to decide whether you should capitalize or expense this expenditure. Include your reasoning to support your decision.

a. You purchase newspaper advertising for the next three weeks, and monthly financial statements are prepared.
b. You purchase newspaper advertising for the next six weeks, and monthly financial statements are prepared.
c. You purchase newspaper advertising for the next six months, and quarterly financial statements are prepared.
d. You enter into a three-year advertising campaign with an advertising agency, and yearly financial statements are prepared.

E6-16 Capitalize or Expense Employee Services?

YOUR PERFORMANCE OBJECTIVE 11a *(page 99)*

Assume that you purchase employee services. Given the following circumstances, use Figure 6-2 to decide whether you should capitalize or expense the following expenditures. Include your reasoning to support your decision.

a. You receive your invoice for employee services for an entire calendar month, pay for them on the last day of that same month, and prepare monthly financial statements.
b. You receive your invoice for employee services for an entire calendar month, pay for them on a bimonthly basis (twice monthly), and prepare financial statements on a quarterly basis.

c. You prepay for a management consultant's services for an entire year, and prepare financial statements on a quarterly basis.
d. You prepay for a management consultant's services for an entire year, and prepare financial statements on a yearly basis.

YOUR PERFORMANCE OBJECTIVE 13
(page 105)

E6-17 Financial Statement Relationships
Refer to the comparative balance sheets shown in Exercise 5-2.
a. Calculate net income given that dividends declared are $8,000.
b. Calculate dividends declared given that net income is $17,000.

YOUR PERFORMANCE OBJECTIVE 18a
(page 239)

E6-18 Cash Basis versus Accrual Basis of Income
The following transactions occurred in April. Determine the amount of expense to recognize in April under both the cash and accrual methods of income measurement. If you believe no expense should be recognized, place a zero in the space provided.

	Cash	Accrual
1. The $3,000 semiannual insurance bill for the period from April 1 to September 30 was paid on April 3.	_______	_______
2. $4,800 of rent for the 4-month period April through July was paid on April 1.	_______	_______
3. $8,000 of dividends were declared and paid on April 15.	_______	_______
4. $25,000 was borrowed from the bank on April 1 by signing a 12%, 90-day note payable.	_______	_______
5. An employee had earned $3,200 during April but had not yet been paid.	_______	_______

YOUR PERFORMANCE OBJECTIVE 18a
(page 239)

E6-19 Cash Basis versus Accrual Basis of Income
The following data present the operating activities of Prentice Wholesale for the years 1, 2, and 3.

	Year 1	Year 2	Year 3
Cash sales	$3,250	$2,250	$2,250
Credit sales	3,750	4,750	6,000
Cash expenses	2,250	2,750	1,250
Accrued (noncash) expenses	3,000	3,500	5,000

Assume that Prentice began operations on January 1, Year 1, and that accounts receivable are collected and accrued expenses are paid entirely within the next year.

Required
Prepare both a cash basis and an accrual basis income statement for the Years 1, 2, and 3.

YOUR PERFORMANCE OBJECTIVE 18a
(page 239)

E6-20 Cash Basis versus Accrual Basis of Income
The Crosby Insurance Agency engaged in the following March transactions:

a. Commissions earned and collected	$14,200
b. Commissions earned but uncollected	4,250
c. Commissions collected on policy whose coverage begins in April	1,000
d. Commissions collected from February sales	2,000
e. Payment of February's utility and telephone bills	850
f. Payment of six months' rent, March through August	7,200
g. Salaries incurred but payable in April	4,800
h. Received bill from carpenter for services performed in March, to be paid in April	100

Required
Prepare both a cash basis and an accrual basis income statement for the month of March for the Crosby Insurance Agency.

Critical Thinking Problems

P6-1 Transaction Analysis

YOUR PERFORMANCE OBJECTIVE 5a
(page 137)

Michael Guttmann is the sole proprietor of the Orpheum Theater, a small movie theater in Aberdeen, South Dakota. The following selected transactions represent what he believes should be reported on his June income statement. Analyze the effects of these transactions on the fundamental accounting equation by using the form provided. Transaction (a) is filled in for you. Use the abbreviation NE for "no effect" if no accounts are affected by the transaction.

Fundamental Accounting Equation							
Transaction	Asset Account Title	Assets	=	Liabilities	+	Owner's Equity	Source of Asset Account Title
a.	Credit Card Receivable	4,240				4,240	Credit Card Sales

NOTE: Both revenue and expense transactions have effects on the fundamental accounting equation. Thus, both revenue and expense transactions also affect the balance sheet.

June Transactions

a. Total credit card ticket sales are $4,240.
b. Employee salaries for June total $7,370, $6,720 of which is paid in cash during the month.
c. Michael Guttmann withdraws $4,000 for personal living expenses.
d. Total cash ticket sales are $16,660.
e. Prepaid $900 for rental costs of movies to be shown during July at a cult film festival.
f. Advertising costs incurred during June total $1,800, $1,450 of which is paid in cash during the month.
g. June concession sales (popcorn, candy and drinks) total $4,850.
h. Film rental costs for June total $8,815, $8,380 of which is paid in cash during the month.
i. Utility costs incurred during June total $1,000, $775 of which is paid in cash during the month.
j. Revenue from local advertisers totals $1,200 during June; $850 of this amount is received in cash.
k. A local church pays $500 for a Sunday morning rental of the theater during July.
l. June concession costs incurred in producing concession sales total $3,430, $2,760 of which is paid in cash during the month.
m. Rental cost for the theater is $2,000 per month.

NOTE: For Problems 6-2 and 6-3, prepare a spreadsheet, where rows represent the transactions and columns represent the transaction numbers and account titles. See the inside back cover of this book for an example. Your columns may not be exactly the same as those shown.

YOUR PERFORMANCE OBJECTIVE 5a
(page 137)

P6-2 Spreadsheet Transaction Analysis

Use a spreadsheet to represent the transactions found in Exercise 5-9.

YOUR PERFORMANCE OBJECTIVE 5a
(page 137)

P6-3 Spreadsheet Transaction Analysis

Use a spreadsheet to represent the transactions found in Problem 6-1.

YOUR PERFORMANCE OBJECTIVES 5a, 5b
(pages 137, 57)

P6-4 Transferring Transaction Effects to T-Accounts

All but a few of the first year transactions of Cards & Memorabilia Unlimited have now been described in the text. Record the effects of Transactions A_1 through A_2 (found in Appendix C) in individual T-accounts as described in this chapter. When you complete this step, arrange the relevant account balances so that you have created a balance sheet at December 31 for CMU's first year of business. Do not use debits and credits in this problem.

YOUR PERFORMANCE OBJECTIVE 10 *(page 95)*

P6-5 Income Statement Calculations

Refer to Problem 6-1 and assume the following information:

a. On June 1, the opening balance of concession inventory is $350. During the month of June, Michael Guttmann, the proprietor of the Orpheum Theater, purchases $4,000 worth of additional concession products. On June 30, his son Paul determines that the cost of concession inventory on hand at the end of the month is $920. Calculate the cost of concessions sold for June.
b. Equipment used in the Orpheum Theater's projection booth cost a total of $48,000 and has an estimated useful life of 10 years. Calculate depreciation for June.

YOUR PERFORMANCE OBJECTIVE 10 *(page 95)*

P6-6 Preparing an Income Statement

Using the recorded effects from Problem 6-4, prepare an income statement for CMU's first year of business ending December 31.

YOUR PERFORMANCE OBJECTIVE 10 *(page 95)*

P6-7 Preparing an Income Statement

Paul Solomon, an accounting professor at New Perspectives University, supplements his income by selling popcorn on campus to students and other faculty members when he is not teaching, holding office hours, doing research, or attending committee meetings. Dr. Solomon has no money invested in his popcorn business other than the money he keeps in his cash drawer and the popcorn wagon he bought three years ago for $1,600. The popcorn wagon contains a popcorn popper, a propane tank, storage space for materials (unpopped corn, butter, and salt), and a compartment for keeping the popcorn warm until it is purchased.

Anticipating a busy Friday of finals week, Dr. Solomon buys an unusually large amount of materials for $480 and places $200 in his cash drawer to make change. His supplier, Mesonznick Confectioners, allows him to charge $200 of his total purchases, and he pays cash for the rest. On Thursday, he buys a two-day supply of propane for $16.

With temperatures in the high 70s, Dr. Solomon sells three-quarters of his purchases for $490 of cash. At the end of the day, he returns home with his unsold popcorn materials with plans to replenish his inventory, pay his supplier bill, and obtain propane fuel for what promises to be another big day for popcorn sales—New Perspectives University spring graduation day.

Required

a. Prepare an income statement to reflect the results of operations for Dr. Solomon's Friday business. List any items that you found difficult to measure.
b. Evaluate Dr. Solomon's relative success in light of the financial opportunities available to most business professors. What might be some of his opportunity costs from engaging in such a part-time business venture? Include both quantitative and qualitative factors in your evaluation.

NOTE: Problem 6-7 is adapted from a classic textbook problem that the author confronted when he was a student. (*Accounting: A Management Approach*, Gordon Shillinglaw, McGraw-Hill/Irwin)

YOUR PERFORMANCE OBJECTIVE 10 *(page 95)*

P6-8 Fantasy Income Statement

You are to creatively reconstruct the summary revenue and expense transactions that would provide a plausible explanation for the following income statement. For example, this income statement reports a $300,000 sales revenue figure. A creative solution would be to hypothesize (fantasize) that a majority of these sales were for cash. Thus, one plausible answer is that cash sales are $240,000 ($300,000 × 0.80), and credit sales account for the $60,000 balance ($300,000 − $240,000). Analyze the effects of these transactions on the fundamental accounting equation by using the form provided. Transaction (a) is filled in for you.

NOTE: If you understand how revenue and expense transactions are recorded and processed to create an income statement, you should be able to work backward from an income statement to reconstruct its underlying revenue and expense transactions. When a problem takes this perspective, it is referred to as a Fantasy Income Statement because solving such a problem requires some creativity on your part.

Trans-action	Asset Account Title	Fundamental Accounting Equation: Assets	= Liabilities	+ Owner's Equity	Source of Asset Account Title
a.	Cash	+240,000			
	Accts. Receivable	+60,000		+300,000	Sales Revenue

NOTE: Assume that Forrester Company is a men's clothing store.

FORRESTER COMPANY
Income Statement
For the Year Ended December 31

Revenues:		
Sales revenue	$300,000	
Interest revenue	10,000	$310,000
Expenses:		
Cost of goods sold	$172,000	
Salaries expense	48,000	
Rent expense	30,000	
Utilities	11,000	
Depreciation expense	6,000	
Office supplies	4,500	
Interest expense	2,500	274,000
Net income		$ 36,000

P6-9 Cash Basis versus Accrual Basis of Income
Prepare income statements on both the accrual basis and cash basis for the Orpheum Theater during June. To work on this problem, you must refer to the information found in Problem 6-1.

YOUR PERFORMANCE OBJECTIVE 18a *(page 239)*

P6-10 Cash Basis versus Accrual Basis of Income
To work on this problem, you must refer to the information found in Problems 6-1, 6-5, and 6-9.

a. Describe how adding the information in Problem 6-5 will change your answer in Problem 6-9.
b. Why must you record both cost of goods sold and depreciation expense during June?

YOUR PERFORMANCE OBJECTIVE 18b *(page 239)*

P6-11 Cash Basis versus Accrual Basis of Income
To work on this problem, you must refer to the information found in Figure 6-6. Compare the accrual basis income statement to the cash basis income statement. Identify both the amount of any differences and the reason for such differences.

YOUR PERFORMANCE OBJECTIVE 18e *(page 237)*

P6-12 Cash Basis versus Accrual Basis of Income
The income statements below present the operating results for a company using both the cash basis and the accrual basis. Study the two income statements and provide a plausible explanation for the differences in each line item.

YOUR PERFORMANCE OBJECTIVE 18e *(page 237)*

	Cash Basis	Accrual Basis
Revenues:		
Sales revenue	$140,000	$163,500
Service revenue	35,000	31,500
Total revenues	$175,000	$195,000
Expenses:		
Cost of goods sold	$ 94,000	$ 86,600
Salaries expense	32,000	36,400
Rent expense	24,000	18,000
Utilities expense	6,500	7,200
Miscellaneous expense	5,100	5,900
Total expenses	$161,600	$154,100
Net income	$ 13,400	$ 40,900

YOUR PERFORMANCE OBJECTIVE 18a
(page 239)

P6-13 Cash Basis versus Accrual Basis of Income

Baylor Data Processing began business operations on March 1 of the current year when Leong Tang, a recent college graduate, contributed $5,000 of cash to finance the business. The following events all took place in March of the current year.

a. Tang purchased a computer costing $20,000 on March 1 by making a $2,000 down payment and signing a 12% note payable for the balance. The first interest payment is due in April. The computer has a useful life of 4 years.
b. Tang paid $1,800 for six months of rent on March 1.
c. Billings of $28,000 for services rendered were sent to clients, but only $20,000 was collected. Of the $20,000 collected, $1,000 was for services that will not be performed until April. This $1,000 amount was not part of the $28,000 March billings.
d. Office supplies of $1,000 were purchased for cash on March 1. On March 31, only $400 of these supplies were still on hand.
e. Although $8,000 of salaries and $1,000 of utilities were both incurred and paid, a $1,000 plumbing bill and a $300 utility bill remained unpaid at the end of March.

Required

Prepare an income statement on the accrual basis for the month of March.

YOUR PERFORMANCE OBJECTIVE 18a
(page 239)

P6-14 Cash Basis versus Accrual Basis of Income

Charles A. Wookiee opened a hair styling and waxing salon on March 1. Wookiee invested $2,000 of his own money and borrowed $5,000 from the local bank. The loan is repayable on June 1 of the current year, with interest at 6% per year.

Wookiee purchased office equipment for $1,200 on account at March 1. This equipment has an expected useful life of 10 years. During the month, he paid $400 on the equipment.

Wookiee purchased $450 of cosmetic supplies on March 2. At the end of March, inventory of these cosmetic supplies totaled $315.

During the month, cash styling revenue totaled $400 and credit styling revenue totaled $250. $100 of the credit sale was collected as of March 31. The cost of salaries incurred and paid in cash by the end of March was $175. The unpaid cost of salaries incurred at the end of March was $45.

Required:

a. Prepare an accrual basis income statement for March. Provide complete numerical support for each income statement element.
b. How much cash basis revenue should be recognized in March?

YOUR PERFORMANCE OBJECTIVES 18a, 18b
(page 239)

P6-15 Cash Basis versus Accrual Basis of Income

Manute Bol, Toni Kukoc, and Sarunas Marciulionis opened a consulting firm called International Sports Management on July 1 of this year. Each partner contributed $5,000 cash to the partnership. In addition, they borrowed $6,000 from a bank on August 1, repayable on July 31 of the following year, at 10% interest per year.

Office space rented for the months of July and August was paid for on July 1. The remaining monthly rental fees of $600 per month were made on the first of each month, beginning September 1. Office equipment with a three-year useful life value was purchased with $3,600 cash on July 1.

Consulting services rendered for clients between July 1 and December 31 of the current year were billed at $14,000. Of this amount, $9,000 was collected by year-end.

Other costs incurred and paid in cash by the end of the year were as follows: utilities, $250; salaries, $5,000; and supplies used, $150. Unpaid bills at the end of the year were as follows: utilities, $50; salaries, $800; and supplies used, $40.

Required

a. Prepare an accrual basis income statement for the six months ended December 31 of the current year.
b. Prepare a cash basis income statement for the six months ended December 31 of the current year.
c. Identify the differences between the two income statements you prepared in problems (a) and (b).
d. Which basis provides a better indication of operating performance of the consulting firm for this period? Why?

P6-16 Cash Basis versus Accrual Basis of Income

YOUR PERFORMANCE OBJECTIVE 18b *(page 239)*

As you learned from this chapter's introduction, the balance sheet was the primary measure of business success until the beginning of the 20th century when the corporate form of business influenced a shift in focus to the income statement. This shift occurred for at least three reasons. First, corporate shareholders began to express more interest in measuring the operating efficiency of their managers than monitoring the changes in their individual equity balances. Second, the Securities Acts of 1933 and 1934 required corporations to prepare annual income statements, using the accrual basis. Third, income tax laws of 1913 and 1918 emphasized the importance of measuring a company's profits and required the proper matching of revenue and expense. After reading the descriptions of both the cash basis and accrual basis of accounting in this chapter, why do you think stockholders, investors, creditors, and the federal government would all prefer to see income statements prepared using the accrual basis? Compare and contrast the two methods and describe at least two reasons why the accrual basis is preferable.

P6-17 Converting a Cash Basis Income Statement into an Accrual Basis Income Statement

YOUR PERFORMANCE OBJECTIVE 18c *(page 240)*

The following income statement is prepared on the cash basis of income measurement.

WHITEWATER RAFTING EXCURSIONS
Income Statement—Cash Basis
For the Year Ended December 31

Revenues:		
Sales revenue	$50,400	
Dividend and interest revenue	5,440	$55,840
Expenses:		
Salaries expense	$ 9,880	
Insurance expense	1,320	
Utilities expense	2,355	
Interest expense	2,590	
Administrative expense	637	
Miscellaneous expense	242	17,024
Net income		$38,816

Additional Information

a. At the end of the year, 10% of all sales revenue was uncollected.
b. Rodham Carter, the proprietor, owns land that has appreciated in value by $12,000 since last year.
c. At the end of the year, $860 of salaries for services rendered was unpaid.

d. Three years of insurance coverage was paid for this year. One year of this coverage was consumed in the current year.
e. At the end of the year, 35% of the administrative expense was unpaid.

Required

Prepare an income statement on the accrual basis.

YOUR PERFORMANCE OBJECTIVE 18c *(page 240)*

P6-18 Tax Effects of Using the Accrual Basis

This morning you received the following e-mail message from a friend, who is the proprietor of a small retail business: "Help! At the end of last year, I was complaining to a friend who also owns a small business that my accountant mentioned that I would have a large tax bill to pay due to an increase in my profits. This friend told me that he avoids this problem by ordering large amounts of supplies and prepaying some bills to increase his expenses when this happens. I took his advice and purchased additional inventory and supplies and prepaid my rent before the end of the year. My accountant just told me that because I use the accrual basis for determining my net income for the year, none of these purchases helped reduce my tax bill. It appears that these are expenditures but not expenses. Is my accountant right? What does this mean? What is the difference between an expenditure and an expense? How come this works for my friend?" Compose an e-mail response to your friend.

YOUR PERFORMANCE OBJECTIVE 18d *(page 240)*

P6-19 Examining the Timing of Cash Flows under the Accrual Basis of Income Measurement

Under the accrual basis of accounting, cash receipts and disbursements may precede, coincide with, or follow the period in which revenues and expenses are recognized. For each case below, provide in words an example of a transaction that corresponds to each of the following conditions:

Case 1: A transaction in which a cash receipt *precedes* the period in which revenue is recognized.

Case 2: A transaction in which a cash receipt *coincides* with the period in which revenue is recognized.

Case 3: A transaction in which a cash receipt *follows* the period in which revenue is recognized.

Case 4: A transaction in which a cash disbursement *precedes* the period in which expense is recognized.

Case 5: A transaction in which a cash disbursement *coincides* with the period in which expense is recognized.

Case 6: A transaction in which a cash disbursement *follows* the period in which expense is recognized.

YOUR PERFORMANCE OBJECTIVES 5a, 10 *(pages 137, 95)*

P6-20 Comprehensive Problem

Peter Kontiagiannis is the sole proprietor of Pete's Deli. The following transactions occurred during the month of April:

a. Paid rent for the month of April.
b. Paid advertising costs for the month of April.
c. Catered a retirement party for a local business. The customer agreed to pay the bill within 30 days.
d. Paid salaries for the month.
e. Recorded credit card sales less a 2% service fee. Pete's Deli allows customers to use Visa and Mastercard.
f. Catered a birthday party for which the customer had paid in advance. The cash payment was received in March.
g. Paid miscellaneous expenses for the month.
h. Cash sales for the month were recorded.
i. Recognized that one month's liability insurance expired.
j. A physical count revealed the amount of inventory sold during the month.
k. At the end of April, Pete owes the employees one week's salary.
l. Recognized one month's depreciation on the store equipment.
m. Received, but did not pay the April utility bill.

Required

a. Analyze the effects of these transactions on the fundamental equation by indicating whether each part of the transaction increases (+) or decreases (−) an element in the equation. Transaction (a) is filled in for you.

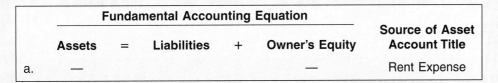

	Fundamental Accounting Equation					Source of Asset Account Title
	Assets	=	Liabilities	+	Owner's Equity	
a.	—				—	Rent Expense

b. Review the list of increases and decreases that you recorded. What observations can you make about the effects of revenue and expense transactions on the fundamental accounting equation? Create a list of general rules to follow when recording these types of transactions.

Research Assignments

A wide variety of interesting Research Assignments for this chapter are available for the following topics at www.mhhe.com/solomon:

R6-1 **How Do Investors and Creditors Use Income Information? (PO 9)**
R6-2 **Income Statement (PO 10)**
R6-3 **Identifying New Income Statement Accounts (PO 10)**
R6-4 **Noncorporate Income Statement (PO 10)**
R6-5 **Fantasy Income Statement (PO 10)**
R6-6 **Income Statement Effects of Balance Sheet Accounts (PO 5 and 10)**
R6-7 **Obtaining a Chart of Accounts (PO 10 and 11b)**
R6-8 **Examining Older Income Statements (PO 10 and 11b)**
R6-9 **Income Statement Comparison (PO 14)**
R6-10 **Creating Next Year's Annual Report (PO 10)**

CHAPTER SEVEN

7 Using the Income Statement to Make Decisions

Also be sure you have mastered the following Performance Objectives from previous chapters. They lay the foundation for the concepts you will learn in this chapter:

PO2
PO3
PO4
PO5a
PO14

PERFORMANCE OBJECTIVES

In this chapter, you will learn the following new Performance Objectives:

PO10 **Prepare** a single-step and/or a multiple-step income statement that reports the results of operations of any entity. (*Modified form of earlier version*)

PO13b From your understanding of financial statement relationships, **analyze** accounting transactions to **determine** their effect—increase, or decrease, understatement or overstatement, or no effect—on the elements of *both* the balance sheet and the income statement.

PO18e **Distinguish between** the accrual and cash basis of income measurement by being able to **explain** how accrual basis net income differs from both the net cash flow from operating activities and the change in the cash balance for the period.

PO19a **Prepare** the adjustments needed at the end of the period using transaction analysis.

PO19b **Determine** the amount of both related balance sheet and income statement accounts after adjustments have been made.

PO20 **Categorize** all income statement accounts into *one* of the following four categories:

a. Primary operating activities that are expected to continue.
b. Peripheral activities that are expected to continue.
c. Primary operating activities that are discontinued.
d. Peripheral activities that are not expected to continue.

PO21 **Discuss** the criteria used to determine when revenue is recognized and then, given specific details about an entity, **apply** these criteria to that entity to **determine** when its revenue should be recognized.

MARY MATHEWS, COMMERCIAL REAL ESTATE AGENT FOR CARDS & MEMORABILIA UNLIMITED

My name is Mary Mathews, and I am a commercial real estate agent. I have worked in commercial real estate since I graduated from college, and I enjoy my job very much. In college I majored in finance and took an introductory accounting course because it was required; but even if it had not been required, my mother would have insisted I take it. She is an accountant and has always told me that understanding accounting would help me succeed, no matter what my career. I didn't believe her.

I resented having to take accounting; but now when I look back, I wish I had worked harder in the course. I know that I could have been much more successful in the course had I paid more attention in class and done the homework regularly.

I don't use accounting every day in my job, but I still use it often to answer questions asked by landlords. Let's take Susan Newman, for example. She called me looking for office space. I carefully questioned her about what type of office space she wanted, such as what square footage, location, and rent amount. Then I took her on a tour of available properties that best met her needs. Once I matched her to a property, the negotiation process with the landlord began. At this point, I helped Susan submit a proposal to the landlord. This proposal outlined what terms she desired in the lease agreement. It included such information as the tenant's name, the nature of her business, the length of the term of the lease, and how she would use the property. The landlord had the option of accepting these terms or negotiating for different terms.

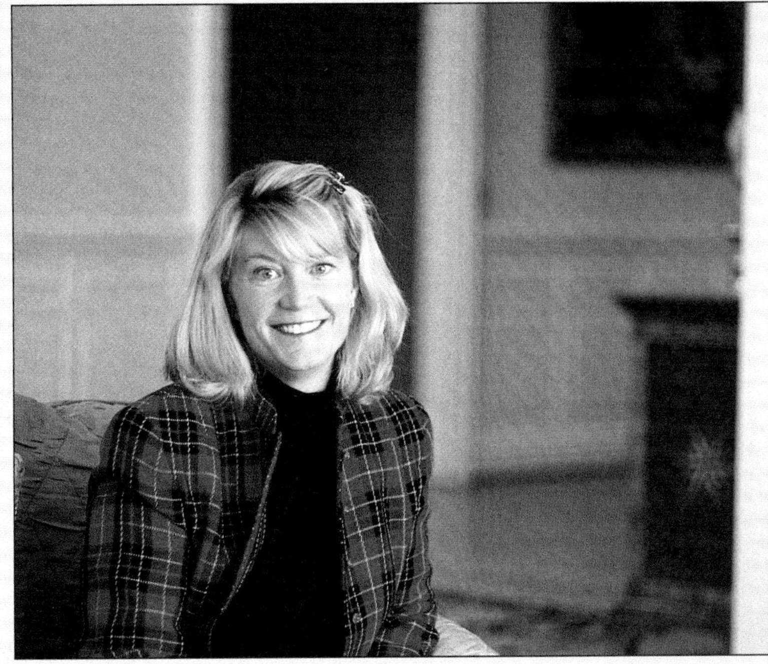

During the negotiation process, landlords almost always want to know more about the tenant. They usually want to see the financial statements of the business, or if it is a new business, projected financial statements. They want to know about the tenant's experience in his/her industry. And they almost always want to see how much rent the tenant is paying in his/her *current* office space. During this phase, landlords will sometimes ask me my opinion about the tenant's financial position, and so my job requires that I use accounting to determine the solvency of a prospective tenant.

I have found that in most careers, and in my industry in particular, the level of professionalism and competitiveness has dramatically increased. I need every tool I can use to keep my competitive edge. So my mother was right after all. I needed that accounting course!

In Chapter 6, you examined the income statement in general and Cards & Memorabilia Unlimited's income statement in particular. You'll learn more about the income statement in this chapter by examining the remaining transactions of Cards & Memorabilia Unlimited. Then you'll examine the form and content of the corporate income statements commonly found in annual reports, determine how entities decide when to recognize revenue, and apply financial statement analysis to the income statement.

Cards & Memorabilia Unlimited: Completing the Income Statement with Adjustments

In Chapter 6, you explored the income statement using transactions M through U. Each of these revenues and expenses was a clearly identifiable or *explicit* transaction entered into by Cards & Memorabilia Unlimited, a sole proprietorship that was later converted into a partnership. Now it is time to learn about some more elusive *implicit* transactions or *adjustments*, which, if unrecorded, will leave an incomplete picture of the entity's results of operations. To better understand how adjustments are the missing links in completing the income statement, let's first explore the critical distinction between explicit transactions and implicit transactions.

Distinguishing between Explicit and Implicit Transactions

All of the transactions you've analyzed so far are explicit transactions. An **explicit transaction** is a transaction that is clearly identifiable for recording purposes because it is derived from a business document that is difficult to overlook, such as a check, a purchase invoice, or a sales invoice. Study Figure 7-1 carefully since it enumerates the specific business documents that underlie each of the CMU transactions introduced so far.

Unfortunately, not all transactions that affect CMU or any business are explicit in nature. **Implicit transactions** or adjustments are not directly derived from a business document and are easily overlooked for recording purposes. They are, nonetheless, considered accounting transactions because they are measurable events that affect both the business and its current financial condition. In fact, the transactions of Cards & Memorabilia Unlimited that you will see in this chapter are five such implicit transactions or adjustments.

Figure 7-2 illustrates how the effects of CMU's explicit income statement transactions in Chapter 6 do not fully account for the amounts reported in CMU's first-year income statement, shown along with CMU's balance sheet in Figure 7-3. If you study Figure 7-2 and the income statement in Figure 7-3 carefully, you will discover that the amounts reported in this annual income statement represent not only the effects of the explicit income statement transactions introduced in Chapter 6 but also the effects of some implicit income statement transactions.

Let's discover the identity of one such implicit transaction. First, consider the miscellaneous expense account balances shown in both Figure 7-2 and Figure 7-3. You might remember that the following adjustment was proposed for this account in the section of Chapter 6 entitled *Income Statement of Cards & Memorabilia Unlimited.*

		Fundamental Accounting Equation					
Date	**Asset Account Title**	**Assets**	**=**	**Liabilities**	**+**	**Owners' Equity**	**Source of Asset Account Title**
12/31						(350)	Miscellaneous Expense
				350			Accounts Payable

FIGURE 7-1 Business documents underlying explicit transactions A_1 through A_2

		Details of Transactions	Document
A_1	01/02	$30,000 cash is contributed by the owner who opens a business checking account.	Bank deposit receipt
B	01/02	$6,000 cash is withdrawn from the checking account to open a business savings account.	Bank transfer receipt
C_1	01/04	$10,000 worth of store equipment is acquired with a credit card.	Invoice/credit card receipt
D	01/06	$15,000 cash is paid to acquire merchandise inventory.	Inventory invoice and check
E	01/09	$2,000 cash is paid to the landlord for the security deposit on the store lease.	Lease contract and check
C_2	02/03	$10,000 cash is paid in full to settle the credit card obligation made on January 4.	Canceled check
F	07/01	$5,000 cash is borrowed with a bank credit line bearing interest at an 8% rate.	Promissory note/deposit receipt
G	07/01–12/1	$18,000 worth of additional merchandise is acquired on account.	Inventory invoice
H	07/01	$7,000 cash is paid to acquire a used van with a 5-year useful life for the business.	Purchase receipt, title certificate, and check
I	11/01	$6,000 cash is collected from customers before any goods or services are provided.	Bank deposit receipt
J_1	07/31–11/30	$12,000 cash is paid to reduce accounts payable.	Canceled checks
J_2	12/31	$6,000 of accounts payable is converted to a 6% interest-bearing note payable due on March 31.	Promissory note
K_1	12/31	$5,000 cash is paid in full to settle the credit line loan made on July 1.	Canceled promissory note and canceled check
L	12/31	$4,000 worth of a computer and printer is acquired by signing a 2-year promissory note.	Purchase invoice and promissory note
M	Daily	$63,200 of cash sales are made to customers throughout the year.	Sales invoice/bank deposit receipt
N	Daily	$20,000 of revenue is earned on account—$19,400 for customer credit sales throughout the year and $600 for teaching a course.	Sales invoice/contract
O_1	12/02	$275 interest is earned from 1/2–12/2 on $6,000 of savings bearing 5% interest.	Savings account statement
P	Monthly	$1,000 cash is paid for office rent due the first day of each month beginning February 1.	Canceled check
Q_1	09/30	$300 of depreciation is recorded to recognize the use of equipment sold on September 30.	Sales contract
R	09/30	$2,000 worth of the store equipment bought on January 4 for $10,000 is sold for $1,350.	Sales invoice/bank deposit receipt
S	12/05	$8,000 cash is paid to employees for work performed through the year's last payday.	Canceled checks
K_2	12/31	$200 cash is paid for interest due on $5,000 borrowed on July 1 at 8% and repaid on December 31.	Canceled check
T	Daily	$4,250 cash is paid for miscellaneous expenses incurred throughout the year.	Purchase invoices/checks
U	12/31	$30,000 of cost of goods sold is determined by taking a physical count of inventory.	Inventory calculations
V	Daily	$15,000 cash is collected from customers throughout the year for amounts owed.	Bank deposit receipt
W	Daily	$8,100 cash is withdrawn from the business by the owner throughout the year.	Bank withdrawal receipts
A_2	12/24	$10,000 worth of merchandise is contributed by an individual for a business interest.	Partnership contract

FIGURE 7-2 Comparing CMU's preadjustment calculations to its year-end calculations for five income statement accounts to determine its adjustments (implicit transactions)

Explicit Transaction	Financial Statement	Account Title	CMU's Pre-Adjustment Calculations	CMU's Year-End Calculations	Amount Needed
O_1	Income statement	Interest Revenue	$ 275	$ 300	$ 25
—	Balance sheet	Interest Receivable	0	25	25
S	Income statement	Salaries Expense	8,000	8,750	750
—	Balance sheet	Salaries Payable	0	750	750
T	Income statement	Miscellaneous Expense	4,250	4,600	350
—	Balance sheet	Accounts Payable	0	350	350
C_1/H/L/Q_1/R	Income statement	Depreciation Expense	300	2,600	2,300
Q_1 & R	Balance sheet	Accumulated Depreciation	0	2,300	2,300
M & N	Income statement	Sales Revenue	82,600	86,600	4,000
I	Balance sheet	Deferred Revenue	6,000	2,000	4,000

As the third transaction in Figure 7-2 suggests, the preceding adjustment is correct since both the Miscellaneous Expense account and its related Accounts Payable account each increase by $350 as a result of an implicit transaction. Apparently, Susan Newman discovered that to properly measure net income in her first year of business, she had to record an additional $350 of miscellaneous expense. Since this expense was not associated with a cash payment on or before December 31, recording an account payable of $350 was necessary to complete this transaction. Recording this liability account is necessary to reflect its anticipated payment sometime after December 31.

Critical Thinking Problem 7-4 asks you to use Figure 7-2 and similar reasoning to determine the identity of the remaining four adjustments. This problem is highly recommended if you have not yet attempted the *Making Business Decisions* case in Chapter 6. Whether or not you attempt the challenge posed by Problem 7-4, be sure to study Figure 7-2 carefully since it helps identify five implicit transactions that must be recorded as of December 31 to properly measure net income for the period.

Now that you understand the distinction between an explicit transaction and an implicit transaction and how both are needed to complete the income statement, let's learn more about the implicit transactions usually called adjustments. First, we will define the term *adjustment*, then describe two central concepts that underlie adjustments, and finally study five implicit transactions (Transactions O_2, X, Y, Q_2, and Z) that Susan overlooked in her recording procedures.

Definition of an Adjustment

An **adjustment** is an implicit transaction recorded at the end of the accounting period to ensure that all revenues and expenses are reported in their proper period. When a business fails to properly record its adjustments, its net income for that period is misstated. Recall that every CMU transaction introduced before Chapter 6 affected only the balance sheet. As you can see in Figure 7-2, however, every adjustment contains both an income statement and a balance sheet account. The systematic steps of gathering information about potential adjustments and then recording the appropriate adjustments or implicit transactions at the end of an accounting period is known as the **adjustment process**.

Concepts Underlying Adjustments: Accruals and Deferrals

Accruals and deferrals are the two primary concepts underlying adjustments. **Accruals** are transactions in which revenues or expenses are recognized in the current pe-

FIGURE 7-3 Cards & Memorabilia Unlimited's income statement and balance sheet prepared by George Wu

CARDS & MEMORABILIA UNLIMITED

CARDS & MEMORABILIA UNLIMITED
Income Statement
For the Year Ended December 31 (Accrual Basis)

Revenues:		
Sales revenue	$86,600[1]	
Service revenue	600	
Interest revenue	300	$87,500
Expenses:		
Cost of goods sold	$30,000	
Rent expense	11,000	
Salaries expense	8,750	
Depreciation expense	2,600	
Miscellaneous expense	4,600	
Interest expense	200	
Loss on equipment sale	350	57,500
Net income		$30,000

CARDS & MEMORABILIA UNLIMITED
Balance Sheet
December 31

Assets		Liabilities and Owner Equities	
Current Assets		**Current Liabilities**	
Cash	$38,275	Accounts payable	$ 350
Accounts receivable	5,000	Salaries payable	750
Merchandise inventory	13,000	Deferred revenue[2]	2,000
Interest receivable	25	Notes payable	6,000
	$56,300		$ 9,100
Investments		**Noncurrent Liability**	
Security deposit receivable	$ 2,000	Notes payable	4,000
Property, Plant, and Equipment		**Owners' Equity**	
Store equipment	$19,000	Contributed capital	40,000
Less: Accum. depreciation	(2,300)	Retained earnings	21,900
Book value of equipment	$16,700		
Total assets	$75,000	Total liabilities and owners' equity	$75,000

[1]($63,200 + $19,400 + $4,000)
[2]Also referred to as Advances from Customers.

riod even though cash will not be collected or paid until a future period. That is, accruals occur when a revenue is earned or an expense is incurred in an earlier accounting period than its related cash effect. The following diagram illustrates how an accrual represents the recognition of an income effect before its related cash effect:

Accrual concept:	Accounting Period 1	Accounting Period 2
	Income effect—an implicit transaction	Cash effect—an explicit transaction

Notice that the accrual is recorded in Accounting Period 1 and is itself the adjustment. This timing can be illustrated by the interest you pay on a credit card account. Although your interest or finance charge accumulates on a daily basis this month, it usually isn't payable until you receive your account statement next month. That is, interest expense is accumulating, or *accruing*, on your account this month despite the fact that you will not pay this interest until the following month. The challenge you face in making this adjustment is that you have to record interest expense in the month preceding the receipt of your interest statement and your interest payment.

Deferrals, on the other hand, are transactions in which cash has been collected or paid in the current period even though the revenues or expenses are not recognized until a future period. That is, deferrals occur when a revenue is earned or an expense is incurred in a period following its related cash effect. Remember that you *defer* or postpone the income effect. The following diagram illustrates how a deferral represents the recognition of a cash effect before its related income effect:

Deferral concept:	**Accounting Period 1**	**End of Accounting Period 1 or Within Accounting Period 2**
	Cash effect—an explicit transaction	Income effect—an implicit transaction

Here, the deferral is recorded in Accounting Period 1 and the adjustment is recorded either at the end of Accounting Period 1 or in Accounting Period 2. This timing can be illustrated by the interest you are required to pay in advance on some student loans. In a process known as discounting the loan,[1] you receive the amount of the loan less the interest. Thus, you effectively pay cash this period and incur interest expense thereafter with the passage of time. That is, interest expense is delayed, or *deferred*, on your account despite the fact that you pay the full amount of interest in advance. The challenge you face in making this adjustment is that you have to record the correct amount of interest expense each month despite the fact that no convenient cash payment reminder is available.

To summarize, accruals always represent immediate adjustments and deferrals always precede their related adjustments. Since there are revenue and expense accruals and revenue and expense deferrals, four types of adjustments exist. Let's now study the general characteristics of these four types and the distinctions among them by focusing on the specific adjustments of CMU.

Adjustments of Cards & Memorabilia Unlimited's Explicit Transactions

Before we begin, here's a hint. In the following discussions, think of the term *accrual* as in accrued revenue and accrued expense without thinking about cash. In fact, the term accrual refers to revenues and expenses that are recorded *before* any cash receipts or payments occur. CMU's Transactions O_2, X, and Y all share this same characteristic—their income effects are recognized in the period preceding their cash effects.

Accrued Revenue An **accrued revenue** is an adjustment transaction in which revenue is earned in the current period even though cash is not collected until a future period. Let's start by analyzing Transaction O_2:

[1] Banks prefer this type of loan since it eliminates student default of interest. It is, however, generally unpopular with students who receive less money than they had anticipated.

Transaction O_2	Assets	=	Liabilities	+	Owners' Equity	Nature of Revenue or Expense
$25 of interest is earned but uncollected on a $6,000 savings account bearing 5% interest.	25				25	Interest Revenue

Analysis: Recall from Transaction O_1 that CMU has already recorded $275 of revenue for interest earned during the period from January 2 to December 2. Since CMU must record the interest that it earned over the period of one year, this adjustment ensures that a full year of interest revenue ($6,000 × 0.05 = $300) is reported in this year's income statement. Using the same concept as a credit sale, CMU must record both a receivable and a revenue. The interest receivable account represents Susan's right to collect interest on January 2 of next year. The interest revenue account, however, represents interest earned between December 3 and December 31 of the current year. Since the interest is collectible as it is earned, CMU must report the interest receivable as a current asset. "Accruing" such interest refers to the process of recording interest revenue before it is collected in cash.

Accrued Expense An **accrued expense** is an adjustment transaction in which expense is incurred in the current period even though cash is not paid until a future period. Let's look at two examples of an accrued expense at CMU—Transaction X and Transaction Y.

Transaction X	Assets	=	Liabilities	+	Owners' Equity	Nature of Revenue or Expense
$750 of salaries expense is incurred but unpaid.			750		(750)	Salaries Expense

Analysis: In the explanation of Transaction S, you learned that Susan paid her employees a total of $8,000 as of Friday, December 5th of the current year, and would not make her next payment to them until Friday, January 4th. In Figure 7-2, you saw that the total salaries expense for the year was $750 higher or $8,750. You were correct if you used these clues to determine that the additional $750 represents employee services provided but unpaid as of December 31. In other words, the additional $750 has accrued during the period from December 6th until December 31. Susan Newman, however, was able to derive the $750 more directly by adding up the hours Peter Nguyen and Steve Wheeler each worked between December 5–31 and multiplying by their respective pay rates.

CMU must report the $750 as an expense under the accrual basis because it has *received* the employees' services, even though it has not yet paid for them. Likewise, CMU must report a liability called Salaries Payable because it owes employees $750 as of December 31. It is not allowed to report the January 4 cash payment because its balance sheet reports only those transactions up to and including December 31. *Accruing salaries* refers to the process of recording salaries expense before it is paid in cash. This same concept is illustrated next with Transaction Y.

Transaction Y	Assets	=	Liabilities	+	Owners' Equity	Nature of Revenue or Expense
$350 of miscellaneous expense is incurred but unpaid.			350		(350)	Miscellaneous Expense

Analysis: In the analysis of *explicit* Transaction T, you learned it was likely that CMU had additional miscellaneous expenses that had not been paid at year-end. In Figure 7-2, you might have realized this additional expense was $350 because the $4,600 total amount reported was $350 higher than the $4,250 reported in Transaction T. Susan was able to derive the $350 more directly, however, by totaling the unpaid bills at year-end from the categories described in the identification of Transaction T. CMU must report the $350 as an expense under the accrual basis, because it has incurred the same types of expense it paid for in Transaction T. Likewise, CMU must report the liability, Accounts Payable, because it owes $350 to various businesses as of December 31. "Accruing" miscellaneous expense refers to the process of recording miscellaneous expense before it is paid in cash.

Deferred Expense (Asset Expiration) A **deferred expense** is a transaction in which cash is paid now or in the future to obtain an asset even though expense will not be incurred until a future period. When such an expenditure is treated as an asset, or *capitalized*, an expense is postponed, or deferred. That is, a *deferred expense* or *asset* is created that will *expire* as goods are sold or services are consumed. Susan's Store Equipment account, based on Transactions C_1, H, L, and R, is just such a deferred expense that must be adjusted at the end of the period to properly measure income. Accordingly, Transaction Q_2 below is not itself a deferred expense but rather an *asset expiration*, an adjustment that records the expiration of an asset's service potential:

Transaction Q_2	Assets	=	Liabilities	+	Owners' Equity	Nature of Revenue or Expense
$2,300 of depreciation is recorded on the use of unsold equipment.	(2,300)				(2,300)	Depreciation Expense

Analysis: As you already know, the portion of equipment cost that is used up during the accounting period is referred to as *depreciation expense*. In Figures 7-2 and 7-3, you learned that the total amount of depreciation expense was $2,600. If you haven't yet calculated this amount, study the allocation of the individual equipment purchase costs to depreciation expense summarized in Figure 7-4. Since $300 of this $2,600 amount has already been recorded in Transaction Q_1, only $2,300 is recorded in Transaction Q_2. Note that Q_2 represents an implicit transaction derived from four explicit transactions (Transactions C_1, H, L, and Q_1), which records this period's use of the asset Store Equipment. Since the consumption of the asset service potential is accumulated in the Accumulated Depreciation account, a contra asset, the asset Store Equipment is ultimately reduced by $2,300 to a book value of $16,700 [($10,000 + $7,000 + $4,000 − $2,000)* − ($300 − $300 + $2,300)].** At the same time, the depreciation expense account is increased, which reduces the owners' equity of the business by $2,300.

* Transactions C_1, H, L, and R, respectively.

** Transactions Q_1, R, and Q_2, respectively.

Transaction	Holding Period	Calculation		Amount
Transaction C_1	$8,000 held all year	$8,000 × 1/5 × 12/12	=	$1,600
Transaction R	$2,000 held till 9/30	$2,000 × 1/5 × 9/12	=	300
Transaction H	$7,000 held since 7/1	$7,000 × 1/5 × 6/12	=	700
Transaction L	$4,000 12/31 purchase	Not applicable		0
				$2,600

FIGURE 7-4

Cards & Memorabilia Unlimited's depreciation calculation

Deferred Revenue Look once more at the definition of *deferral.* How would you define a deferred revenue in your own words? A **deferred revenue** is a transaction in which cash is collected in the current period even though revenue will not be earned until a future period. That is, revenue is postponed, or deferred, whenever the conditions governing revenue recognition have not been met. In fact, *explicit* Transaction I in which Susan received $6,000 of cash on November 1 but had no product to exchange is a deferred revenue. The adjustment, however, is not Transaction I but CMU's Transaction Z shown below:

Transaction Z	Assets	=	Liabilities	+	Owners' Equity	Nature of Revenue or Expense
$4,000 worth of merchandise is delivered to customers who paid in advance.			(4,000)		4,000	Sales Revenue

Analysis: You might recall that Transaction I stated that Susan would deliver $2,000 of goods at the end of both November and December. Nevertheless, it would be easy to overlook its *implicit* adjustment in Transaction Z above unless there was a specific business document reminding you to take action. When Susan spotted this adjustment at December 31, CMU immediately reported $4,000 of sales revenue and eliminated $4,000 of the liability account called Advances from Customers or Deferred Revenue.

It is important to remember that an accrual is itself an adjustment, whereas a deferral is the basis for an adjustment in a later period. Now that you have studied adjustments in some depth, consider Performance Objective 19:

YOUR PERFORMANCE OBJECTIVE 19

a. **Record** the adjustments needed at the end of the period using transaction analysis.
b. **Determine** the amount of both related balance sheet and income statement accounts after adjustments have been made.

Performance Objective 19(a) was demonstrated in Transactions O_2, X, Y, Q_2, and Z. Performance Objective 19(b) represents a variation of Objective 19(a) that focuses your attention on the financial statement effects of adjustments. To apply it to Transaction Q_2, for example, you would determine the amounts of the Store Equipment asset account and the Accumulated Depreciation contra asset account shown on the balance sheet to be $19,000 and $2,300, respectively. Likewise, you would determine that the related Depreciation Expense account amounted to $2,600.

Since adjustments are not as easy to identify as are explicit transactions, before you continue, use Figure 7-5 to solidify your understanding of the accrual and deferral concepts as applied to CMU's five adjustments.

FIGURE 7-5 Accrual and deferral concepts applied to CMU's adjustments

Adjustment	Adjustment Concept	Accounting Period 1	Accounting Period 2
Transaction O_2	Accrued revenue	\$25 Receivable increase \$25 Revenue increase (Transaction O_2)	\$25 Receivable decrease \$25 Cash increase Future transaction
Transaction X	Accrued expense	\$750 Expense increase \$750 Liability increase (Transaction X)	\$750 Cash decrease \$750 Liability decrease Future transaction
Transaction Y	Accrued expense	\$350 Expense increase \$350 Liability increase (Transaction Y)	\$350 Cash decrease \$350 Liability decrease Future transaction
Adjustment	**Adjustment Concept**	**Beginning of Accounting Period 1**	**End of Accounting Period 1**
Transaction Q_2	Deferred expense and asset expiration	\$19,000 Asset increases \$19,000 of offsets (Transactions C_1,H,L,& R)	\$2,300 Expense increase \$2,300 Asset decrease Transaction Q_2
Transaction Z	Deferred revenue and liability reduction	\$6,000 Cash increase \$6,000 Liability increase (Transaction I)	\$4,000 Revenue increase \$4,000 Liability decrease Transaction Z

Financial Statement Relationships Revisited

In Chapter 3 you learned that the statement of owners' equity links the income statement to the balance sheet. Additional evidence of this relationship between the income statement and the balance sheet is the fact that nearly one-half of the first-year transactions of Cards & Memorabilia Unlimited affect not only its balance sheet but also its income statement. Let's now see exactly how an individual transaction can simultaneously affect more than one financial statement and in the process develop your financial analysis skills further.

This skill is particularly useful in evaluating the effect of a proposed transaction on an entity's financial statements. For example, consider the following analysis of a credit sale of merchandise in the table below. Using the terms *increase*, *decrease*, and *no effect*, confirm the answers below.

Transaction	Total Revenue	Total Expense	Net Income	Total Assets	Total Liabilities	Total Owners' Equity
Credit sale	Increase	No effect	Increase	Increase	No effect	Increase

What follows is the underlying reasoning for the financial statement effects listed from left to right in the preceding table. First, since a credit sale increases revenue but has no effect on expense, net income increases. Second, since a credit sale also increases accounts receivable, an asset, but has no effect on liabilities, owners' equity—the opposite side of the fundamental equation—also increases. Notice that you can confirm this increase to owners' equity because an increase to net income also

YOUR PERFORMANCE OBJECTIVE 13

From your understanding of financial statement relationships:

a. **Link** the following related financial statements—balance sheet, income statement, and statement of owners' equity—by being able to **calculate** missing amounts in each of them.
b. **Analyze** accounting transactions to **determine** their effect—increase, or decrease, understatement or overstatement, or no effect—on the elements of *both* the balance sheet and the income statement.

increases owners' equity. Such an analysis is described by Performance Objective 13(b), which requires you to analyze transactions and determine their effects on the balance sheet and the income statement. Notice that Performance Objective 13(a), which you first used in Chapter 3, deals with more global financial statement relationships than does Performance Objective 13(b).

Performance Objective 13(b) can also be used to evaluate the effect of errors and omissions on an entity's financial statements. First, consider the financial statement effects of an error in which a credit sale of merchandise is correctly recorded as an increase to accounts receivable but incorrectly recorded as a decrease to merchandise inventory rather than an increase to sales revenue. Using the terms *overstated*, *understated*, and *no effect*, confirm the answers below.

Recording Error	Total Revenue	Total Expense	Net Income	Total Assets	Total Liabilities	Total Owners' Equity
Credit sale	Understated	No effect	Understated	Understated	No effect	Understated

What follows is the underlying reasoning for the financial statement effects listed from left to right in the preceding table. Since not recording sales revenue understates revenue but has no effect on expense, net income is understated. Since a credit sale increases the asset accounts receivable but doesn't decrease the asset merchandise inventory, assets are understated. Once again, there is no effect on liabilities, and so owners' equity is also understated. Notice that you can confirm this last effect because the understated net income has the effect of understating owner's equity.

Next, consider the financial statement effects of an omission in which a single credit sale is not recorded. Using the terms *overstated*, *understated*, and *no effect*, confirm the answers below.

Recording Omission	Total Revenue	Total Expense	Net Income	Total Assets	Total Liabilities	Total Owners' Equity
Credit sale	Understated	No effect	Understated	Understated	No effect	Understated

What follows is the underlying reasoning for the financial statement effects listed from left to right in the preceding table. Since not recording sales revenue understates revenue but has no effect on expense, net income is understated. Likewise, not recording accounts receivable understates assets but doesn't affect liabilities, so owners' equity is also understated. Once again, you can confirm this last effect because the understated net income has the effect of understating owners' equity.

Your ability to use the preceding reasoning process to analyze significant business transactions is one of the most important user tools provided by this textbook. That is, applying the analytical reasoning embodied in Performance Objective 13(b) is a powerful financial analysis tool as expressed in the following *User Focus*.

A Real-World Application of How Transactions Affect Financial Statements

USER FOCUS

Don't underestimate how important it is to your career to be able to determine the financial statement effects of transactions, errors, and omissions. Everyday, the financial press is full of news about recent and anticipated transactions of well-known businesses. In most cases, however, this news does not spell out the multimillion-dollar financial state-

(continued)

ment effects of these transactions. Such well-known periodicals as *The Wall Street Journal, Barrons, Fortune*, and *Business Week* fail to describe to their readers the logical effects of these transactions on company financial statements. Unfortunately, many readers don't have the analytical skills needed to deduce those effects. Thus, they don't fully appreciate the consequences of these transactions and are left with only a vague notion of their effects. To ensure that you become a more knowledgeable financial statement user, you'll want to use the transaction analysis introduced in the preceding section.

Let's look at the following two articles from an issue of *The Wall Street Journal*[2] to illustrate this useful analysis.

Article 1: "Hitachi to Buy E-Business Unit from Chicago's Grant Thornton"
This article describes how Hitachi, Japan's largest electronics company, plans to purchase the system integration and computer consulting division of Grant Thornton, the fifth largest accounting firm in the United States, for an estimated $175 million. The transaction was part of Hitachi's effort to expand into computer services and Grant Thornton's effort to escape the potential conflict of interest of having consulting and auditing services under one roof. Since this anticipated transaction is significant, let's find out how it affects Hitachi's balance sheet, income statement, and statement of cash flows:

Transaction	Total Revenue	Total Expense	Net Income	Total Assets	Total Liabilities	Total Owners' Equity
Purchase of 500-person e-business consulting group	No effect	No effect	No effect	No effect; Assets increase and decrease by $175 million	No effect	No effect

Balance Sheet: Notice that the nature of Hitachi's assets are affected. It acquires various assets associated with the E-Business Group in exchange for a significant amount of cash.
Income Statement: This transaction does not affect the current income statement of Hitachi, although it might affect its future profitability.
Statement of Cash Flows: Although you have not yet studied this financial statement in great detail, you might recognize that this transaction is classified as a cash outflow from investing activities.

Article 2: "Xerox Seeks to Slash $1 Billion of Expenses and Sell Some Assets"[3]
This article describes how Xerox, the world's largest copier company, plans to cut one billion dollars of expenses and raise two to four billion dollars by selling various assets. Since these transactions were undertaken to reduce Xerox's significant indebtedness and offset recent losses, let's find out what the likely transaction effects will be on its financial statements:

Transaction	Total Revenue	Total Expense	Net Income	Total Assets	Total Liabilities	Total Owners' Equity
1. Expense reductions	No effect	Decrease	Increase	Increase	Decrease	Increase
2. Asset sales	Potential gains	Potential losses	Unclear	Cash increases	No effect	Increase

[2]*The Wall Street Journal*, Dow Jones & Company, New York, N.Y., October 25, 2000, A3, A6, A19.
[3]This title was used on a continuation page. The original title was, "Xerox Pledges to Cut $1 Billion in Costs, Reports a Quarterly Loss of $167 Million."

Balance Sheet: The primary effect of these transactions will be to increase Xerox's assets, especially cash. In addition, some expense-related liabilities will be reduced. Both transactions will increase owner's equity. Since cash will be increased, it could be used to reduce Xerox's indebtedness.

Income Statement: The expense reductions will decrease expenses and have no effect on revenues. The asset sales will create both gains and losses. There is, however, no way of knowing whether net income will be increased or decreased in total.

Statement of Cash Flows: The expense reduction represents a potential operating cash inflow, and the planned asset sales represent a potential investing cash inflow.

Although every accounting student learns about transaction analysis, a large number do not retain their understanding long enough to apply it to real world situations like that described above. Thus, if you desire to be a good business decision maker, you will want to continue using this tool long after this course is over.

Corporate Income Statements Found in Annual Reports

Now that you have completed the income statement for Cards & Memorabilia Unlimited, a partnership, you may be wondering if income statements for sole proprietorships and partnerships differ in any way from corporate income statements. In fact, they do. We now will investigate in detail the income statements of corporations.

Learning to Read the Classified Income Statement

As you have seen, an income statement contains information about the profitability of an entity. Many decision makers consider the income statement an important, if not *the* most important, financial statement in the annual report. Investors, for example, want to know an entity's profitability, or net income, so that they can decide whether or not to invest in that entity. Creditors also look at the profitability of an entity that owes them money to decide if its net income—a source of assets—will produce sufficient cash to repay them. To truly understand the income statement, however, you must look beyond what is known as the bottom line. People use this expression frequently in everyday conversation to mean "get to the point" or "what is the answer?" But if you look only at the bottom line of an income statement, that is, its net income, you are likely to overlook some very important financial information. Knowledgeable decision makers study the complete income statement, not just the final figure, net income—also called **earnings** and **profits**. Such users depend on the **classified income statement**, an income statement that classifies revenues and expenses into several categories.

Informed users of the classified income statement do not treat every reported item equally. Instead, they concentrate on an entity's **primary operating activities**, or transactions, rather than transactions that are peripheral or incidental to the entity. Also, they concentrate on continuing activities or transactions rather than on an unusual event that is unlikely to recur regularly. To help you decide what information in a classified income statement is essential, let's now take a more in-depth look at each of these two important distinctions.

Distinguishing Primary Operating Activities from Activities Peripheral to Operations As just described, primary activities are generally more important in evaluating an entity's operations than peripheral activities. But the distinction between a transaction that is primary and one that is peripheral is not always obvious. To properly classify transactions, you must understand the essential nature of the business entering into those transactions. For example, let's take the sale of a computer printer. This sale is not reported in the same way by Hewlett Packard, an electronics and computer manufacturer, as it is by The Limited, Inc., a collection of brand name retailers whose primary operating activity is to sell casual clothes. The difference, of course, is that the sale of a computer printer by Hewlett-Packard is a primary operating activity that affects both sales revenue and cost of goods sold. In contrast, if The Limited decides to sell its three-year-old computer printer, the sale is considered a transaction that is peripheral to operations and is included in the other gains and losses account. Thus, when you analyze an income statement, you must know more about a company than just its name.

You can determine the essential nature of a business and its primary operating activity by studying its annual report. For example, as described in Chapter 3, the first few pages of an annual report often include this information as does the section detailing the entity's revenue recognition, usually in the Summary of Significant Accounting Policies in the notes to the financial statements. Another good source is the initial information about the nature of the business found in that business's 10-K. Thus, as you have seen from the printer example, it is not difficult to determine activities that are peripheral to an entity once you identify the primary operating activity of that entity.

INSIGHT

What Is the True Nature of Activities Peripheral to Operations?

Examples of activities or transactions that are peripheral to operations include interest revenue (also called interest income), interest expense, dividend revenue, gains and losses on sales of depreciable assets, and income tax expense. Although the Financial Accounting Standards Board (FASB), the rule-making body of the accounting profession, classifies these items as operating activities, you could argue that this group of peripheral income items should be classified as investing or financing activities. For example, a finance professor would classify interest and dividends received and receivable as the result of investing activities. This is because interest is derived from making loans, and dividends are derived from buying stock. In addition, the finance professor could argue that interest paid and payable are directly related to the completion of a financing activity because such interest is incurred from borrowing money. Most accounting professors, however, will classify these items as operating activities, arguing that they have always been reported in the income statement and to exclude them would be misleading to users.

One insight you should gain, therefore, is that although the true nature of these items is actually investing and financing, the accounting profession treats them as activities peripheral to operating activities. To avoid confusion, this textbook follows this practice and presents these items in income statements. We will call such items **peripheral activities** because they are truly not operating in nature.

A second insight you should gain here is that the nature of accounting is more an art than a science. Do not be surprised to learn, therefore, that not all rules and standards followed by the accounting profession agree with other fields of study.

Distinguishing Continuing from Noncontinuing Activities As the words suggest, **continuing activities** are transactions whose effects are reported in the income statement on a fairly regular basis. A gain or loss from periodic sales of equipment used in the business, for example, represents a continuing activity. In contrast, a loss from an oil spill is an event that does not occur on a regular basis and represents an example of a **noncontinuing activity**.

FIGURE 7-6 An example of a significant noncontinuing activity for The Limited, Inc.

THE LIMITED, INC.
Consolidated Statements of Income
(In thousands of dollars except earnings per share)

	2000	1999	1998
Net sales	$10,104,606	$9,766,220	$9,364,750
Costs of goods sold, occupancy and buying costs	6,667,389	(6,443,063)	(6,424,725)
Gross income	3,437,217	3,323,157	2,940,025
General, administrative and store operating expenses	(2,561,201)	(2,415,849)	(2,256,332)
Special and nonrecurring items, net	(9,900)	23,501	1,740,030
Operating income	866,116	930,809	2,423,723
Interest expense	(58,244)	(78,297)	(68,528)
Other income, net	20,378	40,868	59,915
Minority interest	(69,345)	(72,623)	(63,616)
Gain on sale of subsidiary stock	—	11,002	—
Income before income taxes	758,905	831,759	2,351,494
Provision for income taxes	(331,000)	(371,000)	(305,000)
Net income	$ 427,905	$ 460,759	$2,046,494
Net income per share:			
Basic	$1.00	$1.05	$4.25
Diluted	$0.96	$1.00	$4.15

This item amounts to nearly $1.75 billion.

Unsophisticated users often overlook the distinction between continuing and noncontinuing activities. You will be a more informed user of income statements if you study this distinction because it will help you avoid making potentially poor decisions. For example, consider the recent income statements of The Limited, Inc. (Figure 7-6) in which a noncontinuing activity—making Abercrombie & Fitch an independent company—had an exceptionally dramatic effect. In this case, Special and Nonrecurring Items (Line 5) had a nearly one and three-quarter billion dollars effect on the net income of The Limited, Inc. for fiscal year 1998. Would you decide to invest based on its elevated 1998 earnings? Most financial analysts would ignore these earnings when considering how attractive The Limited is for investment. They would instead forecast its future earnings without this information as shown next because none of the special and nonrecurring items are expected to recur:

		(In thousands)	
	2000	**1999**	**1998**
Net income	$427,905	$460,759	$2,046,494
Exclude: Noncontinuing item	9,900	(23,501)	(1,740,030)
Financial analysts' net income	437,805	$437,258	$ 306,464

Thus, in this example, you should concentrate on income from continuing operations labeled "Financial analysts' net income" here, rather than on net income because of the noncontinuing items.

Navigating through the Content of the Income Statement

In Chapter 6 you learned that the elements of an income statement include revenues, expenses, gains, and losses. Now that you have learned some guidelines for analyzing income statement information, you are ready to examine the income statement in even more detail.

Although income statements vary widely, almost every income statement account belongs in one of four possible categories. These are (1) primary operating activities that are expected to continue, (2) peripheral activities that are expected to continue, (3) primary operating activities that are not expected to continue, and (4) peripheral activities that are not expected to continue. In fact, corporations rarely experience the effects of transactions in each of these four categories in a single period. As a result, each category and its most frequently found account titles will be illustrated with the model classified income statement shown in Figure 7-7. Notice that this hypothetical company has the same title, Idealistic Company, as was used in Chapter 4 to illustrate a model classified balance sheet. Refer to this figure carefully in the next few sections and resist the temptation to skim its content. To help you determine Idealistic Company's primary as opposed to peripheral activities, assume that it manufactures instruments used in the biotechnology, chemicals, and plastics industries.

Primary Operating Activities that Are Expected to Continue This income statement category is, by far, the most important. It usually includes items that are found in the top half of the income statement and the great majority of income statement accounts. In Figure 7-7, Idealistic Company's first line item, **net revenues**, includes both the amount billed for product sales as well as the amount billed for services performed. This practice of using one line to summarize two or more sources of revenue is commonly used in annual reports to achieve simplicity.[4] When revenue is solely derived from product sales, however, it is usually called *net sales* or **net sales revenue**. In either case, the word *net* indicates that the total, or gross, amount of sales or revenue has been reduced after accounting for transactions such as customer returns and allowances whose amounts are normally considered too small to report. A notable exception is found in the income statements of the liquor industry because of the unusually heavy taxes they bear relative to other industries. For example, Anheuser-Busch recently reported total sales of over \$13 billion reduced by nearly \$1.7 billion of federal and state excise taxes! Net revenue or net sales is one of the most popular ways used to measure an entity's size. For example, Idealistic Company would be referred to as a one-billion-dollar company because its net revenues are \$1 billion. As large as this revenue figure might seem, it is dwarfed by General Motors' net revenues, which in 2001 alone amounted to over \$177 billion!

The second line item in Figure 7-7, **cost of revenues**, includes Idealistic Company's cost incurred in producing revenue from products and services. Such costs include raw material and labor. When revenue is derived solely from products, however, the account title Cost of Sales or **Cost of Goods Sold**, as it is more commonly called, is reported on the income statement. Whatever its title, this particular expense clearly illustrates the *matching concept*, because revenue is offset by the cost incurred in generating that revenue.

The third line item, **gross margin** or **gross profit**, is an income total determined by deducting cost of revenue or cost of goods sold from sales revenue. You will learn more about this subtotal when you study profitability ratios later in this chapter.

---

[4] In contrast, recall how Cards & Memorabilia Unlimited's revenues were reported in three lines to enhance your understanding as a student.

FIGURE 7-7

A model classified corporate income statement

IDEALISTIC COMPANY
Income Statement
For the Year Ended December 31
(Dollar amounts in thousands except per share amounts)

Net revenues		$1,000,000
Less: Cost of revenues		450,000
Gross margin		550,000
Less: Operating expenses:		
Selling, general, and administrative	$150,000	
Research, development, and engineering	90,000	
Restructuring charges (Note 6)*	(25,000)	215,000
Primary operating income		335,000
Revenue, expense, gain, and loss items:		
Gain on investments	5,000	
Rent expense	(22,000)	
Interest expense (net)	(15,143)	(32,143)
Pretax income from continuing operations		302,857
Less: Federal income tax expense ($302,857 × 0.30)		90,857
Income from continuing operations		212,000
Discontinued activities:		
Loss from operations of business division	(40,000)	
Less: Income tax savings ($40,000 × 0.30)	12,000	
Gain on disposal of business division assets	20,000	
Less: Income tax ($20,000 × 0.30)	(6,000)	(14,000)
Income before extraordinary item		198,000
Extraordinary item: Earthquake loss	(200,000)	
Less: Income tax savings ($200,000 × 0.30)	60,000	(140,000)
Income before cumulative effect of accounting change		58,000
Cumulative effect of change in depreciation method	60,000	
Less: Income tax ($60,000 × 0.30)	(18,000)	42,000
Net income		$ 100,000
Earnings per share ($100,000/10,000)		$ 10.00

**Note 6:* Due to technological obsolescence, certain of the company's inventories were written down below original cost to more accurately represent net realizable value. While such a write-down is an infrequent occurrence in the industry, it is not considered unusual. Thus, this event did not qualify for treatment as an extraordinary item.

The fourth line item, **selling, general, and administrative expenses**, represents a group of operating expense accounts each of which produces revenue but not in as clear-cut a relationship as the matching of cost of goods sold to revenue. Although summarizing these accounts on one line of the income statement is efficient, it does not help this income statement's users to evaluate different aspects of the company's operations. For example, selling expenses usually vary directly with changes in sales, whereas administrative expenses tend to fluctuate little from period to period because they are less affected by changes in sales.

The fifth line item, *research, development, and engineering expense*, is not included in every income statement. It is, however, a reasonable expense for a company that develops, manufactures, and distributes products used in environmental technology, pharmaceuticals, biotechnology, chemicals, plastics, food, agriculture, and scientific research.

The sixth line item, *restructuring charges*, typically represents consolidation or abandonment of operations resulting in loss of asset value and additional costs from the termination or relocation of employees. In Figure 7-7, the restructuring expense relates to inventory that has experienced a loss in value due to technological obsolescence. Such a line item is sometimes referred to as an unusual or **special event**. Unlike an extraordinary event that will be described in a later category, a special event is either *unusual in nature or infrequently occurring*, but not both. In other words, the occurrence of such transactions is not typical but is certainly not rare. Note that footnote disclosure is required of these special events to clarify their nature.

The seventh line item, **primary operating income** or **income from operations**, measures the primary operating activities of an entity by deducting all of the operating expenses from the gross margin. You should pay attention to this income subtotal if you want to learn about the relationship between revenue earned from customers and the expenses incurred in servicing those customers.

Peripheral Activities that Are Expected to Continue As described in an earlier *Insight*, this category includes accounts not associated with how assets are used in operations but that tend to appear each year on the income statement. In the specific case of Idealistic Company, Figure 7-7 reports four line items for this category. They are: gain on investments, rent expense, interest expense (net), and income tax expense. Note that the line item titled "interest expense (net)" is derived by combining an interest revenue account with a larger interest expense account.

At least three points are worth noting about the income tax expense account. First, its appearance confirms that income tax is reported in corporate income statements, unlike sole proprietorship and partnership income statements. Second, unlike the operating expenses, income tax expense is not incurred to produce revenue. Third, this account is usually referred to as **Provision for Income Taxes** in the income statements included in annual reports. Although Idealistic Company uses the title **Pretax Income from Continuing Operations**, the great majority of companies use the simpler but less descriptive title, *Income Before Income Taxes*.

Primary Operating Activities that Are Discontinued (Not Expected to Continue) The financial effects of the preceding two categories—primary and peripheral activities expected to appear in future periods—are represented by the key income statement subtotal entitled **Income from Continuing Operations** in Figure 7-7. Note that this income component includes only the normal and recurring economic activities of the entity. In contrast, the activities in the present category and that which follows are not anticipated to occur on an ongoing basis. Nevertheless, they often have a significant impact on net income and deserve scrutiny.

Generally, a primary operating activity that is discontinued will be reported on the income statement whenever the entity sells a major *business segment* during the year or contemplates that such a sale will occur shortly after the end of the accounting period. A **business segment** is a component of a company, the activities of which represent a separate major line of business or class of customer, such as a subsidiary, division, or department. Usually, a sale or disposal of a business segment involves two separate but related financial effects. The first such effect, titled Loss from Operations of Business Division, Net of Tax in Figure 7-7, is the amount of income or loss from the operation of the discontinued business segment. A notable real-life example was the $10 million loss from discontinued operations reported by PE Corporation when it sold a division that worked on the mirror for the ill-fated Hubble Space Telescope. When the mirror was discovered to be defective, this company decided to pay a settlement fee to the U.S. government to avoid costly legal action. The second financial effect, titled Gain on Disposal of Business Division Assets, Net of Tax in Figure 7-7, is the gain or loss from selling or abandoning the assets of the discontinued business segment. As you can see, these items and their related tax effects are reported separately from income from continuing operations to provide more useful disclosure. In particular, note how discontinued operations are reported net of tax, either by listing the pretax effect, tax effect, and net of tax effect as shown in Figure 7-7 or by the more common practice in which the net of tax effect is reported on a single line of the income statement.

Although this category can disclose significant financial effects, most financial analysts would ignore these transactions when analyzing an entity's investment potential. They would instead forecast its future earnings without this information because none of the items mentioned in this section are expected to recur.

Peripheral Activities that Are Not Expected to Continue The last category of accounts reports events that are peripheral to primary operating activities and that are not expected to appear in the income statement on a regular basis. Do not overlook this category, however, since it often has a major impact on the bottom line. How major an impact? One such transaction had a $21 billion effect on the income statement of General Motors several years ago! The first transaction or event in this category, an **extraordinary item**, rarely appears in financial reporting but can have a significant effect on earnings when it does occur. Examples include losses from earthquakes, hurricanes, or other natural disasters. To qualify as an extraordinary item, the transaction must be relatively significant in amount or "material," unusual in nature, and an infrequent occurrence.

The second transaction or event in this category, **a change in accounting principle** occurs whenever an entity changes from one generally accepted accounting principle to another generally accepted principle (or method) of accounting during the period. A classic example is the not uncommon change from one method of depreciation to another as illustrated in Figure 7-7. Here, the $60,000 difference between the book value of the assets under the old method (the double-declining balance method described in Chapter 12) and the book value of the assets under the new method (straight-line method) represents the cumulative dollar effect of the change. Accordingly, such an item or event is sometimes called the *cumulative effect of a change in accounting principle*.

Note how both the extraordinary item and the cumulative effect of an accounting change in Figure 7-7 are reported net of tax. In fact, this treatment is required of all income statement items reported below the income from continuing operations subtotal.

Now that you have discovered that every income statement account belongs in one of four distinctive categories, review the essential characteristics and most common examples described in Figure 7-8 to master Performance Objective 20.

YOUR PERFORMANCE OBJECTIVE 20

Categorize all income statement accounts into *one* of the following four categories:

a. Primary operating activities that are expected to continue.
b. Peripheral activities that are expected to continue.
c. Primary operating activities that are discontinued.
d. Peripheral activities that are not expected to continue.

What Is the Basic Format of the Income Statement?

Although there are innumerable variations, most income statements in annual reports fit into one of two formats—multiple step or single step.

FIGURE 7-8 Categories used in presenting income statement information

	Continuing Activities	Noncontinuing Activities
Primary operating activities	Creation and/or sale of entity's products and/or services to its customers	Income or loss from discontinued business segment operations and gains or losses from sales of discontinued business segment assets.
Peripheral or incidental activities	Interest revenue, interest expense, dividend revenue, depreciable asset sales, and/or income tax expense	Extraordinary items such as earthquake losses and changes in accounting principles

The format used by Idealistic Company in Figure 7-7 and by more than three-quarters of all companies[5] is the multiple-step income statement. A **multiple-step income statement** format deducts expenses from revenues in a series of income subtotals (steps) that precede income from continuing operations.[6] Notice that in Figure 7-7, these subtotals include gross margin, primary operating income, and pretax income from continuing operations.

In contrast, a **single-step income statement** format reports income from continuing operations as the first income total. Although this format is supposed to deduct all expenses from all revenues in a single step, most companies do not follow this

FIGURE 7-9a

A single-step income statement with a noncontinuing item for General Motors Corporation

GENERAL MOTORS CORPORATION AND SUBSIDIARIES
Consolidated Statements of Income
(Dollars in millions except per share)

	Years Ended December 31,		
	2000	1999	1998
Total net sales and revenues	$184,632	$176,558	$155,445
Cost of sales and other expenses	145,664	140,708	127,785
Selling, general, and administrative expenses	22,252	19,053	16,087
Interest expense	9,552	7,750	6,629
Total costs and expenses	177,468	167,511	150,501
First income subtotal → Income from continuing operations before income taxes and minority interests	7,164	9,047	4,944
Income tax expense	2,393	3,118	1,636
Equity income/(loss) and minority interests	(319)	(353)	(259)
Second income subtotal → Income from continuing operations	4,452	5,576	3,049
Income (loss) from discontinued operations		426	(93)
Net income	4,452	6,002	2,956
Dividends on preference stocks	(110)	(80)	(63)
Earnings attributable to common stocks	$ 4,342	$ 5,922	$ 2,893

Note: Earnings per share information has been excluded for simplicity.

[5] *Accounting Trends & Techniques, 55th edition,* American Institute of CPAs, 2001, p. 289.

[6] When an entity does not have noncontinuing items, income from continuing operations becomes net income.

format completely. They usually report income taxes separately. This creates one more income subtotal, which either precedes income from continuing operations or net income, depending on the presence or absence of noncontinuing income statement items. In Figure 7-9a, for example, General Motors Corporation calls this subtotal *income from continuing operations before income taxes*[7] because its income statement contains income from a discontinued business operation. In Figure 7-9b, however, Wendy's calls this subtotal *income before income taxes* because its income statement does not contain a noncontinuing item, which makes its net income the second and final income total.

Figure 7-10 is designed to help you more easily see the differences between these two forms of income statement. It illustrates the Cards & Memorabilia Unlimited results of operating activities in both formats. When you compare the two formats, notice that the multiple-step format has one advantage over the single-step format: it provides a step-by-step explanation of the financial information and therefore provides the reader more detail. On the other hand, the primary advantage of the single-step format is its simplicity.

FIGURE 7-9b A single-step income statement with no noncontinuing items for Wendy's International, Inc.

WENDY'S INTERNATIONAL, INC. AND SUBSIDIARIES
Consolidated Statements of Income
Years Ended December 30, 2001 and December 31, 2000 and January 2, 2000
(In thousands, except per share data)

	2001	2000	1999
Revenues			
Retail sales	**$1,925,319**	$1,807,841	$1,666,438
Franchise revenues	**465,878**	429,105	400,620
	2,391,197	2,236,946	2,067,058
Costs and expenses			
Cost of sales	**1,229,277**	1,140,840	1,046,380
Company restaurant operating costs	**406,185**	382,963	362,160
Operating costs	**91,701**	86,272	81,706
General and administrative expenses	**216,124**	208,173	192,857
Depreciation and amortization of property and equipment	**118,280**	108,297	97,917
International charges		18,370	
Other expense	**1,722**	5,514	7,193
Interest, net	**20,528**	15,080	10,159
	2,083,817	1,965,509	1,798,372
Income before income taxes	**307,380**	271,437	268,686
Income taxes	**113,731**	101,789	102,101
Net income	**$ 193,649**	$ 169,648	$ 166,585
Basic earnings per common share	**$1.72**	$1.48	$1.37
Diluted earnings per common share	**$1.65**	$1.44	$1.32
Dividends per common share	**$.24**	$.24	$.24
Basic shares	**122,275**	114,341	122,032
Diluted shares	**121,144**	122,483	131,039

This is the same as Income from continuing operations before income taxes.

[7] Although the concept of a minority interest is not relevant to the present discussion, it will be explained in Appendix 10-1.

FIGURE 7-10 Comparing the multiple-step income statement to the single-step income statement

CARDS & MEMORABILIA UNLIMITED

The subtotal gross margin provides important information about an entity's markup of its products'/services' selling price over cost. → Gross margin

The subtotal primary operating income is important because it helps a reader identify an entity's primary operating activities. → Primary operating income

Net income is equivalent to income from continuing operations whenever an entity has no noncontinuing items. → Net income

CARDS & MEMORABILIA UNLIMITED
Multiple-Step Income Statement
For the Year Ended December 31

Primary Operating Activities:		
Sales revenue		$86,600
Cost of goods sold		30,000
Gross margin		56,600
Less operating expenses:		
Rent expense	$11,000	
Salaries expense	8,750	
Depreciation expense	2,600	
Miscellaneous expense	4,600	26,950
Primary operating income		29,650
Peripheral Activities:		
Service revenue	600	
Interest revenue	300	
Interest expense	(200)	
Loss on equipment sale	(350)	350
Net income		$30,000

CARDS & MEMORABILIA UNLIMITED
Single-Step Income Statement
For the Year Ended December 31

Revenues:		
Sales revenue	$86,600	
Service revenue	600	
Interest revenue	300	$87,500
Expenses:		
Cost of goods sold	30,000	
Rent expense	11,000	
Salaries expense	8,750	
Depreciation expense	2,600	
Miscellaneous expense	4,600	
Interest expense	200	
Loss on equipment sale	350	57,500
Net income		$30,000

Income appears by deducting expenses from revenues in a single step. → Net income

Now that you have learned the differences between the single-step income statement and the multiple-step income statement, we need to revise Performance Objective 10:

YOUR PERFORMANCE OBJECTIVE 10

Prepare a single-step and/or a multiple-step income statement that reports the results of operations of any entity.

Deciding When to Recognize Revenue

In Chapter 6 you learned how revenue is *recognized*, and in the preceding section of this chapter, you learned how revenue is presented or *formatted*. Now you need to learn how entities decide which particular point in time to choose, in other words *when*, to recognize revenue.

To answer the question, "How do entities decide when to recognize revenue?" we'll look at an example—revenue from a sale. Most entities recognize revenue at the time a sale is made, but some do not. Chapter 10 takes a more in-depth look at revenue recognition at times other than sale. But no matter when an entity decides to recognize revenue, this decision should not be arbitrary. Each entity must establish specific criteria to justify its decision and must implement this decision consistently. An entity's failure to follow these criteria can result in income being manipulated with unethical income reporting practices.

When Do Entities Generally Recognize Revenue?

In Chapter 6 you learned that, under the accrual basis, revenue is earned or realized in the period in which goods and services are provided. This suggests that revenue should generally be recognized or recorded in the selling phase of the operating cycle rather than the purchasing or collecting phase. More specifically, most businesses record revenue at the point of sale, which is usually interpreted to mean when goods are delivered and services are performed. To determine exactly when a company recognizes revenue, you can look at its annual report in the section usually entitled "Summary of Significant Accounting Policies." Consider, for example, a sampling of the revenue recognition rules that The Walt Disney Company described in its 1999 annual report:

- Revenues from the theatrical distribution of motion pictures are recognized when motion pictures are exhibited.
- Revenues from video sales are recognized on the date that video units are made widely available for sale by retailers.
- Revenues from the licensing of feature films and television programming are recorded when the material is available for telecasting by the licensee and when certain other conditions are met.

Each of these rules recognizes revenue at points in time that are equivalent to delivery of product or performance of service.

For some businesses, it is actually misleading to record revenue at point of sale. Consider, for example, the abbreviated operating cycle or earnings process for the Boston Celtics basketball franchise shown in Figure 7-11. Here, the sale point, the season ticket sale between July and August, is considered too early to recognize revenue. Instead, the annual report indicates that revenue is recognized during the season as each individual game is played. To understand why the Celtics do not recognize revenue sooner, you first have to learn about the criteria entities generally use to recognize revenue.

What Criteria Do Entities Use in Deciding When to Recognize Revenue?

To understand why revenue is usually recognized when goods are delivered and services are rendered, consider the three primary criteria entities use to decide when to recognize revenue—*measurement, performance, and matching*.

1. ***Measurement:*** This criterion assumes that the entity's expected cash inflows (revenues) can be measured objectively, ideally through an exchange of assets.

FIGURE 7-11 The operating cycle and revenue recognition policies for the Boston Celtics

Operating Cycle:

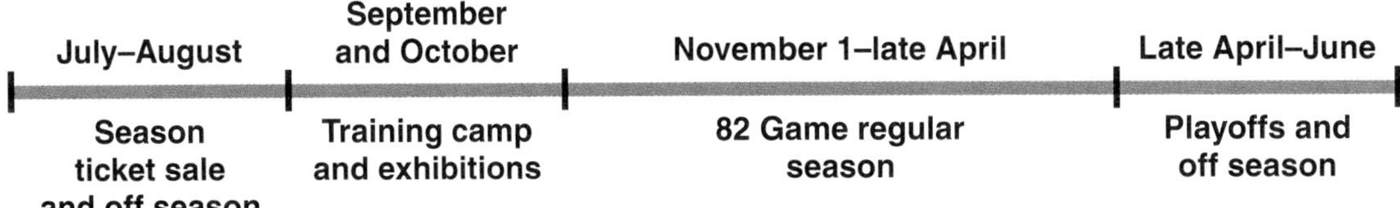

Revenue recognition policies:

1. Revenues, principally ticket sales and television and radio broadcasting fees, are generally recorded as revenues at the time the game to which such proceeds relate is played.
2. Revenues, principally advertising sold to sponsors for commercials during program broadcasting, are recognized when the commercials are broadcast.

2. ***Performance:*** This criterion assumes that the entity has performed all (or a substantial portion) of the critical revenue-producing services it expects to provide. That is, the earnings process has been completed.
3. ***Matching:*** This criterion assumes that most of the entity's expected cash outflows (expenses) associated with the production of the revenue have been incurred. Expenses not yet incurred are either negligible or can be predicted with a reasonable degree of accuracy.

Let's use these criteria to explain the revenue timing decisions of both The Walt Disney Company, a worldwide entertainment corporation, and the Boston Celtics, a professional basketball franchise.

The Walt Disney Company As you saw earlier, Walt Disney's annual report indicated that it records revenue when motion pictures are exhibited or presented. At this point in its operating cycle, Walt Disney has found its customers—movie theater chains—and agreed upon a selling price in return for granting them the right to present its motion pictures (measurement); completed its production—a critical revenue-generating event (performance), and incurred all but a few expenses, such as warranties and bad debts (matching). Both of these expenses, however, can be estimated fairly easily. Thus, Walt Disney has met each of the three criteria.

The Boston Celtics recognizes revenue for season tickets sales game by game, not in August when season tickets are sold.

Boston Celtics Limited Partnership Let's now look at the Celtics. What if you argued that the Celtics should recognize revenue after season tickets and individual game tickets are sold, that is by the end of August. This would meet the measurement criterion but would meet neither the performance nor the matching criteria. Why? Because there might be substantial uncertainty about whether all games will be played due to a players' strike, negotiations of broadcasting rights might be unresolved, and significant travel, medical, and cost of living expenses have not yet been incurred. Thus, the Celtics entity has not performed all of the critical revenue-producing services it expects to provide. Finally, since many player contracts are not guaranteed and injuries can occur, a substantial expense has not been and might never be incurred.

Performance Objective 21 is designed to help use these criteria to determine when revenue should properly be recognized.

YOUR PERFORMANCE OBJECTIVE 21

Discuss the criteria used to determine when revenue is recognized and then, given specific details about an entity, **apply** these criteria to that entity to determine when its revenue should be recognized.

How Income Can Be Manipulated with Unethical Reporting Practices

INSIGHT

In recent years, there has been widespread evidence of income manipulation by companies to increase the attractiveness of their reported earnings. Companies usually engage in these questionable or unethical practices because they face financial difficulty or pressure for greater earnings. The term **earnings management** is used to describe any such financial reporting practice that will improve a corporation's reported earnings. A particularly common motivation for such earnings management is the pressure felt by management to meet or exceed an analyst's forecast of its company's earnings. This chapter's research assignments include opportunities for you to learn more about this controversial topic.

Perhaps the most common unethical practice in revenue recognition is simply recording revenue too early.[8] Here are three ways that this can occur:

1. *Shipping goods before a sales agreement exists.* This practice is particularly common near the end of an accounting period if profits are low. For example, suppose that to justify the recording of revenue, a business ships merchandise before a scheduled delivery date. If customers are expected to place an order in the near future, they are unlikely to return the product; thus, the seller effectively reports next year's sales in this period. Variations of this practice are to send partial shipments of a customer's order when the complete order is unavailable and to ship merchandise on canceled orders.
2. *Recording revenue before it is clear that the buyer will keep the goods or pay for them.* It is inappropriate for textbook publishers to record 100% of the books they sell to college bookstores as revenue, because they expect that a certain percentage of these books will be returned by the bookstore as unsold. Instead, the publisher should reduce its revenue by a reasonable estimate to fairly report returns. Another unethical practice is to record revenue when there is serious doubt about the customer's ability to pay. A classic example is Stirling Homex, a construction corporation that recorded revenues for some of its low income customers, although their ability to pay was in doubt. Another example is the consignment sale, a transaction in which the consignor (seller) arranges with a buyer (consignee) to sell the consignor's inventory with no obligation. That is, the consignee does not pay for a unit of inventory unless the consignee sells the unit. In such a transaction, it is unethical for the consignor to record revenue for goods shipped but not sold.
3. *Recording revenue when cash is received but services are unperformed.* Recall from Transaction I of Cards & Memorabilia Unlimited that advances from customers are properly recorded as a liability *until* goods are delivered or services are performed. An example of an improper practice related to this type of transaction was an overstatement of revenues by Jiffy Lube, the quick oil change franchiser. This entity was sued in a civil lawsuit for recording revenue from all of the initial franchise fees despite the fact that it had not provided all agreed-upon services to these franchisees.

The insight you should gain here is that income can be manipulated by recording revenue before it is actually earned. As a result, even though the financial statements in annual reports have been audited, you cannot assume that they are always a fair and full representation of the entity's transactions. In reality, an audit provides reasonable assurance, not an ironclad guarantee of full and fair disclosure. So, if you desire to be an informed user of financial statements, you must be aware that the reporting of income can be manipulated.

[8]The source of this insight is the book entitled *Financial Shenanigans: How to Detect Accounting Gimmicks and Fraud in Financial Reports,* Howard M. Schilit, McGraw Hill, 1993, pp. 34–47.

Which Ratios Are Used to Analyze the Income Statement?

Despite all you have learned about the income statement, your ability to use its information to make decisions is limited if you do not learn about several ratios that are constructed in part from various items within the income statement. Thus, in the following three sections you'll be introduced to seven more ratios that you can use to more effectively analyze financial statements. These include three activity ratios—the total assets turnover ratio, the accounts receivable turnover ratio, and the inventory turnover ratio; one leverage ratio—the times interest earned ratio (also known as a coverage ratio); and three profitability ratios—the gross margin ratio, the profit margin ratio, and earnings per share. To help reinforce your understanding of these ratios, we will calculate all but one,[9] for Cards & Memorabilia Unlimited. As you study these ratios, don't forget Performance Objective 3:

YOUR PERFORMANCE OBJECTIVE 3

Calculate at least one financial statement ratio within each of the following five categories, **interpret** its meaning, and **discuss** its usefulness and limitations in making decisions:

a. Liquidity—e.g., current ratio and acid test ratio.
b. Activity or turnover—e.g., average collection period.
c. Financial leverage—e.g., debt to equity ratio.
d. Profitability—e.g., return on equity and profit margin ratio.
e. Valuation—e.g., price earnings ratio and dividend yield.

Using Activity Ratios to Evaluate Turnover

If you want to evaluate how efficiently an entity has used its resources or assets, you would use what are called *activity ratios.* **Activity ratios** are so named because they measure how productive a particular asset was in producing sales activity in the entity. The word *turnover* expresses much the same idea. **Turnover** is the number of times, on average, that assets such as accounts receivable and inventory are replaced during the year. Three of the most often used activity or turnover ratios are the asset turnover ratio, the accounts receivable turnover ratio, and the inventory turnover ratio.

Asset Turnover Ratio The *total assets turnover ratio* or simply **asset turnover ratio** indicates how efficiently an entity uses its assets to produce sales during the period. In general, an entity with a high ratio uses its assets more productively than an entity with a low ratio. The formula to calculate the total assets turnover ratio is:

$$\text{Asset Turnover Ratio} = \frac{\text{Net Sales Revenue}}{\text{Average Total Assets}}$$

Since this ratio is designed to measure asset activity *during* the period, it follows that its numerator and denominator must each reflect a period of time rather than a point in time. This condition is met by the amount in the numerator since net sales are accumulated over a period of time. Likewise, the denominator—the result of calculating the average of the beginning and ending asset balances—also defines a period of time. If this is not immediately clear, consider how you might calculate the average temperature *during the day*. One approach is to simply determine the temperature at sunrise (e.g., 52°), the temperature at sundown (e.g., 78°), and calculate the average (52° + 78°)/2 = 65°. 65° is one measure of the average temperature during the day.

[9] Earnings per share is a ratio applicable only to corporations.

CARDS & MEMORABILIA UNLIMITED

Let's now calculate the asset turnover ratio for CMU's first year of business. We'll need its net sales revenue, \$86,600, from Figure 7-3; its total assets of \$40,000 at the beginning of the first year of business (since the first sales were made on January 9, it is reasonable to use the balance of assets as of this date); and its total assets of \$75,000 at the end of the first year of business from Figure 7-3:

$$\frac{86{,}600}{(40{,}000 + 75{,}000)/2} = \frac{86{,}600}{57{,}500} = 1.506$$

This calculation indicates that CMU was able to generate more than \$1.50 of sales from each dollar of assets invested. This activity ratio illustrates the characteristic common to all activity ratios: that the numerator always includes an income statement account that best measures that asset and the denominator always includes the asset account named in the ratio's title.

Consider that this ratio for Apple Computer Inc. and International Business Machines Corporation several years ago was 1.543 and 0.773, respectively. This indicates that Apple was twice as efficient as IBM in using its assets to generate sales. What could IBM do to reduce this difference? You'd be correct if you answered increase sales (ratio numerator) and decrease assets (ratio denominator). It should come as no surprise then that under new management in the following year, IBM did in fact change much of its sales distribution system as well as significantly reduce its assets.

Accounts Receivable Turnover Ratio The **accounts receivable turnover ratio** indicates the relative frequency with which accounts receivable are converted into cash. In other words, it indicates how often the receivable balance "turns over." A high turnover is preferable because it provides quicker access to cash that can earn a return rather than remain unavailable and be an idle use of funds. You calculate this ratio as follows:

$$\text{Accounts Receivable Turnover Ratio} = \frac{\text{Net Credit Sales}}{\text{Average Net Accounts Receivable}}$$

The specific calculation for CMU is:

$$\frac{19{,}400}{(\$0 + \$5{,}000)/2} = \frac{\$19{,}400}{\$2{,}500} = 7.76$$

Note that Susan excluded the \$600 of service revenue she earned from teaching a course (see Transaction N) because it had no relationship to regular customers of CMU. Once again, an average accounts receivable balance in the denominator is used to measure receivable activity during the period.

This ratio's components should make sense to you since only credit sales create an accounts receivable balance. In practice, however, you will discover that companies rarely disclose the amount of their credit sales in annual report income statements. Thus, unless you have contacts within the entity, your only option is to substitute sales revenue or net sales in place of net credit sales. This revised ratio, therefore, becomes:

$$\text{Accounts Receivable Turnover Ratio} = \frac{\text{Sales Revenue}}{\text{Average Net Accounts Receivable}}$$

Although turning over receivables this frequently during the year is considered favorable, it is hard to evaluate unless it is specifically compared to the same ratio of other trading card stores, rather than simply other retailers. For example, CMU's accounts receivable turnover ratio is very similar to the 2001 ratio of 8.26 for Nordstrom, Inc., the well respected, nationwide fashion retailer; but CMU's ratio is significantly lower than the 2001 ratio of 55.69 for Toys "R" Us, the worldwide children's specialty retail chain.

The **average collection period**, sometimes referred to as the average days' sales uncollected, days' accounts receivable outstanding, or the days' sales in receivables, is a turnover measure that expresses the same concept as the accounts receivable turnover ratio, but is easier to interpret. That is, it clearly identifies how much time, on average, passes between sale and collection. The faster the entity collects cash from sales, the more it is able to pay its obligations on a timely basis. This measure is calculated by dividing 365 days by the accounts receivable turnover ratio as shown below:

$$\text{Average Collection Period} = \frac{\text{365 days}}{\text{Accounts Receivable Turnover Ratio}}$$

Although this textbook will use 365 days to achieve greater accuracy, some round off the number of days in a year to 360.

Now, let's calculate this ratio for CMU.

$$\frac{365}{7.76} = 47.04 \text{ days}$$

This calculation shows that, on average, CMU receives payment from customers within 47.04 days from the time of the sale. Although CMU's credit terms require customers to pay within 30 days, Susan Newman is quite happy about this result for two reasons. First, she applied little, if any, collection pressure on her customers and, second, she discovered that her experience was remarkably similar to the average collection period of 44.19 (365/8.26) calculated by Nordstrom in 2001.

Inventory Turnover Ratio Effective inventory management involves a balancing act between having enough inventory on hand to meet the needs of customers, that is, maximizing the opportunity to generate revenue, and tying up cash as a result of not "turning over" the inventory quickly enough. The **inventory turnover ratio** indicates how frequently a business sells its inventory and therefore indicates the relative efficiency of both sales and production or purchasing management. This ratio is calculated as follows:

$$\text{Inventory Turnover Ratio} = \frac{\text{Cost of Goods Sold}}{\text{Average Merchandise Inventory}}$$

Now let's calculate the inventory turnover ratio for CMU.

$$\frac{\$30,000}{(\$15,000 + \$13,000)/2} = \frac{\$30,000}{\$14,000} = 2.1429$$

Although CMU's beginning balance of inventory is zero, the balance as of January 6 is used here to provide a more realistic calculation of the desired average balance for CMU's denominator.

The **average holding period**, sometimes referred to as days' inventories on hand, days' inventory unsold, or days' sales in inventory, is a turnover measure that expresses the same concept as the inventory turnover ratio but is easier to interpret. It is calculated by dividing 365 days by the inventory turnover ratio.

$$\text{Average Holding Period} = \frac{\text{365 Days}}{\text{Inventory Turnover Ratio}}$$

Using this formula, the average holding period for CMU is:

$$\frac{365}{2.1429} = 170.33$$

For Toys "R" Us, the average inventory holding period is 365/3.606, or 101.21 days. Although the trading cards and sports memorabilia industry is different from the toy industry, Susan would definitely want to explore why the average holding period for her cards and memorabilia is so much greater than it is for toys.

Using the Times Interest Earned Ratio to More Fully Evaluate Financial Risk

The **times interest earned ratio** indicates the business's relative protection from being forced into bankruptcy by its failure to meet required interest payments. The formula to calculate this ratio is:

$$\text{Times Interest Earned Ratio} = \frac{\text{Net Income} + \text{Interest Expense} + \text{Income Tax Expense}}{\text{Interest Expense}}$$

You can simplify this numerator by using the equivalent term *Operating Income.* As you will soon see, this ratio indicates how many times interest expense is "covered" by income, and so it is often referred to as a **coverage ratio**.

Assuming CMU is a corporation, you must subtract the $9,000 income tax expense described in Chapter 10 from its $30,000 net income to derive corporate net income of $21,000. Thus, this ratio is calculated as follows:

$$\frac{\$21{,}000 + \$200 + \$9{,}000}{\$200} = 151$$

As this calculation shows, CMU is able to pay its currently required interest payments because it has the earning power to cover its interest payments 151 times. In Chapter 5 you saw that the debt to assets ratio was relatively low, at 17.5%. The large times interest earned ratio just calculated should help reinforce the conclusion that CMU's financial risk is low. This conclusion makes sense when you consider that only a fraction of CMU's financing presently requires interest payments (review Transactions J_2 and L).

Using Profitability Ratios to Evaluate Management's Effectiveness

The last ratios we'll discuss are the **profitability ratios**. Recall that you studied one such ratio, the return on equity, in both Chapters 1 and 3. Three profitability ratios particularly tied to the income statement are the gross margin ratio (also known as the *gross margin rate* or the *gross profit ratio*), the profit margin ratio, and earnings per share. Managers use these ratios to measure their overall effectiveness in generating returns on sales and return on stockholder financing.

Gross Margin Ratio You will discover the concept underlying the **gross margin ratio** if you focus on a small portion of CMU's multiple step income statement in Figure 7-10. Although the amounts needed to calculate this ratio are found in a single-step income statement, the gross margin ratio is much more visible in a multiple-step income statement because gross margin is actually disclosed. Using Figure 7-10, for example, this ratio can be immediately calculated by dividing gross margin by sales revenue as follows:

$$\text{Gross Margin Ratio} = \frac{\text{Gross Margin}}{\text{Sales Revenue}}$$

Calculating for CMU, we have:

$$\frac{\$56{,}600}{\$86{,}600} = 0.65$$

This ratio is very informative because it tells Susan Newman that for every dollar she receives from card and memorabilia sales, 65 cents is available after she pays for her merchandise. With this $0.65 she can cover her other expenses and earn a profit. This relationship can be illustrated as follows:

	Total Dollars	Percentage	Analysis of Each Sales Dollar
Sales revenue	$86,600	100.0%	$1.000
Cost of goods sold	30,000	34.6%	0.346
Gross margin	$56,600	65.4%	$0.654

The gross margin ratios of profitable businesses usually range between 30% and 50% of net sales, depending on the types of merchandise sold. By that measure, CMU seems to be doing well. Once again, however, a financial analyst would compare CMU results to those of other card and memorabilia stores before looking at the ratios of other retailers.

Another analytical tool formed by the complement of this ratio is the ratio of cost of goods sold to sales. (Recall that the complement of any percentage or ratio equals one minus that percentage or ratio.) For every dollar of sales, for example, Susan now knows that she spent $0.35 ($1.00 minus $0.65) on the cost of acquiring her product during CMU's first year of operations.

Profit Margin Ratio The **profit margin ratio**, sometimes called the **return on sales ratio**, indicates how well the entity has controlled the level of its expenses relative to its revenues. This ratio is informative because it focuses management's attention on the relative profitability of sales rather than the absolute dollar amount of sales. When profit margin is low, management may want to consider cost savings measures to curtail expenses. This ratio is similar in concept to the gross margin ratio in that both ratios place a profit measure in the numerator and sales revenue in the denominator. This ratio is calculated as follows:

$$\text{Profit Margin Ratio} = \frac{\text{Net Income}}{\text{Sales Revenue}}$$

Calculating for CMU we have:

$$\frac{\$30,000}{\$86,600} = 0.346$$

The number 0.346 by itself is not informative. To interpret its significance, you must consider the industry in which the entity operates. For example, in the book publishing industry, a 10% to 15% profit margin ratio is considered good, whereas, in retail supermarkets, a 10% profit margin is considered exceptional. For now, let's assume that CMU's profit margin is acceptable.

Earnings per Share **Earnings per share of common stock**, usually abbreviated as **earnings per share**, and also referred to as **basic earnings per common share** for companies with simple capital structures, indicates the relative profitability per share of a common stock investment for the period. This ratio is perhaps the most widely used of all ratios because publicly held companies must disclose their earnings per share in the body of the income statement,[10] usually below net income. Earnings per share is calculated as follows:

[10] This disclosure is required by "Earnings per Share," *Statement of Financial Accounting Standards No. 128,* FASB, 1997, in order to receive a certified public accountant's (auditors') unqualified opinion on the fairness of the entity's financial statements. This pronouncement requires you to supplement the basic earnings per share calculation by a diluted earnings per share calculation whenever the company has a complex capital structure. Note that this more technical calculation is usually treated in intermediate accounting and is outside the scope of this discussion.

Earnings per Share

$$= \frac{\text{Net Income} - \text{Preferred Stock Dividends Declared}}{\text{Weighted Average Common Shares Outstanding during the Period}}$$

To better understand and interpret this ratio, let's first examine its numerator more carefully. The net income is found in the income statement. The preferred stock dividend (recall that preferred stock was described briefly in Chapter 4) is the dollar amount of the year's return to preferred shareholders. By deducting this amount from net income, the numerator then represents the return to common shareholders. Since many companies do not issue preferred stock, the numerator is often net income alone.

As stated in the formula, the denominator is a weighted average rather than a simple average, a difference illustrated in Figure 7-12. In this figure, notice that the hypothetical company has four different holdings of stock during the year for various periods of time. Although 120 shares of common stock are held on December 31, and the simple average is 108.75 shares, an average weighted by the length of time that shares are held is 100 shares. Many companies disclose the denominator used in their calculation, such as Pfizer Inc., as shown at the bottom of Figure 7-13. But when you encounter companies that do not disclose this denominator, it is necessary that you are able to estimate this denominator.

FIGURE 7-12 Illustration of a hypothetical weighted average calculation

Date	Transaction	Number of Shares		Fraction of Year Held		Weighted Average
January 1	75 shares issued	75	×	4/12	=	25
May 1	75 shares issued	150	×	2/12	=	25
July 1	60 shares repurchased	90	×	4/12	=	30
November 1	30 shares issued as stock options	120	×	2/12	=	20
				12/12		100

Total weighted average

Four holdings of stock during the year

Simple Average: $\frac{75 + 150 + 90 + 120}{4} = \frac{435}{4} = 108\frac{3}{4}$

The Limited's 2000 income statement, for example, reports a net income of \$427,905,000 and a basic earnings per share of \$1.00 but reports no weighted average number of shares. Since The Limited has no preferred stock, you can approximate its share denominator by solving for the equation \$427,905,000/shares = \$1.00 and discovering that the shares equal approximately 427,905,000. This number is very close to 427,936,000 [(429,928,000 + 425,943,000)/2], the number of shares calculated by taking the simple average of the company's January 29, 2000 share balance and the February 3, 2001 share balance.

Using Vertical Analysis to Further Evaluate the Income Statement

In addition to ratio analysis, financial analysts and other knowledgeable readers of financial statements use percentage analysis to uncover important relationships and trends. **Percentage analysis** is a technique in which the relative size of particular accounts or line items within financial statements are highlighted to reveal trends that are potentially useful to decision makers. The two most common versions of percentage analysis are called horizontal analysis and vertical analysis. **Horizontal analysis** compares how financial statement items change from year to year. For ex-

FIGURE 7-13

Disclosure of weighted average shares by Pfizer, Inc.

PFIZER, INC.
Consolidated Statements of Income
(Millions, except per share data)

	Year ended December 31		
	2000	1999	1998
Revenues	$29,574	$27,376	$23,231
Costs and expenses:			
Cost of sales	4,907	5,464	4,907
Selling, informational and administrative expenses	11,442	10,810	9,563
Research and development expenses	4,435	4,036	3,305
Merger-related costs	3,257	33	—
Other (income)/deductions—net	(248)	88	1,059
Income from continuing operations before provision for taxes on income and minority interests	5,781	6,945	4,397
Provision for taxes on income	2,049	1,968	1,163
Minority interests	14	5	2
Income from continuing operations	3,718	4,972	3,232
Discontinued operations—net of tax	8	(20)	1,401
Net income	$ 3,726	$ 4,952	$ 4,633
Earnings per common share—basic			
Income from continuing operations	$ .60	$ .81	$ .53
Discontinued operations—net of tax	—	—	.23
Net income	$ .60	$ .81	$ .76
Earnings per common share—diluted			
Income from continuing operations	$ .59	$ .79	$ .51
Discontinued operations—net of tax	—	(.01)	.22
Net income	$ .59	$ .78	$ .73
Weighted average shares—basic	6,210	6,126	6,120
Weighted average shares—diluted	6,368	6,317	6,362

ample, assume net income from 2002 to 2004 is $100, $200, and $300, respectively. One version of horizontal analysis expresses 2003 and 2004 net income as a percentage change in a designated base period such as 2002 so that the percentage changes are 200% and 300%. Another version of horizontal analysis, however, expresses each period's net income in terms of the immediately preceding period's net income; in our example, the percentages become 200% (200/100) and 150% (300/200). You will learn more about horizontal analysis in Chapter 14.

Vertical analysis expresses each item within a particular financial statement as a percentage of a single designated item within the same statement. The most common designated items are total assets in the balance sheet, net sales in the income statement, and the overall change in cash in the statement of cash flows. The term "vertical analysis" is descriptive because the percentage relationships are derived from a single year's information that is usually presented in a vertical column. Figure 7-14, for example, illustrates a vertical analysis of CMU's income statement. Notice how each component of the multiple-step income statement is related to the single designated item of sales revenue.

Two specific profitability ratios described earlier can be derived directly from this vertical analysis. These are the gross margin ratio of 65.4% and the profit margin ratio of 34.6%. In particular, vertical analysis helps a user quickly focus on important relationships. For example, it indicates that CMU's cost of goods sold was almost

FIGURE 7-14

Vertical analysis of CMU's income statement

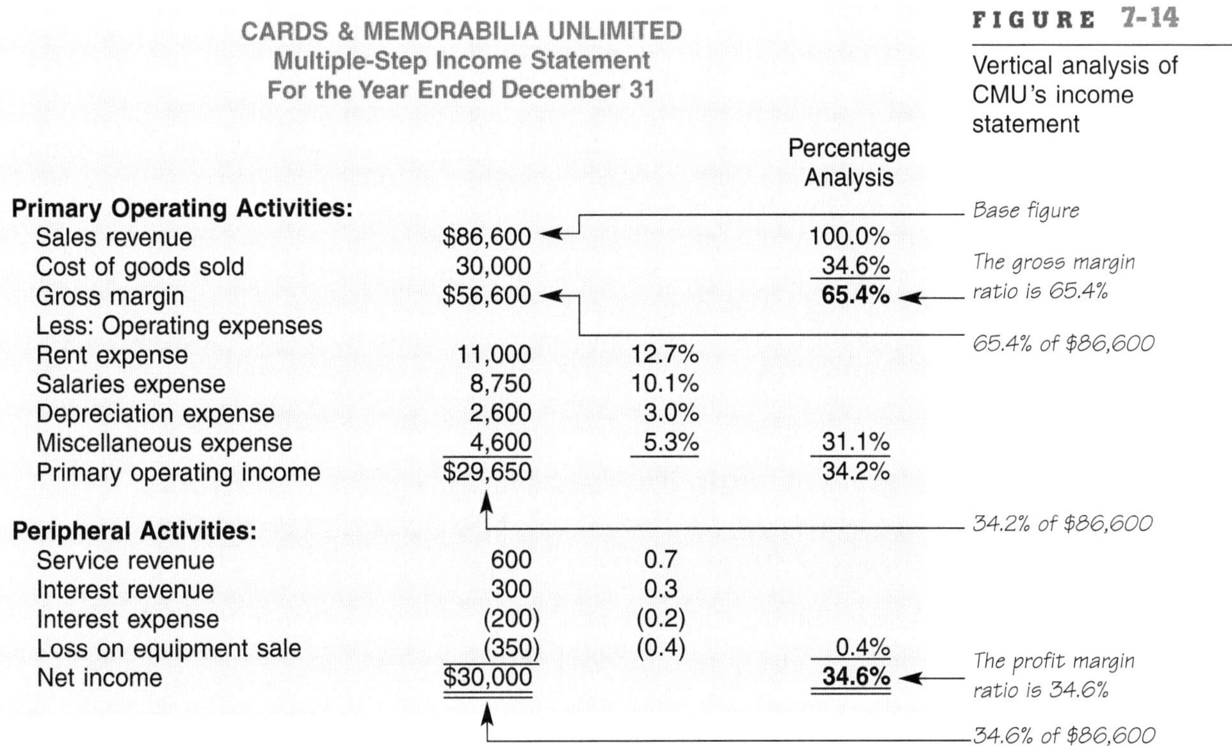

CARDS & MEMORABILIA UNLIMITED
Multiple-Step Income Statement
For the Year Ended December 31

			Percentage Analysis
Primary Operating Activities:			
Sales revenue	$86,600		100.0%
Cost of goods sold	30,000		34.6%
Gross margin	$56,600		**65.4%**
Less: Operating expenses			
Rent expense	11,000	12.7%	
Salaries expense	8,750	10.1%	
Depreciation expense	2,600	3.0%	
Miscellaneous expense	4,600	5.3%	31.1%
Primary operating income	$29,650		34.2%
Peripheral Activities:			
Service revenue	600	0.7	
Interest revenue	300	0.3	
Interest expense	(200)	(0.2)	
Loss on equipment sale	(350)	(0.4)	0.4%
Net income	$30,000		**34.6%**

three times larger than the next largest expense, rent, and that peripheral activities were relatively immaterial factors in this income statement. Feedback of this kind helps decision makers like Susan Newman concentrate on the factors that are most important in maintaining or increasing profitability. With vertical analysis, you can evaluate an entity's performance from year to year as well as compare its current performance to the current performance of other entities within the same industry.

Using Information Not Found in the Income Statement to Make Better Income Statement Decisions

Suppose you wanted to find out as much as you could about a company's income statement. What would you do? If your answer is that you'd look at the income statement in its annual report, you'd be only partly right. And that's because some very valuable information about the income statement is not found in the income statement itself. Instead, this information is found in two other sections of the annual report with which you are already familiar: Management's Discussion and Analysis of Operations (MD&A) and the notes to the financial statements. As we did in Chapter 5 for the balance sheet, let's now examine these annual report sections more closely to find out how they can increase your understanding of the income statement.

How You Can Use the MD&A to Enhance Your Analysis of the Income Statement

No matter what company's annual report you study, the structure of its Management's Discussion and Analysis of Operations or Financial Review section is often quite the same. The MD&A generally begins with a relatively lengthy discussion about the results found on the income statement. This section is usually entitled Results of Operations and generally presents the amount of each major income statement category, reasons for its growth or decline, and a discussion of how its current year performance compares to that of one or even two of the immediately preceding years. Microsoft's 2001 MD&A, for example, includes a two-page discussion of revenue and nearly one-half of a page detailing four components of operating expenses. Although organized somewhat differently, the 2001 MD&As of both Cisco Systems, Inc. and FedEx Corporation also provide much the same information. For example, near the beginning of FedEx Corporation's MD&A section, we discover that "Increased fuel prices negatively impacted. . . . expenses by approximately $160 million for 2001, ..." Thus, the MD&A is an invaluable tool for an in-depth analysis of the income statement because it explains the underlying reasons for a company's performance. Since this information is available to some extent in all annual reports, it is essential that you supplement your ratio calculations with a careful reading of the results of operations discussion found in the MD&A section.

How You Can Use the Notes to the Financial Statements to Enhance Your Analysis of the Income Statement

As you learned in Chapter 5, most annual reports contain from 15 to 20 notes or footnotes, information that documents, supports, or elaborates on specific items within the financial statements. Generally, the first few notes are somewhat general in nature and are followed by notes relating directly to the balance sheet. Information about the income statement is generally found in the Summary of Significant Accounting Policies and in notes providing underlying detail for specific accounts and the earnings per share calculation reported on the income statement.

Summary of Significant Accounting Policies Recall from Chapter 5 that the Summary of Significant Accounting Policies includes the essential accounting principles used by a particular business. One of the more significant principles relating to the income statement is that which describes when a company recognizes revenue, a section described in some detail earlier in this chapter. Under *Revenue Recognition* in the 2001 annual report of FedEx, for example, we learn that "Revenue is recognized upon delivery of shipments. For shipments in transit, revenue is recorded based on the percentage of service completed at the balance sheet date." Both Microsoft and Cisco Systems also include such a heading in their 2001 annual reports but with significantly more detail than FedEx.

Other examples of information relating to the income statement within this section include Cost of Revenue, Property, and Equipment or Depreciation and Amortization; Advertising Costs; Research and Development; and Income Taxes. Thus, you should always look at the Summary of Significant Accounting Policies in your analysis of a company's performance.

Notes Providing Underlying Detail for Income Statement Accounts You might remember that the Summary of Significant Accounting Policies section is generally the first or second of several notes to the financial statements. Although the great majority of the notes that follow this section have balance sheet titles, the information they provide sometimes relates to the income statement as well. For example, the amounts of rent expense under operating leases for 1999, 2000, and 2001 is found under Lease Commitments in the 2001 annual report of FedEx Corporation and under Commitments and Contingencies in the 2001 annual report of Cisco Systems, Inc. Examples of notes that relate directly to the income statement include Income Taxes and Earnings per Share. Thus, if you are interested in a company's performance, be sure to add a careful reading of the notes to your analysis of the income statement and your strategic use of profitability ratios and vertical analysis.

The Relationship between Net Income and Cash Flows

INSIGHT

An entity will encounter financial difficulty if it is unable to generate enough cash at the right times. In fact, it is not unusual for entities, especially new ones, to experience severe cash shortages—or worse, bankruptcy—while reporting substantial earnings. That is, an entity's cash receipts and disbursements are not identical to the revenues and expenses reported in its income statement for the same period. You can readily confirm this fact if you compare the cash amounts column of CMU to its net income amounts column in Figure 7-15. Specifically, the items affecting the cash column are not always the same as the revenue and expense items in the retained earnings column (Transactions M through U and O_2 through Z). That is, the $38,275 cash balance is different from the $30,000 reported net income. Two major reasons account for this $8,275 difference.

1. *Operating activities are not the only source or use of cash.* The amount in the cash accounts at the end of the year, $38,275, was affected by more than revenue and expense transactions. Nonoperating transactions, such as borrowing cash, repaying liabilities, and purchasing assets, will affect the amount of cash without affecting net income. For example, Transaction A_1, an owner contribution of $30,000, represents a financing activity; whereas Transaction H, an investment of $7,000 in equipment not related directly to operations during the period, represents an investing activity. That is, investing and financing activities also generate or use cash. For example, CMU experienced a $4,250 ($21,900 – $17,650) net nonoperating cash increase (Figure 7-16).
2. *Accrual basis net income differs from cash flow from operating activities.* As you know, net income is measured not by the cash effects of transactions but by the accrual basis of income measurement. For example, revenue and expense items such as credit sales and accrued expenses do not affect cash immediately. Conversely, some cash operating events, such as advances from customers, do not affect net income immediately. For these reasons, we expect net income to differ in amount from **net cash flow from operating activities**. This fact is illustrated by comparing the accrual basis income of $30,000 in the top half of Figure 7-3 to the net cash flow from operating activities of $34,025 in Figure 7-16. Also notice in Figure 7-16 that the $38,275 cash balance is a combination of net cash inflow from operating activities of $34,025, net cash outflow from investing activities of $17,650, and net cash inflow from financing activities of $21,900.

These differences between net income and cash flows are expressed by the following performance objective:

YOUR PERFORMANCE OBJECTIVE 18e

Explain how accrual basis net income differs from both the net cash flow from operating activities and the change in the cash balance for the period.

(continued)

FIGURE 7-15

The difference between CMU's cash flows and net income

	Cash Amounts	Net Income Amounts
A_1	$30,000	
B	0 net change	
C_1		
D	(15,000)	
E	(2,000)	
C_2	(10,000)	
F	5,000	
G		
H	(7,000)	
I	6,000	
J_1	(12,000)	
J_2		
K_1	(5,000)	
L		
M	63,200	$63,200
N		20,000
O_1	275	275
P	(11,000)	(11,000)
Q_1		(300)
R	1,350	(350)
S	(8,000)	(8,000)
K_2	(200)	(200)
T	(4,250)	(4,250)
U		(30,000)
V	15,000	
W	(8,100)	
A_2		
O_2		25
X		(750)
Y		(350)
Q_2		(2,300)
Z		4,000
Σ	$38,275	$30,000

The **insight** you should gain here is that an income statement alone does not provide a complete enough picture of a business to justify discontinuing your analysis. Instead, you must consider information from a balance sheet and from the statement of cash flows, which you will learn more about in Chapter 8.

FIGURE 7-16 How Cards & Memorabilia Unlimited's net income differs from its net cash flows from operating activities and change in cash balance

Operating Activities

	Accrual Basis Income Statement	Cash Flow from Operating Activities	
Revenues:			**Cash receipts**
Sales revenue	$86,600	$84,200*	Customer collections
Service revenue	600	0	Trading cards course
Interest revenue	300	275	Interest collections
	$87,500	$84,475	
Expenses:			**Cash disbursements**
Cost of goods sold	$30,000	$27,000†	To merchandise suppliers
Rent	11,000	11,000	For rent
Salaries	8,750	8,000	To employees
Depreciation	2,600	0	
Miscellaneous	4,600	4,250	To miscellaneous suppliers
Interest	200	200	To bank
Loss on sale	350	0	
	$57,500	$50,450	
Net income	**$30,000**	**$34,025**	Net cash flow from operating activities

Net income is not the same as net cash flow from operating activities.

Investing Activities

$ (2,000)	Transaction E
(10,000)	Transactions C_1 and C_2
(7,000)	Transaction H
1,350	Transaction R
$(17,650)	Net cash flow from investing activities

$4,250 of the $38,275 increase in cash is nonoperating in nature.

Financing Activities

$30,000	Transaction A_1
(8,100)	Transaction W
$21,900	Net cash flow from financing activities
$38,275	Final cash balance

This amount is composed of net cash flow from operating activities, net cash flow from investing activities, and net cash flow from financing activities.

*Transactions M, I and V ($63,200 + $6,000 + $15,000)
†Transactions D and J_1 ($15,000 + 12,000)

Summary with Key Terms

You first learned the distinction between **explicit transactions** (268), those described before this chapter, and the remaining CMU transactions introduced here, known as **implicit transactions** (268). You learned that each of these implicit transactions is more often called an **adjustment** (270), a transaction that is recorded to properly measure net income. The end of period activity to record revenues and expenses in the proper period and to complete the income statement is known as the **adjustment process** (270). Adjustments are essentially of two types:

The number in parentheses following each **key term** is the page number on which the term is defined.

accruals (270) and **deferrals** (272). Accrual adjustments are divided into **accrued revenue** (272) and **accrued expense** (273), whereas deferral adjustments are divided into **deferred revenue** (275) and **deferred expense** (274), respectively.

After learning more about financial statement relationships, you examined the form and content of the **classified income statement** (279), commonly found in annual reports. Common synonyms for the net income reported in these income statements include **earnings** (279) and **profits** (279). To effectively read the classified income statement, you must be able to distinguish between **primary operating activities** (279) and **peripheral activities** (280), as well as between **continuing activities** (280) and **noncontinuing activities** (280). These two distinctions produce four possible categories included in the classified income statement. The first category, primary operating activities that are expected to continue, includes: **net revenues** (282) or **net sales revenue** (282); **cost of revenue** (282) or **cost of goods sold** (282); **gross margin** (282) or **gross profit** (282); **selling, general and administrative expenses** (283); and sometimes **special events** (284). The sum of these items produce the income subtotal called **primary operating income** (284) or **income from operations** (284).

The second category, peripheral activities that are expected to continue, includes such items as interest revenue, interest expense, dividend revenue, other gains and losses, and income tax expense, also called **Provision for Income Taxes** (284), in many annual report income statements. This category's income subtotals include **pretax income from continuing operations** (284), or more commonly, income before income taxes and **income from continuing operations** (284). The third category, primary operating activities that are discontinued (not expected to continue), generally includes items derived from discontinued **business segments** (284). The fourth category, peripheral activities that are not expected to continue, includes **extraordinary items** (285), which by definition are rare in nature, and **changes in accounting principle** (285). Finally, you learned how to distinguish between a **multiple-step income statement** (286) and a **single-step income statement** (286).

The next section of this chapter introduced three terms to describe the criteria entities can use to decide when to recognize revenue. These are **measurement** (289), **performance** (290), and **matching** (290). An *Insight* then described how the reporting of income can be manipulated with either questionable or outright unethical reporting practices referred to as **earnings management** (291). One such practice is to simply record revenue too early.

Next, you learned about several ratios that provide further *insight* into results displayed on the income statement. The first such ratio was the **times interest earned ratio** (295), a leverage ratio that is often referred to as a **coverage ratio** (295). Three **activity ratios** (292) measure the concept of **turnover** (292). These are the **asset turnover ratio** (292), the **accounts receivable turnover ratio** (293), and the **inventory turnover ratio** (294). These last two ratios are commonly converted to the more easily interpreted **average collection period** (294) and **average holding period** (294). Finally, you were introduced to three **profitability ratios** (295). These were the **gross margin ratio** (295), **profit margin ratio** (296) or **return on sales ratio** (296), and **earnings per share of common stock** (296), usually abbreviated as **earnings per share** (296). In particular, we examined **basic earnings per common share** (296).

An additional type of financial analysis, **percentage analysis** (297) was introduced in this chapter. This supplement to ratio analysis includes both **horizontal analysis** (297) and **vertical analysis** (298), which is the source of both the gross margin ratio and the profit margin ratio.

The last *Insight* section of this chapter described how accrual basis net income reported in the income statement is rarely identical to an entity's **net cash flow from operating activities** (301) reported in its statement of cash flows.

Making Business Decisions

YOUR PERFORMANCE OBJECTIVE 2
(page 18)

You have just been hired to assist the chief financial officer (CFO) of a newly formed airline, Student Airways. Your first assignment is to help the CFO develop a revenue recognition policy for the company.

Required

a. Discuss the criteria used to determine when revenue is recognized.
b. Apply the criteria you discussed in (a) to determine when Student Airways should recognize revenue. In your answer, describe your assumptions about the essential operations of an airline company.

c. Assume that Student Airways has a frequent flier program.
   1. Identify the assumptions you make about the operation of your frequent flier mileage program. Examples might be the minimum miles traveled before passengers can earn mileage awards and time limits, if any, on the use of a passenger's mileage award.
   2. Apply the criteria again to determine when your company should recognize revenue. In your decision, consider the following items:
      (a) The earning of mileage when passengers purchase tickets.
      (b) The use of earned mileage by passengers.
      (c) The expiration of frequent flier mileage.

Questions

YOUR PERFORMANCE OBJECTIVE 4
(page 22)

7-1 Explain in your own words the meaning of key business terms.
   a. Classified income statement
   b. Earnings or profits
   c. Primary operating activities
   d. Peripheral activities
   e. Continuing activities
   f. Noncontinuing activities
   g. Selling, general, and administrative expenses
   h. Provision for income taxes
   i. Change in accounting principle
   j. Extraordinary items
   k. Turnover
   l. Percentage analysis
   m. Net cash flow from operating activities

7-2 Distinguish between the terms *explicit transactions* and *implicit transactions.* Provide one example of this distinction.

7-3 List at least seven business documents that underlie explicit transactions.

7-4 Describe the purpose of the adjustment process.

7-5 Distinguish between the terms *accrual* and *deferral.*

7-6 Provide one specific example of a transaction that can be classified under each of the following types of adjustments:
   a. Accrued revenue
   b. Accrued expense
   c. Deferred revenue
   d. Deferred expense

7-7 Explain how a deferred expense is related to an asset expiration.

7-8 Describe the four major categories of a classified income statement.

7-9 Distinguish between cost of revenue, cost of sales, and cost of goods sold.

7-10 Distinguish between primary operating income and income from continuing operations.

7-11 Distinguish between a special event and an extraordinary item.

7-12 Distinguish between a single-step income statement and a multiple-step income statement.

7-13 Distinguish between the income statement of a sole proprietorship and the income statement of a corporation. What account(s) would never be found in a proprietorship income statement?

7-14 Describe the criteria entities use to decide when to recognize revenue.

7-15 Discuss how you can determine when a company recognizes revenue.

7-16 In this chapter you learned that the reporting of income can be manipulated. Discuss why this might be a problem from the perspective of the company, the perspective of the company's creditors, and the perspective of the company's investors.

7-17 Why is the times interest earned ratio considered a leverage ratio?

7-18 What is an activity ratio? What is a characteristic common to all such ratios?

7-19 Describe how each of the following ratios is calculated and how you would interpret a high ratio and a low ratio, respectively.
   a. Times interest earned ratio
   b. Asset turnover ratio
   c. Accounts receivable turnover ratio
   d. Inventory turnover ratio
   e. Gross margin ratio
   f. Profit margin ratio
   g. Earnings per share

7-20 Describe the relationship between the accounts receivable turnover ratio and the related average collection period.

7-21 Describe the relationship between the inventory turnover ratio and the average holding period.

7-22 Explain why an average asset balance is used in the calculation of every turnover ratio's denominator.

7-23 Evaluate the following statement: "Earnings per share is not technically a ratio. It is really a net income conversion."

7-24 Explain why net income is seldom identical to net cash flow from operating activities.

Reinforcement Exercises

YOUR PERFORMANCE OBJECTIVE 4
(page 22)

E7-1 Asking the Right Questions: A Group Activity

It's often said that knowing the right answer is not nearly as important as asking the right question. Asking the right question is a problem-solving skill that will help you make sound business decisions. In this exercise, you will review the vocabulary introduced in Chapter 7 by creating questions to match answers—similar to a famous TV show.

Required

a. Given an answer, what's the question?
Choose *three* of the following terms to serve as an answer. Create an appropriate question for each term. For example, if you choose the term *balance sheet*, you might create the question—*What financial statement reports the assets, liabilities, and owners' equity of an entity on a specific date?*

Accruals	Deferrals	Classified income statement
Activity ratios	Business segments	Profit margin ratio
Gross margin	Horizontal analysis	Earnings per share
Adjustments	Vertical analysis	Extraordinary items

b. Are you sure that's the question?
Have each member of your group read aloud the questions they developed in Requirement (a). As a group, decide whether each question is an accurate match for an answer. Once satisfied that all questions are appropriate, the group, as a whole, chooses the three best questions created within the group. Record the three questions chosen (with their answers) on separate pieces of paper or index cards and give them to your instructor.

c. What's the answer?
To ensure that you have learned the vocabulary terms listed in Requirement (a), your instructor will now quiz you on the questions written by all of your classmates.

YOUR PERFORMANCE OBJECTIVE 5a
(page 137)

E7-2 Transaction Analysis

Lawrence Company prepared Balance Sheet 1 after Transaction 1, Balance Sheet 2 after Transaction 2, and so on, as follows:

		1	2	3	4	5	6	7
Assets								
Cash	$ 20	$ 20	$ 50	$ 50	$ 74	$ 74	$ 74	$ 30
Receivables	40	40	86	86	62	62	62	62
Inventory	60	88	46	46	46	46	46	46
Machinery	80	80	80	90	90	90	84	84
	$200	$228	$262	$272	$272	$272	$266	$222
Liabilities and Owners' Equity								
Payables	$100	$128	$128	$128	$128	$150	$150	$106
Owner's equity	100	100	134	144	144	122	116	116
	$200	$228	$262	$272	$272	$272	$266	$222

Required

Identify the seven transactions that caused these changes by using transaction analysis to aid you in your reasoning process.

E7-3 Transaction Analysis

Using the transaction analysis you completed in E7-2,

a. Identify which of the seven transactions are explicit transactions and which are implicit transactions.
b. Determine whether this company uses a periodic or perpetual inventory system based on Transaction 2. Explain your reasoning for this response.

YOUR PERFORMANCE OBJECTIVE 5a *(page 137)*

E7-4 Identifying Adjustments

Gormé Company prepared Balance Sheet 1 after Adjustment 1, Balance Sheet 2 after Adjustment 2, and so on, as follows:

YOUR PERFORMANCE OBJECTIVE 19 *(page 275)*

		1	2	3	4	5	6	7
Assets								
Cash	$ 20	$ 20	$ 20	$ 20	$ 20	$ 20	$ 20	$ 20
Receivables	40	60	60	70	70	70	70	70
Inventory	60	60	60	60	60	48	48	48
Machinery	80	80	80	80	80	80	75	75
	$200	$220	$220	$230	$230	$218	$213	$213
Liabilities and Owners' Equity								
Payables	$100	$100	$115	$115	$120	$120	$120	$110
Owner's equity	100	120	105	115	110	98	93	103
	$200	$220	$220	$230	$230	$218	$213	$213

Additional Information

Adjustment 1 involves interest, Adjustment 2 involves salaries, Adjustment 3 involves rent, Adjustment 4 involves interest, Adjustment 5 involves inventory, Adjustment 6 involves depreciation, and Adjustment 7 involves subscriptions.

Required

Identify the seven adjustments that caused these changes by using transaction analysis to aid you in your reasoning process.

E7-5 Recording Adjustments

Using the transaction analysis you completed in E7-4,

a. Open T-accounts for each account listed to the left of Adjustment (1).
b. Enter the transaction effects of the seven adjustments in the T-accounts opened in part (a).
c. Once you have entered the effects of all seven adjustments, balance the accounts and prove that the accounting equation is in balance.

YOUR PERFORMANCE OBJECTIVE 19 *(page 275)*

E7-6 Identifying Adjustments

Tormé Company prepared Income Statement 1 after Adjustment 1, Income Statement 2 after Adjustment 2, and so on, as follows:

YOUR PERFORMANCE OBJECTIVE 19 *(page 275)*

		1	2	3	4	5	6	7
Revenues								
Sales revenue	$700	$700	$700	$700	$700	$700	$700	$755
Rent	80	80	80	120	120	120	120	120
Interest	40	40	40	40	75	75	75	75
	$820	$820	$820	$860	$895	$895	$895	$950
Expenses								
Cost of goods sold	$300	$300	$300	$300	$300	$325	$325	$325
Salaries	200	200	250	250	250	250	250	250
Depreciation	100	100	100	100	100	100	130	130
Interest	65	85	85	85	85	85	85	85
	$665	$685	$735	$735	$735	$760	$790	$790
Net income	$155	$135	$ 85	$125	$160	$135	$105	$160

Additional Information
Adjustment 1 involves interest, Adjustment 2 involves salaries, Adjustment 3 involves rent, Adjustment 4 involves interest, Adjustment 5 involves inventory, Adjustment 6 involves depreciation, and Adjustment 7 involves subscriptions.

Required
Identify the seven adjustments that caused these changes by using transaction analysis to aid you in your reasoning process.

YOUR PERFORMANCE OBJECTIVE 5a *(page 137)*

E7-7 Classifying Adjustments
Using the transaction analysis you completed in E7-6:
a. Identify for each adjustment whether a cash receipt or cash payment precedes, coincides with, or follows the period when income is recognized.
b. Classify each adjustment as to whether it is an accrued revenue, accrued expense, deferred revenue, or deferred expense.

NOTE: In E7-8 through E7-14, use the following transaction analysis format:

		Fundamental Accounting Equation					
Item	**Asset Account Title**	**Assets**	**=**	**Liabilities**	**+**	**Owners' Equity**	**Source of Asset Account Title**

YOUR PERFORMANCE OBJECTIVE 19a *(page 275)*

E7-8 Classifying and Recording Adjustments
Shapiro & Conrad, Attorneys at Law, provide the following information relating to their monthly adjustments at September 30.
a. Employee salaries of $220 were incurred but unpaid.
b. Interest of $340 was earned but not yet received or recorded.
c. On September 30, office supplies has an unadjusted balance of $900. Office supplies actually on hand were $65.
d. September rent expense includes October rent of $225 paid in advance.
e. September rent revenue includes October rent of $450 received in advance.

Required
a. Identify each transaction (a) through (e) as to whether it is an accrued revenue, accrued expense, deferred revenue, or deferred expense.
b. Record the monthly adjustments needed at September 30 by using transaction analysis.

YOUR PERFORMANCE OBJECTIVE 19a *(page 275)*

E7-9 Classifying and Recording Adjustments
The following information relates to December 31 adjustments for Blake Corporation:
a. Accrued salaries for the week December 27 through December 31 amounted to $10,450.
b. $50,000 was borrowed on October 1 of the current year at an interest rate of 10%.
c. On December 1, rent of $12,000 was paid in advance for six months and recorded as an asset.
d. On December 1, rent of $3,000 was received for three months in advance and recorded as a revenue.

Required
a. Identify each transaction (a through d) as to whether it is an accrued revenue, accrued expense, deferred revenue, or deferred expense.
b. Record the annual adjustments needed at December 31 by using transaction analysis.

YOUR PERFORMANCE OBJECTIVE 19a *(page 275)*

E7-10 Classifying and Recording Adjustments
The following information relates to December 31 adjustments for Edwards Corporation:
a. Weekly salaries total $15,000 for a five-day work week and are payable on Fridays. December 31 of this year is a Wednesday.
b. On October 1, rent for six months was paid and recorded as a $6,000 increase to Prepaid Rent and a $6,000 decrease to Cash.
c. The firm recorded an increase to Service Fee Revenue when it received $800 during December for services to be performed during the following year.
d. Merchandise inventory at January 1 was $18,000. Purchases during the year amounted to $245,000. Merchandise inventory on December 31 was $21,000 from a physical count of merchandise.

Required

a. Identify each transaction (a through d) as to whether it is an accrued revenue, accrued expense, deferred revenue, or deferred expense.
b. Record the annual adjustments needed at December 31 by using transaction analysis.

E7-11 Classifying and Recording Adjustments

YOUR PERFORMANCE OBJECTIVE 19a
(page 275)

The Lopez Memory Enhancement School provides the following information relating to its June 30 adjustments.

a. On June 30, the cleaning supplies account has an unadjusted balance of $1,100. At this date, a physical count of supplies indicates that $400 of supplies are actually on hand.
b. On June 1, $600 is paid to acquire three months' worth of vision insurance coverage. At this date, the prepaid insurance account is increased and the cash account is decreased.
c. On June 1, $3,000 is collected for five months' rental of warehouse space. At this date, both the cash account and the deferred rent revenue account are increased.
d. On June 1, a $12,000, 8%, four-month note is received from a customer. At this date, the notes receivable account is increased and the accounts receivable account is decreased.

Required

a. Identify each transaction (a through d) as to whether it is an accrued revenue, accrued expense, deferred revenue, or deferred expense.
b. Record the annual adjustments needed at June 30 by using transaction analysis.

E7-12 Recording Adjustments

YOUR PERFORMANCE OBJECTIVE 19a
(page 275)

Ito Company has the following account balances at December 31 of the current year before any adjustments have been made:

Office supplies on hand	$ 1,900
Accounts receivable	17,600
Unexpired insurance	360
Salaries expense	11,000
Notes payable	8,000
Unearned commissions revenue	1,500
Commissions revenue	16,000

Additional Data

a. Unexpired insurance at December 31 amounted to $200.
b. Office supplies on hand at December 31 were determined by count to be $1,050.
c. Accrued interest on notes at December 31 amounted to $100.
d. Commissions still unearned at December 31 amounted to $800.
e. Accrued salaries payable at December 31 were $400.

Required

Record the monthly adjustments needed at December 31 by using transaction analysis.

E7-13 Recording Adjustments

YOUR PERFORMANCE OBJECTIVE 19a
(page 275)

Athens Company has the following account balances at June 30 of the current year before any adjustments have been made:

Office supplies on hand	$ 2,200
Accounts receivable	17,600
Unexpired insurance	600
Salaries expense	12,000
Notes payable	10,000
Unexpired rent	900
Rent expense	2,700
Unearned commissions	2,000
Commissions revenue	16,000

Additional Data

a. Office supplies actually on hand amount to $950 at June 30.
b. Unexpired insurance at June 30 amounted to $150.

c. Commissions still unearned at June 30 amounted to $1,000.
d. Interest on the note payable issued on June 1 is unpaid as of June 30. This note bears interest at 12% annually.
e. Accrued salaries payable at June 30 were $800.

Required
Record the monthly adjustments needed at June 30 by using transaction analysis.

YOUR PERFORMANCE OBJECTIVE 19a
(page 275)

E7-14 Recording Adjustments
Sparta Company has the following account balances at December 31 of the current year before any adjustments have been made:

Office supplies on hand	$ 2,740
Accounts receivable	54,000
Prepaid insurance	3,000
Salaries expense	16,000
Prepaid rent	9,000
Deferred service revenue	800

Additional Data
a. Office supplies actually on hand amount to $680 at December 31.
b. The balance in the prepaid insurance account represents the premium on a policy providing three years of coverage. The premium was paid on July 1 of the current year.
c. Fees for delivery services performed but not yet billed to customers amount to $320.
d. Employee salaries accrued at December 31 amount to $770.
e. $550 of the deferred service revenue account balance was earned in the current year.
f. The prepaid rent amount covers a one-year period beginning on October 1 of the current year.

Required
Record the annual adjustments needed at December 31 by using transaction analysis.

YOUR PERFORMANCE OBJECTIVE 10
(page 288)

E7-15 Preparing an Income Statement
Here is a list of income statement account titles taken in random order from an income statement of International Flavors & Fragrances Inc. for the quarter ended September 30 (in thousands):

Cost of goods sold	$176,565
Taxes on income	35,043
Other (income) expense, net	(3,322)
Interest expense	1,359
Selling, administrative and research expenses	73,133
Net sales	341,684

Required
Prepare a single-step income statement and a multiple-step income statement for International Flavors & Fragrances Inc.

YOUR PERFORMANCE OBJECTIVE 10
(page 288)

E7-16 Preparing an Income Statement
Here is a list of income statement account titles taken in random order from an annual report income statement of Silicon Graphics Inc. for the year ended June 30 (in thousands):

Cost of product and other revenue	$ 632,440
Cost of service revenue	87,220
Provision for income taxes	57,004
Interest income and other, net	12,838
Interest expense	8,302
Selling, general and administrative expenses	391,583
Product and other revenues	1,318,693
Service revenue	162,909
Research and development expense	177,217

Required
Prepare a single-step income statement and a multiple-step income statement for Silicon Graphics, Inc.

E7-17 Preparing an Income Statement
Here is a list of income statement account titles taken in random order from an annual report income statement of Nike, Inc. for the year ended May 31 (in thousands):

YOUR PERFORMANCE OBJECTIVE 10 *(page 288)*

Cost of sales	$2,301,423
Income taxes expense	191,800
Other (income) expense net	(8,270)
Interest expense	15,282
Selling and administrative expenses	974,099
Revenues	3,789,668

Required
Prepare a single-step income statement and a multiple-step income statement for Nike, Inc.

E7-18 Preparing an Income Statement
Here is a list of income statement account titles taken in random order from the annual report income statement of Dell Computer Corporation for the year ended January 30 (in thousands):

YOUR PERFORMANCE OBJECTIVE 10 *(page 288)*

Net sales	$2,873,165
Cost of sales	2,440,349
Provision for income taxes (benefit)*	(2,933)
Financing and other income, net	258
Selling, general and administrative expenses	422,906
Research, development, and engineering	48,934

*This item represents a reduction in income taxes; it serves to increase net income.

Required
Prepare a single-step income statement and a multiple-step income statement for Dell Computer Corporation.

E7-19 Ratio Analysis
From the information found in Exercise 7-15, express each item as a percentage of net sales (perform vertical analysis) and then calculate these ratios for International Flavors and Fragrances:

YOUR PERFORMANCE OBJECTIVE 3 *(page 183)*

a. Times interest earned
b. Gross margin
c. Profit margin

E7-20 Ratio Analysis
The following information in thousands represents beginning-of-year and end-of-year balances needed to calculate certain ratios for Silicon Graphics, Incorporated:

YOUR PERFORMANCE OBJECTIVE 3 *(page 183)*

	End of Year	Beginning of Year
Accounts receivable, net	$ 391,271	$ 317,470
Inventories	164,319	156,165
Total assets	1,518,783	1,013,027
Weighted average common shares outstanding	154,486	

Required
With this information and that shown in Exercise 7-16, calculate the following ratios:
a. Times interest earned   b. Asset turnover

c. Accounts receivable turnover
d. Average collection period
e. Inventory turnover
f. Average holding period
g. Gross margin
h. Profit margin
i. Earnings per share

YOUR PERFORMANCE OBJECTIVE 3 *(page 183)*

E7-21 Ratio Analysis
The following information in thousands represents beginning-of-year and end-of-year balances needed to calculate certain ratios for Nike, Incorporated:

	End of Year	Beginning of Year
Accounts receivable, net	$ 703,682	$ 667,547
Inventories	470,023	592,986
Total assets	2,373,815	2,186,269
Weighted average common shares outstanding	75,456	

Required
With this information and that shown in Exercise 7-17, calculate the following ratios:
a. Times interest earned
b. Asset turnover
c. Accounts receivable turnover
d. Average collection period
e. Inventory turnover
f. Average holding period
g. Gross margin
h. Profit margin
i. Earnings per share

YOUR PERFORMANCE OBJECTIVE 3 *(page 183)*

E7-22 Ratio Analysis
The following information in thousands represents beginning-of-year and end-of-year balances needed to calculate certain ratios for Dell Computer Corporation:

	End of Year	Beginning of Year
Accounts receivable, net	$ 410,774	$374,013
Inventories	220,265	303,220
Total assets	1,140,480	927,005
Preferred stock dividends	3,743	
Weighted average common shares outstanding	37,333	

Required
With this information and that shown in Exercise 7-18, calculate the following ratios:
a. Times interest earned
b. Asset turnover
c. Accounts receivable turnover
d. Average collection period
e. Inventory turnover
f. Average holding period
g. Gross margin
h. Profit margin
i. Earnings per share

YOUR PERFORMANCE OBJECTIVE 20 *(page 285)*

E7-23 Categorizing Income Statement Accounts
Categorize all of the income statement accounts included in the income statement of The Limited, Inc., shown in Figure 7-6 of the text, into one of the following four categories. Place the letter of each of these four categories next to the appropriate account.
a. Primary operating activities that are expected to continue.
b. Peripheral activities that are expected to continue.
c. Primary operating activities that are discontinued.
d. Peripheral activities that are not expected to continue.

YOUR PERFORMANCE OBJECTIVE 20 *(page 285)*

E7-24 Categorizing Income Statement Accounts
Categorize all of the income statement accounts included in the income statement of Wendy's International Inc. shown in Figure 7-9b of the text into one of the following four categories. Place the letter of each of these four categories next to the appropriate account.

a. Primary operating activities that are expected to continue.
b. Peripheral activities that are expected to continue.
c. Primary operating activities that are discontinued.
d. Peripheral activities that are not expected to continue.

E7-25 Categorizing Income Statement Accounts

YOUR PERFORMANCE OBJECTIVE 20 *(page 285)*

Categorize all of the income statement accounts included in the income statement of Dreyer's Grand Ice Cream, Inc., shown below, into one of the following four categories. Place the letter of each of these four categories next to the appropriate account.

a. Primary operating activities that are expected to continue.
b. Peripheral activities that are expected to continue.
c. Primary operating activities that are discontinued.
d. Peripheral activities that are not expected to continue.

DREYER'S GRAND ICE CREAM, INC.
Consolidated Statement of Operations
($ in thousands, except per share amounts)

	Year Ended		
	Dec. 25, 1999	Dec. 26, 1998	Dec. 27, 1997
Revenues:			
Sales	$1,099,817	$1,022,335	$970,097
Other income	2,090	3,653	2,994
	1,101,907	1,025,988	973,091
Costs and expenses:			
Cost of goods sold	837,907	827,862	764,551
Selling, general and administrative	235,146	212,151	183,390
Impairment of long-lived assets		44,564	
(Reversal of) provision for restructuring charges	(1,315)	3,300	
Interest, net of amounts capitalized	11,450	13,006	10,695
	1,083,188	1,100,883	958,636
Income (loss) before income tax provision (benefit) and cumulative effect of change in accounting principle	18,719	(74,895)	14,455
Income tax provision (benefit)	7,132	(28,385)	5,681
Income (loss) before cumulative effect of change in accounting principle	11,587	(46,510)	8,774
Cumulative effect of change in accounting principle	595		746
Net income (loss)	10,992	(46,510)	8,028
Accretion of preferred stock to redemption value	424	424	424
Preferred stock dividends	696	696	3,636
Net income (loss) available to common stockholders	**$ 9,872**	**$ (47,630)**	**$ 3,968**

Note: Earnings per share information has been excluded for simplicity.

Critical Thinking Problems

YOUR PERFORMANCE OBJECTIVE 19 (page 275)

P7-1 Recording Adjustments

Sea Cat, Inc., operates a large catamaran that takes tourists at several island resorts on diving and sailing excursions. The company prepares adjustments on a monthly basis. Selected account balances on June 30 after adjustments have been made are as follows:

Prepaid Rent	$ 4,500
Prepaid Insurance	900
Catamaran	42,000
Accumulated Depreciation—Catamaran	7,700
Deferred Passenger Revenue	180

Additional Data

a. Four months' rent had been prepaid on June 1.

b. The prepaid insurance account was recorded on January 1 when a one-year fire insurance policy was purchased.

c. The catamaran is being depreciated over a ten-year useful life.

d. The deferred passenger revenue account represents tickets good for future rides that were sold to a resort hotel for $12 per ticket on June 1. During June, thirty-five of the tickets were used.

Required

a. Answer the following questions:
   1. What is the amount of the monthly rent expense? ________
   2. What is the original cost of the insurance policy? ________
   3. What is the age of the catamaran in months as of June 30? ________
   4. How many tickets were sold to the hotel on June 1? ________

b. Record the adjustments made on June 30 by using the following transaction analysis format below:

		Fundamental Accounting Equation					
Date	Asset Account Title	Assets	=	Liabilities	+	Owners' Equity	Source of Asset Account Title
06/30							

YOUR PERFORMANCE OBJECTIVE 19 (page 275)

P7-2 Recording Adjustments

Abatzoglou Company entered into the following transactions during the current year:

a. Office supplies were acquired for $500 cash at a time when no other supplies were on hand. At the end of the year, the inventory of office supplies amounted to $200.

b. On October 1, cash of $900 was received from customers for services to be performed equally over the next six months.

c. During the year, Abatzoglou paid employees $10,000 cash for their services. At December 31, $250 of unpaid salaries earned by employees during December were unrecorded.

d. A $1,000 note receivable was received from a customer on November 1. The note and interest of 10% per year are due in four months.

Required

Each of the explicit transactions described above is analyzed below using the fundamental equation. Using this initial analysis as a reference, record the adjustment (implicit transaction) necessitated by each explicit transaction. Assume that Abatzoglou's income statement is prepared at December 31.

	Assets		=	Liabilities	+	Owners' Equity	Retained Earnings Account Title
Transaction	**Cash**	**Supplies**					
Explicit (a)	(500)	500	=				
Implicit (a)							
				Advances from Customers			
Transaction	**Cash**						
Explicit (b)	900		=	900			
Implicit (b)							
				Salaries Payable			
Transaction	**Cash**						
Explicit (c)	(10,000)		=			(10,000)	Salaries Expense
Implicit (c)							
		Note/Interest Receivable					
Transaction	**Cash**						
Explicit (d)		1,000	=			1,000	Sales Revenue
Implicit (d)							

P7-3 Determining the Financial Statement Effects of Adjustments

YOUR PERFORMANCE OBJECTIVE 19 *(page 275)*

The following transactions of the Near Side Corporation require adjustment on December 31, the end of Year 3.

a. On April 1, Year 2, the company purchases a three-year insurance policy for $10,800.
b. On September 30, Year 1, the company purchases equipment for $120,000. The equipment is put into use on October 1, Year 1 and has an estimated useful life of eight years.
c. During the current year, the company purchases 8,500 high density computer disks at a total cost of $29,750. There were no disks at the beginning of the period, and 4,500 disks remain at the end of the period.
d. On October 1, Year 2, the firm lends $100,000 to a customer at 14% interest for two years. Interest is due yearly and the principal is due at the end of two years.

Required

For each transaction, calculate the balances of both the relevant balance sheet and income statement accounts on December 31 after all adjustments have been made.

P7-4 Determining the Identity of Four CMU Adjustments

YOUR PERFORMANCE OBJECTIVE 19 *(page 275)*

Using the miscellaneous expense adjustment on page 268 as a model, study Figure 7-2 to determine the identity of the remaining four adjustments made by Cards & Memorabilia Unlimited during its first year of business.

P7-5 Financial Statement Effects

YOUR PERFORMANCE OBJECTIVE 13b *(page 276)*

Study the following transactions entered into this year:

a. Recorded a $500 sale.
b. Recorded the issuance of capital stock.
c. Recorded the payment of a liability account.
d. Recorded the purchase of equipment on account.

Required

Determine the effects of these transactions on each of the accounting elements shown in the following column headings. Use the following symbols:

I = Increased D = Decreased N = No Effect

Trans-action	Total Revenue	Total Expense	Net Income	Total Assets	Total Liabilities	Total Owners' Equity
a.						
b.						
c.						
d.						

YOUR PERFORMANCE OBJECTIVE 13b (page 276)

P7-6 Financial Statement Effects

Study the following errors made this year:

a. Recorded a $500 cash sale using the correct accounts but the incorrect amount of $50.
b. Recorded the issuance of capital stock by increasing cash and a revenue account.
c. Recorded the payment of a liability account by decreasing cash and a revenue account.
d. Recorded the purchase of equipment by decreasing cash and increasing an expense account.

Required

Determine the effects of these errors on each of the accounting elements shown in the following column headings. Use the following symbols:

O = Overstated U = Understated N = No Effect

Error	Total Revenue	Total Expense	Net Income	Total Assets	Total Liabilities	Total Owners' Equity
a.						
b.						
c.						
d.						

YOUR PERFORMANCE OBJECTIVE 13b (page 276)

P7-7 Financial Statement Effects

Study the following omissions that occurred this year:

a. Failed to record depreciation for the year.
b. Failed to record dividends declared this year.
c. Failed to accrue year-end interest on notes payable.
d. Failed to record the collection of an account receivable.
e. Failed to record the payment of an account payable.

Required

Determine the effects of these omissions on each of the accounting elements shown in the following column headings. Use the following symbols:

O = Overstated U = Understated N = No Effect

Omis-sions	Total Revenue	Total Expense	Net Income	Total Assets	Total Liabilities	Total Owners' Equity
a.						
b.						
c.						
d.						
e.						

P7-8 Financial Statement Effects

YOUR PERFORMANCE OBJECTIVE 13b (page 276)

Study the following errors and omissions made this year:

a. Recorded too much depreciation this year.
b. Failed to accrue interest on notes receivable during the year.
c. Recorded too high an amount of dividends declared during the year.
d. Recorded the purchase of office supplies during the year by increasing an expense account. Some of these office supplies were on hand at the end of the period.

Required

Determine the effects of these errors or omissions on each of the accounting elements shown in the following column headings. Use the following symbols:

O = Overstated U = Understated N = No Effect

Error	Total Revenue	Total Expense	Net Income	Total Assets	Total Liabilities	Total Owners' Equity
a.						
b.						
c.						
d.						

P7-9 Preparing an Income Statement

YOUR PERFORMANCE OBJECTIVE 10 (page 288)

Convert The Limited Inc.'s multiple-step income statement found in Figure 7-6 into a single-step income statement. Ignore earnings per share data.

P7-10 Preparing an Income Statement

YOUR PERFORMANCE OBJECTIVE 10 (page 288)

Convert Wendy's International's single-step income statement found in Figure 7-9b into a multiple-step income statement. Ignore earnings per share data.

P7-11 Preparing an Income Statement

YOUR PERFORMANCE OBJECTIVE 10 (page 288)

Convert Pfizer Inc.'s single-step income statement found in Figure 7-13 into a multiple-step income statement. Ignore earnings per share data.

P7-12 Preparing an Income Statement

YOUR PERFORMANCE OBJECTIVE 10 (page 288)

Convert PE Corporation's multiple-step income statement found on page 318 into a single-step income statement.

NOTE: The following descriptions summarize the essential nature of business for companies analyzed in Problems P7-13 through P7-17.
Brown-Forman Corporation is a diversified producer and marketer of fine quality consumer products, including china, crystal, silver, luggage, and alcoholic beverages such as whiskey, wine, and champagne.
The Walt Disney Company is a worldwide provider of quality entertainment through its theme parks, movies, television programming, publications, retail outlets, and consumer products.

P7-13 Timing of Revenue Recognition

YOUR PERFORMANCE OBJECTIVE 21 (page 290)

The Accounting Policies section of a recent annual report from Brown-Forman Corporation states that it "recognizes revenue when goods are shipped." Given what you know about this company, apply the standard criteria used to determine when revenue is recognized to its operation, and discuss whether its policy is reasonable.

P7-14 Timing of Revenue Recognition

YOUR PERFORMANCE OBJECTIVE 21 (page 290)

In the Significant Accounting Policies section of its 1999 annual report, The Walt Disney Company states that "Revenues from the theatrical distribution of motion pictures are recognized when motion pictures are exhibited." Given what you know about this company, apply the standard criteria used to determine when revenue is recognized to its operation, and discuss whether this policy is reasonable.

PE CORPORATION
Consolidated Statements of Operations
(Dollar amounts in thousands except per share amounts)

	For the years ended June 30,		
	1998	**1999**	**2000**
Net revenues	$944,306	$1,216,897	$1,371,035
Cost of sales	431,738	558,813	609,054
Gross margin	512,568	658,084	761,981
Selling, general, and administrative	283,399	364,128	436,911
Research, development, and engineering	115,764	179,275	274,796
Restructuring and other special charges	43,980	6,116	2,142
Acquired research and development	28,850		
Operating Income	40,575	108,565	48,132
Gain on investments	1,605	6,126	48,603
Interest expense	4,905	3,783	3,501
Interest income	5,938	2,869	39,428
Other income, net	3,147	522	3,446
Income before income taxes	46,360	114,299	136,108
Provision for income taxes	25,069	4,140	40,612
Minority interest	5,597	13,362	
Income from continuing operations	15,694	96,797	95,496
Discontinued operations, net of income taxes			
Income (loss) from discontinued operations	40,694	(21,109)	
Gain on disposal of discontinued operations		100,167	
Net Income	$ 56,388	$ 175,855	$ 95,496

YOUR PERFORMANCE OBJECTIVE 21 *(page 290)*

P7-15 Timing of Revenue Recognition
In the Significant Accounting Policies section of its 1999 annual report, The Walt Disney Company states that "Revenues from video sales are recognized on the date that video units are made widely available for sale by retailers." Given what you know about this company, apply the standard criteria used to determine when revenue is recognized to its operation, and discuss whether this policy is reasonable.

YOUR PERFORMANCE OBJECTIVE 21 *(page 290)*

P7-16 Timing of Revenue Recognition
In the Significant Accounting Policies section of its 1999 annual report, The Walt Disney Company states that "Internet advertising revenues are recognized on the basis of impression views in the period the advertising is displayed, providing that no significant obligations remain and collection is probable." Given what you know about this company, apply the standard criteria used to determine when revenue is recognized to its operation, and discuss whether this policy is reasonable.

YOUR PERFORMANCE OBJECTIVE 21 *(page 290)*

P7-17 Timing of Revenue Recognition
In the Significant Accounting Policies section of its 1999 annual report, The Walt Disney Company states that "Revenues from participants . . . at the theme parks are generally recorded over the period of the applicable agreements commencing with the opening of the related attraction." Given what you know about this company, apply the standard criteria used to determine when revenue is recognized to its operation, and discuss whether this policy is reasonable.

NOTE: The following descriptions summarize the essential nature of business for companies analyzed in Problems P7-18 through P7-20.
International Flavors and Fragrances (IFF) is a leading creator and manufacturer of flavors and fragrances used by others to impart or improve flavor or fragrance in a wide variety of consumer products.

(continued)

Silicon Graphics, Inc. is a leading supplier of visual computing solutions and high performance servers targeted for a wide range of technical, scientific, corporate, and entertainment applications.
Nike, Inc. designs and markets a wide variety of athletic footwear, apparel, and related items for competitive and recreational uses.
Dell Computer Corporation is a leading manufacturer, marketer, and distributor of high-performance personal computer systems. It is one of the world's top five personal computer vendors.

P7-18 Ratio Analysis

YOUR PERFORMANCE OBJECTIVE 3c *(page 183)*

Compare the times interest earned ratio of International Flavors and Fragrances (E7-19), Silicon Graphics, Inc. (E7-20), Nike, Inc. (E7-21), and Dell Computer Corporation (E7-22). Which company has the highest financial risk? Discuss how the nature of each company's business might explain its relative financial position.

P7-19 Ratio Analysis

YOUR PERFORMANCE OBJECTIVE 3b *(page 183)*

Compare the full set of activity ratios calculated for Silicon Graphics, Inc. (E7-20), Nike, Inc. (E7-21), and Dell Computer Corporation (E7-22). Use these ratios to evaluate each company's relative turnover. Discuss how the nature of each company's business might explain its turnover results.

P7-20 Ratio Analysis

YOUR PERFORMANCE OBJECTIVE 3d *(page 183)*

Compare the full set of profitability ratios calculated for Silicon Graphics, Inc. (E7-20), Nike, Inc. (E7-21), and Dell Computer Corporation (E7-22). Use these ratios to evaluate each company's relative profitability. Discuss how the nature of each company's business might explain its profitability results.

P7-21 Ratio Analysis

YOUR PERFORMANCE OBJECTIVE 3 *(page 183)*

Listed below are selected financial ratios for IBM Corporation for year 1 and year 2.

	Year 2	Year 1
Times interest earned	13.40	12.99
Asset turnover	0.966	0.941
Accounts receivable turnover	4.71	4.61
Inventory turnover	8.70	7.45
Gross margin	38.99%	40.21%
Profit margin	7.76%	7.15%
Earnings per share	$6.18	$5.12

Required

a. For each ratio listed, explain in which year the company had better results. Be specific, describing the reason for your conclusion.
b. Considering the components of the ratios presented in this chapter, explain what may have caused the change in each of IBM's ratios from year 1 to year 2.

P7-22 Ratio Analysis

YOUR PERFORMANCE OBJECTIVE 3 *(page 183)*

Until a recent merger, Computer 2000 AG was Europe's largest wholesaler of personal computer-related equipment and supplies. German accounting principles and standards are dominated by government rules and regulations. These regulations tend to be more conservative than American accounting standards. Financial statements consist of a balance sheet, income statement, and explanatory notes. In many cases, an auditors' report is required. Financial statements for public companies must always be prepared in German and expressed in Deutsche marks. An income statement must be prepared in the vertical form, and may utilize a sales/cost of sales format. The following excerpt is from Computer 2000's income statement for the year ended September 30, 1997. Some of the account titles have been translated into English for you. All amounts are in thousands of Deutsche marks.

Umsatzerlöse	8,229,729
Umsatzkosten	7,603,718
Bruttoergebnis vom Umsatz (Gross profit)	626,011
Vertriebskosten	250,421
Allgemeine Verwaltungskosten	
(General administrative expenses)	261,859
Sonstige betriebliche Enträge	54,162
Sonstige betriebliche Aufwendungen	
(Other operating expenses)	57,840
Ergebnis aus Betriebstätigkeit	110,053
Zinsergebnis (Interest expense, net)	48,698
Ergebnis der gewöhnlichen Geschäftstätigkeit	
(Operating profit)	61,355
Auβerordentliches Ergebnis	
(Extraordinary expense)	103,999
Steuern vom Einkommen und Ertrag	19,448
Sonstige Steuern (Other taxes)	8,272
Jahresfehlbetrag	(70,364)

Required

a. From the income statements you have studied in Chapters 6 and 7, translate the remaining account titles into plausible English terms.

b. Calculate the following ratios, omitting the extraordinary loss in the calculation:
   1. Times interest earned
   2. Gross margin
   3. Profit margin

c. Compare the results of your calculations in part (b) to the same ratios provided in P7-21 for IBM Corporation. What could account for the differences?

YOUR PERFORMANCE OBJECTIVES 5a, 5b, 10 *(pages 137, 57, 288)*

P7-23 Comprehensive Problem

Now that the full set of Cards & Memorabilia Unlimited's first-year transactions have been described in this textbook and presented in its inside back cover, see if you can prepare both its balance sheet and income statement.

Required

a. Record the effects of Transactions A_1 through Z as described in Chapters 2, 4, 6, and 7 in individual T-accounts.

b. Arrange the relevant account balances to create both a balance sheet and an income statement in good form.

Research Assignments

A wide variety of interesting Research Assignments for this chapter are available for the following topics at www.mhhe.com/solomon:

R7-1 Finding Adjustments in a Small Business (PO 19)
R7-2 Noncorporate Income Statement (PO 10)
R7-3 Classified Income Statement (PO 14)
R7-4 Using the MD&A to Learn More about the Income Statement (PO 14)
R7-5 Using the Notes to Learn More about the Income Statement (PO 14)
R7-6 Using the Notes to Learn More about the Income Statement (PO 14)
R7-7 Earnings Management (PO 21)
R7-8 Ratio Analysis (PO 3)
R7-9 Ratio Analysis (PO 3)
R7-10 Financial Analysis (PO 3, 14, and 20)
R7-11 Comparative Financial Analysis of Computer Companies (PO 3 and 4)
R7-12 Comparative Financial Analysis (PO 3 and 4)
R7-13 Comprehensive Research Assignment (PO 13b and 14)

CHAPTER EIGHT

The Statement of Cash Flows

Also be sure you have mastered the following Performance Objectives from previous chapters. They lay the foundation for the concepts you will learn in this chapter:

PO4
PO7
PO9
PO14

PERFORMANCE OBJECTIVES

In this chapter, you will learn the following new Performance Objectives:

PO1 **Explain** the purposes of budgets and **prepare** both a simple operating budget and a simple cash budget. (*Modified form of earlier version.*)

PO22 **Prepare** in good form a bank reconciliation using the adjusted balance format and **prepare** the adjustments necessitated by this reconciliation.

MANAGING CASH MORE EFFECTIVELY WITH AN ASSIST FROM SCORE

Susan had been in business for eight months and had established a small, but growing, clientele. CMU's cash balance was steadily increasing; but Susan was nevertheless concerned, because her business was young and still vulnerable. She wanted to ensure CMU's continued success by doing all she could to avoid the mistakes small business owners often make. So she telephoned George Wu to see if he might have any advice. George recommended she visit the local SCORE office. He explained that SCORE—Service Corps of Retired Executives—is an all volunteer organization sponsored by the U.S. Small Business Administration (SBA). It provides free counseling and training to small business owners. He told her that SCORE volunteers—or "counselors" as they are called—are men and women from all types of business backgrounds who want to help small business owners make the best business decisions.

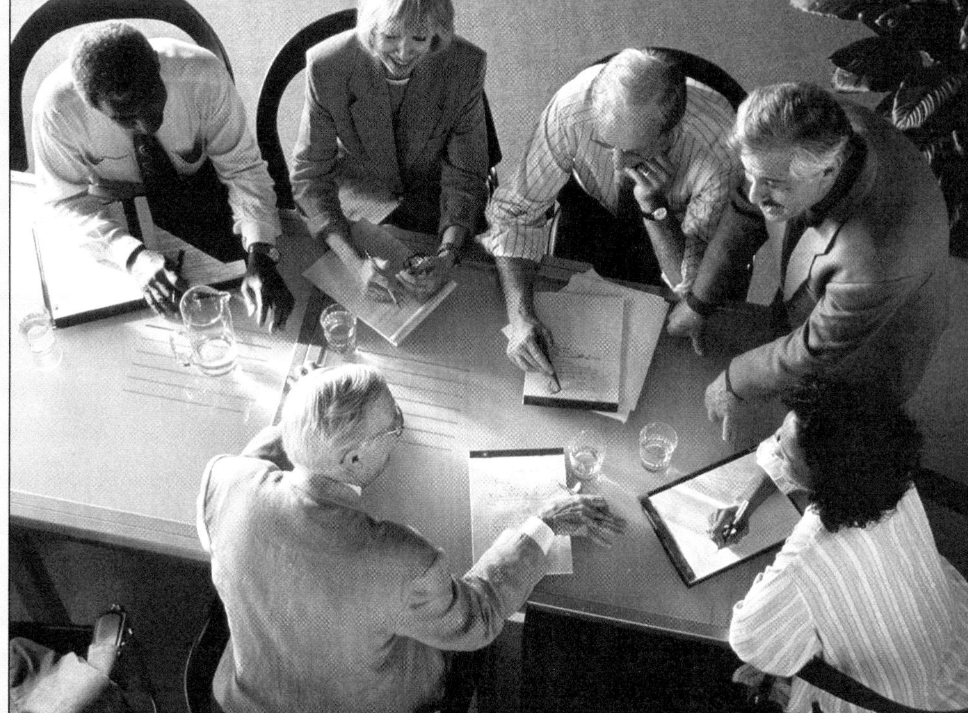

The next day Susan took George's advice by visiting the local SCORE office. When she arrived, she found several counselors sitting in the conference room having their morning coffee. After introducing herself, she told them about her business and explained her concerns. They asked her many questions about CMU and smiled and nodded as she replied. "You don't need us," one of the counselors quipped. "Sounds like you're doing a great job."

Susan was relieved but puzzled. "How could I be doing *everything* right?" she asked. "I'm inexperienced. I must be making some mistakes."

One of the counselors laughed. "I'm sure you are," he said. "But from what you've told us, you're handling your cash well. Poor cash management is the single greatest reason that new businesses fail."

Susan was fascinated. She asked questions, listened, and took notes. After an hour she had three pages of notes—advice based on the more than 200 years of the counselors' combined business experience. She distilled her notes into the following list of five guidelines for cash management.

The Top Five Guidelines for Managing Cash

1. *Before you make any decision, ask yourself "How will this decision affect cash?"* Cash is a critical determinant of success — how much you have, when you have it, how you manage it. If you run out of cash, you're out of business. But also keep in mind — as you saw in Chapter 7's *Insight* entitled "The Relationship between Net Income and

(continued on next page)

(continued from previous page)

Cash Flows" — that all the cash in the world won't make you successful if you don't make a profit.

2. *Plan your use of cash with a cash budget.* Plan conservatively for how much cash you will need and when you will need it. Don't forget to plan for new equipment and other growth. A cash plan like this — called a *cash budget* — helps you determine how much cash you need to follow your business plan and whether you can afford to do more. It's also sometimes a good idea to have another plan for the worst case scenario, so you can see what cash you absolutely must have available for the business to survive.
3. *Use your cash budget.* Analyze your cash position frequently. As you conduct business, monitor how close your actual results are to your cash budget so you can make better decisions. If you consult your budget regularly, you will often be able to anticipate cash problems before they occur and identify possible solutions. Or, if you want to change your business plan and require more cash, you can plug these new cash requirements into your cash budget and see its impact.
4. *Spend cash only when you must.* Obtain as much cash as you can, as soon as you can, and pay out as little as you can and as late as you can. This might seem obvious and oversimplified, but many people commit to leases and other investments and long-term expenses that are unnecessary and, in so doing, tie up their cash.
5. *Expect cash to flow into the business very slowly.* Cash flows into a business much slower than you might think. Even if you have good ideas and a good product, your business will fail if cash inflows don't enter your company fast enough.

Susan was delighted with what she had learned from the SCORE counselors. She had gained a new respect for the role cash plays in the continued success of her business. And as you read Chapter 8—defining key terms, preparing cash budgets, analyzing statements of cash flows, and so on—keep in mind that your understanding of cash, cash management, and the statement of cash flows could be critical to *your* success in business too!

As you can see from Susan's visit to SCORE, cash and cash management are critical factors in the success of a business. In this chapter we'll take a close look at several issues affecting cash—what it is, how it can be managed, and how it is reported in an in-depth fashion through the statement of cash flows, a financial statement to which you were introduced in Chapter 2. You'll learn how the statement of cash flows provides a historical account of cash management, why it is a useful business decision-making tool, and how you can prepare it by analyzing transactions. You'll also learn how to use another essential tool of cash management, a bank reconciliation. And, consistent with earlier chapters, you will examine these tools by using Cards & Memorabilia Unlimited.

Let's begin by taking a closer look at cash—its definition and significance in business decision making.

Cash and Its Significance in Business Decision Making

As you learned in Chapter 4, **cash** represents money and any other medium of exchange that a bank will accept for deposit. The resource unit measured in a statement of cash flows includes not only cash but also cash equivalents. Recall that **cash equivalents** are highly liquid, interest-bearing investments that have maturities of three months or less when purchased. Cash equivalents are readily convertible to known amounts of cash; they include savings deposits, commercial paper, money market funds, and certificates of deposit. Since the purchase and sale of these investments are part of a business's cash management activities, we include cash equivalents when we say "cash."

Cash is a popular financial measure for three reasons:

1. Financial statement users can more easily understand the meaning of a change in cash than, for example, change in working capital or other measures.
2. Cash is recognized by financial experts as important in the decision-making process of business and nonbusiness people alike.
3. Cash clearly measures the relative liquidity of a company's resources. Since no measure is more liquid than cash, information about the cash position of a business enables users to quickly evaluate that business's ability to generate operating cash flows, to determine the advisability of various investments, and to assess the risk of debt and even bankruptcy.

How Is Cash Managed?

If you are now or ever will be a manager, you'll be interested in how to plan future cash flows. The primary vehicle for planning how to obtain and use cash during a future period is a projected statement of cash flows, usually called a *cash budget*.

An equally important aspect of managing cash is how you control it. You can control cash in two ways—by establishing a strong internal control system to prevent unintentional errors and losses from theft and by preparing a bank reconciliation. We'll start our investigation of how cash is managed by looking at the cash budget.

Cash Budgets

In Chapter 1 you learned that a **budget** is a projection or future-oriented plan expressed in financial terms. You might recall that Susan Newman prepared an operating budget, also called a *projected income statement*, to help plan her first year's operations. Many managers also use a **cash budget**, a schedule of expected cash receipts and cash payments, to determine if a company's anticipated cash flow from operations is likely to meet its cash needs during the coming period.

Figure 8-1 shows Cards & Memorabilia Unlimited's cash budget. Susan prepared it when George Wu, her accountant friend, advised her that it was a useful planning tool for anyone running a business. George advised Susan to budget her cash conservatively and not be overly optimistic about the success of CMU's first year. As a result, Susan was pessimistic when she estimated low cash inflow (cash increases) and high cash outflow (cash decreases) for the first year. Notice that Susan's cash budget reflects the following information:

Beginning Cash Balance + Cash Receipts − Cash Payments = End of Cash Balance

This formula, 0 + \$97,500 − \$93,500 = \$4,000, is a concise expression of Figure 8-1. It forecasts that at the end of the period, Cards & Memorabilia Unlimited will have a \$4,000 cash balance. When this balance is negative, it is referred to as a *cash deficit.*

After studying her cash budget, Susan realized that CMU faced a potential cash flow problem because only by borrowing \$5,000 would CMU be able to expect a positive ending cash balance. Given her concern, George suggested several options, such as reducing existing cash balances, postponing payments to suppliers, motivating customers to pay sooner, curtailing nonessential spending, selling assets, reducing payments to owners, or borrowing. Let's evaluate each of these options for CMU.

FIGURE 8-1

Cards & Memorabilia Unlimited's initial cash budget

CARDS & MEMORABILIA UNLIMITED
Cash Budget
For the Year Ended December 31

Cash balance at January 1		$ -0-
Add: Cash receipts		
Cash collections from customers	$62,000	
Owner contributions	30,000	
Borrowing from line of credit	5,000	
Savings account interest receipts	500	97,500
Deduct: Cash payments		
Merchandise purchases	40,000	
Store equipment purchases	16,000	
Store rental	11,000	
Salaries	10,000	
Miscellaneous cash expenses	6,500	
Owner's withdrawal	10,000	93,500
Cash balance at December 31		$ 4,000

Susan can't conserve cash by reducing her cash balances, because her beginning of year cash balance was zero and she doesn't want to finish the year with less than $4,000 cash. Even if she had larger cash balances, reducing them could jeopardize her ability to meet payroll and other obligations. As a new business, CMU does not have an established enough relationship with suppliers to postpone payments on a regular basis—Susan's goal should be to strengthen not weaken CMU's credit rating. Likewise, since her customers are brand new, Susan shouldn't risk offending them by asking them to pay sooner than they had originally planned. Curtailing discretionary spending and selling assets are also unwise options because Susan is trying to expand, not contract, the size of her business. Although Susan's planned withdrawal of $10,000 for personal needs is not excessive, any cutbacks will help increase her $4,000 projected cash balance. Also, since Susan had applied for a loan at Central Bank before she prepared her cash budget, the potential cash shortfall predicted in this budget reinforced her decision to apply for the loan. Despite not being excited about incurring debt, Susan knew that borrowing was justified in light of her projected low cash balance and her rejection of nearly all of the other alternatives.

Now that you have seen how both an operating budget and a cash budget can be used to plan an entity's operations and cash resources, let's modify Performance Objective 1, introduced in Chapter 1, to reflect both an operating budget and a cash budget:

YOUR PERFORMANCE OBJECTIVE 1
Explain the purposes of budgets and **prepare** both a simple operating budget and a simple cash budget.

Although every cash budget presents essentially the same information, there are significant variations in its format depending on the company and the needs of the users. For example, had Susan been more knowledgeable, she could have prepared the equivalent, but more informative, cash budget shown in Figure 8-2. Notice how this format, which focuses on cash flow from operations, helps you immediately detect a problem that can be offset in the short run only by borrowing. Although both cash budgets present the same operating cash flow deficit, Figure 8-2's format is much more informative than Figure 8-1's format. In fact, the format displayed in Figure 8-2 is actually a projected statement of cash flows.

CARDS & MEMORABILIA UNLIMITED Cash Budget For the Year Ended December 31		
Cash flows from operating activities		
Cash collected from customers	$ 62,000	
Cash paid for merchandise purchases	(40,000)	
Cash paid for leased space	(11,000)	
Cash paid for salary expense	(10,000)	
Miscellaneous cash expenses	(6,500)	
Interest received	500	
Net cash provided by operating activities		$ (5,000)
Cash flows from investing activities		
Acquisition of equipment	(16,000)	
Net cash used in investing activities		(16,000)
Cash flows from financing activities		
Cash contribution of owner	30,000	
Borrowing from line of credit	5,000	
Owner withdrawals	(10,000)	
Net cash provided by financing activities		25,000
Net increase in cash		4,000
Cash at beginning of year		–0–
Cash at end of year		$ 4,000

FIGURE 8-2

Cards & Memorabilia Unlimited's initial cash budget presented in a statement of cash flows format

At the end of her first year of business, Susan could have compared this projected statement of cash flows with her actual statement of cash flows (first described in Chapter 3), as shown in Figure 8-3. Comparing an entity's budgeted cash flow to its actual cash flow can be a valuable control device because it provides feedback to managers about the actual cash flows of the entity. This information would be useful to Susan because it would allow her to more closely monitor particular cash flows as well as to prepare a more accurate cash budget for CMU's second year of operations.

Susan appreciated how much the cash budget contributed to her success. It helped reveal a potential cash deficit, which had motivated her to make several decisions to conserve cash that she would not otherwise have made. For example, she used her line of credit, purchased less merchandise and store equipment than planned, deferred some payments to suppliers with a note, and reduced salaries and miscellaneous expenses as well as her own withdrawals. These decisions, along with her unexpectedly higher actual sales, contributed greatly to the significant improvement in CMU's cash position.

The Basic Principles for Internal Control of Cash

You might be impressed by Susan's success in avoiding an anticipated operating cash deficit. But George Wu argued that Susan's cash balance of over $38,000 was far too large for her immediate needs and did not reflect effective cash management. George suggested a more effective cash management strategy would be to use this non-interest-bearing cash to eliminate more of her payables and to earn a greater return from her interest-bearing savings account. He also advised Susan to prepare monthly cash budgets to ensure that she did not maintain excessive amounts of cash in the future. When Susan complained that an emergency could quickly exhaust a low cash balance, George reminded Susan that her bank line of credit was obtained for just this reason.

George, however, did praise Susan's internal control system for preventing unintentional errors and losses from theft. **Internal control** is a process designed to reduce inaccuracy in the accounting information system and discourage unethical behavior

FIGURE 8-3

Cards & Memorabilia Unlimited's actual and projected cash budgets in statement of cash flow format

CARDS & MEMORABILIA UNLIMITED
Statement of Cash Flows
For the Year Ended December 31

	Actual (as of 12/31)	Projected (as of 01/01)
Cash flows from operating activities		
Cash collected from customers	$ 84,200	$ 62,000
Cash paid for merchandise purchases	(27,000)	(40,000)
Cash paid for leased space	(11,000)	(11,000)
Cash paid for salary expense	(8,000)	(10,000)
Cash paid for miscellaneous expenses	(4,250)	(6,500)
Interest received	275	500
Interest paid	(200)	–0–
Net cash provided (used) by operating activities	34,025	(5,000)
Cash flows from investing activities		
Proceeds from sale of equipment	1,350	–0–
Payment of security deposit	(2,000)	–0–
Acquisition of equipment	(17,000)	(16,000)
Net cash used in investing activities	(17,650)	(16,000)
Cash flows from financing activities		
Contributions by owner	30,000	30,000
Proceeds from bank credit line	5,000	5,000
Repayment of bank credit line	(5,000)	N/A
Withdrawals by owner	(8,100)	(10,000)
Net cash provided by financing activities	21,900	25,000
Net increase in cash	38,275	4,000
Cash at beginning of year	–0–	–0–
Cash at end of year	$ 38,275	$ 4,000

Supplemental schedule of noncash investing and financing activities

Computer equipment costing $4,000 was acquired in exchange for a two-year promissory note (Note: Unanticipated at January 1)

among employees and customers. Key features of Susan's formal internal control system include:

1. The functions of handling cash and accounting for cash are separated. That is, none of Susan's employees both handle cash and have access to the accounting records for that cash. As illustrated for CMU, a small business with few employees can implement this feature as long as the owner is actively involved in accounting activities. Unfortunately, many small business owners do not have Susan's time, desire, or knowledge, and their internal control systems suffer as a result. This procedure is relatively easy to implement in a large business because the number of employees allows for a separation between the functions of handling cash and recordkeeping.
2. Every cash receipt is listed immediately when it is received. For example, the moment a cash sale is made, a cash register tape automatically lists its occurrence. Also when Susan opens the mail, she immediately lists any checks enclosed in the envelopes.
3. All cash receipts are deposited daily in the bank account.
4. Susan herself makes all cash payments by check. If she did not, she would have to separate the functions of check approval from check signing. Unlike many businesses, Susan has not needed a petty cash fund for making small payments.

An effective internal control process establishes guidelines for who is authorized to write checks.

5. The bank statement is promptly reconciled with Cards & Memorabilia Unlimited's accounting record of cash. We'll discuss this aspect of internal control in the following section and in the *User Focus* at the end of this chapter.

George and Susan are both confident that if she implements the monthly preparation of cash budgets, her cash management system will be greatly improved.

Bank Reconciliations

To reconcile is to make compatible or consistent. So it makes sense that a bank reconciliation is a financial tool that helps you achieve consistency or agreement between the amount of cash you think you have and the amount of cash the bank thinks you have. More formally, a **bank reconciliation** is a relatively simple schedule that shows exactly how much cash is actually on hand in the entity at a particular point in time.

When an entity entrusts its cash to a bank for safekeeping, two versions of the cash account's balance exist: the bank's version and the entity's version. The bank's balance, referred to as the **balance per bank**, is based on the up-to-date account information known about—that is, recorded—by the bank. The entity's balance, referred to as the **balance per books**, is based on the up-to-date account information known about—that is, recorded—by the entity. These balances are rarely the same at any point in time because the bank and the books seldom learn simultaneously about the transactions that make up these balances. When both the bank and the books know about the identical set of transactions, the bank balance and the book balance of cash are identical. This concept is illustrated in Figure 8-4. In the example shown in this figure, notice that no reconciliation is necessary.

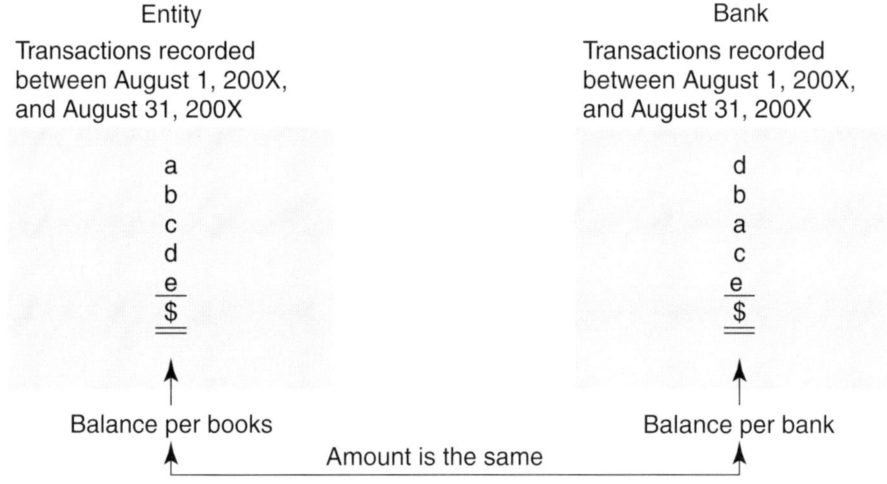

FIGURE 8-4

Two versions of cash with no reconciling items

The two versions of cash will differ and require reconciliation whenever a transaction is recorded by one version of cash but not the other. In Figure 8-5, for example, transactions (b), (c), (d), and (g) fit this description. Since these transactions are not found in both versions of cash, they will account for the difference between the balance per bank and the balance per books. They are called reconciling items because they can be used to reconcile, or balance, the two versions of cash.

If you have access to both the bank's record of the entity's cash and the entity's record of cash at the same point in time, you have complete knowledge of all transactions and are able to prepare a bank reconciliation. Don't let the simplicity of this schedule mislead you into thinking that a bank reconciliation is not a valuable financial decision-making tool. It is a key element of an entity's internal control over cash. For example, during December CMU used the reconciliation process to determine its

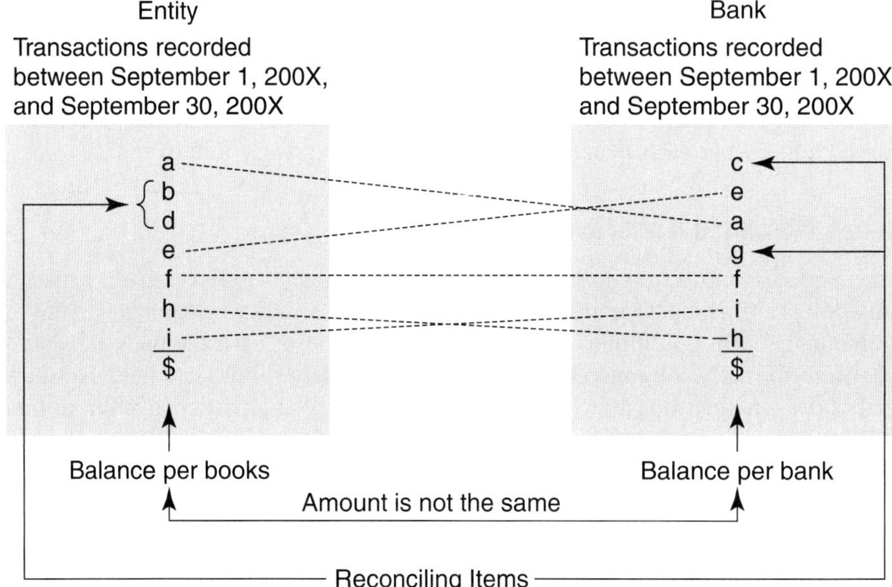

FIGURE 8-5

Two versions of cash with reconciling items

year-ending cash account balance and to learn about a customer check that was dishonored and a check that CMU had recorded incorrectly. In the *User Focus* at the end of this chapter, you will learn how to prepare a bank reconciliation.

What Is the Statement of Cash Flows?

You have now seen that managers have several tools, such as the cash budget and the bank reconciliation, they can use to make decisions about cash and its effect on the activities of an entity. But what information do external decision makers have about an entity's cash flow and its management of that cash flow? External decision makers who want to evaluate a company's cash management do not have access to these internal tools, but they can use the **statement of cash flows**, a financial statement that classifies cash receipts and cash payments into operating, investing, and financing activities.

Although both a statement of cash flows and an income statement summarize activity for a period of time, they differ in two important ways. First, the statement of cash flows generally contains only cash transactions—it is not prepared on an accrual basis as is the income statement. Second, the statement of cash flows classifies these cash transactions into operating, investing, and financing activities, whereas the income statement reports only operating activities.

Although it does not provide information about an entity's present and future cash flows as does the cash budget, the statement of cash flows does report an entity's past cash flows and, along with related disclosures, helps investors, creditors, and other users to evaluate such things as:

- The entity's ability to produce future cash flows.
- The entity's ability to meet its obligations, pay dividends, and finance growth from internal sources.
- The entity's need for external financing.
- The reasons for differences between net income and associated net cash receipts and payments.
- Both the cash and noncash aspects of the entity's investing and financing activities during the period.[1]

[1] "Statement of Cash Flows," *Statement of Financial Accounting Standards No. 95* (Stamford, Conn.: Financial Accounting Standards Board, 1987), paragraph 5.

Let's now take a closer look at the statement of cash flows by revisiting its essential activities and constructing the CMU statement of cash flows in a step-by-step manner. We'll conclude by discussing what you should look for when you examine any entity's statement of cash flows.

What Are the Parts of a Statement of Cash Flows?

You might recognize Figure 8-6 as the statement of cash flows for CMU from Chapter 3. A statement of cash flows contains up to four parts: one part each for the three fundamental business activities that affect cash—operating, investing, and financing—and a possible fourth part, a supplemental schedule businesses use to disclose significant noncash transactions, as shown at the bottom of Figure 8-6.

FIGURE 8-6

Cards & Memorabilia Unlimited's statement of cash flows

CARDS & MEMORABILIA UNLIMITED
Statement of Cash Flows
For the Year Ended December 31

Cash flows from operating activities		
Cash collected from customers	$ 84,200	
Cash paid for merchandise purchases	(27,000)	
Cash paid for leased space	(11,000)	
Cash paid for salary expense	(8,000)	
Cash paid for miscellaneous expenses	(4,250)	
Interest received	275	
Interest paid	(200)	
Net cash provided by operating activities		$34,025
Cash flows from investing activities		
Proceeds from sale of equipment	1,350	
Payment of security deposit	(2,000)	
Acquisition of equipment	(17,000)	
Net cash used in investing activities		(17,650)
Cash flows from financing activities		
Contributions by owner	30,000	
Proceeds from bank credit line	5,000	
Repayment of bank credit line	(5,000)	
Withdrawals by owner	(8,100)	
Net cash provided by financing activities		21,900
Net increase in cash		38,275
Cash in checking account at beginning of year		–0–
Cash in checking and savings accounts at end of year		$38,275

Supplemental schedule of noncash investing and financing activities

Computer equipment costing $4,000 was acquired in exchange for a two-year promissory note.

Figure 8-7 provides the most common cash receipt and cash payment transactions into which operating, investing, and financing activities can be divided. Thus, Figure 8-7 is generic; it is an illustration that can apply to all statements of cash flow.

In Chapter 2, you learned about each of the three fundamental business activities as well as the fact that each activity can be divided into two stages: an initiation stage and a completion stage. Recall that these activities were introduced in the order they

FIGURE 8-7

How all activities can be divided into cash receipt and cash payment transactions*

Operating

Cash receipts

From sale of goods or services

From returns on loans (interest revenue) and investments in stock (dividend revenue)

Cash payments

To suppliers for inventory

To employees for services

To other suppliers for other expenses

To governments for taxes

To lenders for interest expense

Investing

Cash receipts

From sale of property, plant, and equipment

From sale of a business unit

From sale of investments in stocks or bonds (other than cash equivalents)

From collection of loans made by the entity

Cash payments

To acquire property, plant, and equipment

To acquire a business

To acquire investments in stocks or bonds

To make loans to another entity

Financing

Cash receipts

From the sale of capital stock

From the issuance or sale of bonds, mortgages, notes, and other short or long-term borrowings

Cash payments

To acquire treasury stock

To shareholders as dividends

To repay amounts borrowed—includes amounts related to short-term debt, long-term debt, and capitalized lease obligations

*Adapted from Ernst & Whinney Financial Reporting Developments, "Statement of Cash Flows, *FASB Exposure Draft*," Ernst and Whinney, October 1986.

are likely to occur within a business, that is, financing, investing, and operating. Be sure to notice, however, that the statement of cash flows reports these activities in the order of their relative importance to decision makers, that is, operating, investing, and financing. In the following three sections, we'll review these activities, the stages of these activities, and the balance sheet accounts associated with each activity.

Financing Activities

As shown in Figure 8-8, you initiate **financing activities** when you obtain money and other resources from short-term nontrade (e.g., bank) creditors, long-term creditors, and owners. These sources of assets are sometimes called the *capital markets*. The balance sheet accounts created when you initiate financing activities include any current liability account that represents borrowing from a financial institution, noncurrent liability (creditors'), and owner equity (owners') accounts. You complete financing activities when you repay or otherwise settle amounts owed to short-term bank creditors and long-term creditors and when you provide owners with a return on, and a return of, their investment. Financing activities provide money that is used in both investing and operating activities.

FIGURE 8-8 How financing, investing, and operating activities are initiated and completed

(1)

How do you initiate a financing activity?	How do you complete a financing activity?	Balance sheet accounts created by this activity
Obtain money and other resources from short-term nontrade creditors, long-term creditors, and owners	Repay or settle your debts and provide a return **on** and a return **of** the owner investment	Current liabilities such as credit lines and notes; noncurrent liabilities such as notes, bonds, leases, and pensions; all owner equities

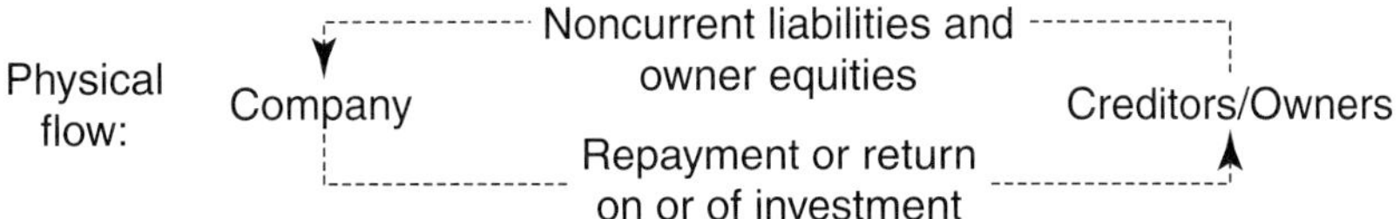

(2)

How do you initiate an investing activity?	How do you complete an investing activity?	Balance sheet accounts created by this activity
Make loans or buy investment securities and property, plant, and equipment	Collect on the loans or sell investment securities and property, plant, and equipment	Noncurrent assets such as notes receivable; investments; property, plant, and equipment

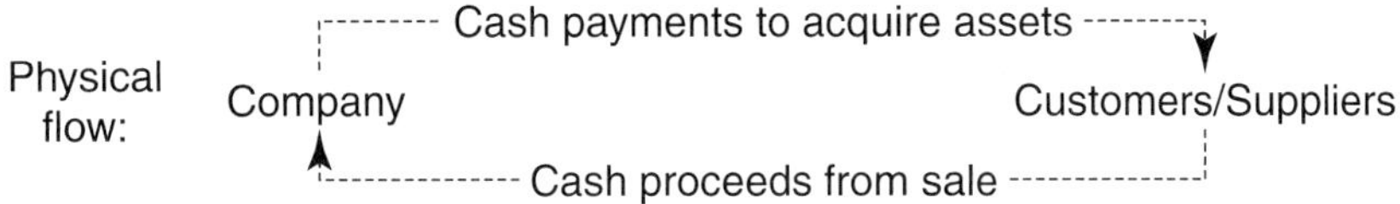

(3)

How do you initiate an operating activity?	How do you complete an operating activity?	Balance sheet accounts created by this activity
Purchase or produce goods and services for sale	Deliver the goods or perform the services as you consume the costs of producing these sales	Current assets and current liabilities such as accounts receivable, inventory, prepayments, accounts payable, advances from customers, and so on

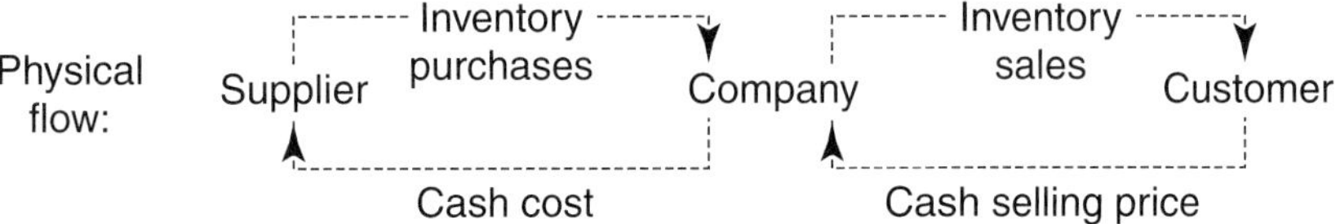

Investing Activities

As shown in Figure 8-8, you initiate **investing activities** when you apply the money obtained from financing activity transactions to long-term, nonoperating activity transactions within the entity, such as making loans or buying investment securities or property, plant, and equipment. For example, a manufacturer's purchase of computers for use in its corporate office represents an investing activity in productive equipment. The accounts that are created when you initiate investing activities are found in the noncurrent asset section of the balance sheet. You complete investing activities either when you collect on the loans you have made or sell investment securities or property, plant, and equipment. Investing activities usually provide the productive capacity or long-term asset base with which to engage in operating activities.

Operating Activities

As shown in Figure 8-8, you initiate **operating activities** when you apply the money obtained from financing activities and the sale of long-term assets obtained in investing activities either to purchase or produce goods and services for sale. The accounts that are created when you initiate operating activities are found in the current asset and current liability sections of the balance sheet. Operating activities are substantially completed when goods are delivered or sold and when services are performed. Cash flows from operating activities are generally the cash effects of transactions and other events that determine accrual basis net income. Don't forget that profitable operating activities reinvested in the business or retained earnings are an additional source of financing. Next, let's examine transactions that simultaneously affect two activities at once.

Noncash Investing and Financing Activities

Most investing and financing activities are associated with the payment or receipt of cash. For example, if you purchase (invest in) a building, you pay cash to the building's owner. Or if you retire a bond issue (financing) you pay cash to the bondholders. Occasionally, however, a firm enters into a noncash transaction that simultaneously involves both an investing activity and a financing activity. When such significant noncash exchanges of assets and/or claims to those assets are made, the accounting profession requires that these **noncash investing and financing activities** be disclosed to ensure that users do not overlook such potentially relevant information. Let's look at three examples of such noncash transactions or what are called direct exchanges to help you distinguish them from the more common investing or financing activities in which cash is involved. A **direct exchange** is any noncash exchange of noncurrent assets and/or noncurrent claims against assets. Whenever you decompose a direct exchange transaction into its fundamental elements, as we do in these three examples, you will discover that a direct exchange is, in substance, an investing and/or financing activity. Although direct exchange transactions do not, by definition, affect cash, they must be disclosed in the statement of cash flows.

Example 1: Exchange of Noncurrent Assets Suppose a sporting goods manufacturer desires to acquire $200,000 of equipment but is short of cash. The manufacturer could sacrifice a portion of its investment in the stock of other companies worth $200,000 to acquire the needed equipment. The transaction analysis of this transaction would be:

Asset Account Title	Assets	=	Liabilities	+	Owner's Equity	Source of Asset Account Title	Activity
Equipment	200,000						Investing
Investment in Stock	(200,000)						Investing

Although this transaction does not affect cash, it does involve the initiation of an investing activity (equipment purchase) and the completion of an investing activity (investment reduction).

Example 2: Exchange of Noncurrent Sources of Assets It is not uncommon for a cash-poor company that needs to retire debt to issue shares of its own stock in return for a reduction of that debt. Assume, for example, that a promising software company issues shares of its stock to a financial institution to settle a two-year $100,000 note payable.

Asset Account Title	Assets	=	Liabilities	+	Owner's Equity	Source of Asset Account Title	Activity
					100,000	Common Stock	Financing
			(100,000)			Notes Payable	Financing

Although this transaction does not affect cash, it does initiate a financing activity (stock issuance) and complete a financing activity (debt liquidation).

Example 3: Noncurrent Asset Exchanged for Noncurrent Source of Assets Since few companies can pay for large asset purchases entirely with cash, it is not uncommon to finance such purchases in part or in whole with debt. Assume, for example, that a manufacturing company acquires land worth $50,000 in exchange for signing a three-year note payable.

Asset Account Title	Assets	=	Liabilities	+	Owner's Equity	Source of Asset Account Title	Activity
Land	50,000						Investing
			50,000			Notes Payable	Financing

Although this transaction does not affect cash, it does initiate an investing activity (purchase of land) as well as a financing activity (incurrence of debt).

It is easier to visualize the true substance of Example 3's exchange of land for a note payable if you imagine that cash is used as an intermediary account in the following hypothetical two-part transaction sequence:

Asset Account Title	Assets	=	Liabilities	+	Owner's Equity	Source of Asset Account Title	Activity
(1) Cash	50,000		50,000			Notes Payable	Financing
(2) Land Cash	50,000 (50,000)						Investing

Although both analyses of Example 3 are correct, the latter two–part analysis shows more clearly that both a financing and an investing activity exist. Nevertheless, the net effect on cash is still zero because the cash borrowed is immediately paid to purchase the land. Although this transaction does not affect cash, it does represent an investing and financing activity, and thus it should be reported in the statement of cash flows.

Creating the Cards & Memorabilia Unlimited Statement of Cash Flows

Now that you have completed the preceding overview of the different parts of the statement of cash flows, you are ready to prepare this statement for CMU.

Classifying Transactions A_1 through Z

Let's begin by revisiting each of Cards & Memorabilia Unlimited's first-year transactions—specifically transactions A_1 to Z—to determine which transactions qualify for inclusion in the statement of cash flows. Once again, you'll use the technique of transaction analysis. This time, however, you will use it to classify CMU's transactions into the three fundamental business activities rather than to analyze assets and sources of assets. Transaction B is the only transaction not falling into one of the three activities because it represents a $6,000 transfer from a checking account to a savings account (recall from earlier in this chapter that a savings account is a cash equivalent).[2] That is, Transaction B represents an internal transfer within the Cash account and is, therefore, not reported in a statement of cash flows.

All remaining CMU transactions can be classified into one of the three fundamental business activities. In fact, all three activities are filled by the time the fourth CMU transaction is considered. First, Transaction A_1 is a cash financing activity in which Susan obtained money to start the business. Next, Transaction C_1 is a noncash investing activity in which store equipment was acquired for long-term use in the business. Last, Transaction D is a cash operating activity in which merchandise was acquired to be resold at a price higher than its cost.

Before you read on, see if you can correctly classify Transactions E through Z into one of the three fundamental business activities and if you can complete the statement of cash flows section of Figure 8-9. First, look at each transaction and decide what kind of activity the transaction represents using Figures 8-7 and 8-8 to help you. If you do not understand the nature of a transaction well enough to immediately connect it to an activity, use the list of noncash balance sheet accounts in Figure 8-8 for help. Recall some current liabilities, noncurrent liabilities, and owner equities represent financing activities; noncurrent assets represent investing activities; and most current assets and current liabilities represent operating activities.

Transaction E: Susan's payment of a lease security deposit in Transaction E is clearly not a financing activity since Cards & Memorabilia Unlimited obtains no money from creditors or owners. Likewise, a deposit that secures a 36-month lease is different in nature from the monthly rental payments that are a regular part of an entity's operating activities. Thus, Transaction E represents a cash investing activity. Suppose, however, that you were not able to use this process of elimination to identify Transaction E. An acceptable, alternative approach would be to recognize that the account Security Deposit Receivable (Other Receivables in Figure 8-9) is a noncurrent asset—it will not be converted back to cash for 36 months—that is created only by initiating an investing activity.

Transaction C_2: Transactions C_1 and C_2 represent the first and second stages, respectively, of an investing activity that has been initiated. In Transaction C_1, Susan acquired the equipment; in Transaction C_2, she paid for the equipment. In other words, Susan does not fully initiate an investing activity until she pays cash for the equipment. If Susan had paid cash at the same time she acquired the equipment, then the initiation of the investing activity would have had one and not two stages. Susan will complete this investing activity when she sells or otherwise disposes of the equipment.

Transactions F & K_1: Susan's borrowing money in Transaction F initiates an obligation with a financial institution, that is, a financing activity; her repayment of that same credit line loan in Transaction K_1 completes the financing activity.

---

[2] To avoid confusion in Chapter 2, we described this transaction as a noncash investing activity because we had not yet defined the term *cash equivalent*. Although we no longer refer to Transaction B as an investing activity, either interpretation is acceptable since neither treatment reports this transaction in a statement of cash flows.

Transaction G: Acquiring merchandise on account represents the first stage of an operating activity. To fully initiate this operating activity, Susan must pay her supplier. To complete this operating activity, Susan must not only sell the merchandise but also collect cash for it.

Transaction H: Acquiring the van in exchange for cash fully initiates an investing activity. This transaction is included in investing rather than operating activities because the asset acquired belongs in the noncurrent asset category called Property, Plant, and Equipment.

Transaction I: Receiving cash advances from customers is an operating activity that has not been initiated (Susan has neither obtained nor paid for the merchandise) and that is not fully completed. That is, cash has been received, but the critical sales event signaling completion of an operating activity has not occurred. You also know that this transaction is classified under operating activities because the Advances from Customers account is a current liability unrelated to borrowing. This transaction will be fully completed when merchandise is delivered or services are rendered.

Transaction J_1: Paying for merchandise acquired on account fully initiates an operating activity that will be completed when the merchandise is sold. You also know that this transaction is classified under operating activities because the Accounts Payable account is a current liability unrelated to borrowing.

Transaction J_2: This transaction represents a reclassification of an old transaction rather than a new transaction. That is, Susan replaces one account associated with an operating activity, Accounts Payable, with another account called Notes Payable. Thus, transaction J_2 is an operating activity.

Transaction L: This transaction represents a noncash financing and investing activity, or *direct exchange*. That is, the purchase of store equipment, a noncurrent asset, represents the initiation of an investing activity, whereas the incurrence of a noncurrent liability represents the initiation of a financing activity.

Since an income statement reports the results of operations, it should come as no surprise that revenue and expense transactions are classified as operating activities. Thus, the great majority of the following transactions are classified under operating activities because they were introduced during Chapter 6's in-depth look at the income statement. Nonetheless, each of these transactions (M to W and A_2) will be analyzed as thoroughly as transactions A_1 to L.

Transaction M: Cash sales of goods or services represent the full completion of an operating activity. Since such sales include cash, they must be reported in the statement of cash flows.

Transaction N: As you have already learned, credit sales of goods or services are reported as revenues in the income statement because they represent substantial completion of an operating activity. You can confirm that a credit sale is classified as an operating activity by noting that a current asset, accounts receivable, is created by this transaction. With few exceptions, current assets and current liabilities are associated with operating activities. A credit sale, however, is not reported in the statement of cash flows because it neither involves cash nor represents a direct exchange.

Transaction O_1: The earnings of $275 derived from the $6,000 in CMU's savings account represents interest revenue and is, therefore, treated as an operating activity. The accounting profession treats interest revenue this way because it is included in the income statement.

Transaction P: The payment of monthly rent enables a business to produce goods and/or services for sale. Thus, this transaction is the initiation of an operating activity. An additional reason to classify Transaction P as an operating activity is because an expense is created.

FIGURE 8-9

Classification of transactions A_1–Z into statement of cash flow activities

	Assets							=	Liabilities				+	Owner Equities		Statement of Cash Flows		
																Activities		
	Cash Checking	Cash Savings	Accts. Recvb.	Mdse. Inven.	Other Recvb.	Store Equip.	Accum. Depr.		Accts. Payb.	Cred. Line Payb.	Advn. From Cust.	Note Payb.		Contrib. Capital	Retained Earnings	Financing	Investing	Operating
A_1	30,000													30,000		√		
B	(6,000)	6,000															NOT APPLICABLE	
C_1						10,000			10,000								√	
D	(15,000)			15,000														√
E	(2,000)				2,000													
C_2	(10,000)								(10,000)									
F	5,000									5,000								
G				18,000					18,000									
H	(7,000)					7,000												
I	6,000										6,000							
J_1	(12,000)								(12,000)									
J_2									(6,000)			6,000[a]						
K_1	(5,000)									(5,000)								
L						4,000						4,000[b]						
M	63,200														63,200			
N			20,000												20,000			
O_1	275														275			
P	(11,000)														(11,000)			
Q_1							(300)								(300)			
R	1,350					(2,000)	300								(350)			
S	(8,000)														(8,000)			
K_2	(200)														(200)			
T	(4,250)														(4,250)			
U				(30,000)											(30,000)			
V	15,000		(15,000)															
W	(8,100)														(8,100)			
A_2				10,000										10,000				
O_2					25										25			
X									750[c]						(750)			
Y									350						(350)			
Q_2							(2,300)								(2,300)			
Z											(4,000)				4,000			
Σ	$32,275	6,000	5,000	13,000	2,025	19,000	(2,300)	=	$1,100	–0–	2,000	10,000	+	$40,000	$21,900			
				$75,000				=			$13,100		+		$61,900			

[a]Reported as current liability; [b]Reported as noncurrent liability; [c]Reported as Salaries Payable

Transaction detail

A_1	$30,000 cash is contributed by the owner who opens a business checking account.
B	$6,000 cash is withdrawn from the checking account to open a business savings account.
C_1	$10,000 worth of store equipment is acquired with a credit card.
D	$15,000 cash is paid to acquire merchandise inventory.
E	$2,000 cash is paid to the landlord for the security deposit on the store lease.
C_2	$10,000 cash is paid in full to settle the credit card obligation made on January 4.
F	$5,000 cash is borrowed with a bank credit line bearing interest at an 8% rate.
G	$18,000 worth of additional merchandise is acquired on account.
H	$7,000 cash is paid to acquire a used van with a 5-year useful life for the business.
I	$6,000 cash is collected from customers before any goods or services are provided.
J_1	$12,000 cash is paid to reduce accounts payable.
J_2	$6,000 of accounts payable is converted to a 6% interest-bearing note payable due on March 31.
K_1	$5,000 cash is paid in full to settle the credit line loan made on July 1.
L	$4,000 worth of a computer and printer is acquired by signing a 2-year promissory note.
M	$63,200 of cash sales are made to customers throughout the year.
N	$20,000 of revenue is earned on account—$19,400 for customer credit sales throughout the year and $600 for teaching a course.
O_1	$275 interest is earned from January 2 to December 2 on $6,000 of savings bearing 5% interest.
P	$1,000 cash is paid for office rent due the first day of each month beginning February 1.
Q_1	$300 of depreciation is recorded to recognize the use of equipment sold on September 30.
R	$2,000 worth of the store equipment bought on January 4 for $10,000 is sold for $1,350.
S	$8,000 cash is paid to employees for work performed through the year's last payday.
K_2	$200 cash is paid for interest due on $5,000 borrowed on July 1 at 8% and repaid on December 31.
T	$4,250 cash is paid for miscellaneous expenses incurred throughout the year.
U	$30,000 of cost of goods sold is determined by taking a physical count of inventory.
V	$15,000 cash is collected from customers throughout the year for amounts owed.
W	$8,100 cash is withdrawn from the business by the owner throughout the year.
A_2	$10,000 worth of merchandise is contributed by an individual for a business interest.
O_2	$25 of interest is earned but uncollected on a $6,000 savings account bearing 5% interest.
X	$750 of salaries expense is incurred but unpaid.
Y	$350 of miscellaneous expense is incurred but unpaid.
Q_2	$2,300 of depreciation is recorded on the use of unsold equipment.
Z	$4,000 worth of merchandise is delivered to customers who paid in advance.

FIGURE 8-10

Classification of transactions A_1–Z into statement of cash flow activities

	Assets							=	Liabilities				+	Owner Equities		Statement of Cash Flows		
																Activities		
	Cash Checking	Cash Savings	Accts. Recvb.	Mdse. Inven.	Other Recvb.	Store Equip.	Accum. Depr.		Accts. Payb.	Cred. Line Payb.	Advn. From Cust.	Note Payb.		Contrib. Capital	Retained Earnings	Financing	Investing	Operating
A_1	30,000													30,000		√		
B	(6,000)	6,000															NOT APPLICABLE	
C_1						10,000			10,000								√	
D	(15,000)			15,000														√
E	(2,000)				2,000												√	
C_2	(10,000)								(10,000)								√	
F	5,000									5,000						√		
G				18,000					18,000									√
H	(7,000)					7,000											√	
I	6,000										6,000							√
J_1	(12,000)								(12,000)									√
J_2									(6,000)			6,000[a]						√
K_1	(5,000)									(5,000)						√		
L						4,000						4,000[b]				√	√	
M	63,200														63,200			√
N			20,000												20,000			√
O_1	275														275			√
P	(11,000)														(11,000)			√
Q_1							(300)								(300)			√
R	1,350					(2,000)	300								(350)		√	
S	(8,000)														(8,000)			√
K_2	(200)														(200)			√
T	(4,250)														(4,250)			√
U				(30,000)											(30,000)			√
V	15,000		(15,000)															√
W	(8,100)														(8,100)	√		
A_2				10,000										10,000		√		
O_2					25									25			√	
X									750[c]						(750)			√
Y									350						(350)			√
Q_2							(2,300)								(2,300)			√
Z											(4,000)				4,000			√
Σ	$32,275	6,000	5,000	13,000	2,025	19,000	(2,300)	=	$1,100	–0–	2,000	10,000	+	$40,000	$21,900			
				$75,000				=			$13,100		+	$61,900				

[a]Reported as current liability; [b]Reported as noncurrent liability; [c]Reported as Salaries Payable

Transaction detail

A_1	$30,000 cash is contributed by the owner who opens a business checking account.
B	$6,000 cash is withdrawn from the checking account to open a business savings account.
C_1	$10,000 worth of store equipment is acquired with a credit card.
D	$15,000 cash is paid to acquire merchandise inventory.
E	$2,000 cash is paid to the landlord for the security deposit on the store lease.
C_2	$10,000 cash is paid in full to settle the credit card obligation made on January 4.
F	$5,000 cash is borrowed with a bank credit line bearing interest at an 8% rate.
G	$18,000 worth of additional merchandise is acquired on account.
H	$7,000 cash is paid to acquire a used van with a 5-year useful life for the business.
I	$6,000 cash is collected from customers before any goods or services are provided.
J_1	$12,000 cash is paid to reduce accounts payable.
J_2	$6,000 of accounts payable is converted to a 6% interest-bearing note payable due on March 31.
K_1	$5,000 cash is paid in full to settle the credit line loan made on July 1.
L	$4,000 worth of a computer and printer is acquired by signing a 2-year promissory note.
M	$63,200 of cash sales are made to customers throughout the year.
N	$20,000 of revenue is earned on account—$19,400 for customer credit sales throughout the year and $600 for teaching a course.
O_1	$275 interest is earned from January 2 to December 2 on $6,000 of savings bearing 5% interest.
P	$1,000 cash is paid for office rent due the first day of each month beginning February 1.
Q_1	$300 of depreciation is recorded to recognize the use of equipment sold on September 30.
R	$2,000 worth of the store equipment bought on January 4 for $10,000 is sold for $1,350.
S	$8,000 cash is paid to employees for work performed through the year's last payday.
K_2	$200 cash is paid for interest due on $5,000 borrowed on July 1 at 8% and repaid on December 31.
T	$4,250 cash is paid for miscellaneous expenses incurred throughout the year.
U	$30,000 of cost of goods sold is determined by taking a physical count of inventory.
V	$15,000 cash is collected from customers throughout the year for amounts owed.
W	$8,100 cash is withdrawn from the business by the owner throughout the year.
A_2	$10,000 worth of merchandise is contributed by an individual for a business interest.
O_2	$25 of interest is earned but uncollected on a $6,000 savings account bearing 5% interest.
X	$750 of salaries expense is incurred but unpaid.
Y	$350 of miscellaneous expense is incurred but unpaid.
Q_2	$2,300 of depreciation is recorded on the use of unsold equipment.
Z	$4,000 worth of merchandise is delivered to customers who paid in advance.

Transaction Q_1: In this transaction, a portion of the store equipment's service potential has expired. The resulting depreciation expense is included in the income statement. Although depreciation expense is therefore classified as an operating activity, it is not a cash outflow. As a result, it is not reported in the statement of cash flows.

Transaction R: A cash sale of equipment fully completes an investing activity that was initiated when the same equipment was acquired. Note that a noncurrent asset, Store Equipment, is affected by this transaction.

Transaction S: Payments to employees for services performed represent an operating activity (refer to Figure 8-7). This classification is supported by the fact that an expense is created.

Transaction K_2: Although a return *of* an amount borrowed is itself clearly a financing activity, the accounting profession classifies a return *on* the amount borrowed as an operating activity. Thus, a cash payment to lenders for interest expense—as in this transaction—represents an operating activity.

Transaction T: Payments to suppliers for miscellaneous expenses reduce several current liabilities and initiate an operating activity as described in Figure 8-7.

Transaction U: Although the recording of the cost of goods sold is clearly an expense transaction and, therefore, classified under the operating activity category, it is not a cash outflow. As a result, it is not reported in the statement of cash flows.

Transaction V: Collection of cash from earlier credit sales affects the accounts receivable account, a current asset (refer to Transaction N), and also represents full completion of an operating activity. Note that this transaction is reported in the cash-basis statement of cash flows but not reported in the accrual-basis income statement.

Transaction W: Since a cash withdrawal by the owner is the exact opposite of a cash contribution by the owner (Transaction A_1), this transaction represents the completion of a financing activity associated with the owner equity Retained Earnings account.

Transaction A_2: Just as with Transaction A_1, this noncash contribution by an owner represents the initiation of a financing activity associated with the owner equity Contributed Capital account. Unlike Transaction A_1, however, this transaction increases merchandise inventory rather than cash. Thus, it will not be reported in the statement of cash flows.

Transactions O_2, X, Y, Q_2, and Z: As you learned in Chapter 7, each of these remaining transactions adjusts various revenue and expense accounts. Thus, they are automatically classified as operating activity transactions. By definition, however, these adjustments are implicit transactions that have no cash effect and, therefore, are not reported in the statement of cash flows. In fact, except for the direct exchange in Transaction L, only the amounts included under the cash column in Figure 8-9 are reported in Cards & Memorabilia Unlimited's statement of cash flows.

The effect of classifying each of Transactions A_1 through Z into its appropriate activity is shown in Figure 8-10. Be sure your own analysis agrees with this figure before you read on.

Reporting Transactions A_1 through Z in the Statement of Cash Flows

Your next step is to prepare the actual statement of cash flows for Cards & Memorabilia Unlimited. To do so, you only need information from five columns in Figure 8-10—the two cash columns, the Financing column, the Investing column, and the Operating column. Notice that Figure 8-11 represents the compression of Figure 8-10 into a more useful format for preparing a statement of cash flows. In particular, Figure 8-11

FIGURE 8-11 Final classification of transactions A_1–Z into statement of cash flow activities

Statement of Cash Flows

	Transactions	Financing (Activities)	Investing (Activities)	Operating (Activities)
A_1	$30,000 cash is contributed by the owner who opens a business checking account.	$30,000		
B	$6,000 cash is withdrawn from the checking account to open a business savings account.	—	—	—
C_1	$10,000 worth of store equipment is acquired with a credit card.		√	
D	$15,000 cash is paid to acquire merchandise inventory.			$(15,000)
E	$2,000 cash is paid to the landlord for the security deposit on the store lease.		$ (2,000)	
C_2	$10,000 cash is paid in full to settle the credit card obligation made on January 4.		(10,000)	
F	$5,000 cash is borrowed with a bank credit line bearing interest at an 8% rate.	5,000		
G	$18,000 worth of additional merchandise is acquired on account.			√
H	$7,000 cash is paid to acquire a used van with a 5-year useful life for the business.		(7,000)	
I	$6,000 cash is collected from customers before any goods or services are provided.			6,000
J_1	$12,000 cash is paid to reduce accounts payable.			(12,000)
J_2	$6,000 of accounts payable is converted to a 6% interest-bearing note payable due on 3/31.			√
K_1	$5,000 cash is paid in full to settle the credit line loan made on July 1.	(5,000)		
L	$4,000 worth of a computer and printer is acquired by signing a 2-year promissory note.	√	√	
M	$63,200 of cash sales are made to customers throughout the year.			63,200
N	$20,000 of revenue is earned on account—$19,400 for customer credit sales throughout the year and $600 for teaching a course.			√
O_1	$275 interest is earned from 1/2–12/2 on $6,000 of savings bearing 5% interest.			275
P	$1,000 cash is paid for office rent due the first day of each month beginning February 1.			(11,000)
Q_1	$300 of depreciation is recorded to recognize the use of equipment sold on September 30.			√
R	$2,000 worth of the store equipment bought on January 4 for $10,000 is sold for $1,350.		1,350	
S	$8,000 cash is paid to employees for work performed through the year's last payday.			(8,000)
K_2	$200 cash is paid for interest due on $5,000 borrowed on 7/1 at 8% and repaid on 12/31.			(200)
T	$4,250 cash is paid for miscellaneous expenses incurred throughout the year.			(4,250)
U	$30,000 of cost of goods sold is determined by taking a physical count of inventory.			√
V	$15,000 cash is collected from customers throughout the year for amounts owed.			15,000
W	$8,100 cash is withdrawn from the business by the owner throughout the year.	(8,100)		
A_2	$10,000 worth of merchandise is contributed by an individual for a business interest.	√		
O_2	$25 of interest is earned but uncollected on a $6,000 savings account bearing 5% interest.			√
X	$750 of salaries expense is incurred but unpaid.			√
Y	$350 of miscellaneous expense is incurred but unpaid.			√
Q_2	$2,300 of depreciation is recorded on the use of unsold equipment.			√
Z	$4,000 worth of merchandise is delivered to customers who paid in advance.			√
Σ		**$21,900**	**$(17,650)**	**$ 34,025**
	Net cash inflows during year		**$ 38,275**	

allows you to clearly see the analytical steps used to report the cash flow effects of Transactions A_1 through Z. These steps are summarized in Performance Objective 7, which you first saw in Chapters 2 and 3.

YOUR PERFORMANCE OBJECTIVE 7

a. **Define** the terms *financing activities, investing activities,* and *operating activities.*
b. **Classify** any accounting transaction into one of these activities or a noncash investing and financing activity.
c. **Classify** any cash receipt or cash payment transaction into the appropriate activity as reported in the statement of cash flows.

Since you have now accounted for every one of Cards & Memorabilia Unlimited's transactions (Performance Objective 7(b)), you are now ready to satisfy Performance Objective 7(c) using Figure 8-11 for reference. Don't forget that Transaction B is merely a transfer of cash between the cash checking account and the cash savings account and its treatment as a cash equivalent prevents it from being treated as an activity.

Study Figure 8-11's Financing column. Note that Transactions F and K_1 are not only related but also involve identical amounts. Although it might be tempting to offset them against one another, you must report them both to comply with the principle of full disclosure. That is, you should include the $30,000 and $5,000 cash inflows as well as the $5,000 and $8,100 cash outflows in the financing section of your statement of cash flows.

Study Figure 8-11's Investing column. Note that Transaction C_2 is a cash outflow that completes the equipment acquisition in Transaction C_1. Since Transaction H also involves equipment acquired with cash, the combined cash effect of Transactions C_2 and H is to include a $17,000 investing activity in the statement of cash flows that should be labeled "acquisition of equipment." Since Transactions E and R are also included in the Investing column, they too must be reported in the investing activity section of the statement of cash flows.

Study Figure 8-11's Operating column. Note that for the convenience of the reader, three separate operating cash inflows (Transactions I, M, and V) should be grouped into the fundamental *cash collected from customers* transaction. Likewise, two separate operating cash outflows (Transactions D and J_1) should be grouped into the *cash paid for merchandise purchases* transaction. Each of the remaining operating transactions—rent payments (Transaction P), salary payments (Transaction S), miscellaneous expense payments (Transaction T), interest received (Transaction O_1), and interest paid (Transaction K_2) are distinct and deserve a separate line in the statement of cash flows. Before you continue, verify that you can fully reconcile the analysis in Figure 8-11 with the completed statement of cash flows in Figure 8-6.

How Is Cash Flow from Operating Activities Reported?

Although cash flow information about each business activity is essential, operating cash flow transactions are generally the most numerous and interesting to users of the statement of cash flows. It is not an accident, for example, that operating cash flows are always reported first in U.S. statements of cash flow.

The accounting profession, through the Financial Accounting Standards Board (FASB), permits two alternative but equivalent methods of presenting operating activities, the direct and the indirect method. Simply stated the **direct method of reporting cash flow from operating activities** converts each accrual basis revenue and expense directly to the cash basis. It presents information about essential transactions such as cash collected from customers, cash paid for merchandise purchases, cash paid to employees, and interest and income taxes paid. The **indirect method of reporting cash flow from operating activities**, begins with accrual basis net income and adjusts it for revenues, expenses, gains, and losses that do not affect

Cash collected from customers	$ xx
Interest and dividends received	xx
Other operating cash receipts	xx
Cash paid to employees and other suppliers	(xx)
Interest paid	(xx)
Income taxes paid	(xx)
Other operating cash payments	(xx)
Net cash provided by operating activities	$ xx

FIGURE 8-12

Generic format of the operating activities section when the direct method is used

cash as well as for operating cash flows that are not reported on the accrual basis income statement. Although equivalent to the direct method, the indirect method's adjustments are less intuitive or logical, hence its name.

Although both the direct and indirect methods include the concept of an accrual to cash conversion, their formats are different. Study Figures 8-12 and 8-13. You should immediately see that the direct method is easier to interpret than the indirect method. For example, the direct method in Figure 8-12 includes recognizable transactions you have already studied (such as cash collected from customers) whereas the indirect method in Figure 8-13 includes little, if any, information that is intuitively understandable. For example, the indirect method essentially adds and subtracts combinations of transactions (such as expenses and losses not using cash) and changes in account balances (such as decreases in noncash current assets) to and from net income. Clearly, the indirect method does not directly present specific operating cash inflows and outflows. Let's now take a closer look at each of these methods.

Net income (accrual NI from income statement)		$xxx
Add: Net income adjustments		
Expenses and losses not using cash	xx	
Decreases in noncash current assets affecting operations	xx	
Increases in noncash current liabilities affecting operations	xx	xxx
		xxx
Deduct: Net income adjustments		
Revenues and gains not providing cash	(xx)	
Increases in noncash current assets affecting operations	(xx)	
Decreases in noncash current liabilities affecting operations	(xx)	(xxx)
Net cash provided by operating activities (Cash Net Income)		$xxx

FIGURE 8-13

Generic format of the operating activities section when the indirect method is used

What Is the Direct Method?

As you have just learned, the direct method of reporting cash flow from operations converts each accrual basis revenue and expense directly to the cash basis. Figure 8-12 illustrates the basic structure of the operating cash receipts and payments reported by the direct method. Because the indirect method has been used for so long, accountants who use the direct method must also present the indirect method in a format equivalent to Figure 8-13.

What Is the Indirect Method?

To review, the indirect method of reporting cash flow from operations begins with accrual basis net income and adjusts it for revenues, expenses, gains, and losses that do not affect cash as well as for operating cash flows that are not reported on the accrual

FIGURE 8-14

The operating activities section under the indirect method for Cards & Memorabilia Unlimited's statement of cash flows

Net income (accrual NI from income statement)		$30,000
Add: Net income adjustments		
Expenses and losses not using cash		
Depreciation expense	$2,600	
Loss on sale of equipment	350	$ 2,950
Decreases in noncash current assets		
Affecting operations		None
Increases in noncash current liabilities		
Affecting operations		
Accounts payable	350	
Salaries payable	750	
Deferred revenue	2,000	
Note payable	6,000	9,100
		42,050
Deduct: Net income adjustments		
Revenues and gains not providing cash		None
Increases in noncash current assets affecting operations		
Accounts receivable	(5,000)	
Merchandise inventory	(3,000)[1]	
Interest receivable	(25)	(8,025)
Decreases in noncash current liabilities affecting operations		None
Net cash provided by operating activities (Cash NI)		$34,025

[1]Although the current asset merchandise inventory actually increases by $13,000, only $3,000 of the increase affects operations. The difference of $10,000 is attributable to Transaction A_2. Recall that this transaction is a financing activity—it does not affect operating activities.

basis income statement. Cash flows from operating activities are the cash rather than accrual effects of transactions included in the determination of net income. Thus, if net income is initially reported, all noncash, accrual effects must be eliminated from it. Figure 8-13 shows the generic reconciliation format that is often used by accountants to report operating cash flows conversions from accrual basis net income (denoted as Accrual Net Income) to cash basis net income.

If you are a user of accounting information, you need only understand the general concept of the indirect method; if you are an accounting major you will learn how to prepare an indirect cash flow from operating activities section in a later course.

Cards & Memorabilia Unlimited: Comparing the Direct Method with the Indirect Method

Now that you have learned about both methods of reporting cash flow from operating activities, look back at Figure 8-6 and decide which method was used for CMU's statement of cash flows. You are right if you identify the direct method. George Wu advised Susan Newman to use the direct method because he knew that she could use it more effectively in evaluating CMU's performance than the indirect method. If Susan had used the indirect method, CMU's statement of cash flows for the first year of operations would look like Figure 8-14.

Compare the total net cash provided by operating activities in Figure 8-6 with the total in Figure 8-14. Notice that the same amount, $34,025, is reported in both the direct and indirect methods. Thus, it is clear that these very different looking formats do provide the same final operating cash figure.

You should now be able to see why the direct method's transactions are much easier to interpret than the miscellaneous account changes shown in the indirect method. For example, it is easy to see why cash collected from customers is added into the statement of cash flows. It is not intuitively obvious, however, why an increase in the accounts receivable account is deducted in a statement of cash flows.

Seeing how counter-intuitive the indirect method is, you might wonder why the indirect method was ever used and/or why it is still used today. Before 1988 the statement of cash flows was not required as part of every annual report. Instead, annual reports included the statement of changes in financial position, which used the indirect method almost exclusively. Due primarily to routine and habit, most companies have ignored the FASB's clear preference for the direct method and continue to use the indirect method.[3] Thus, although the direct method provides a more understandable view of a firm's operating activities and is, therefore, more relevant for decision making, it is seldom used in corporate annual reports. So why study the direct method? The reason, quite simply, is that its clarity allows users to more easily understand an entity's operating cash flows. Hopefully, companies will start to break with tradition and use the direct method more frequently in the future.

Corporate Examples of Statements of Cash Flows

Now that you have seen Cards & Memorabilia Unlimited's statement of cash flows, let's see how larger companies' statements of cash flows found in corporate annual reports might differ. Figure 8-15 is the statement of cash flows for Storage Technology Corporation, a manufacturer of computer hardware and related data communications products. Figure 8-16 is the statement of cash flows for the Target Corporation, America's fourth largest general merchandise retailer. Before you read further, study these two figures. What differences do you notice? *Hint:* Compare each of the fundamental business activities by company.

Congratulations if you noticed that Storage Technology Corporation reports its operating activities using the direct method, whereas Target reports its operating activities using the indirect method. In particular, you should notice that several of the items reported in the operating activities section for Storage Technology Corporation in Figure 8-15 are very similar to those in Figure 8-6 for Cards & Memorabilia Unlimited. The most meaningful difference between Figure 8-6 and 8-15 is that Storage Technology Corporation includes income tax cash flows, which are required in a corporation. Cards & Memorabilia Unlimited, as a partnership, does not itself pay income tax, as explained in the *Insight* titled "The Income Statement Known as Schedule C" in Chapter 6.

[3] *Accounting Trends and Techniques* (AICPA) reported that 593 of 600 companies used the indirect method in 2000.

FIGURE 8-15

An example of the direct method for reporting cash flow from operating activities

STORAGE TECHNOLOGY CORPORATION
Consolidated Statement of Cash Flows

	Year Ended	
	December 28, 2001	December 29, 2000
Operating Activities		
Cash received from customers	$2,083,280,000	$2,085,470,000
Cash paid to suppliers and employees	($1,842,709,000)	($1,773,014,000)
Cash received from (paid for) litigation and other special items	$19,730,000	($25,373,000)
Interest received	$10,189,000	$9,965,000
Interest paid	($5,917,000)	($15,126,000)
Income tax refunded	$1,522,000	$54,858,000
Net cash provided by operating activities	$266,095,000	$336,780,000
Investing Activities		
Purchase of property, plant, and equipment	($57,834,000)	($71,815,000)
Proceeds from sale of property, plant, and equipment	$114,000	$2,053,000
Other assets	$6,417,000	($8,921,000)
Net cash used in investing activities	($51,303,000)	($78,683,000)
Financing Activities		
Proceeds from (repayments of) credit facilities, net	($12,227,000)	($188,472,000)
Proceeds from employee stock plans	$18,043,000	$15,825,000
Proceeds from other debt	$2,305,000	$11,974,000
Repayment of company-owned life insurance policy loans	($30,414,000)	$0
Repayments of other debt	($9,289,000)	($27,729,000)
Repurchases of common stock	$0	$0
Net cash used in financing activities	($31,582,000)	($188,402,000)
Effect of exchange rate changes on cash	($9,724,000)	($5,385,000)
Increase (decrease) in cash and cash equivalents	$173,486,000	$64,310,000
Cash and cash equivalents at beginning of year	$279,731,000	$215,421,000
Cash and cash equivalents at end of year	$453,217,000	$279,731,000

FIGURE 8-16 An example of the indirect method for reporting cash flow from operating activities

TARGET CORPORATION
Consolidated Statements of Cash Flows
(millions)

	2000	1999	1998
Operating Activities			
Net earnings before extraordinary charges	**$1,264**	$1,185	$ 962
Reconciliation to cash flow:			
Depreciation and amortization	**940**	854	780
Deferred tax provision	**1**	75	(11)
Other noncash items affecting earnings	**237**	163	70
Changes in operating accounts providing/(requiring) cash:			
Receivable-backed securities	**(217)**	(184)	(42)
Sale of receivable-backed securities	**—**	—	400
Maturity of publicly held receivable-backed securities	**—**	—	(400)
Inventory	**(450)**	(323)	(198)
Other current assets	**(9)**	(54)	(60)
Other assets	**13**	(65)	(65)
Accounts payable	**62**	364	336
Accrued liabilities	**(23)**	100	75
Income taxes payable	**87**	166	40
Cash flow provided by operations	**1,905**	2,281	1,887
Investing Activities			
Expenditures for property and equipment	**(2,528)**	(1,918)	(1,657)
Proceeds from disposals of property and equipment	**57**	126	107
Acquisition of subsidiaries, net of cash received	**—**	—	(100)
Other	**(4)**	(15)	(5)
Cash flow required for investing activities	**(2,475)**	(1,807)	(1,655)
Net financing (requirements)/sources	**(570)**	474	232
Financing Activities			
Increase/(decrease) in notes payable, net	**245**	564	(305)
Additions to long-term debt	**2,000**	285	600
Reductions of long-term debt	**(806)**	(600)	(343)
Dividends paid	**(190)**	(195)	(178)
Repurchase of stock	**(585)**	(581)	—
Other	**42**	18	38
Cash flow provided by/(used for) financing activities	**706**	(509)	(188)
Net increase/(decrease) in cash and cash equivalents	**136**	(35)	44
Cash and cash equivalents at beginning of year	**220**	255	211
Cash and cash equivalents at end of year	**$ 356**	$ 220	$ 255

USER FOCUS

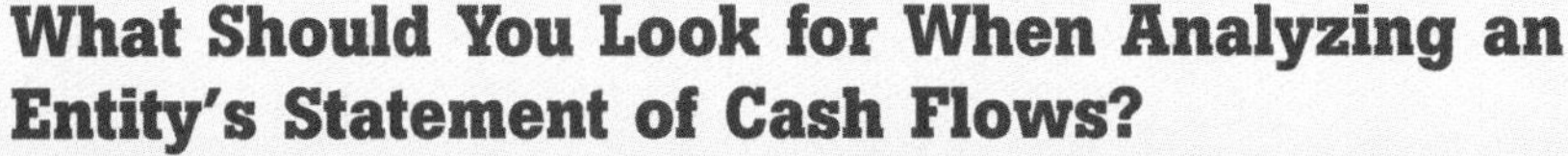

What Should You Look for When Analyzing an Entity's Statement of Cash Flows?

If you are an external user of an entity's financial statements, the first question you should ask when viewing its statement of cash flows is "What is the amount of cash flow from operations?" Answering this question is important because it helps you determine whether the company will be able to pay its bills as they come due solely from operations.

If, for example, cash receipts from operations are much larger than cash payments from operations, then the company is unlikely to consider outside financing. Study Figure 8-16. Target Corporation's cash flow from operations in both 1998 and 1999 was so large that it was able to buy significantly more plant and equipment than it sold and was not forced to incur large amounts of new debt. Likewise Storage Technology Corporation's 2000 cash inflow from operations was large enough for it to make nearly a $200 million repayment on credit facility debt (financing activities) and purchase nearly $72 million of property, plant, and equipment. In 2001, however, its decrease in cash inflows from operating activities forced it to significantly curtail those credit facility debt repayments (only about $12 million).

Thus, if you study a company's cash flow from operations first, you will see that its particular mix of investing and financing transactions is usually directly related to the relative strength of its operations.

As the following *Insight* suggests, you have reason to worry about a company's well-being if it bases its decisions solely on balance sheet ratios instead of supplementing its analyses with information about cash flow from operations.

INSIGHT

How Cash Flow Provides a More Complete Financial Analysis

How can the statement of cash flows help you make better decisions? One way is to use it in conjunction with ratios. Despite their widespread use, ratios *by themselves* are not always reliable measurements of an entity's financial well-being. In particular, do not rely solely upon balance sheet ratios, such as the current ratio (current assets/current liabilities). Why? Since these ratios are calculated as of the beginning and end of the period, they are static and might, therefore, not accurately represent a company's performance during the period.

For example, if Susan knows that Cards & Memorabilia Unlimited has a current ratio of 2.52 and an acid test ratio of 2.31, can she be sure that CMU has an adequate margin of safety? Think about cash flow. What if CMU's cash flow from operations is highly seasonal or actually declining, or what if CMU's operating performance is impaired by consuming current assets to pay off current liabilities? In these cases, relying only on balance sheet ratios is likely to prevent her from correctly assessing CMU's financial well-being.

Thus, in general, you should never rely on a single measure such as net income or the current ratio as a substitute for a comprehensive analysis of a company. In particular, the **insight** you should gain here is that the static, point-in-time components of balance sheet ratios are particularly prone to misinterpretation. If you're going to use these ratios, be sure you supplement your analysis with the statement of cash flows and ratios that include income statement accounts.

How to Prepare a Bank Reconciliation

USER FOCUS

Although you already know about the essential nature of a bank reconciliation, reading this extended *User Focus* will enable you to actually prepare one. Perhaps the most compelling reason to learn how to prepare a bank reconciliation is that it can help you manage your own money. If you have ever avoided balancing a checkbook or struggled to reconcile a checkbook balance with a bank statement balance, you will probably find preparing a bank reconciliation the most valuable personal financial skill you learn in this course.

What Is a Reconciling Item?

The secret of how to easily and quickly prepare a bank reconciliation lies in truly *understanding*, not memorizing, what a reconciling item is. As illustrated by Figure 8-5, a **reconciling item** is a transaction that one version of cash (either the bank's records or the entity's book records) knows about and includes in its cash balance but the other version of cash knows nothing about. There are only two types of reconciling items. The first, a **bank reconciling item**, is any transaction that the entity knows about but the bank doesn't know about as of a particular date. The second, **a book reconciling item**, is any transaction that the bank knows about but the entity doesn't know about as of a particular date. To better understand these two types of reconciling items, let's look at some specific examples.

Bank Reconciling Items

Figure 8-17 illustrates three typical bank reconciling items for a sample entity.

FIGURE 8-17

Bank reconciling items in the adjusted balances bank reconciliation format

SAMPLE ENTITY
Bank Reconciliation
For the Month Ended December 31

Balance per bank			$856
Add:	Deposit in transit		144
Deduct:	Outstanding check	$(300)	
	Bank error: unrecorded payment	(100)	(400)
Adjusted balance per bank			$600

Notice that these three items are placed below the balance per bank of $856—the bank record of cash reported on the monthly bank statement. The first such bank reconciling item occurs quite frequently and is called a **deposit in transit**. If, for example, an entity receives $144 but has either not yet deposited it in the bank or the bank has not yet recorded or posted the entity's deposit to its records, the $144 is a deposit in transit. The entity knows about and has recorded a cash increase of $144. That is, the cash is included in the entity's record of cash, or balance per books. The bank, however, is not yet aware of this $144 cash increase and has not included it in its record of cash, or balance per bank. To update the bank's record of cash with this transaction, you simply need to add it to the balance per bank:

Balance per bank	$ 856
Add: Deposit in transit	144
Adjusted balance per bank	$1,000

Do not simply memorize that deposits in transit are added to the balance per bank. Instead, think as follows: When I add the *deposit in transit* to the balance per bank, I am simply bringing the bank up to date with information about the entity it does not yet have. The entity (or books) has recorded (that is, knows about) the $144 but the bank does not. As soon as both the entity (cash receipt) and the bank (cash deposit) know about this transaction, it is reconciled.

Another commonly used bank reconciling item illustrated in Figure 8-17 is an **outstanding check**. This reconciling item occurs when an entity writes a check that has not yet cleared the bank. In this case, our sample entity knows about and has recorded a cash decrease of $300. That is, it has deducted $300 from its balance per books. The bank, however, does not know about this $300 cash decrease because the check has not yet been presented to it for payment. Thus, the bank has not included it in its record of cash, or balance per bank. To reconcile this transaction, you simply need to deduct $300 from the balance per bank:

Balance per bank	$856
Deduct: Outstanding check	(300)
Adjusted balance per bank	$556

Do not be tempted to memorize that outstanding checks are always deducted from the balance per bank. Instead, think as follows: when I deduct the outstanding check from the balance per bank, I am simply bringing the bank up to date with information it does not yet have. The entity knows about the $300 cash payment, but the bank does not. As soon as both the entity and the bank know about this cash payment, the transaction is reconciled.

As the past two examples illustrate, a bank reconciling item is a transaction that the entity knows about but the bank doesn't as of a particular date. A recording error made by the bank is a variation of this type of reconciling item. In this case, the entity records a transaction correctly that the bank records incorrectly. An example of such an error shown in Figure 8-17 might occur when an entity named Silicon Valley Group records a $100 cash payment to its supplier, but the entity's bank mistakenly records this payment as having been made by Silicon Graphics, Inc. In this case, the entity knows about and records a $100 cash decrease. The bank, however, has not and will not record this cash decrease properly until after the date of the reconciliation when it either detects the error itself or is alerted to the error by either or both of the entities. To properly account for this bank initiated error on your bank reconciliation, you deduct the $100 cash payment from the balance per bank:

Balance per bank	$856
Deduct: Bank error: unrecorded payment	(100)
Adjusted balance per bank	$756

When you deduct the correct cash payment from the balance per bank, you are simply correcting the bank's error. Think of this as though you were recording a transaction that the entity knows about but the bank does not. As soon as both the entity and the bank know about this $100, the transaction is reconciled.

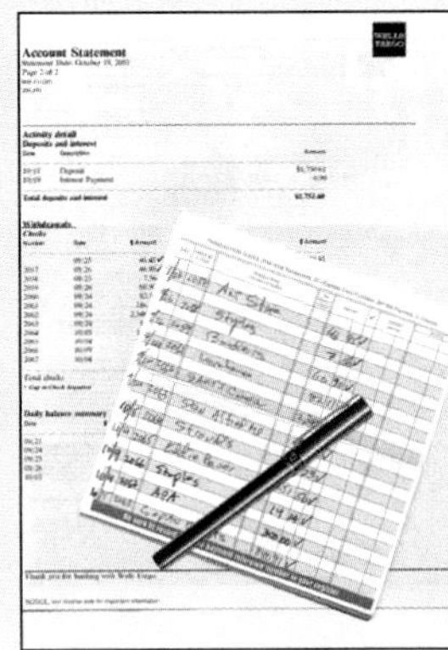

You use your checkbook register to determine your "balance per books" and your bank statement to determine your "balance per bank."

Book Reconciling Items

Recall that the second type of reconciling item is a book reconciling item—a transaction that the bank knows about but the entity doesn't as of a particular date. Figure 8-18 illustrates three typical book reconciling items for our sample entity. The first example is cash of $425 from a note receivable collected by the bank as a service for the entity but unrecorded by the entity because it has not yet been notified of the collection. In this case, the bank knows about and has recorded a cash increase of $425. That is, the cash is included in the bank's record of cash, or balance per bank. The entity, however, is not

FIGURE 8-18

Book reconciling items in the adjusted balances bank reconciliation format

SAMPLE ENTITY
Bank Reconciliation
For the Month Ended December 31

Balance per books			$191
Add:	Cash collected by the bank	$425	
	Error in recording check	9	434
Deduct:	Service charge		(25)
Adjusted balance per books			$600

yet aware of its $425 cash increase and has not included it in its record of cash, or balance per books. To reconcile this transaction, you add $425 to the balance per books:

Balance per books	$191
Add: Cash collected by the bank	425
Adjusted balance per books	$616

When you add the cash received by the bank for the entity, you are simply bringing the entity's records (books) up to date with information it does not yet have. Once both the bank and the books know about this transaction, it has been reconciled.

Another book reconciling item that commonly occurs is a **service charge**—in Figure 8-18 this is a $25 fee charged by the bank that the entity doesn't learn about until it receives its monthly bank statement balance. In this case, the bank knows about and has recorded a cash decrease of $25. That is, the bank has included its effect in balance per bank by deducting $25. The entity, however, does not yet know of this $25 cash decrease and has not included it in its record of cash, or balance per books. To reconcile this transaction, you deduct the $25 from the balance per books:

Balance per books	$191
Deduct: Service charge	(25)
Adjusted balance per books	$166

Do not memorize that service charges are always deducted from the balance per books. Deducting the service charge from the balance per books allows you to bring the entity up to date with information it does not yet have. Think of this as though you were supplying a transaction that the bank knows about but the entity does not. As soon as both the bank and the entity know about this cash decrease, the transaction has been reconciled.

As the past two examples illustrate, a book reconciling item is a transaction that the bank knows about but the entity doesn't as of a particular date. A variation of this type of transaction is a recording error made by the entity. In this case, the bank correctly records a transaction that the entity incorrectly records. An example is a transposition error. For example, our sample entity in Figure 8-18 received a customer's check for $87 but incorrectly recorded it as a cash increase of $78. In contrast, the bank correctly processed the check as an $87 increase to the entity's bank account. The entity is unlikely to detect the error until it receives the bank statement and discovers the $9 ($87 – $78) discrepancy. To properly account for this entity-initiated error on your bank reconciliation, you add $9 to the entity's balance per books:

Balance per books	$191
Add: Error in recording check	9
Adjusted balance per books	$200

(continued)

When you add the $9 amount to the balance per books, you are simply correcting the entity's (book's) treatment of the transaction. When both the bank's and the entity's balances agree, the transaction is reconciled.

Now that you understand bank reconciling items and book reconciling items—and have not merely memorized how to manipulate them—you're ready to prepare a complete bank reconciliation.

Exactly How Is a Bank Reconciliation Prepared?

Recall that a bank reconciliation is a schedule that shows exactly how much cash is actually on hand in the entity at a particular point in time. More specifically, you have learned that it reconciles the entity's version of cash with the bank's version of the entity's cash account. Essentially a bank reconciliation combines the bank reconciling items (Figure 8-17) and book reconciling items (Figure 8-18) together. The reconciling items in Figure 8-19 should look familiar, as they are the examples you saw in the previous section using the adjusted balances format. The **adjusted balances format** adds and subtracts appropriate reconciling items from both the balance per bank and balance per books so that the adjusted balances agree.

FIGURE 8-19

A bank reconciliation using the adjusted balances format

Note that both the adjusted balance per bank and adjusted balance per books reconcile with each other.

SAMPLE ENTITY
Bank Reconciliation
For the Month Ended December 31

Balance per bank			$856
Add:	Deposit in transit		$144
Deduct:	Outstanding check	$(300)	
	Bank error: unrecorded payment	(100)	(400)
Adjusted balance per bank			$600
Balance per books			$191
Add:	Cash collected by the bank	$425	
	Error in recording check	9	434
Deduct:	Service charge		(25)
Adjusted balance per books			$600

Why Should You Use the Adjusted Balances Format?

Although other formats are sometimes used, the adjusted balances format is highly recommended for at least three reasons. First, this format is very logical and intuitively easy to understand. In Figure 8-19, for example, you start with a balance based on a bank's and an entity's available but incomplete information; then you adjust or correct each balance with more up-to-date information. Second, the format automatically leads you to adjusted balances, which represent the entity's correct cash balance ($600 in Figure 8-19) that is reported in the balance sheet. Finally, you can conveniently use the balance per book section of this format to prepare transaction adjustments or corrections as you will soon see.

Now that you are familiar with the adjusted balances format, let's consider Performance Objective 22.

YOUR PERFORMANCE OBJECTIVE 22
Prepare in good form a bank reconciliation using the adjusted balance format and **prepare** the adjustments necessitated by this reconciliation.

These advantages of the adjusted balance format will be more obvious when you learn how to prepare a bank reconciliation and make necessary adjustments and corrections.

Using a Single Question to Direct Your Analysis

When you prepare a bank reconciliation, your first step should be to locate all reconciling items. This is done by comparing the entity's bank statement with the entity's cash account. When you find a transaction (e.g., a service charge) recorded by one version of cash (e.g., the bank) but not the other (e.g., the books), you have found a reconciling item.

Your second step should be to analyze the effect of each reconciling item. An effective way to do this is to ask the question "Who knows about this reconciling item at the date of the reconciliation?" Let's use this question to reanalyze the $144 deposit in transit reconciling item. That is, your answer to the question "Who knows about this deposit in transit at December 31?" should be: "The entity knows about this item at December 31." Since this transaction has been recorded by the entity but not yet by the bank, you must adjust the balance per bank. Specifically, you must add the deposit in transit to the balance per bank because a deposit increases the bank balance.

To be sure you understand how this simple question can help guide your analysis, let's try another example. This time, we'll reanalyze the $25 service charge reconciling item. Your answer to the question "Who knows about this service charge at the date of the reconciliation?" should be: "The bank." If the entity does find out about this service charge near the reconciliation date, it is clear that the bank still knew about it *before* the entity. Since this transaction has been recorded by the bank, but not yet by the entity, you must adjust the balance per books. Specifically, you must deduct the service charge from the balance per books because a service charge decreases the book balance. Notice once again how helpful this simple question is in guiding your analysis.

As described earlier, your third and final step is to add or subtract as appropriate the bank reconciling items from the balance per bank and the book reconciling items from the balance per books. The effect of this step for the six reconciling items already discussed is shown in Figure 8-19.

Determining Transaction Adjustments and Corrections

Once you complete the balance per books section of your reconciliation, you must record its reconciling items. That is, these items, by definition, have not been recorded as of the reconciliation date. If you think about it, you will never want to record the bank reconciling items since the entity has already recorded these items. Thus, you simply need to treat each balance per books reconciling item as an adjustment. Let's now view the adjustments necessitated by the bank reconciliation shown in Figure 8-19. The transaction adjustments and corrections necessitated by a bank reconciliation are shown here:

Date	Asset Account Title	Assets	=	Liabilities	+	Owner's Equity	Source of Asset Account Title
12/31	Cash	425					
	Note Receivable	(425)					
12/31	Cash	9					
	Acct. Receivable	(9)					
12/31	Cash	(25)				(25)	Miscellaneous Expense

Notice that both the $425 and $9 adjustments increase cash, whereas the last adjustment, amounting to $25, decreases cash. These effects of the adjustments are not surprising since the reconciliation directs you to add the first two reconciling items and deduct the last. The only unresolved issue is to decide what account titles will complete each of the three adjustments.

Let's analyze each of these three reconciling items to determine the appropriate account title. Since you now know that the note receivable has been collected, its $425 asset balance must be decreased. Likewise, since the $9 cash collection was understated, so too was the decrease to the Accounts Receivable account. The correction then includes an additional $9 decrease to that account. Finally, a bank service charge represents an expense and must now be recorded by decreasing owner's equity. As you can see, the adjusted balances format provides a straightforward way to record these adjustments and corrections. Recall that all such adjustments must be made to accurately state net income for the period.

Cards & Memorabilia Unlimited Illustration

Susan Newman prepared a bank reconciliation for Cards & Memorabilia Unlimited each month. Figure 8-20 illustrates December's reconciliation and the adjustments it made necessary. Study this figure carefully to determine if you have mastered Performance Objective 22.

FIGURE 8-20

A bank reconciliation and adjustments for Cards & Memorabilia Unlimited

CARDS & MEMORABILIA UNLIMITED
Bank Reconciliation
For the Month Ended December 31

Balance per bank			$28,425
Add:	Deposits in transit		1,885
Deduct:	Outstanding checks		(310)
Adjusted balance per bank			$30,000
Balance per books			$30,350
Add:	Error in recording check #168		270
Deduct:	Dishonored (NSF) check	$600	
	Service charge	20	(620)
Adjusted balance per books			$30,000

Date	Asset Account Title	Assets	=	Liabilities	+	Owner's Equity	Source of Asset Account Title
12/31	Cash	270				270	Sales Revenue
12/31	Acct. Receivable	600					
	Cash	(600)					
12/31	Cash	(20)				(20)	Miscellaneous Expense

Two reconciling items deserve mention. The first is an error by CMU in which a cash sale of $521 is mistakenly recorded as $251, an understatement of $270. To correct this error, the $270 understatement is added to the balance per books. The second item deserving mention is a dishonored check of $600. A **dishonored check,** also called NSF (nonsufficient funds) check, bounced check, bad check, and rubber check, is a customer's check deposited by the entity that is later returned because the customer's bank account had insufficient funds to pay the check. Since the check is invalid, it must be deducted from the balance per books.

Now that you have learned how to prepare a bank reconciliation, let's review the uses of this tool. As you learned at the beginning of this chapter, the bank reconciliation is an important control device in business. For example, it can be used to detect unintentional errors and, in some cases, fraudulent transactions. It is the source of the cash balance reported on the balance sheet. The bank reconciliation can also be an important control device in your personal financial affairs. Even if you never prepare a bank reconciliation for a business, you can certainly benefit from using it to help you manage your own money. When you can reconcile your checkbook balance with your bank statement balance, you will gain control and confidence over your personal financial affairs.

Summary with Key Terms

This chapter began with a discussion about **cash** (324) and its significance in business decision making. You learned, for example, that the resource unit measured in a statement of cash flows includes not only cash but also **cash equivalents** (324). You also learned in this chapter that one aspect of accounting for cash is cash management. Then, after reviewing what is meant by the term **budget** (325), you learned about how cash is planned with a **cash budget** (325) and some basic principles of **internal control** (327) for cash.

In this chapter you examined the **statement of cash flows** (330) in a much more comprehensive fashion than in earlier chapters. As in earlier chapters, the meaning of **financing activities** (332), **investing activities** (333), and **operating activities** (334) was discussed with particular emphasis placed on how you distinguish between initiating and completing an activity. A new concept introduced in this chapter was that of a **direct exchange** (334) in which an entity engages in a noncash exchange of noncurrent assets and/or noncurrent claims against assets. Such transactions must be disclosed in a statement of cash flows under the heading **noncash investing and financing activities** (334).

After classifying each of CMU's transactions into the appropriate activity and excluding any noncash transactions other than direct exchanges, you then prepared CMU's statement of cash flows. In doing so, you used an approach known as the **direct method of reporting cash flow from operating activities** (344). You also learned about an alternative method called **the indirect method of reporting cash flow from operating activities** (344), an approach that is commonly found in annual report presentations of the statement of cash flows. You completed your examination of this statement by looking at corporate statement of cash flow illustrations and receiving guidance in a *User Focus* about what to look for when you begin your analysis of such statements.

The *Insight* section of this chapter discussed the limitations of balance sheet ratios and the importance of supplementing them with the statement of cash flows and ratios that include income statement accounts.

Cash management also includes the use of a **bank reconciliation** (329) to control cash. After an initial discussion, this topic was described in greater detail in the *User Focus* section. This section explained how a bank reconciliation is divided into two sections each of which may contain such classic **reconciling items** (351) as **deposits in transit** (351), **outstanding checks** (352), **service charges** (353), and **dishonored checks** (356). The bank section begins with the **balance per bank** (329), adds and deducts various **bank reconciling items** (351), and ends with the *adjusted balance per bank*. The book section begins with the **balance per books** (329), adds and deducts various **book reconciling items** (351) and ends with the *adjusted balance per books*. This very straightforward format is called the **adjusted balances format** (354).

The number in parentheses following each **key term** is the page number on which the term is defined.

Making Business Decisions

YOUR PERFORMANCE OBJECTIVE 2
(page 18)

Perlin's Clothing for Men and Boys is a small retail shop owned by Bill Perlin. You have worked for Bill during the Christmas season as a cashier for the last five years. This year, he's asked you to work again. Now that you have studied this chapter's section on the basic principles of internal control, you notice several things that happen every year but that you hadn't thought too much about before.

1. Bill's wife, Sally, will often take cash out of the cash register when she wants to go shopping.
2. Gift certificates are kept behind the counter in a stack on the top shelf.
3. Bill will often let people return or exchange gifts after Christmas even if they do not have a receipt.
4. Bill has several tasks to complete at the end of the day, so he always asks you to reconcile cash in the drawer to the cash register total.
5. Citing the need to be efficient with his time, Bill often waits until he has two or three daily deposits of cash before he makes a trip to the bank.
6. Bill doesn't like customers to be inconvenienced, so when there are customers waiting in line who want to pay cash, he takes their money, asks you for the change, and tells you to ring up the sale later.

7. You discover that Bill has not reconciled his bank statements to his accounting record of cash for the last six months.

Consider how each of these seven items is or is not a good example of internal control and explain why it is or isn't. Also for each item, would you advise Bill to make a change? If yes, describe the change you would recommend. If no, explain why not.

Questions

YOUR PERFORMANCE OBJECTIVE 4
(page 22)

8-1 Explain in your own words the meaning of key business terms.

a. Cash equivalents
b. Budget
c. Internal control
d. Statement of cash flows
e. Direct exchange
f. Noncash investing and financing activity
g. Reconciling item
h. Bank reconciliation
i. Deposits in transit
j. Outstanding checks
k. Service charge
l. Dishonored check

8-2 Describe two ways cash can be controlled.
8-3 Distinguish between an operating budget and a cash budget.
8-4 Describe how you might apply any one of the internal control procedures found on pages 327–329 to control your personal financial affairs.
8-5 How does a statement of cash flows differ from an income statement?
8-6 Describe at least three financing activity transactions.
8-7 Describe at least three investing activity transactions.
8-8 Describe at least three operating activity transactions.
8-9 Distinguish between the terms *financing activities*, *investing activities*, and *operating activities*.
8-10 Describe two *related* transactions that initiate and complete a financing activity.
8-11 Describe two *related* transactions that initiate and complete an investing activity.
8-12 Describe two *related* transactions that initiate and complete an operating activity.
8-13 How are the terms *direct exchange* and *noncash investing and financing activity* related?
8-14 Give three examples of noncash investing and financing activities.
8-15 Distinguish between the direct and indirect methods of reporting cash flow from operating activities.
8-16 Why aren't ratios by themselves reliable indicators of an entity's financial health?
8-17 How do a statement of cash flows and a cash budget differ in both content and time frame?
8-18 Distinguish between the balance per bank and the balance per books.
8-19 Distinguish between bank reconciling items and book reconciling items.
8-20 Describe at least three advantages of the adjusted balances format.
8-21 Explain how you can use the following question to guide the analysis in a bank reconciliation: "Who knows about this reconciling item at the date of the reconciliation?"

Reinforcement Exercises

YOUR PERFORMANCE OBJECTIVE 1
(page 326)

E8-1 Preparing Your Own Cash Budget
Prepare a personal cash budget for the month following the current month.

E8-2 Comparing Your Cash Budget to CMU's Cash Budget
Compare and contrast the personal cash budget you prepared in Exercise 8-1 to the cash budget shown in Figure 8-1 for Cards & Memorabilia Unlimited.

YOUR PERFORMANCE OBJECTIVE 1
(page 326)

E8-3 Comparing Your Cash Budget to Your Operating Budget
Compare and contrast the personal cash budget you prepared in Exercise 8-1 to the personal operating budget you prepared in Exercise 1-5.

E8-4 Calculating Cash Collections from Customers

Calculate the cash collected on accounts receivable in each of the following cases:

	Case 1	Case 2	Case 3	Case 4
Sales (all credit sales)	$1,000	$1,000	$1,000	$1,000
Beginning accounts receivable	200	0	200	200
Ending accounts receivable	0	200	200	150

Hint:
Beginning Accounts Receivable + Credit Sales − Cash Collections = Ending Accounts Receivable

YOUR PERFORMANCE OBJECTIVE 1
(page 326)

E8-5 Estimating Cash Payments to Suppliers

Gray Enterprises is preparing its cash budget for the month of November and discovers the following information about its inventory payments:

Cost of inventory on hand, November 1	$ 360
Estimated cost of goods sold for November	1,800
Estimated cost of inventory on hand, November 30	320
Estimated payments in November for purchases prior to November	420
Percentage of November purchases expected to be paid in November	80%

Hint: Beginning Inventory + Inventory Purchases − Cost of Goods Sold = Ending Inventory

Required

Calculate the estimated inventory purchases and the cash payments for inventory in November.

YOUR PERFORMANCE OBJECTIVE 1
(page 326)

E8-6 Asking the Right Questions: A Group Activity

It's often said that knowing the right answer is not nearly as important as asking the right question. Asking the right question is a problem-solving skill that will help you make sound business decisions. In this exercise, you will review the vocabulary introduced in Chapter 8 by creating questions to match answers—similar to a popular TV show.

Required

a. Given an answer, what's the question?
Choose **three** of the following terms to serve as an answer. Create an appropriate question for each term. For example, if you choose the term *balance sheet*, you might create the question—What financial statement reports the assets, liabilities, and owners' equity of an entity on a specific date?

Bank reconciliation	Cash budget	Deposits in transit
Direct exchange	Service charges	Budget
Outstanding checks	Operating activities	Dishonored checks
Balance per bank	Cash equivalents	Balance per books

b. Are you sure that's the question?
Have each member of your group read aloud the questions they developed in Requirement (a). As a group, decide whether each question is an accurate match for an answer. Once satisfied that all questions are appropriate, the group, as a whole, chooses the three best questions created within the group. Record the three questions chosen (with their answers) on separate pieces of paper or index cards and give them to your instructor.

c. What's the answer?
To ensure that you have learned the vocabulary terms listed in Requirement (a), your instructor will now quiz you on the questions written by all of your classmates.

YOUR PERFORMANCE OBJECTIVE 4
(page 22)

Note: Exercises 8-7 and 8-8 test your understanding of internal control, a concept for which a performance objective will be introduced in Chapter 9.

E8-7 Internal Control of Cash

How does the acquisition of an electronic cash register improve an entity's internal control over cash receipts?

E8-8 Internal Control of Cash

Describe how you would apply the basic principles for internal control of cash to the following businesses:

a. Movie theater
b. Dog grooming salon
c. Pizza parlor
d. Bowling alley
e. Post office

YOUR PERFORMANCE OBJECTIVE 7b *(page 64)*

E8-9 Classifying Transactions into Activities

Classify each of the following transactions or events into one of the four categories in the schedule shown here. For the first three categories, indicate the item's effect (increase, decrease, or no effect) by placing a plus (+), a minus (−), or NE (no effect) in the appropriate category. For any noncash effects, insert the word *yes*.

	Categories			
	Operating	**Investing**	**Financing**	**Noncash Effect**
a. Net income				
b. Net loss				
c. Dividend declaration				
d. Dividend payment				
e. Credit sale				
f. Cash sale				
g. Collection of accounts receivable				
h. Depreciation expense				
i. Cash purchase of land				
j. Issuance of capital stock				
k. Cash received in advance from customers				
l. Payment of account payable				
m. Credit purchase of merchandise				
n. Building acquisition through issuance of a mortgage				
o. Conversion of common stock into preferred stock				

YOUR PERFORMANCE OBJECTIVE 7b *(page 64)*

E8-10 Classifying Transactions into Activities

Classify each of the following transactions or events into one of the four categories in the schedule shown here. For the first three categories, indicate the item's effect (increase, decrease, or no effect) by placing a plus (+), a minus (−), or NE (no effect) in the appropriate category. For any noncash effects, insert the word *yes*.

	Categories			
	Operating	**Investing**	**Financing**	**Noncash Effect**
a. Prepayment of insurance				
b. Expiration of insurance				
c. Credit purchase of inventory				
d. Cash purchase of merchandise				
e. Owner withdrawal of cash from business				
f. Equipment acquisition through issuance of long-term note				
g. Recognition of cost of goods sold				
h. Credit sale				
i. Cash sale				
j. Collection of accounts receivable				
k. Depreciation expense				
l. Cash purchase of land				
m. Owner investment in the business				
n. Cash advances from customers				
o. Payment of accounts payable				

E8-11 Classifying Transactions into Activities

YOUR PERFORMANCE OBJECTIVE 7b
(page 64)

Classify each of the following transactions or events into one of the four categories shown in the schedule shown here. For the first three categories, indicate the item's effect (increase, decrease, or no effect) by placing a plus (+), a minus (−), or NE (no effect) in the appropriate category. For any noncash effects, insert the word *yes*.

	Categories			
	Operating	**Investing**	**Financing**	**Noncash Effect**
a. Salaries paid				
b. Interest received				
c. Credit purchase of equipment				
d. Cash purchase of equipment				
e. Credit sale				
f. Net income				
g. Acquisition of land in exchange for investment				
h. Prepayment of rent				
i. Cash sale				
j. Collection of accounts receivable				
k. Depletion expense				
l. Cash purchase of investment				
m. Owner disinvestment in the business				
n. Interest paid				
o. Payment of salaries payable				

E8-12 Preparing a Statement of Cash Flows

YOUR PERFORMANCE OBJECTIVE 7
(page 64)

The following selected transactions of Lovitz Apparel Company represent important business activity during July. Prepare a statement of cash flows using the direct method of reporting cash flows from operating activities for the month ended July 31.

a. Land costing $50,000 is acquired by making a $10,000 down payment and issuing a note payable for the balance.
b. The company buys on credit equipment costing $20,000.
c. The company arranges for a $50,000 line of credit from the bank. No amounts have yet been borrowed.
d. The proprietor, Jon Lovitz, arranges a personal bank loan of $10,000 to increase his financing in the company.
e. Jon Lovitz transfers $8,000 from his personal savings account to his business checking account.
f. The company borrows $25,000 from its line of credit.
g. Inventory costing $10,000 is acquired on credit.
h. The company pays its inventory supplier $10,000.
i. Credit sales amount to 30,000.
j. Collections on credit sales amount to $22,000.
k. Cash sales amount to $16,000.
l. Jon Lovitz withdraws $6,000 from his business checking account for personal use.

E8-13 Preparing a Statement of Cash Flows

YOUR PERFORMANCE OBJECTIVE 7
(page 64)

On January 2, Carl Canola decides to start a business that sells a variety of popcorn and popcorn accessories. The business, called Popcorn Mania, engages in the following transactions during January, the first month of operations. Prepare a statement of cash flows using the direct method of reporting cash flows from operating activities for the month ended January 31.

a. Carl invests $98,000 cash and $2,000 of his personal popcorn poppers to finance his business.
b. A $20,000 purchase of store equipment on January 2 is financed with a one-year bank loan that bears an annual interest rate of 10%.
c. Carl leases a small store at an annual rental of $12,000. Rent for the first six months is paid in advance.

d. Various popcorn accessories costing $15,000 are purchased from a supplier on account.
e. Popcorn accessories costing $25,000 are purchased from suppliers for cash.
f. The company receives cash advances from customers totaling $15,000 for the yet-to-be-delivered Non-Fat Coconut Oil Poppers.
g. An $8,000 installment is paid on the bank loan.
h. The company delivers the Non-Fat Coconut Oil Poppers to two-thirds of its customers who made advance payments.
i. The company pays $7,250 of the remaining account payable.
j. Cash sales amount to $12,000.
k. Credit sales amount to $25,000.
l. Collections on accounts receivable amount to $17,000.
m. Carl withdraws $10,000 cash from his business.

YOUR PERFORMANCE OBJECTIVE 22
(page 354)

E8-14 Proper Treatment of Reconciling Items

Reconciling items are transactions that on a specific date have been included in one but not both of the following balances:

a. The company's record of cash (balance per books).
b. The bank's record of cash (balance per bank).

Required

The adjusted balance bank reconciliation format is shown here. Using numbers 1 through 4 next to each of the items (a) through (j), indicate the proper placement for each of the following items. If you believe an item should not appear, use the number 5.

Balance per bank statement	$xx	Balance per books	$xx
Add:	(1)	Add:	(3)
Deduct:	(2)	Deduct:	(4)
Adjusted bank balance	$xx	Adjusted book balance	$xx

a. Deposits in transit.
b. Proceeds from matured CD held with bank.
c. NSF check.
d. Monthly service charges.
e. A $536 deposit incorrectly recorded on the books as $563.
f. A $536 check incorrectly recorded on the books as $563.
g. A check written to pay monthly rent has been paid by the bank.
h. Charge for printing checks.
i. A deposit the company failed to record.
j. Outstanding checks.

YOUR PERFORMANCE OBJECTIVE 22
(page 354)

E8-15 Preparing a Bank Reconciliation

The following data apply to the Ivy Co. checking account:

Ending company cash balance	$10,274
Ending bank statement cash balance	10,600
Outstanding checks	2,420
Deposits in transit	2,000
Monthly service charge	40
Proceeds from bank collection of note (includes interest of $16)	216

The accountant recorded a deposit of $270 for cash sales twice in error.

Required

Prepare a bank reconciliation as of June 30 of this year.

Critical Thinking Problems

P8-1 Using a Cash Budget as a Basis for Business Decisions

YOUR PERFORMANCE OBJECTIVE 1 (page 326)

Assume that a cash budget you have prepared results in a projected cash deficit. Describe ways in which additional cash may be generated to offset this deficit. For each way, list favorable or unfavorable consequences.

P8-2 Estimating Customer Collections for a Cash Budget

YOUR PERFORMANCE OBJECTIVE 1 (page 326)

Byrd Company has three types of sales. Assume that:

a. Cash sales are 20% of total sales.
b. Sales on account or credit sales are 30% of total sales and are collected as follows: 40% in the first month following the sale, 50% in the second month following the sale, 7% in the third month following the sale, and 3% never collected.
c. Credit card sales are 50% of total sales and are collected in the month following the sale, net of a 4% credit card fee. For example, the credit card fee is $4 on a $100 sale and Byrd company receives $96.

The following information presents Byrd Company's projected sales for the first four months of the current year.

January	$12,500,000
February	16,000,000
March	14,000,000
April	20,000,000

Required

Prepare a portion of the cash budget for Byrd Company by estimating the amount of cash that it will collect from its customers for the month of April.

P8-3 Preparing a Cash Budget

YOUR PERFORMANCE OBJECTIVE 1 (page 326)

The president of Herman Poirot Corporation wants to know the budgeted cash balance at the end of the business day on August 31. You have gathered the following data for the transactions that you believe will occur during the month.

Estimated data for August of the current year:	
Wages incurred	$45,000
Factory expenses to be paid in cash	16,000
Depreciation expense	8,000
Selling and administrative expenses to be paid in cash	8,000
Purchases (all on account)	20,000
Cash sales	19,000
Credit sales	70,000
Payments on accounts payable	34,000
Increase in Accrued Wages Payable account	4,000
Cash received from sale of a machine	15,000
Gain on the sale of the machine	2,000
Expiration of prepaid insurance	700

Additional Information

a. 50% of credit sales are collected in the month of sale.
b. 40% of credit sales are collected in the first month following the month of sale.
c. 10% of credit sales are collected in the second month following the month of sale.
d. Credit sales during June and July were $50,000 and $60,000 respectively.
e. The beginning cash balance on August 1 was $5,000.

Required

Prepare a cash budget for the month of August.

P8-4 Preparing a Cash Budget

YOUR PERFORMANCE OBJECTIVE 1 (page 326)

The first quarter's operating budgets for Buena Vista Company are shown here:

	January	February	March
Sales revenue	$50,000	$60,000	$54,000
Cost of goods sold:			
Beginning inventory	20,000	22,000	22,000
Purchases	40,000	44,000	42,000
Goods available for sale	60,000	66,000	64,000
Ending inventory	22,000	22,000	28,000
Cost of goods sold	38,000	44,000	36,000
Gross margin	12,000	16,000	18,000
Operating expenses:			
Salaries	6,000	7,000	8,000
Rent	500	500	500
Utilities	200	300	350
Depreciation	700	800	800
Insurance	100	120	120
	7,500	8,720	9,770
Net income	$ 4,500	$ 7,280	$ 8,230

Additional Information

a. Cash sales are 20% of total sales revenues in all months.
b. Collections of customer receivables amount to 50% in the month of sale, 40% in the following month, and 10% never collected.
c. Payments for merchandise purchases amount to 30% in the month of purchase and 70% in the following month.
d. 20% of each month's salaries are paid in the following month.
e. Rent is paid six months in advance on both January 1 and July 1.
f. Utilities are paid in the month incurred.
g. A full year of insurance will be prepaid on February 1.
h. New equipment will be purchased for $5,000 cash in February when it is delivered.
i. The cash balance on January 1 is $3,500.
j. The following amounts were reported on the operating budget for the previous December: Sales revenue $56,000, Purchases $38,000, and Salaries $5,500.

Required

Prepare cash budgets for January, February, and March.

Note: Problems 8-5 and 8-6 test your understanding of internal control, a concept for which a performance objective will be introduced in Chapter 9.

P8-5 Internal Control of Cash

Medical Laboratory Service provides laboratory testing of samples from doctors. All work is performed on account with monthly billing to participating doctors. Agnes Bisset, the laboratory accountant, receives and opens the mail. She is required to separate customer checks from the remittance slips that indicate how much each customer has paid. After entering cash receipt information in the customer accounts receivable records, she deposits the checks in the bank. Each day, she calculates the daily cash receipts applied to customer accounts and reconciles this total with that same day's bank deposit slip. This comparison is designed to ensure that all cash receipts are deposited in the bank.

Required

a. Describe the most significant internal control weakness.
b. What fraudulent activity could occur as a result of this internal control system weakness?
c. Identify any other internal control weaknesses existing in Agnes's procedure.

P8-6 Internal Control of Cash

Jodie Whitson works as a cashier in a department store. When she arrives at work each day, she places all of her personal belongings in her employee locker. She then reports to her assigned department and signs on to an electronic cash register while her supervisor observes, uses her employee identification number and password, and verifies the starting cash balance in the register. Jodie is the only employee with access to the cash register during her shift. All cash and credit transactions are rung up on the cash register. For each sale, the customer receives a copy of the register receipt, while the information is also recorded electronically for the store's records. Merchandise returns for cash or credit must be approved by the supervisor before Jodie rings them up on the cash register. Price adjustments for advertised sales are automatically recognized when an item is scanned. Occasionally, Jodie needs to make a price adjustment manually, but can do so only with the supervisor's approval. During breaks, Jodie locks her register before leaving the department. At the end of her shift, Jodie counts the cash in her drawer while observed by her supervisor, signs a form verifying the amount, and then signs off the register.

Required

a. Describe the most significant internal control procedures used in this system.
b. Identify any internal control weaknesses.
c. Compare this system to one you have observed in a local retail store. List the similarities and differences that exist between these systems and explain what you believe is the most important internal control procedure necessary when handling cash transactions.

P8-7 Determining Transaction Effects on a Statement of Cash Flows

YOUR PERFORMANCE OBJECTIVE 7
(page 64)

A simplified statement of cash flows that uses the direct method of reporting cash flows from operations is shown here. Thirteen of the lines in the statement are numbered. Ignore any lines that are subtotals (S) and grand totals (T). Assume that after preparing all of the financial statements, you discover a transaction has been overlooked. You record that transaction in the accounts and correct all of the financial statements. For each of transactions (a) through (n), indicate which, if any, of the numbered lines on the statement of cash flows is affected. Ignore income tax effects.

Statement of Cash Flows for a Period—Direct Method

Cash flows from operating activities		
Cash collected from customers	$ xx	(1)
Interest and dividends received	xx	(2)
Other operating cash receipts	xx	(3)
Cash paid to employees and other suppliers	(xx)	(4)
Interest paid	(xx)	(5)
Income taxes paid	(xx)	(6)
Other operating cash payments	(xx)	(7)
Net cash provided by (used in) operating activities		(S)
Cash flows from investing activities		
Proceeds from sale of noncurrent assets	$ xx	(8)
Acquisition of noncurrent assets	(xx)	(9)
Net cash provided by (used in) investing activities		(S)
Cash flows from financing activities		
Proceeds from sale of debt and equity* securities	$ xx	(10)
Retirement of debt and equity securities	(xx)	(11)
Payment of dividends to shareholders	(xx)	(12)
Net cash provided by (used in) financing activities		(S)
Net increase in cash		(T)
Cash at beginning of year		(T)
Cash at end of year		(T)
Supplemental schedule of noncash investing and financing activities		(13)

*Capital stock

Transactions

a. Depreciation expense for the period is $10,000.
b. A cash dividend of $6,000 is received from an investment in the common stock of another company.
c. Machinery is purchased for $100,000 cash.
d. Machinery is purchased for $100,000 on account.
e. A factory site is acquired by issuing $500,000 of capital stock.
f. A machine that cost $10,000 and that has $7,000 of accumulated depreciation is sold for $4,000 cash.
g. A machine that cost $10,000 and that has $7,000 of accumulated depreciation is sold for $2,000 cash.
h. Cash in the amount of $100,000 is received from the issuance of bonds.
i. Cash of $70,000 is collected from customers on account.
j. Suppliers of merchandise are paid $40,000 on account.
k. Cash in the amount of $80,000 is received from the issuance of common stock.
l. Treasury stock is acquired for $15,000.
m. A cash dividend of $20,000 is declared.
n. A previously declared cash dividend of $20,000 is paid.

YOUR PERFORMANCE OBJECTIVE 7
(page 64)

P8-8 Determining Transaction Effects on a Statement of Cash Flows

A simplified statement of cash flows using the indirect method of reporting cash flows from operating activities is shown here. Nineteen of the lines in this section are numbered. Ignore any lines that are subtotals (S) and grand totals (T). Assume that after preparing all of the financial statements, you discover a transaction has been overlooked. You record that transaction in the accounts and correct all of the financial statements. For each of transactions (a) through (n), indicate which, if any, of the numbered lines in the statement of cash flows is affected. Ignore income tax effects.

Statement of Cash Flows for a Period—Indirect Method		
Net income		(1)
Adjustments to reconcile net income to net cash provided by operating activities		
Add:		
Depreciation Expense		(2)
Amortization of Intangible Assets		(3)
Losses		(4)
Increase in deferred tax liability		(5)
Bond discount amortization		(6)
Decreases in noncash current assets affecting operations		(7)
Increases in noncash current liabilities affecting operations		(8)
Deduct:		
Gains		(9)
Decrease in deferred tax liability		(10)
Bond premium amortization		(11)
Increases in noncash current assets affecting operations		(12)
Decreases in noncash current liabilities affecting operations		(13)
Net cash provided by (used in) operating activities		(S)
Cash flows from investing activities		
Proceeds from sale of noncurrent assets	$ xx	(14)
Acquisition of noncurrent assets	(xx)	(15)
Net cash provided by (used in) investing activities		(S)
Cash flows from financing activities		
Proceeds from sale of debt & equity* securities	$ xx	(16)
Retirement of debt & equity securities	(xx)	(17)

*Capital stock

(continued)

Statement of Cash Flows for a Period—Indirect Method		
Payment of dividends to shareholders	(xx)	(18)
Net cash provided by (used in) financing activities		(S)
Net increase in cash		(T)
Cash at beginning of year		(T)
Cash at end of year		(T)
Supplemental schedule of noncash investing and financing activities		(19)

Transactions

a. Depreciation expense for the period is $10,000.
b. Dividend revenue of $6,000 is reported on the income statement.
c. Machinery is purchased for $100,000 cash.
d. Machinery is purchased for $100,000 on account.
e. A factory site is acquired by issuing $500,000 of capital stock.
f. A machine that cost $10,000 and that has $7,000 of accumulated depreciation is sold for $4,000 cash.
g. A machine that cost $10,000 and that has $7,000 of accumulated depreciation is sold for $2,000 cash.
h. Cash in the amount of $100,000 is received from the issuance of bonds.
i. Cash in the amount of $70,000 is collected from customers on account.
j. Suppliers of merchandise are paid $40,000 on account.
k. Cash in the amount of $80,000 is received from the issuance of common stock.
l. Treasury stock is acquired for $15,000.
m. A cash dividend of $20,000 is declared.
n. A previously declared cash dividend of $20,000 is paid.

YOUR PERFORMANCE OBJECTIVE 7
(page 64)

P8-9 Preparing a Statement of Cash Flows
The March transactions of Kaelin Celebrity Housesitters, Inc. are shown here:

Transaction Detail	Financing	Investing	Operating
1. Land of $300 is acquired by issuing 50 shares of common stock.			
2. Equipment having a cost of $500 and accumulated depreciation of $200 is sold for $200.			
3. A cash dividend of $250 is declared on March 1 and paid in full on March 31.			
4. Equipment having a cost of $650 is acquired with a credit card.			
5. Merchandise inventory in the amount of $2,200 is acquired on account.			
6. The $650 credit card obligation incurred in Transaction 4 is paid.			
7. An amount of $200 is borrowed by accessing an existing bank credit line.			
8. Land with a cost of $100 is sold for cash. The gain on sale amounts to $150.			
9. Interest in the amount of $67 is paid on amounts borrowed with the business credit line.			
10. The amount of $2,350 owed various suppliers of merchandise inventory is paid.			
11. Cash in the amount of $1,250 is collected on amounts owed by customers.			
12. Federal and state income taxes owed in the amount of $333 are paid.			

(continued)

Transaction Detail	Financing	Investing	Operating
13. Cash sales in the amount of $2,300 are made to customers.			
14. March interest in the amount of $25 is incurred but unpaid.			
15. Selling and administrative costs of $900 are paid in cash. An additional $250 of these expenses are incurred but unpaid at March 31.			
16. Cash in the amount of $500 is received from customers before delivery is made.			
17. Credit sales in the amount of $1,700 are made to customers.			
18. $400 worth of goods paid for earlier by customers are delivered.			
19. $150 depreciation is incurred on equipment.			
20. A cost of goods sold of $2,100 is determined using a physical count.			

Required

a. In the columns provided, identify the financing, investing, and operating activities and their amounts, as was done in Figure 8-11.

b. Prepare a statement of cash flows using the direct method of reporting cash flows from operating activities. Assume that the cash balance at the beginning of the month was $300.

YOUR PERFORMANCE OBJECTIVE 7
(page 64)

P8-10 Preparing a Statement of Cash Flows

The March transactions of Heidi's Alpine Resort are shown here:

Transaction Detail	Financing	Investing	Operating
1. Land costing $300 is acquired by issuing 50 shares of common stock.			
2. Equipment having a cost of $500 and accumulated depreciation of $200 is sold for $200.			
3. A cash dividend of $250 is declared on March 1 and paid in full on March 31.			
4. Equipment having a cost of $700 is acquired with a credit card.			
5. $2,300 of merchandise inventory is acquired on account.			
6. The $700 credit card obligation incurred in Transaction 4 is paid.			
7. $150 is borrowed by accessing an existing bank credit line.			
8. Land with a cost of $150 is sold for cash. The gain on sale amounts to $150.			
9. $67 of interest is paid on amounts borrowed with the business credit line.			
10. $2,400 owed various suppliers of merchandise inventory is paid.			
11. $1,350 cash is collected on amounts owed by customers.			
12. Federal and state income taxes owed in the amount of $333 are paid.			
13. $2,300 of cash sales are made to customers.			
14. $25 March interest is incurred but unpaid.			
15. $900 of selling and administrative costs are paid in cash. An additional $150 of these expenses are incurred but unpaid at March 31.			
16. $500 cash is received from customers before delivery is made.			
17. $1,700 of credit sales are made to customers.			
18. $400 worth of goods paid for earlier by customers are delivered.			

(continued)

Transaction Detail	Financing	Investing	Operating
19. $150 depreciation is incurred on equipment.			
20. A cost of goods sold of $2,100 is determined using a physical count.			

Required

a. In the columns provided, identify the financing, investing, and operating activities and their amounts, as was done in Figure 8-11.
b. Prepare a statement of cash flows using the direct method of reporting cash flows from operating activities. Assume that the cash balance at the beginning of the month was $300.

P8-11 Converting from the Direct to the Indirect Method of Reporting Cash Flow from Operations

YOUR PERFORMANCE OBJECTIVE 7 *(page 64)*

The operating activities section of a statement of cash flows, prepared using the direct method, is shown here. Using the additional information provided, prepare the operating activities section using the indirect method.

Cash collected from customers	$131,600
Interest received	1,200
Cash paid to suppliers	(63,800)
Cash paid to employees	(31,700)
Interest paid	(2,400)
Income taxes paid	(8,570)
Net cash provided by operating activities	$ 26,330

Additional Information

	As of 12/31	As of 1/1
Accounts receivable	$31,500	$24,400
Interest receivable	300	500
Accounts payable	23,600	18,900
Salaries payable	1,300	1,000
Income taxes payable	2,900	3,400
Accrual basis net income	21,330	
Depreciation expense	8,500	
Gain on sale of equipment	1,100	

P8-12 Preparing a Statement of Cash Flows

YOUR PERFORMANCE OBJECTIVE 7 *(page 64)*

The financial statements for Mica Furniture Company's first year of business are shown here. Several amounts have been omitted from the statement of cash flows. Study the statements carefully, then fill in the missing amounts to complete the statement of cash flows.

MICA FURNITURE COMPANY
Income Statement
For the Year Ended January 31

Net sales		$171,700
Cost of goods sold		59,620
Gross profit		112,080
Operating expenses:		
Salaries expense	$26,580	
Depreciation expense	12,400	
Other operating expenses	46,340	
Interest expense	2,180	87,500
Net income		$ 24,580

MICA FURNITURE COMPANY
Balance Sheet
January 31

Assets		Liabilities and Owner's Equity	
Current Assets		**Current Liabilities**	
Cash	$ 7,620	Accounts payable	$ 23,740
Accounts receivable	18,170	Salaries payable	4,130
Inventory	41,600	Total current liabilities	27,870
Store supplies	2,160		
Prepaid rent	5,400		
Total current assets	$ 74,950	**Noncurrent Liabilities**	
Property, Plant, and Equipment		Notes payable	43,400
Store equipment	21,900	Total liabilities	71,270
Less: Accumulated Depreciation	(3,600)		
	18,300		
Delivery Equipment	48,400	**Owner's Equity**	
Less: Accumulated Depreciation	(8,800)	Contributed capital	55,000
	39,600	Retained earnings	6,580
Total property, plant, and equipment	57,900	Total owner's equity	61,580
Total assets	$132,850	Total liabilities and owner's equity	$132,850

MICA FURNITURE COMPANY
Statement of Cash Flows
For the Year Ended January 31

Cash flows from operating activities		
Cash collected from customers	$ (1)	
Cash paid for merchandise	(77,480)	
Cash paid for salaries	(2)	
Cash paid for other operating expenses	(53,900)	
Cash paid for interest	(3)	
Net cash used by operating activities		$(2,480)
Cash flows from investing activities		
Cash paid for store equipment	(4)	
Net cash used for investing activities	(5)	
Cash flows from financing activities		
Contributions by owner	55,000	
Repayment of note payable	(6)	
Withdrawals by owner	(7)	
Net cash provided by financing activities		32,000
Net increase in cash		(8)
Cash balance at beginning of year		(9)
Cash balance at end of year		$ 7,620
Supplemental schedule of noncash investing and financing activities		
Delivery equipment acquired by issuance of note payable		$48,400

P8-13 Comprehensive Problem: Statements of Cash Flow

YOUR PERFORMANCE OBJECTIVES 1, 7
(pages 326, 64)

The projected and actual statements of cash flow for Sullivan Optics are shown here. Determine the difference between the actual and budgeted amount in each line item in the statements and provide a plausible reason for the difference. Explain why you believe this difference is good or bad for the company.

SULLIVAN OPTICS
Statement of Cash Flows
For the Year Ended December 31

	Actual 12/31	Budgeted 1/1
Cash flows from operating activities		
Cash collected from customers	$264,336	$240,000
Cash paid to suppliers	(91,412)	(80,000)
Cash paid to employees	(82,134)	(75,000)
Cash paid for other operating expenses	(28,717)	(35,000)
Cash paid for interest	(4,875)	(5,000)
Cash paid for income taxes	(9,439)	(5,000)
Net cash provided by operating activities	47,759	40,000
Cash flows from investing activities		
Cash paid for equipment	(36,488)	(30,000)
Sale of long-term investments	7,256	10,000
Net cash used for investing activities	(29,232)	(20,000)
Cash flows from financing activities		
Proceeds from sale of common stock	30,000	10,000
Repayment of long-term debt	(22,178)	(15,000)
Dividends paid	(12,500)	(5,000)
Net cash used for financing activities	(4,678)	(10,000)
Net increase in cash	13,849	10,000
Cash balance at beginning of year	5,824	6,000
Cash balance at end of year	$ 19,673	$ 16,000

P8-14 Preparing a Bank Reconciliation

YOUR PERFORMANCE OBJECTIVE 22
(page 354)

Singleton Company's bank statement for the month ended August 31 is shown here.

Previous balance as of August 1		$143,880
Add:		
Deposits	$119,004	
Note collected by bank	6,344	125,348
Subtotal		269,228
Deduct:		
Withdrawals	(156,340)	
Monthly checking fees	(200)	(156,540)
New balance as of August 31		$112,688

Additional Information

a. The note collected by the bank includes $344 of interest.
b. Withdrawals include a nonsufficient funds (NSF) check of $2,400 that was received from a customer.
c. The balance in Singleton's cash account on August 31 is $126,692.
d. On August 31, deposits in transit total $53,600 and outstanding checks total $35,852.

Required

a. Prepare a bank reconciliation at August 31 of the current year.
b. Present the adjustments necessitated by the preparation of the bank reconciliation.

YOUR PERFORMANCE OBJECTIVE 22
(page 354)

P8-15 Preparing a Bank Reconciliation
Rohas Corporation's bank statement for the month ended October 31 is shown here.

Previous balance as of October 1		$ 8,600
Add:		
Deposits	$28,000	
Note collected by bank	1,060	29,060
Subtotal		37,660
Deduct:		
Checks cleared	(32,200)	
NSF check from customer	(20)	
Bank service charge	(35)	(32,255)
New balance as of October 31		$ 5,405

Additional Information

a. The note collected by the bank includes $60 of interest.
b. A comparison of deposits recorded by the company with deposits on the bank statement showed deposits in transit of $3,000.
c. Similarly, outstanding checks at the end of October were determined to be $900.
d. A check actually written by Rohas to a creditor for $540 was erroneously recorded on the books as $450.
e. The company cash account in the ledger is shown below:

Cash

Oct. 1	8,220		
Deposits	31,000	32,630	Checks written
	6,590		

Required

a. Prepare a bank reconciliation at October 31 of the current year.
b. Present the adjustments necessitated by the preparation of the bank reconciliation.

YOUR PERFORMANCE OBJECTIVE 22
(page 354)

P8-16 Preparing a Bank Reconciliation
The information shown here pertains to the cash of Highlark Company.

	Sept. 30	Oct. 31
Balance per bank statement	$8,614	$ 8,488
Balance per accounting records	8,134	7,900
Deposits in transit	2,055	3,735
Outstanding checks	2,589	3,045
Service charges	54	72
Deposits shown on October bank statement		$16,764
Charges shown on October bank statement		16,890
Cash receipts in October accounting records		16,194
Cash payments in October accounting records		16,428

Additional Information

a. The bank service charge of any month is not recorded by the company until the following month.
b. The bank collected $2,250 of bond interest for Highlark Company during October. The company earned this interest during October but did not record it.
c. On October 12, the company issued a check for $1,000 for the purchase of land. The check cleared the bank during October but was incorrectly recorded by the company as $1,600.

d. A $1,500 customer's check received on October 23 and recorded by Highlark as a cash receipt the same day is returned in the October bank statement and marked nonsufficient funds (NSF).

Required
Prepare Highlark's bank reconciliation as of October 31.

P8-17 Preparing a Bank Reconciliation

YOUR PERFORMANCE OBJECTIVE 22 *(page 354)*

The bookkeeper for Eisner Company prepared the following bank reconciliation at the end of March. All items and amounts are correctly stated, but the bookkeeper did not know where to place them within the bank reconciliation, resulting in unequal adjusted balances.

Balance per bank		$1,742
Add:		
Cash collected by bank for Eisner Company	$421	
Deposit in transit	310	731
Deduct:		2,473
Check written for $820, entered in Eisner's books for $280		(540)
Adjusted balance		$1,933
Balance per books		$2,438
Add:		
Outstanding checks	$656	
Error by bank, entered $1,000 deposit as $100 in account	900	1,556
Deduct:		3,994
Service charge		(23)
Adjusted balance		$3,971

Required
a. For each item listed in the bank reconciliation, explain who knew about the reconciling item at the date of the reconciliation, the bank or Eisner Company.
b. Using the information described in part (a), list in which section (balance per bank or balance per books) each item should appear on the bank reconciliation and explain why.
c. Prepare a corrected bank reconciliation for Eisner Company.

P8-18 Preparing a Bank Reconciliation

YOUR PERFORMANCE OBJECTIVE 22 *(page 354)*

You are the production accountant for the new TV show, "Grover and Friends" premiering this fall on the Little Kid's Channel. In preparing the bank reconciliation for June 30 of the current year, you have obtained the following information:

Additional Information
a. The general ledger cash account balance as of May 31 is $1,914.
b. The June 10 bank statement deposit of professional fees for $768 is correct. It is found in the cash receipts journal on June 8.
c. The NSF check represents a check received from a customer.
d. The credit memo (CM) represents a note receivable collected by the bank. The interest portion is $16.
e. Outstanding checks at the end of May are #204 for $700 and #205 for $2,000. The deposit in transit at the end of May is $482.

Required
a. Prepare a bank reconciliation at June 30 of the current year.
b. Present the adjustments necessitated by the preparation of the bank reconciliation.

LITTLE KIDS PRODUCTIONS
Bank Statement

Hollywood National Bank
Account Name: Grover and Friends

Account No: 6972-07-8451
Date: June 30

Date June	Checks and Withdrawals	Amount	Deposits	Balance
				$ 4,132
1	#205	$2,000	482	2,614
2	#204	700	1,540	3,454
3	#206	787		2,667
10	#207	1,054	768	2,381
10	#208	2,201		180
11	NSF	150		30
14	#209	1,564	5,362	3,828
18	#212	432		3,396
18	#210	56		3,340
28	#214	2,001	1,400	2,739
30	SC	10	141 CM	2,870

Code: I = Interest; NSF = Not Sufficient Funds; SC = Service Charge;
DM = Debit Memo; CM = Credit Memo

Company Cash Receipts

Date	Cash Debit
6/01	$ 1,540
6/08	786
6/14	5,362
6/25	1,400
6/29	1,256
6/30	1,001
	$11,345

Company Cash Payments

Date	Check	Cash Credit	Date	Check	Cash Credit
6/01	206	$ 787	6/17	212	$ 432
6/08	207	1,054	6/22	213	1,891
6/10	208	2,201	6/25	214	2,001
6/11	209	1,564	6/29	215	1,984
6/16	210	56	6/30	216	102
6/17	211	789			$ 12,861

Research Assignments

A wide variety of interesting Research Assignments for this chapter are available for the following topics at www.mhhe.com/solomon:

R8-1 **How to Read a Statement of Cash Flows (PO 7)**
R8-2 **Examining Older Statements of Cash Flows (PO 7)**
R8-3 **Noncorporate Statement of Cash Flows (PO 7)**
R8-4 **Statements of Cash Flow Comparison (PO 7)**
R8-5 **Statements of Cash Flow Comparison (PO 7)**
R8-6 **How Do Investors and Creditors Use Cash Flow Information? (PO 9)**
R8-7 **Using the MD&A to Learn More about the Statement of Cash Flows (PO 7 and 14)**
R8-8 **Using the MD&A to Learn More about the Statement of Cash Flows (PO 7 and 14)**
R8-9 **Using the Notes to Learn More about the Statement of Cash Flows (PO 7 and 14)**
R8-10 **Comparative Financial Analysis of Pharmaceutical Companies (PO 7 and 14)**
R8-11 **Comparative Financial Analysis (PO 7 and 14)**

CHAPTER NINE

9

The Accounting Process: Manual and Computerized Systems

PERFORMANCE OBJECTIVES

In this chapter, you will learn the following new Performance Objectives:

PO23 **Explain** the basic components of internal control and **describe** the attributes of an effective and efficient internal control system.

PO24 **Explain** the meaning of the words *debit* and *credit* and **use** the debit-credit rules (double-entry method of bookkeeping) in all phases of the accounting process.

PO25 **Select** a likely account title for one-half of a transaction when given the account title for the other half of the transaction.

PO26 **Identify**, **list**, and **perform** in their proper sequence each of the following steps normally followed in the accounting process/cycle for preparation of the principal financial statements:

a. **Identify** accounting transactions and **measure** their effects.
b. **Journalize** transaction entries.
c. **Post** journal entries to the individual accounts in the ledger.
d. **Prepare** an unadjusted trial balance.
e. **Journalize** and **post** adjusting and correcting entries.
f. **Prepare** an adjusted trial balance.
g. **Prepare** the financial statements.
h. **Journalize** and **post** closing entries.
i. **Prepare** a post-closing trial balance.

Also be sure you have mastered the following Performance Objectives from previous chapters. They lay the foundation for the concepts you will learn in this chapter:

PO4
PO11b
PO19a

LIFE AS AN ACCOUNTANT

Are you an accounting major? If you think you might want to be, be prepared for the jokes, the name-calling, and the stereotypes. Bean counters! Number crunchers! You've probably heard these names. And in most movies, the accountant is always the guy wearing glasses and a rumpled suit, with the beat-up briefcase, who loves numbers, doing taxes, and living with his mother.

But today's accountants are very different from the images people conjure up when they hear the word *accountant.* The accounting majors of today are more often female than male. They graduate and get jobs in industry, not just in CPA firms. They don't all do taxes. Some do graduate work, and become accounting educators. And in their day-to-day work, many spend less time with the numbers than you'd think. As you've seen so far in this book, accounting is at the heart of doing business. Every business decision has accounting implications and every accounting decision has implications for the success and efficiency of the business.

Why do people become accounting majors? Some people are "good with numbers" and think that they'll like accounting. Some are encouraged by friends and family to seek a profession that will guarantee them prestige and an attractive income. And others take a course—perhaps like the course you're now taking—and discover that they enjoy using accounting concepts to make business decisions.

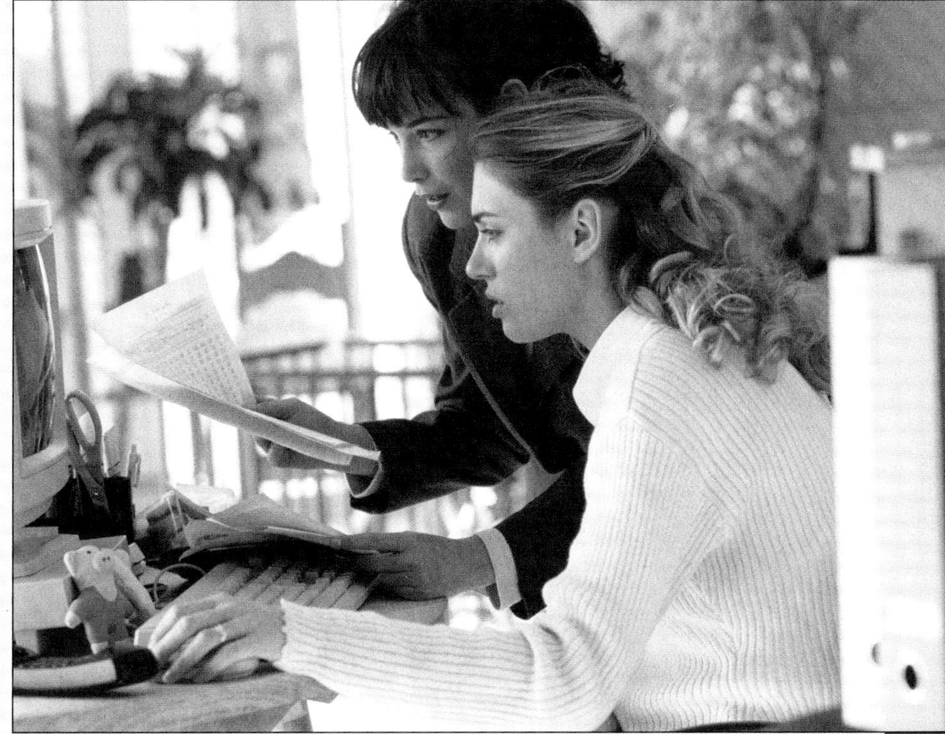

That's what happened to Beverly Alex. After earning a degree in business education, and teaching for a few years, she took a job with IBM as a trainer. The way Beverly describes it, "While working there, I had to take some elective courses at night and chose one in tax. And that was that. I loved it." She readily admits that accounting might not be for everyone, but for her it was a "natural." She liked the research required in tax accounting, the challenge of constantly changing tax laws, and the prospect of helping people who are usually intimidated by the subject matter of taxes. She found accounting stimulating and challenging and fun. Beverly enjoyed her initial taxation course so much that she earned an MS degree in accounting and taxation from the University of Colorado. She worked for the IRS for eight years as a field agent, and then opened her own practice.

The focus of Beverly's accounting practice is to do taxes, but she also consults with her clients to help them computerize their accounting systems and become more efficient. In particular, many of her clients ask about QuickBooks—a software package you'll learn about in this chapter. Using QuickBooks or other accounting software packages, her clients can see where they stand financially on a *daily* basis, something a manual system does not easily allow. When her clients convert from a manual to a computerized system, they can more easily perform activities that they used to hire accountants to do, such as

(continued on next page)

(continued from previous page)

preparing financial statements. Without exception, these clients appreciate how a computerized system can help them save money that they formerly spent on accountants' fees, become more self-sufficient in conducting their business, and make better business decisions.

But Beverly is quick to point out that computerizing her clients' accounting systems does not make her job obsolete. Since her clients seldom have an accounting background, they still need her for tax preparation, for setting up a chart of accounts, and then for continued consultation on accounting issues. For example, most don't know how to properly set up their chart of accounts and what items to include in what accounts. She often tells the story of a client who increased the value of a car he owned whenever he made a car payment! She also helps her clients implement internal controls that improve the efficiency of their operations and often save them the more expensive fees of external auditors.

Beverly is just one example of the thousands of people who own their own accounting practice. Although she took a very traditional route, most accounting majors don't do taxes. Instead, they work with computers in industry and government to process a wide variety of transactions, prepare and interpret reports, and improve the efficiency of their organizations' operation. Many will eventually head up companies because their accounting background helps them understand their businesses so they can make better decisions.

So today, life as an accountant certainly doesn't require that you be a man, wear a rumpled suit, and work alone with numbers!

The Accounting Information System at Cards & Memorabilia Unlimited

When Susan first opened Cards & Memorabilia Unlimited, she decided to use a manual accounting information system. With the help of George Wu, she recorded all of her business transactions by hand on paper. But as her business grew and became more complex, Susan realized that she needed a computerized accounting information system to process the increasing volume of transactions. After discussing the advantages and disadvantages of several accounting software packages with George, Susan decided to purchase QuickBooks, published by Intuit, Inc. George explained that QuickBooks is ideally suited for computerizing the accounting information systems of small businesses. In fact, he heard that it had a very large share of the small business accounting software market. That was good enough for Susan, who bought the software and, again with George's help, began to convert her manual accounting information system into a computerized system.

In this chapter you will learn some basic accounting information systems concepts and, with that foundation, examine Cards & Memorabilia Unlimited's original manual system using debits and credits. Then you will see how Susan implemented her computerized accounting system using QuickBooks.

Information System Concepts

An accounting information system is a specialized part of an entity's overall business information system. Accordingly, this chapter will first define *general* information system concepts such as data, information, input, storage, processing, and output. It will then introduce you to accounting information system concepts. With an understanding of these concepts, you will then see how Cards & Memorabilia Unlimited processed its first-year transactions using both a manual and a computerized accounting information system.

How Is Data Different from Information?

Unless you are a computer professional, you probably use the terms *data* and *information* interchangeably in everyday conversation. In fact, these terms do have very distinct meanings, and understanding this distinction will help you better communicate in the language of business, not just accounting. **Data** is the letters, numbers, and symbols or raw facts and figures that describe people, events, things, and ideas. **Information** is the data that has been transformed into a form useful for decision making.

To better understand this distinction, consider the following example. The letters, numbers, and symbols—100704 SP 5023 crs wmcs $147.59—describe a credit sale transaction that is typical of the data stored in a computer system. When this data is used as the basis for a decision or action, such as mailing customers their invoices, it is more accurately called information. For example, when invoices are prepared by the St. Paul, Minnesota (SP) branch of a large department store, a billing clerk might see the following on the computer screen:

Date	Store Location	Customer Number	Transaction	Department	Amount
10 07 04	SP	5023	crs	wmcs	$147.59

When the bill is printed out and sent to the customer, the letters *crs* and *wmcs* will be converted to credit sale and women's casuals department so the customer will have information to determine whether or not this is a valid invoice. This example also illustrates that 100704 SP 5023 crs wmcs $147.59 can be both data and information depending on its use. If these letters, numbers, and symbols are stored in a computer as raw facts and figures, they are data. If, however, they are acted on or are the basis for a decision, they are information. A convenient way to remember this distinction is that computers use data while humans use information.

What Is an Accounting Information System?

All information systems, whether manual or computerized, and no matter how large or how small, have four components in common: input, processing, storage, and output (Figure 9-1). Understanding these terms is essential to learning how an accounting

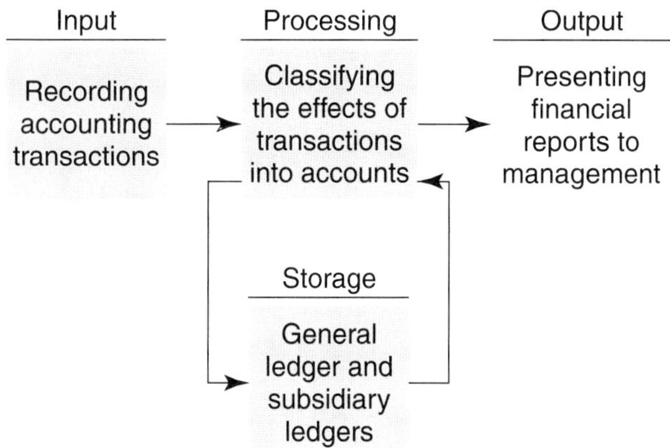

FIGURE 9-1

The four components of an accounting information system

information system functions. So let's examine each of them within the context of an accounting information system.

In an information system, **input** consists of data, that is, letters, numbers, and symbols or raw facts and figures. For example, the credit sale transaction in the previous section represents what some call *input data*. Once this event is considered to be an accounting transaction,[1] it is put into the accounting information system by recording it in the same way you recorded each of CMU's first-year transactions. **Processing** involves activities that transform data into information. For example, when you classify the effects of a day's credit sales transactions into individual accounts receivable and sales revenue accounts, an activity called *posting* in a traditional bookkeeping system, you are processing data. Likewise, when you sort all accounts into assets, liabilities, and owner's equity for their later presentation in a balance sheet, you are processing data. **Storage** is simply the part of an information system that holds data or information for later retrieval and use. For example, evidence of a credit sale (crs) might be *stored* in both a record-keeping system called the *general ledger*, which contains both the Accounts Receivable and Sales Revenue accounts, as well as a record-keeping system called the *accounts receivable subsidiary ledger*, which contains the individual customer's account. The last component, **output**, is the processed data that has been transformed into usable information for decision making. For example, the credit sale (crs) might be included in sales revenue in the income statement or as an uncollected receivable in a report prepared for the credit department. In either case, the information is available to users to help them make decisions.

An **accounting information system (AIS)** is a system that identifies and records accounting transactions (input), processes and stores the effects of these transactions, and communicates their effects in financial reports (output). Every accounting information system is composed of a set of activities that transform the effects of these transactions into financial reports. Although manual and computerized systems share some of the same activities, you will soon learn that they also have unique activities.

Both manual and computerized accounting information systems have at least three record-processing devices in common: a chart of accounts, a general ledger, and one or more subsidiary ledgers. Let's now examine each of these devices as well as distinguish between a transaction cycle and a transaction subsystem.

What Is a Chart of Accounts? One of the first steps required in designing an accounting information system is to develop a chart of accounts. A **chart of accounts** is a complete list of an entity's accounts organized by assigned numbers or codes. Although each entity can design its own numbering scheme, many entities use the following system:

Numbers	Basic Accounts
101–199	Assets
200–299	Liabilities
300–399	Owner Equities
400–499	Revenues
500–599	Expenses

Although the fundamental accounting equation contains only the first three accounts above, subdividing owners' equity into revenues and expenses provides more useful information to both internal and external users. Specifically, it allows you to avoid including revenues and expenses with other transactions that affect owners' equity, such

[1] Recall Chapter 2's discussion of the three conditions necessary for a transaction to qualify as an accounting transaction and, therefore, be recorded in an accounting information system.

as owner contributions and withdrawals. In general, the decision-making needs of a particular entity dictate the way in which the chart of accounts is organized. Thus, the sales revenue account might be subdivided to accommodate several store locations and/or salespersons within each location if, as is likely, the entity needs sales broken into those categories.

Susan Newman's basic code for cash is 101 with 101-01 representing her Cash—Checking account and 101-02 representing her Cash—Savings account. Of course, these CMU account numbers are independent of the account numbers that the bank has assigned to Susan's two accounts. As an entity grows, so, too, does the length of its account numbers. If CMU, for example, added stores in Manchester, New Hampshire, and Dallas, Texas, these same accounts might be organized with prefixes assigned to cities as follows:

	Cash—Checking	Cash—Savings
Manchester	101–01–10	101–02–10
Dallas	101–01–30	101–02–30

Accounts may also be organized by departments within a particular location. Assume, for example, that the Depreciation Expense account is 514, the corporate office code is 111, and the warehouse code is 311. For these same city locations, the applicable numbers are:

	Depreciation Expense	
	Corporate Office	Warehouse
Manchester	514–10–111	514–10–311
Dallas	514–30–111	514–30–311

As you can see, the numbering possibilities are nearly unlimited. In fact, some companies have account numbers in excess of 30 digits.

Although all charts of accounts have similarities, the specific set of accounts used by different businesses varies widely. Compare, for example, the chart of accounts used by a church in Figure 9-2 to the chart of accounts used by a cleaning and janitorial service in Figure 9-3.[2] To minimize differences, various organizations have developed and published uniform account classifications. One such group, the National Association of Public Accountants, has published uniform charts of accounts and accounting information system guidelines for 60 different business types.

What Are a General Ledger and a Subsidiary Ledger? A **general ledger** is a record-keeping device that expresses an organization's chart of accounts in money terms. It contains all of the entity's assets, liabilities, and owner equities including its revenue and expense accounts and is, thus, the basis for the entity's financial statements. In contrast, a **subsidiary ledger** is a more detailed version of a specific general ledger account. For example, the Accounts Receivable account in the general ledger is a controlling, or parent, account for all the individual customer accounts in a subsidiary accounts receivable ledger.

---

[2] Adapted from *Portfolio of Accounting Systems for Small and Medium-Sized Businesses*, National Association of Public Accountants, Third Edition, Prentice-Hall, 1992, pp. 214–215 and 246–247.

FIGURE 9-2 A church's chart of accounts

Account	Description	Account	Description
Current Assets		611	Janitorial and building maintenance supplies
103	Bank account	612	Bulk mailing and P.O. box rent
103-01	General fund	613	Advertising
103-02	Building fund	614	Dues, subscriptions, and memberships
103-03	Missionary fund	615	Social expenses
103-04	Other or designated fund	616	Flowers
Plant, Property, and Equipment		617	Benevolence gifts
140	Land	620	Special speakers expense
141	Land improvements	621	Travel expenses for speakers
142	Buildings	622	Meeting expenses
144	Furniture, fixtures, and equipment	630	Pastor's salary
Liabilities		631	Pastor's allowances
210	Loans payable (Use a separate consecutive number for each loan or note payable)	632	Pastor's insurance
		635	Other salaries and wages
		636	Payroll taxes
Reserves or Net Worth		640	Conference expenses for church members
300	Reserves invested in general funds		
310	Plant, property, and equipment	650	Property maintenance and upkeep
		653	Real estate taxes
Church Operation Accounts		654	Insurance (other than for pastor)
Proceeds		655	Utilities—heat, light, and water
510	Donations received—general fund	656	Telephone
511	Loans received—general fund	670	Loan principal payments (general fund loans only)
512	Expense refund—general fund		
520	Donations received—building fund	675	Interest paid—all loans (It is a general policy that the general fund pay all interest.)
521	Loans received—building fund		
522	Expense refund—building fund		
530	Donations received—missionary fund	700	Land purchases
540′	Donations received—other or designated funds	701	Land improvements
		702	Building costs (initial construction or improvements increasing value of building)
Expenses or Disbursements			
601	Sunday school expenses		
602	Training League expenses	704	Furniture, fixture, and equipment purchases
604	Youth program expenses		
605	Church literature	730	Missionary fund disbursements
610	Office and general supplies	740	Other or designated fund disbursements

In theory, every account in the general ledger can justify having a subsidiary ledger. In practice, however, the most common subsidiary ledgers are those for accounts receivable, accounts payable, payroll, and depreciable assets. Figure 9-4 describes the relationship between a controlling account in the general ledger and its subsidiary ledger.

What Is a Transaction Cycle? Every accounting information system relies on a set of internal control principles to ensure that it operates effectively and efficiently. Rather than examining these controls from transaction to transaction, we'll examine them from the more organized perspective of transaction cycles, which represent the various business activities of the company. A **transaction cycle** is a series or set of related transactions that has an effect on the financial statements. Although financing transactions and investing transactions can be associated with identifiable transaction cycles, the vast majority of any entity's transactions are included in operating activities. In fact, these transactions either directly comprise or support the entity's operating cycle as discussed in Chapter 5. Figure 9-5 shows how individual transactions may be logically grouped into a **spending cycle**, a **conversion cycle**, a

FIGURE 9-3 A cleaning and janitorial service chart of accounts

Account	Name
	Assets
	Current Assets
1000	Cash on hand
1010	Cash in bank—check
1020	Cash in bank—P/R
1030	Accounts receivable
1040	Prepaid insurance
1050	Prepaid interest
1060	Deposits
1070	Supplies inventory
	Plant and Equipment
1110	Vacuums and sweepers
1111	Accumulated depreciation
1120	Wall cleaning machinery
1121	Accumulated depreciation
1130	Autos and trucks
1131	Accumulated depreciation
1140	Office furniture
1141	Accumulated depreciation
1150	Building
1151	Accumulated depreciation
1160	Leasehold improvements
	Liabilities
2000	Accrued payroll tax
2010	FICA tax withholding
2020	Federal withholding
2030	State withholding
2040	City withholding
2050	Uniform deduction
2100	Accounts payable
2110	Loans payable—bank
2120	Loans payable—other
2130	Notes payable—bank
2140	Notes payable—other
2150	Officer loans
	Capital/Stockholders Equity
3000	Owner's capital
3001	Draw, owner
3000	Common stock
3001	Retained earnings
3002	Paid-in capital
	Revenue and Expense
	Revenue
4000	Dusting/polishing fees
4001	Vacuum/sweeping fees
4002	Wall washing
4003	General cleaning
4004	Polishing/waxing floors
4005	Misc. revenue
	Expenses
5000	Wages
5001	Taxes—payroll
5002	Subcontract/temp. help
5003	Depreciation—equipment
5004	Taxes—other
5005	Buckets and brooms
5006	Equipment rental
5007	Auto and truck—gas/oil
5008	M & R equipment
5009	Advertising
5010	Purchases—supplies
5011	Meals and entertainment
5012	Customer gifts
5013	Utilities/gas and electric
5014	Depreciation—autos and trucks
5015	Uniform expense
6000	Salaries—admin. and supervisory
6001	Payroll tax—admin. and supervisory
6002	Legal and accounting
6003	Telephone
6004	Insurance
6005	Depreciation—office furniture
6006	Rent
6007	Office supplies and postage
6008	Interest
6009	Misc. general expense

revenue cycle, and an **administrative cycle** depending on the business documentation used and the types of accounts recorded and reported. For example, the revenue cycle often includes a sales invoice, the recording of changes to the Accounts Receivable and Sales Revenue accounts, and the recognition, or reporting, of revenue.

Further, the concepts of spending, conversion and revenue transaction cycles can help you distinguish among service, merchandising, and manufacturing entities. For example, service entities, such as H & R Block, or Blue Cross/Blue Shield, typically experience a high number of revenue cycle transactions. Merchandising entities, such as Cards & Memorabilia Unlimited or Nordstrom's, require both the revenue and spending cycles to adequately cover their activities. Finally, manufacturing entities, such as Chevron or Apple Computer, require not only the revenue and spending cycles, but also the conversion cycle, which transforms raw materials acquired in the spending cycle into finished goods resold to customers in the revenue cycle.

FIGURE 9-4 The relationship between a controlling account in the general ledger and its subsidiary ledger

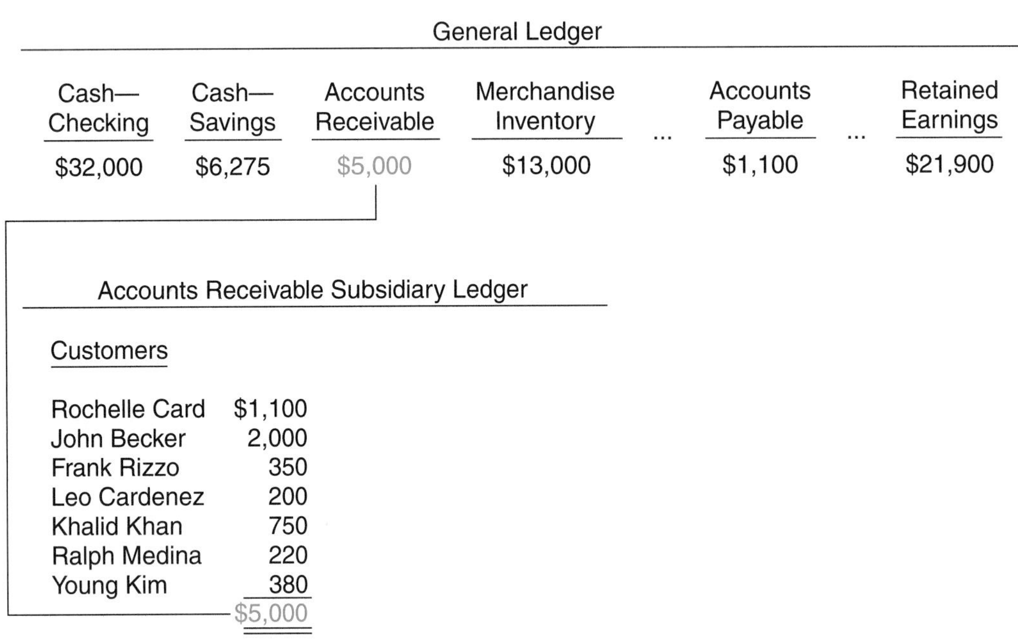

FIGURE 9-5 Transaction cycle model of an accounting information system

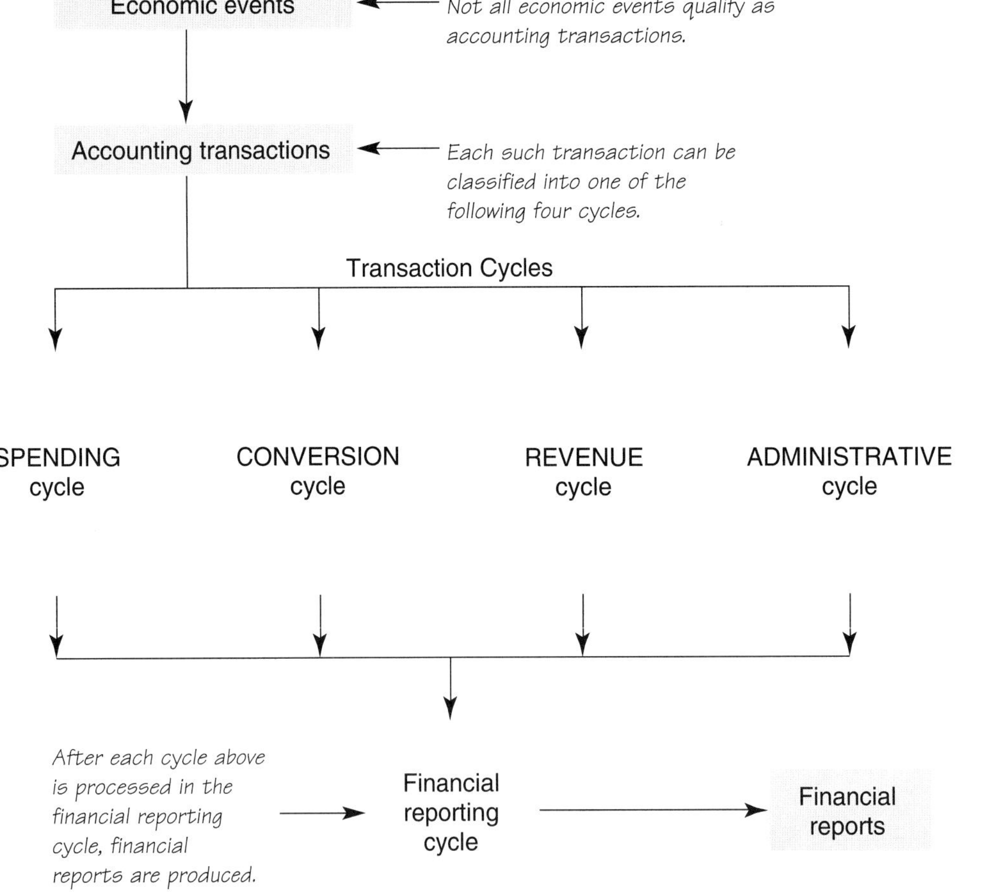

What Is a Transaction Subsystem? Each transaction cycle may be further broken down into transaction subsystems. A **transaction subsystem** is simply a sequence of separate but related activities that together make a complete transaction cycle. For example, the administrative cycle consists of at least four transaction subsystems:

1. A cash management or control system.
2. A property, plant, and equipment control system.
3. A payroll and human resources management system.
4. A general ledger system, which is the ultimate destination of all the entity's transaction effects.

The conversion or production cycle, as it is sometimes called, consists of at least three transaction subsystems:

1. An inventory control system, which controls raw materials acquired from vendors for manufacture. These raw materials pass through the receiving and inspection departments on their way to the inventory storerooms to be readied for production.
2. A production control system, which transforms inputs into desired outputs in the most effective and efficient manner possible.
3. A payroll system, which accurately reports the portion of a product's manufactured cost that is attributable to employee labor and protects the entity from fraudulent payroll practices.

Figure 9-6 illustrates the distinction between a transaction cycle and its transaction subsystems.

Transaction cycle	Administrative cycle
Transaction subsystems	Cash management or control Property, plant, and equipment control Payroll and human resources management General ledger

FIGURE 9-6

Distinguishing between a transaction cycle and its transaction subsystems

What Is Internal Control?[3]

Now that you have a basic understanding of an accounting information system, let's consider how this system is organized to insure internal control. **Internal control** is a process designed to reduce inaccuracy in the accounting information system and discourage unethical and illegal behavior among employees and customers. A properly designed internal control system will affect all aspects of an entity's activities. It is, therefore, essential that internal controls are a fundamental part of the entity, built *into* rather than built *on* the entity's foundation. This is accomplished by having all people at *every* level of the entity implement internal control. Internal control provides assurance that operations are both effective and efficient, financial reporting is reliable, and applicable laws and regulations are followed. Today, an entity can show its

[3] The source of the materials in this section is *Internal Control—Integrated Framework,* Committee of Sponsoring Organizations of the Treadway Commission (COSO), AI CPA, September 1992. These materials are the accounting profession's authoritative source for internal control principles.

commitment to the principles of internal control by declaring in its annual report that it is responsible for the accuracy of its financial statements and the integrity of its control system. Recall from Chapter 3 that this section of the annual report (Figure 9-7) is often called the Report of Management, or Management Statement of Responsibility. No entity's internal control system is flawless; but top management should have confidence that the system is reasonably foolproof.

Internal control consists of five interrelated components that are a fundamental part of the way management runs its business. These components are:

1. ***Control environment:*** In a control environment, management communicates to employees through established codes of conduct that integrity and ethical values cannot be compromised. Such "a tone at the top" is conveyed by Dow Chemical's statement in Figure 9-7 that "Management recognizes its responsibility for fostering a strong ethical climate so that the Company's affairs are conducted according to the highest standards of personal and corporate conduct." Although CMU does not have a written code of conduct, the commitment to integrity and ethical behavior of owner-managers like Susan Newman and Martha Perez is communicated orally—in staff meetings, one-on-one meetings, and dealings with customers and vendors.
2. ***Risk assessment:*** By risk we mean the probability of suffering loss from the occurrence of an event. To evaluate how well the entity's accounting information system reacts to risk, you must first identify what that entity's objectives are. Only then can management identify, analyze, and manage the risks that threaten their achievement. Despite its small size, Cards & Memorabilia Unlimited has established objectives. Recall, for example, that its target market was collectors. What

FIGURE 9-7 Management statement of responsibility for The Dow Chemical Company

Responsibility for Financial Statements and Independent Auditors' Report

Management Statement of Responsibility

The management of The Dow Chemical Company and its subsidiaries prepared the accompanying consolidated financial statements, and has responsibility for their integrity,objectivity and freedom from material misstatement or error. These statements were prepared in accordance with generally accepted accounting principles. The financial statements include amounts that are based on management's best estimates and judgments. Management also prepared the other information in this annual report and is responsible for its accuracy and consistency with the financial statements. The Board of Directors, through its Audit Committee, assumes an oversight role with respect to the preparation of the financial statements.

Management recognizes its responsibility for fostering a strong ethical climate so that the Company's affairs are conducted according to the highest standards of personal and corporate conduct. Management has established and maintains a system of internal control that provides reasonable assurance as to the integrity and reliability of the financial statements, the protection of assets from unauthorized use or disposition, and the prevention and detection of fraudulent financial reporting.

The system of internal control provides for appropriate division of responsibility and is documented by written policies and procedures that are communicated to employees with significant roles in the financial reporting process and updated as necessary. Management continually monitors the system of internal control for compliance. The Company maintains a strong internal auditing program that independently assesses the effectiveness of the internal controls and recommends possible improvements.

Deloitte & Touche LLP, independent auditors, with direct access to the Board of Directors through its Audit Committee, has audited the consolidated financial statements prepared by the Company, and their report follows.

Management has considered recommendations from the internal auditors and Deloitte & Touche LLP concerning the system of internal control and has taken actions that are cost-effective in the circumstances to respond appropriately to these recommendations. Management further believes the controls are adequate to accomplish the objectives discussed herein.

external and internal factors might threaten the achievement of this objective? For example, the major league baseball strike of 1994–1995 seriously dampened the attractiveness of most current baseball cards and memorabilia through the spring of 1996. Compare this external risk with the internal risk to Susan's system of internal controls when she decided to hire part-time help a few months after she began operating. In this case, the expectation that employees other than the owner-manager are expected to safeguard assets and record transactions properly does potentially jeopardize objectives and increases risk.

3. ***Control activities:*** Control activities are the policies and procedures used by an entity to ensure that top management's directives (that is, the control environment) are carried out and that the risks to achievement of the entity's objectives are addressed (that is, risk assessment). They include a wide range of activities such as authorizations, verifications, reconciliations, safeguarding of assets, and segregation of duties. These control activities are needed even in smaller entities, such as CMU. In fact, in such smaller entities, they are often easier to implement. Consider, for example, the principle that duties should be segregated so that one employee does not have control over both the cash received from customers and the customer accounting records. This potential problem does not exist in CMU because only the owner-managers have access to the accounting records.

4. ***Information and communication:*** An effective internal control system enables the entity to identify and capture financial and nonfinancial information so that it can be communicated to people in a reliable and timely manner. At CMU, the effectiveness of the internal control system is facilitated by the frequent day-to-day discussions that the owner-managers have with key customers and suppliers. Likewise, effective communication between the owner-managers and employees, as well as between the owner-managers and customers/suppliers is easier to achieve because of the smaller size of the entity and the easier access to the owner-managers. A rule of thumb is that information is likely to be shared and communicated less effectively as the entity grows larger.
5. ***Monitoring:*** The entire process of internal control must be monitored, and modifications must be made as necessary so the system can react to changes as conditions warrant. In a smaller company such as CMU, there is less need for formal, separate evaluations of the internal control system and more dependence on ongoing monitoring activities. One such monitoring activity might be when Susan takes a physical count of store merchandise and compares it to the amount reported by her accounting records.

How Internal Control Is Implemented in the Revenue Cycle

To give you a more concrete understanding of internal control, we begin with an in-depth look at the revenue cycle, a series or set of related transactions engaged in by nearly all entities. We'll first examine the transaction subsystems of this cycle and the business documents associated with these subsystems. Then, with that background, we'll consider some revenue cycle procedures that can be implemented to increase the effectiveness and efficiency of the internal control system.

Transaction Subsystems and Business Documents The revenue cycle can be divided into at least the three following separate transaction subsystems:

1. *Marketing system:* also known as the *customer order entry system* or simply the *sales system*: capturing and recording sales orders.
2. *Shipping system:* shipping goods and recording cost of goods sold.
3. *Billing and collection system:* billing and recording accounts receivable and sales revenue.

The **marketing system** encompasses events or transactions related to promoting the product, granting credit to customers, and selling the product or service described in a *sales order*. A **sales order** is a document with descriptions and prices of products ordered, as well as such data as customer name, shipping address, and mailing address. Figure 9-8 is an example of a sales order. Marketing transactions begin with the first contact between seller and customer, and end when the goods or services are ready for transfer from seller to customer. The documentation used varies widely but most commonly is initiated with a customer-initiated request for specific

FIGURE 9-8

An example of a sales order

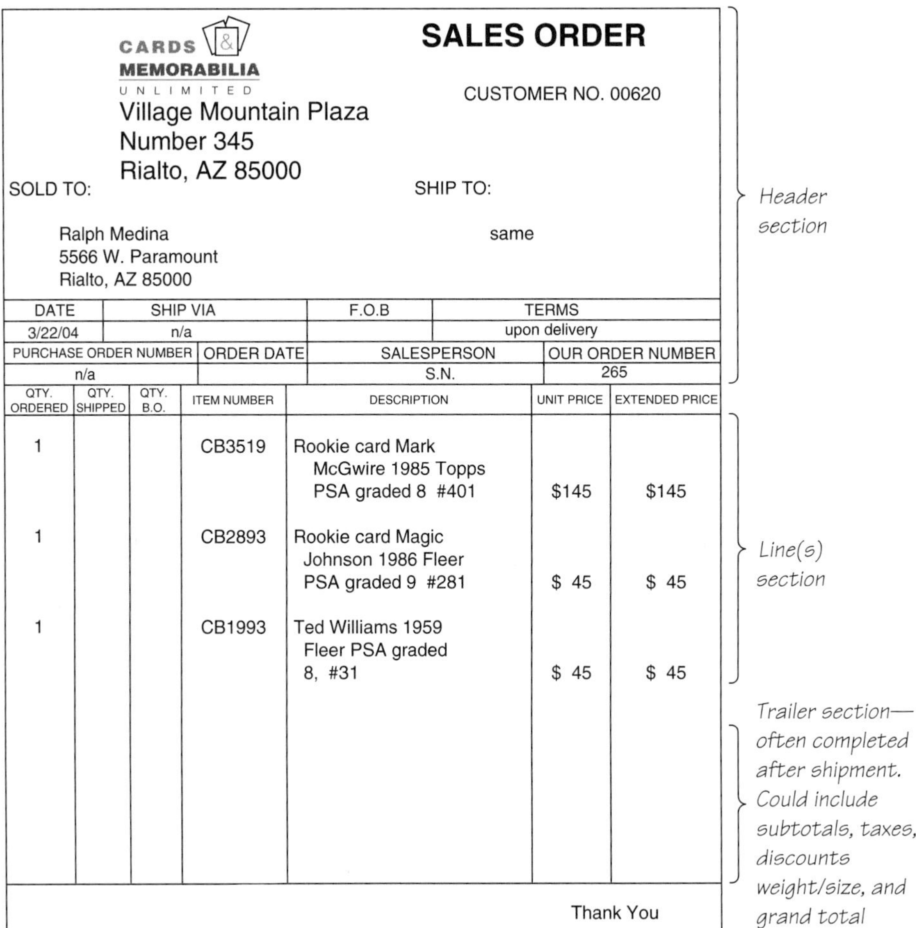

CARDS & MEMORABILIA UNLIMITED
Village Mountain Plaza
Number 345
Rialto, AZ 85000

SALES ORDER

CUSTOMER NO. 00620

SOLD TO: Ralph Medina, 5566 W. Paramount, Rialto, AZ 85000

SHIP TO: same

DATE	SHIP VIA	F.O.B	TERMS
3/22/04	n/a		upon delivery

PURCHASE ORDER NUMBER	ORDER DATE	SALESPERSON	OUR ORDER NUMBER
n/a		S.N.	265

QTY. ORDERED	QTY. SHIPPED	QTY. B.O.	ITEM NUMBER	DESCRIPTION	UNIT PRICE	EXTENDED PRICE
1			CB3519	Rookie card Mark McGwire 1985 Topps PSA graded 8 #401	$145	$145
1			CB2893	Rookie card Magic Johnson 1986 Fleer PSA graded 9 #281	$ 45	$ 45
1			CB1993	Ted Williams 1959 Fleer PSA graded 8, #31	$ 45	$ 45

Thank You

goods or a purchase order. A sales order is prepared by the seller once the customer's credit standing has been checked and approved.

Sellers fill out a shipping order and give it to a shipper, such as Federal Express, who delivers the merchandise to a customer. The customer usually signs the shipping order upon receipt of the merchandise.

The **shipping system** includes events or transactions that are needed to transfer goods from the seller's possession to the customer's possession. The documentation used by the seller almost always includes a shipping order or packing slip, and a bill of lading. A **shipping order** is a document that describes the shipment destination, the expected date of arrival, the mode of transportation, the shipping terms, and the entity responsible for the freight charges. It is prepared by the seller and is received by the customer along with the merchandise. A **bill of lading** is the paperwork exchanged between a shipper and carrier such as a trucking company. The customer, of course, will prepare a receiving document once the goods arrive.

The **billing and collection system** includes events and transactions that begin with the preparation of a sales invoice by the seller and end with the conversion of the customer receivable into cash. A **sales invoice** is the seller's request for payment

FIGURE 9-9 An example of a sales invoice

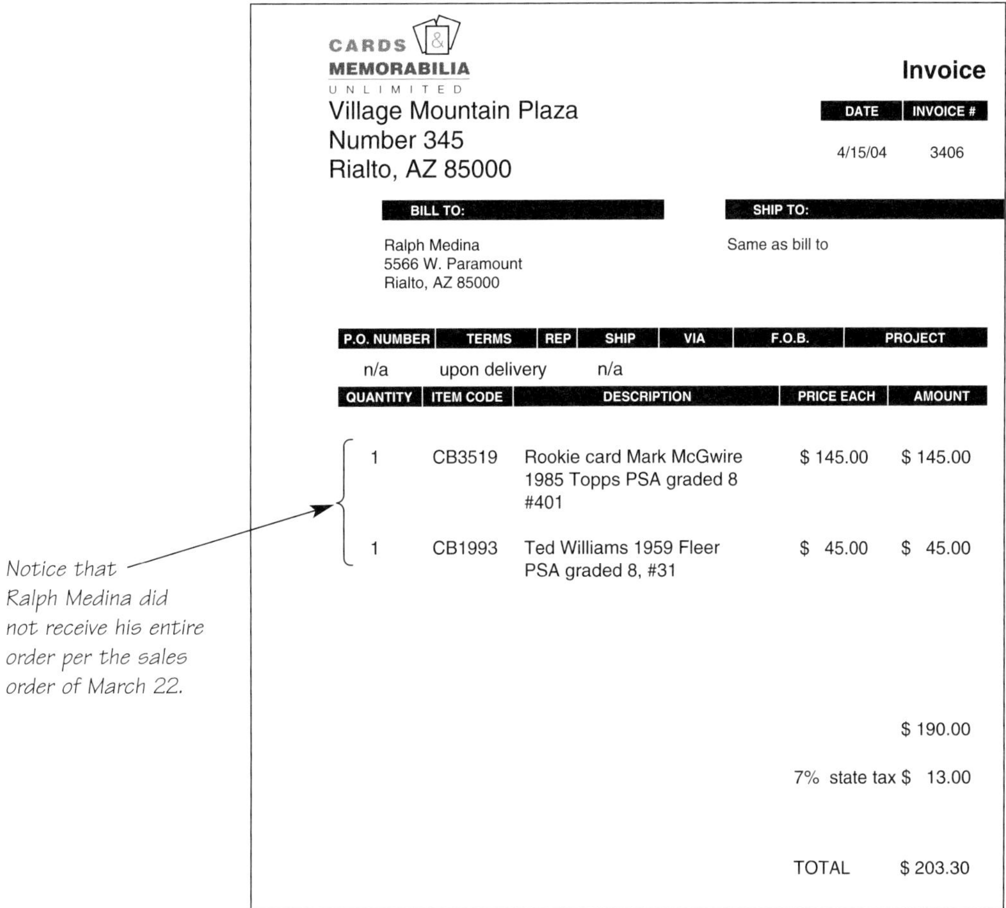

CARDS & MEMORABILIA UNLIMITED
Village Mountain Plaza
Number 345
Rialto, AZ 85000

Invoice

DATE	INVOICE #
4/15/04	3406

BILL TO:	SHIP TO:
Ralph Medina 5566 W. Paramount Rialto, AZ 85000	Same as bill to

P.O. NUMBER	TERMS	REP	SHIP	VIA	F.O.B.	PROJECT
n/a	upon delivery	n/a				

QUANTITY	ITEM CODE	DESCRIPTION	PRICE EACH	AMOUNT
1	CB3519	Rookie card Mark McGwire 1985 Topps PSA graded 8 #401	$ 145.00	$ 145.00
1	CB1993	Ted Williams 1959 Fleer PSA graded 8, #31	$ 45.00	$ 45.00
				$ 190.00
			7% state tax $	13.00
			TOTAL	$ 203.30

from the customer, that is, the seller's bill. An example is Figure 9-9. It often includes more current information than the sales order, because it is usually prepared at the same time that goods are being readied to be shipped.

Notice that Ralph Medina did not receive his entire order per the sales order of March 22.

Internal Control Procedures Now that you have learned the essentials of the subsystems and documents of the revenue cycle, let's look at three internal control procedures related to the revenue cycle—one for each transaction subsystem:

1. *Marketing system:* Prenumbering sales orders and investigating missing documents are necessary to properly capture and record sales orders. This procedure is important because it helps determine whether or not sales orders are lost.
2. *Shipping system:* Comparing the information found on the shipping order to the information found on the sales order is an essential control procedure for the shipping system. This comparison establishes at least three controls—it allows the entity to ship only those products that are authorized for shipment, it promotes the delivery of products in the most efficient manner, and it confirms that all shipments are properly documented. These controls enable necessary documents to be forwarded to accounts receivable on a timely basis.
3. *Billing and collection system:* A control procedure that helps ensure the integrity of this system is be sure that the customer information on a transaction's sales order, shipping order, bill of lading, and sales invoice is identical. By following through on missing or inconsistent information, you can more accurately record invoices for all authorized shipments.

How Internal Control Is Implemented in the Spending Cycle

To further contribute to your concrete understanding of internal control, let's next take an in-depth look at the spending cycle, a series or set of related transactions engaged in by all entities. We'll first examine the transaction subsystems of this cycle and the business documents associated with these subsystems. Then with that background, we'll consider some spending cycle procedures that can be implemented to increase the effectiveness and efficiency of the internal control system.

Transaction Subsystems and Business Documents The spending or expenditure cycle can be divided into the following separate transaction subsystems:

1. *Purchasing system:* Preparing and processing purchase orders.
2. *Receiving system:* Receiving and inspecting goods.
3. *Accounts payable system:* Receiving vendor invoices and recording both purchases and accounts payable.

The **purchasing system** includes events or transactions related to selecting vendors, preparing purchase requisitions, and preparing and processing purchase orders. A **purchase requisition** is an internal request to acquire goods and services. Assume, for example, that the Sporting Life Bar and Grill, a chain of restaurants, wants to buy some sports memorabilia to decorate one of its restaurants. A manager would prepare a purchase requisition and send it to a separate purchasing department within Sporting Life. An employee in the purchasing department would, in turn, prepare a **purchase order**, an external request to purchase goods and services from a vendor as shown in Figure 9-10.

The **receiving system** includes events or transactions that transfer goods from the vendor to the purchaser. The documentation used by the purchaser usually involves a receiving report. A **receiving report** is a business document prepared by the purchaser to describe the content of goods received. This document is first compared to the vendor's packing slip or shipping order to ensure there is agreement between the vendor's shipping department and the purchaser's receiving department. The receiving report is also compared to the purchase order to determine if the actual goods received agree in quantity and characteristics with what had been ordered.

The **accounts payable system** is initiated when the vendor's invoice is received. A **vendor's invoice** or vendor's bill is the vendor's request for payment from the purchaser and is the mirror image of the entity's sales invoice. When both the goods ordered and their invoice are received, the entity has an obligation to pay the vendor. When a comparison of the vendor's invoice to the purchase order and receiving report confirms its accuracy, the entity will create an account payable to reflect that obligation.

Internal Control Procedures Now that you have learned the essentials of the subsystems and documents of the spending cycle, let's look at three internal control procedures related to the spending cycle—one for each transaction subsystem.

1. *Purchasing system:* If you carefully review and approve purchase orders, you are more likely to order items that meet appropriate specifications and are from vendors who are legally qualified and who sell at competitive prices.
2. *Receiving system:* If you monitor the timeliness of your vendors' delivery, you will be able to follow up on poorly performing vendors and improve your chances of receiving items on time in the future.
3. *Accounts payable system:* If you resolve differences between the Accounts Payable Subsidiary Ledger and the Accounts Payable control account, you will enhance the completeness and accuracy of this system. That is, if the combined

FIGURE 9-10 An example of a purchase order

FROM:

The Sp⊘rting Life
Bar & Grill

TO Cards & Memorabilia Unlimited
ADDRESS Village Mountain Plaza
Number 345
Rialto, AZ 85000

DATE May 22, 2004
FOR
HOW SHIP UPS Groundtrak
TERMS
☐ TAXABLE ☐ RESALE _ PERMIT No.
SHIP TO The Sporting Life
ADDRESS 4560 Camelback Blvd
Phoenix, AZ 85261

DATE REQUIRED August 15. 2004

QUANTITY	DESCRIPTION	UNIT PRICE		AMOUNT	
1	Whitey Ford tri-color pinstripe				
	jersey	95	00	95	00
1	Sammy Sosa autographed bat from 1999				
	season	175	00	175	00

IMPORTANT
PLEASE NOTIFY US IMMEDIATELY IF YOU ARE UNABLE TO COMPLETE ORDER BY DATE SPECIFIED

PURCHASING AGENT
Lou Hamlein

totals of your individual supplier accounts do not equal the total of your Accounts Payable general ledger account, there are one or more errors to correct.

The Attributes of an Effective and Efficient Internal Control System

Just as successful entities often have different missions or operating procedures, so too can effective internal control systems vary somewhat between entities. Nevertheless, we can safely generalize about several attributes that most entities have in common—specifically proper authorization, segregation of duties, independent verifications, proper design and use of documents and records, and resource security. In large entities, these activities or procedures are described in written operating manuals. In smaller companies, they are often communicated during the training process. To illustrate the general attributes found in an effective and efficient internal control system, we'll consider them in the context of Cards & Memorabilia Unlimited. To test your familiarity with the basic components of internal control and with the attributes of an effective and efficient internal control system, you will use the following performance objective:

YOUR PERFORMANCE OBJECTIVE 23

Explain the basic components of internal control and **describe** the attributes of an effective and efficient internal control system.

Proper Authorization Some transactions should not be allowed to occur without proper authorization from management. At CMU, employees know that they are authorized to process normal cash sales but are required to receive a manager's approval for other transactions, such as customer checks above $500 or refunds for returned or damaged goods. Authorizations can cover a wide range of transactions. For example, only the owner-managers (Susan and Martha) are allowed to authorize customer layaway purchases in which merchandise is "held" for customers who pay on an installment basis.

Segregation of Duties Duties should be segregated so that one employee does not have control over operating a department, authorizing transactions, handling assets such as cash received from customers, and record keeping. For example, it is very difficult to detect when an accountant prematurely classifies a customer account as uncollectible and steals the cash mailed in by the customer. This potential problem would not materialize at CMU because only the owner-managers have access to the accounting records.

Independent Verifications An employee who records assets should not also handle assets. Further, employees who perform either of these functions should not be responsible for verifying that an asset record accurately reflects the asset itself. Instead, an independent employee should perform this verification. For example, whenever Susan leaves her store for several hours, she always returns by the end of the day to count the cash in the cash drawer. Susan does this to independently verify that the amount of cash agrees with the record of cash reported by the sales terminal. A variation of this control is the rule that employees must take regular vacations—many elaborate embezzlement schemes have been uncovered when replacement employees discover irregularities that cannot be easily explained.

Proper Design and Use of Documents and Records All documents should be prenumbered and all numbers accounted for to ensure that all transactions are recorded. Susan, for example, regularly checks for any gaps in the numbered sequence of her cash sale receipts. This procedure allows her to immediately identify missing documents or other discrepancies. If she didn't use prenumbered cash sales receipts, an employee could destroy the document and steal the associated cash. Thus, the prenumbering control discourages fraudulent activities.

Resource Security Unlike a billing and collection system, the cash sale transaction subsystem has no previous asset record (customer account balance). Thus, accounting control cannot be initiated in a cash sale until a business document has been created. In smaller businesses, this business document is a standardized sales slip or

FIGURE 9-11

A cash sale transaction subsystem

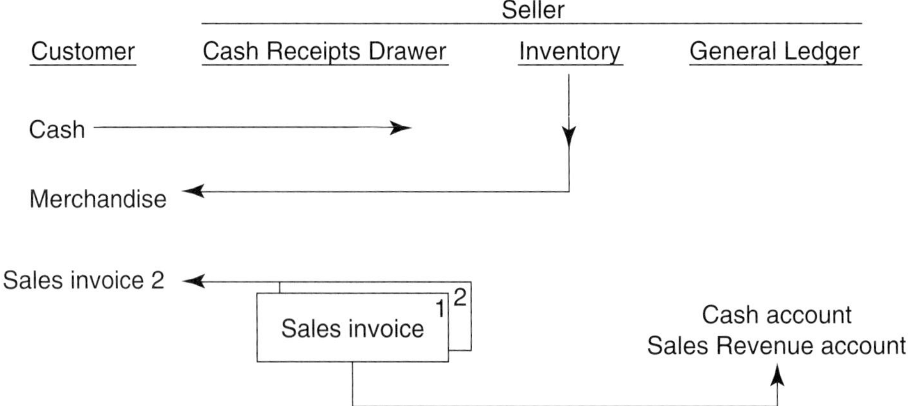

sales invoice prepared by the salesperson. Figure 9-11, for example, illustrates that when merchandise is sold to a customer in exchange for cash, one copy of the sales invoice is given to the customer and another copy is used as the basis for recording the cash sale.

Processing Transactions Manually to Produce Financial Statements

You might well ask why you should study manual transaction processing today when most businesses use computerized systems. One reason is that the accounting concepts you need to grasp are more evident in a manual system than in a computerized system. Another reason is that many small businesses begin their operations with manual accounting systems before they convert to a computerized system. You might, therefore, encounter the essential design and structure of such systems sometime during your career. In addition, you might set up such a system or assist a small business for which you are working adopt a computerized system.

In previous chapters, you learned about the content of and uses for each of the primary financial statements. In fact, you actually prepared these statements for CMU by applying transaction analysis to each of the summary transactions A_1 through Z. Although that transaction analysis approach provides an accurate means for reporting financial information, it is very time-consuming. In fact, businesses use a more efficient approach called the *double-entry bookkeeping system*, a system best known for its trademark terms, *debit* and *credit*. Although this textbook's purpose is not to train you as an accountant, it is difficult to understand the essential workings of an accounting information system without being able to explain the role of debits and credits in such a system. Accordingly, you will now learn how the language of debits and credits is used to process large numbers of business transactions. Once you have learned this language, you will apply it to once more record CMU's transactions and prepare its first-year financial statements.

An Overview of the Accounting Process

The **accounting process**, also known as the **accounting cycle**, is the sequence of steps that transforms the effects of accounting transactions into financial statements. As you learned earlier in this chapter, the accounting information system is a system that identifies and records accounting transactions, processes and stores the effects of these transactions, and communicates their effects in the form of financial statements. If you were to manually process these transactions, you would perform the following nine steps to complete the accounting process:

1. Identify accounting transactions and measure their effects.
2. Record these accounting transactions.
3. Transfer the effects of these recorded transactions to individual accounts in the ledgers.
4. Prepare an unadjusted trial balance from the ledger balances.
5. Record and transfer both transaction adjustments and transaction corrections to the ledgers.
6. Prepare an adjusted trial balance.
7. Prepare the financial statements.
8. Record and transfer to the general ledger the effects of transactions that serve to close the temporary accounts.
9. Prepare a post-closing trial balance.

Each of these nine steps is performed at least once during each accounting period. But before exploring the nine steps in more detail, let's first see how debits and credits streamline the accounting process.

The Double-Entry Bookkeeping System

The fundamental storage device of the double-entry method of bookkeeping is the account. The **account** is simply a financial record that documents increases and decreases in specific assets, liabilities, and owner equities. For example, the Cash account of Cards & Memorabilia Unlimited, Inc. represents a complete record of how the asset Cash was increased and decreased during the period. If transactions are processed manually—that is, by hand—rather than by computer, each account might occupy one page of the general ledger. For analytical and educational purposes, however, the use of a T-account is often more efficient. A **T-account** is an account shaped like the letter T as shown here:

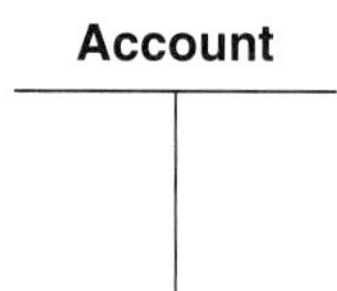

Every account has two sides, a left side and a right side, as illustrated in the following T-account:

Account	
Left side	Right side

Although it is an arbitrary assignment, you will always record increases on the left side of an asset account and decreases on the right side of an asset account as follows:

Asset Account	
Left side Increase	Right side Decrease

Whenever you transfer a number on the asset side of the fundamental accounting equation to the sources of assets side of the equation, you must reverse its sign (plus or minus). In the same manner, you must treat the increase and decrease sides of assets as the exact opposite of the increase and decrease sides of asset sources—as shown here:

Sources of Assets Account	
Left side Decrease	Right side Increase

As you might expect, the two major sources of assets follow this rule:

Liability Account	
Left side Decrease	Right side Increase

Owner Equity Account	
Left side Decrease	Right side Increase

Let's now illustrate the double-entry system by examining how Transaction A_1 of Susan Newman's proprietorship would be recorded:

Cash	
Left side Increase 30,000	Right side Decrease

Contributed Capital	
Left side Decrease	Right side Increase 30,000

Notice that the total amount entered on the left side equals the total amount entered on the right side.[4] To determine if this result can be generalized or not, let's next examine Transaction D in which Susan purchased merchandise inventory by paying cash.

Merchandise Inventory	
Left side Increase 15,000	Right side Decrease

Cash	
Left side Increase	Right side Decrease 15,000

Once again, the entry on the left side is exactly balanced by an entry on the right side. Although there appears to be a rule emerging from these examples, let's first test its applicability by examining Transaction W, a withdrawal of cash from Susan's business.

Cash	
Left side Increase	Right side Decrease 8,100

Retained Earnings	
Left side Decrease 8,100	Right side Increase

If you remain skeptical about this rule, you are encouraged to check additional transactions. You will find, however, that every recorded transaction is characterized by an equal change to both the left and right sides of an account.

You can express this recording equality more easily by using the terms *debit* and *credit*. Although most people mistakenly associate the terms with unfavorable and favorable events, there actually is only one simple definition for each term. The term **debit** (abbreviated as dr. from the Latin *debitum*) is used to refer to the left side of an account while the term **credit** (abbreviated cr. from the Latin *creditum*) is used to refer to the right side of an account. If you substitute these terms into the rule expressed above, you should be able to derive the basic rule of debits and credits.

Assets		=	Sources of Assets	
Left side Debit Increase	Right side Credit Decrease		Left side Debit Decrease	Right side Credit Increase

Basic rule of double-entry bookkeeping: Debits = Credits

[4] A dollar sign is not generally used within a T-account.

You can create the following summary by simply applying this basic debit-credit rule to each of the six major account types:

	Debit	Credit
Asset	+	−
Liability	−	+
Owner Equity	−	+
Revenue	−	+
Expense	+	−
Dividend	+	−

By organizing the preceding account types into two sets of identical increase-decrease patterns, you can create the following summary:

Asset Account

Left side	Right side
Debit	Credit
Increase	Decrease

Expense Account

Left side	Right side
Debit	Credit
Increase	Decrease

Dividend Account

Left side	Right side
Debit	Credit
Increase	Decrease

Liability Account

Left side	Right side
Debit	Credit
Decrease	Increase

Revenue Account

Left side	Right side
Debit	Credit
Decrease	Increase

Owner Equity Account

Left side	Right side
Debit	Credit
Decrease	Increase

When you compare the account patterns in the first row to the account patterns in the second row, it should now be evident that when you debit (that is, enter amounts on the left side) asset, expense, and dividend accounts, you are increasing them. When, instead, you debit liability, revenue, and owners' equity accounts, you are decreasing them. In contrast, you increase liability, revenue, and owners' equity accounts and decrease asset, expense, and dividend accounts by crediting them (that is, entering amounts on the right side). Another way to think of this is that asset, expense, and dividend accounts normally have debit balances whereas liability, revenue, and owner equity accounts normally have credit balances. You can use Performance Objective 24 to master these relationships:

YOUR PERFORMANCE OBJECTIVE 24
Explain the meaning of the words *debit* and *credit* and **use** the debit-credit rules (double-entry method of bookkeeping) in all phases of the accounting process.

If you find it difficult to intuitively understand why expenses and dividends are debited, don't be discouraged; many students do. Instead, let's just examine this rule in more depth. Consider the debit-credit rules for the owners' equity account known as Retained Earnings shown here:

Retained Earnings

Left side	Right side
Debit	Credit
Decrease	Increase

If you recall that revenue transactions increase this account, you will not be surprised to learn that all revenue T-accounts are increased by crediting them. Likewise, since both expenses and dividends decrease retained earnings, debiting an expense account when incurred and a dividend account when declared simultaneously decreases the Retained Earnings account. These ideas are now illustrated with the "parent" retained earnings account and its "children," the expense and revenue accounts.

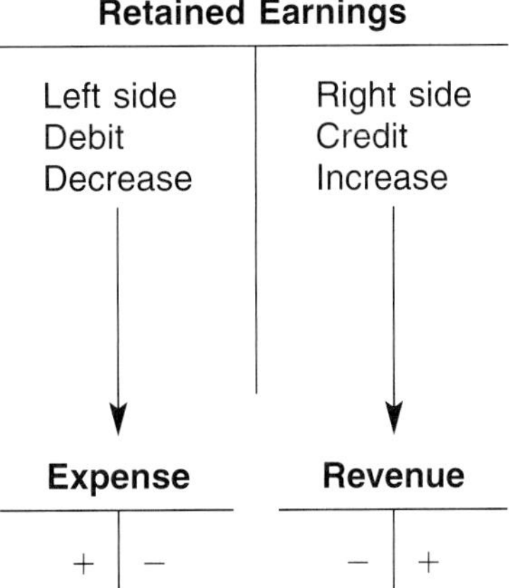

If you think about it, the revenue account is directly related to the retained earnings account, because as the revenue increases, so too does the retained earnings account. Thus, as you credit any revenue account, you simultaneously credit or increase retained earnings. The expense account, however, is inversely related to the retained earnings account, because as the expense increases, the retained earnings account decreases. Thus, as you debit any expense account, you simultaneously debit, or decrease, retained earnings. Notice that the dividend account follows the same debit-credit pattern as the expense account despite the fact that they are different in concept, as you learned in a Chapter 6 *Insight*.

Since these debit-credit rules are applied in nearly every step of the accounting process, let's examine them in more detail by seeing how they apply to CMU's transactions.

Applying the Accounting Process to CMU

Recall that nine steps constitute the manual accounting process. You actually studied the first step—identifying accounting transactions and measuring their effects—in Chapter 2 when you learned that a transaction must meet three conditions before it may enter the accounting information system. What you weren't told then, however, was that you must first gather *input*—letters, numbers, and symbols or raw facts and figures—which are generally drawn from such business documents as receiving documents, purchase invoices, checks, sales invoices, bank deposits, and employee time records. Since you examined several of these business documents earlier in this chapter and are familiar with the three conditions that a transaction must possess to enter the accounting system, let's explore the remaining eight steps of the accounting process. For your convenience, we will group these eight steps into four phases: recording, adjusting, reporting, and closing.

Accounting Process: Recording Phase

The recording phase of a double-entry bookkeeping system includes steps 2 through 5. The second step—recording accounting transactions—is called **journalizing**. The term is derived from the fact that in a manual accounting information system, transactions are usually recorded in a book of original entry called the **journal**. Thus, each such recorded or journalized transaction is referred to as a **journal entry**. The third step—transferring the effects of the journal entries to the individual accounts in the ledger—is called *posting*. The fourth step—preparing an *unadjusted trial balance* from the ledger balances—is designed to test the equality of the debits and credits. As you learned in Chapter 7, journalizing and posting adjusting and correcting entries—the fifth step—is essential if the business is to validly measure and report its net income.

Journalizing A journal entry should use the following general format to communicate transaction information clearly and consistently:

Date	Account debited
	  Account credited
	  Transaction explanation.
		Amount debited	Amount credited

Let's now use this format for the Transaction A_1 journal entry:

01/02	Cash—Checking
	  Contributed Capital
	  $30,000 cash is contributed by the owner who opens a business checking account.
		30,000	30,000

The transaction explanation is traditionally included in a journal entry. In this textbook, however, we will not place the explanation below the journal entry because to do so will be repetitious since the description of the transaction will have already been provided to you.

Recording an entity's transactions in a journal has two primary purposes. First, it provides a chronological record of all transactions in one place. Although Cards & Memorabilia Unlimited uses a single **general journal** for this purpose**,** entities having many repetitive transactions often use special separate journals for purchases, sales, cash collections, and cash payments. Second, the journal reduces but does not eliminate the chance of errors.

When you feel confident that you can correctly journalize transactions, use the details of CMU Transactions A_1 through A_2 found in Appendix C to record them. If you need help in analyzing these transactions, you can use the spreadsheet analysis also found in Appendix C. Then compare your entries with the following entries for correct form and content.

CMU Partnership Transactions in Journal Entry Form

A_1 ***$30,000 cash is contributed by the owner who opens a business checking account.***

01/02	Cash Checking	30,000	
	Contributed Capital		30,000

B ***$6,000 cash is withdrawn from the checking account to open a business savings account.***

01/02	Cash Savings	6,000	
	Cash Checking		6,000

C_1 ***$10,000 worth of store equipment is acquired with a credit card.***

01/04	Store Equipment	10,000	
	Accounts Payable		10,000

CARDS & MEMORABILIA UNLIMITED

D *$15,000 cash is paid to acquire merchandise inventory.*

01/06	Merchandise Inventory	15,000	
	Cash Checking		15,000

E *$2,000 cash is paid to the landlord for the security deposit on the store lease.*

01/09	Security Deposit Receivable	2,000	
	Cash Checking		2,000

C_2 *$10,000 cash is paid in full to settle the credit card obligation made on January 4.*

02/03	Accounts Payable	10,000	
	Cash Checking		10,000

F *$5,000 cash is borrowed with a bank credit line bearing interest at an 8% rate.*

07/01	Cash Checking	5,000	
	Credit Line Payable		5,000

G *$18,000 worth of additional merchandise is acquired on account.*

7/01–	Merchandise Inventory	18,000	
12/01	Accounts Payable		18,000

H *$7,000 cash is paid to acquire a used van with a five-year useful life for the business.*

07/01	Store Equipment	7,000	
	Cash Checking		7,000

I *$6,000 cash is collected from customers before any goods or services are provided.*

11/01	Cash Checking	6,000	
	Advances from Customers (a liability)		6,000

J_1 *$12,000 cash is paid to reduce accounts payable.*

07/31–	Accounts Payable	12,000	
11/30	Cash Checking		12,000

J_2 *$6,000 of accounts payable is converted to a 6% interest-bearing note payable due on March 31.*

12/31	Accounts Payable	6,000	
	Note Payable		6,000

K_1 *$5,000 cash is paid in full to settle the credit line loan made on July 1.*

12/31	Credit Line Payable	5,000	
	Cash Checking		5,000

L *$4,000 worth of a computer and printer is acquired by signing a two-year promissory note.*

12/31	Store Equipment	4,000	
	Note Payable (Long Term)		4,000

M *$63,200 of cash sales are made to customers throughout the year.*

Daily	Cash Checking	63,200	
	Sales Revenue		63,200

N *$20,000 of revenue is earned on account—$19,400 for customer credit sales throughout the year and $600 for teaching a course.*

Daily	Accounts Receivable	20,000	
	Sales Revenue		19,400
	Service Revenue		600

O_1 *$275 interest is earned from January 2 to December 2 on $6,000 of savings bearing 5% interest.*

12/02	Cash Savings ($6,000 × .05 × 11/12)	275	
	Interest Revenue		275

P *$1,000 cash is paid for office rent due the first day of each month beginning February 1.*

Monthly	Rent Expense	11,000	
	Cash Checking		11,000

Q_1 *$300 of depreciation is recorded to recognize the use of equipment sold on September 30.*

09/30	Depreciation Expense	300	
	Accumulated Depreciation		300

R *$2,000 worth of the store equipment bought on January 4 for $10,000 is sold for $1,350.*

09/30	Cash Checking	1,350	
	Accumulated Depreciation	300	
	Loss on Sale of Equipment	350	
	Store Equipment		2,000

S *$8,000 cash is paid to employees for work performed through the year's last payday.*

12/05	Salaries Expense	8,000	
	Cash Checking		8,000

K_2 *$200 cash is paid for interest due on $5,000 borrowed on July 1 at 8% and repaid on December 31.*

12/31	Interest Expense ($5,000 × .08 × 1/2)	200	
	Cash Checking		200

T *$4,250 cash is paid for miscellaneous expenses incurred throughout the year.*

Daily	Miscellaneous Expense	4,250	
	Cash Checking		4,250

U *$30,000 of cost of goods sold is determined by taking a physical count of inventory.*

12/31	Cost of Goods Sold	30,000	
	Merchandise Inventory		30,000

V *$15,000 cash is collected from customers throughout the year for amounts owed.*

Daily	Cash Checking	15,000	
	Accounts Receivable		15,000

W *$8,100 cash is withdrawn from the business by the owner throughout the year.*

Daily	Retained Earnings (Susan Newman, Drawing)	8,100	
	Cash		8,100

Note: If withdrawals are frequently made, a specific contra account entitled Susan Newman, Drawing, might well be used in place of Retained Earnings. This account is closed to the Retained Earnings account at the end of the period.

A_2 $10,000 worth of merchandise is contributed by an individual for a business interest.

12/24	Merchandise Inventory	10,000	
	Contributed Capital		10,000

Now that you have studied how accounting transactions are recorded using debits and credits, you can use Performance Objective 25 to increase your mastery of the account title associations that are so critical in recording these transactions.

YOUR PERFORMANCE OBJECTIVE 25
Select a likely account title for one-half of a transaction when given the account title for the other half of the transaction.

To better understand the value of this performance objective, consider the following example. Assume you are told that a company's cost of goods sold amounts to $90,000. You are then asked to select the most logically related account title to the Cost of Goods Sold account and record the full transaction. Depending on how you record transactions, your answer might look like this:

Stimulus: Cost of Goods Sold
Response: Merchandise Inventory

Transaction Analysis

Account Titles	Assets	= Liabilities	+ Owners' Equity
Cost of Goods Sold			(90,000)
Merchandise Inventory	(90,000)		

(Fundamental Accounting Equation)

Journal Entry

Account Titles	Debit	Credit
Cost of Goods Sold	90,000	
Merchandise Inventory		90,000

Because the ability to rapidly imagine account titles that logically correspond to a given account title is so important to your understanding, you will find two end-of-chapter exercises to develop your skills. In fact, this is a particularly important skill to use with T-account analysis as *Appendix 9–1* will explain.

Posting Although the general journal includes a complete record of an entity's transactions in one place, it does not provide the basis for preparing financial statements. Instead, you must further classify the information found in each transaction into smaller units known as accounts. The ledger, or **general ledger** as it is often called, is a collection of related asset, liability, and owner equity accounts (including revenue, expense, and dividend accounts). The process of transferring data from the journal to the ledger is called **posting**. Let's now see an example of posting using CMU's Transaction C_1.

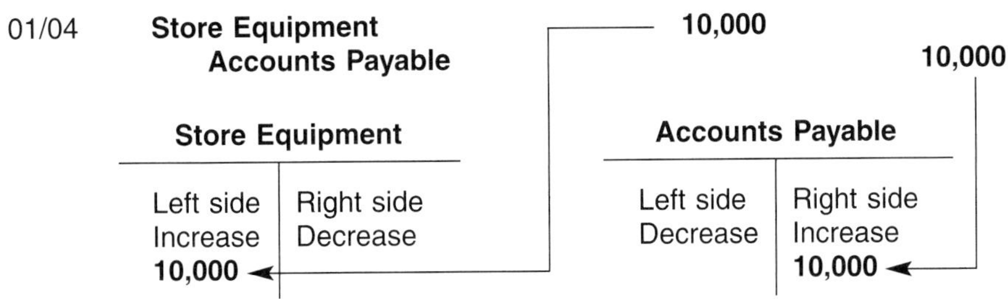

FIGURE 9-12

General ledger accounts for Cards & Memorabilia Unlimited

Cash*

	Debit	Credit	
(A_1)	30,000	6,000	(B)
(B)	6,000	15,000	(D)
(F)	5,000	2,000	(E)
(I)	6,000	10,000	(C_2)
(M)	63,200	7,000	(H)
(O_1)	275	12,000	(J_1)
(R)	1,350	5,000	(K_1)
(V)	15,000	11,000	(P)
		8,000	(S)
		200	(K_2)
		4,250	(T)
		8,100	(W)
	38,275		

Store Equipment

	Debit	Credit	
(C_1)	10,000	2,000	(R)
(H)	7,000		
(L)	4,000		
	19,000		

Accounts Payable

	Debit	Credit	
(C_2)	10,000	10,000	(C_1)
(J_1)	12,000	18,000	(G)
(J_2)	6,000	350	(Y)
		350	

Advances from Customers

	Debit	Credit	
(Z)	4,000	6,000	(I)
		2,000	

Cost of Goods Sold

	Debit	Credit	
(U)	**30,000**		

Rent Expense

	Debit	Credit	
(P)	**11,000**		

Loss on Sale

	Debit	Credit	
(R)	**350**		

Salaries Expense

	Debit	Credit	
(S)	8,000		
(X)	750		
	8,750		

Depreciation Expense

	Debit	Credit	
(Q_1)	300		
(Q_2)	2,300		
	2,600		

Miscellaneous Expense

	Debit	Credit	
(T)	4,250		
(Y)	350		
	4,600		

Accounts Receivable

	Debit	Credit	
(N)	20,000	15,000	(V)
	5,000		

Merchandise Inventory

	Debit	Credit	
(D)	15,000	30,000	(U)
(G)	18,000		
(A_2)	10,000		
	13,000		

Other Receivable

	Debit	Credit	
(E)	2,000		
	2,000		

Interest Receivable

	Debit	Credit	
(O_2)	**25**		

Accumulated Depreciation

	Debit	Credit	
(R)	300	300	(Q_1)
		2,300	(Q_2)
		2,300	

Credit Line Payable

	Debit	Credit	
(K_1)	5,000	5,000	(F)

Salaries Payable

	Debit	Credit	
		750	(X)

Notes Payable

	Debit	Credit	
		6,000	(J_2)
		4,000	(L)
		10,000	

Contributed Capital

	Debit	Credit	
		30,000	(A_1)
		10,000	(A_2)
		40,000	

Retained Earnings

	Debit	Credit	
(W)	**8,100**		

Sales Revenue

	Debit	Credit	
		63,200	(M)
		19,400	(N)
		4,000	(Z)
		86,600	

Service Revenue

	Debit	Credit	
		600	(N)

Interest Revenue

	Debit	Credit	
		275	(O_1)
		25	(O_2)
		300	

Interest Expense

	Debit	Credit	
(K_2)	**200**		

*For simplicity, the Cash—Checking and Cash—Savings accounts are combined here.

In this example, the data in each line of the general journal entry is transferred to a separate account in the general ledger. Figure 9-12 illustrates the posting of all CMU transactions to individual accounts in its general ledger. Before you look at this figure, however, use Appendix C to trace the effects of each transaction to appropriate accounts.

Preparing the Unadjusted Trial Balance The **unadjusted trial balance** is a listing of the ledger account balances immediately before the adjusting journal entries and correcting journal entries are recorded. Its purpose is to test the equality of debits and credits. However, a trial balance will not detect an error if:

- A transaction was omitted.
- A fictitious transaction was included.
- An incorrect amount was recorded for both the debit and credit.
- Offsetting errors were involved.
- The wrong account was debited (or credited) when the correct account should also have been debited (or credited).

In the case of Cards & Memorabilia Unlimited, you must include the effects of all transactions other than Transactions O_2, X, Y, Q_2, and Z. Then, determine if you are able to prepare the unadjusted trial balance for CMU by comparing your answer to the actual unadjusted trial balance shown in Figure 9-13.

FIGURE 9-13

Unadjusted trial balance for Cards & Memorabilia Unlimited

CARDS & MEMORABILIA UNLIMITED
Unadjusted Trial Balance
For the Year Ended December 31

	Debit	Credit
Cash	$ 38,275	
Accounts receivable	5,000	
Merchandise inventory	13,000	
Other receivable	2,000	
Store equipment	19,000	
Accumulated depreciation	–0–	
Accounts payable		–0–
Credit line payable		–0–
Salaries payable		–0–
Advances from customers		6,000
Notes payable		10,000
Contributed capital		40,000
Retained earnings	8,100	
Sales revenue		82,600
Service revenue		600
Interest revenue		275
Cost of goods sold	30,000	
Rent expense	11,000	
Salaries expense	8,000	
Miscellaneous expense	4,250	
Interest expense	200	
Loss on sale	350	
Depreciation expense	300	
Totals	$139,475	$139,475

Accounting Process: Adjusting Phase

The adjusting phase represents step 5 of the accounting process. As you learned in Chapter 7, a business must record adjusting entries at the end of every accounting period to ensure that all revenues and expenses are properly included in the determination of net income. Examples of such adjusting entries for CMU are Transactions O_2, X, Y, Q_2, and Z. This step allows you to convert an unadjusted trial balance (step 4) into an adjusted trial balance (step 6).

Journalizing and Posting To complete the adjusting phase, you must first record each adjustment in the general journal as illustrated here by the following Cards & Memorabilia Unlimited adjusting journal entries:

O_2 ***Accrued revenue adjustment: $25 of interest is earned but uncollected on a $6,000 savings account bearing 5% interest.***

12/31	Interest Receivable	25	
	Interest Revenue ($6,000 × .05 × 1/12)		25

X ***Accrued expense adjustment: $750 of salaries expense is incurred but unpaid.***

12/31	Salaries Expense	750	
	Salaries Payable		750

Y ***Accrued expense adjustment: $350 of miscellaneous expense is incurred but unpaid.***

12/31	Miscellaneous Expense	350	
	Accounts Payable		350

Q_2 ***Deferred expense adjustment or asset expiration: $2,300 of depreciation is recorded on the use of unsold equipment.***

12/31	Depreciation Expense	2,300	
	Accumulated Depreciation		2,300

Z ***Deferred revenue adjustment: $4,000 worth of merchandise is delivered to customers who paid in advance (refer to Transaction I).***

12/31	Advances from Customers (a liability)	4,000	
	Sales Revenue		4,000

Once you have journalized the adjustments shown here, you must post their effects to the relevant general ledger accounts just as we illustrated earlier in our example of Transaction C_1.

Adjusted Trial Balance As its name implies, the **adjusted trial balance** lists ledger account balances immediately after you have recorded the adjusting journal entries and any correcting journal entries. So let's look at the process of posting the adjustment's effect to the ledger by using the depreciation adjustment (Transaction Q_2).

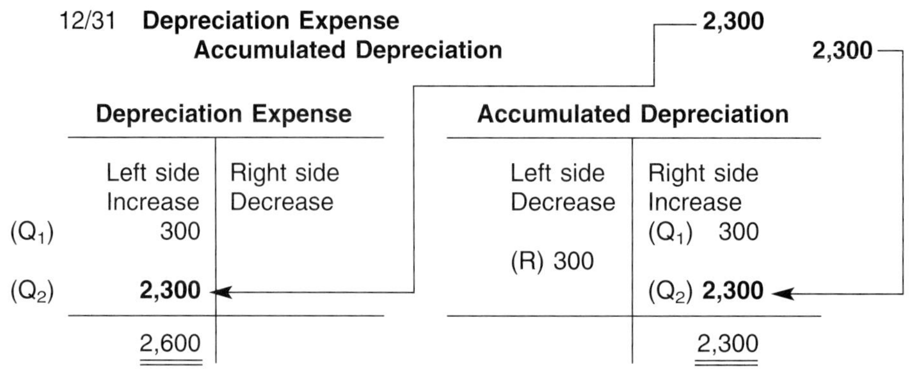

	Unadjusted Trial Balance		Adjusted Trial Balance	
	Debit	Credit	Debit	Credit
Accumulated depreciation				$2,300
Depreciation expense	300		$2,600	

The preceding information shows that the adjusted trial balance is significantly different from the unadjusted trial balance whenever certain accounts are affected by the adjustments process. Study the remaining adjustments carefully to see how their effect is ultimately communicated to the final general ledger balances shown in the adjusted trial balance. Once again, using Appendix C, try to prepare the adjusted trial balance for CMU and then compare your work to Figure 9-14's adjusted trial balance in which all accounts affected by the adjustment process are boldfaced.

The adjustment phase is composed of three steps. First, the transaction is recorded. Second, its effects are posted to the accounts affected. And third, the equality of debits and credits is tested to determine if any errors were made in the immediately preceding adjustment procedure. Although CMU did not have any correcting journal en-

FIGURE 9-14

Adjusted trial balance for Cards & Memorabilia Unlimited

CARDS & MEMORABILIA UNLIMITED
Adjusted Trial Balance
For the Year Ended December 31

	Debit	Credit
Cash	$ 38,275	
Accounts receivable	5,000	
Interest receivable	**25**	
Merchandise inventory	13,000	
Other receivable	2,000	
Store equipment	19,000	
Accumulated depreciation		**2,300**
Accounts payable		**350**
Credit line payable		–0–
Salaries payable		**750**
Advances from customers		**2,000**
Notes payable		10,000
Contributed capital		40,000
Retained earnings	8,100	
Sales revenue		**86,600**
Service revenue		600
Interest revenue		**300**
Cost of goods sold	30,000	
Rent expense	11,000	
Salaries expense	**8,750**	
Miscellaneous expense	**4,600**	
Interest expense	200	
Loss on equipment sale	350	
Depreciation expense	**2,600**	
Totals	$142,900	$142,900

Note: All accounts affected by the adjusting process are boldfaced.

tries in its first year of operations, it is not unusual for a business to also record entries to correct the effect of recording errors made previously that year. Such a correcting entry would be necessary, for example, if Susan had discovered that the amount she recorded as salaries expense had been overstated. Assuming that two weeks earlier she had overstated such a transaction by $150, here is the appropriate correcting entry:

12/31	Salaries Payable	150	
	Salaries Expense		150

Don't forget that the effects of this entry must also be posted to the ledger before an adjusted trial balance is prepared.

Adjustments in General

Recall that an adjustment is an implicit transaction that is recorded at the end of the accounting period to ensure that all revenues and expenses are reported in their proper period. If you review CMU's Transactions O_2–Z, you will be able to verify that every adjustment contains both an income statement account and a balance sheet account.

You now know that year-end adjustments are necessary to precisely measure the net income of CMU or any other business for that matter. So, let's look at an example of each of the four major adjustment types—described in Chapter 7 for CMU—applied to other entities. As you look at each example, remember always to record the initial transaction in such problems. Doing so makes your analysis easier and greatly improves the likelihood of a correct solution. Also note that each of the examples assumes that financial statements are prepared annually, or as is commonly stated, "the books are closed on December 31 of each year."

Accrued Revenue Recall that the accountant must not forget to record any unrecorded revenue that is earned but uncollected at the end of the period. A common example of this accrued revenue adjustment is for interest and rental fees.

Example A 60-day, $1,000 promissory note bearing a 6% interest rate is received from a customer on December 1 in exchange for a sale of goods. For this example, assume there are 360 days in a year.

Initial Transaction

12/01	Notes Receivable	1,000	
	Sales Revenue		1,000

Analysis At the close of the accounting period on December 31, 30 of the 60 days have elapsed. Since interest is earned with the passage of time, the following formula is used to measure the amount of revenue recorded:

$$\begin{aligned}\text{Interest} &= \text{Principal} \times \text{Interest Rate} \times \text{Time}\\ &= \$1{,}000 \times .06 \times 1/12 = \underline{\underline{\$5.00}}\end{aligned}$$

Adjustment Required

12/31	Interest Receivable	5	
	Interest Revenue		5

The interest receivable represents the seller's claim to 30 days of interest earned on December 31, that is, receivable in 30 days.

Subsequent Transaction Although this adjustment is complete, you will better understand this process if you study how the interest receipt and note maturity are treated on January 30 of next year:

01/30	Cash	1,010	
	Note Receivable		1,000
	Interest Receivable		5
	Interest Revenue		5

The $1,010 cash received represents both the $1,000 return *of* principal and the $10 return *on* principal or interest calculated as follows:

$$\text{Interest} = \text{Principal} \times \text{Interest Rate} \times \text{Time}$$
$$= \$1{,}000 \times .06 \times 2/12 = \$10.00$$

Both the note receivable and the interest receivable are eliminated, because full payment of principal and interest is received by January 30. The $5 interest revenue is recorded because 30 days of interest has been earned during the new period ending on January 30.

Accrued Expense An example of another adjustment that must be recorded is an unrecorded expense that is incurred but unpaid at the end of the period. Usually, this accrued expense adjustment occurs with salaries, interest, and property taxes.

Example A total weekly salary of $500 for all employees is paid on Friday, January 2 of Year 2. Assume that the employees earned $100 per day and worked from Monday to Friday.

Analysis Use the following calendar to visualize this problem:

December			January	
Mon.	**Tue.**	**Wed.**	**Thu.**	**Fri.**
29	30	31	1	2

The measurement of expense for the period ending December 31 of Year 1 includes three days of salaries incurred (December 29–31). Net income will be misstated unless $300 ($100 × 3) of salaries expense is recorded in the current period ending December 31.

Adjustment Required

12/31	Salaries Expense	300	
	Salaries Payable		300

Subsequent Transaction Although this adjustment is complete, you will better understand it if you study how the salary payment on January 2 of the next year is treated. Since the adjustment above accounted for all expense through December 31, only two days of salaries expense has accumulated by Friday, January 2. Thus, $200 ($100 × 2) of salaries expense must be recorded. Since full payment of $500 cash is made on January 2, there is no longer an obligation and the $300 balance in the liability account, Salaries Payable, must be eliminated.

01/02	Salaries Expense	200	
	Salaries Payable	300	
	Cash		500

If the adjustment had not been made on December 31, the entire $500 expense would have been recorded on January 2 of Year 2. If these salaries had not been accrued in Year 1, the effect would have been to overstate Year 1 net income and understate Year 2 net income.

Deferred Revenue A deferred revenue adjustment represents the recognition of a previously unrecorded revenue that was collected (in cash) in an earlier period. This adjustment is recorded whenever the conditions for recognizing revenue that were not met before are fully realized. Prime examples of this deferred revenue adjustment are for subscriptions, rental fees, and interest.

Example $24,000 is received from customers on July 1 of Year 1 for a year's magazine subscription to *Modern Romances*.

Initial Transaction When cash is received from subscribers on July 1, the publisher is unable to immediately deliver all 12 issues of the monthly magazine. Thus, the cash is increased and the publisher has an obligation or liability (L) that is titled either Advances from Customers, Deferred Magazine Revenue, Unearned Magazine Revenue, or Magazine Revenue Received in Advance.

07/01	Cash	24,000	
	Deferred Magazine Revenue (L)		24,000

Analysis Since one-half of the issues have been delivered by December 31 of Year 1, the critical revenue-generating event, delivery, has occurred and one-half of all revenue should be recorded.

Adjustment Required

12/31	Deferred Magazine Revenue (L)	12,000	
	Magazine Revenue		12,000

This adjustment is necessary to avoid understating net income for the period ending December 31 of Year 1. On June 30 of Year 2, the same adjustment will be made to complete the transaction.

Deferred Expense (Asset Expiration) A deferred expense adjustment represents the incurrence of a previously deferred expense that was paid in an earlier period. This expense adjustment records the using up of an asset, which is also referred to as an *asset expiration.* Prime examples of this deferred revenue adjustment are for inventory, prepaid assets, and depreciable assets.

Example $500 of office supplies are acquired on account on January 2 of this year. There were no supplies on hand at the beginning of the year and at December 31, $80 of these supplies still remain.

Initial Transaction

01/02	Office Supplies	500	
	Accounts Payable		500

Analysis If $500 of inventory cost was available and $80 remains, $420 must have been used up or expensed, in other words, $500 − $80. Recall that an expense is defined as the cost of goods or services used up in the production of goods or services.

Adjustment Required

12/31	Office Supplies Expense	420	
	Office Supplies		420

The reduction or expiration of the office supplies asset is counter-balanced by a reduction in the owner equity produced by the expense.

Accounting Process: Reporting Phase

The recording and adjusting phases you have just studied include three of the four components of an accounting information system. *Input*, the first component, is derived from business documents to create accounting transactions that enter the system. *Processing*, the second component, involves activities that transform data into

FIGURE 9-15 A manual accounting information system

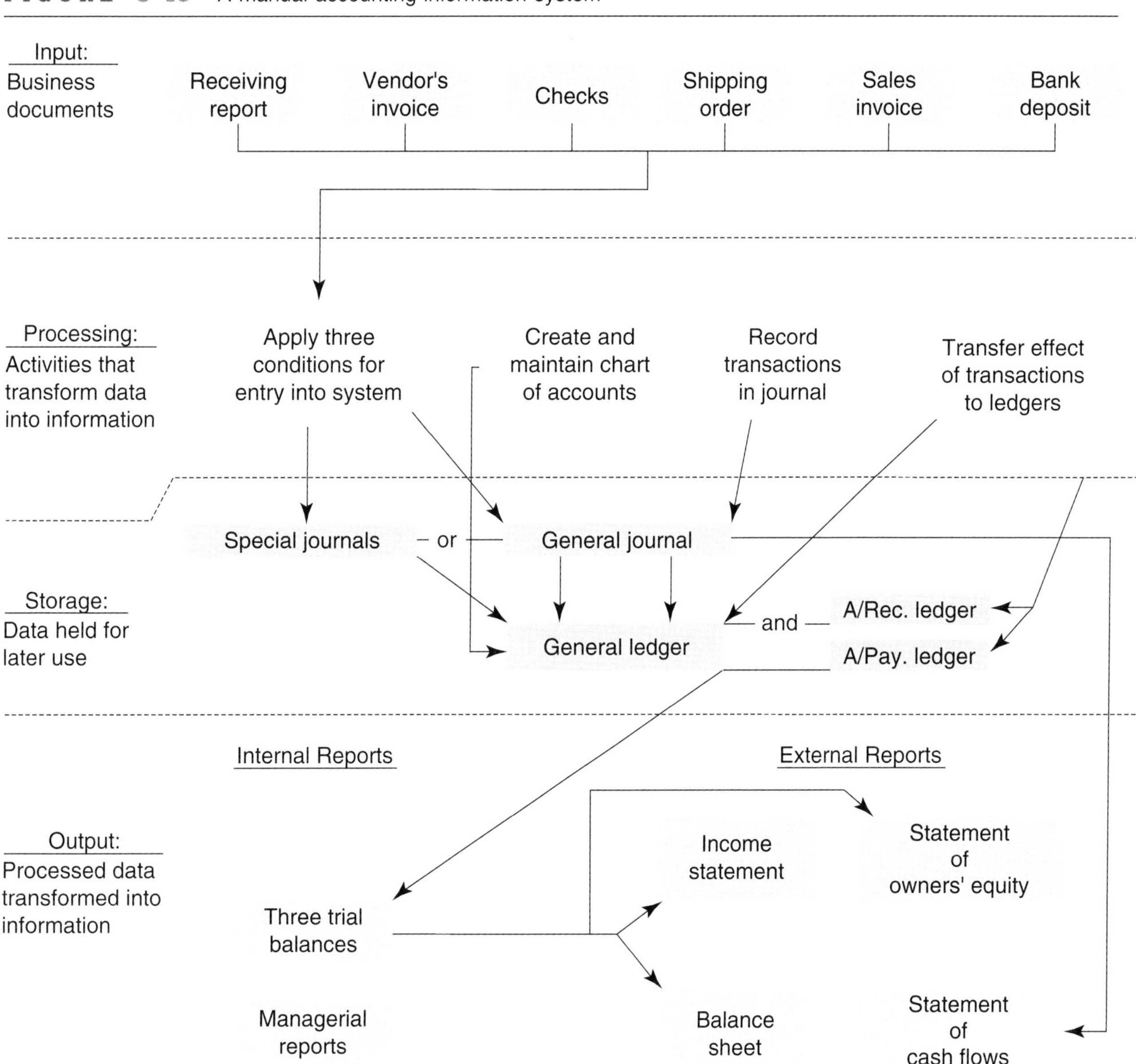

FIGURE 9-16 Financial statements for Cards & Memorabilia Unlimited

CARDS & MEMORABILIA UNLIMITED

CARDS & MEMORABILIA UNLIMITED
Income Statement
For the Year Ended December 31

Revenues:		
Sales revenue	$86,600	
Service revenue	600	
Interest revenue	300	$87,500
Expenses:		
Cost of Goods Sold	30,000	
Rent expense	11,000	
Salaries expense	8,750	
Depreciation expense	2,600	
Miscellaneous expense	4,600	
Interest expense	200	
Loss on equipment sale	350	57,500
Net income		$30,000

CARDS & MEMORABILIA UNLIMITED
Statement of Retained Earnings
For the Year Ended December 31

Retained earnings, 1/2	$ -0-
Add: Net income	30,000
Subtotal	30,000
Deduct: Withdrawals	8,100
Retained earnings, 12/31	$21,900

CARDS & MEMORABILIA UNLIMITED
Balance Sheet
For the Year Ended December 31

Cash	$38,275	Accounts payable	$ 350
Accounts receivable	5,000	Salaries payable	750
Interest receivable	25	Deferred revenue*	2,000
Merchandise inventory	13,000	Note payable	6,000
Total current assets	$56,300	Total current liabilities	9,100
Other receivable	2,000	Long-term note payable	4,000
Store equipment	19,000	Contributed capital	40,000
Less: Accumulated depreciation	(2,300)	Retained earnings	21,900
Total assets	$75,000	Total liabilities and owner's equity	$75,000

*Also titled Advances from Customers

information, such as journalizing and posting both regular and special transactions. *Storage,* the third component, holds data or information for later retrieval or use, such as journals or ledgers. The fourth and final component is *output*—processed data transformed into usable information for decision making. Figure 9-15 illustrates all four of these components from the perspective of a manual system.

Once you record both a business's explicit and implicit transactions for a period, transfer their effects to the ledger, and prepare the adjusted trial balance, you are ready to communicate or report the financial condition and operating results to the outside world. That is, you are creating output and have entered the reporting phase of the accounting process, step 7. In this phase, you prepare the income statement, balance sheet, and statement of retained earnings. Figure 9-16 shows the financial statements, in other words the output or reports for CMU's first year.

Accounting Process: Closing Phase

Finally, closing entries and a post-closing trial balance are prepared to close certain ledger accounts and to test their equality so that they are ready for next period's accounting process. This phase includes steps 8 and 9 of the accounting process.

Recording Closing Entries The first step in the closing phase of the accounting process is often referred to as *closing the books* or simply the *closing process.* Before you can understand this process, however, you must be able to distinguish between permanent accounts and temporary accounts. **Permanent accounts** are accounts whose balances carry over beyond a single accounting period. Examples include asset, liability, and owners' equity accounts. **Temporary accounts** are accounts whose balances pertain only to a single accounting period. Examples include revenue, expense, dividends declared, and income summary accounts.

A **closing entry** enables you to close all temporary accounts so that they are ready for reaccumulation in the next accounting period. The current balances in these temporary accounts are transferred to the Retained Earnings account in a corporation and the Capital account in a sole proprietorship or partnership. (Recall from Chapter 3 that we use a Retained Earnings account for these types of entities.) This transfer assures you that the changes in owners' equity reported in both the statement of retained earnings and the statement of capital actually go into effect in the ledger.

At least two closing entry methods are used to implement the closing process. The **indirect approach**, shown in Figure 9-17(a), is recommended for people less experienced with accounting because it more clearly discloses the individual steps involved in closing the books. A key characteristic of this method is the use of an income summary account. The **Income Summary account** is a temporary account that stores both revenues and expenses in preparation for their ultimate transfer to the Retained Earnings account. Notice that the $30,000 balance in the Income Summary account produced by the closing entries in Figure 9-17(a) represents net income. The amount of net income is then transferred to retained earnings in the following closing entry:

	Debit	Credit
Income Summary	30,000	
Retained Earnings		30,000

The closing process has two objectives. The first objective is to close all temporary accounts. For example, examine the following Cost of Goods Sold and Sales Revenue T-accounts. Note that the letters CL in parentheses represents the effect of a closing entry.

Cost of Goods Sold

Debit	Credit
(U) 30,000	30,000 (CL)

Sales Revenue

Debit	Credit
	63,200 (M)
	20,000 (N)
	4,000 (Z)
(CL) 87,200	87,200

By simply inserting the end of period balance of each account on its opposite side, the net account balance becomes zero and is ready for reaccumulation in the next

FIGURE 9-17(a)

The indirect approach for closing the books

Sales Revenue	86,600	
Service Revenue	600	
Interest Revenue	300	
Income Summary		**87,500**
Income Summary	**57,500**	
Cost of Goods Sold		30,000
Rent Expense		11,000
Salaries Expense		8,750
Depreciation Expense		2,600
Miscellaneous Expense		4,600
Interest Expense		200
Loss on Equipment Sale		350
Income Summary	**30,000**	
Retained Earnings		30,000

Note: The preceding entry produces a zero balance in the Income Summary account so that it, like all other temporary accounts, is now closed for this accounting period. The activity in this account is boldfaced.

Income Summary

Debit	Credit
57,500	**87,500**
30,000	

accounting period. Thus, you must debit the Interest Revenue account and credit all remaining individual expense accounts if you wish to close them.

The second objective of the closing process is to transfer the effect of net income to the Retained Earnings account as illustrated here for CMU.

Retained Earnings

Debit	Credit
	–0–
	30,000 (CL)
	30,000

The **direct approach** shown in Figure 9-17(b) is nothing more than a streamlined version of the indirect approach without the Income Summary account. Study carefully the effects of this approach and you will discover that it ultimately has the very same effect on an entity's accounts as does the indirect approach.

Preparing the Post-Closing Trial Balance The final step in the accounting process involves the preparation of a trial balance to check the equality of debits and credits. This trial balance is called the **post-closing trial balance**, because

FIGURE 9-17(b)

The direct approach for closing the books

Sales Revenue	86,600	
Service Revenue	600	
Interest Revenue	300	
Cost of Goods Sold		30,000
Rent Expense		11,000
Salaries Expense		8,750
Depreciation Expense		2,600
Miscellaneous Expense		4,600
Interest Expense		200
Loss on Equipment Sale		350
Retained Earnings		30,000

it is a listing of all ledger account balances prepared *after* journalizing the closing entries and posting their effects to the ledger. This trial balance includes only permanent accounts, because temporary accounts were closed in the preceding step. Both the adjusted and post-closing trial balances are presented side by side in Figure 9-18 so you can appreciate the differences between them.

FIGURE 9-18

Adjusted and post-closing trial balances for Cards & Memorabilia Unlimited

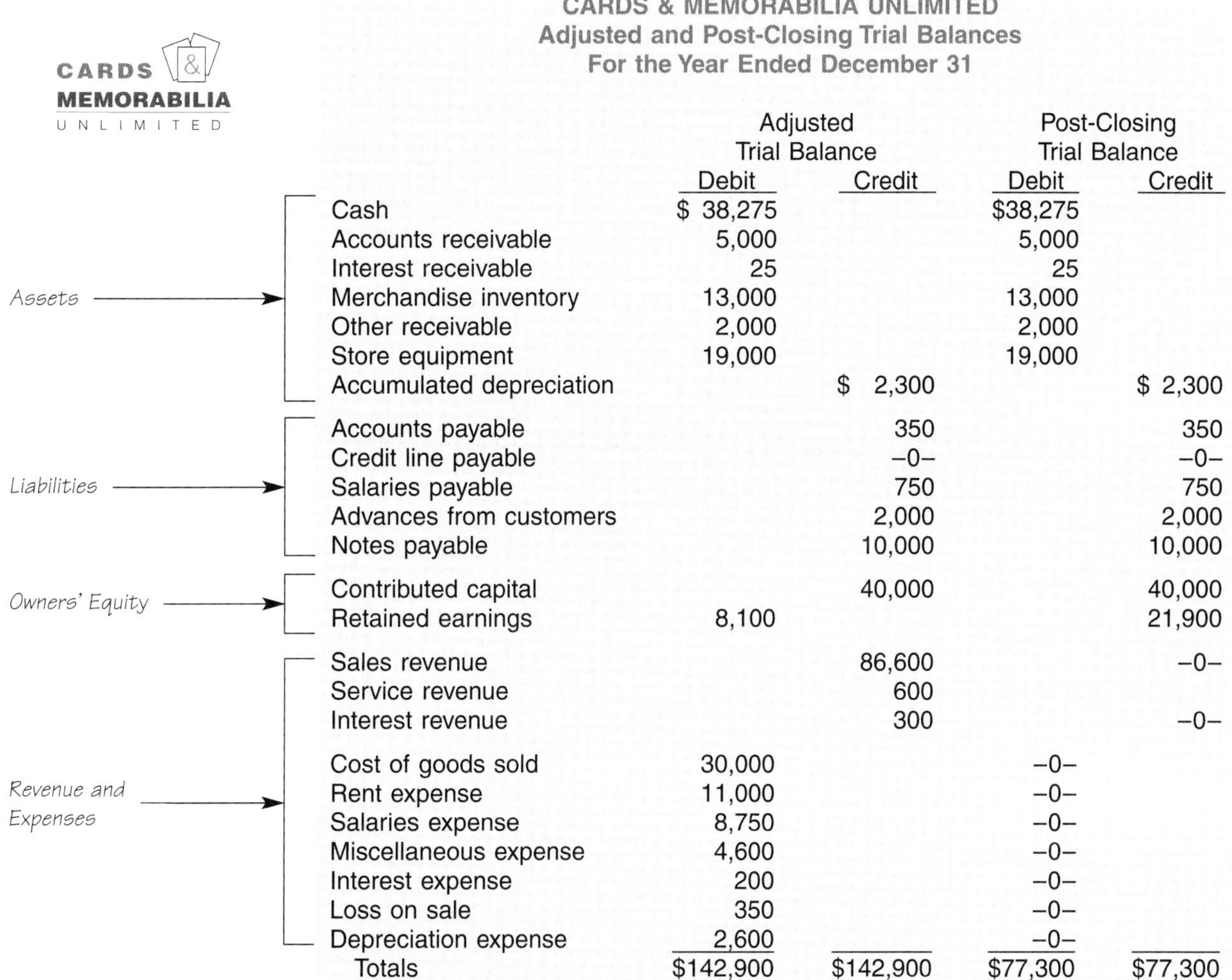

CARDS & MEMORABILIA UNLIMITED
Adjusted and Post-Closing Trial Balances
For the Year Ended December 31

	Adjusted Trial Balance		Post-Closing Trial Balance	
	Debit	Credit	Debit	Credit
Cash	$ 38,275		$38,275	
Accounts receivable	5,000		5,000	
Interest receivable	25		25	
Merchandise inventory	13,000		13,000	
Other receivable	2,000		2,000	
Store equipment	19,000		19,000	
Accumulated depreciation		$ 2,300		$ 2,300
Accounts payable		350		350
Credit line payable		–0–		–0–
Salaries payable		750		750
Advances from customers		2,000		2,000
Notes payable		10,000		10,000
Contributed capital		40,000		40,000
Retained earnings	8,100			21,900
Sales revenue		86,600		–0–
Service revenue		600		
Interest revenue		300		–0–
Cost of goods sold	30,000		–0–	
Rent expense	11,000		–0–	
Salaries expense	8,750		–0–	
Miscellaneous expense	4,600		–0–	
Interest expense	200		–0–	
Loss on sale	350		–0–	
Depreciation expense	2,600		–0–	
Totals	$142,900	$142,900	$77,300	$77,300

Summarizing the Accounting Process Because the accounting process includes a somewhat lengthy set of procedures, you are strongly encouraged to master the following performance objective:

YOUR PERFORMANCE OBJECTIVE 26

Identify, **list**, and **perform** in their proper sequence each of the following steps normally followed in the accounting process/cycle for preparation of the principal financial statements:

a. **Identify** accounting transactions and **measure** their effects.
b. **Journalize** transaction entries.
c. **Post** journal entries to the individual accounts in the ledger.
d. **Prepare** an unadjusted trial balance.
e. **Journalize** and **post** adjusting and correcting entries.
f. **Prepare** an adjusted trial balance.

g. **Prepare** the financial statements.
h. **Journalize** and **post** closing entries.
i. **Prepare** a post-closing trial balance.

Study these steps carefully so that you fully understand the logical nature of the steps one uses to *input* data into the accounting system, *process* it, and later extract usable information from *storage* to produce *output*. But also know that the number of entities that apply these steps in actual practice is dwindling. With the advent of computerized accounting information systems, complete manual systems are no longer found in the larger U.S. businesses. Today, full-scale manual systems are almost extinct! Complete sets of bound working papers, journals, and ledgers are no longer sold. Only very small businesses and students learning the logical steps of the accounting process follow these exact steps. But remember that knowing them provides you a more fundamental understanding of how business transactions are transformed into financial statements.

Using Accounting Software to Produce Financial Statements at Cards & Memorabilia Unlimited

Over the last 15 years, most accounting information systems have been transformed from manual to computerized. So to be sure you're prepared for what you'll find in the world of business, let's learn how a computerized accounting information system differs from the manual accounting information system you have just studied.

What Is an Accounting Software Package?

Application software helps you perform a specific task using the computer. An **accounting software package** is a business applications software package that allows you to computerize the bookkeeping and financial reporting tasks required in most businesses.

Accounting software is usually classified as either "high-end" or "low-end" depending on the characteristics of the user of that software. For example, the more traditional trial balance or general ledger accounting packages were designed for medium to large-scale businesses and generally require accountants to operate and understand them. These software packages are considered high-end and include such well-known products as Great Plains Solomon IV Software and Sage Software. Prices for these packages range from several thousand dollars to more than $100,000! In contrast, low-end accounting software packages are designed for small businesses and focus on the needs of the small business owner/manager—the user of accounting information—rather than on the needs of the accountant—the preparer of accounting information. As a result, these packages provide business management tools such as time tracking and online banking as well as the more standard accounting and audit features. These packages have blossomed into powerful, full-featured programs that are user-friendly even for those business people who know little, if anything, about accounting. Today, the most popular of these accounting software packages include Peachtree Accounting, QuickBooks, M.Y.O.B. Accounting, and Peachtree One-Write Plus, all of which sell for less than $300. Each of these packages enables you to record transactions, print business documents underlying those transactions, maintain a detailed record of all accounts in both the general ledger and subsidiary ledgers, and produce a wide variety of financial reports.

Expansion of the accounting software market is directly tied to the tremendous growth of small businesses as a result of the corporate reengineering and downsizing trends of the 1990s. Just as Susan's entrepreneurial spirit led her to leave her job and start CMU, many business professionals have left large corporations to start or manage small businesses. Since these well-trained professionals are generally not intimidated by the computer, they are anxious to use any computer software that helps them reach their business goals.

How are accounting software packages used to produce financial statements? Let's first compare the operation of an accounting cycle in a computerized system to the operation of an accounting cycle in a manual system. Then, we will take a closer look at QuickBooks, the accounting software package Susan used to produce the financial statements of Cards & Memorabilia Unlimited.

Differences between Computerized and Manual Accounting Information Systems

As you learned earlier, both manual and computerized information systems share four components: input, processing, storage, and output. Both manual and computerized accounting information systems also have at least three record-processing devices in common: a chart of accounts, a general ledger, and one or more subsidiary ledgers. Despite these general similarities, the specific ways in which manual and computerized systems work are often quite different.

Although the input data from source documents is identical, a computerized accounting system requires that it be complete and arranged in specific formats. For example, a transaction might be rejected if an account number is missing.

A more obvious difference is how transactions are processed. In a manual accounting system, each of the steps in the accounting cycle is performed by hand. In a computerized accounting system, however, the amount of manual work is limited to entering transactions on the computer with all other steps performed automatically. Thus, a computerized system is much faster and, at the same time, produces far fewer errors. Moreover, computer processing enables you to perform two or more manual tasks simultaneously. For example, when cash is collected from a customer, accounting software allows you to simultaneously record the transaction and transfer its effects to both the Cash account and Accounts Receivable account in the general ledger, as well as to simultaneously reduce the specific customer's account in the subsidiary ledger. Thus, the computer combines several discrete, time-consuming manual tasks in a single step.

You learned that manual systems often maintain several special journals to record transaction types such as purchases, sales, cash collections, and cash receipts. For example, you might use a cash receipts journal for all events that involve the receipt of cash. A computerized system, however, skips these storage devices.

Another difference is that a computerized accounting system stores information more readily in numerical format than does a manual accounting system, which usually organizes data alphabetically. One reason for this difference is that it is easier to create unique numbers, for example, 111111 versus 111112, than unique names as businesses expand. The common complaint that our ID-number-obsessed society is dehumanizing is understandable when you consider that machines can process these numbers far more easily than people.

Another difference between manual and computerized systems is in the output each produces. A computerized system can produce reports more quickly and in greater variety when compared to a manual system. For example, it enables a decision maker to analyze each product's sales and cash requirements almost instantly as well as to track slow-paying customers on a daily basis. In contrast, the time and cost of manually performing the same analyses would be prohibitive.

INSIGHT

Limitations of Computerized Accounting Information Systems

All of today's popular accounting software packages allow you to process the effects of business transactions and then summarize them in the form of financial statements with the click of a mouse. Nevertheless, the increasingly widespread use of computerized accounting information systems by entities does not *by itself* indicate that these systems are producing more reliable measurements. No matter how sophisticated the equipment, no computer can produce useful information if the input is not good. This idea is described in a well-known acronym, GIGO—garbage-in, garbage-out. Likewise, significant problems can arise unless the employees who operate a computer are well trained. Thus, the **insight** you should gain here is that even computerized systems with numerous features, speed, and efficiency are limited by the people who use them.

A Closer Look at Quickbooks—Cards & Memorabilia Unlimited's Accounting Software

After several hours of study, Susan began to computerize CMU's accounting information system by using QuickBooks Pro 2002 (Figure 9-19). Although QuickBooks does not use journals, ledger accounts, or trial balances as its standard settings, it does process transactions in a manner equivalent to the more traditional manual accounting information system. Intuit, the maker of QuickBooks, offers excellent technical support without accounting-laden terminology and complexity. For example, a QuickBooks user doesn't need to know about debits and credits, journal entries, or closing periods, but they must understand a chart of accounts and the different types of accounts it contains.

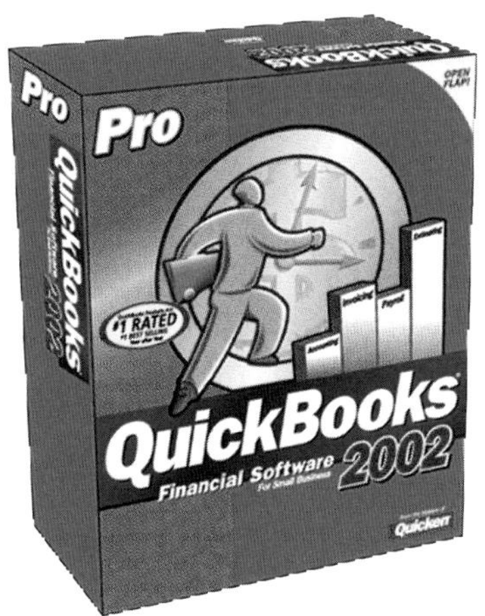

FIGURE 9-19

QuickBooks allows people with no understanding of debits and credits to prepare financial statements

Although our overview of QuickBooks will not be detailed enough to make you an expert user, it will acquaint you with its essential menus and features. Let's begin with menus. When Susan opened QuickBooks for the first time, she recognized such standard Windows menus as *File, Edit, View, Window,* and *Help*. The menus unique to QuickBooks include *Lists, Company, Customers, Vendors, Employees, Banking,* and *Reports*. Each of these menus lists several activities. For example, clicking the

Customers menu produces such activities as *create invoices*, *enter sales receipts* (that is, cash sales), and *receive payments*; clicking the Vendors menu produces such activities as *enter bills* and *pay bills*; and clicking the Banking menu produces such activities as *write checks* and *make deposits*.

QuickBooks has four features that, when combined, help manage the financial activity of a company; produce its balance sheet, income statement, and statement of cash flows; as well as help owner-managers make more effective business decisions. Three of these basic features—lists, forms, and registers—relate to the recording phase of an accounting information system while the fourth feature—reports and graphs—represents the reporting phase. Let's now take a closer look at these features and the particular menus that convert raw transactions into complete financial statements.

Recording Phase In QuickBooks, the **lists** feature is represented by a Lists menu that includes groups of names such as account titles, customers, vendors, and employees, as well as information about these names. Figure 9-20 illustrates such a list, a portion of the chart of accounts for CMU. You can create and edit such a list in several ways. For example, if you want to add a new customer, you can click the *List* menu, click the *Customer* menu, or fill out a form such as an invoice.

FIGURE 9-20 QuickBooks lists feature, showing Cards & Memorabilia Unlimited's chart of accounts

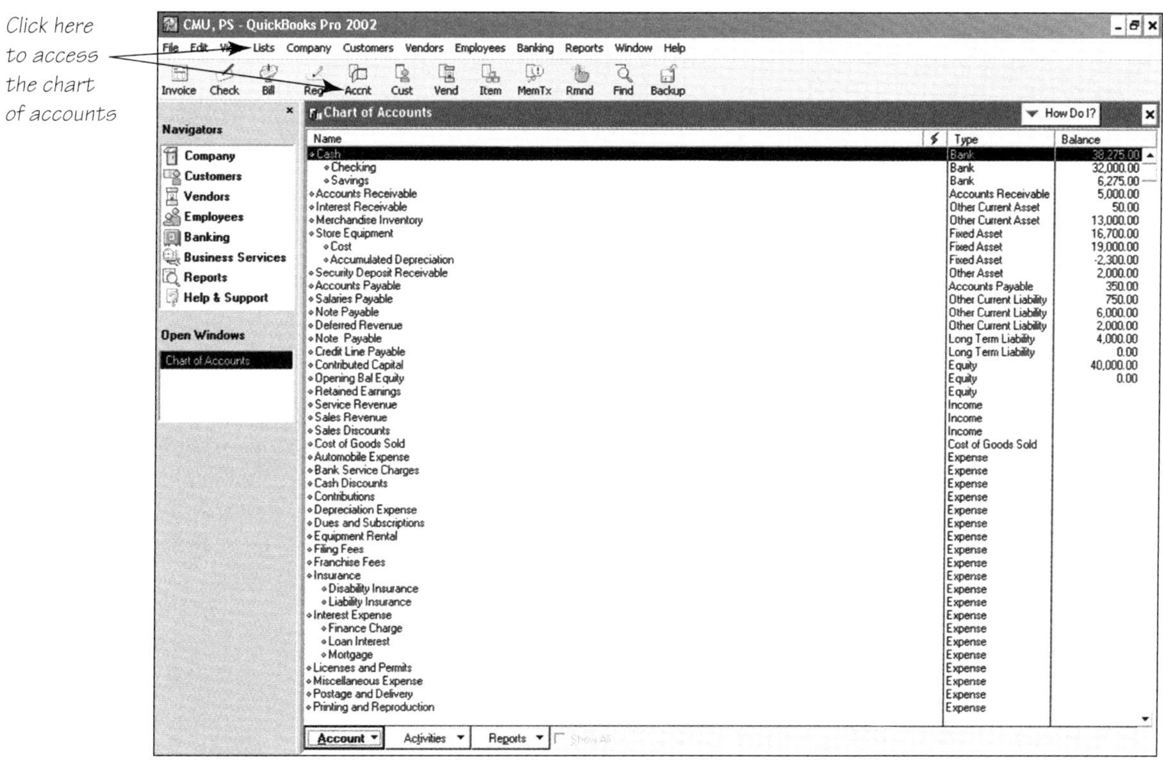

The **forms** feature provides QuickBooks's users electronic representations of the paper forms used to record business activities, such as a customer invoice or a check written to a vendor. Figure 9-21 illustrates such a form—a check written to a CMU vendor. QuickBooks can also track inventory and create purchase orders using CMU's forms on-screen—all without posting, closing, or calculating.

FIGURE 9-21 QuickBooks forms feature, showing a check written to a CMU vendor

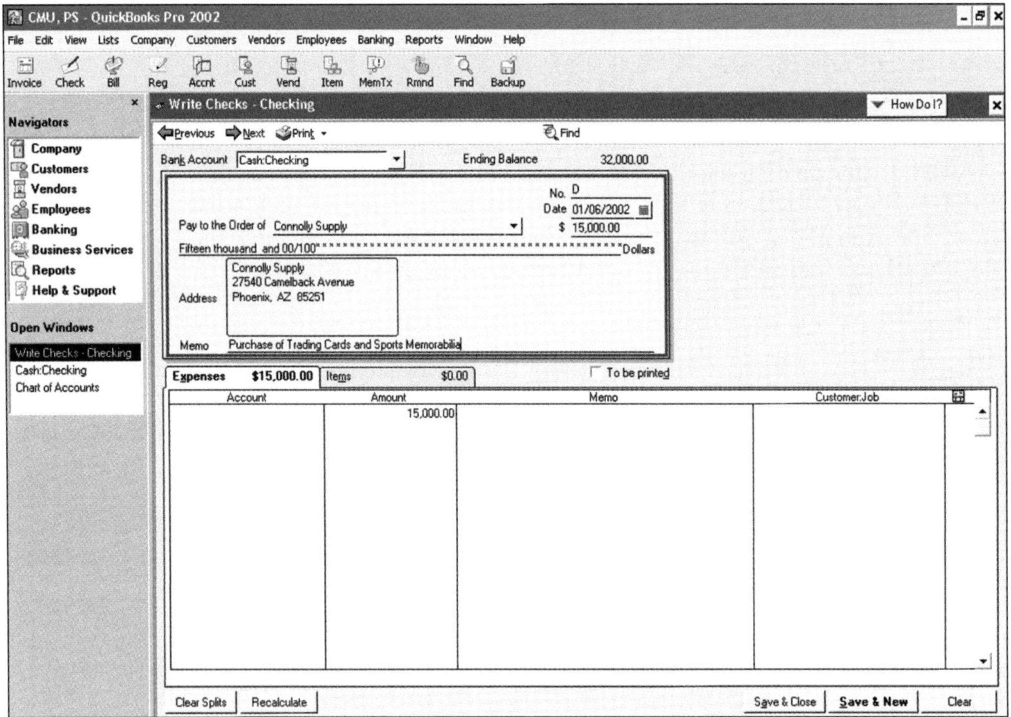

Each **register** is a record of all activity that affects a particular balance sheet account. To access the complete financial history of any asset, liability, or owner equity account, you simply highlight the appropriate account within the chart of accounts, click *Activities*, and then click the words *Use Register*. An account register (illustrated in Figure 9-22b) can be used to enter most transactions (such as checks, bills, and deposits) as well as to maintain the account (such as to make adjustments, void or correct transactions, and so on).

USER FOCUS

How Are Accounting Transactions Recorded in QuickBooks?

One reason for the great success of QuickBooks is that it provides users three distinct but equivalent methods to record transactions. To illustrate each method, let's use CMU's Transaction D in which cash was used to purchase merchandise inventory. The *forms method,* illustrated in Figure 9-22a, is especially popular for users who do not have an accounting background because it automatically records a transaction's effects in the ap-

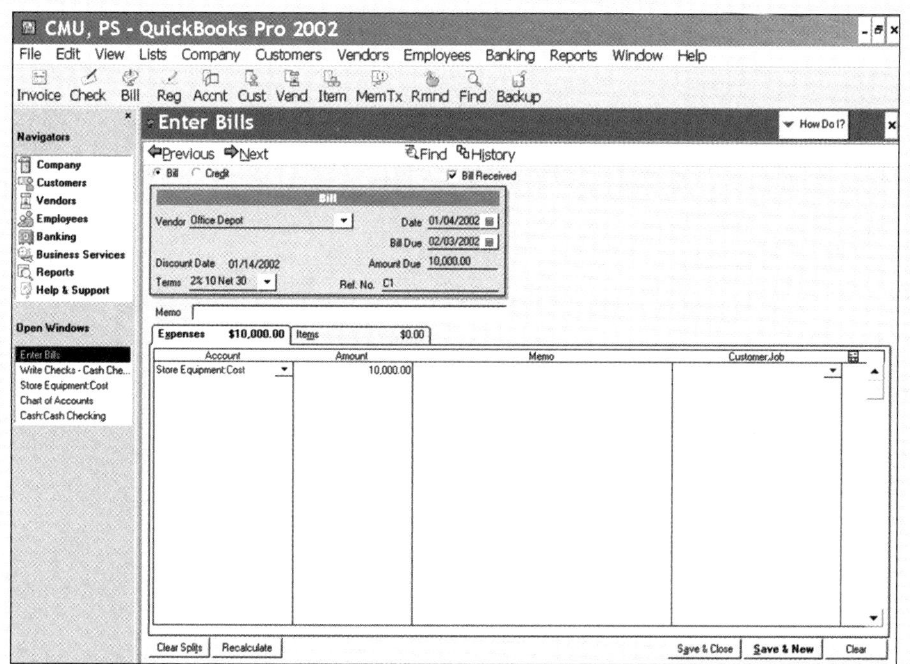

FIGURE 9-22

Three equivalent ways to record transactions in QuickBooks

a. The Forms method

b. The Register method

(continued)

propriate registers when the user fills out a business form or document. The *register method,* illustrated in Figure 9-22b, is accessed through the chart of accounts and uses the same increase-decrease reasoning process as in transaction analysis. The *journal entry method,* illustrated in Figure 9-22c, simply requires the user to enter a transaction's debit-credit effects into the general journal. Thus, QuickBooks provides great recording flexibility.

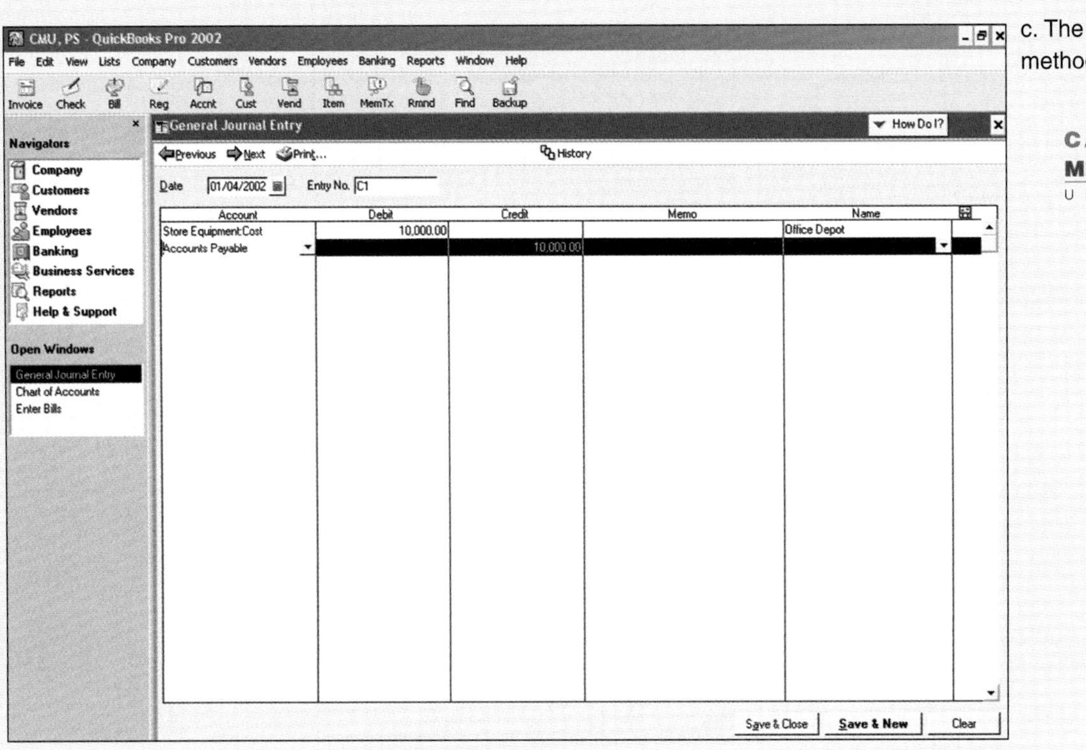

c. The Journal Entr
method

CARDS & MEMORABILI
UNLIMITE

Adjusting and Closing Phases QuickBooks allows you to record adjusting entries in the same way you record transaction entries. That is, whichever of the three equivalent methods you use to input the adjustments on the computer, QuickBooks automatically records and posts this information to ledger accounts. Unlike a manual system, however, QuickBooks automatically completes the closing process.

Reporting Phase You can access the fourth QuickBooks feature, **reports and graphs**, by clicking the Reports menu. This menu provides almost 100 separate financial reports. Included are several versions of the entity's balance sheet (for example, summary versus detailed) and income statement (for example, standard versus comparative), as well as the statement of cash flows. Figure 9-23 shows QuickBooks's version of the manually produced balance sheet that you first saw in Figure 3-2. Likewise, Figure 9-24 illustrates QuickBooks's version of the income statement (QuickBooks uses the title "Profit and Loss") that you first saw in Figure 3-4. This same menu also provides such traditional accounting reports as uncollected customer balances, unpaid vendor balances, a trial balance, a journal, and a general ledger. In addition, every report can be customized so that you can prepare a report for any time period including daily, monthly, and year-to-date.

This menu also allows you to prepare graphs that highlight the significance of financial statement items in ways that make business decision making easier. Figure 9-25, for example, helps illustrate the relative size of each of CMU's expense accounts.

FIGURE 9-23 A portion of CMU's balance sheet in QuickBooks

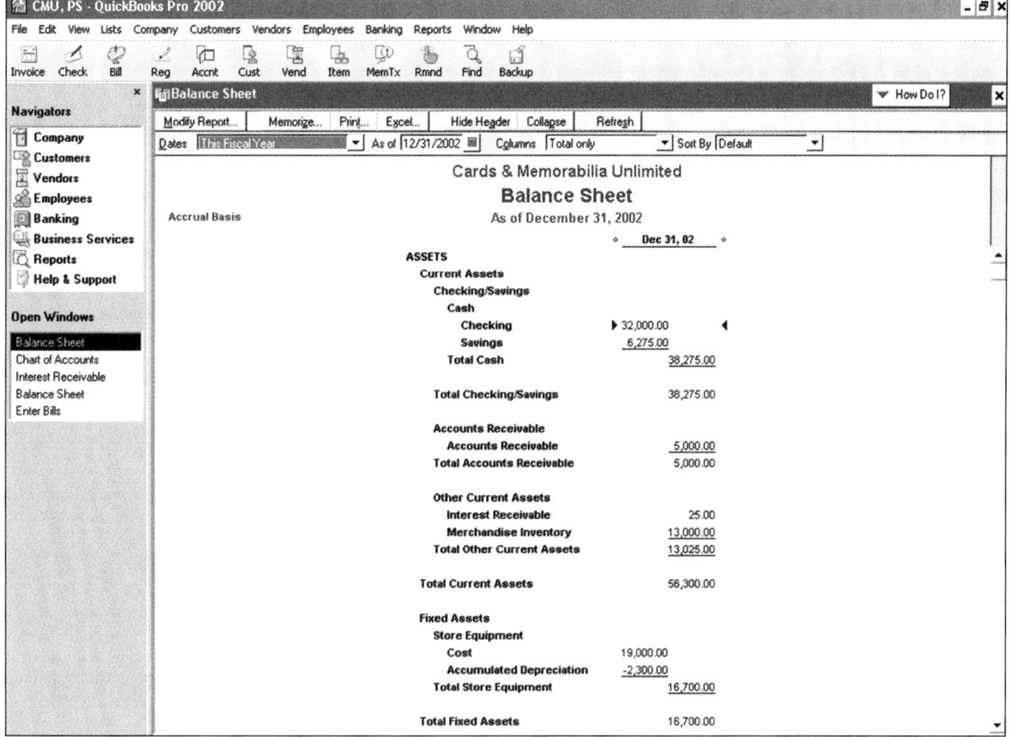

Cards & Memorabilia Unlimited
Balance Sheet
Accrual Basis
As of December 31, 2002

	Dec 31, 02	
ASSETS		
Current Assets		
Checking/Savings		
Cash		
Checking	32,000.00	
Savings	6,275.00	
Total Cash		38,275.00
Total Checking/Savings		38,275.00
Accounts Receivable		
Accounts Receivable		5,000.00
Total Accounts Receivable		5,000.00
Other Current Assets		
Interest Receivable		25.00
Merchandise Inventory		13,000.00
Total Other Current Assets		13,025.00
Total Current Assets		56,300.00
Fixed Assets		
Store Equipment		
Cost	19,000.00	
Accumulated Depreciation	-2,300.00	
Total Store Equipment		16,700.00
Total Fixed Assets		16,700.00

FIGURE 9-24 Cards & Memorabilia Unlimited's income statement in QuickBooks

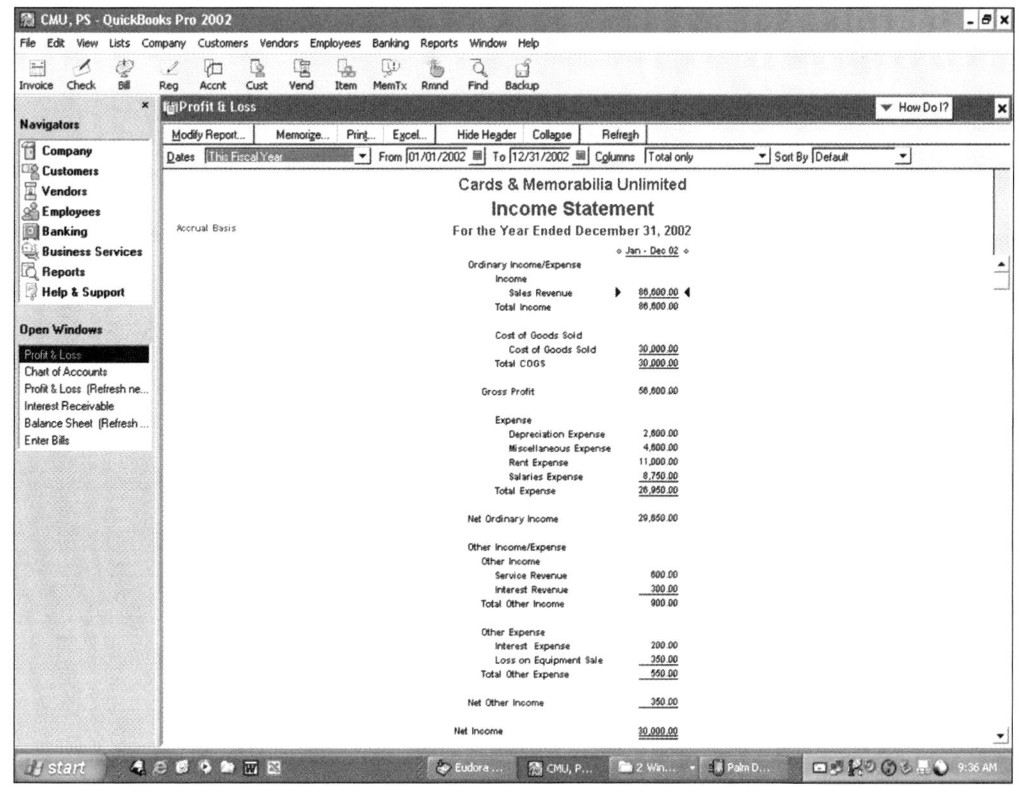

Cards & Memorabilia Unlimited
Income Statement
Accrual Basis
For the Year Ended December 31, 2002

	Jan - Dec 02
Ordinary Income/Expense	
Income	
Sales Revenue	86,600.00
Total Income	86,600.00
Cost of Goods Sold	
Cost of Goods Sold	30,000.00
Total COGS	30,000.00
Gross Profit	56,600.00
Expense	
Depreciation Expense	2,600.00
Miscellaneous Expense	4,600.00
Rent Expense	11,000.00
Salaries Expense	8,750.00
Total Expense	26,950.00
Net Ordinary Income	29,650.00
Other Income/Expense	
Other Income	
Service Revenue	600.00
Interest Revenue	300.00
Total Other Income	900.00
Other Expense	
Interest Expense	200.00
Loss on Equipment Sale	350.00
Total Other Expense	550.00
Net Other Income	350.00
Net Income	30,000.00

FIGURE 9-25 A graphical representation of Cards & Memorabilia Unlimited's expense accounts

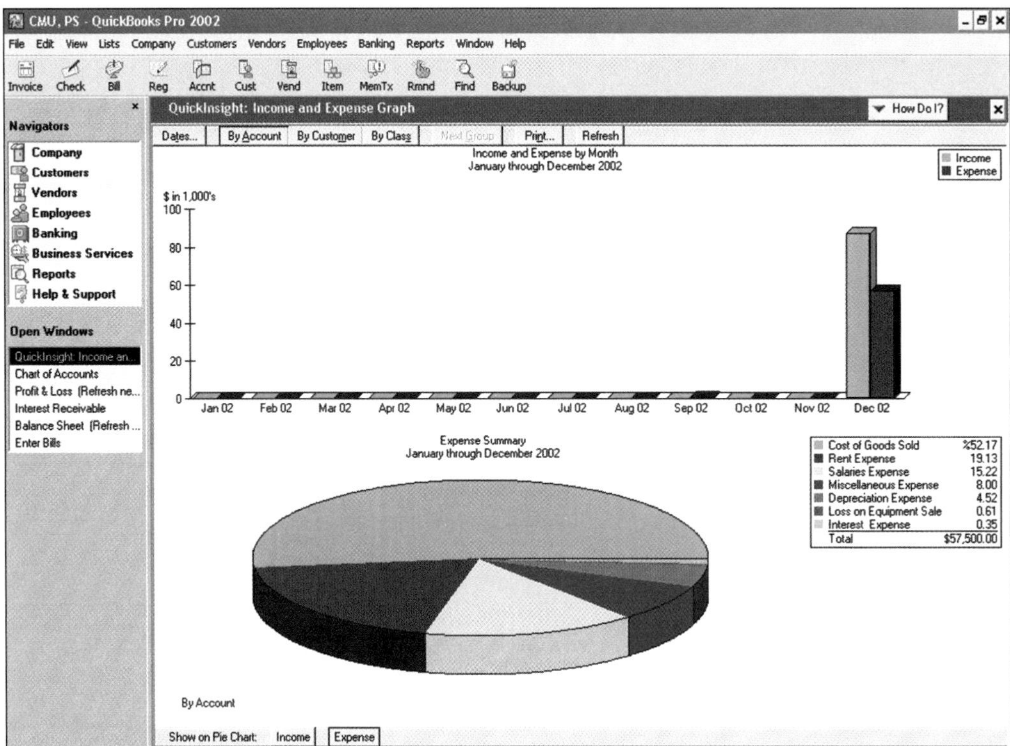

The Benefits of Using QuickBooks This brief introduction to the key features of QuickBooks should whet your appetite to learn more about it or about other popular accounting software packages. The user-friendly features of today's accounting software make it possible for even nonaccountants with no understanding of debits and credits to prepare financial statements. Since you will almost certainly have opportunities to interface with one or more such accounting information systems during your business career, there is no longer good reason to be intimidated by the steps in the accounting process. Using today's accounting software packages, you can take a more active role in the design, operation, and modification of accounting information systems that are designed to facilitate managerial decision making.

APPENDIX

9-1

Learning How to Use T-Account Analysis

PERFORMANCE OBJECTIVES

In this appendix, you will learn the following new Performance Objectives:

PO27 **Apply** T-account analysis to **calculate** the missing amount in an account (i.e., beginning balance, ending balance, increase, or decrease) when three of the four amounts are given, and **record** the transaction that accounts for the missing information.

PO28 **Describe** the nature of the specific transactions whose effects are posted to the increase side and the decrease side of a particular T-account.

PO29 **Prepare** an accrual basis income statement by applying T-account analysis to balance sheet accounts and cash receipts/cash payments information.

T-account analysis is a visual problem-solving technique that can help you master much of the analytical reasoning you will need in this and other accounting courses. Its use of diagrammatic algebra allows you to calculate missing amounts accurately and more rapidly by eliminating the time normally consumed in writing out equations. The purpose of this appendix is not only to demonstrate how T-account analysis works but also to illustrate its usefulness.

T-account analysis has many benefits. Four particularly useful tasks it enables you to do are:

1. Calculate the missing amount in an account.
2. Discern important financial management relationships.
3. Prepare accrual basis income statements from cash basis information.
4. Calculate important cash flows reported in the statement of cash flows.

The last benefit involves converting from the accrual basis to the cash basis, as you will learn in Appendix 14-2. So now we will examine each of the first three benefits more closely.

Calculating the Missing Amount in an Account

You can use T-account analysis to calculate the missing amount in an account in a fast, convenient, and well-documented manner. Compare, for example, the following methods for calculating cost of goods sold:

Method 1

Merchandise Inventory	
14,750	
50,000	?
12,250	

Method 2

Merchandise inventory, 1/1	$14,750
Add: Merchandise purchases	50,000
Cost of goods available for sale	?
Deduct: Mdse. inventory, 12/31	12,250
Cost of goods sold	$?

Although these methods are equivalent in concept, the first method's use of a T-account provides a quicker calculation than does the second method. One reason is that the T-account eliminates the time-consuming reading and/or writing of words. Instead, the T-account identifies such items as beginning or ending inventory, purchases, or cost of goods sold by its specific placement of their numbers. Initially, however, you might feel more comfortable with the second method because its format is more familiar. You can see, for example, that the cost of goods available for sale is $64,750 ($14,750 + $50,000) and, finally, that cost of goods sold is $52,500 ($64,750 − $12,250). Since you will undoubtedly prefer using T-account analysis once you become more familiar with it, let's explore this method in more detail.

Applying T-Account Analysis to an Everyday Example

From our earlier discussion of how T-account analysis is beneficial, it should be apparent that it is a powerful technique. To ensure your complete understanding, let's look at an everyday example with which you can readily identify—carrying money in your wallet. Once you understand this example, you will be ready to tackle the ledger accounts for which T-account analysis was designed.

Suppose you carry your money in a wallet and wish to determine how much you have spent at the end of a day. You begin the day with \$14.75 and end the day with \$12.25. The following T-account portrays this information:

Money in Wallet

Morning 14.75	
Evening 12.25	

Vertical Change Analysis Money in Wallet is a type of daily cash account and must, therefore, be classified as an asset. Since a normal asset balance is a debit, you can see that both the beginning and ending balances of this account have been entered correctly in the T-account above.

The next step is to compare the opening or beginning balance to the closing or ending balance and to calculate a difference or net change in the account for the period. In general, the amount of this change in an account (whether an increase or decrease) is referred to as the **vertical change**. The process of calculating this difference is referred to as **vertical change analysis**, so named because the numbers lie on a vertical plane as shown in the following T-account:

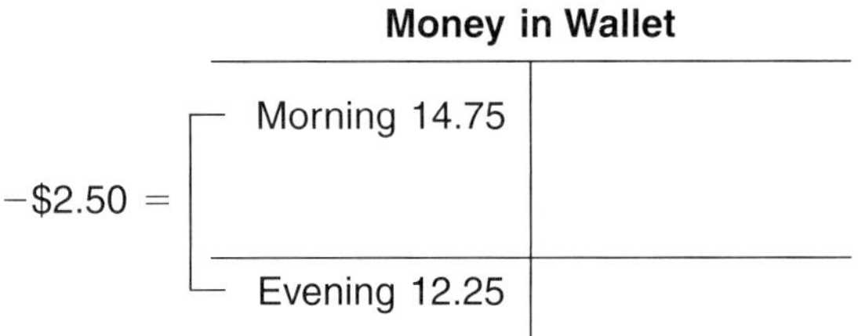

As this T-account discloses, the amount of money in your wallet has decreased by \$2.50 during the day. Note that the vertical bracket on the debit side denotes the vertical change in this T-account. It is calculated by comparing the opening balance to the closing balance and taking the difference between them (\$14.75 − \$12.25 = \$2.50). This \$2.50 amount is then placed outside the vertical bracket. In your analysis, resist the temptation to conclude that \$2.50 was the amount of money actually spent during the day. Instead, remember that money might have been added as well as subtracted from your wallet, netting out to a \$2.50 change.

Horizontal Change Analysis Suppose you recall that a friend gave you \$5 in cash this morning to repay money you loaned her earlier in the week. This sole increase of \$5 to the money in your wallet today represents an increase to an asset and, therefore, must be debited to your Money in Wallet account as shown here:

Money in Wallet

	Morning 14.75	
−\$2.50 =	5.00	
	Evening 12.25	

Now that you know how much cash was received during the day, you will undoubtedly want to know how much cash was paid or disbursed. One approach would be to reason that you had \$19.75 (\$14.75 + \$5.00) in your wallet immediately after being repaid by your friend. If you had \$12.25 at the end of the day, you must have spent \$7.50 (\$19.75 − \$12.25). Although this analysis is correct, it is somewhat cumbersome. An equivalent but more streamlined form of analysis is as follows: If the money in your wallet increases during the day by \$5, but you finish the day with \$2.50 less than you started with, you must have spent \$7.50 during the day. That is, the net change in the account equals \$5.00 − \$7.50, or −\$2.50. The essence of this reasoning process is captured by the rectangle included in the T-account below:

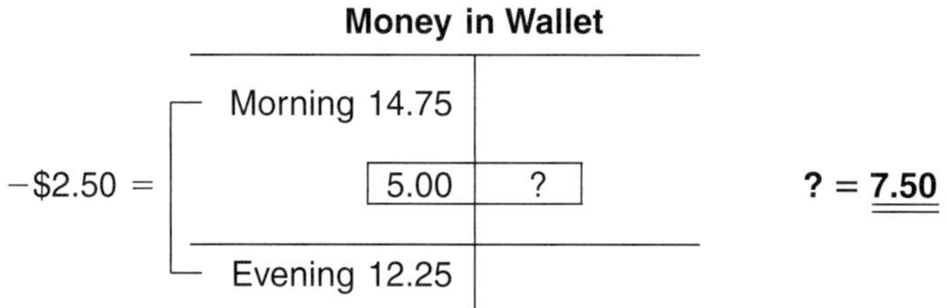

The debit of \$5 and the credit of \$7.50 in the preceding T-account can be referred to as the elements of change. **Elements of change** reflect the activity in an account during a period and should not be confused with the opening balance (\$14.75) or closing balance (\$12.25) of this account. In general, the amount of the difference between these elements of change is referred to as the **horizontal change**. Since this is an asset account and the \$7.50 credit exceeds the \$5 debit, the amount of change is considered to be −\$2.50. The process of calculating the difference between the elements of change is referred to as **horizontal change analysis**, so named because the numbers or elements of change lie on a horizontal plane, that is, the rectangle included in the T-account.

Now, let's introduce some new information to our example. Assume that instead of the \$5 loan, you receive your semimonthly salary of \$1,000 today and immediately cash the check. Despite this addition of cash to your wallet, you end the day with only \$12.25 cash. Under this scenario, you should conclude that \$1,002.50 was either spent or removed from the wallet. Once again, you should compare what was received to what must have been paid to reconcile the net decrease of \$2.50 for the day as shown in the following T-account:

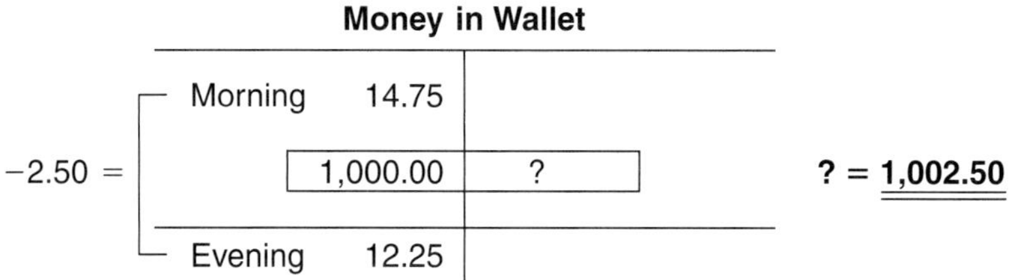

In the preceding analysis, we concentrated on the vertical change (\$14.75 − \$12.25 = −\$2.25) and the known and missing amounts within the rectangle. Specifically, we discovered that a \$1,000 increase to the Money in Wallet account was offset by a decrease to the same account of \$1,002.50, which resulted in a net decrease of \$2.50 to the account. Don't forget that the \$1,000 and \$1,002.50 amounts are referred to as the elements of change and the difference of −\$2.50 between them is referred to as the horizontal change.

The Fundamental Equation of T-Account Analysis The fact that both the vertical and horizontal changes in the preceding T-accounts amount to an identical decrease of \$2.50 is no accident. This equality can be described as the **fundamental equation of T-account analysis**:

Amount of Vertical Change = Amount of Horizontal Change

This equation allows you to calculate a missing amount whenever you have three of the following four T-account amounts: (1) beginning balance, (2) ending balance, (3) increase, and (4) decrease. Note that both the increase and decrease are the elements of change.

The Three-Step Analytical Approach You can summarize our analysis of the preceding T-account with the following three steps:

1. *Calculate the amount of either the vertical or horizontal change.* When you know one such change, you automatically know the other change from the fundamental equation of T-account analysis.

   Example: \$14.75 − \$12.25 = \$2.50 decrease

2. *Identify the known account balance or element(s) of change.*

   Example: \$5.00 increase

3. *Calculate the missing account balance or element of change.*

   Example: If x + \$5.00 = −\$2.50, then x = −\$7.50, or the account decrease = \$7.50

This three-step analytical approach allows you to solve for any missing amount. Assume, for example, that you remember receiving \$5, spending \$7.50, and finding \$12.25 in your wallet at the end of the day. You could then use the following three-step T-account analysis to calculate how much money was in your wallet at the beginning of the day (shown as a question mark in the following T-account):

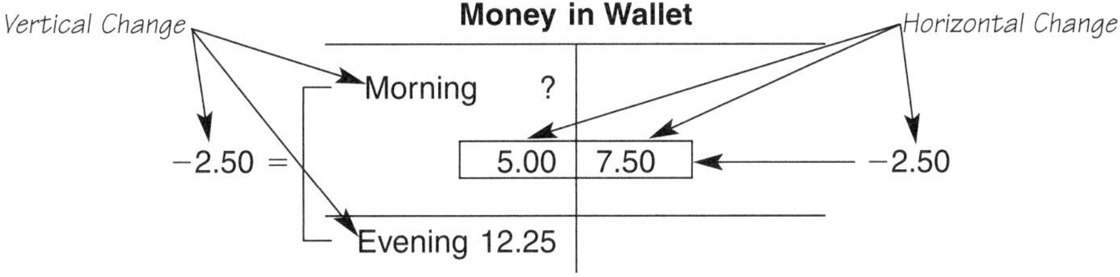

1. *Calculate the amount of either the vertical or horizontal change:*

   \$5.00 + (\$7.50) = \$2.50 decrease

2. *Identify the known account balance or element(s) of change:*

   \$12.25 ending balance

3. *Calculate the missing account balance or element of change:*

   If x + (−\$2.50) = \$12.25, then x = \$14.75, or beginning balance = \$14.75

In the preceding example you solved for a missing amount in a ledger account using T-account analysis. Study Performance Objective 27 so you can solidify your mastery of this skill.

YOUR PERFORMANCE OBJECTIVE 27

Apply T-account analysis to **calculate** the missing amount in an account (i.e., beginning balance, ending balance, increase or decrease) when three of the four amounts are given, and **record** the transaction that accounts for the missing information.

Applying T-Account Analysis to CMU

CARDS & MEMORABILIA UNLIMITED

Let's assume that you knew the beginning balance, ending balance, and increase (represented by credit sales in Transaction N) amounts in CMU's Accounts Receivable account as shown here.

Accounts Receivable

Beginning	–0–	
(N)	20,000	?
Ending	5,000	

Using Performance Objective 27 as a guide, you should be able to determine that the missing fourth amount is a credit to accounts receivable of \$15,000 (0 + 20,000 − 5,000 = 15,000). To record the transaction that accounts for the missing information, you would begin with your credit to the Accounts Receivable account as shown here:

Some Other Account	15,000	
Accounts Receivable		15,000

Then, using Performance Objective 25, you might reason that the likely account title is Cash since the Accounts Receivable account is normally decreased (that is, credited) whenever cash is received.

YOUR PERFORMANCE OBJECTIVE 25
Select a likely account title for one-half of a transaction when given the account title for the other half of the transaction.

The result of the preceding reasoning process is the following transaction:

Cash Checking	15,000	
Accounts Receivable		15,000

You can, of course, verify that this is the correct answer by noting CMU's Transaction V. Now that you understand how you record the transaction that accounts for the missing information in Performance Objective 27, let's turn to another benefit of T-account analysis.

Discerning Important Financial Management Relationships

To understand how T-account analysis can help you discern important financial management relationships, let's look more closely at the inventory data introduced earlier.

Merchandise Inventory

14,750	
50,000	52,500
12,250	

Merchandise inventory, 1/1	\$14,750
Add: Merchandise purchases	50,000
Cost of goods available	64,750
Deduct: Mdse. inventory, 12/31	12,250
Cost of goods sold	\$52,500

The fact that inventory decreased during the period (from $14,750 to $12,250) means that the decreases to this account (credit side) exceed the increases to this account (debit side). Since the debit side represents the cost of inventory purchases and the credit side represents the cost of goods sold, you can also conclude that inventory sales exceeded inventory purchases. This financial management relationship can be very important if it is company policy to always maintain inventory at the same level or if you suspect that additional sales were lost because your company was unable to acquire inventory on a timely basis. Essentially, T-account analysis makes it easier for you to "cut through" the maze of numbers to recognize the critical business relationships with which managers often make their decisions. Use Performance Objective 28 to help you more easily recognize these important financial relationships.

YOUR PERFORMANCE OBJECTIVE 28
Describe the nature of the specific transactions whose effects are posted to the increase side and the decrease side of a particular T-account.

To practice using this performance objective, let's return to our CMU example, in which the Accounts Receivable account increased during the period as shown here:

Accounts Receivable

Beginning	–0–		
(N)	20,000	15,000	(V)
Ending	5,000		

How would you describe the nature of the specific transactions whose effects are posted to the increase side and the decrease side of this account? A complete answer would be that the transactions represented by the increase side are credit sales and the transactions represented by the decrease side are collections of cash from customers. Thus, we should be able to conclude that sales exceeded collections this year. Whether this is favorable—a promising growth in sales or demand for our products—or unfavorable—more customers are either delaying their payments or becoming bad credit risks—might well require further analysis.

Now that you better understand how T-account analysis can enhance your ability to recognize these and other important financial relationships, let's turn to the next benefit of T-account analysis.

Preparing Accrual Basis Income Statements from Cash Basis Information

Perhaps the most beneficial use of T-account analysis is to prepare accrual basis income statements given cash receipts, cash payments, and ledger account balances. This more complex application of T-account analysis is represented by Performance Objective 29.

YOUR PERFORMANCE OBJECTIVE 29
Prepare an accrual basis income statement by applying T-account analysis to balance sheet accounts and cash receipts/cash payments information.

Let's now see exactly how T-accounts can be used to prepare such an income statement.

Using the Six-Step Analytical Approach

Learning how to prepare the accrual basis income statement described in Performance Objective 29 requires more than the ability to solve for a missing amount (Performance Objective 27) or the ability to complete a journal entry when presented with a partial journal entry (Performance Objective 25). Not only must you develop those skills, but you also must be able to describe in words the nature of the transaction whose effect is posted to each side of a ledger account (Performance Objective 28). A six-step analytical approach helps you complete all of these requirements. Let's use the following data to learn this six-step approach:

	January 1	December 31
Debits:		
Accounts Receivable	$1,000	$1,500
Merchandise Inventory	800	1,000
Credits:		
Accounts Payable	$ 400	$ 500
Cash Receipts:		
1. Cash sales	$5,000	
2. Collections from credit customers	2,000	
Cash Payments:		
3. Payments to merchandise suppliers	$2,000	
Assume that there are no cash purchases of inventory.		

Calculating Sales Revenue With this data, let's first use the six-step approach to calculate the amount of accrual basis sales revenue.

Step 1: Identify a target account. The target account is simply the account whose balance is desired. Since Sales Revenue is generally the first account reported on the income statement, it is not surprising that we chose to analyze it first.

Step 2: Identify at least one support account that is related to the target account. Another way of expressing this step is to say that you must find an account that is logically related to, or supports, the target account. One such pairing is a cash sales transaction that includes the Cash account and the target Sales Revenue account. Another familiar pairing is a credit sales transaction that includes the Accounts Receivable account and the target Sales Revenue account. In both cases, you credit the Sales Revenue account. Since you already know that cash sales amount to $5,000, you would check for a missing credit sale transaction. As shown here, the Accounts Receivable account and the related Sales Revenue account are the components of a credit sale:

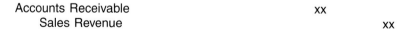

Accounts Receivable	XX	
Sales Revenue		XX

Step 3: Enter the support account's available ledger balances.

Accounts Receivable

Debit	Credit
1,000	
1,500	

The support account is an asset, thus, the beginning and ending balances are inserted on the debit side.

Step 4: Look for evidence of a transaction that is related to the support account and post its effect to that account. In this example, there are three potential transactions from which to choose. Neither the first, cash sales, nor the last, payments to suppliers, affect the Accounts Receivable account. The second transaction, collections from credit customers, does affect this support account as is shown here:

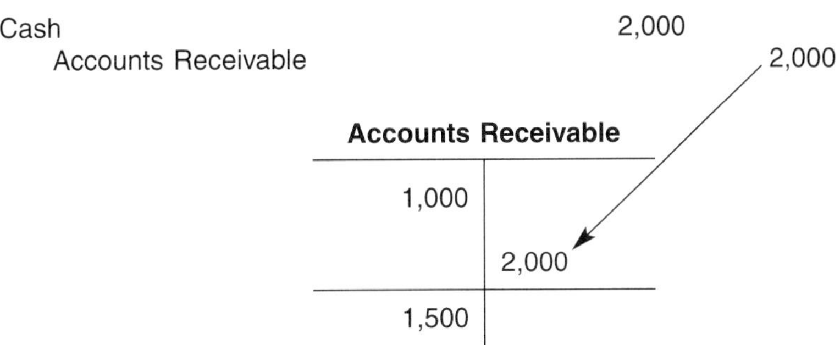

The T-account above illustrates the posting of the $2,000 credit to the support account. There is no reason to post the corresponding debit to the Cash Account because it does not produce information about credit sales.

Step 5: Apply vertical change analysis and horizontal change analysis to the support account to determine the missing amount.

(a) Vertical change analysis:

	Accounts Receivable		
+$500 =	01/01	1,000	
		?	2,000
	12/31	1,500	

When you analyze this T-account vertically, you find there is a net debit increase of $500.

(b) Horizontal change analysis:

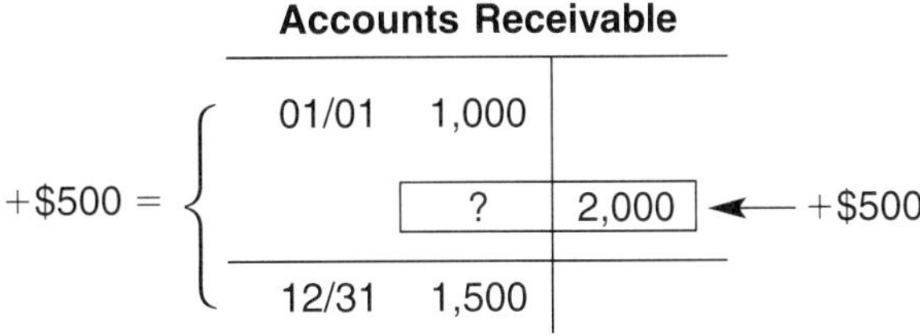

From the fundamental equation of T-account analysis, the combined effect of the elements of change (horizontal change) within the rectangle must also net out to a debit increase of $500. Let's take a closer look to see if that's the case in our example. If the missing (?) − $2,000 = $500, then ? = $2,500. That is, the missing amount is a $2,500 debit to the Accounts Receivable account. Take a look at the revised T-account:

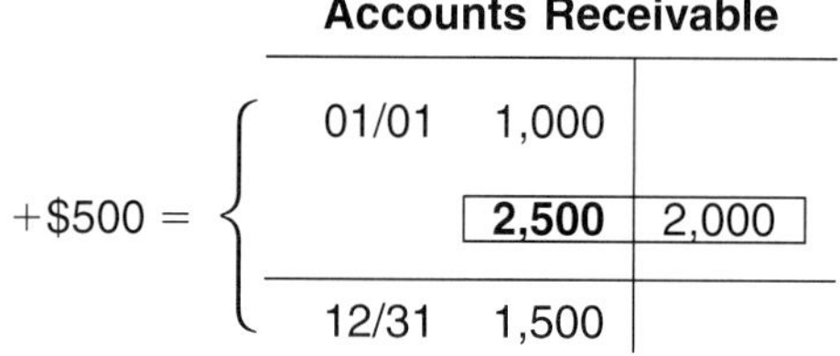

Accounts Receivable
01/01 1,000
+$500 =
2,500
2,000
12/31 1,500

Errors frequently occur at this stage of the horizontal change analysis when one correctly calculates the amount of the vertical or horizontal change, but fails to note whether the amount has increased or decreased. A two-part example of this error follows:

(1) **Accounts Receivable**

	Debit	Credit
	1,000	
$500 =	?	2,000
	1,500	

(2) **Accounts Receivable**

	Debit	Credit
	1,000	
$500 =	**1,500**	2,000
	1,500	

Can you see why the analysis in the second T-account is incorrect? Although there is a $500 difference ($2,000 − $1,500), the placement indicates the account balance has decreased despite the vertical analysis showing a clear increase. To avoid this common error, decide whether the account has increased or decreased by labeling it with pluses and minuses.

Step 6: Post (transfer) this amount to the target account using transaction analysis. Because you just debited the Accounts Receivable account for $2,500 in the preceding step, you must credit its related Sales Revenue account for $2,500 to complete this credit sale transaction:

	Debit	Credit
Accounts Receivable	2,500	
Sales Revenue		2,500

The effect of posting this $2,500 credit to the Sales Revenue account is shown here:

Accounts Receivable

Debit	Credit
1,000	
2,500	2,000
1,500	

Sales Revenue

Debit	Credit	
	5,000	← from cash sales
	2,500	← from credit sales
	7,500	← total sales

The journal entries underlying the $5,000 and $2,500 credits to the sales revenue T-account are as follows:

	Debit	Credit
Cash	5,000	
Sales Revenue		5,000
Accounts Receivable	2,500	
Sales Revenue		2,500

Calculating Cost of Goods Sold Now that we have reconstructed the Sales Revenue account using T-account analysis, let's once again use the six-step analytical approach to determine the balance in the accrual basis Cost of Goods Sold account.

Step 1: Identify a target account. This income statement target is the Cost of Goods Sold account.

Step 2: Identify at least one support account that is related to the target account. The Cost of Goods Sold account is always debited unless it is being corrected or is part of a closing entry. As you debit Cost of Goods Sold, the support account that is simultaneously credited is that of Merchandise Inventory. Notice that you can reach this same conclusion by simply reasoning that the Cost of Goods Sold represents merchandise that is no longer in the firm's inventory because it has been sold. Whatever reasoning process you use, the common transaction linking these accounts together is that shown here:

Cost of Goods Sold	xx	
Merchandise Inventory		xx

What makes the Cost of Goods Sold account unique is the fact that it actually has two support accounts. That is, since the Merchandise Inventory support account is so fundamentally associated with suppliers, the Accounts Payable account must also be included in this analysis.

Step 3: Enter the support accounts' available ledger balances.

Merchandise Inventory (Dr.)	Merchandise Inventory (Cr.)
800	
1,000	

Accounts Payable (Dr.)	Accounts Payable (Cr.)
	400
	500

Step 4: Look for evidence of a transaction that is related to the support account and post its effect to that account. Only one transaction remaining, payments to merchandise suppliers, has a relationship to merchandise inventory, as recorded here:

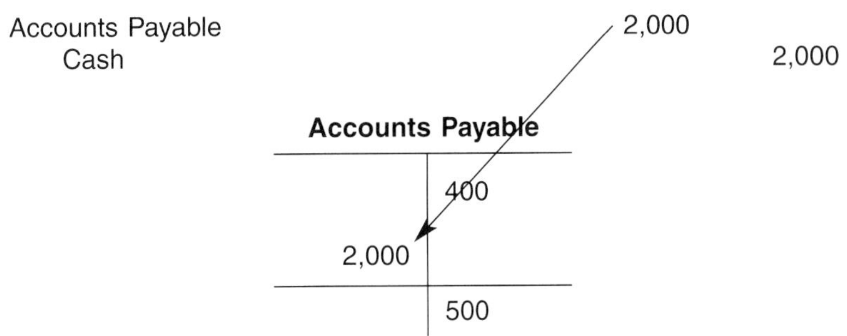

The T-account above illustrates the posting of the $2,000 debit to the Accounts Payable support account.

Step 5: Apply vertical/horizontal change analysis to the support account to determine the missing amount.

(a) Vertical change analysis:

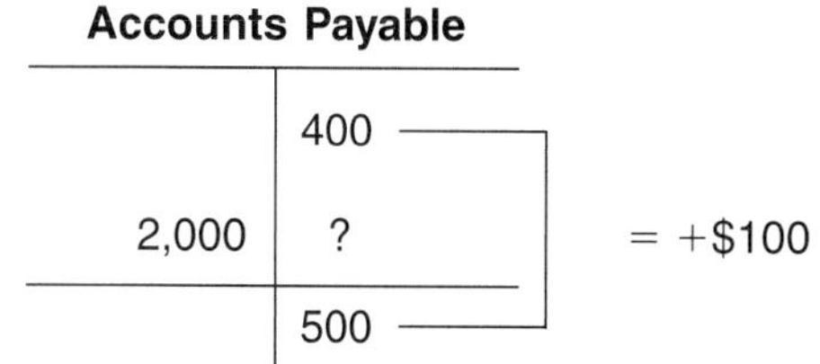

Vertical change analysis of the T-account above indicates a net credit increase of $100.

(b) Horizontal change analysis:

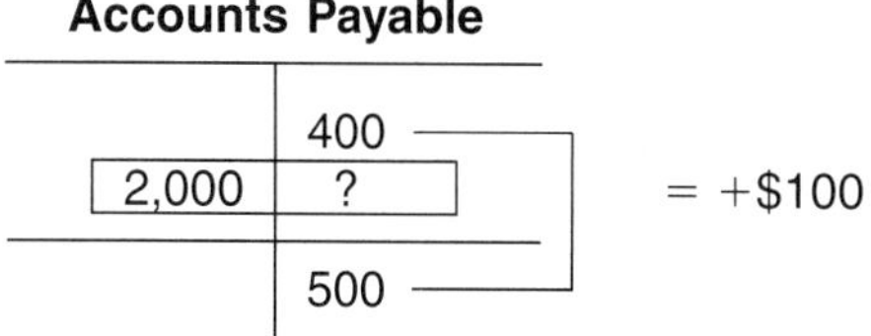

Once again, the combined effect of the elements of change must also net out to a credit increase of $100. If the missing (?) − $2,000 = $100, then ? = $2,100, or the missing amount is a $2,100 credit to the Accounts Payable account. This revised T-account is shown here in correct form.

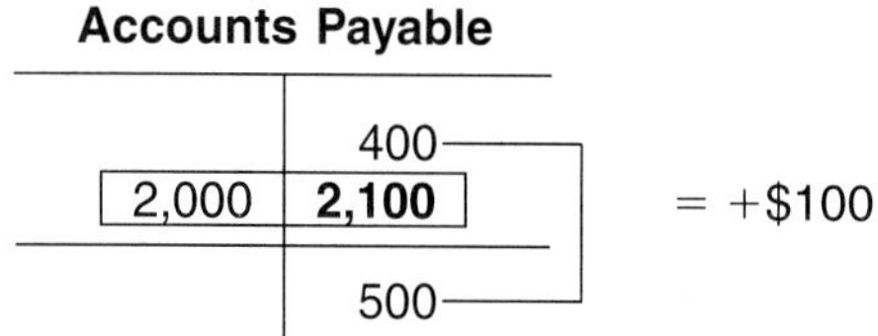

Step 6: Post (transfer) this amount to the target account using transaction analysis. When you credit the Accounts Payable account, the corresponding debit is usually made to the Merchandise Inventory account. Thus, the Merchandise Inventory account becomes a temporary target account as shown here:

Accounts Payable			Merchandise Inventory	
	400		800	
2,000	**2,100**		**2,100**	
	500		1,000	

The $2,100 amount in each account represents a credit purchase of inventory transaction.

At this point, the Accounts Payable account no longer is useful and the Merchandise Inventory account again becomes a support account for the Cost of Goods Sold target account. It is, therefore, necessary to repeat steps 5 and 6 as is shown here:

Step 5: Apply vertical/horizontal change analysis to the support account to determine the missing amount.

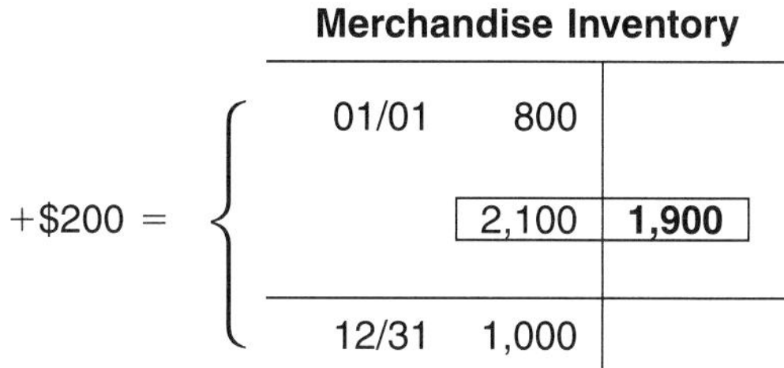

Notice that both vertical change analysis and horizontal change analysis were applied above using one T-account. As you become more comfortable with T-account analysis, you will find that you are able to solve these problems more and more rapidly.

Step 6: Post (transfer) this amount to the target account using transaction analysis.

Merchandise Inventory	
800	
2,100	**1,900**
1,000	

Cost of Goods Sold	
1,900	
1,900	

As shown in the T-accounts above, the amount of Cost of Goods Sold is $1,900.

Once you are confident that you understand the essentials of T-account analysis, be sure you work a good number of the appendix exercises and problems provided at the end of this chapter. As you become more and more comfortable using T-account analysis, you will discover that you no longer need to depend on the three-step and six-step analytical approaches introduced in this appendix. Instead, you will find that the analytical processes you have studied have become second nature to you.

Summary with Key Terms

In this chapter you first learned the definitions of and the distinction between **data** (379) and **information** (379), two important information system concepts. You then were introduced to the four components found in every information system: **input** (380), **processing** (380), **storage** (380), and **output** (380). Collectively, these four elements constitute an **accounting information system** (380), a system that identifies and records accounting transactions or *input*, *processes* and *stores* the effects of these transactions, and communicates their effects in financial reports or *output*.

The number in parentheses following each **key term** is the page number on which the term is defined.

Most accounting information systems, whether manual or computerized, have a **chart of accounts** (380), a **general ledger** (381), and one or more **subsidiary ledgers** (381). These record-keeping devices provide a structure not only for processing but also for reporting. Since these devices process the effects of transactions, you then learned about **transaction cycles** (382) such as the **spending cycle** (382), the **conversion cycle** (382), the **revenue cycle** (383), and the **administrative cycle** (383). Transaction cycles are not the same, however, as the sequence of separate but related activities included in each transaction cycle known as a **transaction subsystem** (385).

No discussion of an accounting information system would be complete without **internal control** (385), a process designed to reduce inaccuracy in the accounting information system and discourage unethical behavior among employees and customers. Internal control consists of five interrelated components: the **control environment** (386), **risk assessment** (386), **control activities** (387), **information and communication** (387), and **monitoring** (387).

The revenue cycle was explored in greater depth by examining its transaction subsystems—a **marketing system** (388), a **shipping system** (388), and a **billing and collection system** (388)—and characteristic business documents—a **sales order** (388), a **shipping order** (388), a **bill of lading** (388), and a **sales invoice** (388).

The spending cycle was also explored in greater depth by examining its transaction subsystems—a **purchasing system** (390), a **receiving system** (390), and an **accounts payable system** (390)—and characteristic business documents—a **purchase requisition** (390), a **purchase order** (390), a **receiving report** (390), and a **vendor's invoice** (390).

The chapter then described the sequence of steps known as the **accounting process** (393), also known as the **accounting cycle** (393), which companies like Cards & Memorabilia Unlimited use to manually transform the effects of accounting transactions into the financial statements. The foundation for this process is the double-entry method of bookkeeping, which distinguishes between the left, or **debit** (395), side and the right, or **credit**, (395) side, of an **account** (394). In a classroom setting an account is represented by a **T-account** (394). Entering a transaction's debit-credit effects, or **journal entry** (398), into a book of original entry, or **journal** (398), is called **journalizing** (397). Small companies may need only a single journal known as a **general journal** (398), whereas larger companies may also need what are called special journals. Transferring the effects of the resulting journal entry to individual accounts in the general ledger is called **posting** (401). The three separate trial balances to test the equality of debits and credits are the **unadjusted trial balance** (403), the **adjusted trial balance** (404), and the **post-closing trial balance** (412). As first explained in Chapter 7, adjusting entries and correcting entries are used to bring the ledger accounts up to date at the end of an accounting period. As its title suggests, a **closing entry** (411) is a journal entry that closes **temporary accounts** (411) but not **permanent accounts** (411) at the end of an accounting period. If you use the **indirect approach** (411), a special **income summary account** (411) will be necessary. Under the **direct approach** (412), however, no such account is needed.

This chapter's *Insight* discussed the limitations of computerized accounting information systems. It concluded that all systems, no matter how impressive, will be compromised if there is bad input or the users are not well trained.

The last portion of this chapter described the nature of an **accounting software package** (414), its classification into high-end and low-end types, and several popular small business packages now available. You then learned some specific details about QuickBooks, the accounting software package used by Cards & Memorabilia Unlimited. Four features of this software package include **lists** (417), **forms** (418), **registers** (418), and **reports and graphs** (420).

Appendix Summary with Key Terms

In T-account analysis, discussed in the appendix, a **vertical change** (425) is the amount of change between the beginning and ending balances of an account, whereas a **horizontal change** (426) is the amount of change between the **elements of change** (426), that is, the account's increase and decrease amounts. The processes of calculating a vertical change and a horizontal change are referred to as **vertical change analysis** (425) and **horizontal change analysis** (426), respectively. The **fundamental equation of T-account analysis** (427) states that the amount of vertical change must equal the amount of horizontal change within the same account.

Making Business Decisions

YOUR PERFORMANCE OBJECTIVE 2
(page 18)

Do you already have an accountant? If not, one day you will probably need one—whether to help prepare your income tax returns, plan your estate, or set up the accounting system for your new business. Your accountant's advice can greatly affect your life, so choosing an accountant is an important decision. As you have seen before in this book, you can make a good decision if you do your homework—plan, think critically, weigh the factors—*before* you make the decision.

So how do you decide who should be your accountant? Is there a guaranteed process, which, if you follow it, will always find you a good accountant? No, of course not. But there are many things you can do to increase the chances that the accountant you choose will provide valuable services.

Your goal in this Decision Case is to develop a 7- to 10-step process on how to choose a good accountant. You will include these steps at the end of a report in which you explain how you developed these steps. To prepare the steps and the report, first perform one or all of the following four activities as directed by your instructor:

1. *Interview an accountant.* Prepare a list of at least 10 questions before the interview and submit this list as part of your report. The goal of this interview is to learn how the interviewee thinks clients can find a good accountant.
2. *Interview at least one friend, acquaintance, or client referred from the accountant in (1) above.* Prepare a list of at least 10 questions before the interviews and submit this list as part of your report. The goal of these interviews is to learn how the interviewees found their accountants; what they like or do not like about their accountants; what they'd do differently the next time they look for an accountant.
3. *Explore two websites thoroughly.* Using a search engine, perform an Internet search for the words "find accountant." Visit several of the sites. Choose the two sites that you think are the most helpful in finding an accountant. Explain why you think these two sites were the most helpful. Quote or refer to each site at least once in your report. Include the appropriate citation.
4. *Use at least one other information source.* This can be advertisements, the yellow pages, newspapers, commercials, the Internet, or any other appropriate source. In your report describe what you learned from this source about how to choose an accountant. Discuss why or why not this source was helpful. Do you think that this source provides reliable information? Why or why not?

Required

After you have completed these activities as assigned, write your report using the following outline. You should adjust the outline to reflect which of the four activities your instructor assigned. You can change the wording of the headings, add names, and so on, but you must follow the general organization. Be sure to end your report with the 7 to 10 steps you derived from all of your research.

I. Introduction
II. Interview of [accountant name]
    a. Who is [accountant name]?
    b. The questions asked and the answers.
    c. A summary of the accountant's information.
III. Interview of friend(s)/acquaintance(s)/client(s)
    a. Who is [Person's Name]?
    b. The questions asked and the answers.
    c. A summary of [person's] information.
IV. Other information sources: Activities (3) and (4) above
    a. A summary of information collected.
    b. The helpfulness of these sources.
    c. The reliability of these sources.
V. The 10 Steps
    a. Analysis of all the information collected.
    b. The method used for determining the 10 steps.
    c. The 10 steps.
VI. Conclusion

Questions

YOUR PERFORMANCE OBJECTIVE 4
(page 22)

9-1 Explain in your own words the meaning of key business terms.

a. Input
b. Processing
c. Storage
d. Output
e. Accounting information system
f. Spending cycle
g. Conversion cycle
h. Revenue cycle
i. Administrative cycle
j. Explain how each of the following components of internal control can be applied to a specific business:
   1. Control environment
   2. Risk assessment
   3. Control activities
   4. Information and communication
   5. Monitoring
k. Marketing system
l. Shipping system
m. Billing and collection system
n. Purchasing system
o. Receiving system
p. Accounts payable system
q. Debit
r. Credit
s. Account
t. Posting
u. Accounting software package
v. Lists
w. Forms
x. Registers
y. Reports
z. Graphs

9-2 Distinguish between the terms *data* and *information.*
9-3 Why is a chart of accounts found in every accounting information system?
9-4 Distinguish between the terms *general ledger* and *subsidiary ledger.*
9-5 What are the advantages of using subsidiary ledgers?
9-6 Describe the relationship between a control account and a subsidiary account.
9-7 Distinguish between the terms *transaction cycle* and *transaction subsystem.*
9-8 What is internal control?
9-9 Distinguish between the following documents usually found in a revenue cycle: sales order, shipping order, bill of lading, and a sales invoice.
9-10 Distinguish between the following documents usually found in a spending cycle: purchase requisition, purchase order, a receiving report, and a vendor's invoice.
9-11 What is the accounting process? List the four phases included in the accounting process.
9-12 What is the basic rule of double-entry bookkeeping?
9-13 Distinguish between an account and a T-account.
9-14 Distinguish among a journal, journal entry, and journalizing.
9-15 Distinguish between a general journal and a special journal.
9-16 What is a ledger? How does it differ from a journal?
9-17 What is a trial balance? Is it a financial statement? Would you expect it to be prepared by an accounting software package?
9-18 Distinguish among an unadjusted trial balance, an adjusted trial balance, and a post-closing trial balance.
9-19 Distinguish between adjusting entries and correcting entries.
9-20 What is the purpose of closing entries?
9-21 Distinguish between temporary accounts and permanent accounts.
9-22 Distinguish between the indirect method and the direct method of closing.
9-23 Describe the role of the income summary account.
9-24 If the income summary account has a credit balance after the revenue and expense accounts have been closed into it, will the entity report a net income or a net loss?
9-25 Distinguish among the following QuickBooks features: lists, forms, and registers.

Appendix Questions

YOUR PERFORMANCE OBJECTIVE 4
(page 22)

A9-1 Explain in your own words the meaning of key business terms.

a. Vertical change
b. Horizontal change
c. Elements of change
d. Vertical change analysis
e. Horizontal change analysis
f. Fundamental equation of T-account analysis

A9-2 Describe at least two benefits of T-account analysis.

A9-3 Distinguish between a vertical change and a horizontal change in a T-account.

A9-4 Describe, in your own words, the nature of the fundamental equation of T-account analysis.

A9-5 What is a target account?

Reinforcement Exercises

E9-1 Asking the Right Questions: A Group Activity

YOUR PERFORMANCE OBJECTIVE 4 *(page 22)*

It's often said that knowing the right answer is not nearly as important as asking the right question. Asking the right question is a problem-solving skill that will help you make sound business decisions. In this exercise, you will review the vocabulary introduced in Chapter 9 by creating questions to match answers—similar to a popular TV show.

Required

a. Given an answer, what's the question?
Choose **three** of the following terms to serve as an answer. Create an appropriate question for each term. For example, if you choose the term *balance sheet*, you might create the question *What financial statement reports the assets, liabilities, and owners' equity of an entity on a specific date?*

Temporary account	Sales order	General ledger	Data
Permanent account	Sales invoice	Subsidiary ledger	Debit
Purchase order	Vendor's invoice	General journal	Credit
Information	Shipping order	Special journal	Posting

b. Are you sure that's the question?
Have each member of your group read aloud the questions they developed in Requirement (a). As a group, decide whether each question is an accurate match for an answer. Once satisfied that all questions are appropriate, the group, as a whole, chooses the three best questions created within the group. Record the three questions chosen (with their answers) on separate pieces of paper or index cards and give them to your instructor.

c. What's the answer?
To ensure that you have learned the vocabulary terms listed in Requirement (a), your instructor will now quiz you on the questions written by all of your classmates.

E9-2 Internal Control Documents

YOUR PERFORMANCE OBJECTIVE 23 *(page 391)*

Briefly describe the purpose of each document listed below and identify the transaction cycle (revenue, spending, conversion, or administrative) to which it would most likely be related.

a. Purchase order
b. Shipping order
c. Inventory control record
d. Sales invoice
e. Receiving report
f. Utility bill

E9-3 Internal Control Documents

YOUR PERFORMANCE OBJECTIVE 23 *(page 391)*

Briefly describe the purpose of each document listed below and identify the transaction cycle (revenue, spending, conversion, or administrative) to which it would most likely be related.

a. Sales order
b. Bill of lading
c. Purchase requisition
d. Vendor's invoice
e. Materials requisition
f. Time slip

E9-4 Internal Control Attributes

YOUR PERFORMANCE OBJECTIVE 23 *(page 391)*

Identify the internal control attribute related to each independent situation described below.

a. Carter Corporation installs a video surveillance camera in its showroom to monitor and protect its inventory.
b. Pestal Company requires its cashiers to have an assistant manager verify the cash count at the end of each shift.
c. Alsop Company prepares all sales invoices in triplicate—one copy for the shipping department, one for the accounts receivable department, and one for the customer.
d. Painter Sales Company requires all returns from customers to be approved by a department manager prior to issuing a refund or sales credit.
e. Champion Finance requires one employee to open all mail and make a list of all checks received and another employee to record the amounts as payments received from customers in the accounts.

YOUR PERFORMANCE OBJECTIVE 23 *(page 391)*

E9-5 Internal Control Attributes

Briefly describe how each of the internal control attributes that were described in this chapter could be employed effectively in the revenue cycle of a service firm.

YOUR PERFORMANCE OBJECTIVE 24 *(page 396)*

E9-6 Debit-Credit Rules

Indicate whether the following increases and decreases should be recorded as debits or credits.

a. Increases in assets.
b. Decreases in assets.
c. Increases in owner equities.
d. Decreases in owner equities.
e. Increases in liabilities.
f. Decreases in liabilities.
g. Increases in expenses.
h. Decreases in expenses.
i. Increases in revenues.
j. Decreases in revenues.

YOUR PERFORMANCE OBJECTIVE 24 *(page 396)*

E9-7 Debit-Credit Rules

Indicate whether the following accounts normally have a debit, credit, or zero balance after the accounting cycle has been completed.

a. Accounts receivable
b. Accounts payable
c. Susan Newman, capital
d. Note payable
e. Cash
f. Retained earnings
g. Rent revenue
h. Salaries expense
i. Interest expense
j. Income summary

YOUR PERFORMANCE OBJECTIVE 24 *(page 396)*

E9-8 Debit-Credit Rules

Indicate whether the following accounts normally have a debit, credit, or zero balance after the accounting cycle has been completed.

a. Interest receivable
b. Prepaid rent
c. Capital stock
d. Mortgage payable
e. Advances from customers
f. Martha Perez, drawing
g. Service revenue
h. Cost of goods sold
i. Interest revenue
j. Merchandise inventory

YOUR PERFORMANCE OBJECTIVE 25 *(page 401)*

E9-9 Account Title Relationships

Select the most plausible account title(s) to accompany these account titles in a journal entry.

a. Accounts receivable
b. Accounts payable
c. Susan Newman, capital
d. Note payable
e. Cash
f. Retained earnings
g. Rent revenue
h. Buildings
i. Salaries expense
j. Interest expense

YOUR PERFORMANCE OBJECTIVE 25 *(page 401)*

E9-10 Account Title Relationships

Select the most plausible account title(s) to accompany these account titles in a journal entry.

a. Interest receivable
b. Prepaid rent
c. Capital stock
d. Mortgage payable
e. Merchandise inventory
f. Interest revenue
g. Cost of goods sold
h. Advances from customers
i. Martha Perez, drawing
j. Service revenue

YOUR PERFORMANCE OBJECTIVES 26a, 26b *(page 413)*

E9-11 Journalizing Transactions

Journalize the following transactions of a proprietorship:

a. Owner invests $37,000 in the business.
b. Merchandise of $20,000 is purchased on account.
c. $12,000 is paid to acquire equipment.
d. $25,000 of credit sales are recorded.
e. $20,000 is paid to suppliers for amounts owed.
f. Monthly rent expense of $5,000 is paid.
g. $10,000 is received from customers for amounts owed.
h. $8,000 is received from customers before goods are delivered.

YOUR PERFORMANCE OBJECTIVES 26a, 26b *(page 413)*

E9-12 Journalizing Transactions

Journalize the following transactions of a partnership:

a. Owners contribute $32,000 to start a business.

b. Supplies are acquired for $20,000 on account.
c. Equipment is acquired for $17,000 cash.
d. Sales of $18,000 are made on account.
e. Pay $10,000 owed to suppliers.
f. Receive $10,000 owed from customers.
g. Merchandise of $12,000 is acquired on account.
h. Owners withdraw $5,000 of merchandise.

E9-13 Journalizing Transactions
Journalize the following transactions of a corporation:
a. Capital stock is issued to shareholders in return for $30,000.
b. $6,000 is received from customers before goods are delivered.
c. Equipment is purchased for $12,000 cash.
d. Credit sales of $15,000 are made.
e. Dividends of $10,000 are declared and paid.
f. $12,000 owed by customers is received.
g. Inventory of $13,000 is acquired on account.
h. $8,000 is paid to suppliers for amounts owed.

YOUR PERFORMANCE OBJECTIVES 26a, 26b
(page 413)

E9-14 Posting Journal Entries to the Ledger and Preparing a Trial Balance
Using Exercise 9-11, transfer the effects of the journal entries to individual T-accounts in the ledger. Then total the account balances and prepare a trial balance.

YOUR PERFORMANCE OBJECTIVES 26c, 26d
(page 413)

E9-15 Posting Journal Entries to the Ledger and Preparing a Trial Balance
Using Exercise 9-12, transfer the effects of the journal entries to individual T-accounts in the ledger. Then total the account balances and prepare a trial balance.

YOUR PERFORMANCE OBJECTIVES 26c, 26d
(page 413)

E9-16 Posting Journal Entries to the Ledger and Preparing a Trial Balance
Using Exercise 9-13, transfer the effects of the journal entries to individual T-accounts in the ledger. Then, total the account balances and prepare a trial balance.

E9-17 Preparing a Trial Balance
Prepare a trial balance using the following information

YOUR PERFORMANCE OBJECTIVE 26d
(page 413)

Account Title	Balance
Accounts payable	$ 5,000
Cash	3,500
David Drake, capital	35,500
Rent expense	2,000
Sales	32,000
Accounts receivable	8,000
Land	15,000
Other expense	2,000
Cost of goods sold	18,000
David Drake, drawing	4,000
Salaries expense	10,000
Merchandise inventory	10,000

E9-18 Journalizing Adjustments
The following is a partial unadjusted trial balance of the Michael Newman Company for the year ending June 30.

YOUR PERFORMANCE OBJECTIVE 26e
(page 413)

	Debit	Credit
Rent revenue		$22,340
Interest revenue		6,780
Salaries expense	$11,340	
Office supplies inventory	900	
Rent expense	2,925	

An analysis of these accounts disclosed the following additional information:

a.	Employee salaries incurred but unpaid	$220
b.	Interest earned but not yet recorded or received	$340
c.	Rent expense includes July rent paid in advance	$225
d.	Rent revenue includes July rent received in advance	$450
e.	Office supplies inventory on hand at June 30	$65

Required

Record adjusting entries as of June 30 by using the preceding information. If the information doesn't warrant an entry, write NO ENTRY.

YOUR PERFORMANCE OBJECTIVE 26e *(page 413)*

E9-19 Journalizing Adjustments

Based on the following information, record the appropriate adjusting journal entries as of April 30.

a. The supplies account has an unadjusted balance of $1,100 on April 30. A physical inventory of supplies on that date indicates $400 worth of supplies are on hand.
b. On April 1, three months of fire insurance premiums for $600 are paid. On that date, Prepaid Insurance is debited and Cash is credited for the full amount.
c. Nonessential warehouse space is rented on April 1 and cash of $3,000 representing five months' rent is received. On that date Cash is debited and Rent Revenue is credited.
d. A $12,000, 8%, four-month note was accepted on April 1 from a customer who could not pay his account. On that date, Notes Receivable was debited and Accounts Receivable was credited for the amount of the principal.

YOUR PERFORMANCE OBJECTIVE 26e *(page 413)*

E9-20 Journalizing Adjustments

Based on the following information from the Hill Company, record the appropriate adjusting journal entries as of December 31 assuming that the company closes its books yearly on December 31.

a. A note receivable for $5,000 at 6% interest was received on November 1. The total interest from the note is to be collected when the note matures on January 30 of the next year.
b. Employees are paid every Friday and were last paid on December 27. The weekly pay amounts to $1,000 for a five-day week, Monday through Friday.
c. Excess warehouse space was rented to another company on November 1 at a monthly rental of $100. On this date, the amount of one year's rent was received in advance and credited to Deferred Rent Revenue (Rent Received in Advance).
d. The Prepaid Rent account has a balance of $3,000 representing rent for one year paid in advance on March 1.
e. A five-year insurance policy was purchased on March 1 for $6,000. This amount was debited to the Insurance Expense account at the time of purchase.

YOUR PERFORMANCE OBJECTIVE 26e *(page 413)*

E9-21 Journalizing Correcting Entries

Record the necessary journal entries to correct the following transactions in which an error has been discovered.

a. Recorded a $500 cash sale using the correct accounts but the incorrect amount of $50.
b. Recorded a $1,000 issuance of capital stock by increasing cash and a revenue account.
c. Recorded the $750 payment of a liability account by decreasing cash and a revenue account.
d. Recorded the $2,000 purchase of equipment by decreasing cash and increasing an expense account.

YOUR PERFORMANCE OBJECTIVE 26e *(page 413)*

E9-22 Journalizing Correcting Entries

Record the necessary journal entries to correct the following transactions in which an error has been discovered.

a. Recorded $8,000 too much depreciation this year.
b. Failed to accrue $500 interest on notes receivable during the year.
c. Recorded $760 in dividends declared during the year rather than the correct amount of $670.
d. Recorded the $100 cash purchase of office supplies during the year by debiting an expense account. $40 of these office supplies were on hand at the end of the period.

YOUR PERFORMANCE OBJECTIVE 26h *(page 413)*

E9-23 Journalizing Closing Entries

Using the following income statement, prepare the related closing entries using (a) the indirect approach and (b) the direct approach.

YAMAMOTO COMPANY
Income Statement
For the Year Ended December 31

Revenues		
Sales revenue	$300,000	
Interest revenue	10,000	$310,000
Expenses		
Cost of goods sold	172,000	
Salaries expense	48,000	
Rent expense	30,000	
Utilities	11,000	
Depreciation expense	6,000	
Office supplies	4,500	
Interest expense	2,500	274,000
Net Income		$ 36,000

E9-24 Journalizing Closing Entries

YOUR PERFORMANCE OBJECTIVE 26h *(page 413)*

Using the following income statement accounts, prepare the related closing entries using (a) the indirect approach and (b) the direct approach.

Cost of product and other revenue	$ 632,440
Cost of service revenue	87,220
Provision for income taxes	57,004
Interest income and other, net	12,838
Interest expense	8,302
Selling, general, and administrative expenses	391,583
Product and other revenues	1,318,693
Service revenue	162,909
Research and development expense	177,217

Appendix Reinforcement Exercises

AE9-1 T-Account Analysis

YOUR PERFORMANCE OBJECTIVE 27 *(page 427)*

Determine the missing amount in each of the following incomplete T-accounts.

(a) Accounts Receivable

Debit	Credit
65,000	
	56,000
56,000	

(d) S. Solomon, Capital

Debit	Credit
	57,000
	12,000
	53,400

(b) Marketable Securities

Debit	Credit
70,000	
	67,000
88,000	

(e) Accounts Payable

Debit	Credit
	56,000
83,000	
	89,000

(c) Interest Receivable

Debit	Credit
5,000	
	3,900
5,300	

(f) Notes Payable

Debit	Credit
	100,000
	40,000
	–0–

YOUR PERFORMANCE OBJECTIVE 27
(page 427)

AE9-2 T-Account Analysis
Determine the missing amount in each of the following incomplete T-accounts.

(a) Accounts Receivable

150,000	
570,000	
210,000	

(e) Interest Receivable

2,500	
	4,000
2,800	

(b) Supplies

8,000	
	10,000
9,200	

(f) Prepaid Insurance

1,400	
6,700	
900	

(c) Salaries Payable

	17,000
44,000	
	15,000

(g) Interest Payable

	900
3,000	
	1,100

(d) Unearned Rent Revenue

	8,200
23,000	
	7,000

(h) Dividends Payable

	2,000
9,000	
	1,500

YOUR PERFORMANCE OBJECTIVES 27, 28
(pages 427, 429)

AE9-3 T-Account Analysis
For each of the following independent situations below, determine the required amount.

a. A company had an $84,000 balance in Accounts Receivable at the beginning of the year and a $92,000 balance in Accounts Receivable at the end of the year. Sales for the year amounted to $635,000. Determine the amount of cash collected from customers during the year.
b. The beginning balance in Income Taxes Payable was $4,300; the ending balance in Income Taxes Payable is $5,100; and income tax expense for the year is $22,400. Determine the amount of cash paid for income taxes during the year.
c. Interest expense reported on the income statement amounted to $6,500; Interest Payable was $875 at the beginning of the year and $625 at the end of the year. Determine the amount of cash paid for interest during the year.

YOUR PERFORMANCE OBJECTIVES 27, 28
(pages 427, 429)

AE9-4 T-Account Analysis
For each of the following independent situations below, determine the required amount.

a. Rent expense reported on the income statement amounted to $28,300; Prepaid Rent was $5,200 at the beginning of the year and $6,300 at the end of the year. Determine the amount of cash paid for rent during the year.
b. Mortgage Payable had a beginning balance of $193,400 and an ending balance of $258,200. During the year, a building was purchased for $90,000 by signing a mortgage note in exchange for the asset. Determine the amount of cash paid on the mortgage during the year.
c. Wages Expense reported on the income statement amounted to $123,300; Wages Payable was $2,350 at the beginning of the year and is $2,875 at the end of the year. Determine the amount of cash paid to employees during the year.

YOUR PERFORMANCE OBJECTIVE 29
(page 429)

AE9-5 T-Account Analysis
The following statement of cash flows and the information presented in the individual T-accounts below have been assembled from the accounting system of Sharman, Inc. for May.

Assume that all merchandise purchases are on account (that is, there were no cash purchases of inventory).

Cash receipts:		
Cash sales	$2,400	
Collections from credit customers	600	$3,000
Cash payments:		
Payments to suppliers	1,000	
Payments to employees	600	
Payment of dividends	900	2,500
Increase in cash balance		$ 500

Accounts Receivable

5/1 900	
5/31 800	

Merchandise Inventory

5/1 300	
5/31 350	

Accounts Payable

	300 5/1
	400 5/31

Salaries Payable

	100 5/1
	150 5/31

Required

Prepare an income statement for the month of May using T-account analysis.

AE9-6 T-Account Analysis

YOUR PERFORMANCE OBJECTIVE 29 *(page 429)*

The following cash flows and the information shown in the T-accounts below have been assembled for the current year from the accounting system of House of Clothes, a chain of sportswear shops. Assume that all merchandise purchases and sales are on account (that is, there were no cash purchases or cash sales).

Cash receipts:		
Collections from credit customers	$2,600	
Proceeds from issuance of common stock	100	$2,700
Cash payments:		
Payments to suppliers	1,000	
Payments to employees	650	
Payment of rent	240	
Payment of taxes	200	
Payment of dividends	100	2,190
Increase in cash balance		$ 510

Accounts Receivable

1/01 280	
12/31 440	

Prepaid Rent

1/01 10	
12/31 80	

Merchandise Inventory

1/01 170	
12/31 140	

Accounts Payable	
	20 1/01
	40 12/31

Salaries Payable	
	35 1/01
	10 12/31

Taxes Payable	
	5 1/01
	80 12/31

Accumulated Depreciation	
	40 1/01
	80 12/31

Required
Prepare an income statement for the current year using T-account analysis.

YOUR PERFORMANCE OBJECTIVE 29
(page 429)

AE9-7 T-Account Analysis
Using the statement of cash receipts and cash payments and the information presented in the individual T-accounts, prepare an income statement for this company. Assume that all merchandise purchases and sales are on account (that is, there were no cash purchases of inventory).

Cash receipts:		
Cash sales	$220,000	
Collections from credit customers	40,000	$260,000
Cash payments:		
Payments to suppliers	90,000	
Payments to employees	70,000	
Payment of taxes	30,000	
Payment of dividends	10,000	200,000
Increase in Cash Balance		$ 60,000

Accounts Receivable	
1/01 70,000	
12/31 60,000	

Merchandise Inventory	
1/01 30,000	
12/31 35,000	

Accounts Payable	
	30,000 1/01
	40,000 12/31

Salaries Payable	
	10,000 1/01
	15,000 12/31

Taxes Payable	
	5,000 1/01
	3,000 12/31

Required
Prepare an income statement for the current year using T-account analysis.

Critical Thinking Problems

P9-1 Internal Control

YOUR PERFORMANCE OBJECTIVE 23 (page 391)

Medcare Laboratory Service provides laboratory testing for samples received from physicians. All work is performed on account and participating physicians are billed monthly. Agnes Fluid, the accountant for this company, receives and opens the mail. When she receives a check from a physician, she is required to list the amount received both on a remittance slip and as a credit to the customer accounts receivable, and later deposit that check in the bank. To ensure that all receipts are deposited in the bank, she compares the total of her remittance slips to the total of the bank deposit slips.

Required

a. Describe the major internal control weakness in this system.
b. List any other weaknesses you believe exist.
c. Can you visualize an accounts receivable fraud that could occur.

P9-2 Internal Control

YOUR PERFORMANCE OBJECTIVE 23 (page 391)

Joanne Sizemore is the owner of a small art dealership, employing three sales staff, a receptionist, a bookkeeper, and a purchasing agent. The purchasing agent attends art shows and auctions to acquire a variety of inventory. He must work within a budget approved by Ms. Sizemore, but otherwise has the freedom to choose any artwork he deems appropriate for the store. He purchases the inventory and provides the bookkeeper with a copy of the bill to be paid to the individual vendors or to be reimbursed for amounts paid at some of the smaller art shows. Once the inventory is displayed in the store, the sales staff can sell the items for as much as the market will bear. The sales staff makes a commission on each item sold. As each sale is made, a receipt is prepared in duplicate, providing the customer with one copy and the bookkeeper with the other. Each salesperson has a receipt book (with blank forms) to use for his or her sales. The sales staff is responsible for approving all credit sales, and informs the bookkeeper of the credit agreements made with each customer. The bookkeeper prepares statements to be sent to the customers on a monthly basis and writes off bad debts as necessary. The bookkeeper is also responsible for recording and paying all expenses, including payroll and sales commissions, and preparing summary reports of inventory, revenues, and expenses each month.

Required

Identify weaknesses in internal control present in Joanne Sizemore's current operation. Briefly describe some methods she could employ to make her internal control more effective and efficient.

P9-3 Debit-Credit Rules

YOUR PERFORMANCE OBJECTIVE 24 (page 396)

Indicate whether the following accounts normally have a debit, credit, or zero balance after the accounting cycle has been completed.

a. Sales returns and allowances
b. Bad debts expense
c. Allowance for bad debts
d. Accumulated depreciation
e. Gain on sale of equipment
f. Loss on sale of land
g. Dividends declared
h. Dividends revenue
i. Patents
j. Income summary

P9-4 Account Title Relationships

YOUR PERFORMANCE OBJECTIVE 25 (page 401)

The ability to determine the second half of a journal entry when you know the first half of a journal entry is important in both the preparation of journal entries and in the analysis of T-accounts. Mastering this skill requires that you reason through the dual effects of the exchange that are present in every transaction.

Each of the following account names represents one-half of a journal entry. Analyze the business transaction involved to determine the missing half of the entry. For example, you might ask what account is debited when the contributed capital account is credited and increases in size. Upon reflection, you should recognize that an owner's contribution is usually accompanied by an increase in cash or other asset. Thus, the cash account is debited.

Required

Select the most plausible account title(s) for the missing half of the following incomplete journal entries.

	Account	Debit	Credit
a.	Merchandise Inventory	XX	
	________________		XX
b.	Salary Payable	XX	
	________________		XX
c.	________________	XX	
	Prepaid Insurance		XX
d.	Dividends Declared	XX	
	________________		XX
e.	________________	XX	
	Accumulated Depreciation		XX
f.	Cost of Goods Sold	XX	
	________________		XX
g.	________________	XX	
	Accounts Receivable		XX
h.	Accounts Receivable	XX	
	________________		XX
i.	________________	XX	
	Accounts Payable		XX
j.	________________	XX	
	Interest Revenue		XX

YOUR PERFORMANCE OBJECTIVES 26a, 26b
(page 413)

P9-5 Journalizing Transactions

Journalize the following transactions of Nate's Auto Parts, a sole proprietorship.

a. The owner, Morris Mesonznick, makes a cash contribution of $100,000 to start the business.
b. $15,000 is borrowed from the bank.
c. $5,000 of the bank loan is repaid.
d. Used auto parts are purchased for $25,000 cash.
e. Used auto parts having a cost of $15,000 are sold for $27,000 cash.
f. Office supplies of $6,500 are purchased on account.
g. Morris withdraws $6,000 to pay personal expenses.
h. $25,000 of equipment is purchased by signing a three-year note.
i. Monthly rent of $1,500 is paid.
j. Equipment used in the business is sold for $4,000 cash.
k. Monthly salaries of $3,000 are paid.

YOUR PERFORMANCE OBJECTIVES 26a, 26b
(page 413)

P9-6 Journalizing Transactions

Journalize the following transactions of Stravinsky Company, a sole proprietorship, that do not include revenue and expense effects.

a. The owner, Igor Stravinsky, makes a cash contribution of $40,000 to start the business.
b. Land is purchased for $50,000, $10,000 of which is paid in cash. A note payable is signed for the balance.
c. Inventory is purchased for $20,000 on credit.
d. A $7,500 liability is paid off.
e. A $30,000 line of credit is obtained from a local bank. No amount has yet been borrowed.
f. Igor wants to make an additional investment in the company in the future and arranges a $10,000 personal bank loan.
g. Cash of $22,500 is borrowed on the line of credit.
h. Igor withdraws $5,000 for personal expenses.
i. Igor invests the $10,000 described in Item (f) in his company.

YOUR PERFORMANCE OBJECTIVES 26a, 26b
(page 413)

P9-7 Journalizing Transactions

Journalize the following transactions of Metaphor Company, a sole proprietorship.

a. The owner made a $75,000 cash investment to start the business.
b. Purchased $24,500 worth of merchandise on account.

c. Sold merchandise costing $10,000 for $16,000 on account.
d. Purchased several items of office equipment for $20,000.
e. Paid $16,500 of the account payable incurred in Item (c).
f. Contributed land worth $25,000 to the business.
g. Collected accounts receivable amounting to $12,000.
h. Paid a yearly insurance premium of $5,000 in advance.
i. Borrowed $10,000 through a bank loan.

P9-8 Journalizing Transactions

YOUR PERFORMANCE OBJECTIVES 26a, 26b *(page 413)*

Journalize the following transactions of Wilkens Lawn Care Company, a sole proprietorship.

a. The owner, Jim Wilkens, made a $65,000 cash contribution to start the business.
b. Lawn care equipment is purchased for $4,000 cash.
c. Lawn care services of $8,000 are provided to customers on account.
d. $5,000 cash is collected on amounts owed by customers.
e. Lawn supplies of $2,000 are purchased on account.
f. Received $6,000 cash from bank loan.
g. Repaid bank loan in full.
h. Replaced 30-day accounts payable (Item e) with a 90-day note.
i. The owner, Jim Wilkens, withdraws $3,000 for his personal use.

P9-9 Journalizing Transactions

YOUR PERFORMANCE OBJECTIVES 26a, 26b *(page 413)*

Journalize the following transactions engaged in by the Seinfeld Company, a sole proprietorship.

a. Seinfeld invests $80,000 cash and $20,000 worth of inventory to start the business.
b. Land and building costing $45,000 are acquired by paying $12,500 cash and assuming a 20-year, 8% mortgage for the balance. The land is reported at $15,000 and the building at $30,000 on the balance sheet.
c. Merchandise inventory costing $36,000 is acquired on account from various suppliers.
d. A $7,200 check is issued for 36 months of insurance coverage.
e. Equipment costing $16,000 is acquired for cash.
f. $200 is paid to National Express Service for delivering the equipment.
g. Cash of $10,000 is received from customers for merchandise to be delivered in one month.
h. Inventory costing $1,000 that was purchased in (c) is returned as defective to the supplier.
i. Invoices totaling $24,000 from the purchases in (c) are paid after deducting a 2% discount for prompt payment. Seinfeld treats cash discounts as a reduction in inventory cost.
j. The remaining invoices from the purchases in (c) are paid after the discount period has ended.

P9-10 Journalizing Transactions

YOUR PERFORMANCE OBJECTIVES 26a, 26b *(page 413)*

Journalize the following January transactions of Travolta's DiscoTech, a sole proprietorship. If you believe that a transaction should not be recorded, write NO ENTRY and your reason.

a. Tony Manero invested $100,000 cash in the company.
b. Paid $1,200 for a two-year insurance policy from Stallone Brothers Mutual.
c. Purchased a building (Odyssey Disco) for $50,000, paying 20% down and signing a mortgage note for the balance.
d. Placed an order for merchandise inventory amounting to $10,000.
e. Purchased merchandise inventory on account for $9,000.
f. Recorded $6,000 of credit sales (private dance lessons for Mark Brando, Steve Rushdie, and Ralph Limbaugh).
g. Recorded $12,000 of cash sales for disco wear (patent leather shoes, polyester clothing, gold chains, and gold jewelry).
h. Recorded the $8,000 cost of the preceding inventory sales.
i. Paid $2,500 owed on inventory purchased in Item (e).
j. Gave the supplier of the inventory in Item (e) a 60-day note for the balance owed. Assume that this note was accepted.
k. Tony Manero withdrew $3,000 cash from the company.
l. Collected $3,000 from a customer (Ralph Limbaugh) on account.
m. Received $3,500 in advance from Stephanie Mangano & Associates for next month's rental of office space in the Odyssey Disco.

n. Paid monthly salaries of $5,000. No entry related to this month's salaries has yet been recorded.
o. Returned $500 of inventory purchased in Item (e) that has not yet been paid for. Refer to Item (j) to determine the account title.

YOUR PERFORMANCE OBJECTIVE 26e
(page 413)

P9-11 Journalizing Adjustments

Every Occasion begins business on January 1 of the current year. Ken Kaelin, the company's founder, asks you to help his accountant, Rosemary Lopez, review the following current year transactions recorded. Your assignment is to help her record any adjustments needed to correctly state net income for the calendar year.

a. *Deferred expense:* On April 1, the firm bought a three-year comprehensive insurance policy for $5,400.
b. *Deferred expense:* During the year, the following purchases of supplies were made:

February 22	$2,300
April 17	1,700
November 3	2,900

At the end of the year, $1,450 of supplies remained available for use.
c. *Accrued expense:* Current year cash payments of $30,000 to employees have been properly recorded. However, $1,400 of salaries for employee work provided but unpaid have not been recorded as of December 31.
d. *Deferred revenue:* During the year, $12,000 cash was received from customers for unperformed services. It was estimated that 80% of these services were performed by the end of the year.
e. *Accrued revenue:* On January 31, a $100,000 note receivable was given by a customer in exchange for services rendered. The note has a 12% interest rate and its principal and interest are due in one year.

Required

Record adjusting or correcting entries on December 31 (the annual closing date). Add new accounts if needed. Provide numerical support for the amount of all journal entries. If you believe no adjustment is necessary, write NONE.

YOUR PERFORMANCE OBJECTIVE 26e
(page 413)

P9-12 Journalizing Adjustments

Great Expectations Maternity Fashions has prepared the following unadjusted trial balance at December 31 of the current year.

	Debit	Credit
Cash	$ 1,800	
Accounts receivable	2,000	
Notes receivable	1,000	
Merchandise inventory	6,000	
Building	20,000	
Accumulated depreciation		$ 5,000
Accounts payable		1,400
Deferred subscription revenue		2,400
Common stock		25,000
Retained earnings		13,700
Sales revenue		32,500
Purchases	29,600	
Salaries expense	12,000	
Insurance expense	3,600	
Miscellaneous expense	4,000	
	$80,000	$80,000

Required
Record adjusting or correcting entries on December 31 (the annual closing date), adding new accounts if needed. Provide numerical support for the amount of all journal entries.

a. The note receivable was received on December 1 in settlement of a customer's account. The note earns interest at a rate of 6% per year and is due on April 1 of the following year.
b. On December 1, $2,400 was collected from customers for a two-year subscription to *Mother's World*, a new magazine published monthly.
c. A three-year insurance policy was purchased on March 1 of the current year for $3,600. At that time, the Insurance Expense account was debited for this amount.
d. Employees earned salaries of $14,000 this year.
e. The year-end physical count of inventory reveals a $4,000 balance.

P9-13 Preparing an Adjusted Trial Balance
Using the information in Problem 9-12, prepare an adjusted trial balance.

YOUR PERFORMANCE OBJECTIVE 26f
(page 413)

P9-14 Comprehensive Accounting Cycle Problem
A complete unadjusted trial balance and an incomplete adjusted trial balance of Poindexter Security Systems at December 31 of the current year are presented below. The periodic financial statements will be prepared as soon as you complete the adjusted trial balance.

YOUR PERFORMANCE OBJECTIVES 26e–26i
(page 413)

	Unadjusted Trial Balance		Adjusted Trial Balance	
	Debit	Credit	Debit	Credit
Cash	$ 12,500		$12,500	
Accounts receivable	24,000		24,000	
Notes receivable	10,000			
Interest receivable	–0–			
Merchandise inventory	75,000			
Prepaid insurance	–0–			
Equipment	35,000		35,000	
Accumulated depreciation		$ 10,000		$10,000
Accounts payable		15,000		
Salaries payable		–0–		
Common stock		40,000		40,000
Retained earnings		15,000		15,000
Sales revenue		120,000		
Interest revenue		–0–		
Cost of goods sold	–0–			
Salaries expense	40,000			
Insurance expense	1,500			
Miscellaneous expense	2,000		2,000	
	$200,000	$200,000	$	$

The following information will help you complete this problem's requirements. Note that December 31 is the annual closing date.

a. The note receivable was received on November 1 in settlement of a customer's account. The note earns interest at a rate of 6% per year and is due on February 1 of the following year.
b. A three-year insurance policy was purchased on January 1 of the current year for $1,500. At that time, the Insurance Expense account was debited for this amount.
c. Employees earned salaries of $45,000 during the current year.
d. A year-end physical count revealed $12,000 of inventory on hand.

Required

a. Journalize and post adjusting and correcting entries.
b. Complete the adjusted trial balance.

c. Prepare the income statement and balance sheet for this company.
d. Journalize and post closing entries using the indirect approach.
e. Prepare the post-closing trial balance.

YOUR PERFORMANCE OBJECTIVES 26h, 26i
(page 413)

Ex

P9-15 Comprehensive Accounting Cycle Problem
The adjusted trial balance of Jedi Jazz and Jive, a cocktail lounge that closes its books on December 31 of each year, is presented here.

Required

a. Journalize the closing entries using the direct approach.
b. Prepare the post-closing trial balance by inserting all relevant amounts in the spaces provided. If one or more account balances must be changed, provide numerical support for the change.

	Adjusted Trial Balance		Post-Closing Trial Balance	
	Debit	**Credit**	**Debit**	**Credit**
Cash	$ 20,000			
Rent receivable	500			
Merchandise inventory	45,000			
Building and fixtures	120,000			
Accumulated depreciation		$ 14,000		
Accounts payable		6,500		
Salaries payable		3,000		
Income taxes payable		1,500		
Common stock		100,000		
Retained earnings		56,500		
Cost of goods sold	110,000			
Salary expense	60,000			
Miscellaneous expense	20,000			
Income tax expense	9,000			
Depreciation expense	2,000			
Sales revenue		175,000		
Rent revenue		30,000		
Totals	$386,500	$386,500		

YOUR PERFORMANCE OBJECTIVE 26
(page 413)

P9-16 Comprehensive Accounting Cycle Problem
Use the transactions in Problem 9-5 to perform steps (a) through (d) in the accounting cycle.

P9-17 Comprehensive Accounting Cycle Problem
Use the transactions in Problem 9-6 to perform steps (a) through (d) in the accounting cycle.

YOUR PERFORMANCE OBJECTIVE 26
(page 413)

P9-18 Comprehensive Accounting Cycle Problem
Use the transactions in Problem 9-7 to perform steps (a) through (d) in the accounting cycle.

YOUR PERFORMANCE OBJECTIVE 26
(page 413)

P9-19 Comprehensive Accounting Cycle Problem
Use the transactions in Problem 9-8 to perform steps (a) through (d) in the accounting cycle.

P9-20 Comprehensive Accounting Cycle Problem
Use the transactions in Problem 9-9 to perform steps (a) through (d) in the accounting cycle.

YOUR PERFORMANCE OBJECTIVE 26
(page 413)

P9-21 Comprehensive Accounting Cycle Problem
Use the transactions in Problem 9-10 to perform steps (a) through (d) and steps (g) through (i) in the accounting cycle.

Appendix Critical Thinking Problems

AP9-1 T-Account Analysis
From the T-accounts listed in Appendix Exercise 9-1, record the transactions that will account for the missing information.

YOUR PERFORMANCE OBJECTIVE 27 *(page 427)*

AP9-2 T-Account Analysis
From the T-accounts listed in Appendix Exercise 9-2, record the transactions that will account for the missing information.

YOUR PERFORMANCE OBJECTIVE 27 *(page 427)*

AP9-3 T-Account Analysis
Information relating to six independent accounts is found below.

a. The beginning balance of the Rent Receivable account is $1,000 and the ending balance is $1,060. During the year, the business had rent receipts of $780.
b. The beginning balance of the Accounts Receivable account is $19,500 and the ending balance is $16,800. During the year, the business recognized $14,100 in credit sales.
c. The beginning balance of the Investments account is $35,000 and the ending balance is $44,000. During the year, the business recorded a $6,000 loss on its sale of capital stock for $52,000.
d. The beginning balance of the Contributed Capital account is $22,800 and the ending balance is $21,360. During the year, the business earned net income of $4,800.
e. The beginning balance of the Accounts Payable account is $11,200 and the ending balance is $17,800. During the year, the business paid $16,600 in settlement of purchases on account.
f. The beginning balance of the Deferred Revenue account is $5,000 and the ending balance is $1,000. During the year, the business received $2,000 in advances from customers.

Required
Record the transactions that will account for the missing information.

AP9-4 T-Account Analysis
McReynolds Company provides the following selected balance sheet and income statement accounts respectively:

YOUR PERFORMANCE OBJECTIVE 27 *(page 427)*

		January 1	December 31
Accounts receivable		$45,000	$63,000
Supplies inventory		40,000	46,000
Salaries payable		8,500	7,500
Deferred rent revenue		16,400	14,000
Sales on account	$171,000		
Supplies used	105,000		
Salaries expense	63,000		
Rent revenue	46,000		

Required
Present the following items reported in the operating activities section of the statement of cash flows.

a. Cash collected from customers
b. Cash paid for supplies
c. Cash paid for salaries
d. Cash collected for rent

AP9-5 T-Account Analysis
McSweeney Company provides the following selected balance sheet accounts and statement of cash flow transactions respectively:

YOUR PERFORMANCE OBJECTIVE 26f *(page 413)*

		January 1	December 31
Interest receivable		$25,000	$28,000
Prepaid insurance		28,000	18,000
Interest payable		9,000	11,000
Dividends payable		10,000	7,500
Interest received	$140,000		
Cash paid for insurance	67,000		
Interest paid	30,000		
Dividends paid	27,000		

Required

Calculate the following accounts reported in the current year's income statement and statement of retained earnings:

a. Interest revenue
b. Insurance expense
c. Interest expense
d. Dividends declared

YOUR PERFORMANCE OBJECTIVE 28
(page 429)

AP9-6 T-Account Analysis

For each side of the ledger accounts listed below, write the name of the specific transaction whose effects are posted to that particular side. The answers for Cash are provided as an example.

Cash	
All cash receipts	All cash disbursements

a. Allowance for Uncollectibles
b. Accounts Payable
c. Prepaid Insurance
d. Equipment
e. Salaries Payable
f. Advances from Customers
g. Capital Stock
h. Accounts Receivable
i. Merchandise Inventory
j. Cost of Goods Sold
k. Insurance Expense
l. Accumulated Depreciation
m. Salaries Expense
n. Sales Revenue
o. Retained Earnings

YOUR PERFORMANCE OBJECTIVE 28
(page 429)

AP9-7 T-Account Analysis

Using the following general ledger of Fulton Company, briefly describe the specific transaction or adjustment that must have occurred to produce the lettered journal entry whose effects are posted to its general ledger. For example, journal entry z—purchased merchandise inventory for cash.

Cash	
(a) 55,000	5,000 (d)
(b) 10,000	12,000 (e)
(c) 20,000	4,000 (k)
	4,500 (z)

Accounts Receivable	
(c) 70,000	

Prepaid Insurance	
(d) 5,000	2,500 (g)

Merchandise Inventory	
(h) 70,000	50,000 (i)
(z) 4,500	

Truck	
(e) 12,000	

Accumulated Depreciation	
	1,500 (j)

Accounts Payable	
	70,000 (h)

Note Payable	
(k) 3,000	10,000 (b)

Interest Payable	
(k) 1,000	1,000 (f)

Capital Stock	
	55,000 (a)

Dividends Payable	
	2,000 (l)

Retained Earnings	
(l) 2,000	35,000 (o)

Sales Revenue	
(m) 90,000	90,000 (c)

Various Expenses	
(f) 1,000	55,000 (n)
(j) 1,500	
(g) 2,500	
(i) 50,000	

Income Summary	
(n) 55,000	90,000 (m)
(o) 35,000	

AP9-8 T-Account Analysis

YOUR PERFORMANCE OBJECTIVES 27, 28
(pages 427, 429)

For each of the following independent situations below, determine the required amount.

a. The beginning balance in the Equipment account is $41,300. Accumulated Depreciation—Equipment is $12,600 at the beginning of the year and $17,700 at the end of the year. The company did not dispose of any equipment during the year and all new equipment was purchased for cash. The ending balance in the Equipment account is $54,500. Determine the amount of cash paid for equipment during the year.

b. Accounts Payable is used to record all purchases of inventory on credit. The Accounts Payable balance at the beginning of the year was $8,300 and $7,400 at the end of the year. The balance in Merchandise Inventory was $32,400 at the beginning of the year and $36,700 at the end of the year. Cost of goods sold reported on the income statement amounted to $188,900. Determine the amount of cash paid for merchandise during the year.

c. Dividend revenue reported on the income statement amounted to $3,100; Dividends Receivable was $700 at the beginning of the year and $400 at the end of the year. Determine the amount of cash dividends received during the year.

d. Dividends declared during the year amounted to $18,800; Dividends Payable was $7,200 at the beginning of the year and $4,800 at the end of the year. Determine the amount of cash paid for dividends during the year.

YOUR PERFORMANCE OBJECTIVE 29 *(page 429)*

AP9-9 T-Account Analysis

Below is the comparative balance sheet for the Mason Company.

MASON COMPANY
Comparative Balance Sheet
For Years Ending December 31, 2001 and 2002

	12/31/02	12/31/01	Change
Cash	$ 6,800	$ 4,000	$2,800
Accounts receivable	7,000	8,000	(1,000)
Equipment	10,000	10,000	–0–
Less: Accumulated depreciation	(3,500)	(3,000)	(500)
Total assets	$20,300	$19,000	$1,300
Salaries payable	$ 1,800	$ 1,600	$ 200
Contributed capital	13,600	12,000	1,600
Retained earnings	4,900	5,400	(500)
Total liabilities and owner's equity	$20,300	$19,000	$1,300

Required

Answer the following questions based on your analysis.

a. Have 2002 cash collections from customers been more or less than 2002 credit sales and by how many dollars?

b. Have 2002 cash payments to employees been more or less than 2002 salaries expense and by how many dollars?

YOUR PERFORMANCE OBJECTIVE 29 *(page 429)*

AP9-10 T-Account Analysis

Below is the comparative balance sheet for the Dixon Company.

DIXON COMPANY
Comparative Balance Sheet
For Years Ending December 31, 2001 and 2002

	12/31/02	12/31/01	Change
Cash	$ 5,200	$ 4,000	$1,200
Accounts receivable	9,000	8,000	1,000
Equipment	10,000	10,000	–0–
Less: Accumulated depreciation	(4,000)	(3,000)	(1,000)
Total assets	$20,200	$19,000	$1,200
Salaries payable	$ 1,400	$ 1,600	$ (200)
Capital stock	14,000	12,000	2,000
Retained earnings	4,800	5,400	(600)
Total liabilities and owner's equity	$20,200	$19,000	$1,200

Required
Answer the following questions based on your analysis.

a. Have 2002 cash collections from customers been more or less than 2002 credit sales and by how many dollars?
b. Have 2002 cash payments to employees been more or less than 2002 salaries expense and by how many dollars?

AP9-11 Preparing an Income Statement from T-Account Analysis

YOUR PERFORMANCE OBJECTIVE 29 *(page 429)*

The following incomplete trial balances as well as a statement of cash receipts and cash payments have been assembled from the accounting system of Russell, Inc. for the current year. Assume that there were no cash purchases of inventory.

	January 1	December 31
Debits		
Cash	$	$
Accounts receivable	38,000	40,000
Merchandise inventory	55,000	50,000
Accrued interest receivable	–0–	2,000
Depreciable assets	50,000	50,000
Total Debits	$	$
Credits		
Accumulated depreciation	$ 8,000	$ 12,000
Accounts payable	46,000	53,000
Salaries payable	1,000	2,000
Mortgage payable	25,000	20,000
Common stock	25,000	25,000
Retained earnings	78,000	
Total Credits	$183,000	$
Cash Receipts:		
1. Cash sales	$ 30,000	
2. Collections from credit customers	144,000	
3. Collection of interest	1,000	$175,000
Cash Payments:		
4. Payments to merchandise suppliers	$124,000	
5. Payments to employees	11,000	
6. Payment of interest	2,000	
7. Repayment on mortgage	5,000	
8. Payment of dividends	3,000	145,000
Increase in cash balance		$ 30,000

Required
Prepare an income statement and a statement of retained earnings for the current year using T-account analysis. *Hint:* Solve for the unknown trial balance amounts first. Then note that this problem's primary objective is to convert information expressed on the cash basis to information expressed on the accrual basis.

AP9-12 Preparing an Income Statement from T-Account Analysis

YOUR PERFORMANCE OBJECTIVE 29 *(page 429)*

Several income statement transactions are recorded in the following T-accounts:
(*Note:* Bal. stands for Balance)

Cash

Debit	Credit
Bal. 10,000	2,000 (b)
(a) 8,000	

Accounts Receivable

Debit	Credit
(c) 5,000	

Inventory

Debit	Credit
Bal. 15,000	7,000 (e)

Prepaid Rent

Bal. 3,000	1,000 (f)

Salaries Payable

	500 (g)

Unearned Revenue

(d) 4,000	Bal. 5,000

Contributed Capital

	Bal. 17,000

Retained Earnings

(b) 2,000	Bal. 6,000
(e) 7,000	(a) 8,000
(f) 1,000	(c) 5,000
(g) 500	(d) 4,000

Required

a. Study the T-accounts above and provide a possible explanation for every journal entry (a) through (g).
b. Identify whether each journal entry made in the accounts increases or decreases the account balance.
c. Calculate the balance in each account and determine if the accounting equation is in balance after these journal entries.
d. Prepare an income statement from the information presented here.

YOUR PERFORMANCE OBJECTIVE 18d *(page 240)*

AP9-13 Cash Basis Vs. Accrual Basis of Income Measurement
Refer to the transactions presented in AP9-12 to respond to the following questions:

a. For each transaction (a) through (g) explain whether a cash receipt or cash payment preceded, coincided, or followed the recognition of the related revenue or expense.
b. Determine whether each transaction (a) through (g) is an example of an implicit or explicit transaction. If it is an explicit transaction, what source document could support the transaction?

YOUR PERFORMANCE OBJECTIVE 29 *(page 429)*

AP9-14 Preparing a Balance Sheet from T-Accounts
The following information relates to Omega Sales Corporation:

Required
Prepare Omega Sales Corporation's December 31 balance sheet using T-account analysis.

OMEGA SALES CORPORATION
Balance Sheet
January 1

Assets		
Cash		$ 17,600
Accounts receivable		22,400
Merchandise inventory		72,700
Furniture and fixtures	$ 75,000	
Less: Accumulated depreciation	(15,000)	60,000
Total assets		$172,700
Equities		
Accounts payable		$ 18,800
Unearned rent revenue		1,500
Interest payable		900
Salaries payable		2,700
Note payable		50,000
Capital stock		70,000
Retained earnings		28,800
Total equities		$172,700

Income Statement
For the Year Ended December 31

Revenues:		
Sales	$246,800	
Rent	18,000	$264,800
Expenses:		
Cost of goods sold	118,400	
Salaries	67,200	
Taxes	24,600	
Interest	5,800	
Depreciation	5,000	221,000
Net income		$ 43,800

Analysis of Cash Flows
For the Year Ended December 31

Cash receipts:		
1. Cash sales	$ 42,700	
2. Collections on accounts receivable	198,300	
3. Collection of rent	18,200	$259,200
Cash payments:		
4. Payments to merchandise suppliers	119,300	
5. Payments to employees	68,500	
6. Payment of taxes	24,600	
7. Payment for new fixtures	7,000	
8. Payment on note payable	5,000	
9. Payment of interest	5,700	230,100
Increase in cash balance		$ 29,100

Note: The Accounts Payable account includes only purchases of merchandise, which amounted to $122,500 during the year.

Research Assignments

A wide variety of interesting Research Assignments for this chapter are available for the following topics at www.mhhe.com/solomon:

R9-1 **Obtaining a Chart of Accounts (PO 11b)**
R9-2 **Obtaining a Chart of Accounts (PO 11b)**
R9-3 **Finding Adjustments in a Small Business (PO 19a)**
R9-4 **Real-World Internal Control Exploration (PO 23)**
R9-5 **Internal Control in a University (PO 23)**
R9-6 **Real-World Internal Control Exploration (PO 23)**
R9-7 **Real-World Internal Control Exploration (PO 23)**
R9-8 **Learning More about Accounting Information Systems (PO 26)**
R9-9 **A Real World Closing Process (PO 26)**
R9-10 **Accounting Software Packages Other than QuickBooks (PO 26)**
R9-11 **Learning More about Accounting as a Career (PO 26)**
R9-12 **Learning More about the CPA Profession (PO 26)**

CHAPTER TEN

10

Comparing Financial Statements by Entity and Industry

Also be sure you have mastered the following Performance Objectives from previous chapters. They lay the foundation for the concepts you will learn in this chapter:

PO3
PO4
PO26

PERFORMANCE OBJECTIVES

In this chapter, you will learn the following new Performance Objectives:

PO30 **Distinguish** among the sole proprietorship, partnership, and corporate forms of entity both as to their characteristics and their respective advantages and disadvantages and **apply** these differences in your preparation of each entity's primary financial statements.

PO31 **Describe** the key differences in the financial statements of merchandisers, manufacturers, construction companies, nonfinancial service companies, and financial service companies and **explain** how these differences reflect the financing, investing, and operating activities of each form of industry.

PO32 **Calculate** net income and **prepare** both the income statements and balance sheets under the percentage-of-completion and completed-contract methods.

PREPARING YOURSELF FOR THE WEST WING

You finally found the courage to run for public office. And you got elected! You are now a proud member of the City Council in a small community with 15,000 people, and you want to implement your ideas for improving its quality of life. You are enthusiastic and full of hope. And then you see it—the city's financial report. Okay, you tell yourself. Nothing to worry about. You took financial accounting in college. You can do this. But as you start reading through the asset section of the balance sheet, you panic when you realize that you don't recognize all of the account titles. You also feel disoriented by the numerous columns, each representing what's called a *fund.* How will you do a good job if you don't understand even the balance sheet?

Even if you are not a real-life elected official, you can see from the asset section of Wheeling, Illinois' balance sheet that government accounting, also called *fund accounting,* is different from traditional accounting. One important difference is that there are several balance sheets because governments allocate their resources to several funds. This is done so that the money received from different sources may be earmarked for different functions. In fact, the various funds of a government function almost as if they were separate companies with their own balance sheets. Another difference is that governments focus on what's available to spend and how much is spent rather than focusing on all expenses involved in running its affairs. As a result of this focus on measuring *current* financial resources, balance sheets for governmental funds primarily report current assets and current liabilities. "Government accounting does not use the full accrual basis in accounting for most of its funds," notes Michael Mondschain, finance director for the Village of Wheeling, a Chicago suburb with a population of about 35,000. "For example, it does not recognize amortization expense on noncurrent assets because they are not *current financial resources.* Moreover, the majority of a community's infrastructure assets such as streets, hydrants, bridges, and the like are not accounted for because they have no value except to the government. Can you imagine anyone" he jokes, "who would want to buy Main Street or the city's traffic lights?" So until recently, communities have neither included these assets in their balance sheets nor depreciated them.

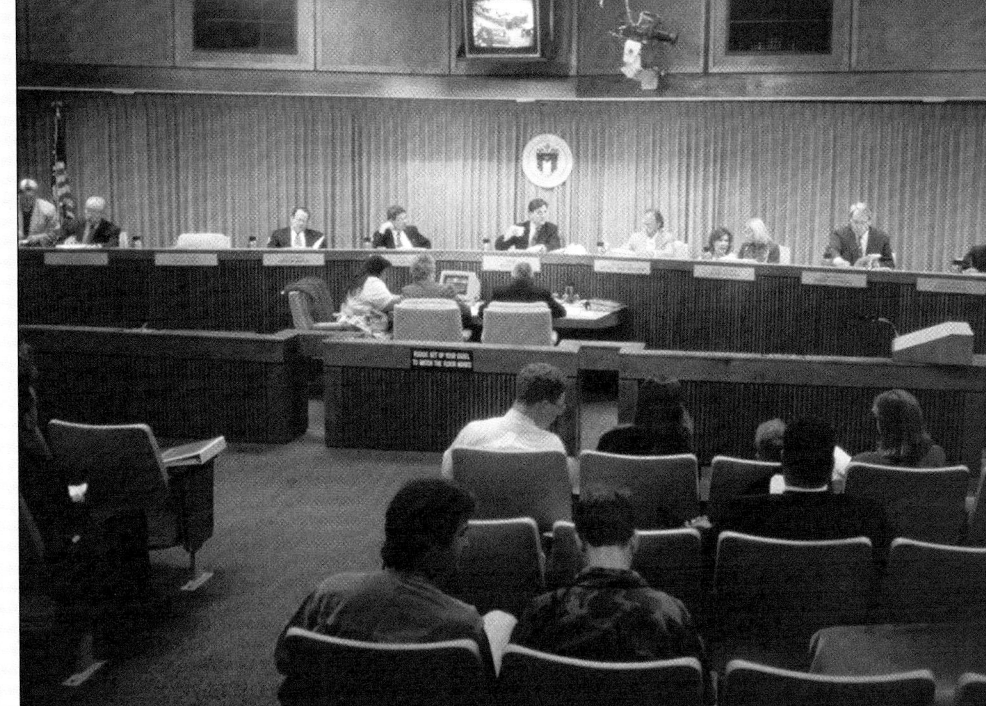

Michael also points out that these differences in how government entities are accounted for often cause difficulties for elected officials. Those who have had an accounting course in college have not been prepared for what they find in government financial statements. Thus, city employees, such as Michael, often help these officials get a better grasp of the basics of government accounting. These officials can also refer to publications, such as *What You Should Know about Your Local Government's Finances: A Guide to Financial Statements,* published by the Government Accounting Standards Board (GASB).

(continued on next page)

VILLAGE OF WHEELING, ILLINOIS

Combined Balance Sheet – All Fund Types and Account Groups

April 30, 2001
(with comparative totals for 2000)

	Governmental Fund Types				Proprietary Fund Types		Fiduciary Fund Type	Account Groups		Totals (Memorandum Only)	
ASSETS AND OTHER DEBITS	General	Special Revenue	Debt Service	Capital Projects	Enterprise	Internal Service	Trust and Agency	General Fixed Assets	General Long-Term Debt	2001	2000
Assets											
Cash and investments	$ 14,561,693	$ 2,834,396	$ 643,665	$ 15,577,546	$ 2,118,447	$ 460,440	$ 40,745,369	$ -	$ -	$ 76,941,556	$ 73,852,064
Receivables (net where applicable of allowance for uncollectibles)											
Property taxes	2,316,260	622,159	650,388	-	-	-	-	-	-	3,588,807	3,790,366
Sales taxes	829,010	72,549	-	-	-	-	-	-	-	901,559	964,225
Income taxes	366,932	-	-	-	-	-	-	-	-	366,932	304,000
Telecommunications tax	208,671	-	-	-	-	-	-	-	-	208,671	194,000
Accounts	-	58,441	-	-	1,206,285	-	-	-	-	1,264,726	1,097,458
Accrued interest	32,656	2,492	-	87,586	1,817	238	20,088	-	-	144,877	182,133
Loans	218,933	-	-	-	-	-	-	-	-	218,933	239,811
Other	125,106	81,921	-	4,156	-	-	7,540	-	-	218,723	213,046
Prepaid items	872,587	64,535	-	-	96,794	50,801	-	-	-	1,084,717	1,153,023
Inventory	85,602	42,238	-	-	311,547	-	-	-	-	439,387	480,978
Due from other governments	54,490	67,167	-	-	-	-	-	-	-	121,657	117,602
Due from IRMA	1,202,692	73,433	-	-	135,783	574,405	-	-	-	1,986,313	1,986,313
Land held for resale	-	-	-	540,000	-	-	-	-	-	540,000	268,000
Advance to other fund	-	-	-	-	250,011	-	-	-	-	250,011	250,011
Fixed assets, net of accumulated depreciation	-	-	-	-	32,155,969	-	-	17,310,679	-	49,466,648	49,438,652
Investment in joint venture	-	-	-	-	37,490,002	-	-	-	-	37,490,002	36,927,646
Other debits											
Amount available for debt service	-	-	-	-	-	-	-	-	643,665	643,665	562,352
Amount to be provided for retirement of general long-term debt	-	-	-	-	-	-	-	-	12,441,335	12,441,335	13,842,648
Total assets and other debits	$ 20,874,632	$ 3,919,331	$1,294,053	$ 16,209,288	$ 73,766,655	$ 1,085,884	$ 40,772,997	$ 17,310,679	$ 13,085,000	$ 188,318,519	$ 185,864,328

But, you might ask, does government accounting really portray a true picture of a city's financial condition? What if, for example, most of the bridges in a town are more than 50 years old? By not reporting the age and expected expenses to repair or retrofit the bridges, is the city making a full and fair disclosure? Apparently not, if the numerous complaints received for so many years about government accounting are any indication. In response, the Government Accounting Standards Board, also known as GASB, has issued *GASB Statement No. 34*, "Basic Financial Statements—and Management's Discussion and Analysis—for State and Local Governments." This pronouncement will change the way state and local governments present financial information to the public. Issued on June 30, 1999 by the Governmental Accounting Standards Board, *GASB 34* requires a government to:

- Report on the overall state of its financial health, not just its funds.
- Include information on its infrastructure assets.
- Show revenues from services provided separately from general government revenues so it can be determined whether a program is paying for itself or being paid for by general tax revenues.
- Prepare an introductory narrative section called "Management's Discussion and Analysis," which will explain the financial statements and describe the major financial transactions made during the year.

GASB 34 will fundamentally change the way governments account for themselves. Governments will have to value their infrastructure by establishing a present day value and then a historic value. They will also now report how much revenue different programs and agencies generate as well as the related costs. For example, tax revenues that are allocated specifically to the fire department can now be tracked so that the report's users will know the cost of running the fire department. Moreover, with *GASB 34* it will be easier to see the long-term impact of short-term decisions. City officials will be able to see what programs and agencies are losing money because revenue will be tied to specific expenditures.

But government isn't alone in having distinctive financial reporting. In this chapter you will learn about other industries and institutions whose financial statements are quite different from traditional statements because of their unique financing, investing, and/or operating activities. Knowing even a little about these differences will broaden your understanding of financial statements and better prepare you as a user of financial statements—whether or not you run for city council!

Broadening Your Understanding of Financial Statements

If you read the title of this chapter and assumed its content was not going to be especially relevant or meaningful to you, you may be in for a surprise. Two of the most important questions asked when starting a business are: What form of entity should I use? and To what industry do I belong? As you will learn in this chapter, these decisions hold major implications for your tax situation, the extent of your legal liability, and the form and content of your financial statements.

The U.S. Census Bureau reports that the vast majority of businesses today are sole proprietorships. Much less often, two or more people start a business together and form a partnership. Often, people create a corporation, a business entity that exists completely separate from them as individuals. If you ever start a business, what steps must you take to properly organize your business and what form of entity will be best for you?

The first section of this chapter helps you to answer these questions. It contains information about the forms of business and their respective advantages and disadvantages. While you might decide later to consult with a lawyer and/or accountant for such advice, this chapter will provide you a solid foundation for making a more informed decision about what form of entity to select.

The second section of this chapter will enhance your understanding of financial statements. Although you have spent considerable time studying the essential concepts underlying the balance sheet, income statement, statement of cash flows, and their relationships, there is more to learn. You might feel confident analyzing the content of some retail or service oriented financial statements, but do you really understand the special accounts found in the construction or banking industries? For example, consider the income statement of Wells Fargo Bank shown in Figure 10-1.

If you feel lost after looking over this statement, don't panic. While you have already learned a great deal about income statements, you were shown this one to convince you that it is now time to learn more about the specialized content found in particular industries. Even if you just skimmed this Wells Fargo income statement, you can't help but have noticed how many account titles were new to you and how accounts you did recognize were often presented in a different order than you expected. The fact is that so far, you've been presented with only standard practices in financial reporting and have not studied many of the variations that do exist.

So this chapter is essential reading if you want to be a more intelligent user of financial statements. In it you will learn more about the three forms of business entities and how the financial statements of these entities differ. You will then learn how the financial statements of different types of industries differ—specifically merchandising, manufacturing, construction, financial services, and nonfinancial services. Armed with this knowledge about forms of entity and types of industry, you'll be much better equipped to meaningfully compare businesses from different industries and, thereby, use financial statements to your advantage.

Different Forms of Business Entities

In Chapter 1 you learned about the essential characteristics of three common forms of business entity—sole proprietorship, partnership, and corporation. Recall that Susan initially established her business as a sole proprietorship. Then in Chapter 6 you saw how, late in her first year of business, Susan decided to convert her business from a sole proprietorship to a partnership with her friend Martha Perez.

From your reading of this textbook so far, you might recall some of the essential characteristics of the three common forms of business entity. Your objective now, however, is to learn more specific information about these entities so that you can satisfy Performance Objective 30:

> **YOUR PERFORMANCE OBJECTIVE 30**
> **Distinguish** among the sole proprietorship, partnership, and corporate forms of entity both as to their characteristics and their respective advantages and disadvantages and **apply** these differences in your preparation of each entity's primary financial statements.

To master this objective, you will now learn more about each entity's characteristics and why businesses decide to adopt a particular form of entity. Then you will see how the transactions and financial reports of Susan and Martha's partnership differ from the transactions and financial reports of Susan's sole proprietorship. Finally, you will see how the transactions and financial reports of a corporation differ from those of both a sole proprietorship and a partnership.

FIGURE 10-1

Income statement of Wells Fargo & Company

Since the term income represents a net concept, a more meaningful term is revenue, which represents a gross concept.

This item is identical in concept to a retailer's gross margin.

Since the term income represents a net concept, a more meaningful term is revenue, which represents a gross concept.

WELLS FARGO & COMPANY AND SUBSIDIARIES
Consolidated Statement of Income
(In millions, except per share amounts)

	Year ended December 31, 2001	2000	1999
Interest income			
Securities available for sale	$ 2,544	$ 2,671	$ 2,533
Mortgages held for sale	1,595	849	951
Loans held for sale	317	418	377
Loans	14,461	14,446	11,823
Other interest income	284	341	250
Total interest income	19,201	18,725	15,934
Interest expense			
Deposits	3,553	4,089	3,166
Short-term borrowings	1,273	1,758	1,127
Long-term debt	1,826	1,939	1,452
Guaranteed preferred beneficial interests in Company's subordinated debentures	89	74	73
Total interest expense	6,741	7,860	5,818
Net interest income	12,460	10,865	10,116
Provision for loan losses	1,780	1,329	1,104
Net interest income after provision for loan losses	10,680	9,536	9,012
Noninterest income			
Service charges on deposit accounts	1,876	1,704	1,580
Trust and investment fees	1,710	1,624	1,366
Credit card fees	796	721	694
Other fees	1,244	1,113	970
Mortgage banking	1,671	1,444	1,407
Insurance	745	411	395
Net venture capital (losses) gains	(1,630)	1,943	1,008
Net gains (losses) on securities available for sale	463	(722)	(228)
Other	815	605	783
Total noninterest income	7,690	8,843	7,975
Noninterest expense			
Salaries	4,027	3,652	3,307
Incentive compensation	1,195	846	643
Employee benefits	960	989	901
Equipment	909	948	928
Net occupancy	975	953	813
Goodwill	610	530	459
Core deposit intangible	165	186	206
Net gains on dispositions of premises and equipment	(21)	(58)	(16)
Other	4,071	3,784	3,396
Total noninterest expense	12,891	11,830	10,637
Income before income tax expense	5,479	6,549	6,350
Income tax expense	2,056	2,523	2,338
Net income	$ 3,423	$ 4,026	$ 4,012
Net income applicable to common stock	$ 3,409	$ 4,009	$ 3,977
Earnings per common share	$ 1.99	$ 2.36	$ 2.32
Diluted earnings per common share	$ 1.97	$ 2.33	$ 2.29
Dividends declared per common share	$ 1.00	$ .90	$ .785
Average common shares outstanding	1,709.5	1,699.5	1,714.0
Diluted average common shares outstanding	1,726.9	1,718.4	1,735.4

Learning More about the Sole Proprietorship and Partnership

The sole proprietorship and partnership forms of business have more in common with each other than either has with the corporation. As a result, we will first study them together and then examine the corporation. This examination will also include information about a new form of partnership, called the *limited liability partnership*.

What Are the Characteristics of a Sole Proprietorship?

As the name suggests, a **sole proprietorship** is an unincorporated business that is owned, and usually managed, by only one person. A major advantage of this form of business is the relative ease with which it may be established. That is, the owner, or *sole proprietor*, often needs only a modest amount of cash and legal work to open the business. Although a sole proprietorship might employ more than one person, only the sole proprietor receives all income or losses and is liable for all business obligations. The proprietorship is the most popular form of business in this country and was the original form of entity for such large and successful corporations as Wendy's and Ford Motor Company.

What Are the Characteristics of a Partnership?

A **partnership** is an unincorporated business that is owned by two or more persons, or *partners*. As we've seen with CMU, a major advantage of this form of business is that it allows the partners immediate access to additional financing. On the other hand, Susan sacrificed some benefits of a sole proprietorship when she went into partnership with Martha because a partnership has three characteristics that a proprietorship does not have: mutual agency, co-ownership of assets, and division of net income. Mutual agency means that the actions of any partner obligate the partnership as a whole. That is, each partner may act on behalf of—that is, serve as agent for—all other partners. For example, if Martha Perez borrows cash from a bank for the business, Susan is obligated by Martha's action, whether or not Martha asked for Susan's advance approval. Co-ownership of assets means that Susan gave up sole ownership of the business assets as soon as the partnership was formed. Division of net income refers to the normal practice of dividing net income between partners in some equitable manner. Susan and Martha should put in writing how they expect to divide the partnership income.

What Are Characteristics Common to Both Sole Proprietorships and Partnerships?

Although partnerships are designed to attract more resources than sole proprietorships and provide unique rules governing the relationships between co-owners, or partners, the partnership and sole proprietorship do share many similarities. Here are some important characteristics that a sole proprietorship and a partnership have in common:

1. They burden their owners with the distinctly dangerous prospect of unlimited liability for business debts. That is, the personal resources of the owner(s) are available to pay off business obligations.
2. Each is relatively easy to form as compared to setting up a corporation. Although Susan worked very hard in researching the card and memorabilia industry and obtaining financing, she had no significant costs and/or legal work to set up her business as either a sole proprietorship or as a partnership.

3. They are commonly used for small businesses in contrast to the corporation, which is nearly always used to organize larger businesses. This is the major reason why Susan did not seriously consider initially organizing her business as a corporation.

4. They require a clear distinction between the transactions of the business and those of its owner(s) for accounting purposes. As you will see, maintaining this distinction, known as the entity concept, is not as important in a corporation, because there is often a clearer separation between management and owners.
5. The business and its owner(s) are one and the same for legal purposes. That is, neither a proprietorship nor a partnership is a separate legal entity. Two consequences of this characteristic are that such businesses:
   a. Tend to have a relatively limited life that is tied to the ongoing participation or life of the owner(s). That is, each is dissolved whenever the sole proprietor or a single partner leaves or dies.
   b. Are not subject to income tax as an entity. For example, the partnership reports its business income on a Form 1065, U.S. Partnership Return of Income, but the income tax itself is not levied until each partner's individual income is passed through to their individual tax return. In other words, the proprietorship and partnership are "pass-through" entities.

Why Did Cards & Memorabilia Unlimited Convert to a Partnership?

Do you recall why Susan Newman decided to convert her sole proprietorship to a partnership? She did it because of the advantages a partnership would bring to CMU. First, she recognized it would be easier to attract additional financing for the future if CMU had the financial resources of more than one owner. Also, she wanted to reduce her exhausting, 60-hour workweek—recall that she could not afford full-time employees and was operating seven days a week to maximize her sales. Finally, she knew that a conversion to a partnership would be relatively easy.

In late November, therefore, Susan approached Martha Perez about becoming her partner. Martha was a CMU customer whose valuable insights into nonsports cards had particularly impressed Susan. Susan reasoned that if Martha took primary responsibility for nonsports cards, Susan could spend more time developing her sports memorabilia market and still handle sports cards. Martha decided to join CMU because she wanted to turn her passion for nonsports cards into a business. She would continue to work as a free-lance computer programmer to supplement her income. On December 24, they signed a partnership agreement giving Martha a 25% interest in CMU. The actual conversion from sole proprietorship occurred December 24, one week shy of the anniversary of CMU's first year in business. Thus, Cards & Memorabilia Unlimited operated as a partnership for the remaining week of the business's first year.

Initial Partnership Transaction Susan and Martha agreed that Martha's initial contribution to the partnership would be entirely in the form of cards, valued at $10,000 as of December 24. Since this textbook has now introduced two methods for recording transactions, we'll use them both in recording Transaction A_2 as follows:

Transaction A_2 $10,000 worth of merchandise is contributed by Martha Perez for a business interest.

Transaction Analysis						Journal Entry		
	Fundamental Accounting Equation							
Account Titles	Assets	=	Liabilities	+	Owners' Equity	Account Titles	Debit	Credit
Merchandise Inventory	10,000					Merchandise Inventory	10,000	
Contributed Capital					10,000	Contributed Capital		10,000

Notice that Transaction A_2 is essentially equivalent to Transaction A_1. In both cases, an owner provides a valuable asset to a business in exchange for an ownership interest in that business. That is, each transaction increases both assets and owners' equity.

Division of Net Income When Martha made this contribution, she and Susan had agreed on how they would share the business income. A partnership's income may be divided equally or allocated according to the provisions of an explicit agreement between the partners. In the case of Cards & Memorabilia Unlimited, Susan and Martha agreed in writing to allocate the partnership net income earned during its first year of business on the basis of their relative share of initial investment and the relative time that Martha was a partner.

One way to determine the relative ownership interest of each partner is to add the fair market value of assets each contributed to the business. In this case, Susan contributed cash of $30,000 and Martha contributed inventory valued at $10,000 for a total owner contribution of $40,000. Thus, it can be argued that Susan has a 75% interest ($30,000/$40,000) and Martha has a 25% interest ($10,000/$40,000).

Since Susan was the sole owner for 51 of 52 weeks, she deserves 100% of CMU's net income for the 51 weeks before the partnership formed. For ease of calculation, assume that net income of Cards & Memorabilia Unlimited is earned equally over time. Susan also deserves 75% of the income earned during the last week of the year. So the calculations are as follows:

$30,000/52	= Income Per Week = $576.9230769	
Susan's Share	= ($576.9230769 × 51) + (.75 × $576.9230769) =	$29,855.77
Martha's Share	= $30,000.00 − $29,855.77 =	144.23
		$30,000.00

Although Martha's share is very small, these calculations demonstrate the relevance of identifying each partner's respective ownership share. As you will see, this most important information is captured in the partnership's statement of capital.

Partnership Financial Statements A partnership's income statement and statement of cash flows do not look significantly different from those of sole proprietorships or corporations. In fact, the financial statement that is affected most by the partnership form of entity is the statement of changes in owners' equity. A more specific title—Statement of Capital—is used when it is prepared for both the sole proprietorship and partnership. Study the following statement of capital for Susan and Martha's new partnership:

CARDS & MEMORABILIA UNLIMITED
Partnership Statement of Capital
For the Year Ended December 31

Susan Newman, Capital, 1/2	$ -0-	
Add:		
Owner Investments	30,000	
Share of net income	29,856	
Deduct:		
Owner withdrawals	(8,100)	$51,756
Martha Perez, Capital, 12/24	-0-	
Add:		
Owner investments	10,000	
Share of net income	144	10,144
Total partners' capital, 12/31		$61,900

After you allocate the partnership net income in some mutually agreeable manner and determine the respective amounts in each partner's capital account, each partner's ending ownership amount in the Statement of Capital is then entered in the owners' equity section of the balance sheet. Such a partnership balance sheet is illustrated here for Cards & Memorabilia Unlimited.

CARDS & MEMORABILIA UNLIMITED
Partnership Balance Sheet
For the Year Ended December 31

Assets		Liabilities and Owners' Equity	
Cash	$38,275	Accounts payable	$ 1,100
Accounts receivable	5,000	Deferred revenue*	2,000
Interest receivable	25		
Merchandise inventory	13,000	Notes payable	6,000
Total current assets	$56,300	Total current liabilities	$ 9,100
Other receivable	2,000	Long-term note payable	4,000
Equipment	19,000		
Less: Accum. depreciation	(2,300)	Partners' capital accounts	61,900
	$75,000		$75,000

* Also titled Advances from Customers, Unearned Revenue, and so on.

Recall that Appendix C lists and analyzes the partnership's first year's transactions.

Although most large U.S. businesses are organized as corporations, there are exceptions, notably the four largest public accounting firms—known as, the Big 4—Ernst and Young, Deloitte & Touche, PricewaterhouseCoopers, and KPMG Peat Marwick. To limit their liability from potential lawsuits, these firms have recently adopted a form of entity known as a **limited liability partnership**, or **LLP**. In this form of entity, partners are generally liable for their own actions but not completely liable for the actions of other partners. Given that these firms provide accounting services to a wide range of clients, it might seem ironic that their own published financial statements disclose little financial information. For example, note that in Figure 10-2, KPMG Peat Marwick LLP uses only one annual report page to describe all of its financial affairs. The justification for this limited disclosure is that a limited liability partnership, unlike a corporation, has no shareholders to which it is accountable.

Learning More about the Corporation

Shortly after Susan and Martha formed their partnership, George Wu encouraged them to educate themselves about the corporate form of business. He reasoned that if CMU grew, Susan and Martha might benefit from converting to the corporate form in the future. Accordingly, we will now examine the characteristics of a corporation, the reasons why entities might want to adopt this form, some hypothetical corporate transactions for CMU, and some different corporate forms that are available. The following section will also introduce a hybrid form of entity known as the *limited liability company*, which has characteristics of both a partnership and a corporation.

What Are the Characteristics of a Corporation?

Susan and Martha learned that a **corporation** is a business that is owned by persons or organizations that have purchased what are called *shares of stock*. Each such share of stock is obtainable by shareholders in return for their resource contributions to the

FIGURE 10-2

Financial information from the KPMG annual report

KPMG INTERNATIONAL
Financial Performance
Balance Sheet at September 30, 2000
(In US$ millions)

	1999	2000
Fixed assets	1,131	1,523
Other assets	467	1,546
	1,598	3,069
Current assets		
Work in progress	782	724
Accounts receivable	2,345	2,726
Other current assets	483	653
Cash and equivalents	938	1,157
Total current assets	4,548	5,260
Accounts payable	(1,369)	(1,988)
Short-term external financing (under one year)	(695)	(692)
Net current assets	2,484	2,580
Total assets less current liabilities	4,082	5,649
Long-term external financing	(792)	(626)
Other liabilities	(909)	(1,275)
Net assets	2,381	3,748
Partners' equity	2,381	3,748
Income Statement		
Client billings	12,200	13,500
Expenses incurred	(1,118)	(1,351)
Net fee income	11,082	12,149
Staff costs (excluding partner remuneration)	(5,334)	(5,757)
Gross margin	5,748	6,392
Other net operating costs	(3,037)	(3,442)
Available for partner income	2,711	2,950

firm. Unlike the sole proprietorship and the partnership, the corporation is legally separate from its owners or *shareholders*. When these ownership interests or shares of stock are widely available to all investors—generally through an organized stock exchange such as the New York Stock Exchange (NYSE) or the National Association of Security Dealers' Automated Quotations (NASDAQ)—they are said to be *publicly traded*. Thus, one advantage of this form is the relative ease with which ownership interests can be transferred. The corporation's greatest advantage, however, is a feature called limited liability. Essentially, **limited liability** refers to the right of shareholders to not be held personally liable for the obligations of the business, unlike the owner(s) in the other forms of business. This and other features make the corporation the most popular form of entity for most of the largest businesses in the U.S.

Why Choose the Corporate Form of Business?

Why do people decide to choose the corporate form of business? And what would motivate Susan and Martha to convert CMU to a corporation? There are several compelling reasons. First, as you already know, corporations are generally more able than sole proprietorships or partnerships to raise large amounts of capital. This is due, in part, to the separation of corporate ownership from corporate management, which allows access to an unlimited number of shareholders. Further, the corporation, at least in theory, has an unlimited life. Changes in ownership interests are easily implemented and don't require forming a new business, as is necessary with partnerships and sole proprietorships. Finally, the limited liability feature is especially attractive to shareholders whose potential loss is usually restricted to the amount that they invest. That is, the corporation is a legal entity separate from its owners. Thus, the personal assets of shareholders are protected and are not legally available for payment of corporate debts.

Corporate Transactions

Susan and Martha believe their partnership will satisfy all resource needs for the foreseeable future and do not want to deal with the legal complications and higher costs associated with the corporation; and so they decide not to organize Cards & Memorabilia Unlimited as a corporation. Nevertheless, to learn more about the unique features of corporate financial statements, let's imagine for now that Susan and Martha do convert their business to a corporation. How would their financial statements change?

Here are the transactions Cards & Memorabilia Unlimited would need if it became a corporation. Note that the first three hypothetical transactions are ownership related and the fourth accounts for how corporate income is taxed differently.

Transaction A 4,480 shares of CMU Inc. capital stock are issued at $10 per share in exchange for the following owner contributions: $30,000 of cash from Susan Newman, $9,200 of merchandise inventory from Martha Perez, and a $5,600 investment in Marvel Corporation stock from George Wu.

Transaction Analysis							Journal Entry		
	Fundamental Accounting Equation								
Account Titles	Assets	=	Liabilities	+	Owners' Equity		Account Titles	Debit	Credit
Cash—Checking	30,000						Cash—Checking	30,000	
Merchandise Inventory	9,200						Merchandise Inventory	9,200	
Investment in Stock	5,600						Investment in Stock	5,600	
Capital Stock					44,800		Capital Stock		44,800

The $44,800 increase in owners' equity, or owners' investment, represents the asset contributions of owners Susan, Martha, and George. In the corporation this investment component is represented by the Contributed Capital account or Capital Stock account.

Transaction W_1 On October 30, the corporation declares $12,900 of dividends to be paid on December 1.

Transaction Analysis							Journal Entry		
	Fundamental Accounting Equation								
Account Titles	Assets	=	Liabilities	+	Owners' Equity		Account Titles	Debit	Credit
Dividends Declared					(12,900)		Dividends Declared	12,900	
Dividends Payable			12,900				Dividends Payable		12,900

Whenever dividends are declared, a corporation reduces its retained earnings and increases Dividends Payable, a liability account. Notice that retained earnings are decreased here by increasing Dividends Declared, a contra retained earnings account.

Transaction W_2 On December 1, the cash dividends are paid to shareholders of record as of November 15.

Transaction Analysis							Journal Entry		
	Fundamental Accounting Equation								
Account Titles	Assets	=	Liabilities	+	Owners' Equity		Account Titles	Debit	Credit
Dividends Payable			(12,900)				Dividends Payable	12,900	
Cash	(12,900)						Cash		12,900

By paying the dividends, the corporation reduces both its cash and liability accounts.

Transaction Z $4,500 of federal income tax is incurred for the year using a tax rate of 15%.

Transaction Analysis							Journal Entry		
	Fundamental Accounting Equation								
Account Titles	Assets	=	Liabilities	+	Owners' Equity		Account Titles	Debit	Credit
Income Tax Expense					(4,500)		Income Tax Expense	4,500	
Income Tax Payable			4,500				Income Tax Payable		4,500

Unlike the sole proprietorship and the partnership, a corporation is a legal entity. Thus, the corporate business entity, Cards & Memorabilia Unlimited, is subject to income tax (assume a 15% tax rate) reported on Form 1120. Since the pretax income is $30,000 from previous income statements, the tax will be $30,000 × 0.15 or $4,500.

Corporate Financial Statements

Now let's consider how corporate financial statements differ from those of sole proprietorships and partnerships. In fact, you will see that only the corporate statement of cash flows is not significantly different from the cash flow statements found in a proprietorship or partnership. The corporate income statement, balance sheet, and statement of owners' equity, however, do differ enough to justify taking a closer look. To appreciate the differences, let's examine the hypothetical corporate financial statements of Cards & Memorabilia Unlimited.

Income Statement Note that in hypothetical Transaction Z, corporate taxation introduces an Income Tax Expense account in the amount of $4,500 to Cards & Memorabilia Unlimited's income statement. Note that in Figure 10-3, this additional expense is subtracted so that corporate net income is $25,500 rather than $30,000. Although the corporate income statement differs in just this one respect, the 15% reduction in income ($4,500/$30,000) makes it a significant difference.

FIGURE 10-3

Cards & Memorabilia Unlimited's corporate income statement

CARDS & MEMORABILIA UNLIMITED, INC. Income Statement For the Year Ended December 31		
Revenues		
Sales revenue	$86,600	
Service revenue	600	
Interest revenue	300	$87,500
Expenses		
Cost of goods sold	30,000	
Rent expense	11,000	
Salaries expense	8,750	
Income tax expense	4,500	
Depreciation expense	2,600	
Miscellaneous expense	4,600	
Interest expense	200	
Loss on equipment sale	350	62,000
Net income		**$25,500**

Statement of Retained Earnings Recall from Chapter 3 that a statement of retained earnings is a financial statement that reports the changes in the Retained Earnings account for a period of time. Recall also from Chapter 3 that its ending balance equals its beginning balance plus net income less dividends declared. In a corporation the investment component is represented by the Contributed Capital or Capital Stock account and the earnings component is represented by the Retained Earnings account. As you study Figure 10-4, note two key differences between the corporate statement of retained earnings and that of other entities. First, corporate net income is $25,500 rather than $30,000; and second, dividends declared rather than withdrawals are reported. As Figure 10-4 illustrates, a statement of retained earnings reconciles the income statement with the balance sheet.

FIGURE 10-4

Cards & Memorabilia Unlimited's corporate statement of retained earnings

CARDS & MEMORABILIA UNLIMITED, INC. Statement of Retained Earnings For the Year Ended December 31	
Retained earnings, 1/2	$ –0–
Add: Net income	25,500
Subtotal	25,500
Deduct: Dividends declared	(12,900)
Retained earnings, 12/31	$12,600

Balance Sheet Recall from hypothetical Transaction A that the Capital Stock account, which is not reported in the statement of retained earnings, amounts to $44,800. Since the ending retained earnings account balance is calculated in the preceding statement of retained earnings, Figure 10-5 illustrates two other essential differences between the corporate balance sheet and its counterparts in the proprietorship and partnership. The corporate balance sheet contains an income tax liability and a Capital Stock account, neither of which are found in the proprietorship or partnership forms of entity.

FIGURE 10-5 Cards & Memorabilia Unlimited's corporate balance sheet

CARDS & MEMORABILIA UNLIMITED, INC.
Balance Sheet
December 31

Cash	$33,475	Accounts payable	$ 350
Accounts receivable	5,000	Salaries payable	750
Interest receivable	25		
Merchandise inventory	12,200	Deferred revenue	2,000
Total current assets	50,700	Notes payable	6,000
		Income taxes payable	4,500
		Total current liabilities	13,600
Other receivable	2,000		
Investment in stock	5,600	Long-term note payable	4,000
Equipment	19,000	Capital stock	44,800
Less: Accumulated Depreciation	(2,300)	Retained earnings	12,600
	$75,000		$75,000

The Investment in Stock account was created from Transaction A. This type of asset can be found, however, in both a proprietorship and a partnership.

Neither account is found in a proprietorship or partnership.

INSIGHT

Corporations Take Many Forms

The form of business entity known as the corporation takes many forms. This means that you must select a specific corporate form if you want to incorporate your business. You can choose the regular corporation, most often referred to as the **C Corporation**, whose name derives from how it is taxed under Subchapter C of the Internal Revenue Code. Or you can choose the closely held corporation, the S Corporation, the nonprofit corporation, or the limited liability company—each of which offers some very viable and attractive options beyond the C Corporation. Each of these additional corporate forms was created to solve a particular set of problems plaguing its owners. Today, as in the past, the corporation continues to evolve as lawmakers respond to the needs and requests of their corporate constituents. Because corporate shareholders continue to face such challenges as tax law changes and emerging legal liability issues, it's very likely that the corporation will take on even more forms in the future.

For most small businesses, a good way to incorporate is to form a **closely held corporation**, also called a *closed corporation.* This type of corporation, often used for family-run businesses, is owned by a relatively small number of stockholders—usually from 1 to 15 in total and never more than 30—who are often actively involved in the management and day-to-day activities of the business. A closely held corporation operates under a shareholder's agreement that enables it to be run as if it were a noncorporate entity. Yet, it is allowed to retain many of the primary advantages of the corporation including limited liability, unlimited life, and ease in transferring ownership. Further, a closely held corporation dispenses with time-consuming and burdensome formalities, such as bylaws and formal board of directors meetings.

Larger businesses often select the **S Corporation**, or **S Corp.**, formerly referred to as the Subchapter S Corporation because of how it is taxed under Subchapter S of the Internal Revenue Code. An S Corporation is usually treated for income tax purposes as if it were a partnership—it doesn't pay federal income tax in the same way as other corporations. Instead, it acts as a conduit, passing through its income and expenses to the shareholders' individual tax returns while limiting the liability of its shareholders. The S Corporation has several advantages. It protects its shareholders from being taxed twice—once on the income of the corporation itself and once on the dividend income reported on the individual tax returns of C Corporation shareholders. Like a C corporation, its shareholders—up to 75 in number—are normally protected from liabilities in excess of their investment. Finally, as in a C corporation, the S Corporation structure enables you to gradually transfer ownership and management to your heirs or successors consistent with effective estate tax planning.

As its name implies, the **nonprofit corporation** is well suited to organizations that engage in charitable, religious, educational, and other activities considered socially beneficial. Its excess of revenues over expenses must be applied to the not-for-profit purpose of the organization. It cannot be distributed to members, officers, or directors of the organization.

Another form of entity that has recently become popular is the **limited liability company**, commonly referred to as the **LLC**. This is a hybrid form of business entity having some attributes of a corporation and other attributes of a partnership. Like an S corporation, the LLC provides its owners limited liability, enables them to participate in management, and avoids double taxation of income by only being taxed at the owner or personal level. Unlike an S corporation, an LLC has no limitations on the number and type of its owners, has no articles of incorporation, and uses the terms *members* and *managers* instead of *officers* and *directors.* Whereas an S corporation must divide income, losses, tax credits, and deductions on a pro-rata basis, an LLC has the flexibility to allocate those items to certain owners. Unlike a corporation, an LLC does not have an unlimited life. In many states, its maximum life span is limited to 30 years and if a manager or member leaves before that time, a new business must be formed, as is necessary with partnerships and sole proprietorships.

Thus, the insight you should gain here is that, today, choosing an appropriate corporate form for a business is a more complicated decision than it was in the past. If you are faced with this decision, you should plan to conduct additional research, and consult with an attorney, an accountant, and your business associates.

Exploring Different Types of Industry

Now that you have learned more about the different forms of business, you can continue to improve your ability to read and interpret financial statements by turning your attention to the different types of industry. Like the form of entity, a business's industry classification usually affects the form and the content of its financial statements. Performance Objective 31 is designed to help you master the unique financial reporting differences found in each industry:

YOUR PERFORMANCE OBJECTIVE 31

Describe the key differences in the financial statements of merchandisers, manufacturers, construction companies, nonfinancial service companies, and financial service companies and **explain** how these differences reflect the financing, investing, and operating activities of each form of industry.

As Performance Objective 31 indicates, you will explore merchandising businesses, manufacturers, construction companies, nonfinancial service companies, and financial service companies. In each case, you will examine the particular financing, investing, and operating activities that produce the distinctive financial statements associated with each industry.

Merchandising

A **merchandiser** buys and resells products; it does not produce them. Merchandisers known as **wholesalers** typically purchase products in large quantities from *manufac-*

NARMS (National Association for Retail Merchandising Services) promotes the benefits of merchandising service companies and establishes industry standards for merchandising performance.

turers, the type of businesses that do produce product. Wholesalers then resell these products in smaller quantities to a merchandiser known as a retailer. **Retailers** usually buy their products from several wholesalers to provide a diverse assortment of products with which to attract consumers. This chain of product distribution is completed when the retailer resells its products to the consumer. The following diagram illustrates what's called a distribution chain and shows that wholesalers are intermediaries between manufacturers and retailers, and retailers are intermediaries between wholesalers and consumers.

You can use Cards & Memorabilia Unlimited to illustrate this distribution chain. Assume you, a consumer, walk into Cards & Memorabilia Unlimited, a retailer, to buy a Mark McGwire rookie card. You might recall from Chapter 1 that CMU works through one wholesaler, Connolly Supply. Connolly Supply, in turn, buys its trading cards from manufacturers, such as Topps, Fleer, and Upper Deck.

Now that you understand some essential facts about merchandisers, let's examine the financial statement effects of merchandisers' operating and investing activities. Although merchandisers certainly engage in financing activities, their financing activities are not easily distinguishable from the financing activities of companies in other industries.

How the Operating Activities of Merchandisers Affect Their Financial Statements

The primary operating activity of most merchandisers is to sell their products to customers. It follows, therefore, that we should look closely at the Accounts Receivable and Sales Revenue accounts created by credit sales, as well as at the related operating activity that simultaneously results in increasing cost of goods sold and decreasing merchandise inventory. In a statement of cash flows prepared under the direct method (Chapter 8), these transactions are prominently disclosed as Cash Collected from Customers and Cash Paid for Merchandise Purchases. Unfortunately, this valuable information is unavailable to you in almost every annual report because the indirect method of reporting cash flow from operations is almost always used. Fortunately, the technique called T-account analysis, described in Appendix 9–1, allows you to reconstruct these amounts.

Accounts Receivable and Sales Revenue Large merchandisers generally have significant accounts receivable from customers. These amounts due from customers arise from credit sales of products or services in which the customer promises to pay in the future. Since not all credit sales will be collected, an estimate of the uncollectible amount is generally deducted from the related receivable to derive a more realistic measurement of what is called the *net receivable*. Recall from Chapter 4 that we call any account that reduces another account a contra account. In this case, the contra asset account might be titled Allowance for Uncollectible Accounts. The fullest disclosure of these accounts and their relationship is shown here.

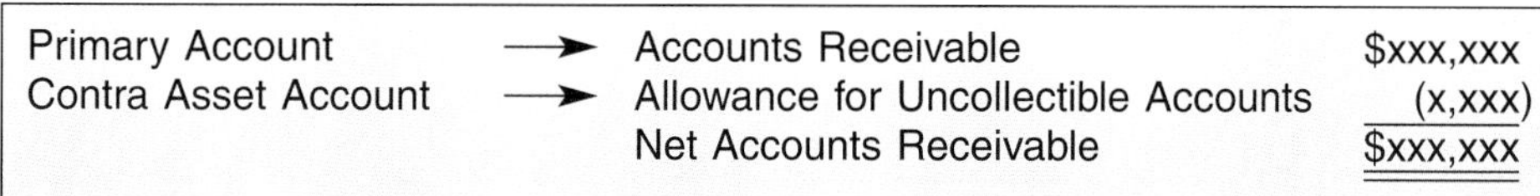

Primary Account	→	Accounts Receivable	$xxx,xxx
Contra Asset Account	→	Allowance for Uncollectible Accounts	(x,xxx)
		Net Accounts Receivable	$xxx,xxx

In this case, the contra asset is placed immediately below and subtracted from Accounts Receivable, its primary asset account.

Seldom will you find examples in which the annual report discloses the three amounts shown above. Instead, both the net receivable and the allowance account might be disclosed, as shown in Figure 10-6 for the Coca Cola Company, or only the net receivable itself might be disclosed, as shown in Figure 10-7 for Nordstrom, the largest independently owned fashion specialty retailer. Far more popular titles than Allowance for Uncollectible Accounts are Allowance for Doubtful Accounts and simply Allowance.[1]

FIGURE 10-6

Presentation of net receivables and allowance amounts

THE COCA-COLA COMPANY AND SUBSIDIARIES
Consolidated Balance Sheets
December 31,
(in millions except share data)

	2001	2000
Assets		
Current		
Cash and cash equivalents	**$ 1,866**	$ 1,819
Marketable securities	**68**	73
	1,934	1,892
Trade accounts receivable, less allowances of $59 in 2001 and $62 in 2000	**1,882**	1,757
Inventories	**1,055**	1,066
Prepaid expenses and other assets	**2,300**	1,905
Total current assets	**7,171**	6,620
Investments and other assets		
Equity method investments		
Coca-Cola Enterprises Inc.	**788**	707
Coca-Cola Amatil Limited	**432**	617
Coca-Cola HBC S.A.	**791**	758
Other, principally bottling companies	**3,117**	3,164
Cost method investments, principally bottling companies	**294**	519
Other assets	**2,792**	2,364
	8,214	8,129
Property, plant and equipment		
Land	**217**	225
Buildings and improvements	**1,812**	1,642
Machinery and equipment	**4,881**	4,547
Containers	**195**	200
	7,105	6,614
Less allowances for depreciation	**2,652**	2,446
	4,453	4,168
Trademarks and other intangible assets	**2,579**	1,917
	$22,417	$20,834

1 *Accounting Trends & Techniques,* AICPA, Section 2.62, 2001.

FIGURE 10-7

A one-line presentation of net receivables and of net land, buildings, and equipment

This is a one-line presentation of accounts receivable less allowance for uncollectible accounts.

This is a one-line presentation of land, buildings, and equipment less accumulated depreciation.

NORDSTROM, INC. AND SUBSIDIARIES
Consolidated Balance Sheets
January 31, 2001 and 2002
(Dollars in thousands)

	2001	2000
Assets		
Current assets		
Cash and cash equivalents	$25,259	$27,042
Short-term investment	—	25,527
Accounts receivable, net	721,953	616,989
Merchandise inventories	945,687	797,845
Prepaid income taxes and other	120,083	97,245
Total current assets	1,812,982	1,564,648
Land, buildings and equipment, net	1,599,938	1,429,492
Available-for-sale investment	—	35,251
Goodwill	39,495	—
Trademarks and other intangible assets	103,978	—
Other assets	52,110	32,690
Total assets	**$3,608,503**	**$3,062,081**
Liabilities and shareholders' equity		
Current liabilities:		
Notes payable	$83,060	$70,934
Accounts payable	466,476	390,688
Accrued salaries, wages and related benefits	234,833	211,308
Income taxes and other accruals	153,613	135,388
Current portion of long-term debt	12,586	58,191
Total current liabilities	950,568	866,509
Long-term debt	1,099,710	746,791
Deferred lease credits	275,252	194,995
Other liabilities	53,405	68,172
Shareholders' equity:		
Common stock, no par; 250,000,000 shares authorized; 133,797,757 and 132,279,988 shares issued and outstanding	330,394	247,559
Unearned stock compensation	(3,740)	(8,593)
Retained earnings	900,090	929,616
Accumulated other comprehensive earnings	2,824	17,032
Total shareholders' equity	1,229,568	1,185,614
Total liabilities and shareholders' equity	**$3,608,503**	**$3,062,081**

An income statement account that is directly related to this allowance account is Uncollectible Accounts Expense, also called Bad Debt Expense or Doubtful Accounts Expense. To properly measure the estimated loss from receivables under the accrual basis, the accountant must record the sales amount for the period that will not ultimately be collected. This periodic matching of the loss on credit sales to the gross sales revenue earned is accomplished by increasing an expense account on the income statement—for example, Bad Debt Expense—and decreasing the net receivable reported on the balance sheet. Such a transaction is treated as an adjusting entry.

Example The uncollectible accounts expense is estimated to be 02.5% of total yearly sales of $20,000, or $500 ($20,000 × .025).

Transaction Analysis					Journal Entry		
	Fundamental Accounting Equation						
Account Titles	Assets	=	Liabilities +	Owners' Equity	Account Titles	Debit	Credit
Bad Debt Expense				(500)	Bad Debt Expense	500	
Allowance for Bad Debts	(500)				Allowance for Bad Debts		500

Simultaneously increasing Bad Debt Expense and the Allowance for Bad Debts as shown here reduces net income and, thus, owners' equity as well as net accounts receivable.

A more correct but seldom used approach is to record a contra sales revenue account (e.g., Sales Contra on Uncollectible Accounts) and a contra receivable account (Allowance for Uncollectible Accounts). Since this approach lowers both net income on the income statement and net receivables on the balance sheet, net income will be the same under either approach. The argument behind using this method is that a loss from uncollectibles is really a reduction of sales revenue not an increase in an expense account.

Because customers are such a critical factor to the success of merchandisers, a merchandiser's accounts receivable balance often represents a higher percentage of total assets than is common in most other industries. In Figure 10-7, for example, 2001 receivables made up 20% of Nordstrom's total assets. To further analyze receivables, you can also use the analytical tool known as a receivable turnover ratio, which you learned about in Chapter 7.

Merchandise Inventory and Cost of Goods Sold As you already know from your study of Cards & Memorabilia Unlimited, merchandise inventory includes finished goods purchased from others whose physical form is not altered prior to their resale to consumers. Often, this account is the largest asset on the balance sheet. Note that a manufacturer's balance sheet differs from a merchandiser's in that it reports *three* inventory accounts—finished goods inventory, work in process inventory, and raw materials inventory.

To help you recall the calculation that underlies the relationship between the asset merchandise inventory and the expense cost of goods, let's review the calculation used to determine the cost of goods sold amount for CMU's Transaction U:

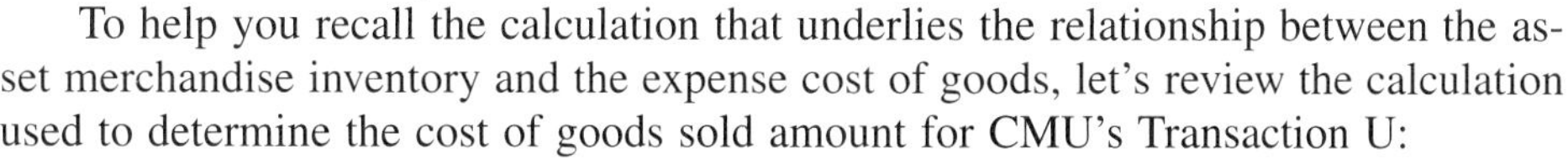

Beginning inventory	$ –0–
Merchandise acquisitions	43,000
Cost of goods available for sale	43,000
Less: Ending inventory	(13,000)
Cost of goods sold	$30,000

As illustrated, cost of goods sold is that portion of the total cost of goods available for sale that is actually sold.

How the Investing Activities of Merchandisers Affect Their Financial Statements

Often, the most important investing activity for wholesalers is to obtain warehouse facilities and for retailers to obtain buildings from which to sell their product. Although this purchase directly affects the balance sheet, it is also prominently disclosed in the statement of cash flows. For example, in Figure 10-8, Nordstrom's capital expenditures—additions to land, buildings, and equipment—represent the largest single line item reported in its statement of cash flows. This investing activity does not itself affect the income statement, but does affect the balance sheet as you'll see next.

FIGURE 10-8 A significant investing activity transaction

NORDSTROM, INC. AND SUBSIDIARIES
Consolidated Statements of Cash Flows
Years Ended January 31, 1999, 2000, and 2001
(dollars in thousands)

	2001	2000	1999
Operating activities			
Net earnings	$101,918	$202,557	$206,723
Adjustments to reconcile net earnings to net cash provided by operating activities:			
Depreciation and amortization of buildings and equipment	203,048	193,718	180,655
Amortization of goodwill	429	—	—
Amortization of trademark and other intangible assets	822	—	—
Amortization of deferred lease credits and other, net	(12,349)	(6,387)	(3,501)
Stock-based compensation expense	7,594	3,331	10,037
Write-down of investment	32,857	—	—
Change in operating assets and liabilities, net of effects from acquisition of business			
Accounts receivable, net	(102,945)	(29,854)	77,313
Merchandise inventories	(128,744)	(47,576)	75,776
Prepaid income taxes and other	(3,889)	(11,777)	15,357
Accounts payable	67,561	51,053	18,324
Accrued salaries, wages and related benefits	16,736	14,942	17,156
Income tax liabilities and other accruals	3,879	965	(4,828)
Other liabilities	(7,184)	7,154	8,296
Net cash provided by operating activities	179,733	378,126	601,308
Investing activities			
Capital expenditures	(321,454)	(305,052)	(306,737)
Additions to deferred lease credits	92,361	114,910	74,264
Payment for acquisition, net of cash acquired	(83,828)	—	—
Investments in unconsolidated affiliates	—	—	(32,857)
Other, net	(5,602)	(9,332)	(2,251)
Net cash used in investing activities	(318,523)	(199,474)	(267,581)
Financing activities			
Increase (decrease) in notes payable	12,126	(7,849)	(184,984)
Proceeds from issuance of long-term debt	308,266	—	544,165
Principal payments on long-term debt	(58,191)	(63,341)	(101,106)
Capital contribution to subsidiary from minority shareholders	—	16,000	—
Proceeds from issuance of common stock	6,250	9,577	14,971
Cash dividends paid	(45,935)	(44,463)	(44,059)
Purchase and retirement of common stock	(85,509)	(302,965)	(346,077)
Net cash provided by (used in) financing activities	137,007	(393,041)	(117,090)
Net (decrease) increase in cash and cash equivalents	(1,783)	(214,389)	216,637
Cash and cash equivalents at beginning of year	27,042	241,431	24,794
Cash and cash equivalents at end of year	**$ 25,259**	**$ 27,042**	**$241,431**

These are additions to land, buildings, and equipment.

Land, Buildings, and Equipment The asset account category Land, Buildings, and Equipment is sometimes referred to as Property, Plant, and Equipment; Fixed Assets; or simply Plant Assets. The contra account, Accumulated Depreciation, like Allowance for Uncollectibles described earlier, reduces its primary asset account—Land, Buildings, and Equipment—from its original cost to its book value as shown here.

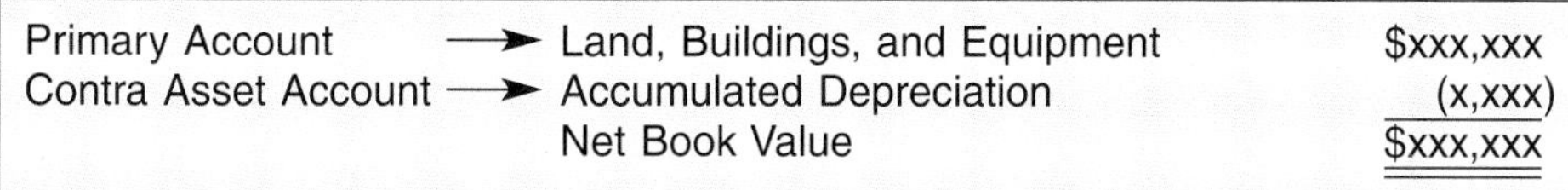

Primary Account ⟶	Land, Buildings, and Equipment	$xxx,xxx
Contra Asset Account ⟶	Accumulated Depreciation	(x,xxx)
	Net Book Value	$xxx,xxx

Notice that Nordstrom in Figure 10-7 presents the net amount of its Land, Buildings, and Equipment in one line rather than in the three lines shown here. Although the one-line format is used most often in annual reports, it does not display the amount of accumulated depreciation and, therefore, limits the usefulness of this information. Instead, the specific amount of accumulated depreciation is usually found in the financial statement notes.

Manufacturing

Unlike merchandisers, **manufacturers** do not buy final products; they produce them. Specifically, they convert raw materials into a wide variety of products or finished goods by applying labor and machines to the raw materials. Once the manufacturer has completed its product, it will attempt to sell it to a wholesaler, a retailer, or a final customer. With these essential facts about manufacturers in mind, we will focus on the financial statement effects of manufacturers' operating activities since their financing and investing activities are not easily distinguishable from the financing and investing activities of companies in other industries.

How the Operating Activities of Manufacturers Affect Their Financial Statements

The primary operating activities of most manufacturers include the purchase and storage of raw materials, the manufacture and storage of both unfinished and finished products, and the resale of these finished products to merchandisers or consumers.

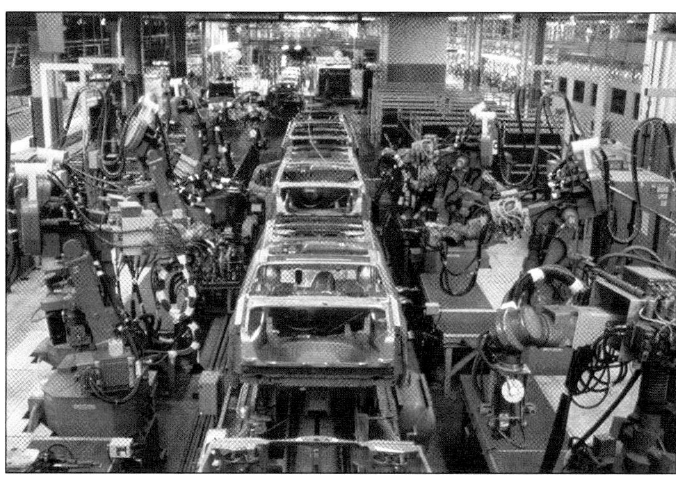

This automobile assembly line is a classic example of how manufacturers produce their products.

Let's now examine each of these phases in more detail to determine just how each phase affects the financial statements. To do so, you need to examine the three major types of cost that go into manufacturing a product as well as the three inventory accounts created by the manufacturing process. As you might imagine, many economic resources are used to manufacture products. These resources are typically divided into three manufacturing or production cost categories—raw materials, direct labor, and manufacturing overhead. Together, they compose what you learned in Chapter 6 are called **product costs**, costs whose expiration is associated with the sale of a product. Let's now examine the first of these product costs.

Raw Materials Cost **Raw materials (RM)** are assets that ultimately are physically incorporated into the final product. These assets are also referred to as **direct materials** because they have a clear and *direct* relationship to the finished product. Examples include such commodities as steel, aluminum, and plastic and such purchased or manufactured components as bolts, computer chips, and leather seats. In all of these examples, the raw materials go directly into making the final product; that is, you can directly trace the incurrence of raw material costs to the form of the final product. When raw materials are added to a product in the manufacturing process, the cost of those raw materials is a product cost, which will ultimately become an expense (cost of goods sold) when the product is sold. Any raw material costs not yet included in the product are reported in a raw materials inventory account. **Raw materials inventory** includes material costs not yet placed into production that will eventually be physically incorporated into the final product. The concept that underlies accounting for raw materials is that of cost of goods sold. Recall that you were introduced to its concept in Chapter 1 and its calculation in Chapter 6. Notice now how this calculation helps you to distinguish between raw materials inventory, which is a balance sheet account, and its related raw materials used, which is a product cost that only becomes an expense when the finished product is sold.

Suppose you begin an accounting period with raw materials valued at $15,000 from the preceding period, purchase $100,000 of the same raw materials during the current period, and determine that you have $12,000 of raw materials on hand at the end of the period. Instead of calculating the cost of goods sold, you use the same concept to calculate the cost of raw materials used during the period as shown here:

Raw materials inventory, 1/1	$ 15,000
Add: Raw materials purchases	100,000
Raw materials available	115,000
Deduct: Raw materials inventory, 12/31	(12,000)
Raw materials used	$103,000

The Raw Materials Inventory account is an asset and will be reported in the end-of-year balance sheet as having a $12,000 balance. The raw materials used of $103,000, however, represent product costs that are reported as assets until the products containing those raw material costs are sold. Only then are these costs of raw materials released to the Cost of Goods Sold account reported in the income statement. Later sections will explain exactly how this process works.

Direct Labor Cost A second major cost category is direct labor. **Direct labor (DL)** includes costs incurred from the work of employees who are *directly* involved in the manufacture of the product. By *directly involved*, we mean that they work by hand on the product or operate machinery that produces the product. This cost category includes the costs of manufacturing salaries, employee benefits such as a company health plan, and even the employer's share of employee payroll taxes. In our ongoing example, the direct labor used amounts to $50,000 during the current period. Once again, this amount represents a product cost and is not reported as cost of goods sold until the products containing these direct labor costs are sold.

Manufacturing Overhead Cost The last major cost category, **manufacturing overhead (MO)** also known as factory overhead, is composed of indirect costs that are essential to the production process. By **indirect costs**, we mean costs that are not directly traceable to individual product units. Examples include heat, light, and power, as well as the yearly depreciation cost of the building within which the manufacturing process is conducted. Other examples include materials such as machine oils, paint, and nails; building costs, such as property taxes, casualty insurance, and depreciation on machinery; and the indirect labor costs of supervisors, janitors, and so on that do not represent direct work on the product. These indirect costs are referred to as *overhead*, a term you can remember by visualizing heat rising, factory lighting above the work floor, or the building as "the roof over your head"—in other words, costs that are literally over your head.

See if you have grasped the concept of manufacturing overhead by determining which of the following six costs are manufacturing overhead:

1.	Depreciation—factory	5,000
2.	Depreciation—office	3,000
3.	Factory utilities	6,000
4.	Sales personnel salaries	17,500
5.	Miscellaneous office expenses	750
6.	Miscellaneous factory expenses	4,000

If you said that costs 1, 3, and 6 are manufacturing overhead, you'd be correct. This is because manufacturing overhead includes only those indirect costs that relate to the manufacturing process. Thus, the correct manufacturing overhead cost, also a product cost, is $15,000 ($5,000 + $6,000 + $4,000).

Total Manufacturing Cost Now that you understand the nature of raw materials cost, direct labor cost, and manufacturing overhead cost, see if you can correctly calculate the total manufacturing cost in our ongoing example. When you are finished, compare your answer to the answer shown here:

Raw materials used	$103,000
Direct labor used	50,000
Manufacturing overhead incurred	15,000
Total manufacturing cost incurred	$168,000

As illustrated here, the three major cost categories are combined to account for the current year's manufacturing cost. To better understand why the $168,000 does *not* represent the amount to be reported in the income statement, we need to examine the concept of cost of goods manufactured.

Cost of Goods Manufactured The second inventory account involved in most manufacturing is work in process inventory. In the following illustration of our ongoing example, study the relationships among this account, total manufacturing cost, and cost of goods manufactured:

Work in process inventory, 1/1		$ 65,000
Add: Total manufacturing costs:		
1. Raw materials used ($15,000 + $100,000 − $12,000)	$103,000	
2. Direct labor used (given)	50,000	
3. Manufacturing overhead incurred ($5,000 + 6,000 + 4,000)	15,000	168,000
Work in process inventory available		$233,000
Deduct: Work in process inventory, 12/31		(70,000)
Cost of goods manufactured		$163,000

From careful study of this illustration, you should conclude that the **Work in Process Inventory (WIP)** account represents costs of raw materials, direct labor, and manufacturing overhead that attach to product units that have not been completely manufactured, what can be called unfinished goods. In contrast, **cost of goods manufactured (COGM)** represents costs of raw materials, direct labor, and manufacturing overhead that attach to product units that have been completely manufactured. In other words, it is a collection of product costs that are ready for sale. Despite its importance, the cost of goods manufactured amount is not itself reported in the income statement. As shown next, that role is reserved for the manufacturing version of cost of goods sold.

Manufacturing Cost of Goods Sold The third and final inventory account involved in the manufacturing process is finished goods inventory. The **Finished Goods Inventory (FG)** account includes the cost of completed but unsold units of product. In our example, the $163,000 cost of goods manufactured represents the cost of manufacturing this period's finished goods. Thus, to calculate the total cost of goods available for sale, you'll need to add the cost of goods manufactured to last period's inventory of finished goods as shown here:

Finished goods inventory, 1/1	$ 30,000
Add: Cost of goods manufactured	163,000
Cost of goods available for sale	$193,000
Deduct: Finished goods inventory, 12/31	(45,000)
Manufactured cost of goods sold	$148,000

This addition might look familiar to you since it is, in fact, equivalent to adding purchases of a merchandiser to its beginning merchandise inventory account. As you study the cost of goods manufactured and sold statement shown in Figure 10-9, remember that the $148,000 amount—not the $103,000, the $168,000, or the $163,000—is the proper expense amount to report in the income statement.

FIGURE 10-9

Cost of goods manufactured and sold statement

HYPOTHETICAL MANUFACTURING COMPANY
Cost of Goods Sold Statement
For the Year Ended December 31

Work in process inventory, 1/1		$ 65,000
Add: Manufacturing costs		
Raw material used:		
Raw material inventory, 1/1	$ 15,000	
Add: Raw material purchases	100,000	
Raw material available	115,000	
Deduct: Raw material inventory, 12/31	(12,000)	103,000
Direct labor used		50,000
Manufacturing overhead incurred		15,000
Work in process inventory available		233,000
Deduct: Work in process inventory, 12/31		(70,000)
Cost of goods manufactured		**$163,000**
Finished goods inventory, 1/1		$ 30,000
Add: Cost of goods manufactured		163,000
Cost of goods available for sale		193,000
Deduct: Finished goods inventory, 12/31		(45,000)
Manufacturing cost of goods sold		**$148,000**

This amount represents product costs that are not yet reported on the income statement.

This entire amount must be reported on the income statement.

Essential to your comprehension of both the concept of cost of goods manufactured and the concept of **manufacturing cost of goods sold (COGS)** is that the entire statement shown in Figure 10-9 is simply the cost of goods sold concept repeated three times as shown in Figure 10-10. Notice the similarity among these three calculations and how similar each calculation is to the cost of goods sold calculation for Transaction U on page 479.

FIGURE 10-10

Repeating the cost of goods sold concept three times

Three-step calculation of a manufacturer's cost of goods sold:

Step 1: Calculate raw materials used		
Raw material inventory, 1/1		$ 15,000
Add: Raw material purchases		100,000
Raw material available		115,000
Deduct: Raw material inventory, 12/31		(12,000)
Raw material used		$103,000
Step 2: Calculate cost of goods manufactured		
Work in process inventory, 1/1		$ 65,000
Add: Total manufacturing costs:		
1. Raw material used	$103,000	
2. Direct labor used	50,000	
3. Manufacturing overhead incurred	15,000	168,000
Work in process inventory available		233,000
Deduct: Work in process inventory, 12/31		(70,000)
Cost of goods manufactured		$163,000
Step 3: Calculate Cost of Goods Sold		
Finished goods inventory, 1/1		$30,000
Add: Cost of goods manufactured		163,000
Cost of goods available for sale		193,000
Deduct: Finished goods inventory, 12/31		(45,000)
Manufacturing cost of goods sold		$148,000

Finally, study the following diagram to see how the manufacturing cost flow process can be described using three steps:

Step 1 Raw Materials Storeroom			**Step 2 Manufacturing Process, Plant, or Assembly Line**			**Step 3 Finished Goods Storeroom/Warehouse**	
Raw materials, 1/1	$ 15,000						
Raw materials purchases	100,000						
Raw materials, 12/31	(12,000)		Work in process, 1/1	$ 65,000			
Raw materials used	**$103,000**	→	**Raw materials used**	**103,000**			
			Direct labor used	50,000			
			Manufacturing overhead incurred	15,000			
$103,000 transferred from Raw Materials Inventory into Work in Process Inventory			Work in process, 12/31	(70,000)		Finished goods, 1/1	$ 30,000
			Cost of goods manufactured	**$163,000**	→	**Cost of goods manufactured**	**163,000**
						Finished goods, 12/31	(45,000)
						Cost of goods sold	$148,000
			$163,000 transferred from Work in Process Inventory into Finished Goods Inventory			$148,000 transferred from Finished Goods Inventory into the Cost of Goods Sold account	

Notice that each step is associated with its own inventory account—Raw Materials Inventory, Work in Process Inventory, and Finished Goods Inventory—and that taken together, these steps result in the calculation of the Cost of Goods Sold account.

Applying Manufacturing Concepts to Real-World Financial Statements Most real-world manufacturing companies include the individual amounts of the three manufacturing inventory accounts in their annual report notes, reporting their total amount in the asset account titled Inventories on their balance sheets. Figure 10-11 provides two examples of this practice with the balance sheet and underlying footnotes of the Gillette Company (Figure 10-11a) and Seagate Technology, Inc. (Figure 10-11b). Notice that the presentation used by these companies is almost identical, with the small exception that Seagate uses the term *components* to more accurately reflect its form of raw *materials*.

FIGURE 10-11a Disclosure of manufacturing inventories for the Gillette Company

The Gillette Company and Subsidiary Companies
Consolidated Balance Sheet
December 31, 2001 and 2000
(Millions, except per share amount)

Assets	2001	2000
Current assets		
Cash and cash equivalents	$ 947	$ 62
Trade receivables, less allowances: 2001—$69; 2000—$81	1,473	2,128
Other receivables	313	378
Inventories	1,011	1,162
Deferred income taxes	481	566
Other current assets	207	197
Net assets of discontinued operations	23	189
Total current assets	4,455	4,682
Property, plant, and equipment, at cost less accumulated depreciation	3,548	3,550
Intangible assets. less accumulated amortization	1,353	1,574
Other assets	613	596
	$9,969	$10,402

SUPPLEMENTAL BALANCE SHEET INFORMATION

Inventories (Millions)	December 31, 2001	December 31, 2000
Raw materials and supplies	$ 130	$ 153
Work in process	183	194
Finished goods	698	815
	$1,011	$1,162

Despite the fact that a manufacturer's calculation of cost of goods sold is more complicated than a merchandiser's, their income statement presentations of this account are usually identical. They both report the title "Cost of Goods Sold" or Cost of Sales" in a single line of the income statement.

FIGURE 10-11b Disclosure of manufacturing inventories for Seagate Technology

SEAGATE TECHNOLOGY

Consolidated Balance Sheets
(In millions, except share data)
Assets

	June 30, 2000	July 2, 1999
Cash and cash equivalents	$ 875	$ 396
Short-term investments	1,140	1,227
Accounts receivable, net	678	872
Inventories	430	451
Deferred income taxes	219	252
Other current assets	167	114
Total Current Assets	3,509	3,312

SEAGATE TECHNOLOGY

Notes to Consolidated Financial Statement

Inventories

Inventories are summarized below:

	2000	1999
	(in millions)	
Components	$142	$143
Work in process	51	54
Finished goods	237	254
	$430	$451

Construction

The construction industry includes both small residential builders or contractors who usually complete their projects in less than a year and large specialized construction companies that often take longer than one year to complete their work. **Long-term construction companies** build aircraft, bridges and dams, skyscrapers, cruise ships, sports stadiums, and other large structures. As you might have guessed, accounting for long-term construction contracts includes accounts that are unlike any you have studied so far. And so, to help you become a more knowledgeable user of financial statements, this section focuses exclusively on these long-term construction companies. As you will see, the key difference between the financial statements of the construction industry and those of other industries is almost exclusively the result of its unique operating activities.

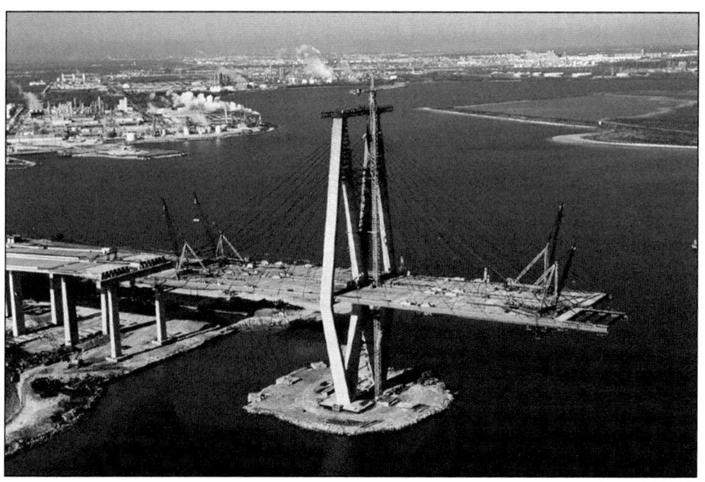

Construction companies, such as the one building this bridge, use some accounting methods that are unique to their industry.

How the Operating Activities of Construction Companies Affect Their Financial Statements

Recall from Chapter 7 that most industries recognize revenue at the point of sale because by that point, most activities necessary for and associated with the production of revenue have been completed. The term *sale* is generally interpreted to mean when goods are delivered or services are performed. When you receive a haircut, for example, the hair stylist can measure and record both the revenue and related expenses by using performance of services as a criterion.

In the construction industry, point of sale occurs when construction is completed. Consistent with the use of point of sale by other businesses, the long-term construction industry does allow revenues and expenses to be recognized when construction is completed under the completed-contract method. However, this method might seriously misstate the contractor's net income for projects that exceed one year in length. Assume, for example, that an ocean liner takes three years to complete. It would be inaccurate to report that no revenue was earned and no expense was incurred for the first two years of construction. Since operating activity takes place well before the point at which the customer takes ownership, the long-term construction industry also allows revenues and expenses to be recognized before delivery or performance of services (that is, completion of construction) under the percentage-of-completion method. This idea should seem reasonable to you, since under the accrual basis, revenue should be reported in the time period it is earned/produced. Let's now examine these two methods in more detail.

Two Income Recognition Methods[2]

You just learned that construction companies may recognize their income at the point of sale by using the completed-contract method. The **completed-contract method** records no project revenues or expenses until the period in which the project is completed. This method is acceptable when there is a lack of dependable estimates available or inherent hazards make forecasts uncertain. But, the accounting profession also allows recognition of income sooner for long-term construction contracts by using the percentage-of-completion method. The **percentage-of-completion method** enables you to record a project's revenues and expenses during production. This method is

[2] In the interest of helping you understand the essential concepts of construction accounting, the transactions used here are less complex than those in actual practice. Once you understand these essentials, more realistic accounting practices will be introduced in this chapter.

preferable when both cost and progress toward completion estimates are reasonably dependable. Let's use the following diagram to distinguish between the timing of income recognition for these methods.

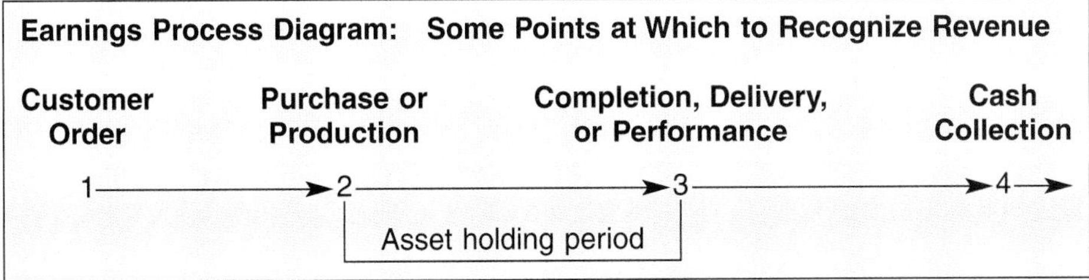

The percentage-of-completion method recognizes income during the period between points 2 and 3, whereas the completed-contract method recognizes income at point 3. To improve your understanding, let's now apply these methods to some examples.

Data Assume that a construction company was formed in Year 1 with capital stock of $1 million contributed in cash. In that same year, the company contracted to build a small corporate jet. The total contract price was $6 million with estimated construction costs of $5 million. Actual cost incurred and cash collections during the two-year contract period were as follows:

	Cash Collected	Costs Incurred and Paid
Year 1	$3,000,000	$4,000,000
Year 2	3,000,000	1,000,000

Mastering Performance Objective 32 will add to your understanding of the two methods used to transform this long-term construction company data into financial statements:

YOUR PERFORMANCE OBJECTIVE 32
Calculate net income and **prepare** both the income statements and balance sheets under the percentage-of-completion and completed-contract methods.

Let's begin by looking at the simpler of the two methods, the completed-contract method. We'll see how this method works by examining its income statements, balance sheets, and statements of retained earnings for the company's first two years.

The Completed-Contract Method

Using our example, here are the income statements generated by the completed contract method:

Completed-contract income statements

Year 1:	No revenue, expense, or net income is reported until completion.		
Year 2:	Revenue	$6,000,000	(All revenue recognized)
	Expense	5,000,000	(All expense recognized)
	Net income	$1,000,000	(Project net income)

Consistent with its title, the completed-contract method does not report revenue or expense in Year 1 because the project is incomplete. When the project is completed in Year 2, the second year income statement includes all of the project's revenues and expenses.

Next, here is the Year 1 balance sheet generated by the completed-contract method:

Completed-contract balance sheet, Year 1			
Cash	$ –0–	Deferred revenue (L)	$3,000,000
Construction in progress	4,000,000	Capital stock	1,000,000
Total assets	$4,000,000	Total liabilities and owners' equity	$4,000,000

You can verify the zero cash balance if you recall that the company began with $1 million cash from issuance of its stock, received $3 million cash, and disbursed $4 million cash ($1,000,000 + $3,000,000 − $4,000,000 = $0). The $4 million **construction in progress** also known as *construction in process* is an asset account created by the incurrence of a $4 million cost that is also paid in cash. Normally, you would record an incurred cost as an expense, but you can't do that until Year 2 under the completed-contract method. Thus, you have to choose another account category. Since these incurred but unexpensed costs represent work that is incomplete or still in process (recall the manufacturing account called Work in Process), we'll use the asset account Construction in Progress. This selection makes perfect sense if you recall that many assets are simply deferred expenses. The transaction analysis and journal entry underlying the $4 million Construction in Progress account are shown here:

$4,000,000 cash payment in Year 1 (in thousands)

Transaction Analysis					Journal Entry		
	Fundamental Accounting Equation						
Account Titles	Assets	= Liabilities	+ Owners' Equity		Account Titles	Debit	Credit
Construction in Progress	4,000				Construction in Progress	4,000	
Cash	(4,000)				Cash		4,000

We recorded an asset rather than an expense in the preceding transaction because the completed-contract method dictates that both revenue and expense are postponed, or deferred, until construction is completed. For this very reason, the cash receipt of $3 million must be offset by a liability account titled Deferred Revenue rather than by a revenue account. The transaction analysis and journal entry underlying the $3 million liability follow.

$3,000,000 cash collection in Year 1 (in thousands)

Transaction Analysis					Journal Entry		
	Fundamental Accounting Equation						
Account Titles	Assets	= Liabilities	+ Owners' Equity		Account Titles	Debit	Credit
Cash	3,000				Cash	3,000	
Deferred Revenue		3,000			Deferred Revenue		3,000

To complete the explanation of the first year balance sheet, a Capital Stock account appears in the amount of $1 million to represent the stock issuance that was used to finance this business. Finally, notice that no retained earnings balance is reported, since a new company has no beginning retained earnings balance, and this company does not report any net income in Year 1.

Now that you understand how the Year 1 balance sheet was prepared, let's study the Year 2 balance sheet prepared under the completed-contract method:

Completed-contract balance sheet, Year 2			
Cash	$2,000,000	Capital stock	$1,000,000
		Retained earnings	1,000,000
Total assets	$2,000,000	Total liabilities and owners' equity	$2,000,000

Since the beginning cash balance of zero was increased by $3 million in cash receipts and reduced by $1 million in cash payments, the ending balance is $2 million. Existing balances in both the Construction in Progress account and the Deferred Revenue account are eliminated because revenue of $6 million and expense of $5 million are recorded in their entirety. To better understand this process, let's look at how the cash payment in Year 2 was recorded:

$1,000,000 cash payment in Year 2 (in thousands)

Transaction Analysis				Journal Entry		
	Fundamental Accounting Equation					
Account Titles	Assets	= Liabilities +	Owners' Equity	Account Titles	Debit	Credit
Construction Expense			(5,000)	Construction Expense	5,000	
Construction in Progress	(4,000)			Construction in Progress		4,000
Cash	(1,000)			Cash		1,000

As you can see, the Construction in Progress account balance of $4 million and the $1 million cash payment are collectively expensed for $5 million. To complete our analysis, let's look at how the cash receipt in Year 2 was recorded:

$3,000,000 cash collection in Year 2 (in thousands)

Transaction Analysis				Journal Entry		
	Fundamental Accounting Equation					
Account Titles	Assets	= Liabilities +	Owners' Equity	Account Titles	Debit	Credit
Cash	3,000			Cash	3,000	
Deferred Revenue		(3,000)		Deferred Revenue	3,000	
Construction Revenue			6,000	Construction Revenue		6,000

Notice that the total revenue is composed of this year's cash sales and the conversion of last year's cash advance from unearned revenue to earned revenue. Since the Deferred Revenue account had a $3 million balance that is reduced by $3 million, it has no balance at the end of the second year.

Now that you have viewed the completed-contract income statements and balance sheets for a two-year period, let's tie all this information together with the completed-contract statements of retained earnings.

Completed-contract statements of retained earnings, Years 1 and 2

	Year 1	Year 2
Retained earnings, beginning	–0–	$ –0–
Add: Net income	–0–	1,000,000
Subtotal	–0–	1,000,000
Deduct: Dividends	–0–	–0–
Retained earnings, ending	–0–	$1,000,000

Since the completed-contract method recognizes no income in years other than the year in which construction is complete, it is reasonable that retained earnings did not increase until Year 2. Let's now see how the percentage-of-completion method differs from the completed-contract method.

The Percentage-of-Completion Method

The elementary concept that underlies the percentage-of-completion method is *the part to the whole*. Whether you realize it or not, you use this concept almost every day. It is likely, for example, that you have already estimated the degree to which you have finished this chapter at least once. That is, you determined the number of pages you had read so far (numerator), determined the total number of chapter pages to read (denominator), compared the numerator to the denominator in the form of a ratio, and calculated the percentage of completion. Think of the many ways you might consciously or unconsciously perform this calculation on a daily basis—length of class time remaining, length of commute remaining between class and home, percentage of exercise completed in miles, repetitions, or sets, and so on.

When you apply this concept to long-term construction projects, you'll find that the dollar cost incurred by the contractor is the unit most often used when calculating a contractor's percentage of completion. That is, if the estimated total cost of construction is \$1,000,000 and the contractor incurs \$250,000 of costs, the percentage of completion is 25% (\$250,000/\$1,000,000). This concept is expressed by the following formula:

$$\text{Percentage of Completion} = \frac{\text{Costs Incurred Each Period}}{\text{Total Estimated Cost}}$$

In other words, you calculate the percentage of completion by dividing the costs incurred each period (numerator) by the total estimated costs to be incurred over the life of the project (denominator). Let's now apply this formula to the two-year construction example we used for the completed-contract method. Once again, let's start with the income statements.

Each of the annual income statements represents a part of a whole, the project's two-year income statement. Avoid the temptation to simply treat each year's income statement as one-half of this two-year income statement, since it is unlikely that the operating activities of each year are equally productive. Instead, use the construction costs as your measure of the percentage of completion. Doing so, you should determine that 4/5, or 80%, of total construction costs are incurred in Year 1 [\$4,000,000/(\$4,000,000 + \$1,000,000)]. The first step in calculating income under the percentage-of-completion method is to view the total project income statement. Then you can multiply both total revenue and expense by 80%[3] to create your Year 1 income statement:

Percentage-of-completion income statements

	The Whole	Percentage of Completion		Year 1 A Part of the Whole
Revenue	\$6,000,000	× .8	Revenue	\$4,800,000
Expense	5,000,000	× .8	Expense	4,000,000
Net income	\$1,000,000		Net income	\$ 800,000

Once you have calculated all but the last year, you can save time by simply subtracting the first year figures from the totals as shown here:

[3] Since an expense may be defined as the cost incurred, you can save one multiplication if you realize that the cost incurred in such problems equals the construction expense.

Year 2		
Revenue	$1,200,000	($6,000,000 − $4,800,000 or $6,000,000 × .2)
Expense	1,000,000	(Cost incurred during year or $5,000,000 × .2)
Net income	$ 200,000	($1,200,000 − $1,000,000 or $1,000,000 − $800,000)

Next, let's look at the balance sheet for the first year of our example.

Percentage-of-completion balance sheet, Year 1			
Cash	$ −0−	Capital stock	$1,000,000
Accounts receivable	1,800,000	Retained earnings	800,000
Total assets	$1,800,000	Total liabilities and owners' equity	$1,800,000

Note that the Cash and Capital Stock account balances are identical to their corresponding balances in the Year 1 completed-contract balance sheet. This is no coincidence, since the choice of income recognition method does not affect such nonoperating accounts. The $800,000 retained earnings balance simply represents the first year percentage-of-completion income that has been transferred to retained earnings at the end of the period. As shown next, the $1,800,000 accounts receivable balance represents the portion of the $4,800,000 percentage-of-completion revenue that was not received in cash.

$3,000,000 cash collection in Year 1 (in thousands)

Transaction Analysis					Journal Entry		
	Fundamental Accounting Equation						
Account Titles	Assets	= Liabilities	+	Owners' Equity	Account Titles	Debit	Credit
Cash	3,000				Cash	3,000	
Account Receivable	1,800				Account Receivable	1,800	
Construction Revenue				4,800	Construction Revenue		4,800

To complete the Year 1 activity, you must also record the following information:

$4,000,000 cost incurred and paid in Year 1 (in thousands)

Transaction Analysis					Journal Entry		
	Fundamental Accounting Equation						
Account Titles	Assets	= Liabilities	+	Owners' Equity	Account Titles	Debit	Credit
Construction Expense				(4,000)	Construction Expense	4,000	
Cash	(4,000)				Cash		4,000

The fact that the choice of income recognition method does not affect such accounts as Cash and Capital Stock is illustrated once more in the Year 2 balance sheet.

Percentage-of-completion balance sheet, Year 2			
Cash	$2,000,000	Capital stock	$1,000,000
Accounts receivable	−0−	Retained earnings	1,000,000
Total assets	$2,000,000	Total liabilities and owners' equity	$2,000,000

The zero balance in accounts receivable results from the $3,000,000 cash receipts being split into a $1,200,000 cash sale and a $1,800,000 collection on accounts receivable in the transaction analysis and journal entry illustrated here.

$3,000,000 cash collection in Year 2 (in thousands)

Transaction Analysis				Journal Entry		
	Fundamental Accounting Equation					
Account Titles	**Assets**	**= Liabilities +**	**Owners' Equity**	**Account Titles**	**Debit**	**Credit**
Cash	3,000			Cash	3,000	
Account Receivable	(1,800)			Account Receivable		1,800
Construction Revenue			1,200	Construction Revenue		1,200

Once again, you must record the expense incurrence and cash paid in Year 2 as shown here:

$1,000,000 cost incurred and paid in Year 2 (in thousands)

Transaction Analysis				Journal Entry		
	Fundamental Accounting Equation					
Account Titles	**Assets**	**= Liabilities +**	**Owners' Equity**	**Account Titles**	**Debit**	**Credit**
Construction Expense			(1,000)	Construction Expense	1,000	
Cash	(1,000)			Cash		1,000

The $1,000,000 balance in retained earnings represents the two-year project net income of $6,000,000 revenue minus $5,000,000 expense or equivalently $800,000 of Year 1 income plus $200,000 of Year 2 income recognized under the percentage-of-completion method. These concepts are more clearly illustrated in the following statements:

Percentage-of-completion statements of retained earnings, Years 1 and 2

	Year 1	Year 2
Retained earnings, beginning	$ –0–	$ 800,000
Add: Net income	800,000	200,000
Subtotal	800,000	1,000,000
Deduct: Dividends	–0–	–0–
Retained earnings, ending	$800,000	$1,000,000

Note that we have restricted our focus to the operating activities of construction companies. Although these companies have significant financing and investing activities, these activities do not vary significantly from the same activities of other industries and, therefore, are not distinctive enough for us to consider here.

INSIGHT

All Income Methods Recognize the Same Income Over Time

Take a few minutes and compare the retained earnings statements under the percentage-of-completion method with those for the completed-contract method. Notice anything interesting? The retained earnings balance under both methods is identical at the completion of the project. That is, the total income recognized in our examples was $1 million under both methods.

Do you know why that is? It's because no matter what income allocation method you use, over long enough time periods, the total income under all methods is the same. Thus, income recognition methods differ only in how they calculate the parts of a whole. Although different income recognition methods might produce markedly different income statement figures from one year to another, no income method reports more or less total income than any other.

The important insight you should gain here is that no matter how total net income (the whole) is divided into yearly net income (the parts of a whole), the same cumulative net income is recognized by all methods. This concept is very important and you will see it reinforced more than once in future chapters of this textbook.

Which Income Recognition Method Is Preferable?

Suppose you were looking at the financial statements of two long-term construction companies. And suppose also that one company used the percentage-of-completion method and the other used the completed-contract method. Although each company could be using the right method for its particular circumstances, the percentage-of-completion method often provides a better measure of performance because it more accurately describes the results of operations than does the completed-contract method. It is relatively misleading, for example, for a contractor to be fully engaged for three years in the construction of a long-term project, but to not report income until Year 3. Yet, this very result can occur if the completed-contract method is properly applied. The clear superiority of the percentage-of-completion method is reflected by its wide–spread popularity. For example, *Accounting Trends and Techniques* reported in 2001 that of the 95 companies reporting long-term construction contracts, 90 companies used the percentage-of-completion method, and only five used the completed-contract method.

The percentage-of-completion method should be used whenever the total contract price or revenue is available and there is relative certainty about the project's future construction costs. The completed-contract method should be used, however, whenever the preceding conditions do not hold or the entity has mostly short-term projects or its long-term projects are evenly distributed over time.

How to Apply Your Understanding of the Construction Industry to Interpret Its Financial Statements

Now that you understand the essential concepts underlying accounting for long-term construction contracts, it is necessary to learn some additional concepts so that you can interpret the financial statements of real construction companies. Since the percentage-of-completion method is by far the more popular method, let's look at the balance sheet of one company and a note to the financial statements of another company, both of whom use it. Figure 10-12 is the balance sheet of the **Boeing Company**, the largest aerospace company in the world and the largest manufacturer of commercial airplanes, military aircraft, and satellites. Figure 10-13 is a note that accompanies the balance sheet of **Harmon Industries, Inc.**, a leading manufacturer of systems and services to freight and transit railroads throughout the world. A careful examination of each presentation yields the following construction related accounts:

The Boeing Company (see Figure 10-12)

Asset: Accounts receivable
Asset: Inventories, net of advances and progress billings
Liability: Advances in excess of related costs

FIGURE 10-12 Construction related accounts of the Boeing Company

THE BOEING COMPANY
Consolidated Statements of Financial Position
for Years 2001 and 2000
(Dollars in millions except per share data)

	2001	2000
Assets		
Cash and cash equivalents	**$ 633**	$1,010
Accounts receivable	**5,156**	5,519
Current portion of customer and commercial financing	**1,053**	995
Deferred income taxes	**2,444**	2,137
Inventories, net of advances and progress billings	**6,920**	6,852
Total current assets	**16,206**	16,513
Customer and commercial financing	**9,345**	5,964
Property, plant, and equipment, net	**8,459**	8,814
Goodwill and acquired intangibles, net	**6,443**	5,214
Prepaid pension expense	**5,838**	4,845
Deferred income taxes		60
Other assets	**2,052**	1,267
Total Assets	**$48,343**	$42,677
Liabilities and Shareholders' Equity		
Accounts payable and other liabilities	**$13,872**	$12,312
Advances in excess of related costs	**4,306**	3,517
Income taxes payable	**909**	1,866
Short-term debt and current portion of long-term debt	**1,399**	1,232
Total current liabilities	**20,486**	18,927
Deferred income taxes	**177**	
Accrued retiree health care	**5,367**	5,163
Deferred lease income	**622**	
Long-term debt	**10,866**	7,567
Shareholders' equity:		
Common shares, par value $5.00—1,200,000,000 shares authorized;		
Shares issued—1,011,870,159 and 1,011,870,159	**5,059**	5,059
Additional paid-in capital	**1,975**	2,693
Treasury shares, at cost—174,289,720 and 136,385,222	**(8,509)**	(6,221)
Retained earnings	**14,340**	12,090
Accumulated other comprehensive income (loss)	**(485)**	(2)
Unearned compensation	**(3)**	(7)
ShareValue Trust shares—39,691,015 and 39,156,280	**(1,552)**	(2,592)
Total shareholders' equity	**10,825**	11,020
Total Liabilities and Shareholders' Equity	**$48,343**	$42,677

Harmon Industries (see Figure 10-13)

Asset: Costs and estimated earnings in excess of billings
Liability: Billings in excess of costs and estimated earnings

Although each of the preceding accounts shown in these figures might appear different, only three distinct accounts are reported—Accounts Receivable, Construction in Progress, and Progress Billings, as the following sections will explain.

FIGURE 10-13

Reporting a construction asset (a) and construction liability (b)

HARMON INDUSTRIES, INC.
10-K 1999-12-31: Footnotes
(Dollars in thousands)

NOTE 2—Contracts in Progress
Contract costs on uncompleted contracts are as follows:

	(a) Costs and Estimated Earnings in Excess of Billings	(b) Billings in Excess of Costs and Estimated Earnings	Total
December 31, 1999:			
Costs and estimated earnings	$190,532	$189,838	$380,370
Billings	162,812	220,630	383,442
	$ 27,720	$ (30,792)	$ (3,072)
December 31, 1998:			
Costs and estimated earnings	$ 30,374	$121,701	$152,075
Billings	20,725	139,194	159,919
	$ 9,649	$ (17,493)	$ (7,844)

Balances billed, but not paid by customers under retainage provisions in contracts amounted to $5,255,000 and $2,643,000 at December 31, 1999 and 1998, respectively. Receivables on contracts in progress are considered to be collectible within 12 months.

Receivable Accounts Notice that in Figure 10-12, the second asset account presented is Accounts Receivable, an account with which you are already well acquainted. In the construction industry, however, it can also be called **Progress Billings Receivable**, *Billings Receivable*, or *Contract Billings*. No matter what title is used, however, it is a current asset that is increased whenever you invoice or bill customers and decreased whenever customers make cash payments on their accounts. In some construction companies, however, the Accounts Receivable account is divided into two components—Contract Billings and Contract Retainage, a less liquid account. As just explained, Contract Billings is simply regular billings less cash collections. *Contract Retainage*, however, represents negotiated amounts held back from the contractor until the customer determines their satisfaction with the quality of the contractor's work.

Construction in Progress Account To take a more in-depth look at how the Accounts Receivable, Construction in Progress, and Progress Billings accounts are treated under the percentage-of-completion method, let's use the identical data from our earlier example and begin with the Construction in Progress account:

Data Assume that a construction company was formed in Year 1 with capital stock of $1 million contributed in cash. In that same year, the company contracted to build a small corporate jet. The total contract price was $6 million with estimated construction costs of $5 million. Actual cost incurred and cash collections during the two-year contract period were as follows:

	Cash Collected	Costs Incurred and Paid
Year 1	$3,000,000	$4,000,000
Year 2	$3,000,000	$1,000,000

First, Construction in Progress, an inventory account, is increased for the costs incurred in completing our project as shown here

Construction costs (in thousands)

Transaction Analysis					Journal Entry		
	Fundamental Accounting Equation						
Account Titles	**Assets**	**=**	**Liabilities +**	**Owners' Equity**	**Account Titles**	**Debit**	**Credit**
Year 1:					**Year 1:**		
Construction in Progress	4,000				Construction in Progress	4,000	
Cash	(4,000)				Cash		4,000
Year 2:					**Year 2:**		
Construction in Progress	1,000				Construction in Progress	1,000	
Cash	(1,000)				Cash		1,000

In actual construction practice, however, this same inventory account is also increased by the amount of income recognized on the project as shown here.

Revenue and expense recognition (in thousands)

Transaction Analysis					Journal Entry		
	Fundamental Accounting Equation						
Account Titles	**Assets**	**=**	**Liabilities +**	**Owners' Equity**	**Account Titles**	**Debit**	**Credit**
Year 1:					**Year 1:**		
Construction Expense				(4,000)	Construction Expense	4,000	
Construction in Progress	800				Construction in Progress	800	
Construction Revenue				4,800	Construction Revenue		4,800
Year 2:					**Year 2:**		
Construction Expense				(1,000)	Construction Expense	1,000	
Construction in Progress	200				Construction in Progress	200	
Construction Revenue				1,200	Construction Revenue		1,200

Thus, under the percentage-of-completion method, the Construction in Progress Inventory account balance of $4,800,000 at the end of Year 1 is composed of costs incurred to date ($4,000,000) plus income recognized to date ($800,000). This practice of increasing an inventory account by the amount of income might well seem confusing given your prior experiences in this course. Nevertheless, the approach is perfectly valid and not unique as the following *User Focus* explains.

USER FOCUS

Not All Assets Are Reported at Cost on the Balance Sheet

Earlier in this textbook, you learned that the accounts receivable balance reported on the balance sheet does not represent historical cost as with most assets but rather uncollected sales revenue. At the point of sale, that is, both the Accounts Receivable and Sales Revenue accounts are increased by an amount equivalent to that product's sales price. Let's use the following hypothetical example to better understand this concept. Assume you have sold a product costing $10 for $12 and have, therefore, earned a $2 profit, or income. Notice that the effect of adding the product's cost to its income is to produce its

Selling price	$12	Cost of product	$10
Cost of product	10	Income realized	2
Income realized	$ 2	Sales revenue	$12

selling price or sales revenue. By definition, sales revenue is composed of both a product's cost and its recorded income ($12 in this example). As you record the revenue and receivable in the amount of its price to customers, you also record an increase to the Cost of Goods Sold expense account and a decrease to the Merchandise Inventory account in the amount of the product's historical cost ($10 in this example).

When we now substitute our construction data after one year for the data in the preceding example, the same concept emerges, namely that whenever cost is added to income, the result is revenue:

Selling price	$4,800,000	Cost of product	$4,000,000
Cost of product	4,000,000	Income realized	800,000
Income realized	$ 800,000	**Sales Revenue**	**$4,800,000**

Thus, construction companies that use the percentage-of-completion method normally report the Construction in Progress account at sales revenue or the dollar measure of the contractor's performance to date (cost plus construction value added). Since the percentage-of-completion method is designed to report income as contract work progresses, both the Construction Revenue account and the Construction in Progress account record an identical amount at the end of the first year of construction, as shown here:

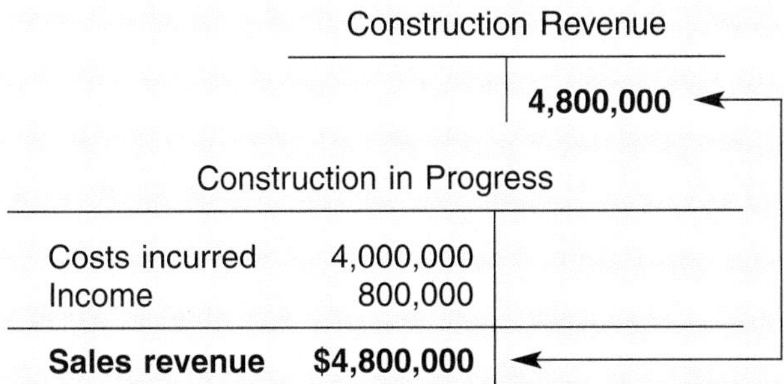

As you can see, the Construction Revenue account balance is the same as the Construction in Progress account balance of $4,800,000 reported on the balance sheet after one year of construction. Operationally, the fact that the Construction in Progress account includes both costs incurred and income calculated to date should confirm for you that it reports sales revenue.

Under the completed-contract method, however, only cost incurred is recorded in the Construction in Progress account as shown here:

Construction in Progress		
Costs incurred	4,000,000	

Since revenue cannot be realized until construction is fully complete and there is formal recognition of a constructed asset, the Construction in Progress account under the completed-contract method is accounted for at cost rather than sales revenue. The justification for this treatment is that revenue emerges from sale rather than production, that is, facts rather than estimates are recorded. Since revenue is not recorded until the project's completion, cost incurred is the valuation basis for the Construction in Progress account under the completed-contract method.

Progress Billings Account Up to now, we have consistently paired the Accounts Receivable account with the Sales Revenue account. We did so, for example, in our simplified percentage-of-completion illustration when $3 million cash was collected. In actual construction industry practice, however, the Accounts Receivable account is instead paired with an account often titled *Progress Billings on Contract* or simply **Progress Billings**, as shown here. Be sure to confirm that Accounts Receivable and Progress Billings are indeed paired in one transaction.

Progress billings (in thousands)

Transaction Analysis					Journal Entry		
	Fundamental Accounting Equation						
Account Titles	Assets	= Liabilities	+	Owners' Equity	Account Titles	Debit	Credit
Year 1:					**Year 1:**		
Accounts Receivable	4,800				Accounts Receivable	4,800	
Progress Billings	(4,800)				Progress Billings		4,800
Year 2:					**Year 2:**		
Accounts Receivable	1,200				Accounts Receivable	1,200	
Progress Billings	(1,200)				Progress Billings		1,200

The Progress Billings account is a contra asset to the Construction in Progress account, its primary account. Notice, in particular, that the Progress Billings account is measured by the amount billed. The following *User Focus* explains just how to interpret these closely related accounts under both the percentage-of-completion and completed-contract methods.

USER FOCUS

How Are Construction in Progress and Progress Billings Reported on the Balance Sheet?

Let's first examine how these accounts are reported on the balance sheet under the percentage-of-completion method. Whenever the balance in Construction in Progress, a current asset measured by the value of the work done or revenue, exceeds the balance in Progress Billings, a contra asset measured by the amount billed, the excess is reported as a current asset. This net asset represents the amount of unbilled future economic benefits that the company has constructed. Some of the titles that are used for this account are *Inventories, Net of Advances and Progress Billings* (Figure 10-12) and *Costs and Estimated Earnings* (that is, revenue) *in Excess of Billings* (Figure 10-13) and the more concisely stated **Revenues in Excess of Contract Billings.** Here is this asset's basic balance sheet presentation:

Current asset		
Revenues in excess of contract billings:		
Construction in progress	xx	
Less: Progress billings	(xx)	xx

When the opposite is true—billed amounts exceed recorded revenues—a current liability is reported. Again, this liability is formed as the combination of two accounts. In this case, there is an implied obligation by the seller to perform services already billed to the customer. That is, if the contractor has billed the customer (progress billings) for more value than the contractor has delivered (construction in progress), the contractor "owes" as yet undelivered services to its customer. Some of the titles used for this account are *Advances in Excess of Related Costs* and *Billings in Excess of Costs* and *Estimated Earnings*—that is, revenue—(refer to Figures 10-12 and 10-13, respectively) and the more concisely stated **Contract Billings in Excess of Revenues**. Here is this liability's basic balance sheet presentation:

Current liability		
Contract billings in excess of revenues		
Progress billings	xx	
Less: Construction in progress	(xx)	xx

In sharp contrast, under the completed-contract method, the corresponding asset title becomes *Costs in Excess of Contract Billings* and the corresponding liability title becomes *Contract Billings in Excess of Costs.*

Now that you are able to calculate net income and prepare both the income statements and balance sheets under the percentage-of-completion and completed-contract methods, you almost certainly will be able to more intelligently read a contractor's financial statements.

Service Companies

When you look at financial statements, how can you distinguish a service company from a merchandiser, manufacturer, or construction company? If you think about it, the typical product of a service company is its *service*—consulting, designing, marketing, and so on. That is, a **service company** is one whose *primary* operating activities involve the sale of services rather than the manufacture or resale of products to its customers. As a result, you would not expect to see either a sales revenue or cost of goods sold account in a service company's income statement. You would, however, expect to see a service revenue account. If, in addition, you find no significant inventory accounts reported on its balance sheet other than for supplies, it is clear that you are looking at a service company. Delta Airlines, for example, reports no significant inventories other than supplies in Figure 10-14.

But exceptions do exist to these rules of thumb. AT&T, for example, is generally considered to be a service company but has somewhat blurred the traditional distinction since it now produces and sells phone equipment. Nevertheless, you can

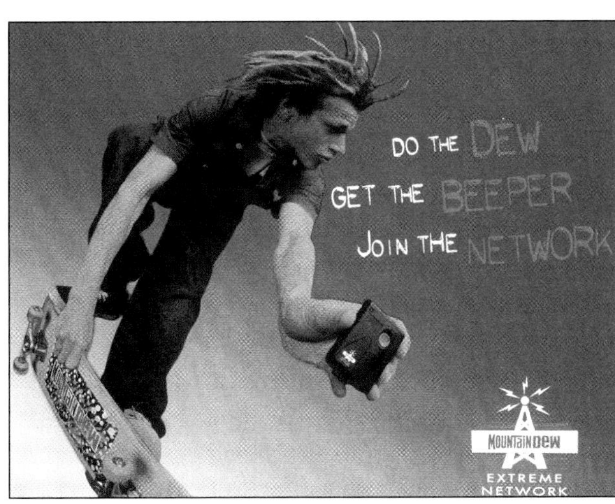

Advertising agencies, such as the one that designed this ad, are companies whose primary operating activities involve the sale of a service.

FIGURE 10-14

A service company reporting no inventory

No inventory listed under current assets

DELTA AIRLINES
Consolidated Balance Sheets
December 31, 2001 and 2000
(in millions)

	2001	2000
ASSETS		
Current Assets		
Cash and cash equivalents	$ 2,210	$ 1,364
Short-term investments	5	243
Accounts receivable, net of an allowance for uncollectible accounts of $43 at December 31, 2001 and $31 at December 31, 2000	368	406
Expendable parts and supplies inventories, net of an allowance for obsolescence of $139 at December 31, 2001 and $124 at December 31, 2000	181	170
Deferred income taxes	518	345
Fuel hedge contracts, at fair market value	55	319
Prepaid expenses and other	230	358
Total current assets	3,567	3,205
Property and Equipment		
Flight equipment	19,427	17,371
Less: Accumulated depreciation	(5,730)	(5,139)
Flight equipment, net	13,697	12,232
Flight equipment under capital leases	382	484
Less: Accumulated amortization	(262)	(324)
Flight equipment under capital leases, net	120	160
Ground property and equipment	4,412	4,371
Less: Accumulated depreciation	(2,355)	(2,313)
Ground property and equipment, net	2,057	2,058
Advance payments for equipment	223	390
Total property and equipment, net	16,097	14,840
Other Assets		
Investments in debt and equity securities	96	339
Investments in associated companies	180	222
Cost in excess of net assets acquired, net of accumulated amortization of $253 at December 31, 2001 and $196 at December 31, 2000	2,092	2,149
Operating rights and other intangibles, net of accumulated amortization of $246 at December 31, 2001 and $236 at December 31, 2000	94	102
Restricted investments for Boston airport terminal project	475	—
Other noncurrent assets	1,004	1,074
Total other assets	3,941	3,886
Total assets	$23,605	$21,931

confirm AT&T's primary identity as a service company by looking at its revenue section in Figure 10-15 and noting that its service revenue is more than twice the size of its product revenue. This example illustrates how important it is to interpret data rather than to mindlessly follow the rules of thumb described earlier.

Service companies cover a much wider range of business operations than do other industries. It is difficult for manufacturing businesses, for example, to vary much since

FIGURE 10-15 A service company having both service and sales revenue

AT&T CORP. AND SUBSIDIARIES
Consolidated Statements of Income
Years Ended December 31, 1995, 1994, and 1993
(Dollars in millions, except per share amounts)

	1995	1994	1993
Sales and Revenues			
Telecommunications services	**$47,277**	$44,600	$42,779
Products and systems	**22,412**	21,161	17,925
Rentals and other services	**6,189**	6,216	6,143
Financial services and leasing	**3,731**	3,117	2,504
Total revenues	**79,609**	75,094	69,351
Costs			
Telecommunications services			
Access and other interconnection costs	**17,618**	17,797	17,772
Other costs	**9,123**	7,873	7,937
Total telecommunications services	**26,741**	25,670	25,709
Products and systems	**16,045**	13,273	10,966
Rentals and other services	**4,098**	3,287	3,319
Financial services and leasing	**2,646**	2,152	1,711
Total costs	**49,530**	44,382	41,705
Gross margin	**30,079**	30,712	27,646
Operating Expenses			
Selling, general and administrative expenses	**25,146**	19,653	18,037
Research and development expenses	**3,718**	3,110	3,111
Total operating expenses	**28,864**	22,763	21,148
Operating income	**1,215**	7,949	6,498
Other income – net	**458**	293	546
Loss on sale of stock by subsidiary	—	—	9
Interest expense	**738**	724	1,032
Income before income taxes and cumulative effects of accounting changes	**935**	7,518	6,003
Provision for income taxes	**796**	2,808	2,301
Income before cumulative effects of accounting changes	**139**	4,710	3,702
Cumulative effects on prior years of changes in accounting for:			
Postretirement benefits (net of income tax benefit of $4,294)	—	—	(7,023)
Postemployment benefits (net of income tax benefit of $681)	—	—	(1,128)
Income taxes	—	—	(1,457)
Cumulative effects of accounting changes	—	—	(9,608)
Net Income (Loss)	**$ 139**	$ 4,710	$ (5,906)
Weighted-average common shares outstanding (millions)	**1,592**	1,564	1,547
Per Common Share:			
Income before cumulative effects of accounting changes	**$ 0.09**	$ 3.01	$ 2.39
Cumulative effects of accounting changes	—	—	(6.21)
Net Income (Loss)	**$ 0.09**	$ 3.01	$ (3.82)

Telecommunication services is more than twice as large as the sales revenue from Products and Systems

they have a common thread—they add to a product's value through the application of material, labor, and overhead. Service companies, however, provide a much more diverse set of services in such varied businesses as banking, insurance, hospitals, airlines, and nonprofit organizations that provide religious, educational, civic, and social services such as Rotary International or Kiwanis.

One very noteworthy type of service company is the **financial service company** such as a bank or other financial institution. As you will see in the next section, banks, in particular, prepare financial statements that are very different from nonfinancial service companies.

Financial Service Companies

The financial services industry includes banks such as Wells Fargo and Bank of America, insurance companies such as State Farm Insurance and Transamerica Corporation, real estate brokerage firms such as Century 21 and Coldwell Banker, and stock brokerage firms such as Merrill Lynch and Charles Schwab. Because the financial services industry is so diverse, we will, for simplicity's sake, concentrate solely on the financial statements of banks and how they differ from those of nonfinancial service industries. Unlike any other industry, the primary operating activity of a bank is to earn interest income on its investments and loans. In contrast, generating interest income in every other industry is considered to be a peripheral operating activity.

Banks engage in a two-step process to produce their interest income. First, they borrow funds from depositors, other banks, and the Federal Reserve. Funds from depositors include three types of deposit accounts: demand, savings, and time deposits. **Demand deposits** are checking accounts, which entitle their owners to withdraw funds on demand, to write checks on the account, and, increasingly common, to earn interest on their balances. Demand deposits may be owned by individuals, government entities, and business organizations and are our society's basic medium of exchange, accounting for about three-fourths of our money supply. **Savings deposits** are the traditional form of savings accounts, which earn interest for individuals, business entities, and nonprofit organizations. The largest source of funds for banks is time deposits. **Time deposits**, unlike demand deposits, are legally due on a specific maturity date and may be owned by both individuals and corporations. Examples include savings certificates, money market certificates, and certificates of deposit. Besides depositors, banks also borrow funds from other banks that act as agents for wholesale money markets and from the Federal Reserve. These two types of borrowed funds are generally for a short term and are used primarily by only large banks.

To illustrate this borrowing process, assume a $1 million transaction in which the bank acquires cash and other liquid assets and incurs liabilities to various creditors as follows:

Bank acquisition of funds (in thousands)

Transaction Analysis						Journal Entry		
	Fundamental Accounting Equation							
Account Titles	**Assets**	**=**	**Liabilities**	**+**	**Owners' Equity**	**Account Titles**	**Debit**	**Credit**
Cash, etc.	1,000					Cash, etc.	1,000	
Deposit Accounts			750			Deposit Accounts		750
Borrowed Funds			250			Borrowed Funds		250

Although the titles Deposit Accounts and Borrowed Funds do not have "Payable" or "Liability" in their titles, they are clearly bank liabilities. Since these liabilities are the basis for the amount of interest expense incurred by the bank, it is often said that the balance sheet "drives" the income statement in banking. The cost of these various types of borrowing arrangements must be recorded as interest expense (assume a 6% interest rate) as shown here:

Bank recognition of interest expense (in thousands)

Transaction Analysis							Journal Entry		
	Fundamental Accounting Equation								
Account Titles	**Assets**	**=**	**Liabilities**	**+**	**Owners' Equity**		**Account Titles**	**Debit**	**Credit**
Interest Expense					(60)		Interest Expense	60	
Interest Payable			60				Interest Payable		60

After taking the first step by borrowing the money, banks then take the second step to earn interest income—they either invest funds in securities or loan them to borrowers. That is, the earning assets of a bank are either classified as investments or loans.

A **loan** is a highly personalized contract that governs the bank's transfer of funds to a borrower in return for eventual repayment of principal and interest. This type of ongoing relationship, tailor-made to the needs of the borrower, is the primary business of most banks and accounts for more than 50% of all bank assets. Loans can be classified as business or commercial, agricultural, financial institution, consumer, and real estate. An **investment**, however, is an impersonal, open-market transaction governed by a standardized contract issued by a variety of large, well-known borrowers, such as state and federal governments or corporations. Banks may resell these investments before their maturity dates. Investments include treasury securities such as U.S. government bonds, government agency securities such as the securities of the Federal Home Loan Mortgage Corporation, and municipal securities such as a bond issue to finance an activity of a city or state. Although bank loans generate the majority of a bank's profitability, they take time to arrange, have a greater risk of borrower default, and are less liquid than most investments. To illustrate this loan and investment process, assume a $1 million transaction in which the bank pays cash and other liquid assets to create a variety of loans and investments as shown here:

Bank acquisition of investments and loans (in thousands)

Transaction Analysis							Journal Entry		
	Fundamental Accounting Equation								
Account Titles	**Assets**	**=**	**Liabilities**	**+**	**Owners' Equity**		**Account Titles**	**Debit**	**Credit**
Investment Securities	400						Investment Securities	400	
Loans Receivable	600						Loans Receivable	600	
Cash, etc.	(1,000)						Cash, etc.		1,000

Since these assets are the basis for the amount of interest revenue earned by the bank, you can again see why the balance sheet is said to drive the income statement in banking. The return from these earning assets must be recorded as interest revenue (assume a 6.6% interest rate) as shown here:

Bank recognition of interest revenue (in thousands)

Transaction Analysis							Journal Entry		
	Fundamental Accounting Equation								
Account Titles	**Assets**	**=**	**Liabilities**	**+**	**Owners' Equity**		**Account Titles**	**Debit**	**Credit**
Interest Receivable	66						Interest Receivable	66	
Interest Revenue			66				Interest Revenue		66

Note that in our ongoing example, the bank will report interest income of $6,000, the difference between interest revenue of $66,000 and interest expense of $60,000. Other substantial sources of bank revenue are the transaction fees for processing loans, automatic teller machine usage, and overdraft charges. These revenues are then offset by such traditional operating expenses as salaries, and by the costs of maintaining office buildings and office equipment.

Unlike some of the industries discussed in this chapter, banking is highly regulated. Banks in some states must adhere to the rules of two or more regulatory agencies including the Federal Deposit Insurance Corporation, the Federal Reserve, state banking charters, and national banking charters. Because these regulatory examinations evaluate the soundness of a bank's decision making, they have a different focus than the independent audit of a public accounting firm, which traditionally evaluates whether the financial statements are a fair representation of the entity's actual financial position and results of operations.

How to Apply Your Understanding of the Banking Industry to Interpret Its Financial Statements

Let's now look more closely at bank financial statements to learn how to interpret them.

A Summary of Essential Banking Transactions To reinforce your understanding of the unique characteristics of the banking industry, study the following summary:

Transaction	Activity	Balance Sheet	Income Statement
Bank borrowing and repayment of funds	Financing activity	Deposits and Other Liabilities	None
Bank's interest cost of borrowing expense	Operating activity	Interest Payable	Interest
Bank purchase and sale of investments and loans	Investing activity	Security and Loan Assets	None
Bank's interest earned from lending	Operating activity	Interest Receivable	Interest Revenue

Also note that assets such as investment securities and loans receivable reported on a bank's balance sheet are reported as liabilities on its customer balance sheets. Likewise, the liabilities reported on a bank's balance sheet are reported as assets on its customer balance sheets. Checking and savings accounts administered by a bank for its customers are examples of bank liabilities.

Types of Assets and Liabilities Found on Bank Balance Sheets Figure 10-16 and Figure 10-17, respectively, illustrate the types of assets, liabilities, and owner equities you can expect to find on the balance sheets of banks, according to the Federal Deposit Insurance Corporation (FDIC) *Historical Statistics on Banking*. From this information, you can see that cash is an insignificant asset unlike both investment securities (17%) and loans (60%), which together constitute the majority of a bank's assets. Likewise, you can see that deposits and other borrowed funds constitute over 90 percent of all liabilities, but that bank owner equity accounts (described as equity capital) are surprisingly insignificant. Figure 10-18 illustrates much the same patterns for Wells Fargo & Company's most recent balance sheet.

FIGURE 10-16 Typical bank asset accounts

FDIC Historical Statistics on Banking Assets
FDIC-Insured Commercial Banks
United States
Balances at Year End
(Dollar amounts in thousands)

Year	No. of Inst.	Cash and Due From	Investment Securities	Total Loans and Leases	Allowance for Losses Loans and Leases	Net Loans and Leases	Other Earning Assets	Bank Premises and Equipment	Other Real Estate	Intangible Assets	All Other Assets	Total Assets
2000	8,297	368,270,912	1,056,991,859	3,787,289,211	63,589,779	3,723,699,433	583,676,160	75,046,336	3,157,766	102,541,513	272,050,447	6,185,434,426
1999	8,562	364,415,847	1,029,302,404	3,465,414,726	58,345,036	3,407,069,690	482,751,272	73,084,675	3,044,685	97,873,822	230,055,849	5,687,598,244
1998	8,756	354,992,282	964,907,744	3,214,858,300	56,843,219	3,158,015,081	562,928,941	70,638,493	3,625,045	80,043,440	205,020,245	5,400,171,270

FIGURE 10-17 Typical bank liability and owner equity accounts

FDIC Historical Statistics on Banking Liabilities and Equity Capital
FDIC-Insured Commercial Banks
United States
Balances at Year End
(Dollar amounts in thousands)

		Liabilities					Equity Capital						
Year	No. of Inst.	Total Deposits	Borrowed Funds	Subordinated Notes	Other Liabilities	Total Liabilities	Perpetual Preferred Stock	Common Stock	Surplus	Undivided Profits	Other Capital	Total Equity Capital	Total Liabilities and Equity Capital
2000	8,297	4,146,038,904	1,026,310,576	86,832,040	400,306,479	5,659,488,000	3,241,873	30,860,761	258,348,188	233,495,608	N/A	525,946,428	6,185,434,426
1999	8,562	3,803,265,269	984,797,006	76,240,168	346,581,578	5,210,884,019	3,045,123	32,463,078	237,901,155	203,304,850	N/A	476,714,208	5,687,598,227
1998	8,756	3,655,102,791	841,189,531	72,578,899	372,334,538	4,941,205,759	2,584,554	34,313,811	216,824,695	205,242,436	N/A	458,965,495	5,400,171,270

Particularly important is the fact that this balance sheet, like those of other banks, is unclassified—it does not classify either its assets or liabilities into current and noncurrent sections. Banks do not present a classified balance sheet because their assets and liabilities are relatively liquid in nature. Because banks present unclassified balance sheets, you must recognize that you will not be able to easily calculate a bank's current ratio or acid test ratio. You can, however, evaluate a bank's liquidity by using the **loan to deposit (LTD) ratio**. This ratio—calculated by dividing a bank's gross loans by total deposits—indicates the percentage of a bank's loans funded through deposits. If you look again at Figure 10-18, you will see that Wells Fargo's loan to deposit ratio for the fiscal year 2001 is .92 ($172,499/$187,266).

Bank Income Statements Let's now return to the income statement that you viewed at the beginning of this chapter. A characteristic that distinguishes bank income statements from those of nonfinancial industries is the placement of bank interest at the top of the income statement. This practice, shown in Figure 10-1, for example, leaves no doubt that the earning and incurrence of interest is Wells Fargo's primary operating activity. This figure indicates that the highest interest revenue is derived from the loans asset, while the highest interest expense is derived from the deposits liability. In contrast, interest is usually one of the last items reported in the income statement of other industries.

FIGURE 10-18

The balance sheet of Wells Fargo Bank

WELLS FARGO & COMPANY AND SUBSIDIARIES
Consolidated Balance Sheet
(In millions, except shares)

	December 31 2001	December 31 2000
Assets		
Cash and due from banks	$ 16,968	$ 16,978
Federal funds sold and securities purchased under resale agreements	2,530	1,598
Securities available for sale	40,308	38,655
Mortgages held for sale	30,405	11,812
Loans held for sale	4,745	4,539
Loans	172,499	161,124
Allowance for loan losses	3,761	3,719
Net loans	168,738	157,405
Mortgage servicing rights	6,241	5,609
Premises and equipment, net	3,549	3,415
Core deposit intangible	1,013	1,183
Goodwill	9,527	9,303
Interest receivable and other assets	23,545	21,929
Total assets	$307,569	$272,426
Liabilities		
Noninterest-bearing deposits	$ 65,362	$ 55,096
Interest-bearing deposits	121,904	114,463
Total deposits	187,266	169,559
Short-term borrowings	37,782	28,989
Accrued expenses and other liabilities	16,777	14,409
Long-term debt	36,095	32,046
Guaranteed preferred beneficial interests in Company's subordinated debentures	2,435	935
Stockholders' Equity		
Preferred stock	218	385
Unearned ESOP shares	(154)	(118)
Total preferred stock	64	267
Common stock—$1⅔ par value, authorized 6,000,000,000 shares; issued 1,736,381,025 shares and 1,736,381,025 shares	2,894	2,894
Additional paid-in capital	9,436	9,337
Retained earnings	16,005	14,541
Cumulative other comprehensive income	752	524
Treasury stock—40,886,028 shares and 21,735,182 shares	(1,937)	(1,075)
Total stockholders' equity	27,214	26,488
Total liabilities and stockholders' equity	$307,569	$272,426

Loan to Deposit Ratio = .9

Since interest is so important to a bank's profitability, analysts often want to know the amount of a bank's net interest income and its net interest margin. **Net interest income**—interest revenue less interest expense ($12,460,000,000 for 2001 in Figure 10-1)—is identical in concept to a retailer's gross margin. **Net interest margin**—net interest income divided by average total earning assets[4] [($12,460/ $220,303.5) = 5.66%]—provides feedback about how well the bank has managed its interest rate decisions. Another indication of a bank's performance is its **loan loss ratio**—loan losses divided by loaned assets. Wells Fargo's loss ratio, calculated from other schedules for example, was 1.09% ($1,780,000,000/$163,302,700,000).

As you can clearly see, the financial statements found in the banking industry are very different from those of other industries. Nevertheless, you have learned much about what is distinctive about a bank's financial statements. And, you also have been introduced to four new but intuitively appealing decision tools—the loan to deposit ratio, net interest income, net interest margin, and the loan loss ratio—to help you evaluate a bank's performance.

[4] Wells Fargo provided this number in another schedule.

APPENDIX

10-1 Learning How to Read Consolidated Financial Statements

PERFORMANCE OBJECTIVE

In this appendix you will learn the following new Performance Objective:

PO33 **Prepare** a consolidated balance sheet given both parent and subsidiary balance sheets and any additional information necessary.

Today, most annual reports of U.S. corporations present consolidated financial statements rather than the statements of the individual entities that make up the corporation. In fact, the Financial Accounting Standards Board requires companies to consolidate financial statements even for subsidiaries having nonhomogeneous operations. Most of the annual report financial statements you have seen in this textbook have been consolidated so let's now take a closer look at their terminology and special accounts.

Consolidated financial statements present the financial effects of the combined transactions of a parent company and one or more of its subsidiary companies. A **parent company** is a company that owns 50% or more of the voting stock of a subsidiary company. A good example of a parent company is Target Corporation. It owns 100% of the voting stock of several subsidiaries, including such well-known retailers as Target Stores, Dayton's, Marshall Field's, Hudson's, and Mervyn's California. A **subsidiary company**, therefore, is controlled by a parent company that owns 50% or more of the subsidiary's voting stock. A subsidiary company is **wholly owned** when the parent company owns 100% of its voting stock, as is true of Target Stores. Another term that is useful to know in the context of consolidated financial statements is net assets. **Net assets** are simply defined as assets minus liabilities. Since net assets (that is, assets minus liabilities) equal owners' equity, you can see why corporate net assets are always equal to the book or recorded value of shareholders' equity.

This appendix will help you become a more knowledgeable user of consolidated statements if you play the role of a preparer of consolidated statements and master Performance Objective 33:

YOUR PERFORMANCE OBJECTIVE 33
Prepare a consolidated balance sheet given both parent and subsidiary balance sheets and any additional information necessary.

How to Prepare a Consolidated Balance Sheet

To help you master Performance Objective 33, you will learn three concepts in the following demonstration problem. You will know that you have mastered these concepts when you are able to reconcile all changes made in each consolidated balance sheet. As you read, pay careful attention to how the balance sheet is affected by each transaction.

Demonstration Problem The individual balance sheets of Parent Company (P) and Subsidiary Company (S) below were prepared just before P gained control of S.

Data just before acquisition

	P Company	S Company
Cash	$300	$ 50
Other assets	200	150
	$500	$200
Capital stock ($1 par)	$300	$100
Retained earnings	200	100
	$500	$200

You will now examine four cases, each of which is used to illustrate important consolidation concepts. In Case 1, you will learn about the concept of consolidation. Case

2 builds on this concept and adds a second important concept, the concept of goodwill. Case 3 introduces the concept of minority interest, and Case 4 introduces the important issue of how consolidated retained earnings is measured subsequent to acquisition. As a result, each succeeding case is more realistic than its predecessor. In all cases, you are to assume that the book value and fair market value of the subsidiary's net assets are equal. This means that the reported net assets of the subsidiary are neither overvalued nor undervalued. To calculate the subsidiary's net assets, you may either subtract liabilities from assets (e.g., $200 − $0 = $200) or simply add up all stockholder equity accounts (e.g., $100 + $100 = $200).

Case 1: The Basic Concept of Consolidation

This simple case will show you how the individual balance sheets of the parent and subsidiary are combined to create a consolidated balance sheet. You will then use the information introduced in this case to build a foundation with which to understand the more realistic data you will be presented with in Cases 2 through 4.

Acquisition Data P Company purchases 100% of S Company shares (on the stock market) for $200 (i.e., at book or recorded value).

Analysis First, the legally separate corporation known as S Company is wholly owned by only one shareholder—P Company—its parent. This gives P Company uncontested control over S's operating and financing policies. If instead, P Company had gained at least 50% ownership of S Company, P Company would be treated as having gained effective control of S Company. Second, the $200 purchase price was paid to the separate accounts of those individuals who owned shares in S Company. That is, from S Company's perspective, P's 100% purchase of S for $200 produced a transfer of ownership but did not increase its cash account. The following transaction is recorded on the books of P Company to reflect its acquisition of S Company.

Transaction Analysis						Journal Entry		
	Fundamental Accounting Equation							
Account Titles	Assets	=	Liabilities	+	Owners' Equity	Account Titles	Debit	Credit
Investment in S Subsidiary	200					Investment in S Subsidiary	200	
Cash	(200)					Cash		200

If you were to prepare balance sheets of the parent and subsidiary immediately after you had recorded this transaction, they would reflect the following balances. As you compare the balance sheets before and after acquisition, study the numerical reconciliation shown here of the changes in P Company accounts occurring as a result of the acquisition.

Data just after acquisition	P Company	S Company	Reconciliation of Changes in P
Cash	$100	$ 50	$300 − $200 = $100
Other assets	200	150	
Investment in S subsidiary	200	—	$0 + $200 = $200
	$500	$200	
Capital stock ($1 par)	$300	$100	
Retained earnings	200	100	
	$500	$200	

Notice in particular that the subsidiary's $200 in resources or net assets (cash of $50 plus other assets of $150) are now reported in two places. That is, P Company reports them as an asset, Investment in S Subsidiary, while S Company reports these same resources under Cash and Other Assets. This reporting approach is not inaccurate when you look at each company as a separate legal entity. After all, P has a 100% interest in these assets while, at the same time, S has possession of these assets.

Why Prepare a Consolidated Balance Sheet? Since, in all cases illustrated, P Company will effectively control the activities of its subsidiary S Company, investors will find it more informative to study the consolidated financial statements of P and S. That is, in substance, P and S represent a single economic entity, while, in form, P and S represent two separate legal entities. Since potential investors prefer complete rather than incomplete financial information—that is, the economic substance rather than the legal form of a transaction—it should not surprise you that consolidated financial statements are considered more relevant to investment decisions.

How to Prepare a Consolidated Balance Sheet To construct a consolidated balance sheet, you must do more than merely add together the amounts in accounts that are common to both parent and subsidiary. To illustrate the basic procedure, study the balance sheet worksheet shown here. It contains the balance sheets of the individual companies, certain adjustments, and the resulting consolidated balance sheet. Note that the consolidated balance sheet found in the far right column is prepared immediately after the acquisition transaction described in Case 1.

Consolidated balance sheet at acquisition

Consolidation	P Company	S Company	Numerical Support	
Cash	$100	$ 50	Simple addition	$150
Other assets	200	150	Simple addition	350
Investment in S subsidiary	200	—	(200)	–0–
	$500	$200		$500
Capital stock ($1 par)	$300	$100	(100)	$300
Retained earnings	200	100	(100)	200
	$500	$200		$500

Notice that the Investment in S Subsidiary and S Company's Capital Stock and Retained Earnings accounts have all been eliminated. These eliminations are represented by the following transaction:

Transaction Analysis							Journal Entry		
	Fundamental Accounting Equation								
Account Titles	Assets	=	Liabilities	+	Owners' Equity		Account Titles	Debit	Credit
Capital Stock (S)					(100)		Capital Stock (S)	100	
Retained Earnings (S)					(100)		Retained Earnings (S)	100	
Investment in S Subsidiary	(200)						Investment in S Subsidiary		200

Decreasing both owner equity accounts and the asset account has the same effect as the earlier subtractions shown in the balance sheet worksheet. An important question, however, remains unanswered. Why must you eliminate these accounts to successfully complete the consolidation?

Why You Must Eliminate the Investment Account and Subsidiary's Owner Equity Accounts during Consolidation The effect of the subtraction shown both in the worksheet and in the recorded transactions above is necessary to avoid double counting the assets and equities of the single economic entity. First, consider the elimination of the Investment account. As pointed out earlier, both the parent and subsidiary report the very same $200 of assets on their respective balance sheets. Reporting the $200 of assets twice is acceptable when presenting individual balance sheets of the parent and subsidiary side-by-side. It is not acceptable, however, when presenting the single economic entity as is done during consolidation. Users of consolidated financial statements evaluate the economic entity by asking how many assets it has accumulated in its dealings with the outside business world. That is, when the economic entity reports its relative success with customers, suppliers, and so on, it is important not to report business dealings within the entity (such as between P Company and S Company).

Just as the single economic entity reports the subsidiary assets only once, it also reports an ownership equity in those same resources once. That is, all ownership equity accounts of S Company must be eliminated because, for consolidation purposes, only the capital stock and retained earnings of the parent are relevant. The entire ownership of the economic entity is associated with P Company not S Company.

Only the acquisition transaction enters the formal accounting information system of the parent company. All of the other transactions you viewed never enter the formal accounting system. Instead, they are worksheet transactions that facilitate the consolidation process.

Although the balance sheet of a consolidated entity is usually called a consolidated balance sheet, you can expect to see some new accounts as well. The first of these accounts is goodwill.

Case 2: Adding the Concept of Goodwill

Goodwill is a noncurrent asset account that you can expect to find on the consolidated balance sheets (or the notes to the balance sheet) of companies that have acquired another company at a price greater than would be expected by looking at the acquired company's balance sheet. In March 1999, for example, Ford Motor Company, acquired a majority interest in AB Volvo, a Swedish manufacturer of luxury cars, by paying $2.5 billion more than the individual fair market values of Volvo's acquired net assets (see Figure 10A-1 for a complete description). That is, Ford initially recorded its goodwill in the amount of $2.5 billion. Since you can now appreciate how significant this type of asset might be, let's take a closer look at how it is created and reported.

Acquisition Data P Company purchases 100% of S Company shares for $210 (i.e., P pays more than book value which is equivalent in our cases to fair market value). Note that if P Company had purchased S Company at its fair market value, it would have paid $200 (100% of S's net assets of $200).

Acquisition Transaction The following transaction is recorded on the books of P Company to reflect its acquisition of S Company:

Transaction Analysis						Journal Entry		
	Fundamental Accounting Equation							
Account Titles	Assets	=	Liabilities	+	Owners' Equity	Account Titles	Debit	Credit
Investment in S Subsidiary	210					Investment in S Subsidiary	210	
Cash	(210)					Cash		210

FIGURE 10A-1

A description of goodwill in a footnote from Ford Motor Company's annual report

Acquisitions: Purchase of AB Volvo's Worldwide Passenger Car Business ("Volvo Car")

On March 31, 1999, we purchased Volvo Car for approximately $6.45 billion. The acquisition price consisted of a cash payment of approximately $2 billion on March 31, 1999, a deferred payment obligation to AB Volvo of approximately $1.6 billion due March 31, 2001, and Volvo Car automotive net indebtedness of approximately $2.9 billion. Most automotive indebtedness was repaid on April 12, 1999. The purchase price payment and automotive debt repayments were funded from our cash reserves. The acquisition has been accounted for as a purchase. The assets purchased, liabilities assumed, and the results of operations, since the date of acquisition, are included in our financial statements on a consolidated basis. The purchase price for Volvo Car has been allocated to the assets acquired and liabilities assumed based on the estimated fair values as of the acquisition date. **The excess of the purchase price over the estimated fair value of net assets acquired is approximately $2.5 billion and is being amortized on a straight-line basis over 40 years.** Value assigned to identified intangible assets is approximately $400 million and is being amortized on a straight-line basis over periods ranging from 12 to 40 years. The purchase price allocation included a write-up of inventory to fair value; the sale of this inventory in the second quarter of 1999 resulted in a one-time increase in cost of sales of $146 million after tax.

The specific information about goodwill is in boldface.

Just What Exactly Is Goodwill? The data in Case 2 are identical to Case 1's data except for the purchase price. Why is the buyer paying more than the fair market value of the individual assets? Apparently, S Company's particular combination of assets has an intangible value that the buyer recognizes and is willing to pay for. Had the assets been purchased other than in combination, buyers would have paid a total of $200 (remember the assumption that book value equals fair market value). In this case, therefore, the whole is greater than the sum of its parts. This phenomenon of synergism is quite common in the worlds of business and sports. That is, many successful sports teams possess exceptional teamwork rather than exceptional individual players.

In a business setting, goodwill, an intangible asset, is the numerical difference between what is paid to acquire a business and what would be paid if the assets were acquired individually. Thus, goodwill must be reported on the consolidated balance sheet when a parent pays more than the fair market value of net assets reported by the company acquired. Until very recently, goodwill had its cost allocated to expense, that is, amortized over a period not to exceed 40 years. The expense was called *amortization expense* and the asset reduction was either accounted for by decreasing goodwill directly or by increasing a contra asset called *accumulated amortization* as shown in Figure 10A-2 for OfficeMax, Inc. As you'll learn in Chapter 12, however, goodwill is now treated as an intangible asset with an indefinite useful life, and is, therefore, not subject to amortization.[5]

The following worksheet contains the individual company balance sheets, certain adjustments, and the resulting consolidated balance sheet prepared immediately after the acquisition transaction for Case 2. Study carefully both this balance sheet worksheet and the numerical formulation of goodwill.

---

[5] "Goodwill and Other Intangible Assets," *Statement of Financial Accounting Standards No. 142* (Stamford, CT: Financial Accounting Standards Board, 2001).

FIGURE 10A-2

Reporting goodwill, goodwill amortization, and a minority interest

The intangible asset, goodwill, and its contra-asset reduction → Goodwill

The shareholders' equity known as minority interest → Minority interest

OFFICE MAX, INC.
Consolidated Balance Sheets
(Dollars in thousands)

	January 27, 2001	January 22, 2000
Assets		
Current assets:		
Cash and equivalents	$ 127,337	$ 73,087
Accounts receivable, net of allowances of $2,766 and $687, respectively	105,666	111,734
Merchandise inventories	1,159,089	1,273,844
Other current assets	110,821	72,910
Total current assets	1,502,913	1,531,575
Property and equipment:		
Buildings and land	36,180	19,292
Leasehold improvements	196,088	188,900
Furniture, fixtures and equipment	599,813	505,345
Total property and equipment	832,081	713,537
Less: Accumulated depreciation and amortization	(397,757)	(311,069)
Property and equipment, net	434,324	402,468
Other assets and deferred charges	55,680	34,333
Goodwill, net of accumulated amortization of $79,902 and $70,039, respectively	300,350	310,168
	$2,293,267	$2,278,544
Liabilities, and shareholders' equity		
Current liabilities:		
Accounts payable—trade	$ 587,618	$ 702,416
Accrued expenses and other liabilities	179,034	143,660
Accrued salaries and related expenses	45,197	50,313
Taxes other than income taxes	67,564	72,966
Revolving credit facilities	220,000	91,800
Mortgage loan, current portion	116	1,300
Total current liabilities	1,099,529	1,062,455
Mortgage loan	1,663	15,125
Other long-term liabilities	141,245	70,895
Total liabilities	1,242,437	1,148,475
Commitments and contingencies	—	—
Minority interest	16,211	14,072
Redeemable preferred shares	52,319	—
Shareholders' equity:		
Common stock without par value; 200,000,000 shares authorized; 124,969,255 and 124,985,364 shares issued and outstanding, respectively	865,319	867,866
Deferred stock compensation	(321)	(304)
Cumulative translation adjustment	(417)	—
Retained earnings	223,415	358,900
Less: Treasury stock, at cost	(105,696)	(110,465)
Total shareholders' equity	982,300	1,115,997
	$2,293,267	$2,278,544

Consolidated balance sheet at acquisition

Consolidation	P Company	S Company	Numerical Support	
Cash	$ 90	$ 50	Simple addition	$140
Other assets	200	150	Simple addition	350
Investment in S Sub.	210	—	(210)	—
Goodwill	—	—	210 − 200	10
	$500	$200		$500
Capital stock ($1 par)	$300	$100	(100)	$300
Retained earnings	200	100	(100)	200
	$500	$200		$500

Consolidated Goodwill = Fair Market Value (FMV) of Subsidiary's Combined Net Assets − FMV of Subsidiary's Individual Net Assets
= Cost of Subsidiary − FMV of Subsidiary's Recorded Net Assets
= $210 − $200 = $10

As in Case 1, another way of showing the changes leading to a consolidated balance sheet is through use of the elimination transaction shown here. Unlike the transaction shown in Case 1, however, this Case 2 transaction not only eliminates double counting but also recognizes the existence of goodwill:

Transaction Analysis					Journal Entry		
	Fundamental Accounting Equation						
Account Titles	Assets	=	Liabilities +	Owners' Equity	Account Titles	Debit	Credit
Goodwill [210 − (100% × 200)]	10				Goodwill [210 − (100% × 200)]	10	
Capital Stock (S)				(100)	Capital Stock (S)	100	
Retained Earnings (S)				(100)	Retained Earnings (S)	100	
Investment in S Subsidiary	(210)				Investment in S Subsidiary		210

Since P Company acquires 100% of S Company's voting stock, S Company ownership must be completely eliminated when the new consolidated entity's financial statements are reported (100% × $200).

Since P Company can effectively control S Company by purchasing 50% or more of its voting stock, parent companies frequently acquire less than 100% ownership of their subsidiaries. In those cases, the group of subsidiary shareholders who retain their stock is referred to as the *minority interest.* Let's now examine the concept of minority interest in Case 3.

Case 3: Adding the Concept of Minority Interest

Acquisition Data P Company purchases 90% of S Company shares for $190, an amount greater than book value. If this purchase had been made at book value, P Company would have paid $180 (.90 × $200).

Acquisition Transaction Below is the transaction recorded on the books of P Company to reflect its acquisition of S Company:

Transaction Analysis					Journal Entry		
	Fundamental Accounting Equation						
Account Titles	Assets	= Liabilities	+	Owners' Equity	Account Titles	Debit	Credit
Investment in S Subsidiary	190				Investment in S Subsidiary	190	
Cash	(190)				Cash		190

Just What Exactly Is Minority Interest? A **minority interest** represents nonparent ownership of voting stock in a less than wholly owned subsidiary company. This concept is reported on a consolidated balance sheet with a special stockholder equity account called Minority Interest. Nevertheless, as illustrated in Figure 10A-2, most companies report this account between liabilities and stockholders' equity on the balance sheet.

Determining the percentage of minority interest is relatively simple. It is the complement of the majority interest, in this case 1 − 90% = 10%. Since minority stockholders have a right to a proportionate share of the subsidiary company assets, the following formula may be used to quantify this ownership equity:

Minority Interest = Minority Interest Percentage × Subsidiary Company Net Assets or Stockholders' Equity at Current Consolidation Date
= MI% × S. Co. Stockholder Equity
= 10% × $200 = $20

The next balance sheet worksheet presents this minority interest amount:

Consolidated balance sheet at acquisition

Consolidation	P Company	S Company	Numerical Support	
Cash	$110	$ 50	Simple addition	$160
Other assets	200	150	Simple addition	350
Investment in S Subsidiary	190	—	(190)	—
Goodwill	—	—	190 − (.9 × 200)	10
	$500	$ 200		$520
Minority interest	$ —	$ —	.10 × 200	$ 20
Capital stock ($1 par)	300	100	(90 + 10)	300
Retained earnings	200	100	(90 + 10)	200
	$500	$ 200		$520

Once again, notice how the Cash account and Other Assets account are simply added together as they were in Cases 1 and 2. Likewise, notice how the goodwill is created in the process of eliminating both the parent's Investment in Subsidiary asset account and the subsidiary's owners' equity amounts above and in the following worksheet transaction:

Transaction Analysis					Journal Entry		
	Fundamental Accounting Equation						
Account Titles	Assets	= Liabilities	+	Owners' Equity	Account Titles	Debit	Credit
Goodwill [190 − (.90 × 200)]	10				Goodwill [190 − (.90 × 200)]	10	
Capital Stock (S)				(90)	Capital Stock (S)	90	
Retained Earnings (S)				(90)	Retained Earnings (S)	90	
Investment in S Subsidiary	(190)				Investment in S Subsidiary		190

This transaction recognizes goodwill (Case 2) and eliminates the double counting of both assets and equities (Cases 1 and 2). That is, 90% of a $100 book value, or $90, is eliminated from each of the $100 subsidiary owner equity accounts since the parent owns 90% of the subsidiary's recorded net assets. In addition, the investment in S Subsidiary account in the amount of $190 is eliminated.

To account for every element in the balance sheet worksheet, however, an additional transaction that simultaneously decreases both capital stock and retained earnings by $10 each (.10 × $100) while recording minority interest is needed. That is, the minority shareholders own the other 10% of the subsidiary's recorded net assets or shareholders' equity of $200 which is expressed here by a minority interest account in the amount of $20.

Transaction Analysis						Journal Entry		
	Fundamental Accounting Equation							
Account Titles	Assets	=	Liabilities	+	Owners' Equity	Account Titles	Debit	Credit
Capital Stock (S)					(10)	Capital Stock (S)	10	
Retained Earnings (S)					(10)	Retained Earnings (S)	10	
Minority Interest (.10 × 200)					20	Minority Interest (.10 × 200)		20

When a consolidated balance sheet is prepared, it is critical that financial statement readers not overlook the existence of a group of shareholders distinct from the parent or controlling shareholder. This distinction is illuminated and preserved by transferring the remaining balances in the subsidiary stockholders' equity accounts to a separate minority interest account as shown for Office Max, Inc. in Figure 10A-2. Thus, the preceding transaction is not an eliminating transaction but rather a *reclassification transaction* in which a 10% ownership interest is transferred from the subsidiary to the minority stockholders.

Case 4: The Concept of a Consolidation Subsequent to Acquisition

Two methods are available to a parent corporation in valuing its investment in a subsidiary at dates subsequent to acquisition—the cost method and the equity method. To avoid unnecessary detail, the following illustration of how to prepare a consolidated balance sheet will be limited to the use of the cost method. Meanwhile, you will learn more about the equity method in Chapter 12.

New Data During the current year, the subsidiary reports a net income of $60 and declares a dividend of $10. Meanwhile, the parent increases its assets and equities by a total of $100.

Analysis Case 4 essentially reexamines Case 3 one period later to illustrate how a consolidated balance sheet is reported subsequent to an acquisition rather than immediately after acquisition. Although the concepts of goodwill and minority interest are still important, pay particular attention now to the calculation of **consolidated retained earnings** as you study the following balance sheet worksheet prepared one year after Company P acquired Company S:

Consolidated balance sheet subsequent to acquisition

Consolidation	P Company	S Company	Numerical Support	
Cash	$125	$ 75	Simple addition	$200
Other assets	285	175	Simple addition	460
Investment in S Sub.	190	—	(190)	—
Goodwill	—	—	190 − (.9 × 200)	10
	$600	$250		$670
Minority interest	$ —	$ —	.10 × 250	$ 25
Capital stock ($1 par)	300	100	(90 + 10)	300
Retained earnings	300	150	[300 + .9(50)]	345
	$600	$250		$670

Consolidated Retained Earnings = Parent Company Retained Earnings + Parent Company Share of Change in Subsidiary Company Retained Earnings Since Acquisition

= 300 + .90(50) = $345

Another way of calculating consolidated retained earnings is to add together the parent and subsidiary retained earnings, e.g. $300 + $150 = $450, and then subtract from this number any decreases to the subsidiary retained earnings account found in the following two transactions. Using this approach you would have $450 − ($90 + 15) = $345.

The following worksheet transactions describe the preceding events. Confirm your understanding of the consolidation process shown under numerical support by studying these transactions carefully. That is, you should be able to both verify each calculation and explain why it was made.

Goodwill recognition and double counting elimination transaction

Transaction Analysis					Journal Entry		
	Fundamental Accounting Equation						
Account Titles	Assets	=	Liabilities +	Owners' Equity	Account Titles	Debit	Credit
Goodwill [190 − (.90 × 200)]	10				Goodwill [190 − (.90 × 200)]	10	
Capital Stock (S)				(90)	Capital Stock (S)	90	
Retained Earnings (S)				(90)	Retained Earnings (S)	90	
Investment in S Subsidiary	(190)				Investment in S Subsidiary		190

Minority interest reclassification transaction

Transaction Analysis					Journal Entry		
	Fundamental Accounting Equation						
Account Titles	Assets	=	Liabilities +	Owners' Equity	Account Titles	Debit	Credit
Capital Stock — S (.10 × 100)				(10)	Capital Stock — S (.10 × 100)	10	
Retained Earnings — S (.10 × 150)				(15)	Retained Earnings — S (.10 × 150)	15	
Minority Interest (.10 × 250)				25	Minority Interest (.10 × 250)		25

Intercompany dividend elimination transactions

Account Titles	Assets	=	Liabilities	+	Owners' Equity	Account Titles	Debit	Credit
	Transaction Analysis					**Journal Entry**		
	Fundamental Accounting Equation							
Dividend Revenue — P (.90 × $10)					(9)	Dividend Revenue — P (.90 × $10)	9	
Dividend Declared — S					9	Dividend Declared		9
Dividend Payable to P			(9)			Dividend Payable to P	9	
Dividend Receivable from S	(9)					Dividend Receivable from S		9

To better understand the nature of the preceding dividend elimination transactions, try to visualize the transactions *actually* recorded on both P Company and S Company books during the year to recognize the declaration of a $10 dividend by S Company to its shareholders.

P Company books

Account Titles	Assets	=	Liabilities	+	Owners' Equity	Account Titles	Debit	Credit
	Transaction Analysis					**Journal Entry**		
	Fundamental Accounting Equation							
Dividend Receivable from S	9					Dividend Receivable from S	9	
Dividend Revenue					9	Dividend Revenue		9

S Company books

Account Titles	Assets	=	Liabilities	+	Owners' Equity	Account Titles	Debit	Credit
	Transaction Analysis					**Journal Entry**		
	Fundamental Accounting Equation							
Dividends Declared					(10)	Dividends Declared	10	
Dividends Payable to P			10			Dividends Payable to P		10

To ensure that only transactions occurring between the consolidated group and outsiders are reported, the preceding transactions remove:

1. The amount added to the parent's Dividend Revenue account (otherwise, the corresponding amount of net income included in the subsidiary's Retained Earnings account will be duplicated).
2. The amount added to the subsidiary's Dividends Declared account (this was not a dividend between the consolidated group and outsiders).
3. The intercompany receivable and payable accounts.

Summary

Essentially, there are two differences between the consolidated balance sheets in Case 3 and Case 4. In Case 4,

1. Minority interest shared in the subsidiary's overall increase in retained earnings and, therefore, increased from $20 to $25.
2. Consolidated retained earnings increased dramatically because of increases in both parent and subsidiary retained earnings.

Now that we have covered how consolidated financial statements are prepared, be sure to use Performance Objective 33 when you solve the consolidation exercises and problems at the end of this chapter.

Summary with Key Terms

The number in parentheses following each **key term** is the page number on which the term is defined.

This chapter began with a thorough discussion about the three most common forms of business entity known as the **sole proprietorship** (466), **partnership** (466), and **corporation** (469). You learned about their unique and shared characteristics, their respective advantages and disadvantages, and the ways in which their financial statements differ from one another. One relatively new partnership form is called the **limited liability partnership**, (469) or **LLP** (469). One particularly important characteristic of the corporation is its **limited liability** (470), which limits a shareholder's potential loss to the amount of their actual investment. This chapter's first *Insight* then explained how corporations might take a different form than the regular corporation or **C Corporation** (474). Alternate forms of the corporation include the **closely held corporation** (474), the **S Corporation** (474), and the **nonprofit corporation** (475). Also discussed was a hybrid form that combines characteristics of both the partnership and the corporation called the **Limited Liability Company** (475), or **LLC** (475).

This chapter then explored different types of industry to help you broaden your understanding of financial statements. The first industry discussed was merchandising. **Merchandisers** (475) include both **wholesalers** (475) and **retailers** (476). The second industry discussed was manufacturing. The **product costs** (482) of **manufacturers** (481) include **raw materials (RM)** (482), also known as **direct materials** (482), **direct labor (DL)** (482), and **manufacturing overhead (MO)** (483), or **indirect costs** (483). You also learned the importance of work in process, **cost of goods manufactured (COGM)** (484), and finished goods in calculating **manufacturing cost of goods sold (COGS)** (485). Finally, you were introduced to three manufacturing inventory accounts—**raw materials inventory** (482), **work in process inventory** (484), and **finished goods inventory** (484), all of which underlie the inventories account in a manufacturer's balance sheet.

The primary focus of the construction industry coverage was **long-term construction companies** (487) and their use of the **completed-contract method** (488) and the **percentage-of-completion method** (488) for recognizing construction income. Although these methods are quite different, an *Insight* section explained that a construction company recognizes the same total income over time no matter what its choice of accounting methods. This chapter then introduced several account titles found in long-term construction company balance sheets including **Construction in Progress** (490), **Progress Billings Receivable** (497), **Progress Billings** (500), **Revenues in Excess of Contract Billings** (500), and **Contract Billings in Excess of Revenues** (501).

You then learned about the nature of a **service company** (501), whose *primary* operating activities involve the sale of services rather than the manufacture or resale of products to its customers. One type of service-based company is the **financial service company** (504) such as a bank or other financial institution.

Three types of liability accounts reported in a bank's balance sheet are **demand deposits** (504), **savings deposits** (504), and **time deposits** (504). Just as **loans** (505) and **investments** (505) are a significant source of any bank's borrowed funds, so too do they constitute the majority of funds provided by banks to their customers. Finally, this chapter introduced four new tools with which you can evaluate a bank's financial performance. These tools are the **loan to deposit (LTD) ratio** (507), **net interest income** (509), **net interest margin** (509), and the **loan loss ratio** (509).

Appendix Summary with Key Terms

The number in parentheses following each **key term** is the page number on which the term is defined.

In the appendix, you learned that **consolidated financial statements** (511) present the financial effects of the combined transactions of a parent company and one or more of its subsidiary companies. A **parent company** (511) is a company that owns 50% or more of the voting stock of a **subsidiary company** (511). A subsidiary is **wholly owned** (511) when the parent company owns 100% of a subsidiary company's voting stock. In a less than wholly owned subsidiary company, the nonparent ownership of voting stock is referred to as a **minority interest** (518) and reported in a stockholders' equity account. When the amount paid by a parent exceeds the individual fair market values of a subsidiary's **net assets** (511), the excess is reported as an intangible asset account called **Goodwill** (514). The last concept introduced to reflect a consolidation subsequent to acquisition was **consolidated retained earnings** (519).

Making Business Decisions

YOUR PERFORMANCE OBJECTIVE 2
(page 18)

During weekends and vacations, you and two of your friends—Laura Hamadi and Jake Swensen—have been taking people on hiking and mountain biking trips in nearby national wilderness areas. Now the three of you have decided to start a more formal business and name it Call of the Wild. You also have decided that the form of this business will be a partnership.

Jake says Call of the Wild needs to do some advertising and buy some liability insurance. Laura agrees, and adds that a dedicated telephone number and a website would be great. Jake has $15,000 that he can invest in the company now, and Laura says she can come up with $10,000 in about three months. You only have $5,000 to invest now but you agree to invest an additional $10,000 when you graduate from college in 15 months. Jake will graduate in three months when he will be able to work full-time (40 hours a week) to help establish and develop the business. You can devote about 20 hours a week to the business for now, but when you graduate you will be able to work full time. Laura is still a sophomore and expects to finish school in about 30 months. She can devote 10 hours per week during that period but is certain she will not stay in the area more than six months after graduation.

In addition, you and Laura are the most experienced tour guides. Jake has only recently joined your group; he would like to lead a few tours, but he really prefers to work on the nontour-business tasks that you and Laura don't enjoy. Jake suggests that your partnership select one of the following profit-sharing arrangements:

1. Net income and net loss are shared equally among all partners.
2. Net income and net loss are allocated on the basis of each partner's initial capital investment.
3. Net income and net loss are allocated on the basis of each partner's total capital investment after one year.
4. 60% of the net income is allocated to a salary allowance for each partner that is based on hours worked in the business with the balance of net income allocated equally among partners.
5. 60% of the net income is allocated to a salary allowance for each partner that is based on hours worked in the business. The remaining balance is then subject to an interest allowance of 10% applied to each partner's capital balance. Finally, any profit or loss deficiency after the salary allowance and the interest allowance is split equally among the partners. This fifth arrangement is calculated by using the following schedule:

Salary Allowance	Interest Allowance	Equal Share of Remaining Profit	Profit Allocated to Each Partner

You know from your business law course that you need to draw up a partnership agreement that lays out the rights and obligations of the partners. You also know that when a change in the composition of the partnership occurs, the partnership must be dissolved and a new partnership agreement drawn up. The three of you decide to begin your partnership three months from now. Thus, you are faced with many important decisions that affect each of you financially. As a group you decide to start by individually considering answers to some of the many questions that have been raised and having a meeting to see what agreements you can reach.

Required

Based on the details given above for Call of the Wild, how would *you* answer the following questions in preparation for your meeting with Laura and Jake?

a. What percentage of this business should each partner own and why?
b. Which of Jake's profit-sharing alternatives do you prefer, assuming the following net income figures are reported?

Year 1	$20,000
Year 2	$36,000
Year 3	$42,000
Year 4	$50,000

c. Propose a profit-sharing arrangement that is different from any of Jake's suggestions.

d. If the business were to be sold within four years, how should the sale price be divided among the partners?
e. How would you answer each of questions (a), (b), and (d) if you were Jake? If you were Laura?
f. If cash from this business is held in a money market account, how should the interest earned on that account be accounted for?
g. Describe one other item that you would want included in this partnership agreement.

Questions

YOUR PERFORMANCE OBJECTIVE 4
(page 22)

10-1 Explain in your own words the meaning of key business terms.
- a. Limited liability
- b. Limited liability partnership (LLP)
- c. C Corporation
- d. Closely held corporation
- e. S Corporation
- f. Nonprofit corporation
- g. Limited liability company (LLC)
- h. Wholesaler
- i. Retailer
- j. Product cost
- k. Long-term construction companies
- l. Construction in Progress
- m. Progress Billings Receivable
- n. Contract Billings
- o. Progress Billings
- p. Revenues in Excess of Contract Billings
- q. Contract Billings in Excess of Revenues
- r. Loan
- s. Investment
- t. Loan to deposit ratio
- u. Net interest income
- v. Net interest margin
- w. Loan loss ratio

10-2 Explain the circumstances in which the use of the term *interest revenue* is preferable to the use of the term *interest income.*

10-3 Describe three characteristics that a sole proprietorship and a partnership have in common.

10-4 True or False? If there is no explicit agreement of how a partnership's net income is to be divided, the net income is divided equally among partners.

10-5 Describe three characteristics of a corporation.

10-6 Explain why the limited liability company (LLC) is such a popular form of entity.

10-7 Distinguish between the following industries: merchandising, manufacturing, construction, and service.

10-8 What are the three primary manufacturing costs?

10-9 Using a manufactured product you are familiar with, describe its raw material, direct labor, and manufacturing overhead components.

10-10 Distinguish between raw materials inventory, work in process inventory, and finished goods inventory. In which of the primary financial statements would these accounts be found?

10-11 Distinguish between direct costs and indirect costs.

10-12 Distinguish between the terms *cost of goods manufactured* and *manufacturing cost of goods sold.*

10-13 Distinguish between the percentage-of-completion and completed-contract methods.

10-14 Describe exactly how a percentage of completion is calculated by a long-term construction company.

10-15 Describe the nature of the income statements generated by a company that uses the completed-contract method.

10-16 If all construction industry income methods recognize the same income over time, why is the selection of a particular method so important?

10-17 At what amount is the construction in progress account reported when:
- a. The percentage-of-completion method is used?
- b. The completed-contract method is used?

10-18 How is a contractor's balance sheet presented when the construction in progress balance exceeds the progress billings balance?

10-19 How is a contractor's balance sheet presented when the progress billings balance exceeds the construction in progress balance?

10-20 Distinguish between a service company and a financial service company.

10-21 Distinguish between the terms *demand deposits, savings deposits,* and *time deposits.*

Appendix Questions

YOUR PERFORMANCE OBJECTIVE 4 *(page 22)*

A10-1 Explain in your own words the meaning of key business terms.
- a. Consolidated financial statements
- b. Parent company
- c. Subsidiary company
- d. Wholly owned
- e. Minority interest
- f. Net assets
- g. Goodwill
- h. Consolidated retained earnings

A10-2 How do consolidated financial statements differ from unconsolidated financial statements?

A10-3 Distinguish between a parent company and a subsidiary company.

A10-4 Explain whether minority interest can exist when a subsidiary company is wholly owned.

A10-5 What role do net assets play in how goodwill is accounted for?

A10-6 How does consolidated retained earnings differ from unconsolidated retained earnings?

Reinforcement Exercises

E10-1 Asking the Right Questions: A Group Activity

YOUR PERFORMANCE OBJECTIVE 4 *(page 22)*

It's often said that knowing the right answer is not nearly as important as asking the right question. Asking the right question is a problem-solving skill that will help you make sound business decisions. In this exercise, you will review the vocabulary introduced in Chapter 10 by creating questions to match answers—similar to a popular TV show.

Required

a. Given an answer, what's the question?
Choose **three** of the following terms to serve as an answer. Create an appropriate question for each term. For example, if you choose the term *balance sheet,* you might create the question *What financial statement reports the assets, liabilities, and owners' equity of an entity on a specific date?*

LLC	Cost of goods manufactured	C Corporation
LLP	Cost of goods sold	S Corporation
Direct labor	Manufacturing overhead	Progress Billings
Indirect costs	Net interest income	Net interest margin

b. Are you sure that's the question?
Have each member of your group read aloud the questions they developed in Requirement (a). As a group, decide whether each question is an accurate match for an answer. Once satisfied that all questions are appropriate, the group, as a whole, chooses the three best questions created within the group. Record the three questions chosen (with their answers) on separate pieces of paper or index cards and give them to your instructor.

c. What's the answer?
To ensure that you have learned the vocabulary terms listed in Requirement (a), your instructor will now quiz you on the questions written by all of your classmates.

E10-2 Comparing Different Forms of Business Entity

YOUR PERFORMANCE OBJECTIVE 30 *(page 464)*

Assume you and a friend are considering forming a new business together and are discussing whether to form a partnership or a corporation. Identify and explain two strengths and two weaknesses of each of these forms of business entity. What additional information would be useful in helping you make this decision?

E10-3 Dividing Partnership Net Income

YOUR PERFORMANCE OBJECTIVE 30 *(page 464)*

Isaac Davis and Victoria Huff are partners who had capital balances of $40,000 and $60,000, respectively, at the start of the year. Mr. Davis contributed an additional $20,000 on April 1 and Ms. Huff contributed an additional $30,000 on September 1. The partnership agreement states that partnership income will be allocated in a ratio of average capital balances. Assuming the partnership net income for this year is $45,000, calculate the amount that will be allocated to each partner's capital account.

YOUR PERFORMANCE OBJECTIVE 30 *(page 464)*

E10-4 Recording Corporate Transactions

The Flemington Company, a corporation, issues 24,000 shares of capital stock on March 23 in exchange for $48,000 in cash. On November 11, the company declares a $6,000 cash dividend to be paid on December 15. On December 15, the company pays the dividend declared on November 11. The company determines that the federal income tax for the year amounts to $18,000.

Required

a. Record the effects of these transactions on the elements of the balance sheet using the following form:

Account Titles	Assets = Liabilities + Owners' Equity

b. Record these transactions in journal entry form.

YOUR PERFORMANCE OBJECTIVE 30 *(page 464)*

E10-5 Corporate Transaction Analysis

Illustrated below are the effects of four corporate transactions on the elements of the balance sheet. Write a possible explanation for each transaction.

Transaction	Assets	=	Liabilities	+	Owners' Equity
a.	80,000				80,000
b.			5,000		(5,000)
c.	(5,000)		(5,000)		
d.			12,000		(12,000)

YOUR PERFORMANCE OBJECTIVES 30, 31 *(pages 464, 475)*

E10-6 Identifying Forms of Business Entity and Type of Industry

Several forms of business entities and types of industries were discussed in this chapter. From your own experience, identify (by company name) specific examples of at least three different business entities and at least four industry types. For example, Kinko's would be a service type business organized as a corporation.

YOUR PERFORMANCE OBJECTIVE 31 *(page 475)*

E10-7 Recognizing Bad Debts

A company, with a year-end accounts receivable balance of $82,000, estimates that 2% of its $360,000 sales will be uncollectible. Analyze the effect of the bad debts on the elements of the balance sheet using the format below. Describe the effect this transaction will have on the balance sheet and income statement.

Transaction	Assets	=	Liabilities	+	Owners' Equity

YOUR PERFORMANCE OBJECTIVE 31 *(page 475)*

E10-8 Disclosing Net Accounts Receivable

In a recent annual report, Pfizer, Inc., a multinational pharmaceutical company, reported the following balance sheet amounts in millions:

	Year 3	Year 2	Year 1
Accounts receivable, less Allowance for doubtful accounts (Year 3—$68; Year 2—$67; Year 1—$35)	$3,864	$2,914	$2,220

For each year shown, what amount was shown in Pfizer's primary accounts receivable account? Why is the reported amount different from the primary account balance?

YOUR PERFORMANCE OBJECTIVE 31 *(page 475)*

E10-9 Calculating Raw Materials Used

Epincott Manufacturing purchases raw materials costing $462,000 during the current year. Assuming the company has $74,000 in raw materials at the start of the year and $86,000 at the end of the year, determine the amount of raw materials available and the amount used during the current year.

E10-10 Identifying Manufacturing Overhead Costs

YOUR PERFORMANCE OBJECTIVE 31 (page 475)

Identify which of the following items are manufacturing overhead costs:

a. Factory rent expense
b. Direct labor
c. Raw materials purchases
d. Depreciation—factory
e. Office salaries
f. Miscellaneous factory expenses
g. Advertising expense
h. Office rent expense
i. Salespeople's salaries
j. Factory utilities
k. Indirect labor
l. Miscellaneous office expenses
m. Depreciation—office
n. Factory machine maintenance
o. Uncollectible accounts expense
p. Factory insurance

E10-11 Calculating Cost of Goods Manufactured

YOUR PERFORMANCE OBJECTIVE 31 (page 475)

Perry Manufacturing used $244,000 in raw materials and incurred $162,000 in direct labor and $321,000 in manufacturing overhead costs. The company has work in process inventory of $88,000 at the start of the year and $72,000 at the end of the year. Calculate Perry's cost of goods manufactured for the year.

E10-12 Calculating Manufacturing Cost of Goods Sold

YOUR PERFORMANCE OBJECTIVE 31 (page 475)

Crown Industries has finished goods inventory of $124,000 at the start of the year and $141,000 at the end of the year. If cost of goods manufactured is $456,000 for the year, determine the manufacturing cost of goods sold.

E10-13 Analyzing Bank Transactions

YOUR PERFORMANCE OBJECTIVE 31 (page 475)

The following transactions relate to a bank:

a. Acquires cash from various sources including $500,000 in demand deposits, $300,000 in savings deposits, and $700,000 in borrowed funds.
b. Invests the cash by lending $800,000 to customers and purchasing investment securities costing $400,000.
c. Incurs interest expense of $100,000.
d. Earns interest revenue of $120,000.

Required

a. Analyze the effect of these transactions on the elements of the balance sheet using the headings below.

Asset Title	Assets	=	Liabilities	+	Owners' Equity	Sources of Assets Title

b. Describe the effect each of the transactions will have on the balance sheet and income statement and identify whether each transaction is an operating, investing, or financing activity.

E10-14 Analyzing Construction Transactions

YOUR PERFORMANCE OBJECTIVE 32 (page 489)

New London Construction agreed to build an office complex for a total contract price of $64 million with estimated construction costs of $48 million. Actual costs incurred and cash collections during the two-year contract period were as follows:

	Cash Collected	Costs Incurred and Paid
Year 1	$36,000,000	$32,000,000
Year 2	$28,000,000	$16,000,000

Required

a. Calculate the amount of net income recognized each year assuming the company uses the completed-contract method.
b. Analyze the effect of the cash collections and costs incurred and paid during each year on the elements of the balance sheet using the headings below.

Asset Title	Assets	=	Liabilities	+	Owners' Equity	Sources of Assets Title

YOUR PERFORMANCE OBJECTIVE 32 *(page 489)*

E10-15 Analyzing Construction Transactions
Assume the information provided in Exercise 10-14, above, remains the same except that New London Construction decides to use the percentage-of-completion method.

a. Calculate the amount of net income recognized each year.
b. Analyze the effect of the cash collections and costs incurred and paid during each year on the elements of the balance sheet using the headings below.

Asset Title	Assets	=	Liabilities	+	Owners' Equity	Sources of Assets Title

Appendix Reinforcement Exercises

YOUR PERFORMANCE OBJECTIVE 33 *(page 511)*

AE10-1 Calculating Goodwill
Calculate the amount of goodwill in each of the following cases:

	Purchase Price	Ownership Percentage	Subsidiary Net Assets
a.	$185,000	90%	$200,000
b.	$160,000	100%	$160,000
c.	$132,000	80%	$150,000
d.	$117,000	70%	$160,000
e.	$150,000	80%	$175,000
f.	$175,000	90%	$180,000

YOUR PERFORMANCE OBJECTIVE 33 *(page 511)*

AE10-2 Calculating Minority Interest
Calculate the amount of minority interest in each of the following cases:

	Ownership Percentage	Subsidiary Net Assets
a.	75%	$120,000
b.	100%	$150,000
c.	90%	$150,000
d.	80%	$175,000
e.	98%	$200,000
f.	90%	$180,000

YOUR PERFORMANCE OBJECTIVE 33 *(page 511)*

AE10-3 Calculating Consolidated Retained Earnings
Calculate the amount of consolidated retained earnings in each of the following cases:

			Subsidiary	
	Parent Company Retained Earnings	Ownership Percentage	Retained Earnings at Purchase	Retained Earnings after Purchase
a.	$120,000	100%	$36,000	$45,000
b.	$135,000	80%	$50,000	$70,000
c.	$ 88,000	90%	$45,000	$45,000
d.	$100,000	75%	$52,000	$60,000
e.	$110,000	100%	$58,000	$53,000
f.	$140,000	80%	$60,000	$90,000

Critical Thinking Problems

P10-1 Dividing Partnership Net Income

YOUR PERFORMANCE OBJECTIVE 30 *(page 464)*

The partnership capital accounts of Churchill Downs, Ernie Equestrian, and Fred Filly have balances of $30,000, $20,000, and $40,000, respectively, on May 1, the beginning of the current fiscal year. Downs invests an additional $5,000 on August 1. Equestrian withdraws $10,000 during the current fiscal year. Their income agreement provides that Equestrian be allowed a yearly salary of $10,000; that each partner be allowed 5% interest on his capital balance at May 1; and that the remaining net income or net loss be divided equally. Assuming the partnership net income for the fiscal year is $17,500, calculate the amount that will be allocated to each partner's capital account.

P10-2 Identifying Forms of Business Entity and Type of Industry

YOUR PERFORMANCE OBJECTIVES 30, 31 *(pages 464, 475)*

The following accounts appear on a company's balance sheet on December 31:

a. Cash and cash equivalents
b. Preferred stock
c. Long-term debt
d. Short-term investments
e. Accounts receivable, net
f. Inventories: Finished goods
g. Dividends payable
h. Goodwill, net
i. Work in process inventory
j. Retained earnings
k. Raw materials and supplies inventory
l. Accounts payable
m. Short-term borrowings
n. Common stock
o. Income taxes payable
p. Post-retirement benefit obligation
q. Treasury stock
r. Property, plant, and equipment, net
s. Deferred taxes
t. Accrued compensation

Based on the preceding account titles, identify the form of business entity and type of industry you believe would characterize this company. Explain how you determined your response. In addition, identify whether each account listed is an asset, liability, or owners' equity.

P10-3 Identifying Forms of Business Entity and Type of Industry

YOUR PERFORMANCE OBJECTIVES 30, 31 *(pages 464, 475)*

The following accounts appear on a company's balance sheet on December 31:

a. Trading account liabilities
b. Loans: Consumer, net
c. Deposits—Interest bearing
d. Common stock
e. Federal funds sold
f. Allowance for loan losses
g. Loans: Commercial, net
h. Cash and cash equivalents
i. Brokerage receivables
j. Short-term borrowings
k. Long-term debt
l. Investments
m. Additional paid-in capital
n. Trading account assets
o. Brokerage payables
p. Acceptances outstanding
q. Non-interest-bearing deposits
r. Retained earnings
s. Premises and equipment, net
t. Preferred stock

Based on the preceding account titles, identify the form of business and type of industry you believe would categorize this company. Explain how you determined your response. In addition, considering the type of industry, identify whether each account listed is an asset, liability, or owner equity.

P10-4 Determining Manufacturing Costs

YOUR PERFORMANCE OBJECTIVE 31 *(page 475)*

In the following data, RM = Raw Materials, WIP = Work in Process, FG = Finished Goods, DL = Direct Labor, MO = Manufacturing Overhead, COGM = Cost of Goods Manufactured, and COGS = Cost of Goods Sold. Using the steps introduced in the chapter, fill in the missing information for (a) through (e):

Raw Materials		Manufacturing Process		Finished Goods	
RM, 1/1	$ 40,000	WIP, 1/1	$110,000	FG, 1/1	$ (d)
RM Purchases	(a)	RM Used	(b)	COGM	(e)
RM, 12/31	48,000	DL	230,000	FG, 12/31	72,000
RM Used	$331,000	MO	134,000	COGS	$718,000
		WIP, 12/31	98,000		
		COGM	$ (c)		

YOUR PERFORMANCE OBJECTIVE 31
(page 475)

P10-5 Determining Manufacturing Costs

In a recent annual report, Pfizer, Inc., a multinational pharmaceutical company, reported the following financial statement amounts in millions:

	Year 2	Year 1
Inventories:		
Finished goods	$ 650	$ 697
Work in process	711	890
Raw materials and supplies	293	241
Cost of sales	2,528	2,094

Assuming direct labor and manufacturing overhead costs amounted to $1,436 in Year 2, determine Pfizer's raw material purchases, raw materials used, and cost of goods manufactured during Year 2.

YOUR PERFORMANCE OBJECTIVE 31
(page 475)

P10-6 Preparing a Cost of Goods Manufactured and a Manufacturing Cost of Goods Sold Statement

Sprewell Corporation had the following inventory levels for 2004 and 2005:

	12/31/04	12/31/05
Raw materials	$18,000	$29,000
Work in process	16,000	46,000
Finished goods	12,000	7,000

The following costs were incurred during 2005:

Purchases of raw materials	$33,000
Direct labor	53,000
Factory overhead	36,000
Cost of goods sold	86,000

Required

Prepare a cost of goods manufactured and a manufacturing cost of goods sold statement for 2005.

YOUR PERFORMANCE OBJECTIVES 3, 31
(pages 183, 475)

P10-7 Financial Statement Analysis of a Bank

Citigroup, Inc., reported the following amounts (in millions) in a recent annual report:

	Year 2	Year 1
Interest revenue	$ 44,900	$ 46,239
Interest expense	24,768	27,495
Gross loans (loaned assets)	244,206	221,951
Credit losses	2,818	2,644
Total deposits	261,091	228,649
Total average earning assets	655,845	607,398

Using the information provided, calculate the following for Year 1 and Year 2 and explain which results were best for each item:

a. Loan to deposit (LTD) ratio
b. Net interest income
c. Net interest margin
d. Loan loss ratio

P10-8 Explaining Revenue Recognition

YOUR PERFORMANCE OBJECTIVE 32 (page 489)

In the notes to the financial statements contained in a recent annual report, Raytheon Company states: "Sales under long-term contracts are recorded under the percentage-of-completion method. Costs and estimated gross margins are recorded as sales as work is performed based on the percentage that incurred costs bear to estimated total costs utilizing the most recent estimates of costs and funding." In your own words, describe what this means and provide examples of which accounts you would expect to find on Raytheon's balance sheet related to these long-term contracts.

P10-9 Calculating Construction Income

YOUR PERFORMANCE OBJECTIVE 32 (page 489)

The Hygenics Company contracted to build a state of the art public restroom for the city of Little Rock. The total contract price was $1,000,000 and the total estimated cost for the construction was $600,000. The actual amounts of costs incurred and cash disbursed and received during the two-year contract period were as follows:

	Cost Incurred	Cash Disbursed	Cash Received
1st Year:	$420,000	$360,000	$500,000
2nd Year:	$180,000	$240,000	$500,000

Required

Providing numerical support where necessary,

a. Calculate net income for each of the two years under the percentage-of-completion and completed-contract methods.
b. Determine the balance in the Accounts Receivable account at the end of year one under the percentage-of-completion method.
c. Determine the balance in the Deferred Construction Revenue account (a liability) at the end of Year 1 under the completed-contract method.
d. Determine the balance in the Retained Earnings account at the end of Year 2 under both these methods (*Note:* assume a zero balance in this account before construction).

P10-10 Analyzing Construction Transactions

YOUR PERFORMANCE OBJECTIVE 32 (page 489)

Phillip Corporation began construction work under a three-year contract this year. The contract price is $1,600,000. Phillip uses the percentage-of-completion method for financial accounting purposes. The following financial statement presentations relate to this contract at December 31 of the first year:

Balance Sheet		
Accounts receivable		$30,000
Construction in progress	$100,000	
Less: Progress billings	(94,000)	
Costs and estimated earnings in excess of billings		6,000
Income Statement		
Pretax contract income recognized in Year 1		$20,000

Required

a. What was the initial estimated pretax income on this contract?
b. How much cash was collected in the first year of this contract?

P10-11 Calculating Construction Income

YOUR PERFORMANCE OBJECTIVE 32 (page 489)

On January 2 of Year 1, the Billy Owens Construction Company contracted to build luxury viewing suites for the Sioux Falls Coliseum Arena. The total contract price was $9,000,000 and the total estimated cost for the construction was $7,200,000. Owens incurred $2,400,000 in construction costs during Year 1, $4,000,000 during Year 2, and $800,000 during Year 3 in completing the luxury suites. The city of Sioux Falls paid $2,000,000 during Year 1, $3,000,000 during Year 2, and the remaining $4,000,000 of the contract price at the time the work was completed and approved in Year 3.

Required

a. Calculate net income for each of the three years under the following methods:
   1. Percentage-of-completion method.
   2. Completed-contract method.
b. Which method do you feel provides a better measure of Owen's performance under this contract? Why?
c. Under what circumstances would the method not selected in (b) above provide a better measure of performance?

YOUR PERFORMANCE OBJECTIVE 32 *(page 489)*

P10-12 Calculating Construction Income

Eastwood Construction Corporation was formed in Year 1 with capital stock of $300,000 contributed in cash. In that same year, the corporation contracted to build a supersonic Firefox jet aircraft for the city of Carmel. The total contract price was $1,800,000, and John Walenda, the manufacturing vice president for the company, estimated the cost of constructing the airplane to be $1,500,000. Actual cost incurred and cash collections during the two-year contract period were as follows:

	Costs Incurred and Paid	Cash Collected
Year 1	$1,200,000	$900,000
Year 2	$ 300,000	$900,000

Required

Construct the income statements and balance sheets for each of the two years under the following alternative income recognition methods:

a. Percentage-of-completion
b. Completed-contract

YOUR PERFORMANCE OBJECTIVE 32 *(page 489)*

P10-13 Calculating Income on a Long-Term Construction Contract

A company has a long-term contract with a total contract price of $186,000,000 and estimated construction costs of $124,000,000. Actual costs incurred and cash collections during the three-year contract period were as follows:

	Cash Collected	Costs Incurred and Paid
Year 1	$44,000,000	$38,000,000
Year 2	$84,000,000	$52,000,000
Year 3	$58,000,000	$34,000,000

a. Assuming the company uses the completed-contract method, calculate the amounts of revenue, expense, and net income that would appear on the company's income statements and the amounts of cash, construction in process, deferred revenue, and retained earnings that would appear on the company's balance sheets each year during the contract period.
b. Assuming the company uses the percentage-of-completion method, and that it bills the customer $62,000,000 per year on the contract, calculate the amounts of revenue, expense, and net income that would appear on the company's income statements and the amounts of cash, progress billings receivable, construction in process, revenues in excess of contract billings, contract billings in excess of revenues, and retained earnings that would appear on the company's balance sheets each year during the contract period.
c. Comparing the results obtained in parts (a) and (b) above, what was the net income (loss) per year and the total increase (decrease) to retained earnings for the contract period under each method?

P10-14 Comprehensive Problem: Journalizing Transactions of CMU Inc.
Below is the complete set of transactions for Cards & Memorabilia Unlimited as a corporation. Record these transactions in journal entry form including any adjustments.

YOUR PERFORMANCE OBJECTIVES 26b, 26e, 30 (pages 413, 464)

A	01/02	4,480 shares of CMU Inc. capital stock are issued at $10 per share in exchange for the following owner contributions: $30,000 of cash from Susan Newman, $9,200 of merchandise inventory from Martha Perez and a $5,600 investment in Marvel Corporation stock from George Wu.
B	01/02	$6,000 cash is withdrawn from the checking account to open a business savings account.
C_1	01/04	$10,000 worth of store equipment is acquired with a credit card.
D	01/06	$15,000 cash is paid to acquire merchandise inventory.
E	01/09	$2,000 cash is paid to the landlord for the security deposit on the store lease.
C_2	02/03	$10,000 cash is paid in full to settle the credit card obligation made on January 4.
F	07/01	$5,000 cash is borrowed with a bank credit line bearing interest at an 8% rate.
G	7/1–12/1	$18,000 worth of additional merchandise is acquired on account.
H	07/01	$7,000 cash is paid to acquire a used van with a 5-year useful life for the business.
I	11/01	$6,000 cash is collected from customers before any goods or services are provided.
J_1	7/31–11/30	$12,000 cash is paid to reduce accounts payable.
J_2	12/31	$6,000 of accounts payable is converted to a 6% interest bearing note payable due on March 31.
K_1	12/31	$5,000 cash is paid in full to settle the credit line loan made on July 1.
L	12/31	$4,000 worth of a computer and printer is acquired by signing a 2-year promissory note.
M	Daily	$63,200 of cash sales are made to customers throughout the year.
N	Daily	$20,000 of revenue is earned on account—$19,400 for customer credit sales throughout the year and $600 for teaching a course.
O_1	12/02	$275 interest is earned from 1/2–12/2 on $6,000 of savings bearing 5% interest.
P	Monthly	$1,000 cash is paid for office rent due the first day of each month beginning February 1.
Q	09/30	$2,000 worth of the store equipment bought on January 4 for $10,000 is sold for $1,350.
R_1	09/30	$300 of depreciation is recorded to recognize the use of equipment sold on September 30.
S	12/05	$8,000 cash is paid to employees for work performed through the year's last payday.
K_2	12/31	$200 cash is paid for interest due on $5,000 borrowed on July 1 at 8% and repaid on December 1.
T	Daily	$4,250 cash is paid for miscellaneous expenses incurred throughout the year.
U	12/31	$30,000 of cost of goods sold is determined by taking a physical count of inventory.
V	Daily	$15,000 cash is collected from customers throughout the year for amounts owed.
W_1	10/30	$12,900 of cash dividends payable on December 1 are declared.
W_2	12/01	$12,900 of cash dividends declared on October 30 are paid on December 1 to shareholders of record as of November 15.
O_2	12/31	$25 of interest is earned but uncollected on a $6,000 savings account bearing 5% interest.
X	12/31	$750 of salaries expense and $350 of miscellaneous expense are incurred but unpaid.
R_2	12/31	$2,300 of depreciation is recorded on the use of unsold equipment.
Y	12/31	$4,000 worth of merchandise is delivered to customers who paid in advance.
Z	12/31	$4,500 of federal income tax is incurred for the year using a tax rate of 15%.

P10-15 Comprehensive Problem: Posting Journal Entries to the Ledger and Preparing Trial Balances

YOUR PERFORMANCE OBJECTIVES 26c, 26d, 26f, 30 (pages 413, 464)

Required

a. Post the journal entries to the ledger for transactions A through W_2 in Problem 10-14 and prepare an unadjusted trial balance.
b. Post the journal entries to the ledger for transactions O_2, X, Y, R_2, and Z in Problem 10-14 and prepare an adjusted trial balance.

P10-16 Comprehensive Problem: Preparing Financial Statements

YOUR PERFORMANCE OBJECTIVES 26g, 30 (pages 413, 464)

Prepare the financial statements for the transactions listed in Problem 10-14. *Note:* This problem requires that you first complete P10-14 and P10-15.

YOUR PERFORMANCE OBJECTIVES 26h, 26i, 30 (pages 413, 464)

P10-17 Comprehensive Problem: Preparing Closing Entries and a Post-Closing Trial Balance
Prepare the closing entries and post-closing trial balance for the transactions listed in Problem 10-14. *Note:* This problem requires that you first complete P10-14 and P10-15.

Appendix Critical Thinking Problems

YOUR PERFORMANCE OBJECTIVE 33 (page 511)

AP10-1 Preparing a Consolidated Balance Sheet
Maximal Security Systems buys 80% of Minimal Risk, Inc. for $360 on January 1. Shown below are the balance sheets of both the parent (Maximal) and the subsidiary (Minimal) just before acquisition. Assume that the book and fair market values of the subsidiary's net assets are equal. During the year, Minimal reported a net income of $100.

	Data Just before Acquisition	
	Maximal	Minimal
Assets	$800	$400
Capital stock	$600	$200
Retained earnings	200	200
	$800	$400

Required
Complete the consolidated balance sheet shown below as of December 31. An asterisk indicates those accounts for which an answer is required.

Consolidation Accounts	Maximal	Minimal	Numerical Support	Consolidated Balance Sheet
Other assets	$560	$500		$1,060
* Investment in Minimal	360	–0–		
* Goodwill	–0–	–0–		
Total assets	$920	$500		$
* Minority interest	$–0–	$–0–		$
* Capital stock	600	200		
* Retained earnings	320	300		
Total equities	$920	$500		$

YOUR PERFORMANCE OBJECTIVE 33 (page 511)

AP10-2 Preparing a Consolidated Balance Sheet
Homestyle Buns buys 90% of Edible Hot Dogs Inc. for $400 on January 1. Shown below are the balance sheets of both the parent (Homestyle) and the subsidiary (Edible) just before acquisition. Assume that the book and fair market values of the subsidiary's net assets are equal. During the year, Edible reported a net income of $90.

	Data Just before Acquisition	
	Homestyle	Edible
Assets	$800	$400
Capital stock	$600	$200
Retained earnings	200	200
	$800	$400

Required
Complete the consolidated balance sheet shown below as of December 31. An asterisk indicates those accounts for which an answer is required.

Consolidation Accounts	Homestyle	Edible	Numerical Support	Consolidated Balance Sheet
Other assets	$500	$490		$ 990
* Investment in Edible	400	–0–		
* Goodwill	–0–	–0–		
Total assets	$900	$490		$
* Minority interest	$–0–	$–0–		$
* Capital stock	600	200		
* Retained earnings	300	290		
Total equities	$900	$490		$

AP10-3 Preparing a Consolidated Balance Sheet

YOUR PERFORMANCE OBJECTIVE 33
(page 511)

The Majestic Corporation acquired control of the Diminutive Corporation on January 4 by purchasing 80% of its outstanding stock at a cost of $85,000. The entire excess of cost over fair market value acquired is attributed to goodwill. Diminutive declares a dividend of $5,000 during the year and reports net income of $20,000 at the end of the year. Diminutive Corporation's stockholders' equity accounts appeared as follows on January 4 and December 31 of the current year:

	January 4	December 31
Common stock	$75,000	$75,000
Retained earnings	25,000	40,000

Additional Information

1. The fair market value of Diminutive's net assets (stockholders' equity) is identical to their book value.
2. Majestic Corporation carries its Investment in Diminutive Subsidiary account on its own books at cost.

Required

a. Record the transaction made by Majestic to recognize the January 4 acquisition.
b. Record the worksheet transactions needed to prepare a consolidated balance sheet at the end of the year.
c. Given the following December 31 single-company balance sheets of Majestic and Diminutive and the work sheet entries from part (b), complete the consolidated balance sheet below.

Consolidation Accounts	Majestic	Diminutive	Numerical Support	Consolidated Balance Sheet
Cash	$ 15,000	$ 25,000		$
Other assets	100,000	90,000		
*Investment in Diminutive	85,000	—		
*Goodwill	—	—		
Total assets	$200,000	$115,000		$
*Minority interest	$ —	$ —		$
*Capital stock	100,000	75,000		
*Retained earnings	100,000	40,000		
Total equities	$200,000	$115,000		$

Research Assignments

A wide variety of interesting Research Assignments for this chapter are available for the following topics at www.mhhe.com/solomon:

R10-1 Comparing Different Forms of Business Entity (PO 30)
R10-2 Determining Specific Transactions of a Corporation (PO 30)
R10-3 Identifying Different Types of Industry (PO 31)
R10-4 Exploring the Financial Statements of Companies in the Same and Different Industries (PO 31)
R10-5 Exploring the Financial Statements of Companies in the Same and Different Industries (PO 31)
R10-6 Exploring a Merchandising Business (PO 31)
R10-7 Exploring a Manufacturing Business (PO 31)
R10-8 Exploring a Construction Business (PO 31)
R10-9 Exploring a Service Business (PO 31)
R10-10 Exploring a Financial Services Business (PO 3 and 31)
R10-11 Exploring a Manufacturing Business (PO 31)

CHAPTER ELEVEN

11 How Operating Activities Affect Financial Statements

Also be sure you have mastered the following Performance Objectives from previous chapters. They lay the foundation for the concepts you will learn in this chapter:

PO3
PO4
PO7
PO8
PO13b
PO14
PO31

PERFORMANCE OBJECTIVES

In this chapter, you will learn the following new Performance Objectives:

PO34 **Identify** the differences between the periodic and perpetual inventory systems, **describe** the effects of transactions appropriate to each system, and **discuss** the situations in which each system is most appropriate.

PO35 **Select** those year-end inventory transactions that should be included and those that should be excluded from the year-end inventory and **calculate** the appropriate cost of all inventory units on hand.

PO36 **Calculate** the balances in ending inventory and cost of goods sold for the specific identification method and the FIFO, LIFO, and average cost-flow assumptions under both a periodic and perpetual inventory system.

PO37 **Identify** the differences between the FIFO and LIFO inventory cost-flow assumptions and **explain** the relative advantages and disadvantages of adopting each as the cost-flow assumption.

PO38 **Determine** the effect (overstatement, understatement, or none) of an inventory error on both balance sheet and income statement amounts.

PO39 **Calculate** the estimated cost of goods sold and cost of ending inventory using the gross margin method.

PO40 **Explain** the principle of conservatism and **apply** it when accounting for inventories and investments with the lower of cost or market method.

PO41 **Distinguish** between the percentage of sales method and the percentage of receivables method for estimating uncollectible amounts in the Allowance for Bad Debts account.

PO42 **Explain** how inventories and accounts receivable can be mismanaged and **describe** how financial statement analysis can be used to evaluate how effectively these resources are being managed.

MANAGING INVENTORY AT CMU

CARDS & MEMORABILIA UNLIMITED

Your backpack broke today, and you need a new one right away because school starts next week. All your friends have ClassPack—the specially designed backpack for college students—and you want one too. So you go to the store at the mall where your friends got theirs. But you can't find ClassPack displayed. You ask the clerk, who tells you that they don't have any in stock. You try three more stores, but none has a single ClassPack in stock.

So, you go on the Internet and check out a few sites. Again, no ClassPack! How could this be happening? And then you find out. Class Corporation, the manufacturer, is completely out of stock of the ClassPack. They misjudged how popular this product would be and didn't manufacture a large enough supply to meet the demand. Bottom line—you're not going to be wearing a ClassPack for three weeks! With regret you check out the sites for other types of backpacks, and you find a new brand called the BackUp—it has all of the features of the ClassPack, a wider color selection, and it's in stock!

Although fictional, this story raises some very real issues. Class Corporation has inventory problems. Customers are clamoring for the ClassPack, which is not in any of the company's warehouses. Class Corporation is losing sales, the stores that carry its backpacks are losing sales, and customers are not happy. Even if the ClassPack is back in stock soon, many customers might be lost forever. All of this occurred because of poor inventory management. This story suggests that poor inventory planning can have serious effects on customer service, revenue, and net income.

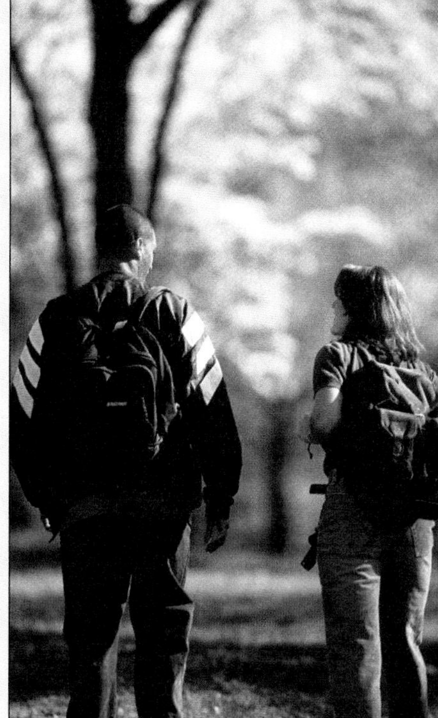

The nature of a company's inventory depends upon its type of business. For example, Class Corporation, a manufacturer, produces backpacks, binders, and organizers, so they have finished goods inventory and work in process inventory, as well as a raw materials inventory containing the materials used to make these items. At CMU, a merchandiser, Susan doesn't manufacture her inventory, but nevertheless has an inventory of trading cards and sports memorabilia. In contrast, service companies, such as advertising firms and banks, are unlikely to have inventory at all.

Companies that do have inventory often use inventory management tools to properly control their inventory. These tools include a set of principles and procedures to simplify the management of inventory. For example, business decision makers are usually concerned about the optimal amount of inventory needed to run a business effectively. If you have too much money tied up in your inventory, cash flow problems can result. If you have too little, you run the risk of poor customer service. How can you run your business effectively and still maintain a reasonable amount of inventory? The cost of carrying inventory itself can be as much as 30% or more of the value of the inventory per year so that holding $10 million of inventory can cost you $3 million per year. One tool sometimes used to deal with this problem is the EOQ or *economic order quantity* formula. Although this and other such tools are outside the scope of this course, be aware that seminars, institutes, consultants, and software abound to help managers manage inventory. You can even earn a CPIM, a certified production and inventory management, designation from APICS, the American Production and Inventory Control Society.

Since Susan faced some of the common inventory issues of other retailers, she decided to research good practices in inventory management. After reading various books, articles, and Internet resources, she developed the following action plan to better manage her inventory at CMU:

- Maintain accurate inventory records: You can't easily sell your inventory unless you know how much you have and where it is. When Susan realized it was important to count her inventory on a regular basis, she implemented a well-designed cycle counting system, which she expected would quickly pay for itself.

(continued on next page)

(continued from previous page)

- Achieve quick turnover time: Susan learned the amount of inventory she carried had little to do with good customer service. The real key was the length of time it took her to replace an item. For example, if a particular item took four weeks to receive, then Susan had to reorder when she had at least four weeks supply, or risk running out of stock of that item.
- Turnover slow-moving inventory: Susan decided she would not try to stock every item anyone could ever want. In addition, Susan decided to reduce her prices on items for which there was little demand so as to reduce the size of her less profitable inventory. She decided to find alternative ways to please her customers and build their loyalty than simply carrying such low demand items.
- Replenish inventory according to demand: Susan decided to replenish her inventory according to customer demand rather than relying solely on static forecasts. These projections can be useful managerial tools, but should always be modified by day-to-day reports of what customers are actually buying.

Based on this list, Susan decided to count all of her inventory and then implement a computerized system that would record every item she sold, keep running totals of each item, and red flag any item when it reached its reorder lead time. She made plans to have twice yearly 20% to 50% off sales to turn over slow-moving inventory. Finally, she began using her computerized system to identify the items most in demand, so she could take steps to ensure that these were always in stock. Susan believed that these inventory management practices would greatly help her manage inventory during CMU's first year of business.

As you just discovered was true of CMU, inventories play an important role in the operating activities of many businesses. As a result, this chapter focuses on the financial statement effects of inventory and other operating activity transactions.

What Are the Financial Statement Effects of Operating Activities?

To ensure that you maximize your learning in this chapter, let's briefly review the financial statement effects of operating activities that were described in earlier chapters. This review will concentrate on the income statement, balance sheet, and statement of cash flows because the primary purpose of the statement of owners' equity is to link the income statement to the balance sheet. As discussed in Chapter 10, the financial statement effects of operating activities vary by type of industry. Since the accounts reported on the financial statements of merchandisers, manufacturers, and service companies are not identical, let's reexamine the financial statement effects of operating activities in each of these industries.

Merchandisers

Merchandise inventory represents finished goods whose physical form is unaltered while being held for future resale. The primary operating activity of most merchandising businesses (both wholesalers and retailers) is not to produce merchandise inventory but, rather, to resell it to customers.

The primary balance sheet effects of a merchandiser's operating activities are on current asset and current liability accounts. For example, there are at least four such effects:

1. The Accounts Receivable account increases with credit sales and decreases with cash collections.
2. The Merchandise Inventory account increases with inventory purchases and decreases with sales.

3. The Accounts Payable account increases with credit purchases of inventory and decreases with cash payments.
4. The Deferred Revenue liability account increases with cash collections from customers before sale and decreases with product deliveries.

In contrast, the primary income statement effects of a merchandiser's operating activities are on the Sales Revenue and Cost of Goods Sold accounts.

The primary statement of cash flow effects of a merchandiser's operating activities are such line items as *cash collected from customers* and *cash paid for merchandise purchases*. Recall that these disclosures are clearly reported only in a statement of cash flows prepared under the direct method of reporting cash flow from operations. This chapter will not discuss how operating activities are reported using the indirect method. This is because those effects—period ending changes in current asset and current liability balances—were discussed in Chapter 8 and are not nearly as intuitive as the transactions reported under the direct method. These general financial statement effects are illustrated in Figure 11-1 while the corresponding financial statement effects for CMU are illustrated in Figure 11-2.

FIGURE 11-1 Financial statement effects of merchandiser operating activity transactions

Operating Activity Transactions	Balance Sheet	Income Statement	Statement of Cash Flows
Cash purchase of inventory	Merchandise inventory Cash	None	Cash paid for merchandise purchases
Credit purchase of inventory	Merchandise inventory Accounts payable	None	None
Cash payments to suppliers	Accounts payable Cash	None	Cash paid for merchandise purchases
Cash sales	Cash Merchandise inventory	Sales revenue Cost of goods sold	Cash collected from customers
Credit sales	Accounts receivable Merchandise inventory	Sales revenue Cost of goods sold	None
Cash collections	Cash Accounts receivable Deferred revenue	None	Cash collected from customers
Product deliveries	Deferred revenue	Sales revenue	None

Manufacturers

The primary operating activities of most manufacturers include the purchase and storage of raw materials, the manufacture and storage of both unfinished and finished products, and the resale of finished products to merchandisers or consumers. As a result, a manufacturer's balance sheet differs from a merchandiser's balance sheet in that it reports *three* primary inventory accounts—raw materials inventory, work in process inventory, and finished goods inventory. Raw material inventory includes raw material costs not yet used up or placed into production that will eventually be physically incorporated into the finished product. Work in process inventory includes the cost of raw materials, direct labor, and manufacturing overhead that attach to product units that are not completely manufactured, or unfinished goods. Finished goods in-

FIGURE 11-2

Primary financial statement effects (shown in color) of Cards & Memorabilia Unlimited operating activities

Balance Sheet
at December 31

Current Assets		Current Liabilities	
Cash	$38,275	Accounts payable	$ 350
Accounts receivable	5,000	Salaries payable	750
Interest receivable	25	Deferred revenue	2,000
Merchandise inventory	13,000	Note payable	6,000
	$56,300		$9,100

Income Statement
For the Year Ended December 31

Revenues		
Sales revenue	$86,600	
Service revenue	600	
Interest revenue	300	$87,500
Expenses		
Cost of goods sold	$30,000	
Rent expense	11,000	
Salaries expense	8,750	
Depreciation expense	2,600	
Miscellaneous expense	4,600	
Interest expense	200	
Loss on equipment sale	350	$57,500
Net income		$30,000

Statement of Cash Flows
For the Year Ended December 31

Cash flows from operating activities:		
Cash collected from customers	$ 84,200	
Cash paid for merchandise purchases	(27,000)	
Cash paid for leased space	(11,000)	
Cash paid for salary expense	(8,000)	
Cash paid for miscellaneous expenses	(4,250)	
Interest received	275	
Interest paid	(200)	
Net cash provided by operating activities		$34,025

ventory, the third and final inventory account involved in the manufacturing process, includes the cost of completed but unsold goods. In contrast to these balance sheet accounts, a manufacturer's income statement accounts and its statement of cash flow line items do not differ significantly from those of merchandisers.

Service Companies

You learned in Chapter 10 that service companies cover a much wider range of business operations than do other industries and provide a diverse set of services that range from banking, insurance, and transportation to education, government, and philanthropy. For the sake of simplicity, we will cover a narrower range of services and say that, in general, a service company's *primary* operating activities involve the sale of services rather than the manufacture or resale of products to its customers. As a result, you would not expect to see either a Sales Revenue account or a Cost of Goods Sold account in a service company's income statement. You would expect to see a Service Revenue account. Likewise, you would not expect to see significant inventory accounts reported on its balance sheet other than for supplies.

The Operating Cycle Revisited

Now that you have reviewed the financial statement effects of operating activities, let's reverse our perspective and return to the initiation of those same activities. To do so, we will use the operating cycle concept introduced in Chapter 5 to examine specific operating activity transactions. As Figure 11-3 shows, the **operating cycle** for a merchandiser is the average length of time it takes a business to move, or cycle, through three major transaction phases—paying cash to purchase merchandise inventory, selling this inventory, and collecting cash from the sale of inventory. That is, the cycle starts with a cash outflow and ends with a cash inflow; it moves from cash back to cash. As you can see, the operating cycle is aptly named. The word *operating* refers to the normal phases of purchasing, selling, and collecting included in the term *operating activities.* The word *cycle* is appropriate because purchasing, selling, and collecting are repetitive phases in the operation of a business.

Suppose it takes Cards & Memorabilia Unlimited an *average* of 20 days to receive its prepaid purchases of merchandise inventory, 45 more days for that inventory to be

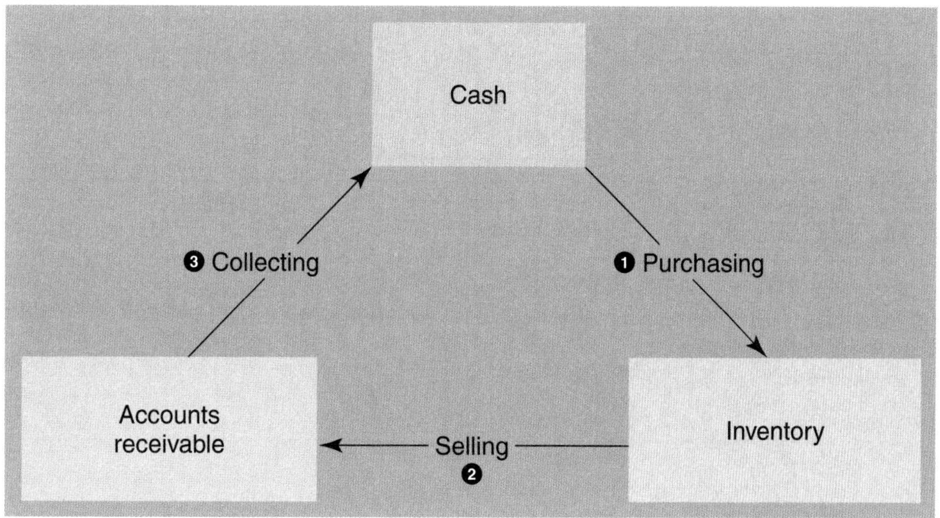

FIGURE 11-3

The operating cycle for a merchandiser

❶ **Purchasing phase:** The first phase of the operating cycle begins at the moment cash is used to acquire merchandise inventory. It ends when this inventory is received from a supplier and is ready for sale.

❷ **Selling phase:** The second phase of the operating cycle begins when the inventory is received and ready for sale. It ends with the sale, that is, delivery of the product to the customer.

❸ **Collecting phase:** The third phase of the operating cycle begins when the customer receives the product. It ends when the seller receives cash, either immediately or later when an account receivable is collected from customers.

sold, and 25 more days to collect outstanding customer balances. The length of this operating cycle is 90 days (20 + 45 + 25). This is the average number of days it takes Cards & Memorabilia Unlimited to generate a return of cash from an investment of cash. Assuming a 360-day year for simplicity, Cards & Memorabilia Unlimited will experience four (360 days/90 days) operating cycles a year. Now, let's briefly review the effects (increase or decrease) on the fundamental accounting equation of the three major transaction phases described above—purchasing, selling, and collecting.

Purchasing Transactions

The first phase of the operating cycle for a merchandiser begins at the moment cash is paid to acquire merchandise inventory. It ends when this inventory is received and ready for sale. From the perspective of Chapter 9, this purchasing phase of the operating cycle is included in what was called the spending cycle. Note that a corresponding phase of the operating cycle for manufacturers is included in what was called the conversion cycle. The spending cycle consists of at least three possible inventory transactions: (a) the cash purchase of inventory, (b) the credit purchase of inventory, and (c) the cash payment of a credit purchase. As you can see from the illustration of these transactions in Figure 11-4, the effect of transaction (a) and the combined effect of transactions (b) and (c) on the balance sheet are the same. In each case, there is an increase in the Merchandise Inventory account and an ultimate decrease in the Cash account. Depending on the terms of the purchase and the particular practices of a company, separate accounts for freight, purchase discounts, and purchase returns and allowances might also be affected. It is also highly likely that the Accounts Payable account will be increased when both the inventory and the vendor's invoice have arrived and decreased when the vendor is paid. Keep in mind, however, that there is no income statement effect during purchasing. The statement of cash flows is affected, however, when the direct method is used. Specifically, the line item *cash paid for merchandise purchases* will be increased as a result of these purchasing transactions.

FIGURE 11-4 The transaction effects of the purchasing phase

	Transaction Analysis				Journal Entry		
		Fundamental Accounting Equation					
	Account Titles	**Assets** =	**Liabilities** +	**Owners' Equity**	**Account Titles**	**Debit**	**Credit**
	Cash purchase						
a.	Merchandise Inventory	xx			Merchandise Inventory	xx	
	Cash	(xx)			Cash		xx
	Credit purchase						
b.	Merchandise Inventory	xx			Merchandise Inventory	xx	
	Accounts Payable		xx		Accounts Payable		xx
c.	Accounts Payable		(xx)		Accounts Payable	xx	
	Cash	(xx)			Cash		xx

The combined effect of these two transactions produces a zero balance in the Accounts Payable account.

Selling Transactions

The second phase of the operating cycle begins when the inventory is received and ready for sale. It ends with the sale, that is, the delivery of the product to the customer. From the perspective of Chapter 9, this selling phase of the operating cycle is included in what was called the revenue cycle. As illustrated in Figure 11-5, this phase of the revenue cycle consists of at least two possible transactions: (a) the credit sale of inventory and (b) the simultaneous recognition of cost of goods sold and the removal of inventory from the company's control. These selling phase transactions put into motion a series of changes in each of the primary financial statements. The first effect on the balance sheet is the direct increase in the Accounts Receivable account. A less obvious, but still important, effect on the balance sheet may take place through the Allowance for Uncollectibles account, which will be described in more detail later in this chapter. Meanwhile, the income statement is effected because the Sales Revenue account is increased when the credit sale is made. If the merchandise conveyed in the credit sale is discounted, returned, or damaged, additional contra revenue accounts will also be created. Since neither of the transactions shown in Figure 11-5 effects cash, the statement of cash flows is uneffected by this phase of the operating cycle.

FIGURE 11-5 The transaction effects of the selling phase

	Transaction Analysis					Journal Entry		
		Fundamental Accounting Equation						
Account Titles	Assets	=	Liabilities	+	Owners' Equity	Account Titles	Debit	Credit
Credit sale								
a. Accounts Receivable	xx					Accounts Receivable	xx	
Sales Revenue					xx	Sales Revenue		xx
COGS recognition								
b. Cost of Goods Sold					(xx)	Cost of Goods Sold	xx	
Merchandise Inventory	(xx)					Merchandise Inventory		xx

Collecting Transactions

The third phase of the operating cycle begins when the customer receives the product. It ends when the seller receives cash, either immediately or later when an account receivable is collected from customers. From the perspective of Chapter 9, this collecting phase of the operating cycle is also included in the revenue cycle. As illustrated in Figure 11-6, this next phase of the revenue cycle consists of at least two possible transactions: (a) the cash sale of inventory and (b) the collection of cash from a credit sale.

FIGURE 11-6 The transaction effects of the collecting phase

	Transaction Analysis					Journal Entry		
		Fundamental Accounting Equation						
Account Titles	Assets	=	Liabilities	+	Owners' Equity	Account Titles	Debit	Credit
Cash sale								
a. Cash	xx					Cash	xx	
Sales Revenue					xx	Sales Revenue		xx
Cash collection								
b. Cash	xx					Cash	xx	
Accounts Receivable	(xx)					Accounts Receivable		xx

Both of these transactions have the effect of increasing the Cash account on the balance sheet and the collection of the credit sale has the effect of reducing the Accounts Receivable account on the balance sheet. Meanwhile, the income statement is effected because the Sales Revenue account is increased when the cash sale is recorded. If the merchandise conveyed in the cash sale is discounted, returned, or damaged, additional contra revenue accounts might also be created. Not surprisingly, both of these transactions affect the statement of cash flows under the direct method of reporting operating activities. Specifically, the line item *cash collected from customers* will increase as a result of either cash transaction.

Now that we have identified the major transactions associated with the operating cycle, let's find out exactly how these specific operating activity transactions create the effects that you see reported in the balance sheet, income statement, and statement of cash flows. We'll start with a detailed look at how the amounts appearing next to inventory on the balance sheet and cost of goods sold on the income statement are compiled.

How Purchasing and Selling Affect Inventory and Cost of Goods Sold

Undoubtedly, you now realize that the inventory and cost of goods sold accounts of merchandising and manufacturing entities usually have a significant effect on their respective financial statements. What you might not realize, however, is just how many distinct inventory methods play a role in the determination of those two account balances. As a result, most of the remaining portion of this chapter focuses on the essential topics associated with accounting for inventories. As you explore several different inventory methods in this chapter, however, your learning will be simplified if you consciously use a single organizing concept—the inventory equation. Because this valuable tool is the single concept common to all inventory methods, it will help you better understand the unique role played by each such inventory method.

The Special Role of the Inventory Equation

In Chapter 6 you were introduced to the use of the inventory equation when we used it to calculate CMU's cost of goods sold expense in Transaction U. Likewise, in Chapter 10 you saw the inventory equation applied to three types of inventories to produce the manufacturing cost of goods sold. You'll soon discover how this same equation can help you better understand more detailed information about inventories. In fact, you will be encouraged to use the inventory equation as the source of your conceptual understanding for each of the inventory methods discussed in this chapter. Before you do so, however, let's revisit how the inventory equation was used first by CMU in Chapter 6 and then by manufacturers in Chapter 10.

Revisiting How CMU Used the Inventory Equation To refresh your memory as to how CMU used the inventory equation, a description of Transaction U, the cost of goods sold calculation, and a brief explanation are provided here:

Transaction U As a result of taking a physical inventory on December 31, the cost of all goods sold (Transactions M, N, and Z) was determined to be $30,000.

Calculation:	
Beginning inventory	$ -0-
Merchandise acquisitions or purchases	43,000
Cost of goods available for sale	43,000
Deduct: Ending inventory	(13,000)
Cost of goods sold	$ 30,000

Explanation Susan treated her beginning inventory as zero because her business did not exist at the end of the preceding year. So no inventory could be carried forward to the beginning of the current year. Susan assigned $43,000 to her inventory purchases by adding the costs from Transactions D ($15,000), G ($18,000), and A_2 ($10,000). In practice, amounts for freight charges and other costs necessary to bring the inventory into its intended location, or **freight-in**, will be added to the invoice cost of these purchases. Likewise, purchase discounts and purchase returns and allowances may also be deducted from the amount labeled *purchases*. When these additions and deductions are made, the result is usually labeled **net purchases**. Finally, Susan took a physical count of all her trading cards and sports memorabilia on hand at December 31 and discovered the ending balance in her merchandise inventory account was $13,000. Since she had $43,000 of inventory costs available to sell and didn't sell $13,000 of those costs, the cost of goods sold must amount to $30,000 ($43,000 − $13,000), that portion of the total cost of goods available for sale that is actually sold. Since the $30,000 represents the cost consumed or sold, it is properly reported in the income statement as an expense. Although you will usually see this equation presented in the vertical format shown earlier, let's now summarize it by looking at its equivalent horizontal format:

Beginning Inventory	+	Net Purchases	−	Ending Inventory	=	Cost of Goods Sold
$0	+	$43,000	−	$13,000	=	$30,000

Revisiting How a Manufacturer Uses the Inventory Equation To refresh your memory as to how a manufacturer uses the inventory equation, let's revisit the example we used in Chapter 10. You probably remember that three manufacturing resources or manufacturing cost categories—raw materials, direct labor, and manufacturing overhead—go into manufacturing a product.

Raw materials (RM), or direct materials, are assets that ultimately will be physically incorporated into the final product. The concept that underlies accounting for raw materials is the inventory equation. As you can see in the example here, this calculation involves a relationship between the Raw Materials Inventory balance sheet account at two different dates, the raw material purchases, and the raw materials used during the period.

Raw material inventory, 1/1	$ 15,000
Add: Raw material purchases	100,000
Raw material available	115,000
Deduct: Raw material inventory, 12/31	(12,000)
Raw material used	$103,000

Notice that you began the accounting period with raw materials valued at $15,000 from the preceding period, purchased $100,000 of the same raw material during the current period, and counted $12,000 of raw materials on hand at the end of the period. You then used the same concept for calculating cost of goods sold to calculate the cost of raw materials used during the period. The Raw Material Inventory account will be reported in the end-of-year balance sheet as having a $12,000 balance. The raw materials used of $103,000, however, represent product costs that are reported as assets until the products containing those raw material costs are sold.

Direct labor includes costs incurred from the work of employees who are *directly* involved—they work by hand on the product or operate machinery that produces the product—in the manufacture of the product. This cost category includes the costs of manufacturing salaries, employee benefits such as a company health plan, and even the employer's share of employee payroll taxes. In our ongoing example, the direct labor used amounts to $50,000 during the current period. Once again, this amount represents a product cost and is not reported as cost of goods sold until the products containing these direct labor costs are sold.

Manufacturing overhead, or indirect cost, is composed of costs essential to the production process but not directly incorporated in the product. Examples include:

- Heat, light, and power.
- The yearly depreciation cost of the building in which the manufacturing process is conducted.
- Indirect material costs such as machine oils, cleaning materials, paint, nails, and bolts often reported on the balance sheet under the account title **Manufacturing Supplies Inventory**.
- Building costs, such as property taxes, casualty insurance, and depreciation on machinery.
- Indirect labor costs of supervisors, janitors, and so on.

In our ongoing example, the total manufacturing overhead costs amount to $15,000.

As illustrated here, the three major cost categories are combined to account for the current year's manufacturing cost.

Raw materials used	$103,000
Direct labor	50,000
Manufacturing overhead	15,000
Total manufacturing cost incurred	$168,000

The $168,000 of total manufacturing or production cost, however, does *not* represent the amount to be expensed in the income statement. Study the relationships among this amount, the work in process inventory balances, and the cost of goods manufactured amount in the second use of the inventory equation shown here:

Work in process inventory, 1/1	$ 65,000
Add: Total manufacturing costs	168,000
Work in process inventory available	233,000
Deduct: Work in process inventory, 12/31	(70,000)
Cost of goods manufactured	$163,000

The $163,000 cost of goods manufactured amount represents costs of raw materials, direct labor, and manufacturing overhead included in the fully completed units of the current period. It is not itself expensed in the income statement. Instead, that role is reserved for the manufacturing version of cost of goods sold.

To calculate cost of goods sold, you must use the inventory equation a third time. You begin by adding last period's finished goods inventory to the cost of goods manufactured which results in the total cost of goods available for sale as shown here.

Finished goods inventory, 1/1	$ 30,000
Add: Cost of goods manufactured	163,000
Cost of goods available for sale	193,000
Deduct: Finished goods inventory, 12/31	(45,000)
Manufacturing cost of goods sold	$148,000

This addition is, in fact, equivalent to adding purchases of a merchandiser to its beginning merchandise inventory account. As you study this third application of the inventory equation, remember that the $148,000 amount—not the $163,000—is the proper expense amount to report in the income statement.

Essential to your comprehension of how a manufacturer uses the inventory equation is the fact that the cost of goods sold concept is repeated three times as shown in the following diagram of the manufacturing cost flow. Notice the similarity among these three calculations.

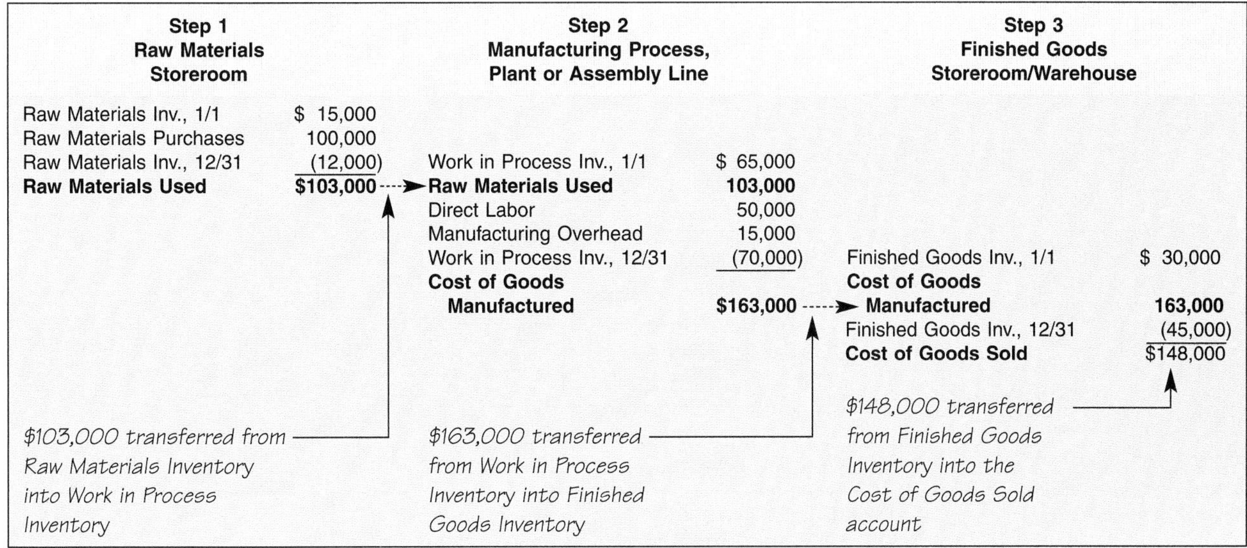

Notice also how each step is associated with its own inventory account—Raw Materials Inventory, Work in Process Inventory, and Finished Goods Inventory—and that taken together, these steps result in the calculation of cost of goods sold. This manufacturing flow of costs is illustrated first with the T-accounts shown in Figure 11-7 and then with the cost of goods manufactured and sold statement shown in Figure 11-8.

As promised, the inventory equation will play a special role in helping you better understand several of the inventory topics that follow. For example, once you have been introduced to the basic distinction between the periodic inventory system and

FIGURE 11-7 A T-Account illustration of manufacturing cost flows

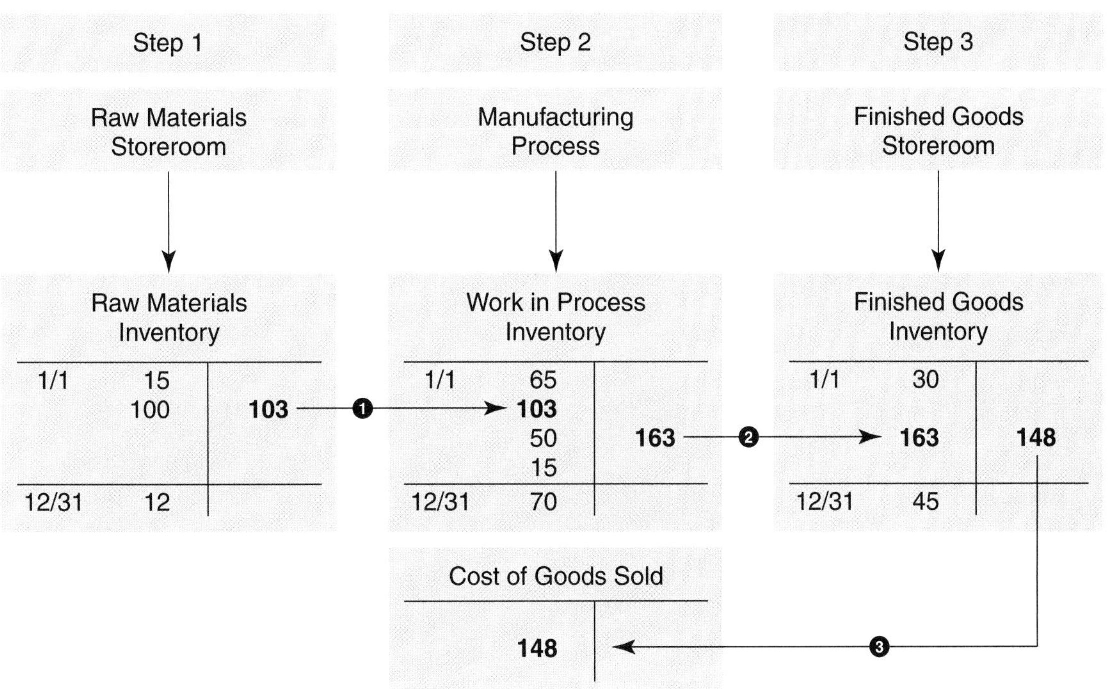

FIGURE 11-8

Cost of goods manufactured and sold statement

This amount represents product costs that are not yet reported on the income statement. (→ Cost of goods manufactured)

This entire amount must be reported on the income statement. (→ Manufacturing cost of goods sold)

HYPOTHETICAL MANUFACTURING COMPANY
Cost of Goods Manufactured and Sold Statement
For the Year Ended December 31

Work in process inventory, 1/1		$ 65,000
Add: Manufacturing costs		
Raw material used:		
Raw material inventory, 1/1	$ 15,000	
Add: Raw material purchases	100,000	
Raw material available	115,000	
Deduct: Raw material inventory, 12/31	(12,000)	103,000
Direct labor used		50,000
Factory overhead incurred		15,000
Work in process inventory available		233,000
Deduct: Work in process inventory, 12/31		(70,000)
Cost of goods manufactured		**$163,000**
Finished goods inventory, 1/1		$ 30,000
Add: Cost of goods manufactured		163,000
Cost of goods available for sale		193,000
Deduct: Finished goods inventory, 12/31		(45,000)
Manufacturing cost of goods sold		**$148,000**

the perpetual inventory system in the next section, the equation will be used to show you how you can calculate the amount of an inventory loss under the perpetual system.

Inventory Systems: A Matter of Timing

Two distinct systems are available for recording a company's cost of goods sold. These are the *periodic inventory system* and the *perpetual inventory system.* Although there are many ways to distinguish between these two systems, their essential difference concerns *when* each system records cost of goods sold. That is, if you want to determine which of these two systems is in use, the key question you should ask is: "When is cost of goods sold recorded?" Although large companies with diverse types of inventory might use hybrid systems—periodic for some inventory and perpetual for other types of inventory—they are distinct systems. No company will apply both systems to the same group of inventory items. Let's begin with the periodic inventory system.

Companies may use one of two inventory systems—periodic or perpetual—to record cost of goods sold.

Periodic Inventory System In a company that uses the periodic inventory system, the answer to the question, "When is cost of goods sold recorded?" is "Once, at the end of the period." That is, a **periodic inventory system** records cost of goods sold only at the end of an accounting period. Under this system, the cost of goods sold amount is derived only indirectly. As shown in the CMU example here, you generally need to first take a physical count of inventory.

Beginning inventory	$ -0-
Add: Net purchases	43,000
Cost of goods available for sale	43,000
Deduct: Ending inventory	(13,000)
Cost of goods sold	$30,000

Recall that when CMU counted its inventory at the end of its first year of business, it discovered the cost of its inventory on hand amounted to $13,000. As you can see, this *unsold cost of inventory* was subtracted from the total cost of inventory available for sale to derive the *sold cost of inventory*, or cost of goods sold. The $30,000 amount represents a periodic calculation that is recorded only once at the end of the period.

Businesses prefer to use a periodic inventory system when they have a large volume of low value per unit items. Although some sports cards and sports memorabilia are high priced, the vast majority of CMU's high volume of inventory items is not expensive. Consider how costly it would be, for example, for Susan to record the cost of goods sold every time she made a sale (as is done under the perpetual inventory system). While the perpetual system is advantageous to use in some business settings, it would be much too time-consuming and expensive an approach to use in the trading card and memorabilia industry. A periodic system is also preferable when the cost of being out of stock is not great. Although Susan could lose a sale if she does not have a particular baseball card of Yankee great Mickey Mantle in stock, her loss is insignificant compared to the loss an exclusive jewelery store would experience if it did not have a particular style of gold watch in stock. Since the periodic system does not provide close control of inventory—it only calculates inventory balances at the end of an accounting period—it is the preferable system to use when inventory is difficult to steal. This criterion is satisfied by CMU since most of its inventory is under glass or not easily accessible to customers. On the basis of these criteria, Susan's decision to choose the periodic inventory system seems well justified.

Perpetual Inventory System Had Susan calculated her cost of goods sold figure by recording costs every time a sale was made, she would have been using the **perpetual inventory system**. This system records cost of goods sold for each and every sale. That is, an expense is recorded *perpetually*, or continually, throughout the accounting period. To help you better visualize this system and how it differs from the periodic inventory system, Figure 11-9 illustrates how a Joe Montana autographed jersey—with an original cost of $50 and selling price of $85 cash by CMU—would be recorded under each system at the time of sale. As you can see, the perpetual inventory system, unlike the periodic inventory system, records the cost of goods sold and the decline in merchandise inventory at the time each sale is made.

No matter how technologically sophisticated a company is, the use of the perpetual system takes more time to maintain than does the periodic inventory system. Thus, there is a cost-benefit trade-off involved in the decision of which system to use. If you value close control of inventory for your business, you might be willing to absorb a higher cost to obtain that control and choose a perpetual system. Generally, businesses prefer to use a perpetual system when: they have a small volume of high

FIGURE 11-9 The primary distinction between the periodic and perpetual inventory systems using a Joe Montana autographed jersey as an example

Transaction Analysis					Journal Entry		
	Fundamental Accounting Equation						
Account Titles	Assets	=	Liabilities +	Owners' Equity	Account Titles	Debit	Credit
Periodic system							
Cash	85				Cash	85	
Sales Revenue				85	Sales Revenue		85
Perpetual system							
Cash	85				Cash	85	
Sales Revenue				85	Sales Revenue		85
Cost of Goods Sold				(50)	Cost of Goods Sold	50	
Merchandise Inventory	(50)				Merchandise Inventory		50

value per unit items, their items are relatively easy to steal, and their customers will not tolerate interruptions in supply. Recently, however, businesses that formerly used only the periodic inventory system are using the perpetual inventory system because technology has made it easier to record transactions.

INSIGHT

Will Technology Make the Periodic Inventory System Obsolete?

Don't make the mistake of assuming that businesses having computerized checkout systems always use a perpetual inventory system. Consider today's supermarket checkout registers known as *point of sale (POS) terminals.* Although these terminals are capable of providing a perpetual inventory system, many large supermarket chains have not found that the benefits of such a perpetual system justify the high costs involved. The decision to not include these terminals in their financial accounting and reporting system does not mean, however, that a supermarket chain is not using POS terminals to provide supermarket store managers with important managerial accounting information. For example, POS terminals can be used to determine item movement, information that is useful in making reorder decisions and in communicating to venders about item popularity. If an item is not turning over rapidly, the store manager might consider enhancement of its shelf presentation, in-store free samples, and sales. If all else fails, the manager might use this information to discontinue the unprofitable item. Furthermore, POS terminals can indicate time of sale, information that is useful in determining employee work schedules, and checker speed, information that is useful in determining which checkers need additional training in operating the terminal.

The **insight** you should gain here is that businesses do not select the periodic inventory system simply because they don't have sophisticated computer systems. Although the cost of record keeping using technology continues to decline, a decision to use the perpetual inventory system should be based on more than simply having access to the technology. Decision makers should make such a selection only when the perceived benefits of an accounting decision match or exceed the actual costs of that decision. Another **insight** you should gain here is that the financial accounting and reporting system and the managerial accounting and reporting system of a business often have very different objectives.

Now that you understand the essential differences between these two systems, consider Performance Objective 34. It will help you master your understanding of these two inventory systems.

YOUR PERFORMANCE OBJECTIVE 34
Identify the differences between the periodic and perpetual inventory systems, **describe** the effects of transactions appropriate to each system, and **discuss** the situations in which each system is most appropriate.

As you have just learned, the perpetual inventory system provides tighter control over inventory because it provides perpetual, or continual, feedback on the cost of goods sold, and therefore, the inventory on hand at any point in time. This is a significant advantage and makes it possible to not take a physical count of inventory (not recommended, however). For example, assume that CMU did use the perpetual inventory system and determined that cost of goods sold did, in fact, amount to $30,000. In that case, the inventory equation would be modified as follows:

Beginning inventory	$ –0–
Add: Net purchases	43,000
Cost of goods available for sale	$ 43,000
Deduct: Cost of goods sold	(30,000)
Ending inventory	$ 13,000

If this equation looks identical to the one presented earlier, look again! Unlike the periodic inventory system, the cost of goods sold is calculated directly; and the inventory can be derived as the difference between the cost of goods available for sale and the cost of goods sold. If you use this system, you'll want to avoid the temptation of not taking a physical count of inventory. Why? The answer is that not taking a physical count of inventory prevents you from benefiting from one of the most important advantages of the perpetual inventory system as described next.

Using the Inventory Equation to Reveal Inventory Losses So far, you have seen the special role the inventory equation plays in asset valuation and income determination. Now that you understand the perpetual inventory system, however, we can expand the usefulness of this equation. Instead of expecting the cost of goods available for sale to either be sold (cost of goods sold) or unsold (ending inventory), a third outcome is possible as illustrated by the following modification of the CMU first year inventory equation:

Beginning inventory	$ –0–
Add: Net purchases	43,000
Cost of goods available for sale	$ 43,000
Deduct: Ending inventory	(11,000)
Deduct: Cost of goods sold	(30,000)
Inventory loss	$ 2,000

In this example, let's assume that a physical count of inventory was taken, as it always should be no matter what system is in use. Notice, however, that this count amounted to $11,000. Since the perpetual records indicate that cost of goods sold is $30,000, the ending inventory should amount to $13,000 ($43,000 − $30,000). Because only $11,000 is found, it is apparent that an inventory loss of $2,000 has occurred. Further investigation is needed to determine why the inventory records ($13,000) differ from the actual count of inventory ($11,000). If this loss is due to normal causes such as breakage, we might adjust the cost of goods sold. If, instead, this loss is due to theft, waste, or an error, we must record an operating expense or loss. In any case, the perpetual inventory system enables you to identify such losses rather than burying them in cost of goods sold, as does the periodic inventory system. Be sure to notice that there are three outcomes for the units associated with the cost of goods available for sale. They can be sold (cost of goods sold), unsold (ending inventory), or lost or destroyed (loss on inventory).

The Proper Content of Inventory

It should now be clear to you that accurately counting the inventory on hand at the end of every accounting period is a necessity if a business is to properly measure its income. Although counting inventory might seem relatively easy, determining the correct number of inventory units and correct cost to assign each unit at period end is often one of the accountant's greatest challenges. Why? Because, at the close of an accounting period, a business might hold inventory it does not own, own inventory it does not hold, include costs that are not part of the inventory, and exclude costs that should be part of the inventory. Let's examine this problem more closely by considering what quantity or number of units should properly be included in inventory and then by considering what dollar costs should be assigned to each inventory unit.

Determining Proper Quantity What items should be included and what items should be excluded from inventory at the end of the accounting period? The general rule is to include all items or goods for which the company holds **legal title** or evidence of ownership, regardless of their location. In practice, this rule is not always followed because determining *exactly* when title or ownership passes can be difficult. Nevertheless, let's try applying this rule to items in transit and consigned items.

When the inventory your company has ordered is located somewhere between your supplier's property and your own property at the close of an accounting period, it is said to be *in transit*. At the same moment, your company might also have inventory it sold in transit between your property and your customer's property. Fortunately, many shipping contracts employ business terminology to reduce this potential confusion. Two such terms are FOB shipping point and FOB destination point.

When a shipment is designated **FOB** (free on board) **shipping point**, title to the items in the shipment legally passes to the purchaser when the seller delivers them to the common carrier, such as an air transport company, a trucking company, or a railroad. Suppose, for example, you, as the seller, ship inventory to a customer by UPS under the terms FOB shipping point. If UPS picks up this inventory from you on December 31, your customer rightfully owns the inventory and should include it in its count of inventory this period; and you, as the seller, should exclude these items from your year-end count of inventory to avoid double counting them. Nevertheless, in the interest of expediency, when amounts are immaterial or small, buyers often wait to record the inventory until it is received.

If this same shipment is designated **FOB destination point**, title will not pass as quickly. In this case, title to these items legally passes to the purchaser when it receives the items from the transportation carrier. Nevertheless, some sellers use shipment as a criterion if it is particularly difficult to determine when the items reach their destination. The following diagram illustrates the relative timing of these terms more clearly.

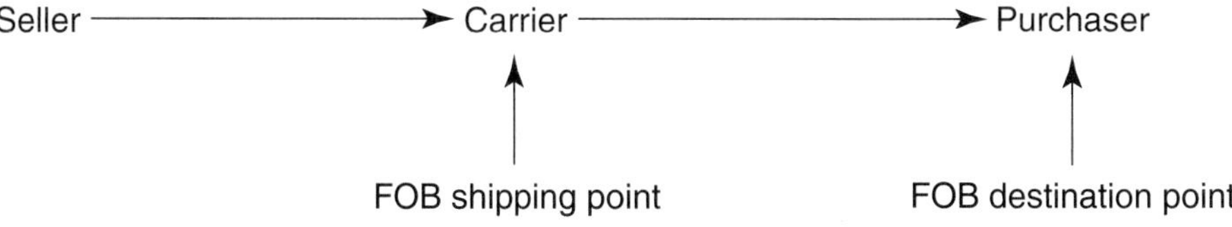

Another situation involving legal title is when goods are sold on *consignment*. To explain the nature and treatment of consigned inventory items, let's use a hypothetical CMU transaction. Assume that Susan Newman wants to sell her cards and sports memorabilia at a popular Phoenix, Arizona, card show but has a conflict and is unable to personally attend. To enable her to still sell her inventory to customers, she decides to sell her inventory on **consignment**, an arrangement in which Susan, the **consignor** or seller, transfers physical possession but not ownership of her inventory to a third party known as the **consignee**. This individual serves as her agent in the potential sale of her goods to the customer. If this consigned inventory is unsold but still in the physical possession of her consignee at the end of the period, Susan still has legal title to it and, therefore, she must account for it as part of her own inventory.

At the end of the accounting period, Susan should include in her inventory both the acquisition cost of any unsold inventory still on consignment and any handling and shipping charges involved in its transfer to the consignee. Susan should exclude these consigned items from her inventory only when they are actually sold by her consignee. At that time, her sales revenue amount should be calculated by multiplying its sales price times units sold less the consignee's commission and any selling expenses incurred by Susan. Notice that the consignee should never include consigned inventory in its own balance sheet because, despite having possession of the goods, it never holds legal title. The following diagram illustrates that the consignor holds title until the inventory is sold to the customer. At that point, it is then the customer who holds legal title.

Determining Proper Cost The general rule for determining the proper cost of inventory is to use either the price paid or the consideration given to acquire the inventory and put it into a condition and position ready for sale. More specifically, this means you should include the invoice price less any cash discounts plus any of the following incidental costs that apply:

1. Freight or shipping.
2. Receiving and storage.
3. Taxes, tariffs, and duties.
4. Insurance during transportation or storage.
5. Aging costs.

As described earlier when we discussed net purchases, freight-in, the cost of freight on purchased inventory, should be allocated to the specific inventory to which it applies. In practice, however, it is often separately recorded as an expense.

Example On December 28, Harvey Department Store purchased goods costing $40,000. The terms were FOB shipping point. Some costs incurred in connection with the sale, delivery, and receipt of the goods were:

Seller's cost of packaging	$ 800
Shipping cost	1,200
Insurance cost during shipping	400
Cost of unpacking and stocking	50

These goods were shipped on December 29 and received on January 2. What amount of inventory cost should be included in Harvey's balance sheet on December 31?

a. $40,000 c. $40,450 e. $42,450
b. $40,050 d. $41,650

Answer $41,650 because legal title passes to the Harvey Department Store, the buyer, at the point of shipment (December 29). All costs incurred from that point on including the invoice cost are properly borne by the buyer. These include all costs except the packaging costs that are borne by the seller.

Since determining the proper content of inventory can have such a significant effect on the financial statements, you can see the benefit of mastering Performance Objective 35.

YOUR PERFORMANCE OBJECTIVE 35
Select those year-end inventory transactions that should be included and those that should be excluded from the year-end inventory and **calculate** the appropriate cost of all inventory units on hand.

Inventory Cost Assignment: The Specific Identification Method

As its title suggests, the **specific identification method** identifies the specific units that are sold during a specific accounting period and the specific units that remain unsold in inventory at the end of a period. To see how this method works, consider the following illustration:

Illustration Local Yokols Superette stocks a limited number of half-gallon cartons of nonfat milk every week. Jerry Yokols, the sole proprietor, has compiled the following information:

Transactions		Carton Dates	Units	Unit Cost	Unit Selling Price
May 1	Balance	May 6	1	$1.20	$1.40
May 2	Purchase	May 8	2	1.25	1.40
May 3	Sale		(3)		
May 4	Purchase	May 10	1	1.28	1.48
May 5	Purchase	May 11	1	1.32	1.48
May 6	Purchase	May 13	2	1.40	1.48
May 7	Sale		(3)		
Ending inventory			1		

Required: Calculate the cost of the ending inventory and the cost of goods sold. Assume for purposes of this part that the single carton remaining is dated May 11.

Solution Let's once again use the inventory equation to solve this problem. For example, here is that equation for the specific identification method:

Beginning inventory = 1 @ $1.20 =	$ 1.20
Add: Purchases = 2 ($1.25) + 1($1.28) + 1($1.32) + 2($1.40)	
= $2.50 + $1.28 + $1.32 + $2.80 =	7.90
Cost of goods available for sale	$ 9.10
Deduct: Ending inventory (recall the date of the carton left)	(1.32)
Cost of goods sold	$ 7.78

Notice that once you know the cost of goods available for sale, it is unnecessary to calculate both the ending inventory and the cost of goods sold. For example, as shown above, if you simply subtract ending inventory (cost of goods sold) from the cost of goods available for sale, the result will be the cost of goods sold (ending inventory). This fact will save you a significant amount of time in your calculations.

The specific identification method is used when individual units (cartons in the preceding example) of inventory sold can be matched with a specific purchase date and cost. In other words, it is used when the exact *flow of goods* is known. In fact, if you asked most people how a business allocates its cost of goods available for sale between its cost of merchandise inventory on hand and its cost of goods sold—referred to as *the flow of costs*, they would intuitively think of the specific identification method. That is, they would assume that a business's *flow of costs* is identical to its actual *flow of goods*.

Despite its accuracy, objectivity, and intuitive appeal, however, the specific identification method is limited to companies whose inventories include a small number of costly and easily distinguishable items such as jewelers and automobile dealers. In fact, this method is very attractive in theory but has some distinct disadvantages—even for those companies for which it is particularly suited. First, its use is subject to income manipulation. How? Visualize a car dealer who makes sure that the specific cars sold to customers are those with the lowest purchase costs. As you have learned, minimizing one's cost of goods sold will maximize the net income reported on one's income statement. Another disadvantage associated with the specific identification method is that it requires detailed and, therefore, costly records.

For businesses whose inventory is composed of a great number of different items, or identical items acquired at different times and different prices, the specific identification method is either impossible or impractical to apply. Consider, for example, how difficult it would be to implement this method at CMU in light of what you know about the nature of its inventory. Even with a computer tracking system, how could you keep track of the tens of thousands of cards? Based on these limitations, it should not surprise you to learn that less than 4.5 percent of a recent sample of nearly 900 companies were found to use this method.[1] These limitations have made it imperative to find some other means to account for the costs of inventory.

Inventory Cost Assignment: Cost-Flow Assumptions

To eliminate the problems associated with the specific identification method, the accounting profession long ago endorsed the use of what are called *inventory cost-flow assumptions*. The profession took the position that the acceptability of these assumptions is not dependent on how accurately they reflect the actual physical flow of goods within the business but rather on how accurately they reflect the periodic income of that business. The profession endorsed three basic assumptions: (1) average cost, (2) first-in, first-out (FIFO), and (3) last-in, first-out (LIFO). Using the Local Yokols Superette data again, let's examine each of these inventory cost-flow assumptions under the following conditions:

a. Assume that Yokols uses an average cost assumption. Calculate both the cost of ending inventory and the cost of goods sold under a periodic and a perpetual inventory system.
b. Assume that Yokols uses a FIFO cost assumption. Calculate both the cost of ending inventory and the cost of goods sold under a periodic and a perpetual inventory system.
c. Assume that Yokols uses a LIFO cost assumption. Calculate both the cost of ending inventory and the cost of goods sold under a periodic and a perpetual inventory system.

---

[1] *Accounting Trends & Techniques*, AICPA, 2001.

Average Cost The **average cost** method can be calculated by using three different averages—a *simple average cost*, a *weighted-average cost*, and a *moving-average cost*. Let's look at each to avoid confusion.

Using the milk carton data introduced previously, you can calculate a simple average by adding the five unit costs ($1.20 + $1.25 + $1.28 + $1.32 + $1.40 = $6.45), and then dividing by five, the number of distinct costs ($6.45/5 = $1.29). Since this calculation is inappropriate because it fails to take into account the different quantities in each purchase, let's try a **weighted-average-cost**. Since a weighted average is really a cost per unit calculation, you must first divide the cost of goods available for sale (COGAS) by the goods or units available for sale (GAS). Recall that you already know the amount of the cost of goods available for sale from the earlier specific identification calculations and you can quickly calculate the units available for sale by consulting the beginning inventory and all purchases:

$$\text{Cost of Goods Available for Sale} = 1(\$1.20) + 2(\$1.25) + 1(\$1.28) + 1(\$1.32) + 2(\$1.40) = \underline{\underline{\$9.10}}$$

$$\text{Units Available for Sale} = 1 + 2 + 1 + 1 + 2 = \underline{\underline{7}}$$

$$\text{Weighted-Average Cost per Unit} = \frac{\text{Cost of Goods Available for Sale}}{\text{Goods Available for Sale}}$$

$$= \frac{\text{COGAS}}{\text{GAS}} = \frac{\$9.10}{7} = \underline{\underline{\$1.30}}$$

Since only one unit remains in inventory and all units are considered to have a cost per unit of $1.30, the cost of the ending inventory is $1.30 (1 × $1.30). Although you could calculate the $7.80 (6 units sold × $1.30 cost per unit) cost of goods sold first, multiplying by the smaller number of units unsold (1) is easier than multiplying by a larger number of units sold (6).

Cost of goods available for sale	= $ 9.10
Deduct: Cost of ending inventory = 1 @ $1.30 =	(1.30)
Cost of goods sold	$ 7.80

So, as you can see from the preceding illustration, the weighted-average cost method is appropriately used under the periodic inventory system.

In contrast, the **moving-average cost** calculation is appropriately used under the perpetual inventory system. Unlike its weighted-average counterpart in which a single average is calculated, the moving average requires you to calculate a new weighted average each time a sale is made. Let's examine how this is done.

Step 1:	5/01	1 @ $1.20	= $1.20	
	5/02	2 @ $1.25	= $2.50	
		3 @ **$1.233**	= $3.70	
	5/03	−3 @ $1.233		
		0 @ $1.233	= $-0-	
Step 2:	5/04	1 @ $1.28	= $1.28	
	5/05	1 @ $1.32	= $1.32	
	5/06	2 @ $1.40	= $2.80	
		4 @ **$1.35**	= $5.40	
	5/07	−3 @ $1.35		
		1 @ $1.35	= $1.35	Ending inventory

Cost of goods available for sale	= $ 9.10
Deduct: Cost of ending inventory	= (1.35)
Cost of goods sold	= $ 7.75

Notice that two separate weighted-average calculations are made. The first calculation in Step 1 produces a weighted-average cost per unit from the May 1 and May 2 purchases. In this case, dividing the cost of goods available for sale of \$3.70 by the three units purchased on those same dates results in a \$1.233 cost per unit. The sale of these three units on May 3 necessitates a recalculation shown in Step 2. As you can see, dividing the new cost of goods available for sale of \$5.40 by four units results in a \$1.35 cost per unit. The final calculation involves subtracting the three units sold, determining the cost of ending inventory (\$1.35), and subtracting this cost from the cost of goods available for sale (\$9.10) to determine the \$7.75 cost of goods sold.

"Got Milk?"

INSIGHT

To make sure that you fundamentally understand the concept underlying the FIFO and LIFO cost-flow assumptions, let's draw from your personal experience. That is, let's go shopping for milk, an experience to which almost everyone can relate.

Try to visualize walking toward the milk section of your local supermarket. When you reach this section, you probably have to crouch to clearly view your choices. Do you simply grab a carton of nonfat milk (your healthiest alternative) and leave? Not if you're at all concerned about the relative freshness of the milk you are going to drink! That is, many shoppers don't leave until they have found a carton with the latest possible date. Be honest! In your quest for the freshest milk, haven't you too been guilty of reaching in towards the back of the display case and selecting the freshest milk? If you have ever had this experience, you will understand the concept of LIFO. By selecting the last possible milk carton to enter the supermarket as your purchase of milk for your home refrigerator, you have consciously implemented a last-in, first-out inventory cost flow. **Last-in, first-out (LIFO)** represents a flow of costs in which the last inventory purchased is treated as the first inventory to be sold. If, however, you are unconcerned about selecting the very freshest milk, it is quite possible that, for you, the physical flow of milk cartons will actually approximate the FIFO cost-flow assumption. Naturally, the milk purchased first is placed closest to the customer's grasp by store employees whose objective is to sell the oldest cartons first so as not to experience spoilage loss. Thus, the store manager consciously tries to implement a first-in, first-out inventory cost-flow assumption. That is, **first-in, first-out (FIFO)** represents a flow of costs in which the first inventory purchased is treated as the first inventory to be sold. This real-life supermarket scenario illustrates a classic conflict between a customer's objective (LIFO) and the store manager's objective (FIFO).

In addition to gaining a better understanding of the concepts of LIFO and FIFO, the insight you should gain here is that the cost-flow assumption chosen for accounting purposes does not have to match the actual flow of goods within a business. That is, you can use LIFO when the actual flow of units is consistent with FIFO—as it is in most retailing businesses. Or, you can use FIFO when the actual flow of units is consistent with LIFO, as it is when an iron ore producer sells its inventory to customers directly from a massive coal pile.

Think of how you buy milk to help you understand the LIFO and FIFO cost-flow assumptions.

First-In, First-Out (FIFO) Now that you have seen the concepts of FIFO and LIFO, let's calculate both the cost of ending inventory and the cost of goods sold in our continuing milk carton example. Under the periodic inventory system and the FIFO cost-flow assumption, the first units purchased are treated as being the first units sold (think of the term *out* as synonymous with the term *sold*). Under this assumption, therefore, the single unit remaining in inventory is the last unit purchased on

May 6 at $1.40. That is, if we first concentrate on ending inventory to simplify our calculations, we are really applying a cost-flow assumption we can call **last-in, still-here** (**LISH**), the mirror image of FIFO. This calculation is shown here:

Cost of goods available for sale	$ 9.10
Deduct: Ending inventory: 1 @ $1.40 =	(1.40)
Cost of goods sold	$ 7.70

Fortunately, the time-consuming calculations required by FIFO under a perpetual inventory system are unnecessary because the calculations under a FIFO periodic inventory system are identical. If you are curious about why this result occurs, you are encouraged to confirm this result in the end-of-chapter exercises and problems that require you to use FIFO.

Last-In, First-Out (LIFO) Under the periodic inventory system and the LIFO cost-flow assumption, the last units purchased are treated as being sold first. Under this assumption, therefore, the single unit remaining in inventory is the very first unit purchased on May 1 at $1.20. Note that by concentrating on ending inventory to simplify our calculations, we are really applying a cost-flow assumption we can call **first-in, still-here** (**FISH**), the mirror image of LIFO. This calculation is shown here:

Cost of goods available for sale	$ 9.10
Deduct: Ending inventory: 1 @ $1.20 =	(1.20)
Cost of goods sold	$ 7.90

Unlike perpetual FIFO, perpetual LIFO by its nature will usually produce a different result than periodic LIFO. So, let's turn to just how the perpetual system concept is implemented under LIFO. Recall that cost of goods sold is recorded continually under the perpetual inventory system. Thus, unlike the periodic inventory system in which the LIFO concept is applied once at the end of the period, you will normally apply the LIFO concept at the date of each sale as shown here in Steps 1 and 2.

Step 1:	5/01	1 @ $1.20	Notice that by selling all units, the normal LIFO reasoning process is not employed here. If only 2 units had been sold on May 3, however, the unit treated as remaining would be the May 1 purchase at $1.20 under the FISH acronym.
	5/02	2 @ $1.25	
		3	
	5/03	−3	
		0	
Step 2:	5/04	1 @ $1.28	In this case, you apply the LIFO concept to determine which of the available 4 units is still on hand after the sale of 3 units. Since the 3 units from the May 5 and May 6 purchases are the first out or sold under LIFO, the May 4 unit costing $1.28 represents FISH.
	5/05	1 @ $1.32	
	5/06	2 @ $1.40	
		4	
	5/07	−3	
		1	

Cost of goods available for sale	$ 9.10
Deduct: Ending inventory: 1 @ $1.28 =	(1.28)
Cost of goods sold	$ 7.82

Now that each of the inventory cost-flow assumptions have been introduced, please study Figure 11-10 carefully. It is particularly valuable because it not only describes the relative differences among the average-cost method, the first-in, first-out method, and the last-in, last-out method but also the differences between the periodic and perpetual inventory systems. Now that you have seen exactly how the Merchandise Inventory and the Cost of Goods Sold accounts are calculated under the specific identification method and the inventory flow assumptions, as well as under both the periodic and perpetual inventory systems, you can appreciate the need for Performance Objective 36.

YOUR PERFORMANCE OBJECTIVE 36
Calculate the balances in ending inventory and cost of goods sold for the specific identification method and the FIFO, LIFO, and average cost-flow assumptions under both a periodic and perpetual inventory system.

Comparing ending inventory

	Periodic Inventory System	Perpetual Inventory System
Last-in, first-out (LIFO)	$1.20	$1.28
Weighted- and moving-average costs	1.30	1.35
First-in, first-out (FIFO)	1.40	1.40

Notice that LIFO produces the *lowest* reported asset amounts, FIFO produces the *highest* reported asset amounts, and the average cost approach produces a reported asset amount in between the LIFO and FIFO amounts. These relationships hold under rising prices because the lower priced, earlier purchased units are included in ending inventory under LIFO and the higher priced, later purchased units are included in ending inventory under FIFO.

Comparing cost of goods sold

	Periodic Inventory System	Perpetual Inventory System
Last-in, first-out (LIFO)	$7.90	$7.82
Weighted- and moving-average costs	7.80	7.75
First-in, first-out (FIFO)	7.70	7.70

Notice that LIFO produces the *highest* reported expense amounts (*lowest* net income), FIFO produces the *lowest* reported expense amounts (*highest* net income), and the average cost approach produces an expense amount and, therefore, also a net income amount in between the LIFO and FIFO amounts. These relationships hold under rising prices because the higher priced, later purchased units are included in cost of goods sold under LIFO and the lower priced, earlier purchased units are included in cost of good sold under FIFO.

FIGURE 11-10

A comparison of the relative differences among inventory cost-flow assumptions and inventory systems based on the milk carton demonstration problem

When calculating FIFO amounts for both ending inventory and cost of goods sold, the periodic and perpetual calculations are identical.

Suggestions to Help Expedite Your Cost-Flow Calculations

Despite the simplicity of our milk carton illustration, it demonstrates how detailed inventory cost-flow assumption calculations can be. Here are some concrete suggestions for making these types of calculations more manageable:

1. Always calculate the cost of goods available for sale (COGAS) first unless the problem already provides this information.

$$\text{COGAS} = 1(1.20) + 2(1.25) + 1(1.28) + 1(1.32) + 2(1.40)$$
$$= \$1.20 + \$2.50 + \$1.28 + \$1.32 + \$2.80 = \underline{\underline{\$9.10}}$$

2. Next, calculate the goods or units available for sale (GAS)

$$GAS = 1 + 2 + 1 + 1 + 2 = 7$$

3. Divide COGAS by GAS to derive average cost per unit information.
4. Always calculate the number of units sold (3 + 3 = 6) and the number of units remaining (7 − 6 = 1).
5. Calculate the ending inventory directly because it generally contains fewer units than does the cost of goods sold. Then, derive the cost of goods sold amount by subtracting the cost of ending inventory from the cost of goods available for sale.
6. Remember that the acronyms FIFO and LIFO describe cost flows for the cost of goods sold rather than the cost of ending inventory.
7. To focus on the calculation of ending inventory cost under FIFO, use the acronym LISH (last-in, still-here). Likewise, to focus on the calculation of ending inventory cost under LIFO, use the acronym FISH (first-in, still-here).

Deciding Which Cost-Flow Assumption to Use As the following table shows, the great majority of companies that account for inventory use either FIFO or LIFO.[2]

Methods	Number	Percentage
FIFO	386	43.5%
LIFO	283	31.9%
Average Cost	180	20.3%
Other	38	04.3%
	887	100.0%

Since FIFO and LIFO are by far the most popular cost-flow assumptions, Performance Objective 37 is designed to help you identify their differences and examine their advantages and disadvantages.

YOUR PERFORMANCE OBJECTIVE 37

Identify the differences between the FIFO and LIFO inventory cost-flow assumptions and **explain** the relative advantages and disadvantages of adopting each as the cost-flow assumption.

Because an advantage of FIFO is generally a disadvantage of LIFO, and vice versa, the following discussion will concentrate on the LIFO cost-flow assumption in the interest of brevity.

LIFO Advantages

1. *LIFO matches current costs with current revenues for a more current or realistic measure of net income.* Since the most recent costs of inventory (that is, last-in) approximate the replacement cost of the sold units (that is, first-out), LIFO can be said to associate or match recent costs with recent revenues. Since the matching concept is one of financial accounting's most valued concepts, it is easy to understand why this matching is considered one of LIFO's primary attributes. In fact, LIFO can be said to measure the value that is added by the marketing process since its gross margin reports only the revenue in excess of replacement cost. In contrast, FIFO's gross margin (a lower cost of goods sold during a period of rising prices) is criticized for including the realized holding gain that occurred when

[2] *Accounting Trends & Techniques*, AICPA, 2001.

the sold items' replacement cost increased while they were in inventory. This prevents managers from being evaluated solely on their marketing performance, which would be the case if FIFO cost of goods sold included only the approximate replacement cost of the units sold.

2. *During a period of inflation, LIFO produces income tax benefits.* This should make sense when you realize that relatively higher costs (that is, last-in) are included in LIFO cost of goods sold during periods of inflation. Since a higher cost of good sold produces a smaller net income, LIFO generates a lower tax. Since managers prefer to pay lower taxes, LIFO is widely used because it allows them to enrich their company's shareholders by reducing income taxes paid. Unfortunately, this clear advantage comes with a significant price to pay as the following *Insight* explains.

The Dilemma of the LIFO Conformity Rule

INSIGHT

Accounting theorists praise LIFO because, by matching current costs with current revenues, it produces the best measure of income. This attribute of LIFO is not very compelling to most managers, however, because they desire to report the highest possible net income to their shareholders. They would prefer to use FIFO on income statements and LIFO on income tax returns because of LIFO's income tax benefits. As you will discover with depreciation in the next chapter, companies often use accounting methods for financial reporting purposes that are different from those used for tax accounting purposes. This should not be surprising since the objectives of financial reporting are quite different from the objectives of federal and state income taxation.

Unfortunately for managers, they are unable to enjoy the best of both the financial reporting and tax reporting worlds because of the *LIFO conformity rule*, which requires companies to use LIFO for financial reporting purposes if they have elected LIFO for tax purposes. Despite the fact that it is rare for a tax reporting election to drive a financial reporting policy, this rule has continued without interruption for over 60 years. The dilemma posed by this rule is that it forces managers to report a lower net income on their income statements if they want to save income taxes and, therefore, increase shareholder wealth.

The insight you should gain here is that the LIFO conformity rule requires managers to tell their shareholders that their earnings are worse off if they desire to actually produce a better cash position by reducing their taxes paid. Thus, most accountants argue that this rule represents a clear shortcoming of generally accepted accounting principles because it impinges on a manager's choice of cost-flow assumption. It is also criticized because it contributes to less rather than more information being provided to shareholders.[3] In recent years, the Securities and Exchange Commission has provided shareholders with some of this information by requiring LIFO users to disclose the FIFO cost of ending inventory in their annual report. You'll learn more about this *LIFO reserve* disclosure next.

[3]"The LIFO Conformity Rule: Do We Really Need It?" Paul Miller and Paul Bahnson, *Accounting Today,* February 12–25, 2001, pp. 12 and 13.

LIFO Disadvantages

1. *LIFO provides an outdated and, therefore, unrealistic balance sheet valuation.* Recall that accounting for the inventory asset with the oldest acquisition costs is expressed by the acronym FISH. After a period of years, these outdated costs may significantly understate the inventory's current replacement cost, which is generally equivalent to its FIFO cost. FIFO, on the other hand, is praised for its more current or realistic measure of balance sheet inventory. Since the current replacement cost of a company's inventory is important information, companies using LIFO generally disclose their current replacement cost, or FIFO cost, in the

notes to their financial statements. A note accompanying the 2000 balance sheet of General Motors, for example, explained that had it used the FIFO method, its reported LIFO inventory of over $7.5 billion would have been higher by $1.1 billion. This difference between the LIFO cost of an inventory and its current replacement cost is often referred to as a **LIFO reserve**. In the case of General Motors, therefore, its LIFO reserve was $1.1 billion.

2. *LIFO provides poor matching if its early layers are liquidated.* That is, whenever inventory quantities on hand at the end of the accounting period decrease, the same outdated layers of low-cost inventory described in the preceding paragraph must suddenly be transferred to the income statement through cost of goods sold. When such outdated costs having no relationship to current fair market value are matched to revenues that reflect current selling prices, cost of goods sold is understated and net income is correspondingly overstated. The irony is that the income tax benefits associated with LIFO are lost whenever quantities decrease during a period. To avoid such a result, companies are more prone to poor buying habits. For a more detailed look at this phenomenon, often called the **LIFO liquidation problem**, see Problem 11-13.
3. *LIFO's cost-flow assumption rarely represents the actual physical flow of inventory in businesses.* As explained in the "Got Milk" *Insight*, the actual flow of units is consistent with FIFO in most retailing businesses. Thus, the LIFO cost-flow assumption is not as intuitively appealing as FIFO because it occurs less often in actual business practice.

Now that you have considered these advantages and disadvantages, you can see how neither FIFO nor LIFO is a perfect method. Under current accounting principles, selecting a cost-flow assumption involves weighing each assumption's relative advantages and disadvantages. Many theorists believe that this inability to simultaneously report current market prices for both inventory and cost of goods sold forces managers to make no-win decisions. Managers who desire a balance sheet that reports the current replacement cost of the inventory (FIFO), for example, have to accept an income statement that does not reflect a current cost of goods sold, and vice versa. As a result, some of these theorists have proposed a method called LIFO/FIFO in which the most recent costs would be reported on both the income statement (as the LIFO cost of goods sold) and the balance sheet (as the FIFO inventory).[4] Figure 11-11 illustrates the hypothetical financial statements produced under this method when applied to our milk carton illustration.

Income Statement Effects of Inventory Errors

From our earlier discussion of the inventory equation, you already know that inventory errors affect both merchandise inventory and cost of goods sold. The effects of such errors are particularly important to understand because, if uncorrected, reported income will be misstated and send inappropriate signals to investors and creditors. To illustrate these financial statement effects, assume that the following company's inventory amounts are correct.

	Year 1	Year 2
Beginning inventory	$ 25,000	$ 30,000
Add: Net purchases	75,000	75,000
Cost of goods available for sale	$100,000	$105,000
Deduct: Correct ending inventories	**(30,000)**	**(25,000)**
Cost of goods sold	$ 70,000	$ 80,000

[4] "Inventory and Cost of Goods Sold: Getting Them Both Right," Paul Miller and Paul Bahnson, *Accounting Today*, February 26–March 18, 2001, pp. 14 and 16.

The LIFO/FIFO method reports LIFO's current cost of goods sold.

Income statement	LIFO/FIFO	LIFO	FIFO
Sales revenue (assumed figure)	$12.00	$12.00	$12.00
Cost of goods sold	7.90	7.90	7.70
Gross margin from marketing	$ 4.10	$ 4.10	$ 4.30
Selling and administrative expenses	1.90	1.90	1.90
Income from continuing operations	$ 2.20	$ 2.20	$ 2.40
Nonoperating income (realized holding gain)	.20	N/A	N/A
Net income	$ 2.40	$ 2.20	$ 2.40
Balance sheet			
All other assets	$20.00	$20.00	$20.00
Inventory	1.40	1.20	1.40
Total assets	$21.40	$21.20	$21.40
Liabilities and other owners' equity	$19.00	$19.00	$19.00
Retained earnings (assume first-year firm)	2.40	2.20	2.40
Total liabilities and owners' equity	$21.40	$21.20	$21.40

The LIFO/FIFO method's net income of $2.40 is broken down into two useful measures of income: a marketing margin of $2.20 as well as a realized holding gain of $.20.

The LIFO/FIFO method reports FIFO's current cost of inventory.

FIGURE 11-11
The hypothetical financial statement effects of the LIFO/FIFO method under a periodic inventory system

Now assume that total sales were $120,000 in each year.

	Year 1	Year 2
Sales revenue	$120,000	$120,000
Deduct: Cost of goods sold	(70,000)	(80,000)
Correct gross margin	**$ 50,000**	**$ 40,000**

Thus, the correct amounts to be reported on the balance sheet are $30,000 for Year 1 and $25,000 for Year 2, while the correct amounts to be reported on the income statement are $70,000 for Year 1 and $80,000 for Year 2.

Effect of an Error in the Amount of Ending Inventory Let's now examine the cumulative effect of an error in ending inventory in Year 1 that is not discovered until after the completion of Year 2. That is, assume that Year 1 ending inventory is *overstated* due to a $10,000 error in taking the physical count. Notice here how this error affects both the amounts reported on the balance sheet and income statement.

	Year 1	Year 2
Beginning inventory	$ 25,000	$ 40,000
Add: Net purchases	75,000	75,000
Cost of goods available for sale	100,000	115,000
Deduct: Incorrect ending inventory in year 1	(40,000)	(25,000)
Cost of goods sold	$ 60,000	$ 90,000

Let's now examine the income effects of such an error by calculating the income component known as gross margin.

	Year 1	Year 2
Sales revenue	$120,000	$120,000
Deduct: Cost of goods sold	(60,000)	(90,000)
Incorrect gross margin	$ 60,000	$ 30,000

Notice that the overstated ending inventory causes income to be *overstated* by $10,000 in Year 1. By virtue of being carried forward as the beginning inventory of the second year, however, the original error in ending inventory has the opposite income effect in Year 2—it causes income to be understated by $10,000 in Year 2. Thus, the income misstatement reverses in the second year. Thus, using the term *direction* to indicate whether the amount is overstated or understated, the following rules of thumb can be derived from the preceding illustration:

Rule 1 *Errors in ending inventory cause income to be misstated in the same amount and same direction.*

Since a $10,000 overstatement in ending inventory caused a $10,000 overstatement in income, both the amount ($10,000) and direction (overstatement) are the same. That is, the overstated ending inventory ($40,000 rather than the correct amount of $30,000) caused an overstated gross margin ($60,000 rather than the correct amount of $50,000).

Rule 2 *Errors in beginning inventory cause income to be misstated in the same amount but opposite direction.*

Since a $10,000 overstatement in the beginning inventory of the second year caused a $10,000 understatement in income, the amount ($10,000) is the same but the direction (understatement) is the opposite. That is, the overstated beginning inventory ($40,000 rather than the correct amount of $30,000) caused an understated gross margin ($30,000 rather than the correct amount of $40,000).

From this illustration, you should be able to see that the effects of these errors are counterbalancing. That is, a single such uncorrected error will misstate income for two periods, but these income misstatements will offset one another so that total two-year income is identical to the amount of reported income had no error occurred. Nevertheless, do not assume that inventory errors are no problem in financial reporting. The effect of such undetected errors on decision making can be significant because the income of *each period* is misstated.

USER FOCUS

Using Arrows to Analyze Inventory Errors

Although the preceding rules are helpful, avoid memorizing their effects. A much more effective reasoning process is to pair your understanding of the inventory equation with directional arrows for overstatement (↑) and understatement (↓), a check mark for a correct amount, and the following symbols to represent the elements of the inventory equation:

Let BI = beginning inventory; PUR = net purchases; COGAS = cost of goods available for sale; EI = ending inventory; COGS = cost of goods sold; S = sales; and GM = gross margin.

Let's now use the following analytical shorthand to confirm the effects of our earlier $10,000 overstatement of ending inventory:

If BI is √ and PUR √, then COGAS is √; if EI is ↑, then COGS is ↓ and GM is ↑ by $10,000.

Notice that this very logical sequential reasoning has led you back to Rule 1. That is, overstatements of ending inventory cause income to be overstated. In the second year, the overstatement of ending inventory can be analyzed as follows: The $10,000 overstatement of ending inventory for Year 1 is carried forward so that Year 2 BI is ↑. If BI is ↑ and PUR √, then COGAS is ↑; if EI is √, then COGS is ↑ and GM is ↓ by $10,000 as you learned before. Figure 11-12 describes this reasoning process in a format that some students prefer.

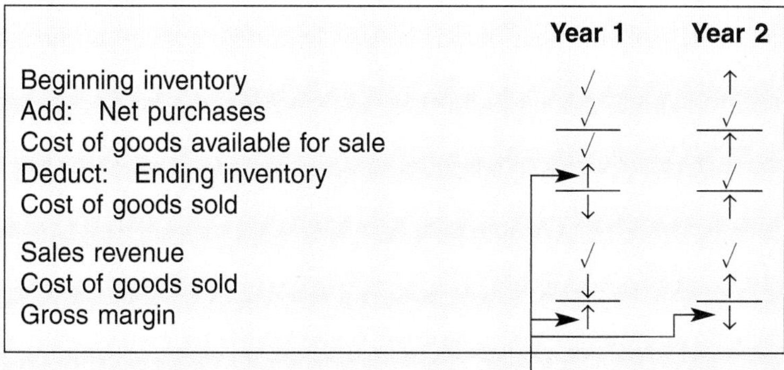

	Year 1	Year 2
Beginning inventory	√	↑
Add: Net purchases	√	√
Cost of goods available for sale	√	↑
Deduct: Ending inventory	↑	√
Cost of goods sold	↓	↑
Sales revenue	√	√
Cost of goods sold	↓	↑
Gross margin	↑	↓

An overstatement in ending inventory in Year 1 causes income (gross margin) to be overstated in Year 1 and understated in Year 2 by the same amount.

FIGURE 11-12

Analyzing the effects of an error in ending inventory using an inventory equation in a vertical format along with arrows

The **insight** you should gain here is that by using the inventory equation with directional arrows, you can more easily analyze the effect of inventory errors on the financial statements. In fact, this approach is far superior to memorizing any rules because it promotes your ability to analyze such effects long after you have taken this accounting course.

Effect of an Error in the Amount of Purchases Let's now examine how you can analyze the effect of an inventory purchase error on the financial statements. Using the same data as before, we now assume that a $3,000 delivery of inventory made on December 29 is not recorded until January 2 when the invoice is received. That is, the amount of purchases in Year 1 is understated and the amount of purchases in Year 2 is overstated. Unlike our original example, however, there is no error in the ending inventory because the inventory purchased on December 29 was counted. Let's begin our sequential analysis by using the inventory equation along with arrows to indicate understatement and overstatement as shown here.

	Year 1	Year 2
Beginning inventory	√	√
Add: Net purchases	↓	↑
Cost of goods available for sale	↓	↑
Deduct: Ending inventory	√	√
Cost of goods sold	↓	↑
Sales revenue	√	√
Cost of goods sold	↓	↑
Gross margin	↑	↓

In other words, an unrecorded purchase of $3,000 that is included in the ending inventory causes net income to be overstated in Year 1 and understated in Year 2 by $3,000. Once again, avoid trying to memorize such effects because subtle variations in how inventory errors occur make such memorization highly ineffective. For example, assume that this same purchase was shipped on December 29 and arrived on January 2 under the terms FOB shipping point. In this case as you learned earlier, the purchaser properly holds title on December 29 despite the fact that the goods are unavailable for the physical count at the end of the year. As presented in Critical Thinking Problem 11-15, this scenario produces at least three different possibilities:

1. The purchase is properly recorded in Year 1 but not included in the year-end count of inventory.
2. The purchase is not recorded until Year 2 but is properly added to the year-end count of inventory.
3. The purchase is not recorded until Year 2 and is not included in the year-end count of inventory.

Add to this set of facts the possibilities created by the terms FOB destination (refer to Critical Thinking Problem 11-16) and you will understand why the sequential analytical reasoning process described here is far more effective in determining the effects of such inventory errors than is memorization. Performance Objective 38 is designed to help you grasp the logical reasoning process presented here.

YOUR PERFORMANCE OBJECTIVE 38
Determine the effect (overstatement, understatement, or none) of an inventory error on both balance sheet and income statement amounts.

Inventory Estimation: Gross Margin Method

Being able to calculate both the cost of inventory and the cost of goods sold without having to take a physical count of that inventory is a particularly useful tool for a business. The **gross margin method**, also called the *gross profit method*, is just such a tool. It estimates these costs by using the ratio formed by dividing gross margin by sales revenue as illustrated here for CMU:

$$\text{Gross Margin Ratio} = \frac{\text{Gross Margin}}{\text{Sales Revenue}} = \frac{\$56{,}600}{86{,}600} = .654$$

A related ratio you can use to directly estimate cost of goods sold is formed by the complement of the gross margin ratio. Since the complement of any percentage or ratio equals one minus that percentage or ratio, this is 1 − .654, or .346, in our example. Thus, this ratio is calculated by dividing the cost of goods sold ($30,000 in this example) by sales revenue.

Although it is always best to base your calculation of inventory and cost of goods sold on a physical count of inventory, situations sometimes arise in which it is useful to estimate both of these costs using the gross margin ratio. Such situations include:

1. Estimating ending inventory for internal use.
2. Testing the accuracy of a physical count of inventory.
3. Testing the validity of reported inventory under the perpetual system without a physical count of inventory being taken (for use in interim financial statements).
4. Establishing the amount of inventory destroyed by fire or other catastrophes or lost through theft when specific cost data are unavailable.

In each of these situations, learning the skills required by Performance Objective 39 will help you estimate inventory cost with the gross margin method.

YOUR PERFORMANCE OBJECTIVE 39
Calculate the estimated cost of goods sold and cost of ending inventory using the gross margin method.

To illustrate just such a gross margin calculation, assume a fire destroys the entire inventory but not the accounting records of CMU late in its second year of business. The following information is available:

Beginning inventory (equivalent to year 1 ending inventory)	$ 13,000
Add: Net purchases	52,000
Cost of goods available for sale	$ 65,000
Sales revenue	$120,000
Ratio of cost of goods sold to sales revenue	.346

Here is how you would calculate the cost of inventory destroyed by the fire:

Cost of goods available for sale	$65,000
Deduct: Estimated cost of goods sold ($120,000 × .346)	(41,520)
Estimated cost of inventory destroyed by fire, or fire loss	$23,480

Real-World Use of the Gross Margin Method

INSIGHT

Because the gross margin method produces only an estimate of ending inventory, it is not recognized under generally accepted accounting principles as an acceptable method for either annual financial reporting or tax purposes. Nevertheless, some small businesses do use it as their primary means of determining annual income. Unlike Cards & Memorabilia Unlimited, for example, it is not uncommon for trading card and sports memorabilia stores to use the gross margin method to avoid the time and expense of an annual physical count of inventory.

Assume, for example, that Superstars, a trading card store, consistently applies a markup percentage of 50% to its sports trading cards and 33.3% to its nonsports trading cards. That is, if Superstars buys $100 worth of sports cards and $60 worth of nonsports cards, it will price these two groups of cards to sell for $150 ($100 × 1.50) and $80 ($60 × 1.333), respectively. If the owner-manager consistently prices the cards in this way, the gross margin percentages for sports cards [($150 − $100)/$150] and nonsports cards [($80 − $60)/$80] will be 33.3% and 25%, respectively. Given that this owner-manager sells $140,000 of sports cards and $90,000 of nonsports cards, the following gross margin and cost of goods sold figures can be calculated:

	Sales	Gross Margin	Cost of Goods Sold
Sports Cards	$140,000 × 33.3% =	$46,667	$140,000 − $46,667 = $ 93,333
Nonsports Cards	90,000 × 25.0% =	$22,500	$ 90,000 − $22,500 = $ 67,500
			$160,833

The first **insight** you should gain here is that although the gross margin method is designed to be used only for inventory and cost of goods sold estimation, some businesses actually use it as their primary means of inventory valuation and income determination. The second **insight** you should gain, however, is that no matter how tempting such practices might appear, they have their limitations. The gross margin method, for example, does not reveal such losses as those from shrinkage or theft. Thus, it is not advisable to use it in place of an actual count of inventory if you value close control of inventory for your business. You also would prefer an actual count of inventory if your financial statements might ever be audited since public accounting firms must follow generally accepted accounting principles.

Inventory Valuation: Lower of Cost or Market Method

Specific identification, LIFO, FIFO, and average cost might be only a starting point for how inventory is reported on the balance sheet. This is because the actual valuation method used to report inventory on the balance sheet is not based on historical cost but rather on the **lower of cost or market method (LOCOM)**. This departure from the historical cost principle is required whenever the future value of inventory is no longer as great as its original cost. The lower of cost or market method applies to losses in inventory value in the normal course of business from such causes as style changes, shifts in demand, and normal wear. In this case, the term **market value** is interpreted to mean replacement cost—the current bid price prevailing at the balance sheet date of the inventory for the particular merchandise in the usual volume purchased.

To illustrate such a loss in inventory value, consider the case of former professional baseball and football player Bo Jackson. When the sports world anticipated that his unique talents in both sports would make him a memorable superstar, the value of his trading cards increased dramatically. These values began to decline when Jackson sustained a serious injury that forced him to give up football. They continued to decline when the same injury led to his untimely retirement from baseball a few years later. Under the lower of cost or market method, card store owners who experienced losses in value on their holdings of Bo Jackson's cards would be required to record a transaction similar to the one shown in Figure 11-13. As you can see, the effect of this transaction is to decrease the amount of the asset and to decrease the amount of net income reported for the period.

FIGURE 11-13 The transaction recorded to implement the lower of cost or market method

Transaction Analysis							Journal Entry		
	Fundamental Accounting Equation								
Account Titles	Assets	=	Liabilities	+	Owners' Equity		Account Titles	Debit	Credit
Loss on Market Decline					(xx)		Loss on Market Decline	xx	
Merchandise Inventory	(xx)						Merchandise Inventory		xx

The assumption underlying the lower of cost or market method is that a decrease in the market value of inventory will be accompanied by a similar decrease in the ultimate selling price of that inventory. If the decline in market value is judged to be temporary, however, the LOCOM treatment is not used. In the interest of fairness to financial statement users, the accounting profession requires that a transaction such as that shown in Figure 11-13 be recorded only if the decline is clearly in prospect. The purpose of this transaction is to properly report inventory on the balance sheet and to record the loss on the income statement in the proper period. To help you better understand this method, let's now examine *conservatism*, the principle underlying this method.

Conservatism: The Underlying Basis for the LOCOM Method

The accounting concept of conservatism should not be confused with our culture's connotation of either political conservatism or social conservatism. Instead, accounting conservatism is a practice that is designed to protect investors and creditors from an overly optimistic interpretation of financial results. Stated in its most straightforward manner, the principle of **conservatism** advises accountants to "anticipate no profit and provide for all losses." That is, whenever accountants evaluate a transaction or a collection of transactions, they are not supposed to anticipate its potential profitability but rather to anticipate its potential for loss. If you think about the implications of this principle, you might argue that it violates another important qualitative accounting principle known as *objectivity*. This not uncommon argument states that since our society depends upon accountants to evaluate financial matters in an unbiased or objective fashion, conservatism promotes a biased judgment that should be rejected. Advocates of conservatism, however, argue that it is an essential safeguard in a world in which exaggerated claims of instant wealth far outweigh those forces in our society that encourage us to be cautious in our financial dealings. Thus, conservatism is a deliberate attempt to balance the natural forces of human optimism and even greed that cloud the thinking of so many of us. When you then consider the unscrupulous individuals who prey on the financial naiveté of so many innocent people, you can probably understand why conservatism has played such an important role in accounting. Moreover, conservatism is not just applied to inventory transactions as you will learn when you study how investments are accounted for in the next chapter. Performance Objective 40 will help you master this very important principle.

YOUR PERFORMANCE OBJECTIVE 40
Explain the principle of conservatism and **apply** it when accounting for inventories and investments with the lower of cost or market method.

How Selling and Collecting Affect Accounts Receivable and Sales Revenue

Much of this chapter has been devoted to examining exactly how the purchasing and selling phases of the operating cycle create the actual balances of both the Inventory account on the balance sheet and the Cost of Goods Sold account on the income statement. Now, let's see how the selling and collecting phases of the operating cycle create the amounts in two other balance sheet accounts—Accounts Receivable and its contra account, Allowance for Uncollectibles—and the amounts in two other income statement accounts—Bad Debts Expense and Sales Revenue.

As you'd expect, merchandisers often have significant accounts receivable that arise from credit sales of products or services that their customers promise to pay in the future. Since not all credit sales will be collected, sellers generally deduct an estimate of the uncollectible amount from the related receivable to derive a more realistic measurement of what is referred to as the *net accounts receivable*. Recall that this contra asset account is either titled **Allowance for Bad Debts**, **Allowance for Uncollectible Accounts**, or **Allowance for Doubtful Accounts**. An illustration of these accounts and their relationship is shown here.

Primary account ⟶	Accounts receivable	$xxx,xxx
Contra asset account ⟶	Allowance for bad debts	(x,xxx)
	Net accounts receivable	$xxx,xxx

In this case, the contra asset is placed immediately below and subtracted from its primary account, Accounts Receivable.

Determining the timing and amount of this uncollectible is the primary obstacle in properly valuing accounts receivable on the balance sheet and precisely measuring net income on the income statement. Let's examine the timing issue next.

When Should Uncollectible Amounts Be Recognized as an Expense?

The essential accounting question to answer is, "When should the expected loss from uncollectibles be properly reported?" Although some small businesses recognize this loss as soon as a specific receivable is deemed unrecoverable, this practice is usually not considered good accounting practice.[5] Instead, under the accrual basis, it is generally agreed that the expense or loss from uncollectibles is incurred not when the loss is discovered but rather when the loss is incurred as shown in Figure 11-14. The reasoning used is that the loss originates with the decision to extend credit to an individual who will later prove to be unworthy of that trust. Had the seller had perfect knowledge and not extended this credit, there would have been no sale and, therefore, no loss. In other words, the loss really occurs at the time the sale is made which, of course, reflects the matching concept described in Chapters 6 and 7.

FIGURE 11-14

A time line for deciding when the expected loss from uncollectibles should be reported

To more easily visualize this time line, assume that you sell merchandise inventory to a customer on January 2 with the expectation of collecting the amount due in 30 days (on or before February 2). After attempting to collect this receivable for 120 days (January, February, March, and April) a decision is made on May 2 that this customer account is uncollectible. Should the loss from uncollectibles be recorded in Period 1, Period 2, Period 3, or later?

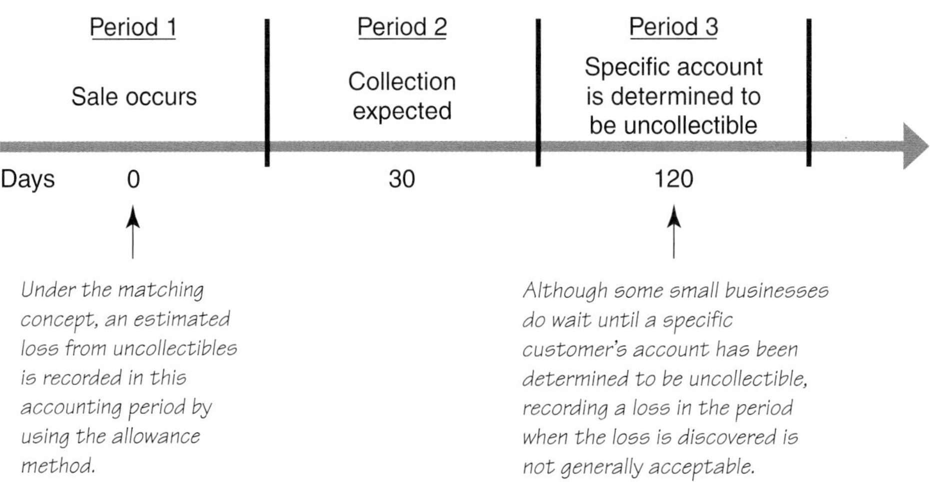

Nevertheless, if actual uncollectible account losses are usually apparent only after the period of sale, how is this matching process possible? The answer is that matching may be accomplished by estimating the expense that will ultimately be discovered. Obviously, this estimate does not involve specific customers or no sale would have been made to them. Instead, businesses that extend credit can generally estimate their losses fairly accurately from year to year based on past experience. These businesses record the uncollectible loss in the period when the related sales are made by estimating their loss with what is called the *allowance method.*

The Allowance Method

Under the **allowance method**, the accountant estimates the amount of sales or receivables that are not expected to be ultimately collected. This yearly matching of the

[5] In this approach called the *direct* or *specific write-off method*, the bad debt expense account is increased and the accounts receivable account is decreased by the amount of the unrecoverable receivable.

loss on credit sales to the gross sales revenue earned is usually accomplished in two parts. First, as described in Chapter 10, an expense account such as **Bad Debt Expense**, also called **Uncollectible Accounts Expense** or **Doubtful Accounts Expense**, is increased. Increasing a contra asset account such as Allowance for Bad Debts simultaneously decreases the net receivable reported on the balance sheet. Because this transaction to record the estimated loss from receivables under the accrual basis is made at the close of each accounting period, it is treated as an adjustment or adjusting entry. The effects of this transaction are shown below:

Transaction Analysis							Journal Entry		
	Fundamental Accounting Equation								
Account Titles	**Assets**	=	**Liabilities**	+	**Owners' Equity**		**Account Titles**	**Debit**	**Credit**
Bad Debt Expense					(xx)		Bad Debt Expense	xx	
Allowance for Bad Debts	(xx)						Allowance for Bad Debts		xx

Simultaneously increasing the bad debt expense and the allowance accounts reduces net income and, thus, owners' equity as well as net accounts receivable.

A more correct but seldom used approach is to record a contra sales revenue account (for example, Sales Contra on Uncollectible Accounts) and a contra receivable account (Allowance for Uncollectible Accounts). Since this transaction lowers net sales revenue on the income statement, net income will be the same under either approach. The argument behind using this approach is that a loss from uncollectibles is really a reduction of sales revenue not an increase in an expense account.

Let's now examine exactly how the amount of the estimated loss from uncollectibles is determined.

Estimating Uncollectible Accounts

The two primary methods used to estimate the loss from bad debts every period are the *percentage of sales method* and *the percentage of receivables method*. Although the form of the transaction shown above is generally the same no matter which of these estimation methods is used, the source of each method's calculation is quite different as you will learn in the following sections.

Percentage of Sales Method The **percentage of sales method** is often referred to as the *income statement approach* because the estimate of bad debts is calculated by multiplying Sales Revenue, an account found in the income statement, by a historical percentage of uncollectibles. That is, its focus is on the proper measurement of income. For example, assume that you have studied the amount of uncollectible accounts receivable losses from past years and have noticed that this loss has generally run about 02.5% of yearly sales. Given that the total yearly sales for the current year are \$20,000, you calculate that the estimated loss from uncollectibles is \$500 (\$20,000 × .025) and record that loss in the current year as shown in the top half of Figure 11-15. The effect of simultaneously increasing Bad Debt Expense and the Allowance for Bad Debts as shown in Figure 11-15 is to reduce net income and, thus, owners' equity as well as net accounts receivable. This method is particularly easy to apply because the estimate itself is also the amount of the adjusting entry as the following T-account demonstrates:

Allowance for Bad Debts		
	xxx ←	Balance before adjustment
	500 ←	Estimate and adjustment
	xxx ←	Balance after adjustment

FIGURE 11-15 Comparing the effects of estimating uncollectibles between the percentage of sales method and the percentage of receivables method

Percentage of sales method

Example: The uncollectible accounts expense is estimated to be 02.5% of total yearly sales or $500 (= $20,000 × .025).

Transaction Analysis							**Journal Entry**		
	Fundamental Accounting Equation								
Account Titles	**Assets**	**=**	**Liabilities**	**+**	**Owners' Equity**		**Account Titles**	**Debit**	**Credit**
Bad Debt Expense					(500)		Bad Debt Expense	500	
Allowance for Bad Debts	(500)						Allowance for Bad Debts		500

Percentage of receivables method

Example: The amount that is estimated to be uncollectible is 7.0% of the December 31 ending accounts receivable balance of $6,000, or $420 (= $6,000 × .07). Note that Allowance for Bad Debts has a credit balance of $200 prior to the recording of this transaction.

Transaction Analysis							**Journal Entry**		
	Fundamental Accounting Equation								
Account Titles	**Assets**	**=**	**Liabilities**	**+**	**Owners' Equity**		**Account Titles**	**Debit**	**Credit**
Bad Debt Expense					(220)		Bad Debt Expense	220	
Allowance for Bad Debts	(220)						Allowance for Bad Debts		220

Allowance for Bad Debts

	200 ← Balance before adjustment
	220 ← Adjustment needed
	420 ← Amount of estimate

This method is intuitively appealing because the source of the estimate—the amount of sales revenue—and the estimate itself—the amount reported in the Bad Debts Expense account or the Sales Contra on Uncollectible Accounts (refer to our earlier discussion)—are all found in the income statement. Thus, as suggested earlier, this method is clearly an income statement approach.

Percentage of Receivables Method The **percentage of receivables method** is often referred to as the balance sheet approach because the estimate of bad debts is calculated by multiplying Accounts Receivable, an account found in the balance sheet, by a historical percentage of uncollectibles. That is, this method focuses on the proper valuation of receivables. For example, assume that you have studied the amount of uncollectible accounts receivable losses from past years and have noticed that this loss has generally run about 7.0% of the ending balance in accounts receivable. Given that your ending accounts receivable balance is $6,000 for the current year, you calculate that the estimated loss from uncollectibles is $420 ($6,000 × .07). Don't be tempted to simply record this $420 amount as the loss from uncollectibles, as we did under the percentage of sales approach. Since the source of this estimate is a balance sheet account (Accounts Receivable), the estimate itself must be reported in a balance sheet account to be consistent. Can you think of what that balance sheet account should be? The only candidate is, in fact, the Allowance for Bad Debts contra asset. To illustrate the process, let's assume that the account has an existing credit balance of $200. Since we want the $420 amount of estimated uncollectibles to be reported in the balance sheet, we must make it the ending balance in the allowance account as shown:

Allowance for Bad Debts

	200 ← Balance before adjustment
	220 ← Adjustment is plugged
	420 ← Estimate inserted here

As shown in the preceding T-account and in the lower half of Figure 11-15, the adjusting entry under the percentage of receivables method is not the estimate itself ($420) but rather the amount ($220) that when added to the beginning allowance balance ($200) equals the amount of the estimate ($420). In other words, under the percentage of receivables method, the allowance account is adjusted to a certain percentage of receivables. The amount of the adjustment is arbitrarily determined by plugging or inserting the number that will achieve the desired estimate.

Just as with the percentage of sales method, the effect of simultaneously increasing Bad Debt Expense and the Allowance for Bad Debts as shown in Figure 11-15 is to reduce net income and, thus, owners' equity as well as net accounts receivable. This method is more difficult to apply because the estimate we calculated does not become the amount of the adjusting entry. The method is appealing, however, because the source of the estimate—the ending balance in accounts receivable—and the estimate itself—the ending balance in the allowance account—are both reported in the balance sheet. Thus, as suggested earlier, this method is clearly a balance sheet approach. Study the lower half of Figure 11-15 to be certain you understand its reasoning process.

Advantages of Using an Aging Schedule

INSIGHT

In estimating bad debts as a percentage of unpaid receivables, some businesses use a more detailed analysis called an *accounts receivable aging schedule.* An **aging schedule** divides a company's existing receivable balance into categories based on how long individual receivables have been unpaid. It is quite likely that you have seen such an aging schedule if you have ever received a medical bill. Such bills anticipate longer collection periods due to the time it often takes health insurance to pay its portion of the amount due.

The general premise underlying any aging schedule is that the probability that an unpaid receivable will never be collected increases with the length of time it has been outstanding. Thus, as shown below for our earlier $6,000 receivable balance, higher uncollectible percentages are assigned to those customer balances that have been outstanding for lengthier periods.

		Amount	×	Uncollectible Percentage	=	Estimated Uncollectible
Current	(0–30 days)	$4,400		.05		$220
Due	(31–60 days)	1,000		.10		100
Past due	(61–90 days)	400		.20		80
Delinquent	(> 90 days)	200		.45		90
		$6,000				$490

As you can see, this more detailed analysis results in an estimate of $490 rather than our earlier estimate of $420. If we believe that this aging schedule is a more accurate analysis of our potential uncollectibles, we will want to insert $490 as the ending balance in the preceding Allowance for Bad Debts account.

(continued)

The **insight** you should gain here is that businesses can often increase the accuracy of their percentage of receivables estimate by using an aging schedule paired with varying uncollectible percentages. Another **insight** you should gain is that even an aging schedule without percentages can be a valuable communication device between the seller and its customers. That is because you, as a customer, are more likely to remit payment when you clearly understand just how long your account has been unpaid.

Now that you have learned about these two distinctive ways of estimating the loss from uncollectible accounts receivable, use Performance Objective 41 to help you master their differences.

YOUR PERFORMANCE OBJECTIVE 41
Distinguish between the percentage of sales method and the percentage of receivables method for estimating uncollectible amounts in the Allowance for Bad Debts account.

Writing Off an Uncollectible Account

In the process of estimating a loss from bad debts in our preceding discussion of the allowance method, you might have noticed that the amount calculated always affected the right-hand side of the Allowance for Bad Debts T-account. In the percentage of sales T-account, for example, notice that the $500 amount on the right-hand side of the account is an estimate. Under the allowance method, the opposite side (left-hand side) of the account is reserved for the specific customer accounts that the company determines will never be collected.

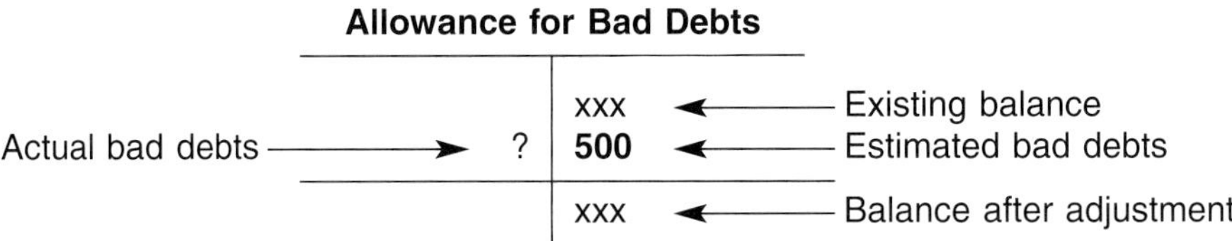

Although the decision of when to write off these customer accounts is a function of particular company credit policies, some fairly universal conditions usually result in the removal of a customer's account from active status. Evidence of such worthlessness includes bankruptcy, death or disappearance of the debtor, and collection barred by a statute of limitations.

Financial Statement Effects of Receivable Write-Offs To illustrate how an account receivable is written off under the allowance method, let's assume that a credit manager decides that an outstanding balance of $100 owed by a particular customer will never be collected. Note that to properly write off this account, you must write off both the specific customer receivable in the accounts receivable subsidiary ledger as well as a $100 amount in the accounts receivable controlling account in the general ledger. Study Figure 11-16(a) to view the transaction recorded in the general ledger to reflect this write off and Figure 11-16(b) to view the effect of this transaction on the financial statements. Notice that this transaction decreases the contra asset, Allowance for Bad Debts, and its primary asset, Accounts Receivable. Since both of these accounts are reduced by an equal amount, the difference between them does not change. That is, as shown in Figure 11-16(b), the actual write-off of a bad debt changes the individual balance sheet accounts but has no net effect on a company's total assets. Since this transaction does not include income statement accounts, the actual write-off has absolutely no effect on income.

FIGURE 11-16 The transaction recorded to reflect a write-off of an account receivable and its financial statement effects

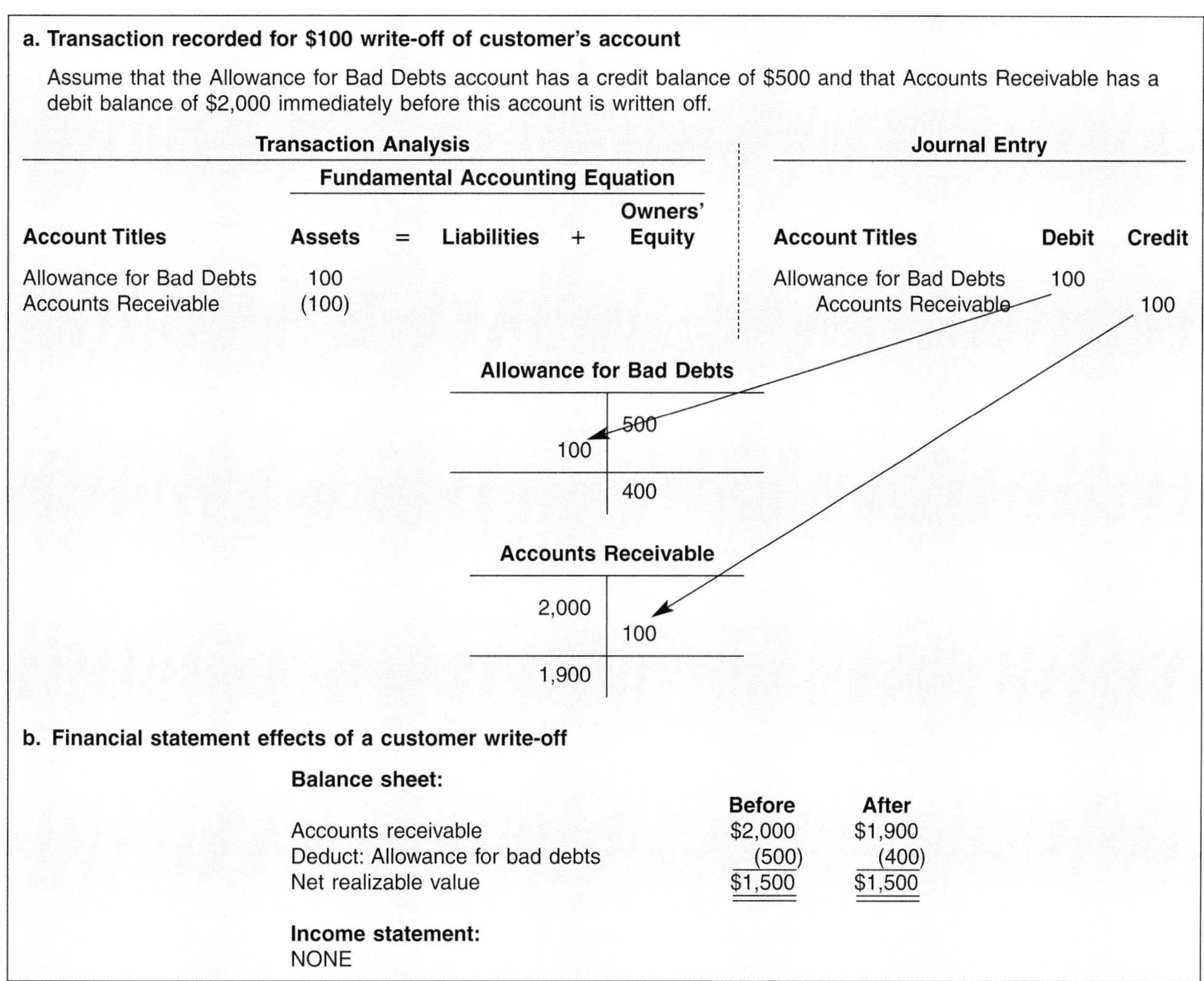

a. Transaction recorded for $100 write-off of customer's account

Assume that the Allowance for Bad Debts account has a credit balance of $500 and that Accounts Receivable has a debit balance of $2,000 immediately before this account is written off.

Transaction Analysis

	Fundamental Accounting Equation				
Account Titles	**Assets**	**=**	**Liabilities**	**+**	**Owners' Equity**
Allowance for Bad Debts	100				
Accounts Receivable	(100)				

Journal Entry

Account Titles	**Debit**	**Credit**
Allowance for Bad Debts	100	
Accounts Receivable		100

Allowance for Bad Debts

	500
100	
	400

Accounts Receivable

2,000	
	100
1,900	

b. Financial statement effects of a customer write-off

Balance sheet:

	Before	**After**
Accounts receivable	$2,000	$1,900
Deduct: Allowance for bad debts	(500)	(400)
Net realizable value	$1,500	$1,500

Income statement:
NONE

Recording the Recovery of a Previously Written-Off Receivable

Occasionally, a previously written-off receivable is recovered when the customer initiates payment of its overdue account receivable. When this relatively rare event occurs, two transactions are necessary as illustrated in Figure 11-17. The first step is to reverse the effect of the previous write-off as shown in Figure 11-17(a). Once the Accounts Receivable account has been reinstated, it is then reduced by recording a standard collection of cash on account as shown in Figure 11-17(b).

Using Financial Statement Analysis to Evaluate the Effectiveness of Operating Activity Management

Now that you understand how operating activities affect financial statements, you are in a better position to evaluate how effectively a company's operating activities have been managed. To conduct such an evaluation, you start with the same financial statement effects you have just studied and pair them with some variations of the activity or turnover ratios you studied in Chapter 7. Recall that activity ratios are so named because they measure how productive particular assets are in generating sales

FIGURE 11-17 Transactions needed to record the recovery of a written-off account receivable

Assumption: The customer whose account was written off in Figure 11-16 sends $100 in full payment of their account receivable.

a. Recovery of previously written-off account receivable

Transaction Analysis					Journal Entry		
	Fundamental Accounting Equation						
Account Titles	**Assets**	**=**	**Liabilities +**	**Owners' Equity**	**Account Titles**	**Debit**	**Credit**
Accounts Receivable	100				Accounts Receivable	100	
Allowance for Bad Debts	(100)				Allowance for Bad Debts		100

b. Collection of outstanding receivable

Transaction Analysis					Journal Entry		
	Fundamental Accounting Equation						
Account Titles	**Assets**	**=**	**Liabilities +**	**Owners' Equity**	**Account Titles**	**Debit**	**Credit**
Cash	100				Cash	100	
Accounts Receivable	(100)				Accounts Receivable		100

activity. Since our focus in this chapter is on operating activities, and more specifically the operating cycle, we are very interested in the relative productivity of our inventories and receivables. Since we can measure the relative efficiency of these assets via the average holding period and the average collection period, let's review these calculations.

Calculating the Average Holding Period

The average holding period, sometimes referred to as days' inventories on hand, days' inventory unsold, and days' sales in inventory, is a turnover measure that expresses the same concept as the inventory turnover ratio but in a more intuitive manner. It includes both the purchasing phase and the selling phase of the operating cycle shown in Figure 11-3 and is calculated by dividing 365 days by the inventory turnover ratio as shown here for CMU:

$$\text{Average Holding Period} = \frac{\text{365 Days}}{\text{Inventory Turnover Ratio}} = \frac{365}{2.143} = 170.33 \text{ Days}$$

Although this textbook will use 365 days to achieve greater accuracy, some round off the number of days in a year to 360.

Calculating the Average Collection Period

The average collection period, sometimes referred to as the average days' sales uncollected, days' accounts receivable outstanding, and days' sales in receivables, is a turnover measure that expresses the same concept as the accounts receivable turnover ratio, but in a more intuitive manner. It is calculated by dividing 365 days by the accounts receivable turnover ratio as shown here for CMU:

$$\text{Average Collection Period} = \frac{\text{365 Days}}{\text{Accts. Rec. Turnover Ratio}} = \frac{365}{7.76} = 47.04 \text{ Days}$$

This calculation shows that, on average, CMU receives payment from customers within 47.04 days from the time of the sale.

Calculating the Length of the Operating Cycle

The length of the operating cycle can be calculated in at least two ways. As described earlier in this chapter, one way is to add the length of time it takes an inventory purchase to move through the purchasing, selling, and collecting phases. Although this approach appears straightforward, it has at least two shortcomings. First, it is very time-consuming and costly to determine the length of time it takes numerous purchases to pass through these phases. Second, the purchase phase calculations are complicated whenever the supplier's credit terms do not require payment until some time after the merchandise has been received and is ready for sale. To better understand this problem, consider the following example.

Example Jordan Company can unpack merchandise and have it ready for sale 3 days after receipt but does not pay for that same merchandise until 30 days after receipt.

Solution The days in this part of the cycle are considered to be a negative 27 days (3 days − 30 days) because the selling phase began a full 27 days before the completion of the purchasing phase.

To avoid these problems, we can calculate the length of the operating cycle by adding the average holding period of inventory to the average collection period of receivables and assume that the time involved in purchasing is zero.[6] As a result, let's now calculate the length of the operating cycle for CMU by using this formula:

$$\text{Operating Cycle} = \text{Average Holding Period} + \text{Average Collection Period}$$

$$217.37 \text{ Days} = 170.33 \text{ Days} + 47.04 \text{ Days}$$

As already discussed, the individual calculations for determining the length of the operating cycle deserve scrutiny. Susan's inventory holding period is simply too high. Hopefully, she can take steps to reduce it so that clear improvement in this efficiency measure is apparent in her second year of business.

The Effect of a Company's Operating Cycle on the Resources Invested in Inventories, Receivables, and Payables

As you learned in Chapter 5, shortening each phase of the operating cycle (for example, cutting in half the length of time a box of trading cards sits on the shelf) has the effect of reducing the amount of assets required to operate the business. Although no retailer wants to incur customer ill will due to inventory shortages, all retailers prefer to turn over large inventory and receivable balances into cash for reinvestment and liquidity needs. In the next section, you will calculate the length of a company's operating cycle so that you can make decisions about its resource needs. Mastering Performance Objective 42 will give you the tools you need to evaluate this operating cycle information.

YOUR PERFORMANCE OBJECTIVE 42

Explain how inventories and accounts receivable can be mismanaged and **describe** how financial statement analysis can be used to evaluate how effectively these resources are being managed.

---

[6] A variation of the accounts payable turnover ratio called *average payment period* or *days' payables* can approximate a negative purchase phase as will be briefly explained in a later *User Focus*.

Note how this performance objective applies to the following illustrations of operating activity management as well as to the *Decision Case* presented at the end of this chapter.

Inventory Management You have learned that the greater the length of the operating cycle, the greater the assets required to operate the business. It also follows that the greater the average holding period of inventory, the greater the balance required in the inventory account. Intuitively, this concept is fairly easy to understand because the slower your inventory moves, the higher the dollar amount you have "sitting," or invested in, that inventory asset. If you begin, instead, to move that inventory more quickly by selling it, you convert the dollars in the inventory asset into cash that can be reinvested throughout your company. Despite its intuitive appeal, the concept that a slow-moving inventory requires a greater investment in inventory is also illustrated by the following numerical example:

Assume a 360-day year and that Cost of Goods Sold is $18,000 in each of these cases.

	Case A	Case B	Case C
Annual inventory turnover	12	9	6

In each case, we calculate the amount invested in the inventory account by using the inventory turnover ratio:

	Case A	Case B	Case C
$\frac{\text{Cost of Goods Sold}}{\text{Average Inventory}} =$	$\frac{\$18{,}000}{\$\ 1{,}500} = 12;$	$\frac{\$18{,}000}{\$\ 2{,}000} = 9;$	$\frac{\$18{,}000}{\$\ 3{,}000} = 6$

Then we calculate the average holding period:

$$\frac{360}{\text{Inventory Turnover}} \qquad \frac{360}{12} = \mathbf{30} \qquad \frac{360}{9} = \mathbf{40} \qquad \frac{360}{6} = \mathbf{60}$$

Notice that this information is organized and presented in Figure 11-18(a). Confirm from your study of this figure that the longer the average holding period, the greater the amount that must be invested in inventory. Since most annual reports contain the preceding information, you generally will be able to compare different companies on how efficiently they manage their inventory. Now let's determine if the same concept applies to receivables.

FIGURE 11-18(a)

Evidence that slow-moving inventory requires a greater investment in inventory

	Case 1	Case 2	Case 3
Average holding period (in days)	30	40	60
Amount of inventory investment	$1,500	$2,000	$3,000

Receivables Management From the preceding discussion, it follows that the greater the average collection period of receivables, the greater the balance required in the receivables account. Intuitively, this concept is fairly easy to understand because the slower your customers pay their balances, the higher the dollar amount you have sitting, or invested in, your receivable asset. If you begin, instead, to collect those receivables more quickly, you convert the dollars tied up in the receivable asset into cash that can be reinvested throughout your company. Despite its intuitive appeal, the concept that slow-moving customer collections require a greater investment in receivables is also illustrated by the following numerical example:

Assume a 360-day year and that Sales Revenue is $24,000 in each of these cases.

	Case A	Case B	Case C
Annual receivable turnover	24	15	10

In each case, we calculate the amount invested in the receivables account by using the accounts receivable turnover ratio:

	Case A	Case B	Case C
$\frac{\text{Sales Revenue}}{\text{Average Receivables}} =$	$\frac{\$24{,}000}{\$\ 1{,}000} = 24;$	$\frac{\$24{,}000}{\$\ 1{,}600} = 15;$	$\frac{\$24{,}000}{\$\ 2{,}400} = 10$

Then we calculate the average collection period:

$$\frac{360}{\text{Receivable Turnover}} \qquad \frac{360}{24} = \mathbf{15} \qquad \frac{360}{15} = \mathbf{24} \qquad \frac{360}{10} = \mathbf{36}$$

Notice that this information is organized and presented in Figure 11-18(b). Confirm from your study of this figure that the longer the average collection period, the greater the amount that must be invested in accounts receivable. Since most annual reports contain the preceding information, you generally will be able to compare different companies on how efficiently they manage their receivables.

	Case 1	Case 2	Case 3
Average collection period (in days)	15	24	36
Amount of receivable investment	$1,000	$1,600	$2,400

FIGURE 11-18(b)

Evidence that slow-moving customer collections require a greater investment in receivables

USER FOCUS

Extending Inventory and Receivable Management Concepts to Payables

Now that you understand why slow-moving inventory and slow-moving customer collections require greater investments in inventories and receivables, you will not be surprised to learn that much the same concept applies to the Accounts Payable account. That is, the more slowly you pay cash to reduce accounts payable, the larger the investment in that account. Unlike inventory and receivable turnover, however, increasing accounts payable turnover does not conserve cash, and is, therefore, not necessarily a good business strategy. To better understand why, let's examine the concept of accounts payable turnover.

The **accounts payable turnover ratio** indicates the relative frequency with which the accounts payable balance turns over. A low turnover is generally preferable because it conserves cash. You calculate this ratio as follows:

$$\text{Accounts Payable Turnover} = \frac{\text{Inventory Purchases}}{\text{Average Accounts Payable}}$$

To illustrate how this calculation is made, assume a 360-day year and that the accounts payable balance is entirely composed of inventory purchases. Also assume the following balances:

Cost of goods sold	$306,000
Beginning inventory	30,000
Ending inventory	36,000
Beginning accounts payable	10,000
Ending accounts payable	16,000

To calculate the numerator or purchases, you would apply the inventory formula as follows:

Beginning inventory	$ 30,000
Merchandise acquisitions or purchases	**312,000**
Cost of goods available for sale	342,000
Deduct: Ending inventory	(36,000)
Cost of goods sold	$306,000

The denominator or average payables would be $13,000 [($10,000 + $16,000)/2]. In this case, the accounts payable turnover ratio is:

$$\text{Accounts Payable Turnover} = \frac{\text{Inventory Purchases}}{\text{Average Accounts Payable}} = \frac{\$312{,}000}{\$13{,}000} = 24$$

Then we calculate the *average payment period of payables*:

$$\frac{360}{\text{Payable Turnover}} = \frac{360}{24} = 15$$

Because this payment period of 15 days represents the number of days in which the payment of cash is delayed, it must be subtracted when calculating the operating cycle. That is, to calculate the length of the operating cycle, you add the days needed to prepare for sale, if any, to the average holding period of inventory and to the average collection period of receivables, and then subtract the average payment period of payables.

For example, assume the following information:

January 2: an inventory unit arrives
- four days are needed to prepare this inventory for sale

January 6: the inventory unit is placed on the shelf for sale (January 2 + 4)
- average payment period is 10 days

January 12: the inventory unit is paid for (January 2 + 10)
- average holding period is 8 days

January 14: the inventory unit is sold (January 6 + 8)
- average collection period is 15 days

January 29: inventory unit's receivable is collected (January 14 + 15)

Using the calculation just described, the length of the operating cycle is:

$$17 = 4 + 8 + 15 - 10$$

You'll soon have another opportunity to work with these concepts in this chapter's *Making Business Decisions* case.

Summary with Key Terms

The number in parentheses following each **key term** is the page number on which the term is defined.

You began this chapter by reviewing the financial statement effects of operating activities in three types of industries introduced in Chapter 10: merchandising, manufacturing, and service companies. One manufacturing financial statement effect that was not described in Chapter 10 is the **Manufacturing Supplies Inventory** account (548). The **operating cycle** (543) was then revisited because of its central role in operating activities.

In describing the special role of the inventory equation and how purchase discounts and purchase returns and allowances are treated, we introduced the element referred to as **net purchases** (547). Then we examined the **periodic inventory system** (551) and the **perpetual inventory system** (551), which are distinguished from one another by virtue of when cost of goods sold is recorded. Another important issue when accounting for inventory is the question of what inventory to properly include and exclude at the end of an accounting period. To help make this determination, it is important to establish who has ownership, or **legal title** (554), to the goods in question at the close of the accounting period. This question is often resolved by finding out whether the terms of sale involve the phrases **FOB shipping point** (554) or **FOB destination point** (554). If the buyer is responsible for these transportation costs, they are called **freight-in** (547) and must be included in net purchases. The determination of who properly should include inventory costs at the end of a period also was illustrated by considering a special type of inventory arrangement called a **consignment** (555). A consignment involves the **consignor** (555), or seller, transferring physical possession but not ownership to a third party known as the **consignee** (555).

A significant portion of this chapter was devoted to how inventory costs can be assigned to specific units of inventory. In this discussion, you learned first about the **specific identification method** (556) and then about three cost-flow assumptions. The first of these cost-flow assumptions, **average cost** (558), is often referred to as **weighted-average cost** (558) under a periodic inventory system and as **moving-average cost** (558) under a perpetual inventory system. You then learned about the two most popular cost flow assumptions, **first-in, first-out**, or **FIFO** (559), and **last-in, first-out**, or **LIFO** (559). Since these terms refer to the calculation of the cost of goods sold, you also learned about FIFO's ending inventory counterpart **last-in, still-here,** or **LISH** (560), and LIFO's ending inventory counterpart **first-in, still-here**, or **FISH** (560). In your exploration of these cost-flow assumptions, you also learned about a disclosure known as the **LIFO reserve** (564) that is intended to overcome one of LIFO's primary disadvantages. Unfortunately, another disadvantage of LIFO known as the **LIFO liquidation problem** (564) is not so easily overcome.

After learning about the financial statement effects of inventory errors, you were presented with the essential characteristics of a popular inventory estimation method known as the **gross margin method** (568). We then ended our coverage of inventory by examining the valuation method known as the **lower of cost or market method**, or **LOCOM** (570), which sometimes allows an inventory's **market value** (570) to be reported on the balance sheet in place of its cost. As you learned, LOCOM is based on the long-standing accounting principle of **conservatism** (570).

This chapter then explained how companies actually account for uncollectible accounts. This process revolves around two primary accounts. The first is that of **Allowance for Bad Debts** (571) also referred to as **Allowance for Uncollectible Accounts** (571) and **Allowance for Doubtful Accounts** (571). The second is that of **Bad Debt Expense** (573) also referred to as **Uncollectible Accounts Expense** (573) and **Doubtful Accounts Expense** (573). To satisfy the matching concept, the **allowance method** (572) is used to record the loss from uncollectibles in the period of sale. Two specific methods for estimating this loss from uncollectibles, the **percentage of sales method** (573) and the **percentage of receivables method** (574), were then illustrated. In particular, an *Insight* described how the accuracy of the percentage of receivables estimate can often be increased by using an **aging schedule** (575) paired with varying uncollectible percentages. You then learned how to record both the write-off of specific customer accounts as well as the recovery of such written-off accounts. This chapter then concluded with an exploration of how operating cycle calculations can be used to evaluate how well any company's inventory and receivable resources are managed. As an extension of this concept, a *User Focus* introduced the **accounts payable turnover ratio** (581) to explain how payments to suppliers can be managed to conserve cash.

Making Business Decisions

YOUR PERFORMANCE OBJECTIVE 2
(page 18)

You have been working for Keating Corporation for three years, and the budget crunch has finally hit. Due to the loss of two large accounts and an economic recession, the company president wants to slash budgets across the board. You don't disagree with her thinking, but you want to take a closer look at how your company manages its inventory and receivables. You know that the slower a company turns over its inventory and receivables, the larger its investment in those current assets. And that whenever a company can reduce its average holding period and its average collection period, it can more effectively manage those resources and invest the additional cash in other areas. So you decide to evaluate the amount of resources that Keating invests in its inventory and accounts receivable. You think that you might be able to offset some of these proposed budget cuts if you perform some analysis and then make some decisions that will save cash.

First, you obtain the following projections for the coming year:

Sales	$800,000
Cost of goods sold	600,000
Beginning inventory	67,500
Ending inventory	82,500
Loss on obsolete inventory	4,000
Beginning accounts receivable	77,000
Ending accounts receivable	83,000
Bad debt expense	6,000
Beginning accounts payable	43,500
Ending accounts payable	38,500

Assume that the accounts payable balance is entirely composed of inventory purchases and that a 360-day year is used.

a. Given this information, what calculations might you perform? Explain why.
b. Perform the calculations from part (a) above.
c. What specific decision affecting only the inventory account could you make that, if successful, could offset a budget shortfall of $15,000? Describe what actions a credit manager might take to implement this decision. Describe another decision the credit manager might make to conserve cash.
d. What specific decision affecting only the Accounts Receivable account could you make that, if successful, could offset a budget shortfall of $30,000? Describe what actions a sales manager might take to implement this decision. Describe another decision the sales manager might make to conserve cash.
e. What specific decision affecting only the Accounts Payable account could you make that, if successful, could offset a budget shortfall of $10,250? Describe what actions a manager might take to implement this decision. Describe any disadvantages associated with this decision.
f. Assume that the budget shortfall is $40,000. Which combination of the preceding solutions would you recommend and why?

Questions

YOUR PERFORMANCE OBJECTIVE 4
(page 22)

11-1 Explain in your own words the meaning of key business terms.

a. Manufacturing supplies inventory
b. Net purchases
c. Legal title
d. FOB shipping point
e. FOB destination point
f. Consignment
g. Freight-in
h. Specific identification method
i. Average cost
j. Last-in, first-out, or LIFO
k. First-in, first-out, or FIFO
l. Last-in, still-here, or LISH
m. First-in, still-here, or FISH
n. Gross margin method
o. Lower of cost or market method, or LOCOM
p. Market value
q. Conservatism

r.	Allowance for bad debts	u.	Bad debt expense
s.	Allowance for uncollectible accounts	v.	Uncollectible accounts expense
t.	Allowance for doubtful accounts	w.	Doubtful accounts expense

11-2 Describe the three phases of the operating cycle.

11-3 Describe a situation in which a phase of the operating cycle could represent negative days.

11-4 Describe the different inventory accounts that a manufacturing company could report on its balance sheet.

11-5 Distinguish between the periodic and perpetual inventory systems.

11-6 Select a business you are very familiar with and discuss which inventory system is probably being used and why.

Indicate whether each of the following statements (Items 11-7 to 11-12) is true or false:

11-7 Ownership of inventory transfers when title to the goods passes from the seller to the buyer.

11-8 Purchases in transit shipped on terms FOB shipping point should be included in the inventory count.

11-9 The higher the cost of ending inventory, the lower the cost of goods sold will be, and the higher the resulting gross margin.

11-10 An overstatement of ending inventory in a period will result in an overstatement of net income for that period.

11-11 An overstatement of ending inventory in a period will result in an understatement of net income in the next period.

11-12 The lower the cost of ending inventory, the higher the net income will be.

11-13 How will an overstatement of ending inventory affect the balance sheet (overstate, understate, or no effect):
a. Of the current year? b. Of the following year?

11-14 Figure 11-10 describes the relative differences between the three inventory cost-flow assumptions introduced in this chapter. Assuming rising prices over time, do the observed differences hold for all forms of inventory or just our milk carton illustration?

11-15 Under what condition will the relationships among average cost, FIFO, and LIFO shown in Figure 11-10 be reversed?

11-16 Discuss the effects on the balance sheet and the income statement of using (a) FIFO and (b) LIFO in a period of rising prices?

11-17 Describe two advantages of using LIFO as a cost-flow assumption.

11-18 Distinguish between a LIFO reserve and a LIFO liquidation.

11-19 Why has the financial reporting practice known as conservatism survived for so long?

11-20 Distinguish between the percentage of sales and percentage of receivables methods for estimating uncollectibles.

11-21 Distinguish between the accounts payable turnover ratio and the average payment period.

11-22 Describe the role that the average payment period plays in calculating the length of the operating cycle.

Reinforcement Exercises

E11-1 Asking the Right Questions: A Group Activity

YOUR PERFORMANCE OBJECTIVE 4
(page 22)

It's often said that knowing the right answer is not nearly as important as asking the right question. Asking the right question is a problem-solving skill that will help you make sound business decisions. In this exercise, you will review the vocabulary introduced in Chapter 11 by creating questions to match answers—similar to a popular TV show.

Required

a. Given an answer, what's the question?
Choose **three** of the following terms to serve as an answer. For each term, create an appropriate question. For example, if you choose the term *balance sheet*, you might

create the question *What financial statement shows the assets, liabilities, and owners' equity of an entity on a specific date?*

Consignee	Consignor	FOB shipping point
Operating cycle	Operating activities	FOB destination point
FIFO	LIFO	Moving-average cost
FISH	LISH	Weighted-average cost

b. Are you sure that's the question?
Have each member of your group read aloud the questions they developed in Requirement (a). As a group, decide whether each question is an accurate match for an answer. Once satisfied that all questions are appropriate, the group, as a whole, chooses the three best questions created within the group. Record the three questions chosen (with their answers) on separate pieces of paper or index cards and give them to your instructor.

c. What's the answer?
To ensure you have learned the vocabulary terms listed in Requirement (a), your instructor will now quiz you on the questions written by all of your classmates.

YOUR PERFORMANCE OBJECTIVE 4
(page 22)

E11-2 Calculating the Length of the Operating Cycle

Calculate the length of the operating cycle in each of the following cases.

a. Kimmel Company bought inventory that was ready for sale 10 days after it was paid for with cash. It sold this inventory 15 days after the inventory was first ready for sale. It collected cash from its customer 20 days after it sold and delivered this inventory.
b. Diamond Company made a cash purchase of inventory that is received and ready for sale on the same day. It sold this inventory later that same day to a customer who paid for the purchase in cash.
c. Ingram Company bought inventory on account and paid for it with cash 15 days after the inventory was ready for sale. It sold this inventory 10 days after the inventory was first ready for sale to a customer who paid 15 days after receiving the inventory.
d. Needles Company bought inventory that was ready for sale 25 days after it was paid for with cash. It sold this inventory for cash 10 days after the inventory was first placed on the shelf and delivered the inventory 20 days later.

YOUR PERFORMANCE OBJECTIVES 7, 13b
(pages 64, 276)

E11-3 Effect of Operating Activity Transactions on a Service Company's Financial Statements

Typical operating activity transactions of a service company are listed below. Describe how each transaction affects the balance sheet, income statement, and/or the statement of cash flows using the direct method. Transaction (a) is completed for you as an example.

Transaction	Financial Statement	Effect of Transaction
a. Cash payment of rent	Balance sheet	Cash decrease
	Balance sheet	Prepaid rent increase
	Income statement	No effect
	Statement of cash flows	Operating cash outflow: cash paid for rent
b. Cash sale of services		
c. Credit sale of services		
d. Receipt of full payment from customer in transaction (c)		
e. Cash payment of salary		

YOUR PERFORMANCE OBJECTIVE 31
(page 475)

E11-4 Calculating Cost of Goods Manufactured

Jacobs Manufacturing used \$23,500 in raw materials and incurred \$20,000 in direct labor and \$26,600 in manufacturing overhead costs. The company has work in process inventory of \$5,000 at the start of the year and \$7,100 at the end of the year. Calculate Jacobs's cost of goods manufactured for the year.

E11-5 Calculating Cost of Goods Manufactured and Manufacturing Cost of Goods Sold

YOUR PERFORMANCE OBJECTIVE 31 *(page 475)*

Camden Yards Corporation started the accounting period with the following account balances:

Cash	$1,000		
Raw materials inventory	300		
Work-in-process inventory	500	Common stock	$ 700
Finished goods inventory	400	Retained earnings	1,500
Total assets	$2,200	Total equities	$2,200

The following information relates to this period:
Purchased $500 worth of raw materials.
Used $600 of raw materials.
Used 90 hours of labor at $5 per hour.
Incurred $300 of factory overhead.
Determined the ending Work-in-Process Inventory balance to be $590.
Determined the ending Finished Goods Inventory balance to be $550.

Required
Calculate the cost of goods manufactured and the manufacturing cost of goods sold for this period.

E11-6 Inventory Systems

YOUR PERFORMANCE OBJECTIVE 34 *(page 553)*

Select the single item below that is correctly described under both inventory systems.

	Item	Periodic	Perpetual
a.	Inventory control	Not as good as perpetual	Very good
b.	Cost to administer	High	Low
c.	Physical count	Must be taken at end of period	Need never be taken
d.	Receipt of inventory	Recorded at end of period	Recorded as received
e.	Cost of goods sold	Recorded at end of period	Recorded at time of sale

E11-7 Inventory Systems

YOUR PERFORMANCE OBJECTIVE 34 *(page 553)*

Two distinct systems are available in accounting for inventory: periodic and perpetual. Determine which inventory system is most likely to be used in each of the following situations and provide logical support for your answer:

a. Automobile dealership.
b. College bookstore.
c. Fur coat department of a retail store.
d. Greeting card department of a retail store.
e. Diamond ring department of a jewelry store.
f. Ballpoint pen department of a jewelry store.
g. Grocery store.

E11-8 Proper Content of Inventory

YOUR PERFORMANCE OBJECTIVE 35 *(page 556)*

In preparing financial statements for the current year ended December 31, you discover the following items relating to inventory, purchases, and sales:

a. Goods costing $4,000 are not included in inventory, but the purchase was recorded. The invoice has been received but the goods have not. The goods were shipped by the supplier FOB destination.
b. Goods costing $4,000 are not included in inventory, but the purchase was recorded. The invoice has been received but the goods have not. The goods were shipped by the supplier FOB shipping point.
c. Goods in transit costing $3,000 are excluded from the inventory. The goods were shipped by the supplier FOB shipping point. The purchase was not recorded.

Required
Complete the following schedule showing any required adjustment of account balances. If there is no effect, write NONE.

	Accounts Receivable	Inventory	Accounts Payable	Sales Revenue	Cost of Goods Sold
Unadjusted amounts	$115,000	$100,000	$80,000	$280,000	$185,000
Adjustments:					
a.					
b.					
c.					
Adjusted amounts	$	$	$	$	$

YOUR PERFORMANCE OBJECTIVE 35 *(page 556)*

E11-9 Proper Content of Inventory

In preparing financial statements for the current year ended December 31, you discover the following items relating to inventory, purchases, and sales:

a. Goods costing $12,000 were sold for $18,000. The sale was recorded and shipped FOB destination. The goods are not included in inventory.
b. Goods costing $12,000 were sold for $18,000. The sale was recorded and shipped FOB shipping point. The goods are not included in inventory.
c. Goods having a cost of $1,500 were shipped on consignment and are excluded from the inventory. The shipment was not recorded as a sale.

Required
Complete the following schedule showing any required adjustment of account balances. If there is no effect, write NONE.

	Accounts Receivable	Inventory	Accounts Payable	Sales Revenue	Cost of Goods Sold
Unadjusted amounts	$115,000	$100,000	$80,000	$280,000	$185,000
Adjustments:					
a.					
b.					
c.					
Adjusted amounts	$	$	$	$	$

YOUR PERFORMANCE OBJECTIVE 36 *(page 561)*

E11-10 Inventory Cost-Flow Assumptions

Use the following data to fulfill the requirements below:

	Units	Unit Cost	Subtotal	Total
Beginning inventory	400	$ 6		$ 2,400
Purchases:	200	6	$1,200	
	100	7	700	
	100	6	600	
	300	8	2,400	
	300	10	3,000	7,900
Cost of goods available for sale				$10,300

According to company inventory records, there were 500 units on hand at the end of the period.

Required

a. Use the first-in, first-out method to calculate the cost of ending inventory.
b. Use the last-in, first-out method to calculate the cost of goods sold.
c. Assume that the inventory data above represent a perpetual inventory system and a year-end physical count reveals only 450 units on hand. Calculate the amount of the inventory loss assuming that a FIFO perpetual inventory system was used.

E11-11 Inventory Cost-Flow Assumptions

Use the following data to calculate the amount of ending inventory in each of the cases below:

YOUR PERFORMANCE OBJECTIVE 36 *(page 561)*

	Units	Unit Cost	Total
Beginning inventory	36	$10	$360
Purchases:	8	11	88
	10	14	140
	6	11	66
	12	10	120
	18	12	216
Available for sale	90		$990

a. Weighted-average method (with sales of 75 units).
b. First-in, first-out method (with sales of 65 units).
c. Last-in, first-out method (with sales of 70 units).
d. Last-in, first-out method (with sales of 50 units).
e. Specific identification method (assume that from the 60 units sold, 30 came from the beginning inventory, 7 came from the first purchase, 8 came from the second purchase, and 15 came from the last purchase of the period).

E11-12 Inventory Cost-Flow Assumptions

Slotsky Company purchased inventory during the current year as follows:

YOUR PERFORMANCE OBJECTIVE 36 *(page 561)*

		Units	Unit Cost
Jan. 1	Beg. inventory	11	$10
Mar. 16	Purchased	20	11
Jul. 23	Purchased	15	12
Oct. 8	Purchased	20	13
Dec. 20	Purchased	14	15

The ending inventory consists of 16 units from October 8.

a. Identify cost-flow assumptions:
   Determine the inventory method being used by Slotsky if the amount assigned to ending inventory is:
   1. $196 3. $208
   2. $165 4. $236
b. Compare cost-flow assumptions:
   Fill in the prices of ending inventory, cost of goods sold, and gross margin in the table below. Assume sales were $1,000 in all cases.

	Average Cost	FIFO	LIFO
Sales	$1,000	$1,000	$1,000
Goods available for sale:	980	980	980
Deduct: Ending inventory			
Cost of goods sold			
Gross margin			

c. Assuming rising prices, which method results in the:
   1. Lowest cost of ending inventory?
   2. Highest profit?
   3. Lowest taxes?
   4. Lowest cost of goods sold?
   5. Largest ending inventory valuation?
   6. Largest net income?

E11-13 Income Statement Effect of Different Cost-Flow Assumptions

YOUR PERFORMANCE OBJECTIVE 37 *(page 562)*

Jackson Company reports its inventory using the LIFO cost-flow assumption. Assume that FIFO's inventory cost was greater than that of LIFO by $200 million at the beginning of the year and $300 million at the end of the year. How much higher or lower would reported income be if FIFO had been used as the cost-flow assumption instead of LIFO?

YOUR PERFORMANCE OBJECTIVE 38 *(page 568)*

E11-14 Effect of Ending Inventory Errors on Reported Net Income
As the newly hired accountant of Morganthal, Inc., you discover the following errors in the ending inventory of 2003–2005:

2003:	$3,000 understatement
2004:	$2,875 overstatement
2005:	$2,200 understatement
2006:	No error

The reported net income for the years 2003–2006 were:

2003:	$60,000
2004:	$76,000
2005:	$68,000
2006:	$83,000

Required
Calculate the correct net income for the years 2002–2006.

YOUR PERFORMANCE OBJECTIVE 38 *(page 568)*

E11-15 Effects of Errors in the Amount of Ending Inventory
An error in a company's physical inventory count results in an overstatement at the end of the current accounting period. Indicate the effect of this error (overstatement, understatement, or none) on the following items, assuming that this error is not detected.

a. 1/1, current period inventory.
b. 1/1, next period inventory.
c. 12/31, current period inventory.
d. 12/31, next period inventory.
e. Cost of goods sold, current period.
f. Cost of goods sold, next period.
g. Net income, current period.
h. Net income, next period.
i. Retained earnings, current period.
j. Retained earnings, next period.

YOUR PERFORMANCE OBJECTIVE 38 *(page 568)*

E11-16 Effects of Errors in the Amount of Ending Inventory
An error in a company's physical inventory count results in an understatement at the end of the current accounting period. Indicate the effect of this error (overstatement, understatement, or none) on the following items, assuming that this error is not detected.

a. 1/1, current period inventory.
b. 1/1, next period inventory.
c. 12/31, current period inventory.
d. 12/31, next period inventory.
e. Cost of goods sold, current period.
f. Cost of goods sold, next period.
g. Net income, current period.
h. Net income, next period.
i. Retained earnings, current period.
j. Retained earnings, next period.

YOUR PERFORMANCE OBJECTIVE 38 *(page 568)*

E11-17 Effects of Errors in the Amount of Inventory Purchases
Assume that an inventory purchase that should be recorded in Period 2 is included in the inventory count of Period 1. Analyze the effects of this error for both periods on purchases, accounts payable, ending inventory, net income, and retained earnings under each of the following conditions:

a. The purchase was recorded in Period 1.
b. The purchase was recorded in Period 2.
c. The purchase was unrecorded in either period.

YOUR PERFORMANCE OBJECTIVE 38 *(page 568)*

E11-18 Effects of Errors in the Amount of Inventory Purchases
Assume that an inventory purchase that should be recorded in Period 1 is excluded from the inventory count of Period 1. Analyze the effects of this error for both periods on purchases, accounts payable, ending inventory, net income, and retained earnings under each of the following conditions:

a. The purchase was recorded in Period 1.

b. The purchase was recorded in Period 2.
c. The purchase was unrecorded in either period.

E11-19 Gross Margin Inventory Method
Holly Company had an inventory balance of $20,000 on June 1 of the current year. In the past, its gross margin percentage has averaged 30% of net sales. The following data are taken from its records for June:

YOUR PERFORMANCE OBJECTIVE 39
(page 568)

Sales	$40,000
Sales returns and allowances	1,700
Sales discounts	1,100
Purchases	50,000
Purchase returns and allowances	600
Purchase discounts	900

Required
What was this company's inventory balance on June 30?

E11-20 Gross Margin Inventory Method
During the current year, Walter Rank, Inc. had sales revenue of $500,000. The balance in its inventory account was $100,000 on January 1 and $75,000 on December 31. On September 1, a fire completely destroyed inventory purchased this year that had a $50,000 cost. This year's cost of goods sold, which does not include the inventory loss, was 60% of sales.

YOUR PERFORMANCE OBJECTIVE 39
(page 568)

Required
What was the cost of purchases made by this company?

E11-21 Lower of Cost or Market Method
High Performance Discount Auto Dealership sells a high profile custom automobile called the Premier for significantly less than comparably equipped luxury cars. High Performance began business on January 1, 2003. Its purchases and sales, as well as its replacement cost of goods on hand at year-end, for its first three years of operations are:

YOUR PERFORMANCE OBJECTIVE 40
(page 571)

	Purchases		Sales		
Year	Units	Unit Cost	Units	Unit Price	Unit Replacement Cost at Year-End
2003	12	$20,000	10	$30,000	$15,000
2004	12	15,000	10	25,000	10,000
2005	6	10,000	10	20,000	5,000

The company states its inventory on a FIFO basis and applies the lower of cost or market inventory rule. Record the effects of the transaction needed to properly reflect the lower of cost or market basis for each of the three years.

E11-22 Basic Accounting for Uncollectibles Transactions
Describe the nature of each of the following four transactions that are associated with accounting for uncollectible accounts:

YOUR PERFORMANCE OBJECTIVE 41
(page 576)

a.

Transaction Analysis						Journal Entry		
	Fundamental Accounting Equation							
Account Titles	Assets	=	Liabilities	+	Owners' Equity	Account Titles	Debit	Credit
Bad Debt Expense					(500)	Bad Debt Expense	500	
Allowance for Bad Debts	(500)					Allowance for Bad Debts		500

b.

Transaction Analysis						Journal Entry		
	Fundamental Accounting Equation							
Account Titles	Assets	=	Liabilities	+	Owners' Equity	Account Titles	Debit	Credit
Allowance for Bad Debts	100					Allowance for Bad Debts	100	
Accounts Receivable	(100)					Accounts Receivable		100

c.

Transaction Analysis						Journal Entry		
	Fundamental Accounting Equation							
Account Titles	Assets	=	Liabilities	+	Owners' Equity	Account Titles	Debit	Credit
Accounts Receivable	100					Accounts Receivable	100	
Allowance for Bad Debts	(100)					Allowance for Bad Debts		100

d.

Transaction Analysis						Journal Entry		
	Fundamental Accounting Equation							
Account Titles	Assets	=	Liabilities	+	Owners' Equity	Account Titles	Debit	Credit
Cash	100					Cash	100	
Accounts Receivable	(100)					Accounts Receivable		100

YOUR PERFORMANCE OBJECTIVE 41
(page 576)

E11-23 Estimating Uncollectible Accounts

As of December 31 of the current year, the unadjusted trial balance of the Carter Company included the following accounts related to its customers:

	Debit	Credit
Accounts receivable	$180,000	
Allowance for uncollectibles		$ 3,000
Bad debt expense	–0–	
Sales (all on credit)		100,000

An analysis reveals that 4% of the credit sales are expected to be uncollectible. Also, one $2,000 account has been determined to be uncollectible because of bankruptcy. Finally, 5% of the ending accounts receivable balance, after any bad debt write-offs, are estimated to be uncollectible.

Required

a. Calculate this year's bad debt expense using the percentage of sales method.
b. Calculate this year's bad debt expense using the percentage of receivables method.

YOUR PERFORMANCE OBJECTIVE 42
(page 579)

E11-24 Managing Inventories and Receivables

The following partial income statement and full balance sheet of Sabino Company are presented for the year just ended:

Partial income statement	
Sales revenue	$900,000
Cost of goods sold	(540,000)
Gross margin	$360,000

Balance Sheet			
Cash	$ 210,000		
Marketable securities	60,000		
Accounts receivable	60,000	Total liabilities	$ 690,000
Inventory	120,000		
Property and equipment	720,000	Owners' equity	480,000
Total assets	$1,170,000	Total equities	$1,170,000

Since the receivable and inventory balance sheet accounts are fairly stable throughout the year, you may treat their ending balances as equivalent to their average balances. Assume that the length of the purchasing cycle is 16 days.

Required

a. Calculate the length of the operating cycle.
b. Calculate the effect on the accounts receivable balance if the average collection period is increased by 36 days.
c. Calculate the effect on the inventory balance if the average holding period is reduced by 20 days.

Critical Thinking Problems

P11-1 Calculating the Length of the Operating Cycle

YOUR PERFORMANCE OBJECTIVES 3, 4
(pages 183, 22)

Calculate the length of the operating cycle for the following cases assuming there are 360 days in a year. Provide documentation for your answer by presenting the days needed to prepare for sale, average holding period, average collection period, and average payment period.

	Cases			
	A	B	C	D
Days needed to prepare for sale	4	3	5	3
Inventory turnover ratio	24	36	12	24
Accounts receivable turnover	12	12	18	9
Days until payment is made	30	0	30	25

P11-2 Effect of Operating Cycle Transactions on a Merchandiser's Financial Statements

YOUR PERFORMANCE OBJECTIVES 7, 13b
(pages 64, 276)

Typical merchandising transactions included in the operating cycle are listed below. Describe how each transaction affects the balance sheet, income statement, and/or the statement of cash flows using the direct method. Transaction (a) is completed for you as an example.

Transaction	Financial Statement	Effect of Transaction
a. Cash purchase of inventory	Balance sheet Balance sheet Income statement Statement of cash flows	Cash decrease Inventory increase No effect Operating cash flow Decrease: cash paid to merchandisers
b. Credit purchase of inventory		
c. Payment of liability for purchase in transaction (b)		
d. Cash sale of merchandise (assume perpetual method)		
e. Credit sale of merchandise (assume perpetual method)		
f. Return of damaged merchandise sold in transaction (d)		
g. Receipt of full payment from customer in transaction (e)		
h. Receipt of cash less discount from customer in transaction (e)		

YOUR PERFORMANCE OBJECTIVE 31 (page 475)

P11-3 Preparing a Cost of Goods Manufactured and Sold Statement
Using the data from Exercise 11-5, prepare a cost of goods manufactured and sold statement for the current year ending December 31.

YOUR PERFORMANCE OBJECTIVE 31 (page 475)

P11-4 Preparing a Manufacturing Income Statement and Balance Sheet
Using the data from Exercise 11-5:

a. Prepare an income statement for the period ending December 31 assuming that sales are $1,500, selling and administrative expenses are $210, and income taxes are $54.
b. Prepare a balance sheet at the end of the period assuming that the Common Stock account is unchanged.

YOUR PERFORMANCE OBJECTIVE 31 (page 475)

P11-5 Calculating Manufacturing Cost of Goods Sold
The following information was taken from Rothstein Company's accounting records for the current year:

Increase in raw materials inventory	$ 15,000
Decrease in finished goods inventory	35,000
Raw materials purchased	430,000
Direct labor payroll	200,000
Factory overhead	300,000
Freight-out	45,000

Required
Calculate cost of goods sold assuming that there was no work in process inventory at the beginning or end of the year.

YOUR PERFORMANCE OBJECTIVE 8 (page 65)

P11-6 Ethical Issues in the Timing of Inventory Purchases
Bryant Industries is a small retail merchandiser planning to apply for a line of credit in February. During the third week in January, the accountant is reviewing the financial statements in preparation for the application. Even though the company would typically replenish stock during

this time, the accountant suggests that no additional inventory be purchased until next month so that the "numbers will look better" on the loan application. Considering the effects of a credit purchase on the financial statements, inventory turnover, average holding period, and length of operating cycle, explain why the accountant might suggest this delay in purchasing inventory. Be specific, using examples as needed. Next, explain why or why not you believe the accountant should make this suggestion.

P11-7 Inventory Systems

YOUR PERFORMANCE OBJECTIVE 34 *(page 553)*

The following inventory information is for Diamond Company:

Beginning inventory	20 units at $10 each
Purchases	100 units at $10 each
Ending inventory	30 units

Sales revenue for the year totaled $1,200.

Required

a. Calculate the cost of goods sold assuming that a periodic inventory system is used.
b. Assume that a perpetual inventory system is used and that 80 units costing $800 were sold for a total of $1,200 of sales revenue. Calculate the amount of inventory shrinkage.
c. Calculate the amount of inventory shrinkage under the periodic inventory system assuming the same set of facts as in part (b).

P11-8 Proper Content of Inventory

YOUR PERFORMANCE OBJECTIVE 35 *(page 556)*

The Lucas Corporation is a wholesale distributor of automotive replacement parts. Initial amounts taken from its accounting records are as follows:

Inventory at 12/31 of the current year*		$125,000
Accounts payable at 12/31 of the current year:		
Vendor	**Term**	**Amount**
Gere Company	2%, 10 days, net 30	$ 26,500
Gibson Company	Net 30	21,000
Hoffman Company	Net 30	30,000
Eastwood Company	Net 30	22,500
Douglas Company	Net 30	—
Crowe Company	Net 30	—
		$100,000
Sales revenue in current year		$900,000

*Based on a physical count conducted in the warehouse on 12/31.

Additional Information (the dates below relate to events that occur either this December or early January of next year):

a. $15,500 of parts received on consignment from Gibson were included in both the physical count of goods in Lucas's warehouse and in accounts payable on December 31.
b. $2,200 of parts, which were purchased from Douglas and paid for in December of the current year, were sold in the last week of the current year and appropriately recorded as sales of $2,800. The parts were included in the physical count of goods in Lucas's warehouse on December 31, because the parts were on the loading dock waiting to be picked up by customers.
c. $3,400 of parts in transit to customers on December 31 were shipped FOB shipping point on December 28. Lucas recorded sales of $4,000 for these parts on January 2 while the customers received the parts on January 6.
d. Retailers held goods on consignment having a cost of $21,000 and a sales value of $25,000 from Lucas, the consignor, at their stores on December 31.

e. Goods having a cost of $2,500 were in transit from Crowe to Lucas on December 31. They were shipped FOB shipping point on December 29.
f. A $200 freight bill, related to merchandise purchased in December but unsold on December 31, was received on January 3. The freight bill was neither included in inventory or in accounts payable on December 31.
g. All purchases from Gere occurred during the last seven days of the year. These items were included in both inventory and accounts payable on December 31 at cost before discount. Company policy is to take advantage of all cash discounts, adjust inventory accordingly, and record accounts payable at net.

Required

Adjust the initial amounts shown below using the format provided. Indicate the effect, if any, of each of the separate transactions. If there is no effect, write NONE.

	Inventory	Accounts Payable	Sales Revenue
Initial amounts	$125,000	$100,000	$900,000
Adjustments: Increase or (decrease)			
a.			
b.			
c.			
d.			
e.			
f.			
g.			
Total adjustments			
Adjusted amounts	$	$	$

YOUR PERFORMANCE OBJECTIVE 36 (page 561)

P11-9 Inventory Cost-Flow Assumptions

Immediately after successful completion of this course, you are hired by Don Pritchard, owner of the With and Swesson Boutique. Your first assignment is to make several inventory calculations based on the following information:

Transactions	Units	Cost per Unit	Total Cost
January 1 balance	10	$ 4.00	$ 40
February 28 purchase	40	6.00	240
May 12 sale	(25)		
July 5 purchase	15	7.00	105
September 21 sale	(35)		
October 2 purchase	35	10.00	350
December 5 sale	(20)		
	20		$735

Required

a. Calculate the December 31 inventory balance using the weighted-average cost-flow assumption (periodic system).
b. Calculate the inventory balance as of May 13 using the moving-average cost-flow assumption (perpetual system).
c. Calculate the December 31 inventory balance using the LIFO cost-flow assumption and a:
   1. Periodic inventory system.
   2. Perpetual inventory system.
d. Calculate the cost of goods sold for the year using the FIFO cost-flow assumption (periodic or perpetual system).

YOUR PERFORMANCE OBJECTIVE 36 (page 561)

P11-10 Inventory Cost-Flow Assumptions

Immediately after successful completion of your accounting course, you are hired by Al

Yankovic, owner of Junk Food Obsessions Buffet and Grille. Your first assignment is to make several inventory calculations based on the following information for the month of May:

Transactions	Units	Unit Cost	Unit Selling Price
May 1 balance	200	$10.00	
May 4 purchase	100	13.00	
May 12 sale	150		$12.00
May 17 purchase	50	15.00	
May 22 sale	120		$14.00
May 26 purchase	100	15.60	
May 29 sale	30		$15.00

Required

a. Assume that Yankovic uses a periodic inventory system. Calculate both the cost of ending inventory and the cost of goods sold for each of the following cost-flow assumptions:
   1. First-in, first-out
   2. Average cost
   3. Last-in, first-out

b. Assume that Yankovic uses a perpetual inventory system. Calculate both the cost of ending inventory and the cost of goods sold for each of the following cost-flow assumptions:
   1. First-in, first-out
   2. Average cost
   3. Last-in, first-out

P11-11 Inventory Cost-Flow Assumptions

YOUR PERFORMANCE OBJECTIVE 36 *(page 561)*

The controller of Spinosa Corporation, a retail company, constructed the following three schedules of gross margin for the first quarter ended September 30, 2003:

	Sales ($10 per unit)	Cost of Goods Sold	Gross Margin
Schedule 1	$280,000	$118,550	$161,450
Schedule 2	280,000	116,900	163,100
Schedule 3	280,000	115,750	164,250

The cost of goods sold calculation was based on the data below:

	Units	Cost per Unit	Total Cost
Beginning inventory, July 1	10,000	$4.00	$40,000
Purchase, July 25	8,000	4.20	33,600
Purchase, August 15	5,000	4.13	20,650
Purchase, September 5	7,000	4.30	30,100
Purchase, September 25	12,000	4.25	51,000

The corporation president cannot understand how three different gross margins can be calculated from the same set of data. As controller, you explain that you prepared these schedules under three cost-flow assumptions: FIFO, LIFO, and weighted average. Educate the president by producing your three ending inventory schedules and identify which cost-flow assumption underlies each schedule.

P11-12 Evaluating the Relative Effect of LIFO and FIFO on Earnings

YOUR PERFORMANCE OBJECTIVE 37 *(page 562)*

Shown below are two sets of inventory figures for General Electric Company: the set on the left represents the actual LIFO ending inventories reported, while the set on the right represents the ending inventory that would have been reported had FIFO been used. The firm's actual pretax income under LIFO is also reported.

GENERAL ELECTRIC COMPANY (amounts in millions)		
End of Year	LIFO Ending Inventory	FIFO Ending Inventory
1	$1,611.7	$1,884.5
2	1,759.0	2,063.1
3	1,986.2	2,415.9
4	2,257.0	3,040.7
5	2,202.9	3,166.6
6	2,354.4	3,515.2
For the Year	Pretax Income under LIFO	Pretax Income under FIFO
2	$ 897.2	?
3	1,011.6	?
4	1,000.7	?
5	1,174.0	?
6	1,627.5	?

Required

Determine the pretax income for Years 2–6, assuming that a FIFO cost-flow assumption was used.

YOUR PERFORMANCE OBJECTIVE 37
(page 562)

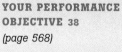

P11-13 LIFO Liquidation Problem

Minoski Corporation accounts for its inventory by using the LIFO periodic basis. On January 1, 2003, it had 2,500 units of inventory on hand, each of which cost $.80. Its inventory purchase and sale information for the years 2003 to 2007 is shown below:

	Units Purchased		Units Sold	
	Units	Unit Cost	Units	Sale Price
2003	5,000	$1.00	5,000	$1.40
2004	5,000	1.20	5,000	1.60
2005	5,000	1.40	5,000	1.80
2006	2,500	1.60	5,000	2.00
2007	7,500	1.80	5,000	2.20

Required

a. Calculate the gross margin for 2003 to 2007.
b. Considering your response to item (a), explain in your own words how a liquidation of a LIFO inventory layer increased pretax income in 2006.
c. Discuss the significance of this income in 2006 from both the perspectives of a manager and a user of the financial statements.
d. Explain how the LIFO cost-flow assumption permits income manipulation.

YOUR PERFORMANCE OBJECTIVE 38
(page 568)

P11-14 Effects of Errors in the Amount of Ending Inventory

On December 30, 2003, Wamopo Company received inventory costing $2,000 and counted it in its December 31 listing of all items on hand. When Wamopo received the invoice for these goods on January 4, 2004, however, it mistakenly recorded the goods as an acquisition of 2004. Assume that Wamopo never discovered the error. Indicate the effect of this error (overstatement, understatement, or none) on each of the following amounts assuming that Wamopo uses a periodic inventory system and ignores taxes.

a. 12/31, 2003 inventory
b. 12/31, 2004 inventory
c. Cost of goods sold, 2003
d. Cost of goods sold, 2004
e. Net income, 2003
f. Net income, 2004
g. 12/31, 2003 accounts payable
h. 12/31, 2004 accounts payable
i. 12/31, 2004 retained earnings

P11-15 Effects of Errors in the Amount of Purchases

YOUR PERFORMANCE OBJECTIVES 36, 38 *(pages 561, 568)*

As discussed in the chapter, assume that a $3,000 purchase of inventory is shipped on December 29 of Year 1 and arrives on January 2 of Year 2 under the terms FOB shipping point. Consider the effects of the following three errors:

1. The purchase is recorded in Year 1 but not included in the year-end count of inventory.
2. The purchase is not recorded until Year 2 but is added to the year-end count of inventory in Year 1.
3. The purchase is not recorded until Year 2 and is not included in the year-end count of inventory in Year 1.

Required

Using the sequential analysis introduced in this chapter, describe the effects of each of these errors on the following elements of the financial statements:

a. 1/1, Year 1 inventory
b. 1/1, Year 2 inventory
c. 12/31, Year 1 inventory
d. 12/31, Year 2 inventory
e. Cost of goods sold, year 1
f. Cost of goods sold, year 2
g. Net income, Year 1
h. Net income, Year 2
i. 12/31, Year 1 accounts payable
j. 12/31, Year 2 accounts payable
k. 12/31, Year 2 retained earnings

P11-16 Effects of Errors in the Amount of Purchases

YOUR PERFORMANCE OBJECTIVES 36, 38 *(pages 561, 568)*

As discussed in the chapter, assume that a $3,000 purchase of inventory is shipped on December 29 of Year 1 and arrives on January 2 of Year 2 under the terms FOB destination. Consider the effects of the following three errors:

1. The purchase is recorded in Year 1 but not included in the year-end count of inventory.
2. The purchase is not recorded until Year 2 but is added to the year-end count of inventory in Year 1.
3. The purchase is not recorded until Year 2 and is not included in the year-end count of inventory in Year 1.

Required

Using the sequential analysis introduced in this chapter, describe the effects of each of these errors on the following elements of the financial statements:

a. 1/1, Year 1 inventory
b. 1/1, Year 2 inventory
c. 12/31, Year 1 inventory
d. 12/31, Year 2 inventory
e. Cost of goods sold, Year 1
f. Cost of goods sold, Year 2
g. Net income, Year 1
h. Net income, Year 2
i. 12/31, Year 1 accounts payable
j. 12/31, Year 2 accounts payable
k. 12/31, Year 2 retained earnings

P11-17 Gross Margin Inventory Problem

YOUR PERFORMANCE OBJECTIVE 39 *(page 568)*

Myong Corporation lost most of its inventory in a fire in December just before the year-end physical inventory was taken. The undamaged inventory had a selling price of $12,000. The corporation's books disclosed the following:

Beginning inventory	$102,000	Sales	$418,000
Purchases for the year	346,000	Sales returns	10,000
Purchase returns	32,300	Gross margin on sales	24%

Damaged inventory with an original selling price of $8,000 had a net realizable value of $1,800. Net realizable value is the amount determined to be the value of this damaged inventory after applying the lower of cost or market method.

Required

Calculate the amount of the inventory loss from fire assuming that the corporation had no insurance coverage.

P11-18 Lower of Cost or Market Method

YOUR PERFORMANCE OBJECTIVE 40 *(page 571)*

Refer to the data presented earlier in Exercise 11-21 and:

a. Calculate the value at which the year-end inventory should be reported on the balance sheet.
b. Calculate income for each of the three years.

c. Comment on the effect of the lower of cost or market method on reported income over time.

YOUR PERFORMANCE OBJECTIVES 34a, 35, 36, 37, 40 *(pages 553, 556, 561, 562, 571)*

P11-19 Comprehensive Inventory Problem

Explain how it may be possible for two retail consumer electronic retailers having an identical supply of televisions at the end of the accounting period to report different inventory amounts on their respective balance sheets.

YOUR PERFORMANCE OBJECTIVE 41 *(page 576)*

P11-20 Estimating Uncollectible Accounts

Mystery Pizza, Inc. has the following balances in its Accounts Receivable and Allowance for Uncollectibles ledger accounts as of December 31, Year 1: $47,000 debit and $6,000 credit, respectively. The firm has decided that a 1.5% estimated uncollectible percentage should be applied to Year 2 sales.

The firm's unadjusted trial balance on December 31 of Year 2 includes the following account balances:

Accounts receivable (debit)	$60,000	
Allowance for uncollectibles (debit)	3,000	
Bad debt expense	—	
Sales revenue (credit)		$700,000

Required

Record all Year 2 receivable and uncollectible transactions. *Hint:* Use T-account analysis to reconstruct these transactions.

YOUR PERFORMANCE OBJECTIVE 41 *(page 576)*

P11-21 Estimating Uncollectible Accounts

The following information from the thirtysomething Advertising Agency is available for the current calendar year. Assume that the firm's books are closed annually on December 31.

Credit sales (billings)	$160,000
Accounts receivable, January 1	30,000
Accounts receivable, December 31	50,000
Cash collections from credit customers	135,000
Allowance for uncollectible accounts, January 1 (credit)	6,200

Required

a. Calculate the bad debt amount written off during the year.
b. Elliot Weston estimates that 5% of agency billings will ultimately be uncollectible. Using the percentage of sales method, record the transaction needed to estimate bad debts.
c. Michael Steadman estimates that 12% of the ending accounts receivable balance will ultimately be uncollectible. Using the percentage of receivables method, record the transaction needed to estimate bad debts.

YOUR PERFORMANCE OBJECTIVE 41 *(page 576)*

P11-22 Estimating Uncollectible Accounts

The following information was taken from the 2003 financial report of Betsyco (dollars in millions), a company using the allowance method of accounting for uncollectible accounts:

	2003
Merchandise sales	$24,811
Credit sales as a % of total sales	61%
Bad debt expense	$ 350
Bad debt write-offs	$ 243

Required

a. Assume that Betsyco used a percentage of credit sales to estimate its Bad Debt Expense account. Calculate the percentage used to record this estimate in 2003.

b. The estimated amount of bad debts clearly exceeds the actual amount of bad debts written off in 2003. Discuss whether or not you would recommend adjusting the rate calculated in part (a) above.
c. Record the effects of transactions that affected the allowance account in 2003.
d. What calculations might you as the credit manager be interested in when analyzing the collectibility of receivables? Limit your answer to no more than three complete sentences.

P11-23 Estimating Uncollectible Accounts

YOUR PERFORMANCE OBJECTIVE 41 *(page 576)*

Historically, Whitefeather Company has estimated that 1.5% of its credit sales will ultimately prove to be uncollectible. Now, however, the company accountant wants to base this estimate on a percentage of receivables, namely the aging schedule of customer receivables. Accordingly, the accountant presents the following aging schedule as of December 31, 2003, based upon past collection experience:

Days Outstanding	Amount	Probability of Collection
Less than 30	$100,000	.98
31–60	50,000	.90
61–90	30,000	.80
91–120	10,000	.60
Over 120	10,000	.50

During 2003 Whitefeather had credit sales of $1.6 million and total sales of $2.2 million. Its Allowance for Uncollectibles account had a credit balance of $25,000 on January 1, 2003. During 2003 the company wrote off uncollectible accounts totaling $18,600.

Required

a. Calculate the uncollectible accounts expense for 2003 if Whitefeather continues to use the percentage of sales method.
b. If Whitefeather uses the percentage of receivables method, calculate the December 31, 2003 account balance in the Allowance for Uncollectibles account after adjustment. Indicate whether this balance is a credit (increase) or debit (decrease).
c. During 2003 Whitefeather received $5,000 for an account that had been written off in 2002. Record the effects of this transaction or transactions.

P11-24 Managing Inventories and Receivables

YOUR PERFORMANCE OBJECTIVE 42 *(page 579)*

Calculate the length of the operating cycle and the required inventory and receivable balances for the following cases assuming that there are 360 days in a year.

	Case A	Case B	Case C
Annual credit sales	$500,000	$500,000	$500,000
Annual cost of goods sold	300,000	300,000	300,000
Purchasing days	–0–	–0–	–0–
Inventory turnover	24	24	18
Accounts receivable turnover	12	8	12

Research Assignments

A wide variety of interesting Research Assignments for this chapter are available for the following topics at www.mhhe.com/solomon:

R11-1 Financial Statement Effects of Operating Activities by Industry (PO 31)
R11-2 Financial Statement Effects of Operating Activities by Industry (PO 31)
R11-3 Financial Statement Effects of Operating Activities by Industry (PO 31)
R11-4 Using the MD&A to Learn More about Inventory (PO 14)

R11-5 **Using the Notes to Learn More about Inventory and Receivables (PO 14)**
R11-6 **Comparative Financial Analysis of Inventory Disclosures (PO 14)**
R11-7 **Comparative Analysis of International Inventory Accounting Practices (PO 14)**
R11-8 **Investigating a Significant Reduction in Inventories (PO 14)**
R11-9 **Financial Analysis of Inventory (PO 14)**
R11-10 **Financial Analysis of Operating Activities (PO 14)**
R11-11 **Ratio Analysis of Operating Activities (PO 3 and 14)**
R11-12 **Real-World Inventory Exploration (PO 34 and 37)**
R11-13 **Real-World Receivable Exploration (PO 41)**

CHAPTER TWELVE

How Investing Activities Affect Financial Statements

Also be sure you have mastered the following Performance Objectives from previous chapters. They lay the foundation for the concepts you will learn in this chapter:

PO3
PO4
PO5a
PO7b
PO8
PO11
PO14
PO17
PO31

PERFORMANCE OBJECTIVES

In this chapter, you will learn the following new Performance Objectives:

PO43 **Determine** which costs should be capitalized and which should be expensed when several costs associated with the purchase of a depreciable or intangible asset are incurred.

PO44 **Describe** how depreciation is calculated and **calculate** depreciation expense for any period desired under each of the following depreciation methods: straight-line, double-declining balance, and sum-of-the-years' digits.

PO45 **Describe** how depletion is calculated using the units-of-production method and **present** the financial statement effects of this calculation.

PO46 **Describe** how amortization is calculated using the straight-line method and **present** the financial statement effects of this calculation.

PO47 **Determine** the proper valuation of both current and noncurrent debt and equity securities at the end of a period, **record** all investment in debt and equity security related transactions, and **present** the complete financial statement effects of this set of transactions.

PO48 **Distinguish** between the cost/fair value method and the equity method of accounting for minority investments in equity securities.

EXPLORING PERSONAL INVESTING ACTIVITIES

401K. Annuity. SEP IRA. Low-load fund. Securities. Stop-limit orders. Is your head spinning yet? If it is, you are not alone. Even the most well-informed individuals could become overwhelmed by the complexity of today's investing world. Nevertheless, there are many tools you can use to help you meet your financial objectives. The Internet, for example, provides access to high-quality information that was previously unavailable to you but now can help you manage your personal investing and finance decisions. For example, the Web provides access to historical data as well as up to-the-minute stock quotes and allows you to buy and sell 24 hours a day, 7 days a week. Or, you might decide that a stockbroker or paid financial advisor is a more comfortable fit for you.

Whatever you decide, you should start investing now, if you haven't already. An early start can make all the difference. For example, suppose you contributed $50 every month from 2003 to 2012, in other words for 10 years—and then nothing more. Or, suppose you contributed $50 every month from 2010 to 2051—in other words for 41 years. You might be surprised to learn that in 2051 you would have about the same amount of money from each of these two separate investments. How is this possible? The answer in one word is "compounding." And in Appendix 12–1 you will see how mastering this concept will help you become a better, more informed investor.

A quick search for personal investing sites using a Web search engine yields an abundance of financial advice. Popular ones are www.iclub.com, www.ibm.com/investor, www.morningstar.com, and the Mutual Fund Education Alliance's site at www.mfea.com. All of the major mutual funds have sites. If you visit the Securities and Exchange Commission site (www.sec.gov), you'll be able to search using the EDGAR archives for public companies' SEC filings, which provide an abundance of valuable information. And unlike the past, more and more information at these investor sites is geared toward novice investors. Many sites have an education feature and include such items as a glossary of terms, reviews of helpful books, primers on investment strategies, and message boards.

But the downside to having so much information is that you can become overwhelmed and have trouble making up your mind. You also can get caught up in information that is not relevant to your decision. So when you surf, have a plan for what you want to learn and stick to it. And remember these basic principles of investing:

- Start by getting your personal finances in order. Look into the best way to pay off any debt you might have. Then, save a "cushion fund"—about three months'

(continued on next page)

(continued from previous page)

income—in a money market account. If you have difficulty saving, consider setting up an automatic savings plan with your bank.

- After your cushion is in place, you can become a little more aggressive with your investing. A good place to begin is with stocks and bonds. Experience has shown that over time, the stock market is a wise investment.
- Develop a long-term investing plan. You can always reconsider this plan, but having a plan in place will help you decide where your money is coming from, and where it is going. You need to know your financial goals to attain them.
- Be informed before you invest. The more informed you are, the better your decisions are likely to be and the more your investments are likely to earn.

Obviously, the effects of implementing these personal investing principles will not be captured in a set of financial statements since most individuals don't prepare them. Nevertheless, your personal investing activities still affect your personal financial position, profitability, and cash flow. Since an individual could trace the effects of their personal investments into financial statements, the effects of personal investing are not entirely different than the effects of business investing as you'll soon discover. So whether you invest on your own, ask friends and family for advice, hire a financial professional, or use any combination of these three, explore your personal investing options. You won't regret it!

Why Do Businesses Engage in Investing Activities?

Recall that you initiate investing activities when you apply the money obtained from financing activities to nonoperating uses within the entity, such as making loans or buying investment securities and productive equipment. The accounts that are created when you initiate investing activities are found in the noncurrent asset section of the balance sheet. You complete investing activities either when you collect on the loans you have made or when you sell investment securities or productive equipment.

From this description, it should be clear to you how essential investing activities are to every business. Just imagine what would happen if a business was unable to engage in investing activities. First, income would be lost because the business would not be making loans or buying investment securities with excess amounts of idle cash. Second, it would be nearly impossible to grow larger and diversify because the business would not be investing in the stock of other corporations and exerting significant influence or control over their operations. More fundamentally, even the smallest business would have difficulty surviving if it didn't have the productive capacity (that is, the long-term asset base) with which to engage in operating activities. That is, without noncurrent assets—integral parts of every entity's earnings process—entities are unable to generate revenues.

What Are the Financial Statement Effects of Investing Activities?

Now that you better appreciate just how essential investing activities can be, let's reexamine the financial statement effects of investing activities that were described in earlier chapters. We'll begin by briefly reviewing our CMU investing transactions and then, just as we did last chapter, study the effects of those transactions on the balance sheet, income statement, and statement of cash flows.

Cards & Memorabilia Unlimited: Investing Activity Transactions

In Chapter 8 we classified all CMU first-year transactions, other than Transaction B, into operating, investing, and financing activities. Transaction B was excluded because a transfer between two types of bank accounts does not qualify as one of these activities. Also, Transaction B was not reported in a statement of cash flows because it did not change total cash. So let's begin by reviewing the CMU transactions that are investing activities.

Figure 12-1 identifies six investing activity transactions—Transactions C_1, E, C_2, H, L, and R. Transactions C_1 and C_2 represent the first and second stage, respectively, of an initiated investing activity. In Transaction C_1, Susan acquires the equipment; in Transaction C_2, she pays for the equipment. Susan completes a portion of this investing activity when she sells $2,000 of this equipment for cash in Transaction R. Transaction E, Susan's lease security deposit, represents a cash investing activity for three reasons. First, it does not provide money from creditors or owners; second, it is different in nature from monthly rental payments; and third, the account created—Security Deposit Receivable—is an interest-bearing noncurrent asset. Transaction H is an investing activity because it represents the cash acquisition of a noncurrent asset. Finally, Transaction L represents a noncash investing and financing activity, or *direct exchange*. That is, the purchase of equipment, a noncurrent asset, represents the initiation of an investing activity, whereas the incurrence of a noncurrent liability represents the initiation of a financing activity.

Cards & Memorabilia Unlimited: Financial Statement Effects of Investing Activities

Let's now review the financial statement effects of each of the CMU transactions described in the preceding section. For simplicity, we will ignore temporary effects such as the one-month effect of first increasing the Accounts Payable account (C_1) and then decreasing it (C_2). These financial statement effects are illustrated in Figure 12-2.

Balance Sheet Effects One balance sheet effect from the preceding investing transactions is to initially establish the noncurrent Store Equipment account at $10,000 (Transaction C_1), increase it first to $17,000 (Transaction H), increase it then to $21,000 (Transaction L) and finally reduce it to $19,000 (Transaction R). Line 2 of the balance sheet in Figure 12-2 shows this effect. The other major balance sheet effect is the $2,000 increase in the Security Deposit Receivable account as the result of Transaction E, as shown in line 1 of the balance sheet.

Income Statement Effects The only income statement effect from the preceding investing transactions is the $350 loss on equipment sale recorded in Transaction R, as shown in the income statement in Figure 12-2. Although depreciation expense is derived from the acquisition of an investing activity transaction and this chapter does explain its measurement in more detail, it is not classified as an investing activity in Figure 12-1 or reported in Figure 12-2's statement of cash flows. Instead, depreciation expense is classified as a noncash operating activity because it measures the use and not the purchase of a noncurrent asset.

Statement of Cash Flow Effects There are at least four individual effects of the preceding investing transactions on the statement of cash flows:

1. The cash inflow from investing activities of $1,350 from the equipment sale proceeds in Transaction R.

FIGURE 12-1 Classification of transactions A_1–Z into operating, investing, and financing activities

	Assets							=	Liabilities				+	Owner Equities		Statement of Cash Flows		
																Activities		
	Cash Checking	Cash Savings	Accts. Recvb.	Mdse. Inven.	Other Recvb.	Store Equip.	Accum. Depr.		Accts. Payb.	Cred. Line Payb.	Advn. From Cust.	Note Payb.		Contrib. Capital	Retained Earnings	Financing	Investing	Operating
A_1	30,000													30,000		√		
B	(6,000)	6,000															NOT APPLICABLE	
C_1						10,000			10,000								√	
D	(15,000)			15,000														√
E	(2,000)				2,000												√	
C_2	(10,000)								(10,000)								√	
F	5,000									5,000						√		
G				18,000					18,000									√
H	(7,000)					7,000											√	
I	6,000										6,000							√
J_1	(12,000)								(12,000)									√
J_2									(6,000)			6,000[a]						√
K_1	(5,000)									(5,000)						√		
L						4,000						4,000[b]				√	√	
M	63,200														63,200			√
N			20,000												20,000			√
O_1	275														275			√
P	(11,000)														(11,000)			√
Q_1							(300)								(300)			√
R	1,350					(2,000)	300								(350)		√	
S	(8,000)														(8,000)			√
K_2	(200)														(200)			√
T	(4,250)														(4,250)			√
U				(30,000)											(30,000)			√
V	15,000		(15,000)															√
W	(8,100)														(8,100)	√		
A_2				10,000										10,000		√		
O_2					25										25			√
X									750[c]						(750)			√
Y									350						(350)			√
Q_2							(2,300)								(2,300)			√
Z											(4,000)				4,000			√
Σ	**$32,275**	6,000	5,000	13,000	2,025	19,000	(2,300)	=	$1,100	–0–	2,000	10,000	+	$40,000	$21,900			
				$75,000				=		**$13,100**			+	**$61,900**				

[a]Reported as current liability; [b]Reported as noncurrent liability; [c]Reported as Salaries Payable

CARDS & MEMORABILIA UNLIMITED

Transaction detail

A_1	$30,000 cash is contributed by the owner who opens a business checking account.
B	$6,000 cash is withdrawn from the checking account to open a business savings account.
C_1	$10,000 worth of store equipment is acquired with a credit card.
D	$15,000 cash is paid to acquire merchandise inventory.
E	$2,000 cash is paid to the landlord for the security deposit on the store lease.
C_2	$10,000 cash is paid in full to settle the credit card obligation made on January 4.
F	$5,000 cash is borrowed with a bank credit line bearing interest at an 8% rate.
G	$18,000 worth of additional merchandise is acquired on account.
H	$7,000 cash is paid to acquire a used van with a 5-year useful life for the business.
I	$6,000 cash is collected from customers before any goods or services are provided.
J_1	$12,000 cash is paid to reduce accounts payable.
J_2	$6,000 of accounts payable is converted to a 6% interest-bearing note payable due on March 31.
K_1	$5,000 cash is paid in full to settle the credit line loan made on July 1.
L	$4,000 worth of a computer and printer is acquired by signing a 2-year promissory note.
M	$63,200 of cash sales are made to customers throughout the year.
N	$20,000 of revenue is earned on account—$19,400 for customer credit sales throughout the year and $600 for teaching a course.
O_1	$275 interest is earned from 1/2–12/2 on $6,000 of savings bearing 5% interest.
P	$1,000 cash is paid for office rent due the first day of each month beginning February 1.
Q_1	$300 of depreciation is recorded to recognize the use of equipment sold on September 30.
R	$2,000 worth of the store equipment bought on January 4 for $10,000 is sold for $1,350.
S	$8,000 cash is paid to employees for work performed through the year's last payday.
K_2	$200 cash is paid for interest due on $5,000 borrowed on July 1 at 8% and repaid on December 31.
T	$4,250 cash is paid for miscellaneous expenses incurred throughout the year.
U	$30,000 of cost of goods sold is determined by taking a physical count of inventory.
V	$15,000 cash is collected from customers throughout the year for amounts owed.
W	$8,100 cash is withdrawn from the business by the owner throughout the year.
A_2	$10,000 worth of merchandise is contributed by an individual for a business interest.
O_2	$25 of interest is earned but uncollected on a $6,000 savings account bearing 5% interest.
X	$750 of salaries expense is incurred but unpaid.
Y	$350 of miscellaneous expense is incurred but unpaid.
Q_2	$2,300 of depreciation is recorded on the use of unsold equipment.
Z	$4,000 worth of merchandise is delivered to customers who paid in advance.

FIGURE 12-2

Primary financial statement effects (shown in color) of Cards & Memorabilia Unlimited investing activities

Balance Sheet
at December 31

Investments:		
Security deposit receivable		$ 2,000
Property, Plant, and Equipment:		
Store equipment		19,000

Income Statement
For the Year Ended December 31

Revenues		
Sales revenue	$86,600	
Service revenue	600	
Interest revenue	300	$87,500
Expenses		
Cost of goods sold	30,000	
Rent expense	11,000	
Salaries expense	8,750	
Depreciation expense	2,600	
Miscellaneous expense	4,600	
Interest expense	200	
Loss on equipment sale	350	57,500
Net income		$30,000

Statement of Cash Flows
For the Year Ended December 31

Cash flows from investing activities:	
Proceeds from sale of equipment	$ 1,350
Payment of security deposit	(2,000)
Acquisition of equipment	(17,000)
Net cash used in investing activities	$(17,650)

Supplemental schedule of noncash investing and financing activities:

Computer equipment costing $4,000 was acquired in exchange for a two-year promissory note.

2. The cash outflow from investing activities of $2,000 from the security deposit payment in Transaction E.
3. The cash outflow from investing activities of $17,000 from the combined cash effects of Transactions C_2 and Transaction H, that each represent a cash payment for store equipment.
4. The noncash investing and financing activity or direct exchange of $4,000 in Transaction L, disclosed because of its significant effect on the business.

So far we have focused on why businesses engage in investing activities, and we have reviewed CMU's investing activity transactions and their effects on CMU's financial statements. We now take a more detailed look at how the balances in the major noncurrent asset accounts and their related income statement accounts are created by investing activities. In particular, we will examine three major noncurrent assets introduced in Chapter 4 beginning with property, plant, and equipment, and then moving to intangible assets and investments in securities.

Accounting for Property, Plant, and Equipment

Recall that the asset category *property, plant, and equipment*, sometimes referred to as *fixed assets* or simply *plant assets*, includes accounts that share three characteristics. They are:

1. Noncurrent—that is, the length of their life exceeds one year.
2. Tangible—that is, they have physical substance.
3. Acquired for active use in the operation of the business rather than held as an investment or for resale.

Account titles included in this general category may be divided into the following types:

- *Property, plant, and equipment subject to depreciation*, or depreciable assets such as buildings, equipment, furniture, and fixtures.
- *Natural resources subject to depletion*, such as oil and gas reserves, mineral deposits, and timber tracts.
- *Property not subject to depreciation or depletion*, such as land.

Before examining depreciable assets, natural resources, and land as separate categories, let's consider how the assets included in property, plant, and equipment as well as intangible assets are recorded when acquired.

Valuation Basis and Cost Measurement

Historical cost is the valuation method generally used to record noncurrent assets. Accordingly, the general rule for determining the proper cost of these assets is no different than the rule used for inventory. The historical cost of acquiring an asset includes all costs, that is, all expenditures or outlays necessary to bring the asset to the condition and location required for its intended use. Specifically, this means you should *capitalize*, or record as an asset, the purchase price less any cash discounts plus any of the following incidental costs that apply:

- Freight or shipping.
- Storage.
- Taxes, tariffs, and duties.
- Insurance during transportation or storage.
- Legal fees.
- Installation.

As with inventory, the cost of freight on a shipment of more than one asset should be allocated to the specific assets to which it applies. In practice, however, it is often recorded separately as an expense.

Determining the proper cost of noncurrent assets has a significant effect on the financial statements, which is why Performance Objective 43 is now introduced.

YOUR PERFORMANCE OBJECTIVE 43

Determine which costs should be capitalized and which should be expensed when several costs associated with the purchase of a depreciable or intangible asset are incurred.

Sometimes, companies will construct depreciable assets such as buildings and equipment for their own use or for sale or lease to others. Usually, these companies borrow money to finance the relatively high cost of these construction projects. A **self-constructed asset**, like a purchased asset, should be recorded at cost and include *all* expenditures needed to construct it and make it ready for its intended use. Under this rule, the interest incurred to construct such an asset is properly included in its cost because the asset would not exist without financing! The interest included in the recorded cost of such self-constructed assets is called **capitalized interest**. Essentially, it represents the portion of your total interest cost that you could have avoided had you not constructed the asset. Fortunately, a more advanced accounting course deals with how to allocate total interest cost between that found on the balance sheet (capitalized interest) and that found on the income statement (expensed interest). What you should understand here is that the cost of interest is not always expensed immediately. Instead, capitalized interest should be recorded initially as an asset. Of course, even capitalized interest will eventually find its way to the income statement in the form of depreciation expense from the self-constructed asset.

When two or more assets are acquired for a single purchase price but their individual prices are unavailable, the single price or cost must be allocated between the individual assets. This situation occurs when more than one building, more than one piece of land, or a building and land are purchased for a single price. You can determine the cost of the individual assets by allocating the total cost between these assets on the basis of their relative fair market values. To illustrate this method, consider the following example of what is known as a *lump-sum purchase* or *basket purchase*:

Example Land and a building are purchased for $600,000. Although the individual prices of the land and building are not available, an appraisal has been conducted that values the land at $200,000 and the building at $1,000,000.

Solution The logical solution to this problem is to use the relative fair market values of the assets.

Allocation

	Appraised Value	Fraction of Appraised Value	×	Joint Cost	=	Allocated Cost
Land	$ 200,000	1/6		$600,000		$100,000
Building	1,000,000	5/6		600,000		500,000
Total	$1,200,000	6/6				$600,000

As this example shows, the underlying assumption of the relative fair market value method is that costs vary in direct proportion to fair market values. Such relative fair market values can be obtained by hiring an independent appraiser or by simply using the most recent insurance appraisal or property tax assessed valuations.

Depreciable Assets

Now we'll refine your understanding of depreciable assets by exploring how two popular accelerated depreciation methods differ from the straight-line depreciation method, how partial years' depreciation is calculated, and how sales of depreciable assets are recorded. First, however, let's review what you have already learned about depreciable assets.

Revisiting Depreciation Terms and Basic Concepts You already know a good deal about depreciable assets. When CMU purchased $10,000 of store equipment (Transaction C_1) in Chapter 1, for example, you learned that it was customary to divide this depreciable asset's cost by its estimated *useful life*, the length of time its future benefits will last. You now know that the result of this calculation ($10,000/5, or $2,000) is called *depreciation expense* and that *depreciation* is the systematic and rational allocation of the cost of a depreciable asset to the periods of time being benefited. Since the equipment was purchased for the purpose of producing sales revenue, a portion of its cost had to be assigned or allocated to expense each year. That is, the $2,000 depreciation expense was the portion of the $10,000 equipment cost used up, or consumed, in producing services or first-year revenues. Recall how this transaction (an adjusting entry) would be recorded at the end of each of the five years of asset life:

Transaction Analysis				**Journal Entry**		
	Fundamental Accounting Equation					
Account Titles	**Assets**	**=** **Liabilities** **+**	**Owners' Equity**	**Account Titles**	**Debit**	**Credit**
Depreciation Expense			(2,000)	Depreciation Expense	2,000	
Accumulated Depreciation	(2,000)			Accumulated Depreciation		2,000

In Chapter 4 you learned about Accumulated Depreciation, an account that includes the cumulative amount of depreciation expense recorded during a depreciable asset's useful life. This account, classified as a contra asset, accounts for the reduction in the original cost of its primary depreciable asset to what is called book value. *Book value* is the difference between a depreciable asset's original cost and its accumulated depreciation, the amount of its cost consumed with the passage of time. Essentially, you account for all property, plant, and equipment accounts (other than land) by first setting up a contra account and then subtracting its balance from the primary account balance. Finally, in Chapter 6, you learned how partial year's depreciation was calculated when you studied Transaction Q_1, and how the sale of a depreciable asset was recorded when you studied Transaction R.

Although nonaccountants often refer to depreciation as a decline in value (for example, the automobile industry estimates of the year-to-year value of different models), depreciation, as reported in financial statements, is a process of cost allocation rather than a process of valuation. Although assets generally experience a decline in value, depreciation expense does not measure that value decline.

Refining Your Understanding of Straight-Line Depreciation

Recall Transaction C_1 in which Susan purchased $10,000 of store equipment having a useful life of five years. Assuming that this asset is not sold, its annual depreciation expense under the straight-line depreciation method would be exactly $2,000. As both its title and the following diagram suggest, the straight-line depreciation method assumes that an asset's usage is constant. That is, an equal amount of the asset's cost is allocated to expense every period.

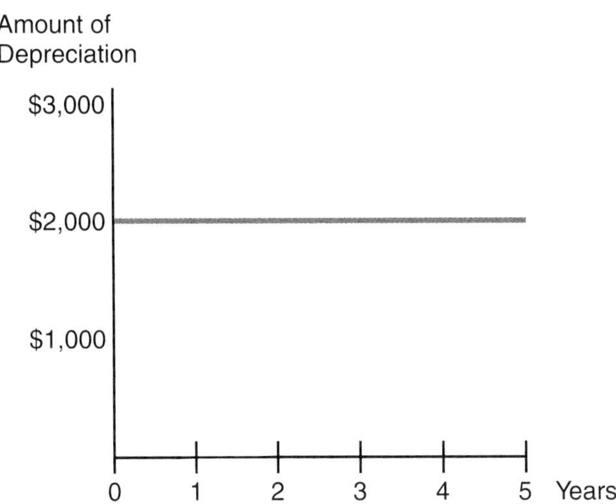

As this diagram indicates, the straight-line depreciation method is so named because its depreciation expense amount produces a straight line when graphed over time. Although you have calculated straight-line depreciation many times during this course, to ease calculations we always assumed that depreciable assets had no remaining value at the end of their estimated useful lives. In fact, this assumption is often unrealistic. It is quite common to recover at least a small cash value, or **salvage value**, when an asset is taken out of service whether to be retired or sold. Perhaps no accounting concept has more acceptable synonyms than does salvage value. For example, it is also referred to as *residual value*, *scrap value*, or *disposal value*. Another useful term is **depreciable cost**, which equals cost minus salvage value. Let's now consider a more formal procedure for calculating straight-line depreciation that incorporates both the terms *salvage value* and *depreciable cost.*

Whenever you calculate depreciation, you must use at least two and sometimes three factors: cost (C), estimated salvage value (S), and estimated useful life (n). The depreciation rate (r), which is derived from n, is a fourth factor we might also use. You calculate r by dividing the number 1 by the number of years of estimated useful life. In other words, you take the reciprocal of the number of years of useful life. For example, an asset with an estimated useful life of 5 years has a 20% depreciation rate (1/5) whereas, an asset with a useful life of 10 years has a 10% depreciation rate (1/10). Let's now apply these factors to calculate an initial straight-line depreciation schedule for the $10,000 of store equipment purchased in Transaction C_1. Although you could simply divide the $10,000 by 5 years to determine the $2,000 depreciation, the more formal approach follows:

Step 1: Determine the depreciable cost or cost minus salvage value.

$$\$10{,}000 - \$0 = \$10{,}000$$

Step 2: Determine the depreciation rate: 1/5 = 20%

Step 3: Multiply the depreciable cost by the depreciation rate to obtain the depreciation expense.

$$\$10{,}000 \times .20 \text{ (or simply } \$10{,}000 \times 1/5) = \underline{\underline{\$2{,}000}}$$

Assume instead that this asset had an estimated $400 salvage value at the end of its useful life. How would your answer change?

Depreciable cost = $9,600 ($10,000 − $400)

Depreciation rate = 20%

Depreciation expense: $1,920 ($9,600 × .20) or ($9,600 × 1/5)

This calculation generates the following depreciation schedule assuming the asset is held for five years:

Year	Depreciation Expense	Cost − Accumulated Depreciation	= Book Value
1	$1,920	($10,000 − $1,920)	$8,080
2	1,920	($10,000 − $3,840)	6,160
3	1,920	($10,000 − $5,760)	4,240
4	1,920	($10,000 − $7,680)	2,320
5	1,920	($10,000 − $9,600)	400

Later in this chapter, we'll use these same calculations to explore how selling such a depreciable asset affects the financial statements.

Using Other Forms of the Straight-Line Method The straight-line method of depreciation used so far allocates cost to expense on the basis of the passage of time. There are at least two variations of the straight-line method, however, that are based on the use of the asset made each period. These are the *units of pro-*

duction method and the *service hours method*. Since these methods are nearly identical, we will illustrate the service hours method below to help you grasp the concept underlying both depreciation methods. We'll then use the units of production method later in this chapter to illustrate how *depletion* is calculated.

You can use the **service hours method** whenever an estimate of the life of the asset expressed in lifetime service hours is available. To illustrate, let's first substitute a large electrical machine for our store equipment but retain the same cost information. Further, assume that the machine is expected to provide 20,000 lifetime hours of service and that it is used for the following lengths of time:

Year 1:	5,000 hours
Year 2:	4,200 hours
Year 3:	4,000 hours
Year 4:	3,800 hours
Year 5:	3,000 hours
Total:	20,000 hours

The depreciation calculations are as follows:

Depreciable cost = $9,600 ($10,000 − $400)
Depreciation rate per hour = $9,600/20,000 hours = $.48 per hour

Depreciation expense:

First year	5,000 × $.48 =	$2,400
Second year	4,200 × $.48 =	$2,016
Third year	4,000 × $.48 =	$1,920
Fourth year	3,800 × $.48 =	$1,824
Fifth year	3,000 × $.48 =	$1,440
Total depreciation expense		$9,600

Both the service hours method illustrated here and the units of production method are useful variations of the straight-line method of depreciation.

Why Estimated Useful Life Is So Critical to Accurate Income Measurement

INSIGHT

You might have noticed that two of the three primary factors needed to calculate depreciation—salvage value and useful life of a depreciable asset—are estimated and not actual amounts. As a result, the depreciation expense calculation represents an accounting estimate rather than an actual amount. Because salvage values are generally small in relationship to an asset's original cost, however, any imprecision of salvage value does not usually pose a problem in calculating depreciation. But let's look at an example of how an imprecise useful life can be significant.

Assume that a small regional airline owns and operates 10 Boeing 737 jets for commuter flights operating in Iowa, Wisconsin, and Nebraska. The following income statement represents the firm's first year of operations:

Revenues:		
Passenger Fares	$21,000,000	
Express Mail & Other Transport Fees	6,000,000	$27,000,000

(continued)

Expenses		
Salaries	10,500,000	
Depreciation	5,000,000*	
Maintenance	3,500,000	
Terminal Charges	2,000,000	21,000,000
Pretax Income		$ 6,000,000

*Calculated by multiplying each plane's depreciable cost of $10,000,000 by the 10 planes in service and then dividing by an estimated useful life of 20 years.

Assume, instead, that U.S. airlines generally depreciate 737 aircraft over a period of 10 years. Now, let's recalculate pretax income.

$10,000,000 × 10 jets = $100,000,000 total depreciable cost

$100,000,000/10 years = $10,000,000 revised depreciation expense

$10,000,000 − $5,000,000 = $5,000,000 increase in depreciation expense

$27,000,000 − $26,000,000 = $1,000,000 revised pretax income

Next, consider these questions: Does the halving of the aircraft's estimated useful life produce an identical 50% change in pretax income? If not, how much of a percentage decrease in pretax income occurs? The answer is no. The 50% decrease in useful life actually causes pretax income to decrease by $5,000,000, or 83% ($5,000,000/$6,000,000).

The preceding calculations illustrate just how important the estimate of useful life can be to a company's bottom line. That is, income measurement is significantly affected by the useful life decision whenever depreciation is a significant expense on the income statement. Although industry guidelines for useful lives are quite reliable measures of physical deterioration, it is very difficult to accurately predict useful life for industries that are especially subject to **obsolescence**—the process of becoming outdated, outmoded, or inadequate due to factors other than physical deterioration. For example, if a short- to medium-range jet airliner is produced that will not only fly at faster speeds but also require 25% less jet fuel, our 737 fleet might be obsolete in 10 years. Thus, the **insight** you should gain here is that if useful life is difficult to reliably estimate, depreciation expense and, most notably, net income might be significantly misstated. A further **insight** is that this difficulty in accurately estimating useful life makes it easier for unethical managers to manipulate net income. That is, if everyone accepts how difficult it is to accurately estimate the useful life of jet aircraft, it is more difficult to control or censure unethical managers who misstate useful life to manipulate, or manage, earnings. Thus, whenever you view a company's reported net income, remember that it might be more a product of accounting estimation than of precise measurement. Keep this limitation in mind especially when you reconsider Performance Objective 17:

YOUR PERFORMANCE OBJECTIVE 17
Identify several limitations of the financial statements found in the annual report.

Examining Accelerated Depreciation The term **accelerated depreciation** refers to a depreciation method in which the greatest amount of depreciation expense is recorded in the first year of use and declines thereafter. This method is used for both tax return purposes and for financial reporting.

In financial reporting, over 82% of companies in 2000 used the straight-line depreciation method when preparing financial statements for their annual report.[1] But

[1] "Depreciation Expense," *Accounting Trends and Techniques*, AICPA, 2001, 3.140.

to develop your business savvy, you should learn the similarities and differences between straight-line and accelerated depreciation methods. The primary rationale for using accelerated depreciation for financial reporting is the matching concept. That is, assets are expected to be most productive (generate higher revenues) when they are new. Thus, to properly match revenues with expenses, it is argued that depreciation should start high and then decline rather than continue with even amounts each year as for straight-line depreciation. Another rationale is that as an asset is used, its depreciation decreases and its maintenance increases so that when combined, a roughly uniform expense is reported for that asset each year.

We'll examine two accelerated depreciation methods, *double-declining-balance method* and the *sum-of-the-years'-digits method.* To better understand the essential steps in calculating depreciation under the **double-declining-balance method (DDB)**, let's illustrate its use with our store equipment example:

1. Determine the asset's book value or declining balance each year

   Example: \$10,000 at the time of purchase

2. Double the straight-line rate ($1/n$, or the reciprocal of estimated useful life)

   Example: Depreciation Rate = $2 \times (1/5) = 2/5 = 40\%$

3. Initially ignore any salvage value, multiply the book value or declining balance (not the depreciable cost!) by the depreciation rate, and do not depreciate beyond the amount of cost minus salvage value.

Figure 12-3 illustrates these steps using our ongoing example. Because the preceding calculations only approximate the actual double-declining-balance depreciation formula, the depreciation amount in the last year must often be adjusted to ensure that the asset is fully depreciated. Just such an adjustment is illustrated in the example shown in Figure 12-3. Note that the little-used theoretical formula for the straight-line depreciation rate is $1 - \sqrt[n]{\text{Salvage}/\text{Cost}}$.

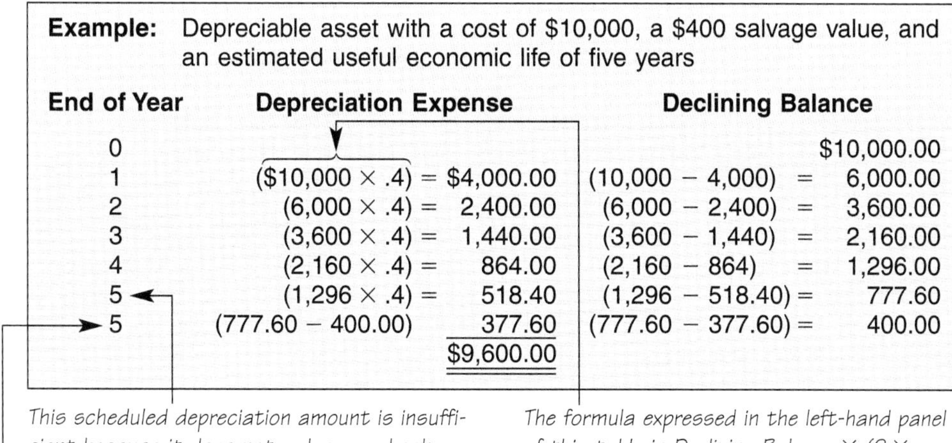

Example: Depreciable asset with a cost of \$10,000, a \$400 salvage value, and an estimated useful economic life of five years

End of Year	Depreciation Expense		Declining Balance	
0				\$10,000.00
1	(\$10,000 × .4) =	\$4,000.00	(10,000 − 4,000) =	6,000.00
2	(6,000 × .4) =	2,400.00	(6,000 − 2,400) =	3,600.00
3	(3,600 × .4) =	1,440.00	(3,600 − 1,440) =	2,160.00
4	(2,160 × .4) =	864.00	(2,160 − 864) =	1,296.00
5	(1,296 × .4) =	518.40	(1,296 − 518.40) =	777.60
5	(777.60 − 400.00)	377.60	(777.60 − 377.60) =	400.00
		\$9,600.00		

This scheduled depreciation amount is insufficient because it does not reduce our book value at the end of the fifth year to \$400.

The formula expressed in the left-hand panel of this table is Declining Balance × (2 × Straight-Line Rate) = Depreciation Expense.

This additional depreciation is added to our scheduled depreciation in the row above to ensure that all remaining undepreciated cost other than salvage value is accounted for (\$9,600 = \$10,000 − 400).

FIGURE 12-3 Double-declining-balance depreciation method calculations

Under the **sum-of-the-years'-digits method (SYD)**, you must calculate a depreciation rate whose numerator changes from year to year and whose denominator is a constant.

Numerator Calculation The first year numerator is the same digit or number as the last year of useful life. In our store equipment example, this number is 5 and it decreases by one each year until it is the number 1 in the fifth year of useful life.

Denominator Calculation The denominator used is the sum of the years' digits—the sum of the numbers representing each year of useful life, that is 5 + 4 + 3 + 2 + 1 = 15. Rather than manually counting these digits, you can use the following formula: $n[(n + 1)/2)] = 5[(5 + 1)/2] = 15$. You then multiply the asset's depreciable cost by this decreasing depreciation rate every year. Figure 12-4 illustrates these calculations assuming the use of our ongoing example.

FIGURE 12-4

Sum-of-the-years'-digits depreciation method calculations

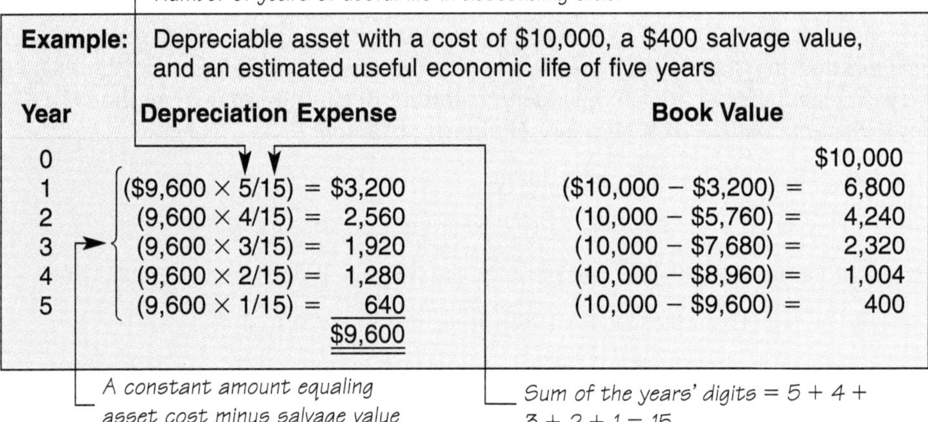

Example: Depreciable asset with a cost of $10,000, a $400 salvage value, and an estimated useful economic life of five years

Year	Depreciation Expense	Book Value
0		$10,000
1	($9,600 × 5/15) = $3,200	($10,000 − $3,200) = 6,800
2	(9,600 × 4/15) = 2,560	(10,000 − $5,760) = 4,240
3	(9,600 × 3/15) = 1,920	(10,000 − $7,680) = 2,320
4	(9,600 × 2/15) = 1,280	(10,000 − $8,960) = 1,004
5	(9,600 × 1/15) = 640	(10,000 − $9,600) = 400
	$9,600	

Unlike our calculation of a partial year's depreciation under the straight-line depreciation method (recall Transaction Q_1 in Chapter 6), with either of these accelerated depreciation methods, you must first calculate a full year's depreciation. Then, you multiply the full year depreciation by the fraction of the year the asset was used. Assume, for example, you sold the store equipment after six months had passed in its third year of use. The appropriate calculations for DDB and SYD are:

Double-declining balance: $1,440 × 1/2 = $720

Sum of the years' digits: $1,920 × 1/2 = $960

Comparing and Contrasting Alternative Depreciation Methods

As the following table indicates, year after year, straight-line depreciation is the most popular choice of depreciation method:[2]

	2000	1999	1998	1997
Straight-line	82.1%	82.3%	82.5%	81.1%
Declining-balance	3.1	3.8	3.6	3.6
Sum-of-the-years'-digits	1.0	1.0	1.3	1.4
Accelerated method—unspecified	7.6	7.6	6.2	7.0
Units-of-production	4.8	4.4	5.1	5.5
Other	1.4	0.9	1.3	1.4
	100.0%	100.0%	100.0%	100.0%

As you study this section, it will be particularly useful to study Figure 12-5 since it summarizes the yearly depreciation amounts that we calculated in our ongoing example for each depreciation method.

[2] "Depreciation Expense," *Accounting Trends and Techniques*, AICPA, 2001, 3.140.

FIGURE 12-5

Summary of alternative depreciation method amounts

Example: Depreciable asset with a cost of $10,000, a $400 salvage value, an estimated useful economic life of five years, and 20,000 lifetime hours of service distributed as follows:

Year 1	5,000
Year 2	4,200
Year 3	4,000
Year 4	3,800
Year 5	3,000

	Straight-Line Methods		**Accelerated Methods**	
Years	**Straight-Line**	**Service Hours**	**Double-Declining-Balance**	**Sum-of-the-Years' Digits**
1	$1,920	$2,400	$4,000	$3,200
2	$1,920	$2,016	$2,400	$2,560
3	$1,920	$1,920	$1,440	$1,920
4	$1,920	$1,824	$ 864	$1,280
5	$1,920	$1,440	$ 896	$ 640
Total	$9,600	$9,600	$9,600	$9,600

The straight-line method's primary advantage is that it is easy to apply. Its primary disadvantage is its assumption that an asset's usefulness remains constant over its entire life. Although the sum-of-the-years'-digits method is seldom used for financial reporting purposes, it is a useful conceptual method to understand and is used more often in tax return depreciation calculations. A clear disadvantage of using the approximation procedure for the declining-balance method is that you must adjust depreciation during the last scheduled year to ensure that the asset is fully depreciated. Note, for example, how depreciation expense in year 5 actually increases in our example. In addition, few use the more precise but awkward theoretical formula.

In comparing and contrasting these methods, the straight-line and the declining-balance methods both apply a constant depreciation rate each year whereas the sum-of-the-years'-digits method applies a constantly decreasing rate. Both the straight-line method and the sum-of-the-years'-digits method subtract salvage value initially, whereas the declining-balance method accounts for the salvage value in an asset's last year of useful life. Despite these period-to-period differences, however, each method is designed to depreciate the same total amount over the life of each asset. Thus, the impact of different depreciation methods on income can be significant from year to year but not as significant when you consider a longer time horizon.

Performance Objective 44 summarizes what you must be able to do to demonstrate your mastery of the detailed depreciation calculations.

YOUR PERFORMANCE OBJECTIVE 44

Describe how depreciation is calculated and **calculate** depreciation expense for any period desired under each of the following depreciation methods: straight-line, double-declining balance, and sum-of-the years' digits.

Recording Gains and Losses on Sales of Depreciable Assets

Now that you have learned how to record the acquisition of a depreciable asset and calculate and record its depreciation, the next logical step is to learn about the sale or disposal of that same asset. To fully appreciate the financial statement effects of selling a depreciable asset, consider the following relevant accounts. They are the result of a $10,000 asset with a $400 salvage value and a five-year useful life being depreciated under the straight-line method:

Store Equipment	
10,000	

Accumulated Depreciation	
	1,920
	1,920
	1,920
	1,920
	1,920
	9,600

The information in these T-accounts indicates that this asset has a book value of $400 ($10,000–$9,600). Recall that when an asset is sold, all balances in accounts associated with that asset must be removed. Thus, both the $10,000 store equipment balance and the $9,600 accumulated depreciation balance must be removed when you record the sale. Keep this information in mind as we record the transaction necessitated by selling the asset at the end of five years in each of the following three independent cases.

1. The store equipment is sold for $800.

Transaction Analysis	Fundamental Accounting Equation					Journal Entry		
Account Titles	Assets	=	Liabilities	+	Owners' Equity	Account Titles	Debit	Credit
Cash	800					Cash	800	
Accumulated Depreciation	9,600					Accumulated Depreciation	9,600	
Store Equipment	(10,000)					Store Equipment		10,000
Gain on Sale					400	Gain on Sale		400

The $400 gain results from selling for $800 an asset with a book value of $400.

2. The store equipment is sold for $400.

Transaction Analysis	Fundamental Accounting Equation					Journal Entry		
Account Titles	Assets	=	Liabilities	+	Owners' Equity	Account Titles	Debit	Credit
Cash	400					Cash	400	
Accumulated Depreciation	9,600					Accumulated Depreciation	9,600	
Store Equipment	(10,000)					Store Equipment		10,000

No gain or loss results because you sold for $400 an asset with a book value of $400.

3. The store equipment is sold for $200.

Transaction Analysis	Fundamental Accounting Equation					Journal Entry		
Account Titles	Assets	=	Liabilities	+	Owners' Equity	Account Titles	Debit	Credit
Cash	200					Cash	200	
Accumulated Depreciation	9,600					Accumulated Depreciation	9,600	
Loss on Sale					(200)	Loss on Sale	200	
Store Equipment	(10,000)					Store Equipment		10,000

A $200 loss results from selling for $200 an asset with a book value of $400.

You might be wondering how you would have recorded the sale if you had sold the asset before its estimated useful life had expired. Suppose for example, that the store equipment is sold for $2,200 after exactly two and one-half years of use. What would you do? Here's a hint: Look at the Accumulated Depreciation account. Notice that two and one-half years of depreciation amounts to $4,800 [($1,920 + $1,920) + .5 × $1,920)] of accumulated depreciation. This amount could also be derived by realizing that two and one-half years represents usage of exactly one-half of the asset's depreciable cost and multiplying $9,600 by 50%. In this case, we calculated the correct amount of accumulated depreciation at the time of sale by multiplying total lifetime depreciation by the amount of useful life consumed. The transaction to record this sale is shown here.

Transaction Analysis						Journal Entry		
	Fundamental Accounting Equation							
Account Titles	Assets	=	Liabilities	+	Owners' Equity	Account Titles	Debit	Credit
Cash	2,200					Cash	2,200	
Accumulated Depreciation	4,800					Accumulated Depreciation	4,800	
Loss on Sale					(3,000)	Loss on Sale	3,000	
Store Equipment	(10,000)					Store Equipment		10,000

Figure 12-6 summarizes the essential calculations for each of the preceding examples of how a sale is recorded. Don't forget that every one of the preceding gains and losses would be reported in the income statement.

Selling Price − Book Value = Gain or Loss

Book Value = Original Cost − Accumulated Depreciation

Cases	Selling Price	Book Value	Gain/(Loss)	Original Cost	Accumulated Depreciation
1	$ 800	$ 400	$ 400	$10,000	$9,600
2	400	400	Not applicable	10,000	9,600
3	200	400	(200)	10,000	9,600
4	2,200	5,200	(3,000)	10,000	4,800

FIGURE 12-6

Summary of depreciable asset gain and loss calculations using formulas

Natural Resources

For a small group of companies, property, plant, and equipment might also include natural resources, also called *wasting assets*. For example, in its 2001 notes, Sonoco Products Company reported over $35 million of timber resources at cost in its property, plant, and equipment account. Timber, mineral deposits, oil fields, and other natural resources, or wasting assets, are subject to what is called depletion. The concept of **depletion** is very similar to depreciation, except that it represents the cost of natural resources allocated to expense, instead of the cost of depreciable assets allocated to expense. Another difference is that depletion is based on the amount of natural resources mined or harvested whereas depreciation is generally based on the passage of time. For example, Sonoco records depletion expense based on the number of trees it cuts down during the year but records depreciation expense for buildings by using useful lives

When companies account for natural resources as part of their property, plant, and equipment, they use the concept of depletion.

of 20 to 30 years. As you might guess, Accumulated Depletion, a contra asset account, is similar to the Accumulated Depreciation account. Unfortunately, most annual reports make it difficult to fully analyze their depletion expense by combining it with depreciation expense. Although the detailed accounting for natural resources will not be covered here, we now take a brief look at how depletion is calculated and reported.

Example Safflower Oil and Gas Company was organized to search, extract, and sell crude oil. Exploration rights were acquired on a parcel of land near the shoreline of Ketchikan, Alaska. Exploration work began soon thereafter and oil was discovered later that same year. Operating data are summarized in the schedule shown below. Assume that all costs are paid in cash and that all cash flows occur at the end of the year.

	Year 1
Acquisition and exploration costs	$18,000,000
Development costs	$ 7,000,000
Production costs	$ 500,000
Barrels discovered	5,000,000
Barrels extracted	500,000
Barrels sold	450,000
Selling price	$ 16

Calculation of Depletion The first step in calculating depletion is to determine the total cost to be depleted. Assuming that the oil field's salvage value will be zero after the last barrel has been removed:

$$\text{Total Depletion Cost} = \text{Acquisition, Exploration and Development Costs}$$
$$= \$18{,}000{,}000 + \$7{,}000{,}000 = \$25{,}000{,}000$$

As described earlier in discussing the straight-line method, the **units of production method** can now be used to calculate depletion:

$$\text{Depletion Cost per Unit} = \text{Total Depletion Cost/Discovered Units}$$
$$= \$25{,}000{,}000/5{,}000{,}000 = \$5.00$$

$$\text{Periodic Depletion Cost} = 500{,}000 \times \$5.00 = \$2{,}500{,}000$$

If all barrels extracted are sold, this $2,500,000 of depletion cost will be expensed. Since 50,000 of the 500,000 barrels extracted are unsold at the end of the year, however, a portion of this depletion cost is not expensed, as shown here.

$$\text{Cost of Goods Sold} = \text{Units Sold} \times \text{Depletion Cost per Unit}$$
$$= 450{,}000 \times \$5.00 = \$2{,}250{,}000$$

$$\text{Inventory Cost} = \text{Units Unsold} \times \text{Depletion Cost per Unit}$$
$$= 50{,}000 \times \$5.00 = \$250{,}000$$

Figure 12-7 illustrates the financial statement effects of this natural resources example. In particular, notice that three assets are reported on the balance sheet. These are the Crude Oil Inventory account, a current asset necessitated by not selling every barrel of oil extracted; the Depletable Natural Resources account, a noncurrent asset that represents the cost of obtaining natural resources; and the Accumulated Depletion account, a noncurrent contra-asset account that represents the cumulative cost extracted. Although our example illustrates the essential concepts underlying accounting for natural resources, we didn't examine several real-life complications. These include how to account for several years of operations and how to account for unsuccessful as well as successful exploration efforts.

Now that you are more familiar with the concept of depletion, you can use Performance Objective 45 to help you master its detailed calculations:

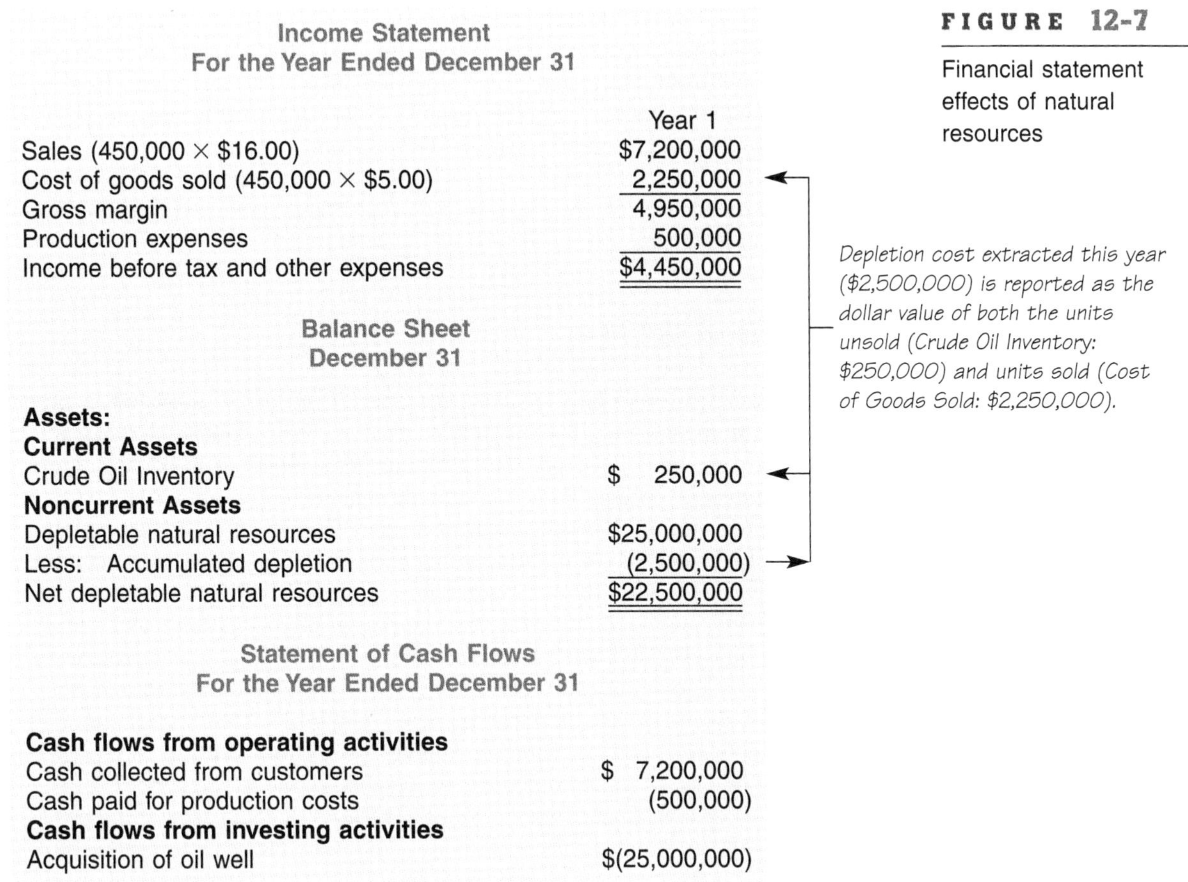

Income Statement
For the Year Ended December 31

	Year 1
Sales (450,000 × $16.00)	$7,200,000
Cost of goods sold (450,000 × $5.00)	2,250,000
Gross margin	4,950,000
Production expenses	500,000
Income before tax and other expenses	$4,450,000

Balance Sheet
December 31

Assets:	
Current Assets	
Crude Oil Inventory	$ 250,000
Noncurrent Assets	
Depletable natural resources	$25,000,000
Less: Accumulated depletion	(2,500,000)
Net depletable natural resources	$22,500,000

Statement of Cash Flows
For the Year Ended December 31

Cash flows from operating activities	
Cash collected from customers	$ 7,200,000
Cash paid for production costs	(500,000)
Cash flows from investing activities	
Acquisition of oil well	$(25,000,000)

Depletion cost extracted this year ($2,500,000) is reported as the dollar value of both the units unsold (Crude Oil Inventory: $250,000) and units sold (Cost of Goods Sold: $2,250,000).

FIGURE 12-7

Financial statement effects of natural resources

YOUR PERFORMANCE OBJECTIVE 45
Describe how depletion is calculated using the units-of-production method and **present** the financial statement effects of this calculation.

Property Not Subject to Depreciation or Depletion

Another type of property, plant, and equipment account is tangible property that is neither subject to depreciation nor depletion. Land, for example, is considered to have an unlimited useful life and, therefore, no depreciation or depletion calculation is possible. Suppose, for example, that in its second year of operation CMU purchased land for a new store location. Assume that CMU paid $16,000 for the land itself and an additional $1,500 for various real estate costs. The transactions accounting for this land—assuming CMU held it for 18 months and then sold it for $20,250—are shown below:

Transaction Analysis							Journal Entry		
	Fundamental Accounting Equation								
Account Titles	Assets	=	Liabilities	+	Owners' Equity		Account Titles	Debit	Credit
a. Land	17,500						Land	17,500	
Cash	(17,500)						Cash		17,500
b. Cash	20,250						Cash	20,250	
Land	(17,500)						Land		17,500
Gain on Land Sale					2,750		Gain on Land Sale		2,750

Notice that the Gain on Land Sale account increases net income and is included in the income statement. Although no depreciation expense is recorded for these land transactions, if Susan had to pay for a sidewalk in front of her store, CMU would have to account for depreciation. The reason is that such land improvements usually have a limited life and, therefore, can be depreciated.

Finally, land held for speculative purposes is usually reported in the investments section of the balance sheet while land held by a land development company is properly included in its inventory.

Accounting for Intangible Assets

Intangible assets differ in only one major respect from assets included in property, plant, and equipment—they are intangible. That is, their value is derived not from their physical substance but from the rights that their possession confers upon their owners. Examples of intangible assets include patents, copyrights, trademarks, franchises, computer programs, certain types of property leases referred to as capital leases in Appendix 13-1, and goodwill. Goodwill is perhaps the most common intangible asset. As you learned in Chapter 4 and Appendix 10-1, goodwill is the cost of acquiring another company over and above the total market price of that company's individual assets less liabilities (net assets). Until recently, nearly all intangible assets were subject to a process known as *amortization*, a process that is identical in concept to depreciation and depletion, except that it involves intangible asset costs rather than tangible depreciable asset costs or natural resource costs. **Amortization** is the systematic allocation of the cost of intangible assets to expense as the future benefits of such assets are used up or consumed. Under current generally accepted accounting principles, intangible assets are divided into two major categories: those with finite useful lives and those with indefinite useful lives. Since intangible assets having finite useful lives are subject to amortization and nearly all intangible assets used to be accounted for in this manner, let's begin our more detailed examination with this category.

Intangible Assets Subject to Amortization

Intangible assets that have finite useful lives include such assets as patents, copyrights, and trademarks. Each of these intangible assets has its own legal life set by federal statute. For example, a *patent* grants its holder the exclusive right to manufacture, sell, or otherwise control an invention for a period of 17 years. A *copyright* grants its holder the exclusive right to reproduce and sell an artistic or published work for the life of the individual plus 70 years. Finally, a *trademark* grants its holder the exclusive right to represent a product or service with a specific name or symbol for 20 years plus an indefinite number of renewal periods as long as the trademark is in use. Capital leases, which are discussed in Appendix 13–1, are also amortized because their lease term is specified by contract. Unlike depreciable assets, intangible assets are almost exclusively amortized on a straight-line basis.

To illustrate how to account for the amortization of such intangible assets, let's suppose that Susan developed a special hologram nonsports card on which she registered a patent that cost CMU $34,000. Assuming that she will use the legal life of this patent, her annual amortization expense would be $34,000/17, or $2,000, recorded as follows:

Transaction Analysis						Journal Entry		
	Fundamental Accounting Equation							
Account Titles	Assets	=	Liabilities	+	Owners' Equity	Account Titles	Debit	Credit
Patent Amortization Expense					(2,000)	Patent Amortization Expense	2,000	
Patent	(2,000)					Patent		2,000

Note that the effect of this transaction is to both decrease net income and total assets. Unlike our accounting for depreciation and depletion, however, a contra intangible asset account is seldom used.

Performance Objective 46 represents this amortization concept:

YOUR PERFORMANCE OBJECTIVE 46
Describe how amortization is calculated using the straight-line method and **present** the financial statement effects of this calculation.

Intangible Assets Not Subject to Amortization

Recently, the Financial Accounting Standards Board, our country's financial reporting standard-setting body, established a significant departure in accounting for certain intangible assets such as **goodwill**.[3] Whenever such assets have indefinite useful lives, they are to be left on the balance sheet until management has evidence that these assets have been *impaired*. That is, such intangible assets are not subject to amortization. One argument for this new approach is that goodwill is an asset that does not decline in value as a function of time but as a function of market conditions. Because the term *impairment* plays such an important role in how this group of intangibles is accounted for, let's examine it in more depth.

What Is Impairment and How Is It Determined? In theory, **impairment** of an asset occurs when it is determined that an asset's market value has declined. Under generally accepted accounting principles, however, you test for impairment by comparing the expected future cash flows of the asset with its book value. If the asset's current book value exceeds the sum of the expected future cash flows, an asset impairment has occurred. Because accounting does not permit assets whose values have declined to remain on the balance sheet at their book values, an impairment loss must be recorded. Note, however, that if the expected future cash flows have declined but still exceed the asset's current book value, an economic loss has occurred, but impairment does not apply.

To illustrate this concept, let's consider an example involving a tangible asset. Suppose that you buy some commercial property for $200,000 from which you expected to collect $1 million in rental revenue over the next 10 years plus $150,000 from its sale after 10 years. Shortly after your purchase, however, you discover that a new highway project will result in a significant loss of future rentals.

Example 1 You now estimate that your land will generate $75,000 of revenue each year for the next six years, at which time it will be sold for $60,000. Since land does not depreciate, its current book value is $200,000. An appraisal sets the land's market value at $160,000. No impairment has occurred in this example because the future cash flows of $510,000 [($75,000 × 6) + $60,000] exceed the land's book value of $200,000. Although no impairment loss would be recorded, you have clearly incurred an economic loss since you paid $200,000 for property that is now worth $160,000 and you have lost $640,000 [($1,000,000 + $150,000) − $510,000] in expected future cash flows.

Example 2 You estimate that your land will generate $35,000 of revenue each year for the next four years at which time it will be sold for $50,000. Just as in Example 1, the land's current book value is $200,000 and its market value is $160,000. In this example, an asset impairment has occurred because the future cash flows of $190,000 [($35,000 × 4) + $50,000] do not exceed the land's book value of $200,000.

[3] "Goodwill and other Intangible Assets," *Statement of Financial Accounting Standards No. 142* (Stamford, CT: Financial Accounting Standards Board, 2001).

To properly record the loss, you would first set the new asset cost equal to market value, remove the land's original cost, and record the $40,000 impairment loss to reduce the book value to its current fair market value. This transaction is shown here:

Transaction Analysis					Journal Entry		
	Fundamental Accounting Equation						
Account Titles	Assets	= Liabilities	+	Owners' Equity	Account Titles	Debit	Credit
Land (new valuation)	160,000				Land (new valuation)	160,000	
Loss on Impairment				(40,000)	Loss on Impairment	40,000	
Land (original cost)	(200,000)				Land (original cost)		200,000

How Are Goodwill and Other Intangibles Accounted for after Initial Acquisition? Now that you understand the basic concept of impairment and how such a loss is both determined and calculated, let's examine how this concept applies to accounting for intangible assets with indefinite lives. Under this non-amortization approach, for example, goodwill is tested for impairment at least annually using a two-step process.[4] The first step of the goodwill impairment test, used to identify potential impairment, compares the fair market value of a reporting entity (an entity that includes the business whose acquisition created the goodwill) with its book or recorded amount, including goodwill. If this fair market value is greater than its book value, goodwill of the reporting entity is considered not impaired and the second step of the impairment test is unnecessary. If the book value is greater than the fair market value, however, the second step is applied.

The second step of the goodwill impairment test, used to measure the amount of the impairment loss, compares the current fair market value of goodwill with the book value of that goodwill. If the book value exceeds the fair market value, a goodwill impairment loss is recorded in the amount of that excess. Here's an example:

Step 1:	Book value of reporting entity	$17,450,000
	Fair market value of reporting entity	16,850,000

Since the book value exceeds the fair market value, step 2 is used. Let's now assume the following values:

Step 2:	Book value of goodwill	$330,000
	Implied fair value of goodwill	295,000
		$ 35,000

Since goodwill has been impaired in the amount of $35,000, the following transaction would be recorded:

Transaction Analysis					Journal Entry		
	Fundamental Accounting Equation						
Account Titles	Assets	= Liabilities	+	Owners' Equity	Account Titles	Debit	Credit
Loss on Goodwill Impairment				(35,000)	Loss on Goodwill Impairment	35,000	
Goodwill	(35,000)				Goodwill		35,000

4 "Goodwill and Other Intangible Assets," *Statement of Financial Accounting Standards No. 142*, paragraphs 19–20, (Stamford, CT: Financial Accounting Standards Board, 2001).

An example of an intangible asset other than goodwill with an indefinite useful life would be an acquired broadcast license that expires in five years. If the business that acquires this license intends to renew it indefinitely and there is no expected challenge to its renewal, the broadcast license would not be amortized until its useful life was no longer considered indefinite. The future economic benefits associated with a company's *research and development costs* also are treated as intangible assets having an indefinite useful life. In this case, however, the accounting profession generally requires that such costs be expensed as incurred because the duration of future benefits from such expenditures are too uncertain to justify recording as assets and then amortizing. The detailed accounting for research and development will be covered in a later accounting course.

Accounting for Investments in Debt and Equity Securities

Now that you have a greater understanding of how the balances in various property, plant, and equipment and intangible asset accounts are calculated, let's look at investments in securities. Recall that you were introduced to these transactions in Chapter 4. In this chapter, you'll learn more about the distinction between debt and equity securities; the distinctions between cash equivalents, marketable securities, and investments; and the financial statement effects of both debt securities and equity securities.

How to Distinguish between Debt and Equity Securities

Companies often invest in the securities of other companies that issue securities to finance their operations. These investments are of two types: debt securities and equity securities. A **debt security**, or *debt investment*, such as a Treasury bill, note, or bond is a financial instrument that allows individuals, companies, or government entities to loan money to other individuals, companies, or government entities. When a company buys a debt security from a borrower, it essentially loans money to the borrower in return for a promise that it will receive a future return *of* the loan along with interest *on* the loan.

When one company invests in the capital stock of another company, the asset acquired is often referred to as an *investment in equity securities*. Up to now, you have used the term *equity* to represent the residual interest of owners after subtracting their liabilities from their assets. Thus, it should not be difficult to understand that an **equity security**, or stock investment, such as shares of common, preferred, or other capital stock, represents ownership interest in a corporation. The return on these equity securities can be dividends and/or an increase in the market price of the stock.

Regardless of whether the security is debt or equity in nature, the investing company is called the **investor** and the owned company is called the **investee**. That is, the investor treats the security owned as an asset and the investee treats the security as a liability.

How to Distinguish between Cash Equivalents, Marketable Securities, and Investments

You might recall that a balance sheet can report investments in securities in as many as three separate asset accounts—cash equivalents, marketable securities, and investments. You can distinguish between these categories by considering: (1) the nature of the security, (2) the security's expected maturity date, and (3) the intention of the security holder.

Nature of the Security One way to distinguish between these security categories is by considering the nature of the security itself. For example, cash equivalents include such highly liquid interest-bearing debt securities as time deposits or savings accounts, certificates of deposit, money market funds, treasury bills, and commercial paper. Although both marketable securities and investments include many of these same items, they also include corporate or government bonds (debt securities) and investments in shares of corporate stock (equity securities). That is, cash equivalents include assets that provide only interest whereas both marketable securities and investments include assets that are able to provide dividends, increases in market value, or interest.

Expected Maturity of Security Another useful way to distinguish between the cash equivalent, marketable security, and investment categories is to consider their expected maturities. For example, **cash equivalents** have maturities of three months or less when purchased, **marketable securities** have maturities of greater than three months to one year, and **investments** have maturities that exceed one year in length.

Intention of the Security Holder Finally, you can distinguish between these security categories by determining why their holder bought them. As you learned in Chapter 4, the intentions of the holder create three categories: trading, available for sale, or held to maturity.[5] As you will soon discover, this classification system not only helps you decide whether the security should be classified as current or noncurrent but also what balance sheet amount you should report for this security. Although this three-category system does apply to cash equivalents, in this chapter we focus on its more important application to marketable securities and investments.

Recall that **trading securities** are debt or equity securities that the company intends to actively trade to profit from short-term differences in price. Because they are held for only a short period of time, trading securities are classified as current assets (marketable securities) and reported on the balance sheet at their **fair value**—a price negotiated at arm's length between a willing buyer and a willing seller, each acting rationally. Trading securities are usually held by businesses whose normal operations involve buying and selling securities, such as banks and insurance companies. In contrast, **available-for-sale securities** are debt or equity securities that the company intends to sell in the future but does not actively trade to profit from short-term differences in price. They can be classified as either current (marketable securities) or noncurrent assets (investments). Although the company must disclose both the cost and fair value of available-for-sale securities, their fair value must be reported on the balance sheet.

The last category, **held-to-maturity securities**, includes debt securities that the company has both the intent and the ability to hold (that is, own) to maturity. Equity securities are not classified in this category simply because they do not have maturity dates. Held-to-maturity securities can be classified as either current (marketable) or noncurrent (investment) assets. Although the company must disclose both the cost and fair value of held-to-maturity securities, their cost is reported on the balance sheet.

As an initial step to learn more about investments in securities, we will use the same example to show how to record typical debt security transactions and how to report the financial statement effects of those same transactions.

---

[5] "Accounting for Certain Investments in Debt and Equity Securities," *Statement of Financial Accounting Standards No. 115*, Financial Accounting Standards Board, May 1993.

How to Account for Debt Securities

To illustrate the essential transactions one would expect from an investment in debt securities, let's assume that your company pays $100,000 plus brokerage commissions of $1,000 for 10-year, 5%, U.S. government bonds on January 1, 2003. For simplicity, we will also assume that the bonds' **face value**—the amount that the borrower (U.S. government) promises to pay at maturity—is $100,000 and that the annual interest of 5% is paid semiannually on January 1 and July 1. To properly account for these bonds, we must record transactions for the acquisition, interest revenue, adjustment to fair value at year-end, and the sale of the bonds as shown in the following sections.

Recording the Acquisition of a Debt Security Generally, this acquisition would be treated as an investment among noncurrent assets because although it can be readily converted into cash, companies purchasing these bonds usually don't intend to do so within one year of their most recent balance sheet. At acquisition, this investment in bonds, like all other assets, is recorded at cost no matter what category of security—trading, available for sale, or held to maturity—is applicable. This cost is equivalent to fair value at acquisition and includes the market price of the security plus any additional costs necessary to complete the purchase. Thus, as shown here, the noncurrent asset Investment in Bonds is recorded at a cost of $101,000.

Acquisition of bonds at 01/01/03:

Transaction Analysis						Journal Entry		
	Fundamental Accounting Equation							
Account Titles	**Assets**	**=**	**Liabilities**	**+**	**Owners' Equity**	**Account Titles**	**Debit**	**Credit**
Investment in Bonds	101,000					Investment in Bonds	101,000	
Cash	(101,000)					Cash		101,000

Note that an appropriate balance sheet title for this noncurrent investment in bonds account might be Investments in Debt Securities or simply Investments. If this same investment had been judged to be a trading security and, therefore, a current asset, an appropriate balance sheet title might be Marketable Debt Securities, or simply Marketable Securities.

Recording the Interest Earned on a Debt Security Since the bonds pay interest twice each year, interest revenue is calculated by multiplying the bonds' face value by the interest rate for a six-month passage of time or $\$100,000 \times .05 \times 1/2 = \$2,500$. Only one interest transaction is recorded on July 1:

Interest revenue at 07/01 of each year:

Transaction Analysis						Journal Entry		
	Fundamental Accounting Equation							
Account Titles	**Assets**	**=**	**Liabilities**	**+**	**Owners' Equity**	**Account Titles**	**Debit**	**Credit**
Cash	2,500					Cash	2,500	
Interest Revenue					2,500	Interest Revenue		2,500

The next transaction, however, is recorded in two parts assuming that our company's accounting period ends at December 31.

Interest revenue at 12/31 of each year:

Account Titles	Assets	=	Liabilities	+	Owners' Equity	Account Titles	Debit	Credit
Interest Receivable	2,500					Interest Receivable	2,500	
Interest Revenue					2,500	Interest Revenue		2,500

Cash receipt at 01/01 of each year:

Account Titles	Assets	=	Liabilities	+	Owners' Equity	Account Titles	Debit	Credit
Cash	2,500					Cash	2,500	
Interest Receivable	(2,500)					Interest Receivable		2,500

What happens, however, if the bonds in the preceding example are purchased between interest dates? That is, assume that your company purchased the bonds at April 1 rather than January 1. How would this transaction be recorded differently?

Recall from our example that on July 1, the bondholder will receive \$2,500 (\$100,000 × .05 × 1/2) cash or six months worth of interest, despite owning the bonds for only three months (April through June). Since the bondholder doesn't deserve six months of interest, the only equitable solution is to require that the bondholder pay the seller of the bonds the accrued interest from January 1 to March 31. This arrangement is accounted for at purchase as shown here:

Acquisition of Bonds at 04/01/03:

Account Titles	Assets	=	Liabilities	+	Owners' Equity	Account Titles	Debit	Credit
Investment in Bonds	101,000					Investment in Bonds	101,000	
Interest Receivable	1,250					Interest Receivable	1,250	
Cash	(102,250)					Cash		102,250

Notice that the \$1,250 in these transactions represents three months worth of interest due the seller for holding the bonds between January 1 and March 31 (\$100,000 × .05 × 3/12). On July 1, you would record the interest revenue as follows:

Interest revenue at 07/01 of the first year:

Account Titles	Assets	=	Liabilities	+	Owners' Equity	Account Titles	Debit	Credit
Cash	2,500					Cash	2,500	
Interest Receivable	(1,250)					Interest Receivable		1,250
Interest Revenue					1,250	Interest Revenue		1,250

The preceding transaction should make sense to you when you consider that the bondholder has earned three months of interest revenue from April 1 to June 30 despite receiving six months worth of interest from January 1 to June 30.

Recording the Adjustment to Fair Value, If Any The real value of the trading, available-for-sale, and held-to-maturity categories is to provide guidance about what, if any, adjustment should be made to an investment at the end of an accounting period. To illustrate, let's examine how the effects of our bond investment would be reported in the balance sheet and income statement under each of these categories.

Trading Securities Although this classification is usually applied to investments of banks or insurance companies, let's illustrate how it works for our example assuming that the bond's fair market value is $101,200 at year-end. Since trading securities must be reported on the balance sheet at their fair value ($101,200) rather than at their cost ($101,000), the following adjustment, in which both the investment account and an unrealized holding gain account are increased by $200, must be recorded.

Adjustment to fair value of $101,200 at 12/31/03:

Transaction Analysis				Journal Entry		
	Fundamental Accounting Equation					
Account Titles	Assets	= Liabilities +	Owners' Equity	Account Titles	Debit	Credit
Investment in Bonds	200			Investment in Bonds	200	
Unrealized Holding Gain			200	Unrealized Holding Gain		200

The account title Unrealized Holding Gain is appropriate because it indicates that the bonds have not been sold and are still held. Unlike the treatment used in the other categories, this gain of $200 is included in net income of the current period. The justification for recognizing income is that, by their nature, trading securities are purchased with the intention of earning income from short-term price fluctuations. The bond would be reported at its fair value of $101,200 on the year-end balance sheet.

Had the bond's fair value been $100,700, the following transaction would have been appropriate:

Adjustment to fair value of $100,700 at 12/31/03:

Transaction Analysis				Journal Entry		
	Fundamental Accounting Equation					
Account Titles	Assets	= Liabilities +	Owners' Equity	Account Titles	Debit	Credit
Unrealized Holding Loss			(300)	Unrealized Holding Loss	300	
Investment in Bonds	(300)			Investment in Bonds		300

The effect of this unrealized holding loss would be to reduce current period income by $300 and the bond would be reported at its fair value of $100,700 on the year-end balance sheet.

Available-for-Sale Securities Let's assume the very same information as in the preceding case except that the bond belongs in the available-for-sale category. This time, we will focus on the assumption that the fair value of the bond is $101,200.

Adjustment to fair value of $101,200 at 12/31/03:

Transaction Analysis				Journal Entry		
	Fundamental Accounting Equation					
Account Titles	Assets	= Liabilities +	Owners' Equity	Account Titles	Debit	Credit
Investment in Bonds	200			Investment in Bonds	200	
Unrealized Holding Gain			200	Unrealized Holding Gain		200

Although this transaction is identical in form to the transaction just illustrated for trading securities and the investment account is still reported in the balance sheet at fair value of $101,200, the financial statement treatment of the $200 gain is dramatically different. The unrealized holding gain or holding loss each period does not affect income immediately, as you'll recall was the case with trading securities. Instead, changes in the fair value of a security are recognized in a separate shareholders' equity account until the security is actually sold. Figure 12-8 illustrates that these changes are not reported in income but rather in the balance sheet of our hypothetical company. The justification for not reporting these changes in income is that, unlike trading securities, available-for-sale securities are not purchased with the intention of earning income from short-term price fluctuations. Another reason for not allowing these gains and losses to affect income is to avoid almost certain earnings volatility from year to year.

FIGURE 12-8

How an unrealized holding gain on an available-for-sale debt security is presented on the balance sheet

Balance Sheet	
Shareholders' equity	
Common stock	$100,000*
Retained earnings	25,000*
Unrealized holding gain on available-for-sale securities	200
Total shareholders' equity	$125,200

Note: An unrealized holding loss would be subtracted from the shareholders' equity accounts above.

*Assumed numbers

Held-to-Maturity Securities Unlike the preceding two categories, held-to-maturity securities are accounted for at cost or, more precisely, amortized cost, an amount that will be explained in Chapter 13. Since fair value is not used, there is no adjustment to make in our illustration. The argument for not reporting our held-to-maturity bond's fair value is that since management has no intention of selling it before maturity, its ongoing fair values provide no useful cash flow information to users of its financial statements. Incidentally, amortized cost for our bond is simply $101,000 because it was issued at that amount.

Recording the Sale of a Debt Security Suppose the U.S. government bond is sold on July 1, 2006, for $101,900. Recording the sale of such a debt security is a very logical process. You record the amount of cash received as well as the removal of the $101,000 cost of your Investment in Bonds account. The difference of $900 is reported on the income statement as a gain on sale of investment in bonds. Here is how the transaction is recorded.

Sale of bonds at 07/01/06:

Transaction Analysis							Journal Entry		
	Fundamental Accounting Equation								
Account Titles	**Assets**	**=**	**Liabilities**	**+**	**Owners' Equity**		**Account Titles**	**Debit**	**Credit**
Cash	101,900						Cash	101,900	
Investment in Bonds	(101,000)						Investment in Bonds		101,000
Realized Gain on Sale					900		Realized Gain on Sale		900

This transaction illustrates a critical distinction in how these securities are accounted for. Only the actual sale of the bond triggered the designation "realized gain." That is, when we recorded a market adjustment at the end of the year in an earlier transaction, the gain was unrealized because we still held the bond. In this case, revenue is truly realized in cash not just anticipated.

How to Distinguish between Different Levels of Stock Ownership

For over 30 years, the accounting profession has used a classification system based on the investor company's relative degree of stock ownership to account for its investments in equity securities. This classification system includes three levels of stock ownership in an investee corporation ranging from little effect to effective control over the investee.[6] For now, we'll refer to these ownership levels in terms of their level of influence:

1. Insignificant
2. Significant
3. Control

Since the terms *significant influence* and *control* are so central to these ownership levels, it is essential to understand their meaning. **Significant influence** is defined as the ability to affect, in an important degree, the operating and financing policies of another company whereas **control** is defined as the ability to determine the operating and financing policies of another company.

Since these terms are so subjective, the accounting profession has established numerical boundaries for these three ownership levels. For example, investments of less than 20% of the voting stock of another company are considered to provide neither significant influence nor control of the investee corporation. Investments of between 20% and 50% of the voting stock of another company are considered to provide significant influence but not control. Investments of greater than 50% of the voting stock of another company, however, are treated as evidence that the investor can exert control over an investee corporation.

Expecting arbitrary percentages to accurately portray a company's degree of ownership of another company is not always realistic. For example, an investor holding as little as a 10% investment in the voting stock of another company could exercise significant influence if the remaining ownership is not unified. It's not unusual, however, for the remaining ownership to band together so as not to sacrifice its influence to another entity. Thus, even a company that obtains a 30% interest in another company as the result of a hostile takeover might be judged to have no significant influence if it has little or no representation on the board of directors and the other stockholders vote in a unified fashion. Thus, companies are expected to treat these percentages as general guidelines rather than absolute rules in determining degree of ownership. Let's now take a closer look at each of these categories.

Equity Investments that Provide Insignificant Influence Investments of less than 20% of the voting stock of another company are generally made with the purpose of earning both dividends and anticipated increases in the stock's market value. Therefore, no matter how these investments are classified—current or noncurrent—the investor owns such a small percentage of the shares of the investee that the investor is unable to exert either significant influence or control over the investee's operating and financing policies. To make this ownership level more distinguishable, we'll refer to a security of this type as a **minority, passive investment**.

---

[6] "The Equity Method of Accounting for Investments in Common Stock," *Accounting Principles Board Opinion Number 18*, Accounting Principles Board, March 1971.

The term *minority* refers to having less than a 50% share of voting stock while the term *passive* refers to the fact that the investor is unable to influence the operating and financing decisions of the investee company in any meaningful way.

Equity Investments that Provide Significant Influence Investments of between 20% and 50% of the voting stock of another company are motivated by the investor's desire to gain a significant influence over the owned company's activities. For example, if CMU had the resources, it might invest in the shares of a card manufacturer to help ensure the continued availability of that manufacturer's products at reasonable prices. A descriptive title for this ownership level is **minority, active investment**. Once again, if this percentage test is met but there is evidence that significant influence cannot be exercised, the company's investments should instead be treated as a minority, passive investment.

Equity Investments that Provide Control Investments of greater than 50% of the voting stock of another company are motivated by an investor's desire to control the investee's broad policies and day-to-day operating decisions. An investment that fits into this category can be referred to as a **majority, active investment**. In this case, the term *majority* means the investor has more than a 50% share of voting stock while the term *active* refers to the fact that the investor can influence the investee's operating and financing decisions in a meaningful way. Evidence that control cannot be exercised, however, is more compelling than simple application of our percentage limit.

Majority, active investments in the stock of another company usually require accounting procedures described in Appendix 10-1 that result in the preparation of consolidated financial statements. As a result, we'll devote our time here to accounting for minority passive investments and minority active investments.

How to Account for Equity Securities

Now that you understand the essential terminology and primary categories associated with investments in equity securities, let's examine how one accounts for these types of transactions. Suppose that at the beginning of its second year of operation, Samson Corporation purchased shares of Thomas, Inc. at $45 a share plus commissions and taxes. Let's now consider how that company would record the acquisition of this stock, the receipt of its dividends, and the sale of the same equity holding under two conditions: the stock purchase represents a minority, passive investment and the stock purchase represents a minority, active investment.

Minority, Passive Investments Let's assume that Samson Corporation purchases 100 shares of Thomas Inc. voting common stock at $45 a share plus brokerage commissions of $100 for a total outlay of $4,600. Since Thomas Inc. has 10,000 shares of common stock outstanding, Samson Corporation's percentage ownership in the voting stock of Thomas Inc. is less than 20%. This determination is important because such investments in stocks are accounted for by using what we will refer to as the cost/fair value method. Under the **cost/fair value method**, the investment in stock account is initially recorded at cost and then reported at fair value at each balance sheet date. Dividend revenue is recorded only when dividends on that stock are declared by the investee.

At Acquisition We will treat this acquisition as a marketable security among current assets because it can be readily converted into cash and the investor is considering doing so within one year of its most recent balance sheet.

Transaction Analysis						Journal Entry		
	Fundamental Accounting Equation							
Account Titles	Assets	=	Liabilities	+	Owners' Equity	Account Titles	Debit	Credit
Investment in Thomas Stock	4,600					Investment in Thomas Stock	4,600	
Cash	(4,600)					Cash		4,600

As shown here, this investment in stock account, like all assets, is recorded at cost when purchased. When reporting this ledger account on the balance sheet, however, it might well be combined with other investments and reported under marketable equity securities.

What if this purchase of stock had been treated as an investment among noncurrent assets because the acquiring company did not intend to convert it into cash within one year of its most recent balance sheet? In that case, it would more appropriately be included in the balance sheet as investment securities or simply investments.

At Declaration of Dividends If Thomas Inc. declares a $1 per share dividend, it is legally obligated to pay that amount to its common stock shareholders at a reasonable future date. Thus, Samson Corporation is justified in recording $100 (100 × $1) of dividend revenue from its holdings of Thomas Inc. as shown here:

Transaction Analysis						Journal Entry		
	Fundamental Accounting Equation							
Account Titles	Assets	=	Liabilities	+	Owners' Equity	Account Titles	Debit	Credit
Dividend Receivable	100					Dividend Receivable	100	
Dividend Revenue					100	Dividend Revenue		100

At Receipt of Dividends If dividends of $100 are then received in cash from the investment in Thomas, Inc. stock, the following transaction would be recorded:

Transaction Analysis						Journal Entry		
	Fundamental Accounting Equation							
Account Titles	Assets	=	Liabilities	+	Owners' Equity	Account Titles	Debit	Credit
Cash	100					Cash	100	
Dividend Receivable	(100)					Dividend Receivable		100

As a peripheral activity that is expected to continue, the dividend revenue is generally reported in the income statement under other revenue and gains.

At Recognition of Investee Net Income Suppose that about six months after the Thomas Inc. stock is purchased by Samson Corporation, Thomas, Inc. reports a significant amount of net income in its annual report. Should our investing company recognize a proportionate increase in its own income to reflect a return on the good fortune of its investee? The answer is no because Samson Corporation's $4,600 investment does not represent even the hint of a significant influence on a large company such as Thomas Inc. In other words, Samson Corporation and Thomas, Inc. are two separate entities. Thus, it would be unreasonable for Samson Corporation to realize income on news of Thomas, Inc.'s earnings.

At Year-End Adjustment to Fair Value, If Any Recall how we used the trading, available-for-sale, and held-to-maturity categories to determine what, if any, adjustment should be made to an investment in debt securities. These same categories can also be used with minority, passive equity investments with one exception. We are unable to use the held-to-maturity category because, as you might remember, equity securities do not have maturity dates. Since there are only two categories in which to place equity securities—trading securities and available-for-sale securities—let's examine how the effects of Samson's Investment in Thomas Stock account would be reported in Samson's balance sheet and income statement under either category.

Trading Securities Let's assume that Thomas, Inc. common stock sells for $51 a share at the end of the accounting period. Since trading securities must be reported on the balance sheet at their fair value of $5,100 (100 × $51) rather than at their cost of $4,600, the following adjustment, in which both the investment account and an unrealized gain account are increased by $500, must be recorded.

Adjustment to fair value of $5,100 at the end of the accounting period:

Transaction Analysis						Journal Entry		
	Fundamental Accounting Equation							
Account Titles	Assets	=	Liabilities	+	Owners' Equity	Account Titles	Debit	Credit
Investment in Thomas Stock	500					Investment in Thomas Stock	500	
Unrealized Holding Gain					500	Unrealized Holding Gain		500

Consistent with the notion that trading securities are purchased to earn net income from short-term price fluctuations, this unrealized gain of $500 is included in Samson's current net income. Meanwhile, Samson's Investment in Thomas Stock account would be reported at its fair value of $5,100 on the year-end balance sheet.

Had the stock been selling for only $42.50 at the end of the year, the following transaction would have been appropriate:

Adjustment to fair value of $4,250 at the end of the accounting period:

Transaction Analysis						Journal Entry		
	Fundamental Accounting Equation							
Account Titles	Assets	=	Liabilities	+	Owners' Equity	Account Titles	Debit	Credit
Unrealized Holding Loss					(350)	Unrealized Holding Loss	350	
Investment in Thomas Stock	(350)					Investment in Thomas Stock		350

The effect of this unrealized holding loss would be to reduce current period income by $350 ($4,600 − $4,250). Meanwhile, the Investment in Thomas Stock account would be reported at its fair value of $4,250 on the year-end balance sheet.

Available-for-Sale Securities Let's assume the very same information as in the preceding case except that Samson's equity security belongs in the available-for-sale category. This time, we will focus on the assumption that the year-end selling price of Thomas, Inc. stock is $51.

Adjustment to fair value of $5,100 at the end of the accounting period:

Transaction Analysis						Journal Entry		
	Fundamental Accounting Equation							
Account Titles	**Assets**	**=**	**Liabilities**	**+**	**Owners' Equity**	**Account Titles**	**Debit**	**Credit**
Investment in Thomas Stock	500					Investment in Thomas Stock	500	
Unrealized Holding Gain					500	Unrealized Holding Gain		500

Although the investment account is still reported in the balance sheet at its current fair value of $5,100, the financial statement treatment of the $500 gain is dramatically different than in our preceding example. In this case, the unrealized holding gain or holding loss each period does not affect income immediately as was the case with trading securities. Instead, such a change in the fair value of a security is recognized in a separate shareholders' equity account until the security is actually sold as illustrated in Figure 12-9.

FIGURE 12-9

How an unrealized holding gain on an available-for-sale equity security is presented on the balance sheet

SAMSON COMPANY
Balance Sheet

Shareholders' equity	
Common stock	$200,000*
Retained earnings	50,000*
Unrealized holding gain on available-for-sale securities	500
Total shareholders' equity	$250,500

Note: An unrealized holding loss would be subtracted from the shareholders' equity accounts above.

*Assumed numbers

At Sale Suppose that Samson sold its 100 shares of Thomas stock exactly 10 months after purchase (with no intervening adjustment to fair value) at a price of $48 per share less brokerage commissions of $125. The net proceeds of this sale would be $4,675 [(100 × $48) − $125] and the sale would be recorded as shown here:

Transaction Analysis						Journal Entry		
	Fundamental Accounting Equation							
Account Titles	**Assets**	**=**	**Liabilities**	**+**	**Owners' Equity**	**Account Titles**	**Debit**	**Credit**
Cash	4,675					Cash	4,675	
Realized Gain on Sale					75	Realized Gain on Sale		75
Investment in Thomas Stock	(4,600)					Investment in Thomas Stock		4,600

As a peripheral activity that is expected to continue, the Realized Gain on Sale account is generally reported in the income statement under other revenues and gains.

Although we have yet to explore how minority, active investments are accounted for, now is a good time to consider Performance Objective 47, a comprehensive objective that will help you master how to account for investments in debt and equity securities.

YOUR PERFORMANCE OBJECTIVE 47
Determine the proper valuation of both current and noncurrent debt and equity securities at the end of a period, **record** all investment in debt and equity security related transactions, and **present** the complete financial statement effects of this set of transactions.

Note that this performance objective also applies to the following type of investment.

Minority, Active Investments Minority, active investments are accounted for under what is called the *equity method.* To illustrate this method, suppose that Thomas, Inc. had 10,000 shares of outstanding common stock and Samson Corporation purchased 2,500 of them. In this example, Samson holds a 25% interest in Thomas. Once again, let's assume that Thomas Inc.'s stock was purchased at $45 a share but that the brokerage commissions of $1,500 were relatively less on a per share basis ($1,500/10,000 = $0.15) than in our preceding example ($100/100 = $1.00). Because Samson Corporation's percentage ownership in the voting stock of Thomas exceeds 20%, we will assume that it has the ability to significantly influence the operating and financing policies of Thomas Inc. Under this scenario, this investment must be accounted for by using the equity method. The **equity method** allows an investor to record its share of an investee's reported net income both as an increase in its own investment in stock account and as investment revenue in its income statement. Since the equity method represents such a dramatic departure from the cost principle, let's take a closer look at how it works.

At Acquisition Since Samson Corporation now holds such a significant share of Thomas, Inc. stock, a more realistic assumption is to treat this acquisition as a noncurrent investment because a sale is not planned for the foreseeable future. The cost to Samson Corporation of this investment in Thomas stock is $114,000 [(2,500 × $45) + $1,500] as shown here:

Transaction Analysis						Journal Entry		
	Fundamental Accounting Equation							
Account Titles	Assets	=	Liabilities	+	Owners' Equity	Account Titles	Debit	Credit
Investment in Thomas Stock	114 000					Investment in Thomas Stock	114,000	
Cash	(114,000)					Cash		114,000

Clearly, the equity method treats the initial purchase of stock in exactly the same way as did the cost/fair value method. That is, this investment in stock account, like all assets, is recorded at cost when purchased.

At Recognition of Investee Net Income The premise of the equity method is that when an investor such as Samson Corporation has the ability to influence the net income of an investee such as Thomas, Inc., it should share in the investee's income. Under the equity method, the investment in stock account includes the cost of the investment plus the investor's share of the investee earnings less the investor's share of investee losses. If Thomas Inc.'s actual reported net income for the year was $80,000, Samson Corporation's 25% share would dictate recording both an increase to its investment in stock account as well as an increase to its investment revenue of $20,000 ($80,000 × .25).

Transaction Analysis					Journal Entry		
	Fundamental Accounting Equation						
Account Titles	Assets	=	Liabilities	+ Owners' Equity	Account Titles	Debit	Credit
Investment in Thomas Stock	20,000				Investment in Thomas Stock	20,000	
Equity in Earnings of Thomas				20,000	Equity in Earnings of Thomas		20,000

The account Equity in Earnings of Thomas is a revenue account and effectively represents a return *on* investment.

At Recognition of Investee Net Loss If Thomas, Inc. were to report a net loss of $18,000 at the end of the second year of Samson's ownership, the exact opposite effect of our preceding transaction would be recorded. That is, instead of increasing the investment account, you would decrease it by Samson's proportionate share of the net loss or $4,500 ($18,000 × .25) as shown here.

Transaction Analysis					Journal Entry		
	Fundamental Accounting Equation						
Account Titles	Assets	=	Liabilities	+ Owners' Equity	Account Titles	Debit	Credit
Equity in Earnings of Thomas				(4,500)	Equity in Earnings of Thomas	4,500	
Investment in Thomas Stock	(4,500)				Investment in Thomas Stock		4,500

In this case, the account Equity in Earnings of Thomas is treated as an expense account and effectively represents a loss *on* investment. For purposes of this illustration, we will assume that no dividend was declared in this second year because of the loss.

At Declaration of Dividends Once again, let's assume that Thomas Inc. declares a $1 per share dividend. Since Samson has already recorded its proportionate share of revenue from the earnings of Thomas, Samson would be double counting income if it also records revenue when Thomas declares a dividend. Thus, Samson Corporation should not record $2,500 (2,500 × $1) of dividend revenue from its holdings of Thomas Inc. If Samson were to record this revenue, it would fail to recognize the classic distinction between return *on* investment (Samson's share of Thomas's earnings) and return *of* investment (Samson's share of Thomas's dividend distribution to its shareholders). Since Samson Corporation should not record revenue from this dividend, its only recording option is to treat the dividend as a return *of* investment by decreasing its Investment in Thomas Stock account as shown here.

Transaction Analysis					Journal Entry		
	Fundamental Accounting Equation						
Account Titles	Assets	=	Liabilities	+ Owners' Equity	Account Titles	Debit	Credit
Dividend Receivable	2,500				Dividend Receivable	2,500	
Investment in Thomas Stock	(2,500)				Investment in Thomas Stock		2,500

At Receipt of Dividends When the dividends are received in cash, the following transaction would be recorded:

Transaction Analysis					Journal Entry		
	Fundamental Accounting Equation						
Account Titles	**Assets**	=	**Liabilities** +	**Owners' Equity**	**Account Titles**	**Debit**	**Credit**
Cash	2,500				Cash	2,500	
Dividend Receivable	(2,500)				Dividend Receivable		2,500

At Sale Before examining the transaction needed to record the sale of this investment, let's first examine the account titled Investment in Thomas Stock.

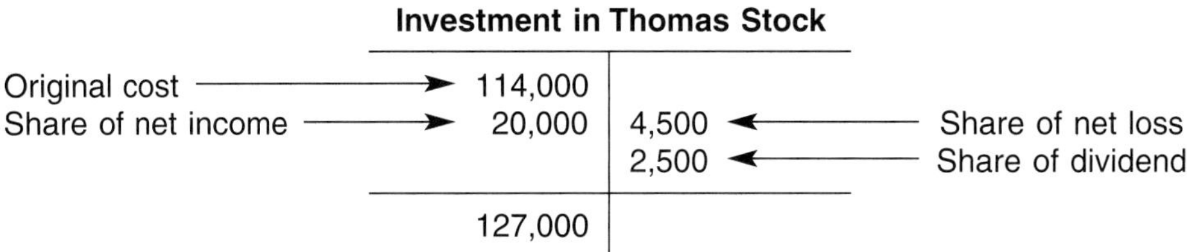

This T-account illustrates that the equity method investment account is composed of the original cost of the investment ($114,000) plus the investor's proportionate share of investee net income ($20,000), minus the investor's proportionate share of investee net loss ($4,500), minus the investor's proportionate share of investee dividends declared. Suppose that our 2,500 shares of Thomas stock were again sold at a price of $48 per share less brokerage commissions of $2,000, or $118,000 [(2,500 × $48) − $2,000]. The sale under the equity method would be recorded as shown here:

Transaction Analysis					Journal Entry		
	Fundamental Accounting Equation						
Account Titles	**Assets**	=	**Liabilities** +	**Owners' Equity**	**Account Titles**	**Debit**	**Credit**
Cash	118,000				Cash	118,000	
Investment in Thomas Stock	(127,000)				Loss on Sale of Investments	9,000	
Loss on Sale of Investments				(9,000)	Investment in Thomas Stock		127,000

As a peripheral activity that is expected to continue, the Loss on Sale account is generally reported in the income statement under Other Expenses and Losses.

Comparing and Contrasting the Cost/Fair Value and Equity Methods Although the cost/fair value method and the equity method are each used to account for equity investments, they differ in the following ways:

1. The cost/fair value method is used with minority, passive equity investments, whereas the equity method is used with minority, active investments.
2. The cost/fair value method assumes that the investor and investee are unrelated business entities, whereas the equity method assumes that the investor can significantly influence the investee's business.
3. The cost/fair value method does not allow an investor to record its proportionate interest in the investee's reported net income, but the equity method does allow this significant departure from standard revenue realization.
4. The cost/fair value method allows the investor to record dividend revenue for its portion of a dividend declared by the investee. In contrast, the equity method treats such a dividend not as revenue but as a decrease to the investment account.

Now that you are more familiar with the differences between the cost/fair value method and the equity method, you can use Performance Objective 48 to help you master their distinctions:

YOUR PERFORMANCE OBJECTIVE 48

Distinguish between the cost/fair value method and the equity method of accounting for minority investments in equity securities.

Real-World Complications of Accounting for Investment Securities

INSIGHT

As you now undoubtedly understand, accounting for debt and equity investments can be a relatively complicated process. In its attempt to provide more useful information, the accounting profession has been unable to find a single valuation method that can be applied to every security in a meaningful way. Instead, at least four relatively distinct valuation methods are currently being used:

1. The amortized cost method for held-to-maturity debt securities.
2. The cost/fair value method for debt and equity securities that are classified as either trading or available for sale.
3. The equity method for minority, active investments in stock.
4. The consolidation method for majority, active stock investments.

If you don't feel confident that you have captured all the fine points of accounting for debt and equity securities, you are not alone. Even accounting professionals have struggled over the years to keep up with the numerous pronouncements issued in this reporting area. Fortunately, the essential concepts relating to investments introduced in this chapter have been organized into a comprehensive figure to help you master them. Use Figure 12-10 to help you integrate all of the recording and reporting rules you have just studied.

FIGURE 12-10 Comprehensive summary of how to account for investments

	Minority, Passive Investments			Minority, Active Investments	Majority, Active Investments
Ownership level		Less than 20%		20%–50%	Greater than 50%
Ability to influence		Insignificant		Significant	Control
Investment categories	Trading	Available for sale	Held to maturity	N/A	N/A
Types of securities	Debt and equity	Debt and equity	Debt	Equity	Equity
Balance sheet classification	Current	Current/Noncurrent	Current/Noncurrent	Current/Noncurrent	Noncurrent
Balance sheet valuation	Fair value	Fair value	Amortized cost	Equity	Consolidation
Accounting requirements					
a. Measurement at acquisition	Cost	Cost	Cost	Cost	Beyond the scope of this textbook
b. Changes in fair value reported?	In income statement	In stockholders' equity in balance sheet	No	No	
c. Revenue reported for	Interest and dividends	Interest and dividends	Interest	Investor's share of of investee earnings or losses	

When these same accounting concepts are applied to a real-world setting, however, several additional complications arise. That is, the preceding textbook examples you studied did not include the following significant complications faced by most, if not all, actual companies:

1. They might own 1,000 or more securities rather than one.
2. They will have to monitor changes in fair value on some securities for several years rather than a single year.
3. They will have to obtain or perform the fair value measurements themselves rather than being simply told the fair value amount.
4. They will have to account for discounts and premiums on most bonds rather than simply recording the bond at its face value. (Chapter 13 will cover both discounts and premiums on bonds.)
5. They will probably transfer securities between portfolios that are accounted for differently such as trading and available-for-sale categories.

Although these issues are dealt with in a more advanced accounting course, let's examine the first issue more closely. The truth is that few, if any, companies operate in the single security world that you encountered. Instead, it is not unusual for medium- and large-size companies to hold thousands and even hundreds of thousands of individual securities. Although the concepts you just studied are applicable to these companies, it is necessary for their accounting staffs to organize securities into several groups that we'll refer to as *portfolios*. Consider Figure 12-11. Although it does not present the volume of securities held by most companies, it does provide a good example of how fair value is

FIGURE 12-11 How the accounting for debt and equity securities might be organized by portfolio for a company having ownership in several securities

Common Stock

Portfolio Designation	Company	Acquisition Cost	Fair Value 12/31/2003	Unrealized Gain (Loss)
Trading	Dell	$ 150,000	$ 130,000	$ (20,000)
	Coca-Cola	200,000	275,000	75,000
	IBM	170,000	185,000	15,000
	General Motors	220,000	255,000	35,000
		$ 740,000	$ 845,000	$ 105,000
Available for sale	Home Depot	$ 160,000	$ 133,000	$ (27,000)
	General Electric	315,000	305,000	(10,000)
		$ 475,000	$ 438,000	$ (37,000)

Bonds

Portfolio Designation	Company	Acquisition Cost	Fair Value 12/31/2003	Unrealized Gain (Loss)
Trading	Exxon	$1,000,000	$1,075,000	$ 75,000
	GMAC	3,000,000	3,200,000	200,000
		$4,000,000	$4,275,000	$ 275,000
Available for sale	Arizona Tax Free	4,000,000	4,250,000	250,000
	New York Municipals	2,000,000	1,780,000	(220,000)
		$6,000,000	$6,030,000	$ 30,000
Held to maturity	Ford	995,000	990,000	(5,000)
	Daimler/Chrysler	1,200,000	1,005,000	(195,000)
		$2,195,000	$1,995,000	$(200,000)

applied to distinct portfolios. Notice, for example, that our hypothetical company divides its securities into two main portfolios, common stock and bonds. Each of these portfolios is further broken down into smaller portfolios on the basis of whether they are trading, available for sale, or held to maturity. If you're interested in seeing if you can correctly apply the concepts you've studied so far, try working Exercise 12-19. It provides practice in determining the appropriate balance sheet and income statement presentations for the information provided by Figure 12-11.

The primary **insight** you should gain here is that no matter how difficult an accounting method introduced in this or any accounting textbook might appear at first glance, applying that same method to the real world is almost certain to present more of a challenge. So, if you think the concepts in this course are challenging, remember that it could be more challenging but also more stimulating to search for solutions in a real-world setting.

APPENDIX

12-1 Mastering Compound Interest Concepts

PERFORMANCE OBJECTIVES

In this appendix, you will learn the following new Performance Objectives:

POCI-1 **Explain** the concept of interest from the perspective of both a borrower and a lender.

POCI-2 **Define** and **distinguish** between simple and compound interest.

POCI-3 **Calculate** both simple and compound interest.

POCI-4 **Define** the terms *future value*, *compound interest*, *time line*, and *interest factor.*

POCI-5 **Distinguish** between the primary (fundamental equation of compound interest) and the secondary future value formulas.

POCI-6 **Apply** the three-step solution approach to solve a future value problem.

POCI-7 **Identify** the appropriate interest rate and number of periods you must use when interest is compounded more frequently than annually.

POCI-8 **Distinguish** between the future value interest concept and the present value interest concept.

POCI-9 **Define** the terms *present value*, *discount rate*, and *discounting.*

POCI-10 **Apply** the three-step solution approach to solve a present value problem.

POCI-11 **Define** the terms *annuity, rent annuity in arrears,* and *annuity in advance.*

POCI-12 **Distinguish** between:

a. An annuity problem and a non-annuity problem.
b. An annuity in arrears and an annuity in advance.
c. A future value of an annuity and a present value of an annuity.
d. The future value of annuity table and the present value of annuity table.

POCI-13 **Determine** which annuity table (future value or present value) is appropriate in a given situation.

POCI-14 **Apply** the three-step solution approach to solve an annuity problem.

Why Study Compound Interest?

Depending on who's talking about it, the compound interest concept is also referred to as *present value analysis*, the *time value of money*, or the *mathematics of finance*. Three of the most compelling reasons to master this concept are:

1. An understanding of the theory and use of compound interest is a necessity in the modern business world. This concept is applied in financial accounting measurement and reporting for such transactions as notes, leases, bonds, and pensions. Also it is frequently used in the managerial decision-making process particularly when business managers evaluate various types of investment alternatives.
2. An understanding of compound interest will be invaluable to you in your personal investment planning. For example, you will be able to determine how much money you must save to accumulate a desired future amount, such as a down payment for a home, and how interest accumulates and principal is reduced in installment loan transactions, such as monthly automobile or mortgage payments.
3. You will encounter the concept of compound interest in many accounting and finance courses, such as introductory financial accounting, managerial accounting, and corporate finance. If you are an accounting major, you can expect compound interest to be covered, to some degree, in almost every accounting course, particularly the intermediate series and managerial/cost courses. For example, capital budgeting is a topic based on compound interest and is covered in both finance and managerial/cost accounting courses at most universities.

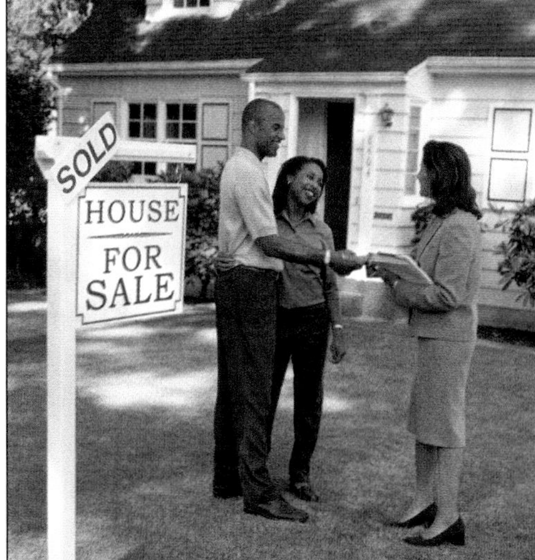

Understanding the concept of compound interest will make you a better informed home buyer.

For all these reasons, you will benefit from learning about and mastering the compound interest concept. Before you can understand the many accounting applications of the compound interest concept, however, you must first understand the basic concepts of interest, future value, and present value. We'll look at each of these next.

The Concept of Interest

Although you dealt with the calculation of interest earlier in this textbook, there is some new information you must learn before you undertake your study of future value and present value. To master the concept of interest, you'll use the first of three performance objectives:

PERFORMANCE OBJECTIVE CI-1
Explain the concept of interest from the perspective of both a borrower and a lender.

Interest represents the time cost of money to a borrower. In other words, if you borrow money for a specific period of time, the cost of using that money is known as interest. Interest also represents the time value of money to a lender. If you lend money for a specific period of time, the value of using that money is known as interest. Thus, every interest transaction has financial effects on both a borrower and a lender.

The fact that there are two types of interest necessitates a second performance objective:

PERFORMANCE OBJECTIVE CI-2
Define and **distinguish** between simple and compound interest.

You may calculate two types of interest—simple and compound. To most efficiently learn how they differ, we'll first focus on Performance Objective CI-3 to learn how they are calculated.

PERFORMANCE OBJECTIVE CI-3
Calculate both simple and compound interest.

To calculate either simple or compound interest, you must use the quantities known as principal and interest rate. **Principal** is the amount of money you borrow or invest and an **interest rate** is a percentage relationship between the amount you borrow and the amount of interest you incur. An interest rate is always expressed on an annual basis. In Transaction F, for example, \$5,000 was the principal and 8% was the interest rate.

Simple Interest

Simple interest is interest that is calculated by using the original principal. The formula for calculating simple interest is:

$$\text{Principal} \times \text{Interest Rate} \times (\text{Investment Period in Days}/360)$$

That is, you calculate simple interest by multiplying the original principal by the interest rate and by the fraction of the time period for which money is borrowed. To simplify calculations, use 360 days to represent one year. When symbols are substituted for these words, the formula for calculating simple interest becomes:

$$I = P \times i \times t$$

where I = Interest, P = Principal, i = Interest Rate, and t = Time (fraction).

Recall that you used this formula in Chapter 6 when you calculated the interest in Transaction K_2 as shown below:

$$\begin{aligned} I &= P \times i \times t \\ &= \$5{,}000 \times .08 \times (180/360) \\ &= \$200 \end{aligned}$$

Although the actual period of time between July 1 and December 31 is 184 days, we'll use 180 days (6 months @ 30 days per month) for simplicity.

Here is some additional practice in calculating simple interest:

Example 1 \$1,000 (P) is invested at 6% per year (i) for a period of four years (t). Calculate the amount of simple interest you earn in Year 1.

Answer:
$$\begin{aligned} I &= P \times i \times t \\ &= \$1{,}000 \times .06 \times (360/360) \\ &= \$60 \end{aligned}$$

Example 2 Calculate the amount of interest you earn in Year 3 by investing \$1,000 at 6% per year.

Answer:
$$\begin{aligned} I &= P \times i \times t \\ &= \$1{,}000 \times .06 \times (360/360) \\ &= \$60 \end{aligned}$$

To calculate interest in both Examples 1 and 2, you used the formula: $I = P \times i \times t$. Next, you substituted the known facts in the formula as follows: $I = \$1{,}000 \times .06 \times 360/360$. The \$60 answer calculated in both Examples 1 and 2 represents the amount of interest earned on the investment for one year and illustrates an important characteristic of simple interest—amounts of simple interest calculated for equal but distinct periods of time (e.g., Year 1 versus Year 3) are identical. In Examples 1 and 2, a full year of simple interest (\$60) is earned on the investment. In our earlier example of Transaction K_2, however, less than a full year of interest was incurred.

An important characteristic of simple interest is that it is calculated on the basis of the original principal. See if you can complete the table below to calculate simple interest for Example 1.

Year	Principal	Interest Rate	Time	Simple Interest
1	$1,000	.06	360/360	___
2	$1,000	.06	______	___
3	$1,000	___	______	___
4	______	___	______	___

Answer: Year	Principal	Interest Rate	Time	Simple Interest
1	$1,000	.06	360/360	$60
2	$1,000	.06	1	$60
3	$1,000	.06	1	$60
4	$1,000	.06	1	$60

Compound Interest

Unlike simple interest, **compound interest** is calculated by using the sum of the principal and accumulated interest. The formula for calculating compound interest is:

(Principal + Accumulated Interest of Past Periods) × Interest Rate × (Investment Period in Days/360)

or

$$I = (P + I) \times i \times t$$

As you can see, the formula for compound interest differs from that of simple interest in only one respect. Namely, the amount of past accumulated interest is added to the original principal.

If you want to calculate the amount of compound interest for one year, you may dispense with the time portion of the compound interest formula just introduced since $t = 1$. For example, a single year of compound interest is calculated by multiplying the sum of the original principal and any past accumulated interest by the interest rate. This idea is expressed in symbols in the formula below:

$$\text{CI} = (P + I) \times i$$

Past accumulated interest means interest that is calculated but not withdrawn. When such interest is added to principal and used in a calculation of interest, it is said to be *compounded*, or interest on interest. Let's now apply this formula to the data from Example 1 assuming we want to calculate compound rather than simple interest:

Example 1 Revisited If $1,000 ($P$) is invested at 6% per year (i) for a period of four years (t), calculate the amount of compound interest you earn in Year 1.

To calculate the first-year compound interest, the formula would appear as follows:

$I_1 = (P + I_0) \times i = (\$1{,}000 + \mathbf{\$0}).06 = \mathbf{\$60}$

where I_1 = Interest accumulated for the first year (year 1)

I_0 = Interest accumulated for the previous year (year 0)

Notice that since no interest accumulates before the first year of the investment, I_0 by definition is zero. Although it is true that the amount ($60) of simple and compound interest are identical in the first year, Example 3 illustrates that simple and compound interest will not be identical in all other years:

Example 3 Calculate the compound interest for the second year using the formula shown below:

$I_2 = \$\_\_\_\_\_\_ = (P + I_1) \times i$

Answer:

$I_2 = (P + I_1) \times i$

$= (\$1{,}000 + \$60).06$

$= (\$1{,}060).06$

$= \$63.60$

When you compare this answer to that for Example 1 and Example 2, you can see that simple interest has a *smaller* time value of money than compound interest.

To solidify your understanding, complete the table below by calculating compound interest for Example 1.

Year	Total Past Principal + Interest	Interest Rate	Compound Interest
1	($1,000 + $0)	.06	$60.00
2	($1,000 + $60)	.06	$63.60
3	($1,000 + $____)	__	____
4	(________)	__	____

Answer:

Year	Total Past Principal + Interest	Interest Rate	Compound Interest
3	($1,000 + $123.60)	.06	$67.42
4	($1,000 + $191.02)	.06	$71.46

Now that you have calculated both simple and compound interest, the following definitions and distinction between simple and compound interest will be much more meaningful. Interest that is calculated on the basis of the original principal is called *simple* interest, whereas interest that is calculated on the basis of the original principal plus the accumulated interest of past periods is called *compound*.

Review of the Concept of Interest

Before you begin your study of the future value concept, study the following performance objectives introduced earlier to determine if you have absorbed the information found in the related summary.

Performance Objective CI-1 **Explain** the concept of interest from the perspective of both a borrower and a lender.

Concept of Interest Interest is a charge for the use of money. It is the time cost of money to a borrower and the time value of money to a lender.

Performance Objective CI-2 **Define** and **distinguish** between simple and compound interest.

Simple versus Compound Interest Simple interest is based on the original principal. Compound interest, however, is based upon the original principal plus the accumulated interest of past periods.

Performance Objective CI-3 **Calculate** both simple and compound interest.

Calculation of Interest

a. **Simple interest** is calculated by multiplying the original principal by the interest rate and by the fraction of the time period for which the money is borrowed.
b. **Compound interest** is calculated by multiplying the sum of the principal and accumulated interest of past periods by the interest rate and by the fraction of the time period for which the money is borrowed.

Now that you fully understand the difference between simple and compound interest, all future discussions will be based on the concept of compound interest.

The Future Value Concept

You will frequently use the terms *future value*, *compound interest*, and *time line* as you study the compound interest concept. The **future value** is the amount the principal becomes when left to accumulate at compound interest for a given period of time. Recall the example in which \$1,000 was invested for four years at an interest rate of 6%. At the end of one year, \$1,060 is the future value of the \$1,000 principal. Thus, a future value amount is *greater* than a principal amount. In fact, **compound interest** is the difference by which the future value amount exceeds the principal or original amount invested. Thus, at the end of the first year, the amount of compound interest for our continuing example is \$60 (\$1,060 − \$1,000).

A **time line** is a visual analysis of a compound interest problem that places the principal and future value in their proper time perspective and identifies the interest rate and number of periods needed for a correct solution. Here is a time line for our continuing example:

Amounts	\$1,000			\$1,060
Time	Now	$i = 6\%$	$t = 1$	1 year later

You might be tempted not to use a time line now because the compound interest problems you've seen so far are quite easy. Avoid this temptation. A time line is an essential analytical tool. Get into the habit of using this tool now, and you will be successful in solving more challenging problems.

The Fundamental Equation of Compound Interest

Once you have prepared your visual analysis of a compound interest problem with a time line, you can use the following specialized formula to solve the future value problem:

$$FV = P + CI$$

where FV = Future Value, P = Principal, and CI = Compound Interest.

For example, in our continuing example, FV equals \$1,060, P equals \$1,000, and CI equals \$60.

Since this formula tells you that future value is calculated by adding the principal to the compound interest, and $CI_1 = P(i)$ where CI_1 = compound interest for Year 1, you should be able to see by substituting terms that $FV = P + P(i)$. If you factor the common term P from both expressions on the right side of this formula, the expression is now transformed into a formula that can be used for all future value problems involving one year.

$$FV = P(1 + i)$$

Inserting the data from our continuing example into this formula gives us:

$$\begin{aligned} FV &= P + P(i) \\ &= \$1{,}000 + \$1{,}000(.06) \\ \text{and } FV &= P(1 + i) \\ &= \$1{,}000(1 + .06) \\ &= \$1{,}000(1.06) \\ &= \$1{,}060. \text{ Thus, the future value is } \$1{,}060. \end{aligned}$$

Here is another problem for your practice.

Example 4 If \$2,000 is invested at 10% compound interest for one year, what is the future value?
Hint: Use the following steps to solve this problem:

Step 1 Draw a time line that identifies known and unknown quantities from your analysis of the problem.

In this step you identify the known and unknown quantities *as you draw the time line*. That is, as you read a problem you mentally identify each quantity and immediately place it on a time line. Be sure to use Step 1 to solve all compound interest problems.

Amounts	\$2,000		?
Time	Now	i = 10%	t = 1

As shown on the time line, the known quantities are P, i, and t (the \$2,000 principal, 10% interest rate, and the time period of one year). The unknown quantity is the future value.

Step 2 Solve for the unknown quantity using $FV = P(1 + i)$.

$$FV = \$2{,}000(1 + .10) = \$2{,}000(1.10) = \$2{,}200$$

Now that you know how to calculate the future value for the first year of an investment, you must learn how to calculate future value for periods greater than one year. For our continuing illustration in which $1,000 is invested at 6% for four years, the future value one year from today (the present) will be $1,060. If you wish to determine the future value of the $1,000 investment two years from now, however, you must calculate the amount of interest earned during the second year using the formula for compound interest. In this case, the formula and calculations are:

$$\begin{aligned} CI_2 &= (\text{Principal} + \text{Year 1 Compound Interest}) \times \text{Interest Rate} \\ &= (P + CI_1) \times i = (\$1{,}000 + \$60) \times .06 = \$1{,}060 \times .06 \\ &= \$63.60 \end{aligned}$$

You now have enough information to calculate the future value of a $1,000 investment two years from now:

Principal (P)	$1,000.00	(P)
1st year interest	60.00	$CI_1 = P(i)$
2nd year interest	63.60	$CI_2 = (P + CI_1)i$
Future value	$1,123.60	

Can you see how the future value of $1,123.60 is the result of adding two years of interest to the principal? Likewise, if you add the corresponding symbols to the right of the preceding calculation, you will derive the following algebraic expression or formula:

$$FV_2 = P + P(i) + (P + CI_1)i$$

An equivalent[1] but more convenient form of the preceding formula is:

$$FV_2 = P(1 + i)^2$$

You can quickly verify that these two formulas are equivalent by completing the following calculation:

$$\begin{aligned} FV_2 &= P(1 + i)^2 = \$1{,}000(1 + .06)^2 = \$1{,}000(1.06)^2 = \$1{,}000(1.1236) \\ &= \$1{,}123.60 \end{aligned}$$

Generalizing from 2 to n periods, the following formula will hereafter be referred to as the **fundamental equation of compound interest**:

$$FV_n = P(1 + i)^n$$

Note that in this equation, n replaces t and represents the number of periods, while i continues to represent the interest rate.

Interest Factors and the Future Value of $1 Table

The quantity $(1 + i)^n$ in the equation $FV_n = P(1 + i)^n$ is known as an **interest factor (IF)**. For example, if you want to calculate the future value of $1,000 invested at 6% for one year, your interest factor would be $(1 + .06)^1$, or 1.06. Likewise, if you want

[1] Understanding the proof below is helpful but not essential to your mastery of this material.

$FV_2 = P + P(i) + (P + CI_1)i$	
$= P + Pi + Pi + CI_1 i$	Multiplying through by i
$= P + Pi + Pi + Pii$	$CI_1 = Pi$
$= P + Pi + Pi + Pi^2$	$ii^1 = i^2$
$= P(1 + i + i + i^2)$	Factoring P
$= P(1 + 2i + i^2)$	Arranging terms
$= P(1 + i)^2$	Factoring $(1 + 2i + i^2)$

to calculate the future value of $1,000 invested at 6% for two years, your interest factor is $(1 + .06)^2$, or 1.1236, the same number appearing in the last solution of the preceding section.

Example 5 Calculate the future value of $1,000 invested at 6% at the end of three years.
Hint: Use the same two-step approach as we did in Example 4.

Step 1 Draw a time line that identifies known and unknown quantities from your analysis of the problem.

Amounts	$1,000		?
Time	Now	$i = 6\%$	$n = 3$

The known quantities are P, i, and n (the $1,000 principal, 6% interest rate, and the time period of three years). The unknown quantity is the future value.

Step 2 Solve for the unknown quantity using $FV_n = P(1 + i)^n$.

$$FV_3 = \$1{,}000(1 + .06)^3 = \$1{,}000(1.06)^3 = \$1{,}000(1.19102) = \$1{,}191.02$$

Although the fundamental equation of compound interest allows you to determine the future value of a principal invested or loaned at compound interest, the calculations are relatively time consuming when $n > 1$. In Step 2 above, for example, several calculations were needed to derive the interest factor of 1.19102. Fortunately, interest tables reduce the time and effort required by these calculations. **Table 1: Future Value of $1** is derived from the fundamental equation of compound interest. Each numerical entry in this table is an interest factor (IF) and represents a unique combination of the two variables interest rate (i) and number of time periods (n). Here is an excerpt from Table 1. You will find the complete Table 1 on page 673.

TABLE 1 Future Value of $1

Primary formula: $FV_n = P(1 + i)^n$
Secondary formula: $FV_n = P(FVIF)$

Periods	Interest Rates = i						
= n	3%	4%	5%	6%	8%	10%	12%
1	1.03000	1.04000	1.05000	1.06000	1.08000	1.10000	1.12000
2	1.06090	1.08160	1.10250	1.12360	1.16640	1.21000	1.25440
3	1.09273	1.12486	1.15763	1.19102	1.25971	1.33100	1.40493
4	1.12551	1.16986	1.21551	1.26248	1.36049	1.46410	1.57352
5	1.15927	1.21655	1.27628	1.33823	1.46933	1.61051	1.76234
6	1.19405	1.26532	1.34010	1.41852	1.58687	1.77156	1.97382
7	1.22987	1.31593	1.40710	1.50363	1.71382	1.94872	2.21068
8	1.26677	1.36857	1.47746	1.59385	1.85093	2.14359	2.47596
9	1.30477	1.42331	1.55133	1.68948	1.99900	2.35795	2.77308
10	1.34392	1.48024	1.62889	1.79085	2.15892	2.59374	3.10585

Now that you know about the interest factor, Performance Objective CI-4 is designed to help you master the four new terms related to the future value concept.

PERFORMANCE OBJECTIVE CI-4
Define the terms *future value, compound interest, time line,* and *interest factor.*

You have just learned that the quantity $(1 + i)^n$ in the equation underlying Table 1 is called an interest factor (IF). You have actually calculated three interest factors included in Table 1—1.06, 1.1236, and 1.19102. These interest factors are associated with the period of time (n) of one year, two years, and three years respectively. Notice that these same interest factors are found under the 6% interest rate (i) column in Table 1.

To use Table 1 and others like it, select a row and a column corresponding respectively to the number of periods and the interest rate found in a problem. For example, suppose that you wanted to know the future value of $1 at the end of three years at 4% compound interest. You'd find the intersection of the 3 period row and the 4% column to be the number 1.12486 as shown below.

	Interest Rates = i		
Periods = n	3%	4%	5%
1	1.03000	1.04000	1.05000
2	1.06090	1.08160	1.10250
3	1.09273	**1.12486**	1.15763

Since $FV_n = P(1 + i)^n = \$1(1.12486)$, a future value of $1.12486 is the correct answer.

Distinguishing between Primary and Secondary Formulas

You have now used the fundamental equation of compound interest, or **primary formula**—$FV_n = P(1 + i)^n$ — to solve future value problems. Let's now consider an alternative form of this future value equation called a **secondary formula**. Since the primary formula's future value interest factor, or FVIF, equals $(1 + i)^n$, it may be validly substituted into the first, or primary, formula to derive the following secondary formula:

$$FV_n = P(FVIF)$$

Recall that in Example 5 the primary formula was used to determine that the future value amounted to $1,191.02. Let's now verify that the answer to that problem is the same when we use the secondary formula and Table 1. For three periods and an interest rate of 6%, the *FVIF* found in Table 1 equals 1.19102. Since the principal is $1,000 and the future value is unknown, the solution using the secondary formula and Table 1 is as follows:

$$FV_n = P(FVIF) = \$1{,}000(1.19102) = \$1{,}191.02$$

Note that both the primary and secondary future value formulas are shown in Table 1. Use the primary formula when you do not have an interest table available. Use the secondary formula when an interest table such as Table 1 is available.

Performance Objective CI-5 will help you grasp the nature of each of these formulas and when to use them:

PERFORMANCE OBJECTIVE CI-5

Distinguish between the primary (fundamental equation of compound interest) and the secondary future value formulas.

Using a Three-Step Solution Approach

You'll now see how the two-step approach used earlier is converted to a three-step approach to include the use of the Future Value of $1 Table.

Example 6 If you invest $2,000 at 10% compound interest for 10 years, what will be the amount of the future value?

Step 1 Draw a time line that identifies known and unknown quantities from your analysis of the problem.

Amounts	$2,000		?
Time	Now	$i = 10\%$	$n = 10$

The known quantities are P, i, and n (the $2,000 principal, 10% interest rate, and the 10-year period). The unknown quantity is the future value.

Step 2 Select the appropriate interest factor from the Future Value of $1 Table.

$$FVIF = 2.59374\ (i = 10\%,\ n = 10)$$

Step 3 Solve for the unknown quantity using the secondary future value formula:

$$FV_n = P(FVIF)$$

$$FV_{10} = \$2{,}000(2.59374) = \$5{,}187.48$$

Despite the convenience of the secondary future value formula, do not forget how to use the primary future value formula because you won't always have access to an interest table. For example, without access to Table 1 in the preceding example, Step 2 can be restated as follows:

Step 2 Solve for the unknown quantity using the primary future value formula:

$$\begin{aligned} FV_n &= P(1 + i)^n \\ &= \$2{,}000(1+.10)^{10} \\ &= \$2{,}000(1.1)^{10} \\ &= \$2{,}000(2.59374) \\ &= \$5{,}187.48 \end{aligned}$$

Performance Objective CI-6 will help you master this three-step solution approach.

PERFORMANCE OBJECTIVE CI-6
Apply the three-step solution approach to solve a future value problem.

Solving for Unknown Quantities Other than Future Value

You've learned that every future value problem includes the following quantities: principal, number of periods, interest rate, and future value. This means that as long as three of these quantities are given (known) in the problem, you can solve for the fourth unknown quantity. For example, future value was the unknown quantity in Examples 4 through 6. If one of the three known quantities is future value, however, you can algebraically manipulate the secondary future value formula $FV_n = P(FVIF)$ and still solve for the unknown. Consider Example 7.

Example 7 What amount must be invested now at 10% compound interest to grow to $379,750 at the end of 14 years?

Step 1 Draw a time line that identifies known and unknown quantities from your analysis of the problem.

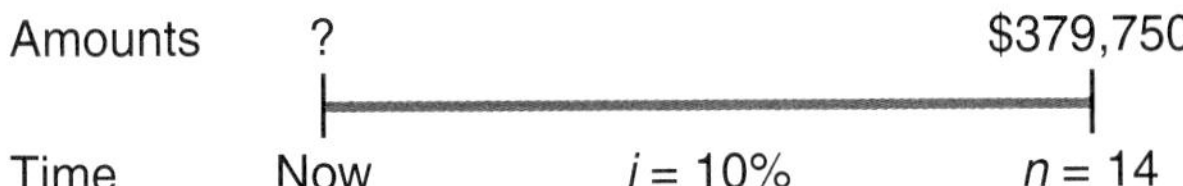

The known quantities are the 10% interest rate, the $379,750 future value, and the 14-year time period. Since the principal is the amount invested now, it should be clear that, in this example, the principal is an unknown quantity.

Step 2 Select the appropriate interest factor from the Future Value of $1 Table at the end of this chapter.

$$FVIF = 3.79750\ (i = 10\%,\ n = 14)$$

Step 3 Solve for the unknown quantity using the secondary future value formula: $FV_n = P(FVIF)$.

Since the only unknown quantity is the principal, you must divide both sides of the equation by *FVIF* to isolate *P*. After performing this operation, the resulting equation is $P = FV_n/FVIF$. You may now solve by substituting the relevant amounts in the equation: $P = FV_n/FVIF = \$379{,}750/3.79750 = \$100{,}000$. Thus, when you invest $100,000 at 10% compound interest, it grows to $379,750 at the end of 14 years.

Example 8 If you have $500 to invest and are able to earn 7% compound interest, how long must you wait until your investment grows to $750? The following column from a Future Value of $1 Table is provided to help you solve this problem:

Periods	Interest Rate 7%
1	1.07000
2	1.14490
3	1.22504
4	1.31080
5	1.40255
6	1.50073
7	1.60578
8	1.71819
9	1.83846
10	1.96715
11	2.10485
12	2.25219

Step 1 Draw a time line that identifies known and unknown quantities from your analysis of the problem.

Amounts $500 $750

Time Now $i = 7\%$ $n = ?$

The known quantities are the $500 principal, the 7% interest rate, and the $750 future value. The unknown quantity is *n* (the number of periods).

In Example 8, you cannot select an interest factor from Table 1 (Step 2) because only one of the two quantities required to determine the future value interest factor

(*FVIF*) is given. Since the *FVIF* is a function of both i and n, and n is unknown, the *FVIF* is also unknown.

Step 2 Solve for the unknown quantity using the secondary future value formula: $FV_n = P(FVIF)$.

Since FVIF is unknown, you must divide both sides of the equation above by P ($FV_n/P = P(FVIF)/P$) to isolate *FVIF*. After performing this operation, you have:

$$FVIF = FV_n/P = \$750/\$500 = 1.50000$$

You can solve Example 8 by scanning down the 7% column for a row corresponding to an interest factor of approximately 1.50000. Since the sixth row is chosen, you can now conclude that \$500 invested at 7% will grow to \$750 in six years.

Solving for Greater than Annual Compounding

Although an interest rate is generally expressed on an annual basis, annual compounding is often not a realistic assumption. That is, interest may be calculated (compounded) several times within a year including quarterly, monthly, and even daily. Thus, we now need to extend our analysis to more frequent than annual compounding. When interest is compounded more frequently than on an annual basis, you must modify both the interest rate and the number of periods you use with a standard interest table like that of Table 1. This modification is necessary because standard interest tables are designed with an assumption of annual compounding. As a result, the next two paragraphs describe how to modify an annual interest rate and how to modify the number of periods, respectively.

When interest is compounded semiannually (twice during the year), *two* six-month interest periods exist within the year. When interest is compounded quarterly, *four* three-month interest periods exist within the year. To generalize, when interest is expressed as an annual rate but the compounding occurs more frequently than once a year (that is, at least twice during the year), you must determine the interest rate for the period (i) that is less than a year. To do so, you must divide the annual interest rate by the number of interest periods within the year. For example, "interest at 8% compounded quarterly" indicates a 2% (8%/4) interest rate for each of four three-month (quarterly) interest periods a year.

When compounding occurs more frequently than once a year, simply modifying the interest rate (i) is not enough. You must also modify the total number of periods (n). To determine the number of periods (n), you must multiply the number of years in the problem by the number of interest periods within the year. For example, "interest at 10% compounded annually for 10 years" provides a 10% interest rate for each of 10 (1 × 10) periods while "interest at 10% compounded semiannually for 10 years" provides a 5% interest rate for each of 20 (2 × 10) periods. This idea is illustrated below by identifying the interest rate per period and the number of periods in each of the following cases:

a. 6% per year, 5 years, compounded semiannually
   Rate per period = 3%; periods = 10 (2 × 5)
b. 12% per year, 5 years, compounded quarterly
   Rate per period = 3%; periods = 20 (4 × 5)
c. 24% per year, 2.5 years, compounded monthly
   Rate per period = 2%; periods = 30 (12 × 2.5)

Performance Objective CI-7 will help you master this calculation.

PERFORMANCE OBJECTIVE CI-7

Identify the appropriate interest rate and number of periods you must use when interest is compounded more frequently than annually.

Review of the Future Value Concept

Before you begin your study of the present value concept, study the following summary of the performance objectives introduced thus far to determine if you have mastered the future value concept:

Performance Objective CI-4 **Define** the terms *future value*, *compound interest*, *time line*, and *interest factor*.

Future Value Future value is the amount the principal becomes when left to accumulate at compound interest for a given period of time.

Compound Interest Compound interest is the difference between the original amount invested (that is, principal) and the future value amount.

Time Line A time line is a picture of a compound interest problem that places the principal and future value in their proper time perspective and identifies the interest rate and number of periods needed for a correct solution.

Interest Factor An interest factor is a number found in an interest table that represents a unique combination of the variables interest rate (i) and number of time periods (n). It is the quantity $(1 + i)^n$ in the formula $FV_n = P(1 + i)^n$.

Performance Objective CI-5 **Distinguish** between the primary (fundamental equation of compound interest) and the secondary future value formulas.

Primary versus Secondary Future Value Formula The primary equation $FV_n = P(1 + i)^n$ is used when no interest table is available while the secondary equation $FV_n = P(FVIF)$ is used when an interest table is available.

Performance Objective CI-6 **Apply** the following three-step solution approach to solve a future value problem:

Future Value Solution Method

a. **Draw** a time line that identifies known and unknown quantities from your analysis of the problem.
b. **Select** the appropriate interest factor from the Future Value of $1 Table using information about the interest rate and number of periods found in the time line.
c. **Solve** the future value problem for the unknown quantity by using the secondary future value formula.

Performance Objective CI-7 **Identify** the appropriate interest rate and number of periods you must use when interest is compounded more frequently than annually.

Interest Rate You must divide the annual interest rate by the number of interest periods within the year.

Number of Periods You must multiply the number of years in the problem by the number of interest periods within the year.

The Present Value Concept

The **present value** is the amount that when left to accumulate at compound interest will grow to become the future value. The term present value is equivalent to what was called the principal in earlier future value problems. Earlier, for example, \$1,060 was referred to as the future value (one year later) of a \$1,000 principal earning 6% interest. In this example, the present value is \$1,000. In general, the amount of principal, or present value, is *less* than the amount of the future value. In future value problems, you are usually given the principal or present value, the interest rate, and the number of periods (that is, known quantities), and you are asked to calculate the amount of future value (unknown quantity). In contrast, present value problems usually provide all quantities except the present value. That is, present value analysis requires that you calculate how much (that is, principal or present value) must be invested today to attain a specified future value at the end of n periods. To summarize, when you solve a future value problem, you are usually given the present value and asked to calculate an equivalent *later value*. When you solve a present value problem, however, you are usually given the future value and asked to calculate an equivalent *earlier value*.

A moment's reflection will indicate that when you calculate the future value, you *add* interest to the principal or present value. In contrast, when you calculate the present value, you *subtract* interest from the future value. Observe the following relationship between present and future values in the following time line:

	Present value = \$1,000		\$1,060
Time	Now	i = 6%	n = 1

Here, interest is being compounded annually at 6% per year.

Recall that the primary formula used to solve a future value problem for n periods is:

$$FV = P(1 + i)^n$$

Since present value is equivalent to principal, you may replace the symbol P in the formula above with the symbol PV. Since the preceding time line included both a future value (\$1,060) and a present value (\$1,000), it follows that both quantities can be expressed in a single formula. That is, the present value formula can be derived from the future value formula. To do so, you must isolate the quantity PV by dividing both sides of the future value equation $FV_n = PV(1 + i)^n$ by the quantity $(1 + i)^n$. The result is shown below:

$$FV/(1 + i)^n = PV(1 + i)^n/(1 + i)^n$$

To summarize, the general formula for present value is:

$$PV = FV_n/(1 + i)^n \quad \text{or} \quad PV = FV_n[1/(1 + i)^n]$$

Interest Factors and the Present Value of \$1 Table

When you now compare the future and present value interest factors below, you will see an interesting relationship:

$$\text{Future value interest factor: } (1 + i)^n$$

$$\text{Present value interest factor: } 1/(1+i)^n$$

Note that these two interest factors have an inverse[2] relationship. That is, each is the reciprocal of the other.

$$1/(1+ i)^n \times (1 + i)^n = 1$$

[2] Every real number a, except 0, has an inverse such that $a(a - 1) = 1$. The number $a - 1$ is equal to $1/a$ and is called the *multiplicative inverse (reciprocal) of a*.

The fact that these two interest factors are inverses of one another reinforces the concept that present value is derived directly from future value. The following example illustrates this point.

Example 9 Calculate the present value of \$1,060 received or paid one year from today at 6% compounded annually.

To solve this problem, use the following two-step approach:

Step 1 Draw a time line that identifies known and unknown quantities from your analysis of the problem.

Amounts	?		\$1,060
Time	Now	$i = 6\%$	$n = 1$

The known quantities are *FV*, *i*, and *n* (the \$1,060 future value, 6% interest rate, and the time period of one year). The unknown quantity is the present value.

Step 2 Solve for the unknown quantity using the formula below:

$$PV = FV_n[1/(1 + i)^n]$$

$$PV = FV_1[1/(1 + i)^1] = \$1{,}060[(1/1.06)^1] \quad \text{Since } 1/1.06 = .943396226$$

$$PV = \$1{,}060(.943396226) = \$1{,}000$$

For $n > 1$, the formula $PV = FV_n[1/(1 + i)^n]$ involves time-consuming calculations. You can avoid these present value calculations, however, by using the following excerpt from Table 2: **Present Value of \$1**. This table of interest factors shows what \$1 due in some future period is worth today or now. You can find the complete table on page 674.

TABLE 2

Present Value of \$1

Primary formula: $PV = FV_n[1/(1 + i)^n]$
Secondary formula: $PV = FV_n(PVIF)$

	Interest Rates = *i*						
Periods = *n*	**3%**	**4%**	**5%**	**6%**	**8%**	**10%**	**12%**
1	.97087	.96154	.95238	.94340	.92593	.90909	.89286
2	.94260	.92456	.90703	.89000	.85734	.82645	.79719
3	.91514	.88900	.86384	.83962	.79383	.75131	.71178
4	.88849	.85480	.82270	.79209	.73503	.68301	.63552
5	.86261	.82193	.78353	.74726	.68058	.62092	.56743
6	.83748	.79031	.74622	.70496	.63017	.56447	.50663
7	.81309	.75992	.71068	.66506	.58349	.51316	.45235
8	.78941	.73069	.67684	.62741	.54027	.46651	.40388
9	.76642	.70259	.64461	.59190	.50025	.42410	.36061
10	.74409	.67556	.61391	.55839	.46319	.38554	.32197

As you learned before, each of the numbers in this table is called an interest factor and represents a unique combination of interest rate (i) and number of periods (n). Since the present value interest factor ($PVIF$) equals the expression $[1/(1 + i)^n]$, you may substitute it into the present value interest formula: $PV = FV_n[1/(1 + i)^n]$. That is:

$$PV = FV_n(PVIF)$$

Notice that $PV = FV_n[1/(1 + i)^n]$ represents the primary present value formula and $PV = FV_n(PVIF)$ represents the secondary present value formula.

You have now been introduced to both the future value concept and the present value concept. Because these differences are important to your overall understanding of compound interest, use Performance Objective CI-8 to master this material.

PERFORMANCE OBJECTIVE CI-8

Distinguish between the future value interest concept and the present value interest concept.

One way you can apply this performance objective is to remember that when you calculate the future value, you add interest to the principal or present value. In contrast, when you calculate the present value, you subtract interest from the future value. Also, recognize that there are now two distinct interest factors. The future value interest factors (FVIF) found in Table 1 are all greater than 1.0 because their function is to transform a smaller, earlier value (principal or present value) into a larger, later value. In contrast, the present value interest factors (PVIF) found in Table 2 are all less than 1.0 because their function is to transform a greater, later value (future value) into a smaller, earlier value.

When working with present value problems, you can use the term **discount rate** to describe the interest rate used and the term **discounting** to describe the process of transforming a future value into a present value by using compound interest. For example, the present value of $1,060 received one year from today and discounted at 6% compound interest is $1,000. The process of discounting is equivalent to subtracting interest. Use Performance Objective CI-9 to master the new terms introduced in conjunction with the present value concept.

PERFORMANCE OBJECTIVE CI-9

Define the terms *present value, discount rate* and *discounting.*

Using a Three-Step Solution Approach

You'll now see how the two-step approach used earlier is converted to a three-step approach to include the use of the Present Value of $1 Table.

Example 10 Calculate the present value of $500 due in five years and discounted at 12% compounded quarterly.

Step 1 Draw a time line that identifies known and unknown quantities from your analysis of the problem.

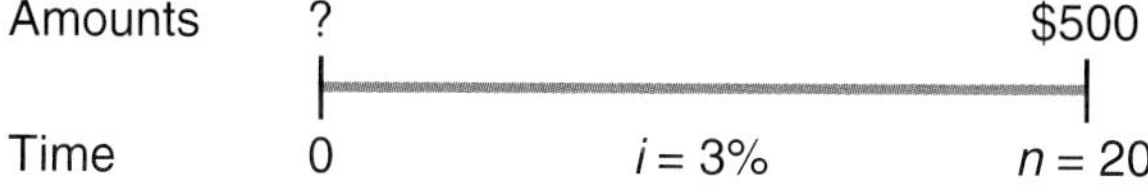

The known quantities are the $500 future value, the 20 three-month periods (5 years × 4 periods per year), and the 3% interest rate per period (12%/4). The unknown quantity is the present value.

Note: Replace the word *now* with the equivalent time of zero for all subsequent time lines you construct.

Step 2 Select the appropriate interest factor from the Present Value of $1 Table on page 674.

$$PVIF = .55368\ (i = 3\%,\ n = 20)$$

Step 3 Solve for the unknown quantity using the secondary present value formula: $PV = FV_n(PVIF)$.

$$PV = \$500(.55368) = \$276.84$$

Use Performance Objective CI-10 to help you become proficient with this three-step solution approach:

PERFORMANCE OBJECTIVE CI-10
Apply the three-step solution approach to solve a present value problem.

Solving for Unknown Quantities Other than Present Value

Any present value problem may be solved if you know at least three of the following four quantities: present value, interest rate, number of periods, and future value. If a quantity other than present value is unknown, simple algebraic manipulation of the secondary present value formula $PV = FV_n(PVIF)$ will allow you to solve the problem. To illustrate, consider the following example:

Example 11 When will a $1,000 future value be received if, when discounted at 6%, its present value is $890?

Step 1 Draw a time line that identifies known and unknown quantities from your analysis of the problem.

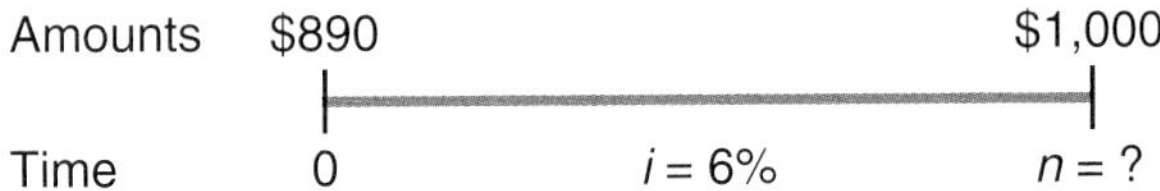

The known quantities are the $1,000 future value, the 6% interest rate and the $890 present value. The unknown quantity is the number of periods.

Step 2 Select the appropriate interest factor from the Present Value of $1 Table.

In this problem, you cannot select an interest factor from Table 2 because only one of the two quantities required to determine the present value interest factor (PVIF) is given. That is, when the PVIF is a function of both i and n and n is unknown, the PVIF is also unknown.

Step 3 Solve for the unknown quantity using the secondary present value formula: $PV = FV_n(PVIF)$.

Since PVIF is unknown, you must divide both sides of the equation above by FV_n to isolate PVIF. After performing this operation, your PVIF will be as follows:

$$PVIF = PV/FV_n = \$890/\$1{,}000 = .89$$

Now, you can solve this example by scanning down the excerpt from Table 2's 6% column for a row corresponding to an interest factor of approximately .89. Verify now that the number of periods corresponding to a PVIF of .89 is 2. That is, the present value of $1,000 received *two* years from now and discounted at 6% is $890.

You have probably noticed that the three-step solution method used in present value problems is very similar to that introduced in the previous chapter for future value problems. Let's now review this solution method.

Step 1 Draw a time line that identifies known and unknown quantities from your analysis of the problem. These quantities include principal or present value, number of periods, interest rate, and future value.

Step 2 Select the appropriate interest factor from the Present Value of $1 Table. To do so, you must use information about the interest rate and number of periods found in the time line.

Step 3 Solve for the unknown quantity using the secondary present value formula: $PV = FV_n(PVIF)$.

Review of the Present Value Concept

Before you begin your study of the annuity concept, study the following summary of the performance objectives introduced in the preceding sections to determine if you have mastered the present value concept:

Performance Objective CI-7 **Identify** the appropriate interest rate and number of periods you must use when interest is compounded more frequently than annually.

Calculation of *i* and *n* When interest is expressed as an annual rate but the compounding occurs more frequently than once a year:

1. Determine the interest rate per period (i) by dividing the annual interest rate by the number of interest periods within the year.
2. Determine the number of periods (n) by multiplying the number of interest periods within the year by the number of years stated in the problem.

Performance Objective CI-8 **Distinguish** between the future value interest concept and the present value interest concept.

Distinctions between Present and Future Value

1. Future value is a later, greater value while present value is an earlier, smaller value.
2. You add interest to the principal or present value to calculate future value while you subtract interest from the future value to calculate present value.

Performance Objective CI-9 **Define** the terms *present value*, *discount rate*, and *discounting*.

1. **Present value** is the amount that when left to accumulate at compound interest will grow to become the future value.
2. **Discount rate** is the interest rate used in a present value problem.
3. **Discounting** is the process of transforming a future value into a present value by using compound interest.

Performance Objective CI-10 **Apply** the three-step solution approach to solve a present value problem.

Present Value Solution Method

Step 1: **Draw** a time line that identifies the following known and unknown quantities from your analysis of the problem: present value, number of periods, interest rate, and future value.

Step 2: **Select** the appropriate interest factor from the Present Value of \$1 Table using information about the interest rate and number of periods found in the time line.

Step 3: **Solve** for the unknown quantity using the secondary present value formula: $PV = FV_n(PVIF)$.

Primary versus Secondary Present Value Formula The primary formula $PV = FV_n[1/(1 + i)^n]$ is used when no interest table is available while the secondary formula $PV = FV_n(PVIF)$ is used when an interest table is available.

The Annuity Concept

Now that you are familiar with both the future and present value of \$1 concepts, it is time to learn about the annuity concept. An **annuity** is a series of equal cash flows (that is, receipts or payments) that occur at regular intervals for a specified number of periods. For example, you have an annuity if you receive \$100 on December 31 of every year for 10 years. Imagine you will receive \$500 on January 31, 2003, \$700 on December 1, 2003, \$90 on February 15, 2004, and \$150 on July 15, 2005. Does this stream of future cash flows represent an annuity? The answer is no because these cash flows are unequal in amount and do not occur at regular intervals. Let's try one more potential annuity situation. Imagine you pay \$5 over a period of five years whenever the temperature is either below 30 degrees or above 70 degrees Fahrenheit. Does this stream of future cash flows represent an annuity? Once again, you should have answered no because these cash flows are equal in amount but do not occur at regular intervals.

Another term regularly used when working with annuities is *rent*. The term **rent** refers to each of the periodic cash flows in an annuity. Use R to symbolize each rent's dollar amount. If you receive \$5,000 annually for five years from an initial investment of \$20,000, the \$5,000 is called a rent. Annuities are of two types: an *annuity in arrears* and an *annuity in advance*. An **annuity in arrears**, or *regular annuity*, is one in which rents occur at the end of all periods whereas an **annuity in advance**, or *annuity due*, is one in which rents occur at the beginning of all periods. For now, you will only work with an annuity in arrears. That is, you will assume that all annuity rents occur at the end of each period.

Now that you have been introduced to the annuity concept, Performance Objective CI-11 will help you master the four new terms just described.

PERFORMANCE OBJECTIVE CI-11
Define the terms *annuity, rent, annuity in arrears,* and *annuity in advance.*

Future Value of Annuity

Besides defining annuity and distinguishing between an annuity and non-annuity problem, and between an annuity in arrears and an annuity in advance, you must be able to analyze and solve both future and present value of annuity problems. For now, let's consider only the future value of annuity concept. The following example provides just such an opportunity.

Example 12 Calculate the future value of a \$1,000, three-year annuity with the \$1,000 rents received on December 31 of each year and with interest compounded at 10% annually. To help you master the new concepts included in this example, the solution will be divided into more than the usual number of steps. Let's begin our analysis by inserting both the relevant cash flows and dates into a time line.

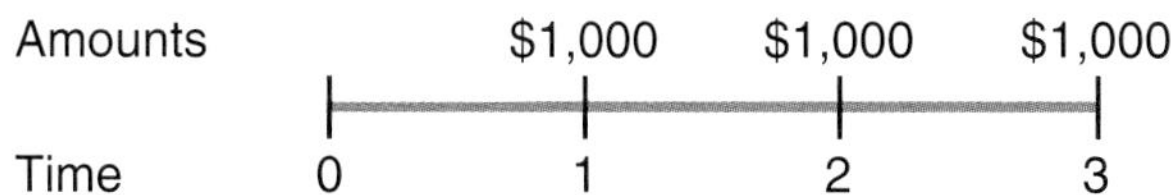

As pictured in this time line, the future value of an annuity in arrears concept requires that you position the first rent at the end of period one. This is equivalent to saying that the point designated as time 0 (that is, the present) precedes the first rent by one period. Our example requires that you calculate the combined future value of the three $1,000 receipts at December 31 of Year 3. Up to now, you have learned how to calculate the future value of only a single amount. How then might you calculate the future value of three such amounts? What if, for example, you calculated the future value of each individual rent and added the results? Let's try this approach by first calculating the future value of the $1,000 rent received at the end of Year 1 using the three-step approach. Note that this rent will earn interest for two periods—from the end of Year 1 to the end of Year 3.

Step 1 Draw a time line that identifies known and unknown quantities from your analysis of the problem.

Amounts $1,000 ?

Time 0 $i = 10\%$ $n = 2$

Note here that the $1,000 rent is treated as a present value by moving one year into the future.

Step 2 Select the appropriate interest factor from the Future Value of $1 Table.

$$FVIF = 1.21000\ (i = 10\%,\ n = 2)$$

Step 3 Solve for the unknown quantity using the secondary future value formula: $FV_n = PV(FVIF)$.

$$PV = \$1{,}000(1.21000) = \$1{,}210.00$$

Now that you have calculated the future value of the first rent, let's next calculate the future value of the $1,000 rent received at the end of Year 2. The number of annual periods for which the $1,000 rent received at the end of Year 2 earns interest is one (from the end of Year 2 to the end of Year 3).

Step 1 Draw a time line that identifies known and unknown quantities from your analysis of the problem.

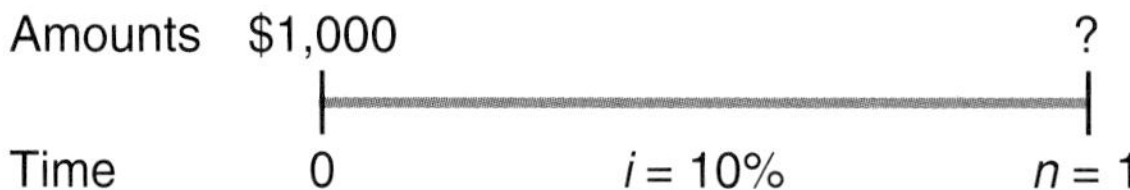

Step 2 Select the appropriate interest factor from the Future Value of $1 Table.

$$FVIF = 1.10000\ (i = 10\%,\ n = 1)$$

Step 3 Solve for the unknown quantity using the secondary future value formula: $FV_n = PV(FVIF)$.

$$PV = \$1{,}000(1.10000) = \$1{,}100.00$$

Now refer back to your time line to view the rent received at December 31 of Year 3. Its future value at December 31 is $1,000 because no interest has had time to accumulate. Here is an illustration of this annuity:

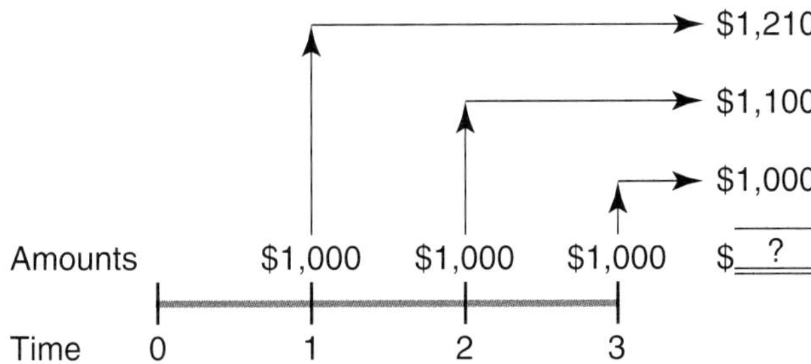

Now that you have calculated these individual future values ($1,210, $1,100, and $1,000), you may add them together to calculate the total future value of the annuity described in Example 12. The future value of this annuity (FVA_n) is:

$1,210
1,100
1,000
$3,310

Using this example, you should be able to confirm that the **future value of an annuity (FVA_n)** is the accumulated total of the future value of each of the original rents earning compound interest. That is, the future value of an annuity ($3,310) results from adding together the individual amounts shown above.

As you just witnessed, you can represent a future value of an annuity problem in a time line. You can also represent this type of problem with the following formula:

$$FVA_n = R\left[\frac{(1+i)^n - 1}{i}\right]$$

where FVA_n = Future Value of Annuity of n rents
R = Rent amount[3]

The essential idea described above is that calculating the future value of each individual rent and adding the results is equivalent to calculating the future value of an annuity. You may simplify such calculations by using the following excerpt from Table 3, the **Future Value of an Annuity of $1 in Arrears Table**. You can find the complete Table 3 on page 675.

TABLE 3

Future Value of an Annuity of $1 in Arrears

Primary formula: $FVA_n = R\left[\frac{(1+i)^n - 1}{i}\right]$

Secondary formula: $FVA_n = R(FVAIF)$

	Interest Rates = *i*						
Rents = *n*	**3%**	**4%**	**5%**	**6%**	**8%**	**10%**	**12%**
1	1.00000	1.00000	1.00000	1.00000	1.00000	1.00000	1.00000
2	2.03000	2.04000	2.05000	2.06000	2.08000	2.10000	2.12000
3	3.09090	3.12160	3.15250	3.18360	3.24640	3.31000	3.37440
4	4.18363	4.24646	4.31012	4.37462	4.50611	4.64100	4.77933
5	5.30914	5.41632	5.52563	5.63709	5.86660	6.10510	6.35285

[3] The following derivation of this primary formula reviews these ideas:

$$FVA_n = R(1+i)n - 1 + R(1+i)n - 2 + \cdots + R(1+i)1 + R(1+i)0$$
$$= R[(1+i)n - 1 + (1+i)n - 2 + \cdots + (1+i)1 + 1]$$
$$= R\left[\frac{(1+i)n - 1}{i}\right]$$

As you already have learned, each of the numbers in Table 3 is called an interest factor and represents a unique combination of number of rents (n) and interest rate (i). When Table 3 is available, you should use the following secondary future value of an annuity formula:

$$FVA_n = R(FVAIF)$$

Let's solve the preceding example again but this time, let's use our Table 3 excerpt.

Step 1 Draw a time line that identifies known and unknown quantities from your analysis of the problem.

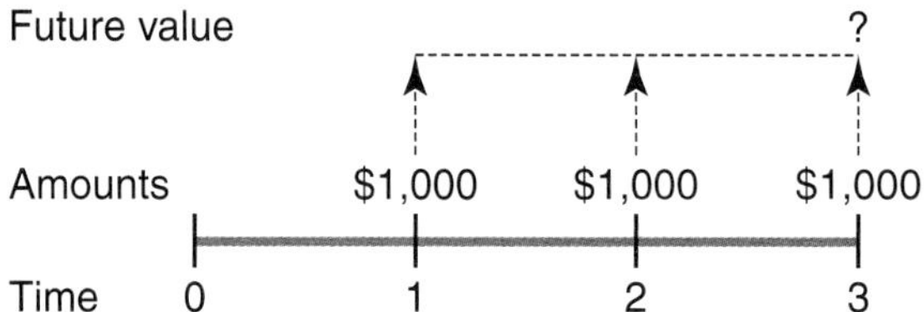

Step 2 Select the appropriate interest factor from the Future Value of an Annuity of $1 Table.

$$FVAIF = 3.31000\ (i = 10\%,\ n = 3)$$

Step 3 Solve for the unknown quantity using the secondary future value of annuity formula: $FVA_n = R(FVAIF)$.

$$FVA_3 = \$1{,}000(3.31000) = \$3{,}310.00$$

Although the solution approaches used to calculate Example 12's answer were somewhat different, the answers obtained were identical. However, the latter solution approach (use of Table 3) is far more efficient because it consists of one interest factor selection and one calculation (a multiplication). In contrast, the first solution approach (use of Table 1) consists of four calculations (three multiplications and an addition). The fact that the answers using either table were identical is no accident. The tables are related as illustrated below:

Table 1		Table 3	
n	i = 10%	n	i = 10%
0	1.00000	3	3.31000
1	1.10000		
2	1.21000		
	3.31000		

What the information above illustrates is that Table 3 consists of cumulative interest factors derived from Table 1. Thus, whenever you deal with a future value of annuity problem, you should use Table 3 rather than Table 1. Incidentally, be sure you understand that the n's in each table are not identical. For example, if you look back to the n in Table 1, you will see that it refers to number of periods whereas the n in Table 3 just presented refers to number of rents. Keep this distinction in mind since it is critical when working with compound interest problems.

Present Value of Annuity

Let's now return to the very same annuity introduced in Example 12 whose future value was just calculated. The only difference now is that we propose to calculate its present value. The **present value of an annuity (PVA_n)** is the total of the individually discounted present values of rents included in the annuity. Here is that example once more.

Example 13 Calculate the present value of a $1,000, three-year annuity with the $1,000 rents received on December 31 of each year and with interest compounded at 10% annually.

Since this example requires you to calculate a present value, you must begin with the appropriate interest factors from the following excerpt from Table 2:

n	*i* = 10%
1	0.90909
2	0.82645
3	0.75131
4	0.68301
5	0.62092

That is, if you calculate each rent's present value and add them together, you can determine the present value of the annuity.

Step 1 Draw a time line that identifies known and unknown quantities from your analysis of the problem.

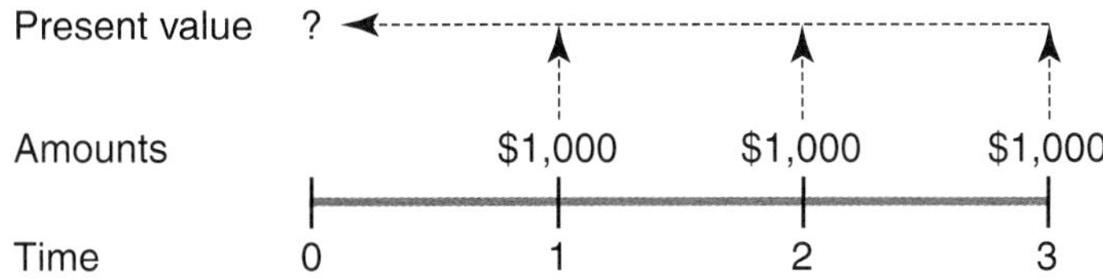

Step 2 Select the appropriate interest factors from this Present Value of $1 Table excerpt:

Present value of $1 received at the end of Year 1 :	.90909
Present value of $1 received at the end of Year 2 :	.82645
Present value of $1 received at the end of Year 3 :	.75131

Step 3 Calculate the present value of the annuity by using the secondary present value formula $PV = FV_n(PVIF)$ to calculate the present value of each rent. Then add these present values together as shown below:

PV = $1,000(.90909) =	$ 909.09
PV = $1,000(.82645) =	826.45
PV = $1,000(.75131) =	751.31
	$2,486.85

Notice that the calculations used in deriving this solution can also be expressed as follows:

$$PVA_n = \$1{,}000(.90909) + \$1{,}000(.82645) + \$1{,}000(.75131) = \$2{,}486.85$$

You may simplify this expression by factoring out the $1,000 rent.

$$PVA_n = \$1{,}000(.90909 + .82645 + .75131)$$

$$PVA_n = \$1{,}000(2.48685) = \$2{,}486.85$$

Notice that this expression represents a secondary present value of an annuity formula. That is, the PVA_n represents a present value of an annuity of n rents, the $1,000 represents a rent (R), and 2.48685 represents a present value of annuity interest factor ($PVAIF$). Such a formula can be used whenever you have access to the **Present Value of an Annuity of $1 in Arrears Table**. An excerpt is shown here.

TABLE 4

Present Value of an Annuity of $1 in Arrears

Primary formula: $PVA_n = R\left[\frac{1 - 1/(1+i)^n}{i}\right]$

Secondary formula: $PVA_n = R(PVAIF)$

	Interest Rates = *i*						
Rents = *n*	**3%**	**4%**	**5%**	**6%**	**8%**	**10%**	**12%**
1	0.97087	0.96154	0.95238	0.94340	0.92593	0.90909	0.89286
2	1.91347	1.88609	1.85941	1.83339	1.78326	1.73554	1.69005
3	2.82861	2.77509	2.72325	2.67301	2.57710	2.48685	2.40183
4	3.71710	3.62990	3.54595	3.46511	3.31213	3.16987	3.03735
5	4.57971	4.45182	4.32948	4.21236	3.99271	3.79079	3.60478

Each of the numbers in Table 4 is called an interest factor and represents a unique combination of interest rate (i) and number of rents (n). This Present Value of Annuity of $1 Table shows what a series of $1 rents due at regular intervals in the future is worth today or now.

Although you will have Table 4 available on page 676 whenever you solve a present value of annuity problem, it will be especially valuable for you to be able to derive an interest factor from this table. For example, this understanding will be particularly useful when you learn about installment loans in Chapter 13. Thus, the formula for deriving any present value of an annuity in arrears interest factor is:

$$PVAIF = \frac{1 - (1+i)^{-n}}{i} = \frac{1 - \frac{1}{(1+i)^n}}{i}$$

where i = Interest Rate
n = Number of Rents (payments or receipts)

Although this formula might look complex to you, it is relatively easy to use as shown by the following illustration for deriving Example 13's present value of annuity interest factor.

The calculation of the interest factor may be derived in the following stages:

1. $(1+i)^n = (1+.10)^3 = (1.1)^3 = 1.331$
2. $\frac{1}{(1+i)^n} = \frac{1}{1.331} = .751314801$
3. $1 - \frac{1}{(1+i)^n} = .248685199$
4. $\frac{1 - \frac{1}{(1+i)^n}}{i} = 2.486851991, \quad \text{or} \quad 2.48685$

Recall that the 2.48645 interest factor derived above is the accumulation of three individual present values (.90909 + .82645 + .75131). That is, Table 4 consists of cumulative interest factors derived from Table 2 interest factors. To confirm this fact, let's solve Example 13 again but this time use Table 4. Since we have already used Step 1 by drawing a time line and Step 2 by selecting an interest factor, we only need to use Step 3:

Step 3 Solve for the unknown quantity using the secondary present value of annuity formula: $PVA_n = R(PVAIF)$.

$$PVA_3 = \$1{,}000(2.48685) = \$2{,}486.85$$

As you can clearly see, the answers obtained from first using Table 2 and now using Table 4 are identical. Nevertheless, given a choice, Table 4 is much easier to use.

Before we consider some refinements of the annuity concept, consider Performance Objective CI-12, which summarizes four key concepts relating to annuities:

PERFORMANCE OBJECTIVE CI-12

Distinguish between:

a. An annuity problem and a non-annuity problem.
b. An annuity in arrears and an annuity in advance.
c. A future value of an annuity and a present value of an annuity.
d. The Future Value of Annuity Table and the Present Value of Annuity Table.

Refining Your Understanding of Annuities

As is true of the future value of annuity table, the element n in the present value of annuity table represents number of rents rather than number of periods. That is, when selecting the appropriate measure of n in an annuity problem, you should always count the number of rents. In contrast, you should count the number of periods when you select the appropriate measure of n in a non-annuity problem.

In general, use a three-step solution approach to solve an annuity problem:

Step 1 Draw a time line that identifies the following known and unknown quantities from your analysis of the annuity problem: present or future value of an annuity, number of rents, and interest rate.

Notice how this step is applied to Examples 12 and 13 below:

Future value of annuity (Example 12)

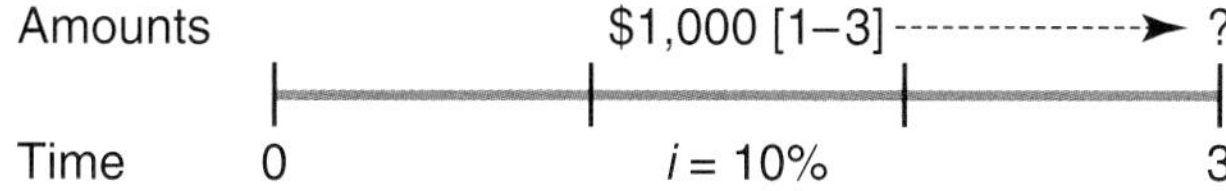

Present value of annuity (Example 13)

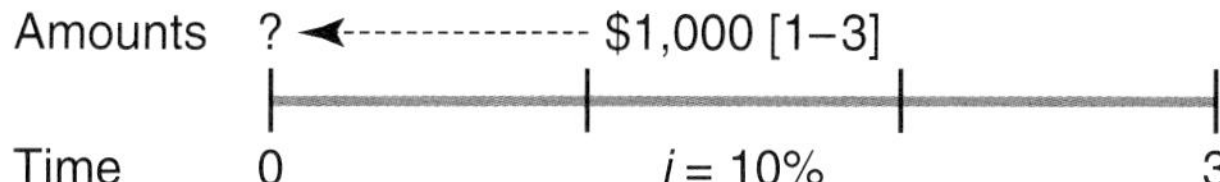

The question mark designates the unknown *future* value of the annuity in the first time line and the unknown *present* value of the annuity in the second time line. Note that in both time lines, the placement of the numbers one to three in braces immediately following the amount of the rent indicates that there are three rents. Any future cash flow is always placed above the time line while the annual interest rate (10% in these cases) is always placed below the time line. We'll use this approach from here on.

Step 2 Select the appropriate interest factor from either annuity table using information about the interest rate and number of rents found in the time line.

Let's now apply this step to Examples 12 and 13. When the combination of i = 10% and $n = 3$ is used to select the correct interest factors from the future value of annuity table and the present value of annuity table respectively, the FVAIF = 3.31000 and the PVAIF = 2.48685. These interest factors and the following simple rules will help you avoid selecting an interest factor from the wrong table:

Rule 1: The future value of annuity interest factor is always greater than n. For example, compare 3.31000 to 3.

Rule 2: The present value of annuity interest factor is always less than n. For example, compare 2.48685 to 3.

Step 3 Solve any annuity problem for its unknown quantity by using one of these secondary annuity formulas: $FVA_n = R\ (FVAIF)$ and $PVA_n = R\ (PVAIF)$.

Applying the secondary annuity formulas results in these solutions:

$FVA_n = R(FVAIF)$	$PVA_n = R(PVAIF)$
$= \$1{,}000(3.31000)$	$= \$1{,}000(2.48685)$
$= \$3{,}310.00$	$= \$2{,}486.85$

As you can see, \$3,310.00 represents the future value of the annuity whereas \$2,486.85 represents the present value of the annuity. An important question you will undoubtedly ask is, "How do I decide which annuity table and formula (future value or present value) to use in a given fact situation." Here are basic rules you can use to answer this question:

Rule 3: If the problem either asks for or provides an amount that *follows* a series of cash flows, you must use the future value of annuity table and formula.

Rule 4: If the problem either asks for or provides an amount that *precedes* a series of cash flows, you must use the present value of annuity table and formula.

To apply these rules, refer back to the time lines that follow the explanation of Step 1. The first time line *asks for* (note the question mark above year 3) an amount that follows a series of cash deposits. Thus, Rule 3 applies and you must use a future value of annuity table and formula. The second time line, however, asks for an amount that precedes a series of cash flows. Thus, Rule 4 applies, and you must use a present value of annuity table and formula. Performance Objective CI-13 is designed to reinforce your mastery of these rules.

PERFORMANCE OBJECTIVE CI-13

Determine which annuity table (future value or present value) is appropriate in a given situation.

Depending on the situation, you will sometimes be given the amount of a future value of an annuity (FVA) or the amount of a present value of an annuity (PVA). If this is the case, your task will be to calculate either the rent amount (R), interest rate (i) or number of rents (n). When this occurs, you can solve for any of the preceding unknown quantities by simple algebraic manipulation of the relevant secondary annuity formula. Example 14 below illustrates this idea.

Example 14 You have \$4,500 available for investment on January 1, 2002. If you purchase an investment that provides six annual receipts beginning on December 31, 2002, what is the amount of each receipt assuming the investment yields an interest rate of 10%?

Step 1 Draw a time line that identifies known and unknown quantities from your analysis of the problem.

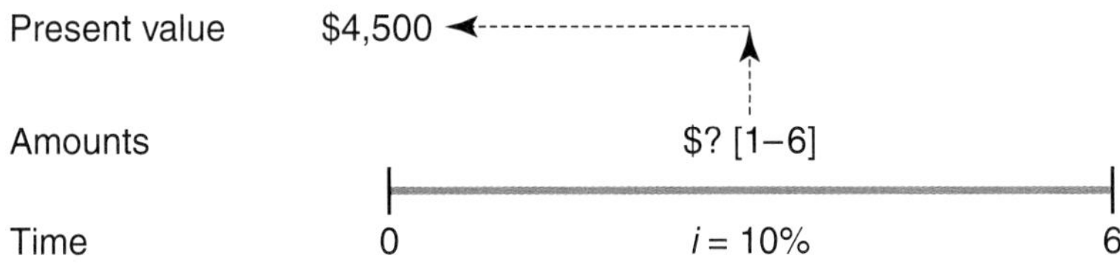

As you can see in the time line above, the $4,500 represents the present value of the annuity and the annual rents are unknown. Since the present value of the annuity, $4,500, is provided and no future value of the annuity is defined—it is neither asked for nor provided—you must use a present value of annuity table and formula in your solution.

Step 2 Select the appropriate interest factor from either annuity table using information about the interest rate and number of rents found in the time line.

If you use Table 4 on page 676, you will discover that your present value of an annuity interest factor is 4.35526 ($i = 10\%$ and $n = 6$).

Step 3 Solve the annuity problem for the unknown quantity by using the secondary annuity formula.

Since the amount of the rents (R) is unknown, you must solve for R in the secondary annuity formula below:

$$PVA_n = R(PVAIF)$$

To isolate R, you must divide both sides of the equation by PVAIF as shown below:

$$PVA_n/PVAIF = R(PVAIF)/PVAIF$$

Since the terms PVAIF cancel, you are left with the expression $R = PVA_n/PVAIF$. By inserting the relevant numbers into this equation, you can determine that the amount of the receipt (R) you would expect each year is $1,033.23, or $4,500/4.35526 = $1,033.23.

Notice that we continue to use a three-step solution approach to solve both future value of annuity and present value of annuity problems. As a result, Performance Objective CI-14 below is designed to help you master this solution approach.

PERFORMANCE OBJECTIVE CI-14
Apply the three-step solution approach to solve an annuity problem.

Review of the Annuity Concept

Study the following summary of the performance objectives introduced in the preceding sections to determine if you have mastered the annuity concept:

Performance Objective CI-11 **Define** the terms *annuity*, *rent*, *annuity in arrears*, and *annuity in advance*.

Annuity An annuity is a series of equal cash flows (that is, receipts or payments) that occur at regular intervals for a specified number of periods.

Rent A rent refers to each of the periodic cash flows in an annuity. Use R to symbolize each rent's dollar amount.

Annuity in Arrears An annuity in arrears or regular annuity is one in which rents occur at the end of all periods.

Annuity in Advance An annuity in advance or annuity due is one in which rents occur at the beginning of all periods.

Performance Objective CI-12 **Distinguish** between (a) an annuity problem and a non-annuity problem, (b) an annuity in arrears and an annuity in advance, (c) a future value of an annuity and a present value of an annuity, and (d) the future value of annuity table and the present value of annuity table.

Annuity Problem and Non-Annuity Problem An annuity problem includes rents whereas a non-annuity problem does not. Furthermore, the variable n represents the number of periods in a non-annuity problem and the number of rents in an annuity problem.

Annuity in Arrears versus Annuity in Advance In the first case, rents occur at the end of all periods, while in the second case, rents occur at the beginning of all periods.

Future Value of an Annuity versus Present Value of an Annuity A future value of an annuity (FVA_n) is the accumulated total of the future value of each of the original rents earning compound interest. In contrast, a present value of an annuity (PVA_n) is the total of the individual present values of rents included in the annuity.

Future Value of Annuity of $1 Table versus Present Value of Annuity of $1 Table Table 3 shows what a series of $1 rents deposited at regular intervals is worth at a specific point in the future. Table 4, however, shows what a series of $1 rents due at regular intervals in the future is worth today.

Performance Objective CI-13 **Determine** which annuity table (future value or present value) is appropriate in a given situation.

Future Value of Annuity Table Use this table and its related formula whenever the problem either asks for or provides an amount that follows a series of cash flows. The future value of annuity interest factor is always greater than n.

Present Value of Annuity Table Use this table and its related formula whenever the problem either asks for or provides an amount that precedes a series of cash flows. The present value of annuity interest factor is always less than n.

Performance Objective CI-14 **Apply** the three-step solution approach to solve an annuity problem.

Step 1: **Draw** a time line that identifies the following known and unknown quantities from your analysis of the annuity problem: present or future value of an annuity, number of rents, and interest rate.

Step 2: **Select** the appropriate interest factor from either annuity table using information about the interest rate and number of rents found in the time line.

Step 3: **Solve** the annuity problem for the unknown quantity by using the secondary annuity formula.

TABLE 1

Future Value of $1

Primary Formula: $FV_n = PV(1 + i)^n$
Secondary Formula: $FV_n = PV(FVIF)$

PERIODS = n	INTEREST RATES = i 1/2%	1%	2%	3%	4%	5%	6%	8%	10%	12%
1	1.00500	1.01000	1.02000	1.03000	1.04000	1.05000	1.06000	1.08000	1.10000	1.12000
2	1.01003	1.02010	1.04040	1.06090	1.08160	1.10250	1.12360	1.16640	1.21000	1.25440
3	1.01508	1.03030	1.06121	1.09273	1.12486	1.15763	1.19102	1.25971	1.33100	1.40493
4	1.02015	1.04060	1.08243	1.12551	1.16986	1.21551	1.26248	1.36049	1.46410	1.57352
5	1.02525	1.05101	1.10408	1.15927	1.21655	1.27628	1.33823	1.46933	1.61051	1.76234
6	1.03038	1.06152	1.12616	1.19405	1.26532	1.34010	1.41852	1.58687	1.77156	1.97382
7	1.03553	1.07214	1.14869	1.22987	1.31593	1.40710	1.50363	1.71382	1.94872	2.21068
8	1.04071	1.08286	1.17166	1.26677	1.36857	1.47746	1.59385	1.85093	2.14359	2.47596
9	1.04591	1.09369	1.19509	1.30477	1.42331	1.55133	1.68948	1.99900	2.35795	2.77308
10	1.05114	1.10462	1.21899	1.34392	1.48024	1.62889	1.79085	2.15892	2.59374	3.10585
11	1.05640	1.11567	1.24337	1.38423	1.53945	1.71034	1.89830	2.33164	2.85312	3.47855
12	1.06168	1.12683	1.26824	1.42576	1.60103	1.79586	2.01220	2.51817	3.13843	3.89598
13	1.06699	1.13809	1.29361	1.46853	1.68507	1.88565	2.13293	2.71962	3.45227	4.36349
14	1.07232	1.14947	1.31948	1.51259	1.73168	1.97993	2.26090	2.93719	3.79750	4.88711
15	1.07768	1.16097	1.34587	1.55797	1.80094	2.07893	2.39656	3.17217	4.17725	5.47357
20	1.10490	1.22019	1.48595	1.80611	2.19112	2.65330	3.20714	4.66096	6.72750	9.64629
25	1.13280	1.28243	1.64061	2.09378	2.66584	3.38635	4.29187	6.84848	10.83471	17.00006
30	1.16140	1.34785	1.81136	2.42726	3.24340	4.32194	5.74349	10.06266	17.44940	29.95992
40	1.22079	1.48886	2.20804	3.26204	4.80102	7.03999	10.28572	21.72452	45.25926	93.05097

TABLE 2

Present Value of $1

Primary Formula: $PV = FV_n[(1/1 + i)^n]$
Secondary Formula: $PV = FV_n(PVIF)$

PERIODS = n	INTEREST RATES = i									
	1/2%	1%	2%	3%	4%	5%	6%	8%	10%	12%
1	0.99502	0.99010	0.98039	0.97087	0.96154	0.95238	0.94340	0.92593	0.90909	0.89286
2	0.99007	0.98030	0.96117	0.94260	0.92456	0.90703	0.89000	0.85734	0.82645	0.79719
3	0.98515	0.97059	0.94232	0.91514	0.88900	0.86384	0.83962	0.79383	0.75131	0.71178
4	0.98025	0.96098	0.92385	0.88849	0.85480	0.82270	0.79209	0.73503	0.68301	0.63552
5	0.97537	0.95147	0.90573	0.86261	0.82193	0.78353	0.74726	0.68058	0.62092	0.56743
6	0.97052	0.94205	0.88797	0.83748	0.79031	0.74622	0.70496	0.63017	0.56447	0.50663
7	0.96569	0.93272	0.87056	0.81309	0.75992	0.71068	0.66506	0.58349	0.51316	0.45235
8	0.96089	0.92348	0.85349	0.78941	0.73069	0.67684	0.62741	0.54027	0.46651	0.40388
9	0.95610	0.91434	0.83676	0.76642	0.70259	0.64461	0.59190	0.50025	0.42410	0.36061
10	0.95135	0.90529	0.82035	0.74409	0.67556	0.61391	0.55839	0.46319	0.38554	0.32197
11	0.94661	0.89632	0.80426	0.72242	0.64958	0.58468	0.52679	0.42888	0.35049	0.28748
12	0.94191	0.88745	0.78849	0.70138	0.62460	0.55684	0.49697	0.39711	0.31863	0.25668
13	0.93722	0.87866	0.77303	0.68095	0.60057	0.53032	0.46884	0.36770	0.28966	0.22917
14	0.93256	0.86996	0.75788	0.66112	0.57748	0.50507	0.44230	0.34046	0.26333	0.20462
15	0.92792	0.86135	0.74301	0.64186	0.55526	0.48102	0.41727	0.31524	0.23939	0.18270
20	0.90506	0.81954	0.67297	0.55368	0.45639	0.37689	0.31180	0.21455	0.14864	0.10367
25	0.88277	0.77977	0.60953	0.47761	0.37512	0.29530	0.23300	0.14602	0.09230	0.05882
30	0.86103	0.74192	0.55207	0.41199	0.30832	0.23138	0.17411	0.09938	0.05731	0.03338
40	0.81914	0.67165	0.45289	0.30656	0.20829	0.14205	0.09722	0.04603	0.02209	0.01075

TABLE 3

Future Value of an Annuity of $1 in Arrears

Primary Formula: $FVA_n = R\left[\frac{(1+i)^n - 1}{i}\right]$

Secondary Formula: $FVA_n = R(FVAIF)$

RENTS = n	INTEREST RATES = i									
	1/2%	1%	2%	3%	4%	5%	6%	8%	10%	12%
1	1.00000	1.00000	1.00000	1.00000	1.00000	1.00000	1.00000	1.00000	1.00000	1.00000
2	2.00500	2.01000	2.02000	2.03000	2.04000	2.05000	2.06000	2.08000	2.10000	2.12000
3	3.01502	3.03010	3.06040	3.09090	3.12160	3.15250	3.18360	3.24640	3.31000	3.37440
4	4.03010	4.06040	4.12161	4.18363	4.24646	4.31012	4.37462	4.50611	4.64100	4.77933
5	5.05025	5.10101	5.20404	5.30914	5.41632	5.52563	5.63709	5.86660	6.10510	6.35285
6	6.07550	6.15202	6.30812	6.46841	6.63298	6.80191	6.97532	7.33593	7.71561	8.11519
7	7.10588	7.21354	7.43428	7.66246	7.89829	8.14201	8.39384	8.92280	9.48717	10.08901
8	8.14141	8.28567	8.58297	8.89234	9.21423	9.54911	9.89747	10.63663	11.43589	12.29969
9	9.18212	9.36853	9.75463	10.15911	10.58280	11.02656	11.49132	12.48756	13.57948	14.77566
10	10.22803	10.46221	10.94972	11.46388	12.00611	12.57789	13.18079	14.48656	15.93742	17.54874
11	11.27917	11.56683	12.16872	12.80780	13.48635	14.20679	14.97164	16.64549	18.53117	20.65458
12	12.33556	12.68250	13.41209	14.19203	15.02581	15.91713	16.86994	18.97713	21.38428	24.13313
13	13.39724	13.80933	14.68033	15.61779	16.62684	17.71298	18.88214	21.49530	24.52271	28.02911
14	14.46423	14.94742	15.97394	17.08632	18.29191	19.59863	21.01507	24.21492	27.97498	32.39260
15	15.53655	16.09690	17.29342	18.59891	20.02359	21.57856	23.27597	27.15211	31.77248	37.27971
20	20.97912	22.01900	24.29737	26.87037	29.77808	33.06595	36.78559	45.76196	57.27500	72.05244
25	26.55912	28.24320	32.03030	36.45926	41.64591	47.72710	54.86451	73.10594	98.34706	133.33387
30	32.28002	34.78489	40.56808	47.57542	56.08494	66.43885	79.05819	113.28321	164.49402	241.33268
40	44.15885	48.88637	60.40198	75.40126	95.02552	120.79977	154.76197	259.05652	442.59256	767.09142

TABLE 4

Present Value of an Annuity of $1 in Arrears

Primary Formula: $PVA_n = R\left[\frac{1 - 1/(1 + i)^n}{i}\right]$

Secondary Formula: $PVA_n = R(PVAIF)$

RENTS = n	INTEREST RATES = i									
	1/2%	1%	2%	3%	4%	5%	6%	8%	10%	12%
1	0.99502	0.99010	0.98039	0.97087	0.96154	0.95238	0.94340	0.92593	0.90909	0.89286
2	1.98510	1.97040	1.94156	1.91347	1.88609	1.85941	1.83339	1.78326	1.73554	1.69005
3	2.97025	2.94099	2.88388	2.82861	2.77509	2.72325	2.67301	2.57710	2.48685	2.40183
4	3.95050	3.90197	3.80773	3.71710	3.62990	3.54595	3.46511	3.31213	3.16987	3.03735
5	4.92587	4.85343	4.71346	4.57971	4.45182	4.32948	4.21236	3.99271	3.79079	3.60478
6	5.89638	5.79548	5.60143	5.41719	5.24214	5.07569	4.91732	4.62288	4.35526	4.11141
7	6.86207	6.72819	6.47199	6.23028	6.00205	5.78637	5.58238	5.20637	4.86842	4.56376
8	7.82296	7.65168	7.32548	7.01969	6.73274	6.46321	6.20979	5.74664	5.33493	4.96764
9	8.77906	8.56602	8.16224	7.78611	7.43533	7.10782	6.80169	6.24689	5.75902	5.32825
10	9.73041	9.47130	8.98259	8.53020	8.11090	7.72173	7.36009	6.71008	6.14457	5.65022
11	10.67703	10.36763	9.78685	9.25262	8.76048	8.30641	7.88687	7.13896	6.49506	5.93770
12	11.61893	11.25508	10.57534	9.95400	9.38507	8.86325	8.38384	7.53608	6.81369	6.19437
13	12.55615	12.13374	11.34837	10.63496	9.98565	9.39357	8.85268	7.90378	7.10336	6.42355
14	13.48871	13.00370	12.10625	11.29607	10.56312	9.89864	9.29498	8.24424	7.36669	6.62817
15	14.41662	13.86505	12.84926	11.93794	11.11839	10.37966	9.71225	8.55948	7.60608	6.81086
20	18.98742	18.04555	16.35143	14.87747	13.59033	12.46221	11.46992	9.81815	8.51356	7.46944
25	23.44564	22.02316	19.52346	17.41315	15.62208	14.09394	12.78336	10.67478	9.07704	7.84314
30	27.79405	25.80771	22.39646	19.60044	17.29203	15.37245	13.76483	11.25778	9.42691	8.05518
40	36.17223	32.83469	27.35548	23.11477	19.79277	17.15909	15.04630	11.92461	9.77905	8.24378

Summary with Key Terms

This chapter began by explaining why businesses engage in investing activities. It then examined the financial statement effects of property, plant, and equipment transactions, often the most prominent investing activity in terms of dollars. One such transaction creates what is known as a **self-constructed asset** (611), a depreciable asset that a company constructs for its own use. The interest included in the recorded cost of such a self-constructed asset is called **capitalized interest** (612).

Although the concept of depreciation had been discussed in previous chapters, several new depreciation terms were introduced. These included **obsolescence** (616) or nonphysical asset deterioration, **salvage value** (614), the amount of cash value remaining at the time an asset is either retired or sold, and **depreciable cost** (614), the difference between the original cost of the asset and the asset's salvage value. This chapter also introduced some depreciation methods including two variations of the straight-line method, called the **service hours method** (615) and the **units of production method** (622) as well as two **accelerated depreciation** (616) methods known as the **double-declining-balance method (DDB)** (617), and the **sum-of-the-years' digits method (SYD)** (617).

The next major investing activity transaction you learned about was **depletion** (621), the cost of natural resources allocated to expense. In particular, you learned how to use the *units of production method* to calculate depletion. A concept similar in nature to depletion is **amortization** (624), the systematic allocation of the cost of intangible assets to expense. You learned that there are two major types of intangible assets, those that are not subject to amortization such as **goodwill** (625) and those that are amortized. The balance sheet amounts reported for assets that are not subject to amortization can, nevertheless, be reduced through a process known as asset **impairment** (625).

The last section of the chapter introduced the detailed accounting for **debt securities** (627) and **equity securities** (627) issued by an **investee** (627) and held by an **investor** (627). In explaining the detailed transactions of the particular debt security known as a bond, the term **face value** (629) was introduced. Several distinctions were explained including those between **cash equivalents** (628), **marketable securities** (628), and **investments** (628). Another set of distinctions having to do with an investor's intentions are **trading securities** (628), **available-for-sale securities** (628), and **held-to-maturity securities** (628). Although **fair value** (628) is disclosed in each of these categories, it is accounted for quite differently. The next distinction involved three levels of ownership for investments in stocks referred to as **minority, passive investments** (633), **minority, active investments** (634), and **majority, active investments** (634). Key terms in determining which of these three categories is appropriate for a particular security are **significant influence** (633) and **control** (633). Investments that are judged to not provide a significant influence to the buyer or investor are accounted for by using the **cost/fair value method** (634). In contrast, you learned that the **equity method** (638) is used for investments in which the investor is able to influence the operating and financing policies of the investee.

The number in parentheses following each **key term** is the page number on which the term is defined.

Appendix Summary with Key Terms

This appendix began by explaining three reasons why it is important for you to master the compound interest concept. Then the concept of interest was introduced by defining three terms: **interest** (645), **principal** (646), and **interest rate** (646). Next, you learned the distinction between **simple interest** (646) and **compound interest** (647).

You then learned that the **future value** (649) is the amount the principal becomes when left to accumulate at compound interest for a given period of time. Then you refined your understanding of compound interest by learning that it is calculated by subtracting the *principal* or original amount invested from the *future value*. You next learned about the visual analysis of a compound interest problem known as a **time line** (649). You were then shown how you can use the **Fundamental Equation of Compound Interest** (651) to generate enough **interest factors** or **IF** (651) to create the **Future Value of $1 Table** (652). A reference used fre-

The number in parentheses following each **key term** is the page number on which the term is defined.

quently in this appendix was the distinction between a **primary formula** (653) such as $FV_n = P(1 + i)^n$ and a **secondary formula** (653) such as $FV_n = P(FVIF)$. Throughout this appendix, you learned the appropriate time to use one and not the other.

The next major topic was **present value** (658) or the amount that when left to accumulate at compound interest will grow to become the future value. One again, you saw how you can use the Fundamental Equation of Compound Interest to develop the **Present Value of $1 Table** (659). Two useful terms to use when working with the present value concept are **discount rate** (660) and **discounting** (660).

After exploring the related concepts of future value and present value, you were introduced to the concept of an **annuity** (663), a series of equal cash flows that occur at regular intervals for a specified number of periods. Based on the timing of cash flows, annuities can be two types: an **annuity in arrears** (663) and an **annuity in advance** (663). Generally speaking, we will use the annuity in arrears in which the **rents** (663) or payments occur at the end of each period. Based on one's decision-making perspective, an annuity can either be a **present value of an annuity (PVA_n)** (666) or a **future value of an annuity (FVA_n)** (665). The corresponding interest tables are referred to as the **Future Value of Annuity in Arrears Table** (665) or the **Present Value of Annuity in Arrears Table** (668). Since it can be confusing as to which annuity concept and annuity table to use in a concrete situation, this appendix provided simple rules to help you make the right choice.

Making Business Decisions

YOUR PERFORMANCE OBJECTIVE 2
(page 18)

In this chapter you spent a lot of time learning about the calculations underlying several investing activity transactions as well as how to record and report them. So you might be left with the impression that investing activities involve a great deal of procedural detail. In fact, however, some very important business decisions underlie the measurement, recording, and reporting of these transactions. And each such decision can have far-reaching effects on the success of a business. How can you grasp the impact that decision making has on investing activities? You can do so by reviewing this chapter and identifying the key decisions that business people have to make before they can measure, record, and report investing activity transactions. For example, consider the calculation of straight-line depreciation for a particular depreciable asset. Underlying this calculation are several different decisions. The first is a business decision relating to which asset should be purchased. That is, why did the business decide to purchase this particular asset? Once this decision is made, one or more accounting decisions must be made, such as what cost amount should be capitalized; what useful life and salvage value should be used; and what depreciation method should be applied? Below is the format you should use to express your answer:

- Chapter section title: Refining Your Understanding of Straight-Line Depreciation
- Business decision(s): Which asset should be purchased?
- Accounting decision(s): What is the amount of cost to be capitalized when recording this asset? What useful life should be selected? What is the proper amount of salvage value? Which depreciation method should be selected?
- Calculation or transaction: Straight-line depreciation

Required

a. For each of the following five calculations or transactions, identify the underlying business decision(s) and any accounting decisions that affected the nature of the calculation or the transaction. Be sure to also identify the chapter title for the section in which the transaction's calculation was explained.
    1. Recording the interest cost for a self-constructed asset.
    2. Recording a gain or loss on the sale of a depreciable asset.
    3. Recording depreciation on land improvements.
    4. Calculating unsold depletion cost.
    5. Recording amortization on an intangible asset.

b. Review the contents of this chapter and select five additional calculations or transactions. Then, apply the same process as described in part (a).

Questions

YOUR PERFORMANCE OBJECTIVE 4
(page 22)

12-1 Explain in your own words the meaning of key business terms.

a. Self-constructed asset
b. Capitalized interest
c. Service hours method
d. Obsolescence
e. Depreciable cost
f. Accelerated depreciation
g. Depletion
h. Amortization
i. Goodwill impairment
j. Debt securities
k. Equity securities
l. Fair value
m. Investee
n. Investor
o. Minority, passive investment
p. Minority, active investment
q. Majority, active investment
r. Cost/fair value method
s. Equity method

12-2 Describe, in your own words, why businesses engage in investing activities.

12-3 Describe, in your own words, the general rule for deciding when to capitalize and when to expense costs associated with the purchase of a depreciable asset.

12-4 Describe the financial statement effects of mistakenly expensing a cost that should be capitalized.

12-5 Describe the financial statement effects of mistakenly capitalizing a cost that should be expensed.

12-6 What is a lump-sum or basket purchase? How do you determine the costs of the individual assets?

12-7 Distinguish between cost, salvage value, and depreciable cost.

12-8 What are the essential differences between straight-line depreciation and accelerated depreciation?

12-9 Compare and contrast the straight-line depreciation method and the double-declining-balance depreciation method.

12-10 Compare and contrast the straight-line depreciation method and the sum-of-the-years'-digits depreciation method.

12-11 Compare and contrast the double-declining-balance depreciation method and the sum-of-the-years'-digits depreciation method.

12-12 Since the units of production method and the service hours method are both derived from the straight-line depreciation method, what makes them different?

12-13 Distinguish between a depreciable asset, a natural resource, and an intangible asset.

Indicate whether each of the following statements (Items 12-14 through 12-17) is true or false:

12-14 The acquisition cost used to record depreciable assets can include invoice price, freight-in, insurance costs during transportation, and installation costs less cash discounts.

12-15 Depreciation, as the term is used in accounting, means the systematic and rational allocation of the cost of natural resources to expense.

12-16 The declining-balance depreciation method initially ignores salvage value in its calculation of periodic depreciation.

12-17 The term *book value* may be defined as acquisition cost minus estimated salvage value.

12-18 Distinguish between cash equivalents, marketable securities, and investments.

12-19 Distinguish between trading securities, available-for-sale securities, and held-to-maturity securities. How is each category of securities reported on the balance sheet?

12-20 Distinguish between an unrealized gain or loss and a realized gain or loss.

12-21 Distinguish between significant influence and control.

12-22 Suppose that an investment in stock's fair value has increased and the gain is reported in an unrealized holding gain account. Describe how this account is presented in the financial statements when it is classified as:

a. A trading security
b. An available-for-sale security

12-23 Suppose that an investment in stock's fair value has decreased and the loss is reported in an unrealized holding loss account. Describe how this account is presented in the financial statements when it is classified as:

a. A trading security
b. An available-for-sale security

12-24 An investor using the equity method treats net income or net loss of an investee differently than if the cost/fair value method had been used. What is that difference?

12-25 An investor using the equity method treats a dividend declared by its investee differently than if the cost/fair value method had been used. What is that difference?

Appendix Questions

AQ12-1 Name the two parties involved in an interest-related transaction.

AQ12-2 Interest represents the time __________ of money to a __________ and the time __________ of money to a __________.

AQ12-3 What term is used to describe a borrower's time cost of money and a lender's time value of money.

AQ12-4 If $1,000 is invested at a 6% rate of interest for one year, it will grow to $1,060. The $1,060 is known as the __________ __________ (two words).

AQ12-5 A picture that describes a compound interest problem in terms of amounts and time is called a __________ __________ (two words).

AQ12-6 Using the information from Example 1, if $CI_1 = \$60$, what are P and i respectively?

AQ12-7 If $FV = P + CI_1$ and $CI_1 = P(i)$, then $FV = P +$ _____.

AQ12-8 Each number in a compound interest table represents a unique combination of __________ __________ and __________ _____ __________.

AQ12-9 Each of the numbers in Table 1 is referred to as an __________ __________.

AQ12-10 The table of interest factors known as the future value of $1 table shows to what value $_____ at compound interest will grow to in the future.

AQ12-11 In the equation $FV_n = P(1 + i)^n$ underlying Table 1, $P =$ _____.

AQ12-12 Using Table 1, select the future value interest factor (FVIF) associated with a period of three years and an 8% interest rate.

AQ12-13 If interest is compounded monthly, there are __________ periods within the year each having a length of __________ month.

AQ12-14 If interest at 10% is compounded semiannually, what are the: interest rate per period, number of interest periods a year, and the length of each period?

AQ12-15 $PV = FV_n/(1 + i)^n$ or $PV = FV_n[1/(1 + i)^n]$

Identify the symbols in the present value formula above.

PV represents ______________________________.

FV_n represents ______________________________.

i represents ______________________________.

n represents ______________________________.

AQ12-16 Distinguish between the secondary future and present value formulas by inserting the appropriate term into the formulas shown below:

$FV_n = PV(\_\_\_\_\_)$ $\quad PV = FV_n(\_\_\_\_\_)$

AQ12-17 When calculating a present value, you must know the future value, number of periods, and the __________ rate.

AQ12-18 The future value interest concept and the present value interest concept discussed so far are closely related in a mathematical sense. That is, the present value interest factor, PVIF, is the __________ of the future value interest factor, FVIF.

AQ12-19 To qualify as an annuity, must cash flows be equal or unequal in amount, occur at regular or irregular intervals, and continue for a specified or unspecified number of periods?

AQ12-20 The formula

$$FVA_n = R\left[\frac{(1 + i)^n - 1}{i}\right]$$

allows you to calculate annuity interest factors when you do not have an interest table available. Is such a formula referred to as a primary or a secondary future value of annuity in arrears formula?

AQ12-21 Identify the present value of an annuity formula.

$PVA_n =$ __________

AQ12-22 In Table 4, what is the interest factor (PVAIF) associated with three rents and a 10% interest rate?

AQ12-23 State the interest rate per period and the number of periods in each of the following cases:

a. 6% per year, for 5 years, compounded annually.
b. 6% per year, for 5 years, compounded semiannually.
c. 6% per year, for 5 years, compounded monthly.

Reinforcement Exercises

E12-1 Asking the Right Questions: A Group Activity

YOUR PERFORMANCE OBJECTIVE 4
(page 22)

It's often said that knowing the right answer is not nearly as important as asking the right question. Asking the right question is a problem-solving skill that will help you make sound business decisions. In this exercise, you will review the vocabulary introduced in Chapter 12 by creating questions to match answers—similar to a popular TV show.

Required

a. Given an answer, what's the question?
Choose **three** of the following terms to serve as an answer. For each term, create an appropriate question. For example, if you choose the term *balance sheet*, you might create the question *What financial statement shows the assets, liabilities, and owners' equity of an entity on a specific date?*

Depreciation	Trading	Debt security
Investor	Amortization	Marketable security
Investee	Equity security	Available for sale
Equity method	Held to maturity	Cash equivalent
Impairment	Obsolescence	Depletion

b. Are you sure that's the question?
Have each member of your group read aloud the questions they developed in Requirement (a). As a group, decide whether each question is an accurate match for an answer. Once satisfied that all questions are appropriate, the group, as a whole, chooses the three best questions created within the group. Record the three questions chosen (with their answers) on separate pieces of paper or index cards and give them to your instructor.

c. What's the answer?
To ensure you have learned the vocabulary terms listed in Requirement (a), your instructor will now quiz you on the questions written by all of your classmates.

E12-2 Goodwill Determination

YOUR PERFORMANCE OBJECTIVE 4
(page 22)

Calculate the amount of goodwill from an acquisition given the following information. *Hint:* Review Appendix 10–1.

Price paid by the purchasing company	$450,000
Book value of the acquired company's individual assets	380,000
Market value of the acquired company's individual assets	420,000
Book value of the purchasing company's individual assets	900,000
Market value of the purchasing company's individual assets	980,000

E12-3 Financial Statement Effects of Investing Activity Transactions

YOUR PERFORMANCE OBJECTIVES 5a, 7a, 11a
(pages 137, 64, 99)

Determine the effects on the balance sheet, income statement, and statement of cash flows from each of the following investing activity transactions. Use NE if you believe that the transaction has no effect on a particular financial statement.

a. Machinery A costing $100,000 is purchased for cash.
b. Machinery B costing $120,000 is purchased on account.
c. Machinery B is paid for by writing a check for $120,000 to the supplier who extended credit in (b).
d. Machinery A with a book value of $85,000 is sold for $90,000.
e. Machinery B with a book value of $100,000 is sold for $92,000.
f. Land worth $200,000 is acquired in exchange for a note payable.

YOUR PERFORMANCE OBJECTIVES 5a, 7a, 11a
(pages 137, 64, 99)

E12-4 Financial Statement Effects of Investing Activity Transactions
Determine the effects on the balance sheet, income statement, and statement of cash flows from each of the following investing activity transactions. Use NE if you believe that the transaction has no effect on a particular financial statement.

a. A $10,000 U.S. government bond is purchased for cash.
b. A $100,000 corporate bond is acquired in exchange for a note payable.
c. The $10,000 U.S. government bond is sold for $10,200.
d. The $100,000 corporate bond is sold for $98,000.

YOUR PERFORMANCE OBJECTIVE 43
(page 611)

E12-5 Determination of Costs to Be Capitalized
Enforcer Corporation purchases a machine to be used in production for an invoice price of $3,000. Shipping costs to transport the machine to the company are $200. When the machine arrives, it is slightly damaged so the seller reduces the invoice price by 2%. The cost of constructing a cement slab to support the new machine is $750. Calculate the proper cost at which to record this machine.

YOUR PERFORMANCE OBJECTIVE 43
(page 611)

E12-6 Determination of Costs to Be Capitalized
Security Corporation purchases a super computer to be used in its accounting department for an invoice price of $300,000. Applicable sales tax was $19,500 and shipping charges were $2,500. Because of the risk of damage during transportation, an insurance premium of $800 was paid. Also, $500 was paid to install this computer and a cash discount of $4,800 was earned because payment was made within 30 days of delivery. Calculate the proper cost at which to record this computer.

YOUR PERFORMANCE OBJECTIVE 43
(page 611)

E12-7 Determination of Costs to Be Capitalized
The Chauncey Gardiner Corporation purchased two machines on January 1, 2004, for $12,000 cash. An independent appraiser provided fair market values for Machine A of $4,000 and for Machine B of $16,000. Allocate the $12,000 price paid between the two machines on the basis of the appraised values.

YOUR PERFORMANCE OBJECTIVE 44
(page 619)

E12-8 Depreciation Calculations
Saginaw Construction Company purchases an industrial crane for $50,000 on January 1 of the current year. This equipment is expected to have a useful life of eight years and a salvage value of $2,000. Calculate its book value at the end of its second year of useful life under the straight-line depreciation method.

YOUR PERFORMANCE OBJECTIVE 44
(page 619)

E12-9 Depreciation Calculations
A company purchased a machine for $20,000 cash on January 1 of the current year. It is estimated that this machine will provide five years of useful life and a salvage value of $800. At the end of the machine's third year of useful life, what will be its book value under the straight-line depreciation method?

YOUR PERFORMANCE OBJECTIVE 44
(page 619)

E12-10 Depreciation Calculations
Maravich Corporation purchased new telephone equipment that was installed and placed in service on January 1 of Year 1. The cost, including installation, was $30,000 with an estimated salvage value of $5,000. The equipment had an estimated useful life of eight years and is to be depreciated using the double-declining-balance method. Calculate the amount of depreciation expense for Year 2.

YOUR PERFORMANCE OBJECTIVE 44
(page 619)

E12-11 Depreciation Calculations
Stephens Corporation purchases new telephone equipment that is installed and placed in service on January 1 of the current year. The cost, including installation, is $30,000 with an estimated salvage value of $5,000. The equipment has a useful life of eight years and is depreciated using the double-declining-balance method. Calculate depreciation expense for the first six years of its life.

YOUR PERFORMANCE OBJECTIVE 44
(page 619)

E12-12 Depreciation Calculations
Silverburg Company purchases a large truck for $50,000 on January 1 of the current year. The truck is expected to have a salvage value of $10,000 after being used for 100,000 miles. Calculate the truck's depreciation expense using the units of production method (a variation of the straight-line method) assuming it is driven 30,000 miles in its first year of use.

E12-13 Depreciation Methods

Warner Company purchases a machine for $35,000 cash on January 1 of the current year. It is estimated that this machine will provide five years of useful life and a salvage value of $5,000. Calculate the depreciation expense for this machine for each of the five years under the following depreciation methods.

a. Straight-line
b. Sum-of-the-years' digits
c. Double-declining balance

YOUR PERFORMANCE OBJECTIVE 44
(page 619)

E12-14 Equipment Sale

Jennifer Company recently sold equipment that had an original cost of $3,000 and accumulated depreciation of $1,600. Record the transaction to account for this sale assuming the following selling prices.

a. $2,000 b. $1,400 c. $ 900

YOUR PERFORMANCE OBJECTIVE 5a
(page 137)

E12-15 Calculation of Depletion

Wonder Cave is purchased for $100,000. It is estimated that the cave will have no salvage value and that the mining operations will unearth 1 million tons of Wonder Yeast, the vital ingredient in Wonder Bread. If 100,000 tons are mined and sold in the first year, what is the depletion cost per unit and how much depletion should be recorded?

YOUR PERFORMANCE OBJECTIVE 45
(page 623)

E12-16 Calculation of Depletion

During the current year, Knight Industries acquired a copper mine for $900,000, of which $300,000 was estimated to be its salvage value. Geological surveys indicate that this mine holds 2 million units of extractable copper. If 600,000 units were extracted and sold this year, what is the depletion cost per unit and how much depletion should be recorded?

YOUR PERFORMANCE OBJECTIVE 45
(page 623)

E12-17 Classifying Account Titles

For each of the following accounts described in this chapter, indicate whether it is an asset, a liability, owners' equity, revenue, or an expense:

a. Accumulated Depreciation
b. Gain on Sale
c. Loss on Sale
d. Land Held for Future Business Use
e. Mining Property
f. Accumulated Depletion
g. Intangible Assets
h. Patent Amortization Expense
i. Goodwill
j. Loss on Goodwill Impairment
k. Investment in Bonds
l. Investment in Stock
m. Dividends Receivable
n. Dividend Revenue

YOUR PERFORMANCE OBJECTIVE 11b
(page 99)

E12-18 Investment in Debt Securities

On September 1, 2004, Becker Company purchased 6%, 10-year, $50,000 face value of bonds dated July 1, 2004, at a price equal to face value. Interest on these bonds is receivable on January 1 and July 1. What is the amount of each of the following?

a. The purchase price of the bonds
b. The total cash paid at the date of purchase (*Hint:* account for interest earned between September 1 and December 31, 2004).
c. Interest received on the bonds during 2004.
d. Interest revenue for the year ended December 31, 2005.
e. Interest receivable as of December 31, 2005.

YOUR PERFORMANCE OBJECTIVE 47
(page 638)

E12-19 Investments in Debt and Equity Securities

Using the information provided by Figure 12-11, determine the appropriate balance sheet and income statement presentations using the cost/fair value method.

YOUR PERFORMANCE OBJECTIVE 47
(page 638)

E12-20 Investment in Equity Securities

Study the following data for the market price per share of two companies' common stock on the given dates in the current year:

YOUR PERFORMANCE OBJECTIVE 47
(page 638)

	Aug. 31	Sept. 30	Oct. 31	Nov. 30	Dec. 31
Neiman Industries	$12	$13	$13	$14	$14
Strauss Inc.	20	16	18	16	25

On August 31, Vincent Corporation purchased 100 shares of Neiman Industries and 50 shares of Strauss Inc. for temporary investment purposes. Then, on November 30, Vincent Corporation sold 25 shares of Strauss Inc. stock.

Using the cost/fair value method, show how Vincent should report its investment in equity securities on both September 30 and December 31 of this year.

YOUR PERFORMANCE OBJECTIVE 47 *(page 638)*

E12-21 Investment in Equity Securities
Transactions involving Ramirez Corporation's available-for-sale marketable securities appear below:

					Fair Values	
Security	Date Acquired	Original Cost	Date Sold	Selling Price	Dec. 31, 2004	Dec. 31, 2005
A	3/05/2004	$ 80,000	—	—	$ 76,000	$ 66,000
B	8/15/2004	150,000	9/16 2005	$156,000	158,000	—
C	11/10/2004	180,000	—	—	186,000	188,000

Required

a. Using the cost/fair value method, present the effects of these transactions on the balance sheet and income statement at December 31, 2004 and December 31, 2005.
b. Repeat part (a) but under the assumption that these are trading securities.

YOUR PERFORMANCE OBJECTIVES 47, 48 *(pages 638, 641)*

E12-22 Equity Method
Nguyen Corporation owns 20% of the voting common stock of Lee, Inc. and carries its Investment in Lee account on the equity basis. Record appropriate transactions for Nguyen as a result of the following 2004 and 2005 events:

a. 2004: Lee, Inc. announces a net income of $250,000 and both declares and pays cash dividends of $100,000.
b. 2005: Lee, Inc. announces a net loss of $30,000 and both declares and pays cash dividends of $10,000.

Appendix Reinforcement Exercises

The following exercises have been designed to test your understanding of compound interest or the time value of money concepts. In analyzing these exercises, always use a time line to help you visualize the timing of the cash flows. Use the compound interest tables found at the back of Appendix 12–1.

YOUR PERFORMANCE OBJECTIVE CI-6 *(page 654)*

AE12-1 Future Value Concept
If you invest $1,000 at 6% compound interest for 5 years, what will be the amount of the future value? Calculate the amount of compound interest earned over this period.

YOUR PERFORMANCE OBJECTIVE CI-6 *(page 654)*

AE12-2 Future Value Concept
On January 2 of this year, Mary Addams invests $6,000 at an interest rate of 8% in the 1st National Bank of Transylvania. If Mary plans no withdrawals, how much money will she have in the bank at the end of five years?

YOUR PERFORMANCE OBJECTIVE CI-6 *(page 654)*

AE12-3 Future Value Concept
Calculate the future value of $558.40 invested today for 10 years at:

a. 6% compounded annually.
b. 6% compounded semiannually.

AE12-4 Present Value Concept
Assuming that the relevant interest rate is 10%, which amount do you prefer—$20,000 received today, January 1, 2004, or $35,000 received on December 31, 2008?

YOUR PERFORMANCE OBJECTIVE CI-10
(page 661)

AE12-5 Present Value Concept
Eight-year-old Hugh Mongus wishes to attend the Wrestling Federation School in exactly 10 years. Assuming that his savings account pays interest at a rate of 6% compounded annually, how much must Hugh's father, "Rabid" Ron A. Mongus deposit now to accumulate the $1,000 entrance fee?

YOUR PERFORMANCE OBJECTIVES CI-6, CI-10
(pages 654, 661)

AE12-6 Present Value Concept
If you are offered an investment opportunity that requires an outlay of $1,000 and returns $2,000 at the end of nine years, what rate of annual interest will you earn? Use either a future value perspective or a present value perspective.

YOUR PERFORMANCE OBJECTIVES CI-6, CI-10
(pages 654, 661)

AE12-7 Present Value Concept
You are offered an investment opportunity that will cost $1,000 and will return $1,500 at the end of six years. What rate of interest does this investment provide? Use either a present value perspective or a future value perspective.

YOUR PERFORMANCE OBJECTIVE CI-10
(page 661)

AE12-8 Present Value Concept
What is the present value today (January 1, 2004) of $1,000 discounted annually at 10% and due on December 31, 2023?

YOUR PERFORMANCE OBJECTIVE CI-10
(page 661)

AE12-9 Present Value Concept
Gomez Addams, your customer, issues a note that will pay you $2,000 four years from today. If discounting is semiannual and the discount (interest) rate is 12%, what is the note worth today (i.e., what is its present value)?

YOUR PERFORMANCE OBJECTIVES CI-12, C1-13, CI-14
(pages 669, 670, 671)

AE12-10 Annuity Concept
If you invest $1,000 at the end of each of 15 consecutive years to earn 8% interest:

a. What amount will your investment accumulate to at the end of the 15th year?
b. How much interest revenue will your investment earn?

YOUR PERFORMANCE OBJECTIVES CI-12, C1-13, CI-14
(pages 669, 670, 671)

AE12-11 Annuity Concept
If you invest $400 at the end of each of 20 consecutive years to earn 12% interest:

a. What amount will your investment accumulate to by the end of the 20th year?
b. How much interest revenue will your investment earn?

YOUR PERFORMANCE OBJECTIVES CI-12, C1-13, CI-14
(pages 669, 670, 671)

AE12-12 Annuity Concept
Mark Foster wishes to attend wrestling school. He decides, however, to accumulate the $1,000 entrance fee by making 10 yearly deposits to a savings account that pays interest at a rate of 6% compounded annually. Calculate the amount of these equal deposits.

YOUR PERFORMANCE OBJECTIVES CI-12, C1-13, CI-14
(pages 669, 670, 671)

AE12-13 Annuity Concept
What is the present value of a 15-year annuity in arrears of $1,000 that earns interest at 8%?

AE12-14 Annuity Concept
What is the present value of a 20-year annuity in arrears of $400 that earns interest at 12%?

Critical Thinking Problems

P12-1 Financial Statement Effects of Minority, Passive Investment Transactions (Accounted for by the Cost/Fair Value Method)
Determine the effects on the balance sheet, income statement, and statement of cash flows of the following transactions from this chapter's illustration of a minority, passive investment in stock. Assume that these particular securities are classified as trading. Use NE if you believe that the transaction has no effect on a particular financial statement.

YOUR PERFORMANCE OBJECTIVES 5a, 7b, 11a
(pages 137, 64, 99)

a. Samson Corporation purchases 100 shares of Thomas, Inc. voting common stock at $45 a share plus brokerage commissions of $100 for a total outlay of $4,600.
b. Thomas, Inc. declares a $1 per share dividend.
c. Samson receives dividends of $100 cash from its investment in Thomas, Inc. stock.
d. Assume the following two scenarios for the value of each share of Thomas, Inc. common stock:
   1. It sells for $51 at the end of the accounting period.
   2. It sells for $42.50 at the end of the accounting period.
e. Ignoring the information in part (d), assume that Samson sells its 100 shares of Thomas stock exactly 10 months later at a price of $48 per share less brokerage commissions of $125.

YOUR PERFORMANCE OBJECTIVES 5a, 7b, 11a
(pages 137, 64, 99)

P12-2 Financial Statement Effects of Minority, Passive Investment Transactions (Accounted for by the Cost/Fair Value Method)
Assuming the very same information as in Problem 12-1 except that Samson's equity security belongs in the available-for-sale category, determine the effects on the balance sheet, income statement, and statement of cash flows. Use NE if you believe that the transaction has no effect on a particular financial statement.

YOUR PERFORMANCE OBJECTIVES 5a, 7b, 11a
(pages 137, 64, 99)

P12-3 Financial Statement Effects of Minority, Active Investment Transactions (Accounted for by the Equity Method)
Determine the effects on the balance sheet, income statement, and statement of cash flows of the following transactions from this chapter's illustration of a minority, active investment in stock. Use NE if you believe that the transaction has no effect on a particular financial statement.
a. Samson Corporation purchases 2,500 shares of Thomas, Inc.'s 10,000 shares of voting common stock at $45 a share plus brokerage commissions of $1,500 for a total outlay of $114,000.
b. Assume the following two scenarios for the reported net income/net loss of Thomas, Inc.:
   1. $80,000 net income
   2. $18,000 net loss
c. Thomas, Inc. declares a $1 per share dividend.
d. Samson receives dividends of $2,500 cash from its investment in Thomas, Inc. stock.
e. Samson sells its 2,500 shares of Thomas stock exactly 10 months later at a price of $48 per share less brokerage commissions of $2,000.
   1. Assume b1 occurred.
   2. Assume b2 occurred.

YOUR PERFORMANCE OBJECTIVE 43
(page 611)

P12-4 Determination of Costs to Be Capitalized
The Reginald Gardiner Corporation purchased two machines on January 1, 2004, for $12,000 cash. An independent appraiser provided fair market values for Machine A of $5,000 and for Machine B of $15,000.

Required
a. Allocate the $12,000 price paid between the two machines on the basis of the appraised values and record the appropriate transaction.
b. Without prejudice to your answer in (a), assume that the cost of Machine A is $3,500. If this machine is depreciated under the straight-line method, has an estimated salvage value of $500, and will have an accumulated depreciation balance of $1,500 at December 31, 2006, what was its estimated useful life at acquisition?

YOUR PERFORMANCE OBJECTIVE 44
(page 619)

P12-5 Depreciation Calculations
A company purchased a machine for $10,000 cash on January 1 of the current year. It is estimated that this machine will provide five years of useful life and a salvage value of $400. At the end of the machine's fourth year of useful life, what will be its book value under the double-declining-balance depreciation method?

YOUR PERFORMANCE OBJECTIVE 44
(page 619)

P12-6 Depreciation Calculations
Maravich Corporation purchased new telephone equipment that was installed and placed in service on January 1 of Year 1. The equipment had a cost, including installation, of $30,000 with an estimated salvage value of $5,000 and an estimated useful life of eight years.

What will be the amount of depreciation expense for Year 6 under the straight-line, double-declining balance, and sum-of-the-years'-digits depreciation methods?

P12-7 Depreciation Calculations

YOUR PERFORMANCE OBJECTIVE 44 *(page 619)*

Assume the accumulated depreciation account has a beginning and ending balance for the current period of $40,000 and $35,000, respectively. If depreciable assets having a cost of $15,000 and book value of $7,000 were sold for $9,000 during the year, calculate the current year depreciation expense. *Hint:* Use T-account analysis.

P12-8 Depreciation Methods

YOUR PERFORMANCE OBJECTIVE 44 *(page 619)*

Wilson Company purchases a machine for $47,000 cash on January 1 of the current year. It is estimated that this machine will provide five years of useful life and a salvage value of $5,000.

Required

a. Record the acquisition of this machine.
b. Calculate the depreciation expense for each year of this machine's useful life under the following depreciation methods.
   1. Straight line
   2. Sum-of-the-years' digits
   3. Double-declining balance
c. Record the sale of this asset for $10,000 at the end of Year 4 assuming the use of the straight-line depreciation method.
d. At the end of this asset's estimated useful life, which depreciation method will have produced the most expense?

P12-9 Depreciation Calculations

YOUR PERFORMANCE OBJECTIVE 44 *(page 619)*

The Machinery and Equipment account from the general ledger of the Sublimation Corporation for Year 1 is shown below:

Machinery and Equipment

		Year 1			
January 1	Balance	123,000	April 25	Disposal*	15,200
March 20	Purchase	14,400			
August 11	Purchase	6,000			
December 31 Balance		128,200			

*The assets disposed of were purchased before the current year.

Required

Calculate the depreciation for the year, assuming use of the straight-line method and an estimated life of 10 years with no salvage value for each of the assumptions shown in parts (a) through (c) below.

a. Depreciation is calculated on acquisitions from the date of purchase to the end of the period and on disposals from the beginning of the period to the date of disposal. Use 365 days for the base.
b. Depreciation is calculated for the full period on the beginning balance in the asset account.
c. Depreciation is calculated on acquisitions from the beginning of the month following acquisition and on disposals to the beginning of the month following disposal.
d. Which of the three methods above is best? Discuss briefly.

P12-10 Income Management

YOUR PERFORMANCE OBJECTIVES 8, 17 *(pages 65, 199)*

Answer the following questions by using this chapter's *Insight* entitled, "Why Estimated Useful Life Is So Critical to Accurate Income Measurement."

a. Which income figure, the original $6,000,000 or the recalculated $1,000,000, is more defensible?
b. Our society assumes that the work of accountants is very precise (that is, accurate to the penny). Is this assumption reasonable when you compare the two pretax income amounts?

c. Why might a company depreciate its jet aircraft over a 20-year useful life? How do you feel about the difference in pretax income produced by the difference in useful life estimates?
d. At what point does ethical financial reporting rather than the nature of accounting estimation become the central issue?

YOUR PERFORMANCE OBJECTIVE 45 *(page 623)*

P12-11 Calculation of Depletion

Naturopathic Cave is purchased by Wellborne Industries for $300,000 at the beginning of Year 1. It is estimated that the mining operations will unearth 1,000,000 tons of Health Bran, the vital ingredient in Healthful Bread. Wellborne mined 50,000 tons and sold 45,000 tons in the first year.

Required

a. What is the depletion cost per unit?
b. How much depletion should be recorded in Year 1?
c. Using Figure 12-7 as your model, present a partial balance sheet and a partial income statement for Wellborne Industries.

YOUR PERFORMANCE OBJECTIVE 45 *(page 623)*

P12-12 Calculation of Depletion

During the current year, Lancelot Industries acquired a copper mine for $1,200,000, of which $200,000 was estimated to be its salvage value. Geological surveys indicate that this mine holds 2 million units of extractable copper. 600,000 units are extracted and 500,000 units are sold this year.

Required

a. What is the depletion cost per unit?
b. How much depletion should be recorded in Year 1?
c. Using Figure 12-7 as your model, present a partial balance sheet and a partial income statement for Lancelot Industries.

YOUR PERFORMANCE OBJECTIVE 11b *(page 99)*

P12-13 Classifying Account Titles

For each of the following investment accounts introduced in this chapter, indicate whether it is an asset, a liability, owners' equity, revenue, or an expense:

a. Unrealized Holding Gain—Trading Securities
b. Unrealized Holding Loss—Trading Securities
c. Unrealized Holding Gain—Available-for-Sale Securities
d. Unrealized Holding Loss—Available-for-Sale Securities
e. Realized Gain on Sale of Investments
f. Realized Loss on Sale of Investments
g. Equity in Earnings of Investee (proportionate share of net income)
h. Equity in Earnings of Investee (proportionate share of net loss)

YOUR PERFORMANCE OBJECTIVE 47 *(page 638)*

P12-14 Investment in Debt Securities

On July 1, 2004, Danson Corporation purchased 6%, 10-year, $100,000 face value of bonds dated July 1, 2004, at a price equal to face value. Interest on these bonds is receivable on January 1 and July 1.

Required

a. Record all bond related transactions between July 1, 2004, and December 31, 2005.
b. Assume that the market price of these bonds on December 31, 2004 and on December 31, 2005 was 97 and 102, respectively. Present the financial statement effects of this investment in bonds on the income statement, balance sheet, and statement of cash flows as of December 31, 2004 and December 31, 2005.

YOUR PERFORMANCE OBJECTIVE 47 *(page 638)*

P12-15 Investments in Equity Securities

On October 1, 2004, Darcy Company purchases common stock of T, U, and V Companies as a short-term investment. The acquisition cost and year-end market values of these securities are as follows:

	October 1, 2004			December 31, 2004	
Company	Number of Shares	Cost per Share	Total Cost	Fair Value per Share	Total Fair Value
T	100	$20	$2,000	$16	$1,600
U	60	15	900	16	960
V	40	30	1,200	29	1,160
			$4,100		$3,720

Events subsequent to December 31, 2004 are as follows:

a. November 1, 2005: sold all V Company shares at $35 per share.
b. December 31, 2005: fair values are: T Company $18/share, U Company $17/share, and V Company $33/share

Record all necessary transactions on:

a. December 31, 2004
b. November 1, 2005
c. December 31, 2005

P12-16 Investment in Equity Securities

YOUR PERFORMANCE OBJECTIVE 47 *(page 638)*

Study the following data for the market price per share of two company's common stock on the given dates in the current year:

	Aug. 31	Sept. 30	Oct. 31	Nov. 30	Dec. 31
Wolcott Industries	$36	39	39	42	42
Thomas Inc.	60	48	54	48	75

On August 31, Vincent Corporation purchased 100 shares of Wolcott Industries and 50 shares of Thomas Inc. for temporary investment purposes. Then, on November 30, Vincent Corporation sold 25 shares of Thomas Inc. stock.

Required

a. Using the cost/fair value method, show how Vincent should report its investment in equity securities on both September 30 and December 31 of this year.
b. Record all necessary transactions for Vincent Corporation during the current year.

P12-17 Investment in Equity Securities

YOUR PERFORMANCE OBJECTIVE 47 *(page 638)*

Transactions involving Arnold Corporation's available-for-sale-marketable securities appear below:

					Fair Values	
Security	Date Acquired	Original Cost	Date Sold	Selling Price	Dec. 31, 2004	Dec. 31, 2005
A	4/15/2004	$120,000	—	—	$114,000	$ 99,000
B	8/10/2004	$225,000	9/22 2005	$234,000	$237,000	—
C	11/17/2004	$270,000	—	—	$279,000	$282,000

Required

a. Using the cost/fair value method, present the effects of these transactions on the balance sheet and income statement at December 31, 2004, and December 31, 2005.
b. Record all possible transactions during 2004 and 2005.
c. Repeat part (a) but under the assumption that these are trading securities.
d. Repeat part (b) but under the assumption that these are trading securities.

YOUR PERFORMANCE OBJECTIVE 47
(page 638)

P12-18 Investments in Debt and Equity Securities

Required

Using the information provided by Figure 12-11:

a. Record the purchase of each bond portfolio assuming each of the securities was purchased on the same date for cash.
b. Record the purchase of each stock portfolio assuming each of the securities was purchased on the same date for cash.
c. Record the necessary adjustments to report the appropriate securities at fair value as of December 31, 2003.
d. Report the appropriate balance sheet and income statement presentations by portfolio using the cost/fair value method.

YOUR PERFORMANCE OBJECTIVES 47, 48
(pages 638, 641)

P12-19 Equity Method

Required

a. Several business transactions are described below. For each event, determine whether it creates a dollar change in the table under each of the following assumptions:
   1. Baker Company uses the cost/fair value method for its investment in the Denson Company.
   2. Baker Company uses the equity method for its investment in the Denson Company.

	Cost/Fair Value Method		Equity Method	
Transactions	**Investment in Denson**	**Dividend Revenue**	**Investment in Denson**	**Equity in Earnings of Denson**
1. At the beginning of Year 1, Baker bought 25% of Denson's common stock at its book value. Total book value of all Denson common stock was $800,000 on this date.				
2. During Year 1, Denson reported $80,000 of net income.				
3. During Year 1, Denson declared and paid $40,000 of dividends.				
4. During Year 2, Denson reported a net loss of $10,000.				
5. During Year 2, Denson declared and paid $10,000 of dividends.				

b. Indicate the Year 2 ending balance in the investment account, and cumulative totals for Years 1 and 2 for dividend revenue and equity in earnings of Denson.

YOUR PERFORMANCE OBJECTIVES 8, 47
(pages 65, 638)

P12-20 Using Investments to Manage Earnings

Under current generally accepted accounting principles, it is possible for a manager to manage reported earnings by holding securities that have experienced losses while selling those that have experienced gains.

Required

a. Describe which one of the three investment categories introduced in this chapter could be used to manage earnings in this way.
b. Explain why this strategy would not work in the case of the other two categories.
c. Do you think this practice is ethical? Why, or why not?

Research Assignments

A wide variety of interesting Research Assignments for this chapter are available for the following topics at www.mhhe.com/solomon:

R12-1 **Financial Statement Effects of Investing Activities by Industry (PO 31)**
R12-2 **Financial Statement Effects of Investing Activities by Industry (PO 31)**
R12-3 **Financial Statement Effects of Investing Activities by Industry (PO 31)**
R12-4 **Using the MD&A to Learn More about Property, Plant, and Equipment (PO 14)**
R12-5 **Using the MD&A to Learn More about Intangible Assets (PO 14)**
R12-6 **Using the MD&A to Learn More about Investments (PO 14)**
R12-7 **Using the Notes to Learn More about Property, Plant, and Equipment (PO 14)**
R12-8 **Using the Notes to Learn More about Intangible Assets (PO 14)**
R12-9 **Using the Notes to Learn More About Investments (PO 14)**
R12-10 **Comparative Financial Analysis of Property, Plant, and Equipment Disclosures (PO 14)**
R12-11 **Comparative Analysis of International Property, Plant, and Equipment Accounting Practices (PO 14)**
R12-12 **Financial Analysis of Property, Plant, and Equipment (PO 14)**
R12-13 **Financial Analysis of Investing Activities (PO 14)**
R12-14 **Financial Statement Disclosure of Investments in Securities (PO 14)**
R12-15 **Real-World Property, Plant, and Equipment Exploration (PO 14)**
R12-16 **Ratio Analysis of Investing Activities (PO 3 and PO 14)**

CHAPTER THIRTEEN

How Financing Activities Affect Financial Statements

Also be sure you have mastered the following Performance Objectives from previous chapters. They lay the foundation for the concepts you will learn in this chapter:

PO3
PO4
PO11b
PO14
PO31
POCI-13
POCI-14

PERFORMANCE OBJECTIVES

In this chapter, you will learn the following new Performance Objectives:

PO49 **Calculate** simple interest on a note payable, **record** the transactions related to its issuance, interest accrual, and payment at maturity, and **present** its financial statement effects.

PO50 **Calculate** all employee and employer amounts related to a company's payroll liability, **record** these amounts, and **present** their financial statement effects.

PO51 **Apply** the present value concept to measure and report the effects of such transactions as credit card accounts, general notes, automobile loans, home loans, leases, bonds, and pensions by being able to:

a. **Calculate** the initial present value of all future cash flows, all subsequent present values (construct an amortization table), and the interest revenue and/or interest expense over the transaction's life.
b. **Record** all transaction-related effects from both perspectives.
c. **Present** the balance sheet, income statement, and statement of cash flow transaction-related effects.

PO53 **Distinguish** between the financial statement effects of the effective interest and straight-line methods of bond amortization.

PO55 **Calculate**, **record**, and **present** the financial statement effects of the following stockholder equity transactions: capital stock issuances and retirements; cash dividends, stock dividends, and stock split declarations; and treasury stock repurchases and reissues.

DISCOVERING THE WORLD OF VENTURE CAPITALISTS

Jack and Tyler Denton are brothers, and they're also business partners. Ten years ago they started Educational Technology Services (ETS), a company that harnesses computer technology to deliver course materials to college classrooms. Over the years, ETS has expanded into the high school, trade school, and corporate training markets. Now, Jack and Tyler are poised to expand ETS to the Internet. They recognize that they must adapt their products for Web-based delivery, or ETS will not survive. But they need a large infusion of cash to do this—probably about $3 million. How will they raise that kind of money?

Getting a bank loan for that amount is impossible, because they don't have enough collateral. They have some friends who have made millions in Silicon Valley. Tyler thinks that a few of them might be "angels," a term often used to describe individuals who, hoping for a large return on their investment, invest in private companies that will eventually go public.

But Jack wants to investigate venture capital firms also known as VCs. VCs generally finance relatively small companies by investing in equity positions and usually receiving common stock or special stock and one or more seats on the company's board of directors. In most cases, besides providing capital, a VC's equity investment raises the company's profile in the marketplace, inspiring confidence among customers, suppliers, bankers, and employees. In addition a VC can bring senior management experience, contacts, and sound advice to the company it helps to finance.

Where do VCs get their money to invest? They establish investment funds from institutional investors, such as insurance companies, pension funds, profit-sharing plans, and also from wealthy families and individuals. They invest in companies that they believe will have a high return on investment. Typically, they want an annual return on each investment of 35% to 50% a year compounded. For example, if a VC wants to receive back five times its original investment in five years, the compound annual rate of return on its investment must be almost 40%.

What kind of companies do VCs consider to be good investments? In most cases VCs invest in products or services that have extraordinarily high growth potential. They are attracted to companies that own proprietary products or services or have something special or distinctive in their strategy, product, market, or process. In other words, the company must have some significant advantage over existing or potential competitors so it can achieve and maintain a dominant position in its industry. Typically, the investments are made in unproven businesses, which pose a higher risk. Venture capitalists are willing to accept these higher risks in return for potentially high returns on their investment. Statistics show

(continued on next page)

(continued from previous page)

that VCs fund fewer than 1 in 100 of the business plans they receive. Of the businesses that are funded, only 1 in 10 is expected to be a great success and less than half of these are expected to survive for a reasonable length of time.

Time frames for venture capital investments vary, but most VCs stay in an investment for three to seven years. How they "exit" an investment depends on various circumstances, such as the company's financial performance, industry, competitive position, and so on. A sale or merger with another company or an initial public offering in which a company offers its stock to the public for the first time are the two most common ways that VCs exit an investment. A third exit strategy is a stock buyback—the company and the venture fund negotiate an agreement allowing the company to repurchase the shares held by the VC.

So Jack and Tyler are faced with a decision that many owners of small technology companies face. And their decision will change ETS forever. Should they try to find an angel? They might not be able to raise $3 million from their "angel" friends. Should they start contacting venture capital firms? ETS meets all of the criteria that VCs require for an investment, but with VCs there are strings attached. Moreover, Jack and Tyler have to find the right VC and negotiate a good deal. It's a tough financing decision.

From a traditional accounting perspective, financing a business using venture capital money is considered unconventional. In this chapter you will learn about the traditional vehicles that businesses use to finance their activities. You will learn, for example, how companies account for financing instruments such as notes and bonds; and you will explore how equity financing is generally accounted for. Then, after you've read the chapter you'll have a better idea of what you think Jack and Tyler should do.

What Are the Financial Statement Effects of Financing Activities?

Now that you better appreciate just how essential financing activities can be, let's reexamine the financial statement effects of financing activities that were described in earlier chapters. We'll begin by briefly reviewing our CMU financing transactions and then, just as we did last chapter, study the effects of those transactions on the balance sheet, income statement, and statement of cash flows.

Cards & Memorabilia Unlimited: Financing Activity Transactions

In Chapter 8 we classified all CMU first-year transactions, other than Transaction B, into operating, investing, and financing activities. So let's begin by reviewing the CMU transactions that are financing activities.

Figure 13-1 identifies six different financing activity transactions—Transactions A_1, F, K_1, L, W, and A_2. Transaction A_1 was a cash financing activity in which Susan obtained money to start the business. Susan's borrowing of money in Transaction F initiated an obligation with a financial institution, which was a financing activity; her repayment of that same credit line loan in Transaction K_1 then completed the financing activity. Transaction L represented a noncash investing and financing activity or *direct exchange*. That is, her purchase of equipment, a noncurrent asset, represented the initiation of an investing activity; whereas her incurrence of a noncurrent liability represented the initiation of a financing activity. Since Transaction W, a cash withdrawal by the owner, is the exact opposite of a cash contribution by the owner (Transaction A_1), it represents the completion of a financing activity associated with the owner equity Retained Earnings account. Finally, the cash contribution by a new owner in Transaction A_2 represents the initiation of a financing activity associated with the owner equity Contributed Capital account. Unlike Transaction A_1,

FIGURE 13-1 Classification of transactions A_1 through Z into statement of cash flow activities

	Assets							=	Liabilities				+	Owner Equities		Statement of Cash Flows		
																Activities		
	Cash Checking	Cash Savings	Accts. Recvb.	Mdse. Inven.	Other Recvb.	Store Equip.	Accum. Depr.		Accts. Payb.	Cred. Line Payb.	Advn. From Cust.	Note Payb.		Contrib. Capital	Retained Earnings	Financing	Investing	Operating
A_1	30,000													30,000		√		
B	(6,000)	6,000															NOT APPLICABLE	
C_1						10,000			10,000								√	
D	(15,000)			15,000														√
E	(2,000)				2,000												√	
C_2	(10,000)								(10,000)								√	
F	5,000									5,000						√		
G				18,000					18,000									√
H	(7,000)					7,000											√	
I	6,000										6,000							√
J_1	(12,000)								(12,000)									√
J_2									(6,000)			6,000[a]						√
K_1	(5,000)									(5,000)						√		
L						4,000						4,000[b]				√	√	
M	63,200														63,200			√
N			20,000												20,000			√
O_1	275														275			√
P	(11,000)														(11,000)			√
Q_1							(300)								(300)			√
R	1,350					(2,000)	300								(350)		√	
S	(8,000)														(8,000)			√
K_2	(200)														(200)			√
T	(4,250)														(4,250)			√
U				(30,000)											(30,000)			√
V	15,000		(15,000)															√
W	(8,100)														(8,100)	√		
A_2				10,000										10,000		√		
O_2					25										25			√
X									750[c]						(750)			√
Y									350						(350)			√
Q_2							(2,300)								(2,300)			√
Z											(4,000)				4,000			√
Σ	$32,275	6,000	5,000	13,000	2,025	19,000	(2,300)	=	$1,100	–0–	2,000	10,000	+	$40,000	$21,900			
				$75,000				=		$13,100			+	$61,900				

[a]Reported as current liability. [b]Reported as noncurrent liability. [c]Reported as Salaries Payable.

(continued)

Transaction Detail

	Date		Description
A_1	01/02	—	$30,000 cash in contributed by the owner who opens a business checking account.
B	01/02	—	$6,000 cash is withdrawn from the checking account to open a business savings account.
C_1	01/04	—	$10,000 worth of store equipment is acquired with a credit card.
D	01/06	—	$15,000 cash is paid to acquire merchandise inventory.
E	01/09	—	$2,000 cash is paid to the landlord for the security deposit on the store lease.
C_2	02/03	—	$10,000 cash is paid in full to settle the credit card obligation made on January 4.
F	07/01	—	$5,000 cash is borrowed with a bank credit line bearing interest at an 8% rate.
G	7/1–12/1	—	$18,000 worth of additional merchandise is acquired on account.
H	07/01	—	$7,000 cash is paid to acquire a used van with a 5-year useful life for the business.
I	11/01	—	$6,000 cash is collected from customers before any goods or services are provided.
J_1	7/31–11/30	—	$12,000 cash is paid to reduce accounts payable.
J_2	12/31	—	$6,000 of accounts payable is coverted to a 6% interest-bearing note payable due on March 31.
K_1	12/31	—	$5,000 cash is paid in full to settle the credit line loan made on July 1.
L	12/31	—	$4,000 worth of a computer and printer is acquired by signing a 2-year promissory note.
M	Daily	—	$63,200 of cash sales are made to customers throughout the year.
N	Daily	—	$20,000 of revenue is earned on account—$19,400 for customer credit sales throughout the year and $600 for teaching a course.
O_1	12/02	—	$275 interest is earned from January 2 to December 2 on $6,000 of savings bearing 5% interest.
P	Monthly	—	$1,000 cash is paid for office rent due the first day of each month beginning February 1.
Q_1	09/30	—	$300 of depreciation is recorded to recognize the use of equipment sold on September 30.
R	09/30	—	$2,000 worth of the store equipment bought on January 4 for $10,000 is sold for $1,350.
S	12/05	—	$8,000 cash is paid to employees for work performed through the year's last payday.
K_2	12/31	—	$200 cash is paid for interest due on $5,000 borrowed on July 1 at 8% and repaid on December 31.
T	Daily	—	$4,250 cash is paid for miscellaneous expenses incurred throughout the year.
U	12/31	—	$30,000 of cost of goods sold is determined by taking a physical count of inventory.
V	Daily	—	$15,000 cash is collected from customers throughout the year for amounts owed.
W	Daily	—	$8,100 cash is withdrawn from the business by the owner throughout the year.
A_2	12/24	—	$10,000 worth of merchandise is contributed by an individual for a business interest.
O_2	12/31	—	$25 of interest is earned but uncollected on a $6,000 savings account bearing 5% interest.
X	12/31	—	$750 of salaries expense is incurred but unpaid.
Y	12/31	—	$350 of miscellaneous expense is incurred but unpaid.
Q_2	12/31	—	$2,300 of depreciation is recorded on the use of unsold equipment.
Z	12/31	—	$4,000 worth of merchandise is delivered to customers who paid in advance.

however, this transaction increases merchandise inventory rather than cash. Thus, you will not find it reported in the CMU statement of cash flows shown in the next section.

Cards & Memorabilia Unlimited: What Are the Financial Statement Effects of Financing Activities?

Let's now review the financial statement effects of each of the CMU financing activity transactions described in the preceding section. The financial statement effects described here are illustrated in Figure 13-2.

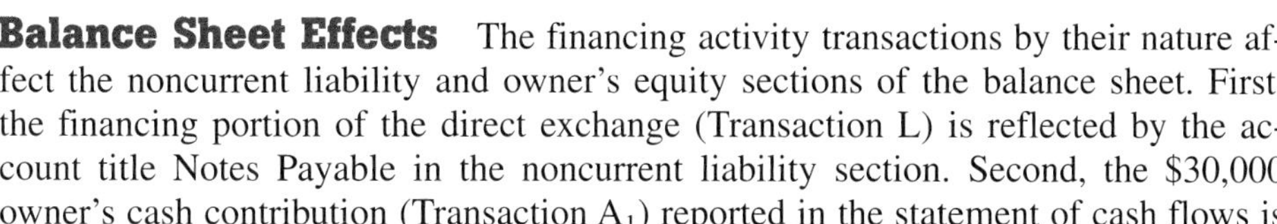

Balance Sheet Effects The financing activity transactions by their nature affect the noncurrent liability and owner's equity sections of the balance sheet. First, the financing portion of the direct exchange (Transaction L) is reflected by the account title Notes Payable in the noncurrent liability section. Second, the $30,000 owner's cash contribution (Transaction A_1) reported in the statement of cash flows is

FIGURE 13-2

Primary financial statement effects (shown in color) of Cards & Memorabilia Unlimited financing activities

Balance Sheet
at December 31

Noncurrent Liability:		
Notes Payable		4,000
Owner's Equity		
Contributed capital	$40,000	
Retained earnings	21,900	61,900

Income Statement
For the Year Ended December 31

Revenues		
Sales revenue	$86,600	
Service revenue	600	
Interest revenue	300	$87,500
Expenses		
Cost of goods sold	$30,000	
Rent expense	11,000	
Salaries expense	8,750	
Depreciation expense	2,600	
Miscellaneous expense	4,600	
Interest expense	200	
Loss on equipment sale	350	$57,500
Net Income		$30,000

Statement of Cash Flows
For the Year Ended December 31

Cash flows from financing activities:		
Contributions by owner	$30,000	
Proceeds from bank credit line	5,000	
Repayment of bank credit line	(5,000)	
Withdrawals by owner	(8,100)	
Net cash provided by financing activities		21,900

Supplemental schedule of noncash investing and financing activities:

Computer equipment costing $4,000 was acquired in exchange for a two-year promissory note.

also included in the account titled Contributed Capital in the owner's equity section of the balance sheet. This $30,000 along with the $10,000 noncash contribution from Transaction A_2 accounts for the $40,000 year-end balance found in the Contributed Capital account. Since the bank credit line is fully repaid by the end of the year, neither the $5,000 proceeds from Transaction F nor the repayment transaction (K_1) are reflected in the year-end balance sheet. Finally, the $8,100 cash withdrawal (Transaction W) found in the statement of cash flows also affects the Retained Earnings account found in the owner's equity section of the balance sheet. That is, the $8,100 reduces the $30,000 balance in retained earnings attributable to net income to its year-ending balance of $21,900 that you see in the balance sheet.

Income Statement Effects Since financing activity transactions by definition do not directly affect the income statement, there are no income statement effects to report.

Statement of Cash Flow Effects As shown in Figure 13-2, the most prominent effects of financing activity transactions on Cards & Memorabilia Unlimited's statement of cash flows are contributions by owner, proceeds from bank credit line, repayment of bank credit line, and withdrawals by owner. Less obvious is the financing portion of the direct exchange of a $4,000 promissory note for equipment.

Thus far we have reviewed CMU's financing activity transactions and their effects on its financial statements. Our next step is to take a more detailed look at exactly how the balances in the major noncurrent liability and owner's equity accounts are created by financing activities. Before we do so, let's first briefly explore current liabilities.

Accounting for Current Liabilities

Recall that current liabilities are obligations that will be eliminated within one year or the operating cycle of the business, whichever is longer. These liabilities are generally settled either by payment from current assets such as cash or by the creation of other current liabilities. Once again, most businesses use one year as the division between current and noncurrent. Although most current liabilities are initiated and completed through operating activities, in the interest of full coverage, we'll next cover the basics on how to account for standard current liabilities. Let's begin with the CMU transactions that created its current liabilities.

As you can see from Figure 13-3, Cards & Memorabilia Unlimited reports four distinct current liability accounts on its year-end balance sheet. These are Accounts Payable, Salaries Payable, Deferred Revenue, and Notes Payable. For now, let's consider the first three of these accounts.

FIGURE 13-3

Current liability section for Cards & Memorabilia Unlimited

CARDS & MEMORABILIA UNLIMITED
Balance Sheet
For the Year Ended December 31

Current Liabilities	
Accounts payable	$ 350
Salaries payable	750
Deferred revenue	2,000
Notes payable	6,000
Total current liabilities	$9,100

Measuring Accounts Payable and Salaries Payable

In Cards & Memorabilia Unlimited, the activity in the Accounts Payable account was created by an equipment purchase, a merchandise purchase (for example, Transactions C_1 and G), and miscellaneous expense incurred but unpaid. Then accounts payable was reduced by repayments of those purchases (for example, Transactions C_2 and J_1) and a conversion of an account payable to a note payable in Transaction J_2. In contrast, the balance in the Salaries Payable account was created by amounts owed but as of yet unpaid to employees. Despite their apparent differences, these two liabilities and various taxes payable accounts are accounted for in similar fashion. First, the amounts of these liabilities are fixed in contrast to contingencies whose amounts are estimated. Second, although employees expect to be paid on particular dates, these liabilities generally have estimated rather than legally fixed payment dates. Perhaps the most important similarity, however, has to do with the valuation method used. In each of these cases, the method used to measure the financial statement effect is the amount of cash due or ultimately payable as summarized in Case 2 of Figure 13-4.

Measuring Advances from Customers

CMU's activity in the Deferred Revenue account was increased by the receipt of cash from customers before the goods had been delivered (for example, Transaction I) and

FIGURE 13-4

Liability classification by degree of uncertainty

Case	Nature of Obligation	Valuation	Examples	Liability Recognition
1	Fixed payment amounts and dates	Present value of amount payable	Note payable, bond payable, capital lease, pension	Noncurrent " " "
2	Fixed payment amounts but estimated payment dates	Amount ultimately payable	Accounts, salaries, and taxes payable	Current " "
3	Estimated payment amounts and dates	Cost of goods or services provided	Contingencies (those that under *SFAS 5* are probable and estimable), warranties, premiums	Usually noncurrent Both Both
4	Partially unexecuted contracts	Amount of cash received	Rental and subscription fees received in advance	Usually current
5	Mutually unexecuted contracts	——	Purchase and employment commitments	Not usually recognized as a liability
6	Loss contingencies	——	Unsettled lawsuits, expropriation threat, loan guarantees	Not usually recognized as a liability

Source: adapted from *Intermediate Accounting,* Davidson, Hanouille, Stickney, and Weil, Dryden Press, fourth edition, 1985.

decreased by the delivery of those same goods at a later date (for example, Transaction Z). Unlike the Accounts Payable and Salaries Payable accounts, such transactions represent partially unexecuted contracts that are measured by the amount of cash received (Case 4 in Figure 13-4). So, whether the Deferred Revenue account is called Advances From Customers, Cash Received in Advance, or Unearned Revenue, the valuation basis for this liability account is actually equivalent to estimated future sales revenue.

Measuring and Reporting Current Notes Payable

Our CMU case study introduced you to two distinct note payable transactions. The first, Transaction J_2, involved a current note payable having a maturity date of three months; the second, Transaction L, involved a noncurrent note payable due in installments over a two-year period. Since generally accepted accounting principles (GAAP) provide for the use of the compound interest concept when dealing with note transactions having maturity dates in excess of one year, we'll examine Transaction L later in this chapter. Before we examine Transaction J_2 to illustrate the accounting for note transactions having maturity dates of one year or less, however, let's first learn more about notes in general.

What Is a Promissory Note? A **promissory note** is a written contract in which one person, known as the *maker*, promises to pay another person, known as the *payee* or *holder*, a definite sum of money. This promise to pay includes a definite future date or dates when the promissory note is due for payment or scheduled to mature known as its **maturity date(s)**. This definite sum of money usually includes the *principal* amount, or *face value*, of the promissory note and the interest that accrues on that principal over the life of the loan.

Figure 13-5 describes the physical flow of events associated with a note transaction. In addition to showing the maker and the payee of the note, this figure illustrates how the note provides for the repayment of the principal as well as the payment of interest. You've already learned how a borrower often gives a promissory note to a lender in exchange for additional cash. Now, using the arrows in Figure 13-5, notice that a buyer/customer can give a promissory note to a seller (payee/holder) in exchange

FIGURE 13-5

Physical flow of events associated with a note transaction

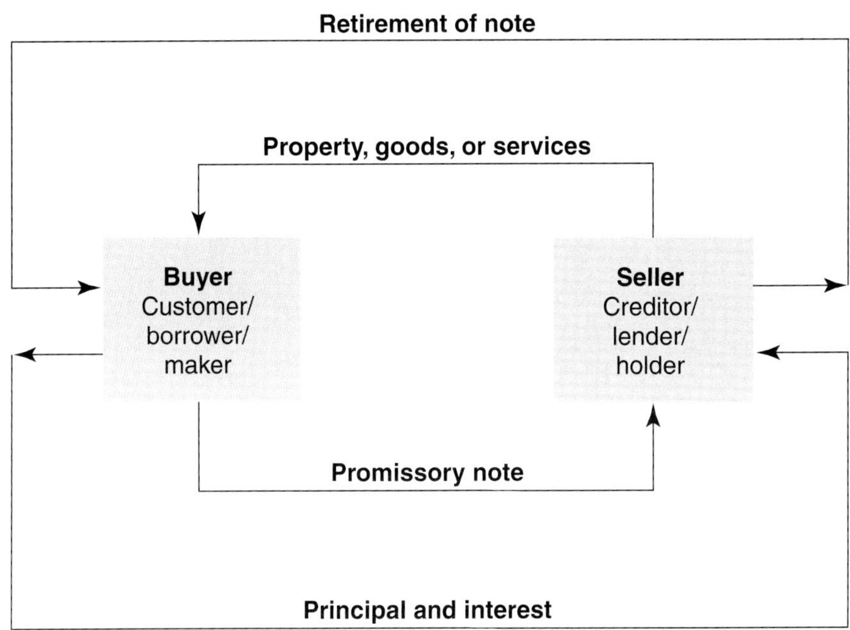

for the seller's goods or services. When you revisit Transaction J_2, you'll discover a buyer/customer can also give a promissory note to a seller to settle the customer's existing account payable.

It is important to be able to distinguish between the buyer's perspective and the seller's perspective of the same note transaction. From the buyer's perspective, agreeing to pay a debt with a note requires the use of the Note Payable account, and interest incurred requires the use of the Interest Expense account. From the seller's perspective, receipt of a note requires the use of the Note Receivable account, and interest earned requires the use of the Interest Revenue account.

Promissory notes may be classified as interest-bearing or non-interest-bearing. An **interest-bearing note** has a stated interest rate and requires that interest be paid in cash at regular intervals. In contrast, a **non-interest-bearing note** does not have a stated interest rate and, therefore, does not pay cash at regular intervals. Instead, the interest is included in the face value of the note and is paid along with the principal when the note reaches its maturity date.

To summarize, a promissory note or, more simply, a **note** has the following four characteristics:

1. It provides for the repayment of the principal as well as the periodic payment of interest.
2. A customer may give it to a seller in exchange for goods or services.
3. A customer may give it to a seller in settlement of an existing account payable.
4. It may be classified as interest bearing or non-interest bearing.

Now that you are familiar with the definition, terminology, physical flow, and characteristics of a promissory note, you are ready to consider how such transactions are accounted for.

Measuring, Recording, and Reporting a Note Transaction You might recall that in Transaction J_2, \$6,000 of accounts payable was converted to a 6% interest-bearing note payable due on March 31 of CMU's second year of business. Since the original debt included in the Accounts Payable account amounted to \$6,000, the amount transferred to the account titled Note Payable was also \$6,000 as shown here.

Transaction Analysis							Journal Entry		
	Fundamental Accounting Equation								
Account Titles	Assets	=	Liabilities	+	Owners' Equity		Account Titles	Debit	Credit
Accounts Payable			(6,000)				Accounts Payable	6,000	
Note Payable—Current			6,000				Note Payable—Current		6,000

Just as was done for accounts payable, GAAP require that the amount borrowed or *ultimately* payable be used to measure a note payable.

Because CMU issued the note on December 31 of the preceding year, the note has a three-month term. CMU must pay monthly interest of 6% on this note. If CMU prepares monthly income statements, three identical transactions for interest of \$30 (\$6,000 × .06 × 1/12) like that recorded on January 31 below will be necessary.

Transaction Analysis							Journal Entry		
	Fundamental Accounting Equation								
Account Titles	Assets	=	Liabilities	+	Owners' Equity		Account Titles	Debit	Credit
Interest Expense					(30)		Interest Expense	30	
Cash	(30)						Cash		30

Assuming that the March 31 interest transaction had been recorded, the retirement of the note on March 31 would be recorded as follows.

Transaction Analysis						Journal Entry		
	Fundamental Accounting Equation							
Account Titles	Assets	=	Liabilities	+	Owners' Equity	Account Titles	Debit	Credit
Note Payable—Current			(6,000)			Note Payable—Current	6,000	
Cash	(6,000)					Cash		6,000

The financial statement effects of this interest-bearing note are as follows:

Balance Sheet In the Notes Payable account, the current liability is reported at its face value of $6,000 until it is retired on March 31.

Income Statement Three monthly interest expense transactions of $30 each would result in the reporting of a $90 interest expense amount in CMU's second year of business.

Statement of Cash Flows Because the interest of $90 recorded as an expense was also paid in cash, it must be reported as interest paid in the cash flows from operating activities section.

Since you have now learned how to account for notes payable classified as current assets, be sure to use Performance Objective 49 to help you master this topic.

YOUR PERFORMANCE OBJECTIVE 49
Calculate simple interest on a note payable, **record** the transactions related to its issuance, interest accrual, and payment at maturity, and **present** its financial statement effects.

Measuring and Reporting Other Current Liabilities

Let's now briefly explore some additional current liabilities. These include payroll tax liabilities, income tax liabilities, and other accrued liabilities.

Salaries and Payroll Tax Liabilities Early in this textbook, you learned how to account for amounts owed to employees by examining Transaction S. Essentially, you learned that a Salary Expense account or a Wage Expense account can be accompanied by a Salaries Payable account until the employee is actually paid. Although accounting for employees is very straightforward in concept, the practical matter of processing a company's payroll can be an exceptionally detailed task. What particularly complicates payroll accounting is that businesses are required to withhold certain taxes from their employees' salaries and then remit those amounts at designated intervals to different government agencies. The most prominent of these withheld amounts are social security taxes (Federal Insurance Contributions Act, or FICA, tax) and federal and state income taxes. Other deductions that the employer is often responsible for withholding from salaries include health insurance premiums and voluntary contributions by the employee to such charities as the United Way or the March of Dimes. In addition to paying employee salaries, the employer is also responsible for paying additional payroll tax expenses such as matching dollar for dollar its employee contributions to social security as well as making payments for both federal and state unemployment compensation taxes. These concepts can be illustrated by the following example.

Example Assume that the following details represent the weekly payroll for Pizza Haven employees:

Gross salary amount		$100,000
Deductions		
Federal income tax withholding	$20,000	
State income tax withholding	2,500	
Social security tax withholding	7,000	
Union dues	400	
Health insurance premiums	3,500	33,400
Net salary amount (take-home pay)		$ 66,600

Once these numbers have been calculated, the following transaction is necessary to record total salary expense, the amounts owed to various governmental agencies, and the net amount payable to employees.

Transaction Analysis				Journal Entry		
	Fundamental Accounting Equation					
Account Titles	Assets	= Liabilities +	Owners' Equity	Account Titles	Debit	Credit
Salaries Expense			(100,000)	Salaries Expense	100,000	
FICA Taxes Payable		7,000		FICA Taxes Payable		7,000
State Income Tax Payable		2,500		State Income Tax Payable		2,500
Federal Income Tax Payable		20,000		Federal Income Tax Pay.		20,000
Health Insurance Payable		3,500		Health Insurance Pay.		3,500
Union Dues Payable		400		Union Dues Payable		400
Salary Payable		66,600		Salary Payable		66,600

The following transaction must be recorded when the employees are actually paid.

Transaction Analysis				Journal Entry		
	Fundamental Accounting Equation					
Account Titles	Assets	= Liabilities +	Owners' Equity	Account Titles	Debit	Credit
Salaries Payable		(66,600)		Salaries Payable	66,600	
Cash	(66,600)			Cash		66,600

Pizza Haven is also responsible for paying the following additional payroll taxes:

Social Security tax matching	$7,000
State unemployment compensation taxes	2,700
Federal unemployment compensation taxes	800

To properly account for these payroll taxes, Pizza Haven must record the following transaction:

Transaction Analysis				Journal Entry		
	Fundamental Accounting Equation					
Account Titles	Assets	= Liabilities +	Owners' Equity	Account Titles	Debit	Credit
Payroll Tax Expense			(10,500)	Payroll Tax Expense	10,500	
FICA Taxes Payable		7,000		FICA Taxes Payable		7,000
State Unemployment Tax Payable		2,700		State Unemployment Tax Payable		2,700
Federal Unemployment Tax Payable		800		Federal Unemployment Tax Payable		800

Now that you have learned about the essential concepts involved in recording a payroll, you can use Performance Objective 50 to ensure your understanding of these concepts.

YOUR PERFORMANCE OBJECTIVE 50
Calculate all employee and employer amounts related to a company's payroll liability, **record** these amounts, and **present** their financial statement effects.

Income Tax Liabilities A business organized as either a sole proprietorship or a partnership does not itself pay federal and state income taxes. Instead, the income tax is levied on the individuals who operate the business. Unlike these forms of business, however, a corporation is a legal entity and must pay federal and state income taxes on its taxable income. Recall the following example from Chapter 10:

Example Assume that the corporation Cards & Memorabilia Unlimited Inc. is subject to income tax (assume a 15% tax rate) reported on Form 1120. Since the pretax income is \$30,000 from previous income statements, the tax will be \$30,000 × 0.15, or \$4,500.

Transaction Z The federal income tax for the year is determined to be \$4,500 (\$30,000 × 0.15).

Transaction Analysis							Journal Entry		
	Fundamental Accounting Equation								
Account Titles	**Assets**	**=**	**Liabilities**	**+**	**Owners' Equity**		**Account Titles**	**Debit**	**Credit**
Income Tax Expense					(4,500)		Income Tax Expense	4,500	
Income Tax Payable			4,500				Income Tax Payable		4,500

Other Accrued Liabilities An accrued liability is recorded whenever an expense is incurred in the current period even though cash is not paid until a future period. In Chapter 7's discussion of accrued expenses, two such accrued liabilities—Transaction X and Transaction Y—were described. Let's review how Transaction Y was recorded:

Transaction Analysis							Journal Entry		
	Fundamental Accounting Equation								
Account Titles	**Assets**	**=**	**Liabilities**	**+**	**Owners' Equity**		**Account Titles**	**Debit**	**Credit**
Miscellaneous Expense					(350)		Miscellaneous Expense	350	
Accounts Payable			350				Accounts Payable		350

As you can see, recording such an accrued liability involves creating an expense and an accrued liability.

Accounting for Noncurrent Liabilities

Generally, the dollar amount included in the noncurrent liability section of the balance sheet is significantly greater than the dollar amount included in the current liability section. By definition, noncurrent liabilities generally have a greater impact on a business's future prospects than do current liabilities. As a result, it is important that you learn just how these financing related accounts are measured and reported. Before we turn to specific noncurrent liabilities, however, let's learn more about why and how the present value concept is used in the measurement and reporting of noncurrent liabilities.

Why Is Present Value Used to Measure and Report Noncurrent Liabilities?

There are at least three reasons why present value is the primary valuation method used to measure and report noncurrent liabilities. The first reason is actually quite simple. Many noncurrent liabilities are characterized by multiple cash flows. Since conventional financial statements can report only a single dollar figure for each liability, we must be able to restate a liability's multiple cash flows into a single dollar amount. The second reason is somewhat similar. Numbers expressed in conventional financial statements represent either current or past amounts. They do not represent future amounts. Thus, we must be able to restate the future dollar amounts associated with liabilities into an equivalent present value.

The third and final reason to use present value as our noncurrent liability valuation method is to more precisely measure income. For example, non-interest-bearing notes often have a face or maturity value that includes both a cash equivalent sales or purchase price—a present value, plus an interest fee or charge for the privilege of deferring collection or payment. That is, the face value of such notes will not equal the present value of the consideration given or received in the exchange. The effect of not recording a note at its present value is to:

1. Misstate sales revenue or income to the seller as well as to misstate asset cost or expense to the buyer in the year of the transaction.
2. Misstate or even ignore interest revenue and interest expense in subsequent periods.

Additional Present Value Tools

Since present value is the valuation method generally used to measure noncurrent liabilities, it is essential that you can apply the compound interest concepts already introduced to transactions that create noncurrent liabilities. You learned about two such tools in Appendix 12–1. Specifically, you can:

1. Draw a time line to represent both cash flow amounts and timing.
2. Calculate the initial present value of all future cash flows.

This chapter will introduce some additional present value tools to help you understand how everyday financing transactions such as borrowing with promissory notes, installment loans, and capital leases (Appendix 13–1, which you can find at www.mhhe.com/solomon) are measured and reported. In addition, these tools will help you better comprehend more significant transactions such as bond issues and pension plan arrangements. Performance Objective 51 summarizes each application of the present value concept presented in this chapter.

YOUR PERFORMANCE OBJECTIVE 51

Apply the present value concept to measure and report the effects of such transactions as credit card accounts, general notes, automobile loans, home loans, leases, bonds, and pensions by being able to:

a. **Calculate** the initial present value of all future cash flows, all subsequent present values (construct an amortization table), and the interest revenue and/or interest expense over the transaction's life.
b. **Record** all transaction related effects from both perspectives.
c. **Present** the balance sheet, income statement, and statement of cash flow transaction-related effects.

You are now ready to examine how interest is calculated when you apply the compound interest concept.

Calculating Interest Revenue and Interest Expense To illustrate how both interest revenue and interest expense are calculated period by period and over the life of the transaction, consider the following example:

Example 1 Suppose you have $4,500 to invest on January 1, 2004, that you use to purchase an annuity yielding a 10% return on investment. The annuity is composed of six annual receipts of $1,033.23 that begin on December 31, 2004.

This time line illustrates all the elements of this annuity.

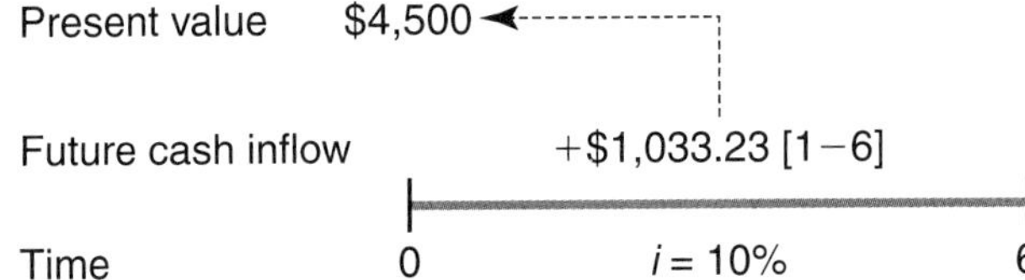

As illustrated by this time line, you paid $4,500.00 at the outset and received a total of $6,199.38 ($1,033.23 × 6) over the life of the investment. The difference of $1,699.38 between cash received ($6,199.38) and cash invested or paid ($4,500.00) represents interest revenue over the life of the investment.

Since you earned interest revenue as the investor in Example 1, it should be clear that you would incur interest expense had you borrowed rather than invested the $4,500. That is, holding an investment provides you with interest revenue while borrowing money places you in the opposite position of incurring interest expense. Thus, the person or organization that borrows your $4,500 incurs interest expense of $1,699.38. To the borrower, interest expense incurred over the life of the transaction is simply the difference ($1,699.38) between cash paid ($6,199.38) and cash borrowed or received ($4,500.00).

In summary, the total interest revenue earned over the life of an investment equals total cash received minus total cash paid. In contrast, the total interest expense incurred over the life of a loan equals total cash paid minus total cash received. We'll next discuss how you calculate each period's (periodic) interest revenue and interest expense.

Amortization Tables Observe that the cash received ($6,199.38) from withdrawing equal payments or rents ($1,033.23) at the end of each of the six years exactly recovers your principal ($4,500.00) and interest earned ($1,699.38). From this perspective, the sixth and last withdrawal brings the balance in your investment to zero. That is, the future value of the annuity has a zero balance immediately after the sixth and last deposit. Be sure to use the following calculations to confirm that your last withdrawal in Example 1 reduces your investment fund balance to zero.

Initial investment (present value at time = 0 or now)	**$ 4,500.00**
Add: Year 1 interest revenue ($4,500 × .10 × 1)	450.00
Balance before withdrawal	4,950.00
Deduct: Year 1 withdrawal or rent (given)	(1,033.23)
Investment fund balance or PV at time = 1	**3,916.77**
Add: Year 2 interest revenue ($3,916.77 × .10 × 1)	391.68
Balance before withdrawal	4,308.45
Deduct: Year 2 withdrawal or rent (given)	(1,033.23)

Investment fund balance or PV at time = 2	**3,275.22**
Add: Year 3 interest revenue ($3,275.22 × .10 × 1)	327.52
Balance before withdrawal	3,602.74
Deduct: Year 3 withdrawal or rent (given)	(1,033.23)
Investment fund balance or PV at time = 3	**2,569.51**
Add: Year 4 interest revenue ($2,569.51 × .10 × 1)	256.95
Balance before withdrawal	2,826.46
Deduct: Year 4 withdrawal or rent (given)	(1,033.23)
Investment fund balance or PV at time = 4	**1,793.23**
Add: Year 5 interest revenue ($1,793.23 × .10 × 1)	179.32
Balance before withdrawal	1,972.55
Deduct: Year 5 withdrawal or rent (given)	(1,033.23)
Investment fund balance or PV at time = 5	**939.32**
Add: Year 6 interest revenue ($939.32 × .10 × 1)	93.93
Balance before withdrawal	1,033.25
Deduct: Year 6 withdrawal or rent (given)	(1,033.23)
Investment fund balance or PV at time = 6	**$ .02**

The format shown above can be called the **future value approach** because the calculations start in the immediate present and proceed into the future. Notice in particular how interest is calculated by focusing on the second year calculations:

Investment fund balance or PV at time = 1	$ 3,916.77
Add: Year 2 interest revenue ($3,916.77 × .10 × 1)	391.68
Balance before withdrawal	4,308.45
Deduct: Year 2 withdrawal or rent (given)	(1,033.23)
Investment fund balance or PV at time = 2	$ 3,275.22

You already know that to properly measure net income, you must calculate and record the amount of interest for each year. For simple interest, that formula was:

Simple Interest = Principal × Interest Rate × Time

In compound interest calculations, however, we must modify one term in the preceding formula as follows:

Compound Interest = **Present Value** × Interest Rate × Time
= $3,916.77 × .10 × 1 = $391.68

This expression is called the **general formula for periodic compound interest**. It suggests that the yearly interest expense for the buyer and the yearly interest revenue for the seller are calculated by multiplying the note's present value by the interest rate and the result multiplied by the appropriate fraction of the year.

As you can see, the direction of movement in the future value approach is from the present into the future. Use it whenever you calculate successive present values, an important procedure in all accounting applications. If you ignore the 2-cent rounding error in our example, the future value of this annuity has a zero balance immediately after the sixth and last deposit. Notice that moving from one present value to a later or successive present value is accomplished by adding interest and subtracting the annual withdrawal. Since each withdrawal far exceeds the interest added, successive present values decline in amount. The fact that the investment balance decreases through time is an important characteristic of every present value of annuity problem. In fact, this systematic reduction of an existing investment or debt balance is called amortization. That is, **amortization** is the process of reducing the investment fund in Example 1 from $4,500.00 to a zero balance over six years.

Besides illustrating the effects of amortization with the future value approach, you can also express those effects in a more visual manner with the use of the graph shown in Figure 13-6. This graph illustrates how the $4,500.00 balance of the six-year investment fund described in Example 1 is reduced year by year until no balance remains. In this graph, the vertical line segments AB and DE represent interest revenue. AB equals the $450 of interest revenue that is added to the initial present value of $4,500, and DE equals the $93.93 of interest revenue that is added to the present value of $939.32 five years later. Likewise, both vertical line segments AC and DF represent the withdrawal or payment of $1,033.23 made at the end of the first year and the sixth year, respectively. Note in Figure 13-6 that while the amount of each withdrawal remains constant, each year's interest revenue becomes progressively smaller as the investment balance declines.

FIGURE 13-6

Graphic representation of amortization in Example 1

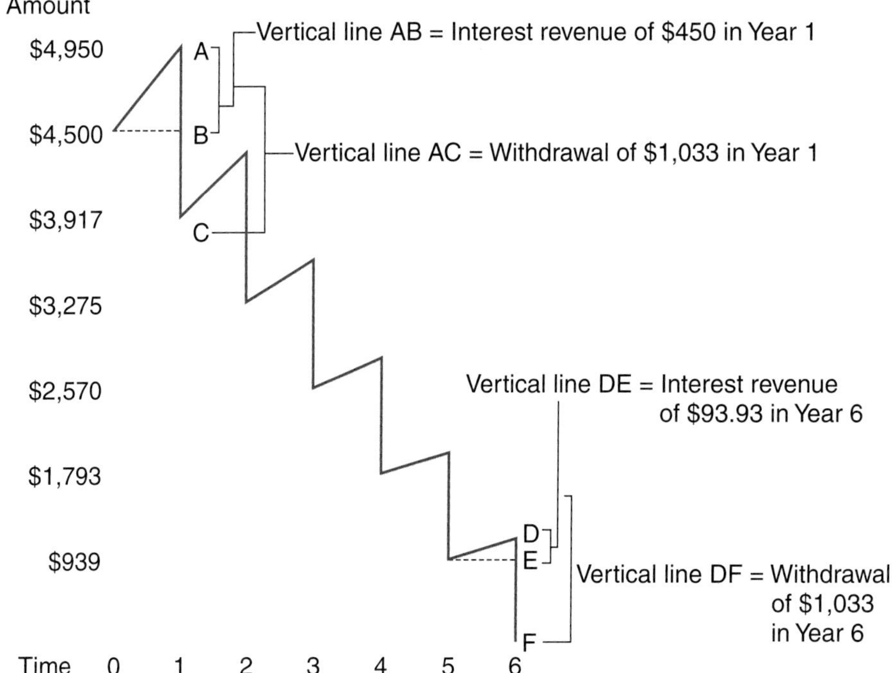

You have now seen two ways to describe the process of amortization: the future value approach and the graphical approach. A third equivalent but more efficient way to describe amortization calculations is to construct the amortization table shown here.

Amortization Table: Calculation of Subsequent Present Values

End of Year	Interest Revenue	Yearly Withdrawal	Investment Balance
0			$4,500.00
1	$ 450.00	$1,033.23	3,916.77
2	391.68	1,033.23	3,275.22
3	327.52	1,033.23	2,569.51
4	256.95	1,033.23	1,793.23
5	179.32	1,033.23	939.32
6	93.93	1,033.23	.02
	$1,699.40	**$6,199.38**	

Study this amortization table carefully. As you move from one present value to the next—as you calculate subsequent present values—you add interest and subtract a payment. Thus, another way of describing an amortization table is to say it represents a calculation of subsequent present values. The amount of amortization for each period equals the amount deducted from the opening balance less the amount added to that same balance. An amortization table displays the interest added, the withdrawal or payment deducted from an existing balance, and the balance itself for all periods affected. Obviously, such a table is much more efficient and understandable than the 25-line calculations necessitated by the future value approach.

The set of calculations used to determine each row of this and all compound interest amortization tables is often referred to as the **effective interest method of amortization**. We'll define the term *effective interest* later in this chapter. For now, think of it as the interest rate underlying all of the present value calculations in an amortization table. The concept of an amortization table can also be applied to a future value of annuity problem as illustrated in Example 2.

Example 2 A company decides to make five annual deposits of $10,000 in a bank to create a debt retirement fund. Each deposit will be made at the end of the year with the fund earning interest at 8% compounded annually. How would you calculate the balance in the debt retirement fund immediately after the fifth deposit is made?

You'd first draw this time line:

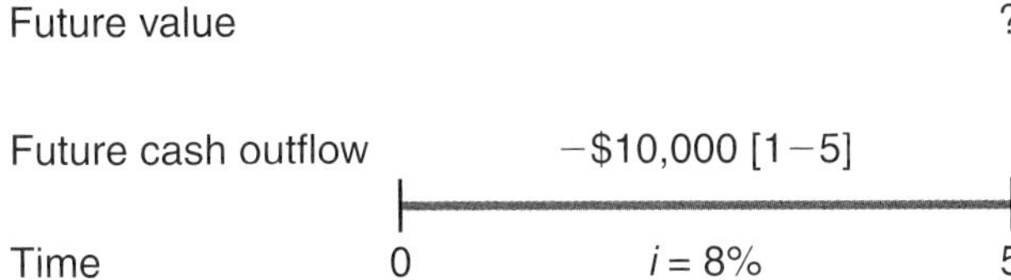

You would then use a future value of annuity table and formula because you are seeking the future value of an annuity. (Review Rule 3 in Appendix 12–1.) As you can see from this annuity's time line, there is no present value. That is, at time zero, no nonzero amount exists. However, the five deposits plus accumulated interest will provide a future value of annuity amount denoted by the time line's question mark.

Using the future value of annuity interest factor (FVAIF) for an 8% interest rate and five deposits or rents with the secondary interest formula, you have $FVA_n = R(FVAIF)$ = $10,000(5.86660) = $58,666. The following amortization table illustrates these calculations more fully.

Amortization Table:
Calculation of Subsequent Present Values

End of Year	Yearly Deposit	Interest Revenue	Investment Balance
1	$10,000	N/A	$10,000.00
2	10,000	800.00	20,800.00
3	10,000	1,664.00	32,464.00
4	10,000	2,597.12	45,061.12
5	10,000	3,604.89	$58,666.01*
	$50,000	$8,666.01	

*1 cent rounding error

From this amortization table, you can see how the $58,666 future value of the annuity is a combination of the five deposits totaling $50,000 plus the accumulated interest of $8,666.00. (Ignore the one cent rounding error.)

Measuring and Reporting Noncurrent Notes Payable

Now that you are acquainted with some basic present value tools required by GAAP for notes with maturity dates exceeding one year, we will examine how noncurrent notes payable are measured and reported. Since an interest-bearing note has already been described in the section "Measuring, Recording, and Reporting a Note Transaction," we'll focus on a non-interest-bearing note.

Non-Interest-Bearing Notes

To illustrate how to account for a non-interest-bearing note transaction, let's move forward in time three years after the opening of Cards & Memorabilia Unlimited. Because of CMU's success, Susan Newman and her partner Martha Perez consider relocating and expanding the business. One option is to buy land and construct a new store. Assume the partners find a parcel of land and are willing to pay $11,664 for it two years from now. The seller, a real estate investment firm that buys and sells land, is willing to accept the $11,664, but offers to discount the price if Susan and Martha promise to pay immediately instead of two years later. What is an acceptable purchase price if the partners are able to borrow the needed funds at an 8% interest rate? To help answer this question, let's use the following time line to illustrate both the amount and timing of cash outflow(s) that apply.

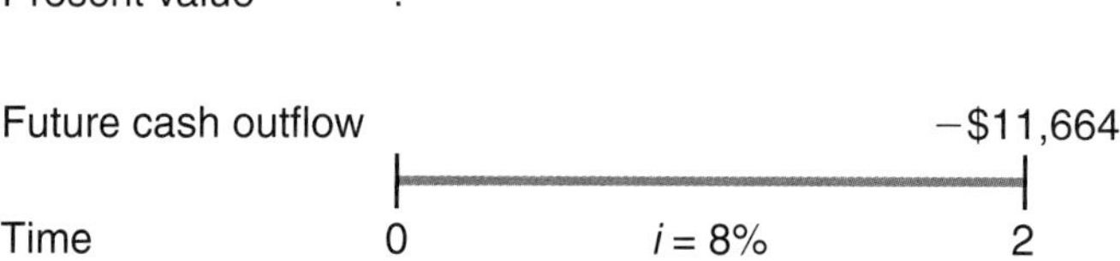

From the information and the time line, it should be clear that our partners must calculate a purchase price for the *present*. That is, they must **discount** or calculate the present value of a cash payment to be made two years from today. Since the interest rate is 8% and the $11,664 will be paid in two years, the appropriate interest factor from the present value of $1 table (Table 2 in Appendix 12-1 on page 674.) is .85734. To determine an acceptable purchase price, that is, the present value of $11,664, we apply the present value formula:

$$PV = FV_2\,(PVIF) = \$11{,}664\ (.85734) = \$10{,}000.00$$ (Ignore the one cent rounding error.)

Thus, an acceptable purchase price rounded to the nearest dollar is $10,000. If CMU pays $10,000 for this piece of land, the following transaction would be recorded at the date of purchase:

Transaction Analysis				Journal Entry		
	Fundamental Accounting Equation					
Account Titles	Assets	= Liabilities +	Owners' Equity	Account Titles	Debit	Credit
Land	10,000			Land	10,000	
Cash [$11,664 × .85734]	(10,000)			Cash [$11,664 × .85734]		10,000

Since Susan and Martha were indifferent as to paying $10,000 today or $11,664 two years from now, there is no reason to believe they would not be willing to issue a non-interest-bearing note in exchange for the land, payable in the amount of $11,664 two years from now, instead of paying cash today. If they did issue such a note, here's how they might record this transaction at the date of purchase:

Transaction Analysis					Journal Entry		
	Fundamental Accounting Equation						
Account Titles	Assets	=	Liabilities	+ Owners' Equity	Account Titles	Debit	Credit
Land	10,000				Land	10,000	
Note Payable			10,000		Note Payable		10,000

Although the nature of this note does not allow it to actually *pay* interest before its maturity date, it does *bear* interest. That is, the note transaction does not represent an interest-free loan, and so CMU must record interest at the end of each accounting period. The following amortization schedule will enable CMU to more easily record this periodic accrual of interest.

Amortization Table: Calculation of Subsequent Present Values

End of Year	Interest Expense (8%)	Cash Payment	Liability at End of Year
0			10,000
1	800	N/A	10,800
2	864	11,664	–0–

With this information available, CMU will record the interest adjustments for this note for Year 1 as follows:

Transaction Analysis					Journal Entry		
	Fundamental Accounting Equation						
Account Titles	Assets	=	Liabilities	+ Owners' Equity	Account Titles	Debit	Credit
Interest Expense				(800)	Interest Expense	800	
Notes Payable—Noncurrent			800		Notes Payable—Noncurrent		800

As you can see from this note's amortization table, the amount of interest expense increases from $800 ($10,000 × .08) at the end of the note's first year to $864 ($10,800 × .08) at the end of the note's second year, the due date of this note.

Transaction Analysis					Journal Entry		
	Fundamental Accounting Equation						
Account Titles	Assets	=	Liabilities	+ Owners' Equity	Account Titles	Debit	Credit
Interest Expense				(864)	Interest Expense	864	
Notes Payable—Noncurrent			864		Notes Payable—Noncurrent		864

The last transaction to record is the retirement of the note.

Transaction Analysis					Journal Entry		
	Fundamental Accounting Equation						
Account Titles	Assets	=	Liabilities	+ Owners' Equity	Account Titles	Debit	Credit
Note Payable			(11,664)		Note Payable	11,664	
Cash	(11,664)				Cash		11,664

The financial statement effects of this note are as follows:

Balance sheet: Notes Payable, a noncurrent liability account, is reported at $10,000 initially and $10,800 at the end of its first year. Although its balance momentarily reaches $11,664, the cash payment eliminates the Note Payable account entirely at the very end of its second year or due date.

Income statement: Interest expenses of $800 and $864 are reported in the first and second years, respectively.

Statement of cash flows: The initial purchase of land in exchange for a note payable is treated as a direct exchange. Interest of $1,664 is reported as interest paid in the cash flows from operating activities section, but not until the second year of the note transaction. Likewise, the retirement of the note is reported in the cash flows from financing activity section as a $10,000 retirement of notes payable.

Installment Loans

You might have already encountered or will encounter a variety of installment loans such as automobile loans, home or building loans, and consumer or equipment loans. Before we consider those loans, however, let's examine a general example.

Generalized Example Suppose a company wants to purchase land selling for $100,000 on January 1, 2004. Since this company needs to conserve cash, it agrees to transfer a $100,000 note payable to the seller in exchange for the land. The note is to be paid off in three equal installments, each of which includes principal plus interest of 8% per year on the unpaid balance. Study the following time line that illustrates both the amount and timing of cash outflows that apply to this installment loan transaction.

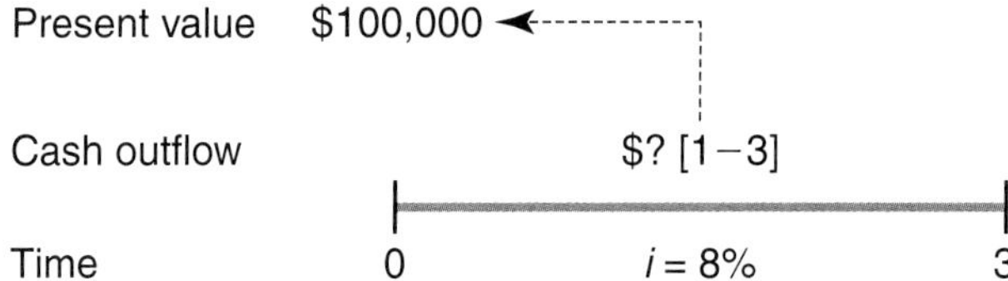

This time line shows that today's $100,000 cash price represents a present value of an annuity since it precedes a series of cash flows. That is, the amount of the note's initial present value is the $100,000 cash price (cash equivalent value) or fair market value of the land on January 1, 2004. This particular annuity has three payments or rents and bears interest at 8%. Confirm that the relevant interest factor from the present value of an annuity of $1 table (Table 4 in Appendix 12–1 on page 676) is $PVAIF$ = 2.57710. Now let's attempt to calculate the amount of each installment payment. Since this amount is unknown, we must isolate the amount of payment or rent (R) in the present value of annuity secondary formula:

$$\begin{aligned} \text{PVA}_3 &= R(PVAIF) \\ \text{Where } R &= \text{Each installment payment} \\ R &= PVA_3/PVAIF \\ &= \$100{,}000/2.57710 \\ &= \$38{,}803.31 \end{aligned}$$

Although this company conserves a significant amount of cash in the first year by financing the purchase, it should determine how much cash it will ultimately have to pay. You can perform this analysis because you know how to calculate the total interest cost that this buyer will bear. Your first step is to calculate the total amount of cash to be paid by financing and compare it to the amount of cash paid had the land been purchased outright. Using the time line, approximately $116,410 ($38,803.31 × 3 payments) will be paid in cash if the buyer finances the land with a note. Had the buyer instead purchased the land immediately, $100,000 of cash would have been paid. The difference of $16,410 ($116,410 cash paid − $100,000 cash equivalent value received), therefore, represents interest expense, the time cost of money to our borrower needed to finance this purchase.

Although we have viewed note transactions from the perspective of the buyer/customer, it is important that you appreciate how the same transaction appears from the perspective of the seller/creditor. From the buyer's perspective, issuance of a note requires the use of the Note Payable account and the incurrence of interest requires the use of the Interest Expense account. From the seller's perspective, however, receipt of a note requires the use of the Note Receivable account and the earning of interest requires the use of the Interest Revenue account. Since the interest calculation is identical from either perspective, the total interest revenue earned by the seller in our earlier land transaction is also $16,410. That is, the seller's perspective is exactly opposite to the buyer's or customer's perspective in a note transaction. Once the interest factor and cash flows have been identified, the January 1, 2004 purchase of land can be recorded.

Transaction Analysis						Journal Entry		
	Fundamental Accounting Equation							
Account Titles	**Assets**	**=**	**Liabilities**	**+**	**Owners' Equity**	**Account Titles**	**Debit**	**Credit**
Land	100,000					Land	100,000	
Note Payable			100,000			Note Payable		100,000

To enable you to record the accrued interest on the note payable (rounded to the nearest dollar) at the end of each year, you must use the general formula for periodic compound interest introduced earlier. Since our present value equals $100,000 and the relevant interest rate is 8%, the calculation is $100,000 × .08 × 1 = $8,000. Since you have discovered that both an interest expense of $8,000 and a cash payment of $38,803.31 must be recorded at the end of Year 1, there must be at least one more account to be recorded. That is, the first installment payment of $38,803.31 consists of both interest on principal ($8,000) and reduction in principal of the note. With this fact in mind, you should be able to reason that the missing amount is, in fact, a reduction in principal of $30,803.31 as shown here:

Transaction Analysis						Journal Entry		
	Fundamental Accounting Equation							
Account Titles	**Assets**	**=**	**Liabilities**	**+**	**Owners' Equity**	**Account Titles**	**Debit**	**Credit**
Interest Expense					(8,000.00)	Interest Expense	8,000.00	
Note Payable			(30,803.31)			Note Payable	30,803.31	
Cash	(38,803.31)					Cash		38,803.31

Notice that the $30,803.31 decrease or debit to the Note Payable account is the difference between the amount of interest expense incurred and the amount of cash paid. Since interest expense for the second and third years cannot be derived without calculating subsequent present values, the following amortization table for the liability, or **debt payment schedule**, will be helpful. Be sure you understand how each table amount is calculated before you read on.

Amortization Table—Calculation of Subsequent Present Values

Time	(Debit) Interest Expense	+	(Debit) Note Payable	=	(Credit) Cash	Unpaid Principal
0						$100,000.00
1	$8,000.00		$30,803.31		$38,803.31	69,196.69
2	5,535.74		33,267.57		38,803.31	35,929.12
3	2,874.33		35,928.98		38,803.31	.14*

*Rounding error.

Notice how this table illustrates the concept that each installment payment is composed of two elements: interest on principal and reduction of the principal. This table's information enables us to now record the interest transactions at the end of Year 2 (12/31/05) and Year 3 (12/31/06).

Transaction Analysis							Journal Entry		
	Fundamental Accounting Equation								
Account Titles	Assets	=	Liabilities	+	Owners' Equity		Account Titles	Debit	Credit
Interest Expense					(5,535.74)		Interest Expense	5,535.74	
Note Payable			(33,267.57)				Note Payable	33,267.57	
Cash	(38,803.31)						Cash		38,803.31

Transaction Analysis							Journal Entry		
	Fundamental Accounting Equation								
Account Titles	Assets	=	Liabilities	+	Owners' Equity		Account Titles	Debit	Credit
Interest Expense					(2,874.33)		Interest Expense	2,874.33	
Note Payable			(35,928.98)				Note Payable	35,928.98	
Cash	(38,803.31)						Cash		38,803.31

Note that the ending balance in the Notes Payable account belongs in the liability section of the balance sheet while the annual amounts in the Interest Expense account belong in the expense section of the income statement.

Since you are quite likely to deal with an automobile loan at sometime during your life, let's next consider a description of this type of installment loan.

A mastery of the compound interest concept will make you more equipped to decide how to finance your automobile.

Automobile Loans Let's assume that Susan Newman buys a new $24,000 car for her business on January 1, 2004. Susan makes a $4,000 down payment and finances the remaining balance with a 12%, five-year, installment car loan. Specifically, she signs a $20,000 promissory note agreeing to pay her dealership equal payments at the end of each of 60 months.

The following series of questions and answers are designed to help you model an analytical approach that will help you solve problems of this type:

Question 1 Does this installment loan represent an annuity or non-annuity problem?

Using a Shortcut to Calculate Subsequent Present Values

INSIGHT

If you need to know the amount of a noncurrent liability's present value several years from now, you don't have to perform laborious, period-by-period calculations to obtain that amount in the liability's amortization table. Instead, you can calculate the present value in a fraction of the time you'd spend preparing an amortization table by simply using a time line and present value tables. This approach is called the **time-line/table approach** because you first construct a *time line* in which the current date is treated as time zero, modify that time line to reflect your target date, and then recalculate the present value from the new perspective by using an interest *table*. For example, carefully compare the two time lines shown below for the preceding present value problem:

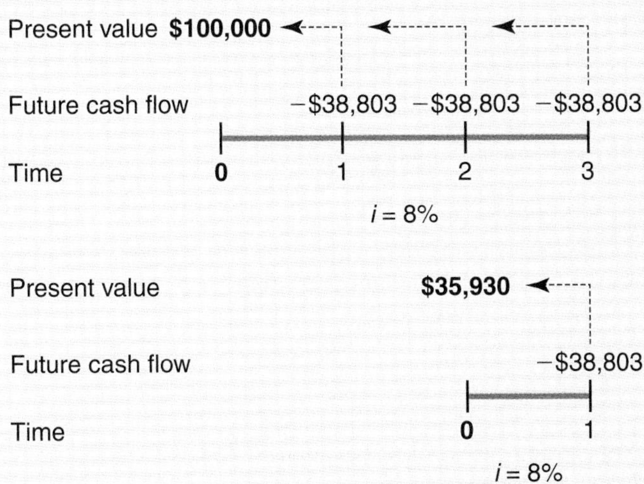

The first time line represents our problem at the moment the land is acquired for $100,000 in exchange for a note payable. The second time line represents this same problem exactly two years later when the subsequent present value is $35,930. Note that you don't have to calculate interest twice, add that total to the $100,000 and then deduct two payments to arrive at the $35,930. Instead, you simply imagine that you have been hurtled two years into the future—to the end of year two. From this perspective, two payments have been made and only one remains—at the end of year three. Under the time-line/table approach, you calculate the present value of this annuity as of the end of the second year as follows:

1. Select a present value of an annuity interest factor for the combination of one payment and 8%: $PVAIF = 0.92593$
2. Use the following secondary annuity formula:
   $PVA_n = R(PVAIF) = \$38,803.31(0.92593) = \$35,929.15$

Notice that there is a $.03 difference due to rounding when you compare this present value balance at the end of Year 2 to the corresponding amount in the amortization table. Nevertheless, the time-line/table approach is equivalent to the approach underlying the amortization table. The insight you should gain here is that you do not have to make laborious calculations to determine what a liability balance will be in the future. The shortcut approach you just learned will be particularly useful in determining what a bond liability will be at various times over its life.

Answer This installment loan represents an annuity problem because Susan's note requires equal payments (unknown for now) at regular intervals (monthly) for a specified period of time (60 months).

Question 2 What are the correct amounts for the interest rate (i) and the number of payments or rents (n)?

Answer

i = 12%/12 months = 1% per month
n = 60 months (given)

Question 3 What does this particular problem's time line look like?

Answer

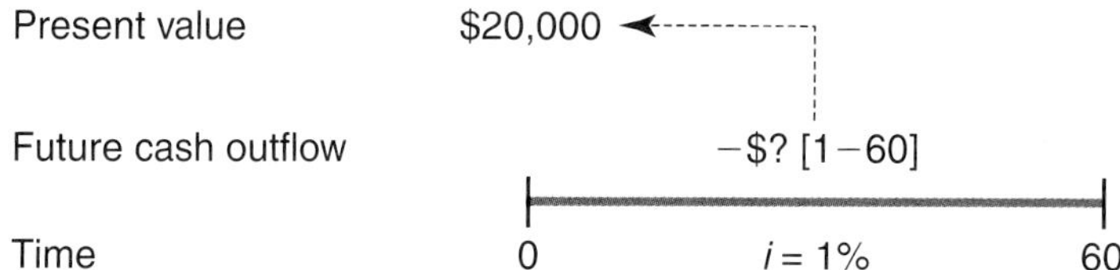

Question 4 Which annuity concept, future or present value, should be used and why?

Answer By studying the time line, you can see that a present value of an annuity must be used because a $20,000 amount preceding Susan's required monthly interest cash payments or outflows is provided.

Question 5 What interest factor should be used for this car loan?

Answer If you attempt to retrieve an interest factor from Table 4 on page 676 you will not find one that corresponds to 1% per month and 60 months. In this situation, you have at least three options. First, you might find another present value of annuity table with more entries. Second, you might use your calculator if it has special compound interest functions. The option that enhances your learning and makes you more self sufficient, however, is for you to derive your own present value of annuity interest factor. This might sound complex but it isn't that difficult if you use the following primary formula for the present value of an annuity interest factor:

$$PVAIF = \frac{1 - (1 + i)^{-n}}{i} = \frac{1 - \dfrac{1}{(1 + i)^n}}{i}$$

where i = interest rate
and n = number of rents

The interest factor is derived in four stages:

1. $(1 + i)^n = (1 + .01)^{60} = (1.01)^{60} = 1.816696699$
2. $\dfrac{1}{(1 + i)^n} = \dfrac{1}{1.816696699} = .550449616$
3. $1 - \dfrac{1}{(1 + i)^n} = .449550384$
4. $\dfrac{1 - \dfrac{1}{(1 + i)^n}}{i} = 44.95503842, \text{ or } 44.95504$

Question 6 What is the amount of the monthly car payment, or R?

Answer To calculate R, you must rearrange terms in the present value of an annuity formula $PVA_n = R(PVAIF)$ so that:

$$R = PVA/PVAIF = \$20{,}000/44.95503842 = \$444.89$$

To complete the time line, you simply have to insert $444.89 as the monthly rent.

Now that we have provided the essential present value calculations, let's apply them to measuring and reporting this installment loan transaction. First, we will use the future value approach to calculate CMU's loan balance at the end of the first and second months, that is, the subsequent present values at $T = 1$ and $T = 2$.

Initial present value of obligation (loan balance)	**$20,000.00**
Add: Month 1 interest expense ($20,000 × .12 × 1/12)	200.00
Loan balance before car payment 1	20,200.00
Deduct: Car payment 1, or rent	(444.89)
Present value of obligation at $T = 1$ (loan balance)	**19,755.11**
Add: Month 2 interest expense ($19,755.11 × .01)	197.55
Loan balance before car payment 2	**19,952.66**
Deduct: Car payment 2, or rent	(444.89)
Present value of obligation at $T = 2$ (loan balance)	**$19,507.77**

Another useful step is to use these calculations to construct an amortization table for the first two months of this car loan.

Amortization Table: Calculation of Subsequent Present Values

(1) Month	(2) Debit Interest Expense	+	(3) Debit Note Payable	=	(4) Credit Cash	(5) Unpaid Liability Balance
0						$20,000.00
1	$200.00		$244.89		$444.89	19,755.11
2	197.55		247.34		444.89	19,507.77

Be sure you understand exactly how these amounts are calculated. Month 1's $200 interest expense in column 2, for example, involves multiplying the initial present value of $20,000 by the interest rate per period of .01 (.12 × 1/12). The $244.89 reduction of the note payable in column 3 is derived by adding the monthly interest expense of $200 and subtracting the monthly cash payment of $444.89. Successive present values in column 5 are generated by applying this monthly reduction to the beginning liability balance of that same period (for example, $20,000 − $244.89 = $19,755.11).

The initial purchase transaction as well as the first two monthly interest transactions can be recorded quite easily with the help of the amortization table above.[1]

January 1, 2004

Transaction Analysis — Fundamental Accounting Equation

Account Titles	Assets	=	Liabilities	+	Owners' Equity
Business Automobile	24,000				
Note Payable			20,000		
Cash	(4,000)				

Journal Entry

Account Titles	Debit	Credit
Business Automobile	24,000.00	
Note Payable		20,000.00
Cash		4,000.00

[1] For ease of calculation, equal months of 30 days have been assumed in this example. In reality, interest is usually calculated on a daily basis to avoid the fact that some months vary in length by as much as three days.

January 30, 2004

Transaction Analysis						Journal Entry		
	Fundamental Accounting Equation							
Account Titles	**Assets**	**=**	**Liabilities**	**+**	**Owners' Equity**	**Account Titles**	**Debit**	**Credit**
Interest Expense					(200.00)	Interest Expense	200.00	
Note Payable			(244.89)			Note Payable	244.89	
Cash	(444.89)					Cash		444.89

February 29, 2004

Transaction Analysis						Journal Entry		
	Fundamental Accounting Equation							
Account Titles	**Assets**	**=**	**Liabilities**	**+**	**Owners' Equity**	**Account Titles**	**Debit**	**Credit**
Interest Expense					(197.55)	Interest Expense	197.55	
Note Payable			(247.34)			Note Payable	247.34	
Cash	(444.89)					Cash		444.89

Since you have learned how the initial present value and the first two months of interest are measured, let's complete the accounting for this business automobile by demonstrating how CMU might report this information on its respective financial statements.

Balance Sheet Presentation of Liability The following Note Payable T-account shows the loan balance from January 1, 2004, to February 29, 2004:

Note Payable

	Debit	Credit	
		20,000.00	← 1/01 present value
Amortization →	244.89		
		19,755.11	← 1/30 present value
Amortization →	247.34		
		19,507.77	← 2/29 present value

Each successive present value would be reported in the noncurrent liability section of CMU's monthly balance sheets. At a minimum, however, the present value for December 31 derived in the same fashion as shown above would be reported in CMU's annual balance sheet.

Income Statement Presentation of Interest Expense The monthly interest expense amounts from January to December would be added together and reported in the year-end income statement. Susan Newman might well prepare monthly income statements, however, for her own feedback in which case the $200 and the $197.55 amounts would each be reported.

Statement of Cash Flows Presentation The initial $4,000 payment would be reported as payment for business automobile, a cash outflow under cash flows from investing activities. The sum of the year's monthly interest payments, however, would be reported as interest paid, a cash outflow under cash flows provided by operating activities.

Building Loans Building loans include home mortgage loans as well as business mortgage loans on buildings and other noncurrent assets constructed or purchased for use in a business. The concept underlying a building loan is very similar to the preceding automobile loan. So what, if any, are the primary differences between an automobile loan and a building loan?

The first difference is the length of the loan. While 36 to 60 months is a common range for automobile loans, building loans often last for at least 30 years. Since monthly payments are the norm in either case, building loans can have a significantly long amortization schedule. For example, an amortization schedule for a standard home loan might contain 360 lines (30 years × 12 months per year). Another difference is the title of the liability account used. As you learned in the preceding section on automobile loans, the asset and liability account titles were Business Automobile and Note Payable; corresponding titles for a building loan might be Building and Mortgage Note Payable.

Cards & Memorabilia Unlimited: Transaction L You might recall that Transaction L involved a direct exchange—CMU's purchase of a computer and printer costing $4,000 in exchange for a two-year note. An examination of the contract underlying this note indicates that the $4,000 price must be paid in monthly installments bearing interest at an annual rate of 12%. The following time line illustrates both the amount and timing of cash outflow(s) that apply to Transaction L:

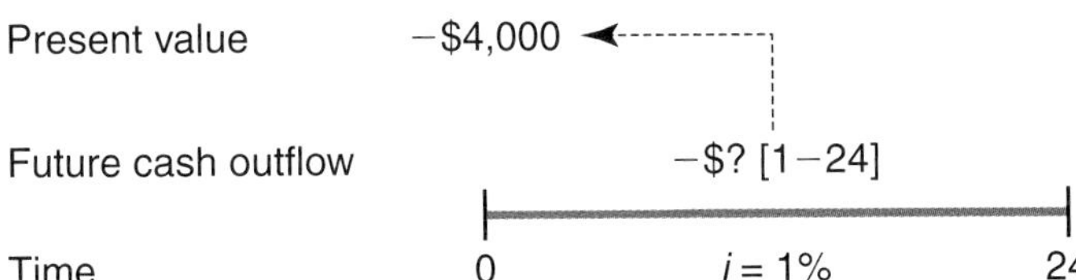

Since the $4,000 present value of annuity, the 1% monthly interest rate (12% yearly interest rate/12 months per year), and the 24 payments are known quantities, only the monthly payment amount or rent is unknown. Because a row for 24 payments is not available in our tables, the precise interest factor using the formula introduced earlier is 21.24338729. When we isolate for the monthly payment or rent R in the formula $PVA = R\ (PVAIF)$, we then have $R = PVA/PVAIF$ = $4,000/21.24338729 = $188.29. That is, CMU must pay $188.29 monthly to fully amortize this note.

We can now evaluate the cost of financing the computer and printer in Transaction L by calculating the total interest expense CMU will bear over the 24 month term of the note.

Cash paid by borrower ($188.29 × 24)	$4,518.96
Cash received by borrower (present value or proceeds)	4,000.00
Interest expense	$ 518.96

Apparently, CMU was willing to pay over $500 in return for conserving cash at the date of purchase. Now let's examine an amortization table for the first three months of this equipment installment loan:

Amortization Table:
Calculation of Subsequent Present Values

(1) Month	(2) Debit Interest Expense	+	(3) Debit Note Payable	=	(4) Credit Cash	(5) Unpaid Liability Balance
0						$4,000.00
1	$40.00*		$148.29		$188.29	3,851.71
2	38.52†		149.77		188.29	3,701.94
3	37.02		151.27		188.29	3,550.67

*$4,000 × .12 × 1/12
†$3,851.71 × .12 × 1/12

The direct exchange is recorded on December 31 of CMU's first year as shown below. Note that the $4,000 purchase price is equivalent to the present value of the equipment and initial liability:

Transaction Analysis						Journal Entry		
	Fundamental Accounting Equation							
Account Titles	Assets	=	Liabilities	+	Owners' Equity	Account Titles	Debit	Credit
Store Equipment	4,000					Store Equipment	4,000.00	
Note Payable—Noncurrent			4,000			Note Payable		4,000.00

Using the amortization table, the monthly interest payment is recorded as follows on January 31, Year 2.

Transaction Analysis						Journal Entry		
	Fundamental Accounting Equation							
Account Titles	Assets	=	Liabilities	+	Owners' Equity	Account Titles	Debit	Credit
Interest Expense					(40.00)	Interest Expense	40.00	
Note Payable			(148.29)			Note Payable	148.29	
Cash	(188.29)					Cash		188.29

The last transaction recorded for Transaction L will be the retirement of the note on December 31 of CMU's third year of business.

The financial statement effects of this note are as follows.

Balance Sheet Notes Payable, the noncurrent liability account, is reported at $4,000 initially and continues to decrease each month until it has no remaining balance at the end of 24 months.

Income Statement The yearly total of this monthly interest expense is reported in CMU's income statements at the end of Years 2 and 3.

Statement of Cash Flows The initial purchase of store equipment in exchange for a note payable is treated as a direct exchange. The interest portion of each cash payment ($40 on January 31) is reported as interest paid in the cash flows from operating activities section each of the two years, whereas the principal reduction of each cash payment ($148.29 on January 31) is reported as payment of notes payable in the cash flows from financing activities section.

While the nature of notes does vary, you now have seen all of the essential tools for applying the concept of compound interest to any note. Likewise, you have the basic foundation for analyzing all other transactions that incorporate the time value of money concept. One such example is a lease that is, in substance, an installment purchase. Such a lease has payments that are composed of two elements, interest on principal and principal reduction. As described in detail in Appendix 13–1 (which you can find at www.mhhe.com/solomon), this transaction is nearly identical in form to the automobile loan.

Measuring and Reporting Bonds

In Chapter 12 you examined some essential transactions related to an investment in bonds. In this chapter our examination of bonds will be more in-depth. You will explore the nature of bonds and how their financial effects are measured, recorded, and reported.

Nature of a Bond

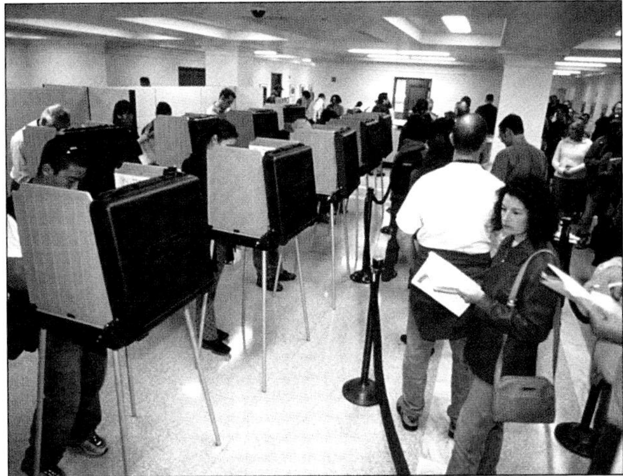

Government bond issues must be approved by voters such as these.

A **bond** is a formal certificate of long-term indebtedness. Because it is used to raise relatively large amounts of cash, it is not a realistic source of financing for individuals or small business owners. Instead, it is more commonly a source of financing for large corporations and governmental units such as school districts. Generally, its loan term is longer than that of a typical promissory note. Also, unlike a note transaction in which there is usually a single borrower and a single investor, bond transactions usually involve a single borrower and a large group of unrelated investors.

Figure 13-7 provides a detailed look at the physical flow of events between the borrower and investors in a typical bond transaction. Notice that the borrower initiates the transaction by issuing bond certificates to investors in exchange for their individual investments of cash collectively referred to as the **proceeds** of the bond issue. The borrower pays interest during the life of the bond issue and principal at its maturity date. When the borrower repays this principal, the bond issue is said to be retired.

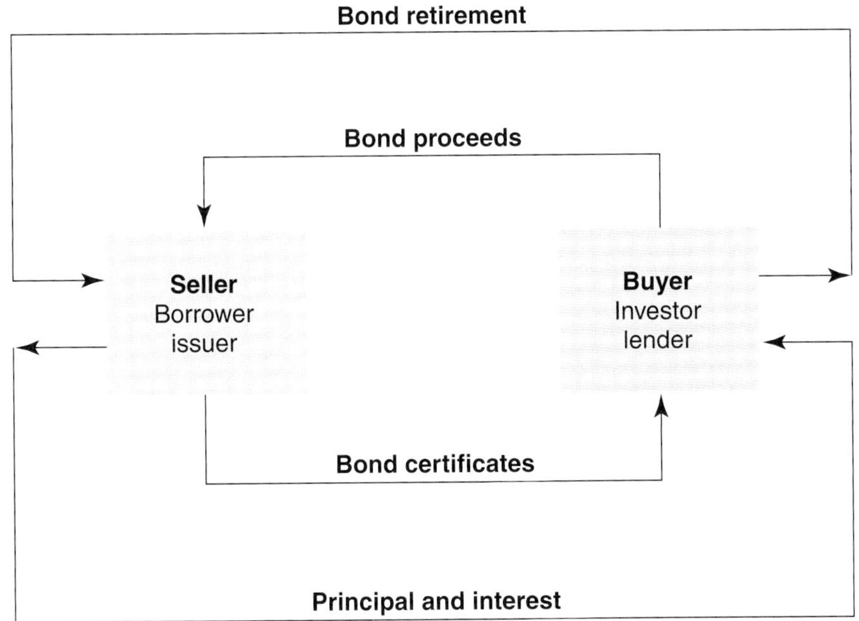

FIGURE 13-7

Physical flow of events associated with a bond transaction

Let's now explore some important terminology associated with bonds.

Essential Bond Terminology

Every bond has at least three key elements, each of which is illustrated in the time line shown in Figure 13-8. These are its *face value*, its *stated interest rate*, and its *effective interest rate*. Because the use of business terminology is not always precise, these three elements are often referred to in different ways as you will soon learn.

Face Value You might recall from earlier discussions of face value in Chapter 12 and in this chapter's treatment of promissory notes that the face value of a bond is the amount that the issuer of the bonds or borrower promises to repay at the bond's maturity date. Face value is sometimes referred to as *principal* or *par*. In Figure 13-8, the face value of the bond issue is $100,000.

FIGURE 13-8

Essential elements found in a bond transaction time line

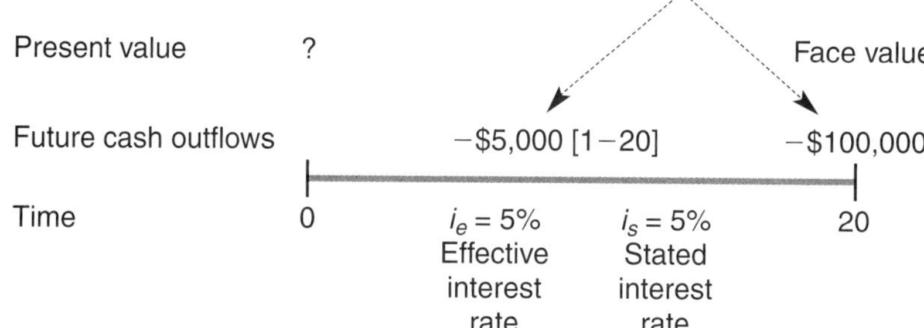

Stated Interest Rate The **stated interest rate** is the rate of interest stated on the face of the bond certificate. It also is referred to as the *coupon interest rate*, the *face rate* or the *nominal interest rate*. In the time line shown in Figure 13-8, the stated interest rate (i_s) is 5%. The stated interest rate is particularly important because it is used to calculate the amount of bond interest paid in cash each period. For example, in Figure 13-8, you can calculate the amount of interest paid in cash each period by multiplying the face value of the bond by the stated interest rate, a simple interest calculation shown here:

Face Value × Stated Interest Rate = Semiannual Interest
$100,000 × .05 = $5,000

Effective Interest Rate The **effective interest rate** is the rate of interest available to investors on the date the bond is issued. It is sometimes referred to as the **market interest rate**, *yield rate*, or *internal rate of return*. In Figure 13-8's time line, the effective interest rate (i_e) is also 5%. You will use this interest rate when you consult the compound interest tables for an appropriate interest factor.

Despite the fact that a bond transaction appears to be different in form than a note or lease transaction, it shares most of their characteristics. As you can see from Figure 13-8, the bond time line includes both an annuity—20 periodic cash outflows for interest of $5,000 each—and a single cash outflow of $100,000, the payment of the bond's principal at the date of maturity. In present value terms, the differences between the bond's time line shown in Figure 13-8 and earlier noncurrent liability time lines is the fact that there is a cash outflow at the bond issue's maturity date and the existence of two interest rates rather than just one interest rate.

INSIGHT

Why Do Bond Transactions Involve Two Interest Rates?

You have just learned that bond issues are associated with two distinct interest rates, the stated interest rate and the effective interest rate. The question you might be asking yourself is "Why do I have to sort out two interest rates rather than just one interest rate?" The answer is less complicated than you might anticipate and can be summed up in one word, timing.

When an organization such as a corporation or school district decides to borrow by issuing bonds, one decision that management and the bond underwriters who help market the bond issue must make is what interest rate to select. Generally, the bond interest rate is set as close as possible to what the prevailing market interest rate is expected to be when the bonds are issued. Since bond interest rates can change daily as a result of market forces outside the company's control, rarely is the stated interest rate printed on the bonds the same as the market rate existing at the date of the bonds' issuance. In fact, several weeks usually pass between the selection of the rate and gaining regulatory agency approval of the bond issue, printing the bond certificates, and completing all marketing efforts.

Now that you understand why two interest rates exist, you can more easily apply each interest rate appropriately. For example, you use the stated rate to calculate the interest cash flows each payment date because the borrower is obligated by law to pay the contract interest rate printed on the bonds. Legally, the periodic interest paid in cash and placed on your time line must be based on the stated interest rate. In contrast, you use the effective or *market* interest rate to evaluate the present value of the bond issue because market forces determine the actual selling price of the bond issue. That is, when you consult present value tables to find the appropriate interest factor or use your financial calculator or an Excel spreadsheet to determine a bond's present value, you must use the effective interest rate.

The first **insight** you should gain here is that simple timing differences between the anticipated market interest rate of a bond issue and the actual market interest rate conspire to make it very unlikely that only one interest rate will apply to a bond issue. Whenever this situation does occur, the bonds are said to be issued at their face value, a case you will learn about shortly. In the more likely case that the interest rate printed on the bond certificate is different from the current market interest rate, the bonds will be issued at a discount or premium as we'll soon explain. The second **insight** to gain here is that understanding the role each of these bond interest rates plays will help you master exactly how bond prices are calculated and also help you interpret the financial statement effects of bonds.

Measuring, Recording, and Reporting Bonds Payable

To illustrate how a bond issue is measured, recorded, and reported, let's consider the following comprehensive bond demonstration problem. This demonstration problem classifies a bond issuance into one of three possible categories:

Case 1 Bonds are issued at face value.
Case 2 Bonds are issued at a discount.
Case 3 Bonds are issued at a premium.

Once again, you are strongly encouraged to consult the systematic process contained in Performance Objective 51 below to help you master the information contained in this demonstration problem.

YOUR PERFORMANCE OBJECTIVE 51

Apply the present value concept to measure and report the effects of such transactions as credit card accounts, general notes, automobile loans, home loans, leases, bonds, and pensions by being able to:

a. **Calculate** the initial present value of all future cash flows, all subsequent present values (construct an amortization table), and the interest revenue and/or interest expense over the transaction's life.
b. **Record** all transaction-related effects from both perspectives.
c. **Present** the balance sheet, income statement, and statement of cash flow transaction-related effects.

Note that for now, we will record the transaction-related effects from only the borrower's perspective. Also, only the first two interest transactions will be shown.

Case 1: Bonds Issued at Face Value

Suppose that bonds having a face value of $100,000 and maturing in 10 years are issued on January 1. Both the stated interest rate (appearing on the bond certificate) and the effective or current market interest rate is 10%. Interest is compounded semiannually and is payable on June 30 and December 31 of each year.

Calculate the Initial Present Value of All Future Cash Flows To calculate the initial present value of all future cash flows, first draw a time line to represent both the amount and timing of cash flows relating to the bond transaction, as shown here:

Present value $100,000

Future cash outflow −$5,000 [1−20] −$100,000

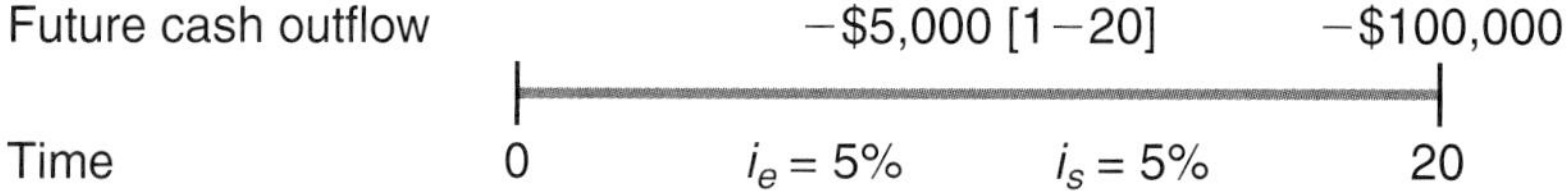

Time 0 $i_e = 5\%$ $i_s = 5\%$ 20

Time Line Explanation

1. When interest is compounded semiannually, you must double the periods to 20 (there are 20 six-month periods because each period is six months in length). You must halve the interest rate to 5% because the interest rate for six months is one-half the 10% annual rate.
2. The interest paid by the borrower to the lender at the end of each six-month period is calculated by multiplying the bond's face value by the legally payable stated interest rate (also known as the coupon, face, or nominal interest rate) for a 6-month period. This calculation is $100,000 × .10 × ½ = $5,000.

With this information in place, you next calculate the initial present value as follows:

PV of $100,000 (*i* = 5% and *n* = 20) = $100,000 ×	.376889483 =	$ 37,688.95
PVA of $ 5,000 (*i* = 5% and *n* = 20) = $ 5,000 ×	12.46221034 =	62,311.05
		$100,000.00

Note that, to eliminate rounding errors, the interest factors used here are more precise than those found in compound interest tables.

Calculate All Subsequent Present Values The next step in our generalized solution procedure is to construct a bond amortization table. Such a table for Case 1 is presented in Figure 13-9. This amortization table makes it relatively easy to generate all bond transactions that must be recorded. Before doing so, however, let's first calculate the borrower's total interest expense (and the investor's total interest revenue).

Calculate Total Interest Expense Just as you have done several times before, here is the calculation of the total interest cost the borrower will bear by issuing the bonds:

Cash Paid by Borrower* [($5,000 × 20) + $100,000]	$200,000.00
Cash Received by Borrower† (Present Value, or Proceeds)	100,000.00
Total Interest‡ Expense, or Total Cost of Financing	$100,000.00

*This amount is more formally referred to as the undiscounted cash flow.
†This amount is more formally referred to as the discounted cash flow.
‡Note that interest can be said to represent the difference between discounting and not discounting future cash flows.

FIGURE 13-9

Bond amortization table for Case 1

Amortization Table: Calculation of Subsequent Present Values

End of Period	Interest Revenue and Expense (5%) (PV × Effective Rate)*	Semiannual Cash Payment (FV × Stated Rate)*	Balance of Bond Asset and Liability
0			$100,000.00
1	$ 5,000.00	$ 5,000.00	100,000.00
2	5,000.00	5,000.00	100,000.00
3	5,000.00	5,000.00	100,000.00
4	5,000.00	5,000.00	100,000.00
5	5,000.00	5,000.00	100,000.00
6	5,000.00	5,000.00	100,000.00
7	5,000.00	5,000.00	100,000.00
8	5,000.00	5,000.00	100,000.00
9	5,000.00	5,000.00	100,000.00
10	5,000.00	5,000.00	100,000.00
11	5,000.00	5,000.00	100,000.00
12	5,000.00	5,000.00	100,000.00
13	5,000.00	5,000.00	100,000.00
14	5,000.00	5,000.00	100,000.00
15	5,000.00	5,000.00	100,000.00
16	5,000.00	5,000.00	100,000.00
17	5,000.00	5,000.00	100,000.00
18	5,000.00	5,000.00	100,000.00
19	5,000.00	5,000.00	100,000.00
20	5,000.00	105,000.00	0.00
	$100,000.00	$200,000.00	

*PV stands for present value. FV stands for face value.

Although you should now be able to calculate this amount yourself, you can confirm your answer by looking at the total of Figure 13-9's Interest Revenue and Expense column.

Record All Bond-Related Transactions for the Borrower Using the information from the amortization table in Figure 13-9, here are the transactions that must be recorded:

Bond issuance at January 1, Year 1

Transaction Analysis						Journal Entry		
	Fundamental Accounting Equation							
Account Titles	Assets	=	Liabilities	+	Owners' Equity	Account Titles	Debit	Credit
Cash	100,000					Cash	100,000	
Bonds Payable			100,000			Bonds Payable		100,000

Notice that the $100,000 cash received, or proceeds of the bond issue, equals both the face value of the bond and its present value.

End of each bond interest period—June 30 and December 31 of each year:

Transaction Analysis						Journal Entry		
	Fundamental Accounting Equation							
Account Titles	Assets	=	Liabilities	+	Owners' Equity	Account Titles	Debit	Credit
Interest Expense					(5,000)	Interest Expense	5,000	
Cash	(5,000)					Cash		5,000

Bond retirement at December 31, Year 10

Transaction Analysis						Journal Entry		
	Fundamental Accounting Equation							
Account Titles	Assets	=	Liabilities	+	Owners' Equity	Account Titles	Debit	Credit
Bonds Payable			(100,000)			Bonds Payable	100,000	
Cash	(100,000)					Cash		100,000

Present the Financial Statement Effects of the Bond Issue

Since we have completed recording the major transactions for this bond issue, let's complete our accounting by presenting the bond-related financial statement effects.

Balance Sheet Here is a partial balance sheet presentation for the borrower:

Long-Term Liabilities	01/01/01	06/30/01	12/31/01
Bond Payable	$100,000	$100,000	$100,000

Income Statement Since interest expense of $5,000 is recorded twice a year, the yearly interest expense is $10,000.

Statement of Cash Flows At the date these bonds are issued, the borrower will include a cash inflow of $100,000 titled Proceeds from Bond Issue in the cash flows from financing activities section. At the date the bonds are retired, the borrower will include a cash outflow of $100,000 titled Retirement of Bond Issue in the cash flows from financing activities section. In addition, the semiannual cash payment of $5,000 will produce a $10,000 amount to be reported as Interest Paid in the cash flows from operating activities section each of the 10 years.

Before turning to Cases 2 and 3, let's first examine the concept of a bond discount and a bond premium.

The Nature of a Bond Discount and a Bond Premium

A **bond discount** is the amount by which the face value of the bond exceeds its issue price or present value. You will soon discover in Case 2, for example, that the

USER FOCUS

An Intuitive Explanation of a Bond Discount and Bond Premium

If you want to quickly determine whether a bond is issued at a discount or premium without actually calculating its present value, you can use the following intuitive reasoning. That is, assume you are an investor who is offered a bond investment that contractually provides a 10% return, its stated rate. You, however, are aware that the current bond market features bonds with equivalent features that offer a 12% return (a market interest rate). Since the bond investment you have just been offered cannot change the interest rate printed on its certificates or stated interest rate, what might its seller do to motivate your purchase when you recognize it has a lower than market interest rate? Actually, you don't need an extensive business or accounting background to intuitively realize that, in this case, the seller or borrower needs to offer his/her bonds at a discount. If, instead, a bond issue you are considering offers you a contractual, or stated, interest rate that is higher than the current market interest rate, wouldn't you be willing to pay a higher than normal price (pay a premium) for those bonds?

A Numerical Explanation of a Bond Discount and Bond Premium

USER FOCUS

So far, two explanations of the nature of bond discounts and bond premiums—definition and intuition—have been presented. If you are still somewhat unclear, the following numerical explanation might be even more helpful. First, remember that it is necessary to offer a discount whenever the market interest rate exceeds the stated interest rate. In Case 2, for example, the amount of the discount is designed to make up the difference between a lower stated interest rate (10%) and a higher market interest rate (12%). Thus, if you calculate today's present value of the interest differential expressed in dollars between the 12% market rate and the 10% stated rate, the following time line from an investor perspective can be constructed:

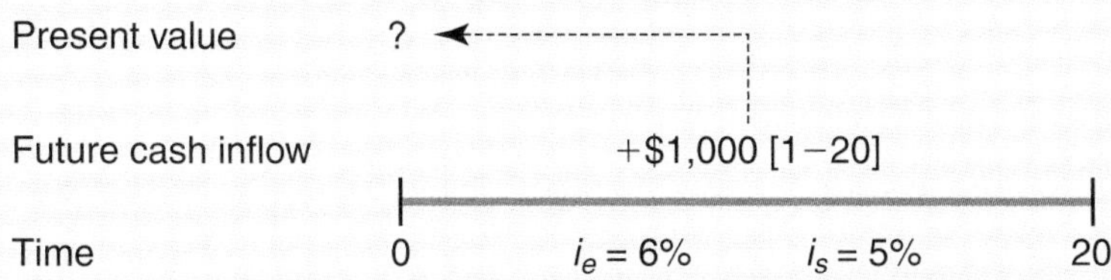

The $1,000 annuity above is calculated by taking the difference between the $6,000 six-month interest payment at 12% ($100,000 × .12 × 1/2) and the $5,000 six-month interest payment at 10% (= $100,000 × .10 × 1/2). That is, if you wanted to know how much of a discount you deserve for accepting a 5% rather than a 6% interest rate every six-month period, you would calculate the present value of the $1,000 interest differential as shown below:

$$\begin{aligned} PVA &= R\,(PVAIF) \text{ for 20 periods at 6\%} = \$1{,}000\ (11.46992) \\ &= \$11{,}469.92, \text{ or } \$11{,}470 \text{ rounded to the nearest dollar.} \end{aligned}$$

Since you can confirm that the bond issued in Case 2 was issued at a price of $88,530 (i.e., $88,530 + $11,470 = $100,000), it is now clear that the preceding calculation provides an accurate numerical explanation of the concept of a bond discount. If you desire equivalent confirmation of the bond premium concept, calculate the interest differential between the 8% market interest rate and the 10% stated interest rate and then discount it at a six-month rate of 4%. Although this approach is useful to understand the concept of a bond discount or premium, do not use it to calculate the present value of a bond.

approximate amount of the discount is $11,470 ($100,000 – $88,530). A discount will arise whenever the prevailing market interest rate is greater than the interest rate stipulated on the bonds being sold (that is, the stated, or face rate). In contrast, a **bond premium** is the amount by which the issue price or present value of the bond exceeds its face value. You will soon discover in Case 3, for example, that the approximate amount of the premium is $13,590 ($113,590 – $100,000). A premium will arise whenever the prevailing market interest rate is less than the stated interest rate on the bonds being sold.

Resist the temptation to memorize the market rate/stated rate relationships to help you identify whether a discount or a premium exists. It is far more effective to focus your energy on developing an accurate time line and calculating both the present value of the annuity representing interest payments and the present value of the single amount representing the bond retirement payment. The sum of those two calculations will either be greater or less than the bond's face value, and you will immediately know whether the bond will be issued at a premium or discount.

Case 2: Bonds Issued at a Discount

In this case, all of the information is identical to Case 1 except that the effective or current market interest rate is 12%.

Calculate the Initial Present Value of All Future Cash Flows

Once again, let's draw a time line to represent the amount and timing of all future cash flows relating to this bond transaction.

Present value +$88,530.08

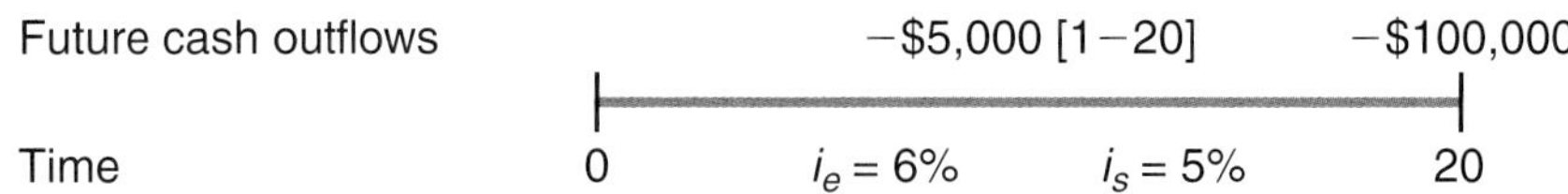

Time Line Explanation:

1. As in Case 1 and Case 3, the semiannual compounding results in 20 six-month periods and a 5% stated interest rate.
2. As in Case 1 and Case 3, the periodic interest is calculated by multiplying the bond's face value by the legally payable stated interest rate or \$100,000 × .10 × ½ = \$5,000.

The next step is to calculate the initial present value:

PV of \$100,000 (i = 6% and n = 20) = \$100,000 × .311804727	=	\$31,180.47
PVA of \$ 5,000 (i = 6% and n = 20) = \$ 5,000 × 11.46992122	=	57,349.61
		\$88,530.08

Since the proceeds of this bond issue are less than the face value of \$100,000, it is clear that these bonds are issued at a discount.

Calculate All Subsequent Present Values The next step in our generalized solution procedure is to construct a bond amortization table. Such a table for Case 2 is Figure 13-10. Once again, you can see that this bond issue has been issued at a discount since the initial present value in the far right column is \$88,530.08. Let's now turn our attention to calculating the total interest expense.

Calculate Total Interest Expense Here is the calculation of the total interest cost the borrower will bear by issuing the bonds:

Cash Paid by Borrower [(\$5,000 × 20) + \$100,000]	\$200,000.00
Cash Received by Borrower (Present Value or Proceeds)	88,530.08
Total Interest Expense or Total Cost of Financing	\$111,469.92

Note that you can confirm this answer by looking at the total of Figure 13-10's Interest Revenue and Expense column.

Record All Bond-Related Transactions for the Borrower Using the information from the amortization table in Figure 13-10, here are the transactions that must be recorded:

Bond issuance at January 1, Year 1

Transaction Analysis					Journal Entry		
	Fundamental Accounting Equation						
Account Titles	Assets	=	Liabilities +	Owners' Equity	Account Titles	Debit	Credit
Cash (Present Value)	88,530.08				Cash	88,530.08	
Bond Discount			(11,469.92)		Bond Discount	11,469.92	
Bonds Payable			100,000.00		Bonds Payable		100,000.00

Since the $88,530.08 of cash collections or proceeds of the bond issue is less than the face value of the bond, a discount exists, which is represented by the contra liability account titled **Bond Discount** or **Discount on Bonds Payable**. The initial balance in this account is amortized over the life of the bond issue using the effective interest amortization method introduced earlier.

End of first bond interest period: June 30, Year 1

Transaction Analysis					Journal Entry		
	Fundamental Accounting Equation						
Account Titles	Assets	=	Liabilities +	Owners' Equity	Account Titles	Debit	Credit
Interest Expense				(5,311.80)	Interest Expense	5,311.80	
Bond Discount			311.80		Bond Discount		311.80
Cash	(5,000.00)				Cash		5,000.00

FIGURE 13-10

Bond amortization table for Case 2

Amortization Table: Calculation of Subsequent Present Values

End of Period	Interest Revenue and Expense (6%) (PV × Effective Rate)*	Semiannual Cash Payment (FV × Stated Rate)*	Balance of Bond Asset and Liability
0			$88,530.08
1	$ 5,311.80	$ 5,000.00	88,841.88
2	5,330.51	5,000.00	89,172.39
3	5,350.34	5,000.00	89,522.73
4	5,371.36	5,000.00	89,894.09
5	5,393.65	5,000.00	90,287.74
6	5,417.26	5,000.00	90,705.00
7	5,442.30	5,000.00	91,147.30
8	5,468.84	5,000.00	91,616.14
9	5,496.97	5,000.00	92,113.11
10	5,526.79	5,000.00	92,639.90
11	5,558.39	5,000.00	93,198.29
12	5,591.90	5,000.00	93,790.19
13	5,627.41	5,000.00	94,417.60
14	5,665.06	5,000.00	95,082.66
15	5,704.96	5,000.00	95,787.62
16	5,747.26	5,000.00	96,534.88
17	5,792.09	5,000.00	97,326.97
18	5,839.62	5,000.00	98,166.59
19	5,890.00	5,000.00	99,056.59
20	5,943.40	105,000.00	0.00**
	$111,469.91	$200,000.00	

* PV Stands for present value. FV stands for face value.
**The $.01 difference is attributable to the effect of rounding.

Notice how this transaction can be broken down into two distinct transactions—the cash payment and the amortization of the bond discount as shown next:

Cash payment

Transaction Analysis						Journal Entry		
	Fundamental Accounting Equation							
Account Titles	Assets	=	Liabilities	+	Owners' Equity	Account Titles	Debit	Credit
Interest Expense					(5,000.00)	Interest Expense	5,000.00	
Cash	(5,000.00)					Cash		5,000.00

Discount amortization

Transaction Analysis						Journal Entry		
	Fundamental Accounting Equation							
Account Titles	Assets	=	Liabilities	+	Owners' Equity	Account Titles	Debit	Credit
Interest Expense					(311.80)	Interest Expense	311.80	
Bond Discount			311.80			Bond Discount		311.80

End of second bond interest period: December 31, Year 1

Transaction Analysis						Journal Entry		
	Fundamental Accounting Equation							
Account Titles	Assets	=	Liabilities	+	Owners' Equity	Account Titles	Debit	Credit
Interest Expense					(5,330.51)	Interest Expense	5,330.51	
Bond Discount			330.51			Bond Discount		330.51
Cash	(5,000.00)					Cash		5,000.00

Another method available for amortizing discounts and premiums is the **straight-line amortization method**. Although less accurate than the effective interest method of amortization, the straight-line method is accepted by GAAP. Using Case 2 as an example, you simply divide the initial discount amount by the number of amortization periods, or $11,469.92/20 = $573.50. This method results in an identical transaction being recorded for each interest payment.

End of each interest period using the straight-line amortization method

Transaction Analysis						Journal Entry		
	Fundamental Accounting Equation							
Account Titles	Assets	=	Liabilities	+	Owners' Equity	Account Titles	Debit	Credit
Interest Expense					(5,573.50)	Interest Expense	5,573.50	
Bond Discount			573.50			Bond Discount		573.50
Cash	(5,000.00)					Cash		5,000.00

Although it is easier to use than the effective interest amortization method, the straight-line amortization method has a major deficiency. By recording a constant interest expense on an ever-changing bond liability balance, the straight-line method ignores the time value of money concept by recording a variable rate of interest. As a result, you are encouraged to use the effective interest amortization method unless there is no appreciable difference between the two methods.

Note that the transaction for recording this bond's retirement is the same as in Case 1 and Case 3.

Present the Financial Statement Effects of the Bond Issue Since we have completed recording the major transactions for this bond issue, let's complete our accounting by presenting the bond-related financial statement effects.

Balance Sheet Here is a partial balance sheet presentation for the borrower with the contra liability account called Bond Discount:

Long-Term Liabilities:	1/01/1	06/30/1	12/31/1
Bond payable	$100,000.00	$100,000.00	$100,000.00
Less: Bond discount	11,469.92	11,158.12	10,827.61
Net carrying/book value	$ 88,530.08	$ 88,841.88	$ 89,172.39

Although the presentation of a contra liability account provides more information, annual report balance sheets rarely disclose the Bond Discount account to conserve space.

Income Statement The interest expense in this case steadily increases as a function of the steadily increasing bond liability balance from which it is derived. In the first year, the interest expense totals $10,642.31 ($5,311.80 + $5,330.51).

Statement of Cash Flows At the date these bonds are issued, the borrower will include a cash inflow of $88,530.08 titled Proceeds from Bond Issue in the cash flows from financing activities section. At the date the bonds are retired, the borrower will include a cash outflow of $100,000 titled Retirement of Bond Issue in the cash flows from financing activities section. In addition, the semiannual cash payment of $5,000 will produce a $10,000 amount to be reported as Interest Paid in the cash flows from operating activities section each of the 10 years.

Case 3: Bonds Issued at a Premium

In this case, all of the information is identical to Case 1 except that the effective or current market interest rate is 8 per cent.

Calculate the Initial Present Value of All Future Cash Flows Here is the time line representing the amount and timing of all future cash flows relating to Case 3:

Present value +$113,590.33

Future cash outflows −$5,000 [1−20] −$100,000

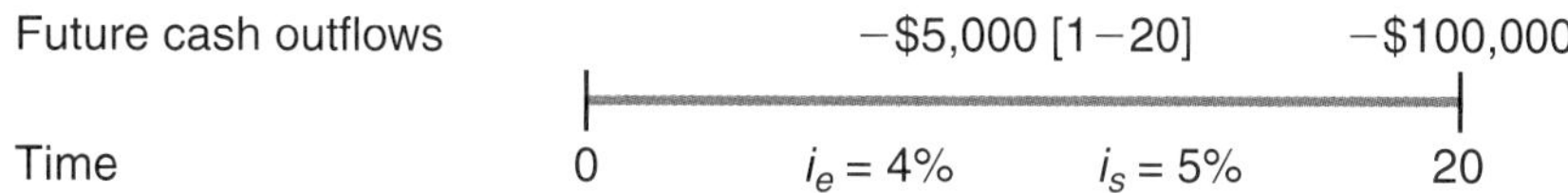

The next step is to calculate the initial present value as follows:

PV of $100,000 ($i$ = 4% and n = 20)	= $100,000 ×	.456386946 =	$ 45,638.70
PVA of $ 5,000 (i = 4% and n = 20)	= $ 5,000 ×	13.59032635 =	67,951.63
			$113,590.33

Since the proceeds of this bond issue are more than the face value of $100,000, it is clear that these bonds are issued at a premium.

Calculate All Subsequent Present Values The next step in our generalized solution procedure is to construct a bond amortization table. Such a table for Case 3 is Figure 13-11. Once again, you can see that this bond issue has been issued at a premium since the initial present value in the far right column is $113,590.33. Let's now turn our attention to calculating the total interest expense.

FIGURE 13-11

Bond amortization table for Case 3

Amortization Table: Calculation of Subsequent Present Values

End of Period	Interest Revenue and Expense (4%) (PV × Effective Rate)*	Semiannual Cash Payment (FV × Stated Rate)*	Balance of Bond Asset and Liability
0			$113,590.33
1	$ 4,543.61	$ 5,000.00	113,133.94
2	4,525.36	5,000.00	112,659.30
3	4,506.37	5,000.00	112,165.67
4	4,486.63	5,000.00	111,652.30
5	4,466.09	5,000.00	111,118.39
6	4,444.74	5,000.00	110,563.13
7	4,422.53	5,000.00	109,985.66
8	4,399.43	5,000.00	109,385.09
9	4,375.40	5,000.00	108,760.49
10	4,350.42	5,000.00	108,110.91
11	4,324.44	5,000.00	107,435.35
12	4,297.41	5,000.00	106,732.76
13	4,269.31	5,000.00	106,002.07
14	4,240.08	5,000.00	105,242.15
15	4,209.69	5,000.00	104,451.84
16	4,178.07	5,000.00	103,629.91
17	4,145.20	5,000.00	102,775.11
18	4,111.00	5,000.00	101,886.11
19	4,075.44	5,000.00	100,961.55
20	4,038.46	105,000.00	0.00**
	$86,409.68	$200,000.00	

*PV stands for present value. FV stands for face value.
**The $.01 difference is attributable to the effect of rounding.

Calculate Total Interest Expense Here is the calculation of the total interest cost the borrower will bear by issuing the bonds:

Cash Paid by Borrower [($5,000 × 20) + $100,000]	$200,000.00
Cash Received by Borrower (Present Value or Proceeds)	113,590.33
Total Interest Expense or Total Cost of Financing	$ 86,409.67

Note that you can confirm this answer by looking at the total of Figure 13-11's Interest Revenue and Expense column.

Record All Bond-Related Transactions for the Borrower Using the information from the amortization table in Figure 13-11, here are the transactions that must be recorded:

Bond issuance at January 1, Year 1

Transaction Analysis					Journal Entry		
	Fundamental Accounting Equation						
Account Titles	Assets	=	Liabilities	+ Owners' Equity	Account Titles	Debit	Credit
Cash	113,590.33				Cash	113,590.33	
Bond Premium			13,590.33		Bond Premium		13,590.33
Bonds Payable			100,000.00		Bonds Payable		100,000.00

Since the $113,590.08 of cash received or proceeds of the bond issue exceeds the face value of the bond, a premium exists, which is represented by the liability account[2] titled **Bond Premium** or **Premium on Bonds Payable**. The initial balance in this account is amortized over the life of the bond issue using the effective interest amortization method introduced earlier, as shown here:

End of first bond interest period: June 30, Year 1

Transaction Analysis						Journal Entry		
	Fundamental Accounting Equation							
Account Titles	Assets	=	Liabilities	+	Owners' Equity	Account Titles	Debits	Credits
Interest Expense					(4,543.61)	Interest Expense	4,543.61	
Bond Premium			(456.39)			Bond Premium	456.39	
Cash	(5,000.00)					Cash		5,000.00

As illustrated in Case 2, we could have recorded the interest expense in two parts here. Instead, we will use the standard recording approach in which both parts are combined.

End of second bond interest period: December 31, Year 1

Transaction Analysis						Journal Entry		
	Fundamental Accounting Equation							
Account Titles	Assets	=	Liabilities	+	Owners' Equity	Account Titles	Debit	Credit
Interest Expense					(4,525.36)	Interest Expense	4,525.36	
Bond Premium			(474.64)			Bond Premium	474.64	
Cash	(5,000.00)					Cash		5,000.00

See if you can verify the amount of the amortized premium under the straight-line interest amortization method in the transaction below:

End of each interest period using the straight-line amortization method:

Transaction Analysis						Journal Entry		
	Fundamental Accounting Equation							
Account Titles	Assets	=	Liabilities	+	Owners' Equity	Account Titles	Debits	Credits
Interest Expense					(4,320.48)	Interest Expense	4,320.48	
Bond Premium			(679.52)			Bond Premium	679.52	
Cash	(5,000.00)					Cash		5,000.00

Now that you have had a chance to compare the effects of the effective interest bond amortization method to the straight-line bond amortization method, you can use Performance Objective 53 to help you grasp these differences.

YOUR PERFORMANCE OBJECTIVE 53
Distinguish between the financial statement effects of the effective interest and straight-line methods of bond amortization.

Present the Financial Statement Effects of the Bond Issue Since we have now completed recording the major transactions for our Case 3 bond issue, let's complete our accounting by presenting the bond-related financial statement effects.

2 Sometimes, this account is called an *adjunct* (add to) account to contrast it with a contra account.

Balance Sheet Here is a partial balance sheet presentation for the borrower with the liability adjunct account called Bond Premium:

Long-term liabilities:	1/01/1	06/30/1	12/31/1
Bond Payable	$100,000.00	$100,000.00	$100,000.00
Add: Bond premium	13,590.33	13,133.94	12,659.30
Net carrying/book value	$113,590.33	$113,133.94	$112,659.30

Although the presentation of a premium account provides more information, annual report balance sheets rarely disclose the Bond Premium account to conserve space.

Income statement The interest expense in this case steadily decreases as a function of the steadily decreasing bond liability balance from which it is derived. In the first year, the interest expense totals $9,068.97 ($4,543.61 + $4,525.36).

Statement of Cash Flows At the date these bonds are issued, the borrower will include a cash inflow of $113,590.33 titled Proceeds from Bond Issue in the cash flows from financing activities section. At the date the bonds are retired, the borrower will include a cash outflow of $100,000 titled Retirement of Bond Issue in the cash flows from financing activities section. In addition, the semiannual cash payment of $5,000 will produce a $10,000 amount to be reported as Interest Paid in the cash flows from operating activities section each of the 10 years.

Figure 13-12 summarizes each of the three time lines used in our bond demonstration problem. Notice that the only element that differs in these time lines is the effective interest rate used to calculate each bond issue's present value. Not surprisingly, therefore, the change in effective interest rates in both Case 2 and Case 3 create a change in their respective present values or bond prices.

FIGURE 13-12

Time lines for Cases 1, 2, and 3

CASE 1: A Bond Issued at Face Value

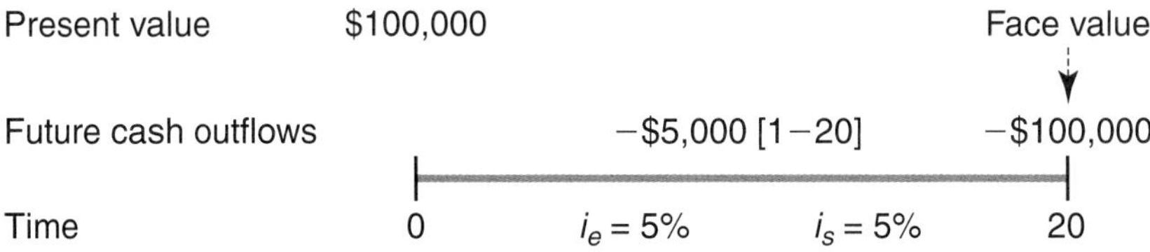

CASE 2: A Bond Issued at a Discount

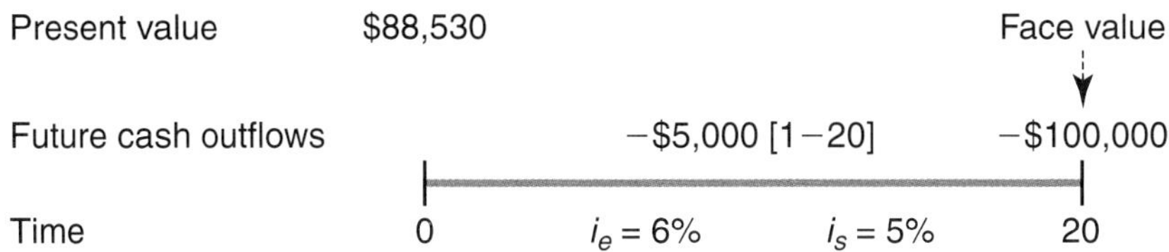

CASE 3: A Bond Issued at a Premium

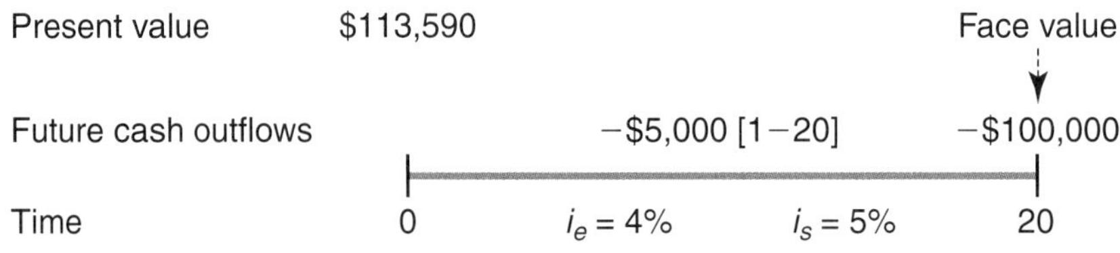

The Existence of a Bond Discount or a Bond Premium Is Unrelated to a Bond's Profitability

USER FOCUS

Some students mistakenly conclude that investing in a bond issued at a premium is preferable to investing in a comparable bond issued at a discount. In fact, the existence of a premium or discount has no bearing on the ultimate profitability or cash flow of a bond issue. In the *User Focus* entitled "An Intuitive Explanation of a Bond Discount and Bond Premium," you learned that the terms *discount* and *premium* only refer to the pricing needed to market a bond issue. That is, you can't expect to sell a bond issue that offers investors a stated interest rate lower than the current market interest rate unless you are willing to discount the selling price of your bond issue to offset its lower interest revenue for investors. Ultimately, the effective interest rate governs profitability—an 8% market interest rate is always more profitable to investors than a 7% market interest rate unless the 7% bond issue is a tax-free municipal bond and the 8% bond issue is a corporate offering. Likewise, it is the stated interest rate that governs cash outflow for the borrower's periodic cash payments.

Investment in Bonds: The Mirror Image of Bonds Payable

Since the focus of this chapter is on financing activities, we have concentrated on the borrower's perspective of how bonds are accounted for rather than that of the investor's perspective. Nevertheless, it is useful to briefly consider some of the key differences. Figure 13-13 shows one such difference in perspective, namely, that the cash outflows in the borrower's time line are the exact opposite of the cash inflows in the investor's time line, and vice versa. That is, when the borrower pays \$5,000 at the end of each six-month period, the investor actually receives that \$5,000.

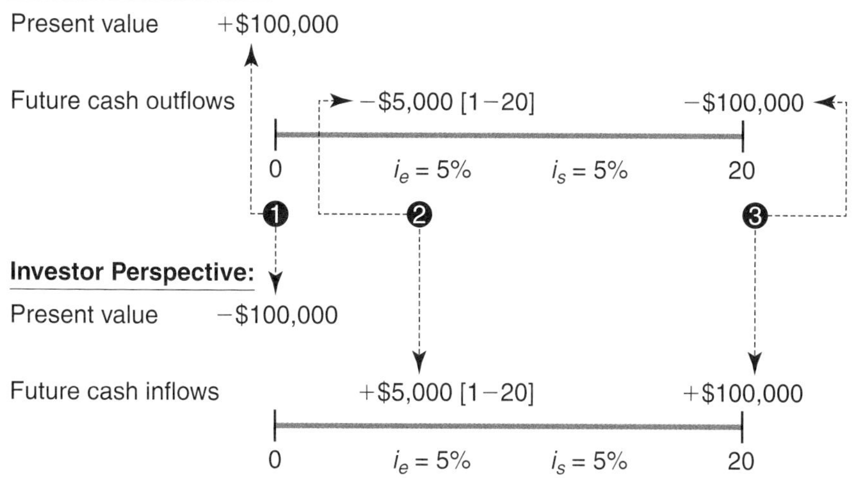

1. At the date of bond issuance, the borrower receives \$100,000 and the investor pays \$100,000.
2. At interest dates, the borrower pays \$5,000 and the investor receives \$5,000.
3. At maturity date, the borrower pays \$100,000 and the investor receives \$100,000.

FIGURE 13-13

A difference in perspective using the Case 1 time lines of a borrower and an investor

FIGURE 13-14 Case 2 bond-related transactions from the investor's perspective

Bond issuance at January 1, Year 1

Account Titles	Assets	=	Liabilities	+	Owners' Equity
Investment in Bonds	88,530.08				
Cash	(88,530.08)				

Journal Entry

Account Titles	Debit	Credit
Investment in Bonds	88,530.08	
Cash		88,530.08

Notice that the $88,530.08 cash paid for the bond issue is less than the face value of the bond. Although its present value is less than face value, no discount account is used.

Effective interest amortization method at June 30, Year 1

Account Titles	Assets	=	Liabilities	+	Owners' Equity
Cash (see time line)	5,000.00				
Investment in Bonds	311.80				
Interest Revenue					5,311.80

Journal Entry

Account Titles	Debit	Credit
Cash	5,000.00	
Investment in Bonds	311.80	
Interest Revenue		5,311.80

Note: Interest revenue: $88,530.08 $\times$ .12 $\times$ $\frac{1}{2}$ = $5,311.80

Effective interest amortization method at December 31, Year 1

Account Titles	Assets	=	Liabilities	+	Owners' Equity
Cash (see time line)	5,000.00				
Investment in Bonds	330.51				
Interest Revenue					5,330.51

Journal Entry

Account Titles	Debit	Credit
Cash	5,000.00	
Investment in Bonds	330.51	
Interest Revenue		5,330.51

Note: Interest revenue: 88,841.88 $\times$ .12 $\times$ $\frac{1}{2}$ = $5,330.51

Effective interest amortization method at June 30, Year 2

Account Titles	Assets	=	Liabilities	+	Owners' Equity
Cash (see time line)	5,000.00				
Investment in Bonds	350.34				
Interest Revenue					5,350.34

Journal Entry

Account Titles	Debit	Credit
Cash	5,000.00	
Investment in Bonds	350.34	
Interest Revenue		5,350.34

Note: Interest revenue: $89,172.39 $\times$ .12 $\times$ $\frac{1}{2}$ = $5,350.34

Straight-line amortization method at June 30, Year 2

Account Titles	Assets	=	Liabilities	+	Owners' Equity
Cash (see time line)	5,000.00				
Investment in Bonds	573.50				
Interest Revenue					5,573.50

Journal Entry

Account Titles	Debit	Credit
Cash	5,000.00	
Investment in Bonds	573.50	
Interest Revenue		5,573.50

Note: Investment in bonds amortization: $11,469.92/20 = $573.50

Another distinction between the borrower's perspective and the investor's perspective relates to the financial statement effects of the bond transaction. As you've learned in this chapter, the borrower views the bond transaction as a noncurrent liability account entitled Bonds Payable that generates the Interest Expense account found in the income statement. As you'd expect, the investor's perspective is the mirror image of the borrower's perspective. Recall from Chapter 12 that the investor views the bond transaction as a noncurrent asset entitled Investment in Bonds that generates the Interest Revenue account found in the income statement.

Now that you understand the conceptual differences between how bonds are accounted for by the borrower and the investor, let's take a somewhat brief but more detailed look at how these differences are reflected in the recording process. Let's use Figure 13-14 to study how the bond issued at a discount in Case 2 might actually be recorded from the perspective of the investor. If you compare the essential Case 2 transactions found in Figure 13-14 to those we discussed earlier, you should reach the following conclusions:

1. At the date of bond issuance, the borrower increases (credits) its Bonds Payable account for the bond's face value whereas the investor increases (debits) its Investment in Bond account for the cost of its investment. These treatments reflect traditional recording differences between assets and noncurrent liabilities. That is, when recording an asset, the focus is on entering cost information, whereas when recording noncurrent debt, it is customary to establish a payable account at face value and then subtract or add any difference between face value and proceeds.
2. As a result of how the bond issue is initially recorded, all later borrower transactions include Bond Discount, a contra liability account, whereas all later investor transactions simply add the amount of the discount to the Investment in Bonds account. In general then, discounts and premiums are recorded in separate accounts when accounting for the liability but not when accounting for the asset.

How You Can Determine a Company's Estimated Pension Liability

USER FOCUS

Accounting for pensions is a complex topic that is usually covered in a course taken only by accounting majors. It also is a highly controversial topic because generally accepted accounting principles do not currently require a pension liability on the balance sheet. Instead, companies with employee pension plans are required to present very detailed information about those plans in their notes to the financial statements. This is significant because it means that in today's world of financial reporting, the pension plan is a form of off-balance-sheet financing.

Despite a pension plan's complexity, knowing the essentials of how the present value concept is applied in measuring a company's pension liability is invaluable in evaluating a company's financial health. So, let's look at the hypothetical case of an employee whom we'll call Simon Chow, the only employee covered by the pension plan of Maxwell Corporation.

Example

(Note that a birthday signifies the successful completion of a year of life. Thus, on your 21st birthday, you have lived exactly 21 full years.) Suppose that each of the following events will take place on Simon's birthday: employment at age 30, retirement at age 65, and death at age 75. Based on his present salary and future salary projections, Simon will receive a $50,000 pension payment annually. The rate of interest underlying pension calculations is 10%.

(continued)

Required

Calculate the firm's pension liability or projected benefit obligation at Simon's 51st birthday.

Solution

As always, it's a good idea to draw a time line to represent both the amount and timing of Maxwell's future pension cash outflows. As you can see, Maxwell Corporation expects to pay Simon a 10-year annuity of $50,000 each year after his retirement.

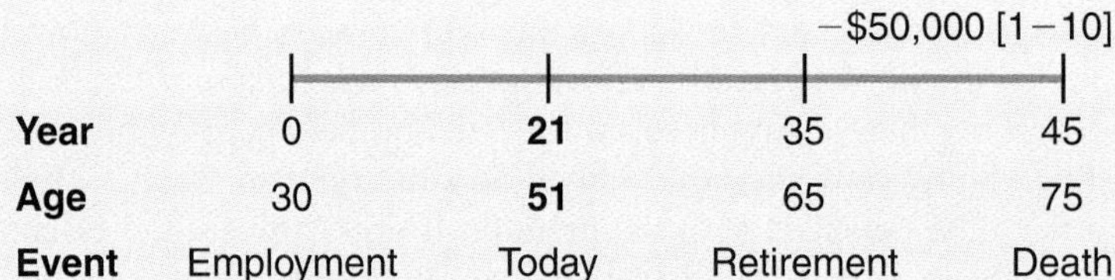

Believe it or not, calculating this employee's pension liability is now a simple two-step process. The first step is to calculate the present value of this 10-year annuity at his retirement at age 65. In other words, let's discount the cash flows in this annuity back to age 65. Since the present value of an annuity interest factor for 10 payments at 10% is 6.14457, the calculation is as follows:

$$PVA = R_{10}\ (PVAIF) = \$50{,}000\ (6.14457) = \$307{,}228.50$$

To complete the second step, let's redraw the time line:

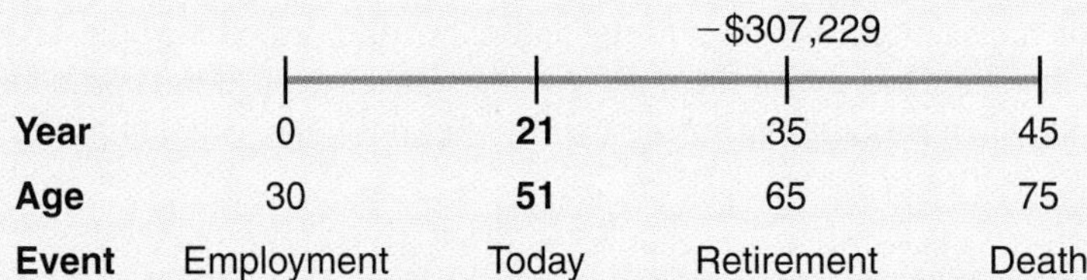

All we have to do is discount the single lump sum at age 65 back to age 51, and we will have calculated the cash equivalent value or present value of the pension liability for Simon when he is 51 years old. Since the present value interest factor for 14 periods (65 − 51) at 10% is .26333, the calculation is as follows:

$$PV = FV_{14}\ (PVIF) = \$307{,}228.50\ (.26333) = \$80{,}902.48$$

This amount represents the current measurement of Maxwell Corporation's pension liability and is referred to as the projected benefit obligation. The **projected benefit obligation** is the present value of estimated future retirement benefits based on future salary levels and resulting from employee services rendered to date. This definition of a pension liability should make sense to you because:

- Our two-step calculation process produced present values.
- The phrase *estimated future retirement benefits based on future salary levels* reflects the $50,000 payments to be received by Simon.
- The phrase *resulting from employee services rendered to date* reflects Simon's 21 years of service.

Although this example was greatly simplified, it does illustrate the concept underlying the determination of pension values. In reality, we can't predict a single individual's date of death; but individuals known as *actuaries* can come amazingly close to estimating the life expectancy of an employee population by using a combination of present value analysis, probability theory, and mortality tables.

Companies with pension plans have legal obligations to pay their employees during retirement. Thus, it is highly desirable that you read the pension footnote of such companies to determine the scale of their financial commitment to future retirees. Look for the projected benefit obligation. For example, Walt Disney reported the projected benefit obligation in its September 30, 2001, annual report to be more than $2.1 billion. And if you think that's large, consider IBM's $38.6 billion estimate of its pension liability (called benefit obligation) in its December 31, 2001, annual report. Although these amounts are estimates and are not currently payable, they are too important for you to overlook.

To learn more about deferred taxes read Appendix 13–2, which you can find at www.mhhe.com/solomon.

Accounting for Stockholders' Equity

In the corporation, significant sources of financing are owner contributions from stockholders and earnings retained in the business. Although stockholder equity transactions can have an important effect on a company's financial statements, the accounting procedures tend to be relatively easier to understand than, for example, those you studied for measuring and reporting bonds. As a result, our coverage here will be brief. We'll begin by examining the essentials of how to measure and report capital contributions by owners, examine the distinction between stock dividends and stock splits and finally, learn how to account for treasury stock.

Measuring and Reporting Capital Contributions

You can expect to find information about capital contributions in at least three locations in the typical annual report. These are the balance sheet, statement of stockholders' equity, and the notes section. Since the balance sheet presentation generally summarizes the detail found in the other two locations, let's look at the two primary balance sheet accounts, namely the generic Capital Stock account and the Additional Paid-In-Capital account.

Nature of Capital Stock When the owners of a corporation contribute cash or other assets to the business, they receive *capital stock*, or ownership shares, in exchange. Capital stock generally is divided into two types: common and preferred. *Common stock* carries both voting rights and the right to share in corporate profits whenever dividends are declared by the board of directors. Although *preferred stock* does not usually carry voting rights, it provides owners of this type of stock a preferred status with respect to dividends and, if the corporation goes out of business, assets. Recall that the number of individual units of capital stock or *shares* owners receive in exchange for their investment is documented with a *stock certificate*.

Each share of both common and preferred stock is often assigned an arbitrary value called **par value** or **stated value**, not to be confused with the market value of the stock. These amounts are used to represent **legal capital**, the threshold portion of contributed capital that must be retained in the business to protect corporate creditors. That is, legal capital restricts the amount of resources that may be withdrawn by stockholders in the form of dividends. Depending on the state laws that apply, this threshold may even extend beyond par or stated value. Suppose, for example, that your company sold 2,000 shares of no-par common stock for $10 per share but without a stated value. In this case, you would record the following transaction in which the entire proceeds become legal capital because there is neither a par value nor a stated value with which to set a boundary between what can be distributed to shareholders and what cannot.

Issuance of 2,000 no-par value common stock with no stated value at $10 per share

Transaction Analysis					Journal Entry		
	Fundamental Accounting Equation						
Account Titles	**Assets**	**=**	**Liabilities +**	**Owners' Equity**	**Account Titles**	**Debit**	**Credit**
Cash (2,000 × $10)	20,000				Cash (2,000 × $10)	20,000	
Common Stock				20,000	Common Stock		20,000

Generally, however, either par or stated value are available and do allow you to confirm the actual dollar amount recorded in either the Common Stock or Preferred Stock accounts found in the balance sheet. For example, if you multiply the $0.75 par value shown in the 2001 balance sheet of Chevron Texaco Corporation by the 1,137,021,057 shares of common stock issued, you will see how the preparers of Chevron Texaco's 2001 annual report calculated the reported common stock dollar amount of $853 million.

Nature of Additional Paid-in-Capital *Additional Paid-in Capital*, also called *Capital Paid in Excess of Par Value*, is the title of the account that measures the amounts invested by owners of common or preferred stock that are in excess of par or stated value. For example, if you were to issue 2,000 shares of $1 par value common stock at $10 per share, you would record the following transaction:

Issuance of 2,000 shares of $1 par value stock at $10 per share

Transaction Analysis					Journal Entry		
	Fundamental Accounting Equation						
Account Titles	**Assets**	**=**	**Liabilities +**	**Owners' Equity**	**Account Titles**	**Debit**	**Credit**
Cash (2,000 × $10)	20,000				Cash (2,000 × $10)	20,000	
Common Stock (2,000 × $1)				2,000	Common Stock (2,000 × $1)		2,000
Additional Paid-in-Capital				18,000	Additional Paid-in-Capital		18,000

In this case, legal capital is only $2,000 instead of the $20,000 in our last example. In its July 31, 2001, balance sheet, Intuit Inc., a software developer, listed both Common Stock and Additional Paid-in-Capital account titles. The common stock was composed of 210,526,239 shares at $0.01 par value, or approximately $2,105,000, whereas the additional paid-in capital was reported at the excess over par of $1,723,385,000.

Measuring and Reporting Retained Earnings

Recall that Retained Earnings is a corporate account title that represents earnings from profitable operations retained in the business. As you learned in Chapter 3, retained earnings consists of accumulated earnings, or net income, reduced by any net losses and dividends declared to date. In its September 30, 2001, statement of stockholders' equity, for example, Walt Disney Company reported that its retained earnings balance of over $12 billion—$12,171,000,000—was composed of a $12,767,000,000 September 30, 2000, balance minus $158,000,000 of net loss minus $438,000,000 of dividends.

Since you have already learned about the effects of net income and dividends (refer to CMU Transactions W_1 and W_2 in Chapter 10) on retained earnings, we next turn our attention to two distinct but commonly confused transactions that each affect stockholders' equity but in a very different way.

Comparing and Contrasting Stock Dividends and Stock Splits

Since there is often confusion over the two transactions known as stock dividends and stock splits, we'll next examine the basic characteristics of each so that we can understand how they are alike and how they are different. Then, we will compare their respective effects on the financial statements.

Stock Dividends A **stock dividend** is, as its name implies, a noncash distribution of additional shares of stock to shareholders. Generally, a corporation will consider issuing a stock dividend when its cash resources are diminished and it wants to maintain shareholder confidence in its ability to not miss a dividend payout. Suppose, for example, you own 100 shares of Pennant Corporation's 10,000 shares of common stock outstanding, when it decides to declare a 5% stock dividend. Since you own 1% (100/10,000) of this company's 10,000 shares before the stock dividend, receiving extra shares will not change your proportionate interest. In fact, your share of the company will still be 1%, which you can confirm by recognizing that your 105 shares [100 shares + (100 × .05)] still represent 1% of the company's new total of 10,500 shares [10,000 + (10,000 × .05)].

Although the preceding example seems to indicate that a stock dividend does not itself convey additional value, some would disagree. One argument is that the expected decline in the market price per share after a stock dividend is declared (5% in our example) does not always take place in practice especially for small stock dividends. Another argument is that if Pennant Corporation decides to resume payment of its regular (say $2.00) per share cash dividend, the stock dividend will indirectly provide additional value of $10 (5 additional shares × $2) to you at every dividend payment date.

Since a larger than 20% stock dividend is recorded in a manner somewhat different from the way a small stock dividend is recorded, we will focus in this textbook on stock dividends of 20% or less. As you will see, the approach we use here for Pennant's 5% stock dividend is very straightforward. Assuming its common stock has a par value of $5 and a fair market value of $20 at the date the stock dividend is declared, the following transaction will be recorded:

Transaction Analysis						Journal Entry		
	Fundamental Accounting Equation							
Account Titles	**Assets**	=	**Liabilities**	+	**Owners' Equity**	**Account Titles**	**Debit**	**Credit**
Stock Dividend Declared					(10,000)	Stock Dividend Declared	10,000	
Common Stock (500 × $5)					2,500	Common Stock		2,500
APIC* (500 × $15)					7,500	Additional Paid-in-Capital		7,500

*Additional Paid-in-Capital

As you can see, Pennant Corporation distributes 500 (10,000 × .05) shares of common stock to its shareholders. Since these shares are currently worth $20 apiece, **Stock Dividend Declared**, a contra retained earnings account, is decreased by the fair market value of the shares distributed. If you think about it, reducing retained earnings by the cash value of these shares is equivalent in concept to reducing retained earnings by the amount of a cash dividend declared.

Stock Splits A **stock split** occurs when a corporation decides to issue additional shares of stock to existing shareholders accompanied by a proportionate reduction in par or stated value. In addition to leaving the total amount of contributed capital unchanged, a stock split usually results in a proportionate reduction in the market price per share. One reason why companies choose to offer stock splits is to lower the stock's market price and, therefore, attract a wider range of potential investors. A high-priced stock might be beyond the reach of many people, but if the share price drops by a half or two-thirds in a three-for-one split, new investors might be attracted.

Suppose, for example, that you own 250 shares of a company's $10 par preferred stock when it announces a 2-for-1 stock split. After this stock split, you will hold 500 shares of $5 par value preferred stock. Your $2,500 of par value is the same, however, both before and after the stock split (250 × $10 versus 500 × $5) which suggests the following classic analogy. In essence, your company has divided its shareholder pie into twice as many slices each of which is half as large as before! Thus, you're not one penny richer because the total value of your shares hasn't changed. You, as a shareholder, can benefit, however, if your stock's price either rises from its post-split level or future cash dividends per share are reduced proportionally less than the increase in shares.

To illustrate how a stock split is recorded, let's assume a corporation has 100,000 shares of $15 par value preferred stock issued and outstanding as it announces a 3-for-1 stock split.

Transaction Analysis				Journal Entry		
	Fundamental Accounting Equation					
Account Titles	Assets	= Liabilities +	Owners' Equity	Account Titles	Debit	Credit
Preferred Stock, $15 par			(1,500,000)	Preferred Stock, $15 par	1,500,000	
Preferred Stock $5 par			1,500,000	Preferred Stock, $5 par		1,500,000

This transaction can be referred to as a reclassification entry since it creates the new Preferred Stock account with 300,000 shares at $5 par value each ($1,500,000) and eliminates the old Preferred Stock account with 100,000 shares at $15 par value each ($1,500,000). Because the amount of contributed capital does not change, some would argue that a simple memorandum entry noting the change in shares and par value is a more efficient way to account for this transaction.

To avoid complexity, this textbook includes stock split examples that are relatively large such as a 2-for-1 stock split (equivalent to a 100% stock dividend) and stock dividend examples that are relatively small such as a 10% stock dividend. When stock splits become more and more indistinguishable from stock dividends, however, recording issues become more difficult. For example, is a 5-for-4 stock split equivalent to a 25% stock dividend?

Since several key dates are important when discussing a stock split, we'll use the Pepsi Bottling Company to illustrate them. First, Pepsi announced its intention to issue a 2-for-1 split on October 11, 2001 (*announcement date*), to those shareholders owning the stock as of December 4, 2001 (*record date*), distributable to shareholders on December 4, 2001 (*payable date*). For Pepsi, the *ex-dividend date*—the date on which it is too late to buy the shares and receive the dividend or split shares—was December 5, 2001.

Comparing the Financial Statement Effects of Stock Dividends and Stock Splits

Balance Sheet If you study the preceding transactions for stock dividends and stock splits, you will realize that neither changes the total dollar amount of stockholders' equity. A stock dividend does change individual balances within retained earnings and contributed capital accounts, but a stock split changes only the par value and number of shares associated with a contributed capital account.

Income Statement No stockholder equity transaction has an effect on the income statement. This should make perfect sense since shareholder transactions are financing activities and should never affect a firm's profitability.

Statement of Cash Flows Stock splits do not have even a remote connection to the statement of cash flows. Stock dividends, however, are sometimes treated as a direct exchange and reported in the supplemental noncash section. The reasoning is that two distinct and somewhat significant financing activities are involved, namely the declaration of a dividend and the issuance of additional shares of stock.

Measuring and Reporting Treasury Stock

Recall that you learned about treasury stock in Chapter 4 when we examined the accounts normally found in a classified balance sheet. We now take a more in-depth look by considering the nature of treasury stock, how it is recorded, and how it is reported in the financial statements.

What Is Treasury Stock? Essentially, **treasury stock** represents a corporation's own shares of stock that have been repurchased by the corporation and taken out of circulation for the present time. Corporations repurchase their stock for many different reasons, including:

- to provide shares for employee stock option and savings plans.
- to reduce outstanding shares so as to increase earnings per share.
- to contract the operations of the business.
- to provide shares for potential acquisition of other companies.
- to buy out a particular ownership interest or protect against a hostile takeover.

How Is Treasury Stock Measured and Recorded? Two methods of accounting, the cost method and the par value method, are used to account for treasury stock transactions. We'll use the simpler of these methods, the cost method, to account for the following facts:

Example The stockholders' equity section of the Williams Corporation before repurchase of shares is as follows:

Common stock, $100 par value, 10,000 shares issued and outstanding	$1,000,000
Additional paid-in-capital	300,000
Retained earnings	400,000
Total stockholders' equity	$1,700,000

Required Record the following transactions:

- *Repurchase:* Williams Corporation acquires 1,000 shares of its own common stock for $125 a share.

Transaction Analysis						Journal Entry		
	Fundamental Accounting Equation							
Account Titles	Assets	=	Liabilities	+	Owners' Equity	Account Titles	Debit	Credit
Treasury Stock					(125,000)	Treasury Stock	125,000	
Cash (1,000 × $125)	(125,000)					Cash (1,000 × $125)		125,000

As its name implies, the cost method increases Treasury Stock, a contra shareholders' equity account, by the $125,000 (1,000 × $125) cost of repurchasing these shares of common stock. Note that the cost method ignores the par value of these shares. If some of these shares are later sold at cost, the effects of the preceding transaction would be reversed and recorded at cost. Let's take a closer look at how you would record reissues that are sold at other than cost.

- *Reissue or sale above cost:* Williams Corporation sells 400 shares of treasury stock at $140.

Transaction Analysis							Journal Entry		
	Fundamental Accounting Equation								
Account Titles	**Assets**	**=**	**Liabilities**	**+**	**Owners' Equity**		**Account Titles**	**Debit**	**Credit**
Cash (400 × $140)	56,000						Cash (400 × $140)	56,000	
Treasury Stock					50,000		Treasury Stock		50,000
APIC—Treasury Stock					6,000		APIC—Treasury Stock		6,000

Since the Treasury Stock account is accounted for at cost, it is decreased here by $50,000 (400 × $125).

- *Reissue or sale below cost:* Williams Corporation sells 400 shares of treasury stock at $120.

Transaction Analysis							Journal Entry		
	Fundamental Accounting Equation								
Account Titles	**Assets**	**=**	**Liabilities**	**+**	**Owners' Equity**		**Account Titles**	**Debit**	**Credit**
Cash (400 × $120)	48,000						Cash (400 × $120)	48,000	
APIC—Treasury Stock					(2,000)		APIC—Treasury Stock	2,000	
Treasury Stock					50,000		Treasury Stock		50,000

Once again, the treasury stock account is decreased by its cost of $50,000 (400 × $125). Note that we could have used the Retained Earnings account in the preceding transaction if the Additional Paid-in-Capital—Treasury Stock had no existing balance. In fact, the Retained Earnings account can be decreased through such transactions but not increased. One explanation for not allowing retained earnings to be increased is accounting's desire to not imply that shareholder transactions in one's own stock generate profit.

How Is Treasury Stock Reported? The stockholders' equity section of Williams Corporation after recording the preceding treasury stock transactions is as follows:

Common stock, $100 par value, 10,000 shares issued and outstanding	$1,000,000
Additional paid-in-capital	300,000
Additional paid-in-capital—treasury stock	4,000
Retained earnings	400,000
Less: Treasury stock, at cost, 200 shares	(25,000)
Total stockholders' equity	$1,679,000

As you can see, the cost of repurchasing shares of treasury stock (200 shares × $125) is subtracted from stockholders' equity as a whole. Obviously, treasury stock is not an asset and is not entitled to receive dividends. Also, its transactions have no effect on the income statement; that is, no gains or losses are recognized.

The preceding presentation is not appreciably different from actual practice. For example, The Walt Disney Company's September 30, 2001, balance sheet reports just such a subtraction of $1.395 billion in its stockholders' equity section from the repurchase of 81.4 million shares.

Comprehensive Performance Objective for Stockholders' Equity

Now that you have learned more about how to measure, record, and report several types of stockholder equity transactions, you can use Performance Objective 55 to help you in your mastery:

YOUR PERFORMANCE OBJECTIVE 55
Calculate, **record**, and **present** the financial statement effects of the following stockholder equity transactions: capital stock issuances and retirements; cash dividends, stock dividends, and stock split declarations; and treasury stock repurchases and reissues.

Summary with Key Terms

This chapter first reviewed the financial statement effects of CMU's financing activities. Then, it began a general examination of how to account for current liabilities, the first of this chapter's financing activity transactions. In our notes payable discussion, you learned that a **promissory note** (700) or simply a **note** (701) is a written contract in which one person promises to pay another person a definite sum of money at its **maturity date** (700). You also learned the distinction between an **interest-bearing note** (701) and **a non-interest-bearing note** (701). In addition, you also learned about salaries and payroll tax liabilities, income tax liabilities, and other accrued liabilities.

The number in parentheses following each **key term** is the page number on which the term is defined.

The greatest portion of this chapter was devoted to noncurrent liabilities. You began by learning how to **discount** (710) future cash flows, how to calculate interest with the **general formula for periodic compound interest** (707) and how to interpret the process known as **amortization** (707). You then went on to use the **effective interest method of amortization** (709) while creating a **debt payment schedule** (713). Two methods of constructing this type of information were presented. These were the **future value approach** (707) and the **time-line/table approach** (715), which was the subject of an *Insight.*

Next, you examined how to account for a **bond** (721), particularly from the perspective of the borrower. Some essential bond terminology includes **stated interest rate** (722) and **effective interest rate** (722) or **market interest rate** (722). Bonds whose **proceeds** (721) are less than face value are said to be issued at a **bond discount** (729), which is accounted for with a **Discount on Bonds Payable** (729) account. Bonds whose proceeds are greater than face value are said to be issued at a **bond premium** (727), which is accounted for with a **Premium on Bonds Payable** (733) account. Generally speaking, the **straight-line amortization method** (730) can be used in place of the effective interest amortization method.

Our present value tools were applied to pensions in a *User Focus* entitled "How You Can Determine a Company's Estimated Pension Liability". In particular, the **projected benefit obligation** (738) is equivalent to the pension liability. Next, in a more in-depth look at stockholders' equity, you were introduced to several new terms, such as **par value** (739), **stated value** (739), and **legal capital** (739). Next, you examined the distinction between a **stock dividend** (741) that is accounted for with a **Stock Dividend Declared** (741) account and a **stock split** (741). Finally, you learned more about the **Treasury Stock** (743) account.

In Appendix 13–1, available at www.mhhe.com/solomon, you learned in greater detail about the **lease** and how to account for its financial effects on both the **lessee** and the **lessor**. You also studied the distinctions between an **operating lease** and a **capital lease**.

In Appendix 13–2, available at www.mhhe.com/solomon, you learned how the account known as **Deferred Income Tax** is created as a result of a **timing difference** between revenue and expense recognition for financial accounting purposes and for tax purposes.

Making Business Decisions

YOUR PERFORMANCE OBJECTIVE 2
(page 18)

You are a part-time student who has just had the unthinkable happen—your car broke down and it is not repairable! Not only do you need a car to get to school but you also need it for your small business, Computer Doctor—a sole proprietorship in which you service the computers of other students.

So today is the day you're going car shopping. Fortunately, you have about $25,000 that you recently inherited from your grandfather. You had planned to invest this money in Computer Doctor after you graduated nine months from now. But now you know that you'll have to spend some of this money on a new car. After searching on the Internet, you find a great deal on a Honda CR-V LX. It lists for $19,150, but you can get it for $17,942. It's sporty and has enough room in the back for your computer equipment. You decide to buy it, but you are faced with a decision. Should you buy it outright, finance it, or lease it?

If you buy it outright, you'll pay $17,942 plus sales tax (8.8%) and about $400 in vehicle and licensing fees. If you finance it, you'll pay 10% down, owe $369.49 per month for a 60-month term, and bear the same fees and sales tax as under the outright purchase. If you lease the car, you'll pay no taxes and fees. The amount due on delivery will be $2,552.58, and you'll pay $250.70 per month. The lease is an *open-end lease*, which means that at the end of the 60 months, you can buy the car for the residual amount—the amount that the car is expected to be worth at the end of the lease period. In this case, the residual amount is $8,031.90. No matter what decision you make, however, you'll also have to buy insurance.

Required

a. Using a 6% discount rate, apply present value calculations to decide whether you should purchase this car outright (100% cash) or finance your purchase with an automobile loan. Document your decision with calculations and time lines, as appropriate, for all options.
b. What qualitative factors relating to these options might change the decision you reached in requirement a?
c. Would your decision change if Computer Doctor were a corporation? Why or why not?
d. (Read Appendix 13–1, which you can find at www.mhhe.com/solomon, before attempting to solve this item.) In your decision, consider leasing the car as an option. Since a lease's residual value is a cash outflow, be sure you include this amount in your time line analysis.

Questions

YOUR PERFORMANCE OBJECTIVE 4
(page 22)

13-1 Explain in your own words the meaning of key business terms.

a. Promissory note or note
b. Maturity date
c. Discount (verb)
d. Debt payment schedule
e. Lease (Appendix 13–1)
f. Bond
g. Proceeds of a bond
h. Projected benefit obligation
i. Deferred income tax (Appendix 13–2)
j. Timing difference (Appendix 13–2)
k. Legal capital
l. Par value
m. Stated value
n. Stock dividend declared
o. Treasury stock

13-2 Describe the characteristics of a promissory note.

13-3 Distinguish between an interest-bearing note and a non-interest-bearing note.

13-4 Identify at least five amounts that might be withheld from an employee's salary.

13-5 Payroll accounting involves two major transactions. Describe the nature of each transaction.

13-6 Why are present value calculations necessary in the valuation of noncurrent liabilities?

13-7 Describe the general formula for periodic compound interest and provide a simple numerical example to illustrate how it is applied.

13-8 Distinguish between asset amortization and liability amortization.

13-9 Distinguish between the future value approach and the time line/table approach for calculating subsequent present values.

13-10 Distinguish between the lessee and the lessor in a lease agreement. (Appendix 13–1)

13-11 Distinguish between an operating lease and a capital lease in the following ways: (Appendix 13–1)
a. Balance sheet presentation
b. Income statement presentation
c. Statement of cash flow presentation

13-12 Distinguish between an operating lease and a capital lease in the following ways: (Appendix 13–1)
a. Rights of ownership transferred.
b. Transaction recorded at the date the lease is signed.
c. Liability measurement using Figure 13-4.

13-13 Why do lessees generally prefer to account for a lease agreement with the operating lease method? (Appendix 13–1)

13-14 Distinguish between a bond's stated interest rate and its effective interest rate. Describe the specific role each interest rate plays in calculating the price of a bond.

13-15 Distinguish between a bond discount and a bond premium.

13-16 As an investor, would you prefer to invest in a bond issued at a discount or at a premium?

13-17 Describe the balance sheet classification of the Discount on Bonds Payable account and the Premium on Bonds Payable account.

13-18 Distinguish between the effective interest method of amortization and the straight-line method of amortization.

13-19 What are the primary differences between common stock and preferred stock?

13-20 What is the primary significance of legal capital?

13-21 Which is the better investment—common stock with a par value of $10 or common stock with a par value of $20?

13-22 You learned in this chapter that total stockholders' equity does not change as a result of either a stock split or a stock dividend. Describe the effects of each action on other aspects of stockholders' equity.

13-23 Contrast the effects of a cash dividend and a stock dividend on a corporation's balance sheet.

13-24 If a stock split transaction does not provide value to a shareholder, explain why it is used by a corporation.

13-25 Describe reasons why a corporation might repurchase its own shares of stock.

Reinforcement Exercises

E13-1 Asking the Right Questions: A Group Activity

YOUR PERFORMANCE OBJECTIVE 4 *(page 22)*

It's often said that knowing the right answer is not nearly as important as asking the right question. Asking the right question is a problem-solving skill that will help you make sound business decisions. In this exercise, you will review the vocabulary introduced in Chapter 13 by creating questions to match answers—similar to a popular TV show.

Required:

a. Given an answer, what's the question?
Choose **three** of the following terms to serve as an answer. For each term, create an appropriate question. For example, if you choose the term *balance sheet*, you might create the question *What financial statement shows the assets, liabilities, and owners' equity of an entity on a specific date*?

Face value	Stock dividend	Non-interest-bearing note
Par value	Stock split	Interest-bearing note
Stated value	Bond discount	Effective interest amortization
Market rate	Bond premium	Straight-line amortization
Coupon rate	Stated rate	Effective rate

b. Are you sure that's the question?
Have each member of your group read aloud the questions they developed in Requirement (a). As a group, decide whether each question is an accurate match for an answer. Once satisfied that all questions are appropriate, the group, as a whole, chooses the three

best questions created within the group. Record the three questions chosen (with their answers) on separate pieces of paper or index cards and give them to your instructor.

c. What's the answer?
To ensure you have learned the vocabulary terms listed in Requirement (a), your instructor will now quiz you on the questions written by all of your classmates.

YOUR PERFORMANCE OBJECTIVE 11b
(page 99)

E13-2 Classifying Account Titles
Indicate how each of the following accounts should be classified:

a. FICA Taxes Payable
b. Federal Income Taxes Payable
c. Accumulated Amortization
d. Additional Paid-in-Capital—Treasury Stock
e. Stock Dividend Declared
f. Treasury Stock
g. Common Stock
h. Preferred Stock
i. Additional Paid-in-Capital
j Bond Discount
k. Bond Premium
l. Investment in Bonds

YOUR PERFORMANCE OBJECTIVE 49
(page 702)

E13-3 Simple Interest Calculation on a Note
Felix Corporation borrowed $100,000 on June 30 of the current year in exchange for a note payable from Jeffries Bank. The loan is for nine months and bears a 6% interest rate. Calculate the amount of interest that must be accrued by Felix on December 31 (the end of its accounting year). What is the total cost of interest expense for Felix? What is the total amount of interest revenue that Jeffries Bank will earn?

YOUR PERFORMANCE OBJECTIVE 50
(page 704)

E13-4 Payroll Liability
In 2004, Wheaton Corporation paid total salaries of $700,000 to its employees, all of which was subject to a 7.65% FICA tax rate. Federal, state, and local income taxes withheld from salaries amounted to $180,000, and health insurance premiums withheld were $24,400.

Required
Provide the transaction necessary to record the salaries expense, the various amounts withheld from employee salaries, and the payment of employee salaries.

YOUR PERFORMANCE OBJECTIVE 51a
(page 705)

E13-5 Credit Card Transaction
You are granted the Nordstrom Preferred Student Credit Card in recognition of your academic achievements at this university. Feeling the stress of your studies, you experience a mental lapse while shopping and accrue a $4,500 account balance before the store temporarily suspends your credit privileges! The annual finance charge on this card is 12% compounded monthly. Anxious to pay off this balance in six months, you give the card to a friend for safekeeping and begin to save money.

a. What equal monthly payment (that is, rent) must you make to Nordstrom's for six consecutive months to retire your $4,500 obligation? *Note:* The present value of an annuity interest factor for $i = 1\%$ and $n = 6$ is 5.79548.
b. Complete the following amortization schedule based on your answer in part (a):

End of Month	Interest Expense	Monthly Payment	Reduction of Obligation	Liability Balance
0	–0–	–0–	–0–	$4,500
1				
2				
3				
4				
5				
6				

YOUR PERFORMANCE OBJECTIVE 51a
(page 705)

E13-6 Automobile Loan Transaction
During the process of negotiating the purchase of a new car, you decide to make a cash down payment of $2,000. Prior to your arrival at the car dealer, you obtain agreement from your bank to finance this purchase at an interest rate of 6% with loan payments due at the end of each of the next 60 months.

Required

a. If the maximum monthly loan payment you can afford is $300, what is the maximum price you will be willing to spend for this car? *Note:* The interest factor for 60 rents and 1/2% interest per period is 51.72556.

b. Assume that you are unable to negotiate a price lower than the price you calculated in (a) above. What steps might you take to reduce your monthly payments below $300 if alternative financing is available? Limit your answer to no more than three complete sentences.

E13-7 Mortgage Loan Transaction

YOUR PERFORMANCE OBJECTIVE 51a *(page 705)*

On January 2, 2003, Cave Creek Realty purchases a building for $2,000,000 and makes a down payment of $400,000. The mortgage is payable monthly over a 30-year term at an annual interest rate of 12%. Use one or more of the following interest factors for 1% and 360 periods to calculate the monthly mortgage payment:

Future value of $1	35.9496
Present value of $1	0.0278
Future value of an annuity of $1	3494.9641
Present value of an annuity of $1	97.2183

Use the amortization schedule shown here to solve Exercises 13-8 to 13-10.

The following amortization schedule of Artful Angles Inc. represents the first 5 years of its 10-year, $100,000 bond issue. Assume that both the payment of interest and the preparation of financial statements take place on December 31 of each year.

End of Year	Interest Expense	Cash Withdrawal	Amount Unamortized	Liability Balance
0	—	—	$702	$9,298
1	$651	$600	651	9,349
2	654	600	597	9,403
3	658	600	539	9,461
4	662	600	477	9,523
5	667	600	410	9,590

E13-8 Bond Transaction

YOUR PERFORMANCE OBJECTIVE 51a *(page 705)*

Since the initial carrying value of these bonds is less than face value, it should be apparent that the bonds are issued at a discount. Describe another way of reaching this conclusion from the amortization schedule above.

E13-9 Bond Transaction

YOUR PERFORMANCE OBJECTIVE 51a *(page 705)*

Using the amortization table shown above, what is the stated, or bond contract, interest rate? What is the effective, or market, interest rate? Describe how you determined these facts.

E13-10 Bond Transaction

YOUR PERFORMANCE OBJECTIVE 53 *(page 733)*

The amortization schedule shown above is based on the effective interest method rather than the straight-line method. Describe how you determined this fact.

E13-11 Bond Payable Transaction

YOUR PERFORMANCE OBJECTIVE 51 *(page 705)*

On January 1, Year 1, the ASAP Corporation issues a $100,000 five-year, 6% bond. Interest is payable semiannually on June 30 and December 31. If the bond is sold to yield 6% compounded semiannually:

a. Draw a time line to represent both the amount and timing of its cash outflows.

b. How much cash will the corporation receive?

c. How much interest expense will be incurred over the five-year period?

d. What is the corporate liability on January 1 of Year 1?

YOUR PERFORMANCE OBJECTIVE 51 *(page 705)*

E13-12 Bond Payable Transaction

On January 1, Year 1, the AWOL Corporation issues a $100,000 five-year, 6% bond. Interest is payable semiannually on June 30 and December 31. If the bond is sold to yield 4% compounded semiannually:

a. Draw a time line to represent both the amount and timing of its cash outflows.
b. How much cash will the corporation receive?
c. How much interest expense will be incurred over the five-year period?
d. What is the corporate liability on June 30 of Year 1?

YOUR PERFORMANCE OBJECTIVE 51 *(page 705)*

E13-13 Bond Payable Transaction

On January 1, Year 1, the TGIF Corporation issues a $100,000 five-year, 6% bond. Interest is payable semiannually on June 30 and December 31. If the bond is sold to yield 8% compounded semiannually:

a. Draw a time line to represent both the amount and timing of its cash outflows.
b. How much cash will the corporation receive?
c. How much interest expense will be incurred over the five-year period?
d. What is the corporate liability on December 31 of Year 1?

YOUR PERFORMANCE OBJECTIVE 51 *(page 705)*

E13-14 Bonds Payable Transaction

On July 1, 2004, Hayden Company issued bonds paying interest on December 31 and June 30 and maturing in 10 years. The following transactions were recorded by Hayden's accountant:

Transaction Analysis							Journal Entry		
	Fundamental Accounting Equation								
Account Titles	**Assets**	**=**	**Liabilities**	**+**	**Owners' Equity**		**Account Titles**	**Debit**	**Credit**
Cash	21,964,000						Cash	21,964,000	
Bonds Payable			20,000,000				Bond Payable		20,000,000
Bond Premium			1,964,000				Bond Premium		1,964,000

December 31, 2004									
	Fundamental Accounting Equation								
Account Titles	**Assets**	**=**	**Liabilities**	**+**	**Owners' Equity**		**Account Titles**	**Debit**	**Credit**
Interest Expense					(1,757,120)		Interest Expense	1,757,120	
Bond Premium			(42,880)				Bond Premium	42,880	
Cash	(1,800,000)						Cash		1,800,000

Required

a. What are this bond's stated interest rate and effective interest rate?
b. What was the amount of the bond liability at December 31, 2004?
c. Calculate the interest expense at June 30, 2005.
d. Calculate the interest expense at December 31, 2005.

YOUR PERFORMANCE OBJECTIVE 55 *(page 745)*

E13-15 Stockholder Equity Transactions

Record the effects of the following common stock transactions:

a. 5,000 shares of $25 par value common stock are issued at $27 per share.
b. 3,000 shares of no-par preferred stock are issued at $21 per share.
c. 10,000 shares of no-par common stock with a $25 stated value are issued at $28 per share.

YOUR PERFORMANCE OBJECTIVE 55 *(page 745)*

E13-16 Stockholder Equity Transactions

Selected accounts from the ledger of Marr Corporation are listed below:

Preferred stock	$70,000
Land	7,000
Cash dividends declared	12,000
Retained earnings	114,000
Organization costs	500
Common stock	100,000
Additional paid-in-capital—treasury stock	4,000
Additional paid-in-capital—from stock dividends	1,500
Treasury stock, at cost	14,000
Stock dividends declared	5,000
Dividends payable	7,000

Assuming that no dividend declared accounts have yet been closed to retained earnings, what is the total stockholders' equity of Marr Corporation?

E13-17 Cash Dividend Transaction

YOUR PERFORMANCE OBJECTIVE 55 *(page 745)*

On January 1, 2004, the stockholders' equity section of Athletic Visionary, Inc.'s balance sheet showed the following balances:

Common stock, no par value, $10 stated value, 20,000 shares authorized, 8,000 shares issued and outstanding	$ 80,000
Additional paid-in-capital—from common stock issuances	20,000
Retained earnings	50,000
	$150,000

Required

a. Record the effects of a $1 per share cash dividend.
b. Present the stockholders' equity section immediately after recording this cash dividend.

E13-18 Stock Split Transaction

YOUR PERFORMANCE OBJECTIVE 55 *(page 745)*

On January 1, 2004, the stockholders' equity section of Athletic Visionary, Inc.'s balance sheet showed the following balances:

Common stock, no par value, $10 stated value, 20,000 shares authorized, 8,000 shares issued and outstanding	$ 80,000
Additional paid-in-capital—from common stock issuances	20,000
Retained earnings	50,000
	$150,000

Required

a. Record the effects of a 2-for-1 stock split.
b. Present the stockholders' equity section immediately after recording this stock split.

E13-19 Stock Dividend Transaction

YOUR PERFORMANCE OBJECTIVE 55 *(page 745)*

Pembroke Corporation's board of directors declared and distributed a stock dividend of one share of common stock for each 20 shares outstanding. Prior to the stock dividend, 20,000 shares were outstanding with a par value of $10 per share. The company recorded the stock dividend at the share's market price of $30 per share.

Required

Describe the effects of this transaction on Pembroke's stockholders' equity section.

E13-20 Stock Dividend Transaction

YOUR PERFORMANCE OBJECTIVE 55 *(page 745)*

On January 1, 2004, the stockholders' equity section of Athletic Visionary, Inc.'s balance sheet showed the following balances:

Common stock, no par value, $10 stated value 20,000 shares authorized, 8,000 shares issued and outstanding	$ 80,000
Additional paid-in-capital—from common stock issuances	20,000
Retained earnings	50,000
	$150,000

Required

a. Record the effects of a 10% stock dividend declared when the market price of the stock was $15 per share.
b. Present the stockholders' equity section immediately after recording this stock split.

YOUR PERFORMANCE OBJECTIVE 55 *(page 745)*

E13-21 Treasury Stock
Hernandez Inc. purchases 10,000 shares of its own previously issued $5 par value common stock for $80,000. Assuming the shares are held as treasury stock, describe the effect of this transaction on:

a. Net income
b. Total assets
c. Additional paid-in-capital
d. Stockholders' equity

YOUR PERFORMANCE OBJECTIVE 55 *(page 745)*

E13-22 Treasury Stock
Assume that the treasury stock held by Hernandez Inc. in Exercise 13-21 is sold for $95,000. Describe the effect of this transaction on:

a. Net income
b. Total assets
c. Additional paid-in-capital
d. Stockholders' equity

Critical Thinking Problems

YOUR PERFORMANCE OBJECTIVES CI-13, CI-14 *(pages 670, 671)*

P13-1 Review of Future Value and Present Value of Annuity Concepts
What amount must be deposited now at 6% compound interest and held for five years to produce an annual withdrawal of $1,000 at the end of each year for years 6 through 10? *Hint:* Work backward starting with Year 10.

YOUR PERFORMANCE OBJECTIVES CI-13, CI-14 *(pages 670, 671)*

P13-2 Review of Future Value and Present Value of Annuity Concepts
Anne Newity is only 12 years old but already aspires to be the chief financial officer at the Whole-Again Holistic Therapy Center. To reach this career goal, she seeks relevant work experience and initiates a college savings program. The money for her savings program comes from two sources:

a. Today, January 1, Year 1, she receives $12,000 from her only rich uncle, Seymour Shrinks. This amount is invested in a special savings account that earns a 10% rate of interest.
b. From her summer job at the Institute for Psychic Catharsis, she will invest an equal amount in her savings account at the end of each year for Years 3–6. These amounts will also earn 10%.

Anne decides that she must withdraw from her savings account exactly $10,000 per year at the end of each year for Years 7–10 to pay for her expected costs at Central State University.

Required
What is the amount of each deposit (or rent) that Anne must make from years 3–6 to accomplish her plan?

YOUR PERFORMANCE OBJECTIVE 49 *(page 702)*

P13-3 Accounting for an Interest-Bearing Note
O'Neill Company borrows $100,000 from Prescott State Bank on June 1 on a six-month, $100,000, 8% note.

Required

a. Record this borrowing transaction on June 1.
b. Prepare the adjustment required on June 30 assuming that interest is recorded monthly.
c. Provide the transaction needed at December 31 to record the note's maturity assuming monthly adjustments have been made to record the note's interest.
d. Provide the transaction needed at December 31 to record the note's maturity assuming monthly adjustments were not made to record the note's interest.
e. What was O'Neill's total interest expense?

P13-4 Payroll Liability

YOUR PERFORMANCE OBJECTIVE 50 (page 704)

Henry Dukamian earns a $105,000 salary per year as an architect. His detailed payroll information is as follows:

Federal income tax withholding	$22,500
State income tax withholding	4,500
Medical insurance withholding	3,000
FICA (social security taxes)	6.20% up to $60,600
Medicare taxes	1.45%
Federal unemployment insurance taxes	0.80% of the first $9,000
State unemployment insurance taxes	5.40% of the first $9,000

Required

From the perspective of Henry's employer,

a. Record a transaction to summarize the payment of Henry's salary during the year.
b. Record a transaction to summarize the payroll taxes and other costs on Henry's salary for the year. Assume the employer pays two-thirds of the total premiums for health insurance.
c. Calculate the total cost to employ Henry for the year.

P13-5 Proper Valuation of a Non-Interest-Bearing Note

YOUR PERFORMANCE OBJECTIVE 51 (page 705)

On January 1, Year 1, Buyer Company acquires a mini-supercomputer from Seller Company in exchange for a $35,000 non-interest-bearing promissory note due in three years. The computer's fair market value of $27,784.13 is used to determine the present value of the note. The interest rate used in this transaction was 8%. The correct journal entries to record the issuance of the note and the first interest accrual are as follows:

01/01/1	Mini-Supercomputer (PV Calculation)	27,784.13	
	Discount on Note Payable (Plug)	7,215.87	
	Note Payable (Face Value)		35,000.00
12/31/1	Interest Expense ($27,784.13 × .08 × 1)	2,222.73	
	Discount on Note Payable		2,222.73

Suppose, however, that the non-interest-bearing note was not recorded at its present value but instead was recorded at its face value as shown here:

Mini-Supercomputer	35,000	
Note Payable (Face Value)		35,000

Required

Explain in specific detail why the preceding journal entry will:

a. Misstate sales revenue or income to the seller as well as misstate asset cost or expense to the buyer in the year of the transaction.
b. Misstate or even ignore interest revenue and interest expense in subsequent periods.

YOUR PERFORMANCE OBJECTIVE 51 *(page 705)*

P13-6 Accounting for a Credit Card Transaction

You are granted the Nordstrom Preferred Student Credit Card in recognition of your academic achievements at this university. Feeling the stress of your studies, you experience a mental lapse while shopping and accrue a $4,500 account balance before the store temporarily suspends your credit privileges! The annual finance charge on this card is 12% compounded monthly. Anxious to pay off this balance in six months, you give the card to a friend for safe-keeping and begin to save money.

a. What equal monthly payment (i.e., rent) must you make to Nordstrom's for six consecutive months to retire your $4,500 obligation? *Note:* The present value of an annuity interest factor for $i = 1\%$ and $n = 6$ is 5.79548.

b. Complete the following amortization schedule based on your answer in part (a):

End of Month	Interest Expense	Monthly Payment	Reduction of Obligation	Liability Balance
0	–0–	–0–	–0–	$4,500
1				
2				
3				
4				
5				
6				

c. Calculate the total interest expense (finance charge) that you will incur over the six-month period.

d. Record the transactions needed at both the end of the first and second months to properly account for interest on and reduction in principal.

e. Present the Credit Card Payable account as it should appear on your balance sheet at the end of the third month.

YOUR PERFORMANCE OBJECTIVE 51 *(page 705)*

P13-7 Accounting for a Credit Card Transaction

On January 2 of the current year, Coach Jerry Kazrakis purchases 24 red suits from Vitale's Big & Tall Mens' Store at a cost of $10,000. Twelve of the suits are for his current varsity basketball players and 12 are for highly recruited players he is now pursuing. Jerry uses a special Red University Booster credit card, which requires monthly payments and carries an 18% finance charge. Jerry plans no further purchases this year and wants to fully pay off the $10,000 credit card balance in one year.

Required

a. Calculate the amount of the monthly payment required. *Note:* Fully document your calculation of the appropriate interest factor needed for this part.

b. Calculate the total interest expense that will be incurred over the term of this loan.

c. Record the transaction needed at both the end of the first and second months to properly account for interest on and reduction in principal.

d. Present the Credit Card Payable account as it should appear on Red University's balance sheet at the end of the third month.

YOUR PERFORMANCE OBJECTIVE 51 *(page 705)*

P13-8 Accounting for an Automobile Loan

On January 2 of the current year, Boris purchases a red KGB Turbo automobile at a price of $20,000. Boris pays $3,045 down and finances the remaining balance with a 12%, five-year installment car loan. Boris signs a promissory note for the loan balance and agrees to make loan payments of $377.15 at the end of each of the next 60 months.

Required

a. Prepare the journal entry that should be recorded on January 2 of the current year.

b. Calculate the total interest expense that will be incurred over the term of this loan.

c. Prepare the journal entry needed at both the end of the first and second months to properly account for interest on and reduction in principal.

d. Present the Installment Note Payable account as it should appear on the balance sheet at the end of the third month.

P13-9 Accounting for an Automobile Loan

YOUR PERFORMANCE OBJECTIVE 51 (page 705)

On January 2 of this year, you purchase the automobile of your dreams for $50,000. You pay $10,000 down and finance the remaining balance with a 12%, five-year installment car loan. You sign a promissory note for the loan balance and agree to make loan payments at the end of each of the next 60 months.

Required

a. Fill in the blanks of the following time line to represent this installment loan.

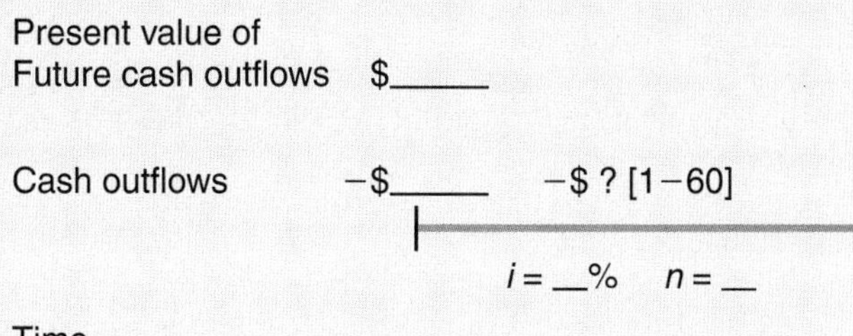

b. Calculate the total interest expense that you will incur over the term of this loan.
c. Prepare an amortization schedule to properly account for interest on and reduction in principal for the first six months of this year.
d. Present the Installment Note Payable account as it should appear on your balance sheet at the end of the second month.

P13-10 Accounting for a Mortgage Loan

YOUR PERFORMANCE OBJECTIVE 51 (page 705)

Michael Wu bought a small home for his parents on January 1, 2005, for $96,750. Michael paid 20% of this price in cash and financed the remaining balance with an 11 3/4%, 30-year, mortgage loan. His monthly mortgage payments are $781.39 and are due on the last day of each month.

a. Complete the time line below representing his mortgage loan.

b. Complete the following amortization schedule to represent the first six months of his mortgage loan.

End of Month	Interest Expense	Monthly Payment	Reduction of Liability	Liability Balance
0	−0−	−0−	−0−	$
1		$781.39		
2				
3				
4				
5				
6				

c. Record all mortgage-related journal entries for January 2005.
d. Present the effects of this mortgage loan on Michael's personal balance sheet prepared as of April 30, 2005.

Notes: The formula for deriving a present value of an annuity in arrears interest factor is shown below:

$$PVAIF = \frac{1-(1+i)^{-n}}{i} = \frac{1-\frac{1}{(1+i)^n}}{i}$$

where i = interest rate and n = number of rents (payments or receipts)

Assume the interest rate changes to 12% for parts (e) through (g).

e. Calculate the appropriate present value of an annuity interest factor for an interest rate of 12% and a period of 360 months. This part requires the use of a calculator with memory and an exponent function.
f. Recalculate the amount of Michael's monthly rental payment.
g. Record the January 31, 2032, journal entry. *Hint:* The term of the mortgage loan will have been completed on December 31, 2034. Thus, 3 years, or 36 months, remain on January 1, 2032. Using the formula above or tables, find the present value on this date.

YOUR PERFORMANCE OBJECTIVE 51 (page 705)

P13-11 Accounting for Bonds Payable
On January 1, Year 1, Li Liang Enterprises issued 10-year, 14% bonds having a face value of $100,000. Interest is payable semiannually on June 30 and December 31 and the bonds were sold to yield the investor 16%.
a. Calculate the total proceeds that Li Liang Enterprises receives from this bond issue. Record the journal entry needed at issuance.
b. Assume in your answer to this part that the proceeds received in (a) above were $90,000. Calculate the total interest expense incurred over the life of this bond issue.
c. Record the journal entries needed on June 30 and December 31 to account for interest and amortization of bond premium or discount. Use the effective interest method and assume that the bond liability as of January 1, Year 1, was $90,000.
d. Present the bond liability as it appears on the balance sheet on December 31, Year 1. Assume that the bond liability as of January 1, Year 1, was $90,000.

YOUR PERFORMANCE OBJECTIVES 51, 53 (pages 705, 733)

P13-12 Accounting for Bonds Payable
The following amortization schedule of Invidious Vectors Inc. represents the first five years of its 10-year, $100,000 bond issue. Assume that both the payment of interest and the preparation of financial statements take place on December 31 of each year.

End of Year	Interest Expense	Cash Withdrawal	Amount Unamortized	Liability Balance
0	—	—	$7,023	$92,977
1	$6,508	$6,000	6,515	93,485
2	6,544	6,000	5,971	94,029
3	6,582	6,000	5,389	94,611
4	6,623	6,000	4,766	95,234
5	6,666	6,000	4,100	95,900

a. Since the initial carrying value of these bonds is less than face value, it should be apparent that the bonds are issued at a discount. Describe another way of reaching this conclusion from the amortization schedule above.
b. The amortization schedule above is based on the effective interest method rather than the straight-line method. Describe how this fact can be determined.
c. What is the stated, or bond contract, interest rate?
d. What is the effective, or market, interest rate?

Do not construct an amortization table to answer parts (e) and (f). *Note:* Interest factors for $i = 7\%$ and $n = 2$ are PVIF = .87344 and PVAIF = 1.80802. Interest factors for $i = 7\%$ and $n = 8$ are PVIF = .58201 and PVAIF = 5.97130.

e. Calculate the total interest expense that will be reported over the 10-year life of this bond issue.
f. Present the complete bond liability as it will appear on the balance sheet at the end of the eighth year.

YOUR PERFORMANCE OBJECTIVES 51, 53 (pages 705, 733)

P13-13 Bond Discount Amortization Methods
Suppose a company issues 20-year, 10% bonds that pay interest annually and are issued at a price that provides an effective interest rate of 12%.

Required
a. Record the issuance of a single $1,000 bond.
b. Record the first and last payments of interest under the:

1. effective interest method of amortization.
2. straight-line method of amortization.

c. For each of these methods, determine the effective rate of interest for both the first and last payments. That is, divide interest expense by the bond liability (bond payable plus the unamortized premium).

P13-14 Bond Discount and Premium Amortization Methods

YOUR PERFORMANCE OBJECTIVES 51, 53 *(pages 705, 733)*

Suppose a company issues 20-year, 12% bonds that pay interest annually and are issued at a price that provides an effective interest rate of 10%.

Required

a. Record the issuance of a single $1,000 bond.

b. Record the first and last payments of interest under the:
   1. Effective interest method of amortization.
   2. Straight-line method of amortization.

c. For each of these methods, determine the effective rate of interest for both the first and last payments. That is, divide interest expense by the bond liability (bond payable plus the unamortized premium).

P13-15 Stockholder Equity Transactions

YOUR PERFORMANCE OBJECTIVE 55 *(page 745)*

The stockholders' equity section from the December 31 balance sheet of Ewe and Eye Seeing-Eye Sheepdogs Company is presented below:

Preferred stock, 5.5% cumulative, $25 par value, 200,000 shares authorized, 160,000 shares issued	$ 4,000,000
Common stock, $5 par value, 5,000,000 shares authorized, 3,000,000 shares issued	15,000,000
Additional paid-in-capital—common stock	5,600,000
Retained earnings	7,500,000
	$32,100,000

As of December 31, all shares issued are outstanding. That is, there are no shares in the treasury.

Required

a. Calculate the total contributed capital on December 31.

b. Assume that the following additional common stock transactions occurred during the year:
   May 1: 90,000 shares of treasury stock are purchased at $14/share.
   June 30: 20,000 shares of treasury stock are sold at $15/share.
   Present the Treasury Stock account as it should appear on the December 31 balance sheet. Be sure to clearly describe how this account relates to the balance sheet (added or subtracted?).

P13-16 Treasury Stock Transactions

YOUR PERFORMANCE OBJECTIVE 55 *(page 745)*

On January 1, 2004, the stockholders' equity section of Athletic Visionary, Inc.'s balance sheet showed the following balances:

Common stock, no par value, $10 stated value, 20,000 shares authorized, 8,000 shares issued and outstanding	$ 80,000
Additional paid-in-capital—from common stock issuances	20,000
Retained earnings	50,000
	$150,000

Required

a. Record each of the following transactions.
   1. 200 shares of treasury stock are acquired at $16 per share.
   2. 80 shares of treasury stock are sold at $19 per share.
   3. 110 shares of treasury stock are sold at $13 per share.

b. Present the stockholders' equity section immediately after recording these transactions.

YOUR PERFORMANCE OBJECTIVE 55
(page 745)

P13-17 Comprehensive Stockholder Equity Transactions
The stockholders' equity section of Ricketts Inc.'s balance sheet showed the following balances:

Common stock, $50 par value, 100,000 shares authorized, 30,000 shares outstanding	$1,500,000
Additional paid-in-capital–from common stock issuances	210,000
Retained earnings	700,000
	$2,410,000

Required

a. Record each of the following transactions that occur this year.
   1. April 1: Declaration and distribution of a 10% stock dividend. The market price was $75 per share at this date.
   2. May 10: Repurchase of 1,000 shares of the company's own stock for $70 per share.
   3. July 3: Common stock was split 2 for 1.
   4. September 15: Declaration and payment of a $.50 per share dividend.
   5. December 1: Sale of all treasury stock at $37 per share.

b. Assuming that Ricketts reported net income for the year ending December 31 was $50,000, present the stockholders' equity section as it would appear on the balance sheet at that date.

Research Assignments

A wide variety of interesting Research Assignments for this chapter are available for the following topics at www.mhhe.com/solomon:

R13-1 Financial Statement Effects of Financing Activities by Industry (PO 31)
R13-2 Financial Statement Effects of Financing Activities by Industry (PO 31)
R13-3 Financial Statement Effects of Financing Activities by Industry (PO 31)
R13-4 Using the MD&A to Learn More about Long-Term Debt (PO 14)
R13-5 Using the MD&A to Learn More about Stockholders' Equity (PO 14)
R13-6 Using the Notes to Learn More about Long-Term Debt (PO 14)
R13-7 Using the Notes to Learn More about Stockholders' Equity (PO 14)
R13-8 Comparative Analysis of Financing Activities (PO 14)
R13-9 Comparative Financial Analysis of Long-Term Debt Disclosures (PO 14)
R13-10 Ratio Analysis of Financing Activities (PO 3 and 14)

At this same website, the following Research Assignments are also available for Appendix 13–1:

AR13-1 Using the Notes to Learn More about Leases (PO 14)
AR13-2 Comparative Analysis of International Lease Accounting Practices (PO 3 and 14)

CHAPTER FOURTEEN

14

Applying What You Have Learned to Analyze The Gap

PERFORMANCE OBJECTIVES

This chapter does not introduce new Performance Objectives. Instead, it is a capstone chapter that tests your mastery of all the Performance Objectives introduced in earlier chapters by performing a comprehensive analysis of both The Gap and The Limited annual reports.

LEARNING ABOUT THE GAP'S ORIGINS AND EVOLUTION

In 1969, Donald and Doris Fisher thought they had a good idea for a business. They had noticed that shopping for jeans was a frustrating experience. Finding both a style that you liked and a size that fit properly was very difficult. Often you had to sort through disorganized piles of merchandise and might still not find your size because of poor inventory control. So Donald and Doris decided to open a small store near what is now San Francisco State University, and they named it "The Gap," after a phrase that had become popular in the 60s—"the generation gap." The Gap specialized in selling a full inventory of jeans that were neatly stacked and organized by size. Eight months later, the Fishers opened a second store in San Jose. By the end of 1970, there were six Gap stores, patronized primarily by teens and college students. The Gap was well on its way to becoming a major player in the retail industry.

By 1983, there were 550 Gap stores, and the Fishers decided to reinvigorate the company by hiring Mickey Drexler, the former president of Ann Taylor. Drexler brought a new vision to The Gap by introducing more brightly colored cotton apparel, consolidating the stores' many private labels into a single Gap brand, changing store layouts, and replacing traditional circular clothing racks with clean-looking white shelves to more neatly stack and display merchandise. In addition to engineering fundamental changes at The Gap stores, he also began to expand the customer base. Under Drexler's leadership, Gap Inc. grew to include Banana Republic, Old Navy, and GapKids.

All of these changes dramatically increased The Gap's success. But with that success, came the sincerest form of flattery—imitation. By the mid-1990s, what had made The Gap successful was also fueling its competitors. Many other retailers successfully copied not only Gap store design but also Gap products and style. Gap's traditional uncluttered look with polished wooden floors and tables with neat stacks of colorful tops was no longer unique. To win back customers, Gap turned to TV advertising, and the unique look and feel of the "Gap" ad campaigns was born—well-known rock musicians shot against a solid white background, twenty-somethings dancing in khakis.

Today, Donald and Doris Fisher—and now their son Robert—still help run the company. Gap Inc. is an international specialty retailer offering clothing, accessories, and personal care products for men, women, children, and babies under The Gap, Banana Republic, and Old Navy brand names. In 1997, Gap Online was launched in the United States followed by the establishment of GapKids and Baby Gap web-based stores in 1998. For the year ending February 2, 2002, overall sales exceeded $13.8 billion. Today, Gap Inc. employs approximately 166,000 people and operates more than 3,700 stores in North America, Europe, and Japan.

Gap's corporate culture is young, upbeat, and fast-paced. Employment opportunities range from student internships to paid employment in a wide variety of departments—marketing, distribution, sales, community relations, corporate communications, product development, production and preproduction, real estate, logistics, and visual merchandising, just to name a few.

If you've seen Gap commercials or walked through their stores, you've seen the Gap image. From jeans and T-shirts to khakis and jackets, Gap's "look" is modern, conservative, and simple. The shopping environment is uncluttered, neatly organized, and easy to navigate. Styles range from the most casual to styles suitable for the casual office. And of course, the convenience of shopping for jeans is still a Gap hallmark. As always, you'll find them at the back of the store neatly stacked on shelves according to style and size. Donald and Doris probably insist on that.

Learning about the Company's Position in the Specialty Retail Industry

Before we perform a financial analysis of The Gap, Inc., we must first learn as much as we can about the nature of its business. To do so, we will use information found in its SEC Form 10-K. Then, we will select a key competitor in the specialty retail industry that we can compare to The Gap for analytical purposes.

Using the 10-K to Learn More about How The Gap Conducts Its Business

As you learned in Chapter 3, companies that are publicly traded, that is, sell stocks or bonds to the public, must issue not only an annual report to shareholders, but also an annual report, known as the 10-K report, to the SEC. Although the 10-K doesn't have the color photographs, modern graphics, or high-quality glossy paper stock found in the annual report, it usually includes a wealth of information about the past, present, and future prospects of an entity. For example, The Gap's 2001 10-K report includes detailed information about its brands and their development; store operations; merchandise vendors; the seasonal nature of its business; advertising strategy; and such business risk factors as its ability to gauge fashion trends and changing consumer preferences, actions of competitors, its success in generating store sales and margins, the acceptance of the capital markets, and changes in its information technology systems. Also included are thumbnail sketches of its executive officers, a listing of its properties, and a detailed description of its legal proceedings. The following sections summarize some key information from The Gap's 10-K report.

Nature of Industry The following excerpt from page 1 of The Gap's 2001 10-K report makes it clear that it is a merchandiser or retailer.

We design virtually all of our products, which in turn are manufactured by independent sources, and sell them under our brands in the following store formats:

Gap: Founded in 1969, Gap stores offer extensive selections of classically-styled, high quality, casual apparel at moderate price points. Products range from wardrobe basics, such as denim, khakis and T-shirts to fashion apparel, accessories and personal care products for men and women aged teen through adult. We entered the children's apparel market with the introduction of GapKids in 1986 and babyGap in 1989. These stores offer casual apparel and accessories in the tradition of Gap style and quality for children aged newborn through teen. We launched GapBody in 1998, offering men's and women's underwear, sleepware and personal care products. As of February 2, 2002, we operated 2,932 Gap brand store concepts at 1,858 locations in the United States, Canada, the United Kingdom, France, Germany, and Japan. Store concepts are any Gap Adult, babyGap or GapBody that meets a certain square footage threshold even when residing within a single physical location.

Banana Republic: Acquired in 1983 with two stores, Banana Republic now offers sophisticated, fashionable collections of dress-casual and tailored apparel and accessories for men and women at higher price points than Gap. Banana Republic products range from apparel, including intimate apparel, to personal care products and home products. As of February 2, 2002, we operated 441 Banana Republic stores in the United States and Canada.

Old Navy: We launched Old Navy in 1994 to address the market for value-priced family apparel. Old Navy offers broad selections of apparel, shoes and

> accessories for adults, children and infants as well as other items, including personal care products, in an innovative, exciting shopping environment. As of February 2, 2002, we operated 798 Old Navy stores in the United States and Canada.

As this information indicates, The Gap is a retailer, which buys and resells products; it does not produce them. Thus, it is not a manufacturer or service business.

Nature of Sales The following excerpt from page 1 of The Gap's 2001 10-K clearly identifies The Gap as a global retailer.

> **General**
>
> We are a global specialty retailer operating stores selling casual apparel, personal care and other accessories for men, women and children under The Gap, Banana Republic, and Old Navy brands. We operate stores in the United States, Canada, the United Kingdom, France, Germany and Japan. . . .

The following excerpt from page 2 describes the nature of the international competition faced by The Gap.

> **International**
>
> We are faced with competition in European, Japanese, and Canadian markets from established regional and national chains. If international expansion is not successful, our results of operations could be adversely affected. Our ability to grow successfully in the continental European market will depend in part on determining a sustainable profit formula to build brand loyalty and gain market share in the especially challenging retail environments of France and Germany.

When you later examine The Gap's balance sheet and that of its competitor, The Limited, you will probably be quite surprised to learn that The Gap reports no accounts receivable, while The Limited reports an accounts receivable amount that represents only about 1.7% of its amount of total assets. Fortunately, the following information from page 2 of The Gap's 10-K explains why accounts receivable are not reported.

> **Store Operations**
>
> Our stores offer a shopper-friendly environment with an assortment of casual apparel and accessories which emphasize style, quality, and good value. The range of merchandise displayed in each store varies depending on the selling season and the size and location of the store.
>
> Our stores generally are open seven days per week (where permitted by law) and most holidays. All sales are tendered for cash, personal checks, debit cards or credit cards issued by others, including Gap, Banana Republic, and Old Navy private label cards which are issued by a third party.

The great majority of store purchases are made either with cash or such credit cards as Visa, Mastercard, or the Discover Card. Thus, it is likely that amounts receivable from the stores' private label cards are relatively small and are probably treated as cash or included in the Other Current Assets balance sheet account.

Nature of Suppliers Although retailers usually buy their products from several wholesalers, the company apparently works directly with manufacturers. To understand this relationship better, let's now examine the following description from pages 2 and 3 of The Gap's 2001 Form 10-K.

Merchandise Vendors

We purchase merchandise from more than 1,000 vendors (suppliers) located domestically and overseas. No vendor accounted for more than 5% of the dollar amount of our fiscal 2001 purchases. Of our merchandise sold during fiscal 2001, approximately 9% of all units (representing approximately 6% of total cost) was produced domestically while the remaining 91% of all units (representing approximately 94% of total cost) was made outside the United States. Approximately 13% of our total merchandise units (representing approximately 16% of total cost) was from China, including Hong Kong, with the remainder coming from more than 50 other countries. Any event causing a sudden disruption of imports from China or other foreign countries, including the imposition of additional import restrictions, could have a material adverse effect on our operations. Substantially all of our foreign purchases of merchandise are negotiated and paid for in U.S. dollars.

We cannot predict whether any of the countries in which our merchandise currently is manufactured or may be manufactured in the future will be subject to additional trade restrictions imposed by the U.S. and other foreign governments, including the likelihood, type or effect of any such restrictions. Trade restrictions, including increased tariffs or quotas, embargoes, and customs restrictions, against apparel items could increase the cost or reduce the supply of apparel available to us and adversely affect our business, financial condition and results of operations. We pursue a diversified global sourcing strategy that includes relationships with vendors in over 50 countries. These sourcing operations may be adversely affected by political and financial instability resulting in the disruption of trade from exporting countries, significant fluctuation in the value of the U.S. dollar against foreign currencies, restrictions on the transfer of funds and/or other trade disruptions.

Although this excerpt requires some careful reading, it provides very useful information to understand more about The Gap. For example, since The Gap has more than 1,000 suppliers, you now know that it is not dependent on a few key supplier relationships as is the case with many companies. It would be foolish, however, to suggest that the large number of suppliers makes The Gap's supply of inventory virtually risk-free, as the following *Insight* explains.

INSIGHT

The Importance of Analyzing the Nature of the Political Environment

The preceding excerpt from The Gap's 10-K implies a potentially serious business risk associated with The Gap's choice of suppliers. Being dependent (to the extent of 91% of all suppliers) on foreign suppliers, some of whom operate in potentially unstable areas of the world, poses a potential threat to The Gap's inventory supply and, therefore, its sales capability. Although The Gap clearly acknowledges the heightened business risk it faces in the light of potential import or trade restrictions, financial analysts must factor this qualitative risk into their evaluation.

By carefully reading this information, you can pick up very subtle nuances most analysts might miss. For example, the following comments were included in the fiscal 1999 Supplier 10-K information but not in the corresponding 2001 Supplier 10-K information you just read:

> The current financial instability in Asia is an example of the instability that could affect some suppliers adversely. Although to date the instability in Asia has not had an adverse effect on the Company's ability to import apparel and therefore the Company's results of operations and financial condition, no assurances can be given that they will not have such an effect in the future.

Apparently, company management believed that this instability in Asia in 1999 was no longer as great in 2001 and removed this passage. Following the tragic events of September 11, 2001, however, you would definitely want to read The Gap's future fiscal year 10-K's to determine if the company acknowledges any vulnerability to terrorist actions. The **insight** you should gain here is that no matter how healthy a company might appear after a comprehensive ratio analysis, an uncertain political environment here in the United States, as well as abroad, should be included in your analysis. Since companies vary in their willingness to fully disclose these risks, it is helpful to compare their 10-K discussion of such risks from year to year as was done here for The Gap.

Nature of Business Risk Factors Pages 3 through 5 of The Gap's 2001 10-K report identify additional risk factors that The Gap acknowledges have the potential to dramatically alter its success.

> **1. We must successfully gauge fashion trends and changing consumer preferences to succeed.**

Within this paragraph is the first serious indication in this 10-K of trouble at The Gap. After some opening sentences, the following passage tells the reader that mistakes have been made:

> A disproportionate part of our recent product offerings may have been too fashion-forward for our broad and diverse customer base. While we believe our current strategies and initiatives appropriately address these issues, continued merchandise misjudgments could have a material adverse effect on our image with our customers and on our operating results.

The following passage from page 4 also adds to the sense that The Gap regrets some recent decisions:

> In the recent past, we did not predict our customers' preferences and acceptance levels of our fashion items with the same accuracy we had previously experienced. In addition, lead times for many of our purchases are long, which may make it more difficult for us to respond rapidly to new or changing fashion trends or consumer acceptance for our products.

The following excerpt from page 4 of The Gap's Form 10-K describes, in detail, the nature of its competition.

2. **Our business is highly competitive and depends on consumer spending patterns.** The global specialty retail industry is highly competitive. We compete with national and local department stores, specialty and discount store chains, independent retail stores and internet businesses that market similar lines of merchandise. We face a variety of competitive challenges including:
   - anticipating and quickly responding to changing consumer demands;
   - maintaining favorable brand recognition and effectively marketing our products to consumers in several diverse market segments;
   - developing innovative, high-quality products in sizes, colors and styles that appeal to consumers of varying age groups and tastes;
   - competitively pricing our products and achieving customer perception of value;
   - providing strong and effective marketing support.

Although the preceding statements do not appear to signal problems, a comment on page 4 clearly acknowledges some serious difficulties.

We have lost market share to some of our competitors in the recent past and if we do not strengthen our competitive position, we may not recover that share and could also lose additional market share in the future.

Although The Gap's unnamed competitors are certainly numerous, one especially prominent and nationally known competitor is The Limited, Inc. The Limited is publicly traded and, like The Gap, has hundreds of stores including such well-known brand names as Bath and Body Works, Victoria's Secret, Lane Bryant, Express, Lerner New York, and The Limited. As a result, we will compare The Limited with The Gap in this chapter.

The following excerpt from page 4 of The Gap's 2001 10-K report is probably the single most important disclosure about The Gap's problems and affects nearly all aspects of its operating results and financial condition discussed later in this chapter. As a result, it is essential that you keep this passage in mind in your continued examination of The Gap in this chapter.

3. **We experience fluctuations in our comparable store sales and margins.** Our continued success depends, in part, upon our ability to improve sales and margins at our stores. . . . Over the past two years, our comparable store sales have decreased each quarter versus the prior comparable period, ranging from decreases of 2% in each of the first two quarters of fiscal 2000 to 16% and 17% in the final two quarters of fiscal 2001. . . . The declines we have experienced in comparable store sales have significantly contributed to a decline in our margins, which have decreased from 42% in fiscal 1999 to 37% in fiscal 2000 to 30% in fiscal 2001 (including a margin of 25% in the fourth quarter). Any failure to meet the expectations of investors, security analysts or credit rating agencies in one or more future periods could reduce the market price of our common stock and cause our credit ratings to decline.

Note that you will have an opportunity to confirm the gross margin percentages described during our comprehensive ratio analysis of The Gap. The last sentence in the excerpt above is particularly important in light of the next business risk stated on page 5 of the 10-K.

4. Recent changes in our credit ratings may have a negative impact on our financing costs and structure in future periods.

As you will learn later in more detail when we discuss the Management's Discussion and Analysis section, the described decline in sales had some serious ramifications for The Gap. These included a downgrade of its credit ratings, increased interest rates, and reduced access to both short-term and long-term borrowing opportunities. The final business risk identified by The Gap appears on page 5 of the 10-K.

5. We are planning certain system changes that may disrupt our supply chain.

Nature of Potential Capital Expenditures The detailed description on page 6 of the 2001 10-K about The Gap's current property holdings provides important information about the significance of The Gap's noncurrent assets and its current and potential use of noncurrent liabilities and additional equity financing. In particular, notice three details that you might find useful in your later analysis. First, The Gap leases almost all of its stores and corporate offices. Second, The Gap has a significant amount of excess office capacity. Finally, The Gap plans to close both a large distribution facility and a warehouse. In the latter two cases, you should be asking why.

Item 2—Properties

We operate stores in the United States, Canada, the United Kingdom, France, Germany, and Japan. The stores operated as of February 2, 2002 aggregated approximately 36.3 million square feet. We lease most of our store premises. Terms generally range from five to 15 years with one or two five-year renewal options. . . . Some leases contain cancellation clauses in our favor if specified sales levels are not achieved.

We currently lease our domestic and international regional offices and part of our headquarters office space, including approximately 495,000 square feet in buildings in San Francisco, California, approximately 265,000 square feet in buildings in San Bruno, California (near the San Francisco Airport), and approximately 350,000 square feet in buildings in New York City. We also have leased an additional office building of approximately 285,000 square feet in San Francisco which is currently under construction and scheduled to be delivered in mid 2002. In San Francisco and San Bruno, we currently have excess office capacity, and are attempting to sublease approximately 565,000 square feet of space on the office sublease market. We also lease approximately 115,000 square feet in Albuquerque, New Mexico that houses our corporate shared services center, as well as approximately 40,000 square feet of office space in Rocklin, California (near Sacramento).

We also lease certain other distribution facilities. Our Eastern Distribution Center/Kentucky Distribution Center complex (EDC/KDC) in Erlanger, Kentucky (near Cincinnati) consists of approximately 725,000 square feet and will be closed in late 2002. Nearby Northern Kentucky facilities include three additional facilities for distribution purposes totaling approximately 1,365,000 square feet. The warehouse/call center consists of approximately 270,000 square feet in Grove City, Ohio (near Columbus) and approximately 425,000 square feet in Groveport, Ohio, both of which service our catalog and online businesses. Our Japan Distribution Center (JDC), approximately 130,000 square feet, in Funabashi City, Chiba, Japan is provided and operated as a component of a distribution agreement with a third-party logistics provider. Our approximately 134,000 square foot warehouse in Basildon, England, will be closed in early 2002.

We own an approximately 160,000 square foot office building and an approximately 540,000 square foot office building in San Francisco. We own office buildings in San Bruno of approximately 190,000 and 270,000 square feet and nearby land which potentially could accommodate an additional building of up to 290,000 square feet, and also own a computer facility of approximately 40,000 square feet in Rocklin, California.

The preceding description of The Gap's properties helps you to anticipate the need for a serious look at the amount of money required to build additional stores, warehouse facilities, and office buildings. Also, given its problems and the fact that in 2000, The Gap doubled its rate of store growth in just two years, a whole set of questions for further analysis are triggered:

1. What impact has this growth in number and size of stores had on the company's amount of cash and other current assets?
2. Have inventory levels changed accordingly?
3. Has depreciation expense changed significantly?
4. Has profitability per store increased or decreased?

In addition, The Gap's significant dependence on leasing necessitates that you study the amount and timing of its future lease commitments.

Learning More about The Gap by Performing a Financial Analysis

The financial statements and related information sources in this textbook are historical and include only information about recent financial performance. They nevertheless provide the basis upon which you can predict future financial performance. Financial analysis helps you organize a vast array of information so that you may more accurately evaluate an entity's past and make better predictions about its performance in the future.

In earlier chapters you have learned financial analysis tools such as ratio analysis, horizontal analysis, vertical analysis, analysis of the MD&A (Management's Discussion and Analysis), and analysis of the Notes to Financial Statements. Now, you will use those tools to evaluate the financial condition and profitability of The Gap. And you will learn new tools of financial analysis to refine your analysis.

The First Step: A Comprehensive Ratio Analysis

You have used ratio analysis throughout this textbook. Now you will use all of the ratios to analyze the 2001 annual reports of The Gap and its competitor, The Limited (as of February 2, 2002). This analysis will help you to fully master Performance Objective 3.

YOUR PERFORMANCE OBJECTIVE 3

Calculate at least one financial statement ratio within each of the following five categories, **interpret** its meaning, and **discuss** its usefulness and limitations in making decisions:

a. Liquidity—e.g., current ratio and acid test ratio.
b. Activity or turnover—e.g., average collection period.
c. Financial leverage—e.g., debt to equity ratio.
d. Profitability—e.g., return on equity and profit margin ratio.
e. Valuation—e.g., price earnings ratio and dividend yield.

Many professionals and academicians in the world of corporate finance are convinced that the analysis you are about to observe is unnecessary. Their rather widely held view is based on a considerable amount of research that securities markets react to financial accounting information in a sophisticated manner. Such research indicates that securities markets are *efficient* with respect to published financial accounting information. That is, stock prices, quickly and without bias, reflect all available and relevant information, including that found in financial statements. So you might ask: Why is ratio analysis a valuable tool? Let's consider this question in the following *User Focus*.

Are These Analytical Tools Really Worthwhile Given the Efficient Market Hypothesis?

USER FOCUS

The implication of what is known as the *efficient market hypothesis* is that the prices of corporate stock accurately reflect the underlying value of their companies and that individuals who use complex tools of financial analysis to guide their decisions seldom have an advantage over those who guide their decisions more on the basis of the market prices of individual companies. If this theory is true, the drop in the market price of The Gap's common stock from $32.12 at year-end 2000 to only $14.10 at year-end 2001, compared with almost no change in The Limited's stock price ($19.81 to $18.45) could be significant. On that basis, for example, one might conclude that The Gap took a significant downturn in fiscal year 2001 whereas The Limited remained relatively stable.

Since the evidence underlying the efficient market hypothesis and the various types of market efficiency is too advanced for an introductory course, it is inappropriate to pursue this concept further. For now, you should appreciate that the type of comprehensive analysis you are about to perform is not universally believed to be worthwhile. So be sure to compare the conclusions we reach through the detailed analysis with the conclusions reached by simply noting price changes in the stock of The Gap and The Limited.

Using Liquidity Ratios to Evaluate Solvency

Let's begin our survey of this traditional analysis with the liquidity ratios. Recall that liquidity ratios are used to evaluate a company's solvency, its ability to meet obligations that mature or come due in the current period. Accordingly, short-term creditors are the user group most concerned with these ratios. A popular but somewhat misleading measure of solvency is working capital, the numerical difference between current assets and current liabilities. Despite the fact that it is not itself a ratio and has limitations as you saw in Chapter 5, we'll begin our analysis with this popular measure.

Let's begin by establishing some basic ground rules for our analysis. First, all of the financial information for The Gap and for The Limited is in Appendix 14–1. Next, remember that the numbers used in our analysis of these companies are expressed in thousands for ease of calculation. Thus, it is critical to not confuse the actual scale of numbers with the equivalent numbers expressed here in thousands that appear smaller. When you compare and contrast any number of companies, make sure that you do so in an equivalent scale. Finally, a ranking has been included to help you compare the relative strength of each company. Below, for example, you can see that The Limited had the highest amount of working capital (ranked number one) and The Gap had the lowest (ranked number 2).

2001	Current Assets	Current Liabilities	Working Capital	Rank
The Limited	$2,682,000	$1,319,000	$1,363,000	1
The Gap	3,044,550	2,056,233	988,317	2

Whenever your analysis reveals a potential problem, it is always desirable to expand your exploration of such a calculation beyond one year. In this case, The Gap's working capital position is not as strong as The Limited's but doesn't seem to be a problem. But let's examine their respective working capital positions one year earlier to gain some perspective. For example, here is the information for the 2000 annual reports (as of February 3, 2001) for comparison:

2000	Current Assets	Current Liabilities	Working Capital	Rank
The Limited	$2,067,798	$1,000,185	$1,067,613	1
The Gap	2,648,050	2,799,144	(151,094)	2

As you can see here, The Gap's working capital position has improved from the previous year. Despite the improvement, knowing that The Gap had a working capital deficit in the previous year is a signal that you probably need to scrutinize its solvency as you continue your investigation. If you are curious, you might even check 1999 to see if this problem is a recent one or has been more persistent.

1999	Current Assets	Current Liabilities	Working Capital	Rank
The Limited	$2,284,755	$1,235,552	$1,049,203	1
The Gap	2,197,790	1,752,879	444,911	2

This additional analysis confirms that The Gap's current working capital position has not been particularly impressive over the last few years. What should you deduce from this? First, you should have a heightened interest in whether this relative weakness is limited to its working capital balance or will turn up in other solvency measures. Second, if this weakness does show up, your attention should shift to asking what are the underlying business factors.

As you learned earlier, an important weakness of working capital is that it does not control for the relative size of the respective companies! We can remove this deficiency, however, if we use what is called the *working capital ratio.* This ratio measures the relative size of working capital by dividing working capital by either current assets or total assets as shown here:

2001	Working Capital	Total Assets	Ratio	Rank
The Limited	$1,363,000	$4,719,000	.289	1
The Gap	988,317	7,591,326	.130	2

Although The Gap's performance on this ratio improved between 2000 (a negative 0.0215) and 2001, The Limited's relative working capital position is both far stronger and more stable (.261 in 2000).

A more useful measure of solvency is the liquidity ratio. As you learned previously, a liquidity ratio measures a company's *relative* ability to meet its maturing current debts, that is, its solvency. Two of the more commonly used liquidity ratios are the current ratio and the acid test, or quick, ratio. The current ratio is a relatively optimistic measure whereas the acid test ratio is a more conservative measure.

Current Ratio Recall that the current ratio is aptly named because to calculate it you simply divide current assets by current liabilities:

$$\text{Current Ratio} = \frac{\text{Current Assets}}{\text{Current Liabilities}}$$

Let's use it to evaluate our specialty retail companies once more.

2001	Numerator Current Assets	Denominator Current Liabilities	Current Ratio	Rank
The Limited	$2,682,000	$1,319,000	2.033	1
The Gap	3,044,550	2,056,233	1.481	2

These current ratio results reinforce our earlier conclusions from using the working capital and working capital ratio calculations. Although The Limited has an advantage in its ability to pay off its short-term debt, let's examine each company's current ratio more closely.

The Limited's current ratio seems impressive since an often used rule of thumb is that a current ratio should be 2.0 or greater. Such a ratio appears to indicate that creditors will be paid in full and on time. Furthermore, The Limited's solvency has remained remarkably consistent over the last two years (a current ratio of 2.067 in 2000). Nevertheless, you wouldn't want to discontinue your analysis here for several reasons. First, a high current ratio can result when a company is holding excessive amounts of cash, accounts receivable, and inventory. Second, a ratio of 2.0 is not that impressive in some industries. In fact, no matter what kind of ratio you use, you should always compare it first to the industry average and then to the corresponding ratios of similar companies in the same industry. Finally, as we just did for 2000, you should also determine if your company's current ratio has changed much when compared with its current ratios of past years. Let's do just that by examining The Gap's current ratio as shown in Figure 14-1 under the heading Financial Position. As you can see by this **horizontal analysis**, The Gap has experienced an almost constant decline in its current ratio since 1995, a clear indication that it is no longer as solvent.

As you've just seen, it is very important to compare a company's current ratio to those of other companies in the same industry and to those it calculated in the past. But if you want to conduct an even more effective analysis of the solvency of these companies, you must use more than the current ratio. For example, the current ratio of 2.067 for The Limited in 2000 indicates that it had adequate resources to meet its current obligations. A closer study of those assets, however, indicates that nearly 56% ($1,157/$2,068) were composed of inventories. Thus, The Limited's case illustrates the primary limitation of the current ratio—it assumes that noncash current assets may be easily converted into cash to cover current liabilities. In many businesses, however, inventories and some receivables are neither quickly converted to cash nor likely to be realized in their full amount. It is highly unlikely, for example, that The Gap would have recovered nearly $2 billion of cash ($1,904,153 × 1,000) if it had been forced to liquidate its inventory on February 3, 2001. Even if it were to somehow have collected 100% of that existing inventory value, it would not have fully met

FIGURE 14-1 Horizontal analysis of The Gap

10-Year Selected Financial Data

	Fiscal Year (in weeks)				
	2001 (52)	2000 (53)	1999 (52)	1998 (52)	1997 (52)
Operating results ($ in thousands)					
Net sales	$ 13,847,873	$ 13,673,460	$ 11,635,398	$ 9,054,462	$ 6,507,825
Cost of goods sold and occupancy expenses, excluding depreciation and amortization	8,905,064	8,025,374	6,360,704	5,013,473	3,775,957
Percentage of net sales	64.3%	58.7%	54.7%	55.4%	58.0%
Depreciation and amortization (a)	$ 799,325	$ 574,068	$ 414,558	$ 304,745	$ 245,584
Operating expenses	3,805,968	3,629,257	3,043,432	2,403,365	1,635,017
Net interest expense	95,875	62,876	31,755	13,617	(2,975)
Earnings before income taxes	241,641	1,381,885	1,784,949	1,319,262	854,242
Percentage of net sales	1.7%	10.1%	15.3%	14.6%	13.1%
Income taxes	$ 249,405	$ 504,388	$ 657,884	$ 494,723	$ 320,341
Net earnings (loss)	(7,764)	877,497	1,127,065	824,539	533,901
Percentage of net sales	(0.1%)	6.4%	9.7%	9.1%	8.2%
Cash dividends paid	$ 76,373	$ 75,488	$ 75,795	$ 76,888	$ 79,503
Net purchase of property and equipment, including lease rights	949,288	1,881,127	1,268,811	842,655	483,114
Per share data					
Net earnings (loss)—basic	$ (0.01)	$ 1.03	$ 1.32	$ 0.95	$ 0.60
Net earnings (loss)—diluted	(0.01)	1.00	1.26	0.91	0.58
Cash dividends paid (b)	0.09	0.09	0.09	0.09	0.09
Shareholders' equity (book value)	3.48	3.43	2.63	1.83	1.79
Financial position ($ in thousands)					
Property and equipment, net	$ 4,161,290	$ 4,007,685	$ 2,715,315	$ 1,876,370	$ 1,365,246
Merchandise inventory	1,677,116	1,904,153	1,462,045	1,056,444	733,174
Total assets	7,591,326	7,012,908	5,188,756	3,963,919	3,337,502
Working capital	988,317	(151,094)	444,911	318,721	839,399
Current ratio	1.48:1	0.95:1	1.25:1	1.21:1	1.85:1
Total long-term debt, less current installments	$ 1,961,397	$ 780,246	$ 784,925	$ 496,455	$ 496,044
Ratio of long-term debt to shareholders' equity (c)	0.65:1	0.35:1	0.35:1	0.32:1	0.31:1
Shareholders' equity	$ 3,009,581	$ 2,928,239	$ 2,233,045	$ 1,573,679	$ 1,583,986
Return on average assets	(0.1%)	14.4%	24.6%	22.6%	17.9%
Return on average shareholders' equity	(0.3%)	34.0%	59.2%	52.2%	33.0%
Statistics					
Number of store concepts opened (d)	587	731	570	356	298
Number of store concepts expanded (d)	311	268	129	135	98
Number of store concepts closed (d)	92	73	18	20	22
Number of store concepts open at year-end (d)	4,171	3,676	3,018	2,466	2,130
Net increase in number of store concepts (d)	13%	22%	22%	16%	15%
Comparable store sales increase (decrease) percentage (52-week basis)	(13%)	(5%)	7%	17%	6%
Sales per square foot (52-week basis) (e)	$ 394	$ 482	$ 548	$ 532	$ 463
Square footage of gross store space at year-end	36,333,400	31,373,400	23,978,100	18,757,400	15,312,700
Percentage increase in square feet	16%	31%	28%	22%	21%
Number of employees at year-end	165,000	166,000	140,000	111,000	81,000
Weighted-average number of shares—basic	860,255,419	849,810,658	853,804,924	864,062,060	891,404,945
Weighted-average number of shares—diluted	860,255,419	879,137,194	895,029,176	904,374,383	922,951,706
Number of shares outstanding at year-end, net of treasury stock	865,726,890	853,996,984	850,498,941	857,960,032	884,549,313

(a) Excludes amortization of restricted stock, discounted stock options and discount on long-term debt.
(b) Excludes a dividend of $.0222 per share declared in January 2002 but paid in the first quarter of fiscal 2002.
(c) Long-term debt includes current installments.

(*continued on next page*)

its current obligations from current assets since its current ratio was .946. The next ratio is designed to avoid the inventory liquidation issue altogether.

Acid Test or Quick Ratio The acid test, or quick ratio, has the very same denominator as does the current ratio—current liabilities. Its numerator, however, differs from the current ratio numerator by eliminating any current assets that are not near

FIGURE 14-1 *(continued)*

10-Year Selected Financial Data

	Fiscal Year (in weeks)				
	1996 (52)	**1995 (53)**	**1994 (52)**	**1993 (52)**	**1992 (52)**
Operating results ($ in thousands)					
Net sales	$ 5,284,381	$ 4,395,253	$ 3,722,940	$ 3,295,679	$ 2,960,409
Cost of goods sold and occupancy expenses, excluding depreciation and amortization	3,093,709	2,645,736	2,202,133	1,996,929	1,856,102
Percentage of net sales	58.5%	60.2%	59.2%	60.6%	62.7%
Depreciation and amortization (a)	$ 191,457	$ 175,719	$ 148,863	$ 124,860	$ 99,451
Operating expenses	1,270,138	1,004,396	853,524	748,193	661,252
Net interest expense	(19,450)	(15,797)	(10,902)	809	3,763
Earnings before income taxes	748,527	585,199	529,322	424,888	339,841
Percentage of net sales	14.2%	13.3%	14.2%	12.9%	11.5%
Income taxes	$ 295,668	$ 231,160	$ 209,082	$ 166,464	$ 129,140
Net earnings (loss)	452,859	354,039	320,240	258,424	210,701
Percentage of net sales	8.6%	8.1%	8.6%	7.8%	7.1%
Cash dividends paid	$ 83,854	$ 66,993	$ 64,775	$ 53,041	$ 44,106
Net purchase of property and equipment, including lease rights	375,838	309,599	236,616	215,856	213,659
Per share data					
Net earnings (loss)—basic	$ 0.48	$ 0.38	$ 0.34	$ 0.27	$ 0.23
Net earnings (loss)—diluted	0.47	0.37	0.33	0.27	0.22
Cash dividends paid (b)	0.09	0.07	0.07	0.05	0.05
Shareholders' equity (book value)	1.79	1.69	1.41	1.15	0.91
Financial position ($ in thousands)					
Property and equipment, net	$ 1,135,720	$ 957,752	$ 828,777	$ 740,422	$ 650,368
Merchandise inventory	578,765	482,575	370,638	331,155	365,692
Total assets	2,626,927	2,343,068	2,004,244	1,763,117	1,379,248
Working capital	554,359	728,301	555,827	494,194	355,649
Current ratio	1.72:1	2.32:1	2.11:1	2.07:1	2.06:1
Total long-term debt, less current installments	—	—	—	$ 75,000	$ 75,000
Ratio of long-term debt to shareholders' equity (c)	N/A	N/A	N/A	0.07:1	0.08:1
Shareholders' equity	$ 1,654,470	$ 1,640,473	$ 1,375,232	$ 1,126,475	$ 887,839
Return on average assets	18.2%	16.3%	17.0%	16.4%	16.7%
Return on average shareholders' equity	27.5%	23.5%	25.6%	25.7%	26.9%
Statistics					
Number of store concepts opened (d)	203	225	172	108	117
Number of store concepts expanded (d)	42	55	82	130	94
Number of store concepts closed (d)	30	53	34	45	26
Number of store concepts open at year-end (d)	1,854	1,680	1,508	1,370	1,307
Net increase in number of store concepts (d)	10%	11%	10%	5%	7%
Comparable store sales increase (decrease) percentage (52-week basis)	5%	0%	1%	1%	5%
Sales per square foot (52-week basis) (e)	$ 441	$ 425	$ 444	$ 463	$ 489
Square footage of gross store space at year-end	12,645,000	11,100,200	9,165,900	7,546,300	6,509,200
Percentage increase in square feet	14%	21%	21%	16%	15%
Number of employees at year-end	66,000	60,000	55,000	44,000	39,000
Weighted-average number of shares—basic	938,579,921	939,866,394	948,699,959	940,287,006	928,417,491
Weighted-average number of shares—diluted	961,351,245	962,443,160	971,144,612	965,110,280	960,903,782
Number of shares outstanding at year-end, net of treasury stocks	926,495,994	971,149,446	977,162,057	980,428,914	973,250,357

(d) Since the beginning of fiscal 2000, Gap brand stores have been reported based on concepts. Any Gap Adult, GapKids, babyGap or GapBody that meets a certain square footage threshold has been counted as a store, even when residing within a single physical location. The number of stores by location at the end of fiscal 2001 and 2000 was 3,097 and 2,848, respectively.

(e) Based on weighted-average gross square footage.

cash (liquid) in nature, such as inventories and prepayments. Since most annual reports do not detail prepayments, it is best to also subtract the account titled Other Current Assets (OCA) along with the Merchandise Inventory account. Thus, its numerator is a much more conservative measure of liquidity than was used in the current ratio.

$$\text{Acid Test Ratio} = \frac{\text{Current Assets} - (\text{Inventories} + \text{OCA})}{\text{Current Liabilities}}$$

As the name *acid test* suggests, this ratio is more certain and dependable than the current ratio. The word *quick* also accurately describes this ratio because the numerator is calculated by considering only cash, marketable securities, and net receivables rather than all current assets.

2001	Numerator Modified Current Assets	Denominator Current Liabilities	Quick Ratio	Rank
The Limited	$1,454,000	$1,319,000	1.102	1
The Gap	1,035,749	2,056,233	0.504	2

Although The Limited's liquidity appears less impressive when this acid test ratio is calculated, its ability to meet its short-term obligations solely from cash and receivables is at least twice as great as The Gap's. To gain additional insight, let's once again determine if The Gap's liquidity position has deteriorated from previous years by examining data from the 2000 annual reports for comparison:

2000	Numerator Modified Current Assets	Denominator Current Liabilities	Quick Ratio	Rank
The Limited	$657,292	$1,000,185	0.657	1
The Gap	408,794	2,799,144	0.146	2

This information only reinforces our earlier conclusion that The Gap has had serious liquidity problems. Notice, for example, that while The Gap's acid test ratio improved significantly from 2000 to 2001, its ratio is still dramatically lower than that of The Limited.

Using Activity Ratios to Evaluate Turnover

Recall that you use activity ratios to evaluate how efficiently an entity has used its resources or assets. Activity ratios are so named because they measure how productive a particular asset was in producing sales activity in the entity. The word *turnover* expresses much the same idea. Turnover is the number of times, on average, that assets such as accounts receivable and inventory are replaced during the year. Four of the most often used activity or turnover ratios are the asset turnover ratio, the inventory turnover ratio, the accounts receivable turnover ratio, and the accounts payable turnover ratio.

Asset Turnover Ratio The asset turnover ratio indicates how efficiently an entity uses its assets to produce sales during the period. In general, an entity with a high ratio uses its assets more productively than an entity with a low ratio. The formula to calculate the asset turnover ratio is:

$$\text{Asset Turnover Ratio} = \frac{\text{Net Sales Revenue}}{\text{Average Total Assets}}$$

Let's use it to evaluate both The Gap and The Limited once more.

2001	Numerator Net Sales	Denominator Average Total Assets	Asset Turnover Ratio	Rank
The Limited	$ 9,363,000	$4,403,500	2.126	1
The Gap	13,847,873	7,302,117	1.896	2

Although The Gap was able to generate nearly $1.90 of sales from each dollar of assets employed, The Limited was more successful. Of even more concern is that The Gap's relative asset turnover has been declining. If you calculate Gap's asset turnover ratio from the data in Figure 14-1 and The Limited's asset turnover ratio from Figure 14-2, you will see that The Gap's asset turnover ratio was actually superior to The Limited's from 1992 through 1999 (verify The Gap's advantage of 2.543 to 2.251 in 1999). Gap's absolute decline in this ratio as well as its decline relative to The Limited should motivate you to investigate further. If you do, you will discover that between 1998 and 2001, Gap's net sales increased by over one-half (compare $9,054,462 to $13,847,873), an impressive growth until you learn that in the same time period, Gap's average total assets actually doubled (compare $3,650,711 to $7,302,117)! Clearly then, this horizontal analysis illuminates The Gap's increasing inability to efficiently produce sales from its use of assets.

Like all clothing retailers, The Gap must manage inventory by taking into account consumer acceptance or lack of acceptance of styles, seasonal demand, price, and other factors.

Inventory Turnover Ratio Effective inventory management involves a balancing act between having enough inventory on hand to meet the needs of customers—that is, maximizing the opportunity to generate revenue—and tying up cash as a result of not *turning over* the inventory quickly enough. The inventory turnover ratio tells you how frequently a business sells its inventory and, therefore, indicates the relative efficiency of both sales and production or purchasing management. This ratio is calculated as follows:

$$\text{Inventory Turnover Ratio} = \frac{\text{Cost of Goods Sold}}{\text{Average Merchandise Inventory}}$$

Now let's calculate this ratio for our companies:

	Numerator	Denominator		
2001	**Cost of Goods Sold**	**Average Merchandise Inventory**	**Inventory Turnover Ratio**	**Rank**
The Limited	$6,110,000	$1,061,500	5.756	1
The Gap	9,704,389	1,790,635	5.420	2

Although The Limited's ratio is superior to The Gap's, the difference is far less significant than our earlier comparisons. Nevertheless, concerns raised about The Gap's health might motivate you to also check the very same ratio from the previous year:

	Numerator	Denominator		
2000	**Cost of Goods Sold**	**Average Merchandise Inventory**	**Inventory Turnover Ratio**	**Rank**
The Limited	$6,667,389	$1,104,027	6.039	1
The Gap	8,599,442	1,683,099	5.109	2

This comparison shows that in 2001 The Gap's ratio improved, whereas The Limited's ratio actually declined. The fact that The Limited's advantage has declined substantially over the past year can only be interpreted as a hopeful sign for The Gap.

FIGURE 14-2 Horizontal analysis of The Limited

FINANCIAL SUMMARY

(Millions except per share amounts, ratios and store and associate data)

	● 2001	★ 2000	● 1999	● 1998	1997	1996	●◆★ 1995	1994	● 1993	1992	◆ 1991
Summary of operations											
Net sales	$ 9,363	$ 10,105	$ 9,766	$ 9,365	$ 9,200	$ 8,652	$ 7,893	$ 7,321	$ 7,245	$ 6,944	$ 6,149
Gross income	$ 3,253	$ 3,437	$ 3,323	$ 2,940	$ 2,736	$ 2,424	$ 2,033	$ 2,108	$ 1,959	$ 1,991	$ 1,794
Operating income	+$ 918	+$ 866	+$ 931	+$ 2,424	+$ 469	+$ 636	+$ 612	$ 796	+$ 702	$ 789	$ 713
Operating income as a percentage of sales	+9.8%	+8.6%	+9.5%	+25.9%	+5.1%	+7.4%	+7.8%	10.9%	+9.7%	11.4%	11.6%
Net income	■$ 519	■$ 428	■$ 461	■$ 2,046	■$ 212	■$ 434	■$ 961	$ 447	■$ 391	■$ 455	$ 403
Net income as a percentage of sales	■5.5%	■4.2%	■4.7%	■21.9%	■2.3%	■ 5.0%	■12.2%	6.1%	■5.4%	■6.6%	6.6%
Per share results											
Basic net income	■$ 1.21	■$ 1.00	■$ 1.05	■$ 4.25	■$ 0.39	■$ 0.78	■$ 1.35	$ 0.63	■$ 0.55	■$ 0.63	$ 0.56
Diluted net income	■$ 1.19	■$ 0.96	■$ 1.00	■$ 4.15	■$ 0.39	■$ 0.77	■$ 1.34	$ 0.63	■$ 0.54	■$ 0.63	$ 0.56
Dividends	$ 0.30	$ 0.30	$ 0.30	$ 0.26	$ 0.24	$ 0.20	$ 0.20	$ 0.18	$ 0.18	$ 0.14	$ 0.14
Book value	$ 6.39	$ 5.44	$ 5.00	$ 4.78	$ 3.64	$ 3.45	$ 4.43	$ 3.78	$ 3.41	$ 3.13	$ 2.60
Weighted average diluted shares outstanding	435	443	456	493	549	564	717	717	726	727	727
Other financial information											
Total assets	$ 4,179	$ 4,088	$ 4,126	$ 4,550	$ 4,301	$ 4,120	$ 5,267	$ 4,570	$ 4,135	$ 3,846	$ 3,419
Return on average assets	■12%	■10%	■11%	■46%	■5%	■9%	■20%	10%	■10%	■13%	13%
Working capital	$ 1,363	$ 1,068	$ 1,049	$ 1,127	$ 1,001	$ 712	$ 1,962	$ 1,694	$ 1,513	$ 1,063	$ 1,084
Current ratio	2.0	2.1	1.8	2.0	2.0	1.9	3.3	3.0	3.1	2.5	3.1
Capital expenditures	$ 337	$ 446	$ 376	$ 347	$ 363	$ 361	$ 374	$ 320	$ 296	$ 430	$ 523
Long-term debt	$ 250	$ 400	$ 400	$ 550	$ 650	$ 650	$ 650	$ 650	$ 650	$ 542	$ 714
Debt-to-equity ratio	9%	17%	19%	25%	33%	35%	21%	24%	27%	24%	38%
Shareholders' equity	$ 2,744	$ 2,316	$ 2,147	$ 2,167	$ 1,986	$ 1,869	$ 3,148	$ 2,705	$ 2,441	$ 2,268	$ 1,877
Return on average shareholders' equity	■21%	■19%	■21%	■99%	■11%	■17%	■33%	17%	■17%	■22%	23%
Comparable store sales increase (decrease)	(4%)	5%	9%	6%	0%	3%	(2%)	(3%)	(1%)	2%	3%
Stores and associates at end of year											
Total number of stores open	4,614	5,129	5,023	5,382	5,640	5,633	5,298	4,867	4,623	4,425	4,194
Selling square feet	20,146	23,224	23,592	26,316	28,400	28,405	27,403	25,627	24,426	22,863	20,355
Number of associates	100,300	123,700	114,600	126,800	131,000	123,100	106,900	105,600	97,500	100,700	83,800

★ Fifty-three-week fiscal year.

● Includes the results of the following companies disposed of up to their separation date: 1) Lane Bryant effective August 16, 2001; 2) Galyan's Trading Co. ("Galyan's") effective August 31, 1999; 3) Limited Too ("TOO") effective August 23,1999; 4) Abercrombie & Fitch ("A&F") effective May 19, 1998; 5) Alliance Data Systems ("ADS") effective January 31, 1996; and 6) Brylane, Inc. effective August 31, 1993.

◆ Includes the results of Galyan's and Gryphon subsequent to their acquisitions on July 2, 1995 and June 1, 1991.

\+ Operating income includes the net effect of special and nonrecurring items of $170 million in 2001, ($10) million in 2000, and $24 million in 1999 (see Note 2 to the Consolidated Financial Statements), $1.740 billion in 1998, ($213) million in 1997, ($12) million in 1996, $1 million in 1995 and $3 million in 1993, Inventory liquidation charges of ($13) million related to Henri Bendel store closings are also included in 1997.

■ In addition to the items discussed in + above, net income includes the effect of the following gains: 1) $62 million related to ADS and Galyan's in 2001; 2) $11 million related to Galyan's in 1999; 3) $9 million related to Brylane, Inc, in 1997; 4) $118 million related to A&F in 1996; 5) $649 million related to Intimate Brands, Inc. in 1995; and 6) $9 million related to United Retail Group in 1992.

Average Holding Period The average holding period is a turnover measure that expresses the same concept as the inventory turnover ratio but in a more intuitive manner. It includes both the purchasing phase and the selling phase of the operating cycle and is calculated by dividing 365 days by the inventory turnover ratio:

$$\text{Average Holding Period} = \frac{\text{365 days}}{\text{Inventory Turnover Ratio}}$$

Although the respective ranks do not change, many people find the average holding period measure of days easier to interpret than the preceding turnover ratios.

2001	Numerator 365 Days	Denominator Inventory Turnover Ratio	Average Holding Period	Rank
The Limited	365	5.756	63.41	1
The Gap	365	5.420	67.34	2

In this case, it takes The Gap almost four days more than The Limited to move its average inventory, another sign that it is not performing as well as The Limited.

Accounts Receivable Turnover Ratio Recall that the accounts receivable turnover ratio indicates the relative frequency with which the accounts receivable balance is converted into cash, or turns over. Companies prefer to have a high turnover because it means relatively quicker access to cash that can earn a return rather than remain unavailable and represent an idle use of funds. You calculate this ratio as follows:

$$\text{Accounts Receivable Turnover} = \frac{\text{Net Credit Sales}}{\text{Average Net Accounts Receivable}}$$

You might recall from Chapter 7 that only rarely do companies disclose the amount of their credit sales in annual report income statements. As a result, we must include total reported sales in our calculations:

2001	Numerator Net Sales	Denominator Average Net Accounts Receivable	Accounts Receivable Turnover Ratio	Rank
The Gap	$13,847,873	not disclosed	N/A	—
The Limited	9,363,000	$86,500	108.243	N/A

Although The Limited does include an accounts receivable balance in its balance sheet, The Gap does not. This is not entirely a surprise since we learned earlier that Gap customers either pay for their purchases with cash or credit card. Thus, we are unable to establish a valid comparison for this ratio.

Average Collection Period The average collection period is a turnover measure that expresses the same concept as the accounts receivable turnover ratio, but in a more intuitive manner. It is the numerical measure of the collecting phase of the operating cycle and is calculated by dividing 365 days by the accounts receivable turnover ratio:

$$\text{Average Collection Period} = \frac{\text{365 days}}{\text{Accounts Receivable Turnover Ratio}}$$

Since there is no way to calculate an accounts receivable turnover ratio for The Gap, we are unable to calculate its average collection period:

2001	Numerator 365 Days	Denominator Accounts Receivable Turnover Ratio	Average Collection Period	Rank
The Limited	365	108.243	3.372	N/A

As you'd expect, the amount of time spent in each step of the operating cycle is largely dictated by industry custom and competitive conditions. The Limited's very short collection period is perfectly reasonable when you consider that its customers either pay for their purchases with cash or a credit card.

Accounts Payable Turnover Ratio As you learned in Chapter 11, the accounts payable turnover ratio indicates the relative frequency with which the accounts payable balance turns over. A low turnover is usually preferable because it conserves cash. You calculate this ratio as follows:

$$\text{Accounts Payable Turnover} = \frac{\text{Inventory Purchases}}{\text{Average Accounts Payable}}$$

Calculating this particular ratio often requires more effort because you must first derive an approximation of the amount of purchases. You do this by first assuming that the accounts payable balance is entirely composed of inventory purchases and locating the balances shown here from the annual report of The Gap:

Cost of goods sold	$9,704,389
Beginning inventory	1,904,153
Ending inventory	1,677,116

To calculate the numerator or purchases, you apply the inventory formula:

Beginning inventory	$ 1,904,153
Merchandise acquisitions or purchases	**9,477,352**
Cost of goods available for sale	11,381,505
Less: Ending inventory	(1,677,116)
Cost of goods sold	$ 9,704,389

The denominator, or average payables, is $1,086,162 [($1,067,207 + $1,105,117) /2]. In this case, the accounts payable turnover ratio for The Gap is:

$$\text{Accounts Payable Turnover} = \frac{\text{Inventory Purchases}}{\text{Average Accounts Payable}} = \frac{\$9,477,352}{\$1,086,162} = 8.726$$

As you compare this ratio for our two companies below, be sure you understand that a low ratio is preferred because it conserves cash:

2001	Numerator Purchases	Denominator Average Accts. Pay.	Accts. Payable Turnover Ratio	Rank
The Gap	$ 9,477,352	$1,086,162	8.726	1
The Limited	5,919,000	259,000	22.853	2

Although this ratio indicates that The Gap conserves cash to a greater extent than The Limited, you might wonder if The Gap's practice of delaying payment of its obligations might adversely affect its relationships with vendors. That is, delaying payment of obligations could be perceived as less than responsible behavior for The Gap especially in light of its highly visible liquidity position. Of course, this discussion is irrelevant if The Gap's accounts payable balance is not composed entirely of inventory purchases.

Average Payment Period The average payment period is a turnover measure that expresses the same concept as the accounts payable turnover ratio, but in a more intuitive manner. It is the numerical measure of the purchasing phase of the operating cycle and is calculated by dividing 365 days by the accounts payable turnover ratio as shown below:

$$\text{Average Payment Period} = \frac{365}{\text{Accounts Payable Turnover}}$$

Consistent with the accounts payable turnover ratio, a higher number of days is generally preferable because it is associated with the conservation of cash. Let's compare our companies:

2001	Numerator 365 Days	Denominator Accounts Payable Turnover Ratio	Average Payment Period	Rank
The Gap	365	8.726	41.83	1
The Limited	365	22.853	15.97	2

By taking more than two and one-half times the number of days it takes The Limited to pay off its accounts payable, The Gap has conserved its cash in this phase of the operating cycle more than has The Limited.

Length of the Operating Cycle Recall that the operating cycle is the average length of time it takes a business to move, or cycle, through three major transaction phases—paying cash to purchase merchandise inventory, selling this inventory, and collecting cash from the sale of inventory, or from cash to cash. Because the average payment period represents the number of days in which the payment of cash is delayed, it must be subtracted when calculating the operating cycle. That is, to calculate the length of the operating cycle, you add the average holding period of inventory to the average collection period of receivables and subtract the average payment period of payables as shown here for The Gap and The Limited.

	Average Holding Period	Average Collection Period	Average Payment Period	Length of Operating Cycle	Rank
The Gap	67.34	undisclosed	(41.83)	25.51	1
The Limited	63.41	3.37	(15.97)	50.81	2

What is most interesting here is that The Gap's policy of slower payments to vendors has played a significant role in its more favorable length of operating cycle than The Limited's. Note that the inability to calculate the average collection period for The Gap does not necessarily invalidate our comparison between The Gap and The Limited. Since customers in the specialty retail industry usually pay for purchases at the time of purchase, it is entirely plausible that The Gap's collecting phase may, indeed, involve no time for cash sales and only a day or two for credit card sales. Thus, The Gap appears healthier than does The Limited from the perspective of this comprehensive measure of activity.

Using Leverage Ratios to Evaluate Financial Risk

Recall that leverage ratios are used to measure the extent to which an entity has been financed by debt. That is, they indicate the degree to which resources or assets have been obtained by incurring liabilities, or debt financing. As a company increases its use of debt financing, it also increases the probability of encountering financial distress, a relationship referred to as *financial risk*. You can monitor this risk by measuring how *leveraged*—the extent to which a business's assets are financed by debt—the business has become. Accordingly, long-term creditors are the user group most concerned with these ratios.

Three ratios are commonly used to evaluate the amount of financial risk borne by a particular entity—the *debt to assets ratio* and the *debt to equity ratio*, both of which derive their elements from the balance sheet, and the *times interest earned ratio*, which most often derives all of its elements from the income statement.

Debt to Assets Ratio The debt to assets ratio is a leverage ratio that indicates the long-run solvency or relative amount of financial risk incurred by a business. Recall the method of calculating this ratio:

$$\text{Debt to Assets} = \frac{\text{Total Liabilities}}{\text{Total Assets}}$$

Let's now use this ratio to evaluate how leveraged our companies are:

2001	Numerator Total Liabilities	Denominator Total Assets	Debt to Assets Ratio	Rank
The Limited	1,798,000	4,719,000	.381	1
The Gap	4,581,745	7,591,326	.604	2

Thus, three-fifths of The Gap's financing is debt and two-fifths is equity. In this case, The Gap's degree of leverage has been fairly stable; it was 58% in 2000, 57% in 1999, and 60% in 1998. Notice how much more leveraged The Gap is than The Limited. Let's now examine another variation of this ratio to see if it reinforces our initial conclusion about The Gap's indebtedness.

Debt to Equity Ratio As its title implies, this ratio is calculated by dividing total liabilities by total owners' equity.

$$\text{Debt to Equity} = \frac{\text{Total Liabilities}}{\text{Total Owners' Equity}}$$

Not unexpectedly, The Gap is again more leveraged than The Limited; and, using this ratio, its degree of leverage seems even greater:

2001	Numerator Total Liabilities	Denominator Total Owners' Equity	Debt to Equity Ratio	Rank
The Limited	1,798,000	2,744,000	.655	1
The Gap	4,581,745	3,009,581	1.522	2

What's more, The Gap's leverage seems to be increasing when we discover that the previous year's ratio for The Gap was 1.395. Since The Gap clearly is highly leveraged in relation to The Limited, let's take a closer look to see if we can better understand The Gap's indebtedness. You might discover one clue to a potential Gap strategy by studying Figure 14-1. Compare the 2001 column with the 2000 column, for example.

Notice that the current ratio has increased by more than 50%, whereas the ratio of long-term debt to shareholder's equity has increased by nearly 100%! How could The Gap effect this change? One way would be to convert a good portion of its current liabilities to long-term liabilities. To verify whether or not this was done, let's refer back to The Gap's balance sheet. There we do indeed find a reduction in current liabilities of more than $700 million coupled with an increase in long-term debt of over $1.2 billion. Since long-term debt is almost always accompanied by an interest cost, the strategy of switching a good portion of debt from short- to long-term debt also increases the amount of financial risk incurred.

Since The Gap seems to be adopting a strategy that will increase its total amount of interest expense, let's consider the times interest earned ratio. Recall, for example, that since this ratio derives its elements, such as interest expense, entirely from the income statement rather than entirely from the balance sheet, it is an excellent tool for evaluating the amount of financial risk borne by a company such as The Gap.

Times Interest Earned Ratio The times interest earned ratio indicates the business's relative protection from being forced into bankruptcy by its failure to meet required interest payments. The formula to calculate this ratio is:

$$\text{Times Interest Earned Ratio} = \frac{\text{Net Income} + \text{Interest Expense} + \text{Income Tax Expense}}{\text{Interest Expense}}$$

Here is this calculation for The Gap:

$$\frac{(7{,}764) + 109{,}190 + (13{,}315) + 249{,}405}{109{,}190} = 3.09$$

An equivalent way to express the numerator is to use the term *operating income.* Since this ratio indicates how many times interest expense is covered by operating income, it is often referred to as a *coverage ratio.* To gain perspective, note that The Gap's times interest earned ratio was 40.40 in 1999 and 19.29 in 2000. Moreover, in both years, The Gap's performance was superior to The Limited's, although The Gap's relative advantage declined in those two years. With the significant increase in long-term debt and, therefore, interest expense in 2001, note how its results changed:

2001	Numerator Operating Income	Denominator Interest Expense	Times Interest Earned Ratio	Rank
The Limited	$918,000	$ 34,000	27.00	1
The Gap	337,516	109,190	3.09	2

The dramatic increase in The Gap's financial risk cannot be minimized. It might explain why its bond ratings were almost universally downgraded and why its stock price plunged. That is, there is strong evidence that the markets did react to these results in an efficient manner.

Thus, it is clear from a number of indicators that The Gap is a highly leveraged company from both the perspective of its balance sheet and, recently, its income statement. Our investigation into its degree of financial risk has done nothing to reduce our concern about the financial well-being of The Gap.

Using Profitability Ratios to Evaluate Management's Effectiveness

Recall that profitability ratios are used to measure the overall effectiveness of managers in generating returns on sales and return on stockholder financing. We will use five such ratios to evaluate The Gap's performance: the return on equity ratio, the return on assets ratio, the gross margin ratio, the profit margin ratio, and the Du Pont Formula.

Return on Equity Ratio (ROE) Recall that Susan Newman calculated this ratio to measure CMU's performance at two different times. In Chapter 1 she divided her projected net income by her initial owner investment to estimate her company's first year performance. In Chapter 3 she compared this same ratio with actual results to evaluate whether her company's performance had failed to match or had surpassed its projected return on equity. To calculate the return on equity for The Gap and The Limited, however, we must use what is called the **return on common stockholders' equity ratio**. This ratio indicates the rate of return earned by investors on their common stock investment. The formula to calculate this ratio is:

$$\text{Return on Common Stockholders' Equity} = \frac{\text{Net Income} - \text{Preferred Stock Dividends Declared}}{\text{Average Common Stockholders' Equity}}$$

Because The Gap incurred a net loss in 2001 and has no preferred stock, its numerator in the majority of the profitability ratios we use here will be a negative number and, therefore, more difficult to evaluate conceptually. For example:

2001	Numerator Net Income − Dividend	Denominator Average Common Stockholders' Equity	Return on Common Stockholders' Equity Ratio	Rank
The Limited	$519,000	$2,530,000	.205	1
The Gap	(7,764)	2,968,910	(.003)	2

Consider that in the preceding year, The Gap actually had a superior return of 34% on this ratio to the 19.1% return of The Limited.

So far, one can't overlook how consistently superior The Limited's performance has been to The Gap's and how The Limited's performance has been dramatically more stable than the erratic performance of The Gap. Let's investigate further and see if this initial advantage in profitability is maintained by The Limited.

Return on Assets Ratio (ROA) The **return on assets ratio** is a variation of the return on equity ratio introduced in Chapter 1. It indicates management's performance in using assets to generate earnings and is calculated as follows:

$$\text{Return on Assets} = \frac{\text{Net Income}}{\text{Average Total Assets}}$$

2001	Numerator Net Income	Denominator Average Total Assets	Return on Assets Ratio	Rank
The Limited	$519,000	$4,403,500	.118	1
The Gap	(7,764)	7,302,117	(.001)	2

Once again the poor showing of The Gap in 2001 is compounded by the fact that The Gap actually outperformed The Limited both in 2000 (14.4% to 10%) and in 1999 (24.6% to 11%).

A reasonable question to ask at this point is: Which rate of return, ROE or ROA, if any, is a better measure of profitability? Although the answers can vary, a strong argument, in the case of The Gap, can be made for the return on assets. The underlying argument is found in the fundamental accounting equation. As you visualize this equation, that is, assets equal liabilities plus owners' equity, recall that The Gap has a significant amount of liabilities. Since a significant portion of The Gap's assets have been financed by liabilities, its owners' equity is relatively small, explaining why its return on that same equity was significantly higher than its return on assets in 1999 (59.2% ROE to 24.6% ROA), 2000 (34.0% ROE to 14.4% ROA), and even 2001 (−.3% ROE to −.1% ROA). What happens is that when you evaluate The Gap's profitability on the combination of its liabilities and owners' equity, as you do with the return on assets measure, its profitability advantage largely disappears. Thus, our most dependable measure of The Gap's profitability for the time being is its return on assets.

Profitability ratios can help evaluate Gap managers' effectiveness in their fast–paced, competitive environment.

Gross Margin Ratio Although the amounts needed to calculate this ratio are available in a single-step income statement such as The Gap uses, the gross margin ratio is more visible in a multiple-step income statement such as The Limited uses because the amount of gross margin is actually disclosed. Recalling that sales revenue is usually reported as net sales, the formula for this ratio is:

$$\text{Gross Margin Ratio} = \frac{\text{Gross Margin}}{\text{Sales Revenue}}$$

2001	Numerator Gross Margin	Denominator Net Sales	Gross Margin Ratio	Rank
The Limited	$3,253,000	$ 9,363,000	.347	1
The Gap	4,143,484	13,847,873	.299	2

Unfortunately, The Gap's 2000 advantage over The Limited in this measure (37.1% to 34%) was lost in 2001.

This ratio is very informative because it tells the managers of The Gap that for every dollar of merchandise sales, nearly $0.30 is available after paying for the merchandise. With the $0.30, The Gap can cover other expenses and earn a profit. This relationship can be illustrated with vertical analysis:

	Total Dollars	Percentage	Analysis of Each Sales Dollar
Sales revenue	$13,847,873	100.0%	$1.000
Cost of goods sold	9,704,389	70.1%	.701
Gross margin	$ 4,143,484	29.9%	$ .299

Prior to 2001, The Gap's gross margin performance was quite acceptable (41.8% in 1999 and 37.1% in 2000), since the gross margin ratios of profitable businesses usually range between 30% and 50% of net sales. Now, however, it is clear that The Gap's core strength, its merchandising ability, is also deteriorating year-by-year.

Profit Margin Ratio Recall from Chapter 7 that the profit margin ratio is sometimes called the return on sales ratio. It indicates how well the entity has controlled the level of its expenses relative to its revenues and helps to focus management's attention on the relative profitability of sales rather than the absolute dollar amount of sales. It is calculated as follows:

$$\text{Profit Margin Ratio} = \frac{\text{Net Income}}{\text{Net Sales Revenue}}$$

Once again, The Limited performs better than does The Gap:

2001	Numerator Net Income	Denominator Net Sales	Profit Margin Ratio	Rank
The Limited	$519,000	$ 9,363,000	.0554	1
The Gap	(7,764)	13,847,873	(.0006)	2

What makes this result even more depressing from the perspective of The Gap is that, once again, it lost the advantage (6.41% to 4.23%) it held over The Limited in 2000.

Although these profit margins might seem modest, to truly evaluate the significance of these numbers, you must consider the industry in which the entity operates. For example, in retail supermarkets, a 10% profit margin is considered exceptional.

Du Pont Formula The **Du Pont Formula** or system of financial analysis has been widely used for many years in American finance. It brings together the asset turnover ratio and the profit margin ratio and shows how these ratios interact to produce the return on assets ratio that was introduced earlier in this chapter. Since this system of analysis was not discussed earlier, let's see how it works for CMU and then compare these measures for The Gap and The Limited:

$$\text{Return on Assets} = \text{Asset Turnover Ratio} \times \text{Profit Margin Ratio}$$

$$\frac{\text{Net Income}}{\text{Average Total Assets}} = \frac{\text{Net Sales Revenue}}{\text{Average Total Assets}} \times \frac{\text{Net Income}}{\text{Net Sales Revenue}}$$

$$\frac{\$30{,}000}{\$57{,}500} = \frac{\$86{,}600}{\$57{,}500^*} \times \frac{\$30{,}000}{\$86{,}600}$$

$$.52 = 1.506 \times .346$$

*($40,000 + $75,000)/2

This system of analysis is helpful in comparing The Gap with The Limited because it allows us to examine each company's return on assets by separating them into two components—asset turnover and profit margin:

2001	Return on Assets	=	Asset Turnover Ratio	×	Profit Margin Ratio
Gap	(.001)		1.896		(.0006)
Limited	.118		2.126		.0554

Although both the return on assets and profit margin ratio included in the Du Pont system are profitability ratios, the combination of these ratios is often classified as a tool for evaluating investing activities via the asset turnover ratio. Since The Gap's negative return in 2001 is somewhat difficult to evaluate, let's instead focus on its more impressive 2000 results:

2000	Return on Assets	=	Asset Turnover Ratio	×	Profit Margin Ratio
Gap	.144		2.241		.0641
Limited	.104		2.460		.0423

Since asset turnover is a measure of how well a company is able to use its assets to sell its products, we can see that The Limited has performed better in this regard than has The Gap. However, The Gap's superior ability to produce profits from its sales measured by the profit margin ratio has allowed it to overtake The Limited with its return on assets ratio. If The Gap's management were looking at this comparison, they might well decide to target their efforts to improve their asset turnover ratio. In contrast, management from The Limited might well be targeting their cost control since a high profit margin company is more efficient in controlling its costs than is a low profit margin company.

As you can see from its 2001 results, The Gap's profitability has shown clear signs of deterioration in all five of the profit measures discussed here. Such results alert the marketplace that The Gap products are less in demand than they were in past years. This fact, coupled with its debt problems makes it imperative that The Gap take serious steps to reverse its declining position.

Using Valuation Ratios to Evaluate the Reception of the Financial Markets

In addition to the ratios we have used so far, investment professionals generally regard one or more of the following ratios to have special value: earnings per share, the price-earnings ratio, the book value per share, and the dividend yield. Let's use each of them in our continuing analysis of The Gap and The Limited.

Earnings per Share Earnings per share (EPS) of common stock, also referred to as *income per common share*, indicates the relative profitability of a common stock investment for the period. It is calculated as follows:

$$\text{Earnings per share} = \frac{\text{Net Income} - \text{Preferred Stock Dividends Declared}}{\text{Weighted-Average Common Shares Outstanding during the Period}}$$

To understand and interpret this ratio, note that: (1) the net income in the numerator is found in the income statement; (2) neither The Gap nor the Limited have a preferred stock dividend to deduct from net income; and (3) the denominator is a weighted average rather than a simple average. Comparisons of earnings per share are generally less useful because companies have different numbers of shares outstanding, and these differences are seldom relevant in their evaluation. Perhaps the most important reason that this measure is calculated is to serve as the denominator of the well-respected price-earnings ratio that we'll discuss next. Nevertheless, The Gap and The Limited are compared here:

	Numerator	Denominator		
	Modified Net Income	Weighted-Average Shares Outstanding	Earnings per Share Ratio	Rank
The Limited	$519,000	428,000	1.213	1
The Gap	(7,764)	860,255	(.009)	2

Once again, the net loss incurred by The Gap makes its earnings per share figure less attractive than The Limited's.

Price-Earnings Ratio The **price-earnings ratio** (P/E ratio) can be expressed in either of the following ways:

$$\text{Price-Earnings Ratio} = \frac{\text{Total Company Market Value}}{\text{Net Income}}$$

OR

$$= \frac{\text{Market Price per Share}}{\text{Earnings per Share}}$$

If you focus on the latter expression, this ratio shows how much an investor is willing to pay for one share of a particular company in excess of what that share currently earns. The P/E ratio of a particular company is heavily influenced by the financial markets' expectations of that company's future performance. That is why a company that has high growth potential will generally sell at a higher multiplier of current earnings or P/E ratio than a no-growth company. Let's now compare the P/E ratios of our companies using market prices provided by Reuters.

	Numerator	Denominator		
2/1/2001	**Market Price per Share**	**Earnings per Share**	**Price-Earnings Ratio**	**Rank**
The Limited	$18.45	$1.213	15.21	1
The Gap	14.10	(.009)	(1,567)	2

Since the negative earnings per share creates an unusually high negative price-earnings ratio, let's look at the 2000 results of these companies so you can see a more typical comparison:

	Numerator	Denominator		
2/2/2000	**Market Price per Share**	**Earnings per Share**	**Price-Earnings Ratio**	**Rank**
The Gap	$32.12	$1.43	22.46	1
The Limited	19.81	1.00	19.81	2

Considering The Gap's price-earnings ratio in 2000, it is not surprising how disappointing its 2001 profit performance was to investment analysts who use the price-earnings ratio as a key indicator in their investment strategies.

Book Value per Share The **book value per share** of a common stock is found by adding up all the assets, subtracting all liabilities and stock issues ahead of the common stock, and then dividing by the number of common shares. The formula to calculate book value per share is as follows:

$$\text{Book Value per Share} = \frac{\text{Common Stockholders' Equity}}{\text{Common Shares Outstanding}}$$

Since this is the first time you have seen this formula, let's apply it to our companies for comparison purposes:

	Numerator	Denominator		
2001	**Common Stockholders' Equity**	**Common Shares Outstanding**	**Book Value per Share Ratio**	**Rank**
The Limited	$2,744,000	429,000	$6.40	1
The Gap	3,009,581	850,499	3.54	2

This calculation is quoted often and is quite popular in the investment community. For example, some analysts believe that the possibility of a hostile takeover of a corporation is greater when its book value exceeds its market value. Nevertheless, the book value per share is not a good measure of the economic or market value of a share of common stock. The reason is that its inclusion of historical book values excludes it from reporting the real market value of the stock. Thus, the fact that The Limited has a higher book value than does The Gap is not of great significance.

Dividend Yield The **dividend yield** is the ratio of the dividend per common share to the market price per common share. This ratio provides investors some idea of the rate of return they will receive in cash dividends from their investment. Companies that retain a relatively high percentage of net income to finance continued growth and expansion have a relatively low dividend yield. Such companies are favored by investors who seek long-term growth.

Here are two equivalent formulas for this ratio:

$$\text{Dividend Yield} = \frac{\text{Cash Dividends Declared}}{\text{Total Company Market Value}}$$

OR

$$= \frac{\text{Cash Dividend per Share}}{\text{Market Price per Share}}$$

It is generally easier to gather data for the second formula as shown for our companies (using market prices provided by Reuters):

	Numerator	Denominator		
2001	Cash Dividend per Share	Market Price per Share	Dividend Yield Ratio	Rank
The Limited	$.30	$18.45	.0163	1
The Gap	.09	14.10	.0064	2

As you can see, The Limited's dividend yield, while not very high, is significantly greater than that of The Gap.

Comparing Financial Statement Ratios with Industry Averages

An essential step in our ratio analysis of The Gap is to compare its key ratios not only with those of The Limited, but also with the average ratios of companies within the same industry. You can view just such a comparison by studying Figure 14-3, which illustrates both The Gap's ratios and a set of its own industry average ratios. To find this information, however, you must first determine The Gap's **Standard Industrial Classification Code (SIC Code)**. This simple coding system established by the U.S. government identifies companies as belonging to one of the following industry groups:

Agriculture, Forestry, and Fishing	01–09
Mining	10–14
Construction	15–17
Manufacturing	20–39
Transport, Communications, and Utilities	40–49
Wholesale Trade	50–51
Retail Trade	52–59
Finance, Insurance, and Real Estate	60–67
Services	70–89
Public Administration (Government)	90–97
Nonclassifiable Companies	99

FIGURE 14-3 Comparison of The Gap's ratios to those ratios representing the industry averages

Ratio Name	(000) Gap's 2001 Ratio Calculation	Industry Norms 80th Percentile	Median	20th Percentile	Strong/Weak or Average Evaluation
Working Capital/Assets	0.130	0.1	0.1	0.1	Average +
Current	1.481	11.0	4.0	2.1	Weak
Quick	0.504	2.9	0.9	0.2	Weak
Asset Turnover	1.896	3.3	2.2	1.5	Weak
Inventory Turnover	5.420	6.5	4.3	2.6	Average +
Holding Period	67.34	56.2	84.9	140.4	Average +
Long-Term Debt to Equity*	0.652	0.50	0.10	0.0	Very Weak
Return on CSE	(0.003)	(0.074)	0.093	0.227	Weak
Return on Assets	(0.001)	(0.019)	0.029	0.096	Weak
Profit Margin	(0.001)	(0.015)	0.023	0.066	Weak
Price Earnings	(1,567)	(4.3)	12.7	20.8	Very Weak

*Since the industry average is based on a numerator of long-term debt, The Gap's calculation here equals 0.652 ($1,961,397/$3,009,581).

SIC Codes use four digits. The first two digits, or Major Group Code, identify the company's broad industry group (for example, 16 is a company in the construction industry). The last two digits, or Product/Service Code, provide a more specific identification of the product or service provided by the company. If the company operates in more than one industry, it is assigned more than one code. In this case, the industry that accounts for the company's largest percentage of sales is represented by the *primary SIC code*. Other industries in which the company participates are then designated by one or more *secondary SIC codes*. If a company has multiple SIC codes, the primary SIC is listed first.

You can locate a company's SIC Code in the reference section of most libraries by consulting either the *Corporate Technology Directory* or *Million Dollar Directory*. You can also determine a company's SIC Code by consulting its profile in what's called the *Compact Disclosure Database*. SIC Codes are easily accessible on such financial websites as Yahoo Finance, CNN Money, and Marketguide. According to these references, The Gap's SIC Code is 5651, which represents family clothing stores. The SIC code system is so detailed, however, that The Limited is actually classified under its own distinct code of 5621, which represents women's clothing stores. Thus, an even more precise financial analysis would be to compare The Gap with a specialty retailer within The Gap's own code.

When you find the company's single or primary SIC code, several resources allow you to compare its ratios to those of comparable companies in the same industry. These include Dun & Bradstreet's *Industry Norms and Key Business Ratios*, *RMA Annual Statement Studies*, and Troy's *Almanac of Key Business Ratios*—books found in the reference section of most libraries. The Dun and Bradstreet reference organizes information by SIC code and provides a median value (midpoint of all companies in the sample) and the upper and lower quartile values (midpoints of the upper and lower halves) for 14 ratios. Another valuable on-line resource is FIS online. In fact, the information found in Figure 14-3 was assembled from both Dun & Bradstreet and FIS online.

Additional Analyses

Recall from Chapters 5 and 7 that some very valuable information about both the balance sheet and income statement is not itself found in those financial statements. Instead, this information is found in two distinctly different annual report sections. These are Management's Discussion and Analysis of Operations, commonly called the MD&A, and the notes to the financial statements. Let's now examine these annual report sections for The Gap to learn more about its financial condition and results of operations. Since the MD&A normally precedes both the financial statements and the notes to the financial statements in an annual report, we'll examine it first.

Using Management's Discussion and Analysis

It should be apparent from this chapter's comprehensive analysis that The Gap, in particular, has experienced some serious declines in its operating performance and financial condition during the last few years. Although such a conclusion might not be apparent from all of the information included in the MD&A, the following income statement and balance sheet related examples make no attempt to hide or minimize the problems:

Cost of Goods Sold and Occupancy Expenses

Cost of goods sold and occupancy expenses as a percentage of net sales increased 7.2 percentage points in fiscal 2001 from 2000 and increased 4.7 percentage points in fiscal 2000 from 1999.

The increase in fiscal 2001 from 2000 was driven by a decrease in merchandise margins and increased occupancy expenses of 4.9 and 2.3 percentage points, respectively. Of the 4.9 percentage points decline in merchandise margins, 4.5 percentage points were attributable to lower margins on regular-priced and marked-down goods and a greater percentage of merchandise sold at markdown. The lower margins and the increase in proportion of goods sold at markdown were driven by poor product acceptance, particularly in the men's division. After a thorough review of our merchandise programs for the fourth quarter of fiscal 2001 and first quarter of fiscal 2002, we cancelled certain product orders in the third quarter of fiscal 2001. This resulted in a $52 million charge which accounted for an additional 0.4 of the 4.9 percentage points decline in merchandise margins. We chose to cancel these programs in order to manage our inventory levels consistent with current business and also as a result of making changes to the product assortment for the fourth quarter of fiscal 2001 and first quarter of fiscal 2002.

Recall from our earlier examination of The Gap's 10-K that its credit ratings were seriously downgraded over the last year as described here in its MD&A:

Summary Disclosures about Contractual Obligations and Commercial Commitments

In response to the deterioration in our operating profitability, Moody's and Standard and Poor's reduced their credit ratings of the Company. On January 14, 2002, Moody's reduced our long- and short-term senior unsecured credit ratings from Baa2 to Baa3 and Prime-2 to Prime-3, respectively. On February 14, 2002, Moody's reduced our long- and short-term senior unsecured credit ratings from Baa3 to Ba2 and from Prime-3 to Not Prime, respectively, with a negative outlook on our long-term ratings, and Standard and Poor's reduced our long- and short-term credit ratings from BBB+ to BB+ and from A-2 to B, respectively, with a stable outlook on our long-term ratings. On February 27, 2002, Moody's reduced our long-term senior unsecured credit ratings from Ba2 to Ba3 and stated that its outlook on our long-term ratings was stable. As a result of the recent downgrades in our long-term credit ratings, the interest rates payable by us on $700 million of our outstanding notes are subject to increase by 175 basis points, effective June 15, 2002, to 9.90 percent per annum on the 2005 notes and 10.55 percent per annum on the 2008 notes. Any further downgrades of our long-term credit ratings by these rating agencies would result in further increases in the interest rates payable by us on $700 million of our outstanding notes. As a result of the downgrades in our short-term credit ratings, we no longer have meaningful access to the commercial paper market. In addition, we expect both the recent and any future lowering of the ratings on our debt to result in reduced access to the capital markets and higher interest costs on future financings.

As you can see, the preceding discussions provide an important supplement to our earlier ratio calculations. If a problem is detectable through ratio analysis, most companies will use the MD&A discussion to offer explanations for why the problem has occurred and what they plan to do about solving that problem for the future.

Using the Notes

The Gap reports 11 notes following its financial statements. The first note is its *Summary of Significant Accounting Policies*. This note describes the nature of Gap's business and the essential accounting principles used by the company, including definitions of cash equivalents and the particular methods or principles used to account for both inventories and depreciation. Note B entitled *Debt and Other Credit Arrangements* confirms the almost twofold increase in long-term debt during the last year, which we discovered during our earlier calculation of leverage ratios. Perhaps the most relevant note, however, is Note D entitled *Leases*. This note details the cash payments that must be made under the terms of noncancelable lease arrangements. This information, of course, represents the amount of Gap's off-balance-sheet financing. Although The Gap does not provide a clear breakdown between its capital leases and its operating leases, it does report that its minimum lease commitment is nearly $5.25 billion! This contractual commitment in which The Gap promises to pay so much in the future might seem alarming, but examination of The Limited indicates a smaller but significant commitment of $3.25 billion. Although the 10-K informed us that The Gap leased almost all of its stores and office facilities, we would almost certainly have been unaware of the financial effect of these leases had we not read the notes to the financial statements. If The Gap were to have a series of bad years, you would definitely want to remember the existence of this sizable future cash commitment and continue to consult the notes to the financial statements for such executory contracts. Of course, leases are a prime example of how companies use off-balance-sheet financing to hide in-substance liabilities from those in the investment community who don't bother to read the footnotes.

Using Horizontal Analysis

Recall that, in addition to ratio analysis, financial analysts and other knowledgeable readers of financial statements use percentage analysis to uncover important relationships and trends. Percentage analysis is a technique in which the relative size of particular financial statement accounts or line items are highlighted to reveal potentially useful trends to decision makers. One percentage analysis tool is horizontal analysis, which compares how financial statement items change from year to year.

You have already viewed two such horizontal analyses. The first was found in Figure 14-1, which included both balance sheet and income statement data of The Gap. The second was found in Figure 14-2, a corresponding 10-year summary of The Limited. Recall that our basic strategy was to use horizontal analysis for a more in-depth analysis whenever we detected a problem in a particular ratio.

Using Vertical Analysis

Recall that vertical analysis expresses each item within a particular financial statement as a percentage of a single designated item within the same statement. The most common designated item within the income statement is net sales. The term *vertical analysis* is descriptive because the percentage relationships are derived from a single year's information that is usually presented in a vertical column. With vertical analysis, you may evaluate an entity's performance from year to year as well as compare its current performance to the current performance of other entities within the same industry.

In fact, we applied vertical analysis when we compared the gross margin ratio of The Gap to that of The Limited earlier in this chapter. In that case, The Gap's income statement in Appendix 14–1 is already in a vertical analysis format.

Looking beyond the Bottom Line

In addition to the ten ratios that were constructed in part from various items within the income statement, you can also extract additional information about the income statement from the annual report to enhance your understanding of The Gap's earnings performance. In fact, some of these additional tools have already been introduced, such as Management's Discussion and Analysis, the notes, and the use of vertical analysis. Another tool is to determine what income statement form is used by companies that you analyze. For example, you already know that The Gap uses a single-step income statement format. Although the simplicity of the single-step income statement is an advantage, our analysis would be easier had The Gap used the multiple-step format as did its competitor, The Limited. Why? Because by providing more of a step-by-step explanation of the financial information, the multiple-step format is usually more informative to the reader. Despite our disappointment, Gap's decision not to use a multiple-step format should in no way reflect poorly on our evaluation of its earnings performance.

Let's now revisit, however, another type of income statement analysis first introduced in Chapter 7. There you learned that it is important to study the complete income statement, not just the final figure, net income, or its bottom line. This means that you should not treat every reported item equally. Instead, you should concentrate on an entity's primary operating transactions, rather than those that are peripheral or incidental to the entity. Likewise, you should concentrate on continuing activities or transactions rather than on an unusual event that is unlikely to recur regularly. To so prioritize what is essential in the income statement involves the ability to classify the income statement into as many as four categories. These are primary operating activities that are expected to continue, peripheral activities that are expected to continue, primary operating activities that are not expected to continue, and peripheral activities that are not expected to continue. We will now use this focus to evaluate both The Gap and The Limited.

Unfortunately, The Gap's income statement in Appendix 14–1 is so heavily condensed, it doesn't provide as much information as we might like. Although it does include two peripheral expenses—interest and income tax—it appears to contain no significant noncontinuing transactions. In contrast, The Limited's income statement is more informative. It allows us to clearly identify such peripheral transactions as interest expense, income tax, and minority interest. Although not shown in Appendix 14–1, The Limited also reported a nearly $1.75 billion dollar nonrecurring item in fiscal year 1998. To more clearly illustrate the idea of how to adjust an income statement for what is really relevant, let's use comparative data from both companies of just a few years ago. To validly compare these income statements, our analytical strategy is very simple. We will attach more significance to primary operating activities that are expected to continue than to the other three categories. Here is an adjusted set of income statements for the year ending January 30 and 31, 1999, that reflects this strategy:

	Gap, Inc.	The Limited
Net sales	$9,054,462	$9,346,911
Cost of goods sold and occupancy expenses	5,318,218	6,375,651
Gross margin	3,736,244	2,971,260
Selling, general, and administrative expenses	2,403,365	2,286,917
Operating income or income from operations	1,332,879	684,343
Net income	$ 824,539	$2,046,494

Notice that the operating income measures the primary operating activities of an entity that are expected to continue. The value of this analysis becomes readily apparent when you compare the operating income to the net income of the two companies. Although it appears that The Limited's earnings were nearly two and one-half times greater than The Gap's, The Gap reported nearly twice as much operating income as did The Limited. Which income figure is more important? As you learned before, the operating income provides a much more accurate indication of future profitability than does the net income. It also tells us more about the relationship between revenue earned from customers and the expenses incurred in servicing those customers.

Although the preceding analysis of primary operating activities that are expected to continue is the most important section of the income statement, studying income from continuing operations might also be potentially helpful to decision makers. This income category includes accounts not associated with how assets are used in operations (that is, peripheral activities) but which nevertheless tend to appear each year on the income statement. Examples include: interest expense that is incurred when assets are financed; interest revenue and dividend revenue that are earned from investments in assets outside the entity; other gains and losses on peripheral sales of assets other than inventory; and income tax expense that is not incurred to produce revenue as are all the operating expenses.

	Gap, Inc.	The Limited
Operating income or income from operations	$1,332,879	$ 684,343
Interest expense	(13,617)	(68,528)
Other income, net		59,265
Income tax expense	(494,723)	(305,000)
Income from continuing operations	824,539	370,080
Net income	$ 824,539	$2,046,494

Notice that The Gap's earnings advantage is actually greater than in our preceding analysis because of the relatively higher income taxes borne by The Limited on its smaller taxable income. Thus, it is clear that adjusting the income statements for nonrecurring items can be a very valuable tool in your financial analysis arsenal.

Analyzing the Statement of Cash Flows

Recall that the statement of cash flows can help you make better decisions by using it in conjunction with ratios. Despite their widespread use, ratios *by themselves* are not always reliable measurements of an entity's financial well-being. Relying solely upon balance sheet ratios, such as the current ratio, is not advisable because these ratios are static and might not accurately represent a company's performance during the period. This is particularly true for companies such as The Gap whose "business follows a seasonal pattern, peaking over a total of about 10 to 13 weeks during the Back-to-School (mid-August through early September) and Holiday (November through December) periods."[1] Since the company's current ratio declined from 1.25 to 0.95 between January 1999 and January 2000, how can we be sure that it has an adequate margin of safety? Think about cash flow. What if the company's cash flow from operations is highly seasonal or actually declining, or what if its operating performance is impaired by consuming current assets to pay off current liabilities? In these cases, relying only on balance sheet ratios might prevent you from correctly assessing the company's financial well-being. Thus, it is essential that you supplement your analysis by using the statement of cash flows tools.

Cash Flows from Operations

The very first question you should ask when viewing The Gap's statement of cash flows is "What is the amount of cash flow from operations?" If you study a company's cash flow from operations first, you will see that its particular mix of investing and financing transactions is usually directly related to the relative strength of its operations. As you can see from The Gap's statement of cash flows, for example, its cash receipts from operations are more than $1.3 billion ($1,317,839,000) larger than cash payments from operations. Moreover, it also generated a positive cash inflow from financing of nearly $250 million. Unfortunately, however, this financing was largely made possible by the issuance of long-term debt of $1.2 billion ($1,194,265,000). So, in the short run, The Gap has augmented its cash flow but added to its leverage problems in the long run. Quite likely, this borrowing was done to cover the payment of nearly $1 billion ($940,078,000) to acquire property and equipment.

Cash Flows from Both Investing and Financing Activities

The following table presents the relative cash flow amounts of the operating, investing, and financing activities of both The Gap and The Limited (expressed in millions of dollars).

	Cash Inflow from Operating Activities	Cash Outflow from Investing Activities	Cash Inflow (Outflow) from Financing Activities	Net Change in Cash
The Gap	$1,317,839	$(950,627)	$271,285	$638,497
The Limited	969,000	(68,000)	(90,000)	811,000

This comparison is informative because it indicates that despite The Gap's ability to generate greater cash inflows from operations than The Limited, The Limited's lower investing and financing needs produced a greater net increase in cash for the period. Nevertheless, The Gap's net change in cash for 2001 was significantly improved over both 2000 and 1999.

Noncash Investing and Financing Activities

In Chapter 8, you learned that the accounting profession requires that significant noncash exchanges of noncurrent assets and/or noncurrent claims against assets be

[1] Form 10-K, The Gap, Inc. February 2, 2001, page 3.

disclosed to ensure that users do not overlook such potentially relevant information. When these direct exchanges are decomposed into their fundamental elements, they become, in substance, an investing and/or financing activity. Although direct exchange transactions do not, by definition, affect cash, they must be disclosed in the statement of cash flows. A good example of just how significant these transactions can be is a nearly $2 billion direct exchange reported by The Limited in 1998 in which previously held Abercrombie & Fitch became an independent company. The Gap, however, reported no such transactions during the year ended February 2, 2002.

Comparing The Gap and The Limited with CMU

How do you think the analysis of a small retailer's ratios would compare to the comprehensive ratio analysis we just completed for our nationally known retailers, The Gap and The Limited? To answer this question, study Figure 14-4, which is a comprehensive ratio analysis of Cards & Memorabilia Unlimited.

FIGURE 14-4

A comprehensive ratio analysis of Cards & Memorabilia Unlimited

Working Capital	$47,200.00
Working Capital Ratio	0.629

Despite having a small absolute amount of working capital, CMU has the highest working capital ratio of our three companies.

Current Ratio	6.187
Quick Ratio	4.758
Asset Turnover Ratio	1.506
Inventory Turnover Ratio	2.143
Average Holding Period	170.32

Although CMU should undoubtedly strive to decrease its inventory holding period, one should not necessarily conclude that Susan Newman is doing a poor job of inventory management since her company is in an entirely different industry than the Gap or the Limited.

Accounts Receivable Turnover Ratio	34.64
Average Collection Period	10.54
Accounts Payable Turnover Ratio	6.6
Average Payment Period	55.3
Length of Operating Cycle	125.56
Debt to Assets Ratio	0.175
Debt to Equity Ratio	0.212
Times Interest Earned Ratio	151.0

It is clear that CMU has financed its operations with much less debt than has The Gap. Using the debt to assets ratio, for example, as a comparison, The Gap's leverage is more than three times as great as that of CMU (.604 to .175).

Gross Margin Ratio	0.654

The gross margin ratios of profitable businesses usually range between 30% and 50% of net sales, depending on the types of merchandise sold. By that measure, CMU *seems* to be doing well. Once again, however, a financial analyst would compare CMU's results to those of other card and memorabilia stores before looking at the ratios of other retailers.

Profit Margin Ratio	0.346

The number .346 by itself, is not informative. To evaluate its significance, you must consider the industry in which the entity operates. For example, in the book publishing industry, a 10% to 15% profit margin ratio is considered good, whereas, in retail supermarkets, a 10% profit margin is considered exceptional. Although further investigation would give us additional confirmation, it is safe to say that CMU's profit margin is acceptable.

DuPont Formula

Return on Assets	=	Asset Turnover Ratio	×	Profit Margin Ratio
.52	=	1.506	×	.346

APPENDIX

14-1

2001 Financial Information for The Gap, Inc. and for The Limited, Inc.

The financial information herein is taken from the Form 10-K Annual Reports filed with the United States Securities and Exchange Commission for The Gap, Inc. and for The Limited, Inc. for fiscal year ended February 2, 2002.

2001 Financial Information for The Gap, Inc.

THE GAP, INC.

CONSOLIDATED STATEMENTS OF OPERATIONS

($ in thousands except share and per share amounts)	52 Weeks Ended Feb. 2, 2002	Percentage to Sales	53 Weeks Ended Feb. 3, 2001	Percentage to Sales	52 Weeks Ended Jan. 29, 2000	Percentage to Sales
Net sales	$ 13,847,873	100.0%	$ 13,673,460	100.0%	$ 11,635,398	100.0%
Costs and expenses						
Cost of goods sold and occupancy expenses	9,704,389	70.1	8,599,442	62.9	6,775,262	58.2
Operating expenses	3,805,968	27.5	3,629,257	26.5	3,043,432	26.2
Interest expense	109,190	0.8	74,891	0.5	44,966	0.4
Interest income	(13,315)	(0.1)	(12,015)	0.0	(13,211)	(0.1)
Earnings before income taxes	241,641	1.7	1,381,885	10.1	1,784,949	15.3
Income taxes	249,405	1.8	504,388	3.7	657,884	5.6
Net earnings (loss)	$ (7,764)	(0.1%)	$ 877,497	6.4%	$ 1,127,065	9.7%
Weighted-average number of shares—basic	860,255,419		849,810,658		853,804,924	
Weighted-average number of shares—diluted	860,255,419		879,137,194		895,029,176	
Earnings (loss) per share—basic	$ (0.01)		$ 1.03		$ 1.32	
Earnings (loss) per share—diluted (a)	(0.01)		1.00		1.26	

See Notes to Consolidated Financial Statements.

(a) Diluted losses per share for the 52 weeks ended February 2, 2002, are computed using the basic weighted average number of shares outstanding and exclude 13,395,045 dilutive shares as their effects are antidilutive when applied to losses.

THE GAP, INC.

CONSOLIDATED BALANCE SHEETS

($ in thousands except share and par value)	Feb. 2, 2002	Feb. 3, 2001
Assets		
Current Assets		
Cash and equivalents	$1,035,749	$ 408,794
Merchandise inventory	1,677,116	1,904,153
Other current assets	331,685	335,103
Total current assets	3,044,550	2,648,050
Property and Equipment		
Leasehold improvements	2,127,966	1,899,820
Furniture and equipment	3,327,819	2,826,863
Land and buildings	917,055	558,832
Construction-in-progress	246,691	615,722
	6,619,531	5,901,237
Accumulated depreciation and amortization	(2,458,241)	(1,893,552)
Property and equipment, net	4,161,290	4,007,685
Lease rights and other assets	385,486	357,173
Total assets	$7,591,326	$7,012,908
Liabilities and Shareholders' Equity		
Current Liabilities		
Notes payable	$ 41,889	$ 779,904
Current maturities of long-term debt	—	250,000
Accounts payable	1,105,117	1,067,207
Accrued expenses and other current liabilities	909,227	702,033
Total current liabilities	2,056,233	2,799,144
Long-Term Liabilities		
Long-term debt	1,961,397	780,246
Deferred lease credits and other liabilities	564,115	505,279
Total long-term liabilities	2,525,512	1,285,525
Shareholders' Equity		
Common stock $.05 par value Authorized 2,300,000,000 shares; issued 948,597,949 and 939,222,871 shares; outstanding 865,726,890 and 853,996,984 shares	47,430	46,961
Additional paid-in capital	461,408	294,967
Retained earnings	4,890,375	4,974,773
Accumulated other comprehensive losses	(61,824)	(20,173)
Deferred compensation	(7,245)	(12,162)
Treasury stock, at cost	(2,320,563)	(2,356,127)
Total shareholders' equity	3,009,581	2,928,239
Total liabilities and shareholders' equity	$7,591,326	$7,012,908

THE GAP, INC.

CONSOLIDATED STATEMENTS OF CASH FLOWS

($ in thousands)	52 Weeks Ended Feb. 2, 2002	53 Weeks Ended Feb. 3, 2001	52 Weeks Ended Jan. 29, 2000
Cash Flows from Operating Activities			
Net earnings (loss)	$ (7,764)	$ 877,497	$1,127,065
Adjustments to reconcile net earnings (loss) to net cash provided by operating activities:			
Depreciation and amortization	810,486	590,365	436,184
Tax benefit from exercise of stock options and vesting of restricted stock	58,444	130,882	211,891
Deferred income taxes	(28,512)	(38,872)	2,444
Change in operating assets and liabilities:			
Merchandise inventory	213,067	(454,595)	(404,211)
Prepaid expenses and other	(13,303)	(61,096)	(55,519)
Accounts payable	42,205	249,545	118,121
Accrued expenses	220,826	(56,541)	(5,822)
Deferred lease credits and other long-term liabilities	22,390	54,020	47,775
Net cash provided by operating activities	1,317,839	1,291,205	1,477,928
Cash Flows from Investing Activities			
Net purchase of property and equipment	(940,078)	(1,858,662)	(1,238,722)
Acquisition of lease rights and other assets	(10,549)	(16,252)	(39,839)
Net cash used for investing activities	(950,627)	(1,874,914)	(1,278,561)
Cash Flows from Financing Activities			
Net increase (decrease) in notes payable	(734,927)	621,420	84,778
Proceeds from issuance of long-term debt	1,194,265	250,000	311,839
Payments of long-term debt	(250,000)	—	—
Issuance of common stock	139,105	152,105	114,142
Net purchase of treasury stock	(785)	(392,558)	(745,056)
Cash dividends paid	(76,373)	(75,488)	(75,795)
Net cash provided by (used for) financing activities	271,285	555,479	(310,092)
Effect of exchange rate fluctuations on cash	(11,542)	(13,328)	(4,176)
Net increase (decrease) in cash and equivalents	626,955	(41,558)	(114,901)
Cash and equivalents at beginning of year	408,794	450,352	565,253
Cash and equivalents at end of year	$1,035,749	$ 408,794	$ 450,352

THE GAP, INC.

CONSOLIDATED STATEMENTS OF SHAREHOLDERS' EQUITY

($ in thousands except share and per share amounts)	Common Stock Shares	Common Stock Amount	Additional Paid-in Capital
Balance at January 30, 1999	997,496,214	$49,875	$349,037
Issuance of common stock pursuant to stock option plans	9,933,713	497	81,456
Net cancellations of common stock pursuant to management incentive restricted stock plans	(73,137)	(4)	2,583
Tax benefit from exercise of stock options by employees and from vesting of restricted stock			211,891
Adjustments for foreign currency translation ($3,305) and fluctuations in fair market value of financial instruments ($2,454)			
Amortization of restricted stock and discounted stock options			72
Purchase of treasury stock			4,276
Reissuance of treasury stock			20,175
Net earnings			
Cash dividends ($.09 per share)			
Balance at January 29, 2000	1,007,356,790	$50,368	$669,490
Issuance of common stock pursuant to stock option plans	13,078,981	654	115,167
Net cancellations of common stock pursuant to management incentive restricted stock plans	(185,563)	(10)	(364)
Tax benefit from exercise of stock options by employees and from vesting of restricted stock			130,882
Adjustments for foreign currency translation			
Adjustments for fluctuations in fair market value of financial instruments, net of tax of $8,131			
Amortization of restricted stock and discounted stock options			45
Purchase of treasury stock			1,873
Reissuance of treasury stock			15,458
Retirement of treasury stock	(81,027,337)	(4,051)	(637,584)
Net earnings			
Cash dividends ($.09 per share)			
Balance at February 3, 2001	939,222,871	$46,961	$294,967
Issuance of common stock pursuant to stock option plans	9,346,228	468	107,130
Net issuance of common stock pursuant to management incentive restricted stock plans	28,850	1	683
Tax benefit from exercise of stock options by employees and from vesting of restricted stock			58,444
Adjustments for foreign currency translation			
Adjustments for fluctuations in fair market value of financial instruments, net of tax of ($5,793)			
Amortization of restricted stock and discounted stock options			
Purchase of treasury stock			
Reissuance of treasury stock			184
Net earnings (loss)			
Cash dividends ($.09 per share)			
Balance at February 2, 2002	948,597,949	$47,430	$461,408

(continued on next page)

(continued)

THE GAP, INC.

CONSOLIDATED STATEMENTS OF SHAREHOLDERS' EQUITY

($ in thousands except share and per share amounts)	Retained Earnings	Accumulated Other Comprehensive Earnings (Loss)	Deferred Compensation
Balance at January 30, 1999	$3,121,360	$(12,518)	$(31,675)
Issuance of common stock pursuant to stock option plans			(9,186)
Net cancellations of common stock pursuant to management incentive restricted stock plans			(3,411)
Tax benefit from exercise of stock options by employees and from vesting of restricted stock			
Adjustments for foreign currency translation ($3,305) and fluctuations in fair market value of financial instruments ($2,454)		5,759	
Amortization of restricted stock and discounted stock options			21,122
Purchase of treasury stock			
Reissuance of treasury stock			
Net earnings	1,127,065		
Cash dividends ($.09 per share)	(75,629)		
Balance at January 29, 2000	$4,172,796	$ (6,759)	$(23,150)
Issuance of common stock pursuant to stock option plans			(4,249)
Net cancellations of common stock pursuant to management incentive restricted stock plans			(919)
Tax benefit from exercise of stock options by employees and from vesting of restricted stock			
Adjustments for foreign currency translation		(24,286)	
Adjustments for fluctuations in fair market value of financial instruments, net of tax of $8,131		10,872	
Amortization of restricted stock and discounted stock options			16,156
Purchase of treasury stock			
Reissuance of treasury stock			
Retirement of treasury stock			
Net earnings	877,497		
Cash dividends ($.09 per share)	(75,520)		
Balance at February 3, 2001	$4,974,773	$(20,173)	$(12,162)
Issuance of common stock pursuant to stock option plans			(5,006)
Net issuance of common stock pursuant to management incentive restricted stock plans			(704)
Tax benefit from exercise of stock options by employees and from vesting of restricted stock			
Adjustments for foreign currency translation			
Adjustments for fluctuations in fair market value of financial instruments, net of tax of ($5,793)		(33,534)	
Amortization of restricted stock and discounted stock options		(8,117)	
Purchase of treasury stock			10,627
Reissuance of treasury stock			
Net earnings (loss)	(7,764)		
Cash dividends ($.09 per share)	(76,634)		
Balance at February 2, 2002	$4,890,375	$(61,824)	$(7,245)

(continued on next page)

(concluded)

THE GAP, INC.

CONSOLIDATED STATEMENTS OF SHAREHOLDERS' EQUITY

	Treasury Stock			
	Shares	Amount	Total	Comprehensive Earnings (Loss)
Balance at January 30, 1999	(139,536,182)	$(1,902,400)	$1,573,679	$ 827,251
Issuance of common stock pursuant to stock option plans			72,767	
Net cancellations of common stock pursuant to management incentive restricted stock plans			(832)	
Tax benefit from exercise of stock options by employees and from vesting of restricted stock			211,891	
Adjustments for foreign currency translation ($3,305) and fluctuations in fair market value of financial instruments ($2,454)			5,759	5,759
Amortization of restricted stock and discounted stock options			21,194	
Purchase of treasury stock	(18,500,000)	(745,056)	(740,780)	
Reissuance of treasury stock	1,178,333	17,756	37,931	
Net earnings			1,127,065	1,127,065
Cash dividends ($.09 per share)			(75,629)	
Balance at January 29, 2000	(156,857,849)	$(2,629,700)	$2,233,045	$1,132,824
Issuance of common stock pursuant to stock option plans			111,572	
Net cancellations of common stock pursuant to management incentive restricted stock plans			(1,293)	
Tax benefit from exercise of stock options by employees and from vesting of restricted stock			130,882	
Adjustments for foreign currency translation			(24,286)	(24,286)
Adjustments for fluctuations in fair market value of financial instruments, net of tax of $8,131			10,872	10,872
Amortization of restricted stock and discounted stock options			16,201	
Purchase of treasury stock	(11,020,038)	(392,558)	(390,685)	
Reissuance of treasury stock	1,624,663	24,496	39,954	
Retirement of treasury stock	81,027,337	641,635	—	
Net earnings			877,497	877,497
Cash dividends ($.09 per share)			(75,520)	
Balance at February 3, 2001	(85,225,887)	$(2,356,127)	$2,928,239	$ 864,083
Issuance of common stock pursuant to stock option plans			102,592	
Net issuance of common stock pursuant to management incentive restricted stock plans			(20)	
Tax benefit from exercise of stock options by employees and from vesting of restricted stock			58,444	
Adjustments for foreign currency translation			(33,534)	(33,534)
Adjustments for fluctuations in fair market value of financial instruments, net of tax of ($5,793)			(8,117)	(8,117)
Amortization of restricted stock and discounted stock options			10,627	
Purchase of treasury stock	(34,500)	(785)	(785)	
Reissuance of treasury stock	2,389,328	36,349	36,533	
Net earnings (loss)			(7,764)	(7,764)
Cash dividends ($.09 per share)			(76,634)	
Balance at February 2, 2002	(82,871,059)	$(2,320,563)	$3,009,581	$ (49,415)

2001 Financial Information for The Limited, Inc.

THE LIMITED, INC.

CONSOLIDATED STATEMENTS OF INCOME

(Millions except per share amounts)	2001	2000	1999
Net sales	$ 9,363	$10,105	$ 9,766
Costs of goods sold, buying and occupancy	(6,110)	(6,668)	(6,443)
Gross income	3,253	3,437	3,323
General, administrative and store operating expenses	(2,505)	(2,561)	(2,416)
Special and nonrecurring items, net	170	(10)	24
Operating income	918	866	931
Interest expense	(34)	(58)	(78)
Other income, net	22	20	41
Minority interest	(64)	(69)	(73)
Gains on sale of stock by investees	62	—	11
Income before income taxes	904	759	832
Income tax expense	385	331	371
Net income	$ 519	$ 428	$ 461
Net income per share:			
Basic	$ 1.21	$ 1.00	$ 1.05
Diluted	$ 1.19	$ 0.96	$ 1.00

THE LIMITED, INC.

CONSOLIDATED BALANCE SHEETS

(Millions except for per share amounts)	February 2, 2002	February 3, 2001
Assets		
Current assets		
Cash and equivalents	$1,375	$ 564
Accounts receivable	79	94
Inventories	966	1,157
Other	262	253
Total current assets	2,682	2,068
Property and equipment, net	1,359	1,395
Deferred income taxes	67	132
Other assets	611	493
Total assets	$4,719	$4,088
Liabilities and Shareholders' Equity		
Current liabilities		
Accounts payable	$ 245	$ 273
Current portion of long-term debt	150	—
Accrued expenses and other	648	581
Income taxes	276	146
Total current liabilities	1,319	1,000
Long-term debt	250	400
Other long-term liabilities	229	229
Minority interest	177	143

(continued on next page)

(continued)

THE LIMITED, INC.

CONSOLIDATED BALANCE SHEETS

(Millions except for per share amounts)	February 2, 2002	February 3, 2001
Shareholders' equity		
Preferred stock—$1.00 par value; 10 shares authorized; none issued	—	—
Common stock—$0.50 par value; 1,000 shares authorized; 432 shares issued in 2001 and 2000	216	216
Paid-in capital	53	83
Retained earnings	2,552	2,168
Less: treasury stock, at average cost; 3 shares in 2001 and 6 shares in 2000	(77)	(151)
Total shareholders' equity	2,744	2,316
Total liabilities and shareholders' equity	$4,719	$4,088

THE LIMITED, INC.

CONSOLIDATED STATEMENTS OF SHAREHOLDERS' EQUITY (Millions)

	Common Stock Shares Outstanding	Common Stock Par Value	Paid-In Capital	Retained Earnings	Treasury Stock, at Average Cost	Total Shareholders' Equity
Balance, January 30, 1999	453	$180	$157	$5,471	$(3,641)	$2,167
Net income	—	—	—	461	—	461
Cash dividends	—	—	—	(130)	—	(130)
Repurchase of common stock, including transaction costs	(30)	—	—	—	(753)	(753)
Spin-off of Limited Too	—	—	—	(25)	—	(25)
Rescission of contingent stock redemption agreement	—	10	8	334	—	352
Exercise of stock options and other	7	—	13	(2)	64	75
Balance, January 29, 2000	430	$190	$178	$6,109	$(4,330)	$2,147
Net income	—	—	—	428	—	428
Cash dividends	—	—	—	(128)	—	(128)
Repurchase of common stock, including transaction costs	(9)	—	—	—	(200)	(200)
Retirement of treasury stock	—	(82)	—	(4,241)	4,323	—
Two-for-one stock split	—	108	(108)	—	—	—
Exercise of stock options and other	5	—	13	—	56	69
Balance, February 3, 2001	426	$216	$ 83	$2,168	$ (151)	$2,316
Net income	—	—	—	519	—	519
Cash dividends	—	—	—	(129)	—	(129)
Exercise of stock options and other	3	—	(30)	(6)	74	38
Balance, February 2, 2002	429	$216	$ 53	$2,552	$ (77)	$2,744

THE LIMITED, INC.

CONSOLIDATED STATEMENTS OF CASH FLOWS (Millions)

	2001	2000	1999
Operating Activities			
Net income	$ 519	$428	$461
Adjustments to reconcile net income to net cash provided by (used for) operating activities:			
Depreciation and amortization	277	271	272
Deferred income taxes	76	46	(78)
Special and nonrecurring items, net	(170)	10	(24)
Minority interest, net of dividends paid	43	47	51
Gains on sale of stock by investees	(62)	—	(11)
Changes in assets and liabilities:			
Accounts receivable	15	15	(37)
Inventories	82	(106)	(54)
Accounts payable, accrued expenses and other	75	53	(20)
Income taxes payable	118	(60)	18
Other assets and liabilities	(4)	65	21
Net cash provided by operating activities	969	769	599
Investing Activities			
Proceeds from sale of subsidiary	280	—	—
Capital expenditures	(337)	(446)	(376)
Net proceeds (expenditures) related to Easton investment	(11)	(22)	11
Net proceeds from sale of partial interest in subsidiary	—	—	182
Decrease in restricted cash	—	—	352
Net cash provided by (used for) investing activities	(68)	(468)	169
Financing Activities			
Repayment of long-term debt	—	(250)	(300)
Proceeds from issuance of long-term debt	—	—	300
Repurchase of common stock, including transaction costs	—	(200)	(753)
Repurchase of Intimate Brands, Inc. common stock	(8)	(31)	(63)
Dividends paid	(129)	(128)	(130)
Dividend received from Limited Too	—	—	50
Settlement of Limited Too intercompany account	—	—	12
Proceeds from exercise of stock options and other	47	55	63
Net cash used for financing activities	(90)	(554)	(821)
Net increase (decrease) in cash and equivalents	811	(253)	(53)
Cash and equivalents, beginning of year	564	817	870
Cash and equivalents, end of year	$1,375	$564	$817

APPENDIX

14-2 Creating a Statement of Cash Flows

PERFORMANCE OBJECTIVE

In this appendix, you will learn the following new Performance Objective:

PO56 Using the technique of T-account analysis, **prepare** or **construct** a statement of cash flows given comparative balance sheets, an income statement, and relevant additional information.

In Chapter 8, you learned how to create a statement of cash flows by analyzing each of the first-year transactions (A_1 to Z) of Cards & Memorabilia Unlimited. But in the real world, it is impractical to analyze each and every transaction of a business for any purpose. Thus, you will next learn an alternative way to create a statement of cash flows derived from comparative balance sheet and selected income statement information. We'll demonstrate this step-by-step approach with a comprehensive problem and solution and the use of T-account analysis. Performance Objective 56 describes how to become proficient at preparing a statement of cash flows.

YOUR PERFORMANCE OBJECTIVE 56

Using the technique of T-account analysis, **prepare** or **construct** a statement of cash flows given comparative balance sheets, an income statement, and relevant additional information.

An Analytical Approach for Creating a Statement of Cash Flows

Recall from Chapter 8 how you used Cards & Memorabilia Unlimited's transactions to prepare its statement of cash flows. Reviewing an entity's entire set of transactions to find only those needed to prepare a statement of cash flows would be both inefficient and costly. Instead, you can prepare the statement relatively easily by using the following three steps:

1. Calculate *what* the change in cash is for the period.
2. Format a complete statement of cash flows.
3. Analyze sequentially all noncash balance sheet accounts to explain in detail *how* cash changed for the period.

You'll now practice these three steps using the comparative balance sheets and income statement of Fairmont Corporation shown in Figure 14A-1 as well as the following additional information:

1. On January 15, Year 2, Fairmont issued 500 shares of its own common stock in exchange for an investment in Longview Corporation stock having a cost of $5,000.
2. On July 1, Year 2, Fairmont sold equipment having an original cost of $5,000 and accumulated depreciation of $3,000.
3. On October 10, Year 2, Fairmont declared a cash dividend of $5,000 on its common stock. $4,000 of this dividend was paid on December 10, Year 2. No other dividends were paid or declared.
4. The Selling and Administrative Expenses account includes depreciation expense as well as insurance expense having a $6,000 account balance.

Now the conditions underlying Performance Objective 56 have been satisfied. That is, you have been provided with a comparative balance sheet, an income statement, and additional information with which to prepare the statement of cash flows.

Required Prepare a statement of cash flows and all related schedules for the year ended December 31, Year 2. Use the direct method for reporting cash flows from operations.

We'll now walk step-by-step through the preparation of a statement of cash flows and all related schedules for the period ended December 31, Year 2.

FIGURE 14A-1

Fairmont Corporation's comparative balance sheets and income statement

FAIRMONT CORPORATION
Balance Sheets
December 31, Year 1 and Year 2

Assets	**Year 1**	**Year 2**	**Increase (Decrease)**
Cash	$ 40,000	$ 60,000	$20,000
Accounts receivable, net	30,000	25,000	(5,000)
Merchandise inventory	70,000	72,000	2,000
Prepaid insurance	12,000	10,000	(2,000)
Long-term investments in stock	–0–	5,000	5,000
Plant and equipment	280,000	290,000	10,000
Accumulated depreciation	(57,000)	(62,000)	(5,000)
Total assets	$375,000	$400,000	$25,000
Liabilities and stockholders' equity			
Accounts payable	$ 60,000	$ 50,000	$(10,000)
Income taxes payable	2,500	4,000	1,500
Dividends payable	–0–	1,000	1,000
Bonds payable	90,000	80,000	(10,000)
Common stock, par value $10	100,000	125,000	25,000
Retained earnings	122,500	140,000	17,500
Total liabilities & stockholders' equity	$375,000	$400,000	$ 25,000

FAIRMONT CORPORATION
Income Statement
For the Year Ended December 31, Year 2

Net sales		$200,000
Operating expenses:		
Cost of goods sold	$115,000	
Selling and administrative expenses	45,000	160,000
Operating income		40,000
Other income (expense):		
Interest expense	(4,500)	
Gain on sale of equipment	2,000	(2,500)
Pretax income		37,500
Income tax expense (40%)		15,000
Net income		$ 22,500

Step 1: Calculate the Change in Cash for the Period

To calculate *what* the change in cash is for the current accounting period, you must compare the beginning and ending Cash account balances found in Figure 14A-1's comparative balance sheet.

	Year 1	**Year 2**	**Increase (Decrease)**
Cash	$40,000	$60,000	$20,000

This comparison indicates that cash has increased by $20,000 during Year 2, a change that must be detailed in the body of the statement of cash flows.

Step 2: Format a Complete Statement of Cash Flows

This step emphasizes form rather than content. That is, all headings for a standard statement of cash flows are prepared leaving sufficient space for the content of Step 3. Thus, you prepare the format or basic structure of the statement before you conduct the analysis of its detailed content as shown in Figure 14A-2. As you study this figure, note that Step 1's cash analysis is included, but the phrases *provided by* and *used in* that label each activity total are not filled in until Step 3.

FIGURE 14A-2

Format for a complete statement of cash flows

FAIRMONT CORPORATION
Statement of Cash Flows
For the Year Ended December 31, Year 2

Cash flows from operating activities:		
Cash collected from customers	$	
Cash paid for merchandise purchases		
Cash paid for prepaid assets		
Cash paid for other operating expenses		
Interest and income taxes paid	______	
Net cash ___________ by operating activities		$
Cash flows from investing activities:		
	$	
	______	
Net cash ___________ investing activities		$
Cash flows from financing activities:		
	$	
	______	
Net cash ___________ financing activities		
Net increase in cash		$20,000
Cash at beginning of year		40,000
Cash at end of year		$60,000

Supplemental schedule of noncash investing and financing activities:

Disclosure of accounting policy:
For purposes of the statement of cash flows, the company considers all highly liquid debt instruments purchased with a maturity of three months or less to be cash equivalents.

Step 3: Analyze Sequentially All Noncash Balance Sheet Accounts to Explain in Detail How Cash Changed for the Period

Since you have calculated *what* the amount of the net change in cash was in Step 1, you now need to describe *how* the amount of this change occurred. This step has two parts. In the first part, you analyze noncash current assets and current liabilities that affect operations thereby creating the operating activities section of a statement of cash flows. In the second part, you analyze all remaining balance sheet accounts for potential cash flows from investing and financing activities as well as significant non-cash activities. If your analysis for these two parts is correct, it should explain *how* the change in cash calculated in Step 1 occurred (the $20,000 cash increase in our illustration). You might recall, however, that some transactions called *direct exchanges* have no cash effect and will not explain the amount of the cash change. These transactions are, nonetheless, important because they often represent significant transactions that would otherwise be overlooked. Notice that these transactions are properly disclosed at the bottom of the statement of cash flows in Figure 14A-2.

Here now is Step 3's detailed analysis of *how* the Cash account increased by $20,000. To explain exactly how cash increased by $20,000 in our comprehensive problem, you must first analyze the noncash current assets and noncash current liabilities that affect operations. You can then create the operating activities section of the statement of cash flows with the results of this analysis. Next, you will analyze all remaining balance sheet accounts for potential cash flows from investing and financing activities as well as significant noncash activities.

Analysis of Noncash Current Assets and Current Liabilities Affecting Operations When you use the direct method of reporting cash flows from operating activities, you must focus on noncash current asset and current liability accounts that directly affect operations of the company. In Fairmont Corporation, the Accounts Receivable, Merchandise Inventory, Prepaid Insurance, Accounts Payable, and Income Taxes Payable accounts all fit this description. We'll exclude Dividends Payable, a current liability account, for now because it does not affect operations. Like the indirect method, the direct method involves a conversion from the accrual to the cash basis. Unlike the indirect method, however, the direct method requires that a complete income statement be provided.

We'll now analyze each of the noncash current assets and current liabilities of Fairmont Corporation to show how the components of cash inflows and cash outflows from operations are calculated under the direct method.

Cash Received from Customers (Equivalent to Cash Basis Sales) You can determine cash received from customers by using the following calculation:

Cash Basis Sales Revenue = Accrual Basis Sales Revenue +
Beginning Accounts Receivable −
Ending Accounts Receivable +
Cash Sales

Avoid memorizing this formula. Instead, employ the following T-account analysis:

Accounts Receivable

30 Credit sales (accrual basis)	Collections on account (cash basis)
25	

The beginning and ending account balances (in thousands) from the balance sheet are entered in this account related to customers. Accrual basis sales are equivalent to credit sales, while cash basis sales are equivalent to collections from customers on account.

Note that cash received from customers includes not only cash collections from customers on account but also cash sales. For Fairmont Corporation, we'll assume that all sales are initially on credit.

Accounts Receivable

30 200	
25	

The net credit sales figure from the income statement ($200 in thousands) is posted as a debit to this account while the credit is made to the Sales Revenue account.

Accounts Receivable	
30	
200	**205**
25	

Since the account balance decreases by $5, the cash collections from customers must exceed the credit sales by $5. Thus, collections equal $205 (in thousands).

Review the format in Figure 14A-2. The analysis presented above would be reflected by reporting cash collected from customers as $205,000. (Remember that three zeros have been dropped to facilitate the analysis.)

Cash Received from Dividends and Interest

Cash Basis Revenue = Accrual Basis Interest/Dividend Revenue + Beginning Receivable − Ending Receivable

Fairmont Corporation does not include this cash inflow. The T-account analysis for this cash inflow is identical to the preceding analysis described for cash received from customers.

Cash Paid to Employees and Other Suppliers

a. Cash Paid to Suppliers of Inventory

Use the following calculations to determine this amount:

Net Purchases = Accrual Basis Cost of Goods Sold + Ending Inventory − Beginning Inventory

Cash Basis Cost of Goods Sold = Net Purchases + Beginning Accounts Payable − Ending Accounts Payable

Once again, however, a T-account analysis approach is recommended in place of memorizing these two formulas:

❶

Inventory		Accounts Payable	
70	Accrual Basis COGS		60
72			50

The Inventories and Accounts Payable accounts are selected because they both are related to suppliers. Once again, the beginning and ending balances from the balance sheet (in thousands) are entered in these accounts.

❷

Inventory		Accounts Payable	
70			60
	115	Cash Basis COGS	
72			50

The cost of goods sold from the income statement is posted as a credit to the Inventory account while the debit is to the Cost of Goods Sold account.

❸

Inventory		Accounts Payable	
70			60
117	115		117
72		50	

Since the Inventory account increases by $2, the inventory purchases must exceed the inventory sales by $2. Thus, inventory purchases equal $117.

❹

Inventory

Debit	Credit
70	
117	115
72	

Accounts Payable

Debit	Credit
	60
127	117
	50

Since the Accounts Payable account decreases by $10, the payments on account must exceed the purchases on account by $10.

Thus, cash paid to suppliers of merchandise amounts to $127,000.

b. Cash Paid for Prepaids

Cash Basis Expenses = Accrual Basis Expenses + Ending Prepaid Assets − Beginning Prepaid Assets

The Prepaid Insurance account shown below is constructed by entering the beginning and ending balances from the balance sheet as debits and the amount of insurance expense (described in item ❹ of Fairmont Corporation's additional information) as a credit.

Step 1

Prepaid Insurance

Debit	Credit
12	
Premium Payments	Expired Benefits
10	

Step 2

Prepaid Insurance

Debit	Credit
12	
?	6
10	

Step 3

Prepaid Insurance

Debit	Credit
12	
4	6
10	

From analysis of the Prepaid Insurance account, it is clear that insurance expirations (that is, accrual basis insurance expense) exceed insurance payments by $2.

Thus, cash paid for insurance during the year amounts to $4,000.

c. Cash Paid for Selling and Administrative (S & A) Expenses

Cash Basis S & A Expenses = Accrual Basis S & A Expenses + Beginning Accrued Liabilities − Ending Accrued Liabilities

Since there is no Accrued Liabilities account, your analysis must differ from the formula shown here. First, only $39 of the $45 Selling and Administrative Expense account balance is used to avoid double counting the already analyzed $6 insurance expense.

S & A Expenses

Debit	Credit
39	
6	
45	

Note that the Selling and Administrative Expenses account (refer to item (4) under Fairmont Corporation's additional information) includes the noncash Depreciation Expense account. To determine the cash paid for selling and administrative expenses, the depreciation expense amount must first be calculated and then subtracted from the $39 balance obtained above.

Accumulated Depreciation

	57
3	**8**
	62

The amount of depreciation expense is determined by analyzing both the Accumulated Depreciation account as well as item (2) under additional information. Since the net change in this account was \$5 and since there was a reduction of \$3 during the period, the account must have been increased by the amount of depreciation expense or \$8. Thus, the cash paid for selling and administrative expenses amounts to \$31,000 (\$39 − \$8).

Selling and Adm. Expenses

31	
8	
39	

d. Interest Paid

Cash Basis Interest Expense = Accrual Basis Interest Expense + Beginning Interest Payable − Ending Interest Payable

Since Fairmont Corporation has no Interest Payable account balance, all interest incurred must have been paid. Thus, cash basis interest expense equals the accrual basis interest expense of \$4,500.

e. Taxes Paid

Cash Basis Tax Expense = Accrual Basis Tax Expense + Beginning Taxes Payable − Ending Taxes Payable

Income Taxes Payable

	2,500
Tax Payment	Tax Expense
	4,000

Income Taxes Payable

	2,500
?	15,000
	4,000

Income Taxes Payable

	2,500
13,500	15,000
	4,000

Here, we confirm that expenses exceed payments in the Income Taxes Payable account by \$1,500. Since the income statement reports an expense of \$15,000, the income taxes paid must be \$1,500 lower or \$13,500.

Summary of Cash Flows from Operating Activities The results of the preceding analysis are shown here. Before going further, look at Figure 14A-3 and verify that this information represents the complete operating activities section of the statement of cash flows.

Cash collected from customers	\$205,000
Cash paid for merchandise purchases	(127,000)
Cash paid for insurance	(4,000)
Cash paid for selling and administrative expenses	(31,000)
Interest paid	(4,500)
Income taxes paid	(13,500)
Net cash provided by operating activities	\$ 25,000

FIGURE 14A-3

Fairmont Corporation's statement of cash flows

FAIRMONT CORPORATION
Statement of Cash Flows
For the Year Ended December 31, Year 2

Cash flows from operating activities:		
Cash collected from customers	$205,000	
Cash paid for merchandise purchases	(127,000)	
Cash paid for insurance	(4,000)	
Cash paid for selling and administrative expenses	(31,000)	
Interest paid	(4,500)	
Income taxes paid	(13,500)	
Net cash provided by operating activities		$25,000
Cash flows from investing activities:		
Proceeds from sale of equipment	4,000	
Acquisition of plant and equipment	(15,000)	
Net cash used in investing activities		(11,000)
Cash flows from financing activities:		
Partial retirement of bonds payable	(10,000)	
Issuance of common stock	20,000	
Payment of cash dividend	(4,000)	
Net cash provided by financing activities		6,000
Net increase in cash		20,000
Cash at beginning of year		40,000
Cash at end of year		$60,000

Supplemental schedule of noncash investing and financing activities:

Additional common stock was issued in exchange for an investment in the stock of Longview Corporation having a cost of $5,000.

Analysis of Remaining Balance Sheet Accounts We'll use the following approach to analyze each of the remaining balance sheet accounts:

1. Determine the dollar change in each remaining balance sheet account.
2. Examine the income statement for any relevant information related to the balance sheet account.
3. Examine the additional information for any details related to the specific balance sheet account.
4. If you are unable to immediately explain how the amount of the dollar change came about, utilize a journal entry and/or T-account to facilitate your analysis.
5. Report the cash effect, if any, in a skeleton statement like that shown in Figure 14A-2. Do not proceed to a new balance sheet account until this step has been completed.

Long-Term Investments in Stock Recall that once you have analyzed all noncash current assets and current liabilities affecting operations, you must turn to all remaining balance sheet accounts. In this case, the next account is Long-Term Investments in Stock. Since both this account and the Common Stock account are described in item (1) under Fairmont Corporation's additional information, they are analyzed together as follows:

	Year 1	Year 2	Increase (Decrease)
Long-term investments in stock	$ –0–	$5,000	$5,000
	Year 1	**Year 2**	**Increase (Decrease)**
Common stock, par value $10	$100,000	$125,000	$25,000

Analysis (#1 refers to item (1) under additional information):

Long-Term Investments in Stock (Given – #1)	5,000	
Common Stock (500 shares × $10 par value)		5,000

This transaction represents an investing and financing activity not involving cash flow or direct exchange. As described in Chapter 8, you do not present such a transaction within the *body* of the statement of cash flows but within a supplemental schedule, specifically the supplemental schedule of noncash investing and financing activities.

Plant and Equipment

	Year 1	Year 2	Increase (Decrease)
Plant and equipment	$280,000	$290,000	$10,000

Analysis Although this account increases by $10,000, examination of both the income statement and item (2) under additional information indicates not only an acquisition but also a sale of a depreciable asset. To analyze these effects, it is essential that you take the time to reconstruct the journal entry for the asset sale as shown here:

Cash	**4,000***	
Accumulated Depreciation (Given – #2)	3,000	
Gain (Given from Income Statement)		2,000
Plant and Equipment (Given – #2)		5,000

*Book value of $2,000 plus gain of $2,000 equals proceeds of $4,000

Initially, the $4,000 might emerge as the amount needed for the journal entry to reflect an equality of debits and credits. Ultimately, however, you should confirm that an asset yielding a gain of $2,000 and having a book value of $2,000 ($5,000 cost − $3,000 accumulated depreciation) has been sold for cash of $4,000. The analysis is completed by posting the $5,000 credit to the T-account below to determine how much cash was paid to acquire plant and equipment.

Plant and Equipment	
280	
15	5
290	

Since this overall account increases by $10, which includes a decrease of $5, the account must have increased by $15 during the period.

Since the Plant and Equipment account is associated with investing activities, the cash effects reconstructed above are reported in the statement of cash flows in Figure 14A-3 as follows:

Cash flows from investing activities:		
Proceeds from sale of equipment	$ 4,000	
Acquisition of plant and equipment	(15,000)	
Net cash used in investing activities		(11,000)

Accumulated Depreciation This account was analyzed earlier to determine the cash paid for selling and administrative expenses. It yields no further relevant information about either cash flows from investing activities or cash flows from financing activities.

Dividends Payable Although the Dividends Payable account is a current liability, it never represents an operating activity because the amount of dividends declared has no effect on the income statement, that is, no effect on operations. In general, a dividend represents a financing activity because it is derived from a purchase of capital stock.

	Year 1	Year 2	Increase (Decrease)
Dividends payable	$ –0–	$1,000	$1,000

Analysis The $1,000 increase in this account is best understood by reconstructing the October 10 and December 10 journal entries described in item (3) under additional information.

Dividends Declared	5,000	
Dividends Payable		5,000
Dividends Payable	4,000	
Cash		4,000

The question here is whether it is the declaration or the payment of a dividend that is relevant in a statement of cash flows. Since the declaration of a dividend does not normally involve an immediate cash flow, it is the *payment of cash* that is relevant.

Thus, the $4,000 payment is included as a cash decrease under the heading *cash flows from financing activities.*

Bonds Payable

	Year 1	Year 2	Increase (Decrease)
Bonds payable	$90,000	$80,000	$(10,000)

Analysis Since there is no additional information outside the balance sheet involving the bond liability, the most logical inference is that the bond liability was reduced by a cash payment during the period. Since the Bond Payable account is associated with financing activities, the $10,000 payment is included under the heading *cash flows from financing activities.*

Common Stock

	Year 1	Year 2	Increase (Decrease)
Common stock, par value $10	$100,000	$125,000	$25,000

Analysis Recall from the analysis of the Long-term Investments in Stock account that the Common Stock account was increased by $5,000. Thus, the question is, "What transaction is responsible for the increase in the Common Stock account here from $105,000 to $125,000?"

Common Stock

	100,000
	5,000
	?
	125,000

Since no additional information is provided, the most logical conclusion is that the missing credit represents an issuance of common stock as described in the following journal entry:

Cash	20,000	
Common Stock ($125,000 − $105,000)		20,000

Thus, the $20,000 proceeds are included as a cash increase under the heading *cash flows from financing activities.*

Retained Earnings

	Year 1	Year 2	Increase (Decrease)
Retained earnings	$122,500	$140,000	$17,500

Analysis Since all activity in this account was previously identified (net income from the income statement and the dividend declared in item (3) under additional information), the function of the T-account shown here is to simply provide one last check on the accuracy of the earlier analyses:

Retained Earnings

		122,500	
#3	5,000	22,500	net income
		140,000	

The cash effects of the analysis that began with the Dividends Payable account and ended with the Common Stock account are reported in the complete statement of cash flows (Figure 14A-3) as follows:

Cash flows from financing activities:		
Partial retirement of bonds payable	$(10,000)	
Issuance of common stock	20,000	
Payment of cash dividend	(4,000)	
Net cash provided by financing activities		6,000

Conclusion

Figure 14A-3 shows the result of our three-step analysis, a completed and properly formatted statement of cash flows. Notice how Performance Objective 56 shown here is satisfied:

YOUR PERFORMANCE OBJECTIVE 56
Using the technique of T-account analysis, **prepare** or **construct** a statement of cash flows given comparative balance sheets, an income statement, and relevant additional information.

To master this Performance Objective with additional practice, refer to the Appendix 14–2 exercises and problems.

Making Business Decisions

YOUR PERFORMANCE OBJECTIVE 2
(page 18)

Congratulations! In this chapter you have worked through a great deal of financial analysis for both The Gap and The Limited. And now suppose that you had to decide in which company you should invest. You are reading this textbook at least one year after Gap and The Limited issued their fiscal year 2001 annual reports. Much can happen in even a few months, so you need to analyze these companies in light of any new information that is now available to you. One factor to consider, for example, is the climate of consumer confidence in the United States in the aftermath of the World Trade Center and Pentagon bombings of September 11, 2001 and the weak economy and stock market of 2002.

Required

1. Go online or contact the companies to secure *current* versions of the 10-K and annual report for The Gap and The Limited.
2. Following the model we used in this chapter, evaluate these businesses by using any analytical tools that you believe are relevant. Be sure to document your analysis with supporting calculations.
3. In which of these companies, if either, would you invest your money? Why?

Making Business Decisions

YOUR PERFORMANCE OBJECTIVE 2
(page 18)

Your friend, Peter Van Holland, has always loved automobiles, especially Mercedes Benz. In school he dreamed about being a mechanic and owning his own auto repair business. After high school, he immediately began working for The Auto Haus, a large, successful Mercedes dealership. Fifteen years later, Peter was living his dream. He had moved up from apprentice to master technician and was a valued member of the Auto Haus staff.

But Peter's dream was not completely fulfilled. He still wanted to own his own business, and now that might happen. Last week, he received a phone call from Jeffrey Wong, a commercial broker, who told him about Bruckner Auto, a small Mercedes dealership that was for sale. Peter knew a little about this dealership. Fritz Bruckner had owned it for about 25 years. The physical plant was sort of run down, and Peter had heard comments from his customers over the years about how Fritz had scaled back his hours and was very selective in the automobiles he chose to work on. A portion of Bruckner Auto's business involved buying and selling foreign cars, but Peter wasn't interested in that aspect of the business. When he heard that Fritz would consider selling just the auto repair business, he told Jeffrey that he was interested. Jeffrey agreed to meet with him and give him copies of Bruckner Auto's financial statements.

When Peter discovered that you had just finished a financial accounting course, he called you to ask for your help in evaluating the merits of this business.

Required

1. Using the accompanying income statement (Figure 14-5), balance sheet (Figure 14-6), statement of cash flows (Figure 14-7), and owner's cash flow worksheet (Figure 14-8), evaluate Bruckner Auto. Use any analytical tools that you believe are relevant. Be sure to document your analysis with supporting calculations.
2. Describe any additional types of information that would have been helpful in evaluating this business.

FIGURE 14-5

BRUCKNER AUTO
Income Statements
For the Years Ended December 31, 2003 and 2004
and for December of each year

	2004		2003	
	December	12 Months	December	12 Months
Revenue				
Sales resale	30.00	7,845.50	76.35	260.35
Sales—parts	11,708.29	122,705.71	6,536.59	95,095.48
Sales—sublet	634.02	5,154.91	192.00	1,620.00
Sales—labor	11,135.00	107,638.37	8,560.70	99,254.10
Sales—auto	23,599.16	112,443.41	2,700.00	85,860.00
Sales other	8.00	998.66	11.40	867.35
Returns and allowances	0.00	287.75	0.00	624.60
Freight income	0.00	0.00	0.00	13.00
Miscellaneous income	0.00	70.13	0.00	0.00
Net sales	47,114.47	356,568.94	18,077.04	282,345.68
Cost of goods sold				
Purchases	5,088.60	79,948.85	3,742.45	65,653.61
Sub contract labor	0.00	4,327.50	900.00	6,375.00
Outside services	0.00	5,295.16	345.00	651.00
Autos	12,842.98	65,324.89	608.66	38,136.67
Freight	0.00	53.95	0.00	132.83
Total cost of goods sold	17,931.58	154,950.35	5,596.11	110,949.11
Gross profit	29,182.89	201,618.59	12,480.93	171,396.57
Expenses				
Salaries	2,588.30	24,959.60	2,088.30	25,059.53
Officer's salaries	3,850.00	46,775.00	3,850.00	42,925.00
Payroll taxes	454.28	5,648.16	454.28	5,492.97
Advertising	139.00	1,165.78	105.00	2,884.76
Alarm maintenance	13.76	249.27	12.00	288.12
Auto expense	300.76	5,758.92	109.15	4,279.74
Bank service charges	261.90	3,613.09	213.53	2,422.47
Cash variations	(136.29)	95.76	(206.77)	(1,271.81)
Contributions	25.00	835.00	880.00	1,110.00
Depreciation	1,000.00	12,000.00	1,000.00	14,628.00
Dues and subscriptions	220.00	1,749.60	54.00	921.74
Education	0.00	0.00	0.00	300.00
Equipment lease	840.60	7,369.61	0.00	76.54
Industrial insurance	0.00	1,707.89	0.00	1,579.78
Insurance	765.41	6,553.75	659.16	7,245.04
Interest expense	764.54	10,849.86	4,175.31	12,611.48
Shop cloths/laundry	146.26	1,563.09	147.89	1,432.96
Licenses	16.00	1,401.65	60.80	1,996.87
Office expense	479.96	2,490.76	173.86	2,768.01
Outside services	126.00	156.00	0.00	5,364.62
Postage	66.00	876.82	79.80	444.44
Professional fees	1,250.00	4,890.00	250.00	3,815.00
Rent	0.00	5,000.00	0.00	2,500.00
Repairs and maintenance	234.94	1,873.61	0.00	1,761.69
Returned checks	0.00	0.00	0.00	162.37
Supplies	412.34	4,471.09	508.91	3,541.09
Small tools	338.50	3,892.39	98.38	5,561.27
Taxes—property	0.00	2,539.89	0.00	2,286.23
Telephone	168.64	4,399.41	439.14	5,151.55
Travel	521.60	2,559.57	0.00	1,446.03
Uniforms	0.00	465.71	0.00	107.59
Utilities	330.69	4,220.15	377.35	5,088.22
Total expenses	15,178.19	170,131.43	15,530.09	163,981.30
Net operating income	14,004.70	31,487.16	(3,049.16)	7,415.27
Other revenue				
Total other revenue	0.00	0.00	0.00	0.00
Other expenses				
Loss on sale of asset	0.00	9,310.20	0.00	0.00
Total other expenses	0.00	9,310.20	0.00	0.00
Income before taxes	14,004.70	22,176.96	(3,049.16)	7,415.27
Net income	14,004.70	22,176.96	(3,049.16)	7,415.27

FIGURE 14-6

BRUCKNER AUTO
Balance Sheet
As of December 31, 2004 and 2003

	12/31/2004			12/31/2003		
			Assets			
Current Assets						
Cash	9,955.44			4,872.58		
Due from stockholders	4,022.22			13,189.00		
Invent.—parts and supplies	4,848.00			4,848.00		
Inventory—Vehicles	22,800.00			19,800.00		
Total current assets		41,625.66			42,709.58	
Fixed Assets						
Machinery and equipment	77,028.04			72,004.63		
Buildings	53,446.66			53,446.66		
Land	45,000.00			45,000.00		
Vehicles	85,110.57			113,907.57		
Improvements	9,822.79			2,961.54		
Accumulated depreciation	(146,387.90)			(119,203.90)		
Total fixed assets		124,020.16			168,116.50	
Other Assets						
Total other assets		0.00			0.00	
Total assets			165,645.82			210,826.08
			Liabilities and Equity			
Current Liabilities						
Customer deposit	5,280.00			1,500.00		
Payroll taxes payable	2,167.42			2,167.48		
Sales tax payable	2,310.32			642.56		
Current portion of notes payable	11,008.42			11,008.42		
Total current liabilities		20,766.16			15,318.46	
Long-Term Liabilities						
Notes payable	74,478.95			127,434.03		
Less: Current portion	(11,008.42)			(11,008.42)		
Total long-term liability		63,470.53			116,425.61	
Total liabilities			84,236.69			131,744.07
Stockholders' Equity						
Common stock		10,000.00			10,000.00	
Addn. paid-in capital		35,000.00			35,000.00	
Dividends		3,842.00			0.00	
Retained earnings		18,074.17			26,666.74	
Current earnings		22,176.96			7,415.27	
Total Equity			81,409.13			79,082.01
Total Liabilities and Equity			165,645.82			210,826.08

FIGURE 14-7

BRUCKNER AUTO
Statement of Cash Flows
For the Periods Ended December 31, 2003 and 2004
Increase (Decrease) in Cash or Cash Equivalents

		12/31/2004		12/31/2003
Cash flow from operating activities				
Net Income (loss)		$22,176.96		$ 7,415.27
Adjustments to Reconcile Cash Flow				
Depreciation	12,000.00		14,628.00	
Decrease (increase) in Current Assets	4,836.00		(13,189.00)	
Increase (decrease) in Current Liabilities	6,947.70		1,988.41	
Total adjustments		23,783.70		3,427.41
Cash provided (used) by operations		45,960.66		10,842.68
Cash flow from investing activities				
Sales (purchases) of assets		15,540.80		(36,417.67)
Cash flow from financing activities				
Cash (used) or provided by Miscellaneous Items		(52,576.60)		20,674.20
Dividends paid		(3,842.00)		0.00
Net Increase (decrease) in cash		5,082.86		(4,900.79)
Cash at beginning of period		4,872.58		9,773.37
Cash at end of period		$ 9,955.44		$ 4,872.58

FIGURE 14-8

OWNER'S CASH FLOW

Business Name Bruckner Auto
Time Period 2004 (12 months)
Net Profit (Sellers Statement) $ 31,487.-

Add Back to Demonstrate "Owners Cash Flow"

Depreciation	$ 12,000.-
Amortization of Other Costs	$ -
Debt Service (Loan Interest)	$ 10,849.-
Owner's Salary (Corporations Only)	$ 46,775.-
Manger's Salary (Adsentee Owned Business Only)	$ -

Personal Expenses and Benefits

Promotions	$ -
Personal Insurance benefits	$ 4,758.-
Travel and Entertainment	$ 2,559.-
Personal Automobile	$ 13,127.-
Other (Specify)	$ -

Expenses Buyer Might Eliminate

Equipment Rental Rent Paid to owner for other space	$ 5,000.-
Discounts and Refunds	$ -
Bad Debt Write-Offs	$ -
Donations (Charitable, etc.)	$ 835.-
Extra Employee(s) (Relatives, etc.)	$ -
Others (Specify) Property Tax Expense	$ 2,539.-

Other Gross Sales, Trades, etc. (Seller to Explain)

$ -

DRAFT

Total "Add Back" Adjustments $ 98,442.-
Owner's Total Cash Flow $ 129,929.-

Owner warrants that the cash flow hereby demonstrated is reasonably accurate for the time period reflected.

Signature Needs seller approval Date
Owner/Seller

3. As Peter's financial advisor, what questions would you ask Fritz Bruckner about his business to provide a more complete picture. *Hint*: What is the nature of "Miscellaneous Items" in the Statement of Cash Flows?
4. Given the data available, make your recommendations to Peter.

Questions

YOUR PERFORMANCE OBJECTIVE 4 *(page 22)*

14-1 Explain in your own words the meaning of each of the following key business terms.
a. Return on common stockholders' equity ratio
b. Return on assets ratio
c. Du Pont Formula
d. Price-earnings ratio
e. Book value per share
f. Dividend yield
g. SIC Code

Capstone Projects

Instead of questions, reinforcement exercises, critical thinking problems, and research assignments, this chapter's end of chapter material includes capstone financial analysis projects, which require similar analyses as were done in this chapter with The Gap.

C14-1 Comparing The Gap to Another Company Having the Same SIC Code
Choose an annual report of a company within SIC Code 5651 and compare this company with The Gap. Write a three- to five-page report in which you analyze this company's financial statements. Be sure to include the MD&A and the Notes in your analysis. Use the headings found in this chapter as a guide to your analysis.

C14-2 Comparing The Limited to Another Company Having the Same SIC Code
Choose an annual report of a company within SIC Code 5621 and compare this company with The Limited. Write a three- to five-page report in which you analyze this company's financial statements. Be sure to include the MD&A and the Notes in your analysis. Use the headings found in this chapter as a guide to your analysis.

C14-3 Analyzing a Company's Financial Statements in Depth
Choose an annual report of a company from an industry other than retailing. Write a three- to five-page report in which you analyze this company's financial statements. Be sure to include the MD&A and the Notes in your analysis. Use the headings found in this chapter as a guide to your analysis.

C14-4 Making an Investment Decision Using an Annual Report
Suppose you had $5,000 to invest in a single company's stock. Choose an annual report of a company in which you might like to invest. Using the entire annual report and paying particular attention to the financial statements, write a two- to three-page explanation of why you would or would not invest $5,000 in this company.

C14-5 Comparing Two Competing Companies
Choose two annual reports of companies who compete against one another in the same type of industry. Examples include Exxon Mobil and Chevron-Texaco, Staples, Inc. and OfficeMax, Inc., or Gateway and Dell Computer Corporation. Write a four- to six-page report in which you explain in detail which of the two companies is financially stronger.

C14-6 Describing How Financial Statement Amounts Are Calculated
Choose the annual report of a company in which you have an interest. Using its balance sheet and income statement, describe how the balance in each major asset, liability, owners' equity, revenue, and expense account is calculated. For example, if the annual report indicates that the company uses straight-line depreciation, you would describe how depreciation expense is calculated given information about the original cost, useful lives, and salvage values of depreciable assets.

Appendix 14-2 Reinforcement Exercises

AE14-1 Calculating Specific Statement of Cash Flow Effects

YOUR PERFORMANCE OBJECTIVE 56 *(page 807)*

The comparative balance sheet of the Heavy Metal Gymnasium showed a balance in the Gym Equipment account at December 31, Year 2, of $2,460,000; at December 31, Year 1, the balance was $2,400,000. The Accumulated Depreciation account showed a balance of $860,000 at December 31, Year 2, and $760,000 at December 31, Year 1. The statement of cash flows reports that cash outflows for gym equipment during the year amounted to $130,000. The income statement reports depreciation expense of $120,000 for the year and a gain of $5,300 from the sale of gym equipment in the determination of net income.

Required

a. Calculate the acquisition cost of the equipment retired during the year.
b. Calculate the accumulated depreciation of the equipment retired during the year.
c. Calculate the proceeds from the sale of the equipment.
d. Present the effects of these transactions as they would appear in the statement of cash flows.

AE14-2 Calculating Specific Statement of Cash Flow Effects

YOUR PERFORMANCE OBJECTIVE 56 *(page 807)*

The following data were taken from comparative trial balances of the Fast Track Runners Corporation:

	December 31	
	Year 1	**Year 2**
Accounts receivable	$150,000	$190,000
Interest receivable	700	500
Inventories	200,000	220,000
Prepaid insurance	1,000	1,800
Accounts payable	190,000	230,000
Other accrued liabilities	10,000	8,000
Net sales		800,000
Interest revenue		1,500
Cost of goods sold		600,000
Insurance expense		2,000
Accrued operating expenses		80,000

In addition, you determined that the firm keeps its books on the accrual basis. Included in operating expenses are depreciation of $2,000 and amortization expense of $1,000.

Required

Determine the following information:

a. Cash basis sales
b. Interest income collected during the year
c. Cash paid for insurance during the year
d. Cash paid for inventory purchases during the year
e. Cash paid for operating expenses during the year
f. Cash generated from operations

Appendix 14-2 Critical Thinking Problems

AP14-1 Preparing a Statement of Cash Flows

YOUR PERFORMANCE OBJECTIVE 56 *(page 807)*

Here are the balance sheets of Tyson Corporation as of December 31, Year 1 and Year 2 and the income statement for the year ended December 31, Year 2.

Balance Sheets

	Year 1	Year 2	Increase (Decrease)
Assets			
Cash	$ 1,200	$ 1,400	$ 200
Accounts receivable, net	3,600	4,000	400
Merchandise inventory	6,300	6,400	100
Land	1,100	1,100	–0–
Buildings and equipment	30,000	31,300	1,300
Less: Accumulated depreciation	(16,000)	(16,700)	(700)
Total assets	$26,200	$27,500	$1,300
Liabilities and Stockholders' Equity			
Accounts payable	$ 4,500	$ 4,800	$ 300
Notes payable (current)	1,400	1,300	(100)
Mortgage payable	4,000	4,000	–0–
Common stock	10,000	10,400	400
Retained earnings	6,300	7,000	700
Total liabilities and owners' equity	$26,200	$27,500	$1,300

Income Statement

Net sales		$40,000
Operating expenses:		
Cost of goods sold	$22,000	
Selling and administrative expense	15,000	37,000
Operating income		3,000
Other income (expense):		
Loss on sale of equipment	(60)	
Interest expense	(440)	(500)
Pretax income		2,500
Income tax expense (40%)		1,000
Net income		$ 1,500

Additional Information

a. Equipment, with $400 of accumulated depreciation and an original cost of $500, was sold.
b. The Selling and Administrative Expense account includes depreciation expense.

Required

Prepare a statement of cash flows for Tyson Corporation.

YOUR PERFORMANCE OBJECTIVE 56
(page 807)

AP14-2 Preparing a Statement of Cash Flows

Here are the balance sheets of Footloose Corporation as of December 31, Year 1 and Year 2 and the income statement for the year ended December 31, Year 2.

Balance Sheets

	Year 1	Year 2	Increase (Decrease)
Assets			
Cash	$ 267	$ 240	$ (27)
Accounts receivable, net	223	325	102
Merchandise inventory	521	671	150
Land	142	153	11
Buildings and equipment	3,364	3,556	192
Less: Accumulated depreciation	(857)	(1,041)	(184)
Total assets	$3,660	$3,904	$244

(continued on next page)

(continued from previous page)

Liabilities and Stockholders' Equity			
Accounts payable	$ 138	$ 231	$ 93
Accrued liabilities	301	392	91
Income taxes payable	117	104	(13)
Bonds payable	995	971	(24)
Common stock	807	827	20
Retained earnings	1,302	1,379	77
Total Equities	$3,660	$3,904	$244

Income Statement

Net sales		$2,400
Operating expenses:		
Cost of goods sold	$1,600	
Selling and administrative expense	543	2,143
Operating income		257
Other income (expense):		
Gain on sale of equipment	3	
Interest expense	(60)	(57)
Pretax income		200
Income tax expense (40%)		80
Net income		$ 120

Additional Information

a. Equipment originally costing $53 was sold for $30. There were no acquisitions of equipment.
b. The Selling and Administrative Expense account includes depreciation expense.
c. The Accrued Liabilities account does not include interest payable.
d. On February 1 of Year 2, Footloose issued common stock with a fair market value of $11 in exchange for land.

Required

Prepare a statement of cash flows for Footloose Corporation.

AP14-3 Preparing a Statement of Cash Flows

Here are the balance sheets of Vincent Corporation as of December 31, Year 1 and Year 2 and the income statement for the year ended December 31, Year 2.

YOUR PERFORMANCE OBJECTIVE 56
(page 807)

Balance Sheets

	Year 1	Year 2	Increase (Decrease)
Assets			
Cash	$ 40,000	$ 70,000	$30,000
Accounts receivable, net	38,000	40,000	2,000
Merchandise inventory	55,000	50,000	(5,000)
Accrued interest receivable	–0–	2,000	2,000
Buildings and equipment	50,000	50,000	–0–
Less: Accumulated depreciation	(8,000)	(12,000)	(4,000)
Total assets	$175,000	$200,000	$25,000

(continued on next page)

(continued from previous page)

Liabilities and Stockholders' Equity			
Accounts payable	$ 46,000	$ 53,000	$ 7,000
Salaries payable	1,000	2,000	1,000
Mortgage payable	25,000	20,000	(5,000)
Common stock	25,000	25,000	–0–
Retained earnings	78,000	100,000	22,000
Total liabilities and owners' equity	$175,000	$200,000	$25,000

Income Statement

Net sales		$176,000
Operating expenses:		
Cost of goods sold	$136,000	
Selling and administrative expense	16,000	152,000
Operating income		24,000
Other income (expense):		
Interest revenue	3,000	
Interest expense	2,000	1,000
Net income		$ 25,000

Additional Information

a. Vincent Corporation pays no income tax.

b. There were no acquisitions or sales of buildings and equipment.

c. The Selling and Administrative Expense account includes only depreciation expense and salaries expense.

Required

Prepare a statement of cash flows for Vincent Corporation.

APPENDIX

Performance Objectives A

YOUR PERFORMANCE OBJECTIVE 1
Prepare a simple operating budget and **explain** its usefulness.

YOUR PERFORMANCE OBJECTIVE 1
Explain the purposes of budgets and **prepare** both a simple operating budget and a simple cash budget.

YOUR PERFORMANCE OBJECTIVE 2
Identify several ways in which financial accounting information is used to make business and personal decisions.

YOUR PERFORMANCE OBJECTIVE 3
Calculate the return on equity ratio and **discuss** its usefulness and limitations in making decisions.

YOUR PERFORMANCE OBJECTIVE 3
Calculate at least one financial statement ratio within each of the following five categories, **interpret** its meaning, and **discuss** its usefulness and limitations in making decisions:

a. liquidity—e.g., current ratio and acid test ratio.
b. activity or turnover—e.g., average collection period
c. financial leverage—e.g., debt to equity ratio
d. profitability—e.g., return on equity and profit margin ratio
e. valuation—e.g., price earnings ratio and dividend yield

YOUR PERFORMANCE OBJECTIVE 4
Explain *in your own words* the meaning of key business terms.

YOUR PERFORMANCE OBJECTIVE 5

Apply the fundamental accounting equation, Assets = Liabilities + Owner's Equity, to:

a. **analyze** the effects of accounting transactions on the elements of the balance sheet and
b. **prepare** a balance sheet that reports the financial condition of any entity.

YOUR PERFORMANCE OBJECTIVE 5a

Analyze the effects of accounting transactions on the fundamental accounting equation, that is, the primary elements of the balance sheet.

YOUR PERFORMANCE OBJECTIVE 5b

Prepare a balance sheet that reports the financial condition of any entity.

YOUR PERFORMANCE OBJECTIVE 6

Identify and **apply** the three conditions necessary for a transaction to qualify as an accounting transaction and, therefore, be recorded in an accounting information system.

YOUR PERFORMANCE OBJECTIVE 7

a. **Define** the terms *financing activities*, *investing activities*, and *operating activities*,
b. **Classify** any accounting transaction into one of these activities or a noncash investing and financing activity, and
c. **Classify** any cash receipt or cash payment transaction into the appropriate activity as reported in the statement of cash flows.

YOUR PERFORMANCE OBJECTIVE 8

Explain what role ethics plays in the preparation of financial statements.

YOUR PERFORMANCE OBJECTIVE 9

Identify the types of decisions investors and creditors make and **describe** what information in the financial statements and/or related disclosures meets the information needs of each group.

YOUR PERFORMANCE OBJECTIVE 10

Prepare an income statement that reports the results of operations of any entity.

YOUR PERFORMANCE OBJECTIVE 10

Prepare a single-step and/or a multiple-step income statement that reports the results of operations of any entity.

YOUR PERFORMANCE OBJECTIVE 11
Differentiate the balance sheet from the income statement by being able to:

a. **distinguish between** transactions that do and do not affect the income statement.
b. **classify** account titles into asset, liability, owners' equity, and income statement accounts.

YOUR PERFORMANCE OBJECTIVE 12
Prepare a statement of owners' equity that reports the changes in owner equity accounts for any entity.

YOUR PERFORMANCE OBJECTIVE 13
Link the following related financial statements—balance sheet, income statement, and statement of owners' equity—by being able to **calculate** missing amounts in each of them.

YOUR PERFORMANCE OBJECTIVE 13
From your understanding of financial statement relationships,

a. **link** the following related financial statements—balance sheet, income statement, and statement of owners' equity—by being able to **calculate** missing amounts in each of them.
b. **analyze** accounting transactions to **determine** their effect—increase, or decrease, understatement or overstatement, or no effect—on the elements of *both* the balance sheet and the income statement.

YOUR PERFORMANCE OBJECTIVE 14
Navigate through and **locate** information in an annual report, so that you can make informed decisions about that entity's financing, investing, and operating activities.

YOUR PERFORMANCE OBJECTIVE 15
Describe how information sources other than the corporate annual report (e.g., quarterly reports and SEC Form 10-K) can be used to learn more about the nature of an entity's business.

YOUR PERFORMANCE OBJECTIVE 16
Describe how the amounts reported on the income statement and balance sheet are determined by:

a. **distinguishing** among the following valuation methods: historical cost, replacement cost, fair market value, and the present value of future cash flows.
b. **identifying** the generally accepted valuation method for each of the major asset and liability accounts.

YOUR PERFORMANCE OBJECTIVE 17
Identify several limitations of the financial statements found in the annual report.

YOUR PERFORMANCE OBJECTIVE 18
Distinguish between the accrual and cash basis of income measurement by being able to:

a. **prepare** both an accrual basis and a cash basis income statement from the same set of facts.
b. **explain** why the accrual basis generally provides a more precise income measurement than does the cash basis.
c. **convert** a cash basis income statement into an accrual basis income statement.
d. **describe** transactions in which cash flows precede, coincide with, or follow the period in which both revenues and expenses are recognized under the accrual basis.
e. **explain** how accrual basis net income differs from both the net cash flow from operating activities and the change in the cash balance for the period

YOUR PERFORMANCE OBJECTIVE 19

a. **prepare** the adjustments needed at the end of the period using transaction analysis.
b. **determine** the amount of both related balance sheet and income statement accounts after adjustments have been made.

YOUR PERFORMANCE OBJECTIVE 20
Categorize all income statement accounts into *one* of the following four categories:

a. primary operating activities that are expected to continue
b. peripheral activities that are expected to continue
c. primary operating activities that are discontinued
d. peripheral activities that are not expected to continue

YOUR PERFORMANCE OBJECTIVE 21
Discuss the criteria used to determine when revenue is recognized, and then, given specific details about an entity, **apply** these criteria to that entity to **determine** when its revenue should be recognized.

YOUR PERFORMANCE OBJECTIVE 22
Prepare in good form a bank reconciliation using the adjusted balance format and **prepare** the adjustments necessitated by this reconciliation.

YOUR PERFORMANCE OBJECTIVE 23
Explain the basic components of internal control and **describe** the attributes of an effective and efficient internal control system.

YOUR PERFORMANCE OBJECTIVE 24
Explain the meaning of the words "debit" and "credit" and **use** the debit-credit rules (double entry method of bookkeeping) in all phases of the accounting process.

YOUR PERFORMANCE OBJECTIVE 25
Select a likely account title for one-half of a transaction when given the account title for the other half of the transaction.

YOUR PERFORMANCE OBJECTIVE 26
Identify, list and perform in their proper sequence each of the following steps normally followed in the accounting process/cycle for preparation of the principal financial statements:

a. **identify** accounting transactions and **measure** their effects
b. **journalize** transaction entries
c. **post** journal entries to the individual accounts in the ledger
d. **prepare** an unadjusted trial balance
e. **journalize and post** adjusting and correcting entries
f. **prepare** an adjusted trial balance
g. **prepare** the financial statements
h. **journalize and post** closing entries
i. **prepare** a post-closing trial balance

YOUR PERFORMANCE OBJECTIVE 27
Apply t-account analysis to **calculate** the missing amount in an account (i.e. beginning balance, ending balance, increase or decrease) when three of the four amounts are given, and **record** the transaction that accounts for the missing information.

YOUR PERFORMANCE OBJECTIVE 28
Describe the nature of the specific transactions whose effects are posted to the increase side and the decrease side of a particular t-account.

YOUR PERFORMANCE OBJECTIVE 29
Prepare an accrual basis income statement by applying T-account analysis to balance sheet accounts and cash receipts/cash payments information.

YOUR PERFORMANCE OBJECTIVE 30
Distinguish among the sole proprietorship, partnership, and corporate forms of entity both as to their characteristics and their respective advantages and disadvantages and **apply** these differences in your preparation of each entity's primary financial statements.

YOUR PERFORMANCE OBJECTIVE 31
Describe the key differences in the financial statements of merchandisers, manufacturers, construction companies, non-financial service companies, and financial service companies; and **explain** how these differences reflect the financing, investing, and operating activities of each form of industry.

YOUR PERFORMANCE OBJECTIVE 32
Calculate net income, and **prepare** both the income statements and balance sheets under the percentage of completion and completed-contract methods.

YOUR PERFORMANCE OBJECTIVE 33
Prepare a consolidated balance sheet given both parent and subsidiary balance sheets and any additional information necessary.

YOUR PERFORMANCE OBJECTIVE 34
Identify the differences between the periodic and perpetual inventory systems, **describe** the effects of transactions appropriate to each system, and **discuss** the situations in which each system is most appropriate.

YOUR PERFORMANCE OBJECTIVE 35
Select those year-end inventory transactions that should be included and those that should be excluded from the year-end inventory and **calculate** the appropriate cost of all inventory units on hand.

YOUR PERFORMANCE OBJECTIVE 36
Calculate the balances in ending inventory and cost of goods sold for the specific identification method and the FIFO, LIFO, and average cost flow assumptions under both a periodic and perpetual inventory system.

YOUR PERFORMANCE OBJECTIVE 37
Identify the differences between the FIFO and LIFO inventory cost flow assumptions and **explain** the relative advantages and disadvantages of adopting each as the cost-flow assumption.

YOUR PERFORMANCE OBJECTIVE 38
Determine the effect (overstatement, understatement, or none) of an inventory error on both balance sheet and income statement amounts.

YOUR PERFORMANCE OBJECTIVE 39
Calculate the estimated cost of goods sold and cost of ending inventory using the gross margin method.

YOUR PERFORMANCE OBJECTIVE 40
Explain the principle of conservatism and **apply** it when accounting for inventories and investments with the lower of cost or market method.

YOUR PERFORMANCE OBJECTIVE 41
Distinguish between the percentage of sales method and the percentage of receivables method for estimating uncollectible amounts in the Allowance for Bad Debts account.

YOUR PERFORMANCE OBJECTIVE 42
Explain how inventories and accounts receivable can be mismanaged and **describe** how financial statement analysis can be used to evaluate how effectively these resources are being managed.

YOUR PERFORMANCE OBJECTIVE 43
Determine which costs should be capitalized and which should be expensed when several costs associated with the purchase of a depreciable or intangible asset are incurred.

YOUR PERFORMANCE OBJECTIVE 44
Describe how depreciation is calculated and **calculate** depreciation expense for any period desired under each of the following depreciation methods: straight-line, double-declining-balance, and sum-of-the-years' digits.

YOUR PERFORMANCE OBJECTIVE 45
Describe how depletion is calculated using the units of production method and **present** the financial statement effects of this calculation.

YOUR PERFORMANCE OBJECTIVE 46
Describe how amortization is calculated using the straight-line method and **present** the financial statement effects of this calculation.

YOUR PERFORMANCE OBJECTIVE 47
Determine the proper valuation of both current and non-current debt and equity securities at the end of a period, **record** all investment in debt and equity security related transactions, and **present** the complete financial statement effects of this set of transactions.

YOUR PERFORMANCE OBJECTIVE 48
Distinguish between the cost/fair value method and the equity method of accounting for minority investments in equity securities.

YOUR PERFORMANCE OBJECTIVE 49
Calculate simple interest on a note payable, **record** the transactions related to its issuance, interest accrual, and payment at maturity, and **present** its financial statement effects.

YOUR PERFORMANCE OBJECTIVE 50
Calculate all employee and employer amounts related to a company's payroll liability, **record** these amounts, and **present** their financial statement effects.

YOUR PERFORMANCE OBJECTIVE 51
Apply the present value concept to measure and report the effects of such transactions as credit card accounts, general notes, automobile loans, home loans, leases, bonds, and pensions by being able to:

a. **calculate** the initial present value of all future cash flows, all subsequent present values (construct an amortization table), and the interest revenue and/or interest expense over the transaction's life;
b. **record** all transaction related effects from both perspectives; and
c. **present** the balance sheet, income statement, and statement of cash flow transaction related effects.

YOUR PERFORMANCE OBJECTIVE 52
Distinguish between the financial statement effects of the operating lease and capital lease methods.

YOUR PERFORMANCE OBJECTIVE 53
Distinguish between the financial statement effects of the effective interest and straight-line methods of bond amortization.

YOUR PERFORMANCE OBJECTIVE 54
Calculate income tax expense, income tax payable and deferred income tax for each period; **record** the related transaction; and **present** the financial statement effects of that transaction.

YOUR PERFORMANCE OBJECTIVE 55
Calculate, record, and **present** the financial statement effects of the following stockholder equity transactions: capital stock issuances and retirements; cash dividends, stock dividends, and stock split declarations; and treasury stock repurchases and reissues.

YOUR PERFORMANCE OBJECTIVE 56
Using the technique of T-account analysis, **prepare or construct** a statement of cash flows given comparative balance sheets, an income statement and relevant additional information.

Compound Interest Performance Objectives for Appendix 12-1

PERFORMANCE OBJECTIVE CI-1
Explain the concept of interest from the perspective of both a borrower and a lender.

PERFORMANCE OBJECTIVE CI-2
Define and **distinguish between** simple and compound interest.

PERFORMANCE OBJECTIVE CI-3
Calculate both simple and compound interest.

PERFORMANCE OBJECTIVE CI-4
Define the terms *future value, compound interest, time line,* and *interest factor.*

PERFORMANCE OBJECTIVE CI-5
Distinguish between the primary (Fundamental Equation of Compound Interest) and the secondary future value formulas.

PERFORMANCE OBJECTIVE CI-6
Apply the three-step solution approach to solve a future value problem.

PERFORMANCE OBJECTIVE CI-7
Identify the appropriate interest rate and number of periods you must use when interest is compounded more frequently than annually.

PERFORMANCE OBJECTIVE CI-8
Distinguish between the future value interest concept and the present value interest concept.

PERFORMANCE OBJECTIVE CI-9
Define the terms *present value, discount rate* and *discounting.*

PERFORMANCE OBJECTIVE CI-10
Apply the three-step solution approach to solve a present value problem.

PERFORMANCE OBJECTIVE CI-11
Define the terms *annuity, rent, annuity in arrears,* and *annuity in advance.*

PERFORMANCE OBJECTIVE CI-12
Distinguish between:

a. an annuity problem and a non-annuity problem,
b. an annuity in arrears and an annuity in advance,
c. a future value of an annuity and a present value of an annuity, and the Future Value of Annuity Table and the Present Value of Annuity Table.

PERFORMANCE OBJECTIVE CI-13
Determine which annuity table (future value or present value) is appropriate in a given situation.

PERFORMANCE OBJECTIVE CI-14
Apply the three-step solution approach to solve an annuity problem.

APPENDIX

B

Commonly Used Account Titles

Assets

Current Assets

Accounts receivable
Advances to employees
Allowance for bad debts/Allowance for uncollectibles/Allowance for doubtful accounts
Cash/Cash equivalents/Cash on hand/Cash checking/Cash savings/Undeposited cash/Petty cash
Commissions receivable
Construction in progress/Construction in process
Deposits
Dividend receivable
Finished goods inventory
Interest receivable
Loans receivable/Notes receivable
Manufacturing supplies inventory
Marketable securities/Short-term investments
Merchandise inventory
Other receivables
Prepaid assets:
- Prepaid insurance/Unexpired insurance
- Prepaid interest
- Prepaid rent/Unexpired rent
- Prepaid supplies
- Prepaid taxes

Progress billings
Raw materials inventory
Rent receivable
Supplies inventory/Office supplies on hand
Work-in-process inventory

Long-Term Investments

Investment in bonds/Investment in debt securities
Investment in stock/Investment in equity securities
Investment securities
- Available-for-sale securities
- Held-to-maturity securities
- Trading securities

Land held for future use
Long-term receivables
Notes receivable
Security deposit receivable

Property, Plant, and Equipment/Fixed Assets/Plant Assets

Accumulated depreciation/Allowance for depreciation
Buildings
Equipment
- Computer equipment
- Manufacturing equipment
- Office equipment
- Store equipment

Furniture and fixtures/Office furniture

Land
Land improvements
Leasehold improvements
Vehicles/Autos and trucks

Natural Resources
Accumulated depletion/Allowance for depletion
Acquisition and exploration costs
Development costs
Mineral deposits
Oil and gas reserves
Production costs
Timber tracts

Intangible Assets
Accumulated amortization/Allowance for amortization
Copyright
Franchise
Goodwill
Leased assets/Capital leases
Organization costs
Patent
Trademark

Liabilities

Current Liabilities
Accounts payable
Accrued liabilities
Advances from customers, Deferred revenue, Unearned Revenue, Revenue received in advance
Bonuses payable
Credit line payable
Current portion of long-term debt
Discount on notes payable
Dividends payable
Estimated tax liability
Federal income taxes payable/Federal withholding payable
Federal unemployment taxes payable
FICA taxes payable
Health insurance payable
Insurance payable
Interest payable
Loans payable—bank
Loans payable—other
Notes payable—bank
Notes payable—other
Property taxes payable
Salaries payable/Wages payable
Sales tax payable
State income taxes payable/State withholding payable
State unemployment taxes payable
Union dues payable
Vacation pay payable
Vouchers payable

Long-Term Liabilities
Bank loan payable
Bond discount
Bond premium
Bonds payable
Capital lease liability/Capital lease obligations
Commitments and contingent liabilities
Deferred income tax
Libel suit payable
Mortgage payable
Notes payable
Pension obligations
Security deposit receivable
Warranty liabilities

Owners' Equity

Contributed Capital
Additional paid-in-capital/Capital paid in excess of par value
Capital stock
  Common stock
  Preferred stock
Contributed capital
Minority interest
Owner's capital
Owner's drawing/Owner's withdrawals

Retained Earnings
Cash dividend declared
  Common stock dividend declared
  Preferred stock dividend declared
Retained earnings
Stock dividend declared

Other Owners' Equity
Treasury stock

Revenues

Commissions revenue
Construction revenue

Consulting revenue
Dividend revenue
Interest revenue
Rent revenue
Royalty revenue
Sales contra accounts: Sales discounts, Sales returns and allowances
Sales discounts lost
Sales revenue/Sales
Scrap revenue
Service revenue
Subscriptions revenue

Expenses

Amortization, Depletion, and Depreciation Expense
Depletion expense
Depreciation expense
Goodwill amortization expense
Patent amortization expense

Selling and Administrative Expenses
Accounting expense
Advertising expense/Marketing expense/Selling expense
Bad debt expense/Doubtful accounts expense/Uncollectible expense
Community service expense/Donations expense
Computer expense
Construction expense
Contribution expense
Delivery expense/Shipping expense/Freight expense/Transportation out
Dues and subscription expense
Education and training expense
Employee expenses/Personnel expenses
Federal income tax expense/Provision for income taxes
Insurance expense
Janitorial expense
Landscaping expense
Legal and accounting expense
Meals and entertainment expense
Medical expense
Medicare expense
Miscellaneous expense/General expense/Other expense
Office supplies expense/Postage and delivery expense
Payroll tax expense
Printing and copying expense
Recruitment expense
Rent expense
Repair and maintenance expense
Research and development expense
Salaries expense/Wages expense
Sales tax expense
State income tax expense
Telephone expense
Travel expense
Utilities expense/Gas and electric expense

Financial Expenses
Bank service charge expense
Cash over and short
Interest expense/Finance charge expense
Purchase discounts lost

Cost of Goods Sold
Cost of goods sold/Cost of sales
Cost of services performed
Purchase discounts
Purchase returns and allowances
Purchases
Transportation-in/Freight-in

Gains and Losses
Equity in earnings of subsidiary
Gain on sale of building
Gain on sale of equipment
Gain on sale of investments
Gain on sale of land
Loss on impairment
Loss on impairment of goodwill
Loss on sale of building
Loss on sale of equipment
Loss on sale of investments
Loss on sale of land
Realized gain on sale
Realized loss on sale
Unrealized holding gain
Unrealized holding loss

Clearing Accounts

Income summary
Revenue and expense summary

APPENDIX

Transactions A_1 through Z for Cards & Memorabilia Unlimited

Details of Transactions A_1 through Z for Cards & Memorabilia Unlimited as a Partnership

A_1	01/02	$30,000 cash is contributed by the owner who opens a business checking account.
B	01/02	$6,000 cash is withdrawn from the checking account to open a business savings account.
C_1	01/04	$10,000 worth of store equipment is acquired with a credit card.
D	01/06	$15,000 cash is paid to acquire merchandise inventory.
E	01/09	$2,000 cash is paid to the landlord for the security deposit on the store lease.
C_2	02/03	$10,000 cash is paid in full to settle the credit card obligation made on January 4.
F	07/01	$5,000 cash is borrowed with a bank credit line bearing interest at an 8% rate.
G	07/1–12/1	$18,000 worth of additional merchandise is acquired on account.
H	07/01	$7,000 cash is paid to acquire a used van with a 5-year useful life for the business.
I	11/01	$6,000 cash is collected from customers before any goods or services are provided.
J_1	07/31–11/30	$12,000 cash is paid to reduce accounts payable.
J_2	12/31	$6,000 of accounts payable is converted to a 6% interest-bearing note payable due on March 31.
K_1	12/31	$5,000 cash is paid in full to settle the credit line loan made on July 1.
L	12/31	$4,000 worth of a computer and printer is acquired by signing a 2-year promissory note.
M	Daily	$63,200 of cash sales are made to customers throughout the year.
N	Daily	$20,000 of revenue is earned on account—$19,400 for customer credit sales throughout the year and $600 for teaching a course.
O_1	12/02	$275 interest is earned from January 2–December 2 on $6,000 of savings bearing 5% interest.
P	Monthly	$1,000 cash is paid for office rent due the first day of each month beginning February 1.
Q_1	09/30	$300 of depreciation is recorded to recognize the use of equipment sold on September 30.
R	09/30	$2,000 worth of the store equipment bought on January 4 for $10,000 is sold for $1,350.
S	12/05	$8,000 cash is paid to employees for work performed through the year's last payday.
K_2	12/31	$200 cash is paid for interest due on $5,000 borrowed on July 1 at 8% and repaid on December 31.
T	Daily	$4,250 cash is paid for miscellaneous expenses incurred throughout the year.
U	12/31	$30,000 of cost of goods sold is determined by taking a physical count of inventory.
V	Daily	$15,000 cash is collected from customers throughout the year for amounts owed.
W	Daily	$8,100 cash is withdrawn from the business by the owner throughout the year.
A_2	12/24	$10,000 worth of merchandise is contributed by an individual for a business interest.
O_2	12/31	$25 of interest is earned but uncollected on a $6,000 savings account bearing 5% interest.
X	12/31	$750 of salaries expense is incurred but unpaid.
Y	12/31	$350 of miscellaneous expense is incurred but unpaid.
Q_2	12/31	$2,300 of depreciation is recorded on the use on unsold equipment.
Z	12/31	$4,000 worth of merchandise is delivered to customers who paid in advance.

Analysis of Transactions A_1 through Z for CMU as a Partnership

	Assets							=	Liabilities				+	Owners' Equity	
	Cash Checking	Cash Savings	Accts. Recvb.	Mdse. Inven.	Other Recvb.	Store Equip.	Accum. Depr.		Accts. Payb.	Cred. Line Payb.	Advn. From Cust.	Note Payable		Contributed Capital	Retained Earnings
A_1	30,000													30,000	
B	(6,000)	6,000													
C_1						10,000			10,000						
D	(15,000)			15,000											
E	(2,000)				2,000										
C_2	(10,000)								(10,000)						
F	5,000									5,000					
G				18,000					18,000						
H	(7,000)					7,000									
I	6,000										6,000				
J_1	(12,000)								(12,000)						
J_2									(6,000)			6,000[a]			
K_1	(5,000)									(5,000)					
L						4,000						4,000[b]			
M	63,200														63,200
N			20,000												20,000
O_1		275													275
P	(11,000)														(11,000)
Q_1							(300)								(300)
R	1,350					(2,000)	300								(350)
S	(8,000)														(8,000)
K_2	(200)														(200)
T	(4,250)														(4,250)
U				(30,000)											(30,000)
V	15,000		(15,000)												
W	(8,100)														(8,100)
A_2				10,000										10,000	
O_2					25										25
X									750[c]						(750)
Y									350						(350)
Q_2							(2,300)								(2,300)
Z											(4,000)				4,000
Σ	$32,000	6,275	5,000	13,000	2,025	19,000	(2,300)	=	$1,100	– 0 –	2,000	10,000	+	$40,000	21,900
				$75,000				=		$13,100			+		$61,900

[a]Reported as current liability; [b]Reported as noncurrent liability; [c]Reported as Salaries Payable

PHOTO CREDITS

P1.1: page 3 © RF / CORBIS
P1.2: page 3 Comstock Images
P1.3: page 4 © Sandy Felsenthal / CORBIS
P1.4: page 6 © David Young-Wolff / PhotoEdit
P1.5: page 7 © David Young-Wolff / PhotoEdit
P2.1: page 58 © RF / CORBIS
P2.2: page 65 Gary L. Fish, CPA, Ed.D., Professor Emeritus, Illinois State University
P2.3: page 71 © Jose Luis Pelaez Inc./ corbisstockmarket.com
P3.1: page 87 © The Image Finders
P3.2: page 97 © David Young-Wolff / PhotoEdit
P3.3: page 109 Courtesy of Merck & Co., Inc.
P4.1: page 135 Courtesy of Yushodo Co., Ltd., Tokyo
P4.2: page 148 © Reuters NewMedia Inc./CORBIS
P4.3: page 158 Courtesy of Hannah and Olivia Blankenship
P5.1: page 175 Susan Solomon, Solomon Communications
P5.2: page 190 Getty Images
P5.3: page 192 "Upper Deck designs and the card/ hologram combination are registered trademarks of The Upper Deck Company, LLC. ©2002 The Upper Deck Company, LLC. All rights reserved. Printed in the U.S.A. Used with Permission."
P6.1: page 217 From The Collection Of The B&O Railroad Museum, Inc.
P6.2: page 218 From The Collection Of The B&O Railroad Museum, Inc.
P7.1: page 267 Susan Solomon, Solomon Communications
P7.2: page 290 NBAE / Getty Images
P8.1: page 323 Bruce Ayres / Getty Images
P8.2: page 328 © DigitalVision / Matton Images
P8.3: page 352 © Bill Aron / PhotoEdit
P9.1: page 377 © Britt Erlanson / Getty Images
P9.2: page 388 © Cindy Charles / PhotoEdit
P9.3: page 416 Courtesy of Intuit Inc.
P10.1: page 461 © Daniel J. Schaefer / PhotoEdit
P10.2: page 476 NARMS www.narms.com
P10.3: page 481 Ken Osburn / Index Stock Imagery
P10.4: page 488 © Bill Pogue / Getty Images
P10.5: page 501 AP / Wide World Photos
P11.1: page 539 Stewart Cohen / Index StockImagery
P11.2: page 550 © Richard Pasley/Stock Boston Inc./ PictureQuest
P11.3: page 559 AP / Wide World Photos
P12.1: page 605 © Reuters NewMedia Inc./ CORBIS
P12.2: page 621 © Dennis MacDonald / PhotoEdit
P12.3: page 645 © Ryan McVay / Getty Images
P13.1: page 714 © Mug Shots / corbisstockmarket.com
P13.2: page 721 © Dwayne Newton / PhotoEdit
P14.1: page 761 © Sion Touhig / Getty Images
P14.2: page 775 © Mark Richards / PhotoEdit
P14.3: page 783 © Tim Boyle / Getty Images

INDEX